WORKERS' COMPENSATION LAW: CASES, MATERIALS, AND TEXT

Fourth Edition

WORKERS' COMPENSATION LAW: CASES, MATERIALS, AND TEXT

Fourth Edition

Lex K. Larson
President Employment Law Research, Inc.

Arthur Larson
James B. Duke Professor Law Emeritus Duke University (1910–1993)

Library of Congress Cataloging-in-Publication Data

Larson, Lex K.
    Workers' compensation law: cases, material, and text/ Lex K. Larson, Arthur Larson.— 4th ed.
p. cm.
    Includes index.
    ISBN 978-1-4224-2259-5 (hard cover)
    1.   Workers' compensation—Law and legislation—United States—Cases.   I.   Larson, Arthur. II. Title.
KF3615.L37   2008
344.7302'1—dc22

2008035917

NOTE TO USERS
To ensure that you are using the latest materials available in this area, please be sure to periodically check the LexisNexis Law School web site for downloadable updates and supplements at www.lexisnexis.com/lawschool.

Editorial Offices
744 Broad Street, Newark, NJ 07102 (973) 820-2000
201 Mission St., San Francisco, CA 94105-1831 (415) 908-3200
www.lexisnexis.com

MATTHEW◆BENDER

(2008–Pub.868)

PREFACE TO THE FOURTH EDITION

This casebook is offered in the conviction that workers' compensation, as a field of law, is big enough and important enough to deserve a place in the curriculum.

It comes as something of a surprise, to students as well as professors, to learn that workers' compensation, by any standard of measurement, is one of the largest areas of American law. Based on on-line legal database searches, there were over three thousand six hundred reported workers' compensation court decisions in calendar year 2007. This is more than the number of automobile negligence decisions, for the same period.

And the reported court-generated compensation decisions are only the tip of the iceberg of lawyer involvement. There are many times that number of cases decided at the administrative agency level, not to mention the numerous additional cases that are settled.

A most striking development is the dramatic increase in the volume of benefit payments. In 1972 total benefit payments nationwide totaled about $4 billion, but by 2000 they had reached $56.0 billion. Actual costs to employers are, of course, much higher.

One of the principal reasons the importance of compensation law in law practice has been underestimated is that a large part of it is concerned not with compensation claims at all, but rather with tort litigation. There are two reasons for this. One is the universal provision making compensation the exclusive remedy against the employer. The other is the third party features of the compensation law, governing the rights of the employer and employee as against third parties. Take the following familiar set of facts: an employee is riding as a passenger in a car driven by a co-employee, and there is a collision with a third party's truck. A personal injury lawyer cannot even begin to analyze the rights of the parties here without a thorough knowledge of compensation law. For a start, the attorney must know whether the employee was within the course of employment, as a prerequisite to determining whether there might be a cause of action against the co-employee or against the employer. And if the accident was covered by the compensation act, the employee's cause of action against the third party may be assigned at once to the employer. A host of detailed questions must be answered and the answers lie within compensation law.

Compensation law is also notable for the rich variety of legal areas it embraces. One could, for example, teach almost a complete course in conflict of laws without ever leaving the field of workers' compensation. And many of the liveliest growth areas of the law are deeply entangled with compensation law, such as products liability, automobile no-fault law, social security disability, and employment discrimination including sexual harassment.

Quite apart from its own particular subject matter, then, compensation law offers unusual opportunities in the law school curriculum. Among other things, it is important to understand the difference between a traditional common law subject, like torts, and a *statute-based* subject like workers' compensation, on which a sort of common law is erected. For this purpose there is no better vehicle than workers' compensation law.

Lex K. Larson
September 2008

ACKNOWLEDGMENTS

In preparing this Fourth Edition and previous editions, I am grateful for the invaluable research and writing contributions of my colleague Thomas A. Robinson: the book has benefited extensively from his talent and from the breadth and depth of his knowledge of Workers Compensation. In addition, I would like to acknowledge the considerable contributions to past editions of Professor Lisa M. Hervatin, who brought to this project her experience teaching with the Second Edition at Loyola Law School (Los Angeles); and of Professor Randy H. Lee of the University of North Dakota School of Law and Professor John Levering of Empire College of Law, Santa Rosa, California, for their most helpful comments. And I am indebted to Roger J. Thompson, of Travelers Medical Management Services, for giving permission to make use of and adapt material he has previously authored on the subject of special injury funds.

Finally, no words can adequately express the invaluable contribution of my father, who authored both the first and second editions. Arthur Larson was unquestionably one of the great legal writers and scholars of the twentieth century. While major revision and updating has taken place with the third edition, the book remains fundamentally a work of Arthur Larson's conception, and much of the writing is still his.

Lex K. Larson
September 2008

BIOGRAPHY

LEX K. LARSON

Lex K. Larson is President of Employment Law Research, Inc., a legal research group located in Durham, North Carolina. A graduate of Haverford College (1962) and Harvard Law School (1965), he practiced law in Washington, D.C. for fourteen years. From time to time he has taught courses as a member of the adjunct faculty of Duke University Law School. In 1991 he assumed the authorship of Larson's Workers' Compensation Law (12 vols. Matthew Bender & Co.) and Larson's Workers' Compensation, Desk Edition (3 vols. Matthew Bender & Co.), and he is author of three other multi-volume treatises on various facets of employment law. In addition, he serves as a member of the North Carolina Industrial Commission Advisory Council. Finally, he has been a certified mediator in the North Carolina court system and past Vice Chairman of the Board of Directors of the Dispute Settlement Center of Durham.

ARTHUR LARSON (1910–1993)

Arthur Larson grew up in Sioux Falls, South Dakota, and received his law degree from Oxford as a Rhodes Scholar. After the Second World War, he became a professor of law at Cornell University, where, in 1952, he authored and published what was then a two-volume treatise on Workers' Compensation. The recognition he received from that publication led to his appointment to the deanship of the law school of the University of Pittsburgh, and then to three high level governmental positions: Undersecretary of Labor, Director of the U.S. Information Agency and special assistant to and speech writer for President Eisenhower.

Dr. Larson arrived at Duke Law School in 1958, where in addition to teaching, he founded the school's Rule of Law Research Center. After retiring from teaching in 1980, Dr. Larson continued to work on his publications, including the workers' compensation treatise, which by the time of his death in 1993 had grown to eleven volumes. His other publications included a treatise on employment discrimination, as well as numerous books and articles on politics, workers' compensation, and international law.

THOMAS A. ROBINSON

Thomas A. Robinson, Durham, N.C., received his B.A., cum laude, for both Economics and History, in 1973 from Wake Forest University , his J.D. in 1976 from Wake Forest University School of Law, where he served as Managing Editor, Wake Forest Law Review, and his M.Div. in 1989 from Duke University Divinity School . From 1976 to 1986, Mr. Robinson was in private practice, where he focused on workers' compensation defense work. From 1987 to 1993, he was research and writing assistant to Professor Arthur Larson. Since 1993, Mr. Robinson has been primary upkeep writer for Larson's Workers' Compensation Law (LexisNexis) and Larson's Workers' Compensation, Desk Edition (LexisNexis). He is a contributing writer for California Compensation Cases (LexisNexis) and Benefits Review Board Service—Longshore Reporter (LexisNexis). He is also a contributing author of New York Workers' Compensation Handbook (LexisNexis) and a contributing editor for Workers' Compensation: The Survival Guide for Business (LexisNexis). Author of numerous short pieces on workers' compensation and employment law, Mr. Robinson has lectured widely on workers' compensation issues. Finally, he is a member of the LexisNexis National Workers' Compensation Advisory Board.

TABLE OF CONTENTS

TABLE OF CONTENTS

TABLE OF CONTENTS

TABLE OF CONTENTS

TABLE OF CONTENTS

TABLE OF CONTENTS

TABLE OF CONTENTS

TABLE OF CONTENTS

TABLE OF CONTENTS

TABLE OF CONTENTS

TABLE OF CONTENTS

TABLE OF CONTENTS

TABLE OF CONTENTS

TABLE OF CONTENTS

TABLE OF CONTENTS

TABLE OF CONTENTS

TABLE OF CONTENTS

TABLE OF CONTENTS

TABLE OF CONTENTS

TABLE OF CONTENTS

Part 1

THE NATURE AND HISTORY OF WORKERS' COMPENSATION

Chapter 1

BASIC FEATURES OF COMPENSATION

§ 1.01 INTRODUCTION

Workers' compensation is a non-fault mechanism for providing cash-wage benefits and medical care to victims of work-connected injuries, and for placing the cost of these injuries ultimately on the consumer, through the medium of insurance, whose premiums are passed on in the cost of the product.

§ 1.02 TYPICAL COMPENSATION ACT SUMMARIZED

The typical workers' compensation act has these features:

(a) The basic operating principle is that an employee is automatically entitled to certain benefits whenever he or she suffers a "personal injury by accident arising out of and in the course of employment" or occupational disease;

(b) Negligence and fault are largely immaterial, both in the sense that the employee's contributory negligence does not lessen his or her rights and in the sense that the employer's complete freedom from fault does not lessen its liability;

(c) Coverage is limited to persons having the status of employee, as distinguished from independent contractor;

(d) Benefits to the employee include wage-loss benefits, usually around one-half to two-thirds of his or her average weekly wage, and hospital, medical, and rehabilitation expenses; in death cases benefits for dependents are provided; arbitrary maximum and minimum limits are ordinarily imposed, usually related to the state's average weekly wage;

(e) The employee and his or her dependents, in exchange for these modest but assured benefits, give up their common-law right to sue the employer for damages for any injury covered by the act;

(f) The right to sue third persons whose negligence caused the injury remains, however, with the proceeds usually being applied first to reimbursement of the employer for the compensation outlay, the balance (or most of it) going to the employee;

(g) Administration is typically in the hands of administrative commissions; and, as far as possible, rules of procedure, evidence, and conflict of laws are relaxed to facilitate the achievement of the beneficent purposes of the legislation; and

(h) The employer is required to secure its liability through private insurance, state-fund insurance in some states, or "self-insurance"; thus, the burden of compensation liability does not remain upon the employer but passes to the consumer, since compensation premiums, as part of the cost of production, will be reflected in the price of the product.

§ 1.03 UNIQUE CHARACTER OF THE AMERICAN SYSTEM

The sum total of these ingredients is a unique system which is neither a branch of tort law nor social insurance of the British or continental type, but which has some of the characteristics of each. Like tort, but unlike social insurance, its operative mechanism is unilateral employer liability, with no contribution by the employee or the state. Like social insurance, but unlike tort, the right to benefits and amount of benefits are based largely on a social theory of providing support and preventing destitution, rather than settling accounts between two individuals according to their personal deserts or blame.

A correctly balanced underlying concept of the nature of workers' compensation is indispensable to an understanding of current cases and to a proper drafting and interpretation of compensation acts. Almost every major error that can be observed in the development of compensation law, whether judicial or legislative, can be traced either to the importation of tort ideas, or, less frequently, to the assumption that the right to compensation resembles the right to the proceeds of a personal insurance policy.

Among lawyers and judges trained in the common law, it has naturally been the tort-connection fallacy that has been most prevalent.[1]

The most familiar and persistent effect is the difficulty lawyers and judges feel in reconciling themselves to the notion that the employee's misconduct causing his or her own injury must really be altogether disregarded. So, in various forms such as added-risk doctrines, and in various troublesome categories, such as assault and horseplay cases, fault concepts have at times crept into both compensation decisions and into the statutory law as well.

Since the concept of compensation as a kind of strict-liability tort has had such widespread acceptance among lawyers and such widespread effects on compensation decisions, most of the following discussion of the inherent nature of workers' compensation has been cast in the form of a demonstration of concrete reasons why compensation cannot properly be so regarded.

---

[1] *See, e.g.,* HARPER, A TREATISE ON THE LAW OF TORTS 415: " . . . it seems clear that the legislature has merely substituted for the old remedies a scheme of liability which, in its broad outline, is fundamentally tort in nature, closely resembling in legal principle and social philosophy, that of common-law strict liability."

§ 1.04   COMPENSATION CONTRASTED WITH TORT

[1]   Introduction

Workers' compensation is fundamentally different from strict tort liability in its basic test of liability — work connection rather than fault; in its underlying philosophy — social protection rather than righting a wrong; in the nature of the injuries compensated; in the elements of damage; in the defenses available; in the amount of compensation; in the ownership of the award; and in the significance of insurance.

[2]   The Test of Liability: Work Connection Versus Fault

The right to compensation benefits depends on one simple test: Was there a work-connected injury? Negligence, and, for the most part, fault, are not in issue and cannot affect the result. Let the employer's conduct be flawless in its perfection, and let the employee's be abysmal in its clumsiness, rashness, and ineptitude: if the accident arises out of and in the course of the employment, the employee receives compensation. Reverse the positions, with a careless and stupid employer and a wholly innocent employee: the same award issues.

Thus, the test is not the relation of an individual's personal quality (fault) to an event, but the relationship of an event to an employment. The essence of applying the test is not a matter of assessing blame, but of marking out boundaries.

[3]   Underlying Social Philosophy

The ultimate social philosophy behind compensation liability is belief in the wisdom of providing, in the most efficient, most dignified, and most certain form, financial and medical benefits for the victims of work-connected injuries which an enlightened community would feel obliged to provide in any case in some less satisfactory form, and of allocating the burden of these payments to the most appropriate source of payment, the consumer of the product.

Let us approach the abstract question of underlying philosophy by taking a typical concrete example of industrial injury. Suppose a claimant has worked for 10 years at a drill press, at a salary that is not enough to permit private accumulation of assets to provide for him or her in the event of loss of ability to work. The rules require the wearing of a safety harness, and, although it is a hot and uncomfortable appliance, the worker has worn it faithfully until the day of the injury, when, in a moment of carelessness, the worker operates the machine without the harness and crushes both hands.

A system of law based in any degree on individual merit at the instant of the accident can see only one result: nonliability. The employee not only was negligent, but violated a safety rule. The employer, on the other hand, had thoughtfully provided a safety device and had done all it could by enforcing a rule requiring the device to be used. To require the innocent employer to pay the "guilty" employee might seem to flout the entire moral basis of law. In an entirely individualistic moral code, this might be so, but let us see what happens when considerations of social morality are introduced.

The society surrounding the disabled person can do one of three things.

First, it can refuse all aid, and let him or her starve in the street, or squat on the sidewalk with a few yellow pencils and beg for pennies from those who were yesterday equals. Since the reign of Queen Elizabeth I, no Anglo-American community has considered this a morally acceptable solution.

Second, it can put that person on relief, or some other form of direct handout. This, while better than the first, is a poor solution in at least two ways: It stigmatizes the person as a pauper, and it places the cost on the political or geographical subdivision where the individual happens to reside, although that subdivision had no connection with the injury.

Third, it can provide workers' compensation, thus preserving the person's dignity and self-respect as an injured veteran of industry. This is psychologically and morally the best of the three solutions, placing the cost where it rightly belongs, on the consumers of the product whose manufacture was the occasion for the injury.

And so, by this simple demonstration of alternatives, we see that workers' compensation, far from being a violation of moral principle, is in fact the only morally satisfactory solution of the problem of the injured worker, once one concedes that morality has a group as well as an individual aspect. The ultimate "social philosophy," then, behind nonfault compensation liability is the desirability of providing, in the most efficient, most dignified, and most certain form, financial and medical benefits which an enlightened community would feel obliged to provide in any case in some less satisfactory form, and of allocating the burden of these payments to the most appropriate source.

It has sometimes been erroneously said that the policy basis for absolute workers' compensation liability resembles the policy basis which gave rise to strict liability in tort — in *Rylands v. Fletcher*,[2] wild-animal cases, blasting, and what the *Restatement of Torts* calls "ultra-hazardous activities." The rationale of strict liability in these latter cases is usually put thus: When a person carries on a hazardous undertaking which has sufficient social utility to prevent the law from forbidding it altogether, the law will permit that undertaking only on condition that the person assume liability without fault for any consequent injuries. So, the argument runs, when an employer embarks on an enterprise, there is a strong probability of personal injuries sooner or later, and accordingly the employer may be made to assume absolute liability for these injuries when they do occur.

The fallacies in this analogy are many, but it will suffice to state the most obvious one: Employment generally is not ultra-hazardous in the sense used in strict-liability tort cases. It is true that, at one time, a handful of statutes, for historical and now invalid reasons having to do with attempts to ensure constitutionality, were on their face limited to "hazardous" employments, but no statutes are now so limited. If employment, regardless of nature, is "hazardous" in this sense (i.e., that accidents will eventually happen), then so is driving a car, operating a household, or perhaps just living at all — and absolute liability should be the rule for all mishaps flowing from these activities. In any case, consistency would demand that an employer's liability to outsiders for all injuries caused by operation of his business be also absolute, for if it is ultra-hazardous for the purpose of strict liability to employees, it must be the same for the purpose of liability to strangers.

Of course, some employments are hazardous, but others are not; and when injury does in fact occur, benefits are just as necessary under the social philosophy of compensation in the latter case as in the former.

[4] Significance of Difference in Defenses

The retention of the defenses of act of God, act of third person and some kinds of contributory negligence in so-called strict tort liability, and their unavailability in compensation law, show that the former is ultimately based on fault, while the latter is not.

While the mistaken grouping of compensation with strict tort liability is due partly to a misunderstanding of compensation, it is also due partly to the erroneous idea that so-called strict tort liability is indeed "absolute liability without regard to fault." The

---

[2] Rylands v. Fletcher, [1865] 3 Hurl. & Colt. 774 [1866] L.R. 1 Ex. 265; [1868] L.R. 3 H.L. 330.

simplest way to show the ultimate fault basis of strict tort liability is to examine the significance of the defenses that remain. Not long after *Rylands v. Fletcher* (which was not believed by the court to announce any new principle of liability), it was decided that act of God[3] and act of third person[4] were good defenses. Consent[5] and "default"[6] of the plaintiff were also recognized as defenses. This means that the boundaries of strict liability must still be described in terms based on fault. To relieve the actor of liability in three instances in which he or she is affirmatively shown to be free of fault in precipitating the harm is to indicate both that the liability is not a true nonfault liability, and that the area in which liability remains probably has some element of fault in it that distinguishes it from the area in which the three defenses create immunity.

So, if an employer, such as a circus, kept a caged tiger, and if lightning or a stranger or the plaintiff caused the release of the tiger, there would under the cases cited be no strict tort liability; but if lightning, a stranger, or a circus employee's own negligence caused the release and resulting injury to the employee, there would be compensation liability. The latter is true liability without regard to fault; the former is not.

[5] Nature of Injuries and Elements of Damage Compensated

In compensation, unlike tort, the only injuries compensated for, as a general proposition, are those which produce disability and thereby presumably affect earning power.

For this reason, some classes of injuries which result in verdicts of thousands of dollars at common law produce no award whatever under a compensation statute.[7] For example, impairment or destruction of sexual potency is not, in classical compensation law, a basis in itself for an award, and, presumably the same result would apply to such an injury as destruction of child-bearing capacity in a woman.

The limitation of compensation to "disability" also runs consistently through all questions of elements of damage. To take a familiar example: There is no place in compensation law for damages on account of pain and suffering, however dreadful they may be. So also in death-benefit cases compensation law refuses to recognize such items as loss of consortium or conscious suffering of the deceased in the interval preceding death.

[6] Amount of Compensation

A compensation system, unlike a tort recovery, does not pretend to restore to the claimant what has been lost; rather, it provides a sum which, added to his or her remaining earning ability, if any, will presumably enable the claimant to exist without being a burden to others.

If our compensation theory is correct, then the amount of compensation awarded may be expected to go not much higher than is necessary to keep the worker from destitution. This is indeed so.

Up to a certain point, the amount of compensation for disability depends on the worker's previous earning level: most acts award a percentage of average wage, somewhere between a half and two-thirds. But practically all acts also set a maximum in terms of dollars per week at a level which, in spite of marked improvements in recent years, represents at most a decent subsistence.

---

[3] Nicholls v. Marsland, [1876] L.R. 2 Ex. D. 1, 259.

[4] Box v. Jubb, [1879] L.R. 4 Ex. D 76.

[5] Att'y-Gen. v. Cory Bros. & Co., [1921] 1 A.C. 521, 539.

[6] Fletcher v. Rylands, [1866] L.R. 1 Ex. 265, *per* Blackburn, J.

[7] *See* Ch. 22, § 22.01, *below,* for discussion of this topic.

[7]   Ownership of the Award

The recipient of installment payments does not ordinarily "own" the unpaid balance of the award so as to entitle his or her heirs as such to any interest in it.[8]

Not only is the award trimmed on all sides — as to kind of injury, elements of damage, and maximum dollar amount — to ensure that it can never exceed the amount necessary to prevent want during disability; but also the award itself is completely cut off in most jurisdictions when, through the death of the worker without dependents, for example, there is no further need to worry about anyone's becoming destitute.

Lack of "ownership" is also seen in the claimant's inability to assign the benefits, and in the usual powerlessness of any court to attach such benefits for such purposes as alimony.[9]

[8]   Significance of Insurance

In compensation theory, liability is not supposed to hurt the employer as it helps the employee, since the loss is normally passed on to the consumer.

Of course, insurance of many kinds of tort liability is a familiar feature of modern law, and we do not, in theory, allow the presence of insurance to alter our conception of the rights and liabilities of the actual parties. But compensation insurance is a little different, for it is normally an integral part of the whole scheme. Most insurance, even where semi-compulsory, is exclusively concerned with providing a fund for possible plaintiffs. Compensation insurance, too, has this primary object, but it is also designed to provide the route whereby the cost of the compensation system is passed on to the consuming public in orderly fashion.

One of the best indications of this distinction is the fact that the impracticability of insuring a particular class of employers, such as private householders, or of employees, such as domestic servants, is usually recognized as reason enough for omitting them from compensation coverage.

Of course, under an experience-rating system the employer may indirectly feel some impact of frequent or large claims in the form of increased insurance premiums, but apart from this, the American compensation system, unlike the tort system, at the moment of creating the liability also creates the means of relieving the employer of the real burden of that liability.

In summary: Tort litigation is an adversary contest to right a wrong between the contestants; workers' compensation is a system, not a contest, to supply security to injured workers and distribute the cost to the consumers of the product.

PROBLEMS

(1) Organized labor sometimes takes the position that workers are really paying for their own compensation because, in the collective bargaining process, if they did not get benefits like workers' compensation they would get an equivalent amount in higher per-hour wages. Therefore, the argument runs, each worker has a right to these benefits comparable to a right to private insurance, and such measures as offsets for social security are unjustifiable. Is this sound economics?

(2) Compare or contrast no-fault workers' compensation with no-fault automobile liability. Is the latter based on a "philosophy" — if so, what is it? Try the same exercise on products liability.

---

[8] *See* Ch. 15, § 15.04, *below.*

[9] *See* Ch. 15, § 15.04, *below.*

(3) If a babysitter suffers an injury that will cost $30,000 a year the rest of his or her life in medical and income benefits, should the future earnings of the person hiring the babysitter be responsible for this?

§ 1.05   AMERICAN SYSTEM DISTINGUISHED FROM SOCIAL INSURANCE

[1]   Introduction

The American workers' compensation system is distinguishable from public social insurance in its essentially private nature, in the question of qualification for and measure of benefits, in the allocation of the burden of payment, in its retention of some relation between hazard and liability, and in its mechanism of unilateral employer liability.

[2]   Private Character of the System

The emphasis above on the features of compensation which distinguish it from tort, such as its social philosophy, its relation of awards to disability rather than loss, and its distribution of the cost to the consumer, may give the impression that the compensation system is virtually a kind of social security or social insurance plan. To restore a balanced impression of the American system, one must contrast it with the systems that are pure social insurance, such as the British plan;[10] this done, it becomes apparent that the present American system is neither tort nor "socialism" but something between.

Though social in philosophy, the American compensation system is largely private in structure, being a matter between employers, insurance carriers, and employees, while, under typical "socialistic" schemes, the government becomes the central figure.

A very brief description of the British plan may be given at the outset, with other details to be added as they become relevant.

The British plan[11] retains the identity of workers' compensation to some extent. Workers' compensation becomes a part of the comprehensive security system, along with retirement, unemployment, sickness, maternity, widows', orphans', family, and death benefits; it is under the same over-all administration by the Ministry of National Insurance; but there is an Industrial Injuries Fund separate from the National Insurance Funds under which most of the other benefits are financed.[12]

The most important difference is the substantially higher benefit for occupational disability than for nonoccupational. The plan calls for contributions by the employer, by the employee, and by the Exchequer, but the fund is, of course, public, and the handling of liability through private insurance or self-insurance is abolished.

By contrast with this type of plan, the American system begins to look conspicuously individualistic. Benefits are keyed (within limits) to the individual's prior earnings, while in Great Britain a flat rate is paid. Except in the few states which require insurance in a state fund, employers are generally free to make private arrangements for securing of their liability, either by carrying liability insurance or by qualifying as

---

[10] For a review of foreign systems, see OCCUPATIONAL DISABILITY AND PUBLIC POLICY (Cheit & Gordon, eds., 1963).

[11] National Insurance (Industrial Injuries) Act, 9 & 10 Geo. 6, Ch. 62 (1946, eff. 1948).

Other parts of the overall legislative scheme are: National Insurance Act, 9 & 10 Geo. 6, Ch. 67 (1946, eff. 1948); Ministry of National Insurance Act, 7 & 8 Geo. 6, Ch. 46 (1944); Family Allowances Act, 8 & 9 Geo. 6, Ch. 41 (1945); and the National Health Service Act, 9 & 10 Geo. 6, Ch. 81 (1946).

[12] As to hospital and medical benefits, as distinguished from cash benefits for wage loss, occupational and nonoccupational injuries alike are covered by the National Health Service program.

"self-insurers." So far as government participation is concerned, while the whole process is under administrative supervision, the government's role is mainly the settlement of disputed claims.

[3] Allocation of Burden, and Relation of Hazard to Liability

Unlike pure social insurance plans, the American compensation system does not place the cost on the "public" as such, but on a particular class of consumers, and thus retains a relation between the hazardousness of particular industries and the cost of the system to that industry and consumers of its product.

It is not quite accurate to say, as is often said, that the public ultimately pays the cost of workers' compensation. In the United States it is more precise to say that the consumer of a particular product ultimately pays the cost of compensation protection for the workers engaged in its manufacture. Between these two apparently similar methods of distributing the cost of protection there is actually a far-reaching difference. Some employments, like logging and lumbering, are highly dangerous; others, of a clerical and sedentary nature, involve a minimum of hazard. Under the American system, the size of the insurance premiums will vary according to the degree of hazard, while in Great Britain, the safe industry will pay taxes at the same rate as the dangerous. The Minister's Report gives a special reason for this feature of its plan: The extra levy for hazardous industries "would fall most heavily on certain important industries which have to meet foreign competition."[13]

In certain competitive situations, the choice of theory here could assume great importance. For example, suppose that two building materials, like stone and brick, are in close competition; the burden of high compensation premiums because of the prevalence of silicosis in the stone-cutting industry might, if that industry bore the full weight of it, drive that product from the market. Under the British plan there would be no such disadvantage.

Where experience rating, i.e., the adjustment of premium on the basis of past accident and liability record, is applied to individual employers, this competitive impact is carried one step further, in that an individual employer with a bad safety record might conceivably in time incur premiums so high that its cost of production would not permit it to compete.

Thus, while by contrast with tort liability, the American compensation system seems to have eliminated all consideration of fault, a comparison with pure social insurance reveals that other systems have gone much further along that road, by relieving not only individual employers but entire industries of all financial responsibility for the extent of injury-producing conditions which, avoidably or unavoidably, they maintain.

[4] Qualification for and Measure of Benefits

The American system does not make actual need the test and measure of compensation; its measure is a compromise between actual loss of earning capacity and arbitrary presumptions of the amount needed for support.

In the sections above, contrasting measure of recovery in compensation and tort, the emphasis was on the many ways in which compensation did not compensate for actual loss in the sense that tort recoveries are supposed to do. But when the comparison is with such plans as that of Great Britain it becomes clear that the compensation system is still far from being a relief system based on actual need.

The present British scale departs sharply from traditional compensation practice by disregarding previous earnings entirely. Benefits are uniform for all individuals, and vary only according to number of dependents.

---

[13] Report of the Ministry of Reconstruction, Social Insurance, Pt. II, ¶ 31 (v).

The typical American compensation act relates the award to the disability or loss of earning capacity, in many injuries fixing arbitrary periods of disability for loss of particular members; and, within the maximum and minimum limits, the amount of the award will be a percentage of and therefore will vary according to previous weekly wages. This reference to previous wage level is the significant point of distinction between the American system and the British, and shows that it is not an outright relief plan, since, within limits, it relates the amount of recovery to the amount of wage loss, makes no inquiry into actual need, and, with a few statutory exceptions, makes no allowance even for presumed degree of need because of number of dependents.

[5]   Retroactive Unilateral Employer Liability

While the objective of American workers' compensation — the protection against wage loss — classes it with other forms of social insurance such as old-age and unemployment insurance, it differs from them in its utilization of the mechanism of employer liability. This distinction has some important practical consequences. In the typical social insurance scheme, the employer's worries are largely over when it makes its regular contributions to the fund. The employee's status as a member of the scheme is usually fixed in advance, often because the system is contributory and the employee is covered only if his or her contributions are on record. By contrast, the workers' compensation claimant's status is determined in retrospect. Many a householder has been startled by being suddenly presented with a workers' compensation claim by someone who had been hired to fix the roof or build a chicken coop.[14] Occasionally an entire category of employees, never thought covered by their employers, are swept retroactively within the compensation act by judicial decision, as when the *Gordon*[15] decision in effect made all full-time commission life-insurance salespeople employees in New York. It is in such situations that the employer is made to realize that the essence of the compensation obligation is not merely to make periodic payments into some social insurance system, but to bear any employer liability that any court may impose under the court's current interpretation of compensation law. If the employer has guessed wrong, and has carried no compensation insurance, the liability it bears will not, from its point of view, look much like social insurance.

The principal practical consequence is that the coverage of an American-type compensation act cannot necessarily be expected to follow wherever the Social Security Act, for example, may lead, such as into the area of domestic service, without some thought on whether the domestic employer's liability can be made both predictable and insurable.[16]

Conclusion: The above pair of contrasts with both tort and social insurance shows that the American system has left behind most traces of tort but, on the other hand, displays significant differences from an all-out public social-insurance plan, and is in no sense a relief system. If this analysis has succeeded, it will aid in preventing the two erroneous extremes of interpretation that run throughout all compensation law. On the one hand, there is the extreme of thwarting the social purposes of the legislation by the importation of common-law restrictions. On the other hand, there is the equally unjustified extreme of indiscriminately resolving difficult questions in favor of the

---

[14] These kinds of claims have invariably been unsuccessful. *See* Ch. 13, § 13.02[3], *below.*

[15] Gordon v. New York Life Ins. Co., 300 N.Y. 652, 90 N.E.2d 898 (1950) (4-3 decision).

[16] *See* Ch. 13, § 13.02[3], *below.*

claimant on the theory that the claimant's position is the same as that of the beneficiary of a personal insurance policy or public relief system.

PROBLEMS

(1) In view of the dramatic increase in the cost of workers' compensation that has occurred in most states since 1980, would it be a good idea to emulate the British and to draw on general tax revenues to take up some of the burden?

(2) How can the financing of workers' compensation be pressed into service to encourage industrial safety?

Chapter 2

HISTORICAL DEVELOPMENT OF WORKERS' COMPENSATION

SYNOPSIS

§ 2.01 COMMON-LAW BACKGROUND

[1] Introduction

The necessity for workers' compensation legislation arose out of the coincidence of a sharp increase in industrial accidents attending the rise of the factory system and a simultaneous decrease in the employee's common-law remedies for his injuries.

[2] Primitive Law

In tracing the origins of the workers' compensation idea in Western law, one is tempted to speculate on the significance of a few fragments of ancient law that might be said to represent a crude equivalent of the modern principle. In the Laws of Henry I, dating from about the year 1100, occurs a passage which may be translated as follows:

> And in some cases a man cannot legitimately swear that another was not, through himself, further from life and nearer to death; among which cases are these: If anyone, on the mission of another, is the cause of death in the course of the errand; if anyone sends for someone, and the latter is killed in coming; if anyone meets death having been called by another. . . .[1]

Similarly, Brunner describes the rule in early Germanic law as follows:

> The master was liable for the *wergeld* of the workman if the latter lost his life in the service, and for the appropriate money-payment if he was injured, — so far as the injury could not be imputed to some third person for whom the master (who had to answer for the misdeeds of his own people) was not responsible. If one who was in the service of another lost his life by misadventure, by reason of a tree or of fire or of water, the accident was imputed to the master as homicidium. If one person sent another away or summoned him on the former's

---

[1] Leges Regis Henrici Primi, XC, 6.

business, and the latter lost his life while executing the order, the former was taken as the *causa mortis*. [2]

This liability was not based on a consciously enlightened social policy, but apparently on the primitive concept of causation. As the first quotation indicates, a person accused of having had some responsibility for a death had to take the oath that the deceased was not, through him, further from life and nearer death. If the accused had sent the deceased on the fatal mission, or had set in motion the employment in which deceased was killed, the accused could not legitimately swear that oath. It was the but-for theory of causation in undiluted form.

[3]   1000–1837

So far as law on the subject of master's liability to his injured servant is concerned, this period seems to be a complete blank. Perhaps the primitive rule met the problem for a time, since this basic concept of responsibility survived into the 15th century.

Beginning about 1700, the principle of vicarious liability of the master for torts of the servant was developed, through a tour de force by Lord Holt in such cases as *Jones v. Hart*,[3] aided by Lord Raymond, who, in his 1743 Reports,[4] converted Holt's hypothetical examples of negligent servants into actual actions brought and decided at Guildhall. Since the statements of the respondeat superior rule at this stage were in sweeping unqualified terms ("the act of a servant is the act of his master"),[5] presumably a master would be liable to a servant injured by the negligence of a fellow-servant. There was nothing in the rule as then stated limiting its benefits to strangers.

[4]   1837–1880: **Contraction of Workers' Remedies**

In 1837, Lord Abinger invented the fellow-servant exception to the general rule of master's vicarious liability, in his famous *Priestly v. Fowler* opinion.[6] In that case, the master, a butcher, was held not liable for the negligence of his servant in overloading a van which broke down as a result and injured the plaintiff, another employee. The decision was based largely on what Abinger called "the consequences of a decision the one way or the other," consisting largely of "alarming" examples of possible master's liability for domestic mishaps due to the negligence of the chambermaid, the coachman, and the cook. If Abinger realized the unhappy effect of his decision on the injured victims of the industrial age which was violently erupting all round him, the opinion does not show it. But when American courts began to follow his lead, as in *Farwell v. Boston & Worcester R. R.*,[7] in Massachusetts, holding a railroad immune from liability to one of its locomotive engineers for injury caused by the negligence of one of its switchmen, it became clear that the real implications of the decision involved not butcher-boys and chambermaids, but trainmen, miners, and factory workers.

"Assumption of risk" is the second of the three common-law defenses of the employer. Its seeds may also be found in *Priestly v. Fowler, above,* where Abinger observed that "the servant is not bound to risk his safety in the service of his master, and may, if he thinks fit, decline any service in which he reasonably apprehends injury

---

[2] Brunner, Deutsche Rechtsgeschichte, II, 549 (1892), cited in Wigmore, *Responsibility for Tortious Acts,* 7 Harv. L. Rev. 315, 383, 442; 3 Select Essays in Anglo-American Legal History, 474, 481.

[3]   Jones v. Hart, [Nisi prius 1698] K.B. 642, 2 Salk. 441.

See Holmes, *The History of Agency,* 4 Harv. L. Rev. 345; 5 Harv. L. Rev. 1; 3 Select Essays in Anglo-American Legal History 368; and Wigmore, n.2, *above.*

[4]   1 Lord Raymond's Reports 739, "as he heard it from 'Magister Place.'"

[5]   Jones v. Hart, [Nisi prius 1698] K.B. 642, 2 Salk. 441, *per* Holt, J.

[6]   Priestly v. Fowler, [1837] 3 M. & W. 1, 150 Reprint 1030.

[7]   Farwell v. Boston, 4 Metc. 49 (Mass. 1842).

to himself; and in most of the cases in which danger may be incurred, if not in all, he is just as likely to be acquainted with the probability and extent of it as the master." The implication is that the employee, being free to do as he or she pleases, and voluntarily undergoing the dangerous conditions of the work, has no standing to complain when injury does occur as a result of these conditions. This idea, based as it is on such phantasms as perfect liquidity of labor, perfect bargaining equality, and perfect knowledge by workers of employment risks and opportunities, needs no refutation in modern times. However, it too, again with the assistance of Judge Shaw in the *Farwell* case, was well established as a defense by the middle of the 19th century.

Contributory negligence, recognized as a defense since *Butterfield v. Forrester* [8] in 1809, became the third employer defense, so that even where direct negligence of the employer could be shown, recovery would be defeated by the negligence — even much smaller in degree — of the employee.

What then remained of employer's liability? Let us analyze the grounds of liability statistically, using German figures for 1907,[9] since the German statistics of the period are unusually full and detailed.

Classification of Causes of Accidents

(1)	Negligence or fault of employer	16.81 %
(2)	Joint negligence of employer and injured employee	4.66 %
(3)	Negligence of fellow-servant	5.28 %
(4)	Acts of God	2.31 %
(5)	Fault or negligence of injured employee	28.89 %
(6)	Inevitable accidents connected with the employment	42.05 %

It is at once apparent that, with (2) and (3) barred by common-law defenses, only under (1) is there any possibility of employer liability; accordingly, the employee at common law was remediless without question in 83 percent of all cases.

What of the remaining 16.81 percent? The defense of assumption of risk might still apply, for even where the employer was at fault, many cases[10] held that the employee, by continuing to work in spite of the defects or dangers created by the employer, consented to waive the employer's obligation.

Moreover, there is quite a difference between classifying an accident as attributable to employer's fault for statistical purposes, and carrying through a fruitful lawsuit based on that fault. The common-law duties of the employer to the employee were of a kind not always easy to assert in court: to provide and maintain a reasonably safe place to work and safe appliances, tools, and equipment; to provide a sufficient number of suitable and competent fellow-servants to permit safe performance of the work; to warn employees of unusual hazards; and to make and enforce safety rules. Even these duties were sometimes weakened by the common-law defenses, for if the unsafe condition of the premises, for example, was due to the negligence of a fellow-servant, the master in some jurisdictions would not be liable.[11] The employer had only to exercise the care of a reasonably prudent master,[12] and if the consequences of the employer's breach of duty should have been obvious to the worker, then it was for the worker to look out for

---

[8] Butterfield v. Forrester, [K. B. 1809] 11 East 60.

[9] Bureau of Labor Bulletin (January 1908).

[10] Russell v. Minneapolis & St. L. Ry., 32 Minn. 230, 20 N.W. 147 (1884); Davidson v. Cornell, 132 N.Y. 228, 30 N.E. 573 (1892).

[11] Armour v. Hahn, 111 U.S. 313, 4 S. Ct. 433, 28 L. Ed. 440 (1884); Henry v. Hudson & M. R., 201 N.Y. 140, 94 N.E. 140, 94 N.E. 623 (1911).

[12] Omaha Bottling Co. v. Theiler, 59 Neb. 257, 80 N.W. 821 (1899).

himself or herself.[13] One need only add that the usual witnesses of the accident, being coemployees, would naturally be reluctant to testify against the employer, to complete the picture of helplessness which characterized the position of the injured worker of the precompensation era.

[5]　Judicial Efforts to Cut Down Common-Law Defenses

It is not surprising that some courts eventually began to try to swing the pendulum in the other direction, and, although the total effect of their efforts was small, this was partly because the task of reform was taken over by legislation. The principal modification of the common-law defenses was the adoption of the vice-principal exception to the fellow-servant rule. In some of the jurisdictions[14] adopting this exception, it took the form of excluding from the fellow-servant category all employees in supervisory capacities, such as foremen. In most jurisdictions,[15] however, it took the broader form of excluding from the fellow-servant category all employees charged with carrying out the common-law duties of the employer. This was, in effect, to say that these duties — of providing a safe place, safe tools, and so on — were nondelegable. The only other instances of softening the common-law defenses by judicial action were the holdings in some but not all states that the employee did not assume the risk of the employer's violation of a safety statute,[16] and the modification of the contributory-negligence rule in three states to confine the effect of contributory negligence to the mitigation of damages.[17]

[6]　Precompensation Legislation

It is important to observe that all legislation prior to the workers' compensation acts accepted the basic common-law idea that the employer was liable to the employee only for the former's negligence or fault or, at most, the fault of someone for whom the employer was generally responsible under the respondeat superior doctrine. These so-called employers' liability statutes did not aspire to create any new principle of liability applicable to the employment relation as such. The most they ever set out to accomplish was the restoration of the employee to a position no worse than that of a stranger injured by the negligence of the employer or of the employer's servants.

The first such acts, beginning with the Georgia Act of 1855,[18] abrogated the fellow-servant defense for railway companies only. In 1880, England, which had judicially rejected the vice-principal rule, legislatively adopted something like it in the Employers' Liability Act,[19] but, what with the exceptions, qualifications, and pitfalls in the act itself, and the prompt judicial holding that a contract waiving an employee's rights under the act was not against public policy,[20] this first legislative effort was largely abortive. However, it did serve as a model for a number of state statutes, and by the time compensation legislation began to take over the field in 1911, 25 states had some kind of employers' liability statute.[21] Many of these statutes abrogated the fellow-servant defense as to railroads only; some abrogated it more generally or altogether;

---

[13]　Ragon v. Toledo, A.A. & N.M. Ry., 97 Mich. 265, 56 N.W. 612, 37 Am. St. Rep. 336 (1893).

[14]　*See, e.g.,* Berea Stone Co. v. Kraft, 31 Ohio St. 287, 27 Am. Rep. 510 (1877).

[15]　*See, e.g.,* Northern Pac. R. R. v. Herbert, 116 U.S. 642, 6 S. Ct. 590, 29 L. Ed. 755 (1886).

[16]　Fitzwater v. Warren, 206 N.Y. 355, 99 N.E. 1042, 42 L.R.A.(n.s.) 1229 (1912).

[17]　*Georgia:* Augusta & S.R. Co. v. McElmurry, 24 Ga. 75 (1858); *Illinois:* Galena & C.U.R.R. v. Jacobs, 20 Ill. 478 (1858); *Tennessee:* L.N. & Gr. S.R.R. v. Fleming, 82 Tenn. 128 (1884).

[18]　Ga. Laws 1855, p. 155.

[19]　Stats. 43 & 44 Victoria, Ch. 42.

[20]　Griffiths v. Earl of Dudley, [1882] 9 Q.B.D. 357.

[21]　*See* Boyd, Compensation for Injuries to Workmen 8 (1913).

some modified it. As to contributory negligence, some adopted instead the comparative-negligence principle, some shifted the burden of proof on the issue of contributory negligence from the plaintiff to the defendant in certain jurisdictions where the plaintiff had had the burden of proving his own freedom from negligence, and some withdrew the defense in case of violation of a safety statute by the employer. As to assumption of risk, some destroyed the defense whenever the risk was caused by the fault of the employer; some destroyed it as to violations of safety statutes; and some modified it so as to make it inapplicable to extraordinary risks, or known defects in plant or machinery, especially in the case of railroads.

The Federal Employers' Liability Act of 1908, applicable to those employees of common carriers who are engaged in interstate or foreign commerce, may be regarded as the high point in this phase of the development of employee protection, for it embodied all the most advanced features of the state acts up to that time. It provided that contributory negligence should only mitigate damages, and that neither this defense nor assumption of risk should apply in case of safety-statute violation. It also made the railroad employer liable for the negligence of all its officers, agents and employees, and for defects due to negligence in track, equipment, engines, and cars, resulting in injury to employees.

To preserve a due sense of proportion when analyzing the overall effect of these legislative and judicial efforts to ameliorate the common law, one should glance again at the German statistics on causes of accidents. Under that table, even if both the fellow-servant defense and contributory negligence were abolished, the effect would be to add only another 10 percent to the cases in which the employer is liable, making a total of about 27 percent of all industrial accidents which could even theoretically form the basis of a recovery. That was the best a common-law system based on fault could possibly hope to do.

To give the employee protection from the inevitable accidents due to no one's fault which accounted for 42 percent of all accidents, some entirely new principle was needed; and to grant the employee benefits for the 29 percent of all injuries which resulted from his or her own fault required, even more obviously, a fundamental departure from the common law.

These German statistics have been used partly because they contain the most relevant breakdown by "fault" of causes of accidents and partly because they cover a rather broad base both as to number of employees and as to duration. While only the 1907 figures are here cited, there are similar figures for 1887 and 1897[22] which vary only slightly in the percentage summaries. The calculation thus covers from 4 to 21 million workers in all kinds of employment over a period of 20 years.

The studies made in America leading up to compensation legislation usually took the form of calculating what injured employees actually received under the old system. The conclusions were invariably shocking. The Illinois commission[23] investigated 5,000 industrial accidents, and found that of 614 death cases, the families received nothing in 214 cases, and were engaged in pending litigation in 111. The other cases were settled for small sums averaging a few hundred dollars. The report of the New York commission[24] contains a number of similar tabulations, of which the table on fatal industrial accidents in New York City in 1908 is typical: Of 74 cases whose disposition was known, there was no compensation in 43.2 percent, and compensation under $500 in 40.5 percent, with only 16.3 percent receiving between $500 and $5,000. Even these figures do not tell the whole story, since attorneys' fees had to come out of these meager sums and averaged a fourth to a third of the amount recovered, according to

---

[22] Zacher, Introduction to Workmen's Insurance in Germany 14.

[23] Report of Illinois Commission, Edwin R. Wright, Secretary.

[24] N.Y. Sen. Docs., Vol. XXV, No. 38, Appendix III (1910).

the New York commission's study. When funeral and other expenses were also deducted, it became clear enough that the precompensation loss-adjustment system for industrial accidents was a complete failure and, in most serious cases, left the worker's family destitute.[25]

§ 2.02   ORIGINS OF WORKERS' COMPENSATION IN EUROPE

Workers' compensation is not an outgrowth of the common law or of employers' liability legislation; it is the expression of an entirely new social principle having its origins in 19th-century Germany.

The story of English and American common law and legislation up to this point has done no more than set the stage for the entrance of the new compensation principle. It explains how an intolerable situation was developed which impelled the English and American jurisdictions, steeped as they were in individualistic traditions, one by one to accept what must at the time have seemed a radical, indeed alien, and even socialistic, innovation. But the story so far does not explain where the compensation principle itself came from; for that, it is necessary to interrupt our chronological sequence and take a fresh start in 19th-century Prussia.

In 1838, one year after Lord Abinger announced the fellow-servant rule,[26] and four years before Judge Shaw of Massachusetts popularized the defense of assumption of risk,[27] Prussia enacted a law making railroads liable to their employees (as well as passengers) for accidents from all causes except acts of God and negligence of the plaintiff. In 1854, Prussia required employers in certain industries to contribute one-half to the sickness-association funds formed under various local statutes. In 1876 an unsuccessful voluntary insurance act was passed, and finally, in 1884, Germany adopted the first modern compensation system, 13 years before England, 25 years before the first American jurisdiction, and 65 years before the last American state.

It is interesting to inquire into the conditions which gave birth to the compensation idea. As to the intellectual origins, both philosophers and politicians played a part. Frederick the Great contributed both a profound conviction that "it is the duty of the state to provide sustenance and support of those of its citizens who cannot provide sustenance for themselves,"[28] and a completely uninhibited view of the state's power and right to bring this protection about by any means. Among the philosophers, probably Fichte was most responsible for propounding the idea that many of the misfortunes, disabilities, and accidents of individuals are ultimately social and not individual in origin, and that the state is therefore "not to be negative nor to have a mere police function, but to be filled with Christian concern, especially for the weaker members."[29] Lassalle, Sismondi, Winkelblech, Wagner, and Schaeffle developed this general conception into insistent and eloquent arguments for the only mechanism which could effectively implement this ideal: industrial insurance. At the same time, especially during the years following the war of 1870–71, Bismarck began to be concerned about the increasing strength shown in elections by the Marxian type of socialists as against the practical socialists of the school of Lassalle, who favored the cooperative association type of development. Accordingly, in 1881 he met the situation by laying before the Reichstag his far-reaching plan for compulsory insurance, which was enacted in various measures between 1883 and 1887.[30] Thus, while workers' compensation has a "socialistic" origin in

---

[25] *See* summary of other studies in BOYD, COMPENSATION FOR INJURIES TO WORKMEN, Ch. V (1913).

[26] *See* Ch. 2, § 2.01[4] n.6, *above.*

[27] *See* Ch. 2, § 2.01[4] n.7, *above.*

[28] *Fourth Special Report of the Commissioner of Labor* 25–26 (1893).

[29] *Fourth Special Report of the Commissioner of Labor* 20 (1893).

[30] Fundamental Law of 1884 (Industry, Transport, Trades, Telegraph, Army and Navy); Agricultural Law, 1886; Building Law, 1887; Marine Law, 1887.

the philosophical sense of the term associated with the views of Fichte and Hegel, it also has an anti-socialistic origin if the term is used in the Marxian sense.

The exact form taken by the German system should be specially noted, because it was significantly different from the English and American systems, and because it is continuing to exert a strong influence on the form taken by social legislation of all kinds. The distinguishing feature of German insurance (apart from its much greater comprehensiveness) was that contributions by the worker were an integral part of the system. Broadly, the German plan fell into three parts: the Sickness Fund (workers contributing two-thirds, employer one-third) paid benefits for the first 13 weeks of either sickness or disability due to accident; the Accident Fund (contributions by employers only) paid for disability after the first 13 weeks; and Disability Insurance (workers contributing one-half) provided for disability due to old age or other causes not specifically covered elsewhere. The plan, though compulsory, was thus essentially based on mutual association. The administration was placed in the hands of representatives of employers and employees under government supervision. The striking resemblance of this plan to the present British system is at once apparent.[31]

It seems paradoxical on the surface that Germany, with its more socialistic philosophical tradition, should produce a system which is more individualistic in the sense that the worker in effect purchases in his own right an insurance policy against sickness and disability, with the employer sharing the premium; while America followed what might appear to be a more radical line by imposing unilateral liability without fault upon the employer, and by making the employer bear the entire burden of any insurance against that liability. There are several reasons for this. The choice of this mechanism in Germany was dictated largely by the existence of already successful schemes on this pattern within the German guilds (Knappschaftskassen). For hundreds of years these guilds had sponsored benefit societies and associations which provided disability, sickness, and death benefits. In a highly developed system, such as the miners' societies, there were benefits on the insurance principle for sickness, accident, and burial, and pensions for orphans, widows, and invalids.[32] The system was administered by a committee made up half of employers and half of employees, and contributions were in the same proportion, with the employer paying the "premium" and deducting the employee's half from the next wage payment.

The New York commission, whose report of March 1910 was the basis for New York's compensation act, studied the German plan, and made the following statement:

> Could we see a practical way to put a scheme of compensation in force in which the employer's share will be the 50 percent of earnings recommended in our bills, and the workmen's contribution say 25 percent. Above that, and the benefits insured to him thereby changed to three-fourths earnings during disability, we would recommend it. The German system on such lines seems admirable. But practically we see no way to accomplish this by force of compulsory law.[33]

The American pattern, then, became that of unilateral employer liability, with no contribution by employees. The issue is by no means dead, however, what with the contributory principle appearing in the British comprehensive system, in the state nonoccupational disability plans that have been adopted,[34] and in the Federal Old Age, Survivors, and Disability Insurance Act. It is significant, therefore, to note that the New York commission rejected the employee-contribution system only because of doubt that compulsory contributions could constitutionally be exacted, and that but for this doubt

---

[31] *See* Ch. 1, § 1.05[2], *above.*

[32] *Fourth Special Report of the Commissioner of Labor* 37 (1893).

[33] At p. 67 of N.Y. Sen. Docs., Ch. 2, § 2.01[6] n.24, *above.*

[34] *See* Ch. 34, § 34.01[1], *below.*

they would have recommended it. No doubt the American pattern was also influenced by the fact that such recovery for industrial injury as the employee had obtained in the past had always taken the form of an adversary imposition of liability upon the employer, so that it was perhaps natural to conceive of even this totally new principle of employee protection in terms of the old mechanism of employer liability.

§ 2.03   ORIGINS OF WORKERS' COMPENSATION IN THE UNITED STATES

By the end of the 19th century, as shown above, the coincidence of increasing industrial injuries and decreasing remedies had produced in the United States a situation ripe for radical change, and when, in 1893, a full account of the German system written by John Graham Brooks was published as the Fourth Special Report of the Commissioner of Labor, legislators all over the country seized upon it as a clue to the direction which efforts at reform might take. Another stimulus was provided by the enactment of the first British Compensation Act in 1897, which later became the model of state acts in many respects.

A period of intensive investigation ensued, carried on by various state commissions, beginning with Massachusetts in 1904, Illinois in 1907, Connecticut in 1908 and a legislatively created commission of representatives, industrialists, and other experts in New York, in 1909. By 1910 the movement was in full swing, with commissions being created by Congress and the legislatures of Massachusetts, Minnesota, New Jersey, Connecticut, Ohio, Illinois, Wisconsin, Montana, and Washington. In 1910 also, there occurred a conference in Chicago attended by representatives of all these commissions, at which a Uniform Workmen's Compensation Law was drafted.[35] Although the state acts which followed were anything but uniform, the discussions at this conference did much to set the fundamental pattern of legislation.

As to actual enactments, the story begins modestly with a rather narrow cooperative accident fund for miners passed by Maryland in 1902,[36] which quietly expired when held unconstitutional in an unappealed lower court decision.[37] In 1909, another miners' compensation act was passed in Montana,[38] and suffered the same fate.[39] In 1908, Congress passed a compensation act covering certain federal employees.[40]

In 1910 the first New York act[41] was passed, with compulsory coverage of certain "hazardous employments." It was held unconstitutional in 1911 by the Court of Appeals, on the ground that the imposition of liability without fault upon the employer was a taking of property without due process of law under the state and federal constitutions.[42]

At the present time, with the constitutionality of all types of compensation acts firmly established, there is no practical purpose to be served by tracing out the elaborate and violent constitutional law arguments provoked by the early acts.[43] One important

---

[35] *See* account of this conference in BOYD, COMPENSATION FOR INJURIES TO WORKMEN 17–22 (1913).

[36] Md. Laws 1902, Ch. 139.

[37] Franklin v. United Rys. & Elec. Co. of Baltimore, 2 Baltimore City Rep. 309 (1904).

[38] Mont. Laws 1909, Ch. 67.

[39] Cunningham v. Northwestern Improvement Co., 44 Mont. 180, 119 P. 554, 1 N.C.C.A. 720 (1911).

[40] 35 Stat. 556 (1908).

[41] Laws of 1910, Ch. 674.

[42] Ives v. South Buffalo Ry., 201 N.Y. 271, 94 N.E. 431 (1911).

[43] *See* BOYD COMPENSATION FOR INJURIES TO WORKMEN, 153–204 (1913).

However, as recently as 1957, New Mexico declared its amended act unconstitutional on the basis of an unlawful delegation of power because the act created a commission whose findings, if supported by substantial

practical result did, however, flow from the preliminary constitutional setbacks: the very fear of unconstitutionality impelled the legislatures to pass over the ideal type of coverage, which would have been both comprehensive and compulsory, in favor of more awkward and fragmentary plans whose very weakness and incompleteness might ensure their constitutional validity. And so, beginning with New Jersey, "elective" or "optional" statutes became common, under which employers could choose whether or not they would be bound by the compensation plan, with the alternative of being subject to common-law actions without benefit of the three common-law defenses. Similarly, a number of states limited their coverage to "hazardous" employments because of doubt as to the extent of the police power. All but one, Wyoming, have since broadened their scope.[44]

In New York, the *Ives* decision was answered by the adoption in 1913 of a constitutional amendment permitting a compulsory law, and such a law was passed in the same year. In 1917 this compulsory law,[45] together with the Iowa elective-type,[46] and the Washington exclusive-state-fund-type law,[47] was held constitutional by the United States Supreme Court.

NEW YORK CENTRAL RAILROAD COMPANY v. WHITE
243 U.S. 188 (1917)

Mr. Justice Pitney delivered the opinion of the court. . . .

Briefly, the statute imposes liability upon the employer to make compensation for disability or death of the employee resulting from accidental personal injury arising out of and in the course of the employment, without regard to fault as a cause except where the injury or death is occasioned by the employee's willful intention to produce it, or where the injury results solely from his intoxication while on duty; it graduates the compensation for disability according to a prescribed scale based upon the loss of earning power, having regard to the previous wage and the character and duration of the disability; and measures the death benefits according to the dependency of the surviving wife, husband, or infant children. Perhaps we should add that it has no retrospective effect, and applies only to cases arising some months after its passage.

---

evidence, were to have the force and effect of a judgment. State v. Mechem, 63 N.M. 250, 316 P.2d 1069 (1957).

More recently, in 1963, North Carolina found it necessary to hold that its compensation act was not unconstitutional because of denial of trial by jury. Huffman v. Douglas Aircraft Co., 260 N.C. 308, 132 S.E.2d 614 (1963).

And to this day there continues to be constitutional challenges to part or all of a workers' compensation law. Statutory changes designed to reduce employers' costs have spurred a number of such challenges:

Texas Workers' Comp. Comm'n v. Garcia, 893 S.W.2d 504 (Tex. 1995). In 1989, Texas completed a major reform of its workers' compensation system that included the utilization of American Medical Association (AMA) impairment guidelines to determine compensability, the establishment of a "designated doctor" whose findings were to be given "presumptive weight," and the removal from jury consideration of most, if not all, factual issues. The Texas Supreme Court held that the amendments were constitutional and did not deny access to a jury trial.

Stephenson v. Sugar Creek Packing, 250 Kan. 768, 830 P.2d 41, 50 (1992). A statutory amendment that provided that repetitive use conditions occurring in opposite upper extremities must be compensated as scheduled injuries rather than as disability to the body as a whole was held to be unconstitutional.

Martinez v. Scanlan, 582 So. 2d 1167 (Fla. 1991).

[44] Wyo. Stat. Ann. § 27-14-102 (LEXIS through 1999).

[45] New York Central R.R. v. White, 243 U.S. 188, 37 S. Ct. 247, 61 L. Ed. 667, L.R.A. 1917D, 1 Ann. Cas. 1917D, 629 (1917).

[46] Hawkins v. Bleakley, 243 U.S. 210, 37 S. Ct. 255, 61 L. Ed. 678 (1917).

[47] Mountain Timber Co. v. Washington, 243 U.S. 219, 37 S. Ct. 260, 61 L. Ed. 685, Ann. Cas. 1917D, 642 (1917).

Of course, we cannot ignore the question whether the new arrangement is arbitrary and unreasonable, from the standpoint of natural justice. Respecting this, it is important to be observed that the act applies only to disabling or fatal personal injuries received in the course of hazardous employment in gainful occupation. Reduced to its elements, the situation to be dealt with is this: Employer and employee, by mutual consent, engage in a common operation intended to be advantageous to both; the employee is to contribute his personal services, and for these is to receive wages, and ordinarily nothing more; the employer is to furnish plant, facilities, organization, capital, credit, is to control and manage the operation, paying the wages and other expenses, disposing of the product at such prices as he can obtain, taking all the profits, if any there be, and of necessity bearing the entire losses. In the nature of things, there is more or less of a probability that the employee may lose his life through some accidental injury arising out of the employment, leaving his widow or children deprived of their natural support; or that he may sustain an injury not mortal but resulting in his total or partial disablement, temporary or permanent, with corresponding impairment of earning capacity. The physical suffering must be borne by the employee alone; the laws of nature prevent this from being evaded or shifted to another, and the statute makes no attempt to afford an equivalent in compensation. But, besides, there is the loss of earning power; a loss of that which stands to the employee as his capital in trade. This is a loss arising out of the business, and, however it may be charged up, is an expense of the operation, as truly as the cost of repairing broken machinery or any other expense that ordinarily is paid by the employer. Who is to bear the charge? It is plain that, on grounds of natural justice, it is not unreasonable for the State, while relieving the employer from responsibility for damages measured by common-law standards and payable in cases where he or those for whose conduct he is answerable are found to be at fault, to require him to contribute a reasonable amount, and according to a reasonable and definite scale, by way of compensation for the loss of earning power incurred in the common enterprise, irrespective of the question of negligence, instead of leaving the entire loss to rest where it may chance to fall — that is, upon the injured employee or his dependents. Nor can it be deemed arbitrary and unreasonable, from the standpoint of the employee's interest, to supplant a system under which he assumed the entire risk of injury in ordinary cases, and in others had a right to recover an amount more or less speculative upon proving facts of negligence that often were difficult to prove, and substitute a system under which in all ordinary cases of accidental injury he is sure of a definite and easily ascertained compensation, not being obliged to assume the entire loss in any case but in all cases assuming any loss beyond the prescribed scale. . . .

§ 2.04   GROWTH OF WORKERS' COMPENSATION IN THE UNITED STATES

[1]   1910–1969

With fears of constitutional impediments virtually removed, the compensation system grew and expanded with a rapidity that has few parallels in comparable fields of law. By 1920 all but 8 states had adopted compensation acts, and on January 1, 1949, the last of the then 48 states, Mississippi, came under the system.

Extension of coverage has taken the form not only of adding jurisdictions, but of broadening the boundaries of individual acts, as to persons, employments, and kinds of injury (particularly occupational disease) covered. At the same time, in those few remaining states where election is permissible, the percentage of employers choosing compensation coverage has increased until, in most states, the nonelecting employer is exceptional.

The principal occupational groups not yet brought within compensation acts are domestic and agricultural workers, who are excluded by many acts. Other exclusions are accounted for by small firms (since some acts exempt employers with less than a stated minimum number of employees), and "casual workers." The percentage of coverage looks slightly better if interstate rail employees are included, since they have the protection of the Federal Employers' Liability Act, which is regarded by some segments of railway labor as preferable to workers' compensation acts.

[2] 1970–1985

The National Commission on State Workmen's Compensation Laws, which was created by Congress in the Occupational Health and Safety Act of 1970, and which consisted of 15 members appointed by the President, submitted its report in July, 1972, after about a year of intensive hearings, studies, staff, analysis, and Commission discussions. The Commission, which was designed to be broadly representative of workers' compensation agencies, business, labor, carriers, the medical profession, compensation experts from the academic community, and the general public, unanimously recommended a set of standards for state workers' compensation that in almost every respect equalled or exceeded the highest standards proposed by various other groups in the past. The essential elements recommended by the Commission were: compulsory coverage in all acts; elimination of all numerical and occupational exemptions to coverage, including domestic and farm labor; full coverage of work-related diseases; full medical and physical rehabilitation services without arbitrary limits; a broad extra-territoriality provision; elimination of arbitrary limits on duration or total sum of benefits; and a weekly benefit maximum that rises from an immediate 66 2/3 percent to an ultimate 200 percent of average weekly wage in the state. As to the crucial question of what role the federal government should play in bringing about adoption of these standards, the Commission recommended that states be given three years to bring their laws into conformity with these recommendations, after which time federal legislation should be passed that would "guarantee compliance" with these standards, the precise mechanism for this guarantee being left somewhat vague in the report.

The decade following the Commission's report was marked by the most dramatic liberalization of state compensation statutes in history. Unlimited medical benefits became universal, as did occupational disease coverage. More than half the states met the 1975 standard of having a weekly maximum benefit of at least 100% of the state's average weekly wage. And the range of employees covered was substantially increased.

During much of this period, various bills were pending in Congress designed to translate into concrete action the Commission's hint of federal intervention. They typically took the form of a set of minimum standards, accompanied by some sort of compliance device if a state failed to conform. No doubt the *in terrorem* effect of these bills contributed to the states' incentive to improve their laws, but the bills themselves never came close to passage, not least because no practical enforcement mechanism could be contrived that would effectively ensure compliance without actually federalizing workers' compensation — a move that has always been and still is politically unthinkable. By about 1980 the federal standards effort had been largely forgotten, and the spotlight moved to specific problems, notably that of asbestos-related diseases, for which it appeared that an *ad hoc* federal solution might be necessary and appropriate.

[3] 1986–Present

A trend of note beginning in the early 1990s is the increasing use of mediation and other forms of alternative dispute resolution in workers' compensation cases. By 1995, at least 17 states had incorporated some form of mediation into their contested claims process. Other approaches include the use of arbitration, and the use of an ombudsman whose role goes beyond being a provider of information and who may actually work to facilitate a settlement or appear in a claimant's behalf.

Second, the interaction of workers' compensation with other areas of federal and state law has been occupying more and more of the time and attention of workers' compensation attorneys. A prime example, addressed in later chapters, is the Americans with Disabilities Act of 1990, which raised such questions as this: can a worker legitimately receive workers' compensation for disability wage loss while claiming under the ADA that he or she is capable of working with reasonable accommodation?

But the most important phenomenon in workers' compensation law in recent years has been the emergence of a wave of legislation, beginning in the mid- to late-1980s with states such as Oregon and Texas, having as its primary goal the curbing of spiraling increases in employer costs. Contributing to this picture were increased costs of medical care, increased number, length, and litigiousness of contested administrative proceedings, greater attorney involvement, and the perception of widespread claimant fraud. By 1997 over two-thirds of the states had, to one degree or another, enacted legislation reacting to these concerns. While there are many differences, changes commonly found in this legislation include (1) restrictions on the right of the claimant to choose his or her medical provider, (2) utilization of managed care, (3) anti-fraud provisions, (4) measures designed to reduce attorney involvement at the administrative level, (5) measures designed to encourage early resolution of claims, and (6) measures designed to reduce duplicate recovery among different reimbursement systems. Also, some of these measures have made it more difficult for claimants to prevail in cases involving preexisting conditions, "mental-mental" or stress cases, or carpal tunnel or other repetitive motion injuries. Termed "reform" legislation by some, the claimant's bar takes issue with this usage, pointing out that, unlike the reforms of the 1970s, these measures have tended to cut back on the right to compensation and on the level of benefits. These battles have often been highly political and polarizing to the groups involved. And they are not over.

Part 2

"ARISING OUT OF THE EMPLOYMENT"

Chapter 3
GENERAL PRINCIPLES AND DOCTRINES

§ 3.01 SUMMARY OF STATUTORY PROVISIONS

The heart of every compensation act, and the source of most litigation in the compensation field, is the coverage formula.

Over 40 states, and the Longshore and Harbor Workers' Compensation Act,[1] have adopted the entire British Compensation Act formula: injury "arising out of and in the course of employment." One state, Utah, changed it to "arising out of *or* in the course of employment."[2] As to variants on the "arising out of" portion, West Virginia preferred "resulting from";[3] Wyoming substituted the phrase "injuries sustained . . . as a result of their employment";[4] Pennsylvania has adopted the phrase "arising in the course of his

---

[1] 33 U.S.C. §§ 901–945, 947–950 (LEXIS through 1999).

[2] Utah Code Ann. § 35-1-45 (1953). Utah has since adopted the typical coverage formula of "arising out of and in the course of employment." Utah Code Ann. §34A-2-102 (LEXIS through 1998).

[3] W. Va. Code Ann., Ch. 23, Art. 4, § 1 (LEXIS through 1998).

[4] Wyo. Stat. §§ 27–49 (III) (1967). Wyoming statutory law now reflects the typical coverage formula of "arising out of and in the course of employment." Wyo. Stat. Ann. § 27-14-102 (LEXIS through 1999). However, Wyoming uniquely interprets it to mean that "arising" and "course" are the same thing. *See* Corean v. State ex rel. Workers' Comp. Div., 723 P.2d 58 (Wyo. 1986).

employment . . . ".[5] As to the "course of employment" concept, 47 states have this phrase; while Wisconsin has, instead, employed the phrase "while performing service growing out of and incidental to his or her employment";[6] the Federal Employees' Compensation Act uses the phrase "sustained while in the performance of duty."[7]

Few groups of statutory words in the history of law have had to bear the weight of such a mountain of interpretation as has been heaped upon this slender foundation. It is not surprising, then, that to make the task of construction easier, the phrase was broken in half, with the "arising out of" portion construed to refer to causal origin, and the "course of employment" portion to the time, place, and circumstances of the accident in relation to the employment. There are plentiful dicta which tell us that each test must be independently applied and met.[8] For the most part, this observation does no harm; but it should never be forgotten that the basic concept of compensation coverage is unitary, not dual, and is best expressed in the term "work connection." In a later chapter, this question will be reopened to show how an uncompromising insistence on independent application of the two portions of the test can, in certain cases, exclude clearly work-connected injuries.[9]

§ 3.02   THE FIVE LINES OF INTERPRETATION OF "ARISING"

[1]   Introduction

Of the two components of the almost-universal coverage formula — "arising out of and in the course of" employment — the "arising out of" test is primarily concerned with causal connection. Most courts in the past have interpreted "arising out of employment" to require a showing that the injury was caused by an increased risk to which claimant, as distinct from the general public, was subjected by the employment. A substantial number have now modified this to accept a showing merely that the risk, even if common to the public, was actually a risk of the employment. An important and growing group of jurisdictions has adopted the positional-risk test, under which an injury is compensable if it would not have happened but for the fact that the conditions or obligations of the employment put claimant in the position where he or she was injured.

The peculiar-risk test, requiring that the source of harm be in its nature (as distinguished from its quantity) peculiar to the occupation, and proximate-cause test, requiring foreseeability and absence of intervening cause, are now largely obsolete.

[2]   Peculiar-Risk Doctrine

Under the peculiar-risk doctrine, which in the early dawn of American compensation law was actually the dominant rule, the claimant had to show that the source of the harm was in its nature peculiar to his occupation. Accordingly, even if the work subjected a claimant to a tremendously increased quantitative risk of injury by heat, or cold, or lightning, that claimant might be turned away with the comment that "everyone is subject to the same weather."

---

[5]   77 Pa. Cons. Stat. § 431 (LEXIS through 1998).

[6]   Wis. Stat. § 102.03(1)(c) (LEXIS through 1998).

[7]   5 U.S.C. § 8102(a), FECA § 1(a) (LEXIS through 1999).

Puerto Rico has a formulation of its own: "Caused by any act or function inherent in their work or employment, when such accidents happen in the course of said work or employment, and as a consequence thereof." P.R. Laws Ann. Tit. 11, § 2 (LEXIS through 1995).

[8]   Ward & Gow v. Krinsky, 259 U.S. 503, 42 S. Ct. 529, 66 L. Ed. 1033, 28 A.L.R. 1207 (1922).

[9]   *See* Ch. 8, § 8.11, *below.*

Thus, in *Robinson's Case*,[10] a laborer froze his foot while working in the public square all night in very cold weather. The court said: "[T]here is nothing to show that the employee was exposed to any greater risk of freezing his foot than the ordinary person engaged in outdoor work in cold weather."[11] But, of course, the ordinary person is not engaged in outdoor work in cold weather; and so to limit the comparison was to rob the claimant's employment of the only distinctive feature it had for present purposes.

[3] Increased-Risk Doctrine

The peculiar risk test gradually achieved a well-deserved oblivion, and was replaced by the increased-risk test. This test differs from the peculiar-risk test in that the distinctiveness of the employment risk can be contributed by the increased *quantity* of a risk that is *qualitatively* not peculiar to the employment.

The increased-risk test is still the prevalent test in the United States today, and, even in states that have accepted the positional-risk doctrine, a prudent lawyer will, in a lightning case for example, begin by trying to prove that the employment increased the risk of exposure to lightning by placing claimant on a height, or near metal, or in contact with an element that conducts electricity.[12]

[4] Actual-Risk Doctrine

Under this doctrine, a substantial number of courts are saying, in effect, "We do not care whether this risk was also common to the public, if in fact it was a risk of *this* employment." It is a more defensible rule than the preceding ones, since there is no real statutory basis for insisting upon a peculiar or increased risk, as long as the employment subjected claimant to the actual risk that injured him. One effect is to permit recoveries in most street-risk cases and in a much greater proportion of act-of-God cases.

[5] Positional-Risk Doctrine

An important and growing number of courts are accepting the full implications of the positional-risk test: An injury arises out of the employment if it would not have occurred but for the fact that the conditions and obligations of the employment placed claimant in the position where he or she was injured. It is even more common for the test to be approved and used in particular situations. This theory supports compensation, for example, in cases of stray bullets, roving lunatics, and other situations in which the only connection of the employment with the injury is that its obligations placed the employee in the particular place at the particular time injury occurred by some neutral force (meaning by "neutral" neither personal to the claimant nor distinctly associated with the employment).

§ 3.03 THE CATEGORIES OF RISK

[1] Introduction

All risks causing injury to a claimant can be brought within three categories: risks distinctly associated with the employment, risks personal to the claimant, and "neutral" risks — i.e., risks having no particular employment or personal character. Harms from

---

[10] Robinson's Case, 292 Mass. 543, 198 N.E. 760 (1935).

[11] Robinson's Case, 292 Mass. 543, 546, 198 N.E. 760, 761 (1935).

[12] For a typical increased-risk lightning award, see Bauer's Case, 314 Mass. 4, 49 N.E.2d 118 (1943). The increased risk included presence on top of an exposed hill, wet clothes, and nearness to an iron bed and electrical wiring.

the first are universally compensable. Those from the second are universally noncompensable. It is within the third category that most controversy in modern compensation law occurs.

[2] Risks Distinctly Associated with the Employment

This group comprises all the obvious kinds of injury that one thinks of at once as industrial injury. All the things that can go wrong around a modern factory, mill, mine, transportation system, or construction project — machinery breaking, objects falling, explosives exploding, tractors tipping, fingers getting caught in gears, excavations caving in, and so on — are clearly in this category and constitute the bulk of what not only the public but perhaps also the original draftsmen of compensation acts had in mind as their proper concern. Equally obviously associated with employment, however, are also the occupational diseases, which as the very name implies, are produced by the particular substances or conditions inherent in the environment of the employment. As far as the "arising" test is concerned, this group causes no trouble, since all these risks fall readily within the increased-risk test and are considered work-connected in all jurisdictions.

[3] Risks Personal to the Claimant

At the other extreme are origins of harm so clearly personal that, even if they take effect while the employee is on the job, they could not possibly be attributed to the employment. If the time has come for the employee to die a natural death, or to expire from the effects of some disease or internal weakness of which he or she would as promptly have expired whether working or not, the fact that this demise takes place in an employment setting rather than at home does not, of course, make the death compensable. Or if the employee has a mortal personal enemy who has sworn to seek the employee out wherever he or she may be, and if this enemy happens to find and murder the employee while the latter is at work, the employment cannot be said to have had any causal relation to the death. The same has been held to be true when (as actually happened in one case)[13] an employee, for reasons of his own, carried a bomb in his bosom, and the bomb went off during business hours.

[4] Neutral Risks

Between these two areas lies the third: that of risks of neither distinctly employment nor distinctly personal character. Illustrations of this category may be drawn from a wide variety of controversial cases. A worker busily engaged in the middle of a factory yard may be hit by a stray bullet out of nowhere, bit by a mad dog, stabbed by a lunatic running amok, struck by lightning, thrown down by a hurricane, killed by an enemy bomb, injured by a piece of tin blown from someone's roof, shot by a child playing with an air rifle, murdered as a result of mistaken identity, felled by debris from a distant explosion, or blinded by a flying beetle.

Another kind of neutral-risk case is that in which the cause itself, or the character of the cause, is simply unknown. An employee may be found to have died on the job from unexplained causes, or may suffer a slip or fall for no reason that anyone, including himself, can explain. An employee may be attacked by unknown persons, whose motives may have been personal or related to the employment.

There are thus three categories of risk; but unfortunately, there are only two places where the loss may fall — on the industry or on the employee. And so the question becomes, which bears the burden of this in-between category of harms?

---

[13] Bogavich v. Westinghouse Elec. & Mfg. Co., 162 Pa. Super. 388, 57 A.2d 598 (1948).

The usual answer in the past has been to leave this loss on the employee, on the theory that it is the employee who must meet the burden of proof of establishing affirmatively a clear causal connection between the working conditions and the occurrence of the injury. More recently, some courts have reasoned in the following vein: Either the employer or the employee must bear the loss; to show connection with the employment, there is at least the fact that the injury occurred while the employee was working; to show connection with the employee personally there is nothing; therefore, although the work connection is slender, it is at least stronger than any connection with the claimant's personal life.

[5] Mixed Risks

Another troublesome problem is that of mixed risks, in which a personal cause and an employment cause combine to produce the harm. The most common example is that of a person with a weak heart who dies because of strain occasioned by the employment. In broadest theoretical outline, the rule is quite simple. The law does not weigh the relative importance of the two causes, nor does it look for primary and secondary causes; it merely inquires whether the employment was a contributing factor. If it was, the concurrence of the personal cause will usually not defeat compensability.

§ 3.04 ACTS OF GOD AND EXPOSURE

[1] Introduction

All courts agree that injury due to lightning, windstorms, earthquake, freezing, sunstroke, and exposure to contagious diseases arises out of the employment if the employment increases the risk of this kind of harm. Some courts will accept a showing that the risk was an actual or positional risk of the particular employment, regardless whether it is greater or less than that of the general public. One exception used to soften the increased-risk rule is the holding that if the harm, though initiated by an act of God, takes effect through contact of claimant with any part of the premises, causal connection with the employment is shown.

[2] Lightning, Tornadoes, Windstorms, Etc.

WHETRO v. AWKERMAN
383 Mich. 235, 174 N.W.2d 783 (1970)

T. G. Kavanagh, Justice.

These cases were consolidated pursuant to our order of September 5, 1968 wherein we granted leave to appeal prior to decision by the Court of Appeals in the case of Emery v. Huge Company, 381 Mich. 774. They were argued together in our April 1969 term.

They turn on the same question, for the damages for which workmen's compensation was awarded in each case were caused by the Palm Sunday 1965 tornadoes which devastated parts of Southern Michigan.

Carl Whetro was injured when the tornado destroyed the residence wherein he was working for his employer and seeks reimbursement for his medical expenses. Henry E. Emery was killed when the motel in which he was staying while on a business trip for his employer was destroyed by the tornado, and his widow seeks compensation for his death.

In each case the hearing referee found that the employee's injury arose out of and in the course of his employment. The award was affirmed by the appeal board in each case and by the Court of Appeals in the Whetro case.

The defendant-appellants in both cases base their defense on the assertion that tornadoes are "acts of God" or acts of nature and injuries which are caused by them do not arise "out of" the employment and hence are not compensable under the Workmen's Compensation Act.

For this reason they maintain that the cases were erroneously decided as a matter of law and the awards should be set aside.

The appellants in each case maintain that the injury did not arise "out of" the employment because that phrase as it is used in the act refers to a causal connection between the event which put in motion the forces which caused the injury and the work itself or the conditions under which it is required to be performed.

Employment as a caretaker-gardener or salesman, they argue, does not include tornadoes as incidents or conditions of the work, and the path of injury is determined by the tornado, not the employment.

Appellants cite a series of Michigan decisions involving injury by lightning; *Klawinski v. Lake Shore & Michigan Southern R. Co.* (1915), 185 Mich. 643, 152 N.W. 213, L.R.A. 1916A, 342; *Thier v. Widdifield* (1920), 210 Mich. 355, 178 N.W. 16; *Nelson v. Country Club of Detroit* (1951), 329 Mich. 479, 45 N.W.2d 362; *Kroon v. Kalamazoo County Road Commission* (1954), 339 Mich. 1, 62 N.W.2d 641, in which compensation was denied and assert that a tornado is like lightning in that it acts capriciously, leaving its victims and the untouched side by side. The decisions in all of these "lightning cases" denied compensation on the ground that the injury did not arise "out of" the employment because the employment did not expose the workman to any increased risk or to a more hazardous situation than faced by others in the area.

The Court of Appeals was able to distinguish between a tornado and a bolt of lightning as a causative force of injury and base its decision affirming the award for Carl Whetro on the reasoning of the Massachusetts supreme court in *Caswell's Case* (1940), 305 Mass. 500, 26 N.E.2d 328, wherein recovery was allowed for injuries received when a brick wall of the employer's factory was blown down on workmen during a hurricane. This "contact with the premises" met the requirement that the injury arise "out of" the employment in the mind of the Court of Appeals.

We are unable to accept the distinction drawn between a tornado and bolt of lightning when viewed as the cause of an injury. As we see it, a tornado, no less than a bolt of lightning or an earthquake or flood is an "act of God" and if the phrase "out of" the employment in the Workmen's Compensation Act necessarily entails the notion of proximate causality, no injury received because of an "act of God" should be compensable.

But we are satisfied that it is no longer necessary to establish a relationship of proximate causality between employment and an injury in order to establish compensability. Accordingly we no longer regard an "act of God" whether it be a tornado, lightning, earthquake, or flood as a defense to a claim for a work connected injury. Such a defense retains too much of the idea that an employer should not pay compensation unless he is somehow at fault. This concept from the law of tort is inconsistent with the law of workmen's compensation.

The purpose of the compensation act as set forth in its title, is to promote the welfare of the people of Michigan relating to the liability of employers for injuries or death sustained by their employees. The legislative policy is to provide financial and medical benefits to the victims of work connected injuries in an efficient, dignified and certain form. The act allocates the burden of such payments to the most appropriate source of payment, the consumer of the product. [*Court's footnote omitted.*]

Fault has nothing to do with whether or not compensation is payable. The economic impact on an injured workman and his family is the same whether the injury was caused by the employer's fault or otherwise.

We hold that the law in Michigan today no longer requires the establishment of a proximately causal connection between the employment and the injury to entitle a claimant to compensation. The cases which have allowed recovery for street risks, increased risks, and on the premises accidents were made without consideration of the proximate causal connection between the nature of the employment and the injury. They have brought the law in Michigan to the point where it can be said today that if the employment is the occasion of the injury, even though not the proximate cause, compensation should be paid.

Such a development of the Michigan law is paralleled by the development of the law in England and Massachusetts — the two jurisdictions which served as Michigan's model in the original legislative drafting and judicial construction of the Workmen's Compensation Act.

The early Michigan case of *Hopkins v. Michigan Sugar Co.* (1915), 184 Mich. 87, 150 N.W. 325, L.R.A. 1916A, 310, imported the "causality" concept into the requirement that the injury must arise "out of" the employment. The court drew this interpretation from the English case of *Fitzgerald v. Clark & Son* [1908] 2 KB 796, and the *McNicol's Case* (1913), 215 Mass. 497, 102 N.E. 697, L.R.A. 1916A, 306. Both of these jurisdictions have since adopted the doctrine of positional risk. *See Powell v. Great Western Railway Co.* (1940), 1 All Eng. Rep. 87, and *Baran's Case* (1957), 336 Mass. 342, 145 N.E.2d 726.

The Massachusetts court said in *Baran's Case*, p. 344, 145 N.E.2d p. 727: "We think that they [recent cases] disclose the development of a consistent course which is a departure from the earlier view expressed, for example in [*McNicol's Case*]. . . . The injury 'need not arise out of the nature of the employment. . . . The question is whether his employment brought him in contact with the risk that in fact caused his death.'"

The English court, in *Powell, above*, held that if the work required the employee to be at the place of injury the accident arose "out of" his employment.

Accordingly, we hold that the employment of Carl Whetro and Henry E. Emery in each case was the occasion of the injury which they suffered and therefore the injuries arose "out of" and in the course of their employment.

The award in each case is affirmed.

For the reasons set forth therein, in keeping with the policy observed in *Bricker v. Green* (1946), 313 Mich. 218, 21 N.W. 2d 105, 163 A.L.R. 697; and *Parker v. Port Huron Hospital* (1960), 361 Mich. 1, 105 N.W.2d 1, the rule of law announced herein will apply to the instant case and all claims for compensation arising after March 12, 1970 the date of the filing of this opinion.

T. M. KAVANAGH and ADAMS, JJ., concurred with T. G. KAVANAGH, J.

BLACK, J. concurred specially.

BRENNAN, CHIEF JUSTICE (dissenting).

The function of the workmen's compensation act is to place the financial burden of industrial injuries upon the industries themselves, and spread that cost ultimately among the consumers.

This humane legislation was developed because the industrialization of our civilization had left in its wake a trail of broken bodies.

Employers were absolved from general liability for negligence, in exchange for the imposition of more certain liability under the act.

But it is a mistake to say that employers were absolved from fault. Liability is the basis of legal remedy. Fault is the basis of moral responsibility.

The workmen's compensation law is society's expression of the moral responsibility of employers and consumers to the workmen whose health and whose lives are sacrificed to industrial and commercial progress and production.

Fault is not the same thing as proximate cause. The compensation law does not use the word *cause*. Rather, it expresses the concept of employer and consumer responsibility in the phrase "arising out of and in the course of" the employment.

The terms "arising out of" and "in the course of" are not redundant. They mean two different things. An adulterous cobbler shot at his last by his jealous wife may be "in the course of" his employment. But the injury does not "arise out of" his job. On what basis of moral responsibility should his injuries be paid for by his employer? By what logic would society decree that his disability should add a farthing to the price of shoes?

The workmen's compensation law is not a utopian attempt to put a price tag on all human suffering and incorporate it into the cost of living.

Lightning, flood, tornados and estranged wives will always be with us, in this vale of tears. They were the occasion of human injury when our forebears were tilling the soil with sharp sticks. They are not a by-product of the industrial revolution, nor are they in any sense the moral responsibility of those who profit by or enjoy the fruits of, our modern industrialized society.

I would reverse without apology for the precedents.

DETHMERS and KELLY, JJ., concurred with BRENNAN, C. J.

PROBLEMS

(1) Do you agree that tornadoes and hurricanes are, for present purposes, indistinguishable from lightning? Does this depend on whether you are applying the increased risk, actual risk, or positional risk theory?

(2) Do you find cogent Chief Justice Brennan's equation of tornadoes and estranged wives in this vale of tears?

[3] Exposure to Heat and Cold

HUGHES v. TRUSTEES OF ST. PATRICK'S CATHEDRAL
245 N.Y. 201, 156 N.E. 665 (1927)

[A section boss had suffered heat prostration while working in a cemetery.]

PER CURIAM. Heat prostration is an accidental injury arising out of and during the course of the employment, if the nature of the employment exposes the workman to risk of such injury. *Madura v. City of New York*, 238 N. Y. 214, 144 N. E. 505. Although the risk may be common to all who are exposed to the sun's rays on a hot day, the question is whether the employment exposes the employee to the risk. *Katz v. A. Kadans & Co.*, 232 N.Y. 420, 134 N.E. 330, 23 A.L.R. 401.

CARDOZO, C. J., and POUND, CRANE, ANDREWS, LEHMAN, and O'BRIEN, JJ., concur.

KELLOGG, J., not sitting.

COMMENT

Note the kind of elegant two-line simplicity you get when your panel is made up of the likes of Cardozo, Pound, et al.

HANSON v. REICHELT
452 N.W.2d 164 (Iowa 1990)

Lavorato, Justice.

This appeal arises out of the death of a farm employee who suffered a heatstroke while working. The Iowa industrial commissioner denied benefits, finding that the employee's injury did not arise out of his employment. In making this finding, the commissioner applied the general public-increased risk rule, a rule this court first approved in a workers' compensation case involving heatstroke more than fifty years ago. . . . The district court affirmed the commissioner's decision.

. . . .

We now adopt the actual risk rule in workers' compensation cases involving injuries from exposure to the elements. . . .

On June 24, 1983, D. Van Maanen agreed to buy some hay from Sherman Reichelt. Reichelt had already baled some of the hay. The remainder of the hay sold to Van Maanen had to be baled, and all of the hay had to be stacked on a hayrack and transported from Riechelt's field.

Reichelt hired Dennis L. Hanson to help with the baling. When the baling operation began, the weather was very hot; the recorded temperature that day reached a high of 95 degrees.

At about 2:30 p.m. on June 24, Van Maanen's wife, Van Maanen, Reichelt, and Hanson began working in the field. Hanson's job was twofold: he stacked bales and drove empty and full hayracks to and from the field. Each bale weighed about sixty pounds. Hanson did this for about an hour and a half. But at no time did he work more than twenty-five minutes without a break.

At some point Hanson quit and sat down in the field. About thirty minutes later, Reichelt drove up in his pickup and found Hanson passed out.

Reichelt called for medical assistance; an ambulance arrived about 5:00 p.m. and took Hanson to a hospital in Newton. The doctors there determined that Hanson had suffered a heatstroke. Later Hanson was transferred to Iowa Methodist Medical Center in Des Moines where he underwent extensive treatment and finally died on July 18, 1983.

Hanson's father and mother were appointed administrators of their son's estate. As such the parents filed a petition with the Iowa Industrial Commission in June 1984. *See* Iowa Code § 85.26(4) (1983). They sought medical and death benefits from Reichelt and Reichelt's insurance carrier.

. . . .

II. In these proceedings the administrators had the burden to prove by a preponderance of the evidence that Hanson had suffered an injury that arose out of and in the course of his employment. *McDowell v. Town of Clarksville*, 241 N.W.2d 904, 907–08 (Iowa 1976). In the context of workers' compensation law, the concept of proximate cause is found in the words "out of." *Crowe v. DeSoto Consol. School Dist.*, 246 Iowa 402, 406, 68 N.W.2d 63, 65 (1955).

The words "in the course of" simply refer to the time, place, and circumstances of the injury. *Id.* So an injury occurs in the course of employment when it happens within the period of employment at a place the employee may reasonably be, and while the employee is doing work or something incidental to it. *Cedar Rapids Community School Dist. v. Cady*, 278 N.W.2d 298, 299 (Iowa 1979).

Both sides agree that Hanson's injury — the heatstroke — arose during the course of his employment. So, as we said, our sole issue is whether Hanson's injury arose out of his employment.

III. In the past this court addressed the issue whether a heatstroke is compensable in workers' compensation cases. *See, e.g.,* Wax v. Des Moines Asphalt Paving Corp., 220 Iowa 804, 263 N.W. 333 (1935); *West v. Phillips,* 227 Iowa 612, 288 N.W. 625 (1939). In *Wax* an employee suffered a heat-stroke while digging a trench in 100+ degree temperatures. The industrial commissioner allowed benefits, and the district court affirmed. Viewing the same facts, we held as a matter of law that the heatstroke did not arise out of the employment. In other words, there was no causal connection between the employment and the injury. *Wax,* 220 Iowa at 865–67, 288 N.W. at 334–35.

In reaching this conclusion, we adopted and applied the general public-increased risk rule which provides that

> [i]f the employment brings with it no greater exposure to injurious results from natural causes, and neither contributes to produce these nor to aggravate their effect, as from lightning, severe heat or cold, than those to which persons generally in that locality, whether so employed or not, are equally exposed there is no causal connection between the employment and the injury. But where the employment brings a greater exposure and injury results, the injury does arise out of the employment.

Id. at 865–66, 288 N.W. at 334. Simply put, the rule permits recovery "only in cases where the [employee] is exposed to conditions of temperature unusual or more intense than those experienced by [employees] of the community in general." *Id.* at 866, 288 N.W. at 334.

Relying on the same rule, we reached an opposite result in *West v. Phillips.* There a bakery employee became ill while working the night shift. The employee died the next day. His doctor testified that the employee showed substantially all the symptoms of heat exhaustion. The doctor performed an autopsy. He found that the employee had severe heart trouble and that the heat exhaustion had hastened the employee's death. *West,* 227 Iowa at 614, 620, 288 N.W. at 629.

In *West* experts testified that heat infiltration from the tar roof, an inefficient fan inside, and artificial heat from the oven combined to make it 10 to 12 degrees hotter inside. During the day, the temperatures outside had reached 108. *Id.* at 617–18; 288 N.W. at 627–28.

We thought that the testimony of the experts was sufficient to sustain a finding "that there was excessive heat in the bakeshop caused by artificial heat." *Id.* at 618, 288 N.W. at 628. Such a finding, of course, met the recovery requirement of the general public-increased risk rule: the employee must be exposed to conditions of temperature unusual or more intense than those experienced by employees of the community in general. In addition, we thought the doctor's testimony was sufficient to establish the necessary causal connection between the employee's death and the heat exhaustion. *Id.*

The facts here are on all fours with the facts in *Wax.* So it is not surprising that the deputy reached the same conclusion as we did in *Wax*: no causal connection between the death and the injury.

One noted authority criticizes the general public-increased risk rule because of the way courts define the general public:

> The heart of the difficulty is almost entirely in defining the general public with which the comparison is made. It is here that many of the negative cases have gone wide of the mark. Clearly, since the object of the comparison between the exposure of this employee and the exposure of the public is to isolate and identify the distinctive characteristics of this employment, the comparison should be made with a broad cross section of the public having no characteristics specially selected because they resemble those of the employment. Because most of these cases arise during extreme hot, cold, rainy, or stormy weather, the most direct way to approach a working rule is to ask: What does the average

man, free of the obligation of any particular employment, do when it is twenty below, or a hundred in the shade, or raining, sleeting or snowing violently? There may be various answers as to what he does, but there is one clear answer as to what he does not do. He does not stay outdoors all day.

1 Larson, Workmen's Compensation Law, § 8.42 (1984).

Larson gives an example of the proper application of the general public-increased risk rule from a Texas sunstroke case in which the court succinctly and clearly summed up the rule:

> In the case before us the very work which the decedent was doing for his employer exposed him to a greater hazard from heatstroke than the general public was exposed to for the simple reason that the general public were not pushing wheelbarrow loads of sand in the hot sun on that day.

Id. (quoting from *American Gen. Ins. Co. v. Webster*, 118 S.W.2d 1082, 1085–86 (1938).

Several jurisdictions have discarded the general public-increased risk rule in cases involving effects of exposure to the elements. In its place, these courts have adopted the actual risk rule. *See, e.g., Hughes v. St. Patrick's Cathedral*, 245 N.Y. 201, 156 N.E. 665 (1927); *Eagle River Bldg. & Supply Co. v. Peck*, 199 Wis. 192, 225 N.W. 690 (1929); 1 Larson at 8.43.

In *Hughes*, the employee suffered heat prostration while working outdoors. In holding for the employee, the court summed up the actual risk rule in two sentences:

> Heat prostration is an accidental injury arising out of and during the course of the employment, if the nature of the employment exposes the workman to risk of such injury. Although the risk may be common to all who are exposed to the suns rays on a hot day, the question is whether the employment exposes the employee to the risk.

245 N.Y. at 202–03, 156 N.E. at 665.

Reaching the same result on similar reasoning in an accidental freezing case, the Wisconsin Supreme Court said:

> The injury in the instant case clearly grew out of and was incidental to the employment. It makes no difference that the exposure was common to all out of door employments in that locality in that kind of weather. The injury grew out of that employment and was incidental to it. It was a hazard of the industry.

Eagle River Bldg. & Supply Co., 199 Wis. at 196, 225 N.W. at 691.

We think the actual risk rule is the better rule and more in line with how we construe our Workers' Compensation Act. We construe the Act liberally in favor of the employee; we resolve all doubts in favor of the employee. *Teel v. McCord*, 394 N.W.2d 405, 406–07 (Iowa 1986).

Moreover, the actual risk rule makes no comparison between risks found by the employee and those found by the general public. So the rule is not subject to the same criticisms that have been voiced against the general public-increased risk rule.

We adopt the actual risk rule in cases involving injuries from exposure to the elements. If the nature of the employment exposes the employee to the risk of such an injury, the employee suffers an accidental injury arising out of and during the course of the employment. And it makes no difference that the risk was common to the general public on the day of the injury.

IV. Because the district court's judgment is based on a rule of law we now renounce, we must reverse. . . .

§ 3.05 THE STREET-RISK DOCTRINE

All courts now agree that street or highway injuries to employees such as traveling salespeople, delivery persons, and solicitors, whose duties increase their exposure to the hazards of the street, arise out of the employment, although the nature of the risk, as distinguished from the degree, is not peculiar to the employment. A large number of courts have gone one step further by holding that injury from such risks is compensable regardless of whether such exposure is continuous or only occasional, so long as the exposure is in fact occasioned by the employment. At the same time, the concept of street risks has been broadened far beyond the original idea of traffic perils, and has been applied to almost any mishap whose locale is the street, including simple falls, stray bullets, falling trees, and foul balls.

The rules that have been followed on street injuries can be classified under three headings: (1) the earliest and strictest application of the increased- *and* peculiar-risk test, which resulted in denials in all cases, on the theory that the *nature* of the hazard was common to all; (2) the increased- (but not peculiar-) risk test, under which those classes of employees whose duties carried them into the street more often than ordinary people were allowed compensation for street injuries, on the theory that while the *kind* of exposure was common to the public, the *degree* of exposure was increased; and (3) the actual-risk test, under which it is immaterial even whether the degree of exposure is increased, if in fact the employment subjected the employee to the hazards of the street, whether continuously or infrequently.

Of these three, the first (1) is obsolete; all courts now are prepared to go as far as the second (2); and the third (3) has achieved the status of majority rule, if full effect is given both to general statements and to the implications of factual holdings by modern courts.

KATZ v. A. KADANS & CO.
232 N.Y. 420, 134 N.E. 330 (1922)

Pound, J.

This is a workmen's compensation case. Louis Katz, the claimant, was a dairyman's chauffeur. On May 7, 1920, when he was driving his employer's car west on Canal street after delivering some cheese, an insane man stabbed him. A lot of people were running after the insane man and he stabbed any one near him. The question is whether claimant's injuries arose out of his employment.

If the work itself involves exposure to perils of the street, strange, unanticipated, and infrequent though they may be, the employee passes along the streets when on his master's occasions under the protection of the statute. This is the rule unequivocally laid down by the House of Lords in England:

> When a workman is sent into the street on his master's business, . . . his employment necessarily involves exposure to the risks of the streets and injury from such a cause [necessarily] arises out of his employment. Finlay, L. C., in *Dennis v. White*, [1917] L. R. App. Cas. 479.

So we have to concern ourselves only with the question whether claimant's accident arose out of a street risk.

Cases may arise where one is hurt in the street, but where the risk is of a general nature, not peculiar to the street. Lightning strikes fortuitously in the street; bombs dropped by enemy aircraft do not expose to special danger persons in a street as distinguished from those in houses. *Allcock v. Rogers*, [1918] House of Lords, 11 B. W. C. C. 149. The danger must result from the place to make it a street risk, but that is enough if the workman is in the place by reason of his employment, and in the discharge of his duty to his employer. The street becomes a dangerous place when street brawlers, highwaymen, escaping criminals, or violent madmen are afoot therein as they sometimes are. The danger of being struck by them by accident is a street risk because it is incident to passing through or being on the street when dangerous characters are abroad.

Particularly on the crowded streets of a great city, not only do vehicles collide, pavements become out of repair, and crowds jostle, but mad or biting dogs may run wild, gunmen may discharge their weapons, police officers may shoot at fugitives fleeing from justice, or other things may happen from which accidental injuries result to people on the streets which are peculiar to the use of the streets and do not commonly happen indoors.

The risk of being stabbed by an insane man running amuck seems in a peculiar sense a risk incidental to the streets to which claimant was exposed by his employment. *Matter of Heidemann v. Am. Dist. Tel. Co.*, 230 N. Y. 305, 130 N. E. 302, does not hold that where the street risk is one shared equally by all who pass or repass, whether in or out of employment, it should be shown that the employment involves some special exposure; that the night watchman is exposed by his employment to the risk of being shot by accident as he nears a sudden brawl which it is his duty to investigate, while the night clerk whose business brings him on the street, but whose duty is not to seek danger, is not so exposed. We decided the case before us and no other, dwelling naturally upon those features of the situation which emphasized the connection between the risk and the employment. But the fact that the risk is one to which every one on the street is exposed does not itself defeat compensation. Members of the public may face the same risk every day. The question is whether the employment exposed the workman to the risks by sending him on to the street, common though such risks were to all on the street. *Moran's Case*, 234 Mass. 566, 125 N. E. 591; *Dennis v. White, above.*

The order should be affirmed, with costs.

Hogan, Cardozo, and Crane, JJ., concur.

Hiscock, C. J., and McLaughlin and Andrews, JJ., dissent.

PROBLEMS

(1) Once "street risks" are expanded to include the Hogarthian picture painted by Pound, with criminals, mad dogs and lunatics running amok, can the concept stop short of:

- stray bullets? *See* Greenberg v. Voit, 250 N.Y. 543, 166 N.E. 318 (1929).
- stubbing one's toe on a curb? *See* City of Chicago v. Industrial Comm'n, 389 Ill. 592, 60 N.E. 2d 212 (1945).
- an apple thrown by a small boy? *See* Crites v. Baker, 150 Ind. App. 271, 276 N.E.2d 582 (1971).

(2) Since lunatics can run amok indoors as well as outdoors, what about the chef who was stabbed by a roving madman who had found his way into the kitchen? *See* Hartford Acc. & Indem. Co. v. Hoage, 66 App. D.C. 160, 85 F.2d 417 (1936).

(3) If being hit by a stray bullet in the street is covered, would the same be true when claimant was cutting across a vacant lot between a garage and the claimant's office building? *See* Auman v. Breckinridge Telephone Co., 188 Minn. 256, 246 N.W. 889 (1933).

(4) Some years ago, fragments of a disintegrating Soviet space vehicle fell in the street of a Wisconsin town. Suppose claimant truck driver had been hit by a fragment — would this have been compensable? Suppose a fragment broke through the window of an office building and hit a secretary 20 feet from the window.

§ 3.06   POSITIONAL AND NEUTRAL RISKS

[1]   Introduction

An increasing number of courts are beginning to make awards whenever the injury occurred because the employment required the claimant to occupy what turned out to be a place of danger. A few frankly state that causal connection is sufficiently established whenever it brings claimant to the position where he is injured. Unexplained falls and deaths occurring in the course of employment are generally held compensable, sometimes on the strength of a presumption, either judicial or statutory, that injury or death occurring in the course of employment also arises out of the employment in the absence of evidence to the contrary.

[2]   Bombs and Terrorist Attacks

According to the New York Workers' Compensation Board, as of June 17, 2004, 10,160 workers' claims had been filed on behalf of those killed or injured as the result of the September 11, 2001 terrorist attacks in Manhattan.[14] New York's use of the "zone of danger" test, combined with the state's actual-risk theory, adds up to something very close to a positional-risk doctrine for workers' compensation claims involving indiscriminate injuries sustained on the street and in nearby business establishments.[15] With this backdrop, one would anticipate that in the vast majority of claims arising from the September 11 terrorist attacks, workers' compensation benefits would be provided without much legal haggling, and the numbers appear to bear this out. Of the more than 10,000 claims filed, only a handful of disputes have reached the appellate courts and few of them involve the issue of compensability. As of January 1, 2008, there was not a single reported decision in which compensability was at issue for an employee who was inside the World Trade Center when the terrorist attack occurred.

Compensability was at issue in a claim filed by a data analyst who worked at the World Trade Center and who was struck by debris when the second tower came down while the employee was still two blocks from the doomed structure.[16] The appellate court affirmed an award, holding that the normal going and coming exception to workers' compensation compensability did not apply. The court acknowledged that ordinarily an employee would not be considered to be within the scope of his or her employment while traveling to and from work. The court indicated that under New York case law, an exception could be made, however, where the employee drew physically nearer to the workplace until he or she could be said to have entered a "gray area" where the risks of travel and the risks from work might be said to merge. In the face of the Board's award of compensation, the appellate court could not say that such a merger had not occurred in the case of the injured employee.

In *Chalcoff v. Project One*,[17] the issue turned on whether the deceased worker was an employee or an independent contractor of Marsh and McLennan, one of the major

---

[14] As reported in a Memorandum to the Members of the U.S. House of Representatives Subcommittee on National Security, Emerging Threats, and International Relations, dated September 2, 2004, from Kristine K. McElroy, Professional Staff Member. According to the Memorandum, according to information supplied the subcommittee by the New York Board, 90 percent of all World Trade Center claims had been resolved by September 2, 2004.

[15] In two early bomb cases, the so-called Wall Street explosion case, Roberts v. Newcomb & Co., 234 N.Y. 553, 138 N.E. 443 (1922) involving a bomb thrown into the street, and the Dunham case, C.A. Dunham Co. v. Industrial Comm'n, 16 Ill. 2d 102, 156 N.E. 2d 560 (1959), involving a bomb planted in an airplane. These two decisions indicate that the street-risk doctrine is sufficiently elastic to embrace these sources of injury.

[16] Tompkins v. Morgan Stanley Dean Witter, 1 A.D.3d 695, 766 N.Y.S.2d 923 (2003).

[17] Chalcoff v. Project One, 784 N.Y.S.2d 738 (App. Div. 2004).

tenants in the World Trade Center. Because the totality of the evidence tended to show that the deceased functioned not as an employee, but as a consultant, Chalcoff's widow was denied benefits. The opposite conclusion, however, was reached in *Wald v. Avalon Partners, Inc.*,[18] where some evidence tended to show that the deceased stockbroker was paid on a commission basis and worked out of his home forty percent of the time, yet other evidence indicated that the purported employer withheld payroll taxes from the deceased earnings, issued an annual W-2 form to him, and had the right to terminate the decedent's services at virtually any time.

The basis for recovery under a positional-risk doctrine is the notion that "but for" the employee's presence at or near the work site, he or she would not have been in a position to suffer injury or death. Hence the question arises: if the worker's position of danger was caused not by bad luck — i.e., being in the wrong place at the wrong time — but by the worker's affirmative action in taking on the risk of harm, should the worker's claim be denied? Several New York decisions have answered the question in the affirmative, particularly where the claim was not for an actual physical injury, but a claim for post-traumatic stress disorder. In one such stress case, benefits were accordingly denied to a Port Authority employee who was home on the morning of the attacks on the World Trade Center and who traveled to the epicenter, where his office had been destroyed, in order assist in rescue efforts.[19] The employee's decision to risk his life and health was his own. Similarly, a New York senior business analyst, who obeyed his employer's order to evacuate its premises located four to five blocks from the World Trade Center, but who, rather than leave the area, instead walked to an adjoining public street in order to observe the destruction from the terrorist acts and who lingered some 20 to 30 minutes before deciding to head north out of lower Manhattan, was held not to have sustained a compensable post-traumatic stress injury.[20]

In the only reported decision involving the ill-fated Flight 93 from Newark to San Francisco, which was hijacked and later crashed in Shanksville, Pennsylvania, a New Jersey appellate court held that a flight attendant, who was originally scheduled to work on the flight, but who several days earlier requested and received the day off, could not recover workers' compensation benefits for post-traumatic stress syndrome.[21] Reversing an award of benefits, the court held that while the injury did arise out of the employment, it did not arise in the course of the flight attendant's employment.

PROBLEM

Consider a hypothetical attorney working as an associate in a small firm whose offices comprise most of the second floor of a nondescript three-story building in a moderate-sized town such as Durham, North Carolina. A terrorist has commandeered a small jet from nearby RDU International Airport. The terrorist has some skill in maneuvering the plane, although not enough to target any specific government or business site. He crashes the plane into the second story of the small building that houses the law firm, killing the attorney. Apart from the positional risk doctrine — which would allow quick recovery under these facts in New York — can the attorney's spouse recover workers' compensation benefits for the death of the spouse? Did the attorney's death arise out of and in the course of the employment?

It is clear from the hypothetical that the attorney's death was in the course of the employment; it occurred at a time and place where the attorney could reasonably have been expected to be as he or she was about the business of the employing law firm. But

---

[18] Wald v. Avalon Partners, Inc., 803 N.Y.S.2d 329 (App. Div. 2005).

[19] Duff v. Port Auth., 787 N.Y.S.2d 175 (App. Div. 2004).

[20] Betro v. Salomon Smith Barney, 8 A.D. 3d 847, 779 N.Y.S.2d 147 (2004).

[21] Stroka v. United Airlines, 364 N.J. Super. 333, 835 A.2d 1247 (2003).

did the attorney's death arise from the employment? Can it be reasonably argued that such an incident was a risk of the attorney's work in that office? Was the attorney at any greater risk of injury or death than anyone else in Durham on that day?

Would it make any difference if instead of the nondescript three-story office building in small-town-America, the attorney worked on a floor near the top of the Sears Tower in Chicago? It could well be argued that the attorney working in the Sears Tower, a highly visible landmark, is at a greater risk than the attorney in Durham. Such increased risk might well make a difference in those jurisdictions which allow recovery where the employment can be said to have placed the employee at a greater risk of death or injury than the general public.

[3]   Unexplained Accidents

COOMES v. ROBERTSON LUMBER CO.
547 S.W.2d 809 (Ky. 1968)

Milliken, Judge.

The Workmen's Compensation Board denied compensation to the appellant, William Gerald Coomes, a forty-eight-year-old employee of the appellee, Robertson Lumber Company, and the circuit court affirmed the Board's decision on appeal. The appeal to us presents the question of whether the Board had to grant compensation to Coomes as a matter of law.

This is a case where no one saw the accident, and little circumstantial evidence was available to suggest exactly how it happened, yet happen it did, and during the course of Coomes' employment with the Lumber Company. Coomes drove a truck for the Company and worked in its lumber yard. On the day of his injury, September 10, 1964, he went home for lunch at noon and returned to his work about an hour later, unloading two-by-fours from a truck. A salesman for the Company saw him after his return to work and testified that Coomes appeared normal at that time, but within an hour later, when the salesman went into the lumber yard for a purpose he could not recall, he saw Coomes stagger to his feet with a bloody forehead, found him dazed, led him to a stack of lumber where he set him down, then telephoned Coomes' wife to come for him. The salesman said he recalled seeing nothing on the ground which would suggest what caused Coomes to fall or what he may have struck when he fell, but there was a truck with lumber on it "and some — a couple of pieces may be pulled out three or four feet."

As heretofore stated, the "in the course of" and "arising out of the employment" factors are not precise concepts. Larson, in his Workmen's Compensation Law, Section 29.10, says these two factors should not be applied entirely independently; that "they are both parts of a single test of work-connection, and therefore deficiencies in the strength of one factor are sometimes allowed to be made up by strength in the other. . . . One is almost tempted to formulate a sort of quantum theory of work-connection: that a certain minimum quantum of work-connection must be shown, and if the 'course' quantity is very small, but the 'arising' quantity is large, the quantum will add up to the necessary minimum, as it will also when the 'arising' quantity is very small but the 'course' quantity is very large. But if both the 'course' quantity and 'arising' quantities are small, the minimum quantity will not be met."

We do not know exactly what caused Coomes' injury, but we do know it occurred in the course of his employment. We do not know whether he fell and was injured or whether one or more of the two-by-fours he was unloading slid and struck him on the head. If a fall was the cause of his injury, we do not know what caused it or what he struck when he fell. We do know that there is not a scintilla of competent evidence in this record to show that any fall he might have suffered stemmed from an innately personal cause. Larson comments in Section 10.31, pages 99 and 100, "In a pure unexplained-fall case, there is no way in which an award can be justified as a matter of causation theory except by a recognition that this but-for reasoning satisfies the 'arising' requirement. In appraising the extent to which courts are willing to accept this general but-for theory, then, it is significant to note that most courts confronted with the unexplained fall problem have seen fit to award compensation." The but-for reasoning referred to is that the injury would not have happened but-for the employment, whatever specifically caused it. The origin of the reasoning is the unanimous opinion of the House of Lords construing the English Workmen's Compensation law (upon which most American acts are modeled) in *Upton v. Great Cent. R.* (1924) A.C. 302 (H.L.) where compensation was awarded for a completely unexplained fall in the course of the employment. For a collection of and analysis of decided cases *see* Larson, Section 10.31, "Unexplained falls." We think this view conforms to our statutory mandate KRS 342.004 to construe our act liberally on the law.

We are not unmindful of our decision in *Stasel v. American Radiator & Standard Sanitary Corp.*, Ky., 278 S.W.2d 721 (1955) where compensation was awarded for an idiopathic fall in the course of the employment, an epileptic fall onto a hot stove, because the employment placed the employee in increased danger of the effects of such a fall for, in the case at bar, we do not find any competent evidence that an idiopathic fall is involved. (*See* Larson, Section 12.11 for a discussion and analysis of idiopathic fall cases; and also *Blair Fork Coal Co. v. Blankenship, Ky.*, 416 S.W.2d 716 (1967).

We conclude that Coomes' injury arose out of his employment whether he was struck by sliding lumber while unloading the truck or whether he suffered an unexplained fall, and that he clearly is entitled to compensation for an extended period of temporary, total disability, and that he may be entitled to an award for permanent disability if the Board so finds. The judgment is reversed and the case referred back to the Board for an award of compensation consistent with this opinion.

WILLIAMS, C. J., and HILL, STEINFELD and PALMORE, JJ., concur.

OSBORNE, J., not sitting.

MONTGOMERY, J., dissents.

PROBLEMS

(1) On what rationale can unexplained-death and unexplained-accident cases be assimilated to the positional-risk doctrine?

(2) An electrical engineer was found dead near electrical equipment he was to inspect. Medical evidence at trial suggested three possible causes of death: diabetes, heart attack, or electrocution. *Compensable? See* Clemmens v. W.C.A.B. 261 Cal. App. 2d 1, 68 Cal. Rptr. 804 (1968).

(3) Claimant, a hospital worker, was found dead after falling from the top floor of a hospital. He was last observed working near a puddle of grease next to the guardrail of the building. There were no witnesses to the accident, and a package of narcotics was found next to his body. An autopsy report revealed evidence of a controlled substance in his system. *Compensable as an unexplained death?*

(4) Suppose, instead of there being an unexplained death within the time and place of employment, the employee, although last seen on the job, simply disappears. *See* Knell v. Maryland Drydock Co., 184 Md. 428, 41 A.2d 502 (1945).

[4] Current Acceptance of Positional Risk Doctrine

It was observed earlier[22] that the positional-risk doctrine had enlisted a growing roster of adherents. Using as a guide either the adoption of the positional-risk rule by name, or the application of it in practice, or both, at least 14 jurisdictions have accepted the positional-risk principle: Colorado, Louisiana, New Jersey, Kentucky, California, Massachusetts, New York, Texas, the Circuit Court of Appeals for the District of Columbia, Hawaii, Idaho, South Dakota, Oklahoma, and the United States Supreme Court.

In addition to this group, there may be mentioned several states in which the acceptance of the positional-risk approach is marginal or inconclusive, because it rests on awards for unexplained risks. North Dakota, New Mexico and Pennsylvania have made awards for unexplained assaults, and Connecticut, Florida, Georgia, North Carolina and Pennsylvania have made awards for unexplained falls.

In judging the growth of the positional-risk principle, one must bear in mind that the kind of fact situation that forces a court to take a stand on this principle is relatively rare. Most cases can be disposed of by finding some morsel of increased risk, for example, creating a slightly greater hazard of exposure to lightning than that of the general public, or by taking refuge in some half-way house such as a street-risk doctrine or the contact-with-the-premises exception. Occasionally a court will hold the positional-risk up to view and then specifically reject it, as Missouri,[23] and Illinois[24] for example, have done. More common is the practice of considering the doctrine and then concluding that, since the award can in any event be affirmed on a less innovative theory, the court will not break new ground when the case in hand does not require it.[25]

---

[22] Ch. 3, § 3.02[2], *above.*

[23] Lathrop v. Tobin-Hamilton Shoe Mfg. Co., 402 S.W.2d 16 (Mo. Ct. App. 1966).

But note that Missouri, on the strength of a statutory amendment, has felt obliged to accept the positional risk doctrine in the limited area of assaults. Allen v. Dorothy's Laundry & Dry Cleaning Co., 523 S.W.2d 874 (Mo. App. D.K.C. 1975).

[24] Brady v. Louis Ruffolo & Sons Constr. Co., 192 Ill. App. 3d. 1, 139 Ill. Dec. 56, 548 N.E.2d 441 (1989), *aff'd* 143 Ill. 2d 542, 578 N.E.2d 921 (1991). Claimant's working table faced a wall beyond which there was a curve in a major highway. A truck, hit by a car, left the curve, which was icy, and smashed into the wall, driving the table into claimant's abdomen. Compensation was denied at every level.

[25] *See, e.g.,* W.T. Edwards Hosp. v. Rakestraw, 114 So. 2d 802 (Fla. App. 1959), where Florida followed this course.

Chapter 4
ASSAULTS

§ 4.01 INTRODUCTION

Assaults resulting in workplace injury give rise to a fascinating and diverse array of questions about work connection. Suppose a fight that breaks out among some workers and one is injured. If the fight is in the workplace, does it matter whether it began with a work-related dispute or a personal dispute? If it began as a work-related dispute, would the injury be compensable even though the fight took place off company property? If the claimant started the fight, should compensation be barred? If the assault is by a superior or by a company official, does this represent intentional rather than accidental injury, thereby taking the matter outside of the world of workers' compensation and into the world of tort recovery? And what of injury due to horseplay — is the horseplay so unrelated to the purposes of the employment as to defeat any work connection? Finally, how should unexplained assaults by strangers who have come into the workplace, or mistaken identity assaults, be handled?

§ 4.02 WORKPLACE ASSAULTS: PERSONAL MOTIVATION

MARTIN v. J. LICHTMAN & SONS
42 N.J. 81, 199 A.2d 241 (1964)

. . . .

Martin was having his lunch in a room in the Lichtman plant customarily used by its employees for that purpose. There were about 18 employees in the room, and Martin was seated between Bradford and Taylor. Martin interpreted a remark made by Bradford to Taylor as meaning that Bradford had a job in addition to his employment with Lichtman, and he said to Bradford "You got two jobs? How can you take care of both jobs?" Bradford did not answer but went to his locker, took out a bottle of soda water, returned to his seat alongside Martin and, a minute or two later and still without saying anything, struck Martin with the bottle, causing the injuries for which Martin seeks compensation. There had been no previous words or difficulties between Bradford and Martin. There is nothing in the record to indicate that they saw each other outside of working hours.

The County Court said "Petitioner's observation or inquiry brought no verbal response. There was an hiatus of some minutes, then the attack. Conceding that the assailant did take umbrage at petitioner's query, and that a period of silent fermentation ensued which produced the attack, how can it be said that the employment had anything to do with it? Apparently, the same query, had it been made off the job, would have produced the same violent result."

That may be true, but the fact of the matter is that it was on the job that Martin ate and talked with Bradford, and Bradford became enraged and struck him. But for the fact that Martin was on the job, he would have had no contact with Bradford and would not have been assaulted by him. As the court said in *Sanders v. Jarka Corp.*, 1 N.J. 36,

41, 61 A.2d 641 (1948), "The employment . . . was the cause in the sense that, but for the employment, the accident would not have happened. . . . "

Lichtman argues that an assault is compensable if it grows out of a quarrel whose subject matter is related to the work, but not when the assault is due only to personal animosity, even though it arose out of the enforced contact of the factory. We hold that there is no longer room for such a distinction under our cases, and that "even if the subject of the dispute is unrelated to the work, the assault is compensable if 'the work of the participants brought them together and created the relations and conditions which resulted in the clash.'" 1 Larson, Workmen's Compensation Law, p. 130 (1952).

. . . .

The assault upon Martin was not motivated by personal vengeance stemming from contact with Bradford outside of the employment, nor did it arise from a purely private relationship entered into by them during the course of their employment, as, for example, if they had embarked on a joint enterprise on the side and fought over it during working hours. *Cf.* Larson, op. cit., *supra*, p. 139. When friction and strain arises between employees because of the enforced contact resulting from the employment and leads to an unjustified assault, the victim's injuries are compensable. Martin's injuries resulted from such an assault. *Crotty v. Driver Harris Co., supra*; *Diaz v. Newark Industrial Spraying Co.*, 35 N.J. 588, 591, 174 A.2d 478 (1961); Larson, op. cit., *supra*, §§ 11.16(a) (c), 11.22. *Cf. Lester v. Elliott Bros. Trucking Co.*, 18 N.J. 434, 114 A.2d 8 (1955).

In *Hartford Accident & Indemnity Co. v. Cardillo*, 112 F.2d 11, 15, 72 App.D.C. 52 (C.A.D.C.1940), cert. denied 310 U.S. 649, 60 S.Ct. 1100, 84 L.Ed. 1415 (1940), cited with approval in *Diaz v. Newark Industrial Spraying, Inc., supra*, at 35 N.J. 591, 174 A.2d at 479, the court said:

> The risks of injury incurred in the crowded contacts of the factory through the acts of fellow workmen are not measured by the tendency of such acts to serve the master's business. . . .
>
> . . . The shift [to compensability] involved recognition that the environment includes associations as well as conditions, and that associations include the faults and derelictions of human beings as well as their virtues and obediences. Men do not discard their personal qualities when they go to work. Into the job they carry their intelligence, skill, habits of care and rectitude. Just as inevitably they take along also their tendencies to carelessness and camaraderie, as well as emotional makeup. In bringing men together, work brings these qualities together, causes frictions between them, creates occasions for lapses into carelessness, and for fun-making and emotional flare-up. . . . These expressions of human nature are incidents inseparable from working together. They involve risks of injury and these risks are inherent in the working environment. . . . (112 F.2d at p. 15)

After reviewing the conflicting views as to the compensability of injuries arising out of on-the-job quarrels, Justice Rutledge said that he considered the better view to be the one which:

> . . . rejects the test of immediate relevancy of the culminating incident. That is regarded, not as an isolated event, but as part and parcel of the working environment, whether related directly to the job or to something which is a by-product of the associations. This view recognizes that work places men under strains and fatigue from human and mechanical impacts, creating frictions which explode in myriads of ways, only some of which are immediately relevant to their tasks. Personal animosities are created by working together on the assembly line or in traffic . . . No worker is immune to these pressures and impacts upon temperament. They accumulate and explode over incidents trivial and important, personal and official. But the explosion point is merely the

culmination of the antecedent pressures. That it is not relevant to the immediate task, involves a lapse from duty, or contains an element of volition or illegality does not disconnect it from them nor nullify their causal effect in producing its injurious consequences. Any other view would reintroduce the conceptions of contributory fault, action in the line of duty, nonaccidental character of voluntary conduct, and independent, intervening cause as applied in tort law, which it was the purpose of the statute to discard. . . . (112 F.2d, at pp. 16–17)

. . . .

PER CURIAM.

The judgment is affirmed for the reasons expressed in the opinion of Judge Gaulkin in the Appellate Division.

For affirmance: CHIEF JUSTICE WEINTRAUB and JUSTICES JACOBS, FRANCIS, PROCTOR and SCHETTINO — 5.

For reversal: JUSTICES HALL and HANEMAN — 2.

DODSON v. DUBOSE STEEL, INC.
159 N.C. App. 1, 582 S.E.2d 389 (2003)

HUDSON, JUDGE.

Defendants Dubose Steel, Inc. (Dubose) and American Manufacturers Mutual appeal an opinion and award entered 18 January 2002 by the North Carolina Industrial Commission that awarded plaintiff medical expenses, death benefits and the statutory $ 2,000 toward burial expenses, for the injury that led to the death of her husband. For the reasons that follow, we affirm.

BACKGROUND

Plaintiff's decedent John Dodson (Dodson), was employed by defendant Dubose as a truck driver, and was driving a load of steel to Virginia for his employer on 27 September 1999. As a result of the events at issue here, Dodson was struck by a vehicle while outside of his truck, and fell to the pavement on his head. After several days without regaining consciousness, Dodson died. His widow Shelby Dodson, the plaintiff, filed claims for workers' compensation benefits due while Dodson was still alive, and for death benefits. . . .

In an opinion and award filed 18 January 2002 by Commissioner Bernadine Ballance, the Full Commission essentially re-wrote the findings of fact and conclusions of law, but awarded the same benefits. Defendants now appeal.

ANALYSIS

. . . Appellants' Arguments

Defendants bring forward three questions presented, organized into two arguments in their brief. In the heading of Argument I, defendants refer to all but one of the nineteen assignments of error. In the body of the argument, however, defendants do not mention any specific findings by number, but argue generally that the evidence does not support that the Commission "found that [Dodson's] injury and subsequent death arose out of his employment." . . .

We do not believe that this argument complies with the Rules of Appellate Procedure sufficiently to bring forward challenges to any of the specific findings of fact, with the possible exceptions of numbers 11, 12 and 14 and conclusions 1, 2 and 4, which read as follows:

11. The root cause of the confrontation between Dodson and Campbell originated when Dodson, while moving with the traffic, merged into Campbell's lane of traffic forcing Campbell out of his lane. Neither Dodson nor Campbell knew each other prior to this incident. There is no evidence that Dodson intended to force Campbell out of his lane of travel. At the time that the root cause incident occurred, Dodson was driving his truck in the ordinary course of his business for defendant-employer, Dubose Steel, Inc. which was the basic nature of his work as a truck driver. Defendants admit that at the time Dodson was struck by Campbell's vehicle he was an employee of Dubose Steel, Inc.

12. John Dodson's injuries and death resulted from an assault upon his person by a vehicle operated by Troy Campbell. Although there had been gestures and verbal exchanges between Campbell and Dodson(which neither of them could hear), based on the greater weight of the evidence, Dodson did not have a wilful intent to injure or kill Campbell when he exited his vehicle and walked toward the driver's side of Campbell's vehicle. Dodson appeared to have acted spontaneously.

* * *

14. Dodson's injury and death arose out of his employment. As a result of his injury and subsequent death, Dodson and now his estate have incurred ambulance and medical bills for treatment for the time that he lived prior to death, as well as burial expenses in excess of $ 2,000 . . .

* * *

CONCLUSIONS OF LAW

1. The injury to John Dodson occurring on September 27, 1999 and the resulting death occurring on October 4, 1999 constituted a compensable injury by accident arising out of and in the course of Dodson's employment with Dubose Steel, Inc. N.C. Gen Stat. §§ 97-2(6); 97-38.

2. John Dodson died as a result of an assault on his person by a vehicle driven by Troy Campbell. The assault originated from an argument based on the manner in which Dodson drove his truck in the course of his employment. *Hegler v. Cannon Mills*, 224 N.C.669, 31 S.E.2d 918 (1944).

* * *

4. Decedent's employment as a long distance truck driver caused him to spend the majority of his working hours traveling on highways and streets. Due to the nature of decedent's work, the risk of driver error causing tempers to flare among strangers on the busy highways was increased. Dodson and Campbell did not know each other so the inciting incident was not due to personal reasons. "Assaults arise out of the employment either if the risk of assault is increased because of the nature or setting of the work, or if the reason for the assault was a quarrel having its origin in the work." A truck driver's risk of being struck by a vehicle is a risk greater than that of the general public. 1 Arthur Larson and Lex K. Larson, *Larson's Workers' Compensation, Desk Edition*, § 8 Scope (2000).

Thus, we will first discuss whether the evidence supports these findings and conclusions.

After a careful review according to the standard articulated by the Supreme Court, we conclude that evidence in the record supports the Commission's findings 11, 12, and 14. First, Troy Campbell, the motorist who hit Dodson, testified that his vehicle and Dodson's tractor-trailer were trying to merge into one lane of travel from the two in which they were traveling, when Dodson's truck forced Campbell off the road, while Campbell was "laying on the horn when he [Dodson] was coming over." At the next stoplight, according to Campbell and witnesses Scott Cash and Mark Davis, Dodson got out of his truck and started walking toward Campbell, banging his fist onto the hood of Campbell's vehicle, at which point Campbell drove forward, striking Dodson. Several days later Dodson died from his injuries. Campbell could not hear what, if anything, Dodson said while walking toward Campbell's vehicle, and Campbell testified that Dodson "really didn't have any kind of facial expression." We believe that this evidence, among much more, fully supports the above findings of fact to the effect that Dodson's injury and death were rooted in the driving incident.

The Full Commission chose to accept certain testimony as credible, which is within its authority, even though there may be evidence from which one could draw a contrary inference. [Citation omitted.] . . . [T]he Full Commission is the "sole judge of the weight and credibility of the evidence" and need not explain its findings of fact to justify which evidence or witnesses it finds credible. We conclude that ample evidence in the record supported the Commission's findings of fact.

Next, we examine whether the findings of fact support the Commission's conclusions of law. We believe that they do. Findings of fact numbers 11, 12, and 14, among others, support the Commission's legal conclusions and award regarding the root cause of Dodson's injury.

In their second "Question Presented," briefed as part B of Argument I, the defendants contend that the Commission erroneously analyzed this case according to the law pertaining to workplace assaults. Defendant's [sic] argue that the Commission's conclusions and award are contrary to applicable law, for three reasons. They contend that (1) the assault cases do not apply; (2) the employer received no "appreciable benefit" from Dodson's actions at the time of the injury according to the so-called Good Samaritan cases; and (3) that Dodson's work did not place him at increased risk of the type of incident in which he was injured.

We conclude, however, that the Commission properly analyzed this case according to the assault cases, because the incident was, we believe, more closely analogous to a workplace assault than to any of the factual scenarios underpinning defendants' proposed alternative theories. In reaching this conclusion we are guided, not only by the standard of review, but also by the clear and oft- articulated mandate of the Supreme Court that, in workers' compensation cases, the statute is to be broadly construed in favor of awarding benefits, in view of the remedial purpose of the Act. [Citation omitted.] . . .

In the assault cases the analysis of "arising out of" turns on whether the assault "originated in" something related to the job. In the opinion and award, the Commission cites *Hegler v. Cannon Mills Co.*, 224 N.C. 669, 31 S.E.2d 918 (1944), as a basis for its conclusion. There, the Supreme Court upheld an award of compensation where the injury and death resulted from an assault that followed a dispute between two cotton mill workers over one's attempt to supervise the other. The Court there pointed out:

> Where men are working together at the same work disagreements may be expected to arise about the work, the manner of doing it, as to the use of tools, interference with one another, and many other details which may be trifling or unimportant. Infirmity of temper, or worse, may be expected, and occasionally blows and fighting. Where . . . as a result of it one injures the other, it may be inferred that the injury arose out of the employment.

Id., 224 N.C. at 671, 31 S.E.2d at 920 (citations omitted). Plaintiff cites a number of cases in which this Court and the Supreme Court have held that an accidental injury is compensable where it results from an assault rooted in the performance of workplace duties. [Citations omitted.]

We believe that the findings of the Commission support the conclusion that Dodson's injury and death originated in the traffic merging incident, which was clearly a dispute about Dodson's driving. Since Dodson's work primarily consisted of driving, and his workplace comprised public roads and highways, including the one upon which he was driving at the time of the merging incident, the findings also support the conclusion that the "assault upon Dodson [by Campbell's vehicle] was rooted in and grew out of his employment," and occurred in his workplace. This case is not similar to those in which a worker has been assaulted because of a personal relationship, unconnected to the employment. [Citations omitted.] Here the Commission has found as fact that the dispute had as its "root cause" the merging incident, which was related to driving and to "the basic nature of his work as a truck driver." Thus, according to the applicable case law, the Commission properly concluded that Dodson's injury and death resulted from an injury by accident arising out of and in the course of his employment.

Defendants argue that the Commission and the Court should analyze this case according to the cases in which an employee on a business trip interrupts his work to engage in personal conduct unrelated to the employer's business, such as the Good Samaritan cases, and that we should employ an "appreciable benefits" or "increased risk" test. [Citations omitted]. Because we have held that the evidence supports the Commission's findings, which in turn support its conclusions to the effect that Dodson's injury and death resulted from a dispute related to his business of driving, we do not believe that these cases apply. In so concluding, we again refer to the standard of review, according to which we are bound by the findings and conclusions of the Commission if there is any evidence to support them. . . .

In Argument II (Question presented 3), defendants contend that the plaintiff is barred from any compensation because Dodson's injury and death resulted from his wilful intention to injure Campbell. However, the Commission accepted as credible the evidence discussed above, and made findings of fact, including finding 12 quoted above, which support its conclusion number 3, that defendant failed to prove "by the greater weight of the evidence that [Dodson's] injury and death resulted from [Dodson's] wilful intention to injure or kill himself or another." Because these findings and conclusion are supported by the evidence even though there may have been evidence to the contrary, we reject this argument.

Conclusion

In sum, we hold that the evidence supports the findings of fact, which in turn support the conclusions of law of the Commission. Since the Commission properly analyzed this case as an assault in the workplace, its conclusions are consistent with the applicable law. For the reasons set forth above, we affirm the opinion and award of the Industrial Commission.

Affirmed.

Judge McGee concurs.

Judge Steelman dissents in part, concurs in part.

Steelman, Judge, dissenting in part and concurring in part.

I respectfully dissent from the majority's decision affirming the portion of the Commission's Opinion and Award concluding Dodson's injury and death arose out of and in the course of his employment and awarding death benefits to plaintiff. Although I concur with the majority's conclusion that Dubose's argument under N.C. Gen. Stat. § 97-12(3) (2001) must fail, I do so on different grounds. The facts in this case are not in dispute; however, I recite additional facts to clarify and support my decision on this matter.

On 27 September 1999, John Dodson ("Dodson") was transporting a load of steel to Virginia for his employer, defendant Dubose Steel, Inc. ("Dubose"). While Dodson was driving in the right lane of a divided highway having two lanes of traffic in each direction,

Troy Campbell ("Campbell") was driving in the same direction in the left lane. The two drivers encountered a disabled recreational vehicle partially blocking the right lane and causing the two lanes of traffic to merge left into a single lane. Dodson moved his truck into the left lane and forced Campbell into a left-turn lane as Campbell blew his horn several times. Dodson returned to the right lane after passing the disabled vehicle.

Campbell pulled up beside Dodson's truck, looked over at him, motioned back and said "you almost hit me back there." Campbell made gestures toward Dodson, who responded by shaking his finger at Campbell. Campbell then moved forward in the left lane to where the vehicles ahead of him were stopped at the traffic signal. While the two vehicles were stopped for the traffic signal, Dodson got out of his truck and walked around the front of Campbell's vehicle, striking the hood with his fist and signaling Campbell to get out of his vehicle. Campbell and other witnesses were under the impression that Dodson was angry as he approached Campbell's vehicle.

When Dodson reached the left front headlight of Campbell's vehicle, Campbell turned the wheels to the left and accelerated in an attempt to move into the left-turn lane. Campbell's vehicle struck Dodson, causing him to fall and to suffer significant head injuries which ultimately resulted in his death on 4 October 1999. . . .

The issue presented in Dubose's appeal to this Court is whether the death of an employee who was engaged in an act of "road rage" at the time of his injury resulting in his death suffered an injury compensable under N.C. Gen. Stat. Chapter 97. In the event that there are procedural inadequacies in Dubose's appeal, I would exercise this Court's authority under N.C.R. App. P. 2 (2003) to suspend the rules and address Dubose's arguments in their entirety.

I.

Dubose first contends the Commission erred in awarding death benefits to plaintiff because the event causing Dodson's injury and resulting death did not arise out of and in the course of his employment with Dubose. Whether an employee's injury arises out of and in the course of his employment is a mixed question of law and fact. [Citation omitted.] This Court's review of the Commission's Opinion and Award is limited to whether its factual findings are supported by any competent evidence and whether its conclusions are adequately supported by its findings. [Citation omitted.]. . . .

A. Background Law

The North Carolina Workers' Compensation Act, N.C. Gen. Stat. § 97-1, *et seq.* (hereinafter "the Act"), defines a compensable, accidental injury under the Act as one "arising out of and in the course of employment. . . . " N.C. Gen. Stat. § 97-2(6) (2001). The phrase "arising out of" relates to the origin of the accident and generally requires a causal connection between the nature of the employment and the injury. *Robbins v. Nicholson*, 281 N.C. 234, 188 S.E.2d 350 (1972). "In the course of employment" refers to the time, place and circumstances giving rise to the injury. *Pittman v. Twin City Laundry & Cleaners*, 61 N.C. App. 468, 300 S.E.2d 899 (1983). Although these elements are interrelated, the claimant has the burden of establishing both to receive compensation. *Pickrell v. Motor Convoy, Inc.*, 322 N.C. 363, 368 S.E.2d 582 (1988). . . .

B. Arising Out of the Employment

There are two lines of North Carolina cases decided under N.C. Gen. Stat. § 97-2(6) which potentially are controlling in our determination as to whether Dodson's injuries arose out of his employment. The first line of cases, relied upon by the majority and the Commission, deals with injuries caused by assaults occurring in the workplace or assaults by co-workers. The second line of cases, relied upon by Dubose, addresses injuries to employees occurring when the employee interrupts his business for his employer to engage in personal conduct unrelated to his employer's business.

1. Assaults in the Workplace

The Commission expressly relied on one of the workplace cases, *Hegler v. Cannon Mills Co.*, 224 N.C. 669, 31 S.E.2d 918 (1944), in finding that Dodson's injuries and death were "rooted in" his employment. In *Hegler*, tensions between two co-workers, Hegler and Smith, developed over the course of a year and culminated in Hegler's complaint to his employer about the quality of Smith's work. *Id.* at 670, 31 S.E.2d at 919. Two days after the complaint, Smith assaulted and killed Hegler at their workplace. *Id.*

Our Supreme Court found that the tension between the two co- workers "had its origin in the employment." *Id.* at 671, 31 S.E.2d at 919. The *Hegler* Court also found that the assault was "directly connected with" and "was rooted in and grew out of the employment." *Id.* at 670-71, 31 S.E.2d at 919. *Hegler* affirmed the Commission's findings and conclusions that the death had occurred in the course of and arose out of the employment. *Id.*

This Court reached a similar conclusion in *Pittman v. Twin City Laundry*, 61 N.C. App. 468, 300 S.E.2d 899 (1983). In *Pittman*, a quarrel between two employees of the laundry service ended in one employee shooting and killing the other at the workplace. *Id.* at 470, 300 S.E.2d at 901. This Court held that the death "had its origin in a risk connected with [Pittman's] employment and that his death was in direct consequence of that risk." *Id.* at 474, 300 S.E.2d at 903. Thus, the *Pittman* Court, citing *Hegler*, found the shooting was causally connected to and arose out of the decedent's employment. *Id.*

Pittman expressly distinguished those cases where the claimant is injured at the workplace by a non-employee assailant who committed the assaults for reasons unrelated to the employer's business. In such cases, our courts have held "that an injury is not compensable when it is inflicted in an assault upon an employee by an outsider as a result of a personal relationship between them, and the attack was not created by and not reasonably related to the employment." *Hemric v. Manufacturing Co.*, 54 N.C. App. 314, 318, 283 S.E.2d 436, 438-39 (1981); *see also, Gallimore v. Marilyn's Shoes*, 292 N.C. 399, 233 S.E.2d 529 (1977) (holding that the employee's death did not arise out of her employment where there was no evidence that the assault was motivated by her employment or that her employment affected her risk of being assaulted). . . .

In the present case, the incident giving rise to Dodson's injury and death was not an assault by a co-worker occurring at the workplace. Therefore, I would hold that this case is not controlled by the decisions concerning assaults in the workplace or assaults by co-workers.

2. Increased Risk Analysis

The facts and issues presented here are more analogous to the cases where an employee interrupts his work for his employer to engage in personal conduct unrelated to the employer's business, such as rendering assistance to a third person. In those cases, our courts primarily have relied on an increased risk analysis to determine whether injuries arose out of the claimant's employment.

The increased risk analysis requires a finding that the employee's injury was caused by an increased risk incidental to the employment. The key determination is whether the injury was "a natural and probable consequence of the nature of the employment." *Gallimore*, 292 N.C. at 404, 233 S.E.2d at 532-33. A contributing proximate cause of the injury must be a risk unique to the nature of the employment and not a risk to which any member of the public would be equally exposed apart from the employment. *Id.* at 404, 233 S.E.2d at 533. . . . This risk also must be one "which might have been contemplated by a reasonable person . . . as incidental to the service when he entered the employment." *Bartlett v. Duke Univ.*, 284 N.C. 230, 233, 200 S.E.2d 193, 195 (1973).

In adopting the increased risk approach, our Supreme Court expressly rejected the "positional risk" doctrine, where an injury arises out of the employment if it " 'has its source in circumstances in which the employee's employment placed him.' " [Citation omitted.] Thus, even when employment provides "a convenient opportunity" for injury, it is not necessarily the contributing proximate cause. [Citation omitted]. . . .

Here, the Commission found that the "root cause" of the *confrontation* occurred when Dodson merged into Campbell's lane while he was driving in the course of his business for Dubose as part of the "basic nature of his work as a truck driver." By finding that Dodson's employment was the "root cause" of his confrontation, the Commission tacitly acknowledged that his employment was merely a remote cause, and not a direct or proximate cause, of his injury.

The Commission also concluded that Dodson's "employment as a long distance truck driver caused him to spend the majority of his working hours traveling on highways and streets." For this reason, the Commission concluded, "the risk of driver error causing tempers to flare among strangers on busy highways was increased." This conclusion is based upon a positional risk analysis, wherein Dodson's employment as a truck driver placed him on the highway more frequently than other drivers and, therefore, increased his risk of confrontations with other drivers. However, our Supreme Court expressly rejected the positional risk doctrine in favor of the increased risk approach.

The Commission further concluded that "[a] truck driver's risk of being struck by a vehicle is a risk greater than that of the general public." While a truck driver may experience an increased risk of being in a collision or accident involving his truck, his employment cannot reasonably be seen as increasing the risk of the driver himself being struck by a vehicle after exiting his truck to confront another driver on the roadside. The risk of confrontations while driving, commonly referred to as "road rage," is not unique to employment as a truck driver. It is something that can occur at anytime to any member of the general public in the normal course of operating a motor vehicle. The mere fact that Dodson drove on the highway more often as a result of his employment may have provided "a convenient opportunity" for exposure to "road rage," but- . . . demonstrating positional risk does not establish a compensable injury.

Furthermore, the facts demonstrate that Dodson's injury was not the natural and probable consequence of his employment. The initial contact between Dodson and Campbell occurred when Dodson merged into Campbell's lane, forcing him into the turn lane. After passing the disabled vehicle, Campbell shouted to Dodson then continued forward to meet the traffic in front of him. At this point, the incident effectively had come to an end. However, Dodson personally chose to renew the confrontation by getting out of his truck to confront Campbell without any additional provocation or contact between the two men or any contact between their vehicles. Once Dodson exited his truck to confront Campbell, his conduct was no longer related to his employment. . . . [I]t was Dodson's independent and voluntary act of getting out of his truck to confront Campbell which created the risk that he could be struck by another vehicle. The risk of injury was not created by the nature of his employment.

The facts as found by the Commission compel the conclusions that the proximate cause of Dodson's injury was his decision to exit his vehicle to confront Campbell in an act of "road rage" and that the risk of such an act is not incidental or unique to nature of his employment as a truck driver but is a risk to which every member of the general public is equally exposed. Therefore, I would hold the Commission's findings do not support the conclusion that Dodson's injuries arose out of his employment with Dubose.

C. In the Course of the Employment

"In the course of employment" refers to the time, place and circumstances giving rise to the injury.

> With respect to time, the course of employment begins a reasonable time before work begins and continues for a reasonable time after work ends. The place of employment includes the premises of the employer. *Where the*

*employee is engaged in activities that he is authorized to undertake and that
are calculated to further, directly or indirectly, the employer's business, the
circumstances are such as to be within the course of the employment.*

Pittman, 61 N.C. App. at 472, 300 S.E.2d at 901-02 (citations omitted) (emphasis added).
The circumstances element is fulfilled when "the employee is doing what a man so
employed may reasonably do within a time which he is employed and at a place where
he may reasonably be during that time to do that thing." [Citation omitted.]

In this case, there was no finding that Dodson's actions occurred at the time or place
of his employment. Further, the incident does not meet the circumstances element.
Dodson was not authorized to exit his truck to confront other drivers, and he was not
engaged in any activity in furtherance of Dubose's business when he got out to confront
Campbell. Dodson was not doing what a truck driver reasonably would do at the time
and place of his employment when the injury occurred. Therefore, I would hold the
Commission's findings do not support its conclusion that Dodson's injuries occurred in
the course of his employment.

II.

In its second argument, Dubose contends the Commission erred pursuant to N.C.
Gen. Stat. § 97-12(3) in awarding death benefits to Dodson where his death was
proximately caused by his own willful intent to injure or kill himself or another. N.C.
Gen. Stat. § 97-12(3) provides that "no compensation shall be payable if the injury or
death to the employee was proximately caused by: . . . (3) his willful intention to injure
or kill himself or another." The employee must intentionally and purposefully intend to
injure another. "Neither acts by the claimant, nor mere words spoken by the claimant
and unaccompanied by any overt act, will be a sufficient bar to compensation unless the
willful intent to injure is apparent from the context and nature of the physical or verbal
assault. [Citation omitted.]

Based on statements by Campbell and other witnesses, the Commission found that
Dodson struck Campbell's vehicle with his fists, pointed at Campbell and generally
seemed angry. The Commission did not find that Dodson verbally threatened Campbell
or that any physical assault on Campbell occurred. The context of this incident does not
make apparent the fact that Dodson willfully intended to injure Campbell, only that he
intended to confront him. I would hold that Dodson is not precluded from receiving
compensation under N.C. Gen. Stat. § 97-12(3).

In summary, because the Commission's findings do not support its conclusions that
Dodson's injuries arose out of and in the course of his employment, I would hold the
Commission erred in concluding that Dodson suffered a compensable injury under N.C.
Gen. Stat. § 97-2(6) and in awarding death benefits.

DODSON v. DUBOSE STEEL, INC.
358 N.C. 129; 591 S.E.2d 548 (2004)

PER CURIAM.

For the reasons stated in the dissenting opinion, the decision of the Court of Appeals
is reversed and the case is remanded to the Court of Appeals for further remand to the
North Carolina Industrial Commission for proceedings not inconsistent with the
dissenting opinion. *Reversed and Remanded.*

PROBLEMS

(1) Under the but-for theory, is it enough that the acquaintance of the assailant and
victim was the result solely of their employment association? Cyrus and Edmonds had
no contacts outside employment. During a break, Edmonds gave Cyrus 34 cents to buy
two packs of cigarettes. (This was 1946.) Cyrus got them for 31 cents, and an argument

developed over the change, in the course of which Edmonds killed Cyrus. Compensable? *See* Cyrus v. Miller Tire Service, 208 S.C. 545, 38 S.E.2d 761 (1946).

(2) On the same question: deceased, while working as a waitress, was asked for a date by a dishwasher, whom she knew only as a coemployee. She declined, none too tactfully, and he shot her. Compensable? *See* Scholtzhauer v. C. & L. Lunch Co., 233 N.Y. 12, 134 N.E. 701 (1922).

(3) Claimant, who had signed a peace petition that was allegedly Communist-inspired, was thrown out of the plant by his coworkers and seriously injured. Compensable? *See* Nash-Kelvinator Corp. v. Industrial Comm'n, 266 Wis. 81, 62 N.W.2d 567 (1954).

(4) Claimant, a police officer, was shot in his sleep by his 12-year-old son. When asked why he did it, the son said that he hated cops. Compensable? *See* Ottawa County v. King, 394 P.2d 536 (Okla. 1964).

(5) Claimant and a coemployee, Erma, were both romantically involved with another coemployee, Donald. Claimant and Erma had no relationship outside of the employment. All three had met at their work. One day Erma noticed a number of coemployees gossiping about them. Armed with a shrimp-peeling knife conveniently supplied by the employment, Erma confronted claimant. In the ensuing fight claimant was stabbed. Compensable? *See* Tampa Maid Seafood Products v. Porter, 415 So. 2d 883 (Fla. App. 1982).

(6) Decedent, a laundry-route driver, was shot by a customer with whose wife decedent had been carrying on an affair during his regular calls for dry cleaning. The signal that the "coast was clear" was a suit hung over the front porch rail. Thus, as decedent approached the place where he was shot, he was also on the direct route he would take to pick up the suit. Compensable? *See* Brookhaven Steam Laundry v. Watts, 214 Miss. 569, 59 So. 2d 294 (1952).

(7) Suppose, in *Brookhaven*, the laundry route driver had been completely innocent — the victim of a totally underserved suspicion. Would the result be different? *See* Bluegrass Pastureland Dairies v. Meeker, 268 Ky. 722, 105 S.W.2d 611 (1967). Do you agree with *Bluegrass*?

(8) Suppose, in *Brookhaven*, the laundry route driver was indeed guilty, but the husband had shot him from ambush in a dark, remote stretch of road where the driver had to pass in the course of his duties. Compensable?

(9) An ex-husband, upon discovering his ex-wife's plans to remarry, decides to kill her. He rents an apartment and, using a false identity, telephones her place of business to order a furniture item (she is in the business of selling furniture). When she appears, he shoots her and then himself. Compensation was awarded on the theory that the work placed the employee in an isolated locale and thus formed part of the husband's scheme to kill her. *Do you agree? See* California Comp. & Fire Co. v. W.C.A.B. (1968) 68 Cal. 2d 157, 65 Cal. Rptr. 155.

§ 4.03   THE AGGRESSOR DEFENSE

STEWART v. CHRYSLER CORP.
350 Mich. 596, 87 N.W.2d 117 (1957)

BLACK, JUSTICE.

. . . [T]he question facing us may in short interrogatory be stated as follows: Was the board justified in finding from the testimony that McCoy, convicted as he has been of manslaughter of Stewart, was the aggressor. I hold for affirmative answer.

Mr. Justice Smith, writing in dissent words that are now authoritative, approaches the variables of "course of employment" this way (*Salmon v. Bagley Laundry Co.*, 344 Mich. 471, 487, 74 N.W. 2d 1, 8):

> We collect these people by the hundreds, even thousands, and we put them to work sometimes amid noise and vibration, sometimes in smoke and steam. They get tired. They get hungry. They get thirsty. They have to go to the toilet. The day wears on and tempers grow short. Relief is sought in horseplay. Trips to the water cooler and the coffee urn grow in number and duration. This is the course of employment. "Course of employment" is not a sterile form of words. It is descriptive of life in the industrial age. These human deviations from the course of the automation do not suspend the employer-employee relationship. They are not departures from employment, but the very substance of it. They are the inevitable concomitants of the working relationship and conditions which produce the product. Its cost must reflect the fatigue, the irritations, and sometimes the blood that went into it. It is here that we find the explanation for the horseplay cases, the curiosity cases, and the assault cases.

Looking at this record of facts, we face appraisal of what in essence is a question of degree[1] of Stewart's fault. Is an ordinary, and understandably provoked, slap of another's face sufficient to break the connection or nexus between employment and countering blow when the degree-comparison lies between a stinging check and a fatally bashed skull? Larson says (1 Larson's Workmen's Compensation Law, § 11.15(c), pp. 126, 127):

> Even the first blow, if it was not a particularly damaging one, or if it was provoked by verbal abuse or by a mistaken idea of attack by a detested co-employee, may be held to fall short of aggression.

> One of the practical difficulties besetting the application of the aggressor defense is the very homely fact that, long after a quarrel is over, it is often almost impossible to determine who really started it. Many a father has come home at six o'clock to find he is expected to sit in belated judgment on this issue between his two children, the testimony consisting of "He hit me"; "Yes, but she called me a stinker"; "But before that he grabbed my comic book"; and so on and on. One cannot read the facts behind the aggressor cases without seeing how closely the average factory scuffle follows this pattern. The difficulty with the defense, as the Massachusetts court concluded, is that it impose s the necessity of selecting one overt act out of a series of hostile verbal, psychological and physical acts as the one which, for compensation purposes, caused the quarrel and elicited the ultimate injury.

Larson refers here, of course, to *Dillon's Case*, 324 Mass. 102, 85 N.E.2d 69, 71, from which I quote with intent of adoption as follows:

> The striking of the first blow is not the sole and ultimate test as to whether the injury arose out of the employment. . . . We must constantly remind ourselves that in compensation cases fault is not a determining factor, whether it be that of the employee alone or that of the employee contributing with the fault of others, unless it amounts to the "serious and wilful misconduct" of the employee which by § 27, as appearing in St. 1935, c. 331, bars all relief to him. Apart from serious and wilful misconduct, the question is whether the injury occurred in the line of consequences resulting from the circumstances and conditions of the employment, and not who was to blame for it. . . . So even

---

[1] *(Court's footnote)* "It is a question of degree whether I have been negligent. It is a question of degree whether in the use of my own land, I have created a nuisance which may be abated by my neighbor. It is a question of degree whether the law which takes my property and limits my conduct, impairs my liberty unduly. So also the duty of a judge becomes itself a question of degree, and he is a useful judge or a poor one as he estimates the measure accurately or loosely." (Mr. Justice Cardozo's "The Nature of the Judicial Process," pp. 161, 162.)

where the employee himself strikes the first blow, that fact does not break the connection between the employment and the injury, if it can be seen that the whole affair had its origin in the nature and conditions of the employment. . . .

In this case the facts as found show that Stewart, in circumstances of annoying provocation, did no more than slap McCoy's face with his hand. What was the severity of the slap? What is a "particularly damaging one"? Did it amount to "a vicious and unprovoked assault," as found in presently considered *Horvath*? Was it of such force as to require our matter-of-law brand of aggressor on Stewart? Surely, and as the signers of this opinion note from the appeal board's essential findings, these are questions for constituted triers of fact rather than questions of law for detached appellate judges.

The analogy of the criminal process is helpful here. Noting again that McCoy was convicted of manslaughter of Stewart, and assuming that the same record of facts was made before the jury when the latter undertook consideration of McCoy's guilt or innocence, would it have been right for the trial judge to instruct that Stewart was the aggressor? I think not (and suspect he did not do so), since the question of identity of the aggressor in personal assault cases, whether the action be one for damages or one brought by the people, invariably becomes one of fact [*Court's footnote omitted*] And, when the question arises in compensation proceedings, it is usually the same: See *Stulginski v. Waterbury Rolling Mills Co.*, 124 Conn. 355, 199 A. 653, 658, where it was said:

> The adoption of a rule, that if an injured employee was the aggressor he could not recover compensation, though the injury arose out of the conditions of the employment, would require a definition of terms which would be extremely difficult. Certainly to hold that no matter what provocation and angry words there might have been between the parties, he who struck the first blow, slight though it might be, would be denied compensation would be neither reasonable nor in accordance with sound principles. That the injured employee was the aggressor would certainly be a factor, in some cases an important factor, to be considered in determining whether the chain of causation between the conditions of the employment and the injury has been broken. But it would have that effect as bearing upon the question whether there had intervened personal motives, designs, or the like, sufficient to constitute an intervening cause. . . .

The appeal board found . . . that McCoy was the aggressor and that Stewart's injury and death at McCoy's blow arose out of and in the course of Stewart's employment. Such finding is fully supported by evidence. The board found:

> McCoy deliberately and in total disregard of decedent's protests removed the steps which had been provided by the employer for the use, convenience, benefit and protection of decedent and other employees in the course of their work. The argument immediately preceding and culminating in the fatal injury arose out of and because of such actions on McCoy's part. This argument would not have occurred but for McCoy's wilful acts in complete disregard of decedent's rights. The acts of McCoy were the first acts of hostility and caused and precipitated the quarrel which resulted in the fatal injury. McCoy was the aggressor. He caused the controversy. The fight arose because McCoy wilfully disturbed, disrupted and interfered with a method and means of ingress and egress incidental to the employment provided, prescribed and approved by the employer. While decedent struck the first blow, this is not the controlling test as to whether the injury arose out of the employment. It did not make decedent the aggressor. Previous acts of aggression on the part of McCoy engendered the enmity and precipitated the actual physical conflict. The disagreement arose out of the employer's work. There was causal relation between the employment and the fatal injury. Acts occurring in the course of work provoked the altercation which brought about the death of decedent. The fatal injury clearly arose out of and in the course of decedent's employment.

. . . .

I vote to affirm.

SMITH, EDWARDS and VOELKER, JJ., concurred with BLACK, J.

DETHMERS, C.J., and SHARPE, KELLY and CARR, JJ., dissented.

PROBLEMS

(1) A minority of jurisdictions now recognize the "aggressor defense" and the number is declining. Do you agree with this trend? What are the pros and cons of having such a defense available?

(2) A self-employed attorney, who was doing an investigation for a client, parked his car on the property of an off-duty deputy sheriff. The deputy sheriff asked him to leave, an argument ensued, and the attorney was injured when the deputy sheriff physically ejected him from the property. Assume you are in a jurisdiction that recognizes the aggressor defense. *Is claimant the physical aggressor?*

(3) A school janitor is playing cards with a co-worker on an authorized break. Suspecting him of cheating, he calls the co-worker a "sonovabitch," whereupon the co-employee grabs the janitor and throws him on the ground, injuring him. *In a jurisdiction recognizing the aggressor defense, who is the aggressor?*

§ 4.04   ASSAULTS BY STRANGERS

WHITE v. ATLANTIC CITY PRESS
64 N.J. 128, 313 A.2d 197 (1973)

PASHMAN, J.

On the morning of April 13, 1971, petitioner John B. White, while driving his automobile to work, picked up two young hitchhikers. They returned his favor by committing acts of felonious assault and robbery upon him. . . .

Petitioner alleges that at the time of the accident, he had been working as a route delivery man, having begun that work in January 1971. His duties encompassed driving a few miles from his residence in Atlantic City to Pleasantville, picking up for delivery 200 of respondent's newspapers, and then delivering them. He would load the daily edition of respondent's papers in his car and drop them off individually by throwing a copy on a customer's front porch or lawn or inserting one in a post box, along a scattered route of 20 to 25 miles in rural Atlantic County. Each morning by 7:00 A.M., the route deliveryman's function would be completed.

Petitioner testified that on the eventful morning of April 13, 1971, he left his home around 5:00 A.M., his usual time, and while still in Atlantic City not too far from his own residence, he picked up two hitchhikers who wanted to be taken to a bus station. Petitioner added that he had never encountered or known of harmful incidents in all the times he picked up hitchhikers. The drive to the bus station necessitated a detour of several blocks from petitioner's customary route but as was evidenced, no appreciable time would have been lost since one could get to Pleasantville by several alternative express roads. While waiting at a red light, one of the hitchhikers pulled a knife and demanded petitioner's money. A fight ensued, and with White losing control, his automobile bounced against several parked cars. Petitioner was hospitalized with lacerations and stab wounds in the face, abdomen and hand, and the assailant was taken into police custody. Petitioner resumed his work a week later. . . .

(The court here ruled that (1) petitioner was indeed an employee, and that (2) the

going and coming exception did not preclude compensability, since the petitioner's employment required the use of his vehicle for the employer's benefit as soon as he left home.)

In Beh v. Breeze Corporation, *supra*, a traveling salesman while driving his car on business for his employer, picked up a hitchhiker during a snowstorm. After stopping for lunch and resuming the journey the passenger attempted to rob the employee at gunpoint and killed him when the latter resisted. The matter of picking up hitchhikers had not been a subject of discussion between employer and employee. The former Supreme Court granted compensation to the decedent's widow, 137 N.J.L. 431, 60 A.2d 273 (1948), pointing out that the act is broad, providing for compensation where the accident or death arises out of and in the course of the employment, except where intentionally self-inflicted or when intoxication is the natural and proximate cause of injury. It declared (at 433, 60 A.2d at 274): We find that the death arose from a risk incidental to the employment and was causally connected therewith because it arose from a risk or hazard incident to the use of the highway. The employee, if he had not stopped for the hitch-hiker, might have been shot anyway. That is one of the risks of travel.

The present Supreme Court reversed. Conceding that the accident had arisen in the course of the employment, it held it had not arisen out of the employment. The Court reasoned that picking up hitch-hikers was not within the employee's express duties nor necessary to their accomplishment; the peril was separable from the employee's line of duty; his duties did not expose him to the danger except through his independent act; and there was no causal connection between the accident and the conditions attending the transaction of the employer's business (2 N.J. at 283, 66 A.2d 156). The accident was not "directly attributable to a risk of the highway to which the decedent's employment exposed him since injuries from an unknown assailant riding as a guest of the driver were not an "ordinary risk of the highway" (*Id.*). The court viewed the pickup as a "charitable incident for the accommodation of the hitch-hiker" from which the employer derived no benefit (*Id.*). Such conduct constitutes a "self-imposed" risk, is commonly known to be dangerous, and is not within the contemplation of the employer at the time of hiring. (2 N.J. at 284, 66 A.2d 156).

We think it clear that the development of the concept of "arising out of the employment" by the decisions of our courts since *Beh* was decided in 1949 is in sharp divergence from the philosophy of that decision as just summarized. The gravamen of Beh is the enlargement of the risks of the employment by voluntary action of the employee beyond those in contemplation by the employer at the time of hiring. However, foreseeability of the incidence of a particular kind of injury to an employee has always been regarded as immaterial in the rationale of compensation law. Larson, *Workmen's Compensation Law*, § 6.50, at 3-7, 3-8 (1972); *Gargiulo v. Gargiulo*, 13 N.J. 8, 97 A.2d 593 (1953). The concept of foreseeability is in the domain of tort law, where fault characteristically plays a role-not in that of workmen's compensation to which it is irrelevant. *Secor v. Penn Service Garage*, 19 N.J. 315, 319, 117 A.2d 12 (1955). The fundamental issue in the latter area is work-connection, Larson, op. cit., at 3-8, and that must be the fulcrum of our inquiry here.

Moreover, the emphasis in *Beh* on the invitation by the employee of the hitchhiker as creative of a "self-imposed risk," as opposed to a "risk of the highway," (2 N.J. at 284, 66 A.2d 156) also clashes with the principle that fault of the employee is basically immaterial in compensation law. Contributory negligence is of course not a defense, and the act carefully delimits the bar of fault, as such, solely to the categories of intentional self-infliction of harm and intoxication as the sole and proximate cause of injury. N.J.S.A. 34:15-7. [*Court's footnote omitted*].

The fountainhead of the inquiry here lies in the question whether the hazard giving rise to petitioner's injury was a "risk that grows out of or is connected with what a workman has to do in fulfilling his contract of service" — a risk which may be "ordinary" or "extraordinary in character, indirectly connected with the employment because of its special nature." *Belyus v. Wilkinson*, Gaddis & Co., 115 N.J.L. 43, 47, 178 A. 181, 184 (Sup. Ct. 1935), *aff'd* 116 N.J.L. 92, 182 A. 873 (E. & A. 1936). But the risk is not beyond the purview of employment connection merely because it is heightened by an act of the employee otherwise within the course of the employment, which might be described as "foolhardy," "negligent," or "foolish," see *Green v. De Furia*, 19 N.J. 290, 297, 116 A.2d 19 (1955); or as a "grossly negligent" act of "mock bravado," see *Secor v. Penn Service Garage, supra* (19 N.J. at 323–324, 117 A.2d 12); and see *Diaz v. Newark Industrial Spraying, Inc.*, 35 N.J. 588, 174 A.2d 478 (1961).

In *Secor, supra*, where a gasoline drenched attendant at a service station, disregarding his employer's direction to change his uniform for the sake of safety, lit a match near his trouser's leg to show that the change was unnecessary and consequently was severely burned, the court allowed recovery as against the employer's contention that the injury resulted from "actions committed by (the employee) not in the course of employment." Speaking for the Court majority, and assuming Arguendo that the employee had acted in a spirit of "mock bravado" Justice Jacobs said (19 N.J. at 324, 117 A.2d at 16): An employee is not an automaton, and, even when he is highly efficient, he will to some extent deviate from the uninterrupted perfomance of his work. Such deviation, if it be considered minor in the light of the particular time, place and circumstance, is realistically viewed by both the employer and the employee as a normal incidence of the employment relation and ought not in this day be viewed as legally breaching the course thereof. Fulfillment of the high purposes of our socially important and ever broadening Workmen's Compensation Act suggests this approach and nothing in the statutory term dictates any narrower position.

In similar vein is the rationale of our decision in *Diaz v. Newark Industrial Spraying, Inc., supra*, where we allowed compensation to an employee who, by repeatedly squirting water on a fellow-employee, provoked the latter into throwing at him what was thought to be water but turned out to be a flammable lacquer thinner, which took fire and burned the skylarking petitioner. Although the employer had no prior knowledge of this kind of frolicking by the employees, *cf.* McKenzie v. Brixite Mfg. Co., 34 N.J. 1, 166 A.2d 753 (1961), recovery was nonetheless granted. We said that "the case requires the application of a realistic view of reasonable human reactions to working conditions and associations with people encountered in the course of employment" (35 N.J. at 590, 174 A.2d at 479); further that in this general area, "the center of inquiry has shifted from insulating the particular act in a vacuum to considering it in the entire nature of the employment, including the risks of human associations and failings and conditions inseparable from the specific work" (at 591, 174 A.2d at 479).

It is in the spirit of such counsel that we must seek the answer to the specific problem which is of present concern. Obviously robbery and assault on a highway are potential hazards of traveling thereon by automobile. *Geltman v. Reliable Linen & Supply Co.*, 128 N.J.L. 443, 25 A.2d 894 (E. & A. 1942). But for the performance by petitioner of his duty to drive to the pickup point in Pleasantville for the newspapers, he would never have encountered the assailants. The analysis thus devolves to the question whether petitioner's succumbing to the instinct of aid to the beckoning couple constituted a "reasonable human reaction," in the language of *Diaz, supra*, even if, Arguendo, "foolhardy" or "grossly negligent." We entertain no doubt that it was such a reaction. It is an act which occurs countless times on the streets and highways, and in the vast majority of instances without harm. The question is not whether it is a prudent act or a commendable one. As noted in the cases cited above, the reasonably expectable range of conduct of workmen in the employment milieu can run the entire gamut from the grossly careless, imprudent, or foolhardy, to the opposite of those characteristics. The teaching of the Secor line of cases is that if the circumstances of the employment can be fairly said to have elicited conduct by the employee which results in his injury, absent what a court would conclude to be substantial deviation from the course of the employment, compensation ordinarily follows regardless of how one might assess such conduct in terms of prudence, judgment, wisdom or human frailty.

We regard the foregoing criteria as here met. The employer placed the petitioner on the highway, and he was thereby subjected to the hazard, albeit apparently not appreciated by him, of the encounter with those who were able to entice him, as they could have many others in similar circumstances, to give them a lift. We hold there was work-connection sufficient to render the ensuing injuries such as arose out of the employment [*Court's footnote omitted*]. . . .

In light of the foregoing conclusions, we need not be detained long by the argument that picking up hitchhikers was a disqualified deviation from the employment. The detour involved was only a few blocks, led to an alternative main route to Pleasantville, and would have taken only a few minutes longer. It was not by any means a serious deviation in terms of comparison with other fact situations we have held not to be fatal to recovery. See, e.g., *Rainear v. Rainear*, 63 N.J. 276, 307 A.2d 72 (1973) and cases cited therein.

For the reasons stated we conclude that *Beh v. Breeze Corporation, supra,* should be and is herewith overruled.

Judgment reversed.

PROBLEMS

(1) Would, or should, the outcome have been different in *White* if the employer had had a flat rule against picking up hitchhikers, and if that rule had clearly been communicated to the petitioner?

(2) A female flight attendant suffers injury when she is raped during a 26-hour "layover" between flights. She met a man on the beach during the layover, and willingly went to his apartment, where the rape occurred. She was paid a salary during the layover, the airline employer paid for her hotel room, and the airline has no rules regarding social activities during layovers. *Compensable? See* Western Airlines v. Workers' Compensation Appeals Board, 155 Cal. App. 3d 366, 202 Cal. Rptr. 74 (1984).

(3) A traveling salesperson stops at a restaurant for lunch between calls on customers. While getting back into his automobile, which is parked on a street near the restaurant, he is deliberately shot and killed by a stranger acting without provocation or discernible reason of any kind, evidently a madman. *Are his dependent spouse and child entitled to death benefits? See* Corken v. Corken Steel Products, Inc., 385 S.W.2d 949 (Ky. 1965).

JORDAN v. FARMERS STATE BANK
791 S.W.2d 1 (Mo. Ct. App. 1990)

PREWITT, JUDGE.

Farmers State Bank of Texas County, the employer of Loretta K. Jordan and James R. Byler, appeals from an award of the Labor and Industrial Relations Commission granting workers' compensation benefits for injuries received by the two employees. The question in both appeals is whether the injuries of James R. Byler and Loretta K. Jordan arose out of and in the course of their employment. As the issues presented are almost identical, the appeals were consolidated.

The relevant facts are not in dispute. James R. Byler was the president of the Farmers State Bank of Texas County, Missouri located in Houston, Missouri. Shortly after he arrived for work on April 24, 1986, he received a phone call from a man, who identified himself as Jay Lewis. Lewis had taken Byler's wife hostage at the Bylers' home. Lewis told Byler that he had "five seconds to get out of the bank, go to Raymondville, and pick up a hundred thousand dollars." There is a branch of the

Farmers State Bank in Raymondville which is located a few miles from Houston.

Byler told Jordan, the vice president of Farmers State Bank, of the call and asked whether she was going with him to get the money. Jordan decided to accompany Byler because he had a history of heart problems. They went to Raymondville and got currency and then went to Byler's home. They placed the money where directed and then Lewis, carrying a firearm, made them go to Byler's garage and lie on the floor. Lewis then shot them.

The Farmers State Bank had anticipated the possibilities of robbery or extortion. The bank had Federal Bureau of Investigation agents and other law enforcement officers talk with the bank employees about what they should do in the event either occurred. If a person was being held hostage the bank employees were to begin preparation for delivery of the sum demanded and to notify another bank official of the threat and the employee's intentions regarding it. They were advised to do as they were told and not to try to be heroic, to follow the procedures and guidelines that they were given, both orally and in writing.

In this proceeding Byler and Jordan sought benefits under the Workers' Compensation Law for the injuries received from the shootings. The Commission, adopting the findings of Chief Administrative Law Judge James H. Wesley II, on the issues here, found that the injuries arose out of and in the course of their employment. Review is of the Commission's Award. *Wilhite v. Hurd*, 411 S.W.2d 72, 76 (Mo. 1967). . . .

For an employer to be liable under the Workers' Compensation Law an employee's injuries must occur by accident "arising out of and in the course of" employment. § 287.120.1, RSMo 1986. "Personal injuries arising out of and in the course of such employment" does not cover workers "except while engaged in or about the premises where their duties are being performed, or where their services require their presence as a part of such service." § 287.020.5, RSMo 1986.

The terms "out of" and "in the course of" are separate tests which must be met for an injury to be compensable. *Davison v. Florsheim Shoe Co.*, 750 S.W.2d 481, 483 (Mo. App. 1988); *Page*, 686 S.W.2d at 532. Case law has defined the phrase "arising out of" to mean the injury is a natural and reasonable incident of the employment; there must be a causal connection between the nature of the duties or conditions the employee is required to perform and the resulting injury.

> "[I]n the course of" is occurring within the period of employment at a place where the employee may reasonably be, while the person is reasonably fulfilling the duties of employment or engaged in doing something incidental thereto. *Parrish v. Kansas City Security Service*, 682 S.W.2d 20, 26 (Mo. App. 1984); *Davison, supra* 750 S.W.2d at 483.

Other cases have worded their analyses of these concepts slightly differently. "An injury 'arises out of' the employment if (1) the injury results from a natural and reasonable incident of the employment, a rational consequence of some hazard connected therewith or a risk reasonably inherent in the particular conditions of the employment and (2) if the injury is the result of a risk peculiar to the employment or enhanced thereby." *Dillard*, 685 S.W.2d at 921. "An injury 'arises in the course of' employment if it occurs within the period of employment at a place where the employee may reasonably be, while engaged in the furtherance of the employer's business or if he is injured in doing an act reasonably incidental to the performance of his duties, of which his employer might reasonably have knowledge or reasonably anticipate." *Id.*

Each case involving whether an accident arose out of and in the course of employment must be decided on its own facts and circumstances, by applying the relevant principles and not by reference to some formula, or by attempting to group compensation problems by fact categories. *Page*, 686 S.W.2d at 533.

Although conceding that the bank having access to large amounts of currency increased the likelihood that Mrs. Byler might be kidnapped, the bank argues that assaults on Byler and Jordan did not arise "out of" their employment and the assaults "were distantly removed in the chain of causation from the presence of money at the bank." It argues that once they arrived at the Byler residence "money was not a contributing cause of their injuries. The assaults occurred because Byler and Jordan were present at a crime scene and could possibly identify the perpetrator." The fallacy in this argument is that they were only present and in the position to identify the perpetrator because they were following guidelines given them in delivering currency which they had access to because of their employment.

The injuries arose out of Jordan's and Byler's employment. There is the hazard that an employee or a member of an employee's family might be held hostage and that currency may have to be delivered to the extortionist at great danger to the employee. The knowledge that banks often have large amounts of currency and that they are sometimes preyed upon by those seeking money through illegal means makes it a natural and a reasonable incident of employment at a bank that an employee could be shot and that shooting would be a rational consequence of the hazard of such employment.

The bank contends that the injuries to Jordan and Byler did not arise "in the course of" employment as it did not occur at the bank nor at any place "where any of the Banks' business ever transpired." They say that the employees were not fulfilling the duties of their employment at the time of the assault but were attempting to secure Mrs. Byler's release.

The injuries were "in the course of" their employment. They occurred during the period of employment at the house of a bank employee whose spouse was being held hostage. In complying with Lewis' instructions Byler was where his employer had instructed him to be. Under the circumstances it was reasonable for Jordan to go with Byler. Indeed, it is doubtful that she would have wanted to expose herself to such danger if it had not been required or expected of her in her employment. It was reasonable for the employees to be there and they were reasonably fulfilling the duties of their employment.

The award is affirmed.

PROBLEMS

(1) An employee was robbed in the employer's parking lot after returning from cashing a personal check. The robber followed her from the bank to the parking lot. *Compensable? See* Rogers v. W.C.A.B. (1985), 172 Cal. App. 3d 1195, 218 Cal. Rptr. 662.

(2) A garbage collector was attacked from behind by an unknown assailant while working alone at 5 a.m. He was injured, and robbed of $3. Is the assault compensable? *See* Pisapia v. City of Newark, 47 N.J. Super. 353, 136 A.2d 67 (1957).

(3) Claimant, an elderly sales clerk, routinely arrives two hours early to work and waits in the employee cafeteria prior to starting her shift. One morning she comes to work and is assaulted and robbed in her employer's parking lot. *Compensable? Was the claimant in the course of employment at the time the injury took place?*

(4) Claimant, a senior director for a charity, worked from her home because the charity had limited office space. She met with co-workers in her home when necessary, had remote access to the charity's computing network and even had an allowance for office supplies. She was attacked in her home during working hours by a neighbor who had been stalking her. *Compensable? Did claimant's injuries arise from the employment? See* Wait v. Travelers Indemnity Co., 240 S.W.3d 220 (Tenn. 2007).

§ 4.05 ASSAULTS STEMMING FROM LABOR DISPUTE

MEO v. COMMERCIAL CAN CORP.
80 N.J. Super. 58, 192 A.2d 854 (1963)

GOLDMANN, S. J.A.D

Meo had been Commercial Can's plant superintendent in charge of production for a number of years at a salary of $450 a week. Although the company had three plants — Brooklyn, Newark and Pittsburgh — his almost sole concern was clearly with the Newark plant. Meo was on call 24 hours a day, day and night — as occasion required — so that plant operations might continue uninterrupted. He had multiple duties, executive as well as physical.

The Brooklyn plant went on strike November 15, 1959. On February 1, 1960 some 80 of the 105 employees at the Newark plant, members of a local affiliated with the Teamsters' Union, went out on strike. Meo was ordered by the company president to keep the Newark operation going, and to this end he, among other things, interviewed and hired workers to replace those who had struck. Among the employees who continued to work were five relatives of Meo, including his son-in-law, John Bellomo. Some of the five were union members; others belonged to management. Meo lived in Fairview, N. J., two doors from Bellomo. The company had provided Meo with a car to travel to and from the plant. Bellomo accompanied him on these trips. Meo testified that during the strike he hired some replacement workers at his home, and there were a number of meetings there to plan work schedules.

The strike was a violent one, attended by active, continuous and disorderly picketing at the plant premises. There were as many as 50 or 60 pickets in the morning, a lesser number in the afternoon, and at times there were as many as 100–150 men on the picket line. There were cursing, name-calling, stone-throwing, and efforts to overturn cars attempting to run the gauntlet of the pickets. A number of persons were hurt and had to be taken to the hospital. The Newark police tried to keep order, and the plant was under constant surveillance.

Meo was the target of constant threats. He testified that shortly after the strike started three union delegates came to his office and said that "if I knew what was good for me that I should close the plant down." He at once called in the Newark police. Meo said that when he would leave the plant with Bellomo to go home, two police motorcycle escorts would accompany them to the Newark boundary line, almost as far as the New Jersey Turnpike. Twice striking employees attempted to run the company-owned car off the Turnpike.

On one occasion when Meo discussed the strike situation with Commercial Can's president, the latter stated that the Newark plant must be kept open despite any violence, and he would personally attend to anything that happened. Soon after the strike started Meo received a call from the president warning him to be careful, never to leave his home alone, and to ask the Fairview police for protection. Meo got in touch with the Fairview police chief and was provided with the necessary surveillance of his home. He received threatening phone calls at his home practically every night, telling him he had better shut down the plant if he knew what was good for him. A typical call was, "You dirty so-and-so; what are you trying to do, take bread and butter out of our mouths? We will get you yet. We are going to spill blood along the road." When his wife answered, the caller would hang up. There was a nightly average of four or five calls, and during the last week or so before he was attacked, he received almost a dozen calls a night.

On the morning of March 30, 1960 Meo arose at about 5:45, dressed and had breakfast, went to the garage, drove the company car out onto the driveway, and then waited for his son-in-law to come over from his home close by so that they could drive to the plant together. A green patch of lawn showing through the snow cover attracted Meo's attention. He got out of the car for a closer look, and as he was looking he heard footsteps, but paid no attention. Suddenly he heard someone say, "Here's the lousy scab," or "Here's that dirty scab." He remembered nothing further; when he regained consciousness he found himself in the Englewood Hospital. He had suffered a broken jaw, bruises to his back, injuries to his head requiring eight stitches, and the loss of three teeth, in addition to other injuries. He could not identify his assailants. Shortly before the attack his wife happened to look out of the kitchen window and saw three men running by, one with a baseball bat in his hands. She testified that she knew that something was wrong, ran outside and, receiving no answer when she called her husband, then found him lying unconscious in a pool of blood, all battered. She had not seen the faces of the assailants, but said they were dressed in working jackets and that they had run to a car on the side street and driven away. Bellomo arrived on the scene moments later and found a wooden bat, some 1 1/2" in diameter and 2" long, lying close by Meo. He testified that as he was coming out of his home he noticed three young fellows come around the corner, but paid no particular attention to them at the time. He, too, was unable to identify any of them.

The company, here as below, states the issue to be, simply: "Does a workman, who is off duty, while leaving his home to go to work, and who is assaulted within the confines of his home, come within the purview of our Compensation Acts?" The matter is incompletely put, for it entirely lacks the frame of reference of the strike and petitioner's responsibilities in the strike setting. It likewise disregards his continuing prior experiences with relation thereto.

One or two preliminary matters should be disposed of before dealing with the core question of whether the injuries which Meo suffered are compensable. In the first place, there is no dispute that an assault may be deemed to be an "accident" within the Workmen's Compensation Act despite its willful or criminal nature. *Cierpial v. Ford Motor Co.*, 16 N.J. 561, 566, 109 A.2d 666 (1954). Nor does the employer dispute that although Meo's assailants were not identified, an inference may reasonably and logically be drawn from the facts and circumstances that those who attacked him were strikers or men sympathetic to their cause.

The company concedes that Meo's injuries resulted from an accident arising "out of" his employment, but vigorously disputes that they arose "in the course of" the employment, and therefore are not compensable. In support of its position it relies heavily upon part of the text appearing in 1 Larson, Workmen's Compensation Law, § 29.21, pp. 447–448 (1952), and 1962 Supp., p. 218:

> If a non-striking employee is assaulted by strikers on his way to [*Enterprise Foundry Co. v. Industrial Accident Commission*, 206 Cal. 562, 275 P. 432 (Sup. Ct. 1929)] or from [*Lampert v. Siemons*, 235 N.Y. 311, 139 N.E. 278 (Ct. App. 1923)] work, even if only two blocks from the employment premises [*Walsh v. Russeks Fifth Avenue*, 266 App. Div. 760, 41 N.Y.S. 2d 145 (Sup. Ct. 1943)], he is denied compensation protection. Or if he is killed in a gun fight a mile-and-a-half from the plant, the same result has been reached, although the strike was the sole occasion for the assault. [*Merz v. Industrial Commission*, 134 Ohio St. 36, 15 N.E.2d 632 (Sup. Ct. 1938)] Even when the employer promises special protection or assumes enlarged responsibility the statutory barrier has remained impermeable. In a New York case [*Bonnafoux v. Downtown Athletic Club*, 268 N.Y. 657, 198 N.E. 543 (Ct. App. 1935), affirming 244 App. Div. 850, 279 N.Y.S. 629 (App. Div. 1935)], the employer furnished a detective escort to a non-striking baker during a city-wide strike. The detective's signal was three rings on the doorbell. One morning when claimant responded to this ring he was met and assaulted by strikers, and lost the sight of one eye. Compensation was denied. And in an English case [*Poulton v. Kelsall*, [1912] 2 K.B. 131, 81

L.J.K.B. 774, 106 L.T. 522] the employer's express agreement to assume responsibility for injuries to a non-striker was held ineffective to enlarge the compensation rights of a claimant assaulted by strikers seven minutes' walk from the employer's premises. Most extreme of all is a Scottish holding that even a strike-breaker injured by stones thrown at him could not recover compensation. [*Murray v. Denholm & Co.*, 48 Sc. L.R. 896 (1911)]

It will at once be observed that the cases cited to the text, and which we have set out in brackets, relate to a past day when courts generally, as indeed many courts still do, held that assaults occurring outside working hours or away from the place of employment were not compensable. The more modern view has long since broken through the barrier of the limited reasoning of these decisions.

The quoted text does not fairly represent Larson's thinking. In his view, there is no class of cases where the basic purposes of compensation law have so far miscarried as in the so-called "delayed injury" cases — work-connected assaults outside regular working hours. The most common examples are those growing out of strikes, and whether one choose to call the claimant a scab or a loyal employee, the fact is that he was assaulted solely because of the performance of his work. Larson points out that looking at the matter from the employer's point of view, if ever an employee deserves compensation for his injuries, it is when he, at considerable personal risk, remains on the job to minimize damage and other loss that might be visited upon his employer. In every case where a court has refused compensation, it was because of the timing of the assault, "which might or might not bring it within the conventional boundaries of course of employment at the irresponsible whim of the assailant." Op. cit., § 29.21, pp. 446–448.

The author notes that sometimes a court is able to find special circumstances enabling it to surmount the "course of employment" obstacle. For example, the employee is attacked near the plant shortly after leaving work, as in *Field v. Charmette Knitting Fabric Co.*, 245 N.Y. 139, 156 N.E. 642 (Ct. App. 1927), where Cardozo, J., found "continuity of cause . . . combined with contiguity in time and space," the ultimate test to be applied being whether "the quarrel from origin to ending must be taken to be one"; *National Union Fire Ins. Co. v. Britton*, 187 F.Supp. 359 (D.C.D.C. 1960); and see *Baggett Transp. Co. v. Holderfield*, 260 Ala. 56, 68 So. 2d 21 (Sup. Ct. 1953) (claimant waited an hour before leaving the plant, but was pursued by strikers, overtaken a mile from the plant, and shot; compensation awarded). Or the assault occurred within the "zone of danger" created by the employment, *Scott v. Industrial Commission*, 374 Ill. 225, 29 N.E.2d 93 (Sup. Ct. 1940); *A. N. Campbell & Co. v. Messenger*, 171 Va. 374, 199 S.E. 511 (Sup. Ct. App. 1938). Or the employee was on 24-hour duty, housed by his employer near the plant, kept on continuous call, or under the employer's protection, *Crippen v. Press Co., Inc.*, 228 App. Div. 727, 239 N.Y.S. 102 (App. Div. 1929), affirmed 254 N.Y. 535, 173 N.E. 584 (Ct. App. 1929); *Malky v. Kiskiminetas Valley Coal Co.*, 278 Pa. 552, 123 A. 505, 31 A.L.R. 1082 (Sup. Ct. 1924). . . .

We have no hesitation in concluding, under the particular facts of this case, that Meo's assault occurred out of and in the course of his employment with Commercial Can. He was on 24-hour duty, and under express direction to keep the plant going at all cost. The area of his employment, and the strike area with it, extended beyond the Newark plant to and into his home in Fairview. What he was doing for his employer brought upon him threats of violence when he was at the plant, on the road home, and within the very confines of his residence. As plant superintendent in charge of production, as the man who defied every effort of the strikers to close the plant, as the person who hired new employees, he was an obvious target for strike violence. His employer knew of the employment hazard attending Meo from the very beginning of the strike at the Newark plant, and in fact warned him of the probability of violence and the necessity of getting police protection.

One is inevitably compelled to the conclusion that the conditions surrounding the labor dispute and the totality of circumstances attending Meo's employment made the assault upon him a natural incident of his work as plant superintendent and, as the county judge observed, a risk occasioned by the nature of his employment in behalf of management. The assault was directly related to his work and is therefore compensable. . . .

Chapter 5
RISKS PERSONAL TO THE EMPLOYEE

§ 5.01 INTRODUCTION

Injuries arising out of risks or conditions personal to the claimant do not arise out of the employment unless the employment contributes to the risk or aggravates the injury. When the employee has a preexisting physical weakness or disease, this employment contribution may be found either in placing the employee in a position which aggravates the effects of a fall due to the idiopathic condition, or in precipitating the effects of the condition by strain or trauma.

When an employee, solely because of a nonoccupational heart attack, epileptic fit, or fainting spell, falls and sustains a skull fracture or other injury, the question arises whether the skull fracture (as distinguished from the internal effects of the heart attack or disease, which of course are not compensable) is an injury arising out of the employment.

The basic rule, on which there is now general agreement, is that the effects of such a fall are compensable if the employment places the employee in a position increasing the dangerous effects of such a fall, such as on a height, near machinery or sharp corners, or in a moving vehicle. The currently controversial question is whether the effects of an idiopathic fall to the level ground or bare floor should be deemed to arise out of the employment.

It should be stressed that the present question, although sometimes discussed in the same breath with unexplained falls, is basically different, since unexplained-fall cases begin with a completely neutral origin of the mishap, while idiopathic fall cases begin with an origin which is admittedly personal and which therefore requires some affirmative employment contribution to offset the prima facie showing of personal origin.

§ 5.02 INTERNAL WEAKNESS CAUSING FALL

GEORGE v. GREAT EASTERN FOOD PRODUCTS, INC.
44 N.J. 44, 207 A.2d 161 (1965)

HALL, J.

In this workmen's compensation case, the employee died from a fractured skull sustained as the result of an idiopathic fall (used in the sense of a fall caused by a purely personal condition having no work connection whatever) "in the course of" his employment. An attack of dizziness, apparently induced by some cardiovascular condition, precipitated the occurrence. He did not strike anything until his head hit the level concrete floor upon which he was standing, bringing about the injury. The Division of Workmen's Compensation dismissed the petitions seeking compensation for the period between the injury and death some few weeks later and for dependency benefits. The Essex County Court reached the same result on appeal and the Appellate Division affirmed in an unreported opinion, holding the case was controlled by this court's 4-3 decision in *Henderson v. Celanese Corp.*, 16 N.J. 208, 108 A.2d 267 (1954), where the pivotal facts were essentially the same. We granted certification. 43 N.J. 261, 203 A.2d 715 (1964). Petitioners urge reconsideration of the rule of Henderson.

In *Henderson,* a case of first impression in this jurisdiction, the majority, in deciding that the accident was noncompensable, conceded the existence of a division of authority in the precise situation among the other states, but determined that the rationale of some of our earlier cases dealing with the statutory language that a compensable injury must also derive from an accident "arising out of" the employment, R.S. 34:15-7, N.J.S.A., dictated the result reached. The underlying thesis was taken from *Spindler v. Universal Chain Corp.*, 11 N.J. 34, 39, 93 A.2d 171, 173 (1952):

> If it [the fall] was occasioned by or was the result of a disease or physical seizure and was not contributed to by "what the workman had to do," it is not compensable. On the other hand, if the fall "would not have occurred but for the services rendered" in the employment, it is covered by the statute.

(The burden of proof to establish the idiopathic cause was placed on the employer. 11 N.J., at p. 38, 93 A.2d 171.) The seeming exclusionary breadth of this thesis was, however, qualified by saying that, even if the inception of the fall was occasioned by a personal condition and non-work connected, the resulting injury was compensable if that injury was caused or contributed to by some added hazard or special condition of the employment. Concrete floors were found not to fall in that category because they are "usual and common in industrial plants" and "[t]he same consequences would probably have been forthcoming had the appellant suffered his seizure in the street or in his home." 16 N.J., at p. 214, 108 A.2d, at p. 270.

The result of the rule is the drawing of an obviously indefinite and, to us, unsatisfactory line. But *cf.* 1 Larson, Workmen's Compensation Law § 12.00, 12.10–12.14 inc. (1964 rev.). If the inception of the fall has the slightest connection with the employment, the resulting injury is compensable. *Freedman v. Spicer Manufacturing Corp.*, 97 N.J.L. 325, 116 A. 427 (E & A 1922) (where an employee became dizzy as a result of an inoculation recommended by the employer and fell to the floor, fracturing his skull); *Hall v. Doremus,* 114 N.J.L. 47, 175 A. 369 (Sup. Ct. 1934) (where an employee watching a cow in parturition was so overcome as to faint and fall to the concrete floor, fracturing his skull). If the employee is caused to fall idiopathically and is located in the course of his employment at even a slight height at the fall's inception or is standing at floor level and on the way down falls into a pit or strikes a table, chair, desk, stove, machinery or some other object situate on the employment premises, the resulting injury is compensable. *Reynolds v. Passaic Valley Sewerage Commissioners,* 130 N.J.L. 437, 33 A.2d 595 (Sup. Ct. 1943), affirmed o. b. 131 N.J.L. 327, 36 A.2d 429 (E & A 1944); *Furda v. Scammell China Co.*, 17 N.J. Super. 339, 86 A.2d 39 (Cty. Ct. 1952); *Williams v. Corby's Enterprise Laundry,* 64 N.J. Super. 561, 166 A.2d 827 (App. Div. 1960), certif. denied 34 N.J. 330, 168 A.2d 693 (1961). Seemingly also, he would be compensated if, through sheer awkwardness, he tripped over his own feet and fell to the floor or, by reason of a congenitally weak back, fell on his head when leaning over to pick up a pencil. But not so, according to *Henderson* and *Stulb v. Foodcraft, Inc.*, 76 N.J. Super. 384, 184 A.2d 673 (Law Div. 1962), if he suffered a spontaneous attack of vertigo and struck nothing but the floor during his descent from a standing posture. The distinctions are neither consistent nor meaningful. Either no consequence of an idiopathic fall should bring compensability or the nature of the result alone should be looked to as the determinant.

We think the latter principle ought to govern as expounded in the rationale so cogently advanced by Judge Clapp in his dissenting opinion in the Appellate Division in *Henderson,* 30 N.J. Super. 353, 360, 104 A.2d 720 (relied upon by the minority in this Court, 16 N.J., at p. 215, 108 A.2d 267). Even at the time *Henderson* was decided, it seemed evident that it was enough, in conjunction with the fundamental principle that "an employer takes an employee as he finds him," to constitute an occurrence an "accident" if either the circumstance causing the injury *or* the result on the employee's person was unlooked for, regardless of whether the inception or the underlying reason for the circumstance or result was personal or work connected. *Neylon v. Ford Motor Co.*, 13 N.J. Super. 56, 59, 80 A.2d 235 (App. Div. 1951), reversed 8 N.J. 586, 86 A.2d 577 (1952), judgment of the Appellate Division affirmed on reargument by an equally divided Court, 10 N.J. 325, 91 A.2d 569 (1952). There can be no question about the proposition at the present time. *Ciuba v. Irvington Varnish & Insulator Co.*, 27 N.J. 127, 134–139, 141 A.2d 761 (1958). Here, as Judge Clapp pointed out, "both the circumstance causing the injury (the striking of the floor) and the consequence upon the employee's person were unexpected." 30 N.J. Super., at p. 361, 104 A.2d, at p. 724. We also completely endorse the second necessary element of his thesis that such an unlooked-for mishap arises "out of" the employment when it is due to a condition of the employment — i.e., a risk of *this* employment, and that the impact with the concrete floor here clearly meets that test. Our conclusion therefore is that *Henderson* was incorrectly decided and should no longer be followed.

Of course, we do not mean to intimate that an employee is entitled to compensation for some idiopathic incident in and of itself, as, for example, where one suffers a non-work connected heart attack or convulsion at work and simply dies at his desk or machine or falls to the floor and suffers no injury from the impact. No such claim is made here.

The judgment of the Appellate Division is reversed and the matter remanded to the County Court for further proceedings consistent with this opinion.

For reversal and remandment: CHIEF JUSTICE WEINTRAUB and JUSTICES JACOBS, PROCTOR, HALL, SCHETTINO and HANEMAN — 6.

For affirmance: None.

PROBLEMS

(1) In *George*, can you articulate a rationale for the case that takes into account the proposition that, if a purely personal weakness is the moving force in the accident, the employment must contribute *something* to the result?

(2) Suppose an epileptic employee of a mattress company has a seizure and falls on an eight-inch thick mattress, breaking his arm. Should the broken arm be compensable, and on what theory?

(3) Is the dictum that "the employer takes the employee as he finds him" an adequate rationale for *George*?

LEON COUNTY SCHOOL BOARD v. GRIMES
548 So. 2d 205 (Fla. 1989)

OVERTON, JUSTICE.

. . . Thelma Grimes was employed by the Leon County School Board as a media technician. The school board knew that she had been afflicted with polio as a youth and thus was required to wear a full-length brace on her right leg. The brace contained a lock which she had to fasten manually each time she stood up. On one occasion while at work, Grimes rose from her desk to reach a file and locked her brace in the usual fashion; however, the brace gave way, causing her to fall and fracture her left ankle. Her left leg was trapped beneath her as she fell on the carpeted floor. It is for the ankle injury that Grimes seeks workers' compensation benefits. It should be noted that evidence was presented that her leg brace had previously given way while she was at home.

The deputy commissioner denied recovery, ruling that "the claimant brought to the job some personal element of risk unrelated to her employment. There was no exertion greater than that normally performed by the claimant during her nonemployment life. The claimant did not sustain an injury from an accident arising out of and in the course of her employment."

On appeal, the First District Court reversed and held that "claimant's employment exposed her to conditions which substantially contributed to the risk of her injury. . . . "

. . . .

The central issue in this case concerns injuries which occur at the place of employment but are the result of a condition personal to the claimant and are not caused by the place of employment. In *Protectu Awning Shutter Co. v. Cline*, 154 Fla. 30, 16 So. 2d 342 (1944), we stated:

> The purpose of the act is to shoulder on industry the *expense incident to the hazards of industry;* to lift from the public the burden to support those incapacitated by industry and to ultimately pass on to the consumers of the products of industry such expense. *Our act affords no relief for disease or physical ailment not produced by industry. Id.* at 31, 16 So. 2d at 343 (emphasis added). Further, we have explained that chapter 440 "was not designed to take the place of general health and accident insurance."

General Properties Co. v. Greening, 154 Fla. 814, 820, 18 So. 2d 908, 911 (1944).

In *Foxworth v. Florida Industrial Commission*, 86 So. 2d 147 (Fla. 1955), we specifically addressed idiopathic falls and noted: "It is well settled that injuries which arise out of risks or conditions personal to the claimant do not arise out of the employment unless the employment contributes to the risk or aggravates the injury." *Id.* at 151. With regard specifically to falls, we stated: "[W]here the idiopathic fall occurring on the job is merely onto a level floor, compensation for effects of the fall is extremely difficult to justify. . . . " *Id.* Previously, in *Protectu Awning*, we permitted recovery where the claimant, as a result of a fainting spell which was attributable to a preexisting heart condition, fell and struck his head against the concrete floor, causing a skull fracture which resulted in his death. In *Foxworth*, we explained our holding in *Protectu Awning*, stating:

> [W]e upheld recovery for effects of a fall caused by the heart attack of the claimant who as a result fractured his skull on the concrete floor. This decision is justified on the basis that the hardness of the floor was an increased hazard attributable to the employment, but that case represents the outer limits of the doctrine. To extend the rule further would be to eradicate completely the statutory requirement that the injury must be one arising out of the employment. The employment in some manner must contribute an increased hazard peculiar to the employment. *Foxworth*, 86 So. 2d at 151. We have regularly applied these *Foxworth* principles. In *Southern Bell Telephone and Telegraph Co. v. McCook*, 355 So. 2d 1166 (Fla. 1977), we denied recovery to an employee who claimed she sustained an injury to her back while bending to pick up toilet tissue while at work, finding it did not arise out of employment where she suffered from an idiopathic condition that manifested itself for the first time during the course of her employment. . . . *(the court here reviews two other similar decisions.)*

To adopt the actual-risk doctrine suggested by the First District Court and *Grimes* would allow recovery in each of the above instances and would require us to overrule each of these cases; further, we would be amending the purpose of chapter 440 to allow compensation to injured employees without regard to whether industry brought about the injury. We find that the legislature, which established this means of compensation, is the proper branch to broaden the purpose of chapter 440.

In the instant case, Grimes fell and suffered the injuries solely as a result of her personal condition. The record supports the deputy commissioner's finding that her employment in no way contributed to her injury. This case is factually distinguishable from *Protectu Awning* because Grimes fell on a carpeted floor, not onto bare concrete. As previously noted, her brace had given way in a similar fashion while she was at home. We find the deputy commissioner had substantial, competent evidence to find that Grimes' employment did not require her to exert herself any more at work than she did while not at work and that her employment conditions did not contribute to her injury. Accordingly, we conclude that the First District Court had no basis to overrule the deputy commissioner's findings. . . .

BARKETT, JUSTICE, dissenting.

. . . [H]ad Mrs. Grimes not worn a brace and merely fallen on the job and injured herself, there is no question that she would be compensated. In this case:

> [C]laimant's job required her to constantly get up and down from her desk, and to work in an area which was considerably more crowded than her home environment. . . . [I]t is less likely that claimant would have fallen at home where she could have better and more selectively controlled her positional changes. . . . [C]laimant's employment exposed her to conditions which substantially contributed to the risk of her injury. . . .

Grimes v. Leon County School Board, 518 So. 2d 327, 329 (Fla. 1st DLA 1987).

§ 5.03 PREEXISTING WEAKNESS AGGRAVATED BY EMPLOYMENT

FRAGALE v. ARMORY MAINTENANCE
24 A.D.2d 302, 265 N.Y.S.2d 793 (1966)

GIBSON, PRESIDING JUSTICE.

Appeal is taken by an employer and its insurance carrier from a decision of the Workmen's Compensation Board which awarded benefits on account of the death of an employee due to a heart attack, caused by "a severe commotion to the chest," as evidenced by fractures of four left ribs and by hemorrhages, all as demonstrated on autopsy; this in the words of claimant's medical expert, whose opinion of causal relation was adopted by the board, and which conclusion, although controverted before the Referee by other medical opinion, seems not to be disputed here; appellants contesting the award solely on the ground that the "accident did not arise out of and during the course of the employment."

The accident occurred during an argument between decedent and a coemployee, the only surviving witness to the affair, who said that after a discussion in which he ridiculed decedent's idea of removing his home to a place nearer his employment, decedent came at him; he pushed decedent, who knocked his hat off; whereupon he again pushed decedent back. The witness continued, "I must have pushed him into the chair, and the chair was one of those type chairs which wobbled around and the thing turned over and he fell on the arm of another chair, a low chair." Claimant died en route to the hospital.

The chairs were furnishings of the small so-called guard's shack in which the incident occurred, had been discarded from use elsewhere on the premises and were described by other witnesses — that into which decedent was first pushed as being a typist's swivel chair, with casters, and the second chair, into which he fell with his body across the arm or arms, as a tubular aluminum chair with wooden arm rests.

. . . .

There is indication in the autopsy report in the case before us that "a roller fell off the [swivel] chair" and the coemployee testified that the swivel chair "wobbled around and . . . turned over", creating a situation closely parallel to that in another case which we analyzed by saying, "If the somewhat unusual height of the stool and the desk or the movement or swiveling of the stool as claimant started to sit down, were ingredient in the occurrence of the fall it may be found accidental even though the claimant's own physiological condition entered into causation"; and in which case we further held that "it was within a fair scope of the board's power to find that the stool, of rather unusual height in the first place, moved or turned when claimant sat in it and that these factors played some contributing part to the accident. In our view that is enough." (*Matter of Stern v. Electrol, Inc.*, 4 A.D.2d 110, 112–113, 164 N.Y.S.2d 682. . . .)

There seems to us no basis in reason or logic or in any previous judicial decision to differentiate the idiopathic fall cases, in which this principle of cooperating cause has been applied, from the factual situation now before us. . . .

If it is to the added employment-connected factors or the "co-operating causes" that we must look (*Matter of Connelly v. Samaritan Hosp.*, 259 N.Y. 137, *supra*, p. 140, 181 N.E. 76, p. 77) it seems impossible to distinguish such an initially impelling force as the thrust of an internal convulsion or the surge of a hemorrhage from the impetus of a playful push or, indeed, a willful assault; or to differentiate the latter from such other forces as an explosion or the collapse of a wall occurring off the premises but causing injuries upon them. . . .

In further seeking a rational basis of distinction, it might be said that in an assault case the initiating cause is a personal one — unlike the off-premises explosion; but the "idiopathic-fall cases in this respect can be closely analogized to the cases of privately motivated assaults. In both instances, the central causal factor is personal — intensely and conspicuously personal — whether it is a diseased heart, or a personal enemy who is determined to shoot the employee wherever and whenever he can find him." (1 Larson, Workmen's Compensation Law, § 12.14, p. 192.16.) The same author argues for the compensability of an injury in a situation which he hypothesizes and which seems closely parallel to that before us, whereby an employee is wounded in the shoulder by a rifle shot directed by his personal enemy and is caused to topple into the cement mixer at which he is working. Professor Larson concludes: "The shoulder wound would be clearly noncompensable, just as the purely internal effects of a heart attack in an idiopathic fall case are not independently compensable. But the added effects of falling into the cement mixer would be compensable, just as if the employee had had an idiopathic fall into a cement mixer." (Larson, op. cit., § 12.14, pp. 192.16–192.17.)

. . . .

Decision affirmed, with costs to the Workmen's Compensation Board.

Taylor, Aulisi and Hamm, JJ., concur.

Reynolds, J., dissents.

PROBLEMS

(1) Suppose Fragale had merely hit the floor. Would the result be different?

(2) Suppose that a claimant was suffering from terminal cancer, from which he would have died in six months at the most. A traumatic injury at work accelerates the cancer and he dies in one month. Should full death benefits be payable? *See, e.g.*, Boyd v. Young, 193 Tenn. 272, 246 S.W.2d 10 (1951).

COWART v. PEARL RIVER TUNG CO.
67 So. 2d 356 (Miss. 1953)

McGEHEE, CHIEF JUSTICE.

This litigation . . . grew out of the death of Rosa May, a Negro woman, who appears to have been at least fifty-five years of age on December 18, 1950, when she died of a "massive cerebrovascular accident" (explained in the testimony as a rupture of a blood vessel on the brain) while actually engaged about the work of her employment in picking up tung (oil) nuts under the trees in the tung orchard of the appellee, Pearl River Tung Company. . . .

In Larson on Workmen's Compensation Law, Section 12.20, p. 170, it is stated: "Pre-existing disease or infirmity of the employee does not disqualify a claim under the "arising out of employment' requirement if the employment aggravated, accelerated, or combined with the disease or infirmity to produce the death or disability for which compensation is sought."

In *Peoria R. Terminal Co. v. Industrial Board*, 279 Ill. 352, 116 N.E. 651, 652, it is said that "Even where a workman dies from a pre-existing disease, if the disease is aggravated or accelerated under certain circumstances which can be said to be accidental, his death results from injury by accident. . . . 1 Bradbury on Workmen's Comp. 385; Elliott's Workmen's Comp. Act (7th Ed.) 9, and citing cases."

. . . .

. . . the sole question presented to the attorney-referee and the commission for decision was whether or not the death of the employee was caused from an injury arising out of and in the course of her employment, whereas the sole question presented to us for decision as an appellate court is whether or not there was such substantial conflict in the testimony as to afford the attorney-referee and commission a reasonable basis for the denial of the claim as the triers of fact. On the issue of whether or not the exertion which was occasioned by the employee stooping and bending to pick up the tung nuts from the ground, had contributed to, aggravated or accelerated the employee's blood pressure so as to precipitate the rupture of the blood vessel on the brain, we do not think there is sufficient conflict in the testimony of the two physicians who testified in the case to justify the denial of the claim for compensation.

It is strongly urged by the appellees that the work in which the employee was engaged was not strenuous, and this contention is correct so far as the carrying of the wire baskets from one tree to another only half-filled with nuts or the actual work of picking up the tung nuts are concerned; that is to say, the half-filled baskets were not too heavy, nor would the picking up of the nuts require any exertion if they had been picked up from a level of approximately waist high to the employee, but the exertion consisted in the stooping and bending by the employee to reach the nuts as they were being picked up from the ground.

We . . . are of the opinion . . . that the proof on behalf of the claimant is to the effect that the stooping and bending in the manner testified about would cause the blood to rush to the head, and would at least contribute to, aggravate or accelerate the blood pressure so as to bring about such an accident as is here complained of; and that the testimony on behalf of the employer to the effect that the accident *could* have happened at a time when the employee was not engaged in strenuous activity is insufficient to substantially contradict the proof on behalf of the complainant as to what was in fact the cause of the accident in this particular case.

The cause must, therefore, be reversed and a judgment rendered here as to liability, and remanded for further proceedings in accordance with the views hereinbefore expressed.

Reversed and remanded.

All Justices concur except HALL, J., who took no part in this decision.

PROBLEM

Within two hours after parking his car and running through his employer's parking lot in order to be on time for work, the employee went into cardiac arrest and later died. Two physicians ultimately attributed his death to a combination of preexisting health conditions, which included heart disease and hypertension, and his physical exertion in running. Should the death claim be compensable? *See* Pagano v. Anheuser Busch, Inc., 301 A.D.2d 977, 754 N.Y.S.2d 700 (3d Dept. 2003).

§ 5.04 IMPORTED DANGER CASES

KENDRICK v. PEEL, EDDY & GIBBONS LAW FIRM
32 Ark. App. 29, 795 S.W.2d 365 (1990)

MAYFIELD, JUDGE.

The appellant in this appeal from the Workers' Compensation Commission is the minor son of Kathy Kendrick, who was shot and killed at her employer's law office by Ronald Gene Simmons on December 28, 1987. It is contended that the child, who was four years old at the time of his mother's death, is entitled to workers' compensation benefits based on the doctrine of positional risk. The Commission did not agree that the doctrine applied and held the evidence failed to establish that decedent's death arose out of and in the scope of her employment.

In *J. & G. Cabinets v. Hennington*, 269 Ark. 789, 600 S.W.2d 916 (Ark. App. 1980), this court said: A claimant before the Workers' Compensation Commission must prove that the injury sustained was the result of an accident arising out of and in the course of employment. The phrase "arising out of the employment" refers to the origin or cause of the accident and the phrase "in the course of the employment" refers to the time, place, and circumstances under which the injury occurred. 269 Ark. at 792–93, 600 S.W.2d at 918.

The doctrine of positional risk relied upon by the appellant in the instant case is explained in 1 Larson, *The Law of Workmen's Compensation* § 6.50 (3/90), as follows: An important and growing number of courts are accepting the full implications of the positional-risk test: An injury arises out of the employment if it would not have occurred but for the fact that the conditions and obligations of the employment placed claimant in the position where he was injured. . . . This theory supports compensation, for example, in cases of stray bullets, roving lunatics, and other situations in which the only connection of the employment with the injury is that its obligations placed the employee in the particular place at the particular time when he was injured by some neutral force, meaning by "neutral" neither personal to the claimant nor distinctly associated with the employment. [Emphasis in Larson.]

Although the positional risk doctrine has not yet been applied in Arkansas to sustain an award of compensation, our cases have indicated that the doctrine would be applied in a proper case. . . .

In the case at bar, the evidence showed that on the morning of December 28, 1987, Kathy Kendrick was killed while performing her duties as receptionist at the law firm where she worked. Brenda Jones, who was seated in the waiting room, testified that Kendrick was in another office when Simmons came in. She said that Kendrick approached Simmons without any sign of recognition and asked, "Can I help you?" At that point, Simmons shot Kendrick several times, then turned around, looked directly at Jones, and walked out of the office. Jones said Simmons did not attempt to go into any of the offices of the attorneys in the firm nor did he make any threatening moves toward her (Jones).

It was stipulated that before Simmons came to the law office he had already killed fourteen of his family members, and that after he shot Kendrick, he went to the Taylor Oil Company where he shot his former employer and another man, then to the Sinclair Mini-Mart where he shot a former co-worker, and finally to Woodline Motor Freight where he shot his former supervisor. It was also stipulated that Kendrick and Simmons had previously worked together at Woodline Motor Freight and that Kendrick left her employment with Woodline on March 2, 1987, and Simmons left his employment there on November 19, 1986.

Vicki Lynn Jackson, a friend of Kendrick's who also worked at Woodline, testified that Kendrick and Simmons were acquainted. She said Kendrick confided to her that Simmons kept asking her (Kendrick) to go out with him but that she refused because he was married; that Kendrick said Simmons wrote her notes, followed her, and would sometimes be found sitting on her doorstep; and that Kendrick said she had told Simmons to just "go away."

Jackson also testified that she saw Simmons come into Woodline and shoot his former supervisor, Joyce Butts, and that he then came into the computer room where Jackson was working, held a gun on her and ordered her to call the police. She said he kept the gun on her until he surrendered to the chief of police, but he did not attempt to hurt her. According to Jackson, Simmons told her "it was all over now, . . . he had gotten everybody that hurt him."

David Eddy, of the appellee law firm, testified that as far as he could determine Simmons had no connection with his law firm or any of its clients. He said none of the attorneys in the firm had ever represented Simmons or were even acquainted with him prior to this incident.

The Commission concluded that the doctrine of positional risk did not apply because the shooting of Kathy Kendrick resulted from a personal vendetta against individuals Simmons felt had harmed him and consequently did not arise out of and in the course of her employment.

(The court rejects arguments that the Commission's decision was not supported by substantial evidence, and that Ms. Jackson's testimony was hearsay and erroneously admitted.)

. . . .

However, even if Jackson's testimony about Kendrick's relationship with Simmons was hearsay and erroneously admitted, we find that when it is completely disregarded, the record contains sufficient evidence to support the Commission's finding that the positional risk doctrine does not apply in this case. It was stipulated that Kendrick and Simmons had worked together and that all but one of the people shot by Simmons were either members of his family or someone he had worked with. (The evidence does not show whether Simmons was acquainted with one of the men shot at Taylor Oil Company.) There is also evidence in the record that Simmons made no attempt to harm several other people who were in close proximity to those killed, and Ms. Jackson testified that while waiting for the police to come get him "he said that it was all over now, that he had gotten everybody that hurt him." Clearly, the evidence does not show that Kathy Kendrick's death resulted from a "neutral" risk which, as we have discussed, means a risk that is "neither personal" to her nor "distinctly associated" with her employment. Certainly it was not like the gust of wind in the Parrish Esso Service Center v. Adams case, *supra*, which affected everything in its path, or like a "roving lunatic," referred to by Larson, who would be expected to kill without the selectivity demonstrated by the evidence in this case.

While the appellant also complains that Ms. Jackson should not have been allowed to testify to the above statement made by Simmons, we disagree. The statement was made within minutes after Simmons had shot at least four people, and we think the statement falls under the hearsay exception of an excited utterance. . . .

. . .

We also point out that while the appellant has relied upon the doctrine of positional risk, there are cases which hold that injuries resulting from an assault are compensable where the assault is causally related to the employment, but not if the assault arises out of purely personal reasons. [citations omitted] This theory is distinguished from the doctrine of positional risk. See 1 Larson, *The Law of Workmen's Compensation* § 11.21(c) (3/90). It is obvious, however, that the evidence in this case would not support a finding that the assault on Kathy Kendrick was causally related to her employment with the appellee law firm. We simply note this in order to explain why we have discussed positional risk only and why the appellant relied only upon that doctrine.

Affirmed.

COOPER and JENNINGS, JJ., agree.

NOTE ON IMPORTED DANGER

The imported danger issue can arise in a variety of ways, beginning with the earlier-mentioned *Bogavich* [1] case in which the deceased, for no known reason, carried a bomb to work beneath his shirt, and it went off. Compensation was denied, as it has been in a number of cases involving employees who have carried guns with them to do some incidental hunting or shooting.

PROBLEMS

(1) Is one's own automobile is a dangerous enough instrumentality to require application of an imported danger rule? Normally, a worker is covered by workers' compensation when going to or coming from work, so long as he or she is on the company premises. But suppose the cause of injury is a defective steering wheel: should one follow the "imported danger" approach would say that the cause of the injury was not the employment but rather a dangerous instrumentality that was brought in to the situation by the worker personally, just like a gun or a bomb? *See, e.g.,* Industrial Comm'n v. Enyeart, 81 Colo. 521, 256 P.314 (1927). On a cold day, claimant was trying to start his car in the employer's parking lot when the battery exploded, injuring him. *Compensable? See* Fisher Body Div., General Motors Corp. v. Industrial Comm'n, 40 Ill. 2d 514, 240 N.E.2d 694 (1968).

(2) And should similar principles apply to food or drink brought to work by the employee that turns out to be tainted or dangerous? Claimant, a butcher, while standing behind the meat counter, choked on a doughnut which he had brought with him to have along with coffee supplied by the employer. He attempted to walk toward a waste basket to spit out the doughnut, blacked out, fell and was injured. Compensable? *See* Williams v. Industrial Comm'n, 38 Ill. 2d 593, 232 N.E.2d 744 (1968).

(3) A truck driver was struck in the eye by the head of a match as he lit a cigarette. Compensable? *See* Hill-Luthy Co. v. Industrial Comm'n, 411 Ill. 201, 103 N.E.2d 605 (1952).

(4) A female employee during an authorized break lit a cigarette in the women's lounge. A spark fell on her fluffy angora sweater causing serious burns. Compensable? *See* Puffin v. General Electric Co., 132 Conn. 279, 43 A.2d 746 (1945).

---

[1] Bogavich v. Westinghouse Elec. & Mfg. Co., 162 Pa. Super. 393, 57 A.2d 698 (1948).

Chapter 6
RANGE OF COMPENSABLE CONSEQUENCES

§ 6.01 INTRODUCTION

When the primary injury is shown to have arisen out of and in the course of employment, every natural consequence that flows from the injury likewise arises out of the employment, unless it is the result of an independent intervening cause attributable to claimant's own intentional conduct.

§ 6.02 ORIGINAL COMPENSABLE INJURY CAUSING SUBSEQUENT INJURY

A distinction must be observed between causation rules affecting the primary injury — which have been the subject of the present chapter up to this point — and causation rules that determine how far the range of compensable consequences is carried, once the primary injury is causally connected with the employment. As to the primary injury, it has been shown that the "arising" test is a unique one quite unrelated to common law concepts of legal cause, and it will be shown later that the employee's own contributory negligence is ordinarily not an intervening cause preventing initial compensability.[1] But when the question is whether compensability should be extended to a subsequent injury or aggravation related in some way to the primary injury, the rules that come into play are essentially based upon the concepts of "direct and natural results," and of claimant's own conduct as an independent intervening cause.

The basic rule is that a subsequent injury, whether an aggravation of the original injury or a new and distinct injury, is compensable if it is the direct and natural result of a compensable primary injury.

The simplest application of this principle is the rule that all the medical consequences and sequelae that flow from the primary injury are compensable. The cases illustrating this rule fall into two groups.

The first group, about which there is no legal controversy, comprises the cases in which an initial medical condition itself progresses into complications more serious than the original injury; the added complications are of course compensable.[2] Thus, if an injury results in a phlebitis, and this in turn leads to a cerebral thrombosis, the effects of the thrombosis are compensable.[3] If the initial injury is followed by the onset of gangrene, necessitating amputation, the amputation is, similarly, a compensable consequence of the injury.[4] The situation is no different when the subsequent complication

---

[1] The problem of suicide caused by a compensable injury, which involves the principles discussed in this section, is separately treated at Ch. 20, § 20.07, *below*.

[2] Freuhauf Trailer Co. v. Industrial Comm'n, 16 Utah 2d 95, 396 P.2d 409 (1964). Claimant developed thrombophlebitis as a result of a compensable accident. He then underwent a gall bladder operation which caused the condition to flare up. This resulted in a pulmonary embolus. The embolus was held compensable.

[3] McCoy v. Cataldo, 90 R.I. 365, 158 A.2d 271 (1960).

[4] Urbancik v. Roseman Estates, Inc., 11 A.D.2d 554, 199 N.Y.S.2d 775 (1960).

takes the form of a neurosis rather than of a physical exacerbation.[5] Moreover, once the work-connected character of any injury, such as a back injury, has been established, the subsequent progression of that condition remains compensable so long as the worsening is not shown to have been produced by an independent nonindustrial cause.[6] This may sound self-evident, but in close cases it is sometimes easy to overlook this essentially simple principle. In a Utah case,[7] claimant had suffered a compensable accident in 1966, injuring his back. Several years later, this condition was triggered by a sneeze into a disc herniation, for which claimant required surgery. The medical testimony was that because of the back condition, it was probable that had claimant not had the sneezing episode, some other major or minor event would have eventually necessitated surgery. The finding that the sneezing episode was the independent cause of claimant's disability, and the resultant denial of compensation, were held to be error, and benefits were awarded on appeal. This result is clearly correct. The presence of the sneezing incident should not obscure the true nature of the case, which is nothing more than that of a further medical complication flowing from a compensable injury. If the herniation had occurred while claimant was asleep in bed, its characterization as a mere sequel to the compensable injury would have seemed obvious. The case should be no different if the triggering episode is some nonemployment exertion like raising a window or hanging up a suit, so long as it is clear that the real operative factor is the progression of the compensable injury, associated with an exertion that in itself would not be unreasonable in the circumstances. A different question is presented, of course, when the triggering activity is itself rash in the light of claimant's knowledge of his condition.[8]

The second group of medical-causation cases comprises the cases in which the existence of the primary compensable injury in some way exacerbates the effects of an independent medical weakness or disease. The causal sequence in these cases may be more indirect or complex, but as long as the causal connection is in fact present the compensability of the subsequent condition is beyond question.[9] For example, if the primary compensable injury makes it impossible to treat the independent condition, the worsening of the independent condition due to lack of treatment is compensable, as when an intestinal perforation followed by infection made it impossible to remove a preexisting cancer of the rectum.[10] Similarly, when the compensable injury produces a condition that interferes with normal curative processes that might have alleviated the preexisting independent condition, the progression of the independent condition is compensable, as when a compensable skull fracture produced a mental condition in

---

[5] Travelers Ins. Co. v. McLellan, 302 F. Supp. 351 (E.D.N.Y. 1969). Claimant developed an occupational loss of hearing, and as a result lost his job. Because of the loss of his job, claimant then developed traumatic conversion hysteria. Psychiatric disability held compensable, as arising out of claimant's occupational hearing loss.

[6] Hayward v. Parsons Hosp., 32 A.D.2d 983, 301 N.Y.S.2d 659 (1969). In 1963 claimant fell and injured her back. Two years later she suffered severe pain while bending forward and to her left while not at work. She was later found to have a herniated disc. On the basis of medical testimony which indicated that the disc was due to the 1963 accident but did not develop until 1965, an award of compensation was affirmed.

[7] Perchelli v. Utah State Indus. Comm'n, 25 Utah 2d 58, 475 P.2d 835 (1970).

[8] See Amoco Chemical Corp. v. Hill, 318 A.2d 614 (Del. Super. 1974).

[9] Waibel v. State Comp. Dep't, 3 Ore. App. 241, 471 P.2d 826 (1970). Claimant suffered from Hodgkin's Disease, and then was involved in an industrial accident which caused an injury to his back. This masked some of the symptoms of further difficulties from the disease, preventing early diagnosis, and thus hastening claimant's total disability. Award for total disability prior to claimant's death held proper.

Drake v. State Dep't of Social Welfare-Larned State Hosp., 210 Kan. 197, 499 P.2d 532 (1972). Decedent suffered from nonoccupational lung disease. He injured his back at work, and medical testimony indicated that back pain prevented decedent from coughing and clearing his lungs, and this contributed to the worsening of the lung condition and eventual death. Award of death benefits affirmed, since the compensable injury complicated decedent's recovery and was causally related to his death.

[10] Strasser v. Jones, 186 Kan. 507, 350 P.2d 779 (1960).

which the decedent could not feel and report the pain of a gall bladder infection which led to his death.[11] Here again the question is purely a medical one, although the causal sequence is somewhat less straightforward than in the first group. Similarly, the strain caused by a shortened or weakened leg,[12] or by the use of prosthesis[13] or simply by hospitalization and confinement to bed,[14] if shown by medical testimony to have aggravated some unrelated and nonemployment condition, is enough to endow the final result with compensable quality.

When we turn from these cases of medical causal relation to the broad question of miscellaneous consequences having some causal connection with the original injury, we enter an area of compensation law where the difficulty of expressing a body of coherent principles is at the maximum.

STATE COMPENSATION INSURANCE
FUND v. INDUSTRIAL ACCIDENT COMMISSION
176 Cal. App. 2d 10; 1959 Cal. App. LEXIS 1438; 1 Cal. Rptr. 73

TOBRINER, JUDGE.

. . . .

We are concerned here with two injuries, their incidence and interrelationship. The first occurred on February 15, 1957, when the respondent Wallin, a carpenter by occupation, born in 1904, suffered an industrial injury to his left eye. A rusty nail which he was driving into the floor flew up and penetrated his eyeball. The next day an iridectomy ("[the] cutting out of a part of the iris" — New Gould Medical Dictionary, p. 519) was undertaken. . . .

The second injury occurred on April 11, 1958. Wallin had not returned to work because he continued to suffer aftereffects from the operation which he described in these bizarre terms: ". . . I could not go back to work then because I was so badly boozed up, [I] [walked] around like I am half drunk. . . . " The commission concluded, however, that the reference was not to the effects of alcohol but to those of the eye condition. . . .

On this date, Wallin was making rough cuts of "junk" lumber at his home for use in his fireplace. Because the wood was too large, he used an electric power hand saw to cut it to proper size. He placed the pieces of lumber on a saw horse and held the longer end of the plank with his knee. After cutting off a piece he would move the board over to sever the next piece. While Wallin was thus sawing the lumber, the saw "jumped and kicked," amputating one of his fingers.

The employee, . . . confronted by the question, "Do you think that your eye affected you in any manner or the condition of your injured eye affected you in any manner in the use of the saw on April 11, 1958?" answered, "I believe so." And again when asked, "Were you suffering from double vision at that time?" he said, "Well, certainly. . . . "

---

[11] Daugherty v. Midland Painting Co., 14 A.D.2d 961, 221 N.Y.S.2d 70 (1961).

[12] Ada Iron & Metal Co. v. Tarpley, 420 P.2d 886 (Okla. 1966). Claimant suffered a compensable back injury and developed thrombophlebitis in his left leg as a result of the treatment. This caused him to shift a disproportionate part of his weight to the right leg, aggravating a preexisting gunshot wound. The entire disability was held compensable.

[13] Webb v. Poirier & McLain Corp., 26 A.D.2d 608, 271 N.Y.S.2d 393 (1966).

[14] Proctor Community Hosp. v. Industrial Comm'n, 41 Ill. 2d 537, 244 N.E.2d 155 (1969). Decedent suffered an injury to his foot which over a period of months became gangrenous, resulting in amputation of a toe. This condition and the required hospitalization was found to have been painful and taxing, to have aggravated decedent's heart condition, and to have become a causative factor in accelerating his death. Award of death benefits reinstated.

The referee found that the injury to the eye on February 15, 1957, proximately caused further disability in the loss of the finger. . . .

. . . we must determine if the record supports the commission's conclusion that "[said] injury proximately resulted in further disability consisting of amputation of the index finger of applicant's right hand on April 11, 1958" . . . and whether or not Wallin was negligent. Finally, assuming such negligence, we must determine if it broke the chain of causation.

To rule as a matter of law that the evidence was insufficient to support this finding we would be compelled to disregard: (1) the testimony that Wallin was suffering from defective vision at the time; (2) the fact that this condition offers at least a more reasonable explanation of the accident than any other, particularly when the employee, an expert in the use of the saw, had never in the many years he had used it undergone any trouble with it, and that he manipulated it here in the usual manner; and (3) his own explanation of the accident. . . .

We turn to the problem of the alleged intervening negligence of the employee. Here the commission states upon the petition for reconsideration that "[it] was not even charged that applicant was guilty of negligence or misconduct, much less proved. . . . "

(The court here reviews various items of evidence supporting the proposition that the applicant's actions were not negligent.)

. . . .

We conclude that sufficient evidence in the record supports the commission's finding that the eye injury proximately caused the loss of the finger; we do not believe the record compelled the commission to find that respondent Wallin was negligent. Even assuming Wallin's negligence, however, we shall point out that in the framework of compensation law such negligence would not insulate the original injury from acting as a contributing cause and that as such it sufficiently supports the award.

Turning to this independent and alternate ground for upholding the award, we believe the definition of causation as applied to the second injury must not be a narrow one of tort law but a broader concept of compensation law. Thus the first injury need not be the exclusive cause of the second but only a contributing factor to it; in this view the presence of contributory negligence in itself would not break the causative connection unless the intervening negligence were the sole and exclusive cause of the injury. So long as the original injury operates even in part as a contributing factor it establishes liability.

Petitioner agrees that "the primary, industrial injury" need not "be the sole proximate cause"; "[it] is sufficient if it is a contributing" cause. But petitioner maintains that, even so, the alleged negligence, as an "intervening" or "superseding" cause "cuts off the chain of causation. . . . " Once, however, the premise of contributing cause is accepted, we submit that causation could be broken only by an intervening act which itself is the sole and exclusive cause of the ultimate injury. Only by such total severance does the original cause become ineffective and cease to "contribute."

This court has recognized that the test of proximate causation in workmen's compensation at least as to the original injury is not identical with that of tort. . . . Indeed the California courts have constantly warned against atavistic attempts to retain common law concepts of tort and negligence in the compensation field. . . . The old and strict concept of proximate causation, followed in many tort cases, which would insist here that the eye injury be the sole cause of the finger injury, conceiving of an intervening negligence as severing causation, should then succumb in workmen's compensation to a more liberal rule that the first injury need be no more than a contributing cause to the second.

. . . .

. . . the employee's negligence actually is as irrelevant in the second injury as it admittedly is in the first. The fact that the workman suffers a secondary consequence of the first injury should not work a mystic change in the nature of the applicable test. While the petitioner argues that the employer is entitled to be protected against secondary injuries which are not the result of "foreseeability" or are the result of the employee's "negligence," this concept should no more be imported here than for the initial injury.

Finally, since the original injury contributed to the second, and operates as an efficient cause of it, the second is a consequence of the first injury. The employee is entitled to protection from such consequence. To deny such protection is to tie compensation into the concept of fault: here, indeed, not the first, but a later negligence. Here, moreover, the negligence is only a partial cause of the injury; hence the importation of the concept is both attenuated and inappropriate. . . .

The award is *affirmed*.

PROBLEMS

(1) Claimant, whose leg is in a cast due to a previous compensable injury, is attending a wedding reception. He tries to catch a child about to fall down the church steps, and because of the cast falls down the steps, injuring himself further. *Is the second injury compensable?* See Kelley v. Federal Shipbuilding & Dry Dock Co., 1 N.J. Super. 245, 64 A.2d 92 (1949).

(2) A claimant whose arm was broken in a compensable accident decides to beat his wife on Saturday night at a time when the arm is not yet healed. The arm is refractured as a result of the weakness attributable to the compensable injury. A man with a normal, healthy arm could have beaten his wife in exactly the same way with no harmful consequences to himself. *Compensable?*

(3) To relieve the pain of a compensable injury, a claimant carelessly takes bichloride of mercury from a bottle labeled "Poison," believing it to be aspirin. *Is injury from the poisoning compensable?* See Brown v. New York State Training School for Girls, 285 N.Y. 37, 32 N.E.2d 783 (1941).

(4) An employee died because he was unable to escape from a fire because of a compensable back injury. *Are death benefits awardable?* See Gerhardt v. Welch, 267 Minn. 206, 125 N.W.2d 721 (1964).

(5) A claimant whose compensable injury is healing well, and who is receiving the finest medical care that science can provide, decides to consult a witch doctor in the woods, who twists his neck and produces total paralysis. *Should the paralysis be compensable?*

(6) A claimant is injured at work and stays home the following day. He is ordered by his employer to visit a doctor in town, and in the course of that journey falls down and further injures himself because he was not looking where he was going. *Is the second injury compensable?*

(7) A man knows that his compensably injured knee is apt to give way without warning, because it had done so on a number of occasions. He nevertheless undertakes to carry an armload of trash down the cellar stairs. His knee collapses and he falls the length of the stairs, striking his head on a drain and breaking his jaw. *Compensable?* See Yarbrough v. Polar Ice & Fuel Co., 118 Ind. App. 321, 79 N.E.2d 422 (1948).

(8) Claimant had previously suffered two compensable knee injuries. As a result of these accidents, his right knee occasionally "locked," rendering the right leg practically useless. While he was driving his automobile his knee locked, he was unable to apply his brakes, and an accident occurred. Were injuries sustained in the automobile accident compensable?

(9) Did the California court in *State Compensation Insurance Fund v. Industrial Accident Commission* above go too far when it ruled that the employee's negligence was not a factor that would break the causation chain? Considering the fact situations in that case and in the problems above, can you suggest a workable principle to govern their outcomes?

§ 6.03   SUBSEQUENT AGGRAVATION OF ORIGINAL INJURY

KLOSTERMAN v. INDUSTRIAL COMMISSION OF ARIZONA
155 Ariz. 435, 747 P.2d 596 (1987)
Reconsideration Denied Sept. 30, 1987

GRANT, PRESIDING JUDGE.

This is a special action review of an Industrial Commission award denying industrial responsibility for a newly torn ligament to a knee which had previously sustained an industrial injury. The parties dispute whether the industrial injury directly and naturally contributed to the tear. Because the uncontradicted medical evidence established this connection and because the reasonableness of the non-industrial activity causing the new injury was not raised, we must set aside the award.

On August 27, 1984, the petitioner employee (claimant) injured his left knee at work. Eugene J. Chandler, M.D., a specialist in knee surgery who had treated the claimant for previous knee injuries, performed arthroscopy and a partial lateral meniscectomy. The claimant made good progress until December 1984, when he noticed increased soreness. At a scheduled examination on December 17th, Dr. Chandler diagnosed a newly torn anterior cruciate ligament and recommended arthroscopy and reconstruction.

The respondent carrier (Argonaut) refused to authorize the additional surgery. Dr. Chandler again requested authorization, informing Argonaut that "the torn anterior cruciate ligament is directly related to the accident of 8/27/84 in that his knee was in a weakened condition and his new injury is directly related to that accident, even though the patient was doing something that he was not supposed to be doing." Argonaut responded by formally denying liability for any subsequent injury. The claimant timely protested, and hearings were scheduled.

At these hearings, the claimant testified that he did not notice an immediate injury while playing frisbee on December 5, 1984, but subsequently developed symptoms. Dr. Chandler was the only medical expert to appear. He testified that the claimant probably tore the ligament while playing frisbee. He also testified, however, that the industrial injury and surgeries, as well as prior injuries, had weakened the left knee. Furthermore, in his opinion the tear on December 5th would not have occurred but for this weakness. Dr. Chandler also noted that jumping or clipping injuries are the most common causes of this type of tear. Finally, he acknowledged that, although the tear could have occurred in several ways, "the frisbee incident did cause it, and if he had done his normal rehabilitation, it probably would not have happened. . . . "

. . . .

Both parties agree on appeal that the correct test is the one delimiting the compensable consequences of a primary industrial injury. Under this test, a new condition is compensable if (1) the primary injury directly and naturally caused it; and (2) the claimant's conduct was not unreasonable so as to break the causal chain. *Dutton v. Industrial Commission*, 140 Ariz. 448, 682 P.2d 453 (App. 1984); *O'Donnell v. Industrial Commission*, 125 Ariz. 358, 609 P.2d 1058 (App. 1980); accord 1 A. Larson, *Workmens' Compensation Law* § 13.11(b) (1985). Argonaut asserts that the causation requirement of the compensable consequences test is unsatisfied and, therefore, that it was unnecessary for the administrative law judge to address the reasonableness of the claimant's conduct. [*Court's footnote omitted*]

Argonaut first argues that the frisbee incident was the sole cause of the new tear. We disagree. It is true Dr. Chandler testified that the frisbee playing had caused the tear. However, he also clearly testified that, but for the weakened state of the knee, caused by the industrial injury and the rehabilitation efforts, the tear would not have occurred. In addition, the claimant testified that he jumped on his right leg, not on his left. He had only a "little collision," not the violent clipping blow which Dr. Chandler testified would be sufficient to injure a completely rehabilitated knee. We therefore reject this argument.

Argonaut argues in the alternative that this is a new injury and that the vulnerability to further injury does not satisfy the direct and natural result requirement. Argonaut cites no authority for its position. This court questioned in East whether a predisposition to injury was "a sufficient causative factor to impose industrial liability for a condition proximately caused by a non-industrial injury." East, 137 Ariz. at 317, 670 P.2d at 422. In that case, however, there was no testimony linking the industrial injury to the petitioner's later injury, and that language was therefore dicta.

This court squarely addressed the issue a year later in *Dutton v. Industrial Commission*, 140 Ariz. 448, 682 P.2d 453 (App. 1984). It rejected a general rule denying the sufficiency of predispositions. See also *Mercante v. Industrial Commission*, 153 Ariz. 261, 735 P.2d 1384 (App. 1987); *O'Donnell v. Industrial Commission*, 125 Ariz. 358, 609 P.2d 1058 (App. 1980) (award denying reopening set aside where claimant suffered new injuries caused by weakened condition remaining from earlier compensable injury). We agree with the reasoning found in Larson: "[E]ven if the employment-weakened member does not actually cause the subsequent accident, it may render the results of that accident compensable if the weakness made the limb more susceptible to refracture. The same principle has been applied to . . . knees made more vulnerable by the compensable injury. . . . " A. Larson, *supra*, § 13.12 at 388–90 (citations omitted). We reject Argonaut's position.

Dr. Chandler's uncontradicted testimony was that the ligament tear would not have occurred but for the knee's weakened condition caused in part by the August 1984 injury. This evidence satisfied the first prong of the compensable consequences test.

However, the administrative law judge failed to make a finding on the second element of the compensable consequences test, i.e., the reasonableness or unreasonableness of the claimant's activities which precipitated the subsequent reinjury. He found only that "the applicant could and did, reasonably or unreasonably, decide that he could play frisbee. . . . "

The parties neither argued at the Industrial Commission nor have raised before this court the issue of whether the claimant has the burden of proving that his frisbee activities were reasonable or whether the carrier has the burden of proving that such activities were unreasonable. Because this issue was not raised, we do not address it. See A.R.S. § 23-951(D).

The award is set aside.

CONTRERAS and FIDEL, JJ., concur.

It is now uniformly held that aggravation of the primary injury by medical or surgical treatment is compensable.[15] Examples include exacerbation of the claimant's condition, or death, resulting from antibiotics,[16] antitoxins,[17] sedatives,[18] anesthesia,[19]

---

[15] Parchefsky v. Kroll Bros., 267 N.Y. 410, 196 N.E. 308, 98 A.L.R. 1387 (1935).

[16] Ryan v. Aetna Cas. & Sur. Co., 161 So. 2d 286 (La. App. 1964). Claimant became partially deaf as a result of streptomycin administered while he was being treated for a compensable injury. Compensation awarded.

[17] City of Austin v. Crooks, 343 S.W.2d 272 (Tex. Civ. App. 1961). The city employee suffered severe reactions to tetanus antitoxin and horse serum administered after he was bitten by a dog. The serum sickness

electrical treatments,[20] immobilization and use of crutches,[21] or corrective or exploratory surgery.[22]

Several cases have held that, when drugs used in the treatment of a compensable disease lead to narcotics addiction[23] or alcoholism,[24] the ensuing consequences are compensable.

§ 6.04 REFUSAL OF REASONABLE SURGERY

COUCH v. SAGINAW MALLEABLE IRON PLANT
42 Mich. App. 228, 201 N.W.2d 683 (1972)

TARGONSKI, JUDGE.

Plaintiff suffered a back injury while employed by the defendant. Voluntary compensation benefits were paid thereafter. On April 8, 1968 plaintiff petitioned for a new injury date and the accompanying higher benefit schedule. The hearing referee, after hearing testimony, granted the plaintiff the higher benefit schedule. On appeal to the Workmen's Compensation Appeal Board, the decision of the hearing referee was reversed by a 4-3 vote. From this decision, the plaintiff brings this appeal. . . .

The Board, in reaching its decision, here relied on the plaintiff's refusal to undergo corrective surgery for his back condition. The medical testimony, including that of the employer's doctor, showed that there was approximately a 50% chance that the surgery could cure persons with the plaintiff's condition, and that the other 50% were not cured. In many cases their condition worsened, some even to the extent of being paralyzed.

The rule is well settled in this state that if the operation is not attended with great danger and the operation offers a reasonable prospect of relief from the incapacity, the employee must submit to the operation or release his employer from the obligation to maintain him. *Coombs v. Kirsch Co.*, 301 Mich. 1, 2 N.W.2d 897 (1942); *Kolbas v. American Boston Mining Co.*, 275 Mich. 616, 267 N.W. 751 (1936); *Dyer v. General Motors Corp.*, 318 Mich. 216, 27 N.W.2d 533 (1947).

However, if the danger is great and there is a considerable chance that the operation will not relieve the disability, the employee is justified in refusing to submit to surgery. In 1 Larson, Workmen's Compensation Law, § 13.22, pp. 3-326–3-327, that author addresses this problem in the following manner:

> But if there is a real risk involved, and particularly if there is a considerable chance that the operation will result in no improvement or even perhaps in a worsening of the condition, the claimant cannot be forced to run the risk at peril of losing his statutory compensation rights.

In the instant case, it cannot be said that there was a reasonable chance of success. When we balance this with the possibility that the claimant's condition could worsen to

---

resulted in physical disabilities and psychoneurosis. Total permanent disability benefits awarded.

[18] Hoffman v. City of New Orleans, 121 So. 2d 12 (La. App. 1960). The deceased suffered a severe head injury on June 23 but continued working until July 11. Terminal causation of death was bronchial pneumonia brought on by heavy medication sedation. Compensation award affirmed.

[19] Spear v. Brockway Motor Co., 9 A.D.2d 799, 192 N.Y.S.2d 766 (1959).

[20] Ortkiese v. Clarson & Ewell Engineering, 126 So. 2d 556 (Fla. 1961). Compensation awarded for cerebral thrombosis disability which resulted from electrical treatments involved in the physiotherapy for a leg injury.

[21] Bergemann v. North Cent. Foundry, Inc., 215 Kan. 685, 527 P.2d 1044 (1974).

[22] Bisonic v. Halsey Packard, Inc., 62 N.J. Super. 365, 163 A.2d 194 (1960).

[23] Ballard v. Workmen's Comp. App. Bd., 3 Cal. 3d 832, 92 Cal. Rptr. 1, 478 P.2d 937 (1971).

[24] Eisele v. Triangle Utilities Inc., 9 A.D. 697, 193 N.Y.S.2d 706 (1959).

the point of paralysis, we must hold as a matter of law that the Board erred in applying this standard to the facts present in this case. . . .

Reversed and remanded for reconsideration in light of this opinion. We do not retain jurisdiction.

WILCUT v. INNOVATIVE WAREHOUSING
2007 Mo. App. LEXIS 915 (June 19, 2007)

NORTON, PRESIDING JUDGE.

Employee was a truck driver for Innovative Warehousing ("Employer"). He was involved in an accident in which he sustained several severe injuries. Employer does not dispute that the accident occurred in the scope of Employee's employment. Employee was taken to a hospital for treatment. He died seven days later.

Employee's treatment was complicated by his refusal to accept a blood transfusion. Employee was a Jehovah's Witness. Members of that faith believe it is a great sin to accept a blood transfusion. Employee was conscious and able to make decisions for himself upon admission to the hospital, and he made it clear that he would not accept the transfusion. This was affirmed by his family and others close to him both before and after losing consciousness. Employee was unable to undergo essential procedures to treat his wounds because he would not accept a blood transfusion, and he died from cardiac ischemia and severe anemia due to the blood lost following the accident.

There was no evidence that Employer objected to the refusal. Employer paid Employee's funeral expenses and paid death benefits to Dependent [Employee's surviving spouse] for nearly two years after the accident. After Employer stopped paying, Dependent filed this action for an award of death benefits commencing from the date they were terminated.

At the hearing in front of the administrative law judge ("ALJ"), doctors testified that Employee's death was preventable if he had accepted the transfusion. A Jehovah's Witness church elder and Employee's family members testified that refusal of blood transfusions is a tenet of the faith and that Employee was a follower of the faith and in good standing with the church. The elder also testified that a Jehovah's Witness may seek forgiveness for sins. The ALJ found, among other things, that Employee's refusal was not unreasonable under section 287.140.5, given his beliefs as a Jehovah's Witness, and therefore he was entitled to benefits.

Employer appealed to the Commission. The Commission adopted the ALJ's findings of fact. The Commission differed with the ALJ, however, in its analysis of the reasonableness of Employee's refusal to accept a blood transfusion. The Commission found the refusal unreasonable both because the physical risk was minimal compared to the near certainty Employee would survive his injuries if he accepted the transfusion, and because Jehovah's Witnesses believe they can seek forgiveness for their sins.

Dependent appeals. . . .

We first closely examine the Commission's decision because of the case's unique facts and the decision's complicated reasoning. The Commission addressed Employee's refusal with the aid of *Martin v. Industrial Accident Commission*, 147 Cal. App. 2d 137, 304 P.2d 828 (Cal. Ct. App. 1956). In *Martin*, an employee sustained a work-related injury. *Id.* at 828–29. The employee and his wife informed hospital authorities and the treating physician that he was a Jehovah's Witness and therefore refused blood transfusions. *Id.* at 829. He died shortly thereafter from complications that arose during a surgical procedure. *Id.* He likely would have survived had a transfusion been part of the treatment. *Id.* California's industrial commission denied compensation because it determined that the refusal was unreasonable, interpreting a statute similar to ours here. *Id.* (quoting "section 4056 of the Labor Code" as it existed in 1956). The California court framed the issue as whether, "in the light of all of the evidence including his religious beliefs, it was unreasonable for him to refuse to accept a treatment necessary to save his life." *Id.* at 830. The court found that it was unreasonable, explaining that the legislature conditioned an employer's liability on finding that the employee's death was not "the result of the voluntary act of the employee in refusing medical attention." *Id.*

Here, the Commission agreed with the court's rationale in *Martin* and considered all facts in the record that it found relevant to its decision, including Employee's beliefs. . . . The Commission concluded that Employee's refusal was unreasonable and "broke the medical causal link between work-related accident and his death." . . .

Our review of Missouri case law, however, reveals no case where the reasonableness of an employee's decision to forego treatment was based on religious beliefs. We must then determine what is meant by "unreasonable" in section 287.140.5. Section 287.140.5 states, in pertinent part, that:

> No compensation shall be payable for the death or disability of an employee, if and insofar as the death or disability may be caused, continued or aggravated by any unreasonable refusal to submit to any medical or surgical treatment or operation, the risk of which is, in the opinion of the division or the commission, inconsiderable in view of the seriousness of the injury.

. . . .

We must determine to what extent the legislature intended an employee's religious beliefs to be considered when analyzing whether a refusal of treatment was unreasonable. Section 287.140.5 does not simply state that any refusal of a low-risk, but beneficial, treatment will result in denial of compensation; the refusal must also be unreasonable in some sense. The section does not provide any further guidance to determine what the legislature might consider "unreasonable." . . .

Some guidance is found in a nearby section of the Worker's Compensation Law. Section 287.140.9 states that "[n]othing in this chapter shall prevent an employee being provided treatment for his injuries by prayer or spiritual means if the employer does not object to the treatment." Dependent cannot claim sanctuary in this section alone in proving the compensability of her claim, however, because Employee and those directing his care chose medical treatment in lieu of the transfusion, including medicines and supplements intended to stimulate blood production.

Nevertheless, the section does show that the legislature contemplated that religious beliefs might impact an employee's decision-making on what treatment to undertake. Necessarily, if section 287.140.5 is to be read harmoniously and liberally construed, sincerely-held religious beliefs must be considered by the Commission. Therefore, when liberally interpreting the phrase "unreasonable refusal [of] . . . treatment" in section 287.140.5 harmoniously with section 287.140.9 to give effect to the legislature's intent, we understand the statute to liberally accommodate an employee's religious beliefs to the extent that they influence his decision to pursue, or not to pursue, a course of treatment.

. . . .

We find that the Commission failed to adequately accommodate Employee's religious beliefs in its decision. While it did recite some of Employee's beliefs, these beliefs received no deference in the final decision. Instead, the Commission followed *Martin* and found that Employee's decision was a voluntary one and broke the causation between his accident and his death. The Commission's reliance on *Martin*, however, is misplaced at best. In addition to being a case from outside this jurisdiction, *Martin* was expressly overruled in Montgomery v. Board of Retirement, 33 Cal. App. 3d 447, 109 Cal. Rptr. 181, 185–86 (Cal. Ct. App. 1973). The court in *Montgomery* found that the court's reasoning in *Martin* was not consistent with the United States Supreme Court's and California courts' interpretations of the constitutional right to freely exercise religion, and the court refused to follow *Martin*. *Id.* at 186.

. . . .

We hold that the Commission's decision was not supported by competent and substantial evidence. The statutory scheme dictates that religious beliefs be liberally considered, and we find that Employee invoked his strong and sincerely held religious beliefs against a transfusion. This refusal was not unreasonable in light of his beliefs, and Dependent is owed death benefits from the date that the benefits were terminated.

. . . .

We reverse the Commission's decision and remand for further proceedings consistent with this opinion.

. . . .

ROMINES, JUDGE (dissenting):

I dissent. This case is not about the exercise of a religious belief — it is about money. The majority opinion confuses the manner of our review and imposes an amorphous standard that is not compelled by Constitution or statute and is not consistent with a court's duty to avoid an analysis of another's religious beliefs.

Initially, the testimony is clear — a blood transfusion and Mr. Wilcut would have survived. This refusal was not a "complication," as the majority suggests. Simply, Mr. Wilcut and his family exercised their religious beliefs — the employer did not seek judicial intervention, nor did the State, to compel a transfusion. . . . As such, there is no religious conundrum for this Court to tackle. . . .

As is patent, Section 287.140.5 requires the Commission to determine if a refusal is unreasonable " . . . in view of the seriousness of the injury. . . . " As is obvious, the injury here was life threatening. This record leaves no doubt that the medical opinion was unanimous — a transfusion was compelled. The medical opinion was correct.

This record is likewise clear that the Wilcut family and medical staff were in contact with Jehovah's Witness counselors who recommended medical treatment that did not include a transfusion of whole blood. This is the record on which the Commission reached the factual conclusion that the refusal was unreasonable, consistent with Section 287.140.5. The Commission reached the only principled conclusion under the facts before it.

The majority, in my judgment, compounds error by then making Section 287.140.9 something more than it is. I read this sub-section to say "pray if you wish," or, "bring in your Pastor, Priest, Practitioner, or Shaman." This section does not justify the Court's straying into a discussion of the principles of a Jehovah's Witness.

. . . .

I suspect that a Jehovah's Witness who reads the Court's doctrinal discussion would find it clumsy and cluttered. Courts cannot base decisions on doctrine. There can be neither a Presbyterian, Christian Science, nor Jehovah's Witness exception to Section 287.140.5; to do so violates the First Amendment to the United States Constitution, and Mo. Const. Art. I, Sections 5 and 7. Inasmuch as I conclude that the majority result violates the First Amendment of the United States Constitution, and Mo. Const. Art. I, Sections 5 and 7, and is contrary to cases thereunder, pursuant to Rule 83.03, I request transfer to the Missouri Supreme Court.

PROBLEMS

(1) McAllister had suffered a compensable heart attack in 1952. His condition became progressively worse. Five years later, he received a phone call at 1:00 a.m. from a friend, who told him that his wife was drinking at a tavern with another man. McAllister rushed to the tavern and became embroiled in a domestic-triangle argument. The emotional experience triggered a fatal heart collapse. Compensable? *See* McAllister v. Board of Educ., Town of Kearney, 79 N.J. Super. 249, 191 A.2d 212 (1963), *aff'd*, 42 N.J. 56, 198 A.2d 765 (1964).

(2) Suppose the compensable injury is severely exacerbated by the malpractice of a physician. Is the added injury compensable? *See* McCorkle v. McCorkle, 265 S.W.2d 779 (Ky. 1954), in which, during an operation for a herniated disc, the employee bled to death because of a slip of the surgeon's knife.

(3) In death cases, should there be a rule on unreasonable refusal of autopsy, analogous to that on unreasonable refusal of surgery? *See* Fish v. Smithville Volunteer Fire Ins. Co., 12 A.D.2d 573, 206 N.Y.S.2d 822 (1960).

(4) Lira, a partially recovered heroin addict, lied about his drug history when applying for his job, because he did not think he would get the job if he told the truth. He injured his back, and the doctors, being unaware of the danger of readdiction, prescribed codeine and other drugs. Lira did indeed become readdicted. Were the consequences compensable? *See* Bludworth Shipyard, Inc. v. Lira, 700 F.2d 1046, 15 BRBS 120 (5th Cir. 1983).

Part 3

COURSE OF EMPLOYMENT

Chapter 7
TIME AND PLACE

§ 7.01 MEANING OF "COURSE OF EMPLOYMENT"

An injury is said to arise in the course of the employment when it takes place within the period of the employment, at a place where the employee reasonably may be, and while he or she is fulfilling his or her duties or engaged in doing something incidental thereto.

The course of employment requirement tests work-connection as to time, place, and activity; that is, it demands that the injury be shown to have arisen within the time and space boundaries of the employment, and in the course of an activity whose purpose is related to the employment. The present chapter deals with questions primarily turning on "time and place" issues; questions on the relation of the activity itself to the employment are dealt with in the following chapter.

Before approaching the specific problems of course of employment, one should observe several general features of the phrase, the importance of which will appear from time to time. First, it does not say, as most people paraphrase it, that the *employee* must have been in the course of employment — although usually it amounts to the same thing; it says that the *injury* must arise in the course of the employment. Second, the usual verb is not to "occur" in the course of employment, but to "arise," which in a close case may make a difference. Third, while the phrase is obviously lifted from the law of vicarious liability of master for the servant's torts, and while perhaps 90 percent of the decisions on course of employment in routine cases are interchangeable between the two fields, the analogy breaks down in certain close cases because of a fundamental difference between the two kinds of liability. In the law of *respondeat superior*, the harmful force is always an act of the servant, or at least an omission which is the equivalent of an act. The inquiry is whether the performance of that act was in furtherance of the master's business. But in many workers' compensation situations, the harmful force is not the employee's act, but something *acting upon* the employee. It is unfortunate that the original drafters of the compensation coverage clause did not seem to be aware of this sharp difference between the impact of a "course of employment" test upon compensation and its impact on vicarious liability. Suppose, for example, a lathe operator, who is required to be present at the lathe even when there is no actual job to do, is engaged during an idle period in the forbidden practice of turning ashtrays out of souvenir shellcases for personal amusement and profit. The course of employment question might arise in several ways: (a) the shell explodes and kills the lathe operator; (b) the same explosion kills a stranger passing by on the sidewalk; (c) the employee while so engaged is struck by an overhead crane solely because he or she is where the employment requires him or her to be. It is immediately apparent that one cannot say categorically that the employee is or is not in the course of employment. Least of all can one assume that the answer to (b) will necessarily be the right answer for (a) or (c).

With these preliminary *caveats*, we may undertake the investigation of some of the most familiar and troublesome course of employment categories.

§ 7.02   GOING TO AND FROM WORK

[1]   Introduction

As to employees having fixed hours and place of work, injuries occurring *on* the premises while they are going to and from work before or after working hours or at lunchtime are compensable, but if the injury occurs *off* the premises, it is not compensable, subject to several exceptions. Underlying some of these exceptions is the principle that course of employment should extend to any injury which occurred at a point where the employee was within range of dangers associated with the employment.

The course of employment is not confined to the actual manipulation of the tools of the work, nor to the exact hours of work. On the other hand, while admittedly the employment is the cause of the workers' journey between home and factory, it is generally taken for granted that workers' compensation was not intended to protect the worker against all the perils of that journey. Between these two extremes, a compromise on the subject of going to and from work has been arrived at, largely by case law, with a surprising degree of unanimity: going to and from work is covered *on the employer's premises*.

[2]   Going to Work

PRICE v. WORKERS' COMPENSATION APPEALS BOARD
37 Cal. 3d 559, 209 Cal. Rptr. 674, 693 P.2d 254 (1984)

Bird, Chief Justice.

Does the "going and coming rule" preclude an award of workers' compensation benefits to an employee who is injured while waiting for his place of employment to open?

I.

Approximately 7:50 a.m. on June 20, 1980, petitioner, Andrew Leo Price, was injured outside his place of employment. Price had arrived at work at 7:45 a.m. Since no lot was provided for employee parking, Price parked his car on the same side of the street as his employer's premises.

Although Price's job officially began at 8 a.m., he generally arrived at work early. Often the premises were open before 8 a.m. If he arrived early and the doors were open, Price would usually begin working. Closing time was 4:30 p.m., regardless of when the employee actually started to work.

The employer's building was half a block wide and fronted directly on the sidewalk. There was no place on the premises where employees could wait if they arrived early. In fact, the employees could not gain access to the premises at all until the doors were unlocked.

On the morning of the accident, Price intended to start work early. However, the doors to the premises were locked and neither his supervisor's nor his boss's car was parked nearby. Since he could not enter the premises, he decided to put a quart of oil into the engine of his car while he waited. As he put the oil into his car, Price straddled the left headlight and extended his right leg to the side. A passing car struck Price's leg. He now seeks compensation for those injuries.

The workers' compensation judge found that Price was injured "in the course of the employment." Although Price was not physically on the employer's premises when the accident occurred, he was waiting to be admitted to work. Further, the workers' compensation judge held that pouring oil into a car was an act of "personal convenience" that did not abrogate the employment relationship.

Upon reconsideration, the Workers' Compensation Appeals Board (board) rescinded the award based on the "going and coming rule." The board relied on the fact that Price was not on the employer's premises when he was injured. Therefore, they concluded that he had not completed his journey to work. (See *General Ins. Co. v. Workers' Comp. Appeals Bd.* (1976) 16 Cal. 3d 595, 600 [128 Cal. Rptr. 417, 546 P.2d 1361] (hereafter *Chairez*).)

II.

An employer is liable under the Workers' Compensation Act (Act) (Lab. Code, § 3201 et seq.) for injuries "arising out of and in the course of the employment." (Lab. Code, § 3600.) The going and coming rule is among the judicially created doctrines that define that statutory requirement. . . . The rule provides that an injury suffered "during a local commute enroute to a fixed place of business at fixed hours in the absence of special or extraordinary circumstances" is not within the course of employment. As such, it is not compensable. . . .

. . . [T]he going and coming rule has had a "tortuous history." . . . Much criticized and subject to numerous exceptions, the rule is difficult to apply uniformly. . . . Neither the rule nor its exceptions are susceptible to "automatic application." . . .

Application of the rule has been especially difficult in "borderline cases" where the employee is hurt close to or on the employer's premises immediately before or after work. . . . In determining whether the going and coming rule bars compensation in a particular case, the courts must abide by the mandate of Labor Code section 3202, which provides that the Act "shall be liberally construed" to protect the injured. . . .

The issue presented here — whether the going and coming rule applies to an employee who has arrived at work but is unable to gain access to the premises — is a question of first impression. The going and coming rule governs injuries incurred "during the course of a local commute" (*Chairez, supra*, 16 Cal. 3d 595, 598) or "while travelling to and from work" (*Parks, supra*, 33 Cal. 3d at p. 588). However, it does not apply to an employee who has arrived at his or her workplace.

When Price found the doors to his employer's premises locked, he was at his place of employment. Thus, he was not injured "in the course of a local commute." Price had finished his journey to work although, because the doors were locked, he had not yet entered his employer's premises. In light of the rule of liberal construction, this court holds that where an employee is injured outside the employer's premises while waiting to be admitted to the workplace, the injury occurs within the course of the employment and is compensable.

This court has often held off-premises injuries compensable. "Although many of our decisions have involved injuries on premises owned or controlled by the employer, we have refused to regard either attribute as a sine qua non for compensation." (*Lewis v. Workers' Comp. Appeals Bd.* (1975) 15 Cal. 3d 559, 562 [125 Cal. Rptr. 353, 542 P.2d 225].) For example, the "special risk" exception to the going and coming rule provides for compensation where a risk associated with the employment causes injury just outside the employer's premises. . . .

Although the special risk exception need not be invoked here because the going and coming rule does not apply, the exception supports by analogy the conclusion that Price's injury occurred within the course of his employment.

"If, prior to entry upon the premises, an employee suffers injury from a special risk causally related to employment, the injury is compensable under the 'special risk' exception to the going and coming rule." (*Chairez, supra,* 16 Cal. 3d at p. 600.) More broadly stated, the special risk exception implies "a zone of employment, varying in distance, measured by the special circumstances of each case and defined by the nature of the employment." (*Lefebvre v. Workers' Comp. Appeals Bd.* (1980) 106 Cal. App. 3d 745, 750 [165 Cal. Rptr. 246].)

The employer's premises were not opened at the same time every morning. Therefore, an employee who wished to start working early, or even promptly, might be forced to wait for the doors to be unlocked after he arrived at the workplace. The employer did not provide a parking area or a place in which his employees could wait. In fact, the employees did not have access to any part of the premises before the doors were unlocked. As the workers' compensation judge stated, "[since] the employer's building is right next to the public sidewalk, it is obvious that applicant could not get onto the employer's premises and wait for the doors to be opened. He had to wait off the premises." Thus, when Price waited near his car for the doors to be opened, he was within the "zone of employment" under the "special circumstances" of this case.

Relying on the *Chairez* case, the board denied compensation on the ground that Price was not on the employer's premises but was out in the street when he was hit by a passing car. The board invoked the so-called "premises line" test. "For [purposes] of the [going and coming] rule, the employment relationship does not begin until an employee enters the employer's premises. Prior to entry the going and coming rule ordinarily precludes recovery; after entry, injury is generally presumed compensable as arising in the course of employment." (*Chairez, supra,* 16 Cal. 3d at p. 598.)

However, the "premises line" test should not preclude compensation here. In *Chairez,* the employee was killed while walking across the street away from his parked car and toward the workplace. He was still on his way to work when the accident occurred because he had not yet reached the employer's premises. (*Chairez, supra,* 16 Cal. 3d at p. 600.) Price, on the other hand, was no longer traveling toward the workplace when the accident occurred. Instead, he had arrived, parked, and observed that he could not gain access to the premises until one of his superiors arrived.

In sum, Price's injury does not fall within the going and coming rule because Price had finished his commute and was waiting to be admitted to his employer's premises when the accident occurred. Price was forced to wait outside the premises because the employer provided no place on the premises for the employees to wait. Moreover, Price's early arrival was usually a benefit to the employer since he worked extra time uncompensated.

The board argues that even if the going and coming rule is inapplicable, Price was not injured within the course of employment. According to the board, Price temporarily abandoned his employment relationship when he decided to put oil in his car while waiting to be admitted to the workplace. Price contends that pouring oil in his car was an act of "personal convenience" and compensable.

"Such acts as are necessary to the life, comfort, and convenience of the servant while at work, though strictly personal to himself, and not acts of service, are incidental to the service, and injury sustained in the performance thereof is deemed to have arisen out of the employment." (*Whiting-Mead Co. v. Indus. Acc. Com.* (1918) 178 Cal. 505, 507 [173 P. 1105, 5 A.L.R. 1518]; accord *Employers' etc. Corp. v. Indus. Acc. Com.* (1940) 37 Cal. App. 2d 567, 573 [99 P.2d 1089] (hereafter *Burnett*).) This court has noted that the personal convenience exception "is not limited to acts performed on the employer's premises." (*State Comp. Ins. Fund v. Workmen's Comp. App. Bd.* (1967) 67 Cal. 2d 925, 927–928 [64 Cal. Rptr. 323, 434 P.2d 619].)

Acts of "personal convenience" are within the course of employment if they are "reasonably contemplated by the employment." (*Pacific Indem. Co. v. Ind. Acc. Com.* (1945) 26 Cal. 2d 509, 514 [159 P.2d 625]; accord *North American Rockwell Corp. v. Workmen's Comp. App. Bd.* (1970) 9 Cal. App. 3d 154, 158 [87 Cal. Rptr. 774] (hereafter *Saska*); *Burnett, supra,* 37 Cal. App. 2d at p. 573.) Courts consider the nature of the act and the nature of the employment, the custom or usage of the employment, the terms of the employment contract, and "other factors." (*Ibid.; Saska, supra,* 9 Cal. App. 3d at p. 158.) In view of the policy favoring employee compensation, doubts as to whether an act is reasonably contemplated by the employment are resolved in favor of the employee. (*Ibid.; Burnett, supra,* 37 Cal. App. 2d at pp. 573–574.)

The evidence presented at the workers' compensation hearing indicated that the doors to the workplace were not opened at the same time every morning. Usually they were opened early, but at times they were not unlocked until after the official starting time of 8 a.m. Waiting outside the employer's premises was, therefore, "reasonably contemplated by the employment."

As the workers' compensation judge noted, "[when] people are waiting for something to happen, they rarely stand in one spot; they 'occupy.' " However, instead of idly pacing, Price made use of the time by adding oil to his car. His act was not "wholly unreasonable" but was "normal, proper and reasonably to be expected." (*Saska, supra,* 9 Cal. App. 3d at pp. 158, 160.) Performing a minor personal task while waiting to begin work is a "normal human response." Therefore, it is within the reasonable contemplation of the employment contract. (*Id.,* at p. 159.) As the court in *Saska* pointed out, "[human] services cannot be employed without taking the whole package." (*Ibid.; Fremont Indemnity Co. v. Workers' Comp. Appeals Bd.* (1977) 69 Cal. App. 3d 170, 177 [137 Cal. Rptr. 847].)

Although Price's conduct was reasonably contemplated by his employment, the board contends that Price's act of "personal convenience" was not within his course of employment because it did not help him to perform his work more efficiently. However, a strong nexus between the personal act and increased efficiency is not a prerequisite to coverage. (*See, e.g., Leffert v. Industrial Acc. Com.* (1934) 219 Cal. 710 [28 P.2d 911] [employee hit by a car while enroute to employer's burned building to retrieve his overcoat]; *Pacific Indem. Co. v. Ind. Acc. Com., supra,* 26 Cal. 2d 509 [agricultural workers drowned in irrigation reservoir while washing up after work]; *Burnett, supra,* 37 Cal. App. 2d at p. 574 [domestic servant "on call" hurt while hemming a dress].) "While [the benefit] rationale is still reflected in the decisions, it is apparent from an examination of the cases . . . that benefit to the employer was presumed and in some cases little more than fiction." (*Saska, supra,* 9 Cal. App. 3d at p. 160.)

. . . .

Moreover, as Price put oil in his car, he provided a benefit to the employer by waiting near the premises so he could enter and begin work as soon as the doors were unlocked. Although Price was engaged in a personal act, he was also serving the employer's interests. Therefore, the injury may be viewed as occurring within the course of employment under the "dual purpose" rule. "[Where] the employee is combining his own business with that of his employer, or attending to both at substantially the same time, no nice inquiry will be made as to which business he was actually engaged in at the time of injury, unless it clearly appears that neither directly or indirectly could he have been serving his employer." (*Lockheed Aircraft Corp. v. Ind. Acc. Com.* (1946) 28 Cal. 2d 756, 758–759 [172 P.2d 1]; accord *Bramall, supra,* 78 Cal. App. 3d at p. 157.)

The dual purpose doctrine generally applies as an exception to the going and coming rule when an employee who is hurt during a local commute is taking work home with him. (*Bramall, supra,* 78 Cal. App. 3d 151, 156.) It is also invoked when an accident occurs in the course of a business trip or errand during which the employee takes care of some personal business. (*Lockheed, supra,* 28 Cal. 2d 756; *Matthews v. Naylor* (1941) 42 Cal. App. 2d 729 [109 P.2d 758].) In addition, the dual purpose doctrine has been applied to hold that an employee's leisure time activity was within the course of employment, where it was reasonably contemplated by the employment and benefited the employer as well as the employee. (*See Dimmig, supra,* 6 Cal. 3d at pp. 864–866, and cases cited.)

. . . .

This case involves elements of both *(the personal convenience and dual purpose)* rules. Pouring a quart of oil into his car while waiting to begin work is an "act of personal comfort or convenience" that is "reasonably contemplated" within the course of Price's employment. In addition, Price's injury falls within the dual purpose doctrine because he was providing a benefit to his employer by arriving at work early. This court need not determine which of the two rules better fits the facts of this case. (*See Fremont Indemnity, supra,* 69 Cal. App. 3d at p. 177.) "[The] point is that the activity was reasonably to be contemplated because of its general nature as a normal human response in a particular situation. . . . " (*Saska, supra,* 9 Cal. App. 3d at p. 159.)

. . . .

Accordingly, the decision of the board is annulled and the cause remanded for further proceedings consistent with the views expressed herein.

LUCAS, JUSTICE, dissenting.

I respectfully dissent.

Applicant Price was injured outside the work premises, before working hours, while engaged in an act of personal convenience. Under such circumstances, his injuries were not compensable under the workers' compensation laws.

The majority holds that all injuries that occur while awaiting entry to the employment premises are compensable. (Ante, pp. 565–566.) I fail to see how the act of awaiting entry before ordinary working hours reasonably may be deemed to arise "out of and in the course of the employment." (Lab. Code, § 3600.) Moreover, I think it is anomalous that compensation must be granted to one, such as applicant, who is injured while attending his parked car, but is denied to an employee who has already left his car and is injured while walking toward his workplace. (*General Ins. Co. v. Workers' Comp. Appeals Bd. (Chairez)* (1976) 16 Cal. 3d 595, 598–600 [128 Cal. Rptr. 417, 546 P.2d 1361] [adopting the "premises line" test].) Surely, in neither case has the ordinary morning "commute" ended, for in neither case has the employee actually entered the work premises. This fact is even more apparent here, where the injury occurred before working hours had commenced.

Nor was any "special risk" created by the employment in this case which might make inapplicable the going and coming rule. Contrary to the majority's characterization, applicant was not "forced" to wait in a place of danger such as the applicant in *Parks v. Workers' Comp. Appeals Bd.* (1983) 33 Cal. 3d 585 [190 Cal. Rptr. 158, 660 P.2d 382] (applicant injured while stuck in usual heavy school traffic outside workplace). There was no indication in the record that applicant herein was regularly subjected to any delay in work access or to any foreseeable risk of injury, or that any prior, similar accidents had ever taken place. In essence, applicant was injured while engaged in an act of personal convenience of no benefit to his employer, prior to his ordinary working hours. Workers' compensation should not be available under those circumstances.

I would affirm the board's decision denying benefits.

PROBLEMS

(1) Are you convinced by the court's distinction between the facts of the case before it and those of the *Chairez* case that it refers to? Does changing the oil in one's car take the personal convenience doctrine one step too far?

(2) Under the general rule that travel from the employer's parking lot to the premises is covered, what about the worker who cannot afford a car, and who is injured in the street between the nearest bus stop and the premises?

(3) Under the "premises rule," where do the "premises" of a university law school begin and end? *See* Warren's Case, 326 Mass. 718, 97 N.E.2d 184 (1951). An apartment construction project consisting of a large number of buildings? Employer's Ins. Co. v. Bass, 81 Ga. App. 306, 58 S.E.2d 516 (1950). A road construction project? Gillette v. Rochester Vulcanite Paving Co., 224 App. Div. 319, 230 N.Y. Supp. 647 (1928). A railroad? Is a railway worker "on the premises" while walking home to dinner along his railway's right-of-way? *See* McInerney v. Buffalo and S.S.R., 225 N.Y. 130, 212 N.E. 806 (1919).

[3]　Leaving Work

HARRIS v. SEARS, ROEBUCK & COMPANY
485 So. 2d 965 (La. Ct. App. 1986)
Writ Denied May 12, 1986

Before CHEHARDY, GRISBAUM and WICKER, JJ. GRISBAUM, JUDGE.

. . . .

The record shows the plaintiff's decedent, Mr. Leroyal Harris, Sr., reported for work at Sears' warehouse on Whitney Avenue on May 3, 1978. By 10 or 10:30 a.m., the warehouse floor area was covered by 14 to 16 inches of standing water; the office area, by 6 to 8 inches. The employees, in the wake of continuing heavy rain, were told they could leave. During the day, water rose as high as the glove compartments of cars parked in the Sears parking lot. Mr. Harris did not leave when he first learned he might but waited around a bit to see what the rain would do. Only after the building was completely flooded did he elect to leave. Mrs. Deanna Horne, Mr. Harris' clerical supervisor, testified that he indicated he was very nervous, that he was going home to his family, that there was some problem at home, and that, despite Mrs. Horne's advising him to wait at least until some Sears repair technicians who were pushing cars to higher ground returned so that they might push him out, Mr. Harris left. Mr. Harris drove his vehicle from the Sears parking lot and down Whitney Boulevard. Within a block of the Sears building, the vehicle began to float and was swept into the Whitney Canal. Mr. Harris crawled atop the vehicle and the Sears technicians, Mr. Alan Sekinger and Mr. Glenn Steib, who had returned from pushing a car, tried to rescue him, but unsuccessfully. He was sucked into a culvert and drowned.

. . . .

ANALYSIS

. . . [T]he United States Supreme Court in *O'Leary v. Brown-Pacific-Maxon, Inc.*, 340 U.S. 504, 71 S.Ct. 470 [95 L.Ed. 483] (1951) held that

> [t]he test of recovery is not a causal relation between the nature of employment of the injured person and the accident. . . . Nor is it necessary that the employee be engaged at the time of the injury in activity of benefit to his employer. All that is required is that the "obligations or conditions" of

employment create the "zone of special danger" out of which the injury arose.
. . . *A reasonable rescue attempt, like pursuit in aid of an officer making an
arrest, may be "one of the risks of the employment, an incident of the service,
foreseeable, if not foreseen, and so covered by the statute." (Citations omitted).*

Id., 340 U.S. at 506, 507, 71 S.Ct. at 471, 472. Lastly, as Justice Sutherland stated in
Cudahy Packing Co. of Nebraska v. Parramore, 263 U.S. 418, 44 S.Ct. 153, 154, [68 L.Ed.
366], "whether a given accident is so related or incident to the business must depend
upon its own particular circumstances. No exact formula can be laid down which will
automatically solve every case."

This Court is of the opinion that it was foreseeable on the part of Sears that certain
of its employees would be injured as a result of the flooding which was invading the
Sears premises and surrounding areas, the "zone of the special danger" referred to in
O'Leary, supra. The mere fact that some Sears employees remained on the premises
while others chose to leave did not reduce or diminish the zone of danger created by the
torrential rain. This Court opines that had decedent not been working for Sears on the
date of the flood (the "obligations or special conditions of employment", *O'Leary, supra*
[sic]), he probably would not have been on or near the Sears premises at the time of the
flood and not have subjected himself to the hazards created by the severe flooding.
Moreover, this Court is of the opinion that the legislative intent behind the Workmen's
Compensation Act was to provide coverage to those employees who were exposed to
risks as a result of their employment. This Court acknowledges that the evidence shows
decedent was probably attempting to go home after being allowed to do so by his
supervisor; however, had the decedent not been allowed to leave, he might not have
drowned. Also, in view of the fact that other Sears employees were helping those
attempting to leave (some employees were guided on foot to a hotel) or move their
vehicles to safer ground and that these helping employees, [sic] were still "working" for
Sears, the actions of those employees, by literally going beyond the Sears premises to
help others, constituted an extension of those premises. Therefore, it can be said that
decedent died "on Sears premises." Had decedent attempted to leave the premises but
risked his life to help another in distress, there would be no doubt that Workmen's
Compensation coverage would be afforded to decedent's family. And so, when decedent
attempted to save his own life, this Court should not equitably deny coverage when only
the bare fact that decedent was not trying to save the life of another distinguishes this
situation from the one alluded to above.

. . . .

The inquiries into nexus generate the general jurisprudential rule that "ordinarily, an
employee injured while going to or returning from work is not entitled to compensation
because the injuries are considered as not arising during the course of the employment
. . . this rule is premised on the employer's lack of supervision and control over the
employee at such times . . . [*any extension of coverage to such times*] . . . must
necessarily be founded on the existence of conditions surrounding the locality of the
employment which makes it more hazardous to the employee than it would have been
had he not been employed." . . .

The exception broached by Justice McCaleb has come to be termed the threshold
doctrine. Most classically, the doctrine means that the worker who, en route to or from
his workplace, rudely encounters a train on tracks situated just beyond the main gates
of his employer's factory will be covered by compensation anyhow. Likewise, the
employee who manages safely to leave the premises only then to be singed by embers
belched from his employer's chimneys. The doctrine as explicated in *Templet, supra*,
requires both (1) a distinctive travel risk for the employee in going to or coming from
work and (2) this risk's existing in an area immediately adjacent to his place of work.
Templet at 80.

In its Reasons for Judgment, quoted above, the trial court relies in part on the threshold doctrine, finding that Mr. Harris was subjected to an elevated flood hazard by virtue of his employment, such hazard being indeed proximate to the place of employment and enveloping the only route of escape therefrom. While we find this reasoning persuasive and, by analogy, instructive as to the proper result, we conclude that the direct application of the threshold doctrine to these facts is unnecessary. The hazard to which Mr. Harris ultimately succumbed — the flooding — presented itself at his place of employment during the time of employment. It follows elementarily, then, that this hazard arose out of and in the course of the employment. The nexus is established notwithstanding that the cause proper devolved from an act of God.

We need, then, only ascertain whether the accident also arose out of and in the course of Mr. Harris' employment. In this context, the defense counsel makes much of the fact that Mr. Harris was no longer on Sears' premises at the time of the accident and was, in fact, probably en route home. Also emphasized is that some employees chose to weather the storm and safely did so by remaining in the Sears warehouse abandoned by Mr. Harris. While these facts are pertinent, collectively they in no manner undercut the conclusion of the trial court. While Mr. Harris had managed safely to exit Sears' parking lot, he clearly had not yet escaped the hazard that had presented itself at his workplace and prompted his departure. Given more time, more distance, more opportunity for the intervention of Mr. Harris' conscious and volitional choice of route, our decision might be different. Here, however, Mr. Harris had left the parking lot by the only available exit and drowned less than a block from his employment premises. That others remained and survived is not determinative: still others sought refuge in a nearby hotel. Mr. Harris is not charged with the omniscient proactive operation of otherwise mortal hindsight. Nor dispositive is that Mr. Harris left probably intending to go home. Confronted with rising flood waters and construing in their wake the need to leave, Mr. Harris of necessity had to go somewhere else. That he chose home in no manner militates against the work-related nature of the hazard from which he fled or of the accident that claimed his life. The accident, arising in such an infinitesimally attenuated context from a hazard that clearly arose out of and in the course of employment, itself possesses sufficient nexus with the employment to produce worker's compensation liability. . . .

For the reasons assigned, the judgment of the trial court is affirmed. All costs of this appeal are to be assessed against the appellant.

Affirmed.

ILLINOIS BELL TELEPHONE COMPANY v. INDUSTRIAL COMMISSION
131 Ill. 2d 478, 137 Ill. Dec. 658, 546 N.E.2d 603 (1989)

STAMOS, JUSTICE.

Claimant, Mary R. Conoboy, was injured when she slipped and fell in a common area of the Woodfield Shopping Mall shortly after leaving her place of employment on the second floor of the mall. . . .

This appeal raises the issue of whether an injury sustained by an employee of a tenant in a multilevel shopping mall building, while in a common area of the mall on her way home from work, arises out of and in the course of her employment.

. . . Claimant testified that at 5 p.m. she finished work and left her employer's premises on the second level of the mall, using the nearest escalator to descend to the first floor of the mall. Upon reaching the first level, she began walking toward one of approximately 10 exits from the mall. When she was about 12 feet from an exit door, her left leg skidded and went out and she fell on her knee. She testified that the floor was waxed and slippery. Claimant then proceeded through the exit, the doors of which were locked; she stated that the mall doors are locked an hour to an hour and a half after the mall closes. The area in which she fell was open to the public when the mall itself was open for business.

Claimant had been employed at Illinois Bell's mall store for six months prior to the accident. She stated that she had used other mall entrances and exits to go to and from work, and testified that she had crossed the area where she fell only about 20 times in the six months she had worked at the mall store. She further stated that Illinois Bell did not require her to use any specific exit or entrance.

An examination of Illinois Bell's lease agreement indicates that the area in which claimant was injured was a "common area." The landlord was solely responsible for the maintenance of the common areas of the mall; the lease also states that the common areas are to be maintained and operated at the sole discretion of the landlord. The landlord also has the right under the lease to prescribe regulations governing the use of common areas and to close temporarily any common area to make repairs or changes. Illinois Bell is required to pay a pro rata share of the expenses of maintaining the common areas.

. . . .

This court has repeatedly held that "when an employee slips and falls, or is otherwise injured, at a point off the employer's premises while traveling to or from work, his injuries are not compensable." (*Butler Manufacturing Co. v. Industrial Comm'n* (1981), 85 Ill. 2d 213, 216, quoting *Reed v. Industrial Comm'n* (1976), 63 Ill. 2d 247, 248–49.) Prior decisions of this court have noted two exceptions to this general rule. Recovery has been permitted for offpremises injuries incurred by an employee when the employee's presence at the place where the accident occurred was required in the performance of his duties and the employee is exposed to a risk common to the general public to a greater degree than other persons. *(citations omitted)* Recovery has also been permitted for injuries sustained by an employee in a parking lot provided by and under the control of an employer. *(citations omitted)*

The facts here do not establish a basis for compensation under the first exception to the general premises rule. In *[Bommarito v. Industrial Comm'n* (1980), 82 Ill. 2d 191, 194]*, which claimant cites, all employees were required to enter and exit the store through a rear door. The court held that the claimant's injuries fell under the Act because of the employer's requirement that employees enter through a particular door and the hazardous risks presented by an alley through which employees had to pass in order to enter through the rear door. The court specifically noted that the case did not involve a situation where a claimant freely chooses to use a certain route and is injured in doing so. (*Bommarito*, 82 Ill. 2d at 196.) Similarly, in *Gray Hill, Inc. v. Industrial Comm'n* (1986), 145 Ill. App. 3d 371, another case cited by claimant, the court upheld compensation because it found that the claimant's presence where she was injured was required by her employer. 145 Ill. App. 3d at 375.

In *Deal v. Industrial Comm'n* (1976), 65 Ill. 2d 234, this court upheld an award of compensation to a claimant who was injured while leaving his employer's premises. The court found that evidence of the actual ownership of the cement apron upon which the claimant was standing when he was injured was not necessary to uphold compensation, because the doorway the claimant exited through was the only practical means of leaving the premises and the position of the exit created a greater degree of risk of injury to the claimant than to the general public.

Claimant in the case at bar testified that she was not required by her employer to use any particular mall entrance or exit and admitted using entrances and exits other than the one she was using when she was injured. For these reasons, we believe that claimant has failed to prove that she was required to be where the accident occurred.

The facts also fail to establish that claimant was exposed to a risk common to the general public to a greater degree than other persons. The common area where claimant slipped was open to the general public during the business hours of the mall. Although claimant testified that the floor was waxed and slippery, there is no evidence in the record that claimant was exposed to a greater risk by walking across the common area than that to which the public was exposed. . . .

In a similar case, *Reed v. Industrial Comm'n* (1976), 63 Ill. 2d 247, the claimant slipped and fell on an icy public sidewalk between her place of employment and a parking lot where employees were allowed to use the lot at a reduced rate. The court applied the general premises rule and denied compensation, noting that the "crosswalk in which the claimant fell is used by patients and visitors entering or leaving the hospital, as well as by employees." (*Reed*, 63 Ill. 2d at 249–50.) Because we find that claimant's employment did not require her to use a particular mall exit and that claimant was not exposed to a risk common to the general public to a greater degree than other persons, claimant is ineligible for compensation under the first exception to the premises rule.

Claimant next argues that because the only possible way for her to get to and from her place of employment was to enter and exit through a mall doorway, and Illinois Bell is a mall tenant, the common area where she fell should be considered the premises of her employer. Claimant apparently seeks to have this court extend the parking lot exception to encompass common areas of malls or buildings in which an employer's office or place of business is located. For the reasons following, we decline the invitation to expand this exception to the general premises rule.

Claimant's argument is based primarily on three decisions of courts of this State. . . .

In *Chicago Transit Authority*, the claimant was injured while riding an elevator from his seventh floor office in the Merchandise Mart in Chicago while on his lunch break. The appellate court stated that in cases involving injuries received by an employee during his lunch hour, the most critical factor in determining whether the accident arose out of and in the course of employment is the location of the occurrence. (*Chicago Transit Authority*, 141 Ill. App. 3d at 869.) The court quoted one authority who has stated that "when the place of employment is a building, an injury incurred by an employee in that building is generally considered to have taken place on the employer's premises so long as the employer 'has some kind of right of passage, as in the case of common stairs, elevators, lobbies, vestibules, concourses, hallways, . . . through which the employer has something equivalent to an easement.' " . . .

In *Master Leakfinding*, the claimant slipped and fell on some icy steps outside his employer's office in a building the employer shared with another tenant. He was found by his wife at the bottom of an incline between the stairs and a parking lot provided by the claimant's employer for its employees. Because the exact location of the injury was unknown, and the evidence conflicted over whether the employer had paid rent for the premises during the time the injury occurred and was therefore a subtenant of the building, the court addressed the employer's two-pronged argument that the claimant was not injured on the employer's premises by making a double finding. The court first stated that the claimant's injuries were compensable under the Act if the claimant fell on the stairs, because there was sufficient evidence to support the conclusion that the claimant's employer was a subtenant of the premises. The court also stated that if the claimant was injured on the parking lot, the claimant's injuries were compensable because it was "permissible to conclude that the accident occurred as a result of conditions on a parking lot provided for . . . employees." *Master Leakfinding*, 67 Ill. 2d at 528, citing *De Hoyos v. Industrial Comm'n* (1962), 26 Ill. 2d 110.

. . . .

Under the facts of this case, we decline to adopt a new exception to the general premises rule for injuries suffered off the premises of the employer in the common area of a mall where claimant's employer is located. Illinois Bell had no control over the common area where claimant was injured. The landlord is solely responsible for the maintenance of the common areas of the mall and even had the right to close temporarily any common area to make repairs or changes. Illinois Bell neither provided nor maintained the common areas of the mall. Although claimant testified that she and others had previously informed Illinois Bell that the common areas were slippery, Illinois Bell had no right to interfere with the landlord's sole discretion to maintain and operate the common areas.

. . . .

We finally note that claimant's citation to *Chicago Tribune Co. v. Industrial Comm'n* (1985), 136 Ill. App. 3d 260, in which the court upheld an award of compensation to a claimant who fell and was injured in a gallery open to the public on the first floor of her employer's building, is inapplicable, because, as the opinion specifically states, the "claim arose out of a slip and fall on respondent's premises" (136 Ill. App. 3d at 261). For all of the above reasons, we find that the decision of the Industrial Commission was against the manifest weight of the evidence. . . .

JUSTICE CALVO took no part in the consideration or decision of this case.

PROBLEMS

(1) What about a fall in a mall parking lot used by both the mall's customers and its employees? *See* Merrill v. J.C. Penney Co., 256 N.W.2d 518 (Minn. 1977).

(2) Add to (1) the fact that the employees were required to use the most distant parts of the lot, so as to leave the closer spaces for customers. *See* Livingstone v. Abraham & Straus, Inc., 524 A.2d 876 (N.J. Super. App. Div. 1987), *aff'd*, 111 N.J. 89, 543 A.2d 45 (1988).

[4]   Meal Breaks and the Like

PALLOTTA v. FOXON PACKAGING CORPORATION
477 A.2d 82 (R.I. 1984)

BEVILACQUA, CHIEF JUSTICE.

. . . Gina Pallotta, hereinafter referred to as the employee, was employed by the Foxon Packaging Corporation, hereinafter referred to as the employer on July 20, 1978, as a press operator. On this day, she punched out for lunch and left through the exit on the west side, the only way to leave the building. She then went to the store across the street, purchased something to eat and returned by means of a driveway located between the employer's building and that of the neighboring owner, Wal-Kar Engraving Company. The employee sat down to eat her lunch approximately six feet away from the entrance to the employer's building. After finishing her lunch, she spoke with a friend. At this time, some company employees were playing baseball, and she was struck on the head by a ball thrown by another employee. [*Court's footnote omitted*] The employee testified that she and other employees ate their lunches in the parking area located directly behind Wal-Kar. She stated that it was customary for employees to eat their lunches and take their coffee breaks in this area, and that the employer had knowledge of this fact. She also testified that she was not paid during her lunch break but that she did receive compensation for coffee breaks. After the incident she returned to work, reporting the accident to the plant manager.

The employee, upon advice of the plant manager, was taken to Roger Williams Hospital. She was examined by Dr. Manoel Falcao, who prescribed treatment. The doctor stated that as a result of the injury, the employee was totally disabled.

. . . .

The sole issue to be considered is whether the employee sustained an injury out of and in the course of her employment. In addressing this issue, the employee argues that the laws of this jurisdiction disregard any rigid "premises" or "off-premises" test, and that all the facts and circumstances must be considered.

In order to recover for injuries sustained, a worker must establish that the injury arose out of and in the course of the employment. . . .

In determining the right to compensation, we do not solely consider the place where the injury was sustained, although a causal connection or nexus is established if the employee can show that his injury occurred within the period of his employment, at a place where he might reasonably have been. *Lomba v. Providence Gravure, Inc.*, 465 A.2d 186, 188 (R.I. 1 983); *Bottomley v. Kaiser Aluminum & Chemical Corp.*, 441 A.2d 553, 554 (R.I. 1 982). To be compensable, the incapacity must result from an injury sustained by the employee in performing an activity that fulfills the duties of employment or is something incidental thereto or to the conditions under which those duties are to be performed. *Tromba v. Harwood Manufacturing Co.*, 94 R.I. 3, 9, 177 A.2d 186, 188 (1962).

. . . .

The employee relies on the case of *Bergeron v. Kilnic Co.*, 108 R.I. 313, 274 A.2d 753 (1971). That case is distinguishable from the case at bar. In Bergeron, the employee was injured on a driveway when she was returning to work after eating her lunch. It was uncontroverted that the only manner of entering the place of employment was by means of this driveway. The employer did not provide a dining area and knew of the employee's practice of going home to eat her lunch. This court held as a matter of law that the employee was injured during the period of employment, at a place where she had a right to be, while doing something that was incidental to her employment and that, therefore, her injury arose out of and in the course of her employment. *Id.* at 319, 274 A.2d at 756.

In the instant case, the facts are not in dispute. The employee was on her lunch break, which was unpaid. There is no evidence in the record to show that the employee in any way benefited her employer during her lunch break while on the premises of the adjoining owner. It was incumbent upon the employee to establish a link between the injury and the conditions of employment. This she failed to do. The record is completely devoid of any evidence that she was, during her lunch break, carrying out any duties of employment. [*Court's footnote omitted*]

The employee's appeal is denied and dismissed, and the decree appealed from is affirmed.

PROBLEM

Should an employee who leaves the premises during a 5 or 10 minute coffee break be treated the same as an employee who has an off-premises lunch-time injury? *See* Jordan v. Western Elec. Co., 1 Or. App. 441, 463 P.2d 598 (1969).

WESTERN GREYHOUND LINES v. INDUSTRIAL ACCIDENT COMMISSION
225 Cal. App. 2d 517, 37 Cal. Rptr. 580 (1964)

TAYLOR, JUSTICE.

. . . On October 3, 1962, the applicant was employed as a bus driver for Greyhound. Her hours of employment were from 5:00 p.m. to 5:00 a.m. At 1:45 a.m., she had completed a trip to San Francisco from Marin County and during her 41 minute layover left the Greyhound bus station at Seventh Street, crossed Seventh and walked about half a block to Foster's Restaurant at the corner of Seventh and Market Streets. She purchased a cup of coffee and sat down at a table where a man unknown to her attempted to converse. Upon her refusal to talk to him, the man attacked applicant causing her disability. She was dressed in her driver's uniform but there is no showing that the assailant was motivated by this fact. The restaurant at the bus depot closes at midnight. However, a snack bar and a coffee vending machine were available on the premises of the depot and a restroom with chairs and benches is located inside the bus terminal. The coffee sold at the snack bar is sometimes good and sometimes bad.

Greyhound bus drivers are permitted to leave the premises during the layover period and they are accustomed to going to Foster's Restaurant for coffee, particularly after the restaurant in the bus depot is closed. Greyhound's operating supervisor knew that drivers went to Foster's for coffee. The Commission found that the applicant's disability arose out of and in the course of employment and made an award for temporary disability.

The petitioner contends that the applicant's errand was entirely for her own pleasure and was unrelated in any way to her employment.

The Commission properly relies on *Western Pipe, etc., Co. of California v. Industrial Accident Commission*, 49 Cal. App. 2d 108, 121 P.2d 35, to support its award. There, the employee, a shipwright-carpenter, was allowed a half-hour off for dinner during a four hour overtime period from 4:30 p.m. to 8:30 p.m., for which he was given double pay. The cafeteria on the premises was closed. The employee left the premises to dine at a restaurant located a few miles away and was killed while crossing the street after having parked his car. The court held, in sustaining the Commission's order granting a death benefit, that it was not indispensable to recovery that the employee should be rendering service to the employer. The opinion relies on a line of cases which hold that where the employer pays transportation to and from work, by implied agreement, the employment may be found to continue from the time the employee leaves home until his return (87 A.L.R. 250). The court also approved the Commission's denial of the employer's petition for a rehearing and commented that the Commission would be justified in finding, as a matter of fact, that a slight deviation, such as crossing the street for cigarettes at the time of the accident, as had been alleged, was reasonably contemplated by the employment and would not take an employee outside his employment. This case has been cited with approval by the Supreme Court on several occasions (*Pacific Emp. Ins. Co. v. Industrial Acc. Comm.*, 26 Cal. 2d 286, 158 P.2d 9, 159 A.L.R. 313; *Reinert v. Industrial Acc. Comm.*, 46 Cal. 2d 349, 294 P.2d 713; *Leffert v. Industrial Acc. Comm.*, 219 Cal. 710, 28 P.2d 911).

We do not agree, as contended by the petitioner, that the holding in *Western Pipe and Steel* hinges upon the payment of double pay for overtime. The court said at page 113 of 49 Cal. App. 2d, at page 38 of 121 P.2d: "Obviously, if an employee is deemed to be acting in the course of his employment in going to or coming from his work when his compensation covers that time, it would seem clear that he is likewise acting within the course of his employment when his hourly wage continues during the time he is permitted to eat lunch or dinner off the premises." (Emphasis added) In *Kobe v. Industrial Acc. Comm.*, 35 Cal. 2d 33, 215 P.2d 736, 737 our Supreme Court approvingly quoted from *Western Pipe and Steel* was follows: "When the employer pays the employee at an hourly rate during his meal hours * * * it seems to be, and is a reasonable inference, that by such an arrangement the employer has impliedly agreed that service will continue during such period." (35 Cal. 2d p. 35, 215 P.2d p. 737.) *(Emphasis added.)* The words "especially when those meals are taken during an overtime period" were pointedly omitted from the quotation.

It has been held that acts of the employee for his personal comfort and gain while at work, even though performed off the employer's premises, may not interrupt the continuity of employment, particularly where the employee's comfort is also of benefit to the employer (*Western Pac. R. R. Co. v. Industrial Acc. Comm.*, 193 Cal. 413, 224 P. 754; *Leffert v. Industrial Acc. Comm.*, 219 Cal. 710, 28 P.2d 911). Here the Commission could well have concluded that it was very much to the advantage of the employer for the bus driver to refresh herself with a cup of coffee at 1:45 a.m. before leaving on the next run.

The petitioner contends that since coffee was readily available on Greyhound's premises, the Commission's order should be nullified. We cannot agree. In *Western Pipe and Steel*, the court placed no particular significance in the fact that the company cafeteria happened to be closed, and it would seem immaterial where the employer consented to the employees leaving the premises during the hours of employment. The evidence was that the coffee at the snack bar was not uniformly good. Not only did Greyhound permit its drivers to leave the station during the layover periods but it was customary for many of them to have coffee at Foster's. In view of the proximity of the restaurant to the depot, it may be inferred that Greyhound was cognizant of this practice. In fact, their operating supervisor admitted that he knew of the custom. Under these circumstances, it would seem unreasonably restrictive to deny employees the benefits of the Workmen's Compensation Act simply because they chose to have coffee in the more relaxing atmosphere of a nearby restaurant rather than from a vending machine or snack bar located on the company premises. . . .

Presumably, the applicant would not have been at Foster's Restaurant at Seventh and Market Streets at 1:45 a.m. had she not been working on a late night shift. She was drinking coffee because she had been driving a bus and would be again in a short time. Thus, she was exposed to the danger she encountered as a Greyhound employee. Since she was paid during this time, her employment continued during such time. . . . We conclude that the applicant's injuries occurred in the course of and arose out of her employment.

The award is *affirmed*.

SHOEMAKER, P. J., and AGEE, J., concur.

PROBLEM

Can *Pallotta* and *Western Greyhound* be distinguished, or are they simply inconsistent approaches to the same problem taken by two different jurisdictions?

GIBBERD v. CONTROL DATA CORPORATION
424 N.W.2d 776 (Minn. 1988)
Heard, considered and decided by the court en banc

KELLEY, JUSTICE.

The ultimate issue for resolution in this case is whether the dependents of an employee, a victim of a random street killing, are entitled to recover workers' compensation benefits from his employer when the victim was killed while away from the employer's premises during his meal break. A compensation judge held that they were not. The workers' compensation court of appeals (WCCA) reversed, and awarded dependency and funeral benefits. We reverse and reinstate the decision of the compensation judge.

Basically, the facts leading up to the killing are undisputed. At approximately 8:30 on the evening of August 26, 1985, Raymond P. Gibberd, an employee of appellant Control Data Corporation (CDC), was shot and killed during the course of an apparent random street assault while walking along a public street some distance from CDC's facility located at 304–306 Dale Street in St. Paul. When assaulted, Gibberd was walking toward the CDC facility. Evidence indicated he had left his work station and checked out of the CDC facility a short time before — apparently on a meal break. No reason has been established for the killing. No personal connection between Gibberd and his assailant has ever been established. There was no evidence that the motive for the killing was robbery. No evidence exists that the assault arose out of anything having to do with Gibberd's employment at CDC. Rather, the police authorities, who conducted an extensive investigation of the incident, have concluded that Gibberd was a victim of a random, senseless, street assault and execution. [*Court's footnote omitted*] . . .

The CDC facility in St. Paul, where Gibberd worked, is known as a World Distribution Center. It is located immediately south of U.S. Interstate 94. At the facility, CDC employs approximately 400 people on the day shift, 20 people on the second shift, and 5 people on the third shift. CDC located the World Distribution Center at its current location as part of a corporate policy favoring building of work facilities in so-called "depressed" inner-city areas. This policy coincides with widely publicized and generally known efforts of St. Paul municipal authorities to address social and economic problems in that same general area by encouraging renovations of commercial and residential buildings located in the area.

The evidence in the case revealed that 12 cities in the United States are roughly comparable in size to the City of St. Paul. Seven of those are considered to have a higher crime rate than does St. Paul. [Court's footnote omitted] In St. Paul the police department has divided the city into 198 "grids." CDC's World Distribution Center is located in "grid 109." In 1985 this "grid" ranked 19th in crime rate in St. Paul. Other "grids" surrounding "grid 109" ranked 5th, 7th, 11th and 30th. In the five years preceding the assault on Gibberd, crime had decreased dramatically in the general area — particularly to the south of the CDC plant. [Court's footnote omitted] Apparently people have been inquiring about and moving with increasing frequency into the general area. [Court's footnote omitted] Although CDC employees had reported to company officials a number of incidents of minor vandalism, purse thefts, and other thefts from employees during the five years preceding this assault, there had been only two assaults on persons reported. [Court's footnote omitted]

CDC provided a cafeteria on its premises for employees. Because most employees worked on the day shift, this cafeteria closed at 3 p.m. Vending machines on the premises provided candy, popcorn, sandwiches, potato chips, etc. A microwave oven was also available for use by employees. CDC had no implied or express policy which required employees to leave the CDC premises to eat out. Management did encourage employees to patronize the cafeteria during the hours it was open, but there existed no policy requiring employees to do so. In fact, CDC management was aware that many employees did take their lunch break away from the premises — particularly at an establishment known as Wendy's Fast Food Restaurant located approximately 7/10 of a mile from the plant.

Gibberd was employed as a computer consultant. He was considered an "exempt" employee. As an "exempt" employee, although his regularly scheduled working hours were 8 a.m. to 5 p.m., he had considerable latitude in setting his own working hours. However, as an exempt employee, any hours worked over 40 hours per week were uncompensated. For some time before and on the day of the assault, Gibberd had been working on a project involving retrieval of information from broken computers. Because demand for computer time was heavy during the regular 8 to 5 shift, when most of the CDC World Distribution Center employees were on duty, during August 1985, while working on this project, Gibberd worked frequently at night and on weekends.

On August 26 at approximately 4:15 p.m. and later about 7:15 p.m., Gibberd informed his family by telephone that he would be working late and not be coming home to eat. In the latter conversation, he mentioned he would shortly go out for a "bite to eat." He actually signed out on CDC's security log at 8:05 p.m. He apparently did not shut down the computer on which he was working because it was found to be running the next morning. Likewise, his briefcase was found open; the lights at his work station were on; and his books and papers were covering his desk.

No CDC employee saw Gibberd after he signed out. However, about one-half hour later, an eyewitness noticed Gibberd walking south on the east side of Dale Street in the direction of and approximately four blocks from the World Distribution Center. Suddenly an unidentified male accosted Gibberd; placed an armlock on his neck; shot him in the head with a pistol; and, after Gibberd was on the ground, shot him a second time in the head.

The time Gibberd signed out from the plant; the state in which he had left his work station; the time the eyewitness observed the assault; plus subsequent autopsy findings revealing partially undigested food estimated to have been ingested within a half hour prior to death; all combined to lead investigating authorities to conclude that he had recently eaten at Wendys.

. . . .

Our inquiry begins, then, by examining whether Gibberd's death is compensable. Minn. Stat. § 176.011, subd. 16 (1984) defines the "personal injury" compensable under the Workers' Compensation Act as one which arises out of and in the course of employment while the employee is engaged in or about the employer's work premises. The same statute excludes from compensation any injury caused by a third person which was intended to injure the employee or was not directed against the employee as a result of the employment. [*Court's footnote omitted*]

. . . .

The very words "arising out of" connote a causal connection, whereas "in the course of" refers to the time, place, and circumstances of the incident causing the injury. . . . In a number of our cases arising prior to 1983, by weighing into the balance the then prevailing precept that the workers' compensation law was to be given a broad and liberal construction in recognition of its supposed remedial purpose, the outer inclusive scope of the definition of the phrase "arising out of" was expanded. *(Citations omitted)* By enactment of 1983 Minnesota Laws, chapter 290, the legislature mandated that no longer should the former rule of liberal construction based upon a perceived remedial basis weigh in the analysis — a factor we must have in mind when using older cases as precedents in deciding cases arising after 1983. [*Court's footnote omitted*]

. . . *(the court here rejects application of several pre-1983 cases that were decided when the liberal construction rule was still in effect)*

. . . A superficial reading of our "meal break" cases might lead one to initially conclude that in this area the court has arrived at seemingly contradictory and inconsistent decisions. In support of their position, respondents, for example, cite such cases as Lassila v. Sears, Roebuck & Co., 302 Minn. 350, 224 N.W.2d 519 (1974); Krause v. Swartwood, 174 Minn. 147, 218 N.W. 555 (1928); Goff v. Farmers Union Accounting Serv., Inc. 308 Minn. 440, 241 N.W.2d 315 (1976); Faust v. State Dep't of Revenue, 312 Minn. 438, 252 N.W.2d 855 (1977); Sweet v. Kolosky, 259 Minn. 253, 106 N.W.2d 908 (1960). In each of those cases the employee's injury which had occurred during a "meal break" was either found by this court to be compensable or an Industrial Commission finding to that effect was affirmed. To the contrary, however, as appellant correctly observes, the court has either denied compensability or affirmed Industrial Commission findings denying compensation in such cases as Bronson v. Joyner's Silver & Electroplating, Inc., 268 Minn. 1, 127 N.W.2d 678 (1964); Callaghan v. Brown, 218 Minn. 440, 16 N.W.2d 317 (1944); and Satack v. State Dep't of Public Safety, 275 N.W.2d 556 (Minn.1978).

Upon closer examination, however, this seeming inconsistency emerges as being, in fact, more apparent than real. Those cases awarding compensation to employees while on a meal break are explainable either because the injury clearly occurred at a place considered to have constituted a part of the employer's working premises or because this court afforded pre-1983 deference to Industrial Commission findings. Thus, in Lassila the employee's injury was incurred in a cafeteria furnished by the employer; in Krause the employee was "on duty" for her employer during a lunch break; in Goff the employee was injured on her way from the office building to a parking lot furnished by the employer; in Faust the state had implicitly encouraged employees to eat lunches in a park it had furnished; [*Court's footnote omitted*] and in Sweet the court, in affirming an Industrial Commission award of compensation, relied heavily on the liberal interpretation rule.

In contrast, absent the existence of a work errand, absent reliance upon the pre-1983 liberal interpretation rule, or when the employee's injury occurred on the public street away from an area not deemed to be the "employment premises," compensation has been denied. . . . The rule to be extracted from the cases appears to be that an employee's injury (or death) incurred during a "meal break" is compensable under the workers' compensation law if (a) it occurred at a place that can reasonably be construed to be a part of the "employment premises," or (b) if it occurred at a time when the employee, in addition to reasons personal to himself, i.e., seeking sustenance, was furthering the employer's interests. If, however, the injury (or death) occurred in a public street and the hazard encountered was no greater than that to which all others not so employed would be exposed if they chose to traverse the way, it is not compensable unless other exceptions to Minn. Stat. § 176.011, subd. 16 (1984) apply.

One of those other exceptions is known as the "special hazard" exception, which respondents contend is applicable. Under that doctrine an employee's injury (or death) may be compensable where the manner in which the injury or death occurred arose from a "special hazard" even though the hazard is physically separated from the employer's premises provided that the hazard is causally connected to the employment and particular to it. See, e.g., *Johannsen v. Acton Construction Co.*, 264 Minn. 540, 119 N.W.2d 826 (1963). It is obvious, of course, that whether the "special hazard" exception is applicable at all depends upon a determination of whether, in fact, a special hazard exists. Even though the basic facts in the instant case are largely without dispute, reasonable persons could draw different inferences from those basic facts — as they did. It cannot be said the compensation judge's implicit finding negating the existence of any special hazard causally connected to and particular to the employment is unreasonable. The evidence of reported incidents of crime comparable with other areas of St. Paul, "downtown" for example, reasonably supports the compensation judge's conclusion. A contrary inference, implicitly drawn by the WCCA, likewise cannot be categorized as being unreasonable. The same reported "incidents of crime" figures showed that other areas of St. Paul had figures lower than the area where this assault occurred. That either inference could reasonably be drawn highlights the conclusion that since the 1983 amendments, now codified in Minn. Stat. § 176.421, subd. 1(3) and Minn. Stat. § 176.441, subd. 1, as interpreted by us in Hengemuhle, the compensation judge's conclusion should not have been set aside.

Additionally, we note the facts in this case differ from those typically present in most of the cases where the "special hazard" exception has been followed. The exception is applicable only if by virtue of the employment the employee is exposed to a hazard which originates on the employment premises, is a part of the working environment, or if it peculiarly exposes the employee to an external hazard which subjects the employee to a greater personal risk than one has when pursuing ordinary personal affairs. . . . The compensation judge observed that adoption of respondent's position would expand the "special hazard" exception to cover risks occurring blocks away from and totally unrelated to the employment activity on CDC's premises where, as here, there exists nothing but the most attenuated nexus between the random street crime and the employment. If the "special hazard" exception is expanded to hold it applicable in this factual setting, no logical reason exists prohibiting its further extension to impose liability on all Minnesota employers whose employees sustain injuries or death on the streets or highways while going to or returning from work. . . .

Finally, respondents claim that Gibberd's death was the result of an assault not caused by reasons personal to him, and that therefore it must be deemed compensable as arising from his employment. The pertinent statutory provision reads: "[a compensable injury] shall not include an injury caused by the act of a third person * * * intended to injure the employee because of reasons personal to him, and not directed against him as an employee, or because of his employment." Minn. Stat. § 176.011, subd. 16 (1984).

In this case all that is known is that Gibberd was assaulted on a public street by a person who obviously intended to injure or cause his death. The compensation judge inferentially found the assault had no nexus with Gibbard's employment. Facts exist from which an inference could be drawn that the assault may have been racially or socially motivated. In contrast, had Gibberd at the time of the assault been displaying or wearing his CDC identification badge, which, at best is conjectural, such fact if it existed might lend support to an inference that the assault was directed against him as a CDC employee. Thus, conflicting but permissible inferences both rest upon speculation. When the facts, and permissible inferences therefrom, support either inference, this court affirms the appropriate fact finder. . . .

The underlying purpose leading to the institution of the workers' compensation system — that employers bear the costs of damages sustained by employees and their survivors for injuries or death arising out of and in the course of the employment relationship — is not furthered by imposing responsibility upon employers for random assaults, having no nexus to the employment and which occur away from the employer's premises at times when employees are in pursuit of their own personal ends. Such expansion, instead, would be antithetical to that basic purpose by converting the statutory workers' compensation system into a compulsory health and accident insurance scheme by which every employer would be made liable for all injuries sustained by employees from the time of leaving for, and returning home from, work. Such a conversion involves policy considerations bearing a number of social, political, and fiscal ramifications that can more appropriately be addressed by the legislature. . . .

We reverse the holding of the workers' compensation court of appeals and affirm the conclusions of the compensation judge that the facts, and inferences reasonably to be drawn therefrom, do not establish that Raymond Gibberd's death arose out of and in the course of his employment.

YETKA, JUSTICE (dissenting) [*Dissent omitted.*]

PROBLEMS

(1) To turn into the employer's premises, the claimant had to make a left turn across traffic at an intersection without a stop light. In making such a turn, he was struck by an oncoming car. Should this be an exception to the premises rule? *See* Husted v. Seneca Steel Service, Inc., 41 N.Y.2d 673, 391 N.Y.S.2d 78, 359 N.E.2d 673 (1976).

(2) Do you agree with the *Gibberd* court that a different decision would convert workers' compensation into a compulsory health and accident insurance scheme? If one's employment places a person in an urban environment with hazards greater than he or she would otherwise be subjected to, and those risks happen to materialize, why shouldn't there be compensation?

(3) Indeed, what would be wrong with simply eliminating the "going and coming" exception entirely and having workers' compensation coverage for all injuries occurring while commuting to or from work? Isn't getting to work necessary to the employment? And isn't it true that injuries occurring on the way to work would not have happened except for the employment?

§ 7.03   JOURNEY ITSELF PART OF SERVICE

The rule excluding off-premises injuries during the journey to and from work does not apply if the making of that journey, or the special degree of inconvenience or urgency under which it is made, whether or not separately compensated for, is in itself a substantial part of the service for which the worker is employed.

Suppose that an employee works at a mine but lives a considerable distance away from it. The employee has as part of his or her job the duty of returning to the mine at night and throwing a switch to turn on the pumps so that the mine will be ready for operations in the morning. The actual work involved consists of a single action which takes but a fraction of a second: the closing of the switch. But the essence of the service performed was the making of the journey to the mine and back at the precise time when the pumps had to be turned on. It follows that the entire journey to and from the mine is in the course of the employment.[1]

Carried to its logical extreme, this principle can be considered the justification for the well-settled rule that traveling workers are generally within the course of their employment from the time they leave home on a business trip until they return, for the reason that the traveling itself is a large part of the job.[2] Several socalled "exceptions" to the basic premises rule on going and coming are applications of this principle: employees sent on special errands; employees continuously on call; and employees who are paid for their time while traveling or for their transportation expenses. The explanation of these exceptions, and the clue to their proper limits, is found in the principle that the journey is an inherent part of the service.

WINN-DIXIE STORES v. SMALLWOOD
516 So. 2d 716 (Ala. Civ. App. 1987)

HOLMES, JUDGE.

. . . .

The employee lived in Russellville, Alabama, where she had worked for approximately five years at the local Winn-Dixie grocery store. The employee was informed by her employer that she would be working the first three days of the following week at the Winn-Dixie store in Moulton, approximately thirty miles from Russellville. She was also informed that an employee from a store in Florence would also be on "temporary assignment" in Moulton and that the two of them should arrange to travel to and from Moulton for those three days together. The two employees made such arrangements and each morning would meet at the Winn-Dixie in Russellville, traveling from there in one car to the Moulton store and then back to the Russellville store at the end of the day.

Although the employee in this case was not compensated for the time she traveled to and from Moulton, she was required to clock in at the distant store in Moulton at her regular time of 7:00 A.M. In her deposition she stated that there had been only one other time during her five-year employment that she had worked at a store other than the one in Russellville.

After her last day on temporary assignment in Moulton, the employee was injured in a car accident as she was returning with the other employee from the Moulton store back to the Russellville store. They had met at the Russellville store that morning to carpool. The accident occurred approximately midway between the two cities in the vicinity of Newburg.

The employee filed suit for workmen's compensation benefits as a result of the injury caused by that accident. As indicated, summary judgment was entered in her favor, the only contested issue being whether the accident arose out of and in the course of her employment.

The employer contends on appeal that the trial court erred in concluding that the accident arose out of and in the course of the employee's employment. We disagree.

It is true, as a general rule, that accidents which occur while the employee is

---

[1] It was so held on similar facts in Cymbor v. Binder Coal Co., 285 Pa. 440, 132 A. 363 (1926). Accord, Traynor v. City of Buffalo, 208 App. Div. 216, 203 N.Y. Supp. 590 (1924), in which claimant had the job of returning to a city park to shut off the water in the fountain at 9 p.m. every night.

[2] See Ch. 8, § 8.06, below.

traveling to and from work are not considered "arising out of and in the course of" his employment. *Barnett v. Britling Cafeteria Co.*, 225 Ala. 462, 143 So. 813 (1932). There are, however, several well-established exceptions to the general rule. See *American Automobile Insurance Co. v. Hinote*, 498 So. 2d 848 (Ala. Civ. App. 1 986).

It has long been the law in Alabama, for example, that, where an employee during his travel to and from work is engaged in some duty for his employer which is in furtherance of the employer's business, accidents occurring during such travel arise out of and in the course of employment. *Patterson v. Whitten*, 57 Ala. App. 297, 328 So. 2d 301 (Ala. Civ. App. 1976).

The employer contends that the instant case does not fall within the exception to the general rule known as the "dual purpose" doctrine. The dual purpose doctrine recognizes that accidents occurring during travel to and from work "arise out of and in the course of employment if the trip involves performance of a service for the employer which would have necessitated a trip by someone if the employee had been unable to perform that service in connection with his personal journey." See *Eddie Wallace's Garage*, 406 So. 2d at 406 (emphasis supplied).

As noted in Professor Larson's treatise on workmen's compensation, Judge Cardozo's formula respecting this dual purpose doctrine has not been improved upon. Judge Cardozo said: "The test in brief is this: If the work of the employee creates the necessity for travel, he is in the course of his employment, though he is serving at the same time some purpose of his own. . . . " See A. Larson, 1 *The Law of Workmen's Compensation* § 18.12, at 4-252 to 253 (1985) (citing Marks' Dependents v. Gray, 251 N.Y. 90, 93, 167 N.E. 181, 183 (1920)).

While we do not necessarily agree that to characterize this case as falling under that exception alone is dispositive, we nevertheless believe that the doctrine has some application to the case at bar. That is, the employer required the employee to travel to the Moulton store when the employee had been living in Russellville for five years and working at the local store there. That trip was necessitated by the furtherance of the employer's business, and that temporary assignment created just that necessity for travel referred to by Judge Cardozo.

We believe, however, that the "special errand" exception is more closely applicable to the instant facts. Larson puts it this way: "The special errand rule may be stated as follows: When an employee, having identifiable time and space limits on his employment, makes an off-premises journey which would normally not be covered under the usual going and coming rule, *the journey may be brought within the course of employment by the fact that the trouble and time of making the journey*, or the special inconvenience, hazard, or urgency of making it in the particular circumstances, is itself sufficiently substantial to be viewed as an integral part of the service itself." A. Larson, id., § 16.11, at 4-124 (emphasis supplied).

In analyzing this "special errand" exception, Larson focuses on several factors that should be taken into account when determining whether a specific case falls within the parameters of the exception. Larson notes that such factors as the irregularity o r unusualness of the special errand, as well as the onerousness of the journey itself, are persuasive facts supporting the application of the special errand rule. See generally A. Larson, id., § 16.13.

He also notes the following: "Although a demonstration that travel time was specifically paid for is one of the most reliable ways of making a case for the compensability of a going or coming trip, and is ordinarily sufficient in itself to support such a finding, the fact that the employee is not paid for his travel does not mean that the trip was not in the course of employment. Payment for time is only one of the evidences that the journey itself was part of the service; other grounds for reaching this conclusion are discussed throughout this section." A. Larson, id., § 16.23 at 4-180.

Among those other grounds is the actual length of the journey itself. To wit: "[W]hen the subject of transportation is singled out for special consideration it is normally because the transportation involves a considerable distance, and therefore qualifies under the rule herein suggested: that employment should be deemed to include travel when the travel itself is a substantial part of the service performed. The sheer size of the journey is frequently a factor supporting this conclusion, as in the successful cases involving trips of eight miles, 20 miles, 22 miles, 30 miles, 50 miles, 54 miles, 60 miles, 105 miles, 120 miles, 130 miles, and 200 miles." A. Larson, id., § 16.31 at 4-181, 200.

Thus, that the employee's temporary assignment in Moulton was not within the regular or usual duties of her employment, that the temporary assignment involved a round trip of some sixty miles each day, and that the employer initiated a carpool for the employee are all pertinent and persuasive facts supporting the conclusion that the employee's accident arose out of and in the course of her employment.

. . . .

In view of the above, the trial court did not err in rendering a summary judgment in favor of the employee in this case.

This case is due to be affirmed.

Affirmed.

BRADLEY, P.J., and INGRAM, J., concur.

PROBLEMS

(1) An employee who lived in Willimantic, Conn., and was employed in Stafford Springs, Conn., was given an extra $90 per day for transportation (in 1917), in the form of a ride in a fellow-employee's car. Is an accident during the journey compensable?

(2) The union contract provided that employees living beyond the single-fare zone should receive the extra trolley fare, which claimant received. An accident occurred in the extra-fare-zone area. Is this case, which was decided by the same Connecticut court, distinguishable from the first case? *Compare* Swanson v. Latham, 92 Conn. 87, 101 A. 492 (1917), *with* Orsinie v. Torrance, 96 Conn. 352, 113 A. 924 (1921).

(3) An employee customarily began work at his home around 8:00 a.m. by working on a computer provided by the employer, after which he would travel to and between the employer's various sales locations to deliver merchandise or for some other business purpose. On the day in question, he logged on to his computer at 7:30 a.m., made a business entry, and then traveled to a shopping mall to work at a company sales kiosk. He sustained injuries in an accident along the way. *Compensable*? *See* Aqua Massage, LLC v. Labor Comm'n, 2005 UT App 143.

§ 7.04 EMPLOYER'S CONVEYANCE

[1] Introduction

When the journey to or from work is made in the employer's conveyance, the journey is in the course of employment, the reason being that the risks of the employment continue throughout the journey.

[2] General Rule Covering Trips in Employer's Conveyance

If the trip to and from work is made in a truck, bus, car, or other vehicle under the control of the employer, an injury during that trip is incurred in the course of employment.[3] The justification for this holding is that the employer itself has expanded

---

[3] *See, e.g.*, Watson v. Grimm, 200 Md. 461, 90 A.2d 180 (1952); Wert v. Tropicana Pools, Inc., 286 So. 2d 1 (Fla. 1973).

the range of the employment and the attendant risks. The employer has, in a sense, sent the employee home on a small ambulatory portion of the premises, just as the sailor on a British ship is conceived to be on a little floating fragment of Britain herself.

The reasoning underpinning the rule on furnishing transportation in a conveyance under the employer's control often differs from that supporting the rule, discussed in the preceding section, on furnishing of travel expense or company automobiles. The latter depends upon the relative importance of travel as a part of the service performed; the supplying of cash or cars is evidence of the status of the journey as part of the compensated employment. The former depends upon the extension of risks under the employer's control. This distinction is important in, say, a case in which the employee pays for the transportation furnished in the employer's conveyance. Since the element of control of the risk in the employer-operated-vehicle case is an independent ground for liability, the employer remains liable for the journey even though it charges the employee an amount for the trip sufficient to cover the employee's cost.[4] Although all trace of extra compensation or reimbursement for the journey disappears, control of the conditions of transportation remains as a ground of liability.

[3] Employers in the Transportation Business

The special position of employers whose very business is the provision of public transportation gives rise to a difficult question on which the available cases are divided. It has been held in Pennsylvania that a streetcar operator boarding a streetcar for a free ride to the car barn where he was to begin his day's duties was in the course of employment.[5] Similar outcomes have occurred in California[6] and in New Jersey.[7] But a New York court has reached a contrary result in a case involving an employee riding on a free subway pass.[8] And in Florida, compensation was denied to a bus company employee for injury sustained while crossing the street to the company shop after alighting from a bus which the employee had utilized under a union contract providing that employees and their spouses could ride the buses free.[9]

PROBLEMS

(1) Applying the distinction discussed in the preceding subsection, which side of this controversy regarding employers in the transportation business has the better argument?

(2) In a California case, an employee of the street railway was entitled to a free ride merely by showing his badge, but on his way to work did not do so, evidently because he was unaware of the privilege, and he paid his fare like anyone else. Due to the negligence of the streetcar company he was severely injured. Should he be entitled to tort damages, as against the exclusive remedy defense? *See* Sullivan v. City and County of San Francisco, 95 Cal. App. 2d 745, 214 P.2d 82 (1950).

(3) Claimant was required to furnish his own automobile for use during the working day, and was reimbursed for his mileage after he reached the premises but not for the going and coming trip. Is the going and coming trip covered? *See* Smith v. W.C.A.B., 69 Cal. 2d 814, 73 Cal. Rptr. 253, 447 P.2d 365 (1968).

---

[4] Peski v. Todd & Brown, Inc., 158 F.2d 59 (7th Cir. 1946).

[5] Brown v. Pittsburgh Rys., 197 Pa. Super. 68, 177 A.2d 5 (1962). Equally divided court.

[6] City & County of San Francisco v. Industrial Acc. Comm'n, 61 Cal. App. 2d 248, 142 P.2d 760 (1943). A streetcar employee riding home on a free pass after completing his duties was in the course of employment.

[7] Micieli v. Erie R.R., 131 N.J. 427, 37 A.2d 123 (1944). A railway employee returning to his home town on a free pass at the end of his day, were within the course of employment.

[8] Lemon v. New York City Transit Auth., 72 N.Y.2d 324, 532 N.Y.S.2d 732, 528 N.E. 2d 1205 (1988).

[9] Jacksonville Coach Co. v. Love, 101 So. 2d 361 (Fla. 1958).

§ 7.05   DUAL-PURPOSE TRIPS

Injury can occur during a trip which serves both a business and a personal purpose. The analytic problems that can arise are well illustrated by a cartoon that appeared in *Esquire* magazine.[10] A young bridegroom at a wedding reception, with his bride on his arm, is receiving the congratulations of his boss — and would he mind, says the boss, looking into several interesting potential industrial sites along the route of the honeymoon?

Now let us suppose that the newlyweds are involved in an accident on the direct route to Niagara Falls, where a bridal suite has been reserved for them. Is this a business trip, for which workers' compensation is appropriate? Even if, at some point in the Niagara Falls stay, some thoughts of hydroelectric power might have come to the employee's mind as he gazed at the falls, probably no one would contend that the honeymoon thereby lost its character as essentially a pleasure trip.

By contrast, suppose that the employer, sometime in April, orders the employee to make a trip to Niagara Falls on June 10th to investigate an industrial site. The employee, who has been engaged for three years but never felt he could afford a wedding trip, sees his opportunity to kill two birds with one stone. He immediately proposes marriage to his betrothed; the date is set for June 9th; and on the 10th the couple sets forth on an expenses-paid honeymoon. Regardless of what might or might not be uppermost in the employee's mind during the journey, the trip remains a business one for compensation purposes.

The dual-purpose problem appears in many forms: an employer calls to an employee just leaving for the day and asks her to drop a letter in the mailbox on her way home; a salesman who has spent the evening in a bar and is injured on his way home contends that he tried to sell the bartender a car in the course of the evening; a sorority house mother suffers a fall while on her way to purchase first-aid supplies and to attend religious services.

All of these widely assorted problems can best be solved by the application of a lucid formula stated by Judge Cardozo in *Marks' Dependents v. Gray* — a formula which, when *rightly understood and applied,* has never yet been improved upon.

MARKS' DEPENDENTS v. GRAY
251 N.Y. 90, 167 N.E. 181 (1929)

Cardozo, C. J.

Award has been made under the Workmen's Compensation Law (Const. Laws, c. 67) to the dependents of Isadore Marks for benefits found to be due by reason of his death. Whether the injury was one "arising out of and in the course of the employment" (Workmen's Compensation Law, § 2, subd. 7; § 10) is the question to be answered.

Marks was a helper in the service of a plumber. His home and his place of business were at Clifton Springs, N.Y. On April 16, 1927, his wife went to visit relatives at Shortsville, where her husband promised to call for her in the family car at the end of the day's work. The employer, hearing that he was to make this journey, asked him to take his tools and fix some faucets that were out of order at a dwelling house in Shortsville. The job was a trifling one, calling for fifteen or twenty minutes of work. There would have been no profit in doing it at the cost of a special trip. It would have been postponed till some other time when it could have been combined with other work, if Marks had not stated that he would make the trip anyhow. He did not use the employer's truck, the vehicle set apart for travel in the course of business. He used his

---

[10] XXXV Esquire 59 (June 1951).

own or his father's car, set aside, it would seem, for the convenience of the family. Nothing was said by the employer about paying him for the job. The expectation was, however, that, for any work that he did, he would be paid at the usual rate for labor after working hours. On the way to Shortsville, when only about a mile from Clifton Springs, he was injured in a wreck and died.

We think the accident did not arise "out of and in the course of" any service that Marks had been employed to render. He was not making the journey to Shortsville at the request of his employer or for the purpose of doing his employer's work. He was making it in fulfillment of a promise to call for his wife at the end of the day, and bring her home in the family car. If word had come to him before starting that the defective faucets were in order, he would have made the journey just the same. If word had come, on the other hand, that his wife had already returned, he would not have made the trip at all. The employment did not bring him on the journey or expose him to its risks. If that is so, it is not "out of the employment" that the injuries arose.

Many cases there are in which the perils of travel on a highway are so related to the employment as to lay the basis for an award. "Street risks" are so varied as to defy enumeration or prediction. The result at times has been that accidents the most bizarre have been held to be incidental to service in the line of duty. *Katz v. A. Kadans & Co.*, 232 N. Y. 420, 134 N. E. 330, 23 A. L. R. 401; *Roberts v. J. F. Newcomb & Co.*, 234 N. Y. 553, 138 N. E. 443. We have no thought to detract from these decisions or to whittle down by exceptions the principle beneath them. They do not touch the case at hand. Unquestionably injury through collision is a risk of travel on a highway. What concerns us here is whether the risks of travel are also risks of the employment. In that view, the decisive test must be whether it is the employment or something else that has sent the traveler forth upon the journey or brought exposure to its perils. A servant in New York informs his master that he is going to spend a holiday in Philadelphia, or perhaps at a distant place, at San Francisco or at Paris. The master asks him while he is there to visit a delinquent debtor and demand payment of a debt. The trip to Philadelphia, the journey to San Francisco or to Paris, is not a part of the employment. A different question would arise if performance of the service were to occasion a detour, and in the course of such detour the injuries were suffered. So here a different question would arise if Marks, after making the trip to Shortsville, had met with some accident while repairing the defective faucets. *Grieb v. Hammerle*, 222 N. Y. 382, 118 N. E. 805, 7 A. L. R. 1075. The collision occurred while he was still upon the highway, a mile or less from home.

In such circumstances we think the perils of the highway were unrelated to the service. We do not say that service to the employer must be the sole cause of the journey, but at least it must be a concurrent cause. To establish liability, the inference must be permissible that the trip would have been made though the private errand had been canceled. We cannot draw that inference from the record now before us. On the contrary, the evidence is that a special trip would have been refused since the pay would be inadequate. The test in brief is this: If the work of the employee creates the necessity for travel, he is in the course of his employment, though he is serving at the same time some purpose of his own. *Clawson v. Pierce-Arrow Motor Car Co.*, 231 N. Y. 273, 131 N. E. 914. If, however, the work has had no part in creating the necessity for travel, if the journey would have gone forward though the business errand had been dropped, and would have been canceled upon failure of the private purpose, though the business errand was undone, the travel is then personal, and personal the risk.

Applying this test, we hold that Marks was not placed upon the highway by force of any duty owing to his employer, and that the risk of travel was his own.

The order of the Appellate Division should be reversed, and the award annulled, with costs against the State Industrial Board in this court and in the Appellate Division.

CRANE, LEHMAN, KELLOGG, and O'BRIEN, JJ., concur.

POUND and HUBBS, JJ., dissent.

Order reversed, etc.

POWERS v. LADY'S FUNERAL HOME
306 N.C. 728, 295 S.E.2d 473 (1982)

MEYER, JUSTICE.

The facts of the case are not in dispute. The claimant, Norwood Glenn Powers, was employed by Lady's Funeral Home as a mortician and embalmer. On 29 July 1978, Mr. Powers began his employment at 8:00 a.m. He was to remain at the Funeral Home or on call at home until 8:00 a.m., the following morning. His duties included visiting the families of the deceased, making funeral arrangements, and embalming bodies. Apart from a one-hour break for supper, Mr. Powers worked at the Funeral Home until 10:30 p.m. on 29 July, when the night man arrived. The night man was not an embalmer. Thus during the remainder of Mr. Powers' shift, he was required to remain at home ready to respond should his services be necessary during the night. During this time he could not leave home, was to respond immediately to a phone call from the Funeral Home and, according to his employer, his "duties would not have ceased on this occasion until 8:00 the next morning. . . ."

Mr. Powers received a call from the night man at about midnight. He immediately dressed, drove to the Funeral Home where he picked up the Funeral Home vehicle, and called on the family of the deceased. He then returned to the Funeral Home to embalm the body. He arrived back at his home at approximately 2:30 a.m. and parked his automobile in the driveway which inclined toward the back door of his home. The automobile rolled down the incline and struck him as he approached the house, knocking him through the door, breaking both of his legs and crushing his ankles.

At the hearing before the Deputy Commissioner, Mr. Powers testified, and the Commissioner found as facts, that after embalming a body it was necessary for Mr. Powers to change clothes and shower; that there were no facilities available at the Funeral Home for this purpose; and that "[u]pon completion of embalming the decedent, the claimant left the funeral home in his personal vehicle in order to return home, shower and await any further calls."

In denying the award, the Deputy Commissioner found that the claimant's injury was sustained by accident, but that, although the journey in response to the call qualified as a special errand, "the journey itself only begins from the time the claimant physically leaves his property or premises . . . and [the journey] only continues thereafter until the claimant physically returns to his property or premises upon completion of his duties, in this case at the time he actually left the public street or highway located adjacent to his residence and was again physically present on his property." The Full Commission affirmed, with one commissioner dissenting. The dissent by Commissioner Coy Vance concluded that "[p]laintiff was on a mission for his employer and had not completed said mission by showering after embalming the body." In an opinion by the Court of Appeals, a majority of the panel adopted the reasoning of the Deputy Commissioner who made the initial findings, conclusions, and award, and affirmed the Full Commission.

In order to justify an award of compensation, a claimant must prove that his injury was caused by an accident; that the injury arose out of the employment; and that it occurred in the course of the employment. G.S. § 972(6). A claimant is injured in the course of employment when the injury occurs during the period of employment at a place where an employee's duties are calculated to take him, and under circumstances in which the employee is engaged in an activity which he is authorized to undertake and which is calculated to further, directly or indirectly, the employer's business. *Clark v. Burton Lines*, 272 N.C. 433, 158 S.E.2d 569 (1968); *Hardy v. Small*, 246 N.C. 581, 99 S.E.2d 862 (1957); *Hinkle v. Lexington*, 239 N.C. 105, 79 S.E.2d 220 (1953).

It is a general rule in this and other jurisdictions that an injury by accident occurring en route from the employee's residence to his workplace or during the journey home is not one that arises out of or in the course of employment. *Humphrey v. Quality Cleaners*, 251 N.C. 47, 110 S.E.2d 467 (1959); *Hardy v. Small*, 246 N.C. 581, 99 S.E.2d 862; *McLamb v. Beasley*, 218 N.C. 308, 11 S.E.2d 283 (1940). Equally as well recognized as the general rule is the "special errand" exception, *seeMassey v. Board of Education*, 204 N.C. 193, 167 S.E. 695 (1933), and 1A Larson, The Law of Workmen's Compensation § 16.10 (1978), which permits coverage of the employee from "portal to portal."

Our research discloses no North Carolina case in which this Court has addressed or interpreted the portal to portal rule,[11] nor do we find it necessary under the present facts to do so here. We hold that while Mr. Powers' journey qualified as a special errand on this particular occasion, his duties did not end at the conclusion of his journey. After embalming a body, claimant was required by his employer to shower and change his clothes in preparation for another call. This requirement was a condition of and incident to his employment and, because shower and change facilities were not available on the premises, this requirement necessitated his returning home from time to time (irrespective of whether the embalming occurred during regular working hours or in response to a night call) to remove the embalming fluid odor from his person. *Gowan v. Harry Butler & Sons Funeral Home*, 204 Kan. 210, 460 P.2d 606 (1969). Not only did the nature of his embalming work give rise to the odor, but the nature of his responsibilities to the family and friends of a deceased made it imperative that he be free of the odor.

Under the circumstances, Mr. Powers' personal appearance was intimately related to his employment and, at least until such time as he had completed his preparations for another call, he remained on duty. The injury by accident occurred in the course of his employment and because the conditions and obligations of the employment required this claimant to be at a place where the accident occurred, subjecting him to additional risks incident thereto, the injury arose out of the employment. *Clark v. Burton Lines*, 272 N.C. 433, 158 S.E.2d 569; *Hardy v. Small*, 246 N.C. 581, 99 S.E.2d 862. Claimant has satisfied the conditions entitling him to an award of compensation. We therefore reverse the decision of the Court of Appeals and remand to that court for further remand to the Industrial Commission for a determination of an appropriate award.

Reversed and remanded.

MARTIN, J., took no part in the consideration or decision of this case.

§ 7.06 WORKING AT HOME

Computers, modems, fax machines and the like have made it possible — and indeed increasingly common — for employees to work at home for at least a portion of the work week. The use of one's home as a second job site creates a variety of concerns as to

---

[11] *(Court's footnote)* Judge (now Justice) Harry C. Martin, in his dissenting opinion in the case before us, rejected the "bright line" interpretation of the portal to portal rule, whereby "certainty is achieved at the expense of justice." 57 N.C. App. 25, 31, 290 S.E.2d 720, 724. This view was subsequently adopted by the Court of Appeals in Felton v. Hospital Guild, 57 N.C. App. 33, 291 S.E.2d 158 (1982), in an opinion authored by Judge Martin.

whether an injury has occurred in the course of employment. The problem can arise either as to the conduct of the work at the home itself, or in the context of travel between the two locations.

When the employee who works at home routinely under an arrangement with the employer suffers an injury arising out of the employment-related duties, compensability is clear. Things become more complex, however, when the source of the injury is more personal.

JOE READY'S SHELL STATION & CAFE v. READY
65 So. 2d 268 (Miss. 1953)

HOLMES, JUSTICE.

This is an appeal from the judgment of the Circuit Court of Harrison County affirming an order of the Workmen's Compensation Commission which affirmed an order of the attorney-referee awarding to the appellee compensation under the Workmen's Compensation Act, Code 1942, § 699801 et seq., for an injury claimed to have been sustained by the appellee in the course of and arising out of her employment. The facts are undisputed, and the only question presented on this appeal is whether or not under the existing facts the injury claimed to have been sustained by the appellee arose out of and in the course of her employment.

The appellee was an employee of Joe Ready's Shell Station and Cafe, located on the coast in Harrison County. She was expressly covered by name in the policy issued by the insurance carrier. In the daytime she performed duties in and about the station and cafe. She was the bookkeeper for the business and performed all of her bookkeeping work at home, and had done so with the knowledge of the insurance carrier and the approval and authority of her employer for a period of about five years. She performed this work in the evening in the living room of her home, which was located some short distance from the station and cafe, working on a small table which was drawn up to a couch in the room. The exact size of the couch is not shown in the evidence but she testified that it was large enough for four people to occupy. She regularly sat on this couch as she did her bookkeeping work on the table. Her husband owned a 16-gauge Browning automatic shotgun which he frequently loaned to his friends. On December 29, 1951, one of his friends who had borrowed the gun returned it to the station. Ben Johnson, an employee of the station who occupied a house trailer on the premises to the rear of the residence of appellee, saw the gun in the station and took it to appellee's home in the afternoon. No one was at the home of appellee and Johnson laid or stood the gun on the couch. The appellee left the station on the evening of said date between 6:00 and 7:00 o'clock, and returned to her home. After reaching there, she prepared and ate her supper, and took a bath, then put on her night clothes with the view, as she said, of being in readiness for bed after she finished her bookkeeping work for the night. After thus preparing herself, she proceeded to sit down on the couch and do her bookkeeping work. The table with her books on it was then drawn up to the couch. She testified: "When I went to sit down in the living room where the table was at that had my papers on it, this gun was laying on the couch, and I had to move the gun to sit down at this table. When I moved the gun it just went off." As a result of the discharge of the gun, Mrs. Ready sustained an injury which necessitated the amputation of her left thumb, and it is for this injury that compensation is claimed.

The case comes within the class of employees who do part of their work at home. The problem presented by this class of employees under the Workmen's Compensation Law has been dealt with by Larson's Workmen's Compensation Law, Vol. 1, pp. 253–254, as follows:

> A common problem in this field is that of the claimant who performs some part of his work at home. Viewed in one way, the trip home of such an employee may be analogized to the trip from one of the employer's buildings to another

via the public streets, which is generally agreed to be within the course of employment . . . *Proctor v. Hoage* [81 F.2d 555, 65 App.D.C. 153 (1935), one of the leading cases granting compensation, presented these facts: claimant insurance agent worked until late one night in the company of his superior, who then ordered him to have his report ready by eight the following morning. They parted after a call in the residential area, and claimant was struck by an automobile while starting for home, where he intended to make out his report. Here it is plain that claimant's work was not done. He had to go somewhere to make out this report. It was late at night and the logical place to go was home. In other words, if we could assume that claimant did not want to go home to sleep, he still would have been required to go home to make out his report, and the basic mixed-purpose test is satisfied.

It is the contention of the appellants that the removal of the gun by the appellee was the performance of a part of her household duties and had no connection with her employment. The facts, however, do not sustain the appellants in this contention. The appellee had been accustomed to doing her bookkeeping work in the living room of her home for five years. She sat on the couch in question and worked at a small table drawn up to the couch and on which table she kept the books of the business. On the evening in question, she returned to her home and prepared her supper and took a bath and put on her night clothes in order to be ready for bed when she finished her book work. She then proceeded to the couch to begin her book work when she observed the gun for the first time on the couch. At that time, she had completed all of her household duties and the only work which remained for her to perform was her book work. According to the undisputed testimony, she had to move the gun in order to sit down on the couch where she was to perform her book work. The presence of the gun, therefore, presented a risk to which her employment then exposed her. Her action in removing the gun was not only necessary but reasonable. In removing the gun preparatory to beginning her work on the books, she was performing an act in furtherance of the work in behalf of her employer. She answered in the affirmative to a question propounded to her on cross-examination, inquiring if in removing the gun, she did not intend to place it in the closet where it was customarily kept. We think it is not material where she intended to put it in order to remove it from the couch, but that the material consideration is that it was necessary to remove it in order to proceed with her work. Since it became necessary to remove the gun in order to proceed with her work, the injury which she received was necessarily connected with the work of her employment. In Larson's Workmen's Compensation Law, Vol. 1, pp. 4 and 5, is found the following:

> The right to compensation benefits depends on one simple test: was there a work-connected injury? Negligence, and, for the most part, fault, are not in issue and cannot affect the result. Let the employer's conduct be flawless in its perfection, and let the employee's be abysmal in its clumsiness, rashness and ineptitude: if the accident arises out of and in the course of the employment, the employee receives his award. Reverse the positions, with a careless and stupid employer and a wholly-innocent employee: the same award issues.

> Thus, the test is not the relation of an individual's personal quality (fault) to an event, but the relationship of an event to an employment. The essence of applying the test is not a matter of assessing blame, but of marking out boundaries.

If the appellee had been doing or about to enter upon the doing of her bookkeeping work in the station or cafe, and the gun had been so left therein as that it was necessary for her to remove it in order to proceed with her work or enter upon her work, and if in removing it the gun had accidentally discharged and injured her, we think it would not be questioned that her injury would be compensable. In our opinion no different result should be reached under the facts of this case merely because the injury occurred in appellee's home. For five years she did her bookkeeping work in her home. Her home in fact had become her workshop so far as her bookkeeping work was concerned, and was therefore a recognized part of the employment premises. "The regularity of the work at home may be a strong factor in favor of bringing the trip within the employment, for this has the effect of making the home a recognized part of the employment premises." Larson's Workmen's Compensation Law, Vol. 1, pages 254 and 255.

Appellee was in the act of engaging in the work on her books when for the first time she observed the gun lying on the couch where she was to sit. It was not only sensible and reasonable but necessary that she remove it in order to proceed with her work. All of her household duties had theretofore been performed and she was then engaged only in the work of her employment. Her injury thus was directly connected with the work of her employment. We think it needs no resort to the rule requiring that a liberal construction be given to our Workmen's Compensation Law, in order to hold appellee's injury compensable under the facts of this case.

We are accordingly of the opinion, under the undisputed facts in this case, that the injury which the appellee sustained is one which is compensable as an injury arising out of and in the course of her employment. . . .

Affirmed.

LEE, ARRINGTON, and ETHRIDGE, JJ., concur in this opinion.

Contra, McGEHEE, C. J., and ROBERDS, KYLE, and LOTTERHOS, JJ.

HALL, J., took no part.

ROBERDS, JUSTICE (dissenting).

This one is just too fantastic. . . .

As to travel between the two locations, an important — and perhaps unintended — by-product of the arrangement is to make compensable virtually any injury sustained in travel between the home and the main business premises. This exception to the going and coming rule assumes an "arrangement" — an actual agreement with the employer that an office in the home be established. The going and coming rule is *not* jettisoned just because the conscientious worker carries work home on a regular basis. As indicated by a New Jersey court, "[h]earthside activity — while commendable — does not create a white collar exception to the going and coming rule."[12]

PROBLEMS

(1) A husband and wife, principal officers of an engineering corporation, maintain an office in their home and often entertain customers in their home. The wife is injured while painting the house. Compensable? *See* Tovish v. Gerber Electronics, 229 Conn. 587, 642 A.2d 721 (1994).

(2) Go back and try out the dual-purpose formula on the four fact situations mentioned in the fourth text paragraph of § 7.05.

(3) Ordinarily the drilling crew foreman delivered a required report to a supervisor fifty miles away at the end of the day. On this occasion he could not, and the deceased employee agreed to do it on his way home. Was the trip covered? Brown v. Arapahoe Drilling Co., 370 P.2d 816 (N.M. 1962).

---

[12] Manzo v. Amalgamated Indus. Union Local 76B, 241 N.J. Super. 604, 575 A.2d 903, 907 (App. Div.), *certification denied*, 122 N.J. 372, 585 A.2d 379 (1990), *quoting* Santa Rosa Junior College v. Workers' Comp. App. Bd., 40 Cal. 3d 345, 220 Cal. Rptr. 94, 708 P.2d 673 (1985).

(4) Claimant, a gradeschool teacher, when injured in a car accident on her way to school, had with her in the car a small bag of thread spools for use in art class, materials graded at home the previous evening, and a few books including her teaching manual. Was the trip covered? *See* Wilson v. WCAB, 16 Cal. 3d 181, 545 P.2d 225, 127 Cal. Rptr. 313 (1976).

(5) A game warden, who had no fixed hours or place of work, and who sometimes slept in his car in the wilder part of the woods while on night patrol, was found dead of monoxide poisoning in his car on a secluded side road. The interior of the car had been made up into a bed, and at the decedent's side was the body of one Chelsea Miami. The bodies were clothed respectively in only shorts and panties. There was no rule forbidding decedent's having company while on duty. Compensable? *See* State Employment Retirement System v. Industrial Acc. Comm'n, 97 Cal. App. 2d 380, 217 P.2d 992 (1950).

(7) Claimant, a senior director for a charity, worked from her home because the charity had limited office space. She met with co-workers in her home when necessary, had remote access to the charity's computing network and even had an allowance for office supplies. She was attacked in her home during working hours by a neighbor who had been stalking her. Compensable? Did claimant's injuries arise from the employment? *See* Wait v. Travelers Indemnity Co., 240 S.W.3d 220 (Tenn. 2007).

(8) The decedent, a financial research analyst whose primary focus was the European retail market, and who occasionally worked from home because of the time differential between the European and American markets, was fatally injured after being struck by a tractor trailer while crossing a street on her way from home to work. The surviving spouse sought death benefits. What factors would be important in determining the compensability of the claim? *See* Kirchgaessner v. Alliance Capital, 39 A.D.3d 1096, 834 N.Y.S.2d 392 (3d Dept. 2007).

§ 7.07 DEVIATIONS

An identifiable deviation from a business trip for personal reasons takes the worker out of the course of employment until the worker returns to the route of the business trip, unless the deviation is so small as to be disregarded as insubstantial. In some jurisdictions, the course of employment is deemed resumed if, having completed the personal errand but without having regained the main business route, the employee at the time of the accident was proceeding in the direction of the business destination. If the main trip is personal, a business detour retains its business character throughout the detour.

The mixed-purpose rule serves to label the overall trip as business or personal. The next question is that of deviations from the main purpose. In Judge Cardozo's illustration of the employee taking a pleasure trip to Paris and calling on a debtor while there, it is beyond question that while actually climbing the debtor's stairs he would be within the course of his employment.

But deviations are seldom as easily defined as this. If an employee, on a business trip from New York to Chicago, drives over to Milwaukee to see his grandmother, it seems quite clear that the round trip from Chicago to Milwaukee is personal. But complications arise when the deviation, instead of being a separable unit, becomes inextricably merged with the main trip, as would happen when, on the same trip from New York to Chicago, the employee visits his uncle in a town a hundred miles south of Chicago, and then, instead of returning to Chicago, starts back toward New York on a different road which angles gently back toward the direct route between New York and Chicago.

BUSH v. PARMENTER, FORSYTHE, RUDE & DETHMERS
413 Mich. 444, 320 N.W.2d 858 (1982)

WILLIAMS, JUSTICE.

This case concerns a claim for workers' compensation benefits for the death of an attorney who was killed after a seven- to eight-hour deviation from his return trip home from a trust and investment seminar. We are asked to determine whether decedent's injuries arose out of and in the course of employment where the wage earner, following "a night out on the town," was shot to death after resuming a course which would have taken him to his house. We hold that decedent's deviation was so extensive and involved such added risks totally unrelated to his employment that decedent had broken the employment nexus and thus had ended the business nature of his trip prior to his death. Therefore, we reverse the Court of Appeals, 79 Mich. App. 49, 261 N.W.2d 51, decision and vacate the compensation award.

I. FACTS

Orrin H. Bush, an attorney specializing in probate and estate planning, was a partner with defendant law firm Parmenter, Forsythe, Rude & Dethmers. On Tuesday, October 5, 1971, Bush left his office in Muskegon to attend a trust and investment seminar in Grand Rapids, some 40 miles away. The seminar, offered by Old Kent Bank, lasted from approximately 4 p.m. to 5 p.m., when the meeting adjourned to an adjoining room for drinks and light snacks provided to the participants by the bank. Bush remained for the cocktail hour, having an estimated two drinks [Aug. 9, 1973 Hearing, Tr 29–31]. He left the seminar about 6 p.m. and drove back to Muskegon. . . . The whereabouts of Bush for the next two hours is unknown. [*Court's footnote omitted*] At 8:15 p.m., he visited Tony's Club, a restaurant-cocktail lounge in Muskegon Heights, [*Court's footnote omitted*] looking for "two or three fellows." Tony Lakos, the owner of the club, noted that Bush did not have anything to drink at his place, nor did the attorney appear to be intoxicated. . . . Bush left Tony's Club immediately after learning that his friends had gone across the street to a nightclub called the Nitehawk. Whether Bush went to a bar in Grand Rapids before returning to Muskegon or stopped along the way is unknown. It is also possible that Bush might have returned to his law office. However, no proof supporting any theory was produced other than the unsubstantiated testimony of Tony Lakos, owner of the first bar Bush was known to have visited, that "[Bush] just got back from Grand Rapids, and he was looking for someone". . . . The three establishments Bush was known to have visited on the ni ght of his death were all within several blocks of each other in Muskegon Heights. Bush's law office was three or four miles north in downtown Muskegon, while Bush's home was a few miles further north, in North Muskegon. Bush was killed shortly after entering the city limits of Muskegon.

Bush arrived at the Nitehawk sometime before 8:30 p.m. and remained there until the nightclub closed at 2:30 a.m. Wednesday, October 6th. During the six hours at the Nitehawk, Bush had several beers and mixed drinks, danced with two or three women and talked with several patrons. . . .

After the Nitehawk closed, Bush drove east for six or seven blocks to Alice's Restaurant, arriving between 2:30 a.m. and 2:45 a.m. He was described by witnesses there as "ornery and mean." Although no one stated that Bush was staggering or had slurred speech, it was apparent that he had been drinking. . . . Bush ordered and consumed a hamburger and a cup of coffee. In the course of the meal, Bush attempted to pick a fight with another customer and with the 14-year-old dishwasher. [*Court's footnote omitted*] He also annoyed a woman patron, despite her requests to be left alone. . . .

Bush also appeared to be forgetful. Upon returning to his seat after the altercation with the customer, he asked the cook for his hamburger and coffee. Despite the fact that Bush had eaten the meal only a few minutes earlier, the cook decided that it would be futile to argue with him, so she cooked a second meal without charge. . . .

Since it was apparent to the employees at Alice's that Bush was in no condition to drive, they tried to get him to take a cab home. At one point they even offered to pay his fare, but he refused. . . . Bush left the restaurant a little after 3 a.m. Wednesday, October 6, 1971.

At approximately 3:10 a.m., Bush was killed in his car three and one-half miles from Alice's Restaurant by a 12-gauge shotgun blast to the right side of his face and head. . . . No one was ever charged with the murder, but the Muskegon Police Department's theory is that Bush was the victim of an attempted armed robbery by one or more unknown assailants. . . . A blood test taken from decedent indicated a 0.21 percent level of alcohol in his blood at the time of death. . . .

. . . .

. . . it is undisputed that decedent was within the course of his employment traveling to, attending and returning from the Grand Rapids seminar. The question remains, however, whether decedent was still in the course of his employment after completing a 7–8 hour deviation within a few miles of his home.

. . . .

The Court of Appeals appears to be relying on a strict and rigid rule: "because decedent was engaged in a trip of special benefit to his employer, it is his employer who must bear the risk for one complete round trip. * * * [U]pon resumption of the * * * return trip the employer's liability recommences." Id. The length and nature of the deviation is immaterial, the Court of Appeals stated, so long as the employee has returned to the path leading to the original destination. If claimant has ended his deviation and is subsequently injured, that Court would ipso facto hold the employer liable.

This Court rejected such a rigid analysis in *Thomas v. Certified Refrigeration, Inc.*, *supra*, 392 Mich. 633, fn. 4, 221 N.W.2d 378, where we noted: "[T]his Court will not follow the path taken by some courts in other jurisdictions which have granted or denied compensation based on rigid rules such as whether the personal mission was completed and the employee was returning to the business route."

While the example given to illustrate this principle was a situation where this Court affirmed compensation for a delivery boy even though he was injured while on an insubstantial detour, *Beaudry v. Watkins*, 191 Mich. 445, 158 N.W. 16 (1916), the principle works equally well in avoiding a rigid rule in favor of compensation. Indeed, we so held in the following paragraph of Thomas, *supra*, 392 Mich. 634–635, 221 N.W.2d 378: "We do not suggest that every authorized use of a company-owned vehicle or deviation from a business route will fall within this triad of cases. [*Burchett v. Delton-Kellogg Schools*, 378 Mich. 231, 144 N.W.2d 337 (1966); *Howard v. Detroit*, 377 Mich. 102, 139 N.W.2d 677 (1966); and *Beaudry, supra.*] An authorized but totally private excursion such as using the company vehicle for weekend personal errands certainly is not covered because such trips lack a dual purpose required by Burchett or 'a sufficient nexus between the employment and the injury' required by Nemeth. If a personal business detour is so great that the deviation dwarfs the business portion of the trip, it no longer can be said that it is 'a circumstance of [the] employment' as required by Howard."

. . . .

The majority view is summarized by Professor Larson: "Any business mission that begins as such from a particular base, such as the employee's home or office, must contemplate both an outgoing and a returning trip." However, the fact that the employee frequently is indeed free to go where he pleases and [d]o what he pleases after the last business chore is completed gives rise to a class of exasperating, complicated and sometimes picturesque fact problems involving employees who, had they gone straight home, would have been entitled to have their homeward journey covered, but who interpolated so many personal diversions between the last business act and the journey home that the ultimate journey home has often been held to have lost its business character somewhere along the line. The case of Mr. Dooley is typical. [*Dooley v. Smith's Transfer Co.*, 26 N.J.Misc. 129, 57 A.2d 554 (NJ Workmen's Compensation Bureau, 1948)] Having the right to travel to and from work at company expense in his own car, he left work at 4:30 p.m., had a few beers, went to the movies, and then was not heard from until he struck a traffic island on his way home at 2 a.m. Although there was no evidence that the accident was due to intoxication, compensation was denied because of the "unreasonable interval." "This kind of case does not generate a set of clear and profound workmen's compensation principles to explain why compensation is denied in some such cases and awarded in others. One thing seems reasonably certain. An employee who has the right to have his homeward journey covered cannot, so to speak, put that right in the bank indefinitely and cash it at whatever future time suits his convenience. The sheer amount of time elapsed is bound to influence courts in these cases. * * * Other factors * * * include the amount of risk added by the personal activities, such as drinking, the nature of the job, and the extent to which there may be found an identifiable moment in time at which work duties end and the clock begins to run on the deviation." 1 Larson, Workmen's Compensation Law, § 19.29, pp. 4-310–4-320 [*Court's footnotes omitted and emphasis added.*]

Thus, merely because Bush was killed after ending his all-night detour does not necessarily mean that he is entitled to benefit. It is possible to break the employment nexus and end the special mission prior to the completion of the "round trip." We must therefore examine the facts to determine whether the business purpose of the return trip was destroyed by the nature and extent of Bush's deviation.

. . . .

Bush left the seminar cocktail reception at approximately 6 p.m. Tuesday, October 5, 1971, and presumably headed directly toward Muskegon. . . . It should have taken decedent an hour more or less to travel the 40 miles of expressway from Grand Rapids to Muskegon. The record is silent as to the whereabouts of Bush until he entered Tony's Club in Muskegon Heights at 8:15 p.m. However, for approximately the next seven hours, decedent was engaged in activity totally unrelated to his employment. Furthermore, he had left his employment-related locale almost 40 miles behind him and was within a few miles of home.

When Bush left Alice's Restaurant shortly after 3 Wednesday morning, he was again headed in the direction of his home. We find that the WCAB's affirmance of the referee's finding that "the evidence establishes that decedent was finally on his way home when he was killed," 1979 WCABO 1356, 1362 [Appellants' App, 132a] is supported by the record. [*Court's footnote omitted.*]

. . . .

This is not a situation in which decedent made a brief stop at the bar after his work mission to have one or two drinks before resuming his travel. Decedent had traveled almost 40 miles home before he spent the rest of the night drinking. His deviation lasted for seven to eight hours, while the seminar was only an hour long plus a two-to three-hour round trip. If Bush had gone directly home or back to his office after the seminar, he should have arrived back in Muskegon around 6:00 to 6:30 p.m. (or 7:00 to 7:30 p.m. if he had gone directly back following the cocktail hour sponsored by the bank) during daylight hours. As it was, he began the last leg of his journey home at 3 a.m. in the dark of night through a high crime area while intoxicated and in a belligerent mood. [*Court's footnote omitted*] To say that this did not substantially increase the likelihood of injury is to ignore reality. To find that such conduct did not "dwarf the business portion of the trip" or break the employment-injury nexus is to create a rule which could never be applied. We decline to do either and hold that, as a matter of law, decedent's extended night out on the town after he had almost reached home terminated the business purpose of the trip so that when Bush was killed Wednesday morning he was not covered by the act. . . .

The decision of the Court of Appeals is reversed, and the award is vacated. . . .

COLEMAN, C.J., and FITZGERALD, RYAN, MOODY, LEVIN and KAVANAGH, JJ., concur.

PROBLEMS

(1) Does the nature of the personal activities matter? Suppose, for example, that Bush's deviation was not for the purpose of drinking but rather in order to work in a program that assists other persons with their chemical dependency problems. *Should the outcome be different?* *See* Kodiak Oilfield Haulers v. Adams, 777 P.2d 1145 (Alaska 1989).

(2) What if Bush had traveled by scheduled commercial airline rather than by automobile? That is, suppose he engages in the same "night out on the town" after the seminar, but the next morning he boards his return flight and is killed when the plane crashes. Assume that he had been scheduled to take that particular flight from the beginning, that it was the first available flight back after the seminar, and that the employer has paid for the tickets. *Should the outcome be different?* Or what if he had been originally ticketed to fly out on the day of the seminar and, in order to allow time for the evening's non-business-related activities, he changes his return ticket to a flight leaving the next day?

(3) What if the employer's policy allowed employees to stay several days after the conclusion of the seminar so as to take advantage of the lowest available roundtrip air fares and, on the day following the conclusion of the seminar, the employee was severely injured in an automobile accident which occurred while he and others were on a personal sightseeing trip? *See* Wisconsin Electric Power Co. v. Labor and Industry Review Comm'n, 226 Wis. 2d 778, 595 N.W.2d 23 (1999).

Chapter 8
ACTIVITY

§ 8.01 GENERAL TEST OF WORK-CONNECTION AS TO ACTIVITY

It is not enough that the injury arise within the time and space limits of the employment. A worker on the employer's premises during working hours who is injured in the course of giving a coemployee a "hotfoot" may well have departed from the employment as effectively as if he or she had left the premises.

In other words, a compensable injury must arise not only within the time and space limits of the employment, but also in the course of an activity related to the employment. An activity is related to the employment if it carries out the employer's purposes or advances its interests directly or indirectly.

It has been well established for many years that work-connected activity goes beyond the direct services performed for the employer and includes at least some ministration to the personal comfort and human wants of the employee. It would be inhuman to snatch away compensation protection from a worker each time he takes a momentary rest from his exertions. On the other hand, one can hardly justify an award to a worker who has been sleeping all day instead of working. The problem is to define a principle which will tell us where the line is to be drawn.

The principle upon which the personal comfort, recreation, and related cases were originally explained was that of indirect benefit to the employer. This idea is perfectly sound as far as it goes, and is adequate to take care of the great bulk of the cases. It is really not as far-fetched as it sounds to say that the employee is acting for the employer's benefit when going to the toilet, for if the employee were not to do so, the work would undoubtedly suffer. The same idea of indirect benefit can readily be applied to such things as getting a drink of water, seeking a breath of fresh air, eating, and the like. Somewhat less readily it can be invoked in the recreational cases, which attempt to find a benefit to the employer in the exercise and morale-building values of both company athletic teams and more casual kinds of recreation permitted or encouraged by the employer.

The "indirect benefit" theory is not completely satisfactory for two reasons. One is that the presumed benefit gets stretched so thin in some cases that it is little better than a fiction, as in the case of the domestic servant who fell off a chair while looking at her skirt hem before going out on a personal shopping mission.[1] The other is that more and more successful cases are appearing in which the activity cannot be said to benefit the employer by any stretch of the imagination, particularly in the "horseplay" field. For example, in a leading New York case,[2] the facts showed that for a long time it had been a common occurrence for waiters when passing each other in the door between the kitchen and dining room to give each other playful jabs and shoves. One such shove somehow resulted in a knife's being pushed into the claimant's side. Here no amount of sophistry can convert the shove into an activity benefiting the employer, but it can honestly be said that the kind of playful nudging and pushing that caused this injury is in fact a common incident of an employment in which employees have to pass and repass each other at close quarters day in and day out. If this is so, there is no compelling reason in the language of the coverage clause to require one to look further. The act does not expressly say that the employee must at the time of injury have been benefiting his employer; it merely says that the injury must have arisen in the course of the employment.

The most important categories in which the course-of-employment issue turns on the nature of the employee's activity at the time of injury will now be examined.

§ 8.02 PERSONAL COMFORT DOCTRINE

Employees who, within the time and space limits of their employment, engage in acts which minister to personal comfort do not thereby leave the course of employment, unless the extent of the departure is so great that an intent to abandon the job temporarily may be inferred, or unless, in some jurisdictions, the method chosen is so unusual and unreasonable that the conduct cannot be considered an incident of the employment.

CLARK v. U. S. PLYWOOD
288 Or. 255, 605 P.2d 265 (1980)

PETERSON, JUSTICE.

This case involves a widow's claim for Workers' Compensation benefits. Her husband, George Clark, was killed while retrieving his lunch, which he had left to be warmed atop a hot glue press. . . . we granted review to consider the extent to which personal comfort activities of a worker will be deemed to arise out of and within the course of employment. . . .

THE FACTS

Clark was employed at a Gold Beach plywood manufacturing plant. He worked a shift which began at 11 p. m. and ended at 7 a.m. During this shift Clark was paid for two 10-minute breaks and a 20-minute lunch period. The lunchrooms provided by the employer contained a table and vending machines, but no facilities for heating food brought by the employees.

On the night of Clark's death, he had brought a lunch which needed to be warmed. About two hours before his lunch break, he approached the assistant operator of a hot glue press and asked him to place Clark's food container on the top of the press to be warmed. The assistant press operator had done this before for Clark, and testified that two or three times a week he placed food on the press for other employees. The hot glue press was about 100 feet from Clark's work station. . . .

Normally the press operator would himself remove a safety chain blocking the three-

[1] Employers' Liab. Assur. Corp. v. Industrial Acc. Comm'n, 37 Cal. App. 2d 567, 99 P.2d 1089 (1940).

[2] Industrial Comm'n (Siguin) v. McCarthy, 295 N.Y. 443, 68 N.E.2d 434 (1946).

foot alley between the press and charger, climb the face of the charger, and place the food on a hot ledge on the top of the press. The chain was connected to an electrical switch, and its removal prevented the charger from moving toward the hot press. A sign stating "DANGER, KEEP AWAY" hung from the chain. On this occasion, however, the assistant press operator was eating, and suggested that Clark could climb up the charger as easily as he could. The operator testified that he told Clark to drop the chain and the charger would not move. Clark did so, climbed the face of the charger, and placed his food on the ledge.

When Clark returned to retrieve his lunch, the charger had just been loaded and the press operator and his assistant were getting ready to move the load into the press. The assistant press operator noticed that Clark was standing at the foot of a ladder which led to the top of the charger and heard him mention something about retrieving his lunch. The assistant press operator testified that he "didn't pay that much attention" to Clark because he had to go around to the back of the press to straighten panels. Nor could the press operator see Clark, because his control panel was on the opposite side of the charger. Clark possibly climbed the ladder, intending to ride the carriage over to the hot press whereupon he would reach over and retrieve his lunch. The press operator activated the charger and Clark was killed when the charger moved across the top of the carriage, crushing Clark between the charger and a stationary cross beam on the front of the carriage. . . .

Most claims for on-premises injuries fall within one of two general categories:

Category 1. Injuries sustained while performing one's appointed task;

Category 2. Injuries sustained while engaged in other incidental activities not directly involved with the performance of the appointed task, such as preparing for work, going to or from the area of work, eating, rest periods, going to the bathroom, or getting fresh air or a drink of water.

Injuries sustained by a worker in doing the appointed task are normally compensable, absent self-inflicted injury. Contributory fault of the employee is no defense. Even when a worker is performing an appointed task in a prohibited manner, injuries are normally compensable. . . .

Lunchtime injuries are normally compensable, if they occur on the premises and arise from premises hazards such as building collapse, tripping on a hole in the floor, or falling on slippery steps. 1A A. Larson, *supra*, § 21.20.

. . . .

In the case at bar, claimant asserts:

(a) The activity of obtaining his lunch was for the benefit of the employer and in furtherance of its interest in having a refreshed employee. . . .

(b) The activity of employees heating lunches on the press was contemplated by the employer and employee at the time of hiring, because it was common for employees to bring lunches needing to be heated and to heat them wherever they could since no facilities were provided.

(c) Since the press was often used to heat lunches (on the average of once or twice a week for over a year before this accident and more frequently before then), placing and retrieving them from the press was an ordinary risk incidental [sic] to decedent's employment.

(d) Decedent was on a paid lunch period at the time of the accident.

(e) The activity was on the employer's premises.

(f) The activity was acquiesced in by the employer in that it was a common, open and visible practice for employees to heat lunches on the press and not objected to or prohibited at the time of the accident.

(g) Decedent was not on a personal mission of his own as this term is generally used in this context, but rather was picking up his lunch so he could refresh himself and return to his duty station within the brief (20 minute) period allowed to eat.

. . . the Court of Appeals denied recovery, stating:

The conduct from which Clark's fatal injuries resulted was so unreasonable that it cannot fairly be considered incidental to his employment. . . . 38 Or. App. at 388, 590 P.2d at 285.

The Court of Appeals' holding that compensability is determined by the reasonableness of the worker's conduct has no foundation in the Workers' Compensation statutes or in Oregon case law. The rule is generally to the contrary: If an act is within the course and scope of employment, and arises therefrom, reasonableness of the employee conduct is irrelevant.

However, as Professor Larson points out, some jurisdictions have held that personal comfort injuries are not compensable if the method chosen is unusual, unreasonable, or abnormal. 1A A. Larson, *supra*, § 21.80. But Larson admits that the test of reasonableness is at best a "rubbery yardstick," and he argues for the substitution of a "somewhat more manageable concept of implied prohibition as the test applicable to borderline situations such as personal comfort . . . , going and coming, recreation, acts outside regular duties and other categories in which active performance of work is not involved." [*(Court's footnote)* 1A A. Larson, *supra*, § 21.84, page 5-67.]

We reject the "reasonableness" test because it is at variance with the purpose of the Workers' Compensation Law — to provide compensation for injuries arising out of and in the course of employment, irrespective of worker fault.

. . . .

Larson opts for a rule that if the injury occurs in a category of activity other than the performance of the task the worker is employed to perform, the injury is compensable unless (1) the employer would have prohibited the method had the subject been addressed, and (2) the employee either knew or should have known of the implied prohibition. [*(Court's footnote)* 1A A. Larson, *supra*, § 21.84, page 5-67.]

We question Professor Larson's "implied prohibition" test for these reasons. First, there is too great an element of hindsight involved. After the accident, the employer will certainly say, in many injury cases, "If Clark had asked or had I known, I would have prohibited him from using the press to heat his lunch."

Second, the difficulty of proving an implied state of mind of the worker which is in turn dependent upon the implied state of mind of the employer creates more than a semantic problem.

Benefits are payable for some on-premises injuries during the lunch hour, even though the ingestion of food may be no less valuable if consumed at home, because (1) the injuries normally result from some kind of on-premises hazard, and (2) the employee is within the time and space limits of the employment as set by the employer, i.e., the employer has expressly or impliedly allowed the conduct in question.

We believe that the compensability of on-premises injuries sustained while engaged in activities for the personal comfort of the employee can best be determined by a test which asks: Was the conduct expressly or impliedly allowed by the employer?

Clearly, conduct which an employer expressly authorizes and which leads to the injury of an employee should be compensated whether it occurs in a directly related work activity or in conduct incidental to the employment. Similarly, where an employer impliedly allows conduct, compensation should be provided for injuries sustained in that activity. For example, where an employer acquiesces in a course of on-premises conduct, compensation is payable for injuries which might be sustained from that activity. Acquiescence could be shown by showing common practice or custom in the work place.

This test squares with the well established requirement that compensation lies for all activities related to the employment if it carries out the employer's purposes or advances the employer's interests directly or indirectly. *Lamm, supra* 133 Or. at 497–498, 277 P. 91 and 1A A. Larson *supra*, § 20. Such a rule is related to the employment environment and the customs and practices of the particular employment and arises from conditions of the employment.

Our statement of the test is in positive terms, rather than in the negative terms of the implied prohibition test suggested by Larson. Although the result in many cases would be the same under either test, we do not intend to necessarily restrict compensability to that which would exist under the implied prohibition test. However, the other prerequisite to recovery must be shown, that is, that the injury arises out of the course of employment.

. . . .

Unless there is no dispute in the evidence, we cannot say, as a matter of law, that the employer expressly or impliedly allowed the conduct which led to Clark's death.

. . . .

We conclude that we cannot say, as a matter of law, whether the claimant should or should not recover. We therefore remand to the Court of Appeals for further proceedings consistent with this opinion. . . .

Reversed and remanded to the Court of Appeals.

HOLMAN, JUSTICE, concurring.

It is my conclusion that the rule of implied authorization set forth in the majority opinion is nothing more than the reverse side of the coin of Professor Larson's rule of implied prohibition and that, in truth, the two rules are the same. I prefer the positive way of stating the rule used in the opinion, rather than Professor Larson's negative way of stating it, but that does not make the rule any different. . . .

PROBLEMS

(1) In *Clark*, what are the relative advantages or disadvantages, if any, of the "implied prohibition" and "implied acquiescence" tests?

(2) Suppose claimant breaks a tooth while eating lunch from his or her own lunch-pail during an unpaid lunch break on the premises. *See* Gelley v. North St. Paul Maplewood School Dist., 241 N.W. 2d 482 (Minn. 1976). What if the claimant chokes on a doughnut? Recall Williams v. Industrial Comm'n, 38 Ill. 2d 593, 232 N.E.2d 744 (1968), Ch. 5, § 5.04 Problem 2, *above. See also* Forsythe v. Inco, 95 N.C. App. 742, 384 S.E.2d 30 (1989), involving choking on a peanut butter sandwich brought from home.

(3) The employer sold food for lunch to his employees. Claimant became ill from spoiled food sold to him, and sued the employer in negligence. Should the action be barred by the exclusive remedy defense? *See* Tscheiller v. National Weaving Co., 214 N.C. 449, 199 S.E. 623 (1938). *See also* Quitmans Knitting Mill v. Smith, 540 So. 2d 623 (Miss. 1989). Claimant, who was taking diet pills, had a cold. She bought a cold tablet from her employer, which resulted in her hospitalization. What result?

(4) Claimant caught his arm in a revolving gear wheel while trying to recover his cigarettes from a pit beneath a conveyor belt under which he was working. *Compensable? See* Natco Corporation v. Mallory, 80 So. 2d 274 (Ala. 1955).

B & B CASH GROCERY STORES v. WORTMAN
431 So. 2d 171 (Fla. Dist. Ct. App. 1983)

LARRY G. SMITH, JUDGE.

. . . Claimant was a member of the employer's ground maintenance crew, which had the responsibility of cleaning and mowing the grounds of the employer's stores and the homes of the owners. Claimant and the other members of the crew drove from site to site in vehicles owned by the employer. The work was hot and dirty and facilities for washing off at the job sites were minimal. It was a regular practice for the boys to cool off by going swimming between jobs at public facilities and private homes. These swimming activities were known to the ground maintenance foreman and to the owners to some extent since the crew members sometimes swam in their pools with their permission.

On June 15, 1982, a very hot day, claimant and his two co-workers were travelling between job sites when they decided to stop at the home of one of the co-worker's parents for the purpose of cooling and washing off in the Alafia River. The home was about a mile and one-half from the direct route between stores. Once there, claimant dove into the water and struck his head on a rock causing a broken neck and quadriplegia.

In addition to the above recited findings by the deputy, the record reveals that claimant and his co-workers were entitled to a fifteen minute break in the morning and afternoon and that the boys had not taken an afternoon break when the accident occurred. Further, there was testimony from at least one of the boys that he worked better after rinsing off between jobs.

We agree with the deputy's conclusion, in finding the accident compensable, that the June 15, 1982 swimming excursion was an insubstantial deviation which was a direct result of the need to wash off caused by claimant's work conditions.

We find that claimant's injury arose out of and in the course of his employment. . . . Evans v. Food Fair Stores, Inc., 313 So. 2d 663 (Fla. 1975). In Evans, the claimant was injured when he was struck by a fellow employee's car which he had helped start on the employer's parking lot. In finding the injury compensable the Supreme Court relied on the fact that claimant's injury occurred on company time, that it was a common practice for the employer's employees to help one another start or work on their cars, that claimant had the implied consent of his supervisor to assist his fellow employee during working hours, and that cooperation like this among employees inured to the morale of the working force and was incidentally beneficial to the employer.

Similarly, claimant's injury in this case occurred while he was on the employer's payroll, when he was engaged in a common practice of the boys on the ground maintenance crew, doing an activity which he had the implied consent of his supervisor to do, which activity increased the productivity of the employees and was incidentally beneficial to the employer.

The fact that claimant was attending to his personal comfort at the time of the injury does not defeat compensability. *Baker v. Orange County Board of County Commissioners*, 399 So. 2d 400 (Fla. 1st DCA 1981); and *Cunningham v. Scotty Home Builders*, 9 FCR 1 (1973), cert. den. 307 So. 2d 182 (Fla. 1974). In Baker, the claimant's employment required his exposure to cold weather and with his employer's knowledge, the claimant began wearing battery operated socks. He was injured when the socks caused severe burns on the bottom of his feet, resulting in gangrene and requiring the amputation of a portion of one foot. This court concluded that the contributing employment conditions and circumstances rendered the claimant's injury one which arose out of his employment. . . .

Nevertheless, the employer/carrier contend that even if swimming in the river under certain circumstances could be held to be within the course and scope of employment, the foolish act of diving headfirst into the river constituted horseplay of such a substantial character as to amount to an abandonment of the employment. *City of Miami v. Granlund*, 153 So. 2d 830 (Fla. 1963). We cannot agree. In *Granlund*, the employee, in the spirit of frolic took what he thought was an empty gun, pointed it at a fellow employee, then placed the barrel at his head and pulled the trigger, killing himself. We find the facts of *Granlund* far removed from this case, in that, among other distinctions, there is no connection between the picking up of a deadly weapon, a revolver (much less the act of placing it to his head and pulling the trigger) and the conditions of the employment, nor was such an act incidental to or a natural consequence of the employment. On the other hand, we think the facts here relate more closely to those in *Times Publishing Company v. Walters*, 382 So. 2d 720 (Fla. 1st DCA 1980). In *Walters*, a fourteen year old newsboy was injured in a foot race which took place during an enforced lull. Examining the extent and seriousness of the deviation, the completeness of the deviation, the extent to which similar activity had either been forbidden or had become an accepted or tolerated practice, and the extent to which such horseplay may have been expected or reasonably foreseeable in the employment, this court concluded that given the totality of the circumstances, the youth had engaged in an insubstantial deviation and his injury was compensable. Similarly, diving into the Alafia River was a momentary deviation without obvious danger, was impliedly tolerated, and was reasonably foreseeable. Compare *Miles v. Montreal Baseball Club*, 379 So. 2d 1325 (Fla. 1st DCA 1980).

Accordingly, the order appealed is *Affirmed*.

ROBERT P. SMITH, C.J., concurs.

THOMPSON, J., dissents with opinion.

THOMPSON, JUDGE, dissenting.

I dissent. To be compensable, an accident must both arise out of and in the course of one's employment. For an injury to arise out of and in the course of one's employment it must be causally connected to the employment, or it must originate in some risk incident to or connected with the employment, or it must flow as a natural consequence from the employment. The injury must occur within the period of the employment, at a place where the employee may reasonably be, and while he is reasonably fulfilling the duties of his employment or is engaged in doing something incidental to his employment.

There is absolutely no causal connection between the claimant diving into the Alafia River and his employment. The claimant's dive into the river did not originate in any risk incident to or connected with his employment, nor did it flow as a natural consequence from his employment. The injury did not occur within the period of employment. Instead, it occurred while the claimant was deviating from his employment for his own personal comfort and benefit and while he was not fulfilling any employment duty, or performing any act for his employer's benefit, or engaged in performing anything incidental to his employment.

The act of diving head first into the edge of the river resulted in an injury to the claimant that neither arose out of nor in the course of his employment. I would therefore reverse the order of the deputy commissioner and remand for the entry of a final order denying the claim.

PROBLEMS

(1) In *Wortman, above*, does the majority or the dissent have the better argument?

(2) A *Newsweek* editor, after a hot day's drive on a mixed business and vacation trip, went for a swim in the ocean. *Covered? See* Davis v. Newsweek Magazine, 305 N.Y. 20, 110 N.E. 2d 406 (1953).

(3) A nighttime security guard and his girlfriend were found dead in his motor home, which he had parked inside his employer's parking lot. Their bodies were found nude and the cause of death was determined to be carbon monoxide poisoning. An investigation revealed that the heater in the motor home malfunctioned. *Compensable under the personal comfort doctrine?*

(4) While a worker on a construction site is smoking marijuana in a portable toilet, a crane lifts the toilet with claimant inside and drops it, injuring him. *Noncompensable as an injury resulting from an act of criminal misconduct?*

(5) A camp counselor suffers paralyzing injuries when she falls while horseback riding at a stable near the camp. She is riding on her own time, after the camp has been closed for the summer. During pre-employment discussions, she had been informed that pay would be minimal, but that camp counselors had opportunities to take advantage of horseback riding activities at reduced rates. *Compensable? See* Reinert v. I.A.C. (1956) 46 Cal. 2d 349, 294 P.2d 713.

§ 8.03   RECREATIONAL AND SOCIAL ACTIVITIES

A comparatively recent development in the "employment environment" is the widespread and increasing prevalence of recreational activities sponsored, encouraged or permitted in varying degrees by employers. These activities range all the way from financing a world-famous basketball team to holding a three-legged race at the company picnic. Although the cases in this field are relatively new, the principles at stake are closely analogous to those which have been discussed in connection with lunch-time injuries, going and coming, and personal comfort cases.

A number of states have recently enacted laws specifically addressing this subject. Nevada, for example, explicitly excludes recreational and social events from coverage unless the worker is paid for participating in it.[3] Illinois requires that the employer have ordered the employee's participation.[4] California has a less restrictive rule, with compensability hinging principally on whether the activity was reasonably expected, or expressly or impliedly required.[5]

FIDELITY & GUARANTY INSURANCE
UNDERWRITERS, INC. v. LA ROCHELLE
587 S.W.2d 493 (Tex. Civ. App. 1979)

ROBERTSON, JUSTICE.

. . . .

. . . [N]ine months before the injury claimed in the present case appellee injured her lower back while working for a different employer. Appellee's injury was diagnosed as a protruding disc. Although surgery was suggested, she opted for several months bed rest and later returned to work. In July of 1976, appellee became an employee of Del-Mar Scientifics, Inc., where she built monitors and detectors for hydrogen-sulfide gas. A ping-pong table was available to the employees for recreation during lunch and various other work breaks during the day. On November 8, 1976, during an afternoon work break, appellee engaged in a game of ping pong in the building next to the one in which she worked, but on her employer's premises. Shortly after the game, she experienced pain in her lower back. Appellee was again treated for a disc condition and this time underwent surgery. During the course of the operation, a degenerated disc condition was discovered, two discs were removed and a fusion was performed.

---

[3] Nev. Rev. Stat. § 616A.265.

[4] 820 Ill. Comp. Stat. 305/11.

[5] Cal. Labor Code § 3600(a)(9).

Appellee initially filed a group-health insurance claim with Del-Mar's insurance carrier and a worker's compensation claim against her former employer, contending that the disc condition was the result of the earlier injury in February 1976. Appellee later filed this worker's compensation suit against Del-Mar and appellant, claiming that she had sustained an "accidental" injury during the course of her employment as a result of the November 8, 1976 ping pong game. . . .

Tex. Rev. Civ. Stat. Ann. art. 8309, § 1(4) (Vernon 1967) defines "compensable injury" to include:

> All other injuries of every kind and character having to do with and originating in the work, business, trade or profession of the employer received by an employee while engaged in or about the furtherance of the affairs or business of his employer whether upon the employer's premises or elsewhere.

The question presented here is whether playing ping pong is an activity "having to do with and originating in the employer's business."

We conclude that a fact issue on this question is presented under the opinion of this court in *Clevenger v. Liberty Mutual Ins. Co.*, 396 S.W.2d 174 (Tex. Civ. App. — Dallas 1965, *writ ref'd n.r.e.*). In that case the plaintiff sustained injuries while playing baseball at a company-sponsored picnic held at a location away from the employer's premises. At trial, the trial court sustained the defendant's motion for instructed verdict holding that the plaintiff was not within the course of his employment at the time of the injury. This court reversed and remanded, stating that the evidence was sufficient to submit an issue to the jury on whether the plaintiff sustained injuries while acting within the course of his employment. This court, quoting with approval Professor Larson in his treatise on Workmen's Compensation, stated the rule: "Recreational or social activities are within the course of employment when (1) they occur on the premises during a lunch or recreation period as a regular incident to the employment. . . . " 396 S.W.2d at 182. Here, appellee's employer Del-Mar gave its employees permission to play ping pong on the premises. The employer regulated where the ping pong table was placed and the times during which the employees could play. Ping pong games occurred regularly. We hold that these facts are sufficient to satisfy the definition of the course of employment approved by this court in *Clevenger* and, thus, the evidence is sufficient to support the jury's finding that the injury occurred in the course of employment.

A factually similar case was before the Supreme Court of Connecticut in *McNamara v. Town of Hamden*, 176 Conn. 547, 398 A.2d 1161 (Conn.1979). In *McNamara*, plaintiff's injuries occurred while he was engaged in a customary and permitted game of ping pong on the employer's premises prior to the appointed hour for the start of the work day, using equipment purchased by the employees. The court held that when determining whether the activity is incidental to the employment, the following rule should be applied: "If the activity is regularly engaged in on the employer's premises within the period of employment with the employer's approval or acquiescence, an injury occurring under those conditions shall be found to be compensable." The Connecticut court found that the plaintiff had been injured in the course and scope of his employment. In language directly applicable to the present case, that court stated:

> The employer sanctioned the games by regulating the permitted playing times by allowing the equipment on the premises, and by setting aside actual work hours in the afternoon for the activity. The games occurred regularly on the premises of the employer. Those facts constitute a sufficient basis on which to conclude that the games were an incident of the employment under the test we now adopt. 398 A.2d at 1166. . . .

Reversed and remanded.

BEAUCHESNE v. DAVID LONDON & CO.
375 A.2d 920 (R.I. 1977)

KELLEHER, JUSTICE.

This employer's appeal from a decree of the Workmen's Compensation Commission awarding benefits to an employee for injuries received at a company-sponsored Christmas party raises an issue of first impression in this jurisdiction. Hereafter we shall refer to the employer as "the company" and the employee by his last name.

The company, whose specialty is the sale of burlap bags and reconditioned barrels, is a family corporation whose ownership and management team consists of a father and his three sons. Beauchesne began working for the company in February of 1974 as a part-time employee and switched to full-time upon his graduation from high school. At the time Beauchesne began his full-time employment, he was 18 years old. On December 24, 1974, he attended the annual Christmas party, which was held in the third-floor offices of the company building, with pizza, soda, beer, and whiskey being supplied by the company. About 2:30 in the afternoon the day's work was put aside, and the festivities commenced.

The employees were told that they could come to the party or leave for the day, as they chose, and that they would be paid for a full day. All the employees (five in number), as well as the London brothers, attended, although one employee left early without telling anyone. The others received a $10 bonus at the party, and the one who left was given his bonus later. Beauchesne apparently partook of the proverbial Christmas cheer, and sometime later in the afternoon became intoxicated. At about 4 p.m. he fell from a third-floor window and suffered a fractured skull, a fractured cervical spine, and severe damage to the arteries and veins in the area of the left knee. Subsequently, his left leg had to be amputated above the knee.

The trial commissioner's findings pertinent to this appeal are that Beauchesne was intoxicated on December 24, 1974; that he sustained his injuries "in the employment of the [company], connected therewith and referable thereto"; and that since December 25, 1974 he has been totally incapacitated. In turn these were affirmed by the full commission.

. . . .

The company maintains that the injury was not in the course of employment because work had ceased for the day and attendance at the party was optional. We feel that these points are not in themselves determinative and that all the facts surrounding the party must be considered. An examination of the cases dealing with injuries suffered by employees while attending or traveling to and from employer-sponsored social or recreational events disclosed that generally jurisdictions are split on the question of recovery, but that basically each case is unique, turning on its own facts. *See* 47 A.L.R.3d 566 (1973).

Perhaps the most lucid opinion on the subject is *Moore's Case*, 330 Mass. 1, 110 N.E.2d 764 (1953). The court there set forth criteria to be examined in determining whether employment and recreational activity are sufficiently related to warrant an award. These factors are: (1) the "customary nature of the activity"; (2) the "employer's encouragement or subsidization" of it; (3) the employer's management or direction of the enterprise; (4) the "presence of substantial pressure or actual compulsion . . . to attend and participate"; and (5) whether the employer expects or receives a benefit from employee participation in the activity. *Moore's Case, supra* at 4–5, 110 N.E.2d at 766–67.[6]

As the court there noted, "[w]hat is required in each case is an evaluation of the

---

[6] *(Court's footnote)* The Moore court did not consider this to be an exhaustive list, nor do we.

significance of each factor . . . in relation to the enterprise as a whole."*Id.* at 5, 110 N.E.2d at 767.

. . . .

. . . Compensation is not to be denied merely because the employee's injury occurred off the premises or at a time other than his regular working hours, but the facts and circumstances of each case will be examined with an eye to ascertaining if the record establishes a nexus or a link between the injury and the employment. *Lima v. William H. Haskell Mfg. Co.*, 100 R.I. 312, 215 A.2d 229 (1965).

It is obvious that when we take the criteria of the *Moore* case and apply them to the company's Christmas party, we find the necessary nexus between Beauchesne's injuries and his employment. The party was held in the plant during a period usually reserved for work and for which the employees were actually paid. While the party may not be classified as an expressed "command performance" for the employees, one can certainly conclude, as did the commission, that their attendance was expected. The testimony giving rise to that inference rests on the facts that the weekly paychecks and the bonus checks were given to all of the employees at the party by one of the London brothers. Additionally, all employees and the three brother-employers attended. As one court has noted, "[l]iteral compulsory attendance at the company's affairs would not have produced the desired employee enthusiasm. . . . It would not be realistic to find that respondent's complete control of the [party] and the inducement to the employees of wages without work while enjoying the affair did not constitute a far greater and more effectual compulsion upon the employees" than mandatory attendance. *Kelly v. Hackensack Water Co.*, 10 N.J. Super. 528, 536, 77 A.2d 467, 471 (1950).

We come now to the question of what, if any, benefit the company might have expected to glean from the party. When the president of the company was asked if the goal of the Yuletide festivities was the promotion of good fellowship, he replied that such an event is a "common thing" and that "[w]e have always had a Christmas party." These responses were a clear indication that management felt that a Christmastime get-together financed by the company did much to create good will between labor and management. Certainly, improved employee relationships, which can and frequently do result from such activities, create a more congenial working atmosphere. *Kohlmayer v. Keller*, 24 Ohio St. 2d 10, 12, 263 N.E.2d 231, 233 (1970). This in turn produces greater job interest and better service. Additionally, the expense of the party may constitute a business expense for income tax purposes and, as the *Kohlmayer* court observed, "[t]angible business benefits are even more likely to be realized where, as here, a small business is involved." *Id.* Thus, we agree with the proposition that benefits may accrue to an employer from a purely social affair. *Id.* at 13, 263 N.E.2d at 233; *Ricciardi v. Damar Prods. Co.*, 45 N.J. 54, 211 A.2d 347 (1965); *Hill v. McFarland-Johnson, Eng.*, 25 A.D.2d 899, 269 N.Y.S.2d 217 (1966). We are sure that almost up until the time the president saw the open window,[7] looked around, and observed Beauchesne lying on the first-floor platform everybody believed that the annual Christmas party was a great vehicle for promoting peace on earth and good will toward men.

The full commission found a nexus, and there is certainly evidence in the record which affords the requisite basis for this finding. In taking this position, we are well-aware of our holding in *Lawrence v. American Mut. Liability Ins. Co.*, 92 R.I. 1, 165 A.2d 735 (1960), where this court upheld the commission's denial of benefits to an employee who was injured while returning home from what he said was an outing given by his employer. The record in *Lawrence*, however, paints an evidentiary picture which differs considerably from that presented by Beauchesne. The outing attended by Lawrence was not sponsored by his employer. It was a joint outing held by two

---

[7] *(Court's footnote)* This was the second time that the president had gone to the window. Minutes before, he had left the executive suite and observed Beauchesne standing on the sill beside the open window. The president forcibly removed Beauchesne from the area and brought him back into the office.

associations of company employees. The employees were not compelled to join either association, and while the employer agreed to make up any deficit incurred by those in charge of the outing, it did not sponsor the event. Indeed, its personnel director, when asked if he thought the outing contributed to the welfare of his company, replied that that event was "a source of concern" to him and many other officers of the company and had been for some time. Thus, the *Lawrence* case affords no support for the position now taken by the company.

The second argument urged by the company is that even if Beauchesne was injured in the course of his employment, G.L.1956 (1968 Reenactment) § 28-33-2 precludes him from recovery. The statute provides that "[n]o compensation shall be allowed for the injury . . . of an employee where it is proved that his injury . . . resulted from his intoxication while on duty." The question before us is whether this provision constitutes an absolute bar to recovery or is unavailable to an employer who has authorized or condoned the drinking. Needless to say, the company favors the former view, citing in support thereof *Hopper v. F. W. Corridori Roofing Co.*, 305 A.2d 309 (Del. 1973), which ruled that the defense of intoxication is complete, leaving no room for estoppel.

The contrary view is exemplified by *McCarty v. Workmen's Compensation Appeals Bd.*, 12 Cal.3d 677, 117 Cal. Rptr. 65, 527 P.2d 617 (1974). California Labor Code § 3600(d) contains a provision comparable to § 28-33-2, and the *McCarty* court reasoned that an employer's approval of and consent to drinking amount to an "implied representation that the employer will not hold it against the employee if he drinks, and will not deprive him of his job or his compensation benefits if he does so." *Id.* at 685, 117 Cal. Rptr. at 70, 527 P.2d at 622.

It seems to us that this latter rationale is more persuasive than that presented in *Hopper*, particularly in this case, which falls squarely within the "course of employment" analysis discussed above, with all the *Moore* criteria, as well as the Larson factors of time and place of the party, militating in favor of the employee. It is only fair to say that when a recreational activity is sufficiently employment-related to allow recovery and the employer permits the use of alcohol, he has elected to shoulder the risks occasioned by such "spirited" activity. We, therefore, conclude that § 28-33-2 does not constitute an absolute bar to recovery and that in this case the company is estopped from raising it as a defense. . . .

The appeal is denied and dismissed, and the decree appealed from is affirmed.

PROBLEM

Claimant had an accident while taking the babysitter home after an office Christmas party. Compensable? *See* Oklahoma National Gas Co. v. Williams, 639 P.2d 1222 (Okla. 1982).

§ 8.04 HORSEPLAY

Injury to a nonparticipating victim of horseplay is compensable. As to instigators or participants, some states permit recovery if such activity has become customary.

The current tendency is to treat the question, when an instigator is involved, as a primarily course of employment rather than "arising-out-of-employment" problem; thus, minor acts of horseplay do not automatically constitute departures from employment but may here, as in other fields, be found insubstantial.

PROWS v. INDUSTRIAL COMMISSION OF UTAH
610 P.2d 1362 (Utah 1980)

WILKINS, JUSTICE.

This is an appeal from an Order of the Industrial Commission (hereafter "Commission") denying the application for Workmen's Compensation benefits by Michael Prows (hereafter "Petitioner").

The facts of this case are essentially undisputed. Petitioner was employed as a truck driver by Respondent Bergin Brunswig Company (hereafter "Bergin"). His duties included loading medical supplies onto his delivery truck and making deliveries to doctors, hospitals, and clinics.

The boxes containing the medical supplies measured approximately eleven and one-half by twenty-four inches, and each box was secured by elastic bands (also described as "rubber bands"). Each rubber band was approximately twelve inches long by three-eighths inch wide.

Testimony before the administrative law judge established that the rubber bands were used by some of Bergin's employees for "rubber bands fights." Petitioner and one of his co-employees testified that the "fights" were an almost daily occurrence. One of Bergin's supervisors testified that he observed such "fights" perhaps two or three times a month, and that when he observed one he discouraged its continuation.

On March 3, 1978, Petitioner was engaged in his usual assigned duties and was loading supplies on his delivery truck. As he was unloading boxes of supplies from a hand truck and onto his delivery truck, he was hit by one or two rubber bands which were flipped at him by two co-employees standing nearby. Petitioner thereupon flipped a rubber band back at his "attacker." One of the co-employees then ripped an approximately eighteen inch long piece of wood off a nearby pallet and came toward Petitioner brandishing the wood like a sword. Petitioner took the wood from his co-employee, placed a rubber band between the handles of his hand truck and attempted to shoot the wood into the air in a slingshot fashion. The piece of wood, instead of sailing into the air, struck Petitioner in the right eye, severely injuring him.

In denying compensation the administrative law judge found, inter alia, that there had been numerous incidents of "horseplay" indulged in by Bergin's employees, including flipping rubber bands, and that this type of activity had been discouraged and was not condoned by Bergin; that the horseplay represented a "complete abandonment of the employee's duties" . . .

. . . .

In his treatise, The Law of Workmen's Compensation (1979), Professor Arthur Larson (hereafter "Larson") lists four "actual or suggested treatments of the problem" of participants in horseplay:[8]

1. The "aggressor defense" which results in the denial of compensation in any case where the injured employee instigated or participated in the horseplay. It is reasoned that by instigating the horseplay the employee has voluntarily stepped aside from his employment. (citation omitted)

2. The New York Rule which permits even an instigator of or participant in horseplay to recover if the horseplay was a regular incident of the employment as distinguished from an isolated act. (citation omitted)

3. The view that an instigator or participant should be treated the same as a nonparticipant since it is the conditions of the employment that induce the horseplay. (citation omitted)

[8] (Court's footnote) 1A Larson § 23.20.

4. The rule proposed by Larson that an instigator or participant should recover if, by ordinary "course of employment" standards, his indulgence in horseplay does not amount to a *substantial deviation* from the employment. *(citation omitted)*

As the basis for the fourth approach above, Larson proposes a four-part test to analyze any particular act of horseplay to determine whether the horseplay constitutes such a substantial deviation as to justify denying compensation to a participant therein. Whether initiation of or participation in horseplay is a deviation from course of employment depends on (1) the extent and seriousness of the deviation, (2) the completeness of the deviation (i.e., whether it was commingled with the performance of duty or involved an abandonment of duty), (3) the extent to which the practice of horseplay had become an accepted part of the employment, and (4) the extent to which the nature of the employment may be expected to include some such horseplay. *(citation omitted)*

This Court has heretofore had only one occasion to examine the issue of horseplay in the workmen's compensation setting. In *Twin Peaks Canning Company v. Industrial Commission, supra,* an award of compensation to the dependents of a worker who was killed as a result of horseplay in which "the deceased was the instigator and the principal, if not the sole actor"[9] was affirmed by this Court. The analysis in *Twin Peaks* turned on whether the deceased employee could be said to have been killed while "in the course of" his employment in light of his activities in using an elevator located on the premises of his employer, the use of which elevator by the deceased was allegedly forbidden by the employer. Although the words "deviation from employment" are nowhere found in the *Twin Peaks* opinion, it is clear that the Court was wrestling with the question of when a deviation from the assigned duties of an employee was sufficient to take that employee out of the course of his employment. In our view, the analysis in *Twin Peaks* though lacking the formal structure of the test proposed by Larson, *supra,* is founded on the same general principles.[10] We therefore adopt Larson's four-part test to determine whether a particular act of horseplay constitutes such a deviation that it can be said that the resulting injury did not arise in the course of the employment and hence is not compensable.

(1) *Extent and seriousness of the deviation.*

. . . .

Recognizing that "a little nonsense now and then is relished by the best of [workers],"[11] it is clear that the better reasoned decisions make allowances for the fact that workers cannot be expected to attend strictly to their assigned duties every minute they are on the job. That is not to say that substantial excursions from job assignments need be tolerated or if injury occurs during such excursions, compensation need be paid. In the case at bar, Petitioner was engaged in the performance of his assigned duties when he was playfully "attacked" by co-workers flipping rubber bands. Petitioner then momentarily set aside his duties and took up the challenge. In an exchange lasting a matter of minutes, Petitioner was injured. As Larson points out:

The substantial character of a horseplay deviation should not be judged by the seriousness of its consequences in the light of hindsight, but by the extent

---

[9] *(Court's footnote)* 57 Utah at 601, 196 P. at 858.

[10] *(Court's footnote)* Mr. Justice Hall in his dissenting opinion distinguishes Twin Peaks from the case at bar and emphasizes that the Court there considered the case borderline. The dissent focuses particularly on the fact that Twin Peaks involved a 14-year-old boy while Petitioner here was almost 22 years old at the time he was injured. A close reading of Twin Peaks reveals that the dicta concerning the worker's age were part of an analysis of the effect of the violation of a rule of the employer and whether the worker's death could be considered to have been "purposely self-inflicted." Twin Peaks, *supra,* 57 Utah at 603–604, 196 P. at 858–859.

[11] *(Court's footnote)* Ognibene v. Rochester Manufacturing Company, 298 N.Y. 85, 80 N.E.2d 749 (1948) (Desmond, J., dissenting, 80 N.E.2d at 751).

of the work-departure in itself. This is not always easy to do, especially when a trifling incident escalates or explodes into a major tragedy.[12]

We think the converse of this principle is likewise true; the fact that a major tragedy has occurred should not dictate an award of compensation when that tragedy resulted from a deviation so extensive and serious that the employment can be said to have been abandoned. However, it is our opinion that the deviation involved in the case at bar was short in duration and when disassociated from the serious consequences which resulted, relatively trivial.

(2) *Completeness of the deviation.*

Petitioner was, at the time he was "attacked" by his co-employees, engaged in the discharge of his duties. Had he not been injured, he would presumably have completed loading the truck and carried on with his deliveries. The horseplay he engaged in was clearly "commingled with the performance of duty" and hence did not constitute an "abandonment of duty." Larson points out:

> . . . the particular act of horseplay is entitled to be judged according to the same standards of exten[t] and duration of deviation that are accepted in other fi[e]lds, such as resting, seeking personal comfort, or indulging in incidental personal errands. If an employee momentarily walks over to a co-employee to engage in a friendly word or two, this would nowadays be called an insubstantial deviation. If he accompanies this friendly word with a playful jab in the ribs, surely it cannot be said that an entirely new set of principles has come into play. The incident remains a simple human diversion subject to the same tests of extent of departure from the employment as if the playful gesture had been omitted.

> At the other extreme, there are cases in which the prankster undertakes a practical joke which necessitates the complete abandonment of the employment and the concentration of all his energies for a substantial part of his working time on the horseplay enterprise. When this abandonment is sufficiently complete and extensive, it can only be treated the same as abandonment of the employment for any other personal purpose, such as an extended personal errand or an intentional four-hour nap.[13] [*Court's footnotes omitted*]

(3) *Extent to which horseplay has become a part of the employment.*

The evidence adduced at the hearing before the administrative law judge was conflicting on the frequency of "rubber band fights," but clearly such "fights" had become a part of the employment, whether the "fights" occurred "daily" or "two or three times a month."

As Larson points out:

> The controlling issue is whether the custom had *in fact* become a part of the employment; the employer's knowledge of it can make it neither more nor less a part of the employment — at most it is evidence of incorporation of the practice into the employment.[14] (italics in original)

We do not consider the fact that apparently no employee of Bergin had ever attempted before to flip a piece of wood with a rubber band as indicating that such a practice could not be considered a part of the employment. The elements of the practice, which must be conceded to have been part of the employment, were not significantly enlarged or so modified so as to no longer constitute a part of the employment.

(4) *Extent to which nature of employment may be expected to include some such horseplay.*

---

[12] *(Court's footnote)* 1A Larson at 5-152.

[13] *(Court's footnote)* *Id.* at 5-142 to 5-143.

[14] *(Court's footnote)* *Id.* at 5-133.

This element of Larson's approach focuses on the foreseeability of horseplay in any given employment environment and on the particular act of horseplay involved. Considerations which may enter into the analysis of this point include whether the work involves lulls in employment activity or is essentially continuous, *(citation omitted)* and the existence of instrumentalities which are part of the work environment and which are readily usable in horseplay situations.[15] This list is not intended to be exhaustive but rather illustrative of the possibilities. In the present case all of the elements which joined to result in Petitioner's injury — the hand truck, the rubber bands, and the piece of wood — were part and parcel of the work environment. It therefore is not difficult to foresee that horseplay of the type engaged in by Petitioner was to be expected.

By adopting the approach suggested by Larson, this Court does not intend the adoption of a test which by mechanical application will in cases involving horseplay dictate a "correct result." Indeed this approach is not susceptible of mechanical application but rather is intended as a method of analysis to assist the Industrial Commission in consideration of future cases coming before it involving horseplay. It is this Court's view that when the underlying policy of the compensation act is effectuated in the light of the analysis suggested herein, a rational result can be expected.

. . . The record herein reveals no substantial evidence supporting the finding of the Commission that by engaging in horseplay, Petitioner "completely abandoned" his duties and hence was not injured in the course of his employment. Therefore the Order of the Commission is reversed. . . .

MAUGHAN and STEWART, JJ., concur.

HALL, JUSTICE, dissents.

PROBLEMS

(1) Claimant, at the parts counter, handed a spool of wire to a coemployee with his left hand and with his right hand simultaneously pulled the coemployee's cap bill over his eyes. In the process, a file flew out of the coemployee's pocket and hit claimant's eye. Had claimant abandoned his employment? *See* Frost v. H.H. Franklin Mfg. Co., 236 N.Y. 649, 142 N.E. 319 (1923).

(2) What about curiosity? A claimant put his hand in front of a new exhaust fan to see how much pull the fan could exert. Simon v. Standard Oil Co., 150 Neb. 799, 36 N.W.2d 102 (1949). An idle mechanic, sitting in a police car, found a tear gas grenade in the glove compartment, and wondered what would happen if he pulled that shiny cotter pin. Jordan v. Dixie Chevrolet, 218 S.C. 73, 61 S.E.2d 654 (1950). A girl on a ship poked her head into an opening in a wall, which proved to be a dumb waiter shaft. Bethlehem Steel Co. v. Parker, 64 F. Supp. 615, 618 (D. Md. 1946).

(3) Would a death in the course of playing Russian Roulette be compensable? *See* Bennett v. Industrial Welding & Fabrication Co., 411 So. 2d 574 (La. App. 1982), in which the only issue was the defense of intentional self-injury. *See* Gibbs v. Orange County Sheriff's Dept., 540 N.Y.S.2d 95 (App. Div. 1989).

§ 8.05   RESIDENT EMPLOYEES

When an employee is required to live on the premises, either by way of contract of employment or by the nature of the employment, and is continuously on call (whether or not actually on duty), the entire period of his presence on the premises pursuant to this requirement is deemed included in the course of employment. However, if the employee

---

[15] *(Court's footnote) See, e.g.,* Johnson v. Loew's Inc., 7 A.D.2d 795, 180 N.Y.S.2d 826 (App. Div. 1958) (involving a situation where an employee shot a paperclip into his own eye with a rubber band). . . .

has fixed hours of work outside of which he or she is not on call, compensation is awarded usually only if the source of injury was a risk associated with the conditions under which claimant lived because of the requirement of remaining on the premises.

It has already been observed, in the case of employees with fixed time and place of work, that such personal activities as eating lunch or indulging in recreation are within the course of employment even when they take place outside strict working hours, if they take place on the employment premises. It has also been shown that all kinds of personal comfort activities within working hours on the premises are covered. It is possible, by an extension of this same idea, to say that when a worker is on the premises night and day all his personal comfort and incidental activities are within the course of employment, including sleeping at night. When the employee is on call at all hours, the reason for this broad coverage is strengthened, since then the position may be analogized to that of an employee who is on duty and paid during his lunch period or rest interval.

If a summary of the current state of the law in this entire area were to be attempted, the following would probably come as close to the mark as any condensed statement could:

> Injuries to employees required to live on the premises are generally compensable if one of the two following features is present: either that the claimant was continuously on call, or that the source of injury was a risk distinctly associated with the conditions under which claimant lived because of the requirement of remaining on the premises.

DOE v. ST. MICHAEL'S MEDICAL CENTER OF NEWARK
184 N.J. Super. 1, 445 A.2d 40 (1982)

KING, J. A. D.

This action was brought by plaintiff against Saint Michael's Medical Center of Newark to recover common-law damages for injuries sustained as a result of a sexual attack and robbery on July 22, 1978, a Saturday morning. Plaintiff, a medical technologist employed at the hospital, was attacked in her room on the third floor of the hospital dormitory, the oldest building in the Saint Michael's medical complex located on Central Avenue in downtown Newark. Plaintiff's claim was predicated on the alleged lack of security at the facility.

Plaintiff had occupied the room for several years under a written lease and had paid $54.16 a month rent which was deducted from her biweekly pay checks. She was not required to live in the dormitory as a condition of employment. The parties stipulated that she lived in the dormitory "because at the time she got the job [in 1974] she did not know where else to live, having no immediate friends or relatives in this area and being unfamiliar with the area at the time she came here. She couldn't then or at any other time have chosen or had the resources to live elsewhere." Only hospital employees could live in the dormitory building. Plaintiff was not on duty or on call the Saturday of the attack. She usually worked in her technologist job Monday through Friday but had worked on Saturday on occasion.

This appeal is taken from a dismissal of plaintiff's complaint following defendant's motion before trial because her exclusive remedy against defendant was under the Workers' Compensation Act.

If the circumstances of plaintiff's injury entitled her to a workers' compensation remedy, she is barred under N.J.S.A. 34:15-8 from bringing a civil action. *See Seltzer v. Isaacson*, 147 N.J. Super. 308, 313, 371 A.2d 304 (App. Div. 1977). The question in this case is whether plaintiff's injury arose "out of and in the course of employment" under N.J.S.A. 34:15-7. Even though in this case the injured employee is resisting compensability, presumably in order to obtain a larger recovery in a civil action, we are bound by the principle requiring liberal interpretation of the Workers' Compensation Act in order to afford a certain remedy. "Consistency requires us to use the same legal yardstick. . . . " *Brooks v. Dee Realty Co., Inc.*, 72 N.J. Super. 499, 508, 178 A.2d 644 (App. Div. 1962).

In holding that plaintiff's accident was compensable the Law Division judge relied primarily on *Barbarise v. Overlook Hospital Ass'n*, 88 N.J. Super. 253, 211 A.2d 817 (Cty. Ct. 1965), which involved a similar situation. In that case a petition for workers' compensation benefits had been filed by a nurse who was injured when she fell on stairs when returning from sun bathing on the roof of the residence hall provided by her employer. She was not required to live in this residence, which her employer had provided for some of its employees. At the time of her injury she was off duty and not on call, but her employer had been known to ask an employee to work after hours if the need arose. In affirming an award of compensation to the employee the court found no basis for distinguishing this case from other cases which had supported compensability for injuries suffered by an employee while engaged in recreational activities sponsored by the employer. *See Ricciardi v. Damar Products Co.*, 45 N.J. 54, 211 A.2d 347 (1965) (petitioner killed while returning home from company picnic); *Cuna v. Avenel Bd. of Fire Com'rs*, 42 N.J. 292, 200 A.2d 313 (1964) (volunteer fireman injured playing on fire company softball team); *Complitano v. Steel & Alloy Tank Co.*, 34 N.J. 300, 168 A.2d 809 (1961), rev'g on dissent 63 N.J. Super. 444, 456, 164 A.2d 792 (App. Div. 1960) (employee injured while playing on company-sponsored softball team). Even though the employees in these cases were not on duty or on call, the injuries were compensable "so long as the activity leading to the injury was 'reasonably incidental to the employment.'" *Barbarise, supra*, 88 N.J. Super. at 258, 211 A.2d 817. That court analyzed a number of cases in which courts had, in one form or another, applied the "mutual benefit doctrine" in determining whether an injury was work-related. *Id.* at 258–261, 211 A.2d 817. Under this doctrine an injury will be found compensable where both the employer and the employee receive benefits from the activity in which the employee was engaged when the injury occurred. *See, also, Strzelecki v. Johns-Manville*, 65 N.J. 314, 317–320, 322 A.2d 168 (1974), where the employee was killed in an auto accident on the way to study for graduate courses encouraged and paid for by the employer.

Applying these same concepts, the *Barbarise* court reasoned:

> Although the petitioner in the instant case was not performing any of her duties as a practical nurse and I find that the evidence does not establish that she was "on call," she was, as respondent concedes, "at a location where she was expected to be" when injured. Residence quarters provided for employees by the employer are, like parking lots provided for employees by the employer, "a part of the *locus* of employment" and an injury sustained by an employee while using such residence facility properly, reasonably and in the manner contemplated by the employer is "reasonably incidental to the employment and compensable." *Cf. Rice v. Pharmaceuticals, Inc., supra*, 65 N.J. Super. [579] at 584 [168 A.2d 201].

> The residence facilities furnished to petitioner by respondent-hospital were mutually beneficial, for it not only made nursing employees such as petitioner more immediately available for service if required, but provided the additional "clear and substantial benefit" of rendering employment by the hospital more attractive to those whose nursing skills are in desperately short supply in the community and in promoting employee morale and good will. [88 N.J. Super. at 261, 211 A.2d 817.]

We find this reasoning equally applicable to the present case. The Supreme Court decisions in *Complitano, supra*, where compensation was awarded to an employee injured while playing softball in a league sponsored by the employer, and *Ricciardi, supra*, where benefits were awarded when an employee was killed on the way home from a company picnic, support the conclusion that the positive effect on employee morale and good will is itself a substantial benefit to the employer. Also in accord is the more recent *Mikkelsen v. N. L. Industries*, 72 N.J. 209, 370 A.2d 5 (1977), where the employee was injured while walking in a parking lot after leaving a union meeting held to ratify a collective bargaining contract. The meeting was held at an inn across the town from the employer's plant. We believe that Saint Michael's in this case was benefitted by furnishing some of its employees with residence facilities. Moreover, it may be assumed that the existence of such facilities rendered the position more attractive to plaintiff, since she was relieved of the necessity of finding housing in an area with which she was unfamiliar.

The leading authority points out that compensability uniformly obtains when the employee is required to live on the portion of the employer's premises where the accident happens. 1A Larson, Workers Compensation Law, § 24.30 at 5-183 (1979). This is the so-called "bunkhouse" rule. The cases are not uniform where residence on the employer's premises is permitted but not required as a condition of employment. Larson, *supra*, § 24.40 at 5-194. "The better view" upholds compensability, especially where there may be "no reasonable alternative . . . or the lack of availability of accommodations elsewhere." *Id.* at 5-197. . . .

Employing the "positional risk" or "but for" test, under which "an injury arises out of employment if the employee's duties and conditions of employment bring him to the place where he is injured at the time of the occurrence," also leads to the conclusion that plaintiff's injury was compensable. *Briggs v. American Biltrite*, 74 N.J. 185, 189, n. 1, 376 A.2d 1231 (1977) (special errand exception to "going and coming" rule). If not for her employment, she would not have been in the place where she was injured because she would otherwise have had no right to live there. . . .

The Law Division judge dismissed plaintiff's action. Rather than a dismissal, the action should have been transferred to the Division of Workers' Compensation.R. 1:13-4(a); *Townsend v. Great Adventure*, 178 N.J. Super. 508, 517, 429 A.2d 601 (App. Div. 1981). We modify the order of dismissal by the trial judge and order the transfer of the claim to the Division. The judgment of the Law Division, as so modified, is affirmed.

STATE COMPENSATION INSURANCE FUND v. WORKERS' COMPENSATION APPEAL BOARD (VARGAS)
133 Cal. App. 3d 643, 184 Cal. Rptr. 111 (1982)

Zenovich, Acting Presiding Justice.

The issue before us in this case is whether the deaths of two employees, Vargas Castellanos and Salvador Macias Vargas, who were shot in a bunkhouse arose out of and occurred in the course of their employment. The Workers' Compensation Appeals Board (Board) denied reconsideration of the trial judge's award of compensability. Petitioner, State Compensation Insurance Fund (petitioner) filed a petition for a writ of review from the Board's decision, which we granted. The case was submitted to the trial judge on an agreed statement of facts (contained in Return to Writ of Review) which we hereby adopt:

"Late Sunday night, 10-8-78, Salvador Vargas, Miguel Castellanos, and Lourdes Mesa, died as a result of gunshot wounds inflicted by either Keith Daniel Williams or Robert Leslie Tyson, or both.

"The assailants, individually or jointly, did not employ the victims, nor were any of the victims fellow employees of either of the assailants at the time of the injuries and deaths. Castellanos and Vargas were employed as dairy milkers by the Soares Family Trust (hereinafter referred to as 'employer'). At the time of their deaths, these two men lived at a bunkhouse located at 1861 No. Highway 99 in Merced, California. These men were shot and killed in their bunkhouse residence. The house is and was owned by the employer, and provided to employees (as in the instant case), rent free as additional compensation for services arising from their employment, and as a convenience to the employer, at the time of the incident of injury. Their bodies were discovered in the bunkhouse the morning following 10-8-78.

"The body of Lourdes Mesa was discovered at a remote location in Tuolumne County on 10-13-78, with three gunshot wounds to the right portion of her back and one gunshot wound in her head. Ms. Mesa may have been living in the bunkhouse and cohabitating with Miguel Castellanos, but his dwelling was not provided to her as compensation for services rendered to the employer, and her employment at the time of the incident of injury is denied.

"On Friday afternoon, 10-6-78, Castellanos, Vargas and Mesa arrived at a garage sale in the area of Galt, Ca. Most of the items being sold at the garage sale had been stolen by Keith Williams and Robert Tyson in September. The items to be sold were brought to the house of Robert and Karen Tyson at 26756 Nichols Road, Galt, California, by Cindy Williams and Betty Farnsworth. Betty and Cindy are allegedly sisters, and Cindy was purportedly a former wife of Keith Williams. Keith, Cindy and Betty had been living at the Tyson home as early as October 4, and they all assisted in the garage sale.

"It was late afternoon when Castellanos, Vargas and Mesa arrived at the garage sale. However, after purchasing a few items there, and discussing prices, Castellanos mentioned to Williams that his car might be for sale. Following this discussion, Keith Williams took the vehicle, a 1973 Plymouth Roadrunner, for a test drive, following which Castellanos and his group left the sale with an understanding they would return the next day to continue negotiations for the car. After the three left the sale, Keith Williams began to tell Robert Tyson how easy it would be to 'blow away' Mexicans. He told everyone in the house how fast the car was and then started mentioning about how he could have forced the people into the trunk of the car and taken them to a field, and could have blown them away because everything that belonged to the car, the pink slip and everything, was inside the glove box of the car.

"On Saturday, 10-7-78, Williams instructed Betty to write out a check for $1,500 from a checkbook that was taken in late September, along with the other stolen items. This was the check that Williams presented to Miguel V. Castellanos when he arrived at the Tyson residence on Saturday. Castellanos subsequently left in another vehicle, but indicated that he would mail back the pink slip as soon as the check had cleared. Following Castellanos' departure, on Saturday, Williams was heard to have commented several times that he could 'blow away niggers and Mexicans' and also to have asked Robert Tyson 'are you with me?' and each time Tyson stated 'Yes'. Williams also remarked that he had seen Castellanos with a big wad of money.

"Saturday night Williams cleaned his gun, and sent Karen and Cindy out to a store for ammunition. When the women returned, Keith Williams and Robert Tyson were discussing their plans to go down to Merced and rob the Mexican people of money, plus anything else that they could find of value. It was important to Williams to get a hold of the bogus check before it cleared the bank.

"At approximately 4:00 PM, on the afternoon of 10-8-78, Keith Williams and Robert Tyson departed the Tyson residence in Galt, Ca. headed for Merced. While traveling to Merced, Williams kept talking about 'killing the Mexicans or blowing them away'. At about 8:00 PM, Williams and Tyson were in the vicinity of the bunkhouse where Miguel Castellanos, Salvador Vargas and possibly, Lourdes Mesa, lived, but were having difficulty finding it.

"Williams then stopped and talked with Joe Scoto, who was a foreman for the employer and lived on the employer's property. Scoto gave Williams directions as to the location of the bunkhouse. Tyson and Wiliams then went to the bunkhouse where Castellanos, Vargas and possibly Mesa lived. At the time they arrived, three other people were also there, Leo Macias, Nadine Padilla and Sylvia Wharton. The earlier sale of the automobile was discussed as well as a discussion about the purchase of a handgun. About 9 or 9:30 PM, the last of the other visitors, Mr. Macias, departed the residence leaving behind Castellanos, Vargas, who was upstairs sleeping, Mesa, Williams and Tyson. After consuming several drinks, Williams drew his gun and held it against Castellanos' throat. Everyone then laughed it off as a joke. Then Tyson and Williams left the bunkhouse and drove to another location and parked. Williams told Tyson he was to make anyone downstairs 'lay down' while Williams would 'take out' the one upstairs. Williams drove the car back to the farm house and then both men, armed with a handgun went inside.

"Miguel Castellanos, who answered the door, was ordered to lay down on his stomach; Tyson stood over him with a drawn handgun. Williams ran upstairs screaming 'where's the money'. Then Williams came downstairs and took Castellanos upstairs with Salvador Vargas and made them lie down on their stomachs. Tyson took Lourdes Mesa to a downstairs bedroom, held a gun on her, and made her sit on the bed. Tyson searched the bedroom drawers for money. Meanwhile, Williams remained upstairs and Tyson could hear doors and drawers upstairs being slammed. About five minutes later, there was one gunshot, then 2 or 3 more. Vargas had been shot once in the back of the head; M. Castellanos had been shot twice and the fatal wound was caused by a gunshot to the back of the head.

"Williams held the gun on Lourdes Mesa while the three of them left the bunkhouse and departed in the car. During the course of their drive in the vehicle, they stopped to purchase some beer and then proceeded to drive somewhere in the Stanislaus or Tuolumne Co. where Williams raped Lourdes Mesa in the back seat of the vehicle as Tyson drove it.

"The car was driven to a rural location near the City of Sonora. The car was stopped and the lights and the motor were turned off and then Williams got out of the car with Mesa and forced her into a remote area where he eventually shot her four times. When Williams rejoined Tyson at the car, he told him that he had had sex with Mesa and then killed her. After that, the two men drove back to Galt. From there, Williams departed for San Francisco with Cindy Williams and Betty Farnsworth."

This ends the "Agreed Statement of Facts."

The workers' compensation judge granted the decedents' survivors death benefits and funeral expenses.

Petitioner then filed petitions for reconsideration alleging that (1) the judge acted without or in excess of his powers in rendering the findings and awards, and (2) the evidence did not justify the findings of fact and awards.

The trial judge recommended that the petitions be denied. He concluded that the Vargas case was compensable for two reasons: (1) because the cause of death was not personal as between decedent and the assailants; and/or (2) because decedent by being provided a farm bunkhouse was placed in a position of danger. Likewise, the Castellanos case was found to be compensable because he was provided a farm bunkhouse and was placed in a position of danger.

Thereafter, the Board, in a two-to-one decision, denied petitioner's petition for reconsideration. In their opinion and order denying reconsideration, the majority held that there was no personal motive to kill Vargas. "The Agreed Statement of Facts does not establish that Vargas participated in any of the negotiations concerning the car sale between Castellanos and the assailants on October 6 and 7, 1978, nor does it establish that Vargas had any other contacts with the assailants before going to sleep on the night of the fatal shooting. Based on our review of the record, including the reasons discussed by the workers' compensation judge in his Report and Recommendation on Petitions for Reconsideration, we are persuaded that the workers' compensation judge was justified in finding no personal motive to kill Vargas."

The majority continued that the judge was justified in finding that there was a work connection which constituted a contributory cause of the injury. In his Opinion on Decision, the workers' compensation judge noted as follows: " . . . Inasmuch as Castellanos was making reasonable use of the bunkhouse at the time of the robbery, and the fact that placing Mexican farm laborers into farm bunkhouses places them in positions of danger, particularly from acts such as robbery, the risk of such incidents is not that remote and unconnected and one that should be borne by the employing farmer. This was true, of course, for Vargas as well as for Castellanos. Connection with the bunkhouse is connection with employment." In his Report and Recommendation on Petition for Reconsideration, the workers' compensation judge noted as follows: "(It) appears that the deaths were industrial. 1. On October 8, 1978, the assailants traveled from Galt to Merced to the bunkhouse of the decedents in part to retrieve a forged check and in part to rob them. 2. At sometime between 8:00 p.m. and 9:00 or 9:30 p.m. on October 8, 1978 the assailants went to the bunkhouse, and while there, discussed the sale of the car and the purchase of a handgun with Castellanos. 3. At about 9:00 or 9:30 p.m. on October 8, 1978, after three other people present at the bunkhouse left, the assailants remained and consumed several alcoholic drinks with one of the decedents. 4. Thereafter, the assailants left the bunkhouse, drove to another location, parked and discussed how the robbery was to take place; they then drove back to the bunkhouse and robbed and killed the occupants. The reasonable inference from this series of events here is that the assailants after seeing the bunkhouse found the occupants vulnerable to robbery and returned to commit it. 'The bunkhouse, and thus the work environment, did contribute to the shootings.' " (Second and third emphases added.)

The dissenting Board member concluded that, for the purposes of the criminal intent and plan of the assailants, the bunkhouse was just another abode and it, as well as the employment relationship, had an extremely remote connection or bearing, if any at all, to the assailants' plan to harm Vargas and Castellanos.

DISCUSSION

Respondents first contend that this court's scope of review is limited "to a finding of whether substantial evidence does exist on the entire record to justify the finding of a lack of 'entirely personal motives.' " Not so.

Respondents are correct that issues not raised in a petition for reconsideration are waived. (U.S. Auto Stores v. Workmen's Comp. App. Bd. (1971) 4 Cal. 3d 469, 476–477, 93 Cal. Rptr. 575, 482 P.2d 199.) However, in the case before us, the petition for reconsideration raised several issues including whether there existed a personal motive for the killings, whether the criminal aspect of the killings may be classified as a neutral cause of death and whether, as a matter of law, the providing of a bunkhouse to Mexican employees places them in a position of increased risk of harm from the danger which ultimately led to their deaths. The Board's decision denying reconsideration touched on these issues. Thus, this court's scope of review is not so limited as respondents contend.

Instead, our review of the Board's award is confined to a determination whether, under applicable principles of law, the award is supported by substantial evidence. . . .

It is well settled that, under Labor Code section 3600, in order to be compensable the injury must arise out of and be in the course of employment. Generally, "in the course of employment" refers to the time and place of the injury. (Argonaut Ins. Co. v. Workmen's Comp. App. Bd. (1967) 247 Cal. App. 2d 669, 676, 55 Cal. Rptr. 810.) The phrase "arise out of employment" refers to a causal connection between the employment and the injury. (California Comp. & Fire Co. v. Workmen's Comp. App. Bd. (Schick) (1968) 68 Cal. 2d 157, 160, 65 Cal. Rptr. 155, 436 P.2d 67.)

Petitioner initially contends that the "bunkhouse rule" establishes only that an injury to an employee making reasonable use of a bunkhouse occurs in the course of employment, yet the injured worker must also establish that his injury, while occurring in the bunkhouse, also arose out of his employment.

Respondents contend that where an employee is shot to death in a bunkhouse the death is compensable unless the evidence clearly establishes that the killing resulted from entirely personal motives. They contend that a separate finding of arising out of employment is not mandated in a bunkhouse case such as this and injuries have been held to be arising out of employment simply because they were sustained during and at the place of employment. We do not think this is the rule for the following reasons.

In our opinion, the bunkhouse rule does not dispense with the requirements of Labor Code section 3600. We find no cases in California indicating that an injury sustained by an employee in a bunkhouse is per se compensable. Our review of these cases reveals that invocation of the bunkhouse rule establishes that the injury occurred in the course of the employment but there also must be some connection between the employment and the injury, [*Court's footnote omitted*] or an injury arising out of the reasonable use of the premises, [*Court's footnote omitted*] or the bunkhouse must place the employee in a peculiar danger. [*Court's footnote omitted*]

It is clear that the bunkhouse rules establish that Vargas and Castellanos were killed in the course of their employment. The real question then is whether the deaths arose out of their employment or, alternatively, when employees who are in a bunkhouse are killed by a third party's intentional act are the deaths compensable?

Generally, an injury which grows out of a personal grievance between the injured employee and a third party does not arise out of the employment if the assault occurred merely by chance during working hours at the place of employment, or if the employer's premises do not place the injured employee in a peculiarly dangerous position. (2 Hanna, Cal. Law of Employee Injuries and Workmen's Compensation (2d ed. 1981 rev.) § 10.03(3), p. 10-15.) Thus, when a third party intentionally injures the employee and there is some personal motivation or grievance, there has to be some work connection to establish compensability [citations omitted]. . . .

The reason for this rule would appear to be that when it is known that the assault was committed out of a personal motivation or grievance, then the chain of causation between the employment and the injury is broken. Thus, when the assault is personally motivated, it could conceivably occur anywhere, thus precluding employer contribution resulting in noncompensability. In other words, the connection between the employment and the injury is so remote that the injury is not an incident of the employment. As stated in Transactron, which involved a personally motivated killing:

However, if the assault is not personally motivated then the injury is compensable. This would comport with the general rule that an injury may still arise out of employment even if the cause of injury is unconnected with the employment in the sense that the employer neither anticipated nor had control over the cause of the injury. [citation omitted]

As stated in California Comp. & Fire Co. v. Workmen's Comp. App. Bd. (Schick), *supra*, 68 Cal. 2d 157, 160, 65 Cal. Rptr. 155, 436 P.2d 67, citing Madin, *supra*, 46 Cal. 2d 90, 292 P.2d 892: "In finding that the injury arose out of the employment, this court held that a sufficient causal connection between the injury and the employment is shown where the employment was a contributory cause of the injury, that where the injury occurs on the employer's premises while the employee is in the course of his employment the injury also arises out of the employment unless the connection is so remote from the employment that it is not an incident thereof, and that an injury can arise out of the employment even though the employer had no connection with or control over the force which caused the injury. It was also held that an injury is compensable where the employee is brought into a position of danger by the employment even though the risk could not have been foreseen by the employer, and, finally, that reasonable doubts as to whether an injury is compensable are to be resolved in favor of the employee."

The Madin court found compensable injuries to 24-hour managers of rental property who were injured when a bulldozer which was being used in the neighborhood was started by some boys and pushed through the walls of the employees' bedroom. The nonpersonally-motivated third party who commits the assault on an employee in the course of his employment would thus be analogous to the bulldozer in Madin.

Based on the foregoing cases, we devine the following principles: Injuries to employees in bunkhouse are not per se compensable; if a third party assaults and injures the employee while in the course of employment (including being in a bunkhouse) and the third party acted out of purely personal motives there is no compensability. However, if the employee can also show there was some employment connection or contribution, i.e., an industrial cause of the injury so as to establish the arising-out-of element, then there is compensability. Such cause need not be the sole cause and need only be a contributing cause. Finally, if the third party's assault causing the injury occurs in the course of employment and is committed for unknown motives or no motive at all, i.e., for nonpersonal motives, the injury is compensable.

In the instant case, the trial judge's conclusion that Vargas was not killed out of a personal motive is unsupported by the evidence. After seeing Vargas and Castellanos at the garage sale, Williams spoke about how easy it would be to "blow away" Mexicans. Although Williams dealt thereafter with Castellanos, he continued to speak about how he could "blow away niggers and Mexicans" and about going to Merced to rob the "Mexican" people. Although it was important for Williams to get ahold of the bogus check from Castellanos before it cleared the bank, at all times Williams and his cohorts intended to commit a racially motivated killing involving the "Mexicans," i.e., Vargas and Castellanos. In our opinion, the Board ignored the racial aspect of the killings but merely focused on the fact that Vargas did not participate in the negotiations for the sale of Castellanos' car. Even though Vargas may have been a virtual stranger to the killers, it is difficult to see how the Board could possibly have concluded that there was no personal motivation for the killing of Vargas. Thus, the racial motive could cut off the causation between the employment and the deaths. The evidence showed that the cause of the deaths was unrelated to employment. The motive was personal and it was unreasonable for the Board to conclude otherwise.

Finding a personal motivation for the killings, we next examine whether there was sufficient evidence of an employer contribution. (Murphy v. Workers' Comp. Appeals Bd., *supra*, 86 Cal. App. 3d 996, 150 Cal. Rptr. 561.)

In the case before us, substantial evidence does not support the Board's conclusion that there was a work connection. First, the trial judge improperly took notice of a fact which was unsupported by the record. The judge stated in part, as quoted by the Board, " . . . the fact that placing Mexican farm laborers into farm bunkhouses places them in positions of danger, particularly from acts such as robbery, the risk of such incidents is not that remote and unconnected and one that should be borne by the employing farmer. This was true, of course, for Vargas as well as Castellanos. Connection with the bunkhouse is connection with employment."

While the trial judge's conjecture about "Mexican" bunkhouses may be true in most instances, we find nothing in the record before us to establish that the bunkhouse was isolated so as to expose the decedents to a peculiar risk and establish a work connection. Simply stated, the record contains no evidence about the bunkhouse's environs. Respondents could at least have introduced pictures of the bunkhouse and its surroundings. For all the record shows, there could have been numerous bunkhouses, thus minimizing the danger due to isolation, rather than one bunkhouse.

Moreover, the trial judge and the Board relied on the fact that the assailants on the night of the killing came to the bunkhouse, left and then returned which supposedly established "(t)he reasonable inference . . . that the assailants after seeing the bunkhouse found the occupants vulnerable to robbery and returned to commit it." Not true. The only reasonable inference on this record is that the assailants' "cased" the bunkhouse and determined that nothing precluded an attack. It was improper for the Board and the trial judge to then make the unreasonable inference that the victims were vulnerable because of the bunkhouse. The fact that the bunkhouse was not a barrier to the intended assault is not the same as facilitating or contributing to the attack.

Third, respondents' argument that the fact that defendants' foreman directed the assailants to the bunkhouse does not support the finding of compensability (Transactron, Inc. v. Workers' Comp. Appeals Bd., *supra*, 68 Cal. App. 3d 233, 238, 137 Cal. Rptr. 142), nor does the characterization of the "bunkhouse" as a "farmhouse" show that it was rural and isolated. Such slender threads do not establish substantial evidence.

Since we find nothing in the record before us to show an employer contribution, i.e., that the bunkhouse's locale contributed to the deaths of the victims at the hands of third parties, the Board's orders in 79 F 44910 and 79 F 44915 are annulled and the matter is remanded to the Board for further proceedings consistent with this opinion.

PAULINE DAVIS HANSON, and CONKLIN, JJ., concur. Assigned by the Chairperson of the Judicial Council.

PROBLEMS

(1) According to the opinion in *Vargas above*, it seems that if an outsider is randomly shooting people, a worker injured as a result would be compensated, whereas if the outsider is randomly shooting blacks and hispanics because of their race, the motivation is "personal," defeating compensability. Is this a satisfactory distinction?

(2) A Caucasian truck driver, on a mission for his employer, drives into a neighborhood during a riot caused by the acquittal of four white police officers for beating an African-American male. The driver is pulled out of his truck and brutally beaten; the motivation behind the beating is racial. *Compensable?*

(3) Resident caretakers in an apartment building are injured when a bulldozer, started up by mischievious boys on an adjoining construction site, comes crashing through their bedroom wall in the middle of the night. *Compensable? See* Madin v. I.A.C. (Richardson) (1956) 46 Cal. 2d 90.

§ 8.06 TRAVELING EMPLOYEES

Employees whose work entails travel away from the employer's premises are held in the majority of jurisdictions to be within the course of their employment continuously during the trip, except when a distinct departure on a personal errand is shown. Thus, injuries arising out of the necessity of sleeping in hotels or eating in restaurants away from home are usually held compensable.

CAUBLE v. SOFT-PLAY, INC.
124 N.C. App. 526, 477 S.E.2d 578 (1996)

WYNN, JUDGE.

The parties stipulate to the following summary of the relevant facts in this matter:

Defendant Soft-Play, Inc., a North Carolina corporation, employed Jamey B. Staton and assigned him as part of an equipment installment crew to a project in Erie County, New York. The company gave all crew members a daily per diem of $30.00 to be used for any purpose, including purchasing meals, and paid directly for their lodging.

While on this assignment, Staton and his supervisor, Thomas Shanahan, drove to a restaurant/bar called the Buffalo Brute Club after working a shift. Shanahan had rented the vehicle subject to reimbursement by defendant Soft-Play. They ate dinner and remained at the sports bar to watch a ball game. Tragically, while returning to their motel late that evening, an accident occurred when another vehicle struck their vehicle as Shanahan attempted to turn left at an intersection controlled by a stoplight. Staton died. The accident occurred approximately 100 yards from their motel.

Both Staton and Shanahan were legally intoxicated at the time of the accident. As a result of the accident, Shanahan pled guilty to criminally negligent homicide and driving while impaired.

Following Staton's death, his mother, plaintiff Elaine Cauble, qualified as the administratrix of his estate. She sought death benefits under the workers' compensation act and requested a hearing before the Industrial Commission. The parties, however, waived the hearing and submitted the case to Deputy Commissioner Laura K. Mavretic on stipulated facts and documents. Thereafter, Deputy Commissioner Mavretic awarded compensation benefits to plaintiff on the grounds that decedent's death was by an accident arising out of and in the course of his employment with defendant Soft-Play. Subsequently, the Full Commission affirmed and adopted the Opinion and Award of the deputy commissioner. Defendants appeal from that decision.

*   *   *

On appeal, defendants challenge the Commission's determination that Staton's death arose out of and in the course of employment.

The Commission's determination that an accident arose out of and in the course of employment is a mixed question of law and fact; thus, this Court may review the record to determine if the findings and conclusions are supported by sufficient evidence. *Williams v. Hydro Print*, 65 N.C. App. 1, 308 S.E.2d 478 (1983), disc. review denied, 310 N.C. 156, 311 S.E.2d 297 (1984). "Moreover, it should be noted that our courts construe the Workers' Compensation Act liberally in favor of compensability." *Chandler v. Nello L. Teer Co.*, 53 N.C. App. 766, 768, 281 S.E.2d 718, 719 (1981), aff'd, 305 N.C. 292, 287 S.E.2d 890 (1982) (citations omitted).

North Carolina adheres to the rule that employees whose work requires travel away from the employer's premises are within the course of their employment continuously during such travel, except when there is a distinct departure for a personal errand. *Martin v. Georgia-Pacific Corp.*, 5 N.C. App. 37, 41, 167 S.E.2d 790, 793 (1969). The rule's rationale is that "an employee on a business trip for his employer must 'eat and sleep in various places in order to further the business of his employer'." Id. at 42, 167 S.E.2d at 794 (quoting *Thornton v. Hartford Acc. & Indemn. Co.*, 198 Ga. 786, 32 S.E.2d 816 (1945)). Therefore, "[w]hile lodging in a hotel or preparing to eat, or while going to or returning from a meal, [a traveling employee] is performing an act incident to his employment." Id. (Emphasis added).

We note at the outset that defendants did not argue in their brief that the fact that Staton's blood alcohol level was above the legal limit of intoxication was sufficient, in and of itself, to bar workers' compensation benefits. (Indeed, intoxication alone will not work a forfeiture of an employee's benefits under N.C. Gen.Stat. § 97-12(1)(1991); rather, he forfeits his benefits only if the injury was proximately caused by the intoxication. *Gaddy v. Anson Wood Products*, 92 N.C. App. 483, 374 S.E.2d 477 (1988). Moreover, even if the employee's intoxication is a proximate cause of his injury, recovery of benefits will not be barred if the intoxicant was "supplied by the employer or his agent in a supervisory capacity to the employee." N.C.G.S. § 97-12(1). In this case, Staton's intoxication was not a cause in fact of the accident which resulted in his death. The accident was caused by Shanahan's negligence. It should also be noted that the alcohol was consumed in the presence and in the company of Staton's supervisor and in effect may have been provided by his employer, defendant Soft-Play, by means of the per diem which employer paid to Staton.). Instead, defendants contend that by electing to remain at the bar after dinner instead of returning to the hotel, Staton's trip became one of a purely personal and social nature and any causal connection to his employment was terminated for the rest of the evening. We disagree.

It is well-established that a traveling employee will be compensated under the Workers' Compensation Act "for injuries received while returning to his hotel, while going to a restaurant or while returning to work after having made a detour for his own personal pleasure." *Chandler v. Teer* , 53 N.C. App. at 770, 281 S.E.2d at 721 (citing *Martin v. Georgia-Pacific Corp.*, 5 N.C. App. 37, 167 S.E.2d 790 (1969); *Clark v. Burton Lines*, 272 N.C. 433, 158 S.E.2d 569 (1968); *Brewer v. Powers Trucking Co.*, 256 N.C. 175, 123 S.E.2d 608 (1962); *Hardy v. Small*, 246 N.C. 581, 99 S.E.2d 862 (1957); *Michaux v. Gate City Orange Crush Bottling Co.*, 205 N.C. 786, 172 S.E. 406 (1934); *Parrish v. Armour & Co.*, 200 N.C. 654, 158 S.E. 188 (1931); *Williams v. Brunswick County Board of Education*, 1 N.C. App. 89, 160 S.E.2d 102 (1968)).

In *Martin v. Georgia-Pacific Corp.*, an out-of-town employee walked several blocks from his hotel to see yachts on the river. He then proceeded to a restaurant to eat dinner and was struck and killed by a car. This Court concluded that although going to see the yachts was a personal detour, once the employee began to proceed to dinner he "had abandoned this personal sight-seeing mission" and was back within the scope of his employment. 5 N.C. App. at 43, 167 S.E.2d at 794. In *Chandler v. Teer*, this Court reversed the Industrial Commission's determination that an out-of-town employee's death was not compensable because he had made a personal detour to set up a soft-ball game while on his way back to his sleeping quarters from a worksite. Judge Becton, writing for the Court, cited Martin and commented: "We do not believe that workers' compensation would have been denied had [the employee in Martin] eaten first, gone to the yacht basin second, and then been killed on his trip back to his hotel." 53 N.C. App. at 770, 281 S.E.2d at 721.

In the instant case, Staton traveled to New York, slept in a motel and ate at restaurants in order to further the business of and at the direction of his employer, defendant Soft-Play. At the time of the accident, he was returning to his motel from the place where he had eaten dinner. Moreover, as pointed out earlier, the parties do not argue that his intoxication was a cause of his death. Based on these facts, we are of the opinion that even if Staton's remaining at the restaurant to drink alcohol and watch a ball game constituted a personal endeavor, sufficient evidence existed to support the Commission's finding that he had rejoined his course of employment at the time of the accident. Accordingly, the Opinion and Award of the Commission is,

Affirmed.

John and McGee, JJ., concur.

SILVER ENGINEERING WORKS, INC. v. SIMMONS
180 Colo. 309, 505 P.2d 966 (1973)

Hodges, Justice.

This is a workmen's compensation case in which the Colorado Court of Appeals in *Silver Engineering Works, Inc. v. Simmons*, 30 Colo. App. 396, 495 P.2d 246 held that a deceased employee met his death under circumstances which made it compensable under terms of the Workmen's Compensation Act. C.R.S. 1963, 81-13-2, requires that the injury or death of an employee must arise out of and in the course of employment before it can be a basis for awarding compensation.

In a petition for certiorari, which we granted, the employer and the insurance company contend that the decedent, who was in travel status for his employer, was outside the scope of his employment when he met his death, and therefore, compensation may not be awarded. We agree, and therefore, reverse the judgment of the Court of Appeals.

A brief resume of the facts will suffice for an understanding of the issue involved here. The decedent, Alden D. Whitmer, who resided in Colorado, was in El Dorado, Mexico on behalf of his employer to assist and be trained in the operation of a continuous diffuser which had been sold by the employer to a Mexican sugar plant. Several days after arriving at El Dorado, Mexico and during the period when the plant was shut down for the Easter weekend, the decedent, and several other employees, drove over a difficult road to a remote beach to swim and fish. The decedent went swimming in the outlet of a river and met his death by drowning. His body was found several miles from the outlet the following morning by fishermen.

A claim for workmen's compensation was filed by the decedent's widow and children. After a hearing, an Industrial Commission referee found that "decedent was outside the course and scope of his employment at the time he met his death" and therefore, the application for compensation was denied. The Industrial Commission reversed the order of the referee and awarded compensation. On appeal, the Colorado Court of Appeals affirmed the award of compensation in this case as previously indicated.

An employee who is away from home on a business trip for his employer is in most circumstances under continuous workmen's compensation coverage from the time he leaves until he returns home. There are exceptions, however, to this general rule. Both the general rule and the exceptions are well described in A. Larson, Workmen's Compensation Law § 25:

> Employees whose work entails travel away from the employer's premises are held in the majority of jurisdictions to be within the course of their employment continuously during the trip, *except when a distinct departure on a personal errand is shown.*(Emphasis added.)

In *Alexander Film Co. v. Ind. Comm.*, 136 Colo. 486, 319 P.2d 1074 (1957), we recognize this qualification to the "traveling employee doctrine" when we set forth that:

> Such an employee is in continuous employment, day and night. This does not mean that he can not step aside from his employment for personal reasons, or reasons in no way connected with his employment, just as might an ordinary employee working on a schedule of hours at a fixed location. He might rob a bank; he might attend a dance; or he might engage in other activities equally conceivable for his own pleasure and gratification, and ordinarily none of these acts would be beneficial or incidental to his employment and would constitute a stepping aside from the employment.

As the above quoted language from the *Alexander* case clearly indicates, the traveling employee is as capable of departing on a personal errand as any other type of employee, thereby losing the right to compensation benefits from accidents occurring during such departures.

We alluded to the exception most recently in *Pat's Power Tongs, Inc. v. Miller*, 172 Colo. 541, 474 P.2d 613 (1970). Compensation was awarded to the traveling employees there because "they had *concluded* their personal activities" at the time the accident occurred. The inference from the opinion was clear that, had the accident taken place while the claimants were still engaged in "their personal activities of the evening," compensation benefits would have been denied.

The undisputed and explicit findings of fact by the *Industrial Commission* referee were sufficient to establish, as a matter of law, that the decedent had indeed stepped aside from his employment and was attending to a matter of personal recreation, which was beyond that necessary to the normal ministration to needs of an employee on a business trip.

Judgment reversed and cause remanded for the purpose of entering a Court of Appeals judgment reversing the award of compensation by the Industrial Commission.

Erickson, J., not participating.

PROBLEMS

(1) In an Arizona case, a traveling man, who went to bed intoxicated, died from suffocation when his head became caught between two metal slats of the headboard. Three years later, the same court was confronted with the case of an agency manager who, after hosting an official cocktail party at a hotel, retired to his hotel room at 4:00 a.m. and while intoxicated set fire to himself while lighting a cigarette. How would you decide these cases? The court reached different results in the two cases. Do you see a distinction? *Compare* Peterson v. Industrial Comm'n, 16 Ariz. App. 41, 490 P.2d 870 (1971) with Pottinger v. Industrial Comm'n, 22 Ariz. App. 389, 527 P.2d 1232 (1974).

(2) In an Oregon case, a longhaul driver, directed to stay overnight in Idaho, went to a tavern, and became involved in a barroom brawl for reasons that are unknown. *See* Slaughter v. SAIF, 60 Or. App. 610, 654 P.2d 1123 (1982).

(3) A traveler got a hairbrush bristle in his eye when the train jolted while he was brushing his eyebrows. *Compensable?* Lief v. A. Walzer & Son, 272 N.Y. 542, 4 N.E. 2d 727 (1936).

§ 8.07 INJURIES AFTER QUITTING OR BEFORE FORMAL HIRING

Injuries incurred by employees while leaving the premises, collecting pay, or getting their clothes or tools within a reasonable time after termination of the employment are within the course of employment, since they are normal incidents of the employment relation. Injuries before actual hiring are not compensable, but hiring is not deemed to depend on paper formalities such as signing the payroll and withholding slips.

NAILS v. MARKET TIRE COMPANY, INC.
29 Md. App. 154, 347 A.2d 564 (1975)

Mason, Judge.

This is an appeal from the judgment of the Circuit Court for Montgomery County denying the Appellant, Peter Nails, compensation for an injury alleged to have been sustained in the course of his employment.

The evidence adduced at trial disclosed that Nails was employed by the Market Tire Co. for approximately ten years. At the time of separation he was the head mechanic and worked on a commission basis. On Thursday, April 22, 1972, Nails was discharged because he recommended certain repairs for a customer's car which the company believed were not needed. On Saturday, April 24th, Nails returned to the company to pick up his tools, which he had been required to furnish as a condition of his employment. When lifting the tools, which weighed about 800 pounds, with the assistance of another employee, he claimed he injured his back. Nails testified further that it was customary to allow employees two or three days to remove their tools.

After a hearing, the trial court ruled, in effect, that Nails was not an employee at the time of the alleged injury and, therefore, the injury did not arise out of and in the course of his employment. No determination was made as to whether Nails' alleged injury resulted from an accident. As framed by the proceedings below, the narrow issue presented on this appeal is whether the alleged injury sustained by Nails after returning to the company to pick up his tools arose out of and in the course of his employment.

We have been unable to find any Maryland case on this point and none has been called to our attention. We believe, however, that the case of *Consol. Engineering Co. v.*

Feikin, 188 Md. 420, 52 A.2d 913 (1947) is instructive and has precedential value as a guide.

In *Feikin*, the claimant was a day laborer, who was only paid for the hours actually worked. After an extended illness, the claimant returned to the job on Monday, July 16th and was assigned to a labor-gang in the hot strip mill. He worked that one day and did not return again until 10:00 a.m. Friday, July 20th, to pick up his one day's pay. It was the custom of the company to distribute pay slips on Friday morning, but require the workmen to pick up their wages at the office between 3:00 p.m. and 4:00 p.m. After receipt of his pay slip, the claimant told the superintendent he would return to work Monday if he felt the same. The claimant then went to the hot strip mill and asked one of the gang leaders where Blair's gang was. He was told they were still working where they were on Monday. At 12:30 p.m. the claimant was found in the strip finishing department severely burned.

The trial court directed a verdict for the claimant, which the Court of Appeals reversed and remanded for a new trial. The Court held that the evidence did not warrant the trial judge ruling as a matter of law that the claimant's disability was the result of an accidental injury arising out of and in the course of his employment. The Court indicated further the jury might have inferred that the claimant, having five hours to idle away before receiving his pay, visited the mill to talk about some personal matter.

Even though the Court of Appeals reversed *Feikin* on the grounds noted above, it adopted the English Rule which holds that where a workman remains on the premises or returns thereto to obtain his pay after work ceases, he is still acting in the course of his employment. As evidence of the adoption of the English Rule, the Court of Appeals said:

> It is acknowledged that a contract of employment is not necessarily terminated when the actual work ceases, but may continue until the workman's wages are paid. This view was announced in England in 1907 in *Lowry v. Sheffield Coal Co.*, 24 Times L.R. 142, 1 B.W.C.C. 1, where a collier quit work on Saturday at 5 a.m., and expected to resume work on Sunday night, but at noon Saturday while walking along a footpath on the employer's premises on the way to the office to get his wages, he was knocked down by an engine moving along a railway line which ran into the employer's premises. The rule was reaffirmed in 1911 in *Riley v. Holland & Sons*, 1 K.B. 1029, 4 B.W.C.C. 155, where a female mill worker, who quit work on Wednesday, went to the mill on Friday, the regular pay day, to get her wages, and was injured when she slipped on her way down the steps from the pay office. In both cases it was held that the injuries arose out of and in the course of employment. . . .
>
> . . . The established custom, under which the workmen are required to appear at the employer's pay office for their wages on or after the regular pay day fixed by the employer, becomes a part of the contract of employment. *Parrott v. Industrial Commission of Ohio* [145 Ohio St. 66, 60 N.E.2d 660]. . . . 188 Md. at 425, 426, 52 A.2d at 916.

In *Lowry v. Sheffield Coal Co., supra*, at 2, the English Court stated:

> In my view it was just as much part of his employment to go to the pay office on that day at that hour as it was to go down the pit the following Sunday night.

In *Riley v. Holland & Sons, supra*, at 157, the English Court observed:

> The contractual obligations of the employers were not terminated or satisfied until the wages due on Wednesday were paid on Friday. . . . Though her employment was at an end on Wednesday night, in the sense that she had ceased to work under the contract, yet the employment continued because of the obligation of the employers to her arising out of the employment and continuing until Friday afternoon.

Arthur Larson in his treatise on *The Law of Workmen's Compensation*, (vol. 1, 1972), supports the English Rule that "the contract of employment is not fully terminated until the employee is paid." Sec. 26.30. He further supports the point that "collecting one's personal effects on leaving employment is logically no different from collecting one's pay, since both are necessary incidents of an orderly termination of the employment relation." Sec. 26.40. We agree and find no rational basis for not applying the principle laid down in *Feikin, supra*, and the cases cited therein, to the circumstances here.

In *Parrott v. Industrial Commission*, 145 Ohio St. 66, 60 N.E.2d 660 (1945), cited with approval in *Feikin, supra*, the employee quit his job on October 23, and commenced working for another company on October 26. He returned to his former employer on October 29, to pick up one week's pay due him. The bookkeeper was at lunch and the employee went to the boiler room to get his work clothes he had left behind. In returning from the boiler room to the timekeeper's office, he fell and sustained an injury to his pelvic bone and hip. The Ohio Supreme Court, in addition to affirming the English Rule regarding an employee returning to pick up wages, said:

> Clearly he was not a trespasser in going to the boiler room for his clothing which he had worn while at work there. He had a right to pick up his own personal property which he was unable to take away with him when he quit work. . . . Acts of an employee done within a reasonable period of time after actual working hours in making the necessary preparations to terminate his employment, are incidents of and within the course of his employment within the meaning and operation of the workmen's compensation laws. 60 N.E.2d at 662.

In *Molloy v. South Wales Anthracite Colliery*, 4 B.W.C.C. 65 (1910), a miner left his job on April 28, 1910, after refusing to do certain work he was ordered to perform. He returned on Monday, May 2, 1910, and was told by the manager he had dismissed himself. The miner obtained leave to pick up his tools, and while down in the mine for that purpose, he was injured by a falling stone. The lower court found that the foreman ordered the miner to fetch his tools and that the accident arose out of and in the course of his employment. The Court of Appeals, England, affirmed. Larson, in commenting on this case, said:

> When a man has been fired, it could indeed be properly said that he is impliedly ordered to clear his personal possessions out of the way to make a place where his successor can hang his hat.

The Law of Workmen's Compensation, Sec. 26.40, at 5-212. Of like import, *see Cowler v. The Moresby Coal Co.* (Company tools), 1 Times Law Reports 575 (Q.B. 1885). *See also Marra Bros. v. Cardillo* (Clothes), 59 F. Supp. 368 (E.D. Pa. 1945), *aff'd*, 154 F.2d 357 (3rd Cir. 1946); *Bardes v. East River Housing Corp.* (Clothes), 14 A.D.2d 939, 221 N.Y.S. 2d 51 (1961); *Mitchell v. Consolidated Coal* (Tools), 195 Iowa 415, 192 N.W. 145 (1923).

There is responsible authority to the contrary. In *Pederson v. Kromrey*, 201 Wis. 599, 231 N.W. 267 (1930), the employee was terminated, apparently on a weekend, and returned to the premises of the employer around 10:00 a.m. Monday to pick up his pay. After receiving his pay, he went to the warehouse to pick up his work clothes and tools. While going downstairs to where the articles were, he slipped and broke a bone in his foot. The Supreme Court of Wisconsin, although conceding that an employee, even after discharge, is covered by the Workmen's Compensation Act, provided he is injured on the employer's premises while present for the purpose of collecting his pay, held that Kromery's return to the warehouse after discharge to pick up his tools and clothes was not referable to his employment contract and was not covered by the Act. *See Parten v. State Industrial Court*, 496 P.2d 114 (Okl. 1972) and *Johnson v. City of Albia*, 203 Iowa 1171, 212 N.W. 419 (1927). Three judges dissented and their opinion is more persuasive and convincing than that of the majority. The dissenting opinion held that:

The appellant was subjected to the hazard that caused his injury solely because of his status as an employee. It was the fact that he was an employee that led him to take his tools and working clothes to the premises of his employer. It was the fact that he was an employee that made it necessary for him to return to his employer's premises in order to secure his property. The removal of his working clothes and tools from the premises was just as essential to end his status as an employee as was the payment of his wages. In either case I believe it should be held that the status continues until he had been paid his wages and has had a reasonable opportunity to remove his personal belongings, taken to his employer's premises in order that he might there use them for the purpose of promoting the business of his employer. . . .

. . . To hold that the status created by the employment is terminated before the employee has a reasonable opportunity after notice of discharge to get his personal belongings seems to me to be a reversal of the policy of the law as it has been interpreted heretofore by this court, and by other courts under similar acts. 231 N.W. at 270, 271.

Whether an accident causing an injury to an employee results from some obligation, condition or incident of the employment depends upon the circumstances of each particular case. *Feikin, supra,* 188 Md. at 424, 52 A.2d 913.

In the present case, the employee returned to the job two days after being discharged to pick up his tools, which he was required to furnish as a condition of his employment. The tools, together with the tool box, weighed approximately 800 pounds and, obviously, required a reasonable time to remove. Moreover, the tools were used for the benefit of the employer's business, and it was customary to allow employees two or three days to remove their tools.

Under the circumstances of this case and the fact that "The Workmen's Compensation Act should be construed as liberally in favor of injured employees as its provisions will permit in order to effectuate its benevolent purposes," *Beth. Sp. Pt. Shipy'd v. Hempfield,* 206 Md. 589, 594, 112 A.2d 488, 491, (1955), we hold that if the employee sustained an accidental injury as alleged, it arose out of and in the course of his employment.

Judgment reversed, case remanded for a new trial, costs to be paid by appellee.

§ 8.08 ACTS OUTSIDE REGULAR DUTIES

An act outside an employee's regular duties which is undertaken in good faith to advance the employer's interests, whether or not the employee's own assigned work is thereby furthered, is within the course of employment.

HOWELL v. KASH & KARRY
264 S.C. 298, 214 S.E.2d 821 (1975)

BUSSEY, JUDGE.

This is a workmen's compensation case wherein the employer and carrier appeal from an order of the circuit court affirming an award of compensation by the Industrial Commission. The facts of the case, as clearly established by the evidence, and/or readily inferable therefrom, are as follows. The employer, Kash and Karry, operates a very large supermarket at the intersection of Buncombe Road and Mulberry Street in Greenville, South Carolina. It maintains a parking lot for its customers across Buncombe Road and another across from Mulberry Street from the actual store.

While traffic upon the sidewalks, immediately adjacent to Kash and Karry, is not restricted solely to its customers, pedestrian traffic is primarily composed of customers of Kash and Karry going to the store and back to the parking lots with grocery carts, the carts of Kash and Karry being frequently parked on the sidewalks themselves.

The claimant, Howell, was a regular employee of Kash and Karry as a checking clerk and stockboy. On the night of December 30, 1971, at about 8:00 p.m., he was sent to the parking lot across Mulberry Street to retrieve a number of gliders or carts. As he was returning to the store Mrs. Clara Belk and her sister were on the Mulberry Street sidewalk approaching the entrance to Kash and Karry, which was immediately around the corner from them on Buncombe Road. Two small boys snatched the purse of Mrs. Belk and Howell gave chase in an effort to overtake the boys and retrieve Mrs. Belk's purse. In doing so he ran into a low fence, fell and broke his arm.

Mrs. Belk and her sister had parked in the Mulberry Street parking lot immediately prior to the altercation and were on their way to Kash and Karry for the purpose of grocery shopping, where Mrs. Belk, at least, had previously shopped and she was familiar with its store and parking lot. They had parked in the parking lot for no other purpose than to enter Kash and Karry. The purse snatchers got all the money that either Mrs. Belk or her sister had to shop with so that they were unable to pursue the intended grocery shopping. There is no contention that it was a part of Howell's regular duties to protect the customers or their property, and no evidence to the effect that Howell, in fact, knew Mrs. Belk or that she was a customer. The circumstances reflected by the evidence, however, are such as would have led Howell or any other reasonable person to believe that Mrs. Belk was at least most probably a customer of Kash and Karry, if under the circumstances of the emergency, he had taken time to reflect thereabout.

Upon the foregoing facts the Commission below as well as the circuit court found, contrary to the contention of the employer-carrier, that the claimant's injury arose out of, and in the course of his employment. We are of the view that the Commission and the circuit court reached the right conclusion and that there is no merit in this appeal. Somewhat similar cases are cited by both appellants and respondent, but no case precisely in point factually is cited by either. The better reasoned decisions clearly support the position of the claimant.

Larson's Workmen's Compensation, section 27.00 states the generally recognized rule as follows:

> An act outside an employee's regular duties which is undertaken in good faith to advance the employer's interest, whether or not the employee's own assigned work is thereby furthered, is within the course of employment.

Here the employee-claimant was in the course of his regular duties when, in his immediate presence a customer who had already parked her vehicle in the store parking lot and was within a few feet of the entrance to the store was hit, pushed and robbed by two purse snatchers. It clearly would have been to the financial interest of the employer, in this case, if the claimant had successfully recovered the purse of the customer. The money that she intended to spend in the employer's store was in the purse that he was attempting to recover. As pointed out by Professor Larson in section 27.22(a), awards have been upheld for injuries occurring in the course of miscellaneous Good Samaritan activities by employees, on the theory that the employer ultimately profited as a result of the good will thus created, and, as he points out, "When the person assisted stands in some business relation to the employer, the employer benefit is relatively obvious."

The time, place and scope of the claimant's actual duties brought him immediately in contact with a customer of his employer who was in sore distress. To assist a customer in any kind of distress is a natural incident of any employee's employment. Would not any reasonable employer expect the nearest employee to go to the rescue of a customer even though rendering assistance was not a part of the regular assigned duty of the employee? Would not every employer want his customers to feel that the employer and his employees would make every reasonable effort to protect them and their purses from juvenile purse snatchers operating in the immediate vicinity of the employer's premises? The only common sense answer to these questions is yes. In view of the current prevalence of purse snatching by juvenile delinquents, there is obvious and substantial benefit flowing to a merchant from knowledge on the part of his customers that the merchant and his employees will make every reasonable effort to protect the customers and their purses from such juvenile delinquents. We have no real difficulty in concluding that the claimant's injury in the instant case arose out of, and in the course of his employment and the judgment of the court below is accordingly,

Affirmed.

MOSS, C. J., and LEWIS, LITTLEJOHN and NESS, JJ., concur.

PROBLEMS

(1) A supervisor drove a worker home who had a bad cold, and was injured during the trip. Compensable? *See* Olson Rug Co. v. Industrial Comm'n, 215 Wis. 344, 254 N.W. 519 (1934).

(2) A tree trimmer working for the telephone company observed a lady in distress. He descended from his immediate duties to help her get her car started, and was injured. Compensable? *See* Gross v. Davey Tree Expert Co., 248 App. Div. 838, 290 N.Y. Supp. 168 (1936).

(3) A law school dean had a heart attack while giving a speech to a legal fraternity. Compensable? *See* University of Denver v. Johnston, 151 Colo. 465, 378 P. 2d 830 (1963).

(4) State board of health regulations required that waitresses undergo a blood test. Is an injury connected with such a test compensable? *See* Industrial Comm'n v. Messinger, 116 Colo. 451, 181 P.2d 816 (1947). *See also* Washington Hosp. Ctr. v. District of Columbia Dep't of Employment Servs., 821 A.2d 898 (D.C. Ct. App. 2003), as to a required measles vaccination.

(5) During World War II, a school teacher, at the request of the employer, was injured while voluntarily acting as a ration book registrant in the school building. The work was being done for a federal agency, and the employer had no legal authority to request such activity. Is the school board liable for compensation? *See* Burton v. Board of Educ., 21 N.J. Misc. 108, 31 A.2d 337 (1942), and Bituminous Cas. Co. v. Industrial Comm'n, 245 Wis. 337, 13 N.W. 2d 925 (1944).

(6) A cotton-gin manager was running for the office of sheriff. Claimant employee was ordered to help put up banners, and in doing so was injured. Result? *See* National Security Corp. v. Kemp, 217 Miss. 537, 64 So. 2d 723 (1953).

(7) Claimant, a die setter, shop steward, and union bargaining agent, had a heart attack after a stormy bargaining session, which took place after regular working hours. Did the injury arise in the course of employment? *See* Salierno v. Miero Stamping Co., 136 N.Y. Super. 172, 345 A.2d 342 (1975).

(8) Decedent, a financial analyst, was attending evening classes, working toward a master's degree in business administration. His employer had agreed that, if decedent successfully completed his course, the employer would reimburse him for his tuition and fees. He was killed while on his way to study in a nearby library. Compensable? *See* Strzelecki v. Johns-Manville Prods. Corp., 65 N.J. 314, 322 A.2d 168 (1974).

(9) The employee, an electrocardiogram technician, received a free flu shot every year on the hospital's premises. One year, she began experiencing vision difficulties soon after the shot and eventually became blind. Compensable? *See* In re Hicks Case, 62 Mass. App. Ct. 755, 820 N.E.2d 826 (2005). *See also* E.I. Dupont de Nemours & Co. v. Faupel, 859 A.2d 1042 (Del. Super. Ct. 2004).

§ 8.09   ACTS IN EMERGENCY

Any emergency or rescue activity is within the course of employment if the employer has an interest in the rescue. Injury incurred in the rescue of a stranger is compensable if the conditions of employment place claimant in a position which requires him or her by ordinary standards of humanity to undertake the rescue. Similarly, when the conditions of employment lead claimant to be pressed into public service to aid in pursuit of fugitives or the like, under circumstances in which claimant must perform the service as a public duty, he or she remains within the course of his or her employment.

BOGGAN v. ABBY FINISHING COMPANY
11 A.D.2d 591, 200 N.Y.S.2d 488 (1960)

Before BERGAN, P. J., and COON, GIBSON, HERLIHY and REYNOLDS, JJ.

MEMORANDUM DECISION.

Appeal by claimant from a decision of the Workmen's Compensation Board dismissing his claim.

The employer was engaged in a business which required the extensive use of highly inflammable materials. For that reason a strict and rigidly enforced rule against smoking in the building was in effect. Claimant went to a washroom in the building, lighted a cigarette, threw the match into a toilet bowl, the contents of which immediately burst into flames. Claimant got a pail of sand and threw it upon the flames, whereupon some of the flaming liquid splashed upon claimant, causing his injuries. It is undisputed that the discovery of a violation of this strict no-smoking rule would result in the immediate discharge of the offending employee. It seems beyond question that when a claimant, in pursuance of a personal act, unconnected with his employment, deliberately violated the rule of which he was aware, he went outside the scope of his employment. (1 Larson on Compensation, §§ 31.11, 31.12). While the attempt to extinguish the flames may have also furthered the employer's interest, it was a continued effort on claimant's part to prevent discovery of his violation of the rule. When claimant left the scope of his employment and, in deliberately violating a rule caused a dangerous situation, to say that an attempt to alleviate the results of his own folly returns him to his employment approaches the ridiculous. Claimant's injuries did not arise out of and in the course of his employment, and are therefore not compensable. Workmen's Compensation Law, § 10.

Decision unanimously affirmed, without costs.

O'LEARY v. BROWN-PACIFIC-MAXON, INC.
340 U.S. 504, 71 S. Ct. 470, 95 L. Ed. 2d 483 (1951)

MR. JUSTICE FRANKFURTER delivered the opinion of the Court.

In this case we are called upon to review an award of compensation under the Longshoremen's and Harbor Workers' Compensation Act. Act of March 4, 1927, 44 Stat. 1424, as amended, 33 U. S. C. § 901 *et seq.* The award was made on a claim arising from the accidental death of an employee of Brown-Pacific-Maxon, Inc., a government contractor operating on the island of Guam. Brown-Pacific maintained for its employees a recreation center near the shoreline, along which ran a channel so dangerous for swimmers that its use was forbidden and signs to that effect erected. John Valak, the employee, spent the afternoon at the center, and was waiting for his employer's bus to take him from the area when he saw or heard two men, standing on the reefs beyond the channel, signaling for help. Followed by nearly twenty others, he plunged in to effect a rescue. In attempting to swim the channel to reach the two men he was drowned.

A claim was filed by his dependent mother, based on the Longshoremen's Act and on an Act of August 16, 1941, extending the compensation provisions to certain employment in overseas possessions. 55 Stat. 622, 56 Stat. 1035, as amended, 42 U. S. C. § 1651. In due course of the statutory procedure, the Deputy Commissioner found as a "fact" that "at the time of his drowning and death the deceased was using the recreational facilities sponsored and made available by the employer for the use of its employees and such participation by the deceased was an incident of his employment, and that his drowning and death arose out of and in the course of said employment. . . . " Accordingly, he awarded a death benefit of $9.38 per week. Brown-Pacific and its insurance carrier thereupon petitioned the District Court under § 21 of the Act to set aside the award. That court denied the petition on the ground that "there is substantial evidence . . . to sustain the compensation order." On appeal, the Court of Appeals for the Ninth Circuit reversed. It concluded that "The lethal currents were not a part of the recreational facilities supplied by the employer and the swimming in them for the rescue of the unknown man was not recreation. It was an act entirely disconnected from any use for which the recreational camp was provided and not in the course of Valak's employment." 182 F. 2d 772, 773. We granted certiorari, 340 U.S. 849, because the case brought into question judicial review of awards under the Longshoreman's Act in light of the Administrative Procedure Act.

The Longshoremen's and Harbor Workers' Act authorizes payment of compensation for "accidental injury or death arising out of and in the course of employment." § 2 (2), 44 Stat. 1425, 33 U. S. C. § 902(2). As we read its opinion the Court of Appeals entertained the view that this standard precluded an award for injuries incurred in an attempt to rescue persons not known to be in the employer's service, undertaken in forbidden waters outside the employer's premises. We think this is too restricted an interpretation of the Act. Workmen's compensation is not confined by common-law conceptions of scope of employment. *Cardillo* v. *Liberty Mutual Ins. Co.*, 330 U.S. 469, 481; *Matter of Waters v. Taylor Co.*, 218 N. Y. 248, 251, 112 N. E. 727, 728. The test of recovery is not a causal relation between the nature of employment of the injured person and the accident. *Thom v. Sinclair*, [1917] A.C. 127, 142. Nor is it necessary that the employee be engaged at the time of the injury in activity of benefit to his employer. All that is required is that the "obligations or conditions" of employment create the "zone of special danger" out of which the injury arose. *Ibid.* A reasonable rescue attempt, like pursuit in aid of an officer making an arrest, may be "one of the risks of the employment, an incident of the service, foreseeable, if not foreseen, and so covered by the statute." *Matter of Babington v. Yellow Taxi Corp.*, 250 N.Y. 14, 17, 164 N.E. 726, 727; *Puttkammer* v. *Industrial Comm'n*, 371 Ill. 497, 21 N.E. 2d 575. This is not to say that there are not cases "where an employee, even with the laudable purpose of helping another, might go so far from his employment and become so thoroughly disconnected from the service of his employer that it would be entirely unreasonable to say that injuries suffered by him arose out of and in the course of his employment." *Matter of Waters v. Taylor Co.*, 218 N.Y. at 252, 112 N.E. at 728. We hold only that rescue attempts such as that before us are not necessarily excluded from the coverage of the Act as the kind of conduct that employees engage in as frolics of their own.

The Deputy Commissioner treated the question whether the particular rescue attempt described by the evidence was one of the class covered by the Act as a question of "fact." Doing so only serves to illustrate once more the variety of ascertainments covered by the blanket term "fact." Here of course it does not connote a simple, external, physical event as to which there is conflicting testimony. The conclusion concerns a combination of happenings and the inferences drawn from them. In part at least, the inferences presuppose applicable standards for assessing the simple, exter nal facts. Yet the standards are not so severable from the experience of industry nor of such a nature as to be peculiarly appropriate for independent judicial ascertainment as "questions of law."

Both sides conceded that the scope of judicial review of such findings of fact is governed by the Administrative Procedure Act. Act of June 11, 1946, 60 Stat. 237, 5 U. S. C. § 1001 *et seq.* The standard, therefore, is that discussed in *Universal Camera Corp. v. Labor Board, ante,* p. 474. It is sufficiently described by saying that the findings are to be accepted unless they are unsupported by substantial evidence on the record considered as a whole. The District Court recognized this standard.

When this Court determines that a Court of Appeals has applied an incorrect principle of law, wise judicial administration normally counsels remand of the cause to the Court of Appeals with instructions to reconsider the record. *Compare Universal Camera Corp. v. Labor Board, supra.* In this instance, however, we have a slim record and the relevant standard is not difficult to apply; and we think the litigation had better terminate now. Accordingly we have ourselves examined the record to assess the sufficiency of the evidence.

We are satisfied that the record supports the Deputy Commissioner's finding. The pertinent evidence was presented by the written statements of four persons and the testimony of one witness. It is, on the whole, consistent and credible. From it the Deputy Commissioner could rationally infer that Valak acted reasonably in attempting the rescue, and that his death may fairly be attributable to the risks of the employment. We do not mean that the evidence compelled this inference; we do not suggest that had the Deputy Commissioner decided against the claimant, a court would have been justified in disturbing his conclusion. We hold only that on this record the decision of the District Court that the award should not be set aside should be sustained.

Reversed.

MR. JUSTICE MINTON, MR. JUSTICE JACKSON and MR. JUSTICE BURTON dissent.

ROCKHAULERS, INC. v. DAVIS
554 So. 2d 654 (Fla. Ct. App. 1989)

JOANOS, JUDGE.

The deceased claimant owned and operated a truck under contract to Rockhaulers, Inc. Under the terms of his contract, claimant was paid a percentage of Rockhaulers' billing for hauling loads of limestone. As a lease operator, claimant called Rockhaulers' dispatch office and received instructions concerning the time and place of the load pick-up, and the load destination. The route traveled by claimant to the load pick-up point and to the drop-off points was not controlled by Rockhaulers. The subject accident occurred at 6:00 a.m. on September 19, 1988, as claimant was traveling on Highway 235 from Alachua County to Jacksonville. Claimant was the first person to arrive at the scene of a head-on collision between a truck and an automobile. He left his truck on the edge of the northbound lane with the emergency lights flashing. Claimant first determined that the driver of the truck was uninjured, and then, as he walked to aid the persons in the automobile, he was struck and killed by another motor vehicle.

The judge of compensation claims found that the deceased employee died from an injury arising out of and in the course of his employment, in that his death occurred within the time period of his employment, at a place where his employer expected him to be, while performing actions incidental to his employment as a truck driver. The employer/carrier contest the compensability determination, contending that claimant's activities were not beneficial to the employer, the employee's injury was not a reasonably foreseeable consequence of fulfilling the duties of his employment, and that the acts of a good samaritan are not compensable in Florida.

We note at the outset that we agree with the judge's determination regarding compensability of the accident. Under section 440.09(1), Florida Statutes (1987), workers' compensation coverage is provided for injuries "arising out of and in the course of employment." The phrase "arising out of" refers to the origin of the cause of the accident, while the phrase "in the course of employment" refers to the time, place, and circumstances under which the accident occurs. *Bituminous Casualty Corp. v. Richardson*, 148 Fla. 323, 4 So. 2d 378, 379 (1941). Therefore, "[t]o be compensable, an injury must arise out of employment in the sense of causation and be in the course of employment in the sense of continuity of time, space, and circumstances." *Strother v. Morrison Cafeteria*, 383 So. 2d 623 (Fla. 1980); *Leonard v. Dennis*, 465 So. 2d 538, 540 (Fla. 2d DCA), review denied, 476 So. 2d 673 (Fla. 1985). *See also Brown v. Winter Haven Citrus Growers Association*, 175 So. 2d 193, 194 (Fla. 1965). Stated another way, for an injury to arise out of employment, (1) it must occur within the period of employment, (2) at a place where the employee may reasonably be, and (3) while he is reasonably fulfilling the duties of employment or engaging in something incidental to it. *Fidelity & Casualty Co. of New York v. Moore*, 143 Fla. 103, 196 So. 495, 496 (1940); *Gray v. Eastern Airlines. Inc.*, 475 So. 2d 1288, 1289 (Fla. 1st DCA 1985), review denied, 484 So. 2d 8 (Fla. 1986); *Cooper v. Stephens*, 470 So. 2d 852, 854 (Fla. 1st DCA), review denied, 480 So. 2d 1296 (Fla. 1985); *Haddock v. Hardwoods of Orlando, Inc.*, 452 So. 2d 97, 98 (Fla. 1st DCA 1984).

The general rule with respect to traveling employees is that an employee whose work takes him away from the employer's premises is within the course of employment at all times during the trip, except for any "distinct departure for a nonessential personal errand." *Gray v. Eastern Airlines*, 475 So. 2d at 1290; *Leonard v. Dennis*, 465 So. 2d at 540; *N & L Auto Parts v. Doman*, 11 So. 2d 270, 271 (Fla. 1st DCA 1959), cert. discharged, 117 So. 2d 410 (Fla. 1960). In *Leonard v. Dennis*, the court noted that "[t]he 'neutral' risk of an automobile accident is always causally related to employment if it involves an employee whose duties increase his exposure to such a hazard." 465 So. 2d at 541.

Somewhat analogous to the traveling employee theory are the theories of compensability pertaining to emergency situations. Professor Larson states that "[i]njury incurred in the rescue of a stranger is compensable if the conditions of employment place claimant in a position which requires him by ordinary standards of humanity to undertake the rescue." 1A Larson, Workmen's Compensation Law § 28.00 (1978). However, Professor Larson emphasizes that there must be a true emergency, as distinguished from a mere benefit to an employer through the act of providing assistance to one in trouble. 1A Larson, at § 28.13. This "true emergency" requirement lies at the heart of the positional risk doctrine. Under this theory, an employee's injury is compensable if it was incurred in the rescue of a complete stranger, provided the employment brought the employee to the place where he observed the situation calling for a rescue attempt. *See O'Leary v. Brown Pacific-Maxon. Inc.*, 340 U.S. 504, 71 S.Ct. 470, 95 L.Ed. 483 (1951); *Murphy v. Peninsular Life Insurance Co.*, 299 So. 2d 3, 4 (Fla. 1974); 1A Larson, § 28.23.

In *Murphy*, the court found the positional risk doctrine inapplicable. The claimant in Murphy was a sales manager trainer of an insurance company, who was injured while accompanying an agent on his rounds in claimant's private car. On the way to the claimant's home, they encountered a truck facing an inclined portion of the road. The truck driver, whose brakes were failing, called for help. He asked claimant to place some blocks under the tires. The claimant climbed atop the truck to throw down the blocks to be placed under the wheels of the truck. The truck's brakes failed, and the truck rolled back striking a utility pole. The claimant injured his leg when he jumped from the truck to avoid being struck by the falling pole. The court found the claimant's injury was not a reasonably foreseeable consequence of fulfilling the duties of his employment.

The differences between the circumstances of this case and the situation in *Murphy* are important. Claimant in this case was the first to arrive on the scene of a "true emergency." In addition, the nature of claimant's employment brought him to the place where a rescue attempt was required by "ordinary standards of humanity." Further the type of action taken by claimant was reasonable and expected behavior. Thus, the positional risk doctrine appears applicable to the facts of this case. In *Murphy* on the other hand, the kind of action taken by the claimant could not have been expected.

In addition, the facts of the case before us appear to fit equally well under the traveling employee theory. Not only did claimant's employment take him away from the employer's premises, but his duties as an over the road truck driver increased his exposure to the risk of traffic related injury. Since the record reflects that claimant's conduct in attempting to aid accident victims was reasonably foreseeable, as well as incidental to his employment as a truck driver, we find no error in the judge's finding of compensability. . . .

PROBLEMS

(1) In *Boggan*, stop the clock at the moment the toilet bowl burst into flames, and ask the question, "If the employer could have been consulted at that moment, what would he have ordered the employee to do?" Looked at in this way, does the idea of the employee's return to his employment appear quite so "ridiculous"?

(2) Claimant, while taking a shower in facilities provided by the employer, saw a cockroach going up the wall. He climbed on a bench to swat it, and the bench fell forward, injuring his leg. Compensable? *See* Chicago Extruded Metals v. Industrial Comm'n, 77 Ill. 2d 81, 32 Ill. Dec. 339, 395 N.E. 2d 569 (1979).

(3) A part-time law clerk was directed by an associate of the firm to help repair the roof on an apartment unit owned by the associate. He had previously performed such errands for the associate as babysitting, taking his children out to dinner, driving his car to a garage for repairs, delivering liquor to the associate's home, changing tires on his car, and acting as night watchman at a warehouse owned by a friend of the associate. Is an injury during the roof repair compensable by the law firm? How about all the other activities of the long-suffering law clerk? *See* Biggs v. U.S. Fire Ins. Co., 611 S.W. 2d 624 (Tex. 1981), *rev'g* 601 S.W. 2d 132 (Tex. Civ. App.). Opinion on remand, 614 S.W. 2d 496.

§ 8.10   "DELAYED-ACTION" INJURIES

GRAYBEAL v. BOARD OF SUPERVISORS OF MONTGOMERY COUNTY
216 Va. 77, 216 S.E.2d 52 (1975)

Before I'Anson, C.J., and Carrico, Harrison, Cochran, Harman, Poff and Compton, JJ.

Carrico, Justice.

In this workman's compensation case, an exploding bomb injured the claimant-employee on his residence premises at night. Although finding that the claimant's injuries arose out of his employment, the Industrial Commission, with Commissioner Miller dissenting, denied compensation because the injuries did not arise in the course of employment. The claimant seeks reversal of the denial of compensation.

The claimant, John Patrick Graybeal, is Commonwealth's Attorney for Montgomery County. In April, 1968, in the course of his duties, he prosecuted Frank H. Dewease, Jr., for murder. As a result, Dewease was convicted of murder of the second degree and sentenced to serve 20 years in the penitentiary.

Thereafter, Dewease vowed revenge upon "everyone having anything to do" with his case and he expressed his desire "to get them all in the courthouse and blow it up." He especially "seemed to want to kill" the claimant. While in prison, Dewease bragged of his knowledge of bomb construction and of his ability to "get dynamite and caps after he got out."

Shortly after his release from prison, Dewease, on the night of December 4, 1973, went to the claimant's home in Christiansburg. There, he placed on the top of the claimant's family automobile, which was parked in the driveway, a "potato chip can" containing a homemade bomb.

On that same evening, the claimant worked in his office at the courthouse preparing for the next day's trial of Commonwealth cases. Completing his work at approximately 11:30 p.m., he drove home in a borrowed automobile. Upon arrival at home, he observed the can on the top of the family car. Believing the can was a toy or an item of groceries, he picked it up. The device exploded, causing the severe and disabling injuries upon which the present claim for compensation is based.

Code § 65.1-7, part of the Virginia Workmen's Compensation Act, defines a compensable accidental injury as one "arising out of and in the course of the employment." We have said that the expressions "arising out of" and "in the course of" are used conjunctively and are not synonymous. Both conditions must be satisfied before compensation can be awarded. Southern Motor Lines v. Alvis, 200 Va. 168, 170, 104 S.E.2d 735, 737 (1958); Dreyfus & Co. v. Meade, 142 Va. 567, 569, 129 S.E. 336 (1925).

As has been noted, the Commission found that the claimant's injuries arose out of his employment. On appeal, that finding is conclusive. Whether the injuries arose in the course of employment is the sole, and novel, question for decision.

In holding that the claimant's injury did not arise in the course of his employment, the Commission relied upon our decision in Conner v. Bragg, 203 Va. 204, 123 S.E.2d 393 (1962). There, we said: "(T)he words 'in the course of' refer to the time, place and circumstances under which the accident occurred. (A)n accident occurs in the 'course of employment' when it takes place within the period of employment, at a place where the employee may be reasonably expected to be, and while he is reasonably fulfilling the duties of his employment or is doing something which is reasonably incidental thereto." 203 Va. at 208, 123 S.E.2d at 396.

Tested by this seemingly rigid rule, the claimant's case might fail. Conner equates "arising" with "occurring." The express requirement that the injury must Occur within the specified time, space, and circumstances of the employment would appear well-nigh insurmountable in the present case.

But the Conner rule was enunciated in and designed for application to a case involving the usual employer-employee relationship and the typical industrial accident. The present case involves neither the usual employer-employee relationship nor a typical industrial accident. Instead, the case involves a public officer charged with the duty of exercising his authority in different places, including his home, and at various times, including evening hours. This officer's public duties, by their very nature, expose him to an increased risk of injury from an atypical accident — an assault by a revenge-seeking criminal who, blaming his plight upon the officer's prosecutorial activities, is apt to seek out the object of his hatred in private places at unexpected times.

It would be both unrealistic and in derogation of the beneficent purposes of the Workmen's Compensation Act to borrow from Conner and apply a rule which is designed for an employment situation with fixed hours of employment, identifiable places of performance, and definable areas of risk, but with no greater nexus between work and injury than exists in the present situation. The present case requires application of a modified rule, one sufficiently flexible to recognize the realities of the claimant's employment situation any yet rigid enough to prevent its extension to unwarranted situations.

A modified rule is permitted, we believe, be the statutory language "arising . . . in the course of the employment." An appropriate rule, limited in application, can be fashioned within the statutory language merely by shifting the emphasis from the word "occurring," which is prominently employed in Conner but is not mentioned in the statute, to the statutory word "arising" and giving it the ordinary meaning of "originating." Under this rule, the claimant's injury would be held to have arisen in the course of his employment if it originated in the course of the employment.

Upon first examination, this rule might appear to constitute a blending into one single test of the dual "arising out of" and "in the course of" requirements. But the "arising out of" requirement refers to causation, only incidentally related to considerations of time and space, and must be satisfied by a showing of causal connection between work and injury. The "course of" requirement, on the other hand, refers to continuity of time, space, and circumstances, only incidentally related to causation. This requirement must be satisfied by a showing of an unbroken course beginning with work and ending with injury under such circumstances that the beginning and the end are connected parts of a single work-related incident.

Considering, then, that in the context of the present case "arising" means "originating," we believe the claimant's nighttime injury from the exploding bomb placed on the top of his family car no less arose in the course of his employment than if he had been shot by his revenge-seeking assailant in the courtroom immediately following the murder trial, or if he had been injured by a bomb triggered to explode in his office upon his return from the courtroom. The difference is in degree only and not in substance. In the realities of the present case, the course from prosecution to desire-for-revenge to injury was unbroken, constituting a single work-connected incident.

For the reasons assigned, the Industrial Commission's denial of compensation will be reversed and the case remanded for the award to the claimant of appropriate compensation.

Reversed and remanded.

PROBLEM

Claimant was laid off from his employment but was kept on the company payroll for two months subsequent to his layoff. Three days before the effective date of his termination, he went to the employer's parking lot and shot himself in his own vehicle. His survivors filed a claim for death benefits. *Compensable? Are injuries resulting from termination of employment compensable as occurring within the course of employment?*

THORNTON v. CHAMBERLAIN MANUFACTURING CORP.
62 N.J. 235, 300 A.2d 146 (1973)

WEINTRAUB, C. J.

Petitioner was denied workmen's compensation benefits upon a finding that his injuries were not sustained in the course of his employment. The County Court agreed, and the Appellate Division affirmed. 118 N.J. Super. 540, 289 A.2d 262 (1972). We granted certification. 60 N.J. 502, 291 A.2d 146 (1972).

The facts are not in dispute. While employed as a production foreman with respondent, petitioner reprimanded an employee named Sozio for repeated failures to wear safety glasses, and several times reported such failures in writing to the employer. On one occasion Sozio told petitioner, "I'll take care of your eyes later." Some nine days after petitioner terminated his employment, he saw Sozio at a bar. As petitioner left, he was attacked by Sozio who said "remember me, remember me." Petitioner's injuries included total loss of vision in the right eye.

The attack obviously had its genesis in the employment in the sense that petitioner's performance of his assigned duty incurred the assailant's enmity and led to the attack. That the injuries were intentionally inflicted does not take them beyond the statute. Had Sozio struck petitioner while he was at work, petitioner would have been entitled to compensation benefits. *Cierpial v. Ford Motor Co.*, 16 N.J. 561, 109 A.2d 666 (1954); *Howard v. Harwood's Restaurant Co.*, 25 N.J. 72, 135 A.2d 161 (1957); *Augelli v. Rolans Credit Clothing Store*, 33 N.J. Super. 146, 109 A.2d 439 (App. Div. 1954). It was the delay in Sozio's violent reaction that created the issue in the case, for petitioner was not at work when he was attacked; in fact his employment relationship had ended some nine days before. Because of those circumstances it was held that petitioner was not injured "in the course of" his employment and therefore not entitled to compensation.

N.J.S.A. 34:15-7 entitles an employee to compensation benefits:

> " . . . for personal injuries to . . . such employee by accident arising out of and in the course of his employment."

Thus there must be injury (1) "by accident," (2) arising "out of" and (3) arising "in the course of" the employment. This test, seemingly simple, has led to volumes of opinions exploring its meaning. The constituent elements readily draw content from the legislative objective one finds in the compensation statute. If the statute is read as a narrow replacement of the common law suit between employee and employer and to continue concepts relevant to that scene, the statute will be restrained in its reach. The coverage is much more expansive if the statutory test is read to reflect a legislative purpose to transfer to the employer's enterprise the human costs reasonably related to that enterprise.

Thus the word "accident" invited disagreement as to whether some external event of an accidental quality was required or whether the unexpected injury was all the Legislature had in mind. If the common law cause of action were the proper reference, some external event would be indicated. But the legislative design to include in the employer's costs those human losses reasonably related to the operation would be furthered if the unexpected injury were itself enough to constitute an accident. That is the view we adopted. *Neylon v. Ford Motor Co.*, 10 N.J. 325, 91 A.2d 569 (1952); *Ciuba v. Irvington Varnish & Insulator Co.*, 27 N.J. 127, 141 A.2d 761 (1958); *see Russo v. Teachers' Pension & Annuity Fund*, 62 N.J. 142, 299 A.2d 697 (1973).

So, too, the phrase "arising out of" could mean different things. It could demand that the risk of injury be a risk peculiar to the job, or if a risk common to the public, that it be present to an uncommon degree in the employment. But again the purpose of the statute would be served if it need appear only that "but for" the employment the employee would not have experienced the injury in question, whether or not the risk of injury was generated or magnified by the employment, unless the risk of injury was personal to the employee. This is the view we embraced. *See Howard v. Harwood's Restaurant Co.*, *supra*, 25 N.J. 72, 135 A.2d 161.

The phrase "in the course of," with which we are here concerned, also lends itself to different views. One could say the employee must be engaged in an assigned duty at the time of the injury. But that reading would unduly limit the statute's coverage. We have found, for example, that an employee on the employer's premises may be "in the course of" the employment before or after work or during a work recess. *Tocci v. Tessler & Weiss, Inc.*, 28 N.J. 582, 147 A.2d 783 (1959). So too we have found exceptions to the proposition that an employee is not "in the course of" his employment in coming to and going from work. *See Hammond v. Great Atlantic & Pacific Tea Co.*, 56 N.J. 7, 264 A.2d 204 (1970); *Bergman v. Parnes Brothers, Inc.*, 58 N.J. 559, 279 A.2d 660 (1971). We found in the cited cases that the injury was sufficiently work-connected to bring the employee within the coverage of the compensation law, on the thesis that the statute "provides protection for employees, not because of fault or failure of the employer, but rather upon the belief that the enterprise itself should absorb losses which inevitably and predictably are an incident of its operations." *Ricciardi v. Damar Products*, 45 N.J. 54, 60, 211 A.2d 347, 349 (1965).

As we have said, the statute would cover petitioner's injury in the present case if the attack had occurred on the employer's premises. The employer concedes that here the injury did arise "out of" the employment, and this because of the undeniable connection between the employment and the attack. But the employer insists the statute requires more than this work-connection, and says that because of the factors of time and place the injury did not arise "in the course of" employment. We think it plain that a denial of benefits in these circumstances could not be reconciled with the thesis we have repeatedly accepted that the Legislature intended the enterprise to absorb the related injuries of its employees. We should not say the statute fails in that objective on the facts of this case unless its language compels that answer. We think it does not.

In *Meo v. Commercial Can Corp.*, 80 N.J. Super. 58, 192 A.2d 854 (App. Div. 1963), petitioner was attacked in front of his home as he was about to drive to work. The attack arose out of a labor dispute. Petitioner, who was the plant superintendent, was on call around the clock in the sense that he was expected to respond at any hour to keep the operation going. The Appellate Division correctly declined to follow decisions elsewhere which denied recovery because the attack, although work-connected in its origin, occurred outside the working place and working hours. In finding for the employee, the court referred to *Field v. Charmette Knitted Fabric Co.*, 245 N.Y. 139, 156 N.E. 642 (1927), where compensation was ordered for the death of the general manager and superintendent of a mill who was attacked by an employee he had just discharged. The discharged employee had moved threateningly toward the deceased within the plant but others pulled him away. The attack occurred later, a few feet outside the plant when the victim emerged to go home. Of interest beyond the result there reached was the concept Chief Judge Cardozo used as the vehicle. He stressed that when the deceased stepped out of the mill he was "confronted by a danger engendered by his work within" and that "Continuity of cause has been so combined with contiguity in time and space that the quarrel from origin to ending must be taken to be one." 156 N.E. at 643. The contiguity in *Field* was quite evident. But the concept is viable beyond the immediate facts of that case. The sense of the concept is that an injury "arises" in the course of employment whenever the work in fact envelops the victim with a danger which goes with him when he leaves the course of his employment. When that is so, the accident has its origin in the course of employment, and that fact may remain decisive notwithstanding that the injurious end accrued after the victim left the physical ambit of his employment.

The subject of "delayed injury" is discussed by Larson in his treatise, 1 Workmen's Compensation Law (1972) §§ 29.21 and 29.22, pp. 452.101, et. seq. He concludes correctly that "something is wrong with the coverage formula" when relief is denied an employee assaulted while not on duty but as the aftermath of resentment incurred in the performance of duty. Sec. 29.21, p. 452.101. The issue of course is not limited to wilful injuries. Larson cites two other cases which reached results startling by present thinking. In one, compensation was denied an employee injured when a steel sliver to which he was exposed at work fell from his eyebrow into his eye while he was en route to his home 15 minutes after the close of working hours. *American Motorists Insurance Co. v. Steel*, 229 S.W.2d 386 (Tex. Civ. App. 1950). In the other case, an employee who forgot to remove a dynamite cap from his pocket was denied compensation because the cap was detonated while he was dressing the next morning. *Gill v. Belmar Construction Co.*, 226 App. Div. 616, 236 N.Y.S. 379 (App. Div. 1929).

The problem of delayed injury arose in *Daniello v. Machise Express Co.*, 119 N.J. Super. 20, 289 A.2d 558 (Cty. Ct. 1972), aff'd o. b., 122 N.J. Super. 144, 299 A.2d 423 (App. Div. 1973). There an employee whose clothing was saturated with jet fuel while at work was injured when the fumes were ignited upon his return to his home. Compensation was denied in the Workmen's Compensation Division but the County Court correctly reversed, finding the accident did arise "in the course of" the employment, and the

Appellate Division affirmed the County Court.

Larson points out that the statute does not speak of an accident "occurring" in the course of employment. Rather the word used is "arising," and that word, in one of its accepted usages, means "originating." Thus an accident may fairly be said to "arise" in the course of the employment if it had its origin there in the sense that it was the end-product of a force or cause set in motion in the course of employment. [*Court's footnote omitted*] Sec. 29.22, pp. 452.108–09. That construction is reasonable and advances the basic purpose of the statute that an enterprise shall absorb the injuries reasonably related to it. Here the injuries were caused in every realistic sense by petitioner's exposure at work. We can think of no reason why the Legislature would want to deny relief because the work-generated force overtook petitioner at one moment rather than another.

We are mindful that in the case at hand the employment relationship itself terminated before the work-initiated hazard ended in injury to him. In this respect, this case goes beyond the authorities cited above. But we see nothing critical in that further fact. In another case that fact might play a decisive role with respect to the work-connection of an injury, but in the case at hand it does not offer a rational basis to say the burden of this injury should not be borne by the enterprise from which it so clearly emerged.

The judgment is reversed and the matter remanded to the Division for the entry of an award in favor of petitioner.

For reversal: CHIEF JUSTICE WEINTRAUB, JUSTICES JACOBS, HALL and MOUNTAIN, and JUDGES CONFORD and SULLIVAN — 6.

For affirmance: None.

PROBLEM

In *Thornton*, did the court treat too cavalierly the problem created by the fact that the claimant had actually changed employers at the time of the attack? Is there an analogy in occupational disease cases, in which all or part of liability is placed on earlier employers whose employment contributed to the harm? *See* Ch. 33, § 33.04, *below*.

LUJAN v. HOUSTON GENERAL INSURANCE COMPANY
756 S.W.2d 295 (Tex. 1988)

RAY, JUSTICE.

The question in this workers' compensation case is whether the death of Abelardo Lujan occurred in the course of his employment. The trial court rendered judgment for Lujan's statutory heirs based on the jury's verdict. The court of appeals reversed and rendered judgment that the Lujan family take nothing. 740 S.W.2d 34. Because we hold that Lujan's death occurred in the course of his employment, we reverse the court of appeals' judgment and render judgment for the Lujan family.

Abelardo Lujan was a painter employed by Ezell Paint & Tank Company in Kermit, Texas. On July 11, 1985, Lujan, along with co-worker Randy Heath, was painting pipe, using a pressurized spray unit to apply paint mixed with thinner. About mid-afternoon, Heath noticed that the unit was leaking. Lujan tried to tighten the connection with a crescent wrench. The unit, which was under ninety pounds of pressure, blew the line off and soaked Lujan with industrial paint.

Lujan used gasoline to remove the paint. He soaked himself with gasoline and wiped off some of the paint and gasoline with paper towels and rags. Lujan decided to go home early to bathe since there were no facilities provided by his employer at the job site for such purposes. On the way back to the shop, Lujan remarked that his skin was burning. In order to reduce the burning, Lujan draped some clothing over himself as protection from the sun.

Lujan closed the shop and went home. Mrs. Lujan testified that when he arrived home, her husband was "full of paint," and that when he took his clothes off, he had paint all over his body. Lujan went into the bathroom to bathe, and the pilot light in the water heater ignited the fumes from his body and caused a flash fire.

When Mrs. Lujan opened the bathroom door, Lujan came out covered with fire. She helped him get the fire out with some clothing, and took him outside, yelling for help. Lujan was taken to the hospital, where he died two days later. The gasoline fumes had triggered the flash fire, but the paint and the thinner, which completely covered Lujan's body, caused the severity of his burns.

The jury's verdict consisted of its answer to one question: whether Lujan's work or the conditions of his employment result in an injury to him which was a producing cause of his death. The jury answered "yes," and the trial court rendered judgment for the Lujan family. . . .

Under the Workers' Compensation Act, an injury is compensable if it is sustained in the course of employment. Tex. Rev. Civ. Stat. Ann. art. 8306, § 3b (Vernon 1967). The Act provides that the term "injury sustained in the course of employment"

> (4) . . . shall include all other injuries of every kind and character having to do with and originating in the work, business, trade or profession of the employer received by an employee while engaged in or about the furtherance of the affairs or business of his employer *whether upon the employer's premises or elsewhere.* (emphasis supplied). Tex. Rev. Civ Stat. Ann. art. 8309, § 1 (Vernon 1967).

Often, the manifestation of an injury occurs later than the precipitating event. In his treatise on workers' compensation law, Larson uses the label "delayed-action" to describe cases in which the risk associated with employment causes an injury after work hours and off the premises of the employer. 1A A. Larson, The Law of Workmen's Compensation § 29.22 (1985); *see also* Larson, Range of Compensable Consequences in Workmen's Compensation, 21 Hastings L. J. 609 (1970). Texas courts have allowed recovery in delayed-action cases. For example, claimants have recovered under the Workers' Compensation Act when a fatal heart attack occurred at home, days or months after the strain or overexertion occurred at work. This is because the injury to the heart originated in the employment, but manifested itself at a later time. *See Stodghill v. Texas Employers Insurance Ass'n*, 582 S.W.2d 102 (Tex. 1979); *Texas Employers Insurance Ass'n. v. Mitchusson*, 515 S.W.2d 168 (Tex. Civ. App. — Eastland 1974, no writ); *Hardware Mutual Casualty Co. v. Wesbrooks*, 511 S.W.2d 406 (Tex. Civ. App. — Amarillo 1974, no writ); *Aetna Casualty & Surety Co. v. Calhoun*, 426 S.W.2d 655 (Tex. App. — Beaumont 1968, writ ref'd n.r.e.); *Lyles v. Texas Employers' Insurance Ass'n*, 365 S.W.2d 819 (Tex. Civ. App. — Texarkana 1963, writ ref'd n.r.e.). These heart attack cases highlight the importance of the "originating in" language of article 8309, section 1. It is the origin of an injury which is crucial, since the real question is whether the event was an industrial accident. The moment of manifestation is almost immaterial. *See* 1A A. Larson, The Law of Workmen's Compensation, § 29.22 (1985).

In *Daniello v. Machise Express Co.*, 119 N.J. Super. 20, 289 A.2d 558 (Atlantic County Ct. 1972), a New Jersey court was confronted with a delayed-action case, the facts of which are similar to those of the case at bar. Mr. Daniello was a truck driver. On the day of his injury, he delivered jet fuel, which splashed on him and permeated his body and uniform. When he arrived home at the end of the work day, his eight year old son was taking trash to the incinerator to be burned. Since he never allowed his son to burn trash, Daniello told his son that he would burn it. When he struck a match, the fire ignited the fumes from the jet fuel on his clothes and body. Based on a similar workers' compensation statute, the New Jersey court of appeals reversed a denial of benefits. The court held that although Daniello's injury occurred at home, he was in the course of employment because the incident originated at his work.

In this case, Houston General Insurance Company urges a strict construction of article 8309, section 1. The carrier argues that because the accident itself, the fire which burned Lujan, did not occur while Lujan was working, he may not recover. It is well settled that the Workers' Compensation Act should be liberally construed in favor of the worker. *Hargrove v. Trinity Universal Insurance Co.*, 256 S.W.2d 73, 75, 152 Tex. 243, 246 (1953). More recently, we have warned that the provisions of the Act "should not be hedged about with strict construction, but should be given a liberal construction to carry out its evident purpose." *Yeldell v. Holiday Hills Retirement & Nursing Center, Inc.*, 701 S.W.2d 243, 245 (Tex. 1985).

The obvious and stated purpose of the Act is to provide compensation to employees whose injuries "hav[e] to do with and originat[e] in the work, business, trade or profession of the employer. . . . " Art. 8309, § 1. Thus, we conclude that the court of appeals erred in holding that Lujan's death is not a compensable injury merely because the injury manifested itself at home. Mr. Lujan was on the job painting when he was soaked with paint. Still on the job, he tried to remove the paint with gasoline. Lujan went home to wash the gasoline and paint from his body. He was severely burned in a flash fire which occurred because of the substances on his body. He became covered with these substances, gasoline, paint, and paint thinner, while he was furthering the business of his employer. Although a delay of the action occurred, reasonable minds cannot differ that his injury "had to do with his work" as a painter, and the cause of his death "originated at his work" when he was covered with gasoline, paint, paint thinner, and surrounded by the fumes attendant to these liquids. The fact that the fumes ignited at home in his bathroom does not preclude the injury from being one sustained in the course of employment. Article 8309, section 1 specifically anticipates that injuries in the course of employment may occur "upon the employer's premises or elsewhere."

An employee is not deprived of the benefits of workers' compensation merely because he was not actually working when the accident occurred. Recently in *Yeldell v. Holiday Hills*, we allowed recovery for a claimant who was on the employer's premises, but was injured while making a personal phone call. We held, as a matter of law, that Ms. Yeldell was in the course of her employment.

In *Yeldell* we noted that often an employee, in the course of employment, reasonably performs acts of a personal nature for purposes of health and comfort. As examples, we listed quenching thirst or relieving hunger. In the case at bar, Lujan went home early to bathe because the gasoline, paint, and paint thinner were causing him personal discomfort and irritation, and needed to be removed from his skin. For this court to deny recovery to Lujan because he could not bathe at his place of employment, even though he was drenched with gasoline on the job, would work an absurd and unjust result. Such a holding would violate the liberal construction rules which favor the employee, and would defeat the obvious, evident, and stated purpose of the Workers' Compensation Act. While ordinarily the issue of course of employment is one for the fact-finder, under the undisputed facts of this case we hold as a matter of law that Lujan was in the course of his employment. . . .

§ 8.11   CONCLUSION: WORK CONNECTION AS MERGER OF "ARISING" AND "COURSE"

In practice, the "course of employment" and "arising out of employment" tests are not, and should not be, applied entirely independently; they are both parts of a single test of work-connection, and therefore deficiencies in the strength of one factor are sometimes allowed to be made up by strength in the other.

The discussion of the coverage formula, "arising out of and in the course of employment," was opened with the suggestion that, while "course" and "arising" were put under separate headings for convenience, some interplay between the two factors would be observed in the various categories discussed.

A few examples may now be reviewed to show that the two tests, in practice, have not been kept in air-tight compartments, but have to some extent merged into a single concept of work connection. One is almost tempted to formulate a sort of quantum theory of work connection: that a certain minimum quantum of work connection must be shown, and if the "course" quantity is very small, but the "arising" quantity is large, the quantum will add up to the necessary minimum, as it will also when the "arising" quantity is very small but the "course" quantity is relatively large. But if both the "course" and "arising" quantities are small, the minimum quantum will not be met.

As an example of the first, a strong "arising" factor but weak "course" factor, one may cite the cases in which recoveries have been allowed off the employment premises, outside business hours, when an employee going to or coming from work is injured by a hazard distinctly traceable to the employment,[16] such as a traffic jam overflowing from the employment premises.[17] Here, by normal course of employment standards, there would be no award, since the employee was not on the premises while coming or going. Yet the unmistakable character of the causal relation of the injury to the employment has been sufficient to make up for the weakness of the "course" factor.

Although the "course" factor is on the borderline when the employee is sound asleep at the time of injury, a strong causal relation of the injury to the conditions of employment — as when a fellow-logger runs amok,[18] or a straw falls into a bunkhouse-inmate's throat from the mattress above,[19] or the employee is trapped in a burning hotel[20] will boost the case over the line to success; while a weak causal connection, as when the salesperson merely slips in the hotel bath[21] coupled with the weak "course" factor due to the absence of any direct service performed for the employer at the time, will under many decisions add up to a quantum of work-connection too small to support an award. It was also shown that when the "course" element is strengthened by the fact that the employee is at all times on call, the range of compensable sources of injury is broader than when the employee, although living on the premises, is not on call.

As an example of the reverse situation, a strong "course" element and a weak "arising" element, one may recall the "positional" cases, as well as the unexplained-fall and other "neutral-cause" cases. Here the course of employment test is satisfied beyond the slightest doubt: the employee is in the midst of performing the active duties of his job. But the causal connection is very weak, since the source of the injury — whether a stray bullet, a wandering lunatic, an unexplained fall or death, or a mistaken assault by a stranger — is not distinctly associated with employment conditions as such, and is tied to the employment only by the argument that the injury would not have occurred to this employee but for the obligation of the employment which placed him in the position to be hurt. Yet, since the "course" element is so strong, awards are becoming increasingly common on these facts.

Incidentally, it may be observed that this "quantum" idea forms a useful yardstick for measuring just how generous a court has become in expanding compensation coverage; for if a court makes an award when a case, by the above standards, is weak both on course of employment and on causal connection, one can conclude that the court is capable of giving the act a broad construction. Thus, an award was made in *Puffin v. General Electric*, [22] where the course element was weak (rest period) and the causal element was weak (setting fire to own sweater while smoking). Both factors were

---

[16] *See, e.g.*, Frisbie v. Dept. of ILHR, 45 Wis. 2d 80, 172 N.W.2d 346 (1969).

[17] Freire v. Matson Nav. Co., 19 Cal. 2d 8, 118 P.2d 809 (1941).

[18] Kaiser Lumber Co. v. Industrial Comm'n, 181 Wis. 513, 195 N.W. 329 (1923).

[19] Holt v. Industrial Comm'n, 168 Wis. 381, 170 N.W. 366 (1919).

[20] Souza's Case, 316 Mass. 332, 55 N.E.2d 611 (1944).

[21] Davidson v. Pansy Waist Co., 240 N.Y. 584, 148 N.E. 715 (1925).

[22] Puffin v. General Electric, 132 Conn. 279, 43 A.2d 746 (1945).

likewise very weak in *O'Leary v. Brown-Pacific-Maxon Inc.*, [23] where the course of employment consisted of a recreation period interrupted by a rescue of a stranger, and the arising factor consisted of drowning in a channel where decedent was prohibited from going. And, in *Martin v. Plaut*, [24] the course of employment factor was weak (a cook dressing in the morning) and the causal factor was also weak (an unexplained fall); yet an award was made in New York.

But another New York case shows that the simultaneous weakness of course and arising factors may reach the point where the requisite quantum is not found. In *Shultz v. Nation Associates*, [25] compensation was denied to an employee who while combing her hair preparatory to going to lunch negligently struck her eye with the comb. Here we see thinness on all fronts: as to course of employment time factor, we have a lunch period; as to the course of employment activity factor, we have care of personal appearance; and as to the causal factor, we have negligence of the employee. Each weakness standing alone — lunch period, care of appearance, negligence — would not be fatal; there are many awards in which one or another of these is present. But when all are present, while an award is not impossible and could be defended on a point by point basis,[26] it can not be relied upon in most jurisdictions by the prudent lawyer.

The total "quantum" of work connection in such cases as the *O'Leary*, *Puffin*, and *Martin* cases just mentioned, by any common-sense standard, is far less than it would be in the case of a supervisor who angers a subordinate during working hours by firing him and later, while asleep on the sand at Jones Beach the following Sunday, is assaulted by the disgruntled ex-employee. Yet insistence on independent satisfaction of the "course" and "arising" tests results in an almost insuperable barrier to compensation for this unquestionably work-connected injury. If it could be openly admitted that very strong causal connection has been allowed in many situations to make up for a very weak course of employment case, a court might be justified in carrying this process to its logical conclusion and awarding compensation on the hypothetical facts just given, where course of employment is virtually non-existent, but causal relation of the injury to the employment is overwhelmingly strong.

---

[23] O'Leary v. Brown-Pacific-Maxon Inc., 340 U.S. 504, 71 S. Ct. 470, 95 L. Ed. 483 (1951), Ch. 8, § 8.09, *above.*

[24] Martin v. Plaut, 293 N.Y. 617, 59 N.E.2d 429 (1944).

[25] Shultz v. Nation Associates, 281 App. Div. 915, 119 N.Y.S.2d 673 (1953).

[26] *See* the dissent in Shultz v. Nation Associates, 281 App. Div. 915, 119 N.Y.S.2d 673 (1953).

Part 4

ACCIDENTAL INJURY AND DISEASE

Chapter 9
"PERSONAL INJURY BY ACCIDENT"

§ 9.01   MEANING OF "PERSONAL INJURY"

"Personal injury" includes any harmful change in the body. It need not involve physical trauma, but may include such injuries as disease, sunstroke, nervous collapse, traumatic neurosis, hysterical paralysis, and neurasthenia. A number of states by statute include injury to artificial members.

Roughly three-fourths of the state statutes use the term "personal injury" in the coverage clause, and about one-fourth use merely "injury." A few go on to define "injury" in various ways, such as "damage or harm to the physical structure of the body and a disease or infection naturally resulting from the damage or harm."[1]

There was at one time some controversy on whether various nontraumatic harms were "injuries," but it is now universally accepted that such injuries as disease and sunstroke come within the general term "injury" or "personal injury."

One of the best general definitions of "injury" was provided in an early Massachusetts opinion:

> In common speech the word "injury," as applied to a personal injury to a human being, includes whatever lesion or change in any part of the system produces harm or pain or a lessened facility of the natural use of any bodily activity or capability.[2]

Apart from special statute, injury to an artificial limb or member is not a personal injury. In *London Guarantee & Accident Company v. Industrial Commission*,[3] injury to the claimant's wooden leg was held to be a property loss, not a compensable harm to part of his person. Some acts specifically make allowance for such injury, and the extension of the concept of injury to prosthetic devices by statutory amendment has been proceeding rapidly. Since 1951, such coverage has been added or enlarged in more than sixteen states, including California,[4] Connecticut,[5] Illinois,[6] Pennsylvania,[7] and Wisconsin.[8]

---

[1] Texas Workmen's Compensation Law, Art. 8309, § 1.

[2] Burn's Case, 218 Mass. 8, 105 N.E. 601 (1914).

[3] London Guarantee & Accident Company v. Industrial Commission, 80 Colo. 162, 249 P. 642 (1926). *Accord*, Southern Elec., Inc. v. Spall, 130 So. 2d 279 (Fla. 1961).

[4] Cal. Laws 1953, Ch. 297.

A familiar and understandable condition of many of these provisions is that the damage to the eyeglasses or other device must have coincided with an otherwise compensable accident.[9] The obvious intent is that the wheels of compensation liability should not be set in motion every time a worker drops a pair of glasses, cracking the lenses.

In view of the high cost of prosthetic appliances, and the direct bearing they have on the performance of essential physical functions, statutes of the type discussed above seems well within the central purpose of compensation legislation.

§ 9.02 MEANING OF "BY ACCIDENT"

[1] Introduction

"By accident," a phrase which in some form is found in most statutes, means "by an unlooked for mishap or an untoward event which is not expected or designed."

[2] Summary of Statutory "By Accident" Provisions

The requirement that the injury be accidental in character has been adopted either legislatively or judicially by all but nine states.[10] The usual statutory phrase, taken from the original British act, is injury "by accident." This phrase occurs in the statutes of a majority of states.[11] Nine states,[12] the District of Columbia, and the Longshore Act use the phrase "accidental injury." A few of these statutes go on to enlarge upon or define the meaning of "by accident" or "accidental," and therefore the general analysis in this chapter of the meaning of these words must be read subject to any such specific definition. The Ohio Code introduces the "accidental" factor by defining injury to include "any injury, whether caused by external accidental means or accidental in character and result." Montana and Washington chose their own wording, the former preferring "unexpected or unforeseen identifiable event or series of events from an unexpected cause" and the latter "any harmful change in the human organism other than normal aging."

In three states, Michigan, West Virginia, and Wyoming, the basic coverage clause contains no explicit accident requirement, but the word "accident" is used elsewhere in the statute, usually as fixing the time from which the period runs in which notice of injury may be given or claim made. The courts of these three states read "accidental" into the coverage clause,[13] but Michigan has virtually read it back out again.[14]

---

[5] Conn., Act 491 (1961) includes damage to eyeglasses if personal injury also results.

[6] Ill., S. 775 (1961).

[7] Pa., Act 440 (1961).

[8] Wis. Laws 1963, Ch. 281, adds damage to a hearing aid if personal injury results from the same accident.

[9] Geiger v. Bell Aerosystems Co. Div., 28 A.D.2d 178, 283 N.Y.S.2d 906 (1967). Claimant bumped his head while at work, and broke his glasses. However, there was no bodily injury. In the absence of injury, the employer was held not liable for the replacement of the glasses.

[10] California, Colorado, Iowa, Maine, Massachusetts, Minnesota, Pennsylvania, Rhode Island, and South Dakota. The United States Employees' Compensation Act also omits the requirement.

[11] *E.g.*, Alabama, Arizona, and Florida.

[12] *E.g.*, Alaska, Arkansas, and Connecticut.

[13] Marlowe v. Huron Mountain Club, 271 Mich. 107, 260 N.W. 130 (1935); Archibald v. Compensation Comm'r, 77 W. Va. 448, 87 S.E. 791, L.R.A. 1916D, 1013 (1916); Pero v. Collier-Latimer, Inc., 49 Wyo. 131, 52 P.2d 690 (1935).

[14] Sheppard v. Michigan Nat'l Bank, 348 Mich. 577, 83 N.W.2d 614 (1957).

[3] Component Elements of the "By Accident" Concept

The basic and indispensable ingredient of "accident" is unexpectedness.[15] The first leading English case, *Fenton v. Thorley & Co., Ltd.*,[16] embodied this factor in the following definition: "an unlooked for mishap or an untoward event which is not expected or designed."

A second ingredient, however, has been added in most jurisdictions: The injury must be traceable, within reasonable limits, to a definite time, place, and occasion or cause. The justification of this widespread addition is not entirely clear. When the phrase "accidental injury" is used, or the equivalent phrase "injury by accident," there is no occasion, as a matter of grammar, to read the phrase as if it referred to "*an* accident," and then proceed to conduct a search for "*the* accident." In the original British formula, "personal injury by accident arising out of and in the course of the employment," and in the many statutes which have adopted this exact wording, the phrase "by accident" clearly is a modifier meaning the same as "accidental."[17] True, the wording in some state acts has been sufficiently altered so that "accident" has become the noun in the formula, itself modified by the "arising" phrase — but this is not true of the formula in its original and commonest version. Of course, once one reads "by accident" or "accidental" as meaning "by *an* accident," it is natural to begin to look for some single incident or event, and this is precisely what many courts have done. One of the pervading problems, then, that cuts through much of the abundant controversy about the meaning of "accident," is the degree to which definiteness of time or occasion characterizes the concept.

The greatest source of controversy, however, lies in the "accidental-cause versus accidental-result" problem. Its most familiar manifestation is the "usual-exertion" case. Consider the example of a man who, for years, has lifted 100-pound sacks many times a day. He suffers a heart attack while lifting one in the usual way, and medical testimony confirms that the heavy lift did in fact cause the attack. At once it becomes apparent that a court can announce a definition of accident as an "untoward event" or "unlooked-for mishap" without necessarily having committed itself on this exact combination of facts. It depends on whether the unlooked-for item is the cause or the effect. If it is the cause — the outward circumstances immediately preceding the injury — nothing unexpected can be shown. But if it is the result on this individual that may be unlooked-for, then the injury can be described as accidental.

A similar two-way meaning is implicit in the requirement of definite time or occasion — although the part played by this ambiguity is less well understood. When a court has said that the injury must be "sustained on some definite occasion, the date of which can be fixed with reasonable certainty," one must again ask the same question: Does the court mean the cause or the effect? The cause may be gradual and imperceptible, as in exposure to dust or poison, leading to a result which is very definite as to time: a sudden collapse at a particular moment. Conversely, the cause may be abrupt, as in a brief exposure to severe chilling, with the result being protracted — gradual succumbing to pneumonia, for example. Or both the cause and result may be gradual, as when the exposure is protracted, and, instead of leading to a clean-cut collapse, it leads only to a dragged-out disease.

The potential component parts of the accident concept, under the usual statutory language, may therefore be broken down as follows:

(1) Unexpectedness

---

[15] "Event without apparent cause, unexpected event; unintentional act, chance, . . . mishap." POCKET OXFORD DICTIONARY, 6 (1926 ed.).

[16] Fenton v. Thorley & Co., Ltd., [1903] A.C. 443.

[17] "It was held that 'injury by accident' meant nothing more than 'accidental injury'. . . . " Lord MacNaghten in Clover, Clayton & Co. v. Hughes, [1910] A.C. 242, 248, 3 B.W.C.C. 775.

    (a)   of cause

    (b)   of result

(2)   Definite time

    (a)   of cause

    (b)   of result

If both parts of both elements are satisfied, one has the clearest example of a typical industrial accident, in the colloquial sense: collisions, explosions, slips, falls, and the like, leading to obvious traumatic injuries.

At the other extreme, if all elements are missing, one sees the typical occupational disease. The cause is characteristic harmful conditions of the particular industry. The result is a kind of disability which is not unexpected if work under these conditions continues for a long time. And the development is usually gradual and imperceptible over an extended period.

Between the two extremes lie the combinations which are the subject of the ensuing sections, and which have produced and are continuing to produce a tremendous volume of litigation in all jurisdictions whose statutes require proof of injury by accident.

[4] Accident and Disease

The place of "disease" in workers' compensation law has always been a troublesome question, with most of the difficulty stemming from the "by accident" requirement. Compensation law has come a long way since the time when some courts apparently thought of "accident" and "disease" as mutually exclusive, so that claims could be ruled out by some such statement as that the injury was the result of disease, not accident. Some of the major categories in which awards for disease figure in the following pages are these: preexisting disease (chiefly heart disease) precipitated by the exertions of the employment; diseases of exposure, brought on by employment conditions such as cold, heat, and dampness; diseases gradually acquired by repeated inhalations or impacts over periods ranging from a few hours to a number of years; infectious or contagious diseases, acquired sometimes suddenly and sometimes gradually; and, finally, occupational diseases caused by exposure over a protracted period to the routine harmful conditions of the particular employment.

The compensability of disease also comes up in two other connections which are not sufficiently controversial to require separate discussion, but which are touched on incidentally. It is generally agreed, either under express statutes or by judicial decision, that any disease is compensable which follows as a natural consequence of an injury which qualifies independently as accidental. This is nothing more than a recognition of the rule that the injury embraces all the results that flow directly from it, whether infection, disease, insanity, or anything else. There may always be controversy on causal relation, of course, when, for example, a person hospitalized by traumatic injury dies of pneumonia; but there is no serious "by accident" issue. The second type of clear case is that in which the disease is the direct result of some identifiable mishap or breakage of equipment on the job, as when a diver's air-line breaks and the diver gets the bends.[18] In such cases, accidental quality is supplied by the obvious external event and compensation is almost invariably awarded without any serious hesitation because of the fact that the injury takes the form of "disease."

---

[18] Beaty v. Foundation Co., 245 Mich. 256, 222 N.W. 77 (1928).

WINN v. HORMEL & CO.
560 N.W.2d 143 (Neb. 1997)

GERRARD, JUSTICE.

Marilyn A. Winn, widow of Larry D. Winn (decedent), petitioned the Nebraska Workers' Compensation Court for benefits because of the decedent's sudden cardiac arrest and death while he was at work at the Geo. A. Hormel & Co. (Hormel) plant in Fremont, Nebraska. Winn alleged that the decedent's death was caused by the Hormel plant nurse's failure to timely diagnose and treat the decedent's symptoms of a heart attack. Following a trial, a single judge of the compensation court dismissed Winn's petition, finding that although the decedent suffered a fatal heart attack while on his employer's premises and during the hours of his employment, the heart attack was not an accident which arose out of and in the course of his employment with Hormel within the meaning of Neb. Rev. Stat. § 48-101 (Reissue 1993). The trial court further found that the term "accident," as defined in the Nebraska Workers' Compensation Act, does not include any omission by the plant nurse with respect to treatment of an accident and injury that has already occurred. A review panel of the compensation court affirmed the trial court's order of dismissal. This appeal follows.

We note that Winn initially filed a cause of action in the district court for Dodge County, alleging common-law negligence on the part of Hormel, by and through its employee-plant nurse for failure to timely diagnose and treat the decedent's symptoms of a heart attack. The district court sustained Hormel's demurrer and dismissed the suit, finding Winn's exclusive remedy to be workers' compensation. Winn appealed the district court's dismissal order, and the disposition of that appeal is pending our determination in the present case.

Thus, the posture of the instant case requires us to decide whether the nurse's alleged negligent medical treatment was an "accident," as defined in Neb. Rev. Stat. § 48-151(2) (Reissue 1993), that caused or contributed to the decedent's death, such that Winn's exclusive remedy is under the Nebraska Workers' Compensation Act. Because we conclude that negligent medical treatment, at an employer's first-aid medical facility, by a trained and qualified professional upon a coemployee may constitute an "accident" upon proof and a finding of such facts, we reverse the compensation court's judgment of dismissal and remand the cause to the compensation court for specific findings of fact in light of our holding.

FACTUAL BACKGROUND

The decedent, Larry Winn, was a longtime employee of Hormel at its hog processing plant in Fremont. On the date of his death, the decedent's shift at Hormel began at 4 a.m., with a lunch break from approximately 10 to 10:36 a.m. After his lunch break, at about 11:30 a.m., the decedent began experiencing symptoms of what he thought was indigestion. The decedent sought treatment from the plant nurse, Lucy Klocke.

At about 11:30 a.m., after attending to another patient at the decedent's insistence, Klocke questioned the decedent about his symptoms. The decedent told Klocke that he thought he had indigestion and reported that he was experiencing chest pressure and aching in his arms. Klocke took the decedent's blood pressure and found it to be higher than normal. However, Klocke found the decedent's respiration and heart rates to be near normal. Klocke said that while in her office, the decedent did not seem to be in distress and that during this time, the decedent conversed normally with other coworkers.

Klocke testified that she told the decedent he was suffering from angina and heart problems, and should contact his doctor. Klocke said she offered to contact the security guards and have them take the decedent to the hospital emergency room. Klocke stated that the decedent refused her offer and instead chose to rest in her office. After about

15 minutes, Klocke again checked the decedent's blood pressure, respiration rate, and pulse rate. Although the decedent's blood pressure was still higher than normal, it had decreased from its former reading. Klocke testified that at approximately 11:50 a.m., the decedent elected to return to work and left her office.

At 11:55 a.m., the decedent was found in the smokehouse, collapsed face down in a caustic soda solution that he had been draining from a tank. Klocke was summoned to the scene and immediately began cardiopulmonary resuscitation on the decedent. The Fremont rescue squad was called, and when it arrived a short time later, emergency medical technicians relieved Klocke and continued resuscitation efforts on the decedent.

Because the decedent had collapsed onto a metal walkway and was lying in a pool of caustic soda liquid, the medical technicians were unable to use their defibrillation equipment to resuscitate him. According to one of the medical technicians, the best course of treatment was to transport the decedent to the hospital emergency room. Upon arrival at the emergency room, the attending physician decided that the decedent had been without a pulse for too long and could not be revived. Thus, the physician did not initiate defibrillation and pronounced the decedent dead.

At the hearing before the single judge, Winn's nursing expert testified that Klocke's care of the decedent was violative of the standard of care for a professional registered nurse. Winn's cardiology expert, Dr. George Sojka, testified that based upon the record, the decedent was suffering a myocardial infarction while he was in the nurse's office and this myocardial infarction precipitated the subsequent cardiac dysrhythmia which resulted in his death. Dr. Sojka stated that the symptoms presented by the decedent to Klocke were the classic symptoms of a heart attack. Dr. Sojka testified that Klocke should have had the decedent stay in her office and should have immediately called the rescue squad or the decedent's physician. Dr. Sojka opined that the decedent's heart attack would have been survivable had he received immediate treatment. Dr. Sojka estimated the decedent's chances for survival at 80 to 90 percent had he received cardiac care prior to the onset of the dysrhythmia. It was Dr. Sojka's opinion that Klocke's failure to call the decedent's physician or the rescue squad immediately upon diagnosing the decedent's heart involvement contributed significantly to his death.

Hormel's cardiology expert, Dr. Thomas Sears, essentially agreed with Winn's expert that the decedent's death resulted from a myocardial infarction followed by dysrhythmia and circulatory arrest and that in all likelihood, it was a recoverable infarction. However, Dr. Sears was critical of the care that the decedent received from the emergency medical technicians and the emergency room physician. A nursing expert testified, on behalf of Hormel, that Klocke met or exceeded the appropriate standard of care for an occupational health nurse because she was still assessing the decedent when he suffered his cardiac arrest and that Klocke was under no duty to persuade the decedent to stay in the nurse's office or to call a physician or the rescue squad.

In its order of dismissal, the trial court found that (1) Winn's evidence was insufficient to establish legal cause because no evidence was adduced indicating the decedent's heart attack was caused by a stress or exertion greater than what the decedent or any other person would have experienced in ordinary nonemployment and (2) the decedent's heart attack was not an accident which arose out of and in the course of his employment with Hormel.

. . . .

ASSIGNMENTS OF ERROR

Summarized and restated, Winn's 15 assigned errors essentially contend that the compensation court erred in (1) determining that the term "accident," as defined in § 48-151(2) and as used in § 48-101, does not include "any omission on the part of a coemployee with respect to treatment of an accident and injury that has already occurred"; (2) failing to consider that the "accident" in the instant case was the plant nurse's failure to timely diagnose and treat the decedent's symptoms of a heart attack; and (3) sustaining certain objections raised in the depositions of the expert witnesses. The disposition of this case requires that we review only Winn's first two assigned errors.

ANALYSIS

Winn first asserts that she was effectively precluded from pursuing her theory of liability because the trial court failed to acknowledge the basis of her claim — that the decedent's injury was his death, and the "accident" which caused this injury was both the negligent nursing care provided by Hormel's employee and the inability of the emergency medical technicians to defibrillate and resuscitate the decedent, occasioned by the conditions of his employment. Winn contends that this is not the typical workers' compensation heart attack case, where the claimant's burden is to show that exertion or stress in his employment contributed in some material and substantial degree to cause the heart injury. See, e.g., *Toombs v. Driver Mgmt., Inc.*, 248 Neb. 1016, 540 N.W.2d 592 (1995).

The dispositive issue in this appeal is whether negligent medical treatment by a trained medical employee upon a coemployee can itself be an "accident," as defined in § 48-151(2). More specifically, the issue is whether a medical employee's negligent failure to diagnose or treat a coemployee's medical condition, regardless of the source of the illness or injury, can be considered an "accident" if there is a sufficient causal connection between the negligence and the death or disability for which compensation is sought. If our answer is in the affirmative, then Winn's exclusive remedy is under the Nebraska Workers' Compensation Act, and the compensation court would be obligated to make further findings of fact determining whether (1) the plant nurse contributed to the decedent's death with negligent medical treatment and (2) the element of causation has been satisfied in the instant case.

The following colloquy, after a relevancy objection early in the trial, is illustrative of the separate paths taken by Winn and the trial court regarding this crucial issue.

[WINN's COUNSEL]: Your Honor, this whole case is based upon a delay of recognizing symptoms and a delay in treatment and a delay that caused death.

[TRIAL] COURT: I understand that, and I've tried to explain to you in my estimation, a review court or review panel of this court or Court of Appeal or Supreme Court may tell me I'm in error, but in my estimation it is not germane.

[TRIAL] COURT: . . . [M]y point is whether there's a nurse, whether there's negligence on the part of the employee, whether there's negligence on the part of the employer or an employee is not germane to this issue. The question is did he have a heart attack, what caused the heart attack, did the heart attack cause his death.

[WINN's COUNSEL]: No, Your Honor, that is not the — what this case is about at all.

[TRIAL] COURT: I understand that we disagree on that, but I've sustained the objection.

Under the provisions of the Nebraska Workers' Compensation Act, compensation is allowed when personal injury is caused to an employee by an accident or occupational disease, arising out of and in the course of his or her employment, if the employee was not willfully negligent at the time of receiving such injury. § 48-101.

Under § 48-151(2), an accident is defined as "an unexpected or unforeseen injury happening suddenly and violently, with or without human fault, and producing at the time objective symptoms of an injury." The "unexpected or unforeseen" requirement of

§ 48-151(2) is satisfied if either the cause was of an accidental character or the effect was unexpected or unforeseen. *Schlup v. Auburn Needleworks*, 239 Neb. 854, 479 N.W.2d 440 (1992).

The second specification of § 48-151(2) requires that an employee's injury must occur "suddenly and violently" to be compensable. This court has held that "suddenly and violently" does not mean instantaneously and with force. The specification of "suddenly and violently" is satisfied if the injury occurs at an identifiable point in time, requiring the employee to discontinue employment and seek medical treatment. *Schlup v. Auburn Needleworks, supra*. See, also, *Sandel v. Packaging Co. of America*, 211 Neb. 149, 317 N.W.2d 910 (1982). We recognized in Sandel that the nature of the human body being such as it is, not all injuries to the body are caused instantaneously and with force, but may indeed nevertheless occur suddenly and violently, even though they have been building up for a considerable period of time and do not manifest themselves until they cause the employee to be unable to continue his or her employment.

Winn claims that the compensation court erred by not analyzing the term "accident" in its correct perspective. We agree. Hormel maintained an emergency first-aid medical facility for the convenience and welfare of its employees. The facility was staffed by a nurse, and care was provided to all employees regardless of the source of their illness or injury. During working hours, the decedent suffered physical distress and went to the nursing office for aid. The visit to Hormel's nursing office certainly is incidental to and arose out of the decedent's employment; i.e., the decedent's contact with Klocke was at a nursing office to which only employees are admitted, and, furthermore, the decedent would not have been examined by Klocke unless he was an employee of Hormel, as was Klocke. See *Dixon v. Ford Motor Co.*, 53 Cal. App. 3d 499, 125 Cal. Rptr. 872 (1975).

We determine that when an employer provides an emergency first-aid medical facility staffed by a licensed medical professional, the employer, by and through its licensed professional employee, owes a duty of reasonable care to those employees that present themselves for emergency medical services at the place of employment. See *Critchfield v. McNamara*, 248 Neb. 39, 532 N.W.2d 287 (1995). This duty of reasonable care is owed to each employee regardless of the source of illness or injury, since healthy workers are of benefit to both the employer and all employees. See *Dixon v. Ford Motor Co., supra*.

The evidence suggests that the decedent was suffering a myocardial infarction while he was first in the nurse's office. However, the injury which is the basis of the instant claim is not the initial myocardial infarction, but, rather, the subsequent cardiac dysrhythmia and circulatory arrest which resulted in the decedent's death.

Certainly, the decedent's cardiac arrest 5 minutes after the decedent had departed from the nursing office was unexpected and unforeseen to both Klocke and the decedent. Further, the cardiac arrest clearly occurred at an identifiable point in time which would have required the decedent to discontinue employment and seek medical treatment had he survived. See *Schlup v. Auburn Needleworks, supra*. The trial court erred when it characterized the alleged negligence of Klocke as an "omission on the part of a co-employee with respect to treatment of an accident and injury that has already occurred." (Emphasis supplied.) The "accident" allegedly occurred when Klocke failed to timely diagnose and treat the decedent's symptoms of a heart attack which, in turn, aggravated, accelerated, or combined with the preexisting heart condition to produce the death for which compensation is sought.

. . . .

We hold that negligent medical treatment, at an employer's first-aid medical facility, by a trained and qualified professional upon a coemployee, may constitute an "accident" as defined in § 48-151(2) upon proof and a finding of such facts. However, in view of the conflicting medical evidence regarding the effect of Klocke's actions, our holding does not conclusively establish that Winn has met the requisite burden of persuasion in this case.

To recover compensation benefits, an injured worker is required to prove by competent medical testimony a causal connection between the alleged injury, the employment, and the disability. *Schlup v. Auburn Needleworks*, 239 Neb. 854, 479 N.W.2d 440 (1992). Further, in a workers' compensation case involving a preexisting condition, the claimant must prove by a preponderance of evidence that the claimed injury or disability was caused by the claimant's employment and is not merely the progression of a condition present before the employment-related incident alleged as the cause of the disability. Such claimant may recover when an injury, arising out of and in the course of employment, combines with a preexisting condition to produce disability, notwithstanding that in the absence of the preexisting condition no disability would have resulted. *Cox v. Fagen Inc.*, 249 Neb. 677, 545 N.W.2d 80 (1996). Thus, the compensation court shall be obligated to make further findings of fact to determine whether (1) Klocke contributed to the decedent's death with negligent medical treatment and (2) the element of causation has been satisfied in the instant case.

CONCLUSION

Because the compensation court erroneously concluded that the term "accident," as defined in § 48-151(2), did not include alleged negligent acts by Hormel's nurse in timely diagnosing and treating the decedent's symptoms of a heart attack, the findings of fact made by the trial court are insufficient to support the order of dismissal in the instant case. Accordingly, we vacate the compensation court's judgment of dismissal and remand the cause to the compensation court with the direction that the judge conducting the initial hearing make new findings of fact and enter an order consistent with those findings on the evidence adduced, and for such further review thereof as the parties may institute under law.

Judgment Vacated, and Cause Remanded with Directions.

§ 9.03   INJURY FROM USUAL EXERTION OR EXPOSURE

The "by accident" requirement is now deemed satisfied in most jurisdictions either if the cause was of an accidental character or if the effect was the unexpected result of routine performance of the claimant's duties. Accordingly, if the strain of claimant's usual exertions causes collapse from heart weakness, back weakness, hernia, and the like, the injury is held accidental. A substantial minority of jurisdictions require a showing that the exertion was in some way unusual, or make other reservations, but this line of decision causes difficulty because of the constant necessity of drawing distinctions between usual and unusual strains. When routine exposure leads to freezing or sunstroke, it is usually held accidental, but when the result is pneumonia, tuberculosis, or other disease caused by exposure, a majority deem the occurrence nonaccidental.

Let us return to the earlier-mentioned fact situation in exertion cases, in which the claimant's duties for years have required the lifting of heavy sacks onto a platform. One day, while lifting a sack of the usual size, the claimant suddenly experiences a severe pain. Medical testimony establishes that the claimant had a weak heart, and that the strain of lifting precipitated the collapse of the heart.

The only question here is whether the collapse is "by accident." Note that, under the facts as given, the injury arose in the course of and out of the employment, since, as shown in an earlier section, it is sufficient in practically all jurisdictions to prove that the employment precipitated the disabling injury, even if the employee had a contributing preexisting weakness.

A long battle has been fought, and is still being fought, in the United States on this issue. The issue, in theoretical terms, is whether a court in construing "by accident" will require an accidental cause or will be satisfied with an accidental result. In practical terms, the issue is whether injury is accidental when it is the unexpected consequence of the usual exertion or exposure of the particular employee's job: A delivery person's routine heavy lift produces a hernia; a freight loader accustomed to handling heavy boxes suffers a cerebral hemorrhage while lifting a normal-sized box; a police officer runs after a fugitive and has a coronary thrombosis; a firefighter becomes encased in ice while fighting a fire in winter and dies of pneumonia.

As a matter of theory, it might be thought that each jurisdiction would take its stand on this cause-result issue, so that one could make up a neat list saying: The following jurisdictions accept as accidental any routine exertion or exposure leading to unexpected harm, and the following do not, and therefore the one or the other is the majority rule. Unfortunately this cannot be done. The reason is that the two parts of the accident concept — unexpectedness and definiteness — do not in practice seem to remain distinct. Logical or not, a usual exertion leading to a clean-cut result such as a rupture may be held accidental while an identical usual exertion leading to some more generalized result such as "heart failure" may not. Similarly, a usual exposure causing sunstroke or freezing may be held accidental while an identical usual exposure leading to pneumonia may not. The preponderance of the authorities on whether the effects of the usual conditions of employment can be considered accidental varies according to the definiteness of the harm produced.

GUIDRY v. SLINE INDUSTRIAL PAINTERS, INC.
418 So. 2d 626 (La. 1982)

CALOGERO, JUSTICE.

Plaintiff's husband, an industrial painter, died shortly after suffering a heart attack on his job. It was an acute myocardial infarction secondary to atherosclerotic heart disease.

The narrow question in this workmen's compensation case is whether the admitted accident (heart attack) which caused Mr. Guidry's death, to be compensable, must in some degree have been causally related to physical stress, strain, or exertion of the job; and if so whether Guidry's heart attack was related, in part, to work stress, strain, or exertion.

Alcide Guidry, a fifty-three-year-old industrial painter, suffered an acute myocardial infarction secondary to atherosclerotic heart disease minutes after pausing for a smoke break while at work. After a trial on the merits, the judge denied recovery both for compensation benefits and for penalties and attorney's fees.

We affirm the Court of Appeal judgment in favor of plaintiff. . . .

This burden of plaintiff's is to show by a preponderance of the evidence that the work effort, stress or strain in reasonable probability contributed in some degree to the heart accident. Anything less and it can hardly be said that the accident arose out of the employment or that the employment in any measure contributed to the accident.

If the physical exertion, stress, or strain on the job, and preceding the infarction, is no more than the worker would likely have experienced in a non-work situation, the attack may be the result of the natural progression of the pre-existing disease rather than the result of the employment activity.

This reality has led Professor Larson to suggest a rule which we draw upon to resolve this amorphous legal problem. *See generally:* 1B. A. Larson, Workmen's Compensation § 38.83, 7-233 (1980)

For the heart accident to arise out of or be connected with the employment, the exertion stress or strain, acting upon the *pre-existing* disease, must be of a degree greater than that generated in everyday non-employment life.[19] (*e.g.*, as compared to

---

[19] *(Court's footnote)* In particular, Professor Larson notes at 7-237:

If there is some personal causal contribution *in the form of a previously weakened or diseased*

the more or less sedentary life of the average non-worker).

In other words if the activities in which the worker with a pre-existing heart disease is engaged, whether for his job usual and customary or not, entail exertion, stress or strain greater than would be involved in everyday non-employment life and he experiences a heart accident, he has made a prima facie showing that the accident arose out of or was connected with, the employment.

However, simply being at work on the job is not enough, since at the time of and for an appreciable period before the accident such worker (i.e., with a pre-existing heart disease) may not have been engaged in his usual stressful activities, or his usual work may have been of a sedentary nature, or may have involved no physical stress or exertion beyond that generated in everyday non-employment life. In either of these latter cases, it is difficult to say that the accident arose out of the worker's employment rather than that the accident arose out of or was prompted simply by the pre-existing heart disease.

Now we turn to the facts of this case. Guidry was fifty-three years old. He had done manual work most of his life. He was employed as an industrial painter through the union by Sline Industrial Painters and assigned to Cities Service Refinery in Calcasieu Parish, Louisiana. On December 28, 1979, the day he sustained the myocardial infarction Guidry had reported for work at 7:30 a.m., as was customary. He and a Mr. Duplechain were assigned the task of painting large rolling doors on a warehouse. They were using a single ladder ten to twelve feet tall. The top portions of the doors which were out of reach to a painter working on the ground were painted by Duplechain, Guidry's role being to brace the ladder to assure Duplechain's safety, and to move the ladder as required. The areas of the doors accessible from the ground were painted by the two men. The pair had worked non-stop from 7:30 a.m. until the noon lunch break, with only a ten minute break during that time at 10:00 a.m. The pair again commenced working after the lunch break and worked until approximately 2:00 p.m.

At 2:00 p.m. the pair, along with some of the other workmen in the area, went inside the building that was being painted to a rest area for a work break. It was at this time that Guidry suffered the heart attack. It caused him to fall from his chair to the ground, unconscious. Mr. Guidry never regained consciousness and died seven days later in the hospital.

Guidry's co-workers, in testifying, stated that Guidry seemed in good health that day and showed no signs of illness. Guidry did not regain consciousness after the incident, so he was unable to tell anyone of any ill feelings he might have been having earlier in the day.

The trial court relied upon the testimony of the treating physicians, Drs. Reichert, Seale and Turner, who were of the opinion that the heart attack was not causally related to the decedent's usual and customary actions or exertions on the job. However, Drs. Reichert and Seale are not heart specialists, the former being a specialist in family practice and the latter a surgery specialist. And Dr. Turner, a heart specialist, when presented with a more accurate hypothetical of Mr. Guidry's activities on the day in

heart, the employment contribution must take the form of an exertion greater than that of nonemployment life. . . . Note that the comparison is not with *this employee's* usual exertion *in his employment* but with the exertions of normal *nonemployment* life of this or any other person.

If there is no personal causal contribution, that is, if there is no prior weakness or disease, *any* exertion connected with the employment and causally connected with the collapse as a matter of medical fact is adequate to satisfy the *legal* test of causation. This is the heart-case application of the actual risk test: *This* exertion in fact causally contributed to *this* collapse.

In both situations, with or without prior personal weakness or disease, the claimant must also show that *medically* the particular exertion contributed causally to the heart attack.

question, admitted that there *could* be some relationship between the described physical activity and the heart attack.

Furthermore, the testimony that the heart attack was not work related was contradicted by the testimony of a cardiovascular specialist presented by plaintiff, Dr. Fastabend. Dr. Fastabend stated that in his opinion the physical exertion of the decedent on that day was such that there was no question in his mind but that the physical activity in which the deceased had been involved triggered the heart attack. Although it is true that Dr. Fastabend was not the decedent's treating physician, he was no less qualified than the other medical witnesses to render an opinion concerning stress and exertion, infarction, and the causal relationship, particularly inasmuch as the patient's unconsciousness and inability to communicate following the accident would tend to reduce the advantage a treating physician might otherwise have had.

Guidry came to work early that morning. He had performed physical and fairly strenuous work for most of the day. He had returned to his duties right after lunch and he continued to work until minutes before the attack. Our appreciation of the evidence in this case prompts us to conclude that Guidry's activities while working on the fateful day of his heart attack, were marked by stress, exertion, and strain greater than that generated in everyday non-employment life, and greater than that generated in the more or less sedentary life of the average non-worker.

We conclude that Guidry's myocardial infarction, and ensuing death, arose out of his employment. His widow, the plaintiff, is therefore entitled to such workers' compensation benefits as the law provides.

PROBLEMS

(1) The author's proposed test in heart cases, cited in *Guidry* at N.19, *above*, has been criticized on the ground that a heart attack cannot happen as a result of exertion unless there is prior heart disease. Appraise the validity of this criticism.

(2) What is the distinction between medical causation and legal causation in the heart, back, and related cases?

(3) How is the disposition of these cases affected by whether the state's coverage formula contains the words "by accident"?

§ 9.04 DEFINITE TIME VERSUS GRADUAL INJURY: CUMULATIVE TRAUMA

[1] Introduction

Most jurisdictions will regard the time of accident as sufficiently definite if either the cause is reasonably limited in time or the result materializes at an identifiable point. In the absence of definiteness in time of either cause or effect, as when repeated impacts or inhalations gradually produce disability, many courts find accident by treating each impact or inhalation as a separate accident.

[2] Repeated Exposure to Harmful Substances

MARQUEZ v. INDUSTRIAL COMMISSION
110 Ariz. 273, 517 P.2d 1269 (1974)

STRUCKMEYER, JUSTICE.

On May 30, 1968, Ramon Marquez died, and thereafter his widow, Maria, filed a claim for death benefits under Arizona's Workmen's Compensation Act. Her claim was denied by the Industrial Commission, and she brought certiorari. The Court of Appeals affirmed the award of a non-compensable claim, Marquez v. Industrial Commission, 19 Ariz. App. 139, 505 P.2d 577 (1973). We accepted review. Decision of the Court of Appeals vacated and the award of the Industrial Commission set aside.

Ramon Marquez worked for Magma Copper Company, San Manuel Division, continuously from October 1955 until shortly before his death on May 30, 1968. Prior to working for Magma, decedent had worked as an underground miner at a number of copper, lead and zinc mines. He worked for Magma underground from October 1955 until the middle of May 1958, about 832 shifts. During this time he was exposed to harmful quantities of silicon dioxide dust. Thereafter, and until May 17, 1968, Marquez worked above-ground as a laborer, where he was not exposed to harmful quantities of dust. Marquez died of heart failure described medically as corpulmonale. The cardiac failure was concededly induced by the undue strain placed upon the heart because of the long-standing fibrotic condition of the lungs.

Silicosis is classified by the Legislature as an occupational disease, A.R.S. § 23-1102, but to be compensable the statute (§ 23-1107 B) requires exposure to harmful quantities of silicon dioxide dust for 1200 work shifts within the ten years immediately preceding the death. Since the Commission denied Maria compensation for death benefits, it must have found the heart failure caused by the fibrotic condition of the lungs was not a compensable industrial accident under Arizona's Workmen's Compensation Law.

By the Constitution of Arizona, Article 18, § 8, A.R.S., compensation must be paid to a workman engaged in manual or mechanical labor and to his dependents in case of his death "if in the course of such employment personal injury to or death of any such workman from any *accident* arising out of and in the course of, such employment,. . . . " (Emphasis added.) The precise question presented, therefore, is whether a physical condition of a workman defined by the Legislature as a disease, which is caused, at least in part, by the workman's employment, can be considered accidental so as to compel payment of compensation under Arizona's Constitution.

We first note that a disease is defined in general as any departure from a state of health. *See* The American Illustrated Medical Dictionary, Dorland (22d Ed.). So that the categorization of a condition as a disease by the Legislature does not necessarily exclude the condition as compensable under the Constitution, Article 18, § 8. As Larson says:

> Compensation law has come a long way since the time when some courts apparently thought of "accident" and "disease" as mutually exclusive, so that claims could be ruled out by some such statement as that the injury was the result of disease, not accident. . . . It is generally agreed, either under express statutes or by judicial decision, that any disease is compensable which follows as a natural consequence of an injury which qualifies independently as accidental. This is nothing more than a recognition of the rule that the injury embraces all the results that flow directly from it, whether infection, disease, insanity, or anything else. There may always be controversy on causal relation, of course, when, for example, a man hospitalized by traumatic injury dies of pneumonia; but there is no serious "by accident" issue. Vol. 1A Workmen's Compensation Law, § 37.30.

This Court held in *Dunlap v. Industrial Commission*, 90 Ariz. 3, 6, 363 P.2d 600, 602 (1961), that pneumonia contracted through the inhalation of tractor fumes was compensable, saying:

> At an early date a majority of jurisdictions in this country steadfastly held that to constitute an "accident" within the meaning of the usual Workmen's Compensation Act there must have been a sudden, unexpected or violent event resulting in injury. This was the rule in Arizona after *Pierce v. Phelps Dodge Corporation*, 42 Ariz. 436, 26 P.2d 1017, which held that the word "accident" referred to a sudden and unexpected event which must have occurred to give

rise to the right of compensation. However, the case of *In re Mitchell, supra,* [61 Ariz. 436, 150 P.2d 355] later liberalized this restrictive rule and held that although accidental injury usually involved a sudden happening caused by some violent or external means such as traumatic injury, an industrial accident need not be an instantaneous happening and violence is not a prerequisite of the right to compensation.

And we also said:

The terms "disease" and "accident" are no longer considered mutually exclusive. Any disease is compensable under our statute which follows as a natural consequence of any injury which has qualified independently as accidental. *Dunlap, supra,* 90 Ariz. at 8, 363 P.2d at 603.

As early as 1944, in *In re Mitchell,* 61 Ariz. 436, 150 P.2d 355 (1944), this Court held that the inhalation of carbon tetrachloride causing death through necrosis of the liver and other damage to vital organs was compensable as an accident although there was no instantaneous mishap which, taken by itself, could be recognized as an accident. In *English v. Industrial Commission,* 73 Ariz. 86, 237 P.2d 815 (1951), this Court held that the inhalation of nitric oxide and sulphur dioxide fumes causing an illness was compensable within the contemplation of the Workmen's Compensation Act, notwithstanding there was no sudden or external violence. In *Mead v. American Smelting and Refining Company,* 90 Ariz. 32, 363 P.2d 930 (1961), it was held that there was a causal connection between the petitioner's asthma and pulmonary emphysema, or at least an aggravation thereof through the claimant's inhalation of dust and smoke, and that this was compensable under the Workmen's Compensation Act.

We conclude that while it is to be recognized that there is authority to the contrary, this State has clearly been committed to the view over many years that the inhalation of poisonous compounds and dust having a detrimental effect upon the lungs and other vital organs is compensable under Article 18, § 8, of Arizona's Constitution. We think this is true where there has been a sudden onslaught of damage from silicon dust, as in *Pero v. Collier-Latimer, Inc.,* 49 Wyo. 131, 52 P.2d 690 (1935), or where there is a gradual deterioration through protracted exposure and an accident has been found by treating each impact or inhalation of silicon dust as a miniature accident in itself leading to the ultimate disability, *Brown v. St. Joseph Lead Company,* 60 Idaho 49, 87 P.2d 1000 (1939). *See also, Tri State Ins. Co. v. Employers Mutual,* Ark., 497 S.W.2d 39 (1973), and *Batesville White Lime Co. v. Bell,* 212 Ark. 23, 205 S.W.2d 31 (1947).

The award is ordered *vacated.*

CAMERON, V. C. J., and LOCKWOOD, J., concur.

HAYS, CHIEF JUSTICE (dissenting).

I dissent.

This case is a perfect example of the statement that hard cases make bad law. One cannot help having great sympathy for the widow who is seeking death benefits for her husband's death. Obviously, the majority has brought this case into the purview of the Workmen's Compensation Act because our Arizona Occupational Disease Act fails to provide a much needed relief.

While conceding that the Occupational Disease Act is archaic and greatly in need of change, we cannot go along with judicial legislation in this area. This is a matter for the legislature, and for that reason I dissent.

HOLOHAN, J., concurs.

[3] Carpal Tunnel Syndrome and Other Repetitive Motion Injuries

PEORIA COUNTY BELWOOD NURSING HOME v. THE INDUSTRIAL COMMISSION OF ILLINOIS
138 Ill. App. 3d 880, 93 Ill. Dec. 689, 487 N.E.2d 356 (1985)

BARRY, JUSTICE.

The critical issue in this appeal is whether an injury sustained as the result of work-related repetitive trauma is compensable under the Workers' Compensation Act absent one precise, identifiable incident which a court may label an "accident." Based upon the purpose of the Workers' Compensation Act (Ill. Rev. Stat. 1983, ch. 48, par. 138.1 et seq.) (hereafter the Act) and recognizing the new and changing nature of the employment environment, we hold that such injuries, when the claimant's burden of proof has been met, are compensable under the Act. . . .

This appeal is brought by the claimant's employer, Peoria County Belwood Nursing Home (hereafter Belwood). The claimant, Wanda Cagle, filed a claim for compensation under the Act on August 24, 1979. The claimant alleged that she developed carpal tunnel syndrome in her left wrist in the course of her job in the laundry room of Belwood. She had been employed by Belwood for 12 years. She worked in the laundry room for the six years prior to her injury. Her duties in the laundry room consisted of sorting laundry and loading the laundry into two 200-pound capacity washing machines. Each machine was operated six times a day and was loaded by operating a spring-loaded door into each of three compartments. She was also required to carry laundry bags weighing from 25 to 50 pounds.

The claimant initially identified the date of her injury as October 5, 1976. At trial, she testified that she noticed pain, numbness and tingling for a substantial period of time prior to October 5. Her testimony was confused as to exactly how long she experienced symptoms, but she did experience symptoms on October 4, 1976. On October 5, 1976, she consulted Dr. McLean, a neurologist, regarding her symptoms. She continued to work until August 23, 1977, when she underwent outpatient surgery for carpal tunnel syndrome.

Based on this evidence, the arbitrator amended the application for benefits to reflect a date of injury of October 4, 1976. The arbitrator awarded benefits for temporary total disability and for 25% permanent total disability. The Industrial Commission affirmed the award. The circuit court of Peoria County confirmed the Commission's decision. Belwood brings the instant appeal.

Belwood raises two interrelated issues. It asserts, first, that the Industrial Commission's finding that the claimant sustained an accidental injury is contrary to the manifest weight of the evidence. In a related argument, the employer asserts that the claim for benefits is barred by the statute of limitations.

The arbitrator and Commission found that the claimant had sustained an accidental injury as a result of repeated trauma to her wrist in operating the two large washing machines. The employer argues that because there was no specific incident by which the claimant's injury could be traced to a definite time, place and cause, the injury was not an "accidental injury" under the Act. The Commission's finding that the claimant suffered an "accidental injury" is, according to Belwood, contrary to the manifest weight of the evidence.

The crux of this issue, then, is what constitutes an "accidental injury" under the Act. The Illinois Supreme Court has held that an injury is "accidental" within the mean ing of the Act if it is traceable to a definite time, place and cause. (*International Harvester Co. v. Industrial Com.* (1973), 56 Ill. 2d 84, 305 N.E.2d 529.) The employee in *International Harvester* developed emphysema as a result of his employment. Barred from recovery under the Workmen's Occupational Diseases Act, the employee sought recovery under the Workmen's Compensation Act. The Illinois Supreme Court noted that aggravation of a pre-existing disease was compensable under the Act where the "employee's existing physical structure, whatever it may be, gives way under the stress of his usual labor and he is suddenly disabled." (56 Ill. 2d 84, 90, 305 N.E.2d 529, 533.) The court thus reasoned that either the cause or the effect of the aggravation of disease must be traceable to a specific time, place and cause in order for an employee to recover under the Act.

The court in *International Harvester* observed that the Act and the Workmen's Occupational Diseases Act are complimentary. Indeed, a claim submitted under one statute may be considered under the other if the facts of the case demonstrate that the other is the more appropriate law. Following the decision in *International Harvester*, the Workmen's Occupational Diseases Act was amended to provide recovery for disease arising out of repeated exposure. The legislature thereby nullified the rule in International Harvester that the aggravation of a pre-existing disease must be traceable to a specific time, place and cause. The legislature has obviously seen no need to address the question of whether a physical injury must be similarly traced. The Illinois courts, however, have retained the definition of "accidental" in *International Harvester* in resolving claims brought under the Act for work-related physical injury.

The requirement that an accidental injury be traceable to a definite time, place and cause was reiterated in *General Electric Co. v. Industrial Com.* (1982), 89 Ill. 2d 432, 433 N.E.2d 671. The claimant in *General Electric* sought compensation for carpal tunnel syndrome sustained as the result of work-related repetitive trauma. *General Electric* argued that there was no accidental injury because the claimant's injury was not traceable to a definite time, place and cause. The supreme court held that the claimant sustained an accidental injury despite the fact that the injury was the result of repeated trauma because there was a precise identifiable incident in which her physical structure gave way under the stress of her usual work tasks.

Thus, the rule has evolved that in order to demonstrate an "accidental injury," a claimant must trace the injury either to a specific accident identifiable as to time and place or to the specific moment of collapse of one's physical structure, identifiable as to time and place. Under the present interpretation of the Act, it is not sufficient for a claimant to show that a bodily structure eroded over time to the point of uselessness as a result of employment. Instead, a claimant must demonstrate a precise moment of collapse and dysfunction.

We consider the implication of this rule for all of the employees, factory workers, supervisors, managers, secretaries, salespeople and others, working in Illinois in this technological age. In real life, the erosion of a bodily structure to the point of uselessness translates into arms that cannot lift, legs that cannot walk, knees that cannot bend, lungs that cannot breathe, and eyes chronically irritated or worse. But evidence of such work-related injuries alone is not sufficient under the prior interpretations of "accidental injury." Instead, useless limbs, damaged organs and disabled bodies must be pushed to a precise moment of collapse and dysfunction. Then, and only then, according to these interpretations, may a court of this State find an employee eligible for compensation under the Act.

The time has come to abandon an interpretation of "accidental" which fails to address documentable and medically recognizable risks faced by the individuals in connection with their employment. The risk of injury from repeated trauma and exposure endured by truck drivers, CRT operators, chemists and others must be recognized. The judicial interpretation of "accident" must be refined to reflect the purpose of the Act and the reality of employees obligated to perform repetitive tasks. . . .

Like the courts of Illinois, the Supreme Court of Ohio had historically interpreted the term "accidental" in its worker's compensation statute (Ohio Rev. Code Ann. sec. 4123.01(C) (1980)) to require a showing of a sudden mishap occurring at a particular time and place. In *Village v. General Motors Corp.* (Ohio 1984), 15 Ohio St. 3d 129, 472 N.E.2d 1079, the court noted that its efforts to define "accidental" had resulted in a tortuous line of cases, culminating in holdings that disabilities which developed over time were not compensable because they lacked the essential features of suddenness, unexpectedness and unforeseeability. The *Village* court rejected these holdings, finding that the distinction between gradual and abrupt causation frustrated the clear purpose of the statute, which was to compensate workers injured as a result of the requirements of their employment.

In his concurring opinion, Justice Holmes acknowledged that difficult questions would be presented in the application of the *Village* decision. He noted, however, that it remained the claimant's burden to establish that his injury was caused by a "working condition with a definite time span." 15 Ohio St. 3d 129, 135, 472 N.E.2d 1079, 1084.

We concede that similar issues of law and fact will arise because we today recognize gradual injury due to repetitive trauma as compensable under the Act. However, as Justice Holmes also noted, a claimant must fulfill his obligation of proof and show that his injury is work-related and not the product of the aging process.

An employee alleging injury based on repetitive trauma must meet the same standard of proof as claimants alleging a single, definable accident. The difficulty in proving that injury resulting from repeated trauma arose out of and in the course of employment will pose a serious burden for a claimant. The difficulty of resolving any such issues should not prevent this court, like Ohio, from considering just compensation for all employees so injured.

The Illinois Supreme Court has noted that the word "accident" is not a technical legal term. (*E. Baggot Co. v. Industrial Com.* (1919), 290 Ill. 530, 125 N.E.2d 254.) Indeed, the word "accidental," as used in the Act, "is a comprehensive term almost without boundaries in meaning as related to some untoward event." *Ervin v. Industrial Com.* (1936), 364 Ill. 56, 60, 4 N.E.2d 22, 24.

Like the Ohio court in *Village*, this court finds that an employee may be "accidentally injured" under the Act as the result of repetitive, work-related trauma even absent a final, identifiable episode of collapse. We reject an interpretation of "accidental" which forces injured employees needing the protection of the Act to choose between foregoing that protection, "creating" one identifiable incident, or pushing their now-injured bodies to the point of collapse or dysfunction. The elimination of this too narrow definition of "accidental injury" will effectuate the purpose of the Act and provide equal protection for all manner of employees of this State.

Absent the narrow construction of "accident" in the case at bar, the evidence was sufficient to prove that the claimant sustained an accidental injury arising out of and in the course of her employment. Although the date of injury alleged by the claimant differed from the date of injury assigned by the arbitrator, the claimant established by her testimony that she was injured during her employment. (*See generally Interlake Steel Co. v. Industrial Com.* (1985), 136 Ill. App. 3d 740.) The claimant testified that she experienced pain and tingling in her left arm. While she worked a regular work schedule on October 4, on October 5, she informed her physician that she experienced extreme difficulty in gripping the washer doors due to the severity of her symptoms. Both the claimant and Dr. Rivero related the symptoms to her employment. The medical testimony as to the claimant's condition was uncontroverted. We find that the claimant proved that she sustained an "accidental injury" under the Act.

Because we so find, we must now consider whether the claim was timely filed. Belwood argues that the claim is barred by the statute of limitations.

Section 6(c)(2) of the Act provides, in relevant part, that a claim for compensation must be filed within three years after the date of the accident. (Ill. Rev. Stat. 1975, ch. 48, par. 138.6(c)(2).) To determine whether the filing of the claim was timely, we must first determine the date of the claimant's accident.

Professor Larson suggests that the date of an "accident" in cases of repetitive trauma be defined as "the date on which the disability, manifests itself." (1B Larson, Workmen's Compensation sec. 39.50 (1985).) The Supreme Court of Maine utilized this definition to determine when a worker was disabled by carpal tunnel syndrome in *Ross v. Oxford Paper Co.* (Me. 1976), 363 A.2d 712. The employee Ross had received treatment from the employer's first aid department over a period of years for continuing numbness in his hands. Finally, on March 17, 1974, the worker was no longer able to perform his job and ceased working. The court in *Ross*, relying on the rule set forth in Larson's treatise, fixed the date of disability at March 17, 1974.

Two alternative criteria are set forth by Larson for fixing the date when the injury manifests itself. The first is the time at which the employee can no longer perform his job. Inability to perform one's work was the criteria used in *Ross*.

The alternate criteria set forth by Larson is the onset of pain which necessitates medical attention. In *Consolidated Gas Utilities Corp. v. Jeter* (Okla. 1951), 238 P.2d 804, the claimant's injury resulted from repeatedly striking her keypunch keyboard with her fingers. On December 27, 1950, she notified her employer that she was experiencing pain in her fingers because of an unusually heavy workload. She then sought medical treatment. She continued to work for several weeks. The supreme court of Oklahoma fixed the date of the claimant's injury as December 27, the day she experienced pain sufficiently intense to cause her to seek medical care.

We adopt the rule propounded by Larson and find that where an employee in Illinois suffers a work-related injury due to repeated trauma, the date of the accidental injury is the date on which the injury "manifests" itself. Manifest means to show plainly or make palpably evident. (Webster's Third New International Dictionary 1375 (1971).) We further find that an injury has manifested itself when both the fact of the injury and the causal relationship between the injury and the employment are plainly evident.

The time at which both the fact of the injury and the causal relationship became plainly evident will be a question of fact. The claimant may demonstrate the manifestation of the injury with divers facts. The criteria suggested by Larson, the onset of pain and the inability to perform one's job, are among the facts which may be introduced to establish the date of injury.

In sum, in the instant case the claimant experienced symptoms on October 4, 1976. On October 5, 1976, she sought medical attention, at which time the doctor confirmed that her injury was caused by the conditions of her employment. Thus, the arbitrator correctly set forth the date of the claimant's injury as October 4, 1976, the last day on which she worked before the fact of the injury and the causal connection became apparent. On that date, both the fact of her injury and the causal relationship were plainly evident. The claimant filed her application of claim on August 24, 1979. The claim for benefits under the Act was, therefore, filed within the three-year statute of limitations.

The claimant was awarded benefits by the arbitrator and the Commission. The award of benefits was confirmed by the circuit court. We affirm the judgment of the circuit court of Peoria County.

Affirmed. . . .

PROBLEMS

Can carpal tunnel syndrome be compensated as an occupational disease?

(1) Some workers' compensation legislation in the 1990s has explicitly addressed the problem of carpal tunnel syndrome and other repetitive motion trauma. For example, in 1997 Virginia amended its occupational disease definition to provide that "[h]earing loss and the condition of carpal tunnel syndrome are not occupational diseases but are ordinary diseases of life. . . . "[20] In order to recover benefits for either condition as an "ordinary disease of life" a claimant in Virginia must now establish, by clear and convincing evidence, [1] that the disease exists and arose out of and in the course of employment and did not arise from causes outside the employment and [2] that the disease or condition [a] follows as an incident of occupational disease, [b] is an infectious or contagious disease contracted in the course of one's employment in a hospital or other specified health care facility, or in the course of employment as an emergency rescue personnel and those who volunteer for such duty, or [c] is characteristic of the employment and caused by conditions peculiar to the employment.

Before this statutory change, the Virginia Supreme Court had ruled that cumulative trauma was not compensable either as accidental injury or as occupational disease. *See* The Stenrich Group v. Jemmott, 251 Va. 186, 467 S.E.2d 795 (1996). Hearing loss was similarly ruled noncompensable. *See* Allied Fibers v. Rhodes, 474 S.E.2d 829 (Va. Ct. App. 1996).

After the new Virginia statute, recovery is still denied for all types of cumulative trauma other than hearing loss and carpal tunnel. *See* United Airlines, Inc. v. Walter, 482 S.E.2d 849 (Va. Ct. App. 1997).

Louisiana, by statute, now creates a presumption that carpal tunnel arising within the first twelve months of employment with an employer did not arise out of that employment. Benefits have been denied based on that presumption; *See* Dvorak v. Melvin Jones Framing Contractors, 688 So. 2d 94 (La. Ct. App. 1997).

(2) Is there any justification for Virginia's applying a "clear and convincing" standard to a carpal tunnel or hearing loss claim but not to other kinds of compensation claims? What is the significance of requiring a showing that carpal tunnel is a disease characteristic of the particular employment? Why are legislatures like that in Virginia making it so hard for a worker suffering from work-induced repetitive stress injury to be compensated?

---

[20] Va. Code Ann. § 65.2-400(c).

Chapter 10
DISEASE

§ 10.01 INFECTIOUS DISEASE AS AN "ACCIDENT"

The contraction of disease is deemed an injury by accident in most states if due to some unexpected or unusual event or exposure. Thus, infectious disease may be held accidental if the germs gain entrance through a scratch or through unexpected or abnormal exposure to infection.

Infectious diseases are usually subjected to both of the tests discussed in the preceding sections — unexpectedness and definiteness of time — and in addition have certain special obstacles to surmount under particular statutes. A number of statutes cover diseases following upon injury,[1] and some expressly rule out all other diseases.[2] Even when this exclusion is not express, it is sometimes implied under the doctrine *expressio unius exclusio alterius.*[3] Other statutes contain such requirements as violence to the physical structure of the body,[4] or traumatic injury,[5] or injury producing objective symptoms.[6]

CONNELLY v. HUNT FURNITURE CO.
240 N.Y. 83, 147 N.E. 366 (1925)

Cardozo, J.

Claimant's son, Harry Connelly, was employed by an undertaker as an embalmer's helper. In the line of his duty, he handled a corpse, which by reason of the amputation of a leg had become greatly decayed and was full of gangrenous matter. Some of this

---

[1] This group includes, among others, Arizona, Georgia, Indiana, Maryland, New York, Pennsylvania, South Carolina, Texas, and Virginia.

[2] *E.g.*, Mont. Rev. Codes Ann. § 39-71-119(4) states that "Injury" or "injured" does not include a disease that is not caused by an accident.

[3] Richardson v. Greenburg, 188 App. Div. 248, 176 N.Y. Supp. 651 (1919): "This express mention of a disease which is the consequence of injury would seem to exclude all diseases which are not."

[4] *E.g.*, Nebraska.

[5] *E.g.*, Kentucky, Montana, and Washington.

[6] *E.g.*, Louisiana, Missouri, and Nebraska.

matter entered a little cut in his hand, and later spread to his neck, when he scratched a pimple with the infected finger. General blood poisoning set in, and caused his death. His dependent mother obtained an award for death benefits. The Appellate Division reversed, and dismissed the claim.

" 'Injury' and 'personal injury' mean only accidental injuries arising out of and in the course of employment and such disease or infection as may naturally and unavoidably result therefrom." Workmen's Compensation Law (Consol. Laws, c. 67) § 2, subd. 7. A trifling scratch was turned into a deadly wound by contact with a poisonous substance. We think the injection of the poison was itself an accidental injury within the meaning of the statute. More than this, the contact had its occasion in the performance of the servant's duties. There was thus not merely an accident, but one due to the employment. We attempt no scientifically exact discrimination between accident and disease, or between disease and injury. None perhaps is possible, for the two concepts are not always exclusive, the one of the other, but often overlap. The tests to be applied are those of common understanding as revealed in common speech. *Lewis v. Ocean Accident & Guarantee Corporation*, 224 N.Y. 18, 21, 120 N. E. 56, 7 A.L.R. 1129; *cf. Van Vechten v. Am. E. F. Ins. Co.*, 239 N.Y. 303, 307, 146 N. E. 432.

We have little doubt that common understanding would envisage this mishap as an accident, and that common speech would so describe it. Germs may indeed be inhaled through the nose or mouth, or absorbed into the system through normal channels of entry. In such cases their inroads will seldom, if ever, be assignable to a determinate or single act, identified in space or time. *Matter of Jeffreyes v. Sager Co.*, 198 App. Div. 446, 233 N. Y. 535, 135 N. E. 307. For this as well as for the reason that the absorption is incidental to a bodily process both natural and normal, their action presents itself to the mind as a disease and not an accident. Our mental attitude is different when the channel of infection is abnormal or traumatic, a lesion or a cut. If these become dangerous or deadly by contact with infected matter, we think and speak of what has happened as something catastrophic or extraordinary, a mishap or an accident (*cf. Lewis v. Ocean A. & G. Corp.*, *supra*, at page 21, 120 N. E. 56), though very likely a disease also. "A common-sense appraisement of everyday forms of speech and modes of thought must tell us when to stop." *Bird v. St. Paul F. & M. Ins. Co.*, 224 N.Y. 47, 51, 120 N.E. 86, 87, 13 A. L. R. 875.

If Connelly's death was the outcome of an accident, as we think indisputably it was, only a strained and artificial terminology would refuse to identify the accident with the pernicious contact and its incidents, and confine that description to the scratch or the abrasion, which had an origin unknown. On the contrary, when a scratch or abrasion is of itself trivial or innocent, the average thought, if driven to a choice between the successive phases of the casualty, would find the larger measure of misadventure in the poisonous infection. The choice, however, is one that is needless and misleading. The whole group of events, beginning with the cut and ending with death, was an accident, not in one of its phases, but in all of them. If any of those phases had its origin in causes engendered by the employment, the act supplies a remedy.

We think this reading of the statute is well supported by authority. The earlier cases on the subject are decisions by the House of Lords. *Brintons, Ltd. v. Turvey*, [1905] A. C. 230, held that there was an "injury by accident" where a bacillus passed from wool to the eye of a workman, and infected him with anthrax. That judgment, in some of its aspects, was quoted with approval by this court in *Lewis v. Ocean Accident & G. Corp.*, *supra*, where the controversy had to do, however, not with a claim under the statute, but with a policy of insurance. There was reiteration and extension of the ruling in *Innes v. Kynoch*, [1919] A. C. 765, a case identical in its essentials with the one before us now. An abrasion of the knee, the origin of which was unknown, became infected in the course of work, and a remedy was sustained. In our own court, *Horrigan v. Post Standard Co.*, 224 N.Y. 620, 121 N.E. 872, was a case where a workman who had cut one of his fingers was poisoned through an infection suffered while cleaning out a urinal, and *Hart v. Wilson & Co.*, 227 N.Y. 554, 124 N.E. 898, a case where a puller of wool, suffering from eczema of the hands, became a sufferer from tetanus as the result of germs which entered the system through the cracks in his skin.

Matter of Jeffreyes v. Sager Co., 198 App. Div. 446, 191 N.Y.S. 354, affirmed, on opinion below, 233 N.Y. 535, 135 N. E. 307, is cited to the contrary, but it differs in important features. There the employee of a photographer, who dipped her hand in a developing solution many times a day for more than a week, was poisoned and lost a finger through the gradual action of the chemicals. The claim was disallowed. The contacts were voluntary, and the process of absorption was through channels of entry both natural and normal. More important, however, "the injuries resulted from no occurrence which is referable to any particular moment of time which is definite." 198 App. Div. 447, 191 N.Y.S. 355. The ensuing injuries were thought to be an occupational disease.

We make little progress when, viewing infection as an isolated concept, and ignoring its channels of attack or the manner of its coming, we say, upon the authority of science, that infection is a disease. It may be this, and yet an accident, too. This is distinctly recognized in section 48 of the statute, if it might otherwise be doubtful. Sunstroke, strictly speaking, is a disease, but the suddenness of its approach and its catastrophic nature have caused it to be classified as an accident. *Ismay, Imrie & Co. v. Williamson*, [1908] A. C. 437, 441; *Gallagher v. Fidelity & Casualty Co.*, 163 App. Div. 556, 148 N.Y.S. 1016; *Id.*, 221 N.Y.664, 117 N. E. 1067; *Matter of Murray v. Cummings Construction Co.*, 232 N.Y. 507, 134 N. E. 549. Tuberculosis is a disease, yet, if it results from the sudden inhalation of poisonous fumes, it may also be an accident. *Matter of O'Dell v. Adirondack Electric Power Co.*, 223 N.Y. 686, 119 N.E. 1063. A like ruling has been made where some extreme and exceptional exposure has induced pneumonia or rheumatism. *Coyle v. Watson, Ltd.*, [1915] A.C. 1; *Glasgow Coal Co., Ltd., v. Welsh*, [1916] 2 A.C. 1, 10.

Nor does it clarify the problem much to characterize the act as voluntary, unless we can also say of the volition that involved in it there was foresight of the peril and acceptance of the consequences. *Messersmith v. Am. Fidelity Co.*, 232 N.Y. 161, 165, 166, 133 N. E. 432, 19 A.L.R. 876. If Connelly had knowingly injected a germ into the cut, then indeed there would have been a volition inconsistent with an accident. A finding might then be made that there was a "willful intention of the injured employee to bring about the injury." Workmen's Compensation Act, § 10. As it is, there is no evidence of his appreciation of the danger, and none that the contacts, so far at least as they included the scratch and the pimple, were designed and deliberate, rather than heedless or inadvertent. The range of accident would be reduced, indeed, to vanishing dimensions, if we were to take out of the category every case in which the physical movement had been willed without advertising to the consequences. *Messersmith v. Am. Fid. Co., supra*. The laborer who cut the poison ivy and was awarded compensation (*Plass v. Central N. E. R. R. Co.*, 169 App. Div. 826, 155 N.Y.S. 854; *Id.*, 226 N.Y. 449, 123 N. E. 852) intended to cut grass, though he did not know that it was poisoned. The undertaker's helper intended to embalm a corpse, and found to his undoing that he had been impregnated by putrefying matter adhering to his hand.

An argument is built upon the wording of the statute. Workmen's Compensation Law, § 2, subd. 7. The statute speaks, as we have seen, of "accidental injuries arising out of and in the course of the employment," and also of "such disease or infection as may naturally and unavoidably result therefrom." The point is made that infection is here coupled with disease as something other than an accident or an injury, though a possible concomitant. We think the intention was by the addition of these words to enlarge and not to narrow. Infection, like disease, may be gradual and insidious, or sudden and catastrophic. It may be an aggravation of injuries sustained in the course of the employment and arising therefrom, in which event it enters into the award, though its own immediate cause was unrelated to the service. It may be an aggravation of injuries which in their origin or primary form were apart from the employment, in which event, if sudden and catastrophic and an incident of service, it will supply a new point of departure, a new starting point in the chain of causes, and be reckoned in measuring the award as an injury itself.

The order of the Appellate Division should be reversed, and the award of the State Industrial Board affirmed, with costs in this court and the Appellate Division.

POUND, CRANE, and LEHMAN, JJ., concur.

HISCOCK, C. J., and McLAUGHLIN and ANDREWS, JJ., dissent, and vote to affirm the order of the Appellate Division on opinions of Kellogg and Van Kirk, JJ., below.

Order reversed, etc.

§ 10.02 OCCUPATIONAL DISEASE

[1] Introduction

All states now provide general compensation coverage for occupational diseases. For the purpose of defining the affirmative inclusion of diseases within this term, the older definition distinguishing occupational disease from accident has been largely abandoned, with its stress on gradualness and on prevalence of the disease in the particular industry. Jurisdictions having general coverage of occupational disease now usually define the term to include any disease arising out of exposure to harmful conditions of the employment, when those conditions are present in a peculiar or increased degree by comparison with employment generally. Thus, even a disease which is rare and which is due to the claimant's individual allergy or weakness combining with employment conditions will usually be held to be an occupational disease if the increased exposure occasioned by employment in fact brought on the disease.

[2] Summary of Occupational Disease Statutes

The fifty states, Puerto Rico, Guam, the District of Columbia, the Federal Employees' Act, and the Longshoremen's Act now have general coverage of occupational disease; that is, they cover all occupational diseases, sometimes by general definition of the term,[7] sometimes under a broad use of the term "injury,"[8] sometimes under an unrestricted coverage of disease,[9] sometimes by a catch-all provision following a list of named diseases,[10] and sometimes by an entirely separate act.[11]

In almost all states, the benefits for occupational diseases, and the conditions controlling compensability, are now the same as for other kinds of disability.

[3] Background of Occupational Disease Legislation

Occupational disease coverage historically lagged far behind "accident" coverage in the United States. There were various reasons for this lag. One was the early opinion in some jurisdictions that, while accidental injuries were known to the common law and could be made the subject of an action for damages in appropriate circumstances, the

---

[7] *E.g.*, Alabama, Florida, Hawaii, Oregon.

[8] *E.g.*, Massachusetts, California, Federal Employees' Act.

[9] *E.g.*, Wisconsin, North Dakota, and California.

[10] *E.g.*, New York, North Carolina, Ohio, and Nevada.

[11] *E.g.*, Illinois, Indiana, and Pennsylvania.

concept of occupational disease was a stranger to the precompensation-era common law.[12] To the extent that compensation acts were thought of as substituting nonfault liability for the kind of injuries that were potential subjects of fault liability, there was thought to be no place for occupational diseases due to general workplace conditions, as opposed to the specific negligence of the employer.[13] But the most persistent obstacle was the argument that the heavy incidence of certain diseases in particular industries or areas would make their full coverage an impossible burden on the compensation system.

The earliest kind of occupational disease coverage in the United States took the form of general inclusion within the term "injury," in the Massachusetts,[14] Federal Employees' and California acts, or within the term "disease," in the California and Wisconsin acts. It was not until 1920 that New York adopted the first schedule-type act, following the English practice of listing not only particular diseases but the process in which they are acquired. While the schedule method was widely copied, the trend has been toward expansion into general coverage, either by abandoning the schedule altogether, or, as was done in New York, Ohio, and, more recently, Nevada and North Carolina, by leaving the list intact while saying that the act also covers all other occupational diseases.

[4] Definition of "Occupational Disease"

Definitions of "occupational disease" should always be checked against the purpose for which they were uttered.

Among the purposes for which definitions have been formulated are these:

(1) Defeating compensation because an injury is "not an accident but an occupational disease," in jurisdictions which, at the time of the decision, had no occupational disease coverage;

(2) Getting around the exclusive coverage provisions of the compensation act so as to sue for damages under a statute relating to safe working conditions;

(3) Limiting benefits in those states where special restrictions are placed on occupational diseases as against accidents; and,

(4) Getting awards for occupational disease under general definitions of the term, as against the contention that the disease is an ordinary nonindustrial illness.

Of these, only the last is presently in point. The rest are concerned with the contrast between accident and occupational disease, largely for the purpose of establishing noncompensability. With the expansion of occupational disease legislation, this contrast between accident and occupational disease has largely lost its importance, and awards are frequently made without specifying which category the injury falls in.

Under general definitions of occupational disease in statutes granting compensation for such disease, how much is affirmatively included? The important boundary becomes now, not that separating occupational disease from accident, since compensability lies on both sides of that boundary, but the boundary separating occupational disease from diseases that are neither accidental nor occupational, but common to mankind and not

---

[12] Boshuizen v. Thompson & Taylor Co., 360 Ill. 160, 195 N.E. 625 (1935).

[13] Adams v. Acme White Lead & Color Works, 182 Mich. 157, 148 N.W. 485 (1914): "We are not able to find a single case where an employee has recovered compensation for an occupational disease at common law." However, when the disease was attributable to the employer's negligence, every state except Michigan and Illinois that passed on the question recognized the possibility of an action for damages. *See* Banks, "Employer's Liability for Occupational Diseases," 16 Rocky Mt. L. Rev. 60, 61, n.5 (1944).

[14] Hurle's Case, 217 Mass. 223, 104 N.E. 336, 1916A, L.R.A. 279, 1915C, Ann. Cas. 919 (1914). "Injury" interpreted to include blinding by long exposure to coal gas.

distinctively associated with the employment. For this purpose a new set of standards must be used.

A number of statutes contain detailed definitions of the term "occupational disease," and these statutory definitions give the clue to the distinction which is controlling for present purposes. The common element running through all is that of the distinctive relation of the particular disease to the nature of the employment, as contrasted with diseases which might just as readily be contracted in other occupations or in everyday life apart from employment. It will be observed at once that this test resembles the original "peculiar-risk" test for the "arising out of employment" requirement.

A representative definition, containing phrases which reappear in a number of statutes, is Nebraska's:[15]

> The term occupational disease shall mean only a disease which is due to causes and conditions which are characteristic of and peculiar to a particular trade, occupation, process, or employment and shall exclude all ordinary diseases of life to which the general public is exposed.

Another representative definition is Connecticut's:[16]

> "Occupational disease" means any disease which is peculiar to an occupation in which an employee was or is engaged and which is due to causes, in excess of the ordinary hazards of employment which are attributable to such occupation. . . .

Most statutory definitions are in substance similar to these, and, when the statute contains no definition at all, the judicial definition designed to describe the inclusiveness of the term will be found to stress the same elements.[17]

WILDERMUTH v. B. P. O. ELKS CLUB (LODGE 621)
5 A.D.2d 911, 170 N.Y.S.2d 874 (1958)

MEMORANDUM DECISION.

Appeal by employer and its insurance carrier from a decision and award of the Workmen's Compensation Board.

Claimant worked as a waiter in a club eight or nine hours daily, and occasionally longer, for 25 years. He said that he was required to be on his feet continuously, walking on hard-surfaced floors. He developed in one leg a condition of varicose veins, with ulceration, which required surgery.

The board has properly awarded for occupational disease. The medical testimony related the varicosities themselves, as well as their subsequent aggravation, to claimant's work on his feet for a long period of time. Appellants seem to contend that because the condition could occur to any one who is on his feet a great deal it was not an incident of claimant's occupation. However, "The conditions of employment which distinguish the occupational disease from the ordinary diseases of life" are sufficiently distinctive if "familiar harmful elements are present in excessive degree." (1 Larson on Workmen's Compensation Law, § 41.50). We have previously held that the question as

---

[15] Neb. Rev. Stats., Ch. 48, Art. 1, § 48-151(3).

[16] Conn. Gen. Stats., Ch. 573, Tit. 31, § 396.

[17] *E.g.*, Harman v. Republic Aviation Corp., 298 N.Y. 285, 82 N.E.2d 785, 786 (1948):

> An ailment does not become an occupational disease simply because it is contracted on the employer's premises. It must be one which is commonly regarded as natural to, inhering in, an incident and concomitant of, the work in question. There must be a recognizable link between the disease and some distinctive feature of the claimant's job, common to all jobs of that sort.

to whether varicosities of the legs might constitute an occupational disease was an is sue of fact and thereupon affirmed an award for disability thus caused. *Vines v. Lazar Motors, Inc.*, 277 App. Div. 1083, 100 N.Y.S.2d 735.

Appellants' additional contention is that the medical proof was only of aggravation of a condition which disabled claimant some years before and that his later disability due to such an aggravation is not compensable. This does not follow from *Detenbeck v. General Motors Corp.*, 309 N.Y. 558, 132 N.E.2d 840, 842, upon which appellants rely. There it was held that the test of "a recognizable link between the disease and some distinctive feature of the claimant's job" is not met "where disability is caused by an aggravation of a condition which is not occupational in nature." Here, as we have held, the work activity was sufficiently distinctive and, upon the record, the condition was occupational in nature. Further, while the direct examination of the only physician who testified was limited to the question of aggravation, on cross-examination he related the original condition itself to claimant's work in this same employment and said that the condition is a progressive one and continued in this case until ulceration occurred, necessitating surgery and resulting in the disability for which the award was made.

Decision and award affirmed, with costs to the Workmen's Compensation Board.

BOOKER v. DUKE MEDICAL CENTER
297 N.C. 458, 256 S.E.2d 189 (1979)

On plaintiffs' petition under G.S. 7A-31(a) to review the decision of the Court of Appeals reversing an award of the North Carolina Industrial Commission in plaintiffs' favor, 32 N.C. App. 185, 231 S.E.2d 187 (1977), docketed and argued as Case No. 9 at the Fall Term 1977.

This proceeding was begun before the Industrial Commission as a compensation claim for death benefits filed by the widow and four minor children, the sole dependents of Robert S. Booker (Booker), deceased employee of Duke University Medical Center.

Stipulations and plaintiffs' evidence show the following facts:

Booker began working for Duke Medical Center on 24 October 1966. From that date until the first part of July 1971 he worked as a laboratory technician in the Clinical Chemistry Laboratory, where he performed various chemical determinations on serum blood, blood serum, whole blood, and other body fluids. In the process he manually tested blood samples and, although he was a careful and experienced employee, he routinely spilled blood upon his fingers. Each day one or more of the blood samples he tested was infected with serum hepatitis. These samples bore no diagnostic label when they came in or went out, and the lab technicians never knew whether the patient's blood was diseased. The blood samples tested were divided about equally between Duke's in-patients and out-patients. The first of July 1971 Duke began to label all diagnosed hepatic patients' blood which came to the lab, but not all infected blood had been diagnosed.

On 3 July 1971 Booker, who had been totally asymptomatic up until 3 or 4 days prior to that date, developed symptoms which caused him to consult Dr. Joe B. Currin, a specialist in internal medicine. Dr. Currin ascertained that Booker was suffering from serum hepatitis and hospitalized him for ten days. Thereafter Booker, who had worked continually with blood samples, ceased handling blood and worked in the lab as an "electronical engineer."

In July 1972 Dr. Michael E. McLeod of the Department of Medicine at Duke Hospital, Duke Medical Center, took Booker as a patient and treated him for serum hepatitis until Booker's death on 3 January 1974. During this interim Booker was "in and out" of the hospital on sick leave. About 1 October 1973 he became unable "to sustain his performance" at the lab, and on 15 October 1973 Dr. McLeod certified that Booker was no longer able to work. The autopsy, performed 3 January 1974 at Duke Medical Center, showed that Booker "died of a disease due to serum hepatitis."

Initially, Booker filed a claim with the Industrial Commission in his own behalf. A hearing was held before Commissioner William H. Stephenson on 18 October 1973. Thereafter, on 14 December 1973 an order was entered resetting the case on 1 March 1974 for the taking of additional evidence. Because of Booker's death on 3 January 1974 the case was removed from the hearing docket. On 16 December 1974 the plaintiffs filed their claims for death benefits, and Commissioner Stephenson conducted a hearing on 10 September 1975. At that time plaintiffs offered sufficient evidence to establish the facts summarized below.

Serum hepatitis is a virus disease of the liver which is transmitted when any amount of blood from one infected with the disease is introduced into the blood of another. It is usually transmitted by transfusions, injections, or contact with blood or blood products through some point of entry such as nicks, cuts, and scratches on the skin. It might also be transmitted by the handling of feces or orally, as for example, by the use of unsterilized instruments in a dentist's office. An accidental contact with an "almost microscopic" amount of contaminated blood can transmit serum hepatitis. Dr. McLeod testified, "Even with our assay of the hepatic antigen, which is the most sensitive assay, one can dilute the blood a million times and still transmit the illness serum hepatitis." It takes only one exposure to contaminated blood to originate the disease. Dr. Currin testified that "the incubation period of serum hepatitis is generally considered to be six weeks to six months."

Serum hepatitis is not a disease limited to persons who handle blood. Members of the general public are from time to time afflicted with this disease. Thus, it was not possible for Booker himself or the medical experts and chemist who testified for plaintiffs to state with absolute certainty the time or place at which Booker became infected. . . .

SHARP, CHIEF JUSTICE.

For an injury or death to be compensable under our Workmen's Compensation Act it must be either the result of an "accident arising out of and in the course of the employment" or an "occupational disease." The Court of Appeals concluded that Booker's injury was not the result of an "accident" because no specific incident could be identified which led to his contracting the disease. *Booker v. Medical Center*, 32 N.C. App. 185, 231 S.E.2d 187 (1977). None of the parties to this appeal assigned that conclusion as error. The question before us therefore is whether or not his death was the result of an "occupational disease." Because serum hepatitis is not expressly mentioned in the schedule of diseases contained in G.S. 97-53, it is a compensable injury only if it falls within the general definition set out in G.S. 97-53(13). . . .

Effective 1 July 1971, and applying "only to cases originating on and after" that date, subsection (13) of G.S. 97-53 was amended to read as follows:

> Any disease, other than hearing loss covered in another subdivision of this section, which is proven to be due to causes and conditions which are characteristic of and peculiar to a particular trade, occupation or employment, but excluding all ordinary diseases of life to which the general public is equally exposed outside of the employment. . . .

Since the dependents' right to compensation under G.S. 97-38 does not arise until the employee's death, the date of his death logically governs which statute applies. . . .

For an occupational disease to be compensable under the amended version of G.S. 97-53(13) two conditions must be met: (1) It must be "proven to be due to causes and conditions which are characteristic of and peculiar to a particular trade, occupation or employment;" and (2) it cannot be an "ordinary disease of life to which the general public is equally exposed outside of the employment."

Before attempting to apply G.S. 97-53(13) to the facts of the instant case, it will be helpful to review briefly the circumstances which led to its enactment. Occupational disease coverage in the United States has always lagged far behind "accident" coverage.

1B A. Larson, Workmen's Compensation Law § 41.20 (1978). The first worker's compensation laws were constructed to afford relief only to those persons who suffered an unexpected, employment-related accident during the working day. Even well-known diseases of the workplace, such as lead and arsenic poisoning, were not covered by the early laws. Solomon's, *Workers' Compensation for Occupational Disease Victims: Federal Standards and Threshold Problems*, 41 Alb. L. Rev. 195, 197 (1977). When North Carolina passed its Workmen's Compensation Act in 1929 it borrowed the phrase "injury by accident" from the original British Act to describe the type of injury covered. Note, *Development of North Carolina Occupational Disease Coverage*, 7 Wake Forest L. Rev. 341, 342 (1971). No specific coverage was provided for occupational diseases. 1929 N.C. Pub. Laws, ch. 120. In 1935 the General Assembly amended the Act to provide coverage for specified occupational diseases. 7 Wake Forest L. Rev. at 344; 1935 N.C. Pub. Laws, ch. 123. In the thirty-five years following the enactment of G.S. 97-53 only two new occupational diseases (undulant fever and psittacosis) were added to the schedule of coverage. 7 Wake Forest L. Rev. at 352.

The great disadvantage of schedule-type coverage is its failure to keep pace with the development of new disabling exposures in the industrial process. Sears and Groves, *Worker Protection Under Occupational Disease Disability Statutes*, 31 Rocky Mtn.L. Rev. 462, 467 (1959). While the schedule method was widely used at first, the definite trend has been toward expansion into general coverage, either by abandoning the schedule altogether or by leaving the list intact while providing for coverage of all other occupational diseases. 1B A. Larson, Workmen's Compensation Law § 41.20 (1978). The clear intent of the General Assembly in enacting the current version of G.S. 97-53(13) was to bring North Carolina in line with the vast majority of states by providing comprehensive coverage for occupational diseases.[18]

The Court of Appeals held that an illness is compensable under G.S. 97-53, whether mentioned specifically in the statute or falling within the general definition in subsection (13), only if it also comes within "well understood definitions of the term 'occupational diseases.'" 32 N.C. App. at 192, 231 S.E.2d at 192. The definitions to which the court referred are those found in *Henry v. Leather Co.*, 234 N.C. 126, 66 S.E.2d 693 (1951). In this case, decided long before adoption of the current version of G.S. 97-53(13), this Court made the following remarks:

> The Legislature, in listing those diseases which are to be deemed occupational in character, was fully aware of the meaning of the term "occupational disease." Indeed, it in effect, defined the term in G.S. 97-52 as a diseased condition caused by a series of events, of a similar or like nature, occurring regularly or at frequent intervals over an extended period of time, in employment. The term has likewise been defined as a diseased condition arising gradually from the character of the employee's work. These are the accepted definitions of the term. *Cannella v. Gulf Refining Co. of La.*, 154 So. 406; *Barron v. Texas Employers' Ins. Assoc.*, 36 S.W.2d 464. *See also* Words & Phrases, "Occupational Diseases."

An injury by accident, as that term is ordinarily understood, "is distinguished

---

[18] *(Court's footnote)* As of 1978 forty-one states including North Carolina provided for general coverage of occupational diseases, i.e., they covered all occupational diseases. Nine states covered specified diseases ranging from as few as twelve in Kansas to as many as forty-seven in Colorado. 1B A. Larson, Workmen's Compensation Law § 41.10 (1978). For a list of specific statutory provisions, see E. Blair, Reference Guide to Workmen's Compensation Law § 8 (1974). In many states language substantially similar to that used in G.S. 97-53(13) provides the sole definition of occupational disease. *See, e.g.*, Conn. Gen. Stat. Ann. § 31-275 (1972); Neb. Rev. Stat. § 48-151(3) (1974). Other states have converted from a "scheduled" to a "comprehensive" system by amending their respective schedules to include a catch-all provision embracing any disease arising out of employment. *See, e.g.*, Nev. Rev. Stat. §§ 617.440,.450 (1973); N.Y.Work.Comp. § 3(2)(30) (McKinney Cum. Supp. 1978-79); Ohio Rev. Code Ann. § 4123.-68(BB) (Page 1973); R.I. Gen. Laws § 28-34-2(33) (1968); Utah Code Ann. § 35-2-27(28) (1953).

from an occupational disease in that the former rises from a definite event, the time and place of which can be fixed, while the latter develops gradually over a long period of time." 71 C.J. 601 (*see* cases in note)." 234 N.C. at 130–31, 66 S.E.2d at 696.

Similar definitions of the term "occupational disease" can be found in *Watkins v. Murrow*, 253 N.C. 652, 661, 118 S.E.2d 5, 11–12 (1961) and *MacRae v. Unemployment Compensation Comm.*, 217 N.C. 769, 775, 9 S.E.2d 595, 599 (1940).

Because serum hepatitis is not a disease which develops gradually through prolonged exposure to harmful conditions but instead is an illness caused by a single exposure to a virus, the Court of Appeals concluded that it was not compensable as an occupational disease. For the reasons which follow we disagree.

We begin by noting Professor Larson's admonition that "[d]efinitions of 'occupational disease' should always be checked against the purpose for which they were uttered." 1B A. Larson, Workmen's Compensation Law § 41.31 (1978). Because the first workmen's compensation acts usually provided coverage for accidental injuries while denying or limiting it for victims of occupational disease, the tendency in early court decisions construing these acts was to expansively define the term "accident" while narrowly construing the term "occupational disease." As jurisdictions amended their laws to provide coverage for all occupationally related illnesses, these older definitions became less viable:

> The present problem of definition is: Under general definitions of occupational disease in statutes granting compensation for such disease, how much is affirmatively included? The important boundary becomes now, not that separating occupational disease from accident, since compensability lies on both sides of that boundary, but the boundary separating occupational disease from diseases that are neither accidental nor occupational, but common to mankind and not distinctively associated with the employment. For this purpose a new set of standards must be used. *It is of little value, and, indeed, may be quite misleading, to quote indiscriminately from old definitions whose only purpose was distinguishing accident.* 1B A. Larson, Workmen's Compensation Law § 41.32 (1978) (Emphasis added.)

In all of the North Carolina cases cited earlier, the term "occupational disease" was defined solely for the purpose of distinguishing it from an "injury by accident." In *Watkins v. Murrow, supra*, for example, claimant was a truck driver who was permanently disabled by carbon monoxide poisoning when he parked his truck and went to sleep with the motor running. The carbon monoxide entered the cab from a faulty exhaust pipe. Noting that an occupational disease is one which "develops gradually over a long period of time," the Court agreed with the Industrial Commission that claimant had suffered an accidental injury. 253 N.C. at 661, 118 S.E.2d at 11–12. In none of these cases was any attempt made to inclusively define the term "occupational disease." To use the definitions for that purpose is to carry them beyond their intended scope.

The Court of Appeals' construction, moreover, would work a judicial repeal of a portion of the statute. In holding that an illness is compensable only if it falls within prior judicial definitions of the term "occupational disease," the Court noted that even a disease listed by name in G.S. 97-53 would be noncompensable under that statute if it were the result of "a single event" as opposed to being the "cumulative effect of [a] series of events." 32 N.C. App. at 192–93, 231 S.E.2d at 192–93. Of the occupational diseases listed by name in the statute, however, at least three — anthrax, psittacosis, and undulant fever — are infectious diseases which are contracted, like serum hepatitis, by a single exposure under optimum conditions to the virus or bacteria causing the disease. Steadman's Medical Dictionary (22nd ed. 1972); G.S. 97-53(1), (26), (27). The Court of Appeals' construction would in effect read these diseases out of the statute.

Finally, the Court of Appeals' interpretation must be rejected as inconsistent with the overriding legislative goal of providing comprehensive coverage for occupational diseases. Except for those diseases specifically named in the statute, it is our view that the legislature intended the present version of G.S. 97-53(13) to define the term "occupational disease." To the extent that this statute conflicts with prior judicial definitions of the term "occupational disease," the older definitions must give way.

As Professor Larson points out, the "element of gradualness, so heavily stressed in definitions contrived to distinguish accident, loses its importance when the sole question is the inclusiveness of an occupational disease statute. If the inherent conditions of employment produce outright infection, . . . it may be treated as an occupational disease although the process is much more sudden than that described in the older definitions." 1B A. Larson, Workmen's Compensation Law § 41–40 (1978).

If an employee contracts an infectious disease as a result of his employment and it falls within either the schedule of diseases set out in the statute or the general definition of "occupational disease" in G.S. 97-53(13), it should be treated as a compensable event regardless of the fact that it might also qualify as an "injury by accident" under G.S. 97-2(6).

Other jurisdictions faced with the same issue have reached a similar result. *See, e.g., Board of National Missions v. Alaska Industrial Board*, 14 Alaska 453, 116 F.Supp. 625 (1953) (tuberculosis contracted by missionary ministering to persons with that disease deemed an "occupational disease"); *Mills v. Detroit Tuberculosis Sanitarium*, 323 Mich. 200, 35 N.W.2d 239 (1948) (tuberculosis contracted by dishwasher at Sanitarium); *Otten v. State*, 229 Minn. 488, 40 N.W.2d 81 (1949) (contraction of tuberculosis by nurse); *Herdick v. New York Zoological Society*, 45 A.D.2d 120, 356 N.Y.S.2d 706 (1974) (zookeeper contracted tuberculosis from handling infected animals).

Having concluded that G.S. 97-53(13) is to be interpreted independently of any prior definitions of "occupational disease," we turn now to its construction. To be compensable under subsection (13) a disease must, *inter alia*, be "characteristic of and peculiar to a particular trade, occupation or employment."

A disease is "characteristic" of a profession when there is a recognizable link between the nature of the job and an increased risk of contracting the disease in question. *See Harman v. Republican Aviation Corp.*, 298 N.Y. 285, 82 N.E.2d 785 (1948). Appellees argue, however, that serum hepatitis is not "peculiar to" the occupation of laboratory technician since employees in other occupations and members of the general public may also contract the disease.

Statutes similar to G.S. 97-53 have been examined by the courts of many states. Conn. Gen. Stat. § 5223, for example, defined an occupational disease as "a disease peculiar to the occupation in which the employee was engaged and due to causes in excess of the ordinary hazards of employment as such." (Current version at Conn. Gen. Stat. Ann. 31-275 (West 1972)). In *LeLenko v. Wilson H. Lee Co.*, 128 Conn. 499, 503, 24 A.2d 253, 255 (1942) that statute was construed as follows:

> The phrase, "peculiar to the occupation," is not here used in the sense that the disease must be one which originates exclusively from the particular kind of employment in which the employee is engaged, but rather in the sense that the conditions of that employment must result in a hazard which distinguishes it in character from the general run of occupations (*see* Oxford Dictionary: Funk & Wagnalls Dictionary). . . . To come within the definition, an occupational disease must be a disease which is a natural incident of a particular occupation, and must attach to that occupation a hazard which distinguishes it from the usual run of occupations and is in excess of that attending employment in general. *Glodenis v. American Brass Co.*, 118 Conn. 29, 40, 170 A. 146, 150.

In *Ritter v. Hawkeye-Security Insurance Co.*, 178 Neb. 792, 795, 135 N.W.2d 470, 472 (1965) the Nebraska Supreme Court examined a statute almost identical to our own. *See* Neb. Rev. Stat. § 48-151 (1974). In upholding a disability award to a dishwasher who developed contact dermatitis as a result of the use of cleansing chemicals in his work, the court made the following remark:

> The statute does not require that the disease be one which originates exclusively from the employment. The statute means that the conditions of the employment must result in a hazard which distinguishes it in character from employment generally.

Similarly, in allowing an award to a nurse's aide who contracted tuberculosis from her patients, the Supreme Court of Maine in *Russell v. Camden Community Hospital*, 359 A.2d 607, 611–12 (Me.1976) said:

> The requirement that the disease be "characteristic of or peculiar to" the occupation of the claimant precludes coverage of diseases contracted merely because the employee was on the job. For example, it is clear that the Law was not intended to extend to an employee in a shoe factory who contracts pneumonia simply by standing next to an infected co-worker. In that example, the employee's exposure to the disease would have occurred regardless of the nature of the occupation in which he was employed. To be within the purview of the Law, the disease must be so distinctively associated with the employee's occupation that there is a direct causal connection between the duties of the employment and the disease contracted.

Courts in other jurisdictions have likewise rejected the proposition that a particular illness cannot qualify as an "occupational disease" merely because it is not unique to the injured employee's profession. *Young v. City of Huntsville*, 342 So. 2d 918 (Ala. Civ. App. 1976), *cert. denied*, 342 So. 2d 924 (Ala. 1977); *Aleutian Homes v. Fischer*, 418 P.2d 769 (Alaska 1966); *State ex rel. Ohio Bell Telephone Co. v. Krise*, 42 Ohio St. 2d 247, 327 N.E.2d 756 (1975); *Underwood v. National Motor Castings Division*, 329 Mich. 273, 45 N.W.2d 286 (1951).

In the light of these principles we turn now to an examination of the evidence presented to the Industrial Commission. The record indicates that from 1966 until 1971 Booker manually tested blood samples in the laboratory at Duke Medical Center. Some of the blood would routinely spill on his fingers. His supervisor testified that he came in contact with blood samples containing hepatitis associated antigen at least once a day. Dr. Michael McLeod, a medical expert specializing in internal medicine, stated that in his opinion the conditions "that Mr. Booker worked under put Mr. Booker at a much, much higher risk to contract the disease serum hepatitis than other employees in the hospital and people who are not employed in the hospital." Similarly, Dr. Joe Currin testified that "the public is generally not nearly as exposed to the hazard."

It is clear from this evidence that a distinctive relation exists between Mr. Booker's occupation and the disease serum hepatitis. The evidence amply supports the Commission's determination that Booker's job exposed him to a greater risk of contracting the disease than members of the public or employees in general. This finding of fact supports its legal conclusion that serum hepatitis is a disease "characteristic of and peculiar to his occupation of lab technician." We note that many other states have similarly recognized that hospital employees may face an increased risk of contracting communicable diseases. *See* Note, *Occupational Diseases and the Hospital Employee — A Survey*, 5 Mem. St. U.L. Rev. 368 (1975) and cases cited therein.

Appellees also argue that serum hepatitis is an "ordinary disease of life" and is therefore noncompensable. They cite in particular Dr. Michael McLeod's statement on cross-examination that "[s]erum hepatitis is not a disease which is limited to persons who handle blood. Members of the general public from time to time are [also] afflicted with this disease." Clearly, serum hepatitis *is* an "ordinary disease of life" in the sense that members of the general public may contract the disease, as opposed to a disease like silicosis or asbestosis which is confined to certain trades and occupations. Our statute, however, does not preclude coverage for all ordinary diseases of life but instead only those "to which the general public is *equally exposed* outside of the employment." G.S.

97-53(13) (Emphasis added). The testimony of Dr. McLeod and Dr. Currin cited earlier supports the Commission's conclusion that the public is exposed to the risk of contracting serum hepatitis to a far lesser extent than was Mr. Booker.

As the Michigan Supreme Court observed when faced with a similar argument in *Mills v. Detroit Tuberculosis Sanitarium*, 323 Mich. 200, 209, 35 N.W.2d 239, 242 (1948):

> [T]he statute does not place all ordinary diseases in a non-compensable class, but, rather those "to which the public is generally exposed outside of the employment." The evidence in this case indicates that the plaintiff was exposed in his employment to the risk of contracting tuberculosis in a far greater degree and in a wholly different manner than is the public generally.

The greater risk in such cases provides the nexus between the disease and the employment which makes them an appropriate subject for workmen's compensation.

The final requirement in establishing a compensable claim under subsection (13) is proof of causation. . . .

The Commission's findings of fact based on the foregoing evidence substantially exclude the possibility that Booker contracted the disease outside of his employment. It is also perfectly obvious that his occupation exposed him to a greatly increased risk of contracting serum hepatitis for each day he handled unmarked vials of blood infected with the disease. These findings are sufficient to sustain the Commission's conclusion that Booker's disease was caused by his employment. . . .

For the reasons stated, the decision of the Court of Appeals is reversed and the case is returned to the Court of Appeals with directions that it be remanded to the North Carolina Industrial Commission for the implementation of its award.

Reversed and Remanded.

BRITT and BROCK, JJ., took no part in the consideration or decision of this case.

[5] Individual Allergy and Occupational Disease

FARMERS RURAL ELECTRIC COOPERATIVE CORPORATION OF GLASGOW v. COOPER
715 S.W.2d 478 (Ky. Ct. App. 1986)

GUDGEL, JUDGE.

These consolidated appeals stem from a judgment entered by the Barren Circuit Court which affirmed an opinion and award of the Workers' Compensation Board. The board awarded appellee benefits for a 50% occupational disability, and apportioned liability for one-fifth of the award against the employer and the remainder against the Special Fund. Appellants contend that the board's award is not supported by substantial evidence. For the reasons indicated in this opinion, we reverse and remand for further proceedings.

Appellee Brenda Cooper went to work for appellant Farmers Rural Electric Cooperative Corporation (Farmers) in 1968. In 1974, the company began installing computer terminals in a portion of its offices. By 1976, Mrs. Cooper, a billing clerk who was assigned to work with the new computer terminals, began experiencing symptoms of shortness of breath, sore throat, and numbness and tingling sensations over her body when the terminals were turned on. She consulted several physicians about her problems but none of them were able to diagnose their etiology. Finally, in 1981, her physician referred her to an allergist, Dr. A. F. White. Although Dr. White was of the opinion that Mrs. Cooper's adverse physical symptoms resulted from her work exposure to the computer terminals, he was unable to identify what irritating substance was emanating from the terminals. Subsequently, at Mrs. Cooper's request, Farmers switched her job to one which was located in an area of the office which had no computer terminals. Between August 1981 and December 1982, Mrs. Cooper worked at Farmers without any further problems. At the end of 1982, however, Farmers installed computer terminals in all areas of its offices, and Mrs. Cooper again began experiencing symptoms. After an episode of illness on February 2, 1983, Mrs. Cooper went home, and she has not returned to work since.

Mrs. Cooper's application for adjustment of her claim, filed on July 11, 1983, alleged that she had contracted an occupational disease. The proof adduced by the parties was directed solely towards that issue. The board, however, in an opinion and award rendered December 10, 1984, concluded that Mrs. Cooper sustained a work-connected injury on February 2, 1983, and that as a result of the injury she is 50% occupationally disabled. Moreover, the board apportioned liability for its award pursuant to the subsequent injury statute, KRS 342.120, concluding that Mrs. Cooper's February 2 injury aggravated a preexisting condition. The Special Fund was adjudged liable for four-fifths of the award. The circuit court, on review, affirmed the board's award. These appeals followed.

Appellants contend the board's award is not supported by substantial evidence. We are constrained to agree. During these proceedings, Mrs. Cooper never claimed that she sustained a work-connected injury. Rather, she claimed that she suffers an allergic reaction to chemicals which emanate from computer terminals, and hence, that she is entitled to an award of benefits as a result of having contracted an occupational disease. Further, all the proof adduced was directed to the issue of whether she frequently got sick at work because she was allergic to some unidentified chemical substance which emanates from computers. No evidence, much less any substantial evidence, was adduced to show that Mrs. Cooper sustained a work-connected injury or that she suffered from a preexisting dormant disease or condition which was aroused into disabling reality by a subsequent injury. The board's ultimate findings in this case, therefore, clearly are not supported by substantial evidence. Hence, they must be set aside. On remand, the board should make new findings comporting with the dictates of KRS 342.316, the occupational disease statute.

Although we are constrained to reverse the board's award, we deem it appropriate in the interest of judicial economy to address the underlying issue in this case of whether the inability of Mrs. Cooper's expert medical witnesses to identify the particular chemical irritant or substance, which is found in or emanates from computer terminals and causes her to suffer an allergic reaction, dictates that her occupational disease claim should be dismissed. The controlling case on this issue is *Princess Manufacturing Company v. Jarrell*, Ky., 465 S.W.2d 45 (1971). In *Princess*, the claimant had "an inherent inability to withstand exposure to unlaundered fabrics used in the employer's plant. As a result she suffered an allergic reaction and broke out in a rash." *Id.* at 47. According to the court, the medical evidence adduced merely showed that the claimant was highly sensitive to the fabrics used in the plant. Although the incidence of such allergic reactions among garment workers generally was not shown to be unusual, the claimant's problem was not commonly associated with the garment workers' occupation. Significantly, although the court's opinion seems to indicate there was evidence that certain fabrics are generally recognized to be allergens insofar as some members of the general population are concerned, it did not indicate that there was any evidence identifying by name the particular irritating substance in the fabric. The court also indicated that in determining whether a particular allergic reaction may be an occupational disease within the meaning of KRS 342.316, the board may apply a subjective test to determine how the particular employee is affected by the conditions of employment.

In the instant case, there was ample evidence that Mrs. Cooper suffered an allergic reaction every time she was exposed to computer terminals in her work environment.

Doctors White, Tapp, and Wrenn all indicated by letter that they were satisfied that she adversely reacted to some unknown chemical irritant emanating from the computers. Further, Doctors White and Simon, both allergists, testified by deposition that they were satisfied Mrs. Cooper suffered an allergic reaction to computer terminals in the work place, and Dr. Crook testified that he has treated other persons who have had an adverse reaction to chemicals emanating from computers.

Given the fact that, pursuant to *Princess*, the board need only apply a subjective test to determine how the conditions of the employment affected Mrs. Cooper, we fail to perceive that her failure to adduce evidence identifying by name the allergen emanating from the computers necessarily dictates that her occupational disease claim must be dismissed. In short, since the offending fabric substance in the *Princess* case was not required to be identified, we conclude that there was no necessity that Mrs. Cooper identify the chemical irritant which emanated from computer terminals in the instant action.

The court's judgment is reversed and this case remanded with directions that it be returned to the board for further proceedings consistent with the views expressed in this opinion. . . .

All concur.

SCHOBER v. MOUNTAIN BELL TEL.
96 N.M. 376; 630 P.2d 1231 (N.M. Ct. App. 1980)

LOPEZ, JUDGE.

This suit is the result of plaintiff's attempts to secure compensation under the Workmen's Compensation Act, §§ 52-1-1 to 52-1-69, N.M.S.A. 1978. Plaintiff, formerly an engineer with Mountain Bell, collapsed at work, in November, 1976 and on January 24, 1977, allegedly as a result of his continued exposure to cigarette smoke in his work area. His recovery from the second collapse took four months, by which time he had lost his job. . . .

In May of 1977, he was fired for excessive absences. The absences resulted from Schober's collapse at work in January 1977, allegedly due to his allergy to cigarette smoke. He started noticing this allergy when his work area changed from one in which there was relatively little tobacco smoke, because the area housed Mountain Bell's sensitive machinery, to an open office area in which about half the employees smoked. As this discomfort increased, he began consulting physicians. Dr. Woodward, the phone company's physician, recommended that he see Dr. Field, an allergy specialist. Dr. Field determined that Schober was allergic to tobacco smoke, and recommended that he avoid the substance, avoidance being the only treatment known. Eventually, he consulted a psychiatrist, Dr. Hovda, and made three trips to National Jewish Hospital in Denver, all in the hope that someone could cure his allergy. The prescription was the same — avoidance of cigarette smoke. By prohibiting smoking in his home, installing a special filtration system there, and avoiding smoky public places, he could eliminate smoke from his personal environment; but he had no control over it at work where he was subjected to it every day. He offered to install a filter at work if Mountain Bell would provide him with a small enclosed space. They would not do so. In August of 1975, Schober took a demotion from engineering back to the plant in order to get out of the smoky area. By this time, however, he had become so sensitized to cigarette smoke, that even exposure to minute quantities triggered nose, throat, and chest pains. He continued to work until January 24, 1977, when he collapsed for the second time at work and was hospitalized. His first collapse at work was in the preceding November. His second recovery took four months, by which time he had been fired. . . .

Disability is compensable only if it results from an accidental injury "arising out of" and occurring "in the course of" the worker's employment. Section 52-1-9(C), N.M.S.A.

1978. Mountain Bell argues that Schober's collapse was due to idiopathic sensitivity to tobacco smoke and not to any risk inherent in his employment. Consequently, it asserts, the injury did not arise out of the employment.

The question of whether a fall from a motor scooter by a meter reader was an accident arising out os his employment was discussed in *Williams v. City of Gallup*, 77 N.M. 286, 421 P.2d 804 (1966). The court said:

> For an injury to "arise out of" the employment, there must be a showing that the injury was caused by a risk to which the plaintiff was subjected by his employment. The employment must contribute something to the hazard of the [injury]. . . . Compensation has been denied where the risk was common to the public, and where the risk was personal to the claimant. (Cites omitted.)

The difficulty is not in defining the test, but in applying it. *Id.* at 289, 421 P.2d at 806. *See also*, Gutierrez v. Artesia Public Schools, 92 N.M. 112, 583 P.2d 476 (Ct.App. 1978).

In *Berry v. J. C. Penney Co.*, 74 N.M. 484, 485, 394 P.2d 996, 997 (1964), the Supreme Court wrote:

> There must not only have been causal connection between the employment and the accident, but the accident must result from a risk incident to the work itself. . . .
>
> [A]n employee who has a pre-existing physical weakness or disease may suffer a compensable injury if the employment contribution can be found either *in placing the employee in a position which aggravates the danger due to the idiopathic condition*, or where the condition is aggravated by strain or trauma due to the employment requirements. . . . (Emphasis added.)

Id. at 486, 394 P.2d at 997. The parties recognize that whether any disability on plaintiff's part arose out of an accident depends upon the evidence. *See, Berry, supra*; *Christensen v. Dysart*, 42 N.M. 107, 76 P.2d 1 (1938).

Defendants contend: (a) the evidence shows that the cause of plaintiff's injury was not any hazard created by the nature of the employment; (b) every reasonable effort was made to accommodate plaintiff's peculiar sensitivity to tobacco smoke; (c) the air quality in the buildings where plaintiff worked was better than any other office building in town; (d) plaintiff was subjected to significantly less tobacco smoke than he would have encountered in the average office building.

We agree there is evidence to support defendants' contentions and evidence that would have supported a conclusion that the injury did not arise out of the employment. There is also evidence however, that the accident did arise out of plaintiff's employment; and it is the function of the trier of fact, and not of this court, to weigh the evidence. *See, Marez, supra*.

It is uncontroverted that the areas where Schober worked contained tobacco smoke. Any and everyone who worked there was subjected to the smoke and to the risk that they might be or become allergic to it. Although cigarette smoke exists other places than at Mountain Bell, the evidence indicates that Schober was continuously exposed to it there, and that he encountered a minimal amount of smoke elsewhere, due to extraordinary precautions on his part. For Schober, employment at Mountain Bell where others smoked contributed something to the hazard that he would ultimately collapse as his tolerance to cigarette smoke decreased. There were two causes of Schober's collapse; first, his allergic reaction to tobacco smoke; and second, that he was continuously exposed to that substance at work. Dr. Casebolt testified, to a medical probability, that plaintiff's working eight hours a day, five days a week, in an area that contained tobacco smoke "was the major contributing factor to his problem today." This evidence meets the test quoted above from *Berry, supra*, and supports the conclusion that plaintiff's accident and injury arose out of his employment. . . .

The judgment of the trial court is affirmed in all respects, except in its finding and order that the disability payments cease on February 9, 1978. The cause is remanded and the court below is instructed to order payments for 30% disability to continue until and unless changed pursuant to § 52-1-56, N.M.S.A. 1978. Plaintiff is awarded $1,500 for the services of his attorney on this appeal.

It is so ordered.

WOOD, C.J., LEILA ANDREWS, J., concur.

PROBLEMS

(1) Should partial loss of hearing as a result of continual loud noise on the job be compensable as an occupational disease? *See* Slavinski v. J.H. Williams & Co., 298 N.Y. 2d 545, 81 N.E.2d 93 (1948), and Green Bay Drop Forge Co. v. Industrial Comm'n, 265 Wis. 38, 60 N.W.2d 409 (1953).

(2) Decedent died of hypersensitivity to Alternaria fungus. His physician testified that this was one of only two cases of such hypersensitivity in his experience. Is this an occupational disease? *See* Consolidated Papers, Inc. v. Department of ILHR, 76 Wis. 2d 210, 251 N.W.2d 69 (1977).

(3) Suppose claimant's preexisting condition is not an allergy but an actual nonindustrial disease, like bursitis, which is aggravated by employment conditions. Should the resulting disability be compensated *as an occupational disease*? *See* Beaudry v. Winchester Plywood Co., 255 Or. 503, 469 P.2d 25 (1970).

(4) Can severe asthma attacks caused by claimant's allergic reactions to cigarette smoke in the workplace be compensated as accidental injury under the repeated trauma theory? *See* Johannensen v. New York City Dept. of Housing Preservation and Development, 154 App. Div. 2d 753, 546 N.Y.S.2d 40 (1989).

(5) Claimant contends that her employment as a key punch operator, which caused her to sit in a fixed position for long periods of time with her neck in extended positions while making repetitive strokes on the keyboard, caused or exacerbated a cervical condition. *See* Malloy v. AT&T Consumer Prods., 475 So. 2d 80 (La. Ct. App. 1985).

(6) Can work-related depression allegedly caused by extended contact with dying cancer patients be compensated as an occupational disease? *See* Lewis v. Duke Univ., 163 N.C. App. 408, 594 S.E.2d 100 (2004).

§ 10.03   SPECIAL PROBLEMS OF CERTAIN RESPIRATORY DISEASES

[1]   Introduction

Several respiratory diseases have, for varying reasons, created special problems in the adaptation of traditional worker's compensation to their particular characteristics. In the case of "black lung," the backlog of unmet needs of pneumoconiosis victims was so large that federal legislation was found necessary. As to asbestos-related diseases, the sheer volume of both compensation and tort claims has swamped both systems, and this, complicated by long-latency problems such as short statutes of limitations, identification of the responsible employer and carrier, etc., prompted calls for a federal solution here also. Another pervading issue affecting these diseases, including byssinosis, is that of dual causation, when the final disability is the product of both industrial exposure and smoking; the normal rule is that, if the employment contribution is significant, full compensation without apportionment is payable.

[2] The Black Lung Act

Dissatisfaction with restrictions and inadequacies of state compensation acts in the area of pneumoconiosis resulted in an extraordinary resort to federal power to rectify the situation or induce the states to do so. The Federal Coal Mine Health and Safety Act of 1969, while primarily designed to establish nationwide health and safety standards for the coal-mining industry, also included an income-maintenance provision that is of unusual interest, since it for the first time gave the federal government responsibility in a traditional area of state workers' compensation. Monthly cash benefits are provided for coal miners who are "totally disabled" because of pneumoconiosis ("black lung" disease) and for their dependents and survivors, when death either was due to pneumoconiosis or occurred while the miner was totally disabled by pneumoconiosis. Full medical benefits were added by the 1972 amendments.[19]

The Black Lung Benefit Act of 1972 was held constitutional in *Usery v. Turner Elkhorn Mining Co.*[20] The main attack by the mine operators was based on the due process clause, and was directed at the establishment of various definitions, presumptions, and limits on rebuttal evidence, and at provisions requiring payment of benefits to miners who left employment before the effective date of the Act and to their survivors. Irrebuttable presumptions upheld included (1) the presumption of total disability due to black lung if there is clinical evidence of the presence of the disease in its final stage; and (2) the presumption that, in such cases, death and total disability at time of death were due to black lung.

Rebuttable presumptions upheld included several involving death or disability of miners who have been employed a stated number of years and who have suffered or died from respiratory impairments. The definition of total disability, which covers inability to work in a mine or in comparable employment, was also sustained. The employers had objected that former miners who were employable in other lines of work were deemed disabled under this definition. As to the retroactivity issue: the court said that liability for disabilities before the passage of the Act was justifiable "as a rational measure to spread the costs of the employees' disabilities to those who have profited from the fruits of their labor — the operators and the coal consumers."

[3] Asbestos-Related Diseases

HALVERSON v. LARRIVY PLUMBING & HEATING CO.
322 N.W.2d 203 (Minn. 1982)

Todd, Justice.

Wallace Halverson was exposed to asbestos fibers over a period of years while employed by a series of employers. He was ultimately diagnosed as suffering from asbestosis and as a result of the disease was forced to quit working. The Workers' Compensation Court of Appeals overturned the compensation judge's finding that the last employer was liable for all compensation and found that the second-to-the-last employer should pay the benefits. We affirm.

Wallace Halverson was employed for 30 years as a plumber. In 1948 he went to work as a plumber's helper for respondent A. G. O'Brien where he worked with asbestos insulation. From that year until 1960 he worked at various times for O'Brien, Young & Krause Plumbing and Heating, and Sher Plumbing and Heating. He worked around dust and insulation during those years. In 1960 and 1961 Halverson did general

---

[19] P.L. 91-173, 83 Stat. 742, 30 U.S.C. 801 et seq.

[20] Usery v. Turner Elkhorn Mining Co., 428 U.S. 1, 96 S. Ct. 2882, 49 L. Ed. 2d 752 (1976).

plumbing for two other employers. From 1962 to 1970 he was employed solely by Sher Plumbing doing general plumbing and heating. There he was subject to daily asbestos exposure.

From 1970 through 1975 Halverson was employed solely by relator Larrivy Plumbing and Heating Company. In October of 1976 he began working for both Larrivy and respondent A. G. O'Brien. From February, 1977 until he stopped working completely in May or June of 1979 he was employed only by O'Brien. During the time that Halverson was employed by Larrivy and O'Brien he worked on individual projects for each employer and was exposed to asbestos at each job site.

The employee first noticed that he had trouble breathing during a swimming outing in 1975. Thereafter he experienced occasional breathing problems. In August of 1977 Halverson went to the doctor and complained that he had suffered from shortness of breath during the past two years. In September he went to see a pulmonary specialist, Dr. Clark. Dr. Clark diagnosed Halverson as having asbestosis, a condition caused by scarring of the lungs by asbestos. The employee did not work from September of 1977 to January of 1978. He went back to work for O'Brien Plumbing half days until he finally quit work completely in May or June of 1979.

A hearing was held on January 22, 1980 before a compensation judge. The judge found Halverson to have suffered a 40% permanent partial disability of the lungs as a result of asbestosis. A. G. O'Brien, as the place of last exposure, was ordered to pay benefits to Halverson. The Workers' Compensation Court of Appeals, in a unanimous decision, vacated in part the finding and determination of the compensation judge and substantiated its finding that Halverson's employment with Larrivy Plumbing substantially contributed to his disability and its determination that Larrivy was liable for all compensation.

The issue on appeal is whether the record supports the court of appeals' finding that Larrivy, the second-to-the-last employer, was liable for the full amount of the compensation because the exposure to asbestos while employed by O'Brien, the last employer, was not a substantial contributing factor.

We have held that, in occupational disease cases, the employer and the insurer on the risk at the time the employee becomes disabled is responsible for Workers' Compensation Benefits. *Robin v. Royal Improvement Co.*, 289 N.W.2d 76 (Minn. 1979). Apportionment of liability may be allowed only in those rare cases in which medical testimony permits a precise allocation of liability among different employers. *Michels v. American Hoist & Derrick*, 269 N.W.2d 57, 59 (Minn. 1978). However, one exception to the "last employer" rule must be recognized: for an employer and insurer to be liable for benefits, there must be some causal connection between the employee's occupational disease and the work which he performed for the employer. An "occupational disease" is defined as "a disease arising out of and in the course of employment . . . ," and the disease arises out of the employment "only if there be a direct causal connection between the conditions under which the work is performed." Minn.Stat. 176.011, subd. 15 (1980). Liability is most often assigned to the insurer on the risk at the time the employee becomes disabled "if the employment at the time of disability was of a kind contributing to the disease." 4 A. Larson, Workmen's Compensation Law § 95.21 (1981).

We have not yet expressly defined the extent to which an employee's disability or death from an occupational disease must be causally related to his last employment. In non-occupational disease cases we have held that an employer may be assigned liability as long as the employment can be said to have been "an appreciable or substantial contributing cause" of the employee's disability, *Roman v. Minneapolis Street Railway Co.*, 268 Minn. 367, 380, 129 N.W.2d 550, 558 (1964), or a "substantial contributing cause of his death." *Palmquist v. Meister*, 277 N.W.2d 376, 380 (Minn. 1979). In the present case the court of appeals properly applied a "substantial contributing cause" test in establishing employer and carrier liability.

The court of appeals relied on expert medical testimony regarding the latency period of asbestosis in determining that the employment with O'Brien was not a substantial contributing cause of the disability here. The scope of our review of that finding is to determine whether it is based on credible evidence and it will not be disturbed "unless it is manifestly contrary to the evidence" or unless the evidence "would clearly require reasonable minds to adopt a contrary conclusion." *Lockwood v. Tower Terrace Mobile Homes*, 279 N.W.2d 51, 53 (Minn. 1979).

The medical evidence in this case consists of the deposition testimony of Dr. Terrance Clark, a board certified pulmonary specialist who examined and treated Wallace Halverson in 1977. Dr. Clark testified that Wallace Halverson's current lung and chest disease was caused by exposure to asbestos during the period from 1952 through August of 1977. In response to the question of whether the exposure from 1976 to August, 1977 aggravated or accelerated the development of the lung condition, Dr. Clark stated that an x-ray taken in 1975 already showed signs of the disease but that it was possible that the later dust exposure aggravated the problem such that the employee became clinically ill in 1977. However, when questioned by opposing counsel, Dr. Clark stated that the latency period for asbestosis is 5 to 40 years, depending upon the intensity of the exposure. He testified that the recent exposures would not affect the asbestosis until at least 5 years in the future:

> Clark: [T]he disease that we measure now reflects predominantly those exposures that occurred fifteen or twenty years ago. Any subsequent exposures are likely to produce disease which we cannot yet measure.

> Attorney: And would not yet affect him or impair his ability until they reach the point where you can measure them?

> Clark: Yes.

The medical evidence indicates that the exposure during the time Halverson was employed by O'Brien may aggravate the disease but that the effects of that exposure will not be measurable for at least 5 years, and that the employee's present condition is the result of exposure 5 to 20 years ago. The court of appeal's finding that O'Brien is not liable for compensation is supported by sufficient evidence and is affirmed.

PETERSON, J., took no part in the consideration or decision of this case.

[4]   Byssinosis

RUTLEDGE v. TULTEX CORP./KINGS YARN
308 N.C. 85, 301 S.E.2d 359 (1983)

EXUM, JUSTICE.

The questions for decision are whether the Industrial Commission applied the wrong legal standard in its order denying benefits to claimant and whether there is evidence from which the Commission could have made findings, using the correct legal standard, that would support a conclusion that claimant contracted an occupational disease. We answer both questions affirmatively.

After hearing evidence for claimant and defendants, Deputy Commissioner Denson concluded that claimant had not contracted an occupational disease. This conclusion was based in part on the following factual findings, which are summarized unless quoted, to which no exception has been taken: Plaintiff, born 8 August 1935, has a tenth grade education and now lives in Georgia. She has smoked cigarettes from about age fifteen until February 1979 at the rate of approximately one pack per day. She has worked for four textile mills: (1) United Merchants in Buffalo, South Carolina, from 1953 until 1971 as a weaver; (2) Milliken at Union, South Carolina, from 1971 to 1973 as a "dry cleaner";

(3) Aleo Manufacturing, Rockingham, North Carolina, from 1975 to 1976 as a weaver; and (4) for defendant from 25 October 1976 until 12 January 1979 as a winder and then as a spinner. She was absent "for bronchitis" from 28 January 1977 until 13 May 1977. She "retired" on 12 January 1979.

All the plants where plaintiff worked "had a lot of cotton dust and lint" but defendant's premises, both in the weaving and spinning areas, were "relatively clean." Defendant's mill processed essentially 50 percent cotton blend materials and occasionally blends made of even a smaller percentage of cotton. "Although there was respirable cotton dust in [defendant's] weave room, there was much less than . . . in other premises." Plaintiff began developing a cough at work in 1969 or 1970. "[H]er cough was associated with her presence at work. Her shortness of breath became severe in December of 1976 and she has had various bouts with it since that time having to be out of work. . . . Plaintiff suffers from chronic obstructive pulmonary disease [with elements] of pulmonary emphysema and chronic bronchitis. . . . Plaintiff is disabled, because of her pulmonary impairment from all but sedentary . . . work which must be in a clean environment because of her reaction to cotton dust and other such irritants."

Deputy Commissioner Denson also made certain findings to which claimant excepted. The first was that in 1971 claimant "began developing a shortness of breath." Second was the following which the Deputy Commissioner included in the findings of fact:

> 6. . . . Cigarette smoking and recurrent infection have played prominent roles in the pulmonary impairment. Cotton dust may aggravate it, but since plaintiff was showing her symptomatology in problems prior to her employment with defendant employer, *exposure at defendant employer has neither caused nor significantly contributed to plaintiff's chronic obstructive pulmonary disease.*
>
> . . . .
>
> 8. Plaintiff has not contracted chronic obstructive lung disease as a *result of any exposure while working with defendant employer.* [Emphasis added.]

The Full Commission, with one commissioner dissenting, adopted Deputy Commissioner Denson's findings, conclusions, opinion and award as its own.

The Court of Appeals concluded that although the Commission erred "in requiring plaintiff to prove that her last employment was the cause of her occupational disease," the error was harmless since there was insufficient evidence before the Commission to show that plaintiff had ever contracted an occupational disease during her working life. *Rutledge v. Tultex Corp./Kings Yarn,* 56 N.C. App. 345, 350, 289 S.E.2d 72, 74 (1982).

Because of the italicized portions of findings 6 and 8, it does appear that the Commission thought that in order successfully to claim against defendant, claimant's last employer, claimant must establish that her exposure there either caused or significantly contributed to her chronic obstructive pulmonary disease. This is not the law. That part of G.S. 97-57 pertinent to this case provides:

> In any case where compensation is payable for an occupational disease, the employer in whose employment the employee was last injuriously exposed to the hazards of such disease, and the insurance carrier, if any, which was on the risk when the employee was so last exposed under such employer, shall be liable.

Under this statute, consequently, it is not necessary that claimant show that the conditions of her employment with defendant caused or significantly contributed to her occupational disease. She need only show: (1) that she has a compensable occupational disease and (2) that she was "last injuriously exposed to the hazards of such disease" in defendant's employment. The statutory terms "last injuriously exposed" mean "an

exposure which proximately augmented the disease to any extent, however slight."
Haynes v. Feldspar Producing Company, 222 N.C. 163, 166, 169, 22 S.E.2d 275, 277, 278
(1942). . . .

[C]hronic obstructive lung disease may be an occupational disease provided the
occupation in question exposed the worker to a greater risk of contracting this disease
than members of the public generally, and provided the worker's exposure to cotton dust
significantly contributed to, or was a significant causal factor in, the disease's development. This is so even if other non-work-related factors also make significant contributions, or were significant causal factors.

Significant means "having or likely to have influence or effect: deserving to be
considered: important, weighty, notable." Webster's Third New International Dictionary (1971). *Significant* is to be contrasted with *negligible, unimportant, present but not
worthy of note, miniscule, or of little moment.* The factual inquiry, in other words,
should be whether the occupational exposure was such a significant factor in the
disease's development that without it the disease would not have developed to such an
extent that it caused the physical disability which resulted in claimant's incapacity for
work. . . .

In *Smith v. Fieldcrest Mills, Inc.*, 224 Va. 24, 294 S.E.2d 805 (1982), claimant Smith,
employed as a textile worker for more than thirty-four years and exposed to "large
quantities" of cotton dust, was diagnosed as having "severe chronic obstructive
pulmonary disease." Medical testimony was that the disease's components were
emphysema, chronic bronchitis, and that "chronic byssinosis is a significant component
of [Mrs. Smith's] pulmonary problem." Medical testimony showed that byssinosis was
"more likely than not [an] etiologic factor in the evolution of chronic bronchitis" and
"cigarette smoking may be a relative causative factor." *Id.* at —, 294 S.E.2d at 806–07.
The Virginia Industrial Commission denied an award on the ground that "it is just as
probable that [Mrs. Smith's condition] resulted from a noncompensable cause (smoking)
as that it resulted from a compensable cause (cotton dust exposure)." *Id.* at —, 294
S.E.2d at 807. The Virginia Supreme Court, in an opinion by Chief Justice Carrico,
reversed the Commission and remanded the matter for further proceedings. The Court
relied on its earlier case of *Bergmann v. L. & W. Drywall*, 222 Va. 30, 278 S.E.2d 801
(1981), in which the worker had suffered a back injury at work. Following this injury the
worker was stricken with a nonoccupational neurological disorder which, together with
the back injury, rendered him incapable of working. The Industrial Commission denied
any benefits on the ground that the neurological disorder was just as probable a cause
of the incapacity for work as the work-related back injury. The Virginia Supreme Court
reversed this ruling, stating that it was not necessary that the work-related injury be the
sole cause of the worker's incapacity for work but that full benefits would be allowed
when it is shown that "the employment is a contributing factor to the disability." *Id.* at
32, 278 S.E.2d at 803. In *Smith*, the lung disease case, the Court said that the same rule
should apply. It remanded the matter to the Commission in order for it to determine
whether Mrs. Smith's exposure to cotton dust, i.e., her byssinosis, was "a contributing
factor" to Mrs. Smith's ultimate disability. 224 Va. at —, 294 S.E.2d at 808.

Cases from jurisdictions other than Virginia with statutes like ours support our
holding here. *Newport News Shipbuilding & Dry Dock Co. v. Director*, 583 F.2d 1273
(4th Cir. 1978), *cert. denied*, 440 U.S. 915, 99 S.Ct. 1232, 59 L.Ed.2d 465 (1979); *Pullman
Kellogg v. Workmen's Compensation Appeals Bd.*, 26 Cal. 3d 450, 161 Cal. Rptr. 783, 605
P.2d 422 (1980); *McAllister v. Workmen's Compensation Appeals Bd.*, 69 Cal. 2d 408, 71
Cal. Rptr. 697, 445 P.2d 313 (1968); *Thornton Chevrolet, Inc. v. Morgan*, 148 Ga. App.
711, 252 S.E.2d 178 (1979); *Riley v. Avondale Shipyards*, 305 So. 2d 742 (La. App. 1975);
Langlais v. Superior Plating, Inc., 303 Minn. 213, 226 N.W.2d 891 (Minn. 1975); *Bolger
v. Chris Anderson Roofing Co.*, 112 N.J. Super. 383, 271 A.2d 451 (1970), *aff'd* 117 N.J.
Super. 497, 285 A.2d 228 (1971); *Mueller v. State Accident Ins. Fund*, 33 Or. App. 31, 575

P.2d 673 (1978). *See generally* 1B Larson, Workmen's Compensation Law, § 41.64(a)–(c) (1982).

In these cases cigarette smoking together with the inhalation of occupational substances produced either lung disease, *see Newport News Shipbuilding, Pullman Kellogg, Thornton Chevrolet, Riley, Langlais* and *Mueller,* or lung cancer, *see McAllister* and *Bolger.* The courts concluded in all cases, however, that because there was evidence that inhalation of occupational substances contributed to the diseases, the diseases were compensable occupational diseases. The courts, therefore, either affirmed compensation awards, as they did in *Newport News Shipbuilding, Pullman Kellogg, Thornton Chevrolet, Riley, Langlais* and *Bolger,* or reversed denials of awards by administrative agencies, as they did in *McAllister* and *Mueller.*

Indeed, the significant contribution principle which we adopt puts upon the claimant in these lung disease cases a somewhat heavier burden than our sister states seem to require or that we require in industrial accident cases. Our purpose in adopting this principle is to strike a fair balance between the worker and the employer in the administration of our Workers' Compensation Act as it is applied to the difficult lung disease cases. To hold that the inhalation of cotton dust must be the sole cause of chronic obstructive lung disease before this disease can be considered occupational establishes too harsh a principle from the standpoint of the worker and the purposes and policies of our Workers' Compensation Act. This Act "should be liberally construed so that the benefits under the Act will not be denied by narrow, technical or strict interpretation." *Stevenson v. City of Durham,* 281 N.C. 300, 303, 188 S.E.2d 281, 283 (1972). On the other hand, to hold the causation requirement is satisfied if cotton dust exposure contributes to the slightest extent, however miniscule or insignificant, to the etiology of chronic obstructive lung disease, places too heavy a burden on industry. This holding would compromise the valid principle that our Workers' Compensation Act should not be transformed into a general accident and health insurance law.

In determining whether a claimant's exposure to cotton dust has significantly contributed to, or been a significant causative factor in, chronic obstructive lung disease, the Commission may, of course, consider medical testimony, but its consideration is not limited to such testimony. It may consider other factual circumstances in the case, among which are (1) the extent of the worker's exposure to cotton dust during employment, (2) the extent of other non-work-related, but contributing, exposures and components; and (3) the manner in which the disease developed with reference to the claimant's work history. *See Booker v. Duke Medical Center, supra,* 297 N.C. at 476, 256 S.E.2d at 200.

In the case before us it is clear that claimant suffers from chronic obstructive lung disease, which prevents her from doing anything but sedentary work. The Commission has so found. There is also evidence that claimant's exposure to cotton dust in her employment "probably was a cause" of her lung disease, that cigarette smoking "was one of the more probable causes . . . after taking into consideration her exposure to cotton dust," and that "emphysema" and "chronic bronchitis" were components of the disease. Further evidence, largely from the claimant herself, detailed her twenty-five years of exposure to cotton dust and the gradual development during those years of her breathing difficulty to the point where it simply rendered her so physically disabled that she could no longer work at the only trade she knew and for which she was qualified. There was also evidence that textile workers, such as claimant here, are "at an increased risk of contracting chronic obstructive pulmonary disease" and that her exposure to cotton dust at Kings Yarn would have aggravated claimant's pulmonary condition existing at the time she went to work there. There was also some evidence that claimant's exposure to cotton dust played an insignificant role in the development of claimant's lung disease. Dr. Williams, as already noted, said: "It is not possible to completely exclude cotton dust as playing some role in causing an irritative bronchitis but she does not give a classical history of byssinosis."

From this evidence the Commission could have found as facts, although it would not have been compelled to find, that: (1) claimant has chronic obstructive lung disease; (2) the two primary causes of this disease are the inhalation of cotton dust for twenty-five years while claimant was a textile worker and the inhalation of cigarette smoke over a similar period of time; (3) the disease also has components of chronic bronchitis and emphysema; (4) the disease developed gradually over the period of claimant's working life until by 1971 claimant had developed a breathing difficulty; (5) by 1977 her breathing difficulty began to affect her ability to do her job because it caused her to be too fatigued to work; (6) by January 1979 claimant's lung disease had rendered her physically unable to work in the textile industry; (7) the disease would not have developed to this extent had it not been for her exposure to cotton dust and her inhalation of cigarette smoke, both of which significantly contributed to, or were significant causative factors in, the development of the disease; (8) because of her age, limited education, and her lifetime of employment in the textile industry, claimant is neither trained nor qualified to do other kinds of work and, at this time, is not able to be gainfully employed; (9) claimant's chronic obstructive lung disease was aggravated to some extent by her exposure to cotton dust at Kings Yarn; and (10) claimant's job in the textile industry exposed her to a greater risk of contracting chronic obstructive lung disease than members of the public generally.

These findings of fact, if made by the Commission, would support the following legal conclusions: (1) claimant's chronic obstructive lung disease is due to causes and conditions characteristic of and peculiar to the textile industry under G.S. 97-53(13); (2) claimant's chronic obstructive lung disease is not an ordinary disease of life to which the general public not employed in the textile industry is equally exposed under G.S. 97-53(13); (3) claimant's chronic obstructive lung disease is, therefore, an occupational disease under G.S. 97-53(13); (4) claimant is totally incapacitated for work under G.S. 97-29, 97-54, and 97-2(9); (5) claimant's total incapacity for work results from her occupational disease under G.S. 97-52; and (6) claimant's last injurious exposure to the hazards of her occupational disease were in the employment of defendant Kings Yarn under G.S. 97-57. These conclusions of law would, in turn, support an award against defendants and in favor of claimant for workers' compensation benefits for total incapacity for work by reason of an occupational disease.

On the other hand there is some testimony from Dr. Williams which would have supported a finding that claimant's exposure to cotton dust played an insignificant causal role in, or did not significantly contribute to, the development of Ms. Rutledge's lung disease. If the Commission so finds, it would have to conclude that the disease is not an occupational disease in this case.

The Court of Appeals relied on *Walston v. Burlington Industries, supra,* 304 N.C. 670, 285 S.E.2d 822, *amended on rehearing,* 305 N.C. 296, 285 S.E.2d 822, for its conclusion that the evidence was insufficient to show claimant had an occupational disease. In *Walston* the principal medical witness could testify only that claimant's exposure to cotton dust "could *possibly* have played a role in the causation of his pulmonary problems." *Id.* at 672, 285 S.E.2d at 827 (emphasis supplied). This Court held, 304 N.C. at 679, 285 S.E.2d at 828:

> While smoking "was almost certain[ly] the primary etiologic agent," there was only a "possibility" that any portion of plaintiff's disability was caused by the inhalation of cotton dust. Such evidence supports the findings and conclusions of the Commission that plaintiff failed to meet his burden of proof, i.e., failed to prove that he had an occupational disease defined in G.S. 97-53(13). A mere possibility of causation is neither "substantial" nor sufficient.

In the case at bar the medical witness testified claimant's exposure to cotton dust "*probably was* a cause" (emphasis supplied) of her chronic obstructive lung disease. Therein lies the difference in this case and *Walston. See Moore v. Stevens & Co.,* 47 N.C. App. 744, 752, 269 S.E.2d 159, 164, *disc. review denied,* 301 N.C. 401, 274 S.E.2d 226

(1980) (physician's opinion that "referred to 'possibility' rather than 'probability'" justified Commission's finding that "plaintiff's chronic pulmonary disease 'is not due to her exposure to cotton dust and lint in her employment'"); *see also, Lockwood v. McCaskill*, 262 N.C. 663, 668–69, 138 S.E.2d 541, 545–46 (1964) ("The 'could' or 'might' as used by Stansbury [in discussing hypothetical questions propounded to expert witnesses] refers to probability and not mere possibility. . . . If it is not reasonably probable . . . that a particular effect is capable of production by a given cause . . . the evidence is not sufficient to establish *prima facie* the causal relation. . . . "; the Court stated that testimony showing a particular causal relation is a mere possibility or conjecture should have been excluded).

We conclude that the Court of Appeals correctly determined that the Industrial Commission decided this case under a misapprehension of applicable law and that the Court of Appeals erred in determining that there was no evidence from which the Commission could make findings sufficient to support a conclusion that claimant suffered from an occupational disease. The decision of the Industrial Commission, therefore, is vacated and the case is remanded to the Commission for a new determination of claimant's entitlement to benefits under the legal principles herein set out.

The dissent argues that there is evidence that claimant had other physical ailments unrelated to her pulmonary disease which might have contributed independently of this disease to her incapacity for work. It is true that there was some evidence of these other ailments. The Commission, however, has found that plaintiff's incapacity for work is due entirely to her pulmonary disease. This finding is supported by the evidence and forecloses the argument in the dissent that these other ailments might have contributed to the claimant's incapacity for work. By our remand of the case, therefore, we do not intend to suggest to the Commission that it re-open this aspect of the case. The only question for reconsideration by the Commission is whether the pulmonary disease is an occupational disease when the legal principles set out in this opinion are applied to the facts.

Affirmed in part; reversed in part and remanded.

MEYER, JUSTICE, dissenting.

I respectfully dissent. The majority today, although without expressly so stating, has subtly but effectively reversed the position of this Court, adopted so recently in *Morrison v. Burlington Industries*, 304 N.C. 1, 282 S.E.2d 458 (1981); *Hansel v. Sherman Textiles*, 304 N.C. 44, 283 S.E.2d 101 (1981), and *Walston v. Burlington Industries*, 304 N.C. 670, 285 S.E.2d 822 (1982). . . .

PROBLEM

A two-year claim period, if dated from last exposure, in the case of most asbestos-related diseases destroys the remedy before the claim exists. Is this constitutional? *See* National Gypsum Co. v. Bunker, 441 N.E.2d 8 (Ind. 1982), *rev'g* 426 N.E.2d 422 (Ind. App. 1981).

Chapter 11
MENTAL AND NERVOUS INJURY

§ 11.01 INTRODUCTION

Efforts by many states to control the costs of their workers' compensation systems have coincided with a period of advancement in the acceptance, understanding, and treatment of mental illness. The nature of the American workplace is also changing in emphasis away from industrial production toward technology and information. In a world of computer cubicles and global competition, stress-related disability is no longer a rare, exceptional occurrence.

At the intersection of these social trends lies a difficult question: How should job-related stress and mental illness fit within a workers' compensation system?

§ 11.02 THE CALIFORNIA EXPERIENCE

Beginning in the 1970s, judicial decisions and legislative standards developed for so-called "mental-mental" or "stress" cases, creating a variety of tests and outcomes. California is a case in point, and the demise of that state's permissive standards for stress cases is well-documented.[1]

In 1982, the California Court of Appeals let stand an award for mental stress caused by the claimant's "honest misperception of job harassment which interact[ed] with [her] preexisting psychiatric condition."[2] The breadth of coverage implied by the court's holding is hard to overstate: Compensability was judged purely on the claimant's subjective perception of work stressors, not objective reality. In addition, the claimant's acute susceptibility to mental stress, due to a preexisting psychiatric condition, was not considered an alternative cause of her injury.

Predictably, California employers reported a jump in the number of workers' compensation stress claims filed from 1,282 in 1980, to 4,236 in 1984, to 6,812 in 1986, with the actual number of claims filed possibly 10 times as high.[3] Another troublesome trend to emerge was the high cost of these claims, in relation to the amount of benefits actually paid out to claimants.[4]

In an effort to control costs and reduce claims fraud, the California legislature enacted a series of reforms beginning in 1989. By 1993, the following statutory provisions were in place limiting relief for mental-mental workers compensation claims: (1) a claim must be based on "actual" employment conditions, which must be shown to be a "predominant cause" of the mental injury; whereas exposure to a violent act need only be a "substantial cause" thereof; (2) claims must be proved by a preponderance of

---

[1] *See, e.g.*, Aya V. Matsumoto, *Reforming the Reform: Mental Stress Claims Under California's Workers' Compensation System*, 27 Loy. La. L. Rev. 1327, 1330–50 (1994).

[2] Albertson's, Inc. v. Workers' Comp. App. Bd., 131 Cal. App. 3d 308, 310, 182 Cal. Rptr. 304, 305 (1982).

[3] *See* Larson, Workers' Compensation Law, § 56.06[1][a]; Matsumoto, *above* n.1, at 1330 & n.12.

[4] Matsumoto, *above* n.1, at 1330–31 & ns. 17–20.

the evidence; (3) mental illnesses are evaluated according to the diagnostic standards developed by the American Psychiatric Association; (4) no mental injury claims may be filed until the employee has worked for the employer for six months; (5) no mental injury claim may be founded on a good faith personnel action such as discharge or demotion; and (6) the post-employment filing of claims is sharply limited.[5]

§ 11.03 STATUTORY DEVELOPMENTS IN OTHER STATES

Other states such as Oregon, Alaska, and West Virginia have amended their workers' compensation laws in the face of state court decisions establishing liberal standards for stress claims. These amendments run the gamut from minor restrictions or evidentiary requirements to a complete denial of relief for stress claims.

A surefire way to minimize the burden of stress cases on workers' compensation systems is to exclude them from coverage completely. Kentucky, which adopted this approach in late 1996, now defines "injury" in its workers' compensation statute "not [to] include a psychological, psychiatric, or stress-related change in the human organism, unless it is a direct result of a physical injury."[6] Kentucky thus joined states such as Florida, Oklahoma, Wyoming, and West Virginia, which allow no relief for mental-mental claims.

Perhaps the strictest jurisdiction in this regard is Montana, which appears to deny coverage for mental injury even when accompanied by disabling physical injury.[7] In May 1997, the Montana Supreme Court took this statutory exclusion to its logical extreme, denying compensation to a firefighter who suffered post-traumatic stress disorder after he was struck by an exploding ball of fire in a burning home.[8] The claimant had suffered first and second degree burns on his hands and face, which had required emergency medical treatment and had caused him to miss work for two and a half weeks. Nevertheless, the state court denied compensation for his permanent disability, holding that it had been caused not by the actual physical impact of the fireball, but rather by the mental shock and fright induced thereby.

Other state legislatures have enacted a variety of limitations governing stress claims short of absolute bar. These restrictions fall into five broad categories: (1) requiring a set amount or type of stress;[9] raising the standard of causation;[10] (3) increasing the burden of proof;[11] (4) imposing specific diagnostic guidelines;[12] and (5) limiting benefits.[13]

Most jurisdictions continue to allow recovery for stress claims, but courts in some of these states, lacking specific statutory guidance, have nevertheless devised special standards for workers' compensation stress cases. Despite the equivalent treatment of

---

[5] *See* Cal. Lab. Code § 3208.3.

[6] Ky. Rev. Stat. § 342.0011(1) (enacted Dec. 12, 1996). Injury "shall not include a psychological, psychiatric, or stress-related change in the human organism, unless it is a direct result of a physical injury."

[7] Mont. Code Ann. 39-71-119(3).

[8] Yarborough v. Montana Municipal Ins. Auth., 938 P.2d 679 (Mont. 1997), *reh'g denied* (June 19, 1997).

[9] *See, e.g.*, Ariz. Rev. Stat. § 23-1043.01 provides that the work stress must be "unexpected, unusual or extraordinary" and must be a "substantial contributing cause" of the injury.

A common provision excludes from coverage any claim arising from good faith personnel actions, such as a demotion or discharge. *See, e.g.*, Conn. Gen. Stat. § 31-275(16)(B)(iii); Me. Rev. Stat. Ann. tit. 39A § 201(3).

[10] *See, e.g.*, Col. Rev. Stat. Ann. § 8-41-302. In Colorado, stress claims are not compensable "unless it is shown by competent evidence that such mental or emotional stress is proximately caused solely by hazards to which the worker would not have been equally exposed outside the employment."

[11] *See, e.g.*, La. Rev. Stat. Ann. §§ 23:1021 (7)(b), 23:1031.1(D).

[12] *See, e.g.*, Ark. Code Ann. § 11-9-113(a)(2), which mandates use of criteria established in the most current issue of the Diagnostic and Statistical Manual of Mental Disorders.

[13] Ark. Code Ann. § 11-9-113(b)(1) limits benefits for mental injuries to 26 weeks.

mental and physical harm in Wisconsin's workers' compensation law, the Wisconsin Court of Appeals has articulated a more demanding stress requirement in mental-mental claims.[14] If a mental stimulus results in a physical injury, the claimant need only show that his or her work activity precipitated, worsened, or hastened the condition. To raise a successful mental-mental claim, however, a worker must show that the mental injury was caused by "unusual stress" — i.e., a "situation of greater dimensions that the day-to-day emotional strain and tension which all employees must experience."[15]

There are still some states, including Maryland and North Carolina, for example, where courts award benefits for mental-mental claims under the general accidental injury and occupational disease standards without differentiating between mental and physical injuries.

§ 11.04   PHYSICAL TRAUMA PRODUCING MENTAL INJURY

WATSON v. MELMAN, INC.
106 So. 2d 433 (Fla. 1958)

PEARSON, JUDGE.

The claimant in a Workmen's Compensation proceeding petitions for certiorari. She complains of an order of the Florida Industrial Commission which set aside the deputy commissioner's order allowing her claim and directed that her claim be denied. The burden of the petition is that the full commission in its order, reversing the order of the deputy commissioner, misapplied section 440.02(19), Fla. Stat., F.S.A.[16] The petition is well founded and the order of the full commission is reversed.

The deputy commissioner made the following findings: While the claimant was working at a sewing machine in her employer's place of business a fellow employee picked up a cardboard spool weighing eight and one-half ounces and tossed it towards the claimant, intending that it should go over her head and into a trash receptacle some fifteen feet away. The edge of the spool struck the claimant immediately behind her ear. Other than a slight discoloration of the skin, no sign was left upon the area where the blow struck.

The deputy commissioner further found:

> That, by reason of the accidental death of her teen-age son by being struck a blow upon his head, an injury of such a nature as the claimant sustained was of sufficient connotation to the claimant to constitute the "symbolic significance" described by Dr. Gilbert, and that, having been divorced in her later years of life and required to engage in strenuous labor to provide for herself and her daughter, and to thereafter sustain an injury of "symbolic significance" was sufficient to constitute a significant threat to her financial security as also described by Dr. Gilbert, and that by reason of her industrial accident of May 25, 1956, the claimant, although incurring no organic disability whatsoever, did incur a traumatic neurosis whereby she is now and has been since the aforesaid date temporarily and totally disabled.

---

[14] United Parcel Serv., Inc. v. Mutual Insurance Co., 208 Wis. 2d 306, 560 N.W.2d 301 (Wis. Ct. App. 1997).

[15] 560 N.W.2d at 305.

[16] *(Court's footnote)* " 'Accident' shall mean only an unexpected or unusual event or result, happening suddenly. A mental or nervous injury due to fright or excitement only or disability or death due to the accidental acceleration or aggravation of a venereal disease or of a disease due to the habitual use of alcohol or narcotic drugs, shall be deemed not to be an injury by accident arising out of the employment. . . . " Section 440.02(19), Fla. Stat., F.S.A.

As to this finding the full commission held:

> The Deputy Commissioner has made a finding that "although incurring no organic disability whatsoever, (she) did incur a traumatic neurosis." The finding the Deputy made with respect to claimant's suffering from no "organic disability" is supported by competent substantial evidence; however, we are of the opinion that the Deputy has misconstrued the law in respect thereto. Apparently Section 440.02(19), Florida Statutes [F.S.A.], which states, in part, "A mental or nervous injury due to fright or excitement only . . . shall be deemed not to be an injury by accident arising out of the employment," has been unintentionally overlooked or deemed inapplicable.

The conclusion reached by the full commission is simply "[S]aid claim should be dismissed, in that fright alone does not constitute an injury by accident."

There is no doubt that the claimant sustained "an accident arising out of and in the course of her employment." The only question is whether compensation is barred by the provisions of section 440.02(19), Fla. Stat., F.S.A.

The full commission placed strong emphasis upon the deputy commissioner's finding of "no organic disability." It should be pointed out that the deputy commissioner did not say "no organic *injury*." Disability is defined by the Workmen's Compensation Act:

> "Disability" means incapacity because of the *injury* to earn in the same or any other employment the wages which the employee was receiving at the time of the injury. (Emphasis added.) Section 440.02(9), Fla. Stat., F.S.A.

Therefore the only significance of the finding of "no organic disability" is that the claimant was found not to be incapacitated for work by reason of an organic condition. Nevertheless, the commissioner found that she did suffer an injury to her body and that as a direct result of the injury she was at the date of the hearing temporarily and totally disabled.

The question then, when reduced to its essentials may be stated as follows: Is compensation for a purely nervous condition, resulting from accident arising out of and in the course of employment, recoverable under the Florida Workmen's Compensation Act? We think that this question has already been answered for the claimant by the Supreme Court in *Superior Mill Work v. Gabel*, Fla. 1956, 89 So. 2d 794, 795:

> that "when there has been a physical accident or trauma, and claimant's disability is increased or prolonged by traumatic neurosis or hysterical paralysis . . . the full disability including the effects of the neurosis is compensable." Larson's Workmen's Compensation Law, 1952, Sec. 42.22. In this state, as in some others, there must be an actual physical injury upon which to predicate compensation for a neurosis. *See City Ice & Fuel Division v. Smith*, Fla. 1952, 56 So. 2d 329; Larson, *ibid.*, Sec. 42.23.

It is true that having laid down this principle the Supreme Court went further to find that the claimant's neurosis in that case did not result directly and immediately from his injury.

Section 42.22 of Larson's Workmen's Compensation Law, quoted with approval in *Superior Millwork v. Gabel, supra*, continues in part, "As in other connections, a pre-existing weakness in the form of a neurotic tendency does not lessen the compensability of an injury which precipitates a disabling neurosis."

It will also be noted that in the case of *City Ice & Fuel Division v. Smith*, Fla. 1952, 56 So. 2d 329, the court was careful to point out that the claimant suffered emotional shock only and that his trouble was not aggravated by trauma.

The problem in the instant case is not whether there was an injury, because the deputy commissioner found that there was a blow, although not of itself disabling. He further found that there was a "traumatic neurosis," which by definition includes an injury. Nor is the problem whether there is a causal connection between the injury and the neurosis, as in *Superior Millwork v. Gabel, supra,* because the deputy commissioner found such a connection, and the full commission does not mention this finding. A review of the record reveals competent, substantial evidence, as a basis for the finding, in the testimony of several of the doctors who testified before the deputy commissioner.

The conclusion reached by the Industrial Commission could only be reached by a determination that there was no injury, and such a conclusion is exactly contrary to the finding of the deputy commissioner who is the trier of fact.

Accordingly, certiorari is granted, the order reviewed is quashed, and the cause remanded for further proceedings not inconsistent herewith.

CARROLL, CHAS., C. J., and HORTON, J., concur.

PROBLEMS

(1) In *Watson*, suppose the claimant had not been hit by the spool, but had *almost* been hit by it, and that the incident had triggered the same neurosis. Should the result be different?

(2) In an unreported Florida case, claimant, in the course of her employment, had been mugged by a black man, who stole her purse and knocked her to the ground, fracturing a vertebra. Since then she has had an irrational fear of black men, which disables her for any normal employment. Compensation was awarded by the Judge of Compensation Claims. The award was upheld by a state court, and the U.S. Supreme Court declined to hear the case. The employers have filed a suit in federal court, particularly relying on the constitutional argument that the award conflicts with equal rights guarantees of the U.S. Constitution. What result would you favor?

(3) Claimant was injured by an electric shock. He took this to be a form of supernatural punishment, and had the idea that his continuing disability would end only when he got a suitable settlement, proving that God had overthrown the devil. Is this reason enough for such a settlement? *See* Moses v. R.H. Wright & Son, Inc., 90 So. 2d 330 (Fla. 1956).

§ 11.05   MENTAL TRAUMA PRODUCING MENTAL INJURY

SEITZ v. L & R INDUSTRIES, INC.
437 A.2d 1345 (R.I. 1981)

WEISBERGER, JUSTICE.

This is an appeal from a final decree of the appellate commission awarding compensation to Beulah Seitz (employee) for total disability resulting from a personal injury of a psychological nature allegedly arising out of the course of her employment during a period of approximately sixteen working days beginning September 15, 1975, and ending on October 3, 1975. The case was initially argued before four members of the court on March 4, 1981. This argument resulted in a per curiam opinion in which the final decree of the appellate commission was affirmed by an equally divided court. *Seitz v. L & R Industries, Inc.*, R.I., 428 A.2d 788 (1981). Thereafter, a petition for reargument was granted, and the case was reargued before a five-member court on October 5, 1981. The posture in which this case comes before us presents legal and factual issues of first impression in this state. The facts as found by the appellate commission are as follows.

The employee had worked as secretary to the vice president and general manager of the Worcester Pressed Aluminum Corporation (Worcester) for approximately six years. The place of employment during this period was Worcester, Massachusetts. In

1975 portions of the Worcester enterprise were placed on the market for sale. One of the divisions known as Palco Products Division was sold to L & R Industries, Inc. (employer). At some time during the month of September 1975, the employer ordered the Palco operations to be moved from Worcester, Massachusetts, to Smithfield, Rhode Island. This change necessitated physical movement of office equipment, furniture, inventory, records, invoices, and machinery. The moving operation began on a Friday afternoon and was completed in a thirty-six-hour period. The employee and a former vice president of Palco Products Division, one Francis Maguire, were active in supervising and implementing the moving activities.

When Palco Products, under the new ownership, began operation on the following Monday, conditions in the new location were confusing and abnormal to a marked degree. Records were unavailable, the telephone service was inadequate, the previous tenants had not vacated the premises, and personnel were untrained. The employee sought to perform duties as office manager and secretary to Mr. Maguire but was also required to do janitorial and cleaning work and to protect office equipment from potential damage due to a leaking roof. She encountered difficulties in interpersonal relations with other employees in the new location. Her authority as office manager was not recognized, and office protocol was not satisfactory to her. She attempted to arrange a meeting with Mr. Maguire and other key personnel in order to work out these difficulties and to improve the organization of the employer's business at the new location. The meeting was scheduled for October 3, 1975, but because of the intervention of another employee, the meeting did not take place. As a result, the employee became so upset that she terminated her employment on the afternoon of October 3, 1975, and has not returned to work since that time.

Dr. Elliot R. Reiner, a psychiatrist who practices in the city of Worcester, had earlier begun treatment of the employee on June 10, 1967, for a condition he described as a depressive neurosis. After three office visits, the employee was discharged. The employee next visited the doctor on October 9, 1975, and described the emotional disruption she had experienced in association with occupational problems and conflicts during the period she had worked with the employer in Smithfield. The doctor diagnosed the employee's condition as an "obsessive compulsive personality disorder." The doctor stated, and the commission found, that the employee's rigid personality characteristic had been of long standing but had been aggravated by her employment from September 15, 1975 to October 3, 1975. The doctor testified that the employee had sustained an emotional trauma but had not experienced any physical trauma as the result of her employment.

The commission found that this aggravation qualified within the terms of G.L. 1956 (1979 Reenactment) § 28-33-1 as a "personal injury arising out of and in the course of [her] employment." Although the commission determined the aggravation to be entirely psychic, it found as a matter of fact and held as a matter of law that the conditions under which the employee had been required to work resulted in a malfunction of the body which gave rise to an incapacity to perform her customary work. Therefore, the appellate commission, with one dissenting member, sustained the decree of the trial commissioner and ordered that compensation for total disability be paid to the employee. We reverse.

Professor Larson in his treatise on The Law of Workmen's Compensation has set forth an analysis of three broad types of psychic injury.[17] The first type is a physical injury caused by mental stimulus. An analysis of case law on this subject leads Professor Larson to conclude that the "decisions uniformly find compensability." [(Court's footnote) 1B Larson, supra at § 42.21.] There appears to have been only one case reported to the contra in the last twenty-five years, Toth v. Standard Oil Co., 160 Ohio St. 1, 113 N.E.2d 81 (1953). In that case the Supreme Court of Ohio determined

---

[17] (Court's footnote) 1B Larson, The Law of Workmen's Compensation §§ 42.21–.23 (1980).

that an injury must be physical or there must be a traumatic damage of an accidental character. Professor Larson criticizes this opinion as unnecessary under the Ohio statute and as *contra* to the great weight of authority. [*Citations omitted*] Rhode Island has no reported cases in respect to such injuries.

The second broad type of psychic injury is that caused by physical trauma. The courts, including this court, have almost universally awarded compensation for this type of physically produced psychic injury upon an appropriate showing of causal connection. *Greenville Finishing Co. v. Pezza*, 81 R.I. 20, 98 A.2d 825 (1953) (neurosis produced by traumatic loss of eye); *Imperial Knife Co. v. Calise*, 80 R.I. 428, 97 A.2d 579 (1953) (incapacity from a fear complex following severe and painful fractures of fingers while operating a power press); *Wareham v. United States Rubber Co.*, 73 R.I. 207, 54 A.2d 372 (1947) (anxiety neurosis following back injury). *See also* cases cited from numerous jurisdictions under § 42.22, 1B Larson, *The Law of Workmen's Compensation* (1980).

The third type of psychiatric injury mentioned by Professor Larson is a mental injury produced by mental stimulus in which there are neither physical causes nor physical results. Professor Larson finds "a distinct majority position supporting compensability in these cases" but concedes that "[t]he *contra* view, denying compensation in the 'mental-mental' category continues, however, to command a substantial following." *Id.* § 42.23 at 7-628. [*Citations omitted*]

In this field, of course, it is difficult to compare holdings in various jurisdictions because of the variation among the statutory provisions. Some statutes require accidental injuries. Other statutes, such as that of Rhode Island, require "personal injury" without the necessity of an accident.

A number of the states that have approved compensation for psychic injuries produced by mental stimulus have done so on the basis of dramatic psychological trauma. For example, in *Bailey v. American General Insurance Co.*, 279 S.W.2d 315, 154 Tex. 430 (1955), characterized by Professor Larson as "[o]ne of the most impressive of the earlier decisions," the claimant and another workman were on a scaffold when one end gave way. The other workman plunged to his death in view of the claimant. The claimant thought he was about to be killed but was caught in a cable and did not fall. He managed to jump to the roof of another building. After this experience, the claimant was unable to continue in this employment as a structural steelworker. He would blank out and freeze, undergoing complete paralysis when attempting work in a high place. On these facts the Supreme Court of Texas reversed the Court of Civil Appeals and determined that the psychic injury was compensable.

In *Wolfe v. Sibley, Lindsay & Curr Co.*, 36 N.Y.2d 505, 369 N.Y.S.2d 637, 330 N.E.2d 603 (1975), after many years of rejecting the compensability of "mental-mental" injuries, the Court of Appeals of New York ordered the award of compensation based upon a dramatic set of facts. The employee had served as secretary to the security director of a department store. By reason of job pressures, the security director became increasingly nervous and withdrawn. The female employee sought to assist her boss by relieving him of some of the duties of his position and by serving as a confidante. However, one day she entered the office and found the security director dead of a self-inflicted gunshot wound. The shock of this encounter caused the employee to enter into a condition of severe depression which left her unable to work for about a year. In awarding compensation, the court noted, "There is nothing talismanic about physical impact. . . . " *Id.* at 510, 330 N.E.2d at 606, 369 N.Y.S.2d at 642. In spite of the drama of this occurrence, Chief Judge Breitel in dissent made the following observation:

> In an era marked by examples of overburdening of socially desirable programs with resultant curtailment or destruction of such programs, a realistic assessment of impact of doctrine is imperative. An overburdening of the compensation system by injudicious and open-ended expansion of compensation

benefits, especially for costly, prolonged, and often only ameliorative psychiatric care, cannot but threaten its soundness or that of the enterprises upon which it depends. *Id.* at 513–14, 330 N.E.2d at 608, 369 N.Y.S.2d at 644.

A third illustrative state in which this category of injury has been found compensable is Illinois. In *Pathfinder Co. v. Industrial Commission*, 62 Ill.2d 556, 343 N.E.2d 913 (1976), an employee who was engaged in instructing a fellow worker in the operation of a punch press saw her coworker's hand being caught in the press. When the employee sought to extricate her coworker's hand, she found it already severed at the wrist. The employee fainted and was taken to the hospital. Upon return to work, she suffered from psychic and neurotic symptoms which disabled her from employment. The Supreme Court of Illinois, in ordering compensation, expressed the opinion that its holding would not encourage filing of claims by malingering employees but suggested that the Illinois Industrial Commission should continue to be "vigilant in the assessment of claims that might be easily fabricated or exaggerated." *Id.* at 567, 343 N.E.2d at 919.

As an example of a contrary conclusion, one might consider the case of *Ayer v. Industrial Commission*, 23 Ariz. App. 163, 531 P.2d 208 (1975), in which a switchboard operator was denied compensation for mental problems that she claimed to be the result of the increase in the duties of her employment and a consequent buildup of emotional stress over a period of time. The court determined that this kind of disabling mental condition — one not caused by an unexpected traumatic event — was not compensable. The court suggested that to determine otherwise would literally be to open Pandora's Box by "permitting compensation to any disgruntled employee who leaves [her] job in a huff because of an emotional disturbance." *Id.* at 166, 531 P.2d at 211.

The Supreme Court of Wisconsin has succinctly encapsulated the distinction in *School District No. 1 v. Department of Industry, Labor & Human Relations*, 62 Wis. 2d 370, 215 N.W.2d 373 (1974), in which it stated:

> Thus it is the opinion of this court that mental injury nontraumatically caused must have resulted from a situation of greater dimensions than the day-to-day emotional strain and tension which all employees must experience. Only if the "fortuitous event unexpected and unforeseen' can be said to be so out of the ordinary from the countless emotional strains and differences that employees encounter daily without serious mental injury will liability . . . be found. *Id.* at 377–78, 215 N.W.2d at 377.

In *School District No. 1*, compensation was denied to a school guidance teacher who suffered psychic injury in the form of an acute anxiety reaction upon seeing a recommendation from a group of students that she be dismissed from her position as a member of the guidance counseling staff of the school.

Our neighboring state of Massachusetts in *Fitzgibbons' Case*, 374 Mass. 633, 373 N.E.2d 1174 (1978) allowed compensation to a supervisory corrections officer who had reacted to a violent scuffle that brought about the death of a subordinate officer. This incident gave rise to an acute anxiety reaction on the part of Fitzgibbons which ultimately led to his committing suicide. The Supreme Judicial Court noted that this injury stemmed from a single traumatic event and not from response to everyday-employment stress. Thereafter, in *Albanese's Case*, 378 Mass. 14, 389 N.E.2d 83 (1979), the Supreme Judicial Court awarded compensation to a foreman who had reacted to conflicting orders from his immediate superior over a considerable period to the point where he was thoroughly discredited and confused. He had ultimately experienced such stress in attempting to accommodate the conflicting demands of both his subordinates and the plant manager that he became totally unable to perform his duties. The court held that this was a personal injury arising out of and in the course of employment. The court noted, however, that Albanese's injury was not "the result of everyday stress or '[b]odily wear and tear resulting from a long period of hard work.' " *Id.* at —, 389 N.E.2d at 86.

Although it might be possible to multiply examples of cases in which compensation has been allowed as well as cases in which compensation has been withheld, there seems to be an elusive thread of consistency woven among them which may be discerned.

The courts are reluctant to deny compensation for genuine disability arising out of psychic injury. However, since screening of such claims is a difficult process, the courts recognize the burden that may be placed upon commerce and industry by allowing compensation for neurotic reaction to the ordinary everyday stresses that are found in most areas of employment. Indeed, it is a rare situation in which some adverse interpersonal relations among employees are not encountered from time to time. Employers and managers must admonish their subordinates and correct perceived shortcomings. The stress of competitive enterprise is ever present and attendant upon all types of commercial and industrial activity.

Great care must be taken in order to avoid the creation of voluntary "retirement" programs that may be seized upon by an employee at an early age if he or she is willing or, indeed, even eager to give up active employment and assert a neurotic inability to continue.

It is all very well to say that the adversary system will expose the difference between the genuine neurotic and the malingerer. We have great fears that neither the science of psychiatry nor the adversary judicial process is equal to this task on the type of claim here presented. An examination of the evidence in the instant case discloses that the employee's psychiatrist largely accepted her statement that she was unable to return to work. The patient, who had exhibited neurotic tendencies, arising out of family relationships as early as 1967, apparently suffered an aggravation during her sixteen-day period of employment with the employer. An analysis of the testimony in the case would clearly indicate that this stressful period contained conditions that, though scarcely tranquil did not exceed the intensity of stimuli encountered by thousands of other employees and management personnel every day. If psychic injury is to be compensable, a more dramatically stressful stimulus must be established. Otherwise, the fears expressed by Chief Judge Breitel dissenting in *Wolfe v. Sibley, Lindsay & Curr Co., supra*, would be most applicable in terms of the potential burdens to be imposed upon the Rhode Island compensation system.[18]

---

[18] *(Court's footnote)* Our brother Kelleher argues eloquently in dissent that principles of statutory interpretation mandate that compensation be awarded to an employee who receives a personal injury produced by a mental stimulus related to situations arising out of job stress. He further suggests that any relief from such statutory interpretation should be sought from the Legislature rather than from this court. It is worthy of note that the term "personal injury," as opposed to "person injury sustained by accident," was first introduced into our workers' compensation statute by provisions of P.L. 1949, ch. 2282. At the time of enactment of this statute, not a single case can be found which awarded compensation for mental injuries or aggravation produced by gradually accumulated job stress. An examination of the cases compiled in 97 A.L.R. 3d 161, 184 (1980), allowing compensation for mental disorder resulting from nonsudden stimulus, discloses that the earliest case set forth in the compilation appears to be Carter v. General Motors Corp., 361 Mich. 577, 106 N.W.2d 105 (1960). An examination of the cases set forth under § 42.23(b) of 1B Larson, The Law of Workmen's Compensation, fails also to disclose any case awarding compensation for gradual stimulus causing nervous injury prior to 1960. As a consequence, the decisional context in which our Legislature adopted the statutory term "personal injury" did not include any interpretation that would have alerted the Legislature to the ramifications of compensation for mental injury caused by gradual, nondramatic stimulus. We should, therefore, suggest that in the event the Legislature desired to make such injuries compensable, a more definite expression of intention than the words "personal injury" should be manifested. Consequently, although we agree that any change in the statute should be made at the State House rather than in the court house, we are of the opinion that interpretation of the words "personal injury" should be made in the legal context in which these words were first adopted rather than to confer upon them a judicial gloss from certain other selected jurisdictions applied long after the Legislature had initially spoken.

CANDELARIA v. GENERAL ELECTRIC COMPANY
105 N.M. 167, 730 P.2d 470 (1986)

ALARID, JUDGE.

Defendants appeal from the judgment of the district court in favor of Robert Lee Candelaria (plaintiff). This appeal raises issues of first impression: whether and under what circumstances psychological disability predicated upon psychological injury that arises from work-related stress is compensable under the New Mexico Workmen's Compensation Act (Act), NMSA 1978, Sections 52-1-1 to -69 (Orig. Pamp. and Cum. Supp.1985). . . .

FACTS

Plaintiff is forty-three years old and has been married for seven years. He has a high school education and was in the service for three years. He testified that he had no problems in the service and was honorably discharged. He then began work as a "plater." Eventually, he became a foreman supervising platers and later became a plant manager overseeing a substantial number of employees. He held this position for thirteen or fourteen years until, in 1977, the owner sold the plant, leaving plaintiff without a job. Plaintiff came to New Mexico to look for work and had to settle for a janitor job. Subsequently, plaintiff worked as a laborer and for a company making roof trusses. He testified that he had no problems with these jobs and had no clashes with his supervisors. Plaintiff then went to work for General Electric (G.E.), as a janitor, hoping that he could advance to a plating job.

Plaintiff first worked as a janitor for G.E., but soon became a forklift operator. Thereafter, he began to work as a "process varied" preparing jet engine parts for plating. According to plaintiff, he had no emotional difficulties with his supervisors during this period of time. At first, plaintiff worked during the night shift under Gianini for a period of between six months and a year. Plaintiff testified that except for one instance where he had refused to take a shortcut requested by Gianini, he had no problems while he worked the night shift.

Plaintiff described the process of his work. Basically, he prepared various components of jet engines for plating. The parts would be cleaned and then placed in acid, cleanser chemical or plating baths for various periods of time. A timer would go off when the part was to be removed from the bath. More than one part would be going through this process at any given time. Plaintiff testified that this was a full-time job.

Plaintiff's problems began when he was transferred to the day shift and began working under the supervision of Jewett. At first, plaintiff had basically the same job. After a few weeks, however, Jewett began to assign more duties to plaintiff. An employee with a different job classification quit, and plaintiff was required to perform this employee's job in addition to his own. Plaintiff testified that he received no help from other employees in performing these additional tasks. The performance of these additional tasks was complicated by the fact that parts were being timed while plaintiff was doing these tasks and by the fact that Jewett would tell plaintiff to drop everything in order to work on the "hot" (priority) items.

Plaintiff complained to Jewett, but was told that he had to do the work assigned to him. Plaintiff then went to the union and various plant officials, but nothing was done. Plaintiff then went to the Labor Board, but was told to talk to the plant manager. Plaintiff did talk to the plant manager and was told a new worker would be hired in three weeks. Three weeks passed, and no new worker was hired.

On or about May 13, 1981, plaintiff again went to see the plant manager. The manager said he had been too busy and needed additional time. Plaintiff returned to his work station and was told to go outside to steam clean some parts. Plaintiff felt nervous. Jewett came outside and started giving plaintiff more orders. Plaintiff started shaking and felt like killing Jewett. Plaintiff formed an intent to kill Jewett but changed his mind. Plaintiff ran inside the building he was crying, sweating and had chest pains. Plaintiff went home where he was later found by his wife still crying and shaking. His wife called the family doctor.

A series of hospitalizations began for psychological problems. First, plaintiff was hospitalized for three months at Vista Sandia on a voluntary basis. He then returned to G.E., was again placed under Jewett and asked to perform the same tasks. Soon, plaintiff was suffering from nervousness, sweating and chest pain. He was again hospitalized at Vista Sandia for three months. Plaintiff returned to work at G.E., again was placed under Jewett and asked to perform the same tasks. According to plaintiff, "Jewett didn't slack off one bit." Plaintiff had a nervous breakdown and was again hospitalized at Vista Sandia. This happened again and again for a total of four times. Plaintiff told officials at G.E. that he would work as a janitor, if necessary, if they would not place him under Jewett again. After the fourth hospitalization, plaintiff was finally placed under another supervisor. However, after attending a deposition, plaintiff saw Jewett, got chest pains and began to hyperventilate. He was then hospitalized for the fifth time in January 1983. . . .

1. Compensability of Psychological Injury Caused by Emotional Stress

A. Recognition of the Cause of Action

Defendant's arguments on appeal are related to the issue of whether a workman may recover compensation benefits where he has sustained disability predicated upon a psychological injury, caused by emotional stress, which is unrelated to any accompanying physical injury. Although this question has been raised previously in this jurisdiction, recovery has been denied based upon the facts of each particular case. *See Kern v. Ideal Basic Industries*, 101 N.M. 801, 689 P.2d 1272 (Ct. App. 1984) (a mental breakdown suffered as a result of termination was not an injury "arising out of" employment because it was not related to the performance of the employee's employment duties). No case has held or suggested that a psychological injury caused by stress arising out of and in the course of employment would not be compensable. There is a divergence of opinion as to whether workmen's compensation benefits are payable due to the disability or death of a workman caused by shock, excitement or emotional disturbance unaccompanied by physical impact or violence on the workman's body. *See, e.g., State Compensation Fund v. Industrial Commission*, 24 Ariz. App. 31, 535 P.2d 623 (1975) (mental or emotional shock resulting in disability is compensable without physical injury) *Burlington Mills Corp. v. Hagood*, 177 Va. 204, 13 S.E.2d 291 (1941) (recognizing recovery without physical impact). Contra *In re Loague*, 450 P.2d 492 (Okla.1969); *In re Korsun's Case*, 354 Mass. 124, 235 N.E.2d 814 (1968); *Samolin v. Trans World Airlines, Inc.*, 20 App. Div. 2d 160, 245 N.Y.S.2d 628 (1963); *Liscio v. S. Makransky & Sons*, 147 Pa. Super. 483, 24 A.2d 136 (1942).

A "distinct majority" of out-of-state courts have held that an emotional or mental stimulus can produce a compensable "nervous" injury. 1B A. Larson, Workmen's Compensation Law, § 42.23 (1985). *See, e.g., American National Red Cross v. Hagin*, 327 F.2d 559 (7th Cir.1964); *Carter v. General Motors Corp.*, 361 Mich. 577, 106 N.W.2d 105 (1960); *Wolfe v. Sibley, Lindsay & Curr Co.*, 369 N.Y.S.2d 637, 330 N.E.2d 603 (1975); *Bailey v. American General Insurance Co.*, 279 S.W.2d 315, 154 Tex. 430 (1955). *See also* Annot., 97 A.L.R. 3d 161 (1980 & Supp. 1985). An substantial number of courts, however, still deny recovery in these cases. *Id. See, e.g.,* Jacobs v. Goodyear Tire & Rubber Co., 196 Kan. 613, 412 P.2d 986 (1966); *Johnson v. Hartford Accident & Indemnity Co.*, 196 So. 2d 635 (La. App. 1967); *Vernon v. Seven-Eleven Stores*, 547 P.2d 1300 (Okla. 1976). The majority of courts that have dealt with the question have held that this emotional or mental stimulus may be gradual. Larson, *supra*, § 42.23(b). *See, e.g., American National Red Cross Carter.*

New Mexico law points us in the direction toward recognizing that an emotional or mental stimulus can produce a compensable psychological injury. In a series of cases involving physical injuries at the workplace, the supreme court has held that a resulting psychological disability is compensable. *Webb v. Hamilton*, 78 N.M. 647, 436 P.2d 507 (1968), overruled on other grounds, *American Tank & Steel Corp. v. Thompson*, 90 N.M. 513, 565 P.2d 1030 (1977), *Ross v. Sayers Well Servicing Co.*, 76 N.M. 321, 414 P.2d 679 (1966), *Jensen v. United Perlite Corp.*, 76 N.M. 384, 415 P.2d 356 (1966) overruled on other grounds. Gonzales v. Gackle Drilling Co., 70 N.M. 131, 371 P.2d 605 (1962). In a series of cases involving physical disabilities, both the supreme court and this court have held that an injury caused by emotional stress at work is compensable. *Salazar v. County of Bernalillo*, 69 N.M. 464, 368 P.2d 141 (1962) (cerebral hemorrhage caused by stressful events at work), *Little v. J. Korber & Co.*, 71 N.M. 294, 378 P.2d 119 (1963) (emotional upset at work caused heart attack), *Crane v. San Juan County, New Mexico*, 100 N.M. 600, 673 P.2d 1333 (Ct. App. 1983) (work stress caused high blood pressure which caused hemorrhage in eye). Thus, existing case law has established that a psychological disability is a "disability" within the meaning of the Act, and that physical disabilities resulting from work-related emotional stress are compensable. If both physical trauma leading to psychological disability, and emotional stress, leading to physical disability are compensable, it follows that emotional stress leading to psychological disability comes within the Act. We hold that a psychological disability caused by stress arising out of and in the course of employment is compensable. *See Townsend v. Maine Bureau of Public Safety*, 404 A.2d 1014 (Me.1979).

Implicit in our holding is the recognition that a gradual, non-traumatic emotional condition arising from stress may be an accidental injury under Section 52-1-28 of the Act. This section makes "an accidental injury arising out of, and in the course of . . . employment" a pre-condition to coverage. *Id.* The language makes no distinction between physical and mental injuries. An accidental injury is merely an unlooked-for mishap, or untoward event, that is not expected or designed. *Bufalino v. Safeway Stores, Inc.*, 98 N.M. 560, 650 P.2d 844 (Ct. App. 1982). An accident is not limited to a sudden injury, nor is it limited to any time test. *Gilbert v. E.B. Law & Son, Inc.*, 60 N.M. 101, 287 P.2d 992 (1955). Such injury, moreover, may be produced gradually and progressively. *Webb v. New Mexico Publishing Co.*, 47 N.M. 279, 141 P.2d 333 (1943). The statutory language does not operate to bar an emotional condition arising from stress.

The language serves as a reflection of the basic purpose of the Act, which is to ensure that industry carry the burden of personal injuries suffered by workmen in the course of their employment. *Gonzales v. Chino Copper Co.*, 29 N.M. 228, 222 P. 903 (1942), *Casillas v. S.W.I.G.*, 96 N.M. 84, 628 P.2d 329 (Ct. App. 1981). Our inclusion of a gradual, non-traumatic emotional injury does no more than track that purpose. In *Royal State National Insurance Co. v. Labor and Industrial Relations Appeal Board*, 53 Haw. 32, 487 P.2d 278 (1971), the Hawaii Supreme Court eloquently articulated why this is so. That court interpreted "accidental injury" in a statutory provision similar to Section 52-1-28, and concluded:

> HRS [Hawaii Revised Statutes] § 386-3 makes no differentiation between organic and psychic injuries arising out of the employment relationship and we do not believe this court should impose such a distinction. The legislature has chosen to treat work-related injuries as a cost of production to be borne by industry and, ultimately, through the consumption process, by the community in general. (Citation omitted). In today's highly competitive world it cannot be doubted that people often succumb to mental pressures resulting from their employment. These disabilities are as much a cost of the production process as physical injuries. The humanitarian purposes of the Workmen's Compensation Law require that indemnification be predicated not upon the label assigned to the injury received, but upon the employee's inability to work because of

impairments flowing from the conditions of his employment. *Id.* at 38, 487 P.2d at 282 (citation omitted). *See also* Annot., 97 A.L.R.3d at 168–69.

Defendants are in error, therefore, when they assert that plaintiff suffered no accidental injury. Substantial evidence supported the trial court in finding that an accidental injury took place on May 13, 1981 (the first hospitalization), and before each subsequent hospitalization.

B. "Arising Out Of" Employment

Our holding, however, raises other issues argued on appeal. We must, in recognizing a new basis for recovery, determine what is required for the psychological injury to "arise out of" the particular employment. Section 52-1-28. We first discuss the "arising out of" component in New Mexico and its relationship to the present case. We next discuss the approach of other jurisdictions, and the approach we will adopt.

It is unnecessary that a workman be subjected to an unusual or extraordinary condition for an injury to be compensable. *See, e.g., Lyon v. Catron County Commissioners,* 81 N.M. 120, 464 P.2d 410 (Ct. App. 1969), *Webb v. New Mexico Publishing Co.; Alspaugh v. Mountain States Mutual Casualty Co.,* 66 N.M. 126, 343 P.2d 697 (1959). In order to arise out of employment, an injury need only be causally related to the performance of the job duties. *See Wilson v. Richardon Ford Sales, Inc.,* 97 N.M. 226, 638 P.2d 1071 (1981). In New Mexico, however, it is not sufficient that the injury occurs at work the disability must have resulted from a "risk incident to work itself" or "increased by the circumstances of the employment." *Kern,* 101 N.M. at 802, 689 P.2d at 1273.

To the extent, therefore, that plaintiff's disability was due to stress associated with the performance of his work duties, it "arose out of" his employment. *Salazar v. County of Bernalillo; Little v. J. Korber & Co.; Crane v. San Juan County.* Whether plaintiff's stress, resulting from the conflicts with Jewett, arose out of the employment depends upon whether the conflicts were related to work. *Cf. Perez v. Fred Harvey, Inc.,* 54 N.M. 339, 224 P.2d 524 (1950) (jury question whether shooting by fellow employee was personally motivated or motivated by work-related quarrel). Jewett denied any conflict with plaintiff. Plaintiff's testimony, set forth above, was that the conflict arose from Jewett's assignment of work duties. Plaintiff's testimony was substantial evidence that the stresses identified by Drs. Fredman and Sacks as the cause of the disability did arise from plaintiff's employment.

Certain jurisdictions have expressed concern over applying the normal interpretation of "arising out of" to cases involving gradual psychological injury. This concern grows out of the traditional reluctance of courts to allow recovery for any mental suffering unaccompanied by physical impact or injury. The reluctance is based on a fear of fraudulent claims and the lack of judicial expertise for evaluating injury unaccompanied by observable physical manifestations. *See Townsend.* Where a psychological injury "occurs rapidly and can be readily traced to a specific event . . . there is a sufficient badge of reliability to assuage [any] Court's apprehension. Where, however, a mental injury develops gradually and is linked to no particular incident, the risk of groundless claims looms large indeed." *Id.,* 404 A.2d at 1018.

As a response to the difficulties inherent in the evaluation of psychological injury, the Supreme Court of Wisconsin, in *School District 1 v. Department of Industry, Labor & Human Relations,* 62 Wis. 2d 370, 377, 215 N.W.2d 373, 377 (1974), enunciated the following interpretation of "arise out of" employment:

> [I]t is the opinion of this court that mental injury non-traumatically caused must have resulted from a situation of greater dimensions than the day-to-day emotional strain and tension which all employees must experience. Only if the "fortuitous event unexpected and unforeseen" can be said to be so out of the

ordinary from the court less emotional strains and differences that employees encounter daily without serious mental injury will liability . . . be found.

The plaintiff in *School District* was employed as a school guidance counselor. She received a list of recommendations from high school students that asked for the removal of several staff members, including herself. The Department of Industry found that receipt of this list, and conversations with students concerning the list, constituted the accident "arising out of" plaintiff's employment which caused subsequent "acute anxiety reaction" and resulting disability. *Id.* at 372–373, 215 N.W.2d 374–375. The court, however, after formulating its interpretation of "arise out of," concluded that the receipt of the list "could not be deemed to be so out of the ordinary from the countless emotional strains and differences that employees encounter daily without serious mental injury." 60 Wis. 2d at 378, 215 N.W.2d at 377. Her application for compensation was dismissed.

Arkansas, Rhode Island and Wyoming have adopted the School District interpretation of "arising out of." *See Owens v. National Health Laboratories,* 8 Ark. App. 92, 648 S.W.2d 829 (1983), *Seitz v. L. & R. Industries, Inc., etc.,* 437 A.2d 1345 (R.I.1981), *Consolidated Freightways v. Drake,* 678 P.2d 874 (Wyo. 1984). Defendants ask this court to adopt *School District* and overrule the trial court on that basis.

In *Townsend,* the Supreme Court of Maine modified *School District* because it perceived a problem with its application. The Townsend court announced the following standard:

> While this rule [in *School District*] would be appropriate in the vast majority of gradual mental injury cases, it would not compensate an individual who, for example, developed a psychological disability resulting from the simple day-to-day stresses of an assembly line. . . . Our Act, however, is not merely objective covering the average person it is also subjective and protects even the eggshell. With adequate safeguards to shield the employer, even those predisposed to mental injury should be able to recover for ordinary work-related stress to which others would not succumb. We conclude that ordinary work-related stress and stain could be compensable if it were shown by clear and convincing evidence that the trauma generated by the employment predominated in producing the resulting injury. [*Court's footnote omitted.*] Any less showing, however, would be insufficient adequately to protect an employer. 404 A.2d at 1019–20. *Townsend* recognized the higher level of stress required under *School District* for most cases but, at the same time, permitted a subjective standard for the measurement of stress designed to protect those workers predisposed to mental injury.

Another group of jurisdictions allow compensation based on a gradual mental injury resulting from day-to-day work-related stress without the higher standard of proof imposed in *Townsend. Baker v. Workmen's Compensation Appeals Board,* 18 Cal. App. 3d 852, 96 Cal. Rptr. 279 (1971); *Royal State; Carter.* This approach is premised on the view that the basic purpose of a worker's compensation system mandates that a worker disabled as a result of work-related stress receive treatment identical to a worker disabled by a work-related physical injury. *Carter.*

We realize the competing interests involved with any approach. On the one hand, there is the goal of maintaining a progressive worker's compensation system. *Carter.* On the other, there is the goal of reducing fraudulent claims in order to financially preserve the system. *Townsend.* It is, however, the province of the legislature to make changes in the provisions of coverage under the Act. *Varos v. Union Oil Co. of California,* 101 N.M. 713, 688 P.2d 31 (Ct. App. 1984).

Section 52-1-28 does not distinguish between a physical and mental injury, nor does any provision of the Act condition compensation on an injury resulting from unusual or extraordinary working conditions. *Webb Lyons.* The application of the *School District* rule would mean that a mental injury, to be compensable, must result from an extraordinary working condition, whereas a physical injury, to be compensable, need only result from the usual conditions of employment. Application of the higher standard of proof in *Townsend* would also differentiate between physical condition that makes him more susceptible to physical injury is not subjected to a higher standard of proof than a worker not so disposed. *Salazar v. County of Bernalillo*. However, a worker predisposed to mental injury from day-to-day stress would have to establish, by clear and convincing evidence, the causal connection between the trauma generated by the employment and the resulting disability. The basis for such differentiation is not present in our Act. We must deter to the legislature. *Varos. See McGarrah v. State Accident Insurance Fund Corp.*, 296 Or. 145, 675 P.2d 159 (1983).

We conclude that a psychological injury resulting from a sudden or gradual emotional stimulus "arises out of" employment when it is causally related to the performance of job duties. This standard is in keeping with the letter, and purpose, of the Act. This standard also makes no distinction between those workers predisposed to mental injury and those not so disposed. Plaintiff, through the recited testimony, has met this standard.

Our conclusion presupposes the existence of an actual job condition which causes the stress (actual stress), rather than a perceived condition that does not exist (imagined stress). Actual stress is that stress traceable to real working conditions imagined stress exists when a worker honestly perceives that some event, or events, occurred during the course of his employment to cause injury when, in fact, no such event or events occurred. *See McGarrah.* In this case, defendants contend that plaintiff testified about occurrences existing only in his mind. They base their contention on testimony that plaintiff's disorders could cause him to distort reality. They challenge the trial court's finding of actual stress.

Substantial evidence supports this finding. *Garcia v. Genuine Parts Co.*, 90 N.M. 124, 560 P.2d 545 (Ct. App. 1977). First, there was no evidence that plaintiff had trouble coping with other situations. Logically, this supports an inference of actual stress at work. Second, there was a flare-up in plaintiff's symptoms each time he returned to work. Third, Jewett had a reputation as the type of foreman who would "ride on a person." Fourth, Dr. Fredman testified that even paranoid ideations have some basis in reality. Fifth, Dr. Sacks testified that there was not condition suffered by plaintiff that would cause him to misperceive reality. The trial court's finding of actual stress will not be overturned.

We do not, at this time, address the complex issue of whether the effect of the perceived work environment on the worker, i.e., imaginary stress, is sufficient to establish an injury "arising out of" the employment. Such a discussion is not necessary in the present case because there is evidence of the effect of the actual work environment. *See McGarrah* and *Williams v. Western Electric Co.*, 178 N.J.Super. 571, 429 A.2d 1063 (1981), for a discussion of actual versus imaginary stress.

Any plaintiff must still demonstrate that, as a medical probability, any disability is a natural and direct result of the accidental injury. Section 52-1-28. Expert medical testimony is required to establish this causal connection. *Id.* The testimony of Drs. Fredman and Sacks provided substantial evidence on causation for plaintiff in this case. . . .

The judgment of the district court is affirmed.

It is so ordered.

DONNELLY, C. J., and MINZNER, J., concur.

PROBLEMS

(1) Should the sheer fear of dying because of exposure to radiation or asbestos be compensable in the absence of actual physical injury? Courts in several states have faced this question, with varied results. *See, e.g.,* Martinez v. University of California,

601 P.2d 425 (N.M. 1979); Cooper v. Workers' Comp. App. Bd., 173 Cal. App. 3d 44, 218 Cal. Rptr. 783 (1985); and McMahon v. Anaconda Co., 678 P.2d 661 (Mont. 1984).

(2) In the "mental-mental" category, is the distinction between sudden psychic trauma and gradual stimulus a valid one? *Cf.* Bailey v. American Gen. Ins. Co., 279 S.W.2d 315, 154 Tex. 430 (1955) with Transportation Ins. Co. v. Maksyn, 580 S.W.2d 334 (Tex. 1979). Is the "floodgates" argument a valid legal consideration?

(3) Suppose the psychiatric testimony establishes clearly (a) that claimant is totally disabled by his compensation neurosis, and (b) that as soon as an award is made the disability will clear up. What should the referee do?

(4) Claimant filed a mental stress claim as a result of his employer's investigation into conduct that he engaged in forging customers' signatures on contracts. *Should compensability depend upon whether claimant in fact engaged in forgery? See* Pacific Tel. & Tel. Co. v. W.C.A.B. (Blackburn), 114 Cal. App. 4th 1174, 8 Cal. Rptr. 3d 467, 69 Cal. Comp. Cases 21 (2004).

(5) Claimant contended that worry related to the potential insolvency of his employer constituted a compensable mental injury. Compensable? *See* Pacific Gas and Elec. Co. v. W.C.A.B. (Bryann), 112 Cal. App. 3d 241 (1980).

(6) As research in biochemistry and psycho-pharmacology continues, the traditional distinction between mental and physical cause and effect blurs. Can our workers' compensation systems afford to abandon the distinction between stress claims and other injuries, however outdated it may be from a scientific perspective, and could they possibly absorb a full dose of the monumental health care costs tied to employment-related stress — estimated by one study at about $300 billion annually?[19] Or is this an area where the prohibitive costs of such a sea-change requires the law to ignore scientific truth in favor of pragmatism, or, to paraphrase Justice Holmes, where a page of history (or economics) is worth a volume of medical insight?

---

[19] Patricia Pattison & Philip E. Varca, *Workers' Compensation for Mental Stress Claims in Wyoming*, 29 LAND & WATER L. REV. 145, 147 (1994), citing Michelle Osborn, *Stress: Can't Take It Anymore*, USA TODAY Sept. 8, 1992, at 1B. This estimate includes the costs of worker absenteeism and turnover.

Part 5
STATUTORY COVERAGE

Chapter 12
EMPLOYMENT STATUS

§ 12.01 "EMPLOYEE" DEFINED

The term "employee" is defined by most statutes to include every person in the service of another under any contract of hire, express or implied. Judicial application of this definition to workers' compensation status problems generally follows the tests worked out by common law distinguishing servants from independent contractors for vicarious liability questions. However, a recognition of the difference between compensation law and vicarious liability in the purpose and function of the employment concept has been reflected both in statutory extensions of the term "employee" beyond the common law concept and in a gradual broadening of the interpretation of the term to bring within compensation coverage borderline classes for whom compensation protection is appropriate and practical.

CERADSKY v. MID-AMERICA DAIRYMEN, INC.
583 S.W.2d 193 (Mo. App. 1979)

Shangler, Presiding Judge.

The dependents of Ceradsky, a workman killed as he operated a truck owned by one Percell used to haul milk to Mid-America Dairymen for manufacture into cheese, appeal from a judgment to affirm denial of workmen's compensation by the Industrial Commission. The final award of the Commission rested on the determination that Percell, otherwise regularly employed by Mid-America Dairymen as a field man, operated the milk route as an independent contractor, and therefore Ceradsky was not an employee of Mid-America Dairymen within the Workmen's Compensation Law.

The claim was heard by the referee on deposition testimony. The facts from the evidence are not in dispute and frame but one issue: was the workman Ceradsky an employee of Mid-America Dairymen [then Bethany Cheese Company] at the time of his death within the coverage of the Workmen's Compensation Law? The referee determined that Ceradsky was in fact an employee and awarded benefits to the claimants-dependents. The Industrial Commission found anew from the same evidence that *Ceradsky was neither an employee in fact nor a statutory employee* of Mid-America Dairymen and entered a final award to deny compensation. In other — and more essential — terms, the decision of the Industrial Commission determined that Percell, in his role as milk drayer, was not an employee of Mid-America Dairymen and so did not impart such a status to Ceradsky on principles of agency. [See *Gingell v. Walters Contracting Corporation*, 303 S.W.2d 683 (Mo. App. 1957)].

The appeal from the judgment of the circuit court to affirm the final award of the administrative body poses to this court the question of law: whether the determination by the Industrial Commission that Ceradsky was not an employee of Mid-America Dairymen rests on sufficient competent evidence. *Maltz v. Jackoway-Katz Cap Co.*, 336 Mo. 1000, 82 S.W.2d 909, 918[7–9] (1935). And where, as in the case at bench, no dispute concerns the facts which bear on the status of employee, or not, the conclusions on the evidence adopted by the administrative body do not bind a court of review. *Corp v. Joplin Cement Company*, 337 S.W.2d 252, 258[7] (Mo. banc 1960).

The evidence shows conclusively that Percell was employed by Mid-America Dairymen [then the Bethany Cheese Company] as a field man and office help five days a week on a fixed schedule and for a fixed salary from which taxes and benefits money were withheld. In that role he was an *employee* of the Cheese Company [and later of Dairymen] within the intendment of § 287.020, RSMo 1969, and of the coverage of the Workmen's Compensation Law. The fieldman entailed duty as a solicitor of farmer business and troubleshooter to them on quality control and other incidents of milk production. The field man also advised the farmers on equipment and sold them supplies, particularly filter disks to cleanse the production sold to the company. The employment as field man, however, was augmented by a separate oral undertaking between Percell and Bethany Cheese to pick up milk from farmers within numerous counties in northwest Missouri and southern Iowa for delivery to the factory for process into cheese. This dual capacity of service continued for about eleven years and even after Mid-America Dairymen bought out Bethany Cheese.

It is the relationship of Percell as milk drayman for Bethany Cheese and successor Mid-America Dairymen, and not his duty as field man, which determines the status of Ceradsky on the claim for compensation. If Percell in the capacity of milk hauler was an employee of the cheese company, on principles of agency Ceradsky was within the coverage of the Workmen's Compensation Law; but if Percell was an independent jobber, Ceradsky does not stand to claim the benefits of an employee.

To operate the milk route Percell purchased a truck and hired a succession of drivers. Percell paid for the insurance and all maintenance on the vehicle. Ceradsky was hired at a regular salary to service the territory, outlined by the company as Route N in the agreement with Percell. Percell paid the wages, withheld the taxes, furnished Ceradsky the W-2 forms and paid contributions for unemployment compensation. Ceradsky received no payments from the company.

The cheese company paid the farmers per hundredweight for the milk and paid Percell a commensurate fee. The company checks were delivered to the farmers by Ceradsky and the other drivers.

Ceradsky ran the route six days a week from about midnight to eight in the morning. It was his procedure to leave empty milk cans [furnished by the company] with the farmer, pick up the full cans, unload them at the milk plant, and then to return home with the Percell truck to run the route anew the next morning. On occasions when the farmers left with the milk cans an order for supplies [generally, filter disks], Ceradsky remitted the purchase requests to the company and delivered the goods on the next round. There was intimation that in case of farmer discontent on the route, plant manager Hunt [and major shareholder of Bethany Cheese] felt free to reprimand Ceradsky, but the farmers dealt with Percell on milk matters and it is clear that Percell managed Ceradsky.

The truck owned by Percell and used by Ceradsky had an insulated bed for the transportation of the milk. That component bore the Bethany Cheese identification decal. The company had furnished Percell an insulated bed for the truck when the one in use was condemned by health inspectors. On the occasion when the Percell truck was disabled from damage, the company furnished a substitute, but Percell paid the cost of operation.

Ceradsky was killed one morning during the operation of the Percell milk truck along Route N. It is acknowledged that the death was out of and in the course of that duty. Only the question of status remains: whether Percell as milk hauler — and hence Ceradsky — was in the service of Dairymen within § 287.020.1 and so entitled to benefits of the Workmen's Compensation Law.

The final award of the Industrial Commission to deny compensation to the dependents rests on the determination that Percell was an independent contractor. That adjudgment rests on the rationale, simply, that as to Percell in the occupation of milk drayman, the cheese company exercised no control nor enjoyed right of control. The evidence allows acceptance without cavil only to the ultimate conclusion of direct control. That absent an observable right of control there can be no employment status for workmen's compensation, however, mistakes the law.

The definition of employment status, as the preeminent authority on Workmen's Compensation Law observes, almost of necessity, takes the form of a distinction between an employee from an independent contractor.

> The reason is simple. If one wants to get something done without doing it oneself, there are really only two ways open: to hire an employee to do it, or to contract out the work to an independent entrepreneur. The employee-independent contractor distinction is not an artificial dichotomy invented by legal minds interested in fine distinctions for their own sake. It is a fundamental fact of business life which could not be abolished by the most grandiose legislation. Larson, *The Law of Workmen's Compensation.* (1978) § 43.20.

Our courts, as virtually all others, have adapted the definition of *servant* worked out for vicarious tort liability purposes by Restatement of the Law of Agency Second [§ 220] to derive a definition of *employee* for workmen's compensation or other statutory purposes. *Cline v. Carthage Crushed Limestone Company,* 504 S.W.2d 102, 105[1, 2] (Mo. 1973); *Lawrence v. William Gebhardt, Jr., & Son,* 311 S.W.2d 97, 102[1] (Mo. App. 1958); *Pratt v. Reed & Brown Hauling Company,* 361 S.W.2d 57, 62 (Mo. App. 1962):

Section 220. Definition of Servant

(1)   A servant is a person employed to perform services in the affairs of another and who with respect to the physical conduct in the performance of the services is subject to the other's control or right to control.

(2)   In determining whether one acting for another is a servant or an independent contractor, the following matters of fact, among others, are considered;

(a)   the extent of control which, by the agreement, the master may exercise over the details of the work;

(b)   whether or not the one employed is engaged in a distinct occupation or business;

(c)   the kind of occupation, with reference to whether, in the locality, the work is usually done under the direction of the employer or by a specialist without supervision;

(d)   the skill required in the particular occupation;

(e)   whether the employer or the workman supplies the instrumentalities, tools, and the place of work for the person doing the work;

(f)   the length of time for which the person is employed;

(g)   the method of payment, whether by the time or by the job;

(h)   whether or not the work is a part of the regular business of the employer;

(i)   whether or not the parties believe they are creating the relation of master and servant; and

(j)   whether the principal is or is not in business.

Where the evidence shows that a person to whom a service is rendered has a right to control the performance of the person who renders the service, the relationship of employer and employee is essentially established. *Tokash v. General Baking Company*, 349 Mo. 767, 163 S.W.2d 554, 555[3] (1942). That is the sense of subsection (1) of the Restatement § 220. Where the evidence lacks such a conclusiveness, however, whether the one who renders the service for the other acts as employee or independent contractor depends upon all the circumstances of the work relationship — so that control becomes only one indicium weighted with the several others to determine the true status. That is the sense of subsection (2) of the Restatement § 220. Larson, op. cit., *supra*, § 43.10; *Lawrence v. William Gebhardt, Jr., & Son, supra*, l. c. 102[1].

The term *servant* in Restatement § 220, however, formulates a common law purpose not altogether compatible with the *employee* status under our Workmen's Compensation Law. *Kourik v. English*, 340 Mo. 367, 100 S.W.2d 901, 905[3–7] (1937). The *servant* concept at common law delimits the vicarious tort liability of the master for harm done to the extent to which the employer has the right to control the servant activity. The compensation law, rather, concerns not injury by the employee to another but to himself — and not only from controlled activity but also from the activity of others beyond the control of the employer. Larson, op. cit., *supra*, § 43.42; Restatement of Agency Second, § 220, Comment on Subsection (1)g: Statutory interpretation. The scheme of workmen's compensation, however, discards the common law system of fault as an inadequate redress for worker disability and accepts such injury as inherent to the industrial process and — as a matter of urgent public welfare — allocates the risk to the industry which gives it occasion. *Maltz v. Jackoway-Katz Cap Company, supra*, 82 S.W.2d l. c. 912 [2–6]. In such a scheme, the right to control the detail of the work activity has no such immediate relevancy as in a case of vicarious tort liability. It is within the compelling purpose of the Workmen's Compensation Law — which has shed the defenses and disabilities of the common law to ameliorate the economic consequences of injury to the worker — that the employee status of the decedent Ceradsky must be determined. *Bethel v. Sunlight Janitor Service*, 551 S.W.2d 616, 618[1] (Mo. banc 1977).

The Workmen's Compensation Law [§ 287.020] defines *employee*[1] to mean

every person in the service of any employer . . . under any contract of hire, express or implied, oral or written, or under any appointment or election.

. . . .

The employer-employee relationship by the statutory definition rests on *service*, construed by judicial definition to mean *controllable service*.[2] *Rutherford v. Tobin Quarries, supra* [n.1], 82 S.W.2d l. c. 923; *Maltz v. Jackoway-Katz Cap Company, supra*, 82 S.W.2d l. c. 912[2–6]. Where actual control or right of control of the work performance [and hence the presumptive employer-employee relationship] is not readily demonstrable from the evidence, our decisions have applied the secondary test for *servant* of

---

[1] *(Court's footnote) Independent contractor* is not defined in the Workmen's Compensation Act. The term has been given the judicial definition: "An 'independent contractor' is one who, exercising an independent employment, contracts to do a piece of work according to his own methods, without being subject to the control of his employer, except as to the result of his work." Vaseleou v. St. Louis Realty & Securities Company, 344 Mo. 1121, 1122, 130 S.W.2d 538, 539 [2–4] (1939). The decisions hold invariably that whether the work status is that of employee or independent contractor depends on the facts in the particular case. Rutherford v. Tobin Quarries, 336 Mo. 1171, 82 S.W.2d 918, 921[4] (1935).

[2] *(Court's footnote)* The judicial introduction of the element of *control* into the employee status under the Workmen's Compensation law rests on the construction that "the framers of the act had in mind the law of master and servant and the relationship, duties, rights, and limitations arising out of the same." Maltz, *supra*, 82 S.W.2d l. c. 911[2–6].

subsection (2) of Restatement § 220 [whether the employment is a distinct occupation, the length of time of employment, whether the work is a part of the regular business of the employer, etc.] without doctrinaire rigidity and so as to give practical effect to the remedial purpose of the statute. As example, the factor (g) as to "the method of payment, whether by time or by the job," when by the hour gives "very strong evidence of the employment status" [*Pratt v. Reed & Brown Hauling Company, supra*, l. c. 64] yet when by the job [*Horn v. Asphalt Products Corporation*, 131 S.W.2d 871, 872[5] (Mo. App. 1939)] or without payment altogether [*Lawson v. Lawson*, 415 S.W.2d 313, 319[6] (Mo. App. 1967)], is nevertheless consistent with the status of compensable employment according to the nature of the service. As further example, that a worker is engaged for no definite period of time [factor (f)] and is therefore subject to dismissal at will is "more conclusive" of control — and hence employment — than any other single circumstance [*Maltz v. Jackoway-Katz Cap Company, supra*, 82 S.W.2d l. c. 918] yet the unrestricted right of the employer to terminate the service "does not of itself make the relation one of agency" [*Rutherford v. Tobin Quarries, supra*, 82 S.W.2d l. c. 922[8, 9]], according to the amalgam of circumstances. Even as to control of the details of the work activity [factor (a)] frequently posed as the dominant proof of the employment relationship [*Fisher v. Hennessey*, 329 S.W.2d 225, 228 (Mo. App. 1959); *Hackler v. Swisher Mower & Machine Company*, 284 S.W.2d 55, 58[2–4] (Mo. App. 1955)], that proof is satisfied when a *right* to control is implicit in the circumstances of the relationship. [*Gingell v. Walters Contracting Corporation*, 303 S.W.2d 683, 686[2] (Mo. App. 1957); *Maltz v. Jackoway-Katz Cap Company, supra*, 82 S.W.2d l. c. 918]. The factors of the subsection (2) Restatement § 220 test for *servant* which remain — whether or not the worker employed is engaged in a distinct occupation [factor (b)], the kind of occupation [factor (c)], the skill required [factor (d)], whether the employer or the worker supplies the instrumentalities [factor (e)], and the others — bear on the ultimate issue of employment according to whether they show an integrated relationship of service between the worker and the activity served.

That is to say, on analysis, *the right to control the detail of the work* factor given predominance as proof of the employee status[3] shows through as merely an euphemism for worker activity of such a nature as to be a regular and continuous part of the manufacture of the product or other service. Thus, that the work activity is of a kind necessary in the operation of the business so that if not done by the claimant would be done by a direct employee of the business, essentially establishes the renderer of the service an *employee* within the purposes of the compensation law. *Maltz v. Jackoway-Katz Cap Company, supra*, l. c. 917[22]; *Lawson v. Lawson, supra*, l. c. 319; *Pratt v. Reed & Brown Hauling Company, supra*, l. c. 64; *Tokash v. General Baking Company, supra*, 163 S.W.2d l. c. 556[7]; *Horn v. Asphalt Products Corporation, supra*, l. c. 872[5]; *Gingell v. Walters Contracting Corporation, supra*, l. c. 686[2]; *Vaseleou v. St. Louis Realty & Securities Company, supra*, 130 S.W.2d l. c. 540[5]. In such case, the purpose of the Workmen's Compensation Law does not expect a worker, otherwise without

---

[3] *(Court's footnote)* The right of control which satisfies the conditions for employee status can be so attenuated as to be satisfied from an inference from the evidence of "apparent necessity" for the exercise at all. Thus in Maltz v. Jackoway-Katz Cap Company, *supra*, a hat salesman who worked on a commission basis in an assigned territory, used and paid for his own automobile expenses, who was given an order book and samples but was not required to report at any time nor was subject to the dictations of the employer as to the method of sale was an employee within the compensation law because he could be terminated at any time and so the *right of control*, albeit unexercised, remained in the employer. An almost equally attenuated right of control did not prevent the employee status, and compensation, in Schultz v. Moerschel Products Co., 142 S.W.2d 106 (Mo. App. 1940). The sense of these cases, and our many others, is best stated in the dissent of Conford, J. [later adopted as the unanimous opinion of the Supreme Court of New Jersey in Marcus v. Eastern Agricultural Ass'n, 32 N.J. 460, 161 A.2d 247 (1960), reversing and adopting the dissenting opinion in 58 N.J. Super. 584, 157 A.2d 3, 10 (1959): "[T]he requirement of control is sufficiently met where its extent is commensurate with that degree of supervision which is necessary and appropriate, considering the type of work to be done and the capabilities of the particular person doing it."

feasible means, to bear the burden of industrial injury but casts that risk upon the process of manufacture and, ultimately, on the cost of the product.[4] *Bethel v. Sunlight Janitor Service, supra,* l. c. 618[1].

The *ad hoc,* case by case, reasonings of our decisions as to whether the control test of the Restatement § 220 was met where the evidence was close to balance and the ultimate status of employee or independent contractor not clearly drawn, fall readily into the systematic treatment which Larson calls *the relative nature of the work test.* That analysis does not discard the traditional requirement of control: the presence of control conclusively proves the employment status. Where by the very nature of the work relationship or other circumstance, however, control is not conspicuous, the right to direct the detail of the work becomes only one indicium of control among others and the inquiry turns to the economic and functional relationship between the nature of the work and the operation of the business served. The inquiry, moreover, tends away from technical common law definitions to the public purpose of the scheme for workmen's compensation.[5]

The treatment by Larson rests on the theory of workmen's compensation legislation that [§ 43.51]

> the cost of all industrial accidents should be borne by the consumer as a part of the cost of the product.[6] It follows that any worker whose services form a regular and continuing part of the cost of that product, and whose method of operation is not such an independent business that it forms in itself a separate route through which his own costs of industrial accident can be channelled, is within the presumptive area of intended protection.[7]

Where the element of control in the work relationship does not emerge clearly, the relative nature of the work test determines employee status [for purposes of workmen's compensation] by [§ 43.52]

---

[4] *(Court's footnote)* The principle of risk distribution underlies, also, and for analogous reason, the workmen's compensation liability to a *statutory employee* under § 287.040 which deems as an employer

> [a]*ny person who has work done under contract* on or about his premises *which is an operation of the usual business which he there carries on.*[Emphasis added.] Liability for workmen's compensation results under the statute despite that the injured worker, by common law definition, may be an independent contractor and not an employee. Schwandt v. Witte, 346 S.W.2d 50, 52[3] (Mo. 1961). That is because the public policy of the statutory employee provision is to prevent an enterprise, through the guise of agreements with independent contractors of doubtful fiscal responsibility, to evade workmen's compensation [and even common law] liability for injury to a worker performed in the usual and ordinary business enterprise work. Ferguson Air-Hydraulics Company, 492 S.W.2d 130, 136[6] (Mo. App. 1973); Pruitt v. Harker, 328 Mo. 1200, 43 S.W.2d 769, 772 (1931).

[5] *(Court's footnote)* A progression of jurisdictions have adopted *the relative nature of the work test* either by announced theory or by effect. *See, e.g.,* Marcus v. Eastern Agricultural Association, Inc., *supra,* (N.J. 1960); Biktjorn v. Worley Homes, Inc., 12 A.D.2d 540, 206 N.Y.S.2d 744 (1960); Seals v. Zollo, 205 Tenn. 463, 327 S.W.2d 41 (1959); Samson v. Borden Co., 92 So. 2d 152 (La. App. 1957); Woody v. Waibel, 276 Or. 189, 554 P.2d 492 (1976). See also, the cases cited in Larson, op. cit., *supra,* §§ 43.53–43.54 and the discussion citations by Dean Stern in Comment, 10 U.C.L.A.L.Rev. 161, 173 et seq. (1962). Our decisions, Maltz v. Jackoway-Katz Cap Company, Pratt v. Reed & Brown Hauling Company, Horn v. Asphalt Products Company, and the others cited, *supra,* as we have noted, give effect to the relative nature of the work principle without attribution by terminology or theory to accord employee status within a theory of industrial risk distribution where the right of control is attenuated, and, sometimes, only supposed.

[6] *(Court's footnote)* That statutory purpose is declared as a matter of public welfare by Hickey v. Board of Education of the City of St. Louis, 363 Mo. 1039, 256 S.W.2d 775, 777[2–5] (1953); Bethel v. Sunlight Janitor Service, *supra,* and numerous other Missouri decisions.

[7] *(Court's footnote)* Such, we have noted, is the theory of decision of Pratt v. Reed & Brown Hauling Company, Horn v. Asphalt Products Company and the several others cited on that discussion.

the character of the claimant's work or business — how skilled it is, how much of a separate calling or enterprise it is, to what extent it may be expected to carry its own accident burden and so on — and its relation to the employer's business, that is, how much it is a regular part of the employer's regular work, whether it is continuous or intermittent, and whether the duration is sufficient to amount to the hiring of continuing services as distinguished from contracting for the completion of a particular job.[8]

On the principles of subsection (2) of the Restatement § 220 and of the relative nature of the work test alike, the determination by the Industrial Commission that Percell as milk hauler was an independent contractor, first of Bethany Cheese and then of Dairymen, is without substantial support in the evidence. Rather, the undisputed proof constitutes Percell an employee and, hence, the Ceradsky dependents entitled to the benefits they claim. . . .

The judgment is reversed and remanded with directions that the circuit court further remand the proceedings to the Industrial Commission with directions that an award for compensation be entered for the Ceradsky dependents.

All concur.

§ 12.02   CONTRACTOR DISTINCTION: RIGHT TO CONTROL DETAILS

The traditional test of the employer-employee relation is the right of the employer to control the details of the work. It is the ultimate right of control, under the agreement with the employee, not the overt exercise of that right, which is decisive. If the right of control of details goes no further than is necessary to ensure a satisfactory end result, it does not establish employment. The principal factors showing right of control are (1) direct evidence of right or exercise of control; (2) method of payment; (3) the furnishing of equipment; and (4) the right to fire.

It is almost always said, both in the common law of master and servant and in workers' compensation law, that the fundamental test of employment relation is the right of the employer to control the details of the work, and that other tests are subordinate and secondary.

It is indeed unfortunate that, of the list of tests, the "primary" one should also have to be the only one that is seldom a demonstrable fact. The other "subordinate" tests are usually based on provable features of the employment: the method of payment can be proved to be by the piece or by the hour; the right to fire or quit is usually quite clear; and there is seldom any factual dispute on who furnishes equipment. But the right to control the details of the work is most often an inference from these and other tangible facts, rather than a solid fact in itself.

CAICCO v. TOTO BROTHERS, INC.
62 N.J. 305, 301 A.2d 143 (1973)

CONFORD, P. J. A. D. (temporarily assigned).

This is a workmen's compensation case in which the sole issue is whether petitioner Caicco's deceased husband was an independent contractor rather than an employee of respondent Toto Brothers, Inc. at the time of his accidental death. The Division of

---

[8] (*Court's footnote*) Once again, considerations of a continuous work service of a function normally discharged by employees of the business, the skill necessary to the work performance and, implicitly, the economic feasibility to require the worker to assume the burden of the injury loss all, to some measure, bear on the decisions which find the employee status, and hence coverage, in Maltz, Horn, Pratt, Gingell, and those other decisions we have mentioned recurrently, *supra*.

Workmen's Compensation found decedent to be an employee, and awarded petitioner compensation benefits. On appeal the County Court found to the contrary and dismissed petitioner's claim. The Appellate Division affirmed in an unreported *per curiam* opinion. This court granted certification. 62 N.J. 67, 299 A.2d 65 (1972).

Decedent Luigi Caicco was accidentally electrocuted on June 6, 1968 when the dump truck he was operating came in contact with high tension wires. The accident occurred at the job construction site of L. Zimmerman & Sons, Inc. on Woodbridge Avenue near the interchange of Routes 95 and 440 in Edison, New Jersey. At the time of the accident decedent was delivering a load of landfill for respondent which had subcontracted to supply landfill at the site.

The dump truck used by decedent was his own and he maintained it at his own expense. The landfill had been loaded on the truck at respondent's sand pit several miles from the job site. The loading was accomplished by means of a "caterpillar" loader operated by one of respondent's regular employees. Respondent's operations, from pick-up of loads to dumping at the construction site, were in effect from seven in the morning until lunchtime and from after lunch to three or three-thirty in the afternoon. This work schedule was in effect five days a week, exclusive of weekends and holidays. In addition to decedent's truck the hauling operation was serviced by four other dump trucks owned by respondent and driven by respondent's regular employees and by ten to fifteen "hired trucks" such as decedent's. The trucks took one of two routes to the job site where they would be directed by respondent's employees where to unload.

Decedent's employment with respondent was on a day-to-day basis and depended on such circumstances as weather conditions and available work. He was generally paid by the load but on occasion was paid by the hour. He could be fired at any time, but according to respondent, he could also quit at any time. He never used any employees of his own.

There was no written contract. However, as in the case of all of respondent's "hired drivers," decedent was required as a condition of employment to supply respondent with a letter in a form prescribed by respondent stating that he would be responsible for his own federal income taxes and that he was self-employed. Similarly, decedent was required to furnish respondent with proof of insurance for vehicle liability and workmen's compensation.

Decedent for his part held himself out as self-employed. Painted on the side of his truck was the name "C. L. Trucking," together with a telephone number. The name was not registered as a trade or business name, nor was the business incorporated. In addition to the dump truck decedent maintained a small pick-up truck for incidental use in his business. Decedent maintained a telephone answering service, entertained business associates and sponsored a "Little League" team. His 1967 and 1968 income tax returns listed his occupation as that of a self-employed trucker, and, as such, he paid his income tax directly. Nothing was withheld by respondent. Decedent billed respondent and others for whom he did trucking by invoice in the name of "C. L. Trucking."

Beginning December 18, 1967 respondent became decedent's prime source of work and so remained until his death. From the commencement of that relationship about 81% of decedent's work-days were devoted to respondent and 19% to four other customers. About 85% of decedent's billings for work done during that period were to respondent.

The evidence as a whole justifies the inference, which we draw, that during the five to six month period of his association with respondent decedent made himself primarily available to respondent, and did trucking for others practically only when respondent had no work for him.

We need not here recanvass the extensive consideration given to the criteria of employment vis-a-vis independent contractorship for workmen's compensation purposes in the Appellate Division opinion which we adopted in affirming recovery in *Tofani v. Lo Biondo Brothers Motor Express, Inc.*, 83 N.J. Super. 480, 200 A.2d 493 (1964), aff'd o. b. 43 N.J. 494, 205 A.2d 736 (1964), and in the dissenting opinion in the Appellate Division in *Marcus v. Eastern Agricultural Ass'n, Inc.*, 58 N.J. Super. 584, 596, 157 A.2d 3 (1959), which we adopted in reversing in that case, 32 N.J. 460, 161 A.2d 247 (1960). Both the "right to control" and "relative nature of the work" criteria, fully discussed in those decisions, here point strongly to a legal conclusion of employment and compensability.

Concerning respondent's right to control, it is evident that decedent had to adapt the details of his performance to the specifications of respondent's requirements. He had to appear at the loading point about 7:00 A.M., haul his load to the dump site; there coordinate the dumping of the load with the activities of the other trucks which inferably were at the same time performing the same function for respondent as decedent, all under superintendence of respondent; take his lunch when convenient to respondent, and close out his day when respondent's work-day ended at about 3:30 P.M. There was thus both actual control and right of control of the details of the work in respondent, at least to the extent that such control of details was functionally relevant to respondent's requirements. *See Piantanida v. Bennett*, 17 N.J. 291, 294, 111 A.2d 412 (1955).

The "relative nature of the work" criterion of employment, 1A Larson, The Law of Workmen's Compensation (1967), §§ 43.52, 43.53, *Marcus, supra*; *Hannigan v. Goldfarb*, 53 N.J. Super. 190, 204–206, 147 A.2d 56 (App. Div. 1958); *Brower v. Rossmy*, 63 N.J. Super. 395, 164 A.2d 754 (App. Div. 1960), certif. den. 34 N.J. 65, 167 A.2d 54 (1961), is that which is most pertinent here. The hauling of materials performed through decedent's labor was a cog in the wheel of respondent's operation as a subcontractor of Zimmerman in as realistic a sense as the hauling being done by respondent's regular employees. Decedent had made himself substantially dependent on respondent, economically, during the period in question. The fact that he sought work from others during slack periods with respondent does not derogate from that fact. Nor does the circumstance that he maintained the superficial trappings of an independent businessman so long as substantial economic dependence on respondent and functional integration of operations persisted. *See Tofani, supra* (83 N.J. Super., at 493, 200 A.2d 493). Compensation has frequently been awarded notwithstanding the employee maintained some sort of independent business concomitant with the relationship held to constitute employment in the particular case. *See Piantanida v. Bennett, supra*; *Glens Falls Indemnity Co. v. Clark*, 75 Ga. App. 453, 43 S.E.2d 752 (Ct. App. 1947); *Schneider v. Village of Shickley*, 156 Neb. 683, 57 N.W.2d 527 (Sup. Ct. 1953); *Christopherson v. Security State Bank of Oklee*, 256 Minn. 191, 97 N. W.2d 649 (Sup. Ct. 1959); *Brademeyer v. Chickasaw Bldg. Co.*, 190 Tenn. 239, 229 S.W.2d 323 (Sup. Ct. 1950).

The authorities sometimes allude to the factor as to whether the alleged employer, as opposed to the alleged employee, is better able to provide protection of the worker for occupational injury. Larson, op. cit. *supra* §§ 43.51, 43.52. This criterion is broadly useful in the overall approach but cannot be mechanically applied as a determinant in a particular case. In the present instance decedent was able to and did purchase workmen's compensation insurance, but it was useless for present purposes as it was issued to decedent as a self-employed individual.[9]

Respondent's insistence on decedent supplying it with various documents ostensibly

---

[9] *(Court's footnote)* Had the insured under the policy been a corporation of which decedent was an employee, even though its principal owner and officer, there would have been coverage for the accident. See Henk v. Eastern Air Taxi, Inc., 91 N.J. Super. 317, 220 A.2d 200 (App. Div. 1966), *certif. den.* 48 N.J. 110, 223 A.2d 490 (1966).

indicative of an independent contractor relationship cannot affect the result if in substance, as we find the fact to be, the relationship was that of employment in the workmen's compensation context. *Tofani, supra* (83 N.J. Super. at 494, 200 A.2d 493).

We conclude that the basic relationship between the parties here is sufficiently similar to that which obtained in *Tofani, supra,* to make that decision controlling for recovery. The fact in *Tofani* that the workman's vehicle and, in effect, his personal services, were contracted exclusively to the hiring party for successive 30-day periods does not, for reasons already stated, constitute a sufficient distinction to warrant a difference in result.

In sum, the relationship of decedent to respondent was, on the whole, one such as evokes application of the underlying philosophy of the statute that injuries arising from labor rendered in an industrial enterprise are properly compensable by the proprietors of that enterprise. *See Thornton v. Chamberlain Mfg. Corp.,* 62 N.J. 235, 300 A.2d 146 (1973).

The judgment of the Appellate Division is reversed and the decision of the Division of Workmen's Compensation reinstated.

For reversal: CHIEF JUSTICE WEINTRAUB, JUSTICES JACOBS, HALL and MOUNTAIN and JUDGES CONFORD and LEWIS — 6.

For affirmance: None.

HANSON v. BCB, INC.
114 Idaho 131, 754 P.2d 444 (1988)

BAKES, JUSTICE.

The appellants, Harold and Jesse Hanson, are husband and child of the deceased Patrice Hanson. Patrice Hanson (Hanson) was shot and killed in the parking lot while leaving the Hide-Out Saloon (Saloon) where she had been performing as an exotic dancer. Appellants appeal a decision of the Industrial Commission (commission) which found that Patrice Hanson was an independent contractor and not an employee of the Hide-Out Saloon and thus not covered by the Workmen's Compensation Law. We reverse and remand.

Hanson began dancing at the saloon after answering an ad in the Idaho Statesman and passing an audition with the owner. There was no written employment contract. Hanson was paid no wages as such. Her compensation was based entirely on a share of the cover charge (all of which was divided solely among the dancers), tips, and one free drink per night. The saloon supplied the music for the performances. The dancers supplied their own costumes. The saloon received no part of the cover charge or tips. The dancers did not report the amount of their earnings to the bar, and there was no arrangement for withholding any taxes or other withholdings from their earnings.

The testimony before the commission regarding the scheduling of dancing was conflicting. Hanson's husband testified that the deceased danced three to five nights per week at the discretion of the owner. The owner, on the other hand, testified that there was a calendar in the dressing room, and the dancers put their names on the days they wanted to perform; she then transferred this information onto a separate sheet of paper and posted it on the jukebox. The owner also testified that the deceased usually danced three nights a week at the bar and that she frequently came in later than 4:00 p.m., the usual starting time, and went home before 1:00 a.m., the quitting time. According to the owner, 4:00 p.m. was the suggested starting time because that was when the cover charge was in effect and the bouncer was on duty.

Both the deceased's husband and the owner testified that employees were not disciplined for failure to report to work. There was testimony that if dancers did not want to work on a night for which they had signed up, they could obtain their own substitute. Also, if a dancer was scheduled to dance, but never showed up, the owner would call one of the others to obtain a substitute, but the other dancer was not obligated to substitute if she did not want to.

The owner required dancers to wear pantyhose to ensure compliance with the Idaho Code and reserved the right to fire noncomplying dancers.

Although the commission found some indicia of an employer/employee relationship, the commission ultimately determined that the preponderance of the evidence indicated that Hanson and the saloon had an independent contractor/principal relationship. The commission applied the "right to control" test as required by this Court's decision in *Ledesma v. Bergeson*, 99 Idaho 555, 585 P.2d 965 (1978). The commission reasoned from the facts that Hanson was an independent contractor because (1) the saloon "did not assume the right to exercise direction and control over the time, manner, method and details of work performed by Deceased"; (2) the dancers chose their own days and hours of work; (3) the dancers supplied the major items of equipment (i.e., their costumes and their bodies); (4) the method of pay was consistent with that of an independent contractor. On balance, the commission found that Mrs. Hanson was not an employee, and that therefore the claimants were not entitled to benefits.

On appeal the main issue is whether the Industrial Commission's finding that Hanson was an independent contractor is supported by substantial evidence in the record.[(*Court's footnote*) Appellants' appeal is based primarily on the allegation that the factual record does not support the commission's findings. They also argue that this Court should adopt a different test, the "nature of the work" test as described in 1B Larson, Workmen's Compensation Law § 45.10. That test involves an analysis of two factors: (1) whether the work being done is an integral part of the regular business of the employer, and (2) whether the worker, relative to the particular employer, furnishes an independent business or professional service. However, the "right to control" test is supported by a long line of Idaho decisions, *infra*, and we decline the invitation to overrule such a well established line of precedent. Furthermore, the factors to be considered in the "right to control" test, as adopted by this Court in Ledesma v. Bergeson, *supra*, encompass much the same factors which would be considered in the "nature of the work" test.] This Court's ability to review factual questions is limited. "Our review of the decisions of the Industrial Commission is limited by Article 5, § 9 of the Idaho Constitution to questions of law and to determination [of] whether the commission's findings are supported by substantial and competent evidence." *Cahala v. OK Tire Store*, 112 Idaho 1020, 1021, 739 P.2d 319, 320 (1987); *Parker v. St. Maries Plywood*, 101 Idaho 415, 419, 614 P.2d 955, 959 (1980), citing Idaho Const. Art. 5, § 9; *Booth v. City of Burley*, 99 Idaho 229, 580 P.2d 75 (1978).

The commission correctly acknowledged that, "The determination of whether an injured party is an independent contractor or an employee is a factual determination to be made from full consideration of the facts and circumstances established by the evidence" *(citations omitted)*.

. . . .

Larson has explained in Workmen's Compensation Law that:

§ 44.00 The traditional test of the employer-employee relation is the right of the employer to control the details of the work. It is the ultimate right of control, under the agreement with the employee, not the overt exercise of that right, which is decisive. If the right of control of details goes no further than is necessary to ensure a satisfactory end result, it does not establish employment. The principal factors showing right to control are (1) direct evidence of right or exercise of control; (2) method of payment; (3) the furnishing of equipment; and (4) the right to fire.

Larson, Workmen's Compensation Law § 44.00 (emphasis deleted). "[T]he right to control the details of the work is most often an inference from these and other tangible facts, rather than a solid fact in itself." *Id.*, § 44.00. The weight to be given any one of these factors must, of necessity, vary with the specific circumstances of any individual case. None of these elements in and of itself is controlling. Although it was essential that the commission look at all relevant facts in light of these four elements, the commission was not required to find facts meeting each element.

Nevertheless, in this case we conclude that the commission erroneously applied the third factor in the "right to control" test, i.e., the furnishing of major items of equipment. The commission accepted the referee's finding that "the dancers supplied the major items of equipment (i.e., their bodies, skills and costuming)." However, in a case involving personal services, in deciding whether or not the worker is an employee or an independent contractor, the worker's body is not a major item of equipment within the meaning of the third element of the "right to control" test. Major items of equipment include such things as tools, machinery, special clothing, parts, and other similar items necessary for the worker to accomplish the task to be performed. For example, a plumber, hired to perform plumbing repairs on a building, usually brings the tools, the parts, and often special equipment in the form of augers, pipe cutters and threaders, etc., in order to perform the service. Those are the sorts of items which constitute the "major items of equipment" under the third element of the right to control test. The fact that the plumber also supplies the body doing the work is true whether he is acting as an employee or as an independent contractor. Accordingly, we think the referee's finding, adopted by the commission, placing emphasis on the fact that the dancers' bodies were "major items of equipment" was an erroneous application of the test.

The commission's decision in this case is not unlike the case of *Ross v. Fiest*, 105 Idaho 119, 666 P.2d 646 (1983), where the Industrial Commission, conversely, found that a worker was an employee rather than an independent contractor because the ownership of timber cutting rights by a person who hired a sawyer to cut the timber was analogous to the ownership of major items of equipment for the purpose of the third factor in the "right to control" test. In remanding that case to the commission, we stated:

> [T]he commission erred in its conclusion that, Fiest's timber cutting rights were analogous to the ownership of equipment. Every principal contractor necessarily extends to a subcontractor the right to do work on the involved premises, and the principal does not thereby necessarily change the status of a subcontractor to the status of an employee. Therefore, the commission's rationale, i.e., that Fiest's ownership of timber cutting rights was a factor in determining the employment status, was erroneous.

105 Idaho at 120, 666 P.2d at 647. Conversely, in this case, the worker's body could not be considered the "furnishing of major items of equipment" within the meaning of the test. Rather, for the purposes of this test, the commission should be looking at items such as tools, machinery, parts, special clothing (such as costumes, which the dancers provided for themselves), etc.

In *Ross* we held that: "When erroneous evidence is considered in arriving at a factual decision, particularly where the ultimate factual issue is as close as the issue in this case, the cause should be remanded to the factfinding to reconsider the factual issue without the erroneous evidence." 105 Idaho at 120, 666 P.2d at 647.

As in *Ross*, we conclude that this matter should be remanded to the Industrial Commission to reconsider its factual findings and conclusions without considering Hanson's body as a "major items of equipment" provided by her. We re-emphasize that while the commission must consider all of the four elements of the "right to control" test, none of these elements in and of itself is controlling and, indeed, one or more of the four may not be met on the facts of any given case. Rather, the commission must balance each of the elements present to determine the relative weight and importance of each. The commission should then make its determination of whether or not, considering all of the facts and circumstances in the case, Hanson was an employee or an independent contractor.

Reversed and remanded for further findings consistent with this opinion. Costs to appellant. No attorney fees on appeal. . . .

§ 12.03   CONTRACTOR DISTINCTION: RELATIVE NATURE OF WORK

The modern tendency is to find employment when the work being done is an integral part of the regular business of the employer, and when the worker, relative to the employer, does not furnish an independent business or professional service.

S.G. BORELLO & SONS, INC. v. DEPARTMENT OF INDUSTRIAL RELATIONS
48 Cal. 3d 341, 256 Cal. Rptr. 543, 769 P.2d 399 (1989)

EAGLESON, JUSTICE.

We ordered review to decide whether agricultural laborers engaged to harvest cucumbers under a written "sharefarmer" agreement are "independent contractors" exempt from workers' compensation coverage. [footnote omitted] Our answer has implications for the employer-employee relationship upon which other state social legislation depends. [footnote omitted]

The grower claims the "sharefarmer" harvesters are independent contractors under the statutory "control-of-work" test, because they manage their own labor, share the profit or loss from the crop, and agree in writing that they are not employees. After taking evidence on the nature of the work relationship, the Division of Labor Standards Enforcement (Division) of the Department of Industrial Relations rejected these contentions. The superior court found that the Division's decision was supported by the evidence. However, these rulings were reversed by the Court of Appeal.

Like the Division and the superior court, we find the grower's arguments unpersuasive. The grower controls the agricultural operations on its premises from planting to sale of the crops. It simply chooses to accomplish one integrated step in the production of one such crop by means of worker incentives rather than direct supervision. It thereby retains all necessary control over a job which can be done only one way.

Moreover, so far as the record discloses, the harvesters' work, though seasonal by nature, follows the usual line of an employee. In no practical sense are the "sharefarmers" entrepreneurs operating independent businesses for their own accounts; they and their families are obvious members of the broad class to which workers' compensation protection is intended to apply.

We therefore conclude as a matter of law on the undisputed facts that the "sharefarmers" are "employees" entitled to compensation coverage. Accordingly, we reverse the judgment of the Court of Appeal.

FACTS

On August 14, 1985, a deputy labor commissioner issued a stop order/penalty assessment against S.G. Borello & Sons, Inc. (Borello), a Gilroy grower, for failure to secure workers' compensation coverage for the 50 migrant harvesters of its cucumber crop. (Lab.Code, §§ 3700, 3710.1, 3722. [footnote omitted]) Borello appealed the citation to the Division. At the administrative hearing, Borello admitted the failure to secure coverage. It contended only that the workers were independent contractors excluded from the workers' compensation law. (§§ 3351, 3353.)

A preprinted agreement signed by the heads of harvester families was introduced in evidence. The agreement, printed in English and Spanish, designates the signatory worker as a "Share Farmer" and states that his function is to "prepare for and harvest the cucumbers." Borello agrees to "furnish and prepare the land; plant the crop; cultivate, spray, and fertilize the crop; and pay all the costs incurred with respect thereto." The grower also agrees to furnish the boxes and bins into which cucumbers will be loaded, and to transport the harvest to the buyer.

The "Share Farmer" agrees "to furnish himself and the members of his family, but *only* the members of his own family, to harvest the crop. . . . " (Italics in original.) "Harvest is agreed to mean the placing of the crop, clean and free from rubbish and debries [sic], in the boxes or bins supplied by [Borello]." The method and manner of accomplishing this task are left "solely" to the "Share Farmer," who nonetheless "agrees to utilize accepted agricultural practices in order to provide for the maximum harvest . . . and . . . to devote the necessary time to accomplish the harvest." The "Share Farmer" must supply his own tools and his own transportation to and from the field.

The agreement further provides that the crop harvested by the "Share Farmer" will be sold to a buyer "acceptable to both parties." Borello will retain title to the crop until it is sold, but the "Share Farmer" and Borello will split the gross proceeds equally. The contract specifies that the amount of the proceeds will depend exclusively upon price, weight, and grading data developed by the buyer. Copies of this data will be furnished to both parties. Borello undertakes to keep all necessary weight, grade, and price records, which shall be open to the "Share Farmer's" inspection.

Finally, the agreement recites that the parties deem themselves principal and independent contractor rather than employer and employee; that the "Share Farmer" is self-employed; that he will follow all child labor laws; that Borello will not withhold taxes; that the "Share Farmer" must file separate tax returns; and that Borello will not provide workers' compensation or disability insurance coverage. The contract is deemed personal and nonassignable except with the other party's consent.

Richard and Johnny Borello, principals of the company, testified as follows: Borello grows a number of crops, including cucumbers. All the other crops are harvested by employees on a wage basis. In recent years, the only local market for cucumbers is the Vlasic pickle company. Vlasic unilaterally determines the cucumber varieties it will accept and sets the prices it will pay. "The smaller the cucumber, the higher the price" per ton.

The growing cycle for cucumbers is 60 days. Borello plants and cultivates the crop at its own expense, using its own pipe irrigation system and applying pesticides under Vlasic's direction.

The harvest workers — 14 migrant families during the 1985 season — arrive around "2–3 weeks" before the harvest begins. They "[want] to go on a sharefarming basis" because "they make a lot more money." Some families have returned to work under the system for several years running, and it is commonly employed for cucumber harvest in the Gilroy area. Vlasic supplies the preprinted "Share Farmer" contract form, which Borello has a family head sign. The contract is read and explained to the workers, in Spanish if necessary.

The sharefarmers may contract for the amount of land they wish to harvest on a first-come, first-served basis. One or two acres or twenty to forty rows is common. The workers are "totally responsible" for the care of the plants in their assigned plots during the harvest period. Besides hoeing and weeding, the harvesters must prevent the vines from growing into the furrows between the rows where they might be stepped on and damaged. The latter task is accomplished simply by laying any errant vine into the proper position. The sharefarmers also collectively decide when to irrigate during this period, but Borello controls the water supply.

Borello maintains no field supervisor and does not direct the harvesters' work. They may set their own hours. The workers decide when to pick each cucumber at the correct size to maximize the profit. Profit incentive is the only guaranty of performance and quality control. Borello's only field employee is a tractor driver. He supplies empty boxes or bins, coded for each sharefarmer, and removes them to a loading area when full. The workers "could" transport their own harvest to Vlasic, but Borello handles the transportation because that is what Vlasic prefers.

Based on the code system, Vlasic keeps records of each sharefarmer's harvest. At Borello's request, the weekly check for the sharefarmer's share of proceeds is issued directly by Vlasic, though Richard Borello "physically" hands over the check and a copy of Vlasic's documentation. The sharefarmer then splits his share as he chooses with other family members working under him.

Borello's witnesses insisted that they have no right to discharge a sharefarmer or his workers during the harvest, and no recourse if the harvesters abandon the field. Despite contract terms which prohibit assignment of the sharefarmer agreement or employment of workers outside the sharefarmer's family, several sharefarmers have unilaterally assigned or sublet their plots when family emergencies arose. The workers leave once the cucumber harvest is over and do not harvest any other crops for Borello. Richard Borello conceded the grower provides no food or sanitary facilities for its cucumber harvesters.

On this evidence, the Division concluded that because of Borello's predominant control over the cultivation, harvest, and sale of its cucumbers, and the workers' lack of investment in the crop, they cannot be deemed "sharecroppers in the true sense." Hence, it ruled, they are employees rather than independent contractors. The penalty assessment/stop order was affirmed. [Footnote omitted].

Borello sought mandamus to review the Division's order. (Code Civ. Proc., § 1094.5.) After a hearing, the trial court found the Division's finding supported by the evidence and denied the writ.

The Court of Appeal reversed. It concluded that Borello's relinquishment of control over the harvesters' work, its lack of authority to discharge them at will, their responsibility for furnishing necessary tools, the "result" method of compensation, the temporary nature of the work, and the mutual understanding embodied in the written contract all combine to render the sharefarmers independent contractors as a matter of law.

DISCUSSION

The Worker's Compensation Act (Act) extends only to injuries suffered by an "employee," which arise out of and in the course of his "employment." (§§ 3600, 3700; see Cal. Const., art. XIV, § 4 (former art. XX, § 21).) "Employee[s]" include most persons "in the service of an employer under any . . . contract of hire" (§ 3351), but do not include independent contractors. The Act defines an independent contractor as "any person who renders service for a specified recompense for a specified result, under the control of his principal as to the result of his work only and not as to the means by which such result is accomplished." (§ 3353.)

The determination of employee or independent-contractor status is one of fact if dependent upon the resolution of disputed evidence or inferences, and the Division's decision must be upheld if substantially supported. (*Germann v. Workers' Comp. Appeals Bd.* (1981) 123 Cal. App. 3d 776, 783, 176 Cal. Rptr. 868.) If the evidence is undisputed, the question becomes one of law (Tieberg v. Unemployment Ins. App. Bd. (1970) 2 Cal. 3d 943, 951, 88 Cal. Rptr. 175, 471 P.2d 975), but deference to the agency's view is appropriate. The label placed by the parties on their relationship is not dispositive, and subterfuges are not countenanced. (*Kowalski v. Shell Oil Co.* (1979) 23 Cal. 3d 168, 176, 151 Cal. Rptr. 671, 588 P.2d 811 [other citations omitted]) The Act must be liberally construed to extend benefits to persons injured in their employment. (§ 3202.) One seeking to avoid liability has the burden of proving that persons whose services he has retained are independent contractors rather than employees. (§§ 3357, 5705, subd. (a).)

Borello and its amici (collectively the growers) urge that the Court of Appeal properly found independent contractorship as a matter of law. By agreement and in actual practice, the growers urge, Borello retains the cucumber sharefarmers for a "specified result" — completed harvest — relinquishing all "control" over the "means" by which the task is accomplished. Moreover, the growers note, the sharefarmers are paid a "specified recompense" based entirely on results. The growers stress that the harvesters furnish their own tools, exercise specialized skill, cannot be discharged, and have expressly accepted their independent status with its attendant risks and benefits. We disagree both with the growers' premises and with their conclusions.

The distinction between independent contractors and employees arose at common law to limit one's vicarious liability for the misconduct of a person rendering service to him. The principal's supervisory power was crucial in that context because " . . . [t]he extent to which the employer had a right to control [the details of the service] activities was . . . highly relevant to the question whether the employer ought to be legally liable for them. . . . " (1C Larson, *The Law of Workmen's Compensation* (1986) § 43.42, p. 8-20; see also 2 Hanna, *Cal. Law of Employee Injuries and Workmen's Compensation* (2d ed. 1988) § 3.01[2], p. 3-4.) Thus, the "control of details" test became the principal measure of the servant's status for common law purposes.

Much 20th-century legislation for the protection of "employees" has adopted the "independent contractor" distinction as an express or implied limitation on coverage. The Act plainly states the exclusion of "independent contractors" and inserts the common law "control-of-work" test in the statutory definition. The cases extend these principles to other "employee" legislation as well. Following common law tradition, California decisions applying such statutes uniformly declare that "[t]he principal test of an employment relationship is whether the person to whom service is rendered has the right to control the manner and means of accomplishing the result desired. . . . " (*Tieberg, supra,* 2 Cal. 3d at p. 946, 88 Cal. Rptr. 175, 471 P.2d 975 [unemployment insurance]; *see also, e.g., Isenberg v. California Emp. Stab. Com.* (1947) 30 Cal. 2d 34, 39, 180 P.2d 11 [same; drawing direct analogy to workers' compensation law]; *Perguica v. Ind. Acc. Com.* (1947) 29 Cal. 2d 857, 859–861, 179 P.2d 812 [workers' compensation]; *Empire Star Mines Co. v. Cal. Emp. Com.* (1946) 28 Cal. 2d 33, 43–44, 168 P.2d 686 [unemployment insurance].)

However, the courts have long recognized that the "control" test, applied rigidly and in isolation, is often of little use in evaluating the infinite variety of service arrangements. While conceding that the right to control work details is the "most important" or "most significant" consideration, the authorities also endorse several "secondary" indicia of the nature of a service relationship.

Thus, we have noted that "[s]trong evidence in support of an employment relationship is the right to discharge at will, without cause. [Citations.]" (*Tieberg, supra,* 2 Cal. 3d at p. 949, 88 Cal. Rptr. 175, 471 P.2d 975, quoting *Empire Star Mines, supra,* 28 Cal. 2d at p. 43, 168 P.2d 686.) Additional factors have been derived principally from the Restatement Second of Agency. These include (a) whether the one performing services is engaged in a distinct occupation or business; (b) the kind of occupation, with reference to whether, in the locality, the work is usually done under the direction of the principal or by a specialist without supervision; (c) the skill required in the particular occupation; (d) whether the principal or the worker supplies the instrumentalities, tools, and the place of work for the person doing the work; (e) the length of time for which the services are to be performed; (f) the method of payment, whether by the time or by the job; (g) whether or not the work is a part of the regular business of the principal; and (h) whether or not the parties believe they are creating the relationship of employer-employee. (*Tieberg, supra,* at p. 949, 88 Cal. Rptr. 175, 471 P.2d 975; *Empire Star Mines, supra,* 28 Cal. 2d at pp. 43–44, 168 P.2d 686; see Rest.2d Agency, § 220.) "Generally, . . . the individual factors cannot be applied mechanically as separate tests; they are intertwined and their weight depends often on particular combinations." (*Germann, supra,* 123 Cal. App. 3d at p. 783, 176 Cal. Rptr. 868.)[footnote omitted]

Moreover, the concept of "employment" embodied in the Act is not inherently limited by common law principles. We have acknowledged that the Act's definition of the employment relationship must be construed with particular reference to the "history and fundamental purposes" of the statute. (*Laeng v. Workmen's Comp. Appeals Bd.* (1972) 6 Cal. 3d 771, 777–778, 100 Cal. Rptr. 377, 494 P.2d 1.)

The common law and statutory purposes of the distinction between "employees" and "independent contractors" are substantially different. While the common law tests were developed to define an employer's liability for injuries caused by his employee, "the basic inquiry in compensation law involves which injuries to the employee should be insured against by the employer. [Citations.]. . . . " (Id., at pp. 777–778, fn. 7, 100 Cal. Rptr. 377, 494 P.2d 1 [italics in original]; 1C Larson, *supra,* § 43.42, pp. 8-20, 8-21; 2 Hanna, *supra,* § 3.01[2], p. 3-4, & fn. 14.)

Federal courts have long recognized that the distinction between tort policy and social-legislation policy justifies departures from common law principles when claims arise that one is excluded as an independent contractor from a statute protecting "employees." Where not expressly prohibited by the legislation at issue, the federal cases deem the traditional "control" test pertinent to a more general assessment whether the overall nature of the service arrangement is one which the protective statute was intended to cover. (*E.g., Bartels v. Birmingham* (1947) 332 U.S. 126, 130–132, 67 S.Ct. 1547, 1549–1551, 91 L.Ed. 1947 [other citations and footnote omitted].)

A number of state courts have agreed that in worker's compensation cases, the employee-independent contractor issue cannot be decided absent consideration of the remedial statutory purpose. Several state cases have so concluded despite statutes, like California's, which emphasize "control" of the work as the governing distinction between employees and independent contractors. [Citations omitted]. . . .

We agree that under the Act, the "control-of-work-details" test for determining whether a person rendering service to another is an "employee" or an excluded "independent contractor" must be applied with deference to the purposes of the protective legislation. The nature of the work, and the overall arrangement between the parties, must be examined to determine whether they come within the "history and fundamental purposes" of the statute. (*Laeng, supra,* 6 Cal. 3d at p. 777, 100 Cal. Rptr. 377, 494 P.2d 1.)

The purposes of the Act are several. It seeks (1) to ensure that the cost of industrial injuries will be part of the cost of goods rather than a burden on society, (2) to guarantee prompt, limited compensation for an employee's work injuries, regardless of fault, as an inevitable cost of production, (3) to spur increased industrial safety, and (4) in return, to insulate the employer from tort liability for his employees' injuries. [Citations omitted].

The Act intends comprehensive coverage of injuries in employment. It accomplishes this goal by defining "employment" broadly in terms of "service to an employer" and by including a general presumption that any person "in service to another" is a covered "employee." (§§ 3351, 5705, subd. (a); see *Laeng, supra,* 6 Cal. 3d at pp. 776–778, 100 Cal. Rptr. 377, 494 P.2d 1.)

The express exclusion of "independent contractors" is purposeful, of course, and has a limited but important function. It recognizes those situations where the Act's goals are best served by imposing the risk of "no-fault" work injuries directly on the provider, rather than the recipient, of a compensated service. This is obviously the case, for example, when the provider of service has the primary power over work safety, is best situated to distribute the risk and cost of injury as an expense of his own business, and has independently chosen the burdens and benefits of self-employment.

This is the balance to be struck when deciding whether a worker is an employee or an independent contractor for purposes of the Act. We adopt no detailed new standards for examination of the issue. To that end, the Restatement guidelines heretofore approved in our state remain a useful reference. The standards set forth for contractor's licensees in section 2750.5 [Citations omitted] are also a helpful means of identifying the employee/contractor distinction. The relevant considerations may often overlap those pertinent under the common law. (See *Laeng, supra,* 6 Cal. 3d at pp. 777–778, fn. 7, 100 Cal. Rptr. 377, 494 P.2d 1.) Each service arrangement must be evaluated on its facts, and the dispositive circumstances may vary from case to case.

We also note the six-factor test developed by other jurisdictions which determine independent contractorship in light of the remedial purposes of the legislation. Besides the "right to control the work," the factors include (1) the alleged employee's opportunity for profit or loss depending on his managerial skill; (2) the alleged employee's investment in equipment or materials required for his task, or his employment of helpers; (3) whether the service rendered requires a special skill; (4) the degree of permanence of the working relationship; and (5) whether the service rendered is an integral part of the alleged employer's business. (*Real v. Driscoll Strawberry Associates, Inc.* (9th Cir. 1979) 603 F.2d 748, 754 [Fair Labor Standards Act].)

As can be seen, there are many points of individual similarity between these guidelines and our own traditional Restatement tests. . . . We find that all are logically pertinent to the inherently difficult determination whether a provider of service is an employee or an excluded independent contractor for purposes of workers' compensation law.

By any applicable test, we must dismiss the growers' claims here. Despite Borello's elaborate effort to deal with the cucumber harvesters as independent contractors, the indicia of their employment are compelling.

The issue has arisen on several occasions elsewhere. There, as here, growers claimed that migrant harvesters of their cucumber crops were self-employed "sharefarmers," who contracted for a finished job, applied skill and judgment, controlled their own work, and were compensated only for results. Hence, the growers urged, the harvesters were not "employees" for purposes of protective legislation, but excluded "independent contractors."

With one exception, the cases have rejected such contentions. The decisions emphasize that the growers, though purporting to relinquish supervision of the harvest work itself, retained absolute overall control of the production and sale of the crop. Moreover, the cases note, the workers made no capital investment beyond simple hand tools; they performed manual labor requiring no special skill; their remuneration did not depend on their initiative, judgment, or managerial abilities; their service, though seasonal, was rendered regularly and as an integrated part of the grower's business; and they were dependent for subsistence on whatever farm work they could obtain. Under these circumstances, the authorities reason, the harvesters were within the intended reach of the protective legislation. [Citations omitted] Similar considerations are dispositive here.

The growers emphasize that, with respect to the cucumber harvest, Borello contracts only to obtain a "specified result" for a "specified recompense," retaining no interest in the details of the work. They stress that the sharefarmers work free of Borello's interference, have all legal and actual power over the means of accomplishing their work, and are paid for their production rather than their labor. The job involves considerable skill and judgment, the growers urge, because the crops require final hoeing, weeding, and irrigation; the vines must be "trained" out of the furrows; and care is necessary to pick each maturing cucumber at the most marketable size. Hence, the growers assert, the factor of "control" weighs against a finding of employment.

We are not persuaded. In the first place, Borello, whose business is the production and sale of agricultural crops, exercises "pervasive control over the operation as a whole." (*Lauritzen, supra,* 835 F.2d at p. 1536.) Borello owns and cultivates the land for its own account. Without any participation by the sharefarmers, Borello decides to grow cucumbers, obtains a sale price formula from the only available buyer,[footnote omitted] plants the crop, and cultivates it throughout most of its growing cycle. The harvest takes place on Borello's premises, at a time determined by the crop's maturity. During the harvest itself, Borello supplies the sorting bins and boxes, removes the harvest from the field, transports it to market, sells it, maintains documentation on the workers' proceeds, and hands out their checks. Thus, "[a]ll meaningful aspects of this business relationship: price, crop cultivation, fertilization and insect prevention, payment, [and] right to deal with buyers . . . are controlled by [Borello]." [Citation and footnote omitted]

Moreover, contrary to the growers' assertions, the cucumber harvest involves simple manual labor which can be performed in only one correct way. Harvest and plant-care methods can be learned quickly. While the work requires stamina and patience, it involves no peculiar skill beyond that expected of any employee. [Citations omitted] It is the simplicity of the work, not the harvesters' superior expertise, which makes detailed supervision and discipline unnecessary. Diligence and quality control are achieved by the payment system, essentially a variation of the piecework formula familiar to agricultural employment.

Under these circumstances, Borello retains all necessary control over the harvest portion of its operations. A business entity may not avoid its statutory obligations by carving up its production process into minute steps, then asserting that it lacks "control" over the exact means by which one such step is performed by the responsible workers. [Citations and footnote omitted]

Other factors also show convincingly that the worker's compensation statute places the risk and cost of work-related injuries upon Borello, rather than the farmworkers themselves. The harvesters form a regular and integrated portion of Borello's business operation. Their work, though seasonal by nature, is "permanent" in the agricultural process. Indeed, Richard Borello testified that he has a permanent relationship with the individual harvesters, in that many of the migrant families return year after year. This permanent integration of the workers into the heart of Borello's business is a strong indicator that Borello functions as an employer under the Act. (*See, e.g., Lauritzen, supra,* 835 F.2d at pp. 1535–1538; *Kokesch, supra,* 411 N.W.2d at pp. 562–563; 1C Larson, *supra,* § 45.00, p. 8-174 ["The modern tendency is to find employment when the work being done is an integral part of the regular business of the employer, and when the worker, relative to the employer, does not furnish an independent business or professional service."].)

By the same token, the sharefarmers and their families exhibit no characteristics which might place them outside the Act's intended coverage of employees. They engage in no distinct trade or calling. They do not hold themselves out in business. They perform typical farm labor for hire wherever jobs are available. They invest nothing but personal service and hand tools. [footnote omitted] They incur no opportunity for "profit" or "loss;" like employees hired on a piecework basis, they are simply paid by the size and grade of cucumbers they pick. [footnote omitted] They rely solely on work in the fields for their subsistence and livelihood. Despite the contract's admonitions, they have no practical opportunity to insure themselves or their families against loss of income caused by nontortious work injuries. [footnote omitted] If Borello is not their employer, they themselves, and society at large, thus assume the entire financial burden when such injuries occur. [footnote omitted] Without doubt, they are a class of workers to whom the protection of the Act is intended to extend. [footnote omitted]

The growers suggest that by signing the printed agreement after full explanations, the sharefarmers expressly agree they are not employees and consciously accept the attendant risks and benefits. However, the protections conferred by the Act have a public purpose beyond the private interests of the workers themselves. Among other things, the statute represents society's recognition that if the financial risk of job injuries is not placed upon the businesses which produce them, it may fall upon the public treasury. (See discussion, ante.) Of course, a worker's express or implied agreement to forego coverage as an independent contractor is "significant." (See *Tieberg, supra*, 2 Cal. 3d at p. 952, 88 Cal. Rptr. 175, 471 P.2d 975.) However, where compelling indicia of employment are otherwise present, we may not lightly assume an individual waiver of the protections derived from that status.

Moreover, there is no indication that Borello offers its cucumber harvesters any real choice of terms. Richard Borello testified only that the family heads sign the preprinted contract. He conceded that recent seasons have brought a surplus of workers to the local cucumber harvest, suggesting further that no real bargaining takes place. Nor is there evidence that nonsignatory members of the sharefarmer's family have accepted Borello's disclaimer of employment responsibilities. The record fails to demonstrate that the harvesters voluntarily undertake an "independent" and unprotected status. [footnote omitted]

A conclusion that the sharefarmers are "independent contractors" under the Act would suggest a disturbing means of avoiding an employer's obligations under other California legislation intended for the protection of "employees," including laws enacted specifically for the protection of agricultural labor. These include the Agricultural Labor Relations Act (§ 1141 et seq.), statutes requiring the licensure and bonding of farm labor contractors (§ 1682 et seq.), laws governing minimum wages, maximum hours, and (as illustrated in this case) employment of minors (§ 1171 et seq., § 1285 et seq.), the antidiscrimination provisions of the Fair Employment and Housing Act (Gov.Code, § 12940 et seq.), and provisions governing employee health and safety (*see, e.g.*, Lab. Code, § 6300 et seq. [Occupational Safety and Health Act]; Health & Saf. Code, § 5474.20 et seq. [imposing duty, not followed here, to provide toilet and washing facilities for each 40 or fewer field "employees"].) [footnote omitted]

We therefore hold as a matter of law that Borello has failed to demonstrate the cucumber sharefarmers are independent contractors excluded from coverage under the Act. Accordingly, the judgment of the Court of Appeal, directing the superior court to grant Borello's petition for writ of mandate, is reversed.

LUCAS, C.J., and MOSK, BROUSSARD and ARGUELLES, JJ., concur.

KAUFMAN, JUSTICE, dissenting. [dissenting opinion omitted]

RE/MAX OF NEW JERSEY, INC. v. WAUSAU INSURANCE COMPANIES
304 N.J. Super. 59, 697 A.2d 977 (1997), *aff'd* 316 N.J. Super. 514; 720 A.2d 658

GIBSON, J.S.C.

These are consolidated cases in which Re/Max of New Jersey and several of its franchisees seek a declaratory judgment that their sales agents be deemed independent contractors for the purpose of calculating workers' compensation premiums. Defendants are various insurance carriers which have supplied workers' compensation coverage to plaintiffs. The carriers contend that the agents should be deemed employees. This issue appears to be one of first impression and is before the court procedurally based on stipulated facts and cross motions for summary judgment.

Findings of Fact

Plaintiff, Re/Max of New Jersey, Inc. (hereafter Re/Max) is a subfranchiser of Re/Max International Inc. The various Re/Max offices in New Jersey are franchisees of Re/Max of New Jersey. All are engaged in the business of providing real estate services to the public. Defendants, Employers Insurance of Wausau, Aetna Life & Casualty, Travelers Insurance Company, New Jersey Re-Insurance Company and Pennsylvania Insurance Company (hereafter carriers) are the insurance companies which service the Re/Max offices. At some point, each of those carriers determined that Re/Max agents should be considered employees for purposes of the workers' compensation act and began to charge premiums accordingly. Plaintiffs objected and contended that the agents were independent contractors. Unable to resolve those differences, this action was instituted.

Each of the Re/Max offices in New Jersey consists of a licensed broker and at least one sales agent. As part of the franchise agreement, all Re/Max brokers are required to have their sales agents sign an "Independent Contractor Agreement" which sets forth their rights and obligations and contains a variety of provisions intended to underscore the agents' independent contractor status. Included among those provisions is the agent's right to set his own hours, engage in his own advertising and to enjoy the benefits of the so-called "100% Concept." Under the 100% Concept, Re/Max agents are entitled to retain the entire commission earned from any sale rather than splitting the commission with the broker, as is common in other real estate agencies. In consideration of the agent's services and the fees paid, the broker agrees to make available, on a non-exclusive basis, office and desk space plus access to listings, forms, telephone and other means of communication.

Although Re/Max agents are not required to share a commission, the agents are obligated to pay to the broker a variety of fees and expenses. Those sums include a security deposit, a one-time initiation fee and a monthly management fee representing a proportionate share of the office expenses. The office expenses include so-called fixed expenses (proportionately shared among the agents), miscellaneous shared expenses and finally personal expenses such as postage and advertising. The actual amount of the monthly expenses may vary from agent to agent and from month to month. At times, individual agents may not generate enough sales to meet their monthly expense obligation. To accommodate those situations, Re/Max offers an Alternative Payment Program which allows agents to reduce the amount they need to pay toward monthly expenses by taking an advance against future commissions.

Re/Max agents generally work full time, but they are not compelled to spend any minimum amount of "floor time" in the office. They also supply their own vehicle and control their own advertising but all advertising must include the Re/Max logo and name and conform with other guidelines. Franchisees hold regular meetings to inform agents regarding real estate topics, but attendance is voluntary. Agents are also required to maintain their personal appearance and provide dependable, efficient, courteous and professional service and Re/Max retains the right to immediately terminate any agent for cause; either party may terminate without cause upon sixty days written notice.

All Re/Max agents agree to work exclusively for the Re/Max office, to maintain loyalty to Re/Max and to abide by the various statutory requirements of the Real Estate Brokers and Salesman Act, N.J.S.A. 45:15-1-29.5. In accordance with that Act, it is only the broker that can bring an action to collect a commission. Although plaintiffs contend that the broker simply acts as a conduit, the consequences are the same; that is, no agent has the ability to enforce a commission agreement without the help of the broker. Finally, although the actual control exercised varies among offices, the agreement gives the broker the right to supervise and control the performance of every agent.

Conclusions of Law

Before addressing the merits, it should be noted that the purpose of a declaratory judgment is to end uncertainty about the legal rights and duties of parties to litigation. . . .

As for the merits, given the fact that the financial benefits under the workers' compensation act extend only to employees, N.J.S.A. 34:15-1, the question of whether a Re/Max sales agent is an employee or an independent contractor is crucial to the determination of whether the brokers are required to maintain coverage and, in turn, whether these carriers may legitimately include the agents in calculating premiums. *Kertesz v. Korsh*, 296 N.J. Super. 146, 152, 686 A.2d 368 (App. Div. 1996). *See generally*, 38 New Jersey Practice, Worker's Compensation Law § 5.1 through § 5.9 (1994). Although there are no reported cases which have decided this issue, this court is not without guidance. For example, under the Worker's Compensation Act, the term "employee" is given a broad definition and includes "all natural persons . . . who perform services for an employer for financial consideration." N.J.S.A. 34:15-36. It is also clear that the term "employee" is to be liberally construed so as to bring as many persons as possible within the coverage of the Act. *Hannigan v. Goldfarb*, 53 N.J. Super. 190, 195, 147 A.2d 56 (App. Div. 1958). As a consequence, a variety of working relationships have been held to be covered by the Act, including those not necessarily confined to traditional employment settings. *Ibid; Marcus v. Eastern Agricultural Ass'n, Inc.*, 58 N.J. Super. 584, 590, 157 A.2d 3 (App. Div. 1959), *rev'd on dissent*, 32 N.J. 460, 161 A.2d 247 (1960).

In addressing the employee/independent contractor issue in other factual settings, our courts have applied two tests; the so-called "control test" and the "relative nature of the work test." *Ibid; Tofani v. Lo Biondo Brothers Motor Express, Inc.*, 83 N.J. Super. 480, 484–92, 200 A.2d 493 (App. Div.), aff'd o.b., 43 N.J. 494, 205 A.2d 736 (1964). The "control test" is the older of the two and, in general, is based on the notion that when an individual is an independent contractor, that person carries on a separate business and contracts to do work according to his or her own methods, without being subject to the control of an employer, except as to the results. When the relation is that of employer and employee, on the other hand, the employer not only retains the right to control what is done but also to direct the manner in which the work is completed. *Kertesz v. Korsh, supra*, 296 N.J. Super. at 152, 686 A.2d 368 citing *Cappadonna v. Passaic Motors, Inc.*, 136 N.J.L. 299, 55 A.2d 462 (N.J. Sup. 1947), aff'd, 137 N.J.L. 661, 61 A.2d 282 (N.J. Err. & App. 1948). Significantly, our courts have held that the "control test" is satisfied so long as the employer has the right of control, and it is not necessary to prove its actual exercise. *Brower v. Rossmy*, 63 N.J. Super. 395, 405, 164 A.2d 754 (App. Div. 1960), *certif. denied*, 34 N.J. 65, 167 A.2d 54 (1961).

As for the "relative nature of the work test," not only is it the more modern of the two, it is also believed to be the more realistic test in terms of the objectives of the workers compensation act, *Kertesz v. Korsh, supra*, 296 N.J. Super. at 154, 686 A.2d 368 Larson, Workmen's Compensation Law, § 43.50 at 8–10. As characterized by the Appellate Division dissent, adopted by the Supreme Court.

The test . . . [is] essentially an economic and functional one, and the determative criteria [are] not the inclusive details of the arrangement between the parties, but rather the extent of the economic dependence of the worker upon the business he serves and the relationship of the nature of his work to the operation of that business.

[*Marcus v. Eastern Agricultural Ass'n, Inc., supra*, 58 N.J. Super. at 603, 157 A.2d 3 (Conford, J.A.D. dissenting).]

A critical focus is the workers' degree of independence and whether his or her work is an integral part of the regular business of someone else. *Kertesz v. Korsh, supra*, 296 N.J. Super. at 154, 686 A.2d 368.

In assessing the relationship of Re/Max agents under the "control test", I am sensitive to the fact that the brokers and the agents have themselves defined their relationship as independent contractors and their agreement includes a variety of provisions which purport to underscore that point. For example, the agents are on a 100% commission basis, they set their own hours and conduct their own advertising. On the other hand, the agents must comply with an elaborate set of guidelines and quality controls. Also, although agents handle their own advertising, the advertising must contain the Re/Max logo and must depict them as part of the Re/Max organization. Even the written contract makes it clear that the agents are subject to the supervision and control of Re/Max and/or their local broker. And, of course, it is the Re/Max brokers that supply the listings, office, the phones, and other services needed to implement an agent's sales efforts. Thus, although workers and employers may make whatever contractual arrangement they wish, any arrangement which thwarts the purposes of the workers' compensation legislation by manipulating labels will not be sanctioned. *Marcus v. Eastern Agricultural Ass'n, Inc., supra*, 58 N.J. Super. at 594, 157 A.2d 3.

Similar reasoning was applied by the court in *Hannigan v. Goldfarb, supra*, 53 N.J. Super. at 196, 147 A.2d 56. In that case, the court concluded that a taxicab driver who paid a set fee to operate a cab on his own for twelve hour shifts, but who did not own the cab, was nevertheless an employee for the purposes the Workers Compensation Act. The court concluded that since the driver was operating the cab through the defendant association, was identified with the association by its logo and received his fees through a central office which managed the overall operation, there was sufficient control to justify labeling the driver an employee. *Ibid.* The court reached the same conclusion by applying the relative nature of the work test. *Id.* at 204–208, 147 A.2d 56. In *Tofani v. Lo Biondo Brothers Motor Express, Inc., supra*, the court applied a similar analysis to conclude that a decedent who owned his own tractor, leased it to the defendant and drove it while hauling a trailer owned by defendant was the defendants employee for coverage purposes. Most recently, the Appellate Division concluded that even though a sheetrocker operated his own business, he was nevertheless an employee of a real estate developer for workers compensation purposes where that developer hired the sheetrocker three or four times a month, supervised the work through his foreman and supplied the materials. *Kertesz v. Korsh, supra*, 296 N.J. Super. at 157, 686 A.2d 368. Although the worker brought his own tools to the job, it was the builder who had the right to control the nature of the work. *Id.* at 153, 686 A.2d 368. Based on the above, I am satisfied that Re/Max agents would be considered employees under the control test.

Even if this court were to conclude that the "control test" supported plaintiffs' position or that the test was inconclusive, the absence of control would not preclude a finding that these agents are employees. *Ibid.* A clear showing of control will, of course, lead to the conclusion that an employer-employee relationship existed. However, given the variety of situations in which control is not dispositive, our courts have placed greater reliance upon the "relative nature of the work test." *Pollack v. Pino's Formal Wear*, 253 N.J. Super. 397, 407, 601 A.2d 1190 (App. Div.), *certif. denied*, 130 N.J. 6, 611 A.2d 646 (1992). An application of this test to the instant case further supports the conclusion that Re/Max agents should be considered employees for workers' compensation purposes. As noted, under this test, one looks to the extent of the economic dependence of the worker upon the business served, as well as the relationship of the nature of the person's work to the operation of the business as a whole. *Marcus v. Eastern Agricultural Ass'n, Inc.*, 58 N.J. Super. at 603, 157 A.2d 3 (Conford, J.A.D. dissenting). Stated differently, the key question is whether the nature of the work done by the individual is an integral part of the regular business of the employer and/or whether the worker is economically dependent on that business. *Kertesz v. Korsh, supra*, 296 N.J. Super. at 154, 686 A.2d 368, 1C Larson, Workmen's Compensation Law, *supra*. In the case at bar, there is no question that the agents are economically dependent on the broker. The broker provides the listings, the office, the equipment and the support staff. In addition, the agents work for the Re/Max office exclusively. Beyond that, the agents' dependence has a statutory basis. For example, under N.J.S.A. 45:15-3, it is only the broker that can lawfully enforce a client's obligation to pay a commission. In sum, Re/Max agents do not have the ability to act independently.

In addition to the two tests discussed above, New Jersey Reinsurance Company, has raised a contractual argument based on language in the insurance policy. For example, paragraph 5(c)(2) of the standard form policy authorizes the carrier to calculate premiums based on payroll and to include all other persons engaged in work that "could make" the carrier liable for workers' compensation benefits. It is the carrier's contention that such a classification is quite broad and would include the Re/Max sales agents regardless of whether they are independent contractors. In view of the traditionally strict reading applied to insurance contracts, however, this court chooses not to rely on this argument, and given the above analysis, it need not do so.

Conclusion

In view of the broad definition of "employee" under the workers' compensation act, the liberality with which coverage issues are to be treated, and the weight of the case law supporting a broader application of the Act, I am satisfied that Re/Max sales agents should be considered employees for these purposes. The nature of the Re/Max operations gives the office managers sufficient control over the sales people to obviate a claim of independence. More importantly, the integration of the agents' work with the business of the brokers, both economically and from an operational perspective, makes any further claim of independence difficult to sustain. [Court's footnote omitted]

Judgment will therefore be entered on behalf of defendants and against plaintiffs.

PROBLEMS

(1) Claimant was injured while umpiring a softball game, when attacked with a bat by an irate player. The Softball Umpires Association made game assignments, but, although claimant had to umpire a certain number of games per year, he had no obligation to accept any particular assignment. Disputed decisions could be appealed to the Association, but otherwise claimant's officiating was completely under his own control. Was he an employee of the Association? *See* Gale v. Greater Washington Softball Umpires Ass'n, 19 Md. App. 481, 311 A.2d 817 (1973).

(2) Claimant, a jockey, owned all his own equipment, and got his check from the race track office. The owner gave the jockey pre-race instructions, but otherwise exercised no control. Was the jockey an employee of the owner? *See* Clark v. Industrial Comm'n, 54 Ill. 2d 311, 297 N.E. 2d 154 (1973). Of the trainer? *Cf.* Gross v. Pelican, 65 N.J. Super. 386, 167 A.2d 838 (1961). Of the track operator? *See* Haggard v. Industrial Comm'n, 278 App. Div. 31, 103 N.Y.S. 2d 457 (1951).

(3) Moynihan, an attorney with over twenty years' general law practice, had his own law office in Monroe, Colorado, where he employed two other lawyers. The Oliver Power Co. of Paonia, Colorado, paid him a retainer of fifty dollars a month, which gave the company the right to consult the office on the legal aspects of its going policies. For any extra work, payment was *per diem* with expenses. A considerable part of Moynihan's job was appearing before the Utilities Commission to get certificates of convenience and necessity. It was on a trip of this kind of business that he was injured. Compensable? *See* Industrial Comm'n v. Moynihan, 94 Colo. 438, 32 P.2d 802 (1934).

(4) When silicosis became compensable in Wisconsin, it was discovered that practically all granite cutters had the disease in some stage. As a result, the compensation premium actually became greater than the payroll. Since neighboring states had not yet recognized silicosis as compensable, the Wisconsin monument works all had to shut down. Schlimgen, who had a small monument works employing four men, tried to figure out an arrangement to get the four men back to work, and the

workers, after consulting their own lawyer, agreed to it. There were two instruments: a partnership agreement between the four workers under which they advanced equal capital, shared profits equally, had drawing accounts, and kept partnership books; and a lease of the Schlimgen shop to the partnership at 22 1/2% of the gross volume of business transacted, under which the partnership was to process products at job rates for Schlimgen, and the latter was to be the sole sales agent of the products. One of the partners later attempted to claim compensation. What result? *See* York v. Industrial Comm'n, 223 Wis. 140, 269 N.W. 726, 107 A.L.R. 841 (1936).

(5) Shortly after *York*, a Wisconsin granite company, confronted with the same problem, organized its 50 employees into a partnership, which leased the quarry from the employer. Instead of fluctuating profits, however, they received wages. What result in the Wisconsin Supreme Court? *See* Montello Granite Co. v. Industrial Comm'n, 227 Wis. 120, 278 N.W. 391 (1938).

(6) Claimant, a CETA worker, was hired by the County, but assigned to work for the Town. County paid claimant with funds supplied by the federal government. The Town had complete control of the details of the work. The County, pursuant to a federal requirement, carried compensation insurance; the Town did not. Can the County be held liable for workers' compensation to claimant on some kind of estoppel theory? *See* Godley v. County of Pitt, 306 N.C. 357, 293 S.E.2d 167 (1982).

§ 12.04　DELIBERATE AVOIDANCE OF EMPLOYMENT RELATION

Whether the deliberate substitution of the independent contractor for the employee relation is effective to avoid compensation liability depends on whether the actual facts of the relationship, as distinguished from the legal name and form given it, are shown by the parties' contract and conduct to constitute independent contractorship.

§ 12.05　NECESSITY FOR "CONTRACT OF HIRE"

[1]　Introduction

The compensation concept of "employee" is narrower than the common law concept of "servant" in one important respect: Most acts require that the service be performed under a contract of hire, express or implied. Among the more important consequences of this requirement are the following:

(a) Persons who perform services and receive some kind of payment, but not under the usual contract between persons equally free to bargain and contract, such as prisoners and relief workers, have in the majority of cases been denied compensation;

(b) Gratuitous servants are not employees, since the element of "hire" is lacking; but payment may be found in anything of value, such as board and lodging, and an agreement to pay is usually implied when the parties have omitted to make an express agreement on payment;

(c) Persons employed under illegal contracts of hire are usually denied compensation if the illegality results from the obligation of performing punish able acts, but not if it arises merely from a prohibition against making the contract, as in the case of minority.

[2]　Reason for "Contract" and "Hire" Requirements

Up to this point, the discussion of status has shown that the compensation "employee" concept has expanded beyond the common law "servant" concept in its actual application. There is, however, one respect in which the compensation concept is narrower than that of the common law: Most acts insist upon the existence of a "contract of hire, express or implied," as an essential feature of the employment relation. At common law, it is perfectly possible to strike up a master-servant relation without a contract, so far as vicarious liability is concerned.[10] An infant, a prisoner, a slave, a helpful house guest — all might impose vicarious liability on one who accepted their services performed subject to the master's control.

The reason for the difference between the two concepts is readily explained by the difference between the nature of the two liabilities involved. The end product of a vicarious liability case is not an adjustment of rights between employer and employee on the strength of their mutual arrangement, but a unilateral liability of the master to a stranger. The sole concern of the vicarious liability rule, then, is with the master: Did the master accept and control the service that led to the stranger's injury? If so, it is of no particular importance between the master and the stranger whether the servant enjoyed any reciprocal or contractual rights vis-a-vis the master. Accordingly, the *Restatement of Agency (Second)* says plainly that the master must consent to the service,[11] but nowhere requires that the servant consent to serve the master[12] or even know who the master is.[13]

Compensation law, however, is a mutual arrangement between the employer and employee under which both give up and gain certain things. Since the rights to be adjusted are reciprocal rights between employer and employee, it is not only logical but mandatory to resort to the agreement between them to discover their relationship. To thrust employee status on someone who has never consented would not ordinarily harm that person in a vicarious liability suit by a stranger against his employer. But it might well deprive that person of valuable rights under the compensation act, notably the right to sue the employer for common law damages.

There is also a sound reason for the requirement that the employment be "for hire." In a vicarious liability suit, payment is not a requisite of servant status, since the stranger's rights against the master could not possibly be affected by the presence or absence of financial arrangements between the master and servant. But in a compensation case, the entire philosophy of the legislation assumes that the worker is in a gainful occupation at the time of injury. The essence of compensation protection is the restoration of a part of the loss of wages which are assumed to have existed. Merely as a practical matter, it would be impossible to calculate compensation benefits for a purely gratuitous worker, since benefits are ordinarily calculated on the basis of earnings.

[3] Lack of Voluntary Bilateral Contract of Hire

POLK COUNTY v. STEINBACH
374 N.W.2d 250 (Iowa 1985)

McCormick, Justice.

We hold that a person who participates in a county work program to repay the county for general relief assistance may be an employee of the county for workers' compensation purposes. Respondent Lavern Steinbach was injured while working to repay Polk County for a $75 rent voucher. The county denied he was an employee, and

---

[10] Restatement (Second) of Agency § 221, comment c; Mechem, Outlines of the Law of Agency 328 (3d ed. 1923).

[11] Restatement (Second) of Agency § 221.

[12] *See* § 224, subjecting to master-servant type liability one who accepts services from another who performs them under duress or compulsion of law.

[13] § 222, making undisclosed principal liable for acts of a servant, even if the servant does not know who his master is.

he initiated claim proceedings. The industrial commissioner awarded him benefits, and the county petitioned for judicial review. The district court reversed the commissioner, and Steinbach appealed. We reverse the district court.

Principles governing our review are summarized in *Rouse v. State*, 369 N.W.2d 811, 812–15 (Iowa 1985). The crucial issue is whether Steinbach proved he was a county employee at the time of his injury. To do so it was necessary for him to establish that he had a contract of hire, express or implied, with the county. *Id.* at 814. The determination is ordinarily one of fact. *Id.* at 813. We are bound in our review by findings of fact of the commissioner that are supported by substantial evidence.

The parties stipulated to the relevant events. Steinbach applied to the Polk County Department of Social Services for general relief assistance on December 17, 1980. Pursuant to authority under Iowa Code section 252.27 (1979), the county conditioned relief on a promise by the recipient to repay the relief either in cash or by working it off at the prevailing wage rate in a county work program. Steinbach received rent vouchers of $75 each for two separate two week periods. In order to repay the county for the first voucher, he executed an agreement to work in the county's work experience program at the minimum wage for seven days and one and one-fourth hours.

The work coordinator assigned Steinbach to the county emergency housing unit, located on leased premises in Des Moines. Steinbach reported to the county employee who managed the premises. The manager supplied him with a bucket of water, sponge and other cleaning materials and instructed him to wash walls and woodwork in a stairwell. The manager had authority to remove Steinbach for poor performance or if another person were endangered by Steinbach's performance. Approximately one-half hour after starting work, Steinbach fell over a bannister to the floor below and was injured.

This court has addressed the eligibility of a relief worker for workers' compensation benefits in three cases. In *Hoover v. Independent School District*, 220 Iowa 1364, 264 N.W. 611 (1936), the court discussed the issue in dicta, asserting that an employer and employee relationship has uniformly been held not to exist in situations where the public body provides relief assistance whether the recipient works or not. The workers in Hoover were not relief workers but were denied workers' compensation from the school district because they were employees of the federal civil works administration merely on loan to the district. In *Oswalt v. Lucas County*, 222 Iowa 1099, 270 N.W. 847 (1937), a relief worker was denied workers' compensation on the ground the agreed facts did not show he was employed by the county. Relief was paid from federal and state funds, and the work program was administered and supervised by a state agency. The court noted that relief workers were denied workers' compensation benefits in some jurisdictions when the worker had the right to obtain relief without working for it. *Id.* at 1107, 270 N.W. at 851 ("He would receive the relief whether he worked or not."). In *Arnold v. State*, 233 Iowa 1, 6 N.W.2d 113 (1943), the *Hoover* and *Oswalt* cases were distinguished and a relief worker was declared eligible for workers' compensation. When he applied to the county for relief, the worker was found to be employable and was given a choice of working for the county at a specified price to pay for grocery orders or of not receiving them. He agreed to work and while working on the courthouse roof was fatally injured. The court found that, as a matter of law, a contract of employment existed:

Claimant undertook, at the direction of representatives of the county, to do certain work at a stipulated price. That payment was to be made in groceries instead of cash seems to us to make no difference in the application of underlying legal principles. *Id.* at 4, 6 N.W.2d at 115. *Hoover* and *Oswalt* were distinguished on their facts. *Id.*

The industrial commissioner applied the Arnold principles in the present case, and he was right in doing so. The stipulated facts support the commissioner's finding that the county could refuse Steinbach relief if he did not agree either to work it off or pay it back. Thus the case is distinguishable from those in which relief workers are denied workers' compensation because benefits must be paid whether the recipient works or not. *See* 1C A. Larson, The Law of [Workers'] Compensation, § 47.32 at 8-250–8-251 (1982). In those cases the worker is treated as a charitable ward of the public body rather than as a person who must provide a quid pro quo for relief assistance. *See County of Los Angeles v. Workers' Compensation Appeal Board*, 179 Cal. 3d 391, 401–02, 179 Cal. Rptr. 214, 219–20, 637 P.2d 681, 686–87 (1981).

In determining whether Steinbach had a contract of hire, the commissioner employed the five-factor employment test enunciated in our cases. *See, e.g.*, Henderson v. Jennie Edmundson Hospital, 178 N.W.2d 429, 431 (Iowa 1970). *The county's right of selection is supported by the evidence that the county selected Steinbach as a person who could repay the county for relief assistance by working. In this respect the case is indistinguishable from Usgaard v. Silver Crest Golf Club*, 256 Iowa 453, 457, 127 N.W.2d 636, 638 (1964), where the golf club, which selected its members, required each member to assist the club by paying a five dollar assessment or by working five hours. Moreover, the county's right of discharge parallels that of the club in *Usgaard. Id.* at 459, 127 N.W.2d at 639. No dispute exists concerning the other factors: the county's responsibility for giving Steinbach credit at the agreed wage rate, the right of the county to control the work, and the county's role as the authority in charge of the work.

Substantial evidence supports the commissioner's finding that Steinbach was an employee of the county for workers' compensation purposes. We need not decide whether as in Arnold the evidence compelled that conclusion as a matter of law. It is sufficient to hold, as we do, that the district court erred in upsetting the commissioner's decision on the ground relied on. . . .

Reversed.

[4] Necessity for Payment

CHARLOTTESVILLE MUSIC CENTER, INC. v. McCRAY
215 Va. 31, 205 S.E.2d 674 (1974)

I'ANSON, JUSTICE.

Plaintiff, Ollie T. McCray, administrator of the estate of Jeffrey A. McCray, deceased, instituted this action against the defendant, Charlottesville Music Center, Inc., to recover for the wrongful death of plaintiff's decedent. Judgment for the plaintiff in the sum of $25,500, of which $500 was for funeral expenses, was entered on the jury's verdict, and the defendant is here on a writ of error to the judgment.

Defendant contends the court below erred (1) in not holding that Jeffrey McCray was an employee of the defendant within the purview of the Virginia Workmen's Compensation Act. . . .

The evidence shows that during the afternoon of Wednesday, June 23, 1971, fifteen-year-old Jeffrey McCray was killed as he operated a cargo hoist to assist two of his young friends in erecting shelves in defendant's Staunton, Virginia, store.

One of the decedent's friends, Calvin (Chip) Jarvis, Jr., had arrived at defendant's store on the morning of Monday, June 21, 1971, to erect some shelving which had been purchased from Chip's father. Later that day Jeffrey McCray, the decedent, after performing volunteer work at Western State Hospital, came by the store to offer his services to Chip and another boy who were working on the shelving. The store manager was aware of each boy's presence and gave his tacit approval to McCray's working with them. There was no promise of compensation by the manager to any of the boys, and they did not expect to receive any.

In the rear of defendant's Staunton store was a wooden cargo hoist, which was used for moving merchandise and equipment to and from the first floor stockroom and the basement. The car, or cage, was propelled by an electric motor which was attached to a roof beam by a hook and connected to the car by a chain. The motor was activated by pulling one rope to lower the hoist and another to raise it. The ropes could be pulled by an operator of the hoist standing outside of the car. On one side of the car there was a two-by-four which pivoted on a bolt, and this assembly was referred to as "the brake," for when the bottom of the two-by-four was rotated outward the car could not move. The decedent operated the hoist on both Monday and the following Wednesday to move equipment between the basement and the first floor. On the fateful Wednesday, decedent was unable to get the cargo car to descend to the basement. He called down to Chip, who, along with another of decedent's friends, was in the basement, and told him of the situation. Chip replied, "Try the brake." Almost immediately the car, the decedent and the motor fell to the basement floor. As a result, the decedent was fatally injured. . . .

Defendant first contends that the court erred in overruling its special plea that the plaintiff's decedent was its employee within the purview of the Virginia Workmen's Compensation Act, and thus could not maintain this action.

Code § 65.1-4, in material part, defines an "employee" for Workmen's Compensation purposes as:

> . . . every person, including a minor, in the service of another under any contract of hire or apprenticeship, written or implied, except one whose employment is not in the usual course of the trade, business, occupation or profession of the employer. . . .

Defendant concedes that there was neither a written contract of hire nor an expressed oral contract of hire in the instant case. However, it argues that there was an implied relationship of employment between the decedent and defendant; that in determining whether a person is in an implied contractual relationship of employment with another, and thus an employee under the Workmen's Compensation Act, a court is governed by common law principles; and that under common law principles the determining factor is the right of control, not compensation.

Defendant's reliance in the instant case on cases involving common law elements necessary for the relationship of master and servant is misplaced. Whether decedent was an "employee" under Code § 65.1-4 turns on whether he performed work under an implied contract of hire with the defendant as the employer. *See Board of Supervisors v. Lucas*, 142 Va. 84, 92–93, 128 S.E. 574, 576 (1925).

The Virginia Workmen's Compensation Act, Title 65.1, Chapter 1, does not define the phrase "contract of hire" as used in Code § 65.1-4. Hence we must give the phrase its ordinary or obvious meaning. *See* Commonwealth v. Community Motor Bus, 214 Va. 155, 157, 198 S.E. 2d 619, 620 (1973); *Board of Supervisors v. Boaz*, 176 Va. 126, 130, 10 S.E.2d 498, 499 (1940).

A "contract of hire" is usually defined as an agreement in which an employee provides labor or personal services to an employer for wages or remuneration or other thing of value supplied by the employer. 1A Larson, The Law of Workmen's Compensation, § 47.10 at 8-145–8-149 (1973); 9 Words and Phrases, Contract of Hire or Hiring, at 546–550.

Since the word "hire" connotes payment of some kind, decisions under a Workmen's Compensation Act have uniformly excluded from the definition of "employees" workers who neither receive nor expect to receive remuneration of any kind for their services. 1A Larson, The Law of Workmen's Compensation, *supra*, § 47.41 at 8-162–8-164.

An implied contract of hire exists where one party has rendered services or labor of value to another under circumstances which raise the presumption that the parties intended and understood that they were to be paid for, or which a reasonable man in the position of the person receiving the benefit of the services or labor would or ought to know that compensation or remuneration of some kind was to be exchanged for them.

See Fitzgerald and Mallory Const. Co. v. Fitzgerald, 137 U.S. 98, 112, 11 S.Ct. 36, 34 L.Ed. 608 (1890), *(quoting Pew v. Bank*, 130 Mass. 391, 395 (1881)*); 58 Am. Jur., Work and Labor, § 4 at 512.*

When services or labor are rendered voluntarily without a promise of compensation or remuneration of any kind, express or implied, then the one providing the services or labor has supplied them gratuitously, and is not covered by the Act. Other jurisdictions with statutory provisions similar to our Code § 65.1-4 have adopted this view. *See, e.g., Van Horn v. Industrial Accident Commission*, 219 Cal. App. 2d 457, 463, 33 Cal. Rptr. 169, 172 (1963); *Hall v. State Compensation Insurance Fund*, 154 Colo. 47, 50, 387 P.2d 899, 901 (1963).

Here the circumstances do not permit a presumption that decedent and defendant, by their conduct, intended that decedent would be paid for his work. Decedent of his own volition came to the store to help his friend. There was no evidence that decedent expected any payment or remuneration or that he had received any. Hence, the decedent was not an employee of the defendant within the purview of the Workmen's Compensation Act, and the trial court properly overruled the special plea. . . .

For the reasons stated, the judgment of the court below is

Affirmed.

CONVEYORS' CORPORATION v. INDUSTRIAL COMMISSION
200 Wis. 512, 228 N.W. 118 (1929)

The appeal is from a judgment of the Dane county circuit court affirming an award by the Industrial Commission of compensation to Josephine Galko under the Workmen's Compensation Act for the death of her husband, who died as a result of exposure to poisonous gases while attempting to remove the body of an employee of the plaintiff corporation from the tank of an ash conveyor in process of installation by the plaintiff corporation for the defendant corporation. The corporations are hereinafter called, respectively, the "Conveyors' Corporation" and the "Body Corporation." At the time of the accident the Conveyors' Corporation was making some changes required before the conveyor would be accepted by the Body Corporation. The conveyor was being installed at and in connection with the Body Corporation's power plant. Collins, an employee of the Conveyors' Corporation, was a workman engaged in making the changes. Becker, also an employee of the Conveyors' Corporation, had come from Chicago with detailed plans to supervise the changes. On reaching the plant he hunted up Collins and found him lying in the bottom of the tank overcome by gas. He did not know whether Collins was beyond resuscitation. He could not remove him alone and went for help to the nearest place where help could be procured, which was the boiler room of the Body Corporation's power plant. He called to the head fireman that Collins was in the bottom of the tank. The head fireman repeated the word to his helper, Galko, and went to the engine room and repeated it to a workman, Bethe, who was there employed. Becker and Galko had started for the tank to rescue Collins and Bethe followed them. The three went down a ladder to the bottom of the tank but could not get Collins up the ladder. Becker then went for a rope and more help. A rope was let down, and Galko and Bethe fastened it around Collins and were both overcome while he was being lifted up. Bethe recovered, but Galko died as a result of his exposure to the gas in the tank.

FOWLER, J. The Workmen's Compensation Act, hereinafter referred to as the "act," defines an "employer" as one who has any person in service under any contract of hire, express or implied, oral or written, and an "employee" as one who is in the service of another under any such contract but not one whose employment is not in the usual course of the business of his employer. Sections 102.04(2); 102.07(4), Wis. Stats. Section 102.03(2) provides for compensation of an employee where at the time of the accident he is performing service growing out of and incidental to his employment.

The contentions of the Conveyors' Corporation fall under two general heads: (1) That it is not liable because Galko was not its employee, but the employee of the Body Corporation, if at the time of accident he was an employee at all within the meaning of the act; and (2) that if Galko was its employee, it is not liable because he was not injured in the usual course of the corporation's business.

Under the first head, the Conveyors' Corporation attempts, inferentially at least, to shift liability for compensation, if any exists, to the Body Corporation. That Galko was an employee of the Body Corporation does not subject that corporation to liability, unless at the time of his accident he was performing a service for that corporation incidental to his employment. The workman must be performing a service for the company employing him when injured, and the service must be incidental to his duties to that company. Collins was not an employee of the Body Corporation. The Body Corporation owed no duty to him. It was under no duty as an employer to rescue him from his position of danger. Galko in assisting to rescue Collins was performing no service for the Body Corporation, and his act towards rescue was in no sense incidental to his duties under his contract of employment with that corporation. Upon no theory could the Body Corporation be held liable.

Under this head the claim is also made that Galko was not an employee at all because no contract of hire existed for performing the work of rescue. There was no express contract of hire for that work and no agreement to pay a wage therefor. But there was a contract of employment by implication, and that contract was with the Conveyors' Corporation. This arises from the following considerations: It is the duty of an employer to rescue his employee from a position of imminent danger in an emergency. *Dragovich v. Iroquois Iron Co.*, 269 Ill. 478, 109 N.E. 999; *Bessemer L. & I. Co. v. Campbell*, 121 Ala. 50, 25 So. 793, 77 Am. St. Rep. 17; *United States F. & G. Co. v. Industrial A. Comm.*, 174 Cal. 616, 163 P. 1013. Any other rule would be inhuman and unthinkable. Our statute imposes such duty. It requires that the employer "shall do every other thing reasonably necessary to protect the life" of the employee. Section 101.06. Collins was an employee of the Conveyors' Corporation and was in a position of imminent danger, and it was the corporation's duty to rescue him. The corporation could only act through its agents or employees. Becker, also an employee of the corporation, was the only agent of the corporation who was present. There was no one else to act for his employer when he found Collins overcome in the bottom of the tank. It was his duty towards his employer to act immediately and with greatest possible speed to rescue Collins, who was not known to be beyond resuscitation. It was as much his duty to rescue Collins as it was the employee's duty to rescue the employer's property from fire in *Belle City Co. v. Rowland*, 170 Wis. 293, 297, 174 N. W. 899, 7 A. L. R. 1071. Becker could not remove Collins alone. In the emergency he was by necessary implication authorized to procure assistance. *St. Louis & S. F. R. Co. v. Bagwell*, 33 Okl. 189, 124 P. 320, 40 L. R. A. (N. S.) 1180; 18 Ruling Case Law, p. 580; *State ex rel. Nienaber v. Dist. Court*, 138 Minn. 416, 165 N. W. 268, L. R. A. 1918F, 200. Those whom he procured were during the rescue acting for the employer of Collins and Becker, the Conveyors' Corporation. Compliance with the request of Becker for assistance under the circumstances constituted them employees of that corporation. One so complying is not a volunteer, but an employee within the meaning of the act, whether the employee making the request has express authority to procure help or an emergency exists from which authority is implied. 28 Ruling Case Law, pp. 760, 761; *West Salem v. Industrial Comm.*, 162 Wis. 57, 155 N. W. 929, L. R. A. 1918C, 1077.

Little remains to be said under the second general contention of the Conveyors' Corporation that if Galko was an employee he was not injured in the usual course of the company's business and thus without the act. As already stated, it is the duty of an employer to rescue an employee from a position of imminent danger into which he gets in the course of his employment. One employee attempting the rescue of his fellow employee is engaged in the performance of a duty incumbent on a manufacturer in the conduct of his business. Although such emergencies do not regularly occur, they do occur at times in the usual course of any manufacturing business, and an employee engaged in such rescue may properly be held to be engaged in the usual course of his employer's business.

It thus appears that Galko was for the time being an employee of the Conveyors' Corporation, employed for and in the special work of rescuing Collins. He was injured while performing a service growing out of and incidental to his such employment, and his widow is entitled to compensation. The Conveyors' Corporation claims that there is no testimony from which the Commission could fix the amount of the award. Galko was engaged as a helper of the fireman of a power plant. His compensation as such was $42 per week. The basis for computation of the compensation, however, is not his such earnings, but the earnings of one engaged in the work at which he was employed when injured. *West Salem v. Industrial Comm., supra.* There was no wage fixed for his such work, and his compensation must be computed on the reasonable value of the work. The ordinary wage paid for such work as is involved is ordinarily the basis of fixing recovery on quantum meruit. But as matter of common knowledge there is no customary wage for such rescue work as is here involved. No direct testimony could from the nature of the case be produced as to the reasonable value of such work. But compensation should not be denied for this reason. The amount paid may be arrived at indirectly by analogy. The Commission took $1,400 per year as the basis of the award. Galko was a common laborer and his wage as such was a half more than the Commission took as basis for the award. The Commission, in absence of testimony to the value of the same kind of service as he was doing, might take testimony of the wage of similar service. Work in the tank of the ash conveyor, where hot ashes such as Galko handled in his ordinary work were frequent, might not unreasonably be considered as similar to his regular work. It is common knowledge that common labor commands $5 a day in some lines at least, and we think the Commission might properly take that wage as a basis of computation.

The judgment of the circuit court is *affirmed.*

[5] Illegal Employment

BOWERS v. GENERAL GUARANTY INSURANCE COMPANY
430 S.W.2d 871 (Tenn. 1968)

DYER, JUSTICE.

This case presents the question of whether an employee under our Workmen's Compensation Statutes, T.C.A. § 50-901 *et seq.,* is entitled to benefits for accidental injuries received when employee was performing an act made illegal by the penal statutes of this State.

There is no dispute as to the facts and those necessary to note are as follows:

R. E. Cutshall, doing business as the J & R Tavern (employer), held a valid license for the retail sale of beer at a certain location in Greene County, Tennessee. On the premises at this location there are two buildings about eighty feet apart. In one of these buildings known as the Tavern legal sales of beer are made, and in the other building known as the old house sales of liquor are made, which sales are in violation of our penal statutes.

Hobart H. Bowers (employee) was employed to work as a salesman both at the Tavern and the old house, apparently making it necessary for him to go from one building to the other. On December 29, 1966, in the course of making a sale at the old house the employee was assaulted, which resulted in serious injuries for which he claims benefits under our Workmen's Compensation Statutes.

The chancellor found the employee at the time of the assault was knowingly violating the penal statutes of this State and by reason thereof the injuries received were not within the scope and purview of our Workmen's Compensation Statutes.

The employee takes the position he is covered under the language of T.C.A. § 50-902(b) wherein it is said:

"Employee" shall include every person, including a minor, whether lawfully or unlawfully employed, . . . in the service of an employer,. . . .

In 1A Larson's Workmen's Compensation Law, Section 47.51, at page 788, it is stated:

Although it could be argued technically that a requirement of a "contract of hire" can be satisfied only by showing a legal contract, the cases have generally drawn a distinction between contracts that are illegal in the sense that the making of the contract itself violates some prohibition, and contracts that call for the performance of acts that are themselves violations of penal laws. The former will ordinarily support an award of compensation; the latter will not. For example, it was illegal under Pennsylvania law for claimant, an elected official, also to be employed as a supervisor, but claimant, injured while working in his capacity as supervisor, was held entitled to workmen's compensation. And compensation was awarded a nightclub hostess in spite of the existence of a statute prohibiting the very contract under which she was hired, since the duties she was required to perform — the mere encouraging of patrons to drink, on a commission — did not themselves constitute violations of a penal statute. But compensation has been uniformly denied to bartenders hired during prohibition, and even to a beer deliveryman.

We think it was the intent of the Legislature by the above quoted language of T.C.A. § 50-902(b), defining an employee entitled to coverage to distinguish between contracts for hire, the making of which is prohibited (such as employment in certain cases of minors) and those contracts for hire which call for performance of acts which are themselves violations of our penal statutes. We construe this language to provide coverage to an employee even though the contract of employment be prohibited by statute or otherwise, if the duties required of the employee are themselves legal. We do not construe this language to provide coverage on an employee employed even under a legal contract of hire if the acts required of the employee are themselves a violation of our penal statutes and the employee receives injuries in the performance of the required illegal acts.

The judgment of the lower court is *affirmed.*

BURNETT, C. J., and CHATTIN, CRESON and HUMPHREYS, JJ., concur.

STOVALL v. SALLY SALMON SEAFOOD
306 Or. 25, 757 P.2d 410 (1988)

LENT, JUSTICE. . . .

The second issue is whether the later employer can avoid payment of compensation under the doctrine of equitable estoppel because claimant falsely stated on her pre-employment application that she had never had any hand, wrist or arm trouble. We hold that the employer cannot defeat claimant's right to compensation by the defense of equitable estoppel. . . .

Claimant was employed at Sally Salmon Seafood (Sally) for about one year prior to June 5, 1984. She did not work every day or even all day on some days that she did work. On the other hand, she sometimes worked up to 12 hours per day and more than 40 hours in a week. Her work was shaking crab, which required her at times to strike her wrist against a pan or bench to loosen the crab meat from the shell. She also filleted fish and shucked oysters. Her work caused her to experience pain and swelling in her wrist and hand. She did not lose work on that account. She did not seek medical treatment but alleviated her discomfort and the swelling by home treatment, utilizing a kind of liniment and ice packs. Her work with Sally ended on June 5, 1984, but not because of any disability.

On July 28, 1984, she became employed at Hallmark Fisheries (Hallmark). Prior to gaining this employment, she filled out a "Pre-Employment Application" on a form provided by Hallmark. On that form she checked the "No" space in answering the question: "Have you ever had — 1. Hand, wrist, or arm trouble?"

Her primary work at Hallmark was as a black cod scraper. This required her several hundred times per day to scrape the blood from fish backbones. For approximately the first two weeks she did this work without discomfort. From then on she again experienced discomfort and swelling in the wrist and hand.

She continued to work until midday on September 6, 1984, when she left her job because of the pain and other symptoms in her forearm, wrist and hand, and on the next day she first sought medical treatment for her condition. The doctor diagnosed "[p]robable carpal tunnel syndrome," and later tests confirmed this diagnosis. A few weeks later she had surgery for the condition.

We summarize some important facts. Claimant did not leave her employment at Sally because of the trouble that she was having in her forearm, wrist and hand. She had made no claim, even for medical benefits, under the Workers' Compensation Law before she was employed at Hallmark. She was not disabled at the time she applied for work at Hallmark. She performed the duties of her job at Hallmark for over two months before she became disabled.

Claimant filed claims against both Sally and Hallmark for workers' compensation. Each employer denied her claim. She requested hearings and successfully asked that the hearings be consolidated.

At the hearing, both employers conceded that her claim was compensable, but each contended that the other employer was responsible for payment of compensation. In addition, Hallmark contended that she was estopped from asserting a claim against Hallmark because of her false statement that she had not had previous hand, wrist or arm trouble.

At the hearing, claimant conceded that her answer on the application form was false. Hallmark's plant supervisor testified that had she answered the question truthfully, he would have made inquiry into her work history, and had he learned that she had been having the trouble she did have while working at Sally, he would not have "considered her physically fit for the kind of work for which you were going to hire her." He was not asked directly whether he would have hired her, either at all or for other work. . . .

In its purer sense the doctrine of estoppel operates to prevent a person from taking a position contrary to that earlier taken; it prevents a person from proving the truth where that is opposed to a false position earlier taken that caused another to rely on the false position and thereby to choose a course of action.

> [Equitable estoppel is] employed to prevent one from proving an important
> fact to be something other than what by act or omission he has led another party
> justifiably to believe.

Wiggins v. Barrett & Associates, Inc., 295 Or. 679, 689, 669 P.2d 1132 (1983). When used in that sense, the doctrine would be of no avail to Hallmark. This is because claimant's case does not rest on proving now the true history of her arm, hand and wrist trouble. In other words, her case does not rest on denying the truth of what she represented on the application form.

It is fair to say, however, that the doctrine is not as narrow as the above authorities would suggest. For instance, this court has said:

> This doctrine of equitable estoppel or estoppel *in pais* is that a person may be precluded by his act or conduct, or silence when it was his duty to speak, *from asserting a right* which he otherwise would have had. (Emphasis added.)

Marshall v. Wilson, 175 Or. 506, 518, 154 P.2d 547 (1944).

> The doctrine of estoppel is only intended to protect those who materially change their position in reliance upon another's acts or representations.

Bash v. Fir Grove Cemeteries, Co., 282 Or. 677, 687, 581 P.2d 75 (1978). It is on the rule as thus stated that Hallmark must rely. In other words, Hallmark here contends that claimant cannot assert her right to compensation by reason of her false statement and Hallmark's reliance thereon, which we have assumed arguendo.

In that broad sense Hallmark would ordinarily be entitled to rely on the doctrine of estoppel to defeat this claim, but we shall now turn our attention to whether a workers' compensation claim may be barred by estoppel.

While acknowledging that the case did not involve an issue whether a claimant may be estopped from successfully presenting a claim, Hallmark contends that our discussion of equitable estoppel in *Frasure v. Agripac*, 290 Or. 99, 104–107, 619 P.2d 274 (1980), shows that the doctrine is applicable to workers' compensation cases. In that case the Court of Appeals had held that one employer's insurer, by paying benefits, was estopped by its conduct from later denying a claim on the basis that it was not compensable. We held, in this respect, only that the insurer was not estopped. We did not discuss whether the doctrine of estoppel is available to any party in a workers' compensation case. Finally, we noted on this issue that the insurer had not made a representation normally associated with estoppel.

In answer to questions submitted by this court to decide whether to allow review on this issue, claimant acknowledged that Professor Larson has written:

> (e) A false statement in an employment application does not of itself make the employment contract invalid. Benefits are barred only if (1) the employee knowingly and wilfully made a false representation as to his physical condition; (2) the employer relied on the representation and the reliance was a substantial factor in the hiring; and (3) there was a causal relation between the false representation and the injury.

1C Larson's Workmen's Compensation Law 8-284, § 47.00 (1986). In elaborating on this "black letter" statement, Larson continues:

> § 47.53 False statements in employment application
>
> On the basis of the distinction stated in § 47.51, it has been held that employment which has been obtained by the making of false statements — even criminally false statements — whether by a minor or an adult, is still employment; that is, the technical illegality will not of itself destroy compensation coverage. What seems to be emerging, in place of a conceptual approach relying on purely contractual tests, is a common-sense rule made up of a melange of contract, causation, and estoppel ingredients. The following factors must be present before a false statement in an employment application will bar benefits: (1) The employee must have knowingly and wilfully made a false representation as to his physical condition. (2) The employer must have relied upon the false representation and this reliance must have been a substantial factor in the hiring. (3) There must have been a causal connection between the false representation and the injury. (Footnotes omitted.)

Id. at 8-394. In support of this text the author cites in footnote 24 a lengthy list of cases, continuing into the 1987 supplement. We have examined those cases. Some of them are apparently the source of the rule stated by Professor Larson. Others are cases in which the rule, as stated by him, was applied to various fact situations. In some cases application of the rule worked to deny compensation and in others worked not to deny compensation.

These cases are discussed in terms of fraud except for those from Tennessee. *Foster v. Esis, Inc.*, 563 S.W.2d 180, 182 (Tenn 1978), seems to say that the Tennessee court would deny benefits by application of the doctrine of estoppel; however, the court does not discuss why it chose to apply "estoppel" rather than fraud or misrepresentation. The cases from the many other jurisdictions cited in the footnote do not mention estoppel but discuss whether the claimant must be barred from recovery by reason of fraud or misrepresentation.

The Tennessee court in *Foster v. Esis, Inc., supra*, in applying the doctrine of estoppel, purported to rely on *Federal Copper & Aluminum Company v. Dickey*, 493 S.W.2d 463 (Tenn 1973). In that case the court found a public policy declared by the legislature to support adoption of Professor Larson's test. The court noted that Tennessee statutes provided for waiver of workers' compensation coverage for a prospective employee "who is susceptible to an occupational disease or has a history of heart disease." *Id.* at 464. The court did not use the word "estoppel" at all in its decision except as it appears in the quotation of Larson's test. It held that one is usually prohibited from "profiteering" from his fraud or wilful misrepresentation and that the result should be no different just because the legislature had not anticipated the "problem" presented by such misrepresentation. We are not quite sure how the *Foster v. Esis, Inc.* court translated this into estoppel.

As discussed by both Professor Larson and by the court in *Teixeira v. Kauikeolani Children's Hosp.*, 3 Haw. App. 432, 652 P.2d 635 (1982), there is a split of authority as to whether misrepresentations will bar a claim and, if so, in what circumstances. Some of the courts that permit a claim to be barred have found policy in their respective state statutes that, although not exactly in point, have led the courts to bar claims. Other courts have found no bar because there is no legislative policy one way or the other. Courts which have not referred to legislative policy have split on whether there should be a rule such as that phrased by Professor Larson.

We do not find any decision, not resting on statute, that persuades us one way or the other whether Oregon should follow either line of authority. Especially we find nothing in the cases that would lead us to recognize a defense of estoppel.

VI.

This brings us to what this court should do, now faced for the first time with a contention that the doctrine of estoppel should be employed to defeat a claim. We believe the better approach to be an attempt to discern public policy as expressed by the legislature.

The legislature has made it clear that an employer cannot obtain a valid release of a worker's right to benefits for injury under the Workers' Compensation Law. ORS 656.236(1) provides:

> No release by a worker or beneficiary of any rights under ORS 656.001 to 656.794 is valid.

By ORS 656.804 this provision is applicable to claims under the Occupational Disease Law.

The fear that employers or private insurers might attempt to use releases to defeat claims was the reason for inclusion of ORS 656.236(1) in the 1965 major revision of the Workers' Compensation Law. Skelton, The 1965 Oregon Workmen's Compensation Law, 45 Or. L. Rev. 40, 47 (1965). It would appear that the policy underlying the legislative injunction against obtaining releases of a worker's rights would extend to forbidding a waiver of those rights if such were sought as a precondition of employment. This policy points in the opposite direction from the Tennessee statute examined in

Federal Copper & Aluminum Company v. Dickey, supra.

It must be kept in mind that court decisions in cases arising under the Workers' Compensation Law interpret that statutory law. This seems to have been lost on some of the courts whose decisions are cited by Professor Larson, *supra*. Some of those courts obviously arrived at decisions denying benefits because those courts believed that they were free to engraft on the statutory schemes of their respective states the courts' ideas of what the common law or equity might require in the circumstances.

It also must be remembered that the passage of workers' compensation legislation, while giving to the worker the right to compensation regardless of fault, deprived the worker of the right to maintain an action for damages for injuries suffered by reason of the employer's fault. Early on, this court deemed the legislation was for the benefit of the worker. Whether or not it was exclusively so, that concept led this court to pronounce many times over the years that Oregon's statutory workers' compensation scheme was to be construed liberally in favor of the worker-claimant. *See, e.g., Fossum v. SAIF*, 289 Or. 787, 792–93, 619 P.2d 233 (1980):

> [A]ny such ambiguity must be construed in favor of compensation, just as ambiguous provisions of insurance policies are construed in favor of the beneficiaries, particularly in view of the long-established rule in Oregon that the Workers' Compensation Law must be liberally construed in favor of the worker and compensation. [Citing cases.]

In short, we understand the philosophy of the Workers' Compensation Law to be that if a person is hired and is, in fact, working for an employer in the role of an employee and becomes disabled as a result of being so employed, the cost of the worker's disability is to be borne by the economy through the employing enterprise and not to be borne by the worker. That statutory policy should not be vulnerable to reopening the way in which a worker in fact obtained the employment when the worker is injured or contracts a disabling occupational disease on the job, perhaps months or years after the event of hiring.

VII.

We conclude that public policy as expressed by the legislature weighs in favor of not defeating a claim for benefits by application of a doctrine not endorsed by the legislature. If false representations by a worker to obtain employment are to defeat a claim for benefits under the doctrine of equitable estoppel, we leave it to the legislature so to provide.

The decision of the Court of Appeals is *affirmed*.

GILLETTE, J., dissents. . . .

FARMER BROTHERS COFFEE v. WORKERS' COMPENSATION APPEALS BOARD (RUIZ)
133 Cal. App. 4th 533, 35 Cal. Rptr. 3d 23 (2005)

HASTINGS, J.

We issued a writ of review on April 4, 2005, with regard to two workers' compensation matters and consolidated them for argument and decision. Each petition contends that the Immigration Reform and Control Act of 1986 (IRCA), title 8 United States Code section 1101 et seq., preempts Labor Code section 1171.5, which provides that immigration status is irrelevant to the issue of liability under state labor and employment laws, and Labor Code section 3351, which includes aliens in the definition of "employee," even those unlawfully employed. In each case, it was undisputed that the employee was an alien, unauthorized to work in the United States at the time of the injury. We have subsequently severed the two matters, and now proceed only with the petition of Farmer Brothers Coffee.

. . . .

On November 5, 2004, the workers' compensation judge issued an opinion and the following finding: "Applicant is an employee per Labor Code Sections 3351 [subdivision] (a) and 3357."

Farmer Brothers then filed a petition for reconsideration by the Board on the grounds of federal preemption and its contention that Ruiz obtained employment and his expectation of benefits by means of fraud, in violation of Insurance Code section 1871.4. The Board rejected the contentions, and denied the petition for reconsideration on December 22, 2004. . . .

Petitioner [Farmer Brothers] contends that sections 3351 and 1171.5 have been preempted by the employment provisions of the IRCA (8 U.S.C. § 1324a).

Section 3351, subdivision (a), defines "employee" as "every person in the service of an employer under any appointment or contract of hire or apprenticeship, express or implied, oral or written, whether lawfully or unlawfully employed . . . " including aliens. Section 1171.5 reads, in relevant part:

> The Legislature finds and declares the following:
>
> (a) All protections, rights, and remedies available under state law, except any reinstatement remedy prohibited by federal law, are available to all individuals regardless of immigration status who have applied for employment, or who are or who have been employed, in this state.
>
> (b) For purposes of enforcing state labor and employment laws, a person's immigration status is irrelevant to the issue of liability, and in proceedings or discovery undertaken to enforce those state laws no inquiry shall be permitted into a person's immigration status except where the person seeking to make this inquiry has shown by clear and convincing evidence that the inquiry is necessary in order to comply with federal immigration law.
>
> (c) The provisions of this section are declaratory of existing law. . . .

Under the IRCA, it is unlawful to hire or continue to employ an alien the employer knows to be an "unauthorized alien," defined as one who is not lawfully admitted for permanent residence, or authorized to be so employed by federal immigration and nationality law or by the United States Attorney General. (8 U.S.C. § 1324a(a)(1)-(2), (h)(1).) The statute provides for graduated civil penalties for violations, and criminal penalties for employers who are found to have engaged in a pattern or practice of hiring unauthorized aliens in violation of the law. (8 U.S.C. § 1324a(e)(4)-(5), (f)(1).) It is also a crime to knowingly accept a false immigration document for purposes of satisfying the requirements of the statute. (8 U.S.C. § 1324c(a)(2); 18 U.S.C. § 1546(b).)

"Article VI of the Constitution provides that the laws of the United States 'shall be the supreme Law of the Land; . . . any Thing in the Constitution or Laws of any state to the Contrary notwithstanding.' Art. VI, cl. 2. Thus, . . . state law that conflicts with federal law is 'without effect.' [Citation.] Consideration of issues arising under the Supremacy Clause 'start[s] with the assumption that the historic police powers of the States [are] not to be superseded by . . . Federal Act unless that [is] the clear and manifest purpose of Congress.' [Citation.]" (*Cipollone v. Liggett Group, Inc.* (1992) 505 U.S. 504, 516 [112 S. Ct. 2608, 120 L. Ed. 2d 407] (*Cipollone*).)

Examples of historic police powers include "[c]hild labor laws, minimum and other wage laws, laws affecting occupational health and safety, and workmen's compensation laws. . . . " (*De Canas v. Bica* (1976) 424 U.S. 351, 356-357 [96 S. Ct. 933, 47 L. Ed. 2d 43].) "States possess broad authority under their police powers to regulate the employment relationship to protect workers within the State." (*Ibid.*) "Accordingly, ' "[t]he purpose of Congress is the ultimate touchstone" ' of pre-emption analysis.

[Citations.] Congress' intent may be 'explicitly stated in the statute's language or implicitly contained in its structure and purpose.' [Citation.] In the absence of an express congressional command, state law is pre-empted if that law actually conflicts with federal law, [citation], or if federal law so thoroughly occupies a legislative field ' "as to make reasonable the inference that Congress left no room for the States to supplement it." ' [Citations.]" (*Cipollone, supra*, 505 U.S. at p. 516.)

There is no preemption language in the IRCA expressly affecting state workers' compensation laws. The only express preemption provision states: "The provisions of this section preempt any State or local law imposing civil or criminal sanctions (other than through licensing and similar laws) upon those who employ, or recruit or refer for a fee for employment, unauthorized aliens." (8 U.S.C. § 1324a(h)(2).)

. . . .

We conclude that preemption of state workers' compensation laws was not the " 'clear [or] manifest purpose of Congress.' [Citation.]" (*Cipollone, supra*, 505 U.S. at p. 516.) Thus, we must consider whether California's workers' compensation law actually conflicts with the IRCA, or whether the IRCA so thoroughly occupies the same field " ' "as to make reasonable the inference that Congress left no room for the States to supplement it." ' [Citations.]" (505 at p. 516.)

"Power to regulate immigration is unquestionably exclusively a federal power. [Citations.] . . . [But] standing alone, the fact that aliens are the subject of a state statute does not render it a regulation of immigration. . . . " [Citation omitted.] Since the IRCA does not provide for or prohibit compensation for injured workers, Congress has not occupied the field of workers' compensation. We therefore turn to the issue of actual conflict.

To imply preemption, there must be "such actual conflict between the two schemes of regulation that both cannot stand in the same area . . . " because the state law " 'stands as an obstacle to the accomplishment and execution of the full purposes and objectives of Congress,' [citation]." (*Florida Avocado Growers v. Paul* (1963) 373 U.S. 132, 141 [83 S. Ct. 1210, 10 L. Ed. 2d 248].)

California law has expressly declared immigration status irrelevant to the issue of liability to pay compensation to an injured employee. (§ 1171.5.) Were it otherwise, unscrupulous employers would be encouraged to hire aliens unauthorized to work in the United States, by taking the chance that the federal authorities would accept their claims of good faith reliance upon immigration and work authorization documents that appear to be genuine. Other jurisdictions have come to the same conclusion with regard to their workers' compensation laws. (See, e.g., *Dowling v. Slotnik* (1998) 244 Conn. 781, 791 [712 A.2d 396], *cert. den., Slotnik v. Considine* (1998) 525 U.S. 1017 [119 S. Ct. 542, 142 L. Ed. 2d 451]; *Mendoza v. Monmouth Recycling Corp.* (N.J.Super. 1996) 672 A. 2d 221, 224-225.)

If compensation benefits were to depend upon an alien employee's federal work authorization, the Workers' Compensation Appeals Board would be thrust into the role of determining employers' compliance with the IRCA and whether such compliance was in good faith, as well as determining the immigration status of each injured employee, and whether any alien employees used false documents. Benefits would be denied to the undocumented injured employee for the sole reason that he is undocumented. Thus, the remedial purpose of workers' compensation would take on an enforcement purpose, in direct *conflict* with the IRCA. (See 8 U.S.C. § 1324a(h)(2).)

Petitioner contends that the United States Supreme Court's decision in [*Hoffman Plastic Compounds, Inc. v. NLRB* (2002) 535 U.S. 137, 149, 122 S. Ct. 1275, 152 L. Ed. 2d 271] has placed the states in just such a position of enforcement. *Hoffman* held that the policies underlying the IRCA prohibited the National Labor Relations Board from awarding backpay as a remedy for unfair labor practices to illegal aliens. (535 U.S. at pp. 149-151.) Backpay in such a case would reward *unperformed* work in a job that could not lawfully have been obtained, and in essence, may provide the illegal alien a bonus due to his or her inability to mitigate damages by working in the United States. (*Ibid.*)

Section 1171.5 was enacted by the California Legislature in response to *Hoffman*. (See *Rivera v. NIBCO, Inc.* (9th Cir. 2004) 364 F.3d 1057, 1073.) The Legislature sought to avoid any conflict with the IRCA by providing that an employee's immigration status was irrelevant to his or her workers' compensation claim, as provided under existing law, except with regard to the issue of reinstatement, since the employer would be committing a federal crime by reinstating the undocumented employee. . . .

Section 1171.5, subdivision (b), avoids conflict with *Hoffman*'s backpay prohibition by making an exception to the exclusion of evidence of the employee's immigration status "where the person seeking to make this inquiry has shown by clear and convincing evidence that the inquiry is necessary in order to comply with federal immigration law," and by excluding any reinstatement remedy prohibited by federal law. Under existing law, backpay is not recoverable by an employee who would not be rehired regardless of any employer misconduct. (*Rivcom Corp. v. Agricultural Labor Relations Bd.* (1983) 34 Cal.3d 743, 773-774 [195 Cal. Rptr. 651, 670 P.2d 305].) Thus, where reinstatement is prohibited by federal law, section 1171.5 would also prohibit backpay, which was the intent of the Legislature in passing section 1171.5 and related statutes. (See Sen. Com. on Labor and Industrial Relations, Rep. on Sen. Bill No. 1818, *supra*, as amended May 14, 2002; Civ. Code, § 3339; Gov. Code, § 7285.)

We conclude that the Workers' Compensation Act, with the addition of section 1171.5 prohibiting reinstatement remedies to undocumented aliens, is not in conflict with the IRCA and comports with the reasoning of *Hoffman, supra,* 535 U.S. 137, since prohibited remedies necessarily include backpay. . . .

Petitioner contends that Ruiz does not come within the definition of "employee" set forth in section 3351, subdivision (a), as "every person in the service of an employer under any appointment or contract of hire or apprenticeship, express or implied, oral or written, whether lawfully or unlawfully employed, [including aliens]."

Petitioner suggests that by including the phrase *unlawfully employed*, the Legislature intended to exclude *illegal* employees from the definition. Petitioner contends that *unlawfully employed* must mean only that the *employer* is guilty of hiring the worker in violation of federal law. (See 8 U.S.C. § 1324a.) When it is the *employee* who has violated the law by using fraudulent documents, petitioner reasons, he or she cannot be considered as coming within the definition set forth in section 3351, subdivision (a).

Before hiring an employee, an employer is required to examine specified identification documents, and if applicable, immigration and work authorization documents, and to report under penalty of perjury on a federal form that it has verified that the individual is not an unauthorized alien. (8 U.S.C. § 1324a(b)(1)(A).) Employers may be subject to civil or criminal penalties for failures to comply in good faith, and employees may be subject to civil and criminal penalties for using false documents. (See 8 U.S.C. § 1324a(e)(4)-(5), (f)(1); id., § 1324c(a)(1)-(3); 18 U.S.C. § 1546(b); *Hoffman, supra,* 535 U.S. at p. 148.)

There is no language in the statute to indicate that the Legislature intended "unlawfully employed" to have such a complex meaning or to incorporate federal immigration law, and our task in construing the statute is simply "to ascertain and declare what is in terms or in substance contained therein, not to insert what has been omitted, or to omit what has been inserted . . . ." (Code Civ. Proc., § 1858.)

The sole authority cited by petitioner to support its questionable logic is a dissenting opinion in a Pennsylvania Supreme Court case, urging the court "to announce, as a matter of public policy consistent with federal immigration law, that unauthorized aliens are not eligible for workers' compensation benefits [because] [o]ne who obtains employment in a manner contrary to federal law should not benefit from that illegal employment relationship." (*Reinforced Earth Co. v. W.C.A.B., supra,* 810 A.2d at pp.

111-112 (dis. opn. of Newman, J.), fn. omitted.) The majority refused to do so, leaving that task to the Pennsylvania Legislature. (See *id.* at p. 105.)

In California, as in Pennsylvania, the Legislature establishes public policy. [Citation omitted.] Once it has done so, the courts may not simply fashion a policy more to their liking. We therefore decline petitioner's suggestion that we insert such a policy into the statute.

In any event, assuming for discussion that the California Legislature meant "unlawfully employed" to refer only to the employer's violation of its reporting obligations under title 8 United States Code section 1324a(b)(1)(A), petitioner has failed to point out evidence that it did or did not comply with its federal reporting obligations, and our review has revealed none. Since petitioner did not dispute Ruiz's claim that he performed work at its request, it was petitioner's burden to prove that Ruiz was not an employee for purposes of the Workers' Compensation Act. (See § 3357; *Schaller v. Industrial Acc. Com.* (1938) 11 Cal.2d 46, 51 [77 P.2d 836].) Since petitioner did not prove otherwise, we assume that it did not comply with federal requirements, and therefore, petitioner's own definition of "unlawfully employed" has been met.

. . . .

Petitioner contends that Ruiz's use of a fraudulent Social Security card and fraudulent green card to obtain employment, and then putting a false Social Security number on his workers' compensation claim form, violated Insurance Code, section 1871.4, which makes it a criminal offense to make a knowingly false or fraudulent material representation for the purpose of obtaining workers' compensation benefits.

A claimant *who has been convicted* of a violation of Insurance Code section 1871.4 is barred from receiving or retaining any compensation obtained as a *direct result* of the fraudulent misrepresentation. (*Tensfeldt v. Workers' Comp. Appeals Bd.* (1998) 66 Cal.App.4th 116, 123-124 [77 Cal. Rptr. 2d 691]; Ins. Code, § 1871.5.) There is no evidence of a conviction in this record. Further, Ruiz was not required to be a lawfully documented alien to be an employee entitled to workers' compensation benefits. (See §§ 3351, 3357.) It was employment, not the compensable injury, that Ruiz obtained as a direct result of the use of fraudulent documents.

The Board's order denying reconsideration is *affirmed.*

EPSTEIN, P. J., and CURRY, J., concurred.

PROBLEMS

(1) A juror was injured when she fell as she was leaving the jury box during her first week of "mandatory" jury duty. Compensable? The mandatory period was 25 days, but a juror could voluntarily serve longer. Suppose the injury occurred on the 30th day of service. Would this make a difference? *See* Lockerman v. Prince George's County, 281 Md. 195, 377 A.2d 1177 (1977).

(2) What about a minor child working for his or her father in the father's business at regular wages? *See* Williams v. Williams, 91 N.J. Super. 273, 219 A.2d 895 (1966).

(3) An Iowa statute excludes from coverage children of employers, and children and relatives of farm employers. Is this constitutional? *See* Ross v. Ross, 308 N.W. 2d 50 (Iowa 1981).

(4) A professional dancer volunteered to act as a hostess at a servicemen's canteen during World War II. She was injured dancing with a marine. Compensable? *See* Edwards v. Hollywood Canteen, 27 Cal. 2d 802, 167 P.2d 729 (1946).

(5) A florist and an undertaker had an arrangement in which each worked for the other whenever they had time, the only compensation being the reciprocal services. The florist was injured removing a vault lid. Compensable? *See* Alexander v. J.E. Hixon & Sons Funeral Home, 44 So. 2d 487 (La. 1950).

(6) Claimant was injured while participating in an agility test which was part of a tryout competition for the position of refuse crew worker with the city. He had not, at the time of his injury, been selected as an employee. Compensable? *See* Laeng v. Workers' Comp. App. Bd., 100 Cal. Rptr. 377, 494 P.2d 1 (1972).

(7) Injured worker is offered work as a vehicle driver but is unable to obtain driver's license because of his illegal status. Is this a sufficient refusal of work that worker is disqualified from additional disability benefits? *See* Martines v. Worley & Sons Constr., 278 Ga. App. 26, 628 S.E.2d 113 (2006).

(8) A Michigan statute provides for the suspension of weekly wage loss benefits when the employee is unable to obtain or perform work because of the commission of a crime. Would the statute operate to temporarily suspend any award of weekly wage loss benefits to illegal aliens? *See* Sanchez v. Eagle Alloys, Inc., 254 Mich. App. 651, 658 N.W.2d 510 (2003), *order granting leave to appeal vacated*, 471 Mich. 851, 684 N.W.2d 342 (2004).

(9) Injured worker sustains severe injuries and receives PD rating of 65 percent. He is deported because of his illegal status and the employer petitions to terminate continued payment of disability benefits on the ground that it cannot offer employment to the worker because he cannot legally re-enter the United States. Must the employer continue paying disability? *See* Wet Walls, Inc. v. Ledezma, 266 Ga. App. 685, 598 S.E.2d 60 (2004).

§ 12.06　LENT EMPLOYEES AND DUAL EMPLOYMENT

When a general employer lends an employee to a special employer, the special employer becomes liable for workers' compensation only if:

(a) The employee has made a contract of hire, express or implied, with the special employer;

(b) The work being done is essentially that of the special employer; and

(c) The special employer has the right to control the details of the work.

When all three of the above conditions are satisfied in relation to both employers, both employers are liable for workers' compensation.

Employment may also be "dual," in the sense that, while the employee is under contract of hire with two different employers, his activities on behalf of each employer are separable and can be identified with one employer or the other. When this separate identification can clearly be made, the particular employer whose work was being done at the time of injury will be held exclusively liable.

ANTHEUNISSE v. TIFFANY & COMPANY, INC.
229 N.J. Super. 399, 551 A.2d 1006 (1988)

Gruccio, J.A.D.

Plaintiff Susan Antheunisse appeals from a judgment dismissing her complaint for personal injuries allegedly sustained while working for defendant Tiffany & Company, Inc. The trial judge granted defendant's motion for summary judgment, concluding that defendant was a special employer and that the claim was governed by the Workers' Compensation Act. On appeal plaintiff contends that the motion for summary judgment was improperly granted. We agree with the trial judge's determination and affirm.

The record establishes that the Pat Shea Personnel Agency orally contracted to provide defendant with temporary help during the holiday season. Defendant's personnel department screened all the applicants sent by Pat Shea before selecting and assigning them to its various departments. Once the applicants were hired, Pat Shea's role was restricted to processing their paychecks. Defendant, however, retained the power to supervise, discharge or recall a temporary employee until the end of the employment period. When the holiday season ended, the temporary employees would return to the agency for new assignments.

Plaintiff was hired by defendant on October 29, 1984, to work in its packing department until December 21, 1984. On November 28, 1984, while at work, plaintiff sustained serious injuries to her knee. She claims that a foreign object on defendant's floor caused her to slip and fall. Plaintiff subsequently filed a claim against Pat Shea for workers' compensation benefits and a separate tort claim against defendant for personal injury. . . .

Our jurisdiction allows an employee, for the purpose of workers' compensation to have two employers, both of whom may be liable in compensation. However, recovery against one bars the employee from maintaining a tort action against the other for the same injury. *Blessing v. T. Shriver and Co.*, 94 N.J. Super. 426, 429–430 (App. Div. 1967). "Whether the common law action is precluded is thus dependent upon a determination that the borrower of an employee is, in fact, a special employer." *Id.* at 430. Professor Larson, in his treatise on Workmen's Compensation formulates a three-pronged test in order to establish employment within the terms of the act regarding "Lent Employees and Dual Employment":

> When a general employer lends an employee to a special employer, the special employer becomes liable for workmen's compensation only if
>
> (a) the employee has made a contract of hire, express or implied, with the special employer
>
> (b) the work being done is essentially that of the special employer and
>
> (c) the special employer has the right to control the details of the work.
>
> When all three of the above conditions are satisfied in relation to both employers, both employers are liable for workmen's compensation.
>
> Employment may also be "dual," in the sense that, while the employee is under contract of hire with two different employers, his activities on behalf of each employer are separate and can be identified with one employer or the other. When this separate identification can clearly be made, the particular employer whose work was being done at the time of injury will be held exclusively liable. [1C Larson, Workmen's Compensation (1986), § 48.00, p. 317.]

In *Blessing*, we considered two other co-equal factors, namely, whether the special employer: (1) pays the lent employee's wages, and (2) has the power to hire, discharge or recall the employee. *Blessing*, 94 N.J. Super. at 430.

Plaintiff first contends that there was no contract between herself and defendant. She contends that in order to find the existence of one, there must be a showing of her deliberate and informed consent. Plaintiff relies on the holding in *M.J. Daly Co. v. Varney*, 695 S.W.2d 400 (Ky.1985), in support of her contentions. We find the facts of *Daly* distinguishable. There, plaintiff was employed by a labor service company and was on assignment to defendant. The plaintiff in *Daly*, however, explicitly refused to enter into any employment contract with defendant, preferring to stay on the service company's payroll. The court held that plaintiff had elected to retain his common-law rights to sue defendant in tort rather than under workers' compensation. *Ibid.*

We find the facts of *Whitehead, et al. v. Safway Steel Products, Inc.*, 304 Md. 67, 497 A.2d 803 (1985), more analogous to the matter before us. *Whitehead* involved a worker, employed by a temporary services agency, who brought a negligence action against the company to which he was provisionally assigned. *Id.* 497 A.2d at 805. The court granted the company's motion for judgment n.o.v. and held that the worker was an employee of both the temporary agency and the company and that his exclusive remedy was under workers' compensation law. *Ibid.* The court ruled that the test of whether an express or implied contract of hire existed is satisfied if the employee consents to the special employment relationship. *Id.* 497 A.2d at 812. The court concluded that plaintiff had voluntarily submitted to the employer's direction and control. *Ibid.*

Moreover, in *Chickachop v. Manpower Inc.*, 84 N.J. Super. 129 (Law Div.1964), the court stated that the most "important criterion to be scrutinized is the requirement of a contract between the employee and the special employer." *Id.* at 137. The court found the work being performed by the lent employee was "essentially that of the special employer and said employer controlled the details of the work." The court held that "the employee knew he would be hired out to special employers and accepted such employers just as he accepted the general employer." *Ibid.*

Here, plaintiff knew that Pat Shea would hire her out to various employers and accepted the terms of her employment with defendant. She was apprised of the name of her potential employer, the nature of the work and had the opportunity to refuse the job without fearing any reprisal from the agency. Plaintiff impliedly contracted with defendant when she reported voluntarily to work, complied with store policies and accepted the training and guidance provided by defendant. Plaintiff was also aware that she would be terminated from her employment if she failed to submit to defendant's direction and control. Unlike the claimant in *Daly*, plaintiff acquiesced to contract with defendant.

Plaintiff concedes that her assigned task of packing china and crystal is definitely part of defendant's regular business. Plaintiff also concedes that defendant had the right to control the details of her work and had the power to hire, discharge or recall her. The interrogatories clearly indicate that defendant's personnel department screened all of the applicants sent by Pat Shea before making its final selection assigned each employee to a specific department, trained and supervised them. The interrogatories also indicate that defendant had the power to discharge any employee whose performance failed to meet company standards. It is of no consequence that plaintiff could remain in the agency's employ even after being discharged by defendant. As we stated in *Blessing*, 94 N.J. Super. at 426 an employee may have two employers.

Plaintiff also contends that Pat Shea paid her wages and her workers' compensation insurance. We disagree. The interrogatories indicate that the agency would submit to defendant invoices which listed the number of hours plaintiff had worked. Defendant would then submit payment to the agency who in turn processed plaintiff's paycheck. The amount Pat Shea billed defendant ($ 6.65 per hour) for its use of the temporary employee was greater than what it paid plaintiff ($ 5 per hour). This extra cost undoubtedly helped cover, besides the agency's profit margin, such expenses as payment of plaintiff's workers' compensation insurance. Thus, defendant actually contributed to the insurance protection of one of its employees. *See Chickachop*, 84 N.J. Super. at 139 *Whitehead*, 497 A.2d at 809. The money Pat Shea used to pay plaintiff's compensation benefits came directly from the fee paid by defendant and was one of the expenses included in calculating that fee. *See Renfroe v. Higgins Rack Coating & Manufacturing Co.*, 17 Mich. App. 259, 169 N.W.2d 326, 330 (1969).

We find that defendant was plaintiff's special employer at the time of the accident and that the claim is governed by the Workers' Compensation Act. Consequently, we find no genuine issue as to any material facts and find the grant of summary judgment proper.

Affirmed.

RUBLE v. ARCTIC GENERAL, INC.
598 P.2d 95 (Alaska 1979)

PER CURIAM.

In June 1975, appellant Roy Ruble was working on the state funded Airport Road Extension Project in Fairbanks, Alaska. Ruble sustained injuries when the belly plate of a road scraper which he was operating became disengaged, causing the vehicle to come to an abrupt halt. He brought a tort action against Arctic General, Inc. (hereinafter "Arctic"), the owner-lessor of the road scraper; contending that Arctic was negligent in maintaining the machine. The superior court, acting on Arctic's and Ruble's cross-motions for summary judgment, dismissed Ruble's complaint, on the ground that he was an employee of Arctic and hence limited to his remedies under workers' compensation. AS 23.30.055. Ruble has appealed this dismissal. We affirm the judgment of the superior court.

On May 30, 1975, JIJ Nelson, Joint Venture (hereinafter "JIJ"), the contractor for the highway project, entered into an agreement with Arctic for the use of several pieces of road equipment. The agreement called for Arctic to maintain the equipment and supply operators. Accordingly, Ruble was dispatched from the union hiring hall to work for Arctic. He was put on Arctic's payroll and instructed in the use of the road scrapers by Bud LaFon, a part-owner of Arctic. Sometime in the next few days the state asked JIJ either to put Arctic's operators on its payroll or to make Arctic a subcontractor, in order to comply with state and federal law. JIJ and Arctic agreed on the former, and on June 2, Ruble was transferred to the JIJ payroll. His wages, however, were remitted by Arctic to JIJ after JIJ paid the equipment rental fees specified in the May 30 agreement. Ruble also continued to be accountable to and supervised by LaFon.

As a result of the accident, Ruble was dismissed from his job on June 16.[14] Three weeks later, he filed a workers' compensation claim against JIJ, and received benefits under that claim. In September, he began the action which is the subject of this appeal.

Both parties discuss at great length the various tests that we have used in the past to determine whether a person was an employee for workers' compensation purposes.[15] Those tests, however, were designed to differentiate employees from independent contractors, and have not proved useful here, where the question is whose employee Ruble was, rather than whether or not he was an employee at all.

In his text on workers' compensation law, Professor Larson discusses factors to be considered in determining the employer in situations involving joint employers and joint employment. According to Larson, a special employer[16] such as JIJ, becomes liable for workers' compensation only if the employee, here Ruble, has made a contract of hire, express or implied, with the special employer, the work being done is essentially that of the special employer, and the special employer has the right to control the details of the work.[17] In the usual case involving multiple employers, the employee is seeking to hold a particular employer liable for workers' compensation.[18] In such cases, the liberal purpose of the workers' compensation act, to benefit the employee,[19] and the presumption that a claim comes within the provisions of the act[20] apply. In this case, however, an employee is seeking to hold the "general employer" liable as a third party. When an employee, who has coverage under the compensation act, seeks to hold his original employer liable as a third party, policy considerations are more evenly balanced. Thus, there are neither presumptions for or against finding tort liability on

[14] (Court's footnote) The record does not show if he was formally dismissed by Arctic or by JIJ.

[15] (Court's footnote) The doctrines discussed by the parties include the "nature of the work" test, adopted in Searfus v. Northern Gas Co., 472 P.2d 966, 969–70 (Alaska 1970); the "contract of employment" test, relied on in Selid Constr. Co. v. Guarantee Ins. Co., 355 P.2d 389, 393 (Alaska 1960); and the "right of control" test, which we used in Cordova Fish & Cold Storage Co. v. Estes, 370 P.2d 180, 184 (Alaska 1962).

[16] (Court's footnote) When one employer borrows an employee having an existing employment relation with another employer, the former is known as a "special employer," the latter as the "general employer." See 1B A. Larson, Workmen's Compensation Law § 48.10, at 8-208, 8-209 (1978) (hereinafter cited as Larson). In the case at bar, Arctic General is the general employer.

[17] (Court's footnote) 1B Larson, supra note 3, § 48.00, at 8-205.

[18] (Court's footnote) See, e.g., Raymond Concrete Piling Co. v. Industrial Comm'n, 37 Ill.2d 512, 229 N.E.2d 673 (1967); Bradshaw v. Richardson Trucks, Inc., 467 S.W.2d 945 (Mo. 1971).

[19] (Court's footnote) Hood v. State, Workmen's Comp. Bd., 574 P.2d 811, 813 (Alaska 1978); S.L.W. v. Alaska Workmen's Comp. Bd., 490 P.2d 42, 43 (Alaska 1971).

[20] (Court's footnote) AS 23.30.120(1).

behalf of the third party, nor presumptions for or against finding an employment relation with respect to a particular employer.[21]

The issue before us quite simply, is whether the evidence presented indicates that the initially established employment relation between Arctic and Ruble had terminated at the time of Ruble's injury. Applying the Larson tests, it does not appear that Ruble entered into a contract of hire, express or implied, with JIJ.[22] The work was benefitting both Arctic and JIJ and was not essentially for JIJ any more than for Arctic, and all control was exercised by Arctic through LaFon, although JIJ had a right to designate the type and location of work to be performed by the scraper.

There is no dispute that Ruble was an Arctic employee until June 2, 1975. What effect, then, did his transfer to the JIJ payroll have? LaFon testified in his deposition that neither JIJ nor Arctic contemplated any significant change because of the payroll switch,[23] and no modifications were made to the written agreement. Arctic, by reimbursing JIJ, was, in reality, still paying Ruble's full salary after the transfer. Professor Larson states:

> The element of who pays the employee shrinks into comparative insignificance in lent-employee problems, because the net result is almost invariably that the special employer ultimately pays for the services received and the employee ultimately gets his wages. But whether the special employer pays the general employer who in turn pays the employee, which is the typical procedure in the Manpower-type cases, or whether the special employer pays the employee direct, the difference for present purposes is one of mechanics and not of substance. *Of course, if this is not so — that is, if either the general employer or the special employer pays the employee and is not reimbursed — the fact of payment is strong evidence that the payor is the employer.*[24]

---

[21] (*Court's footnote*) With reference to a somewhat similar situation, Professor Larson states:

> What gives the lent-employee cases their special character, however, is the fact that they begin, not with an unknown relation, but with an existing employment relation. The conflict of interest becomes one not between employer and employee (who is assured of recovering from someone) but between two employers and their insurance carriers. There is here no place for presumptions based on the beneficent purposes of the act. The only presumption is the continuance of the general employment, which is taken for granted as the beginning point of any lent-employee problem.1B Larson, *supra* note 3, § 48.10, at 8-210 to 8-211 (footnote omitted).

[22] (*Court's footnote*) We do not imply that the Workmen's Compensation Board erred in holding that JIJ was an employer under the Compensation Act. Because of the factors in workers' compensation law discussed above, JIJ could be considered such an employer. In Cradic v. Eastman Kodak Co., 202 F. Supp. 590 (E.D. Tenn. 1962), an excavation contractor leased a large piece of construction equipment, known as a "wobble-wheel," and an operator for the machine to Kodak. The operator sustained injuries while performing work under Kodak's control and supervision. The operator, who received a workers' compensation judgment against the excavation contractor, brought a common law negligence action against Kodak. The court dismissed the complaint, holding that the operator was an employee of Kodak, the "special employer," as well as the excavation contractor, the "general employer." In Lewis v. S. M. Byers Motor Car Co., 102 Pa.Super. 434, 156 A. 899 (1931), a truck distributor furnished a truck with a driver to a gasoline delivery company. The driver was killed when an explosion occurred during the delivery of gasoline. The driver's wife sought workers' compensation against both companies, and the court held that the truck distributor, alone, was the employer. *Id.* 156 A. at 901. In a later suit arising out of the same facts, a widow of a third party killed by the explosion sought to recover damages from both the truck distributor and the gasoline company based on the deceased driver's negligence. The Supreme Court of Pennsylvania held that both companies were vicariously liable, giving no weight to the compensation decision. Gordon v. S. M. Byers Motor Car Co., 309 Pa. 453, 164 A. 334, 336 (1932).

[23] (*Court's footnote*) He referred to it as "a token thing."

[24] (*Court's footnote*) 1B Larson, *supra* note 3, § 48.30, at 8-248 to 8-250 (emphasis added, footnotes omitted).

According to Larson, the factor that seems to play the largest part in lent-employee cases is that of furnishing heavy equipment.[25] He cites many cases holding that a general employer furnishing operators and equipment continues to be regarded as the employer when the employee is injured.[26] Discussing the "right to control" factor, Larson states:

> [T]he majority of the decisions have been influenced by the arguments both that the general employer would naturally reserve the control necessary to ensure that his equipment is properly used, and that a substantial part of any such operator's duties would consist of the continuing duty of maintenance of the equipment.[27]

We believe that these factors are persuasive here. The lease between Arctic and JIJ involved six pieces of heavy earth-moving equipment which Arctic agreed to operate and maintain. Arctic also retained the authority to see that its equipment was properly used and not abused.[28]

Further, several JIJ officials stated in affidavits that they never considered Ruble to be a JIJ employee, and Ruble himself in his deposition expressed unequivocally that he believed himself an Arctic employee.[29] He received all of his orders from LaFon and reported his injury to him. Given these facts, we cannot find that Ruble's status as an employee of Arctic ended on June 2.

Ruble relies heavily on the determination of the Alaska Workmen's Compensation Board that he was a JIJ employee, and on Arctic's failure to participate in those proceedings. The Board's determination, however, cannot be binding on Arctic, as Arctic was not a party to those proceedings.[30] Since Ruble filed his worker's compensation claim against JIJ, we will not attribute any weight to Arctic's unwillingness to intervene.[31] Finally, while we do not condone Arctic's failure to comply with its statutory duty to file a report with the Workmen's Compensation Board within ten days after learning of an employee's injury,[32] we do not believe this fact is of significance in the determination of whether there was an employment relationship between Arctic and Ruble.

The trial court found that Ruble was an employee of both Arctic and JIJ. Larson writes:

> Joint employment occurs when a single employee, under contract with two employers, and under the simultaneous control of both, simultaneously performs services for both employers, and when the service for each employer is the same as, or is closely related to, that for the other. In such a case, both employers are liable for workmen's compensation.[33]

---

[25] (*Court's footnote*) *Id.* at 8-250.

[26] (*Court's footnote*) *Id.* at 8-250 to 8-251.

[27] (*Court's footnote*) *Id.* at 8-253.

[28] (*Court's footnote*) Bud LaFon testified in his deposition: Well, I did have control over [Ruble] on the way he handled the machine. If I felt that he was abusing the machine, or dangerous, I would have control.

[29] (*Court's footnote*) Under questioning by his own attorney, Ruble backed off somewhat from that flat assertion.

[30] (*Court's footnote*) We note that the Board's determination is not necessarily inconsistent with Arctic's position: the Board may have concluded that Ruble was a joint employee, or JIJ may have decided not to raise its possible non-employer defense.

[31] (*Court's footnote*) While the record indicates that Arctic had notice of Ruble's injury shortly after it occurred, nothing in the record indicates that Arctic was aware of the workers' compensation proceeding against JIJ.

[32] (*Court's footnote*) AS 23.30.070(a).

[33] (*Court's footnote*) 1B Larson, *supra* note 3, § 48.40, at 8-253.

Because this appeal involves the limited issue of Arctic's relationship to Ruble, we do not reach the question of whether Ruble was also an employee of JIJ or a joint employee.

Ruble's arguments emphasize form over substance. Even though his check was issued by JIJ, the money came from Arctic, and his employment was in every way more closely linked to Arctic then to JIJ. The judgment of the superior court dismissing the action is

Affirmed.

BURKE, J., not participating.

PROBLEMS

(1) The U.S. Forest Service told the corporation's manager that there was a fire on national forest land and that he was to send two water trucks and two tractors to the fire. The manager told the foreman to take the equipment to the fire. The foreman's salary was paid by the U.S. government for the work done fighting the fire. He injured his back. Is the U.S. Government liable for compensation? The corporation? *See* Argonaut Ins. Co. v. Industrial Acc. Comm'n, 54 Cal. 2d 740, 8 Cal. Rptr. 438, 356 P.2d 182 (1960).

(2) A policeman was temporarily assigned to stand at the door of a dance hall and admit only those who had tickets. Should the city be liable for compensation for an injury during this activity? *See* Rainbow Gardens v. Industrial Comm'n, 186 Wis. 223, 202 N.W. 329 (1925). *But cf.* United States Fire Ins. Co. v. City of Atlanta, 135 Ga. App. 390, 217 S.E. 2d 647 (1975).

(3) The Aircraft Corporation rented to the Pictures Corporation an airplane and pilot by the day. The Pictures Corporation was to give him his orders as to the flight to be made in connection with the filming of a picture sequence. After a trial run, the Pictures Corporation told the pilot he would have to fly lower. He hesitated, objecting that it would be dangerous, but finally acquiesced. While flying at seventy-five feet he struck an airpocket and crashed. Two representatives of the Aircraft Corporation were present, and could have vetoed the instruction to fly lower, but said nothing. Should the Pictures Corporation be liable for compensation? The Aircraft Corporation? Both? *See* Famous Players Lasky Corp. v. Industrial Comm'n, 194 Cal. 228, 228 P. 5, 34 A.L.R. 765 (1924).

Chapter 13
SPECIFIC INCLUSIONS OR EXEMPTIONS

§ 13.01 "STATUTORY EMPLOYEES"

Most statutes impose a special compensation liability upon an employer who gets part of its regular work done by the employees of a contractor under it, if the intermediate contractor's compensation liability is uninsured. Since one purpose of these statutes is to prevent evasion of compensation coverage by the subcontracting of the employer's normal work, the test of applicability is the question whether the work being done under the contractor would ordinarily be done by employees, in view of this employer's past practices and the practices of employers in comparable businesses.

Attempts are also being made to extend protection to specific classes of workers, such as newspaper deliverers and caddies, whether strictly employees or not; but constitutional doubts have been cast on the legislature's power to declare the existence of a contract of hire where it has not actually been made by the parties themselves.

The preceding chapter has dealt with questions of status turning entirely on the definition of the term "employee." The present chapter is concerned with the instances in which specific categories of conceded nonemployees are deliberately brought within the coverage of the act, and in which specific categories of conceded employers and employees are excluded or exempted from the act.

Over three-quarters of the states[1] have adopted "contractor-under" statutes, imposing on the general employer compensation liability to the employees of contractors (in most instances uninsured contractors) under it. Not uncommonly, the liability so created is referred to as that of the "statutory employer" to a "statutory employee."

The purpose of this legislation was to protect employees of irresponsible and uninsured subcontractors by imposing ultimate liability on the presumably responsible principal contractor, who has it within its power, in choosing subcontractors, to pass upon their responsibility and insist upon appropriate compensation protection for their workers. This being the rationale of the rule, in the increasingly common situation displaying a hierarchy of principal contractors upon subcontractors upon sub-subcontractors, if an employee of the lowest subcontractor on the totem pole is injured, there is no practical reason for reaching up the hierarchy any further than the first insured contractor. Thus, in *In re Van Bibber's Case*,[2] an insured general contractor

---

[1] Examples of states *not* included are California, Delaware, Iowa, and West Virginia.

[2] *In re* Van Bibber's Case, 343 Mass. 443, 179 N.E.2d 253 (1962).

engaged an insured subcontractor who in turn engaged an uninsured sub-subcontractor. The subcontractor was held liable for the compensation payable to an injured employee of the sub-subcontractor. The general contractor was held not liable.

The statute also aims to forestall evasion of the act by those who might be tempted to subdivide their regular operations among subcontractors,[3] thus escaping direct employment relations with the workers and relegating them for compensation protection to small contractors who fail to carry (and, if small enough, may not even be required to carry) compensation insurance.

Practically all of the cases of general interest interpreting this type of statute are addressed to one question: When is the subcontracted work part of the regular business of the statutory employer? The statutory language lying behind this question varies somewhat; some acts speak of work which is "part of or process in" the employer's trade or business,[4] perhaps excluding for good measure, work which is "merely ancillary and incidental" to such trade or business,[5] some use the phrase "any work which is a part of his trade, business or occupation,"[6] and there are many other variants. But, with a surprising degree of harmony, the cases applying these assorted phrases agree upon the general rule of thumb that the statute covers all situations in which work is accomplished which this employer, or employers in a similar business, would ordinarily do through employees.

Of course, when the statute says expressly (as many do) that a contractor who subcontracts any part of its own contract becomes the statutory employer of the subcontractor's employees, the question whether the subdivided work is part of the principal contractor's work usually answers itself. The very fact that it is a parcelled-out fraction of the main job is proof enough. In such a case, as when a building contractor subcontracts the plumbing work, it would be no defense on the part of the building contractor that it is customary to get such work done through independent contractors.[7]

PROBLEM

Wisconsin passed a statute declaring that any person on a golf course for purposes of caddying was deemed to be an employee of the golf course. New Jersey passed a statute legislating *out* of the act all persons selling newspapers, magazines or periodicals or delivering them directly to the public. Are these statutes constitutional? *See* Wendlandt v. Industrial Comm'n, 256 Wis. 62, 39 N.W.2d 854 (1949), and De Monaco v. Renton, 18 N.J. 852, 113 A.2d 782 (1955).

§ 13.02   NONBUSINESS EMPLOYMENTS

[1]   Introduction

Various categories of employment may be specifically excluded by statutory provision, as is usually the case for domestic servants, or it may be excluded under a general provision exempting employments that are casual and not in the employer's trade or business. For example, it is implied from the word "business" that construction or work done for private householders is not covered; but if the work is of such regularity and duration as to be no longer casual, it may be covered even when done for

---

[3] Dubois v. Soule Mill, 323 Mass. 472, 82 N.E.2d 886 (1948).

[4] *E.g.*, Conn. Gen. Stat. Ann. § 31-154 (1958). Connecticut, following the British Act (Sec. 4, 6 Edw. 7 (1906)), and in common with several other states, also requires that the work be performed on or about premises under the control of the employer.

[5] *E.g.*, Mass. Workmen's Compensation Law § 18 (1965).

[6] *E.g.*, Va. Code Ann. § 65-27 (1950).

[7] Huffstettler v. Lion Oil Co., 110 F. Supp. 222 (W.D. Ark 1953), *aff'd*, 208 F.2d 549.

a householder, since the exemption demands a showing of both casualness and nonbusiness character. As to charitable, religious, and other non-profit employers, there is a marked divergence of opinion, with the majority holding them covered by the general terms "employer" and "business" unless specifically exempted.

[2] Summary of Categories Exempted by Statute

Domestic service is excluded in about half of the states.[8]

Casual employment is excluded in about three-fifths of the states.[9]

Employment not in course of employer's trade, business or profession is excluded in over two-thirds of the states.[10]

Agricultural employment is excluded in about one-fifth of the states.[11]

Employers with *less than a specified minimum number of employees* are excluded in about a quarter of the states.[12]

Nonprofit employers are excluded in at least one state, namely Hawaii, and charitable or religious employers are excluded in at least two states, namely Arkansas and Mississippi.

There is an assortment of other exemptions; for example, newspaper deliverers are excluded in at least two states, including California and Mississippi.

[3] General Nonbusiness Exemptions

The purpose behind the various exemptions which have in common the nonbusiness character of the employer's activity can best be approached by imagining a set of facts which could easily happen to any average householder. Let us suppose that you are a lawyer, owning a modest home, and living on a modest income, and that you have hired a neighbor boy to mow your lawn for five dollars an hour. While the boy is attempting to adjust the bed of the power mower with the blades turning, his screwdriver slips and both his hands are badly cut by the blades. Complications develop, and both hands are lost, making the boy totally and permanently disabled. Would you, as a lawyer — with, we will assume, a special consciousness of compensation law — expect to assume workers' compensation liability in the circumstances, amounting to perhaps five hundred thousand dollars? If not, what statutory provisions stand between you and this financial catastrophe?

The injured person is admittedly an employee who has suffered an accident in the course of his employment and who presents exactly the same social problem as the injured factory worker. The question is whether he is within the letter or the spirit of compensation legislation, and if not, why not.

FINCHAM v. WENDT
59 Or. App. 416, 651 P.2d 159 (1982)

JOSEPH, CHIEF JUDGE.

The sole issue in this case is whether a worker engaged in remodeling a cold storage room in a building located on a "hobby farm" is subject to workers' compensation

---

[8] Examples: Arkansas, Arizona, Florida, Indiana, Nebraska, Pennsylvania, and Virginia.

[9] Examples: California, Colorado, Connecticut, Idaho, Minnesota, Nevada, New Mexico, North Carolina, Ohio, Oregon, Utah, and Virginia (as well as the District of Columbia).

[10] Examples: see n.9, immediately *above*, and, in addition, Georgia, Illinois, Massachusetts, Nebraska, and Wisconsin.

[11] Examples: Arkansas, Georgia, Indiana, Kentucky, Mississippi, and New Mexico.

[12] Examples: Alabama, Florida, Georgia, Mississippi, New Mexico, North Carolina, and Virginia.

coverage. Claimant seeks judicial review of a determination by the Workers' Compensation Board that he is a nonsubject worker under the householder exemption. ORS 656.027 provides in relevant part:

All workers are subject to ORS 656.001 to 656.794 except those nonsubject workers described in the following subsections:

. . . .

(2) A worker employed to do gardening, maintenance, repair, remodeling or similar work in or about the private home of the person employing the worker.

Employer lives on a 25-acre farm, where he grows peaches, pears, apples, cherries, grapes and berries. He occasionally has hired teenagers to help pick the fruit. Some of the crop is sold to commercial outlets; the rest is sold from a self-service fruit stand. Gross sales in 1980 were about $8,000. Although it has shown a profit at times in the past, the farm is not generally a profitable activity. Employer has regular full-time employment elsewhere; he regards the farming as a hobby that enhances the family's enjoyment of the property as their home.

In September, 1980, employer hired claimant, a 17-year old high school student, to pick fruit for two days. On October 18, 1980, employer hired claimant again, this time to expand a cold storage room in a building located 65 feet from employer's residence. The building houses farm machinery, tractors, tools and a mechanical repair shop, as well as other cold rooms for storing peaches and apples intended for sale. Claimant worked on the project after school for about two weeks. On November 2, 1980, he injured his head in a fall from a ladder while he was engaged in the work.

The referee found that claimant was not an independent contractor; the employer does not contend otherwise. The only issue before us is the applicability of the quoted householder exemption; thus, if the exemption is inapplicable, claimant is a subject worker under ORS 656.027. The Board, in reaching its conclusion that the exemption was applicable, reasoned:

As noted, we have found that the employer was not really engaged in farming as a business, but as a hobby, and that the claimant was not hired as a general farm laborer. That being the case, we find that the employer is not a subject non-complying employer, as did the Referee, due to the exception contained in ORS 656.027(2).

Employer contends that this case is disposed of by a mechanical reading of the statutory language "in or about the private home." By his reading, the construction work was "about" the home for no other reason than that the building was in the vicinity of the home. We agree that the statutory language can be construed to include outbuildings. Remodelling done not "in" but "about" a private home might well include renovation of an outbuilding, such as an attached or detached garage housing the family car. Under the interpretation urged by employer, however, remodeling of a commercial machine shop that happened to be located adjacent to the private home of the machine shop owner could be considered to be in the vicinity of and, hence, "about" the private home, and the employment would thus fall within the exemption. That result is clearly wrong. A mechanical reading of the statute must therefore fail.

The dispositive concept in this statutory provision is the term "private," which must be distinguished from the concept of business or commercial premises. The basis of the householder exemption is the character of the home as a private place, not as business premises. Outbuildings are included in the exemption only because they are extensions of the home and, as such, share the same character as the home. In order for work done on outbuildings to fall within the exemption, the outbuildings must be of a private character rather than business or commercial.

The record shows that the building in question here was used to store tractors, tools, farm equipment and fruit intended for sale. It was evidently not used to house personal automobiles of the employer.[13] Certainly, the cold storage room that claimant was building was directly related to the fruit sales. We conclude that the construction claimant was engaged in was not work on an extension of the private home but rather on the premises of a farm operation.

The Board and employer have taken the position that the fruit selling operation was not "really" a business, because it was not the primary source of income of the employer. We rejected a similar contention in *Carlile v. Greeninger*, 35 Or.App. 52, 580 P.2d 588, *rev. den.* 283 Or. 235 (1978), where the issue was whether the employee was an independent contractor or servant. There, the primary business of the employer was rock crushing, but he was also trying to start a cordwood business. We said:

> Defendant argues that cordwood cutting is not a regular part of his business, which was rock crushing, and that the claimant's job was merely temporary with no prospect for continued employment. Defendant is essentially arguing that under the "relative nature of the work' test put forth in *Woody v. Waibel*, 276 Or. 189, 554 P.2d 492 (1976), claimant does not qualify as an employe. [Footnote omitted.]

> While it may be that woodcutting was not defendant's primary business, it was a business of his, and the falling and bucking of trees was an essential part of that enterprise. Further, there was a prospect of continued employment although it was contingent upon defendant's ability to acquire more timber. 35 Or. App. at 54–55, 580 P.2d 588.

While selling fruit grown on his small farm may not have been the employer's primary business, we conclude, as in *Carlile*, that it was nonetheless a business or commercial activity.

---

[13] *(Court's footnote)* The employer's testimony suggests that the vehicles in the "garage" were farm tractors:

Q. . . . What building was it that the remodeling work was to be done in?

A. It was the garage — existing garage — that's been there since 1943.

Q. And what did you use that building for?

A. Well, it's a shop and garage and cars.

Q. Did you park your vehicles in it?

A. Tractors.

Q. And when you say shop —

A. One part of it.

Q. Did you have mechanical parts — excuse me — mechanical tools and things like that in the building?

A. Yes.

. . . .

Q. Do you keep all of your farm equipment and tractors in this garage?

A. Yes.

Q. Do you also do your work on them in there?

A. Some of them, yes.

Q. Do you keep the tools that you work for picking the fruit in this building?

A. Yes.

Q. Do you keep or store the fruit in any other location, besides the cold storage rooms in this building?

A. No.

Similarly, we reject the argument that a business effort must show a profit in order to constitute a business. As stated by Larson:

> On one point a fair degree of unanimity seems to have emerged. In the absence of a 'pecuniary-gain' requirement, the concept of trade or business does not necessary [sic] embrace the element of profit-seeking. It is true that the word "profit' turns up here and there in general definitions of 'business' as distinguished from nonbusiness activities, but when the showdown comes, the court may explain that this was not really an essential part of the definition. For example, although Washington had held that the Red Cross was not covered because it was not in business for profit, it managed to hold later that a cafeteria run on a nonprofit basis by a corporative Naval Supply Depot was indeed a business.

> This is a sound result. The test is not whether the employer is in business for profit, but whether he is in business at all. If he supplies a product or service, it is immaterial what he does with his profits, or whether he expects or gets any profits at all.

I Larson, Workers' Compensation Law, § 50.44(9) (1980). [Footnotes omitted.]

We concur with this view. The record here indicates that the employer's fruit selling business was sometimes profitable, sometimes not. Workers' compensation coverage does not depend on the profit and loss statements of the employer.

The Supreme Court has held that statutes governing workers' compensation are to be interpreted to effectuate the purposes of the law. *Woody v. Waibel*, 276 Or. 189, 197, 554 P.2d 492 (1976). In *Woody*, the two chief purposes of workers' compensation law were recognized to be to further a social bargain (giving up the right to litigation for that of limited compensation) and as social insurance (allocation of financial risk to the ultimate consumer). The court quoted from a law review article explaining the social insurance purpose:

> The second principal social policy purpose was the social insurance form through which workmen's compensation was to operate. [Footnote omitted.] This would be its risk distribution aspect. The fact that modern industrial life will inevitably generate work-related injuries and possibly death is one of the major premises underlying workmen's compensation. . . . Therefore, the cost of these injuries and fatalities is to be distributed throughout society and viewed as a cost of doing business.' Note, Employer or Independent Contractor: The Need For a Reassessment of the Standard Used Under California's Workmen's Compensation, 10 U.San.Fran.L.Rev. 133, 136–37 (1975). 276 Or. at 194 n. 6, 554 P.2d 492.

Larson directly relates the purpose of the householder exemption to the social insurance purpose of workers' compensation law:

> It has always been assumed, rightly or wrongly, that the cost of compensation protection did not become a burden upon the employer directly, since he was expected to pass the cost along to the consumer in the price of the product. There are those who argue that this does not go to the essence of the compensation idea, and perhaps does not really work out at all; but the fact remains that for decades the compensation principle has been made acceptable to employers (and, to some extent, also to skeptical courts) on the argument that the cost could be passed along through the medium of insurance whose premiums are reflected in the cost accounts on which the price is based. Whether or not Lloyd George ever really said that 'the cost of the product should bear the blood of the working man,' it was in the setting provided by this idea that the principle became established of the business employer's unilateral non-contributory liability without fault toward anyone who might retroactively be determined by a court to have a claim upon him for compensation.

When a similar liability is imposed upon the householder, however, who produces and sells no goods or services that can bear the cost of compensation insurance, the law has gone one step further and said that any employer, solely because he stands in the employment relation to an employee, is liable without fault for the latter's injuries and must assume and absorb the entire ultimate cost himself.

. . . .

. . . [S]imply to impose workmen's compensation liability on householders, whether by judicial decision or by statutory extension, would mean, first, that the employer would bear all the cost of protection in this category of wage-loss, and, second, that he could never be quite sure in advance whether he needed compensation insurance and what his potential future liability might be. No closer questions can be found in the entire shadowy realm of employee status than the very questions that would face the householder many times every year: the status of directly hired window washers, repairmen, snow shovelers, grass mowers, babysitters, and all the army of artisans whose visits are a normal and frequent incident in the life of a house owner. No one would dare to let a handyman climb to his precarious perch on a stepladder and remove a storm window without first taking out compensation insurance for the day.

I Larson, Workers' Compensation Law, § 50.25 (1980).

In this case, we draw the line between subject and nonsubject worker status, not on the basis of the physical proximity of the worker's employment to the private home of the employer, but rather in light of the fundamental purposes of workers' compensation law. In the context of this case, the employer was a producer, rather than a consumer like the ordinary householder. The fruit selling operation is within the stream of commerce, whether or not employer was always able to make the business a financial success. Claimant was not engaged in construction on an extension of the private home, but rather on the premises of and in connection with a business. Hence, the remodelling was not "about the private home" within the meaning of ORS 656.027(2), and claimant was a subject worker.[14]

Reversed and remanded with instructions that the claim be accepted as compensable.

[4] Domestic Servants

GRIEBEL v. INDUSTRIAL COMMISSION OF ARIZONA
133 Ariz. 270, 650 P.2d 1252 (Ariz. App. 1982)

EUBANK, PRESIDING JUDGE.

Petitioner Eleanor Griebel filed a claim for widow's benefits alleging that the death of her husband on March 6, 1980, was compensable under the Arizona Workmen's Compensation Act. Because no insurance carrier was involved, the Industrial Commission undertook the initial evaluation of petitioner's claim. An award was issued denying compensability. This award was protested, and formal hearings were held. On May 29, 1981, an award was issued denying compensation on the grounds that Mr. Griebel's employer was not covered by the compensation act. Alternatively, the

---

[14] *(Court's footnote)* In Anfilofieff v. SAIF, 52 Or.App. 127, 132, 627 P.2d 1274 (1981), we interpreted the phrase "employed to do . . . work" in the householder exemption, ORS 656.027(2), to signify the overall nature of the employee's duties rather than the specific task. We held that repair of a bath house on the premises of the employer's private residence was work incidental to the overall nature of the claimant's employment as a carpenter on a housing project and, hence, that the claimant was not *employed* to repair or remodel the bath house. That case is inapplicable to this one, for claimant here had no other regular employment relationship with the employer.

administrative law judge found that Mrs. Griebel's claim was foreclosed because she had settled a claim for third party liability without approval of the Industrial Commission.

The record shows that Mr. Griebel was employed as a groundskeeper and handyman for the Morning Star ranch of Mr. and Mrs. Rector. After Mr. Rector's death, Mr. Griebel continued his duties at Morning Star, although Mrs. Rector had moved into a townhouse in the city. Mr. Griebel assisted Mrs. Rector with the moving, and also assisted Mrs. Rector's daughter when she moved to Phoenix. Since Mr. Griebel was such a fine groundskeeper and handyman, Mrs. Rector allowed him free reign in his upkeep of the Morning Star ranch, and occasionally requested his services at the other properties owned by the Rector family.

After Mr. Rector's death, Mrs. Rector had become engaged to Mr. Dayton, who is now her husband. Mr. Dayton was renovating an old ranch on a leased mining claim, and requested Mr. Griebel's assistance on an electrical problem. Mr. Griebel agreed to help, but on the third day of this project, he was killed in an automobile accident in transit from the Morning Star ranch. It is unclear whether Mr. Griebel's destination was the mining claim or Mrs. Rector's townhouse, but in any event, there is no question that Mr. Griebel was killed within the course and scope of his employment for Mrs. Rector. The only question for our consideration is whether Mrs. Rector was an "employer" of Mr. Griebel within the meaning and coverage of the Workmen's Compensation Act, A.R.S. § 23-902(A).

The administrative law judge correctly concluded that it was petitioner's burden to show the "employer" status of Mrs. Rector under A.R.S. § 23-902(A). *See Lewis v. Industrial Commission*, 93 Ariz. 324, 326, 380 P.2d 782, 783 (1963). A.R.S. § 23-902(A)[15] reads as follows:

> A. Employers subject to the provisions of this chapter are the state, each county, city, town, municipal corporation, school district and *every person who has in his employ any workmen or operatives regularly employed in the same business or establishment under contract of hire, except domestic servants.* Exempted employers of domestic servants may come under the provisions of this chapter by complying with its provisions and the rules and regulations of the commission. For the purposes of this section "regularly employed" includes all employments, whether continuous throughout the year, or for only a portion of the year, in the usual trade, business, profession or occupation of an employer. (Emphasis added).

Based on the requirements of this statute, the administrative law judge made two findings of fact. First, that Mrs. Rector was not engaged in *any* trade, business, profession or occupation. Second, that Mr. Griebel was a "domestic servant." The sufficiency of either finding precludes petitioner's recovery of a widow's benefit.

Petitioner takes exception to both of these findings. She contends that her husband was not a "domestic servant" such as a maid or housekeeper. Furthermore, she contends that Mrs. Rector and Mr. Dayton were in the "business" of holding properties for their appreciating values. Because we believe that these issues are intertwined both in fact and in law, we shall address them conjunctively.

Although a term of common usage, "domestic servant" has been subject to varying and inconsistent definitions. Some authorities have attempted to define it by virtue of the employee's residence; that is, whether the employee lives within or without the master's residence. *See* Toole Furniture Co. v. Ellis, 5 Ga. App. 271, 274, 63 S.E. 55, 57 (1908) (negligence action involving the master-servant relationship; citing Bouvier's Law

---

[15] *(Court's footnote)* The legislative history indicates that this section was adopted from Utah. We note that Utah recently removed "domestic servant" as an exemption and substituted a basis of hours worked and wages paid the employee. U.C.A. § 35-1-42 (Supp. 1981).

Dictionary); Black's Law Dictionary (Rev. 4th ed. 1968). Of this concept, the Minnesota supreme court stated:

> This distinction dates back to Blackstone and other ancient authorities on the common law of England. It was said that a domestic servant must live "*intra moenia*" or "within the walls." It had its origin in feudal conditions which no longer exist, and which never have existed in Minnesota.

Anderson v. Ueland, 197 Minn. 518, 520, 267 N.W. 517, 518 (1936). Certainly, the same thing can be said about Arizona. *Cf. Johnson v. Industrial Commission*, 5 Ariz. App. 185, 424 P.2d 833 (1967).

Similarly, contentions have been raised that "domestic servant" should be defined according to the nature of the work done. Such is the case of *Barres v. Watterson Hotel Co.*, 196 Ky. 100, 244 S.W. 308 (1922), wherein a hotel maid filed a claim for workmen's compensation and the hotel defended on the grounds that a maid was a "domestic servant." The court stated:

> She was, to be sure, engaged in an employment or occupation similar in many of its aspects to that generally pursued by domestics in the home. We apprehend, however, that the business of running a hotel is industrial in its nature and not domestic in the general meaning of that word.

Id. at 101–02, 244 S.W. at 309. *See also*, Fitzpatrick v. Crestfield Farm Inc., 582 S.W.2d 44 (Ky. App. 1978).

These cases, we believe, show the fallacy of drawing distinctions based on antiquated definitions of domestic service. We agree that a "domestic servant" must be employed in or about the home or residence (although not necessarily within the walls), performing domestic tasks such as handymen, yardmen, gardeners, maids and so forth. *See Torres v. Industrial Commission*, 10 Ariz.App. 210, 457 P.2d 750 (1969); *Johnson v. Industrial Commission, supra.* For workmen's compensation purposes, however, we believe the most important inquiry is the use to which the master puts his servant's labor. As stated in *Jack v. Belin's Estate*, 149 Pa.Super. 531, 534, 27 A.2d 455, 457 (1942):

> Agricultural workers are those who are engaged in an enterprise conducted by the employer for his profit. House servants merely contribute to the personal needs and comfort of the employer. Between the two groups are the outservants, who in strictness do not fall within either class. And yet there is much better reason for excluding gardeners, caretakers and the like, than agricultural workers, for they are not engaged in commercial enterprise and their services all relate to the home life. Our conclusion, in construing the act, is that the place where the services are performed does not determine the nature of the employment. Cooks and house maids are domestic servants, not because they work indoors, but because they serve the needs of the household. Similarly, one who drives an automobile in bringing supplies from market or in disposing of waste materials or who raises vegetables and produce for use on the estate is a domestic servant in the broader sense contemplated by the act. Growing flowers for the delight and pleasure of the family of the owners is the same kind of service. Where, as here, the grounds, though extensive, are maintained as the curtilage to the mansion house and for the comfort and pleasure of the occupants, they who thus minister to the needs of the owners, according to the standard of living established by them, are domestic servants within the purview of the act.

See also, Gunter v. Mersereau, 7 Or. App. 470, 491 P.2d 1205 (1971) (concluding that a live-in nurse's aide was excluded from coverage as a domestic servant); 1C Larson, Workmen's Compensation Law §§ 50.21, 50.30 (grouping domestic service with other "nonbusiness" employments, and explaining the policy reasons for exclusion from

Workmen's Compensation coverage).[16]

We believe the rule to be that if the master is regularly using his servant's labor in a commercial enterprise, that is, attempting to profit in an entrepreneurial capacity from the labor of the servant, then the master is an "employer" within the A.R.S. § 23-902(A) definition, *supra*, notwithstanding the place where the servant works or the nature of his duties. On the other hand, if the master is the sole consumer of the servant's labor, and that labor is directed to the construction, maintenance or repair of the master's private properties or care of the master's family, and that labor is not within the usual trade, business, profession or occupation of the master, then the servant is a "domestic servant" under the A.R.S. § 23-902(A) exemption.

This conclusion, we believe, is mandated by the familiar principle that the purpose of workmen's compensation is to place the burden of injury from industrial causes upon industry. *See Lewis v. Industrial Commission*, 93 Ariz. 324, 327, 380 P.2d 782, 783–84 (1963). Thus, in *Lewis*, a servant hired to remodel the master's residence for aesthetic pleasure and not for resale was held to be excluded from compensation coverage. Also, in *Cooper v. Industrial Commission*, 74 Ariz. 351, 355, 249 P.2d 142, 145 (1952), a part time yardman was not counted as an "employee" in determining his employer's status under the compensation law. In *Stephens v. Industrial Commission*, 26 Ariz. App. 192, 194, 547 P.2d 44, 46 (1976), a master who hired a servant to build a prefabricated personal residence was held not to be an "employer" under A.R.S. § 23-902(A). In *Torres v. Industrial Commission, supra*, a domestic servant was held exempt even though she worked several days a week at her employer's business. Finally, in *Johnson v. Industrial Commission, supra*, we affirmed an award finding that the employee with both inside and outside duties was an exempt domestic servant under the statute. It is upon the spirit of these cases that we rely for our definition of "domestic servant."

Having defined domestic service in this manner, we turn to the evidence of record presented herein. All testimony indicates that Mrs. Rector had no trade, business or occupation. She was simply a wealthy woman whose financial circumstances allowed her to own several personal residences. She employed her handyman as needed about these residences with no intent to exploit his labor by reselling the homes at a profit. Under these circumstances, we hold that the evidence supported the administrative law judge's determination that Mr. Griebel was a "domestic servant" under this exemption.

Petitioner contends that the mere fact that Mrs. Rector loaned her servant to her fiance Mr. Dayton was enough to take Mr. Griebel out of the domestic servant category. This might be true, if Mr. Dayton had intended to exploit Mr. Griebel's labor for financial gain. The record shows, however, that Mr. Dayton's mining claim was not even a saleable piece of property; it had no value except as a recreational home for the Daytons. Thus, Mr. Griebel was no less a domestic servant in Mr. Dayton's service than in Mrs. Rector's. Further, the evidence did not establish that Mr. Griebel was traveling to Mr. Dayton's mining claim at the time he was killed.

On review, we find that the findings of the administrative law judge were supported

---

[16] *(Court's footnote)* Larson, in his treatise, considers the following cases:

The courts have consistently held that compensation acts do not apply in such instances. The examples that can be drawn from decided cases cover a range as varied as the hypothetical cases just suggested: a carpenter helping to build or remodel the employer's own residence; a practical nurse called in to look after the employer's husband; a handyman working on a country estate; a plasterer redecorating the employer's home; a carpenter building a chicken coop on the employer's residential premises; a caretaker looking after a summer home for the owner; a horse trainer working for an owner of a private stable; a chauffeur repairing the owner's car; a repairman fixing a leak in the roof of the employer's house; a man sawing logs for the use of himself and his neighbors; a man helping a farmer store ice for the farmer's own use; a painter painting a barn on the employer's residential premises; and a gamekeeper employed by the lessee of hunting privileges to guard against poaching. (Footnotes omitted).

by the evidence and the law of Arizona.[17] Therefore, the award is affirmed.

CONTRERAS and FROEB, JJ., concur.

§ 13.03   CASUAL EMPLOYMENT NOT IN COURSE OF USUAL BUSINESS

Employment is "casual" when it is irregular, unpredictable, sporadic, and brief in nature. Under most statutes, even if casual, it is not exempt unless it is also outside the usual business of the employer. Under this test, most maintenance and repair activities, as well as even remodeling and incidental construction, have been held to be within the usual course of a business.

Since the keeping of accounts and payroll records, the systematic provision of insurance, and the proof of past earnings all assume regular and sustained employment, about three-fifths of the states have felt it necessary for administrative reasons to attempt some exemption of "casual" employment.[18] Most states, but not all, apply the exemption only when the employment is both casual and outside the usual business of the employer.

PROBLEMS

(1) The classical theory that householders and other nonbusiness employers should be exempt from workers' compensation because they do not have a "product" through which to pass the cost of compensation insurance to the consuming public does not enjoy universal acceptance. *See, e.g.*, Riesenfeld, Forty Years of Workmen's Compensation, 7 NACCA L.J. 15, 20. Appraise the merits of this theory in the light of contemporary conditions and expectations.

(2) Is a church a "business"? *See* Gardner v. Trustees of Main St. Episcopal Church, 217 Iowa 1390, 250 N.W. 740 (1933), in which the court recalled that early in his career the Head of the Christian Church said, "I must be about my Father's business."

(3) Is the student manager of the football team at Northeast Louisiana University an employee? *See* Shepard v. Louisiana Power & Light Co., Inc., 369 So. 2d 1196 (La. App. 1979).

(4) Claimant, a 70-year-old woman on Social Security, earned about $700 a year as a baby-sitter. She had worked for the defendant on eight occasions over a period of two months, because of the defendant's recent move to a new home. She was staying with the children for a five-day period when she was injured. The statute excludes casual employment, defining it, if it is not in connection with the employer's "business," as "employment not regular, periodic or recurring. . . . " Compensable? *See* Herritt v. McKenna, 77 N.J. Super. 409, 186 A.2d 694 (1962).

§ 13.04   MINIMUM NUMBER OF EMPLOYEES

Under numerical-minimum exemption statutes, the controlling number of employees is determined in the light of the employer's established mode or plan in the operation of its business. If it regularly employs the requisite number, the employer remains covered although the number employed falls temporarily below the minimum. Ordinarily only such employees as would themselves be subject to the act are included in the count. Details of interpretation should be controlled by the underlying purpose of the exemption, which is to avoid administrative inconvenience to very small employers.

---

[17] *(Court's footnote)* Because of our disposition of this appeal, we need not address the alternative finding that Mrs. Griebel waived her right to workmen's compensation by the unauthorized settlement of third party liability.

[18] Ch. 13, § 13.02[2] n.9, *above*.

Typically, the critical number of employees, under which an employer is exempt, is three (*e.g.*, North Carolina and Virginia[19]), four (*e.g.*, Rhode Island), or five (*e.g.*, Florida, Mississippi, and Tennessee). There are sometimes "exceptions to the exception"; for example, in Florida, the minimum does not apply in the construction industry, where all employers who employ one or more employees are covered.

In most states, employers of one or more employees are covered. However, in some of these states a "small employer" exception is geared to the size of the payroll. For example, in Kansas, employers are exempt if they have not had payroll for the preceding year, and anticipate a payroll of the less than $20,000. Similarly, in South Carolina employers with a total payroll in the previous year of less than $3,000 are not covered.

Also there are other limited purpose exceptions, such as those in Illinois,[20] and Michigan.[21]

§ 13.05   FARM LABOR

The exemption of farm labor is construed according to the character of the work regularly performed by the employee, not according to the nature of the employer's business. But if a process performed on the farm is merely the first stage in the processing of a commodity by an industrial employer, such as a cannery or sugar refinery, the work may be held nonagricultural. Excessive specialization, commercialization, or marketing by the farmer may cause the work to lose its agricultural standing. Occasional excursions into or out of agricultural duties are disregarded when the employee by virtue of his regular employment has status as either a covered or exempt employee.

As previously noted, about a fifth of the states generally exclude farm or agricultural labor.[22]

The particular conditions limiting agricultural coverage in other states vary widely, sometimes, for example excluding employees with less than a certain amount of

---

[19] Uninsured Employer's Fund v. Gabriel, 272 Va. 659, 636 S.E.2d 408 (2006). The decedent and Preble formed a management consulting firm and incorporated the business in Virginia, where decedent lived at the time. The decedent was named president and treasurer of the company. Preble, who lived in Massachusetts, was named Vice-President and Secretary. The corporation conducted the bulk of their business in airports and clients' offices and used laptop computers. Financial and corporate records were maintained in Virginia, at a home office of decedent. The corporation also employed two other employees, one in Virginia, who assisted decedent, and one in Massachusetts, who assisted Preble.

The decedent was a passenger on the plane that struck the Pentagon in the terrorist attacks of September 11, 2001. The corporation did not maintain a policy of workers' compensation insurance at the time of decedent's death. The issue was whether Preble was "regularly in service" in Virginia. If he was not, then the corporation was not required to have insurance and, under appropriate circumstances, the uninsured fund would not be liable for death benefits. The court of appeals affirmed a finding that Preble had sufficient contacts to be considered "regularly in service" in Virginia. For the limited facts of the case, the court held that a presumption existed that a corporate officer and director of a Virginia corporation had sufficient corporate responsibilities to be regularly in service within the state.

On further appeal, however, the state supreme court reversed. The evidence suggested that Preble had been in Virginia only four times. The court indicated further that Preble's status as an officer did not render him "regularly in service" within the state. Since the corporation did not have three employees regularly in service within the Commonwealth, the Commission had no jurisdiction over the matter.

[20] A numerical exemption of two or less employees applies for "carriage by land, water, or aerial service and loading or unloading in connection therewith."

[21] A numerical exemption of three or less employees applies unless at least one is employed by the same employer for thirty-five hours per week for thirteen weeks or longer during the preceding fifty-two weeks.

[22] Ch. 13, § 13.02[2] n.11, *above.*

Other countries, such as Great Britain, France, and Germany, generally cover farm labor.

earnings.[23] In addition, a few states cover agricultural workers in certain circumstances, most commonly when employed in hazardous work or in the use of machinery or power equipment.

Of course, under most acts it is possible for the employer to elect compensation coverage even if exempt, and in actual practice many of those who employ farm labor on a large scale have found it advisable to follow this course.

Many reasons, of varying degrees of validity, have been given to explain the agricultural exemption. The principal one is the practical administrative difficulty that would be encountered by hundreds of thousands of small farmers in handling the necessary records, insurance, and accounting. If this is the reason, it ought to follow that the exemption should be confined to small farmers and not at the same time relieve from compensation responsibility the great fruit, truck, sugarcane, dairy, and wheat farms which have much more in common with industry than with old-fashioned dirt farming.

Less convincing is the argument that the farmer cannot, like the manufacturer, add his compensation cost to the price of his product and pass it on to the consumer. This might be true if an isolated state attempted compulsory coverage, but if all states extended coverage to farm labor, there would be no competitive disadvantage so far as the domestic market is concerned.

Least convincing of all is the assertion that farm laborers do not need this kind of protection. Whatever the compensation acts may say, agriculture is one of the most hazardous of all occupations. In 1964, of 4,761,000 agricultural workers, 3,000 were fatally injured, while of 17,259,000 manufacturing employees, the number of fatalities was 2,000.

It is important to ask what valid reason lies behind the exemption, in order to have some guide in construing the notoriously troublesome terms "farm" and "agriculture."

HINSON v. CREECH
286 N.C. 156, 209 S.E.2d 471 (1974)

On 3 December 1971 deceased, Nannie Mae Hinson, was fatally injured in a motor vehicle accident while operating a truck belonging to her employers and while she was engaged in delivering eggs for her employers.

Plaintiff, the surviving spouse and administrator of the estate of the decedent, filed notice of the accident with the employers pursuant to G.S. § 97-22 and filed claim with the Industrial Commission as required by G.S. § 97-24. On 30 May 1972, a hearing was held before Chief Deputy Commissioner Delbridge of the Industrial Commission.

The uncontradicted evidence presented at the hearing showed that defendants John W. Creech and wife Jean Creech, trading as Eugene Jackson Egg Service (employers), were engaged in the production and sale of eggs. Employers bought baby chicks and raised them until they began laying eggs, and when the hens were no longer productive, they were removed from the premises. There were twelve laying houses on the premises, and defendants had purchased a $5,000 egg grader. The eggs were cleaned, graded, and packaged on premises leased by employers and were then delivered to various customers, including stores, restaurants, institutions, and individuals. Brokers also purchased eggs from employers and transported them from the premises. Employers purchased all the chicken feed used in the operation. They also raised hogs on the premises.

Decedent's duties consisted of cleaning, grading, packaging, and delivering eggs. She also kept records of sales and collected for the eggs that she delivered.

It was stipulated that decedent was employed by employers and received an average weekly wage of $50. It was further stipulated that decedent died as a result of injuries

---

[23] *E.g.*, Washington.

sustained in an automobile-truck wreck on 3 December 1971; that on that date employers had five or more employees; and that employers had no Workmen's Compensation Insurance. Evidence was submitted concerning decedent's medical and burial expenses.

After finding facts substantially in accord with the above-recited evidence and stipulations, Chief Deputy Delbridge concluded that "[t]he defendants are engaged in an agricultural pursuit, and the employees of the defendants, including the deceased employee, Nannie Mae Hinson, are farm laborers. The defendants are exempt from the North Carolina Workmen's Compensation Act. . . ."

The claim was dismissed, and plaintiff appealed to the full Commission for further review. The full Commission adopted the opinion and award of Chief Deputy Commissioner Delbridge as its own and affirmed the results of the opinion and award. Plaintiff appealed from the award and opinion of the full Commission, and the North Carolina Court of Appeals affirmed. We allowed plaintiff's petition for writ of certiorari to review the decision of the Court of Appeals on 30 August 1974. . . .

BRANCH, JUSTICE.

We first consider whether plaintiff's intestate was a farm laborer within the meaning of G.S. § 97-13(b), which provides, in relevant part: "This Article shall not apply to . . . farm laborers. . . ."

The "farm labor" exemption has generally received a more narrow interpretation than the exemption of "agricultural labor" from the definition of employment under the various Workmen's Compensation Acts. 99 C.J.S. Workmen's Compensation § 33, page 195; *Gwin v. J. W. Vestal & Son*, 205 Ark. 742, 170 S.W.2d 598. Whether an employee is a farm laborer depends, in a large degree, upon the nearness of his occupation to the planting, cultivation, and harvesting of crops. *Mulanix v. Falen*, 64 Idaho 293, 130 P.2d 866; *see* Note, 16 Tex. L. Rev. 608. In considering the question of whether an employee is a farm laborer, a majority of the jurisdictions have placed emphasis upon the nature of the employee's work rather than upon the nature of the employer's business. 1A A. Larson, The Law of Workmen's Compensation § 53.31.

The prevailing rule is aptly stated in *H.J. Heinz Co. v. Chavez*, 236 Ind. 400, 140 N.E.2d 500:

> . . . [A]lthough the character of the 'employment' of an employee must be determined from the 'whole character' of his employment and not upon the particular work he is performing at the time of his injury, nevertheless the coverage of an employee under the Act is dependent upon the character of the work he is hired to perform and not upon the nature and scope of his employer's business. . . .

Accord, Bob White Packing Co. v. Hardy, 340 S.W.2d 245 *(Ky.)*; *Peterson v. Farmers State Bank*, 180 Minn. 40, 230 N.W. 124.

In reaching its decision, the Court of Appeals relied heavily upon *Department of Labor and Industries v. McLain*, 66 Wash. 2d 54, 401 P.2d 211. There the Court held that a chicken farm constituted "farming" within the meaning of the Washington statute. *McLain* is factually distinguishable from instant case in that there the claimant was on the premises of the farm shoveling snow from the roof of a chicken house. The duty that he performed was obviously a necessary farm chore connected with the raising of chickens and production of eggs.

The Court of Appeals also relied upon *Fleckles v. Hille*, 83 Ind.App. 715, 149 N.E. 915, which stated that agriculture includes the "raising, feeding and management of livestock and poultry," and upon *Davis v. Industrial Commission*, 59 Utah 607, 206 P. 267, which contains the following language: "Every standard authority that defines the word "agriculture' includes in the definition the rearing and care of live-stock."

We have no quarrel with the holdings in these cases; however, they furnish no authority for decision of the question here presented. In instant case there is no evidence that plaintiff's intestate was ever engaged in duties which included the "raising, feeding, care and management of livestock or poultry." To the contrary, the uncontradicted evidence shows that plaintiff's intestate regularly used employers' automobile to deliver employers' eggs to retail customers on a regularly maintained schedule. Her other duties consisted of cleaning, grading, and packaging the eggs. She also kept records and collected for the eggs delivered to various retail customers, including stores, restaurants, institutions, and individuals.

We hold that the duties of plaintiff's intestate were sufficiently removed from the normal process of agriculture to prevent her exclusion from coverage under the Workmen's Compensation Act as a "farm laborer."

We next turn to the question of whether the employment relationship under the facts of this case constituted agriculture within the meaning of G.S. § 97-2(1), which exempts "agriculture" from the definition of "employment" under the Workmen's Compensation Act.

Traditionally, agriculture has been broadly defined as "the science or art of cultivating the soil and its fruits, especially in large areas or fields, and the rearing, feeding, and management of livestock thereon, including every process and step necessary and incident to the completion of products therefrom for consumption or market and the *incidental* turning of them to account." 3 Am. Jur. 2d Agriculture § 1 (emphasis supplied); *see Keeney v. Beasman*, 169 Md. 582, 182 A. 566. This traditional definition has been extended to encompass the storage and marketing of agricultural products. *H. Duys & Co. v. Tone*, 125 Conn. 300, 5 A.2d 23; *Bucher v. American Fruit Growers Co.*, 107 Pa. Super. 399, 163 A. 33; *see generally* 3 C.J.S. Agriculture § 2. The same general definition of agriculture has obtained under the various Workmen's Compensation Acts, *see generally* 1A A. Larson, The Law of Workmen's Compensation § 53.30, and at least one court has construed such a definition to include egg-producing operations. *Department of Labor & Industries v. McLain, supra.*

It must be recognized that the line of demarcation between agricultural and non-agricultural employment often becomes "extremely attenuated." *Mulanix v. Falen, supra; see generally* 1A A. Larson, The Law of Workmen's Compensation § 53.33 and cases there cited. The question in marginal factual situations must frequently turn upon whether the employment is a separable, commercial enterprise rather than a purely agricultural undertaking. *See* Davis, Death of a Hired Man, 13 S.D.L. Rev. 1.

In *Crouse v. Lloyd's Turkey Ranch*, 251 Iowa 156, 100 N.W.2d 115, defendant was engaged in business under a trade name and operated a turkey and chicken operation on a six-acre tract. When the poultry was ready for market, he processed about half the turkeys by slaughtering and dressing them in his own processing plant located on the premises. Plaintiff, a seasonal worker in the processing plant, was injured when she slipped on the floor in the processing plant and brought an action to recover Workmen's Compensation benefits. The Court held that the employee was not engaged in agriculture within the meaning of the agricultural exclusion. Although the Iowa statute contains wording somewhat different from our own, we nevertheless consider the reasoning helpful in instant case. The Court there stated a test for inclusion in doubtful situations:

> The determination of where agriculture stops and commercial processing begins is not easy. The defendant thought it more profitable to process as many of his turkeys as he could sell; but this is no way answers the question. Grains must be harvested, and fruits and vegetables must be garnered and put in condition for marketing; and these are properly a part of agriculture. But the problem before us goes one step further. It involves the question of a process, not necessary but perhaps more profitable, in marketing. . . .

In *Barbour v. State Hospital*, 213 N.C. 515, 196 S.E. 812, a State employee suffered fatal injuries while driving a tractor in the cultivation of food crops on State land. His representative filed a claim with the North Carolina Industrial Commission, and defendant contended that it was exempt from the provisions of the Workmen's Compensation Act. The full Commission ruled in favor of plaintiff, and the Superior Court, in affirming the award of the full Commission, *inter alia*, concluded " . . . [t]hat the statute's exemption of farm laborers was intended for the protection of farmers as an occupational class, and a farm laborer in contemplation of the statute is a man hired to till the soil or do other agricultural work by one whose occupation is that of a farmer. . . . "

In affirming the opinion and award of the full Commission, this Court stated:

> . . . The question involved: Is the death of a State employee, arising out of and in the course of his employment, while driving a tractor in the cultivation of food crops on the lands of the State used by the State Hospital at Raleigh compensable under the Workmen's Compensation Act? We think so.
>
> This and other courts of the United States have held that the various compensation acts should be liberally construed so that the benefits thereof should not be denied upon technical, narrow and strict interpretation. The primary consideration is compensation for injured employees. We think the judgment of the court below correct — that the State Hospital employee, Tessie Barbour, deceased, was not a 'farm laborer' in contemplation of the statute.

The rule of liberal construction stated in *Barbour v. Hospital, supra*, is supported by a host of decisions in this jurisdiction. *See, e.g.*, Stevenson v. City of Durham, 281 N.C. 300, 188 S.E.2d 281; *Hollman v. City of Raleigh*, 273 N.C. 240, 159 S.E.2d 874; *Cates v. Construction Co.*, 267 N.C. 560, 148 S.E.2d 604; *Guest v. Iron & Metal Co.*, 241 N.C. 448, 85 S.E.2d 596. We concede that the production of eggs is an agricultural pursuit. Nevertheless, in the case *sub judice*, when employers formed a business association with a registered trade name and sought to increase the profits of the business by selling and delivering eggs over stated routes to stores, institutions, and individuals, they subjected their employee to the daily hazards of operating a motor vehicle upon the highways to places far removed from the farm. Applying the above-stated rule of liberal construction to the facts of this case, we conclude that employers' business ceased to be agriculture and became part and parcel of the activities of the marketplace.

By this decision we do not intend to hold that the ordinary marketing of produce by a farmer or the incidental sale of eggs, poultry, or other farm products should be in any way affected. It is only when a farmer departs from his agricultural pursuits and clearly enters into a service business or another business remote from the direct production of agricultural products that his services cease to be "agriculture" within the meaning of G.S. § 97-2(1).

We hold that the Court of Appeals erred in affirming the conclusion of law adopted by the full Commission that "[t]he defendants are engaged in an agricultural pursuit, and the employees of the defendants, including the deceased employee, Nannie Mae Hinson, are farm laborers. The defendants are exempt from the North Carolina Workmen's Compensation Act. . . . "

This cause is remanded to the Court of Appeals with direction that it be returned to the North Carolina Industrial Commission with order for entry of opinion and award in accord with this opinion.

Reversed and remanded.

BOBBITT, C. J., not sitting.

PROBLEMS

(1) Michigan at one time excluded seasonal farm laborers. This was attacked as unconstitutional on grounds, among others, that most seasonal farm workers were members of ethnic minorities. What result? *See* Gutierrez v. Glaser Crandell Co., 388 Mich. 654, 202 N.W.2d 786 (1972). *But cf.* Eastway v. Eisenga, 420 Mich. 410, 362 N.W.2d 684 (1984).

(2) The operator of a farm, who raised tobacco, hay, cattle, and thoroughbred yearlings, also boarded thoroughbred horses, which accounted for 73% of his income. Does the agricultural exemption apply? *See* Fitzpatrick v. Crestfield Farms, Inc., 582 S.W.2d 44 (Ky. App. 1978). How about running a mink farm? Collins v. Moyle, 83 Idaho 151, 358 P.2d 1035 (1961). A beekeeping and honey production operation with a thousand hives? Morel v. Thompson, 225 N.W.2d 584 (N.D. 1975). Breeding and raising hunting dogs. *See* Partello v. Stipa, 115 Idaho 522, 768 P.2d 785 (1989). Treating high quality cows so that they would super-ovulate and produce multiple embryos which could then be implanted in "surrogate mother" cows. 23 Ark. App. 58, 742 S.W. 2d 124 (1988).

§ 13.06   EXECUTIVES AND PARTNERS

Corporate officers are generally covered by workers' compensation, not only as to typical "employee" work but also as to managerial activities. However, when corporate office is combined with controlling stock ownership to such an extent that the corporation is in effect the alter ego of the stockholder, coverage is often denied, but even here an exception is sometimes made when the duties involved were typical "employee" duties. True members of a partnership, however, apart from a few special statutes, cannot be employees, even if they do extra work for which they receive payment beyond their share of the profits, since there is no separate business entity that can be called the employer, and since all partners normally have equal rights in management.

FRATERNAL ORDER OF EAGLES v. KIRBY
6 Ark. App. 198, 639 S.W.2d 529 (1982)

COOPER, JUDGE.

This is a workers' compensation case. Appellee was chairman of the Board of Trustees of the Fraternal Order of Eagles in Midway, Arkansas. As a trustee and chairman, he was required to attend meetings, oversee the general business activity of the lodge, and to take care of the lodge building. He was paid $1.00 per year. Appellee was injured on March 19, 1980, when he suffered a high voltage electrical shock while he was inspecting the roof of the lodge building for leaks. The administrative law judge found that the activity that appellee was doing at the time he was injured was expected and routine, and was an important part of the successful operation of the lodge. He further found that the injury arose out of and in the course of appellee's employment. The full Commission affirmed the administrative law judge's opinion, adopting it as their own. From that decision, comes this appeal.

On appeal, the appellants argue that there is no substantial evidence to support a finding that appellee was an employee at the time of the injury, or that the injury was causally connected to the incident. . . .

Arkansas Statutes Annotated § 81-1302(a) (Repl. 1976) defines "employer" as any individual, partnership, *association*, or corporation carrying on any employment. "Employment" is defined according to whether the employer has the minimum number of employees in order to subject that employer to the requirements of the Workers' Compensation Act. Ark. Stat. Ann. § 81-1302(c) (Repl.1976). Arkansas Statutes Annotated § 81-1302(b) (Supp. 1981) defines "employee" as:

> [A]ny person, including a minor, whether lawfully or unlawfully employed in the service of an employer under any contract of hire or apprenticeship, written or oral, expressed or implied, but excluding one whose employment is casual and not in the course of the trade, business, profession or occupation of his employer. The term "employee" shall also include a sole proprietor or a partner who devotes full time to the proprietorship or partnership and who elects to be included in the definition of "employee" by filing written notice thereof with the Division of Worker's Compensation. . . .

Ordinarily, whether a person is an "employee" can be determined by the position that person occupies and its relationship to the alleged employer. However, in those cases where a person occupies more than one position, it becomes necessary to consider the type of work that was actually being done by that person at the time of his injury. *See Brook's Inc. v. Claywell*, 215 Ark. 913, 224 S.W.2d 37 (1949).

In 1B A. Larson, The Law of Workmen's Compensation § 54.21 (1979), Professor Larson discusses the circumstances under which a corporate officer can be found to be an employee and then states:

> With very little difficulty, the courts also extended coverage to corporation officers when their duties were of a *supervisory character*, such as those of a foreman, superintendent of construction, superintendent of a department, and even, with near unanimity, a *general manager*, since these are all jobs that, in ordinary circumstances, would make the holder an employee. [Emphasis added.]

This Court has quoted the above section with approval in *Continental Ins. Co. v. Richard*, 268 Ark. 671, 596 S.W.2d 332 (Ark. App. 1980), and *Benefield Real Estate v. Mitchell*, 269 Ark. 607, 599 S.W.2d 445 (Ark. App. 1980).

We believe that the standard we have applied to corporate officers is likewise applicable to the executive officers of associations, at least where the sole question is whether the officer is an "employee."[24]

At the time of injury, appellee and the roofer were on the roof of the lodge building attempting to find a leak in the roof. While examining the roof, appellee came in contact with an air conditioning unit. The appellee suffered an electrical shock from the unit, and immediately left the roof. The type of work that appellee was performing at the time of his injury, is generally associated with the duties of a general manager. Therefore, we affirm the Commission's decision which finds that the appellee was an employee.[25]

---

[24] *(Court's footnote)* We realize that the liability of members in a partnership and an association are similar in some ways, and that a partner cannot be an "employee" of a partnership, unless an election has been made to be included as such under the definition. See Brinkey Heavy Hauling Co. v. Youngman, 223 Ark. 74, 264 S.W.2d 409 (1954); Ark. Stat. Ann. § 81-1302(b) (Supp. 1981). However, it is not argued before this Court that the appellee cannot be an "employee" of the association because at once he is an employer and an employee, and thus a contradiction of liability. It should be pointed out that the Youngman case was decided by the Arkansas Supreme Court in 1954, with four justices in the majority and three justices dissenting.

[25] *(Court's footnote)* The only argument presented in this Court against appellee's status as an employee, was that he was performing executive or supervisory duties at the time of his injury. No question has been raised as to the existence of a "contract of hire."

. . . .

HAYS v. WORKERS' COMPENSATION DIVISION
768 P.2d 11 (Wyo. 1989)

MACY, JUSTICE.

In this worker's compensation case, appellant Martin L. Hays, deceased, through his surviving widow and children, appeals from the denial of his motion for a new trial and for relief from judgment under W.R.C.P. 59 and 60.

We affirm.

Appellant presents the following issues:

1. Whether a partner whose business is classed as extrahazardous is an "employee" as defined by W.S. § 27-12-102(a)(viii)(1977 Repub. Ed.) and, therefore, entitled to coverage under the Wyoming Worker's Compensation Act if injured while actually subject to the hazards of the business.

2. If the Wyoming Worker's Compensation Act is construed to deny coverage to a partner, does that construction deny equal protection of the law, in violation of the Fourteenth Amendment of the United States Constitution and Article 1, § 34 of the Wyoming Constitution.

On October 25, 1986, appellant fell from a scraper that he was cutting into scrap metal with a blow torch. He suffered fatal head injuries and died within a few hours of the fall.

On December 8, 1986, appellant's widow, Tammy S. Hays, filed an employee's report of injury, alleging that appellant was a laborer for Hays Transportation Co. and that his death was a result of his employment. This report was followed by an application for death benefits filed by Mrs. Hays on December 30, 1986, on behalf of herself and appellant's two minor children. The district court approved the application and on January 12, 1987, awarded an aggregate sum of $ 100,223.05 in death benefits plus costs of the last hospitalization and funeral service for appellant. . . .

Appellant's representatives assert that, despite his status as a partner, he was nevertheless an employee and, therefore, he and his survivors are entitled to benefits under the Act. To recover death benefits under the Act, the decedent must have been an "employee" involved in extrahazardous work as that term was defined in § 27-12-102(a)(viii). Thus, the first question to be addressed is whether a member of a partnership, the business of which was classified as extrahazardous, was an "employee" within the meaning of § 27-12-102(a)(viii). This determination involves the statutory interpretation of § 27-12-102(a)(viii). Our rules of statutory interpretation have often been cited and need not be reiterated here except to note that, when a statute is clear and unambiguous, this Court will not resort to rules of statutory construction and the words will be given their plain and ordinary meaning. *State Board of Equalization v. Jackson Hole Ski Corporation*, 737 P.2d 350, on reh'g 745 P.2d 58 (Wyo. 1987), *Wyoming Insurance Department v. Avemco Insurance Company*, 726 P.2d 507 (Wyo. 1986).

Section 27-12-102(a)(viii) defined an "employee" as

any person who has entered into the employment of or works under contract of services or apprenticeship with an employer engaged in an extrahazardous occupation, except a person whose employment is purely casual and not for the purpose of the employer's usual trade or business, or those engaged in clerical work and not subject to the hazards of the business. "Employee" also includes the officers of a corporation, the business of which is classed as extrahazardous, if the officers are actually subject to the hazards of the business in the regular performance of their duties, and the employer elects to come under the provisions of a this act by notifying the division by registered mail at least thirty

(30) days prior to the effective date of the coverage. Coverage remains effective until withdrawn by written notice to the division. Any reference to an employee who has been injured and dies, includes his dependents or his legal representatives, or his guardian or next friend if the employee is a minor or incompetent. No minor employee shall be denied the benefits of this act for the sole reason that his employment is in violation of the labor laws governing the employment of minors[.]

The plain and unambiguous language of § 27-12-102(a)(viii) mandates the conclusion that partners could not receive benefits as "employees" under the Act. The language specifically defined an "employee" as one who had "entered into the employment of or works under contract of services or apprenticeship with an employer." To accept appellant's argument that a partner was an employee under the Act would be to ignore the plain language of § 27-12-102(a)(viii) and the legal characteristics of a partner. The language of the statute clearly anticipated that an employer and employee would be separate legal entities. Thus, a partner-employer could not be included in the language of the statute as one covered under the Act, as the Act was intended to cover employees only. Although this Court has held that worker's compensation statutes are to be construed so that industry, rather than an injured workman, bears the burden of an industrial accident, *Robinson v. Bell*, 767 P.2d 177 (Wyo. 1989), we nevertheless are not permitted to ignore clear statutory language so as to extend coverage and benefits to situations that do not reasonably fall within the intended ambit of the statutes. *Lehman v. State ex rel. Wyoming Workers' Compensation Division*, 752 P.2d 422 (Wyo. 1988). Here, the statutory language cannot be construed so as to extend employee benefits to a partner/employer.

. . . .

Benefits for injuries to partners have traditionally been denied under worker's compensation acts because of the legal characteristics of partners and partnerships. A partnership is not an entity separate from its partners. 1C A. Larson, *supra* at § 54.31. "Therefore, since the partnership is nothing more than the aggregate of the individuals making it up, a partner-employee would also be an employer." *Id.* at 9-253, quoted in *Ryder's Case*, 341 Mass. 661, 171 N.E.2d 475, 477–78 (1961). The worker's compensation acts cannot be presumed to have envisioned any such combination of employer and employee. . . .

In view of the overwhelming weight of authority and the clear and unambiguous language of the statute, we align ourselves with the majority of jurisdictions in holding that members of a partnership, the business of which was classified as extrahazardous, were not employees as that term was defined in § 27-12-102(a)(viii) and, therefore, were not entitled to compensation under the Wyoming Worker's Compensation Act for injuries received while they were actually subjected to the hazards of the business.

Appellant argues that, if § 27-12-102(a)(viii) is construed to mean that partners were not "employees" under the Act and thereby were not entitled to the Act's benefits, then § 27-12-102(a)(viii) violated the Equal Protection Clauses of the Fourteenth Amendment to the United States Constitution and article 1, section 34 of the Wyoming Constitution. Appellant makes this argument on the basis that, in the statute's specific classification, officers of a corporation were "employees" entitled to receive benefits under the Act while members of a partnership were not classified as such. [*(Court's footnote)* Wyo. Const. art. 1, § 34 provides for equal protection in the following language:

All laws of a general nature shall have a uniform operation.] . . .

The Equal Protection Clauses of the Fourteenth Amendment of the United States Constitution and article 1, section 34 of the Wyoming Constitution guarantee that "similar people will be dealt with similarly and that people in different circumstances will not be treated as though they were similar." *Bell*, 693 P.2d at 771. In an attempt to fulfill the burden to show that no rational basis existed for the different treatment of officers of a corporation as opposed to members of a partnership, appellant argues that the legal distinctions between officers and partners were not sufficient to permit unequal treatment under the statute. We do not agree.

A corporation has a separate legal existence, distinct from its officers. The corporation, as a separate entity, is the employer, and the officers are employees. *Barnette v. Doyle*, 622 P.2d 1349 (Wyo. 1981). A partnership, however, is fundamentally unlike a corporation. A partnership is merely the aggregate of the individuals comprising it, and it is not an entity distinct from its members. 1C A. Larson, *supra* at § 54.31. The partners' status is one of both employer and employee. Professor Larson has observed that, in cases

> in which a partner (or someone claiming compensation on the strength of his status) is the claimant, . . . the almost insuperable conceptual obstacle is encountered of having the same person appear as employer and employee.

Id. at 9-255. Thus, an officer of a corporation and a member of a partnership are not similarly situated. A partner is an employer and employee, whereas an officer is simply an employee. A rational basis exists, therefore, for the disparate treatment afforded under the Act to partners as opposed to corporate officers, and appellant's equal protection challenge of the statute must fail.

We hold that a member of a partnership was not an employee within the definition of § 27-12-102(a)(viii) and was not entitled to benefits under the Wyoming Worker's Compensation Act. Further, appellant has failed to demonstrate that the Act unconstitutionally discriminates between partners and corporate officers in such a manner as to offend the Equal Protection Clauses of United States and Wyoming Constitutions.

Affirmed. . . .

§ 13.07   PUBLIC EMPLOYMENT

Most states now make compensation available to public employees, but of these the majority exclude "officials." Officials are usually distinguished from employees in that they exercise some portion of sovereign power.

BOLIN v. KITSAP COUNTY
114 Wash. 2d 70, 785 P.2d 805 (1990)

UTTER, JUSTICE.

Bjorn Viking Bolin, appellant in this matter, seeks compensation under the Industrial Insurance Act for injuries incurred while returning home from jury service. The Board of Industrial Insurance Appeals reversed a proposed decision in Bolin's favor by an industrial appeals judge and found no coverage. The trial court, in turn, affirmed the board's decision. We reverse the trial court and find that Bolin is covered under the Industrial Insurance Act and is entitled to compensation.

Bjorn Bolin served as a juror for the Superior Court for Kitsap County. On April 18, 1984, following jury service, he drove directly home and was seriously injured in an automobile accident enroute. Kitsap County paid Bolin $ 14.35 for mileage at the rate of 20.5 cents per mile, and $ 10 per day for jury service.

This appeal presents two issues — whether Bolin was an employee of Kitsap County when serving as a juror, and whether Bolin was injured in the course of his employment. We find that he was an employee of Kitsap County while serving as a juror and that the car accident occurred in the course of his employment.

The liberality of Washington's workers' compensation statute forces the conclusion that jury service is employment under the act. Washington's workers' compensation law defines "employee" to include "all officers of the state . . . counties . . . or political subdivisions" and all workers. RCW 51.08.185. The statute defines "every person . . . in the employment of an employer" as a worker. RCW 51.08.180. Our act states:

There is a hazard in all employment and it is the purpose of this title to embrace all employments which are within the legislative jurisdiction of the state.

This title shall be liberally construed for the purpose of reducing to a minimum the suffering and economic loss arising from injuries and/or death occurring in the course of employment. RCW 51.12.010. Unlike many states which list or define employments *included*, our act lists only employments *excluded*. *See* RCW 51.12.020. Jury service is not within the list of those employments excluded. In addition, our Industrial Insurance Act has been construed liberally, subject to reasonable limitations. *Scott v. Department of Labor & Indus.*, 77 Wn.2d 888, 890, 468 P.2d 440 (1970), *Sacred Heart Med. Ctr. v. Carrado*, 92 Wn.2d 631, 635, 600 P.2d 1015 (1979).

The question of whether jurors are covered differs from most other workers' compensation issues inasmuch as jurors are involuntary workers, rather than workers subject to traditional employment relationships based on consent of both parties. We have implicitly held that involuntary service may be employment under the *Industrial Insurance Act. See Rector v. Cherry Valley Timber Co.*, 115 Wash. 31, 196 P. 653 (1921) (holding that a soldier ordered to work on private land was voluntarily employed, covered by workers' compensation, and barred from common law remedies). The view that jurors are not covered because their employment is involuntary cannot be reconciled with the cases in this jurisdiction and those of our sister states that citizens impressed into various kinds of civic service may recover. *Accord* Note, Jurors as Nonvoluntary Employees under Workmen's Compensation Law, 74 Dick. L. Rev. 334–46 (1969).

Because Bolin's entire service was involuntary, this court's recent decision in *Novenson v. Spokane Culvert & Fabricating Co.*, 91 Wn.2d 550, 588 P.2d 1174 (1979) does not control this case. In *Novenson*, this court enunciated a 2-part test to determine whether an employment relationship existed for purposes of the Industrial Insurance Act. We held that "an employment relationship exists only when: (1) the employer has the right to control the servant's physical conduct in the performance of his duties, and (2) there is consent by the employee to this relationship." *Novenson*, at 553.

Novenson dealt with a question substantially different from that before the court in this case. The plaintiff there worked for a temporary agency, Kelly Labor of Northwest, Inc., which assigned him to Spokane Culvert. While working at Spokane Culvert's plant he injured his hands. He collected workers' compensation from Kelly Labor, and then sued Spokane Culvert. Spokane Culvert obtained summary judgment as an employer covered by workers' compensation and therefore immune from tort suit.

On appeal this court reversed, stating that a worker has an election of remedies when injured by one "not in the same employ." *Novenson*, at 552. That case revolved around the nature of liability between an employer and a third party, the issue then before the court. For those purposes, the law requires the employee's consent, lest an employment relationship be implied without his consent to deprive him of his right to sue at common law. In that context, consent is necessary.

In cases involving jurors, however, the claimant has no common law remedy. The doctrine of judicial immunity still protects the county and the state from tort liability for the acts of judicial and quasi-judicial officials. *Creelman v. Svenning*, 67 Wn.2d 882, 885, 410 P.2d 606 (1966). To apply the *Novenson* consent requirement to the facts of this case does not serve the purpose the *Novenson* court sought. It does not protect the claimant from involuntarily relinquishing his rights, but instead deprives him of his only means of redress.

. . . .

Numerous cases in other states have held that workers' compensation does not cover jurors (*itations omitted*). These cases are not persuasive. As we have previously indicated, many states' statutes list or define the employments included our state lists only employments excluded. . . .

This court must interpret Washington's statute, not those of other states. Under the language, statutory scheme, and cases construing our act, we conclude that jurors are employees. The more difficult question is whether jurors are employees of the county.

Jurors are employees of the county by virtue of their responsibility to the superior court. Superior court judges are officials of both the state and county as this court has repeatedly held. *See In re Salary of Superior Court Judges*, 82 Wash. 623, 144 P. 929 (1914) *State ex rel. Edelstein v. Foley*, Wn.2d 444, 448, 107 P.2d 901 (1940) *State ex rel. Lawler v. Grant*, 178 Wash. 61, 34 P.2d 355 (1934) *State ex rel. Pischue v. Olson*, 173 Wash. 60, 65, 21 P.2d 516 (1933). *See also Neal v. Wallace*, 15 Wn. App. 506, 508, 550 P.2d 539 (1976) (prosecuting attorney represents judge in mandamus action because the judge is a county and state officer). The county pays half of their salaries, and the county pays all of the costs of providing them with bailiffs, sheriffs, and the like.

Respondents have pointed out that this court's decision in *Kildall v. King Cy.*, 120 Wash. 472, 207 P. 681 (1922) supports the conclusion that the county is not the juror's employer. In that case, this court held that the county was not liable in tort for a bailiff's negligence because it exercised no control over the bailiff. Respondents urge that we apply the reasoning of this case by analogy to jurors. The judge, not the county commissioners, controls both the juror and the bailiff.

The *Kildall* court's holding must be examined in the context of the tort setting in which it arose. In that context, judicial immunity requires that the court hold neither the county nor the judge liable on a theory of a respondent superior for torts. *See Kildall*, 120 Wash. at 476.

When the juror seeks workers' compensation, the purposes of the statute are better served by treating the county as the juror's employer. A judge is not a servant of the county, as the *Kildall* court pointed out. This precludes holding the county liable in tort for a judge's actions or those of a juror under his control. But a judge is an official of the county as well as of the state, and jurors under a superior court judge's control are county employees for purposes of the Industrial Insurance Act.

The sole remaining issue is whether Mr. Bolin was injured in the course of his employment. Mr. Bolin was injured while returning directly to his home after a day of jury service. Under Washington's statute, employees receive compensation only for injuries "in the course of . . . employment." RCW 51.32.010. Thus, Bolin can only receive workers' compensation if his travel to his home was within the course of employment as a juror.

The statute defines acting in the course of employment as "acting at his or her employer's direction or in the furtherance of his or her employer's business". RCW 51.08.013.

Generally speaking, a worker's commuting is not in the course of his employment. *See Aloha Lumber Corp. v. Department of Labor & Indus.*, 77 Wn.2d 763, 766, 466 P.2d 151 (1970); *Westinghouse Elec. Corp. v. Department of Labor & Indus.*, 94 Wash. 2d 875, 880, 621 P.2d 147 (1980). An exception exists, however, when the employer has a customary or contractual obligation to furnish the transportation. *See Westinghouse*, 94 Wash. 2d at 880, 621 P.2d 147. If the employer has such an obligation, commuting injuries may be within the scope of employment, regardless of whether the employer fulfills his obligation directly, or by compensating the employee for transportation expenses. *See Aloha*, 77 Wash. 2d at 772, 466 P.2d 151; *Westinghouse*, 94 Wash. 2d at 880, 621 P.2d 147.[*(Court's footnote)* The Westinghouse decision dealt with two cases in which union contracts provided for reimbursement for mileage. See *N.A. Degerstrom, Inc. v. Department of Labor & Indus.*, 25 Wn. App. 97, 604 P.2d 1337 (1980), *overruled, Westinghouse*, 94 Wn.2d at 882 *Westinghouse Elec. Corp. v. Department of Labor &*

Indus., 25 Wn. App. 103, 604 P.2d 1334 (1980), *aff'd, Westinghouse*, 94 Wn.2d at 882.]

The Court of Appeals in *Degerstrom* held that a contractual provision providing transportation expressly as a fringe benefit did not bring commuting within the course of employment. *Westinghouse* overruled this holding and placed great weight on the contractual nature of the obligation to provide transportation expenses.

Kitsap County did not have a contractual obligation. It did have a statutory obligation created by RCW 2.36.150, which establishes a custom of paying jurors' transportation. This is sufficient to bring Bolin's accident within the scope of employment.[26]

Compensation for mileage benefits the recipient. The question then regarding whether there was a mutual benefit must focus on the benefit to the payor. Jurors can be excused from service upon a showing of "undue hardship" or "extreme inconvenience." RCW 2.36.100. Compensation for mileage expedites trials by taking away excuses, which in turn benefits the county.

The trial court is reversed and the case remanded for a determination of the amount of compensation.

---

[26] *(Court's footnote)* Kitsap County argues that the statutory obligation does not rise to the level of the contractual obligations at issue in Westinghouse and Aloha. As respondents point out, the Westinghouse court placed great reliance on the fact that the obligation "was for the mutual benefit of employee and employer" in concluding that the obligation to reimburse mileage at issue brought travel to and from work within the course of employment. 94 Wash. 2d at 881, 621 P.2d 147.

Part 6

BENEFITS

Chapter 14

DISABILITY: WAGE LOSS VERSUS MEDICAL INCAPACITY

§ 14.01 INTRODUCTION

Compensable disability is inability, as the result of a work-connected injury, to perform or obtain work suitable to the claimant's qualifications and training. The degree of disability depends on impairment of earning capacity, which in turn is presumptively determined by comparing pre-injury earnings with post-injury earning ability; the presumption may, however, be rebutted by showing that post-injury earnings do not accurately reflect claimant's true earning power. When a claimant has been found disabled in spite of receiving some post-injury wages from his or her former employer, the employer may be credited with the amount of compensation due for the weeks in which wages at least equal to such compensation were paid if, in all the circumstances, it can be said that the wages were intended to be in lieu of compensation.

Total disability may be found, in spite of sporadic earnings, if the claimant's physical condition is such as to rule out regular employment in the labor market. Conversely, when the claimant is unable to obtain employment because of a physical condition, medical evidence that the claimant could perform such work if he or she could get it will not detract from the status of total disability.

§ 14.02   KINDS AND ELEMENTS OF DISABILITY

[1]   Basic Principles

Workers' compensation benefits fall initially into two categories: benefits to the worker for physical injury, and benefits to dependents in case of death. Benefits for physical injury, in turn, are of two kinds: wage-loss payments based on the concept of disability; and payment of hospital and medical expenses occasioned by any work-connected injury, regardless of wage loss or disability.

It has been stressed repeatedly that the distinctive feature of the compensation system, by contrast with tort liability, is that its awards (apart from medical benefits) are made not for physical injury as such, but for "disability" produced by such injury. The central problem, then, becomes that of analyzing the unique and rather complex legal concept which, by years of compensation legislation, decision, and practice, has been built up around the term "compensable disability."

The key to the understanding of this problem is the recognition, at the outset, that the disability concept is a blend of two ingredients, whose recurrence in different proportions gives rise to most controversial disability questions: The first ingredient is disability in the medical or physical sense, as evidenced by obvious loss of members or by medical testimony that the claimant simply cannot make the necessary muscular movements and exertions; the second ingredient is *de facto* inability to earn wages, as evidenced by proof that claimant has not in fact earned anything.

The two ingredients usually occur together; but each may be found without the other: A claimant may be, in a medical sense, utterly shattered and ruined, but may by sheer determination and ingenuity contrive to make a living. Conversely, a claimant may be able to work, but awareness of the injury may lead employers to refuse employment. These two illustrations expose at once the error that results from preoccupation with either the medical or the wage-loss aspect of disability. An absolute insistence on medical disability in the abstract would produce a denial of compensation in the latter case, although the wage loss is as real and as directly traceable to the injury as in any other instance. At the other extreme, an insistence on wage loss as the test would deprive the claimant in the former illustration of an award, thus not only penalizing his laudable efforts to make the best of misfortune but also fostering the absurdity of pronouncing a man nondisabled in spite of the unanimous contrary evidence of medical experts and of common observation. The proper balancing of the medical and the wage-loss factors is, then, the essence of the "disability" problem in workers' compensation.

Disabilities are traditionally divided into four classifications: (1) temporary total, (2) temporary partial, (3) permanent partial, and (4) permanent total. Among these classifications the relative prominence of the two factors is markedly different. *Temporary total* (although the majority of claims are in this group) and *temporary partial* occasion relatively little controversy, since they are ordinarily established by direct evidence of actual wage loss. In the usual industrial injury situation, there is a period of healing and complete wage loss, during which temporary total is payable. This is followed by a recovery, or stabilization of the condition, and probably resumption of work, and no complex questions arise. *Permanent partial schedule awards*, by contrast, are based on medical condition after maximum improvement has been reached, and ignore wage loss entirely. Fixed payments for loss of specified members are due even if the claimant during the period is back at work at higher wages than before. The arbitrary character of this type of benefit gives rise to special problems which are the subject of the next section. It is, then, the two fields of *nonschedule partial* disability and *total permanent* disability which occasion controversy because of the constant interplay of medical and wage-loss factors; and it is mainly to these two categories that analysis of the disability concept is addressed.

[2]　Earning Impairment Versus Physical Impairment

One of the current controversies in the area of workers' compensation concerns the movement to restore the centrality of the earnings-impairment principle.

Workers' compensation in its origins had a well-understood function: it was to provide support for industrially-disabled workers during periods of actual disability, and for their dependents in the event of occupationally-related death, together with hospital, medical and funeral expenses. Over the years, in a number of jurisdictions, this function has imperceptibly given way to a process of paying cash for physical impairment as such, regardless of either actual or presumed loss of earning capacity, and often in a lump sum, until in some states this cash-for-injury operation has come to predominate both as to the costs entailed and as to the administrative and legal time consumed. This in turn has recently generated a strong reaction among those who view this trend as an unfortunate and expensive distortion of the real mission of workers' compensation. The most dramatic expression of this reaction was Florida's adoption in 1979 of a completely overhauled statute[1] that virtually eliminated cash payments for "permanent partial" impairments as such, and concentrated on paying benefits during weeks of actual wage loss, with a minimum of administrative and legal involvement.

By contrast, Minnesota in 1974 amended its statute to carry the opposite trend — that of paying for physical impairment as such — to what is probably the furthest extreme of any state so far. The amendment declared in no uncertain terms that permanent partial benefits were payable for impairment of function, distinct from and in addition to any other payment.[2] Minnesota's "schedule," to which this rule applies, also may well be the most inclusive on record, extending as it does, not only to the usual losses of members and disfigurements,[3] but also to head injuries, injuries to internal organs, back injuries, burns, and loss of the voice mechanism[4] (and, in case anything has been overlooked, to any other permanent partial disability not enumerated).[5]

[3]　The Competing Theories of Disability Defined

At the outset of the analysis of this controversy, it is important to define with some precision the "schools of thought" that are the protagonists in this struggle.

For some years, it has been customary to identify three such "schools": the actual "wage loss theory," the "earning capacity theory," and what was once called the "whole man theory," but currently is more readily recognized as the "physical impairment theory." For purposes of the present controversy, however, it is more useful to use a two-way division, turning on whether the essence of what is being compensated for is medical or economic. Under this division, the first two theories may be combined under the name of the "earning impairment theory," in contrast to the "physical impairment theory."

A pure wage-loss statute would do no more than compare actual post-injury and pre-injury earnings, and then pay appropriate compensation for weeks in which actual earnings were either nonexistent or less than pre-injury earnings. It would, of course, have no "schedule" at all. All the earliest compensation acts were of this kind, but no

---

[1] Fla. Stat. § 440, as amended Ch. 79-40, 1979 Fla. Laws 215. *See* Ch. 14, § 14.02[10], *below*, for detailed analysis of the amendments.

[2] Minn. Stat. § 176.021(3) (1978 & Supp. 1979).

[3] Minn. Stat. § 176.101 Subd. 3., paras. (1)–(37) and (41).

[4] Minn. Stat. § 176.101 Subd. 3., paras. (38–48).

[5] Minn. Stat. § 176.101 Subd. 3., para. (49).

such "pure" statute exists in America today. Even the 1979 Florida wage-loss reform makes a few limited concessions, including an extremely narrow "schedule."

The important question now becomes: how many such concessions can a basically "wage-loss" or "earning-capacity" statute make, and still be entitled to be identified as an "earnings-impairment" statute? These concessions fall into two categories: adjustments of the pre- and post-injury earnings to make the comparison more realistic, and limited applications of the schedule principle.

As to the first, it is certainly not inconsistent with the central earnings-impairment principle to temper the cold arithmetical comparison of actual earnings before and after injury when necessary to get a true calculation of loss. Particularly in times of double-digit inflation, allowances may be necessary for changes in wage levels; other familiar adjustments are those for changes in the claimant's age, training, or hours, for distortions of wage by employer sympathy, and for the impermanence of particular post-injury earnings.

Moreover, a limited schedule is not inconsistent with the earnings-impairment principle, provided that the items included are such that the conclusive presumption of probable actual wage loss is realistic and not fictitious. In addition, the loss must be obvious enough so that the reason for indulging the presumption — administrative convenience and prevention of litigation — is also realistic.

[4] Historic Centrality of the "Wage-Loss Principle"

As stated earlier, the system had, in its beginnings, a purely wage-loss-replacement function. This generalization may not be accepted as self-evident by some people, particularly those who have become so accustomed to the physical-impairment approach that they believe it to be the normal form of the system. Indeed, many people, including compensation specialists, appear to think of the Florida amendments as a radical innovation, when in fact they are an attempt to return to the original compensation approach.

Indeed, as of 1911, of the 22 statutes enacted in foreign countries and provinces, and the 10 enacted in the United States, all but two were of the pure wage-loss type, and only one had a "schedule." This is by no means to suggest that that all states should, out of deference to history, immediately rush out and emulate Florida. Realistically, the choice between the Florida approach and the Minnesota approach will be made, not on historic grounds, but on pragmatic considerations of efficiency in doing the job the state wants done.

Still, the reference to history is something more than a debating point. When a system, all of whose features are keyed to a wage-loss function, is changed, whether absent-mindedly or deliberately, into a physical impairment system, with no corresponding adjustment of these wage-loss-related features, there is bound to be trouble. To take only the most obvious illustration, because compensation was originally concerned with wage loss, the *amounts* paid were tied to prior wage; but if what is being compensated for is physical impairment, it makes no sense at all to pay the high-salaried worker more than the low-wage earner.

[5] Meaning and Origin of the "Schedule Principle"

The story from this point on takes the form of the gradual erosion of the wage-loss principle in many jurisdictions by the schedule principle. It becomes important, therefore, to pause at this point and define precisely what the term "the schedule principle" means in a workers' compensation context.

The concept ordinarily contains two components:

The first has to do with the way the amount of disability (and therefore compensation) is reckoned. In a typical American schedule, this takes the form of a list describing various members of the body, and prescribing a fixed number of weeks of compensation for their loss or loss of use.

The second component has to do with the fundamental rule of liability. Normally, the fixed amount of compensation for a schedule loss is paid regardless of actual wage loss. This can cut both ways. A worker who has lost an eye, but has returned to work at his regular wages, is nevertheless entitled to the scheduled amount. Conversely, if the fixed benefits expire and the worker remains unemployed because of disability, the benefits stop. This latter "exclusiveness" rule was never universal, and has been giving way to both judicial and legislative assaults in more recent times.

It has often been observed that the origins of the "schedule" seem to have been lost in the mists of history.[6] The search for origins is eased somewhat by considering separately the two components just identified.

In the sense of a tabulation of fixed amounts of compensation for particular physical losses, the first schedules were probably those in individual insurance policies, which began to appear in the second half of the nineteenth century.[7]

Belgium's industrial accident schedule was closely associated with comparable compensation for war wounds, as was also France's original schedule.[8]

These historical fragments, while helpful in understanding where the first component came from, are of no use at all in explaining the origin of the second component: the complete independence from actual wage loss, within an over-all wage loss system, of one particular group of injuries.

The historical evidence is quite clear that the schedule was never intended to be a departure from or an exception to the wage-loss principle. The typical schedule, limited to obvious and easily-provable losses of members, was justified on two grounds: the gravity of the impairment supported a conclusive presumption that actual wage loss would sooner or later result; and the conspicuousness of the loss guaranteed that awards could be made with no controversy whatever.

When the Pennsylvania act was under study by the Pennsylvania Industrial Accident Commission, the commission had the benefit of the talents of Professor Francis H. Bohlen, of the University of Pennsylvania Law School, who was probably the most brilliant workers' compensation analyst of his time. In an address to the Law Association of Philadelphia, on November 15, 1912, he summed up in one sentence the dual justification for including in the Commission's proposed draft a very limited schedule covering only loss of a hand, an arm, a foot, a leg, or an eye, or two or more of these:

> The *determining consideration* was that by rendering the amount definite *litigation would be prevented* and certainty attained, since whenever a mutilation of this sort occurred there could be no question as to the *extent of disability* of the sufferer or the amount payable to him.[9]

Note the absoluteness of the terms chosen. In adducing administrative convenience as a justification, he did not say that litigation would be reduced, or simplified, or discouraged. He said that it would be "prevented." On the disability issue, there would be "certainty," and "no question of the extent," and hence no room for litigation at all.

As to the other component, the presumption of wage loss, his argument took the form of explaining why the schedule was confined to major members, and why the New Jersey example of including minor members had been rejected:

---

[6] *See, e.g.*, GEERTS, KORNBLITH, & URMSON, COMPENSATION FOR BODILY HARM: A COMPARATIVE STUDY 110 (1977).

[7] *See, e.g.*, GEERTS, KORNBLITH, & URMSON, COMPENSATION FOR BODILY HARM: A COMPARATIVE STUDY 110 (1977).

[8] *See, e.g.*, GEERTS, KORNBLITH, & URMSON, COMPENSATION FOR BODILY HARM: A COMPARATIVE STUDY 112 (1977).

[9] *Duke Univ. Law Library Pamphlets*, vol. 121, No. 15. Emphasis supplied.

The Commission rejected the idea of similarly valuing the lesser injuries which are valued in both the Federal[10] and New Jersey Acts. While certainty would thus be attained, it would be a certainty of injustice. In the case of serious mutilations, while the effect of disability in a few cases may be greater or less than that provided in the act, yet the Commission believes that a fair average has been struck which will cover with approximate justice the great bulk of such cases. On the other hand, the effect of minor injuries varies so enormously with the trade of the individual, that no average can be struck that will give a fair general result. The average would not fairly represent the usual or average case, but would be a mere mean between widely divergent extremes. A typesetter or engraver who loses one joint of the index finger of his or her right hand becomes thereby incapable of practicing his or her trade and must learn late in life a new vocation; in such a case the payment of one-half wages for 25 or 40 weeks would be manifestly inadequate. On the other hand, a teamster or any worker doing unskilled labor, would, in a great majority of cases, suffer no loss of earning power except during the period when he or she is actually being treated for his or her injury, such period usually not exceeding two weeks to a month. In such case the compensation would be manifestly excessive. . . .

The idea that the schedule in any way represented compensation for physical impairment as such was emphatically disavowed — so much so that Prof. Bohlen regarded any such provision as a downright curiosity:

In Illinois, a curious provision occurs, whereby a servant who suffers any serious disfigurement to his hands and face, though not actually incapacitating him, is entitled to a reasonable . . . amount of compensation, not exceeding one-quarter the amount payable in the event of death. Such sums are awarded by way of damages for the sentimental loss entailed, and, having no relation to the earning power of the sufferer, and being given in addition to compensation for the loss thereof, have no place, in the opinion of the Commission, in a compensation act, the sole object of which is to protect, in part at least, the injured workmen and those dependent upon them from the economic sufferings entailed by the total or partial destruction of their earning power.

The tying-in of the schedule with the wage-loss principle by the conclusive presumption of wage loss from major impairments was a realistic one — even more obviously so in earlier times than now. It must be recalled that, in 1912, none of the developments had occurred that would later soften the impact of such handicaps on employment prospects. There were no Second Injury Funds.[11] There were no hire-the-handicapped programs comparable to those existing today. There were no mandatory laws prohibiting employment discrimination based on handicap, such as Section 503 and 504 of the Rehabilitation Act of 1973.[12] Rehabilitation techniques, benefits, and programs were, by modern standards, primitive or nonexistent. The presumption that a one-armed or one-legged worker would suffer eventual actual wage loss, then, was no fiction, nor was it a facade behind which to distribute payments for physical impairment.

---

[10] It may be noted here that any federal acts at this period were not true workers' compensation acts, and accordingly are omitted from the present discussion. Since the federal plans were merely provisions by the government for its own employees, they were more comparable to private plans voluntarily adopted by private employers.

[11] A majority of states now have such a fund. Although they vary widely, they share the common purpose of relieving the employer of liability for the amount by which the final disability of an already-impaired worker exceeds the disability that would have been produced by the instant injury alone on an unimpaired worker. *See* Ch. 16, § 16.03, *below*.

[12] 41 U.S.C. § 793 and § 794 (Supp. V 1975), applicable to government contracts and government grants, respectively. There are also other federal and state laws on the subject. *See* LARSON, EMPLOYMENT DISCRIMINATION, vol. 4, §§ 107 and 108.

[6]   Gradual Erosion of the Wage-Loss Principle Through Expansion of the Schedule Principle

It was noted earlier that, up to the end of 1911, of the 32 statutes enacted throughout the world, including 10 in the United States, only one, New Jersey, had a schedule.[13] For some reason, perhaps in part because of the New Jersey example, schedules began to proliferate at about this time. In 1912, three states, Michigan,[14] Rhode Island,[15] and Maryland,[16] passed original statutes containing very limited schedules. Even more significantly, a number of states whose original statutes had had no schedules added them within a few years; this occurred in Ohio,[17] Wisconsin,[18] Nevada,[19] Massachusetts,[20] Illinois,[21] and, in modified form, California.[22]

Most of these schedules, and of those that appeared in the next few years, were quite narrow — sometimes limited to major members and often limited to "loss" or even "loss by severance," thus excluding not only partial loss but partial and even total loss of use.[23]

The expansion of the schedule principle from these very restricted beginnings can be summarized by identifying categories of extension that occurred, sometimes gradually, sometimes abruptly, and in no particular chronological sequence.

One form of expansion was from relatively major members to smaller and smaller members, such as portions of fingers.[24]

Complete loss of use was added to loss or loss by severance, on the quite reasonable argument that a person may, if anything, be better off with an amputation (thus permitting use of a prosthesis) than with a dangling arm or leg that not only is useless but gets in the way.

But the next extension, to "partial loss of use," opened the floodgates of controversy and litigation. Total loss was ordinarily self-evident, and total loss of use, under the standard definition of "no better off with the member . . . if the member had been

---

[13] N.J. Laws 1911, c.95.

[14] Mich. P.A. 1st Exec. Sess. 1912, Act No. 10, p.20, part II, § 10. The schedule listed only "loss," not loss of use or partial loss.

[15] R.I. Pub. Laws 1912, c.831. The limitation here is even clearer than that in the Michigan act, N.14 immediately *above*, since it refers to "loss by severance." Payments were "in addition to all other compensation."

[16] Maryland Acts 1912, Sec. 5, covering only loss by actual separation of hand or foot, or loss of eye. The loss was treated as one-half of total disability.

[17] Ohio, 1913 Senate Bill No. 127, Gen Code § 1463–37 et seq. This schedule was in § 33, and referred only to "loss."

[18] Wis. Laws 1913, c.599, § 2394–9(5), and Laws 1915 c.241. This was a rather broad provision, followed by a catch-all clause for impairments not listed.

[19] Nev. Stat. 1915, p.279, c.190. The schedule spoke only of "loss." It was followed by a catch-all provision, which however, was tied to the wage-loss presumption by providing that such factors as occupation and age should be taken into account in judging the extent of the disability.

[20] Mass. Ch. 571, Sec. 2 Acts of 1912. The list was rather short, and referred to losses by severance. The payments were to be "in addition to all other compensation."

[21] Ill. Hurd's Rev. St. 1915–16, p.1272, § 8(e), referring to "loss."

[22] Cal. Laws 1913, c.176. There was no schedule-type list of members. The provision is cast in terms of percentages of total disability, with age and occupation to be considered, along with physical injury, in determining the percentages. § 15(b)(5) and (7). The California formula thus displayed its kinship to the presumed wage-loss principle and its rejection of the physical-impairment principle.

[23] *See* NS. 13–22, *above*, this subsection.

[24] A few schedules went this far in their earliest forms. The present summary is only intended to depict in broad strokes the steps in the expansion process.

severed,"[25] was not much more difficult to observe and prove. But "partial loss of use" set the stage for the innumerable numbers games to be played by doctors, lawyers, administrators and judges, endlessly quarreling about whether the loss of use of an arm was 15 percent or 22 percent or 39 percent.

The next step was to extend the schedule beyond members, to include the back, the internal organs, the head, the voice mechanism, the body as a whole, and, for good measure, a catch-all clause including anything else that might have been overlooked. Combine this with partial loss of use, and it is no wonder that the problems both of disability evaluation and of proof became unmanageable.

When upon all this is superimposed the practice of lump-summing, all resemblance to a wage-loss system is lost. If a worker is given $20,000 for some internal organ damage that has no conceivable effect, actual or presumptive, on earning capacity, it is no longer possible to pretend that this is still somehow only an extrapolation of the wage-loss principle aided by the conclusive presumption of eventual wage loss.[26]

Of course, once a state deliberately severs the earning-capacity connection with a particular category of benefits, as Minnesota did in 1975 in the case of permanent partial awards, the anti-lump-summing rationales no longer apply. Minnesota accordingly has made lump-summing of permanent partial awards not only permissible but mandatory when return to work occurs prior to four weeks from the date of injury; in other permanent partial cases, the award is spread out into four installments at four week intervals, unless temporary disability ceases or the claimant returns to work sooner, in which case the full amount is payable.[27]

[7] Express Adoption of Physical-Impairment Theory by Minority of States

Minnesota's dramatic statutory legitimizing of the physical-impairment principle only serves to highlight the fact that, until very recently, the expansion of the schedule principle just sketched was not accompanied by any corresponding abandonment of the earning-capacity principle as a theoretical or doctrinal matter. Most states insisted throughout the process that the schedule was based on presumed loss of earning capacity. For example, until Minnesota's amendment, in spite of Minnesota's extremely broad schedule, the Minnesota courts had staunchly clung to the earning-capacity theory.[28] Indeed, this was why the amendment was thought necessary.

In addition, several states judicially broke ranks: for example, a Kansas court came right out and said that the primary purpose of that the Act was to compensate an injured worker for his physical injuries.[29]

[8] Practical Problems Attending Physical Impairment Theory

[a] Introduction

These statutory and judicial departures may have the advantage of reconciling theory with actual practice in states where the expansion of the schedule principle has reached an advanced stage. But this abrupt attempt to transform long-established underpinnings of the system with no corresponding adjustment of its remaining

---

[25] Steele v. Darlington Fabrics Corp., 78 R.I. 272, 81 A.2d 424 (1951).

[26] *See* Ch. 31, § 31.08[7], *below*, for discussion of lump-summing.

[27] Minn. Stat. Ann § 176.021 subd. 3.

[28] *See, e.g.*, Boquist v. Dayton-Hudson Corp., 297 Minn. 14, 209 N.W.2d 783 (1973).

[29] Cody v. Jayhawk Pipeline Corp., 222 Kan. 491, 565 P.2d 264 (1977).

structure or details was bound to generate serious problems, three of which will now be examined.

[b] Fallacy of Basing Amount of a Non-Earning-Capacity Award on Prior Earnings

Suppose A's previous average weekly wage was $400 and B's was $150. Suppose each suffers work-connected loss of his voice mechanism. In Minnesota, A would get an award at the maximum rate of $197 a week, B's award would be based on 66 2/3% of $150, or $100. For 500 weeks, A would get $98,500. B would get $50,000. Why? If what is being compensated for has nothing to do with loss of earning capacity, of what relevance are prior earnings? Indeed, it takes no vivid imagination to construct possible combinations in which the disparity is not merely senseless but outrageous. A may be in private life a recluse who never talks to anyone anyway. B may be an amateur opera singer. A still gets almost twice as much as B.

Suppose X is a 78-year-old executive making $5000 a week, and Y is a young manual worker getting only $60 a week. Suppose both lose their testicles in industrial accidents. There being no minimum on permanent partial in Minnesota, X would get five times as much for his loss as would Y.

Compounding the preposterousness of results of this kind is the added fact that, under the exclusive remedy clause, each loses any common-law right he might have to sue the employer in tort, if employer negligence was involved. Y's tort damages would obviously be much higher than X's — certainly at least 10 times higher. The injustice to Y is thus not just five-fold, but at least thrice five-fold.

If a case presenting anything like these hypothetical examples were to arise, it might well be that the magnitude of the injustice, unsupported by any rational state purpose, would raise this discrimination to the level of unconstitutionality.

[c] Impossibility of Rationally or Fairly Rating "Disability" When the Tie With Earning Capacity Is Severed

The schedule approach, exemplified by the Minnesota statute, presupposes that there is an abstract and uniform measure of "disability" that is valid and fair for all persons, apart from their activities or occupations.

What, for example, does "loss of use" of three fingers mean? Loss of use for what purpose? For typesetting or for unskilled labor?

This is a problem that has haunted compensation administrators for years — indeed ever since the schedule strayed beyond loss of major members. It is precisely the problem so presciently foreseen by Professor Bohlen,[30] and indeed to this day accounts for a large amount of compensation litigation. The controversy will not die. In 1979, the New York Appellate Division was confronted with a textbook example of the problem. A court reporter had fallen and injured his left ear, and he was left with a 19.2% loss of hearing in that ear. This loss was enough, however, to disqualify him completely as a court reporter. New York had for many years operated under a rule that hearing losses must be treated as schedule losses.[31] But the Appellate Division here, evidently determined to find some way round the gross miscarriage of compensation law purpose that a strict application of this rule would produce, found its solution by holding that the condition was still "unsettled." It is elementary, of course, that schedule awards are not made when the condition has not yet stabilized, or when its effects extend beyond the member to other parts of the body. But here there was no physical instability, or

---

[30] *See* text accompanying Ch. 14, § 14.02[5] n.9, *above.*

[31] Rowe v. McGovern, Inc., 254 App. Div. 432, 5 N.Y.S.2d 626 (1938). The court expressly stated that the actual loss of earning capacity was immaterial.

swelling, or radiating pain. The percentage of hearing loss was clearly established by an otologist's testimony. The only "unsettled" item adduced by the court was the fact that claimant had been inquiring about more effective hearing aids. The court upheld the referee's decision that the injury was not schedulable, and that continuing benefits for total disability should be paid.[32]

The difficulty of evaluating disability in the absence of any standard, such as effect on work performance, is obvious enough when members like fingers, hands, eyes or ears are involved. When extended to internal organs and the like it passes beyond the bounds of any rational solution.

Until 1979, the Minnesota statute stated that compensation for loss of internal organs was to be in an amount "for that proportion of 500 weeks which is the proportionate amount of disability caused to the entire body by the injury. . . . "[33]

To take only one actual reported example: what is the proportionate disability to the entire body represented by the loss of a kidney? The claimant argued that 100% loss of a kidney should yield an award for the entire 500 weeks. The compensation court found him 50 percent permanently partially disabled and awarded 250 weeks. The Supreme Court agreed that a percentage determination could not be made by simply looking to the percentage of the organ lost, and directed the compensation judge to look at the percentage of permanent partial disability the claimant had suffered.[34]

But is the "entire body" of a person who has lost one kidney really fifty percent disabled? Indeed, as long as the other kidney is functioning normally, is the person disabled at all? Disabled to do what?

[d]   Physical-Impairment Awards Carried to Their "Logical" Conclusions

Sometimes a striking way to test the soundness of a principle is to see what happens when it is carried to its logical conclusion.

In *Bagge's Case*,[35] decedent lived 17 to 24 minutes, in a coma, after being struck on the head. His dependents were awarded full death benefits. In addition, they were awarded full permanent partial benefits for loss of both eyes, both ears, both arms, both legs, other bodily functions, and disfigurement. The court felt compelled to do this by the statutory provision, present in the Massachusetts act from its inception, that schedule awards are payable "in addition to all other compensation,"[36] and a 1951 amendment making the unpaid balance of such compensation payable to dependents.[37]

Suppose instead of 17 or 24 minutes, the employee lives one minute. Should this random fact of sixty-second survival rather than instantaneous death determine whether relatives get a four-hundred-thousand dollar windfall? Or if one minute, why not one second? How often, one wonders, is accidental death absolutely instantaneous?

Even if the employee does not die, there is the possibility of enormous cumulations of schedule payments, as in the Minnesota case of *Lerick v. Thermo Systems, Inc.*[38] The claimant sustained a compensable injury to his spinal cord which rendered him a quadriplegic, with 100% permanent partial disability to his spine, both arms, and both legs. The court determined the liability to be the total number of weeks for loss of use

---

[32]   Cecere v. County of Niagara, 7 A.D.2d 759, 419 N.Y.S.2d 315 (1979).

[33]   Minn. Stats. Ann. § 176.101 Subd.3 (40).

[34]   Getter v. Travel Lodge, 260 N.W.2d 177 (Minn. 1977).

[35]   Bagge's Case, 338 N.E.2d 348 (Mass. 1975).

[36]   Mass. Gen. Laws, c.152, § 36, St. 1949, c.519.

[37]   Mass. Gen. Laws, c.152, § 36A, St. 1951, c.494.

[38]   Lerick v. Thermo Systems, Inc., 292 N.W.2d 741 (Minn. 1980).

of each arm, loss of use of each leg, and 100% permanent partial disability to the spine, all increased by 15% under a simultaneous injury provision.

[9] Motives Behind the Movement to Restore the Wage-Loss Principle.

There are two main motives behind the present movement to restore the wage loss principle. The first is reducing waste of the compensation dollar on nondisabling losses. The second is reducing waste of administrative, legal, and judicial time and resources.

As to the first, the beginning-point is that the fund available for compensation payments is not infinite. If, for example, 80 percent of the compensation dollar is frittered away on small schedule awards for conditions that are in no sense disabling, inevitably the ability of the system to do its real job, that of taking adequate care of the really disabled, is damaged.

That this relationship is no mere theory is demonstrated by what happened in Florida. Before the wage-loss reform, the maximum weekly benefit was $130; with the reform it became 100 percent of average weekly wage, or $211, rising to $288 in 1984.

Again, it should not be necessary to belabor the argument that, assuming a given amount of benefit money available, this $81 differential is much better used in preventing destitution among actually-disabled workers for whom it is probably the sole source of income, than in scattering cash awards among workers who in many cases are still employed at full wages.

As to the second motive, reducing litigation, it should be remembered that this was one of the principal reasons for replacing common-law remedies with compensation in the first place. And, as to the schedule specifically, recall that, according to Professor Bohlen, *the* purpose was not merely to reduce, but to "prevent," litigation.[39]

The paradox is that this very feature, the schedule as distorted over the years, is now of all issues the largest producer of litigation. In Florida, for example, before the 1979 reform, it was estimated that quarreling about disability evaluation consumed 79 percent of administrative and legal time.

[10] The Florida "Wage-Loss Reform" Amendments of 1979

The trends toward converting workmen's compensation increasingly into a system paying for physical impairment rather than wage earning impairment finally produced in 1979 a sharp reaction, in the form of a set of amendments to the Florida compensation act designed to reestablish the centrality of the wage-loss principle.[40] A second, and closely related, purpose of the amendments was to simplify administration, increasing the claimants' ability to recover compensation without legal assistance, increasing the direct responsibility of administrators, employers, and carriers for seeing that claimants are promptly compensated, and discouraging shotgun claims, needless hearings, and excessive use of lawyers.

The "wage loss" approach is here used to refer to a system which pays income benefits only for periods during which there has been in fact a reduction or loss of earnings.

The original Florida plan contains only two relatively minor exceptions to the principle. Having abolished the conventional category of "permanent total," it did retain that designation for the very limited category involving loss of two major members, in the absence of conclusive proof of a substantial earning capacity.[41] The most significant

---

[39] Ch. 14, § 14.02[5] n.9, *above.*

[40] CSSB 188, eff. July 1, 1979.

[41] Fla. Stats. § 440.15(1)(b)

changes were found in the new subsection on "permanent impairment and wage-loss benefits."[42] The amendments abolished the "permanent partial," "schedule benefits," and "disability ratings." This subsection contained the second small concession to the past. In a limited group of losses including only permanent impairment due to amputation, loss of 80 percent or more of vision, after correction, or serious facial or head disfigurement, falling short of the permanent total category, a token "up-front" payment is made of fifty dollars for each percent of permanent impairment of the body as a whole up to 50 percent, and one hundred dollars for each percent above 50. From there on, everything depends on actual wage loss.

In 1990, the Florida Legislature enacted new legislation that contained extensive workers' compensation reforms. While the legislation preserved the wage-loss principle, an impairment schedule was adopted by which the employee's injury was to be evalauted and assigned a permanant disabiltiy rating which was then utilized to determine the duration of benefits.[43] In 1993, the Florida Legislature again passed workers' compensation reform legislation. An impairment schedule was adopted which provided that for each percentage point of impairment an injured worker was entitled to three weeks of compensation at the rate of 50 percent of the employee's average weekly temporary total disability benefit.[44] In addition, an injured employee who has suffered a 20 percent or greater impairment and is earning less than 80% of his or her pre-injury weekly wage as a direct result of their injury is entitled to supplemental benefits. These benefits are payable at a rate of 80 percent of the difference between 80 percent of the employee's average weekly wage before injury and the weekly wages the employee has earned since the injury.[45] While legislation passed by the Florida Legislature in the 1990s has modified the original Florida plan, the Florida Compensation Act is still guided by the wage-loss principle.

The "back to wage-loss" movement is by no means confined to Florida. In recent years, a number of states have enacted modified wage-loss type of statutes.[46]

§ 14.03   EARNINGS AS CREATING PRESUMPTION OF EARNING CAPACITY

OLSON v. MANION'S INC.
510 P.2d 6 (Mont. 1973)

DALY, JUSTICE.

This appeal is from a decision of the district court of the eleventh judicial district, Flathead County, affirming an order of the Industrial Accident Board denying benefits to plaintiff Duane Olson.

On January 23, 1962, Olson in an industrial accident sustained injuries which impeded his movement and ability to assume certain positions. A claim was filed by Olson and accepted by the Industrial Accident Board under Plan 2 of the Workmen's Compensation Act, carried by his employer Manion's Inc., a car dealership and garage in Kalispell. At that time temporary total disability compensation was paid for a period of 9 and 4/7ths weeks. In 1967 the Industrial Accident Board on rehearing determined that Olson had suffered permanent partial disability from 5% of the back to 20% of the body as a whole. Later that year, a subsequent application for rehearing was denied by

[42] Fla. Stats. § 440.15(3).

[43] Fla. Stats. § 440.15 (3)(a).

[44] Fla. Stats. §440.15 (3)(a).

[45] Fla. Stats. §440.15 (3)(b).

[46] La. Rev. Stat. Ann. 23:1221; N.H. Rev. Stat. Ann. 281-A:31. W. Va. Code 23-4-9.

the Board and Olson appealed the Board's order to the district court.

After several continuances, the district court on July 5, 1972, ruled against Olson, adopting the Board's findings of fact and conclusions of law which denied admissibility of certain evidence offered by Olson on the ground it was without legal effect.

The additional evidence offered by Olson and refused by the Board and the district court was: (1) At the time Olson sustained the compensable injury in 1962 he was earning $2.60 per hour but the same job at Manion's paid $4.60 per hour in 1972. (2) Olson's present job, which pays $3.80 per hour, is substitute employment because he is physically unable to perform the job he held prior to injury.

On appeal the sole issue is whether the Industrial Accident Board and the district court erred in refusing to admit and consider the offered evidence of impairment of earning capacity.

Section 92-703, R.C.M. 1947, establishes the amount of compensation to be paid in cases of permanent partial disability. It provides for a fixed percentage (subject to a stated maximum):

> . . . of the difference between the wages received *at the time of the injury* and the wages that such injured employee *is able to earn thereafter.* . . . (Emphasis added.)

Olson relies on cases decided by this Court applying section 92-703, in which the terms "loss of earning capacity" and "loss of ability to earn in the open market" were used: *Shaffer v. Midland Empire Packing Co.*, 127 Mont. 211, 259 P.2d 340; *Mahlum v. Broeder*, 147 Mont. 386, 412 P.2d 572. He also cites section 92-838, R.C. M.1947, which states:

> Whenever this act or any part or section thereof is interpreted by a court, it shall be liberally construed by such court.

It is fundamental to the issue of this case to keep in mind that the workmen's compensation system is not based on common law tort liability concepts, but rather depends upon the particular statutes which the legislature enacts to create and administer the system. 2 Larson's Workmen's Compensation Law § 57.10, pp. 2, 3 states:

> It has been stressed repeatedly that the distinctive feature of the compensation system, by contrast with tort liability is that its awards (apart from medical benefits) are made not for physical injury as such, but for "disability" produced by such injury. The central problem, then, becomes that of analyzing the unique and rather complex legal concept which, by years of compensation legislation, decision, and practice, has been built up around the term "compensable disability."

What constitutes a "compensable disability" is not a static concept, particularly in the instance of permanent partial disability. Section 92-830, R.C.M. 1947, empowers the Board at any time after an award is made, to review, increase or diminish that award. Possible bases for review include: changes in the job market affecting the availability of jobs which the disabled can perform; changes in technology or method in a particular job field so as to preclude a disabled person from performing; or, a determination that subsequent wages earned were based on consideration of sympathy or relationship. None of these situations apply in the instant case. Essentially, Olson is contending that he has a compensable disability based on his inability to do his old job.

99 C.J.S. Workmen's Compensation § 295, p. 1031, states:

> *Earning power in same or other employment.* It has been held under, apart from, or without reference to, statutes so providing, that the test of an injured employee's right to compensation is his inability by reason of the injury to work and earn wages in the employment at which he was engaged when injured, so that the earning capacity remaining to the employee in other callings cannot be

considered. *However, it is otherwise under statutes which impose no such limitation*, or where the compensation is measured by the loss of ability to earn in any suitable employment, or in the same or any other employment. . . .

The fact that claimant might have been earning more had he been able to resume, and been promoted in, the employment he was engaged in when injured does not affect the determination. Where the average weekly wages which claimant is able to earn are not limited to those he could earn in the same employment but include the whole monetary result of a reasonable use of all his powers, mental and physical, whether working for himself or for others and whether or not his earnings are called wages in common speech, no compensation can be had where talents previously undiscovered produce an earning capacity greater than that enjoyed prior to the injury. (Emphasis added.)

In Montana's Workmen's Compensation Act we find no limitation of consideration to a disabled's earning ability in the same employment, or the same type of employment he was engaged in when injured. *Dosen v. East Butte Copper Min. Co.*, 78 Mont. 579, 254 P. 880; *McKinzie v. Sandon*, 141 Mont. 540, 380 P.2d 580.

The New Hampshire court in *Desrosiers v. Dionne Bros. Furniture, Inc.*, 98 N.H. 424, 101 A.2d 775, 778, decided under a similar statutory provision an analogous fact situation, and stated:

In some jurisdictions earning capacity refers only to the employee's capacity to earn in the employment or trade in which he was working at the time of the accident so that for compensation purposes the earning capacity remaining to him in other callings is not considered. . . . Section 23 of our act imposes no such limitation nor has it been so interpreted. . . .

The test of compensable disability under our statute is not the employee's ability or disability because of his injury to do his old job. Nor is it what the claimant could have earned but for his injury in the employment or trade in which he was working at the time of the accident. . . . It is the difference between "his average weekly wage before the injury and the average weekly wage *he is able to earn thereafter*" with his injury in suitable work under normal employment conditions.

We hold that the test of compensable disability under the Montana Workmen's Compensation Act is "the difference between the wages received at the time of the injury and the wages that such injured employee is able to earn thereafter" in any suitable field of employment or profession he subsequently enters under normal conditions, whether or not his earnings in that field of employment or profession are commonly called "wages."

Olson's contention that this rule makes no provision for "inflation" or "parity" is correct. He makes a meritorious argument supporting the desirability and practicality of such a provision, and we take judicial notice of the fact that prevailing wage scales have risen in the period between 1962 and 1972. However, it is neither the function nor prerogative of this Court to rewrite the Workmen's Compensation Act to include such a provision. That is the function of the legislature.

The courts of this state have followed the directive set forth in section 92-838, R.C.M. 1947, in liberally construing the provisions of the Act, particularly in the interpretation of the terms "in the course of" and "arising out of". But we see no room for interpretation of the words "wages received at the time of injury." As this Court said in *Mont. Ass'n of Tobacco and Candy Distributors v. State Board of Equalization*, 156 Mont. 108, 114, 476 P.2d 775, 778:

Where the language of a statute is plain, unambiguous, direct, and certain, the statute speaks for itself and there is nothing left for the court to construe.

The judgment of the district court is *affirmed*.

JAMES T. HARRISON, C. J., and HASWELL, CASTLES and JOHN C. HARRISON, JJ., concur.

§ 14.04   REBUTTING PRESUMPTION BASED ON EARNINGS

MAXEY v. MAJOR MECHANICAL CONTRACTORS
330 A.2d 156 (Del. Super. 1974)

BIFFERATO, JUDGE.

This is an appeal from a decision of the Industrial Accident Board [hereinafter Board] by Cyrus Maxey. Mr. Maxey was injured in a compensable industrial accident on September 3, 1969. In addition to total disability, he incurred permanent injury to his left arm. He could no longer function as a non-licensed plumber, a position which, at the time of the accident, paid him $180 per week, $4.50 per hour. He subsequently obtained employment at a gas station in July of 1970, and received a salary of $500 per month for a 50-hour week, approximately $2.50 per hour. He was awarded compensation for permanent partial disability in the amount of $50 per week by the Board pursuant to 19 Del.C. § 2325.[47]

In April of 1973, Mr. Maxey was made supervisor of the Kayo Gas Station in Elsmere. His wages were $700 per month for a 50 hour week, the equivalent of $3.22 per hour, and he was subject to 24-hour call. On October 10, 1973 Maxey was transferred to another Kayo Station in Twin Oaks, Pennsylvania, where he served as manager. There he earned wages of $625 per month for a 50-hour week, approximately $3.10 per hour, but he was no longer subject to 24-hour call.

The employer, appellee herein, on July 5, 1973, petitioned the Board to reduce Maxey's weekly compensation. Mr. Maxey urged the Board to deny this request on the ground that inflation accounted, in part, for his increased wages and, considering the inflationary factor, his compensation should remain $50 per week.

At the hearing before the Board, held on November 13, 1973, David Golland, Research Analyst Chief of the Delaware Department of Labor, testifying on behalf of Mr. Maxey, stated that one of his duties was to compute the average weekly wage of covered employees[48] in the State of Delaware and that such average weekly wage has increased from $143 a week in 1969 to approximately $170 a week in 1973. This demonstrates an inflationary trend of approximately 19%.

The Board refused to take into account the change in wage scales since 1969. It estimated the hourly differential between Maxey's pre-injury and post-injury wages and, based on a 40-hour week, computed a weekly loss of $51.20 for the period between

---

[47] *(Court's footnote)* 19 Del.C. § 2325, as it read at the time of the accident, provided:

"For injuries resulting in partial disability for work, except the particular cases mentioned in subsections (a)–(g) of section 2326 of this title, the compensation to be paid shall be 66 2/3 percent of the difference between the wages received by the injured employee before the injury and the earning power of the employee thereafter, but such compensation shall not be more than $50 per week. This compensation shall be paid during the period of such partial disability for work, not, however, beyond 300 weeks. In construing the words 'earning power of the employee thereafter' as those words appear in this section, the Board shall take into consideration the value of gratuities, board, lodging and similar advantages received by the employee in a subsequent employment."

[48] *(Court's footnote)* Covered employees are those employees within the State who are covered by the unemployment insurance law. These employees comprise 75–80% of the total work force in the State.

April, 1973 and October 10, 1973 and a weekly loss of $64.80 for the compensable period subsequent to October 10, 1973. It therefore determined that Maxey was entitled to compensation in the amount of $34.13 per week for the period between April, 1973 and October 10, 1973 and $43.80 per week for the compensable period thereafter.

Maxey contends that the Board erred as a matter of law in failing to consider the increase in wage levels since 1969. He argues that in order to properly calculate his compensation either his pre-injury wages must be adjusted upward or his post-injury wages adjusted downward to reflect the wage level change since 1969. Maxey relies on the testimony of Mr. Golland to demonstrate said change.

The term "earning power," as viewed in 19 Del. C. § 2325, is not synonymous with actual earnings. Rather, it is synonymous with earning capacity or earning ability. *Ruddy v. I. D. Griffith & Co.*, 237 A.2d 700 (Del. Supr. 1968); *Globe Union, Inc. v. Baker*, 310 A.2d 883 (Del. Super. 1973). While post-injury compensation *per se* may, in some instances, constitute an adequate reflection of earning power, it is, under other circumstances, an unfair criterion thereof. Certain factors must be taken into account in evaluating the accuracy of post-injury compensation as a measure of earning power. In *Ruddy, supra*, the Supreme Court, citing 2 Larson, Workmen's Compensation, delineated the following factors:

(1) The employee may be the beneficiary of a mere gratuity and does not actually earn his wages;

(2) The employee, by education and training, may have fitted himself for more remunerative employment;

(3) The employee worked longer hours than he did before his injury, his hourly remuneration having decreased;

(4) A general change in wage scale may have taken place for the type of work or in the industry in general;

(5) The new wages are intended as an inducement to the employee to refrain from pursuing a claim;

(6) The employee before his injury was younger or a minor;

(7) The employment in which the employee was employed after his injury was of uncertain duration.

In discussing the aforementioned factors, Larson states:

The ultimate objective of the disability test is, by discounting these variables, to determine the wage that would have been paid in the open labor market under normal employment conditions to claimant *as injured, taking wage levels, hours of work, . . . as of exactly the same period used for calculating actual wages earned before his injury.* Only by the elimination of all variables except the injury itself can a reasonably accurate estimate be made of the impairment of earning capacity to be attributed to that injury. 2 Larson, Workmen's Compensation, § 57.21. [Emphasis supplied.]

See, also, Osborne v. Johnson, 432 S.W.2d 800 (Ky.1968); *Arizona Public Service Co. v. Industrial Comm.*, 492 P.2d 1212 (1972). Referring specifically to changes in wage levels, Larson emphatically states:

In determining loss of earning capacity, earnings after the injury must be corrected to correspond with the general wage level in force at the time pre-injury earnings were calculated. 2 Larson, Workmen's Compensation, § 57.32.

On the basis of the factors delineated in *Ruddy*, and the construction thereof espoused by Larson, the Court believes that appellant's point is well taken in that his post-injury earnings should be adjusted to the 1969 wage scale in order to adequately reflect earning power. In refusing to do so, the Board erred as a matter of law.

The employer contends that *Ruddy* is inapposite insofar as it dealt with a situation wherein an employee subsequent to his injury was earning wages which were higher than his pre-injury compensation. In the instant case, appellant is earning less than his pre-injury compensation. Certainly, the preponderance of authority adopting the view that wage level increases must be considered in determining earning capacity does deal with situations wherein the employee is earning an amount equal to or greater than his pre-injury compensation. *See, e.g., Ruddy v. I. D. Griffith & Co., supra; Marmon v. Union Collieries Company,* 135 Pa. Super. 582, 7 A.2d 156 (1939); *Kurtz v. Wall,* 182 So. 2d 618 (Fla. 1966); *Rennard v. Rouseville Cooperage Co.,* 141 Pa. Super. 286, 15 A.2d 48 (1940); *Lombard v. Uhrich,* 102 Kan. 780, 172 P. 32 (1918). *See generally* Annotation, 92 A.L.R. 1188. However, the Court has neither found nor has its attention been called to any authorities presenting a logical reason why an increase in wage levels should only be a factor in determining earning power in instances where an employee, after his accident, earns as much as or more than his pre-injury compensation. Moreover, Larson, in concluding that post-injury earning capacity must be measured by wage levels in effect at the time of the injury, relies heavily on the case of *Whyte v. Industrial Commission,* 71 Ariz. 338, 227 P.2d 230 (1951), which, in fact, dealt with an employee who was earning wages which were *less* than his pre-injury compensation. *See, also,* 58 Am. Jur., Workmen's Compensation § 316.

The figures proffered by appellant, through his witness, Mr. Golland, demonstrate that, in general, covered employees in 1969 earned approximately 84% of what they earned in 1973. However, these figures do not specifically reflect the change in wage scale for the industry in which Maxey is now employed or for the type of work he now performs, to wit, gas station manager, and, therefore, are not probative under the test enunciated in *Ruddy.*

This case is therefore remanded to the Board with the instruction that, assuming appellant introduces evidence of the 1969 wage scale of a manager of a comparable gas station, the Board must apply said 1969 wage scale, rather than appellant's current wages, in order to determine his compensation under 19 Del.C. § 2325. It is so ordered.

§ 14.05   THE "ODD-LOT" DOCTRINE

GUYTON v. IRVING JENSEN COMPANY
373 N.W.2d 101 (Iowa 1985)

McCormick, Justice.

In this case of first impression we adopt the "odd-lot doctrine" in workers' compensation cases. The court of appeals reversed the district court's affirmance of the industrial commissioner's disability decision on the ground the evidence showed as a matter of law that petitioner was totally rather than partially disabled. We believe an issue of fact was presented on the extent of petitioner's industrial disability. Nevertheless we believe the commissioner erred in failing to apply the odd-lot doctrine in this case. Therefore we vacate the decision of the court of appeals, reverse the district court, and remand the case to the industrial commissioner for appropriate additional proceedings.

Petitioner Frank Guyton, Jr. began this action by filing a petition for review-reopening pursuant to Iowa Code section 85.26(2) (1979). He hurt his back on May 5, 1978, while working for respondent Irving Jensen Company in Sioux City, when he was struck in the left hip by a cement truck. Workers' compensation benefits were paid during three months in 1978. In the review-reopening proceeding, he sought benefits for permanent disability, and the dispute concerns the extent of his compensable disability.

The industrial commissioner, acting through a deputy assigned to make the agency decision in accordance with Code section 86.3, determined Guyton's disability to be twenty percent. Upon Guyton's petition for judicial review, the district court affirmed the commissioner. When Guyton appealed to this court, we transferred the case to the court of appeals. That court reversed the district court after holding that Guyton proved total disability as a matter of law. We granted the employer's petition for further review.

Guyton raises essentially two questions in seeking to upset the commissioner's ruling. He contends that the commissioner applied an incorrect rule of law in determining the extent of his industrial disability. He also contends that the commissioner erred in failing to find him totally disabled because the evidence compels such a finding as a matter of law.

I. *The applicable law.* The commissioner acknowledged that a worker's physical impairment is only one factor in determining the extent of the worker's industrial disability. He also acknowledged that the worker's inability to find suitable work after bona fide efforts to do so may demonstrate total disability. In his analysis of the evidence, however, the commissioner framed the standard differently. In relevant part he said:

> The question of disability remains the same for this claimant as for any other claimant: what does the evidence show that he can or cannot do? The evidence clearly shows what he cannot do due to his non-physical limitations, and the medical testimony shows that he indeed has some physical limitations which stem from the injury. However, the photographic evidence shows that his physical limitations are not so complete as to totally incapacitate him from work.

There are some 90 pictures in the exhibits (some are duplicates) which are discussed in the testimony of the private investigator. These pictures and that testimony clearly establish that on the first three days of June, 1982, claimant was able to load a box spring and other miscellaneous items onto his pickup truck, drive it to a landfill, and dispose of the items there. Also, he was able single-handedly to lift a heavy roto tiller onto the pickup. He was observed doing this work, driving the pickup, and other normal activities. It is true that claimant obtained paid medication after doing this work, but it is also true that he apparently continued to do such work because, as of the week of the hearing, the private investigator found that claimant's vehicle was again loaded with "junk." From that fact, one takes the inference that claimant continued his loading, hauling and unloading activities.

The testimony and pictures show that claimant can do work which is within his capabilities for extended periods of time. That being the case, he cannot be said to be permanently and totally disabled. In his findings of fact, the commissioner said:

Although claimant has a permanent partial impairment to the body as a whole of 15 to 20 percent, he is able to perform such activities as loading light to moderately heavy items onto a pickup and is at times able to load an item as heavy as a roto tiller onto a pickup and is able to drive a pickup. The commissioner also said:

> Claimant is disabled to the extent of 20 percent of the body as a whole because of the injury of [May 5, 1978]. In accordance with these findings, the commissioner awarded Guyton benefits based on a twenty percent industrial disability.

Thus the commissioner equated Guyton's ability to obtain employment with his ability to perform physical activity in "junking." In this context, Guyton's industrial disability was determined to be approximately the same as his fifteen to twenty percent functional disability. The availability of suitable employment was not discussed.

The commissioner did not in his analysis address any of the other factors to be considered in determining industrial disability. Industrial disability means reduced earning capacity. Bodily impairment is merely one factor in gauging industrial disability. Other factors include the worker's age, intelligence, education, qualifications, experience, and the effect of the injury on the worker's ability to obtain suitable work. *See Doerfer Division of CCA v. Nicol*, 359 N.W.2d 428, 438 (Iowa 1984). When the combination of factors precludes the worker from obtaining regular employment to earn a living, the worker with only a partial functional disability has a total industrial disability. *See McSpadden v. Big Ben Coal Co.*, 288 N.W.2d 181, 192 (Iowa 1980).

Abundant evidence concerning the other factors was adduced in this case. Guyton is a black man approximately 40 years old who does not know his age. He grew up in Mississippi where he had about one month of formal education. He cannot read or write or make change. The evidence included results of psychological tests administered for social security disability purposes. The tests showed Guyton to be mildly retarded. Considering his retardation with his lack of education and illiteracy, the examiner concluded Guyton "will be limited in competitive employment to jobs of an unskilled, repetitive nature requiring no literacy."

Guyton's employment history before his injury included work as a farm hand in Mississippi, fertilizer bagger in Waterloo, laborer in a Waterloo bottling plant for six years, city garbage man, and janitor at the Waterloo sewage plant. He was working as a laborer on highway construction when he was injured.

The uncontroverted medical evidence was that Guyton received a lower back sprain in the truck mishap, resulting in some percentage of permanent physical impairment due to recurrent pain. Substantial evidence supports the commissioner's finding that this impairment is fifteen to twenty percent of the body. Guyton's physician testified that he would have good days and bad days but could not do any job on a regular basis that involved bending, prolonged sitting, or even lifting as little as ten or fifteen pounds. He believed Guyton could not perform the work in the kind of jobs he previously had.

Testimony was received from a vocational counselor. Based on the medical and psychological data and her study of the job market, she said that before his injury Guyton could expect to obtain elemental employment in the bottom ten percent of the job market. After his injury she did not believe he could even obtain jobs of that type. She said Guyton might find work in a sheltered workshop that would pay approximately $1430 a year. In a normal economic climate, she believed most employers would eliminate him as a job applicant. If he were hired, she thought he would be put in a "last hired, first fired" category. His physical and mental limitations would combine to screen him out of job opportunities. She concluded that Guyton had "little, if any, possibility of job placement in substantial gainful activity." As a result, she said she considered him to be 100 percent vocationally disabled.

The record contains substantial evidence of Guyton's efforts since his injury to find employment. He applied for work with the assistance of a friend at numerous places in the Waterloo area and up to 150 miles away. He had not found employment in this period of more than four years. He subsisted by earning small amounts through his junking activities and through social security disability compensation. There was no evidence that jobs were available to persons with his combination of impairments.

The question is more than the one posed by the commissioner concerning what the evidence shows Guyton "can or cannot do." The question is the extent to which the injury reduced Guyton's earning capacity. This inquiry cannot be answered merely by exploring the limitations on his ability to perform physical activity associated with employment. It requires consideration of all of the factors that bear on his actual employability. *See New Orleans (Gulfwide) Stevadores v. Turner*, 661 F.2d 1031, 1042 (5th Cir. 1981) (are there jobs in the community that the worker can do for which he could realistically compete?). Although the commissioner correctly identified the issue as one of industrial disability, he did not apply that concept in all of its essential aspects to the evidence in this case. We conclude that he misapplied the law. *See* Iowa Code § 17A.19(8)(e).

In determining the correct rule of law to be applied to this record we must address Guyton's contention that Iowa recognizes the "odd-lot doctrine." He argued this contention before the commissioner and in district court. The commissioner believed that doctrine is implicit in the industrial disability standard enunciated in our cases, and we agree. We now formally adopt the doctrine.

Under that doctrine a worker becomes an odd-lot employee when an injury makes the worker incapable of obtaining employment in any well-known branch of the labor market. An odd-lot worker is thus totally disabled if the only services the worker can perform are "so limited in quality, dependability, or quantity that a reasonably stable market for them does not exist. . . . " *Lee v. Minneapolis Street Railway Co.*, 230 Minn. 315, 320, 41 N.W.2d 433, 436 (1950). A person who has no reasonable prospect of steady employment has no material earning capacity. *Id.* at 320, 41 N.W.2d at 436–37. This concept was recognized in *McSpadden*, 288 N.W.2d at 192 ("a claimant's inability to find other suitable work after making bona fide efforts to find such work may indicate that relief should be granted"). It is recognized in virtually every jurisdiction. *See* 2 A. Larson, The Law of [Workers'] Compensation, § 57.51 at 10-164.24 (1983). The evidence in the present case would permit the finder of fact to find Guyton is an odd-lot employee.

In most jurisdictions, the odd-lot doctrine involves an allocation of the burden of production of evidence that has not been addressed in our prior cases. Professor Larson states the general rule as follows:

> A suggested general-purpose principle on burden of proof in this class of cases would run as follows: If the evidence of degree of obvious physical impairment, coupled with other facts such as claimant's mental capacity, education, training, or age, places claimant prima facie in the odd-lot category, the burden should be on the employer to show that some kind of suitable work is regularly and continuously available to the claimant.

Certainly in such a case it should not be enough to show that claimant is physically capable of performing light work, and then round out the case for non-compensability by adding a presumption that light work is available. It is a well-known fact of modern economic life that the demand for unskilled and semiskilled labor has been rapidly declining with the advent of the age of mechanization and automation, and that the great bulk of the persistent hard-core unemployment of the United States is in these categories. 2 A. Larson, *supra*, at 10-164.95 to 10-164.113. Our cases make it clear that the burden of persuasion on the issue of industrial disability always remains with the worker. *See Doerfer Division of CCA*, 359 N.W.2d at 438. The cases, however, have distinguished between burden of persuasion and burden of production in other workers' compensation situations. *See, e.g., McDowell v. Town of Clarksville*, 241 N.W.2d 904, 907 (Iowa 1976) *Nelson v. Cities Service Oil Co.*, 259 Iowa 1209, 1214–15, 146 N.W.2d 261, 263–64 (1966). Before today we were not required to decide whether a presumption exists that suitable work is available to an odd-lot employee or whether evidence must be adduced on that subject.

We adopt the burden of proof allocation enunciated in Professor Larson's statement of the general rule. We emphasize that this rule merely allocates the burden of production of evidence. It is triggered only when the worker makes a prima facie case for inclusion in the odd-lot category:

> It is normally incumbent upon an injured [worker], at a hearing to determine loss of earning capacity, to demonstrate a reasonable effort to secure employ-ment in the area of . . . residence. Where testimony discloses that a reason-able effort was made, the burden of going forward with evidence to show the availability of suitable employment is on the employer and carrier. *Employers Mutual Life Ins. Co. v. Industrial Commission*, 25 Ariz. App. 117, 119, 541 P.2d 580, 582 (1975). The evidence allocation is justified on the ground that the employer ordinarily is in a better position than the worker to determine whether the labor market offers opportunities to persons in the odd-lot

category. *See Ham v. Chrysler Corp.*, 231 A.2d 258, 262 (Del. 1967). The overriding reason for requiring evidence of employment opportunities is because there is no presumption that merely because the worker is physically able to do certain work such work is available. *See Niles Police Dept. v. Industrial Commission*, 83 Ill. 2d 528, 534–35, 416 N.E.2d 243, 246 (1981).

We therefore hold that when a worker makes a prima facie case of total disability by producing substantial evidence that the worker is not employable in the competitive labor market, the burden to produce evidence of suitable employment shifts to the employer. If the employer fails to produce such evidence and the trier of fact finds the worker does fall in the odd-lot category, the worker is entitled to a finding of total disability.

II. *The evidence in this case.* The court of appeals, without using the burden-shifting aspect of the odd-lot employee doctrine, nevertheless found Guyton carried his burden to prove total disability as a matter of law. We do not agree. Even under the odd-lot doctrine that we adopt today the trier of fact is free to determine the weight and credibility of the evidence in determining whether the worker's burden of persuasion has been carried. Only in an exceptional case would evidence by sufficiently strong to compel a finding of total disability as a matter of law. The evidence in the present case is not that strong. As demonstrated in the analysis of the commissioner, a dispute existed in the evidence concerning the effect of Guyton's injury on his ability to hold and keep a job. Although Guyton clearly made a prima facie case that he is totally disabled, the evidence was not strong enough to compel that holding as a matter of law. The evidence would permit a finding that his inability to obtain employment was attributable to unsatisfactory work history unrelated to his injury.

Upon remand, in view of the burden-shifting aspect of the odd-lot doctrine we adopt today, the commissioner shall give the parties an opportunity to offer such additional evidence as they wish on the issue of availability of suitable employment for Guyton. The Commissioner shall make new findings of fact and conclusions of law in accordance with today's holding.

Decision of Court of Appeals vacated. Judgment of District Court reversed and remanded.

All justices concur except Wolle, J., who takes no part.

§ 14.06   INABILITY TO GET WORK BECAUSE OF INJURY AS DISABILITY

POWERS v. DISTRICT OF COLUMBIA DEPARTMENT OF EMPLOYMENT SERVICES
566 A.2d 1068 (D.C. App. 1989)

Before NEWMAN, BELSON and STEADMAN, ASSOCIATE JUDGES.

STEADMAN, ASSOCIATE JUDGE:

Powers suffered a back injury at work and could no longer perform all the duties required by his old job with the National Geographic Society. Nevertheless, the Society retained him in a light-duty job at his former wage level. Several months later the employee resigned in order to take a higher-paying job with the U.S. Postal Service. After a few weeks, he quit because the duties of the new job were too rough on his injured back. The Society refused to rehire him. It took Powers about five months to find new employment. Powers filed a claim for workers' compensation benefits covering this five-month period, which was denied by the Director of the Department of Employment Services (DOES). He appeals to this court.

Section 36-301(8) of the D.C. Workers' Compensation Act denies "disability" as incapacity because of injury which "results in the loss of wages." D.C. Code 36-301(8) (1988). "Wages" in turn are defined as "the money rate at which the service rendered is recompensed under the contract of hiring in force at the time of the injury." D.C. Code § 36-301(19) (1988). The Director reasoned that since subsequent to the injury Powers was receiving from the Society the same wages as at the time of the injury, he was suffering no "loss of wages" on account of the injury and hence was not "disabled" within the meaning of the Act.[49] Thus, at the time Powers decided to resign, he occupied the same position as any other employee who voluntarily determines to leave his or her employment. Furthermore, the Act provides that "if an employee voluntarily limits his income . . . then his wages after becoming disabled shall be deemed to be the amount he would earn if he did not voluntarily limit his income." D.C. Code § 36-308(3)(V), (5). Powers' departure from his job with the Society, voluntarily entailing a risk of wage diminution as a result of subsequent events, was considered as failing within this general principle.[50]

Some of the most complex disability questions arise when claimant first gets some kind of employment after his injury and later becomes unemployed. Claimant's subsequent unemployment may be a combination of the physical disadvantage, general economic conditions, the operation of union seniority rules, and perhaps other factors, such as his discharge for misconduct or his voluntary quitting of his job. 2 A. Larson, Workmen's Compensation Law § 57.62 (1987). On the precise question presented here, the Director correctly notes that some other jurisdictions have held that there is no right to compensation benefits when an employee resigns, not for reasons related to the injury or disability, but for economic reasons to take a better paying job. Otherwise put, any casual link is thereby severed. See Larson, supra, at § 57.64(b); Bryant v. Industrial Comm'n, 21 Ariz. App. 356, 519 P.2d 209 (1974); Pearl v. Builders Iron Foundry, 73 R.I. 304, 55 A.2d 282 (1947).[51]

"The agency's interpretation of the statute it administers is binding on this court unless it conflicts with the plain meaning of the statute or its legislative history. Indeed, we must sustain the agency's interpretation even if a petitioner advances another reasonable interpretation of the statute or if we might have been persuaded by the alternate interpretation had we been construing the statute in the first instance." Smith v. Nonscheduled of Employment Services, 548 A.2d 95, 97 (D.C. 1988) (referring to the Workers' Compensation Act) (citations omitted). Pursuant to this standard, the decision

---

[49] (Court's footnote) Petitioner argues that he was in any event disabled at the point he resigned because he could not then compete in the open labor market, but no such construction is necessarily compelled or controlling in a situation involving a voluntary departure as here.

[50] (Court's footnote) This voluntary limitation of income analysis was that applied by the hearing examiner and adopted by the Director in his original decision. On remand from this court for clarification, the Director issued an amended decision emphasizing the statutory definition of "disability." However, the amended decision also "affirmed, adopted, and incorporated by reference herein" the hearing examiner's decision. Of course, as the amended decision observed, the instant case does not involve "traditional" voluntary limitation of income problems, such as refusal to accept appropriate employment or to undertake vocational rehabilitation.

[51] (Court's footnote) "One difficulty with the rule in the Pearl case is that the claimant, having resumed his employment, apparently must cling to the same job forever, for if he leaves it, even an admitted combination of medical disability and inability to get work as a result will never again entitle claimant to an award." Larson, supra at § 57.64(c). Accordingly, some cases have approved a more ameliorated approach. See Bajdek's Case, 73 N.E.2d 253 (Mass. 1947); Continental Insurance Co. v. Lamar, 147 Ga. App. 487, 249 S.E. 2d 304 (1978).

of the Director must be affirmed.

PROBLEMS

(1) Formulate a rationale that would justify a limited and modest schedule within a basically "wage-loss" statute.

(2) Claimant schoolteacher continued teaching a year after his injury in order to reach thirty years' service for retirement. Does this fact of itself disprove disability? *See* American Sur. Co. v. Kizer, 212 Tenn. 328, 369 S.W.2d 736 (1963).

(3) No state has as yet attempted to contrive a specific formula to deal with the problem in *Powers* — i.e., how to decide, under a wage-loss system, whether post-injury unemployment is due to the injury, or to independent causes such as business conditions, the employee's misconduct, or the employee's good-faith quitting to get a better job. Try your hand at formulating a statutory provision covering this problem. Consider whether there should be one rule for the initial inability to get any job at all after the injury, and subsequent inability to get a job after having held some kind of employment and lost it for reasons other than the injury.

Chapter 15
SCHEDULE BENEFITS

SYNOPSIS

§ 15.01   INTRODUCTION

If an injury has left the claimant with a "scheduled" permanent bodily impairment, compensation for a specified number of weeks is payable without regard to presence or absence of wage loss during that period. For loss (and usually also loss of use) of members, arbitrary schedules of the number of weeks for which compensation is payable are provided; for other permanent impairments, a calculation of percentage of total permanent disability is usually made. Although in many jurisdictions the schedule award is the exclusive remedy whenever applicable, some courts are beginning to treat the loss of specific members as amounting to percentage disabilities of larger members or of the entire body, or as total disability, when this more fairly reflects the actual effect of the injury.

§ 15.02   NATURE OF SCHEDULE BENEFITS

Schedule benefits for permanent partial disability are authorized by the statutes in all American jurisdictions.

The typical schedule provides that, after the injury has become stabilized and its permanent effects can be appraised, benefits described in terms of regular weekly benefits for specified numbers of weeks shall be paid, ranging, for example, from 312 weeks for an arm, 288 for a leg, and 160 for an eye to 38 for a great toe and 7 1/2 for one phalange of the little finger.[1] These payments are not dependent on actual wage loss. Evidence that the claimant has had actual earnings, or has even been regularly employed at greater earnings than before, is completely immaterial.[2]

This is not, however, to be interpreted as an erratic deviation from the underlying principle of compensation law — that benefits relate to loss of earning capacity and not to physical injury as such. The basic theory remains the same; the only difference is that the effect on earning capacity is a conclusively presumed one, instead of a specifically proved one based on the individual's actual wage-loss experience. The effect must necessarily be a presumed one, since it would be obviously unfair to appraise the impact of a permanent injury on earning capacity by looking at claimant's earning record for some relatively short temporary period preceding the hearing. The alternative is to hold every compensation case involving any degree of permanent impairment open for a lifetime, making specific calculations of the effect of the impairment on claimant's earnings each time claimant contends that his earnings are being adversely affected. To

---

[1] These illustrative figures are taken from the schedule in the N.Y. Workmen's Comp. Law § 15(3) (1965).

[2] Alaska Indus. Bd. v. Chugach Elec. Ass'n, 356 U.S. 320, 78 S. Ct. 735, 2 L. Ed. 2d 795 (1958). "The lump-sum awards for total or permanent disability under this [Alaska's] Compensation Act ignore wage losses. Whatever the employee may have made before, whatever his wages may be after the injury, the award is the same. To that extent it is an arbitrary amount. But it is the expression of a legislative judgment that on average there has been a degree of impairment and whatever may be the fact in a particular case, the lump sum should be paid without more." 356 U.S. at 323–324.

avoid this protracted administrative task, the apparently cold-blooded system of putting average-price tags on arms, legs, eyes, and fingers has been devised.

§ 15.03 EXCLUSIVENESS OF SCHEDULE ALLOWANCES

VAN DORPEL v. HAVEN-BUSCH COMPANY
350 Mich. 135, 85 N.W.2d 97 (1957)

VOELKER, JUSTICE.

On December 22, 1948 Peter Van Dorpel a 65-year old widower without dependents was working at the job he had followed for upwards of five years: painting steel beams and angle irons for his employer. When painting heavy steel beams it was the practice to rest a number of beams on steel shop horses, attaching the one being painted to an overhead electric chain hoist, which from time to time could be operated for ease in maneuvering or turning the beam on which a man was working. On the day in question, as one of the beams was being turned on the chain hoist, the chain broke and the beam fell, striking the right leg of Peter Van Dorpel and forcing another beam against his right hand, with which he painted.

In the accident the right leg was badly crushed and the four fingers of the right hand were dismembered at the palm. During subsequent hospitalization it was deemed necessary on January 18, 1949 to amputate the leg above the knee. In due course Mr. Van Dorpel was paid compensation on the basis of specific losses of members of the body in accordance with the schedules as they then existed, namely, for the loss of four fingers and a leg. At the expiration of this period the payments were stopped and Mr. Van Dorpel applied for further compensation. In an award dated May 10, 1955 the hearing officer found that the claimant "has a further total disability above and beyond the specific losses suffered in the accidental personal injury" of December 22, 1948, and further compensation was ordered.

From this award the defendant company and its insurer sought review, and on April 13, 1956 a divided appeal board affirmed the award, modifying it to provide that compensation should not exceed 750 weeks from the date of injury. From this decision the defendants applied to this Court for leave to appeal, which was granted. For convenience hereafter the two corporate appellants will be referred to in the third person singular.

The material facts as to the injury and extent of disability are not in dispute. The thumb was not involved and there were no other injuries or complications. Healing recovery from the amputation was normal. There was medical and other testimony that the claimant had lost the industrial use of his hand and had difficulty in walking, dressing and feeding himself. No question is presented as to whether or not Peter Van Dorpel is in fact totally and permanently disabled from any further industrial employment. All are agreed that he is. The sole question for our determination is the narrow legal one of whether or not recovery for specific losses under part II, section 10 of the act operates as a legal bar to any additional recovery under section 9.

Since its enactment in this state in 1912, section 9 of part II of the workmen's compensation act has provided for compensation for total incapacity and section 10 has provided for compensation for partial incapacity and also for enumerated specific losses of members of the body, certain enumerated combined losses also there being declared to result in total disability. Despite occasional amendments to both sections, the basic design of each has remained substantially unchanged.

At the time of this accident the applicable portion of section 9, after stating the weekly payments for total incapacity for work, read as follows:

> and in no case shall the period covered by such compensation be greater than
> 500 weeks from the date of the injury, nor shall the total amount of all

compensation exceed $10,500.00, except for permanent and total disability, when the compensation shall be paid for 750 weeks from the date of the injury." Comp. Laws 1948, § 412.9.

Likewise section 10:

> In cases included by the following schedule, the disability in each such case shall be deemed to continue for the period specified, and the compensation so paid for such injury shall be as specified therein, to wit: Comp. Laws 1948, § 412.10.

There then follows the list of specific losses of members of the body coming within the schedule for which payment must be made for a specified number of weeks depending upon the particular member or members lost. In December 1948 this schedule provided for a total of 100 weeks for the loss of the first, second, third and fourth fingers, and further provided for 200 weeks for the loss of a leg.

It is the contention of the appellant that the payment of compensation for the scheduled number of weeks provided by section 10 for the specific loss of four fingers of the right hand and the loss of the right leg acts as a permanent legal bar and limitation to the allowance of any further or other compensation whatever to the claimant, regardless of his condition or state of recovery or inability to work at the end of that time. In other words appellant claims that these provisions of section 10 set both the maximum as well as the minimum of compensation payments allowable and that in no event may a claimant later seek recovery for total disability for such injuries and losses under section 9.

In support of his position he cites as bearing on this point five cases. They are: *Limron v. Blair*, 1914, 181 Mich. 76, 147 N.W. 546; *Curtis v. Hayes Wheel Company*, 1920, 211 Mich. 260, 178 N.W. 675; *Addison v. W. E. Wood Company*, 1919, 207 Mich. 319, 174 N.W. 149; *Stackhouse v. General Motors Corporation*, 1939, 290 Mich. 249, 287 N.W. 452; and *Clements v. Chrysler Corporation*, 1948, 321 Mich. 558, 33 N.W.2d 82.

In his brief and argument appellee attempts to distinguish appellant's cases; he also hints but does not quite bring himself to say that some of them are bad law; and he further attempts to differ his situation from that of the *Curtis* case by urging that here we have multiple grave cumulative losses from a common accident, amounting in fact to admitted total disability, whereas there was but the loss of a single member. He also claims that he is entitled to recover total disability under section 10 for the combined loss of a hand and leg, a proposition anticipated, argued and denied by the appellant.

Of the cases cited by appellant we believe the *Curtis* case, decided in 1920, is the one most squarely in point. There the applicant suffered an injury to his leg necessitating amputation between 4 and 5 inches below the knee joint. Agreed compensation was paid for the specific loss of a foot for the total number of weeks then provided. Following this the applicant filed a petition for further compensation, alleging non-recovery and continued incapacity to work. After a hearing the board found that total incapacity to work existed and made an award accordingly.

In vacating that portion of the award allowing compensation beyond the number of weeks then allowed for specific loss under section 10, this Court there said (211 Mich. at page 264, 178 N.W. at page 676):

> . . . This leads to a careful consideration of the several provisions of sections 9 and 10 [part 2] of the act, (sections 5439, 5440, 2 Comp. Laws 1915, as amended by Pub. Laws 1919, No. 64). Section 9 provides for compensation in cases where the incapacity for work is total. Applicant is entitled to recover under it until the time when his foot was amputated. Thereafter his claim comes under the provisions of section 10, which specifically allows 'for the loss of a foot, sixty per centum of average weekly wages during one hundred and twenty-five weeks.' As soon as the amputation was performed, he became disabled by the loss of his foot. He suffered no other injury than that which resulted in the amputation. As

the act provides specific compensation for the loss of a foot, we are of the opinion that all liability of [defendants] ceased when payment was made for the full term of 125 weeks. These specific items of compensation fixed by the act must control when no other disability than such as results from the removal of the member exists. To hold otherwise would, so far as the employer is concerned, render this provision nugatory and of no effect. Should the employee recover from the effects of the amputation in a few weeks and be able to resume his employment, the payments secured to him on account thereof are in no way affected, but continue during the term fixed. *To hold that when his recovery is not fully completed at the expiration of the stated term he may present a claim for further compensation under section 9, would give him an advantage not contemplated in the act. . . .* (Italics ours.)

At the outset we must record the fact that the Court which signed the unanimous opinion in the *Curtis* case had already done much to promulgate a broad and liberal interpretation of the workmen's compensation act and continued to make many notable contributions in that direction after the *Curtis* case was decided. Both fairness and candor demand that this be freely acknowledged. But few courts are infallible, especially when they are construing comparatively new legislation; and sometimes the full implications of a given interpretation of a statute can best be appraised only by living with it. Judges are no less fallible than other men and no originality is claimed when we suggest that sometimes in this area, as in other areas of life, experience is often the best teacher. In the light of this acknowledgment and these observations, then, we shall proceed to appraise the *Curtis* case.

After 37 years we now make bold to ask: a contrary rule gives the luckless amputee an "advantage" over whom? Did the *Curtis* case mean to announce some sort of rule of "turn-about-is-fair-play" in that since, fortunately, many injured workmen do recover and are able to return to work before the minimum number of weeks allowed for specific loss runs out that therefore those who do not should cheerfully accept their fate in order to roughly balance out a presumed inequity? Or did it mean to suggest that amputees possess some mysterious "advantage" over those unfortunate injured workmen who are denied the heady distinction and presumed aesthetic delight inherent in a neatly executed surgical amputation? And in what way would a different rule have rendered section 10 "nugatory"? In what way would a different rule have given an unrecovered or disabled amputee an "advantage" over his brother workers who were hardy enough or fortunate enough to recover and return to work at the time or even before their minimum number of weeks had run out? How can any workman who cannot work ever possess any "advantage" over one who can?

These are some of the questions which we are afraid were not hinted at much less grappled with in the *Curtis* case. Rather is it not true that under such a rule as there declared all the advantage lies instead with those injured workmen who are stubborn or better advised or lucky enough to refuse or escape amputation? Rather did not the *Curtis* case itself, however unwittingly, in one swoop "amputate" an important area of the act and render it "nugatory"?

There is more to be said. We mean to cast no aspersion on a dedicated and hard-working medical profession when we suggest that such a rule does little or nothing to discourage employers and their insurers from favoring a prognosis of early amputation. It also cannot help but compel some surgeons to at times feel not unlike reluctant commercial sculptors. That way, too, long and expensive therapy to save injured members may thus be avoided. And, as we have suggested, the rule of the *Curtis* case tends likewise to encourage stubborn, brave — or well-advised — injured workmen to grin and bear it, and to cling at almost any cost in pain and suffering to their injured members for economic rather than medical reasons. None of this is healthy or good for anyone concerned, least of all for the injured employee. Thus Peter Van Dorpel in this case would have been economically better off if he would have grinned and borne it and in his state of shock and confusion refused or managed to avoid amputation of his crushed leg — just as, under the "hand" decisions of this Court, he would have been economically better off if the fateful steel girder which bore his name had struck his hand a few inches higher. Under the *Curtis* case, too, he would have been better off if he had received in addition a slight concussion or strain or wrench or blow — or else dreamed one up; something, anything, to take the curse off his singular misfortune in merely neatly losing a leg and four fingers of his working hand, slick and clean, and then daring to come in and swear that that was all.

We can conceive of many situations in which the workman who receives injuries resulting in specific losses aggregating less than a statutory finding of total disability may in fact be totally disabled. Thus the piccolo player or tailor or night club pianist or anyone else who must normally use all his fingers may be forever out of business over the loss of a few of the wrong fingers (and yet fall far short of the statutory combination of declared total disability). Again that same individual may instead lose both legs (thus gaining total statutory disability) and actually be able at an early date to go on with his usual work unperturbed. Now we do not mean to quarrel with the notion of statutorily declared minimums up to total disability, which has much to commend it; rather we seek to demonstrate that the only fair and sensible rule in cases of non-recovery or inability to work following specific loss of members that may fall short of declared total disability is, as in all other cases, to inquire into the facts in each case: can the injured workman in fact continue to work and earn wages in the employment at which he was engaged when injured? *See Levanen v. Seneca Copper Corp.*, 227 Mich. 592, 601, 199 N.W. 652.

As we have already noted, plaintiff not only seeks to distinguish the *Curtis* case on its facts but to offer a rather novel distinction between that case and those — such as this one — where there are multiple specific losses resulting from a common accident. To such lengths has the *Curtis* case driven imaginative and zealous counsel. We admire plaintiff's resource and appreciate his ingenuity, but we refuse to grasp at this shyly proffered legal straw. In our view the ultimate question in this case and in all situations akin to this one is not — and never should be — whether the injured workman suffered one or a dozen specific losses. In our view the sole question in all of these cases should be: after the passage of the number of weeks allowed for the specific loss or losses falling short of declared total disability, can the injured workman go back to work? If he can — and fortunately he usually does — then well and good; if he can't, and if there are competent proofs to support his claim of continuing disability, then his compensation should be continued. It is as simple as that, and we do not hesitate to brush aside those decided cases which hold or appear to hold to the contrary, including at long last the unfortunate *Curtis* case.

Such a construction as was made in the *Curtis* case is to import into the act a rigidity and disregard for the common experience of mankind and the endless variety of jobs that men must perform to earn a living which we cannot believe the members of the legislature ever intended. We cannot believe that by section 10 a legislative body sitting in Lansing meant so cavalierly and irrevocably to separate the wounded industrial sheep from the goats; to appear to say so surely that the loss of so many inches or pounds of human flesh and gristle and bone shall entitle one man to one thing and no more, regardless of his condition and ability to work at the end of that time, and that the loss of so many other inches or pounds would entitle the next man to a finding of so many more weeks up to total disability, regardless of his original and subsequent condition and ability to work. Did the legislature mean to be lavishly liberal on the one hand and deliberately niggardly on the other? Or rather did it not there intend to consult broad industrial experience and lay down an irreducible minimum number of weeks allowable for certain common specific losses — thus removing the issue from costly and delaying litigation at a time when the workman was most helpless and his need the greatest — leaving the question of further disability and compensation to be determined on proofs made at a hearing in an orderly manner (in which the healed workman could be present and intelligently participate) in the light of his recovery or lack of it, having due regard for the nature and extent of the injuries, the then capacities and general condition of the workman, and the kind of a job he had before his injury? It is our educated guess that it meant the latter.

"The usual statute provides for both total disability and specific loss- . . . without expressly saying that either shall be exclusive," Larson says beginning on page 45 of volume 2 of his work on workmen's compensation. "It could therefore be argued that, since the act must be given a liberal construction," he continues, "destruction of the more favorable remedy should not be read into the act by implication in a case where claimant is able to prove a case coming under either heading. . . . To refuse total disability benefits in such a case . . . has the effect of ruling out the inability-to-get-work element in a listed group of injuries which just happen to take the form of a neatly classifiable loss of a member. . . . Logically there is no reason to make the distinction [whether total disability exists] turn on the physical extension of effects beyond the lost member. . . . The above reasoning was followed in *Cox v. Black Diamond Coal Mining Company*, D.C.E.D.Tenn., 93 F.Supp. 685, which disposed of the issue as a straightforward matter of statutory construction, there being two parallel benefits provided for uncomplicated loss . . . and the rule of liberal construction requiring that claimant be allowed the more favorable."

In his conclusion the appellant argues forcefully and at length that legislative silence and inaction for 37 years after the *Curtis* case amounts to a tacit recognition of its soundness by which we must irrevocably be bound. Now this beguiling doctrine of legislative assent by silence possesses a certain undeniable logic and charm. Nor are we oblivious to the flattery implicit therein; double flattery, in fact: flattery both to the profound learning and wisdom of the particular supreme court which has spoken, and flattery to a presumably alert and eagerly responsive state legislature. One pictures the legislators of our various states periodically clamoring and elbowing each other in their zeal to get at the pearls of wisdom embalmed in the latest decisions and advance sheets of their respective supreme courts — and thenceforth indicating their unbounded approval by a vast and permanent silence.

Yet there are several dark shadows in this picture. For one, it suggests a legislative passion for reading and heeding the decisions of our supreme courts which we suspect may be scarcely borne out by the facts. For another, pushed too far such a doctrine suggests the interesting proposition that it is the legislatures which have now become the ultimate courts of last resort in our various states; that if they delay long enough to correct our errors those errors thus become both respectable and immutably frozen; and, finally, the larger and more dismal corollary that if enough people persist long enough in ignoring an injustice it thereby becomes just. We reject as both un-Christian and legally unsound the hopeless doctrine that this Court is shackled and helpless to redeem itself from its own original sin, however or by whomever long condoned.

Courts throughout the land have long split over this doctrine of legislative acquiescence by silence. The usual arguments for recognizing it are that it gives stability and sureness to the law; that "rights" thus acquired can thus only be disturbed at regular and predictable intervals by but one branch of the government, the legislative; and, finally, that to disregard the doctrine amounts to judicial legislating. Now we recognize that a court should not lightly overrule an interpretation of a statute that has been the law for 37 years, but we also see little justice or utility in continuing to give stability or sureness to an unfortunate rule of law; nor do we understand that employers or their insurance carriers have gained any vested "rights" in the interpretation of this statute; nor do we think that the reinterpretation of a statute in the light of long experience with an unfortunate interpretation constitutes judicial legislating.

This case involves an interpretation of a statute which is silent on the precise issue involved. This Court 37 years ago decided what it thought the correct interpretation should be. We happen to disagree with that old interpretation and wish to make a new interpretation, for the reasons herein stated. It is suggested that we should not do this because, whether the original interpretation was right or wrong, inaction by the legislature since it was handed down constitutes a sort of informal post-enactment declaration of legislative assent thereto possessing the binding effect of law; and that any new and variant interpretation here and now would on that account constitute "judicial legislation."

To our mind the doctrine implicit in this kind of reasoning constitutes a surrender of the judicial function to a legislative body. In the final analysis the objection may fairly be stated thus: Our Court interprets a statute; whether right or wrong our decision henceforth becomes judicially immutable and we are powerless to change it; there is only one way it can be changed; if we are wrong we must wait for the legislature to tell us so; if by its long silence and inaction the legislature does not speak out and tell us we are wrong then it has perforce by the same token told us we are right; in any case this Court is forever fettered and powerless to reinterpret the statute in question. We have instead delegated that function to the legislature. This curious doctrine can be boiled down even more: right or wrong in the *Curtis* case, we are helpless to change it.

Such a doctrine is to squarely place the legislature in the position of a super supreme court. We also consider it an abdication of judicial responsibility. We reject such a doctrine flatly along with the sort of mechanistic thinking that can arrive at such an ironic impasse. This doctrine has irreverently been called the "one shot" theory of legislative interpretation. We ourselves brand it a Rip Van Winkle doctrine of judicial stagnation and inertia. We happen strongly to disagree with it and in this we are not alone.

. . . .

A little sense of proportion and realism in this area might not be amiss. The plain fact is that courts of last resort everywhere constantly engage in a form of "judicial legislating" when they are confronted — as they so often are — by statutory or other provisions of ambiguous or uncertain meaning. Such judicial interpretations often in effect add words to a statute. Must we act at our peril that we might possibly be wrong? Some judges solemnly declare that we must. Yet far from being the doctrine of humility and keeping our places that they would have it appear, isn't this essentially to preach the gospel of judicial infallibility? Scarcely a term of this Court passes that all of us are not obliged to interpret unclear statutes. Occasionally we must reinterpret them. It is one of our primary functions; that's what we're here for. It is only when a judge ignores or flies in the face of a positive and unambiguous statutory enactment that he may justly be accused of judicial legislating, in the bad sense. That is not our case.

No living man can possibly measure the amount of poverty and pain and human indignity suffered by Michigan workmen and their families because of the unfortunate *Curtis* case. It has lain across the jugular vein of workmen's compensation far too long. Rather than attempt to distinguish that case — as we are aware we might — we prefer to sweep away the last vestiges of the *Curtis* case and at long last align Michigan squarely behind the more modern and liberal decisions which refuse to limit workmen's compensation benefits to the scheduled allowance. We believe it is time for the *Curtis* case to go.

In the final analysis we have here — as Larson has pointed out — a situation where the legislature has not clearly expressed its intent. It is unfortunate that the highest court in one of the greatest industrial states in the nation should 37 years ago have adopted a narrow construction of that unexpressed intent. We have long conceived the workmen's compensation acts to be one of the great pioneer landmarks in humanitarian social legislation in the Anglo-American world. In the bold sweeping away of ancient legal cobwebs and in the grandeur of its concepts and declared purposes these acts were almost as revolutionary, in their way, as was the surging Industrial Revolution itself that preceded their inevitable birth. These acts set the pace and led the way for much salutary social legislation that followed. It is not too much to say that they charted a whole brave new legal world.

In our view it should go almost without saying that as new interpretative issues should arise judicially under these acts all fair and reasonable doubts should be resolved in favor of upholding the basic purposes of the legislation, in this case compensating in some measure the broken and injured workman who cannot work.

. . . .

In view of our decision we shall not consider the interesting companion question whether recovery might have been had here under section 10 for the combined loss of a leg and a hand. The award of the appeal board is affirmed with costs. The appellant should of course have credit for compensation already paid.

SMITH, EDWARDS and BLACK, JJ., concurred with VOELKER, J.

SHARPE, KELLY and CARR, JJ. and DETHMERS, C.J., dissented.

GENERAL ELECTRIC CO. v. INDUSTRIAL COMMISSION
89 Ill. 2d 432, 433 N.E.2d 671 (1982)

SIMON, JUSTICE.

. . . .

While working for another employer 10 years earlier, [claimant] developed a wrist problem known as carpal tunnel syndrome, had a surgical procedure called carpal tunnel release, and received a compensation award. Her latest job was with G.E. It consisted of picking up coils weighing about three pounds each, inserting them in a machine for processing, and removing them, by which time they would weigh about seven pounds. When she began the job, she could do it without difficulty and in general had no problem with her arm, but after a few months her arms started giving her some trouble at work. One day she felt a sharp pain in her wrist while picking up a coil, and she reported to the nursing station. She continued working for several months with the help of a wrist bandage, and her condition worsened until she could no longer do her job. She had once more developed carpal tunnel syndrome and required more surgery.

. . . (the court here rejects the contention that the claimant was not injured in the course of her employment.)

Section 8(e) begins: "For accidental injuries in the following schedule, the employee shall receive compensation for the period of temporary total incapacity * * * and shall receive in addition thereto compensation for a further period for the specific loss herein mentioned, but shall not receive any compensation under any other provisions of this Act." (Emphasis added.) (Ill. Rev. Stat. 1975, ch. 48, par. 138.8(e).)

However, in Springfield Park District v. Industrial Com. (1971), 49 Ill. 2d 67, 273 N.E.2d 376, this court held that the italicized language did not establish section 8(e) as the exclusive remedy for all scheduled injuries, but was intended only to prevent double recovery; that is, if a claimant receives an award under section 8(e), he is not eligible for any other compensation except for temporary total incapacity. In particular, Springfield Park District held that if an injury listed in section 8(e) permanently and completely disables an employee for work, he is entitled to a total disability award under section 8(f) (Ill. Rev. Stat. 1969, ch. 48, par. 138.8(f)).

In Pruiett v. Industrial Com. (1976), 65 Ill. 2d 240, 2 Ill. Dec. 377, 357 N.E.2d 544, on the other hand, this court barred recovery under section 8(d) for earnings loss in cases of scheduled injuries not producing total disability, holding that recovery was to be exclusively under section 8(e). The reasoning of Pruiett was that section 8(d), as it then read, expressly applied "except in cases covered by the specific schedule" of paragraph (e) (Ill. Rev. Stat. 1971, ch. 48, par. 138.8(d)).

The Act, however, has been amended since the accident that was the subject matter of Pruiett. The exception that formerly read "except in cases covered by the specific schedule" has been changed to read "except in cases compensated under" paragraph (e) (emphasis added) (Ill. Rev. Stat. 1975, ch. 48, par. 138.8(d)(1)). This court has never interpreted the new language.

The change in language must have been intended to change the law, especially because the same act that effected the change (Pub. Act 79-79) also added a new provision to section 8(d), namely section 8(d)(2), dealing with serious and permanent injuries "not covered by" paragraphs (c) and (e) (emphasis added) (1975 Ill. Laws 224, 252). The legislature did not simply like the sound of "compensated" better than "covered"; it continued to use "covered" when it meant "covered," but amended section 8(d)(1) to use a different word. The obvious meaning of section 8(d)(1)'s amended language ("except in cases compensated under" paragraph (e) (emphasis added)) is that compensation under section 8(d)(1) is barred only if compensation is actually awarded under section 8(e), not simply because an injury is listed in the schedule as compensable under paragraph (e). Compensation may be proper under either section, though not both at once.

The change in the law accomplished by this amendment is in line with a nationwide trend. Professor Larson summarizes: "Although it is difficult to speak in terms of a majority rule on this point, because of significant differences in statutory background, it can be said that at one time the doctrine of exclusiveness of schedule allowances did dominate the field. But in recent years there has developed such a strong trend in the opposite direction that one might now, with equal justification, say that the field is dominated by the view that schedule allowances should not be deemed exclusive * * *." 2 A. Larson, Workmen's Compensation sec. 58.23, at 10-257 (1981).

This trend is supported by sound reasons. Scheduled awards are often not fair. For example, partial loss of use of a finger may be an annoyance to some workers, but a catastrophe for a violinist. Nor are scheduled allowances always fast and certain. It is often easier to calculate how much a claimant's earnings have decreased since the accident than to assign a percentage partial loss of use. Exclusive scheduled awards cannot be justified as a kind of liquidated damages, an unchallengeable estimate of earnings loss. Rather, the schedule represents a presumed minimum loss, looking toward the uncertainties of future employment prospects. The law recognizes that the loss of a body part will probably catch up with a worker sooner or later, even if his current work happens to be only slightly impeded by the injury. The worker is allowed to recover the scheduled amount without having to demonstrate how the expected eventual loss of earnings will come about. If, however, he can prove an actual loss of earnings greater than the schedule presumes, there is no reason why he should not recover that loss. In theory, the basis of the workers' compensation system should be earnings loss, not the schedule.

We conclude that the Act, as amended, authorizes awards under section 8(d)(1) even for injuries enumerated in section 8(e). The Industrial Commission's decision to award compensation under section 8(d) was not improper. . . .

The judgment is *affirmed*.

§ 15.04 ATTACHABILITY OR GARNISHABILITY OF BENEFITS

GENERAL MOTORS ACCEPTANCE CORP. v. FALCONE
130 N.J. Super. 517, 327 A.2d 699 (1974)

LONGHI, P. J. D. C.

On April 22, 1974 plaintiff obtained judgment against defendant in the sum of $623.89 plus costs. The judgment not having been paid, plaintiff executed on the judgment and on June 22, 1974 levied on $145.39 in defendant's checking account. Plaintiff now seeks an order directing the bank to pay over to the constable the monies levied upon. Defendant resists the order on the ground that the funds levied upon derive solely from social security and workmen's compensation benefits and are exempt.

Defendant's sole means of support, for himself and his family, are a monthly social security check in the amount of $518.10 and semi-monthly workmen's compensation checks in the amount of $160.00.

While on the date of the bank levy there was only $145.39 in defendant's checking account, his total deposit for June, up to the date of levy, were $900.10. Of these monies $518.10 represented social security benefits and $342.00 represented the residue of workmen's compensation checks.

It is clear that monies obtained from social security benefits are exempt from execution, levy, attachment, garnishment or other legal process, even after they have been paid to the debtor. 42 U.S.C.A. § 407; *Philpott v. Essex County Welfare Board*, 409 U.S. 413, 93 S.Ct. 590, 34 L. Ed.2d 608 (1973).

The question presented to the court is whether the exemption provided in the Workmen's Compensation Act applies to monies after payment to a debtor.

The relevant portion of the Workmen's Compensation Act, N.J.S.A. 34:15-29 provides:

> Claims or payments due under this chapter shall not be assignable, and shall be exempt from all claims of creditors and from levy, execution or attachment.

At issue is the meaning to be given the phrase "Claims or payments due," but more specifically the word "due." Plaintiff urges that once payments have been made they are no longer "due" and thus the exemption no longer applies. In support of his position plaintiff cites *Beierlein v. Faulkner*, 15 Misc. 313, 190 A. 853 (Dt. Ct. 1937).

Beierlein involved a similar factual pattern. The court there construed the phrase "Claims or payments due" in its strictest sense. The court viewed the purpose behind the exemption as administrative in nature, intended to avoid confusion in the Workmen's Compensation Division, thereby relieving the Division of extra bookkeeping duties and conflicting claims of ownership. *Beierlein* has not been followed and has more or less withered on the vine. In any event I feel that the result in *Beierlein* is wrong and contrary to the intent and purpose of the Workmen's Compensation Act.

The purpose of statutory construction is to bring the operation of the statute within the apparent intention of the Legislature. *Nagy v. Ford Motor Co.*, 6 N.J. 341, 78 A.2d 709 (1951).

Exemptions as the term is used in connection with the rights of creditors seeking to secure their debts can be said to be the right of a debtor to retain a portion of his personal property free from seizure under judicial process. 31 Am. Jur. 2d, Exemptions, § 1. Exemptions did not exist at common law and are mere creatures of statute or constitutional enactment. They are granted on grounds of public policy for a humane purpose.

It is the policy of the State of New Jersey to favor exemptions in those situations where they exist by statute. *See Hoffman v. Hoffman*, 8 N.J. 157, 162–163, 84 A.2d 441 (1951); *Freedom Finance Co., Inc. v. Fleckenstein*, 116 N.J.Super. 428, 282 A.2d 458 (Cty. Dt. Ct.1971).

The Workmen's Compensation Act is social legislation designed to accomplish a humane and generous purpose. The award is "in lieu of wages." *Williams v. Newark Dept. of Welfare*, 43 N.J. Super. 473, 477, 129 A.2d 56 (Cty. Ct. 1957). *See also, Kozielec v. Mack Mfg. Corp.*, 29 N.J. Super. 272, 102 A.2d 404 (Cty. Ct. 1953); *King v. Western Electric Co.*, 122 N.J.L. 442, 448, 5 A.2d 490 (Sup. Ct. 1939). Workmen's compensation affords an injured worker a measure of economic security during the period of time he is recuperating from a work-related accident, and further compensates him for permanent disability which reduces his future earning capacity. *See Naseef v. Cord Inc.*, 48 N.J. 317, 325, 225 A.2d 343 (1966); *Sanders v. Jarka Corp.*, 1 N.J. 36, 42, 61 A.2d 641 (1948), *Electronic Associates, Inc. v. Heisinger*, 111 N.J. Super. 15, 19, 266 A.2d 601 (App. Div. 1970). The obvious intent of the Legislature is to keep the injured worker from becoming a burden to the public.

It is ludicrous to give the exemption provided in the Workmen's Compensation Act a meaning that merely promotes "the convenience of the state by withdrawing the occasion for conflicting claims of ownership." *Surace v. Danna*, 248 N.Y. 18, 22, 161 N.E. 315, 316 (Ct. App. 1928).

I would point out that the logical application of plaintiff's position would permit a creditor to attach, levy or execute upon the entire workmen's compensation monies after they were paid to an injured worker — a result he could not obtain if he were garnishing the wages of a noninjured worker. 15 U.S.C.A., §§ 1671 to 1677; N.J.S.A. 2A:17-50 to 56. Such a result is clearly unjust.

I find that the intent of the exemption in the Workmen's Compensation Act, N.J.S.A. 34:15-29, is not limited to monies before payment to a petitioner but also to funds actually paid to him and deposited in a bank account, insofar as said funds are traceable to workmen's compensation benefits.

The motion for an order to turn over the bank account is denied and the levy is vacated.

PROBLEMS

(1) Oregon has an express statutory provision exempting compensation benefits from garnishment. Claimant failed to make child support and alimony payments. Can a court make an exception to the statute in such a case? *See* Calvin v. Calvin, 487 P.2d 1164 (Or. App. 1971).

(2) In New Jersey, a year after *Falcone*, a wife in a divorce settlement sought to have included in the property available for equitable distribution any award her husband might receive in a pending compensation claim. What result? *See* Hughes v. Hughes, 132 N.J. Super. 559, 334 A.2d 397 (1975).

Chapter 16
SUCCESSIVE DISABILITIES

§ 16.01 INTRODUCTION

The total effect of two successive injuries may be much greater than the sum of schedule allowances for the parts, the commonest illustration being the loss, by a person blind in one eye, of the remaining eye. In a few states, by statute, the loss may be apportioned, with the employer paying only for such disability as would have resulted in the absence of the prior disability. Under such statutes it is important to distinguish such prior disability (which means the kind of definite loss of a member or permanent impairment of the body that would be recognized as a disability for compensation purposes if work-connected) from prior predisposing weakness or disease which, although not disabling at the time of injury, is precipitated by the industrial injury and contributes to its effects. Apart from apportionment statutes, the employer is generally held liable for the entire disability resulting from the combination of the prior disability and the present injury. To prevent the unfair impact of this rule on employers and the discrimination against impaired workers in hiring policy that results, most modern statutes have created a special fund which pays something like the difference between what the employer pays under this rule and what it would pay under an apportionment statute.

§ 16.02 FULL-RESPONSIBILITY RULE

The successive-injury problem arises from the obvious fact that the combined effect of two physical disabilities is often far greater than would be reflected by merely adding together the schedule allowances for each injury existing separately. The loss of a leg, which would ordinarily mean only partial disability to a normal person, results in total disability to the person who has already, from whatever cause, lost the other leg.

There are three approaches to the resulting dilemma:

(1) The "full-responsibility" rule, imposing liability for the entire resulting disability upon the employer;

(2) Apportionment statutes, under which the employer pays only for the single member lost in his or her employment; and

(3) Second-injury funds, which ensure that the employee receives the full disability benefits but reimburses the employer for the difference between this sum and what he or she would pay under an apportionment statute.

In the absence of an apportionment statute, the general rule is that the employer becomes liable for the entire disability resulting from a compensable accident.[1] So, if an

---

[1] *See, e.g.,* Perry v. Workers' Comp. Appeals Bd., 66 Cal. App. 3d 887, 136 Cal. Rptr. 309 (1977).

employee already had only one eye, or ear, or leg, or hand, the employer becomes liable as for total disability or deafness upon the loss of the remaining eye or ear or leg or hand.

The full-responsibility rule applies to temporary total disability, even in a state which permits apportionment of permanent disability.[2] And this principle is by no means confined to combinations that result in total disability: the full-responsibility rule also governs when the combined effect of the injuries is a permanent partial disability.[3]

Several states,[4] however, have special apportionment provisions in their statutes, under which an employee with a prior disability receives for a subsequent disability only what he or she would have been entitled to for the latter disability considered alone.

FORD MOTOR COMPANY v. HUNT
26 Va. App. 231, 494 S.E.2d 152 (1997)

BENTON, JUDGE.

Ford Motor Company appeals from the commission's award of disability benefits to Larry I. Hunt. Ford argues that Hunt's activity restrictions were unrelated to his compensable injury, that the commission improperly applied the "two causes" rule, and that Hunt failed to adequately market his residual work capacity. We affirm the commission's award.

I.

Hunt suffered an injury to his right knee while working in a Ford assembly plant. He was treated by Dr. Sheldon Cohn, who placed Hunt on work restrictions, including no crawling, squatting, or lifting over thirty pounds. When Ford accepted the claim as compensable, the commission awarded Hunt benefits from March 30, 1993 until May 16, 1993.

Hunt returned to work at Ford in a light duty capacity and continued to experience pain in his knee for several months. In October 1993, Dr. Cohn performed an "arthroscopic partial medial meniscectomy and open lateral release of [Hunt's] right knee" and reported that Hunt was unable to work. On February 25, 1994, Dr. Cohn released Hunt for limited duty and noted that Hunt was "not to squat, crawl, or climb." In March and April, Hunt participated in a work-hardening program which also recommended limits "on prolonged standing/walking." In a report dated April 8, 1994, Dr. Cohn "released [Hunt] with permanent work restrictions of limited squatting, climbing, crawling, and not to stand over four hours at a time." Several weeks later, Hunt returned to Dr. Cohn complaining of pain. Dr. Cohn gave him injections and removed him from work until April 27. When Hunt returned to work, Dr. Cohn continued his work restrictions.

In July, Dr. Cohn noted that Hunt was experiencing pain while at work and removed him from work until August. In a report dated August 1994, Dr. Cohn again noted that Hunt was not to stand or walk for prolonged periods; was not to stoop, climb, squat, crawl, or kneel; and could not carry heavy materials. However, after several weeks, Dr. Cohn removed the restrictions on prolonged standing and walking and noted that "otherwise, his work restrictions are the same."

When Hunt returned to work in a modified light duty capacity, he drove a forklift for three months until Ford moved the job to another plant. Hunt then drove a forklift for

---

[2] American Can Co. v. Industrial Acc. Comm'n, 196 Cal. App. 2d 445, 16 Cal. Rptr. 424, 26 Cal. Comp. 203 (1961).

[3] Belth v. Anthony Ferrante & Son, 47 N.J. 38, 219 A.2d 168 (1966).

[4] *E.g.*, California and North Carolina.

two weeks until he was taken off that job because of Ford's seniority policy.

Hunt returned to Dr. Cohn on April 5, 1995, complaining of swelling in the right knee. Dr. Cohn diagnosed Hunt with arthrosis of the right knee and stated, "I do not believe his present condition is related to his previous work related injury."

Ford had no positions within Hunt's restrictions and released Hunt in December 1995. In a December 12, 1995 letter written in response to Ford's request for information regarding Hunt's restrictions, Dr. Cohn stated that, although Hunt's work restrictions barred squatting, crawling, or climbing, "[a]ny further restrictions, which would include the walking and standing restrictions, would be due to arthrosis of his knee, not related to a work injury." A month later, Dr. Cohn noted:

> At this time, I will continue his permanent work restrictions of no squatting, crawling, or climbing. These are work related. At this time, I will make his nonwork related restrictions, which is mainly for arthritis, of not to stand over 30 minutes at one time with 10 minute breaks in-between.

Hunt filed an application alleging a change in his condition due to temporary total disability as of December 6, 1995. At the evidentiary hearing, Hunt testified that he did not have arthritis in his right knee prior to his 1993 work injury or the surgery that was performed on his knee. He also testified that he did not have arthritis at any place except in his injured knee. In addition, the evidence at the hearing proved that Hunt sought a second opinion from Dr. Michael T. Longstreet on May 28, 1996. Dr. Longstreet opined that the knee injury was not arthritis and that the injury to Hunt's knee was work-related.

The deputy commissioner ruled that Hunt's current partial disability was the result of two causes, one work-related and one non-work-related. Applying the "two causes" rule, the deputy commissioner ruled that Ford was liable for the entire resulting disability. The deputy commissioner also found, however, that Hunt failed to adequately market his residual capacity and, therefore, denied Hunt any benefits.

Hunt and Ford each requested review by the commission. The commission applied the "two causes" rule and found that the evidence sufficiently established that Hunt's work injury was a contributing factor to the disability because the standing and walking restrictions were partly caused by Hunt's work-related injury. In holding that the restrictions were not exclusively caused by the arthritis condition, the commission cited Dr. Cohn's January 23, 1996 letter and stated that "[i]f the claimant's restrictions result 'mainly' from his arthritis, some portion of it must result from his industrial injury." The commission also relied on the proof that the two injuries were to the same body member, the right knee. In addition, the commission upheld the deputy commissioner's finding that Hunt failed to market his residual capacity and was not entitled to benefits from December 1995 to April 28, 1996. The commission found, however, that Hunt was entitled to temporary partial disability benefits beginning on April 29, 1996 when he found employment within his residual capacity.

II.

The standard of our review of the commission's findings of fact is well established.

We do not retry the facts before the Commission nor do we review the weight, preponderance of the evidence, or the credibility of witnesses. If there is evidence or reasonable inference that can be drawn from the evidence to support the Commission's findings, they will not be disturbed by this Court on appeal, even though there is evidence in the record to support contrary findings of fact. *Caskey v. Dan River Mills, Inc.*, 225 Va. 405, 411, 302 S.E.2d 507, 510–11 (1983). The commission's interpretation of the medical evidence is a finding of fact. See *Ohio Valley Constr. Co. v. Jackson*, 230 Va. 56, 59, 334 S.E.2d 554, 556 (1985).

Viewed in the light most favorable to Hunt, see *R.G. Moore Bldg. Corp. v. Mullins*, 10 Va. App. 211, 212, 390 S.E.2d 788, 788 (1990), the evidence proved that in 1993 and in

1994, Dr. Cohn limited Hunt from stooping, climbing, squatting, crawling, kneeling, carrying heavy objects, prolonged standing, and prolonged walking. All of those restrictions were caused by Hunt's work-related injury. In August of 1994, Dr. Cohn removed the restrictions on prolonged walking and standing. However, he noted that Hunt still had "permanent work restrictions of no squatting, crawling, or climbing," which flowed from his work-related injury.

In 1995, Dr. Cohn also noted that Hunt then had a restriction on his standing "which is mainly from arthritis." Interpreting Dr. Cohn's explanation of the restrictions, the commission found that because Hunt's standing restriction in 1995 was not based solely on his arthritis, a portion of that restriction resulted from Hunt's work-related injury, which was the only other source of his knee disability. Credible evidence supports that factual finding. The commission's interpretation of Dr. Cohn's report is based on the reasonable inference that Dr. Cohn understood that "mainly" means "in the principal respect" or "for the most part." Webster's Third New International Dictionary 1362 (Unabridged, 1965).

The principle is well established that when medical evidence is not conclusive, it "is subject to the commission's consideration and weighing." *Hungerford Mechanical Corp. v. Hobson*, 11 Va. App. 675, 677, 401 S.E.2d 213, 215 (1991). As the trier of fact, the commission is also free to consider "[t]he testimony of a claimant . . . in determining causation, especially where the medical testimony is inconclusive." *Dollar General Store v. Cridlin*, 22 Va. App. 171, 176, 468 S.E.2d 152, 154 (1996). Although the evidence proved that in 1995 the restriction against standing for prolonged periods was "mainly" based on Hunt's arthritis, which Dr. Cohn deemed a non-work-condition, the evidence also proved that on several occasions prior to 1995 Dr. Cohn barred Hunt from "prolonged standing/walking" because of his work-related injury. The commission's interpretation of Dr. Cohn's 1995 report was made within the context of Hunt's medical history and Hunt's testimony that, apart from his work-related injury and his arthritis, he had no other physical ailments that contributed to the problems with his knee. Credible evidence proved that Hunt's only other disability to that same knee was a work-related injury. Accordingly, we hold that the commission's finding is supported by credible evidence.

III.

The principle is well established that "where a disability has two causes: one related to the employment and one unrelated [to the employment] . . . full benefits will be allowed." *Bergmann v. L & W Drywall*, 222 Va. 30, 32, 278 S.E.2d 801, 803 (1981). The evidence proved that Hunt suffered disability in the knee from both a work-related injury and a non-work-related condition. Thus, the evidence proved Hunt's disability to the knee resulted from two causes. Accordingly, we affirm the commission's finding regarding Hunt's disability.

IV.

Hunt testified regarding the job search he conducted after being released from Ford. He spoke with Ford and his union representatives several times, he contacted the employers listed on his Work Search Contacts Record, he contacted potential employers verbally, and he checked the newspaper employment advertisements. Eventually, on April 29, 1996, Hunt obtained a part-time position as a painter's helper earning an average of $125 per week. Prior to his release, Hunt had been earning approximately $614 per week at Ford.

The evidence proved that in April 1996, Hunt obtained employment that he could perform consistent with his restrictions. The commission made the following findings regarding Hunt's efforts to locate that employment:

In April 1996, he found a part-time job with J.M. Jolly, painting contractor, earning $125 per week. The claimant, who is 49 years old, has worked for his preinjury employer in an assembly plant for 16 years. There is no information in the record concerning his education or training. The claimant indicated that he looked in the want ads but could not perform the required job duties due to his restrictions. . . . Considering the evidence before us concerning the nature and extent of his disability and his experience, we find that he has found suitable employment within his residual capacity.

Unlike the facts in *National Linen Service v. McGuinn*, 8 Va. App. 267, 380 S.E.2d 31 (1989), where the employee "did not attempt to find any other job," id. at 270, 380 S.E.2d at 33, the evidence proved, and the commission found, that Hunt sought other employment. Because the record contains credible evidence to support the commission's findings, we affirm the ruling that Hunt made reasonable efforts to market his residual work capacity.

For these reasons, we affirm the commission's award.

§ 16.03   SECOND INJURY FUNDS

[1]   Summary and Background

State Second Injury Funds (SIFS) were created to encourage employers to hire and retain workers who have physical impairments and to provide certain economic relief to those employers should a second injury occur. Prior to the creation of SIFs, when an injury in the course of employment occurred to a previously handicapped worker-resulting in increased or perhaps permanent total disability — either the worker was penalized by having any compensation benefits limited to the disability directed associated with the second injury or, the employer was penalized by having to pay for the combined resulting disability. This latter possibility provided a strong economic incentive for employers to refuse to hire or retain physically impaired employees.

So state SIF laws represent an ingenious device to prevent injustice to either the employer or the injured worker. They allow for compensation to be paid to the injured worker for the total disability resulting from the combined injuries, but the employer is responsible only for the compensation associated with the second injury, the balance being payable from the SIF.

While a number of states experimented with such legislation during the 1920s and 1930s, World War II served as the catalyst for legislative action on a wide scale. It was then, while hospital ships were returning thousands of disabled veterans from Europe and Asia, that many groups worked together to get second injury fund laws adopted around the country.

Following enactment of these original laws, criticism quickly developed regarding the narrowness of coverage; i.e., requiring loss of a major body member and the combined effect resulting in permanent total disability. To respond to those criticisms, many states began to experiment with broader legislative provisions in an attempt to lower the threshold of access.

Some efforts at lowering the access threshold involved the recognition of pre-existing impairment "from any cause or origin" rather than the complete loss of a major body member.

Others had to do with easing the requirement that the combined result culminate in permanent and total disability. Consequently, a number of states, such as New York and South Carolina, now have "low access" thresholds to their funds, while others, like Illinois, North Carolina, and Pennsylvania, retain the older "high threshold" approach.

Since 1992, almost a dozen states, including for example Alabama, Colorado, Connecticut, and Florida, have repealed or abolished their funds for claims arising after a certain specified date. States with high access thresholds question whether the original purpose of such funds are being met when the potential for recovery is so limited. At the opposite extreme, states with low access thresholds question whether or not their funds are simply becoming "dumping grounds" for problem cases and are no longer serving their original purpose of encouraging the hiring of the disabled. The availability of remedies under the Americans With Disabilities Act of 1990 is also regularly cited as a reason why SIF's are no longer necessary.

[2] Claims on Special Injury Funds

NORRIS v. IOWA BEEF PROCESSORS, INC.
224 Neb. 867, 402 N.W.2d 658 (1987)

KRIVOSHA, C.J., and BOSLAUGH, WHITE, HASTINGS, CAPORALE, SHANAHAN, and GRANT, JJ.

SHANAHAN, JUSTICE.

Iowa Beef Processors, Inc., now IBP, Inc., appeals the award obtained by Larry J. Norris in the Nebraska Workers' Compensation Court. Also, the Nebraska Workers' Compensation Court dismissed the action against the State of Nebraska, Second Injury Fund, impleaded by IBP. Norris cross-appeals on issues regarding the degree of Norris' permanent disability determined by the Nebraska Workers' Compensation Court, and compensation from the Second Injury Fund. We affirm.

In his petition Norris alleged that as a result of his employment at IBP, he had sustained bodily injuries, and sought compensation for injuries to his legs, shoulders, right arm, and back. IBP filed a "claim against the Second Injury Fund," and the State of Nebraska, Second Injury Fund, was impleaded in the action.

Born on March 23, 1949, Larry Norris, at age 4, sustained accidental injury to his right eye and, since age 7, has had a prosthesis in his right eye socket. Norris has corrected vision in his left eye but has some trouble with peripheral vision in that eye. On account of Norris' loss of sight in the right eye, some prospective employers declined to hire Norris at the risk of possible total blindness resulting from employment. In his written application to IBP for employment in 1976, Norris stated: "I'm blind in my right eye." Similar statements about the absence of sight in Norris' right eye appear in other records of IBP, establishing IBP's knowledge of the disability when IBP hired Norris.

From 1978 through the fall of 1983, IBP employed Norris as a "beef lugger," a job which required Norris to unload trucks and carry quarters of beef which had an average weight of 185 pounds. The lightest pieces of beef weighed 135 pounds, and the quarters had a normal maximum weight of 235 pounds. Norris carried an average of 480 pieces of beef per day, thus daily bearing an average weight of more than 88,000 pounds of beef. While a truck was being unloaded, "fronts" of beef dropped a distance of 2 feet from the delivery truck onto Norris' shoulders. Occasionally, workers slipped and fell on the plant floor, which was slick with animal fat and blood.

In 1980, Norris slipped and fell at IBP, underwent six separate surgical procedures on his knees (three procedures on each knee), and eventually required a patellectomy (removal of kneecap) of his right knee in 1984. Norris also suffered a carpal tunnel syndrome (nerve entrapment at the wrist or elbow) in his right arm, restricting mobility and repetitive work involving Norris' right arm.

As a consequence of his employment at IBP, Norris sustained various bodily injuries resulting in his inability to be on his feet for any prolonged duration; shoulder problems experienced when Norris pushed or reached with his arms; inability to lift more than 40 pounds; limitations in pushing and pulling leg controls on machinery or equipment; and general difficulty in squatting and crawling or climbing stairs. Loss of sight in the right eye never interfered with Norris' job at IBP.

Since 1981 Dr. John J. Dougherty, an orthopedist, has treated Norris' various injuries. Dr. Dougherty expressed his opinion that Norris has sustained permanent partial disability in five areas on account of injuries sustained at IBP, namely, disability of 1 percent of the right arm, 20 percent of the right knee, 5 to 10 percent of the left knee, and 1 to 2 percent in each shoulder. Referring to the American Medical Association, Guides to the Evaluation of Permanent Impairment (2d ed. 1984), and as an additional evaluation based on the five separate areas of Norris' disability, Dr. Dougherty extrapolated percentages of permanent disability to Norris' body as a whole. According to Dr. Dougherty, Norris sustained the following permanent partial disability to the body as a whole: 1 percent as the result of the arm injury; 8 percent from injury to the right knee; 4 percent on account of injury to the left knee; and 1 percent attributable to each shoulder injury. Dr. Dougherty further extrapolated Norris' disabilities and expressed an opinion that, as an overall disability or combined value of permanent disabilities or impairment, Norris had sustained 36 percent disability of the body as a whole, that is, 24 percent for the loss of sight in the right eye and 12 percent attributable to the other disabilities to Norris' body as a whole. . . .

On rehearing, the three-judge panel found that Norris had sustained a 20-percent permanent partial disability to his right leg, a 10-percent permanent partial disability to his left leg, a 1-percent permanent partial disability to his right arm, and, as a consequence of the shoulder injuries, a 5-percent permanent partial disability to Norris' body as a whole. The Workers' Compensation Court found that Norris had failed to prove any disability to his back and denied recovery referable to the back problem alleged by Norris. The Nebraska Workers' Compensation Court ordered payment of weekly benefits, as well as payment of medical and hospital expenses, and determined that Norris was entitled to vocational rehabilitation.

In denying the claim against the Second Injury Fund, two members of the panel (one judge dissenting) stated:

> While it is true that the plaintiff has vision in one eye only, and that this has been true during the whole of his employment by the first named defendant and was reflected on the plaintiff's application for employment with the first named defendant, the Court does not believe that the degree or percentage of disability suffered by the plaintiff today is substantially greater than that which would have resulted from the knee, shoulder and arm injuries considered alone and of themselves.

In his dissent, one judge expressed:

> Translating each of the injuries into whole body impairments, all of which are charged to Iowa Beef Processors, Inc., other than the loss of the eye, the defendant Iowa Beef Processors, Inc., would pay 42.8 per cent of the total disability compensation and the Second Injury Fund would pay 57.2 per cent. . . .

Payment from the Second Injury Fund is governed by Neb. Rev. Stat. § 48-128 (Reissue 1984), which provides in part:

> If an employee who has a preexisting permanent partial disability whether from compensable injury or otherwise, which is or is likely to be a hindrance or obstacle to his obtaining employment or obtaining reemployment if the employee should become unemployed and which was known to the employer prior to the occurrence of a subsequent compensable injury, receives a subsequent compensable injury resulting in additional permanent partial or in permanent total disability so that the degree or percentage of disability caused by the combined disabilities is *substantially greater* than that which would have resulted from the last injury, considered alone and of itself; and if the employee is entitled to receive compensation on the basis of the combined disabilities, the

employer at the time of the last injury shall be liable only for the degree or percentage of disability which would have resulted from the last injury had there been no preexisting disability, and for the additional disability the employee shall be compensated out of a special trust fund created for that purpose, which sum so set aside shall be known as the Second Injury Fund. (Emphasis supplied.)

For liability of the Second Injury Fund, statutory predecessors of the present § 48-128 required that the combined injuries must result in "total disability," *see* § 48-128 (Reissue 1968), whereas, by amendment, *see* § 48-128 (Reissue 1974), the present statute relates to claims based on additional permanent partial disability or permanent total disability.

Under the statutory scheme of § 48-128, the amount payable from the Second Injury Fund is, ordinarily, the difference between the weekly benefits payable for permanent disability from a second injury which is compensable and the weekly benefits payable for the combined permanent disabilities from a previous injury and such second injury. *See* 2 A. Larson, The Law of Workmen's Compensation § 59.34(a) (1986).

To recover from the Second Injury Fund, § 48-128, a claimant must prove by a preponderance of evidence (1) a prior permanent partial disability, (2) a second or subsequent injury which is compensable, causing permanent disability, and (3) the combination of permanent disabilities existing after such second or subsequent injury is substantially greater in degree or percentage than permanent disability from the second or subsequent injury, considered by itself and not in conjunction with the prior permanent disability.

One claiming against the Second Injury Fund has the burden to prove that the combination of permanent disabilities is substantially greater in degree or percentage than the permanent disability from the second or subsequent compensable injury considered by itself. *Flansburg v. Giza*, 284 Minn. 199, 169 N.W.2d 744 (1969). *See also, Benson v. Barnes & Barnes Trucking*, 217 Neb. 865, 354 N.W.2d 127 (1984) (on employer's claim for apportionment of benefits and payment by the Second Injury Fund, burden of proof is on employer).

Whether a combination of permanent disabilities, within the purview of § 48-128, is substantially greater than permanent disability from a second or subsequent compensable injury is a question of fact. *See Matter of Garcia v Brassiere Rest.*, 66 A.D.2d 930, 411 N.Y.S.2d 448 (1978).

. . . .

Weekly benefits for total disability are determined in accordance with Neb. Rev. Stat. § 48-121(1) (Reissue 1984) of the Nebraska Workers' Compensation Act. For partial disability, weekly benefits are determined by § 48-121(2), except in cases of a specific "schedule injury" classified in § 48-121(3).

An analysis of the bases for payment of weekly benefits is contained in *Jeffers v. Pappas Trucking, Inc.*, 198 Neb. 379, 253 N.W.2d 30 (1977):

> Section 48-121 . . . provides for compensation for three categories of job-related disabilities. Subdivision (1) sets the amount of compensation for total disability; subdivision (2) sets the amount of compensation for disability partial in character, except in cases covered by subdivision (3); and subdivision (3) sets out "schedule" injuries to specified parts of the body with compensation established therefore. Disability under subdivisions (1) and (2) refers to loss of employability and earning capacity, and not to functional or medical loss alone . [Citations omitted.] Thus losses in bodily function, so far as subdivisions (1) and (2) are concerned, are important only insofar as they relate to earning capacity and employability. [Citation omitted.]

> For claims falling under subdivision (3), however, it is immaterial whether an industrial disability is present or not. [Citation omitted.] . . . There is, how-

ever, an exception to this rule. Where "an employee has suffered a schedule injury to some particular member or members, and some unusual or extraordinary condition as to other members or any other part of the body has developed," he may be compensated under subdivision (1) or (2) of section 48-121. [Citations omitted.]

. . . [I]f an employee suffers a schedule injury which falls under subdivision (3), of section 48-121 . . . he is entitled only to the compensation provided for in that subdivision, unless some unusual or extraordinary condition as to other members or other parts of the body has developed. The presence or absence of industrial disability is immaterial in cases falling under subdivision (3). If the injury falls under either subdivision (1) or (2), however, a determination must be made as to the employee's loss of employability or earning capacity, and loss of bodily function is not at issue.

Id. at 384–85, 253 N.W.2d at 33–34.

"Earning power," as used in Neb. Rev. Stat. § 48-121(2) . . . is not synonymous with wages, but includes eligibility to procure employment generally, ability to hold a job obtained, and capacity to perform the tasks of the work, as well as the ability of the workman to earn wages in the employment in which he is engaged or for which he is fitted.

Akins v. Happy Hour, Inc., 209 Neb. 236, 239, 306 N.W.2d 914, 916 (1981).

Franzen v. Blakley, 155 Neb. 621, 52 N.W.2d 833 (1952), involved an employee's claim against the Second Injury Fund. Franzen's first accident, nonindustrial in origin, caused permanent partial disability to Franzen's right wrist. A subsequent and compensable injury caused permanent partial disability of Franzen's left hand. After the second accident, Franzen was "not able to do the work of her former employment, or any other kind of work that required the effective use of her hands." *Id.* at 624, 52 N.W.2d at 836. A physician testified that Franzen was unemployable as the result of the condition of her hands. In *Franzen*, this court stated at 628, 52 N.W.2d at 838:

[P]laintiff's disability to her right hand is not, as such, a compensable injury under section 48-121. . . . It is a fact condition which becomes material in applying the provisions of section 48-128. . . . [T]he Legislature in section 48-128 . . . was not undertaking to provide compensation for a previous disability other than one caused by disease, as such, but rather was undertaking to provide compensation for permanent total disability resulting from a combination of the previous fact condition with a compensable injury.

. . . *(The court here reviews two more prior decisions to like effect.)*

From the foregoing cases, a rule has evolved concerning a claim against the Second Injury Fund, § 48-128: With the exception of increased disability resulting from additional injury to the same specific member of the body, as classified by § 48-121(3), *disability* for the purpose of § 48-128 means the decrease or loss of earning power (capacity) or diminished employability. Frequently, "disability" is expressed in terms of a percentage of disability to the body as a whole, that is, anatomical loss of function. As a practical matter, in the absence of other evidence, such percentage of disability of "the body as a whole" may be accepted as the index for determination of weekly benefits under § 48-121(2). *See Jeffers v. Pappas Trucking, Inc.*, 198 Neb. 379, 253 N.W.2d 30 (1977).

However, in addition to establishing an employee's decrease or loss of earning power or diminished employability, a claimant seeking payment from the Second Injury Fund must also establish that, after the second or subsequent compensable injury, an employee's combined permanent disabilities are *substantially greater* than the permanent disability from the last compensable injury considered by itself.

Under § 48-128, a combination of permanent disabilities is "substantially greater" than permanent disability from the second or subsequent injury when the resulting permanent disability from all causes combined is substantially greater than the disability resulting solely from the second or subsequent compensable injury. *See Rex E. Lantham Co. v. Indus. Comm'n of Utah*, 717 P.2d 255 (Utah 1986).

For the combination of permanent disabilities necessary to sustain a claim against the Second Injury Fund, the prior permanent partial disability or disabilities must interact with the effects of the second or subsequent compensable injury and enhance the permanent disability that otherwise results from the later compensable injury alone. *See* Bordo Citrus Products v. Varnadore, 395 So. 2d 260 (Fla. App. 1981). *See, also, Davis v. Conger Life Insurance Company*, 201 So. 2d 727 (Fla. 1967), where the Florida Supreme Court, construing a former statute substantially similar to Nebraska's § 48-128, held that the combined disabilities must have the "total effect of creating a greater degree of disability to the body as a whole and a claimant's wage-earning capacity than would have resulted from the last injury considered by itself and not in conjunction with a previous injury." 201 So. 2d at 729.

As expressed in 2 A. Larson, The Law of Workmen's Compensation § 59.32(g) at 10-447 (1986):

> Although the prior impairment need not combine with the compensable injury in any special way, it must add something to the disability before the Special Fund [Second Injury Fund] can become liable. In other words, it is not enough to show that the claimant had some kind of handicap, if that handicap contributed nothing to the final disability.

Norris has unquestionably experienced problems in locomotion, lifting, reaching, and standing for protracted periods. We recognize, and do not minimize or disregard, those limitations consequent to Norris' injuries involving his knees, arm, and shoulders. The question is not whether those injuries are serious. The gravity of those individual injuries is obvious and beyond question. Rather, the issue is whether Norris' disability from loss of sight, when combined with the permanent disability from injuries to his knees, arm, and shoulders, resulted in permanent disability *substantially greater* in degree or percentage than would have resulted from Norris' injuries at IBP, considered by themselves and apart from Norris' loss of sight.

Dr. Dougherty rendered his opinion about Norris' permanent disabilities and expressed his evaluation in terms of percentages of disability sustained in specific areas of Norris' body, as well as an overall disability or combined value for disability resulting from all injuries. On the basis of Dr. Dougherty's extrapolations, the loss of sight in Norris' eye accounted for 24 percent out of the 36 percent resulting from the overall disability or combined value of all permanent disabilities sustained by Norris. One might reasonably conclude that 36 percent (combination value of all disabilities) is substantially greater than 12 percent (disability from injuries at IBP) and that 24 percent (loss of sight) is a substantial contribution to Norris' overall disability or combined value of disabilities. As a simple arithmetical expression, when the various and individual percentages assigned to loss of function ("body as a whole") are added together, the sum of permanent partial disabilities for Norris' body as a whole is 42 percent — 24 percent attributable to Norris' loss of sight, 18 percent to the injuries at IBP. From a purely mathematical analysis, one might conclude that 42 percent (combined disabilities) is substantially greater than 18 percent (disability from injuries at IBP).

. . . .

The rehabilitation counselor, Stricklett, testified that Norris' "job options as well as his earnings potential have been affected by his numerous injuries at Iowa Beef Processors," and also testified that the combination of injuries and resultant disability "would affect [employability] to *some* extent." (Emphasis supplied.) The compensation court may have concluded that the rehabilitation counselor's nebulous and equivocal statements about Norris' particular employability fail to supply a sound basis for comparison of Norris' disabilities; that is, a failure to establish that Norris' loss of earning power or employability, as the result of combined disabilities, is "substantially greater" than would have resulted from injuries sustained at IBP when such injuries at IBP are considered by themselves and apart from Norris' loss of sight. The Iowa rehabilitation evaluators indicated their inability to "identify problems specifically resulting" from the loss of sight in Norris' right eye as a hindrance to future employment.

Under the standard of review imposed on this court, we are unable to conclude that the findings of the Nebraska Workers' Compensation Court are clearly incorrect. . . .

Affirmed.

[3] Interplay between SIF statutes and the Americans With Disabilities Act

In many states with second injury funds the employer may benefit from the fund only if it knows about the prior disability; in some states a written record of the pre-existing impairment is required. The Americans With Disabilities Act of 1990 (ADA), on the other hand, prohibits pre-employment inquiries as to medical condition or as to the existence or nature of a job applicant's disability.[5] This potential conflict has been resolved by the Equal Employment Opportunity Commission in its ADA regulations by providing for a two-stage hiring process.[6] At the initial hiring phase, medical inquiry is forbidden, but after the employer has made a "conditional" job offer, it is possible for the employer to obtain information about disability, both to determine what kind of accommodation of the disability might be needed, and to satisfy Second Injury Fund requirements as well. Employers may also submit information along this line to workers' compensation regulatory bodies or to second injury funds without violating medical confidentiality requirements.[7]

§ 16.04 EFFECT OF SUCCESSIVE INJURIES ON MAXIMUM AMOUNT ALLOWABLE

DENNIS v. BROWN
93 So. 2d 584 (Fla. 1957)

O'CONNELL, JUSTICE.

Dennis, the employer, and his carrier petition this Court for writ of certiorari to review a compensation order of the Florida Industrial Commission. The Commission's order affirmed the order of a deputy commissioner awarding payment of compensation to the respondent, U. L. Brown, for temporary total disability.

In 1949, Brown, the respondent claimant, was seriously injured in the course of his employment with petitioner Dennis. Because of those injuries, claimant was adjudicated totally and permanently disabled and Dennis, through his carrier at that time, paid claimant the maximum benefits then recoverable under the Workmen's Compensation Act, F.S.A. § 440.01 *et seq.* Medical treatment was continued to be furnished claimant by his employer and the carrier.

In February of 1954, claimant again became employed by the same employer, Dennis. It was necessary for him to wear a brace and use a cane. He could not work outside of the store, as he had done previously as a salesman. He could work only a part

---

[5] 42 U.S.C. 12112(d)(2)(A).

[6] 29 CFR § 1630.14(b)

[7] 29 CFR Part 1630, Interpretative Guidance on Title 1 of the Americans With Disabilities Act, Section 1630.14(b).

of each day. Nevertheless, according to his employer, he was earning the pay he received. On September 30, 1955, claimant fell on a freshly waxed floor and reinjured his back. Dennis' new carrier, National Surety Corp., furnished medical treatment but controverted claim for compensation. The carrier contended claimant had already been compensated by the same employer for permanent total disability and that therefore no further benefits were payable.

The deputy commissioner found the claimant had regained a certain wage earning capacity and was entitled to compensation for temporary total disability due to the second injury, in spite of the previous award of maximum benefits under the Act. Dennis and his carrier applied for review to the full commission. The order of the deputy was affirmed by the full commission, whereupon this petition for writ of certiorari was filed.

Petitioners maintain that claimant was given employment and that he received his earnings out of the generosity, helpfulness and sympathy of his employer and patronizing friends. They say he could not and did not sustain any loss of earning capacity due to the second accident, because at the time thereof he had no earning capacity. Yet they do admit the claimant was selling enough merchandise to earn his salary.

The deputy commissioner found claimant's situation created an enigma. He felt the answer was sought in the 1955 amendment to our Workmen's Compensation Law [which appears now as Section 440.15(5), Subsequent Injury; Special Disability Fund] but that a full answer did not result. He cited in support of his conclusion one case which he felt in point to the instant claim. In that case the claimant had received a 100 per cent permanent disability rating, but the California court allowed compensation for a subsequent accident, upon its interpretation of that state's subsequent injuries legislation. *Smith v. Industrial Accident Comm.*, 1955, 44 Cal. 2d 364, 282 P.2d 64. The court stated, 282 P.2d on page 68:

> If an employee may properly be rated at 100 per cent disability to qualify him for the basic form of workmen's compensation, even though his earning power has not in truth, for practical purposes, been impaired, it should be at least equally permissible to penetrate the fiction of 100 per cent disability and accept the truth of his remaining earning ability so that the further truth of a subsequent injury with increased actual disability may be compensated from the fund set up for that purpose.

However, in California a showing of loss of earning power is not a prerequisite to compensation for permanent disability. This fact is stated in the *Smith* case and its truth is readily ascertained from referring to the quoted portion set out above. Compensation is based on the physical injury rather than actual loss of earning power, in that state, and therefore we should not rely too heavily on that case in support of the commission's finding. It is settled in this state that the disability is determined not by the functional loss, but by the loss of wage earning ability. *Ball v. Mann*, Fla. 1954, 75 So. 2d 758. However, even in our state we have a schedule of certain injuries which automatically constitute permanent total disability, irrespective of loss in earning power. Section 440.15(1)(b).

Petitioners cite several cases in other jurisdictions which hold that a man cannot be more than totally disabled. *O'Brien v. Albert A. Albrecht Co.*, 1919, 206 Mich. 101, 172 N.W. 601, 6 A.L.R. 1257; *Van Tassel v. Basic Refactories Corp.*, 1926, 216 App. Div. 774, 214 N.Y.S. 491; *Harrington v. Department of Labor and Industries*, 1941, 9 Wash. 2d 1, 113 P.2d 518.

In the *Harrington* case, the rule of the *Van Tassel* case is cited. The court, in the *Harrington* case, said that the mere fact that a workman may recover from an injury which has been classified as a permanent total disability for which he has been fully compensated does not negate the fact he has already received all the benefits allowed for permanent total disability. This statement was made immediately after a statement by the court that the theory upon which compensation is allowed is that the workman has sustained a loss of earning power. An opposite holding was cited by the court in the case of *Asplund Const. Co. v. State Industrial Comm.*, 1939, 185 Okl. 171, 90 P.2d 642, but the Washington court felt a statutory distinction brought such about. It quoted [9 Wash. 2d 1, 113 P.2d 520] the applicable Washington statute as providing "should a further accident occur to a workman who has been previously the recipient of a lump sum payment under this act, his future compensation shall be adjudged according to the other provisions of this section and with regard to the combined effect of his injuries and his past receipt of money under this act." Rem. Rev. Stat. § 7679(g). The applicable statute in Oklahoma was quoted as providing "the fact that an employee has suffered previous disability, or received compensation therefor, shall not preclude him from compensation for a later injury; but in determining compensation for the later injury his average weekly wages shall be such sum as will reasonably represent his earning capacity at the time of the later injury." 85 O.S.1951 § 22, subd. 6. The Washington court pointed out that the Oklahoma statute made no distinction as to degrees of disability to which it applied and made no exception of permanent total disability. Because its statute contained language substantially different, the Washington court refused to consider the *Asplund* case as authority on the question.

It will be noted that the statute in Oklahoma referred to above is quite similar to the language used in our own Workmen's Compensation Act. *See* Sec. 440.15(5) (c).

The *Asplund* case was decided in 1939. The question before the court was whether a claimant who had on one date received an injury for which he had been awarded compensation for permanent and total disability could thereafter receive an award for temporary total disability for a second injury. The second injury occurred some sixteen years after the first, while claimant was working for a second employer. For eight years previous to the second injury he had been working at various mechanical and manual labor jobs. The court found the question to be one of first impression and adopted its holding upon its construction of that state's workmen's compensation law. It found the statute did not except a previous permanent total disability when it provided an employee might receive an award even though he had previously received compensation for a prior injury. It therefore concluded the workman was entitled to the additional compensation. In reaching that conclusion it considered that the previous adjudication of total disability by the Industrial Commission was, and of necessity, must have been based upon opinion evidence by doctors. The court said it could not, however, overlook the recuperative powers of nature which in the case of the first injury constituted the final arbiter. The court found the claimant had an earning power, irrespective of the prior adjudication of total permanent disability, and that industry saw fit to use this earning capacity. It concluded that the second award was not erroneous because of the first award for permanent total disability.

We favor the reasoning of the court in the *Asplund* case. Our statute, while similar in part to that applicable to the *Asplund* case, goes further, however. It provides that an employee who is suffering from a previous disability shall not receive compensation for a later injury in excess of the compensation allowed for such injury when considered by itself and not in conjunction with the previous disability. Sec. 440.15(5)(c). In the instant case the second injury resulted in a temporary total disability when considered alone. We have held, in *International Paper Co. v. Merchant*, Fla.1955, 77 So. 2d 622, that where a claimant had been paid for a permanent partial disability and thereafter developed an occupational disease which left him totally disabled, he was entitled to full compensation for permanent total disability without deduction of payments made on account of the prior injury. We are of the opinion the reasoning of that case may be extended to the circumstances of this case and no violation of Sec. 440.15(5) (c) results.

The following comments are found in 2 Larson's Workmen's Compensation Law, Sec. 59.41–59.43:

> There is sound and practical reason for the generally accepted rule that awards for successive or concurrent permanent injuries should not take the form of weekly payments higher than the weekly maxima for total disability. A man can be no more than totally disabled, and if he is allowed to draw weekly benefits simultaneously from a permanent total and a permanent partial award, it will probably become more profitable for him to be disabled than to be well — a situation which compensation law always studiously avoids in order to prevent inducement to malingering.

The author comments, however, in a footnote, that such argument is open to question, since a schedule award continues to run even if claimant resumes his normal earnings. Therefore, he says, a potential malingerer's choice is between total compensation benefits (some percentage of his wages) plus partial benefits, on the one hand, and full wages plus partial benefits on the other. He goes on to say, immediately after the quotation above:

> However, no such policy applies when, as in many states, there is a maximum-number-of-weeks limit on disability payments *including even total disability payments, and a claimant receives, concurrently or successively, an injury constituting total disability and another constituting partial.* . . . Putting the allowances "end-to-end," so to speak, permits full allowance for the specific losses without the criticized feature of making any weekly payment greater than the wages claimant would get if actually working. (Emphasis ours.)

> The capacities of a human being cannot be arbitrarily and finally divided and written off by percentages. The fact that a man has once received compensation as for 50% of total disability does not mean that ever after he is in the eyes of compensation law but half a man, so that he can never again receive a compensation award going beyond the other 50% of total. After having received his prior payments, he may, in future years, be able to resume gainful employment. If so, there is no reason why a disability which would bring anyone else total permanent disability benefits should yield him only half as much.

Finally, Larson comments, concerning an over-all dollar limit on benefits:

> If the maximum is to have any effect, it must be understood to set a limit on the allowance that can be made for a specific damaging result to a particular member manifested at a particular time. As noted above, after time healing and training have done their work, an injured member may again be susceptible to injury for which maximum compensation is appropriate.

It is our view that the foregoing comments lend direct support to our finding in this case. Where necessary the author's comments are susceptible to an extension applicable to the circumstances of the present case. We are of the opinion that an employee, although previously adjudicated permanently and totally disabled and fully compensated therefor, may thereafter acquire a wage earning capacity. If he suffers a subsequent injury which deprives him of such newly acquired wage earning capacity, he may be entitled to compensation for such loss.

Workmen's compensation acts are but statutory creations. Few statutes have achieved perfection in accomplishing their purpose. The statutes themselves may not evince a perfect logic. For instance, many provide that for a permanent and total disability a man shall be compensated at a percentage of his salary for a certain maximum number of weeks, instead of a period based upon some formula with respect to his remaining life expectancy. Due to the impossibility or impracticality of providing for every conceivable factual situation, application of the statute to achieve a known purpose of legislation may sometimes create a technical inconsistency. We feel that workmen's compensation acts were designed to remove from the workman himself the burden of his own injury and disability and place it on the industry which he served. Such acts should be liberally construed with the interest of the working man foremost.

Many acts have provided for subsequent injuries, as ours has done. Special disability funds have been created. Such legislative action was no doubt inspired by desire to encourage employment of handicapped workers. In our state, we have also provided for rehabilitation of injured workers. Sec. 440.49, Fla. Stats. 1955, F.S.A. This provision includes the case of those previously adjudicated permanently and totally disabled. It contemplates the possibility of one so adjudicated again becoming gainfully employed. To construe our law to be that one who has become gainfully employed as a result of rehabilitation, whether through his own efforts or with the aid of the Commission, may not be entitled to compensation for loss of such rehabilitated wage earning capacity due to a subsequent injury is, in our opinion, contrary to what we believe to have been the Legislature's intent, and is contrary to common sense.

The petition for writ of certiorari is therefore denied. However, there appears to be some error in the Commission's computation of the 350 week period of compensation for the injury sustained on April 14, 1949. Our calculations indicate said first period of compensation should be computed to have expired on the 9th day of January, 1956, rather than on the 15th day of March, 1956, assuming the commencing date to have been April 18, 1949, in accordance with the four-day waiting period. If the Commission finds its calculation to be incorrect, it is directed to modify its order accordingly.

THOMAS, ACTING C. J., and DREW and THORNAL, JJ., concur.

Chapter 17
CALCULATION OF BENEFIT AMOUNTS

§ 17.01 INTRODUCTION

The normal unit by which benefits are measured consists of a fixed statutory percentage, usually between one-half and two-thirds, of "average weekly wage." The computation of average weekly wage is frequently based upon actual wages during the preceding year, if claimant's employment has been substantially continuous, and upon the wages of employees in similar work if it has not.

Since the entire objective is to arrive at as fair an estimate as possible of the claimant's future earning capacity, a claimant who has made only part-time earnings should have the wage basis figured on part-time wages only if the employment is inherently part-time and likely to remain so; otherwise the relevant earnings should be converted to a full-time basis.

When an employee, who regularly holds two concurrent jobs, is injured in one of them, the wage will usually be based on actual earnings in both if they are in a similar line of work. If they are not, a numerical majority of states will not combine the wages, but a strong and growing minority will combine them in all cases.

§ 17.02 THE CONCEPT OF "AVERAGE WEEKLY WAGE"

In almost every jurisdiction, the beginning point in calculating the amount of benefits is the "average weekly wage." This, when the fixed statutory percentage of roughly between one-half and two-thirds has been applied to it, becomes the unit of benefit by which practically all compensation, excluding disfigurement allowances and medical payments, is measured. Awards for greater or less disability are usually adjusted, not by changing the number of dollars per week, but by changing the number of weeks for which the fixed weekly benefit is payable. The crucial importance of the original "average weekly wage" figure is thus apparent.

The commonest type of wage basis statute is in three parts:

(1) the first paragraph usually says that, if the claimant has worked in the kind of employment in which he or she was injured for substantially the whole of the preceding year, the average annual earnings shall consist of, say, 300 times the average daily wage as a six-day worker, and 260 times the average daily wage as a five-day worker, which the claimant shall have earned while so employed;

(2) the second paragraph typically says that, if the claimant did not work in such employment during substantially the whole of the year, the same formula shall be applied to the wage of an employee of the same class working substantially the whole of the year in the same or similar employment in the same or a neighboring place on the days when so employed; and

(3) the third paragraph contains some general formula to be used if either of the foregoing methods cannot fairly be applied, such as the following: such sum as, having regard to the previous earnings of the injured employee in the employment in which he or she was working at the time of the injury, and of other employees of the same class, etc., or in other employment or self-employment of such employee, shall reasonably represent the annual earning capacity of the injured employee.

The average weekly wage is then set at one-fifty-second part of the average annual earnings so computed.

Many of the litigated cases in this area begin with the question whether the first can fairly be applied or whether resort to the second or third is appropriate.[1] Typically, the necessity for the latter approach exists when the duration of the employment has not been substantial enough to supply an accurate guide, or when the employment itself, or claimant's relation to it, is inherently intermittent, discontinuous, or part-time, for in such cases the multiplication of average daily wage by 300 would not accurately reflect annual earning capacity in that employment.

In computing actual earnings as the beginning point of wage-basis calculations, there should be included not only wages and salary but any thing of value received as consideration for the work, for example, tips,[2] bonuses,[3] room and board,[4] a car allowance,[5] or anything else constituting real and direct economic gain to the employee.[6] As to benefits, it has been held that "average wage" should include the value of free day care services[7] and employer contributions to medical insurance,[8] but not employer contributions to a union health and welfare fund.[9] Nor are retirement[10] or unemployment benefits[11] themselves includable as wages.

The necessity of approximating future earning capacity is often recognized both by judicial decisions and by statutes in the special case of young workers or apprentices. For example, a student nurse whose only compensation at the time of injury was board and room, but who was on the verge of obtaining and later did obtain the regular nurse's wage of $7 a day was awarded compensation on the $7 basis.[12] Some states[13] expressly provide by statute that, when the employee is of such age and experience that his

[1] *E.g.*, P & L Construction Company, Inc. v. Lankford, 559 S.W.2d 793 (Tenn. 1978).

[2] Petrafeck v. Industrial Commission, 554 P.2d 1097 (Colo. 1976).

[3] Richmond v. Weiss & Goldring, Inc., 124 So. 2d 601 (La. App. 1960).

[4] Waldroupe v. Kelley, 189 Kan. 99, 367 P.2d 77 (1961).

[5] Weingarten v. Democrat & Chronicle, 19 A.D.2d 566, 239 N.Y.S.2d 980 (1963).

[6] Harvey Auto Supply, Inc. v. Industrial Comm'n, 542 P.2d 1154 (Ariz. App. 1975). When the claimant, an employee of a closely held family corporation, exercised the option of taking part of his $1,000 a month salary in stock, the entire $1,000 was the proper wage basis.

[7] Jess Parrish Memorial Hospital v. Ansell, 390 So. 2d 1201 (Fla. App. 1980).

[8] Agrico Chemical Co. v. Laws, 384 So. 2d 722 (Fla. App. 1980).

[9] Morrison-Knudsen Construction Co. v. Director, OWCP, 103 S. Ct. 2045 (1983).

[10] Florida Department of Transportation v. London, 380 S. 2d 554 (Fla. App. 1980).

[11] Strand v. Hansen Seaway Service, Ltd., 614 F.2d 572 (7th Cir. 1980).

[12] Nosowich v. Central Islip State Hosp., 274 App. Div. 1080, 85 N.Y.S.2d 674 (1949).

[13] *E.g.*, Massachusetts and Wisconsin.

earnings may under natural conditions be expected to increase, that fact may be taken into account in determining the weekly wages.

PROBLEMS

(1) A school bus driver worked during the nine months of the school year. How should his weekly wage be calculated: total nine-months' earnings divided by the 39 weeks of the school year? Nine-months' earnings divided by 52 weeks? Nine-months' earnings divided by 39 weeks less Christmas vacation and other school holidays? *See* Breeland v. Colleton County, 216 S.C. 147, 57 S.E.2d 63 (1950).

(2) A maintenance and custodial worker at a private school received free tuition for his three children. Should this benefit be considered in the computation of his average weekly wage? *See* Blackwelder v. Faith Heritage School, 27 A.D.3d 1004; 811 N.Y.S.2d 225 (3d Dept. 2006).

§ 17.03   WAGE BASIS IN CONCURRENT EMPLOYMENT

AMERICAN UNIFORM & RENTAL SERVICE v. TRAINER
262 So. 2d 193 (Fla. 1972)

BOYD, JUSTICE.

This cause is before us on petition for writ of certiorari to the Florida Industrial Relations Commission. The question presented is the proper method of determining under Florida Statutes § 440.14, F.S.A., the average weekly wage of an employee who holds concurrent but dissimilar part-time and full-time jobs and is injured in the course of his part-time employment.

Claimant, a 54-year-old man suffered an injury by accident in the course of his employment with American Uniform and Rental Service, petitioner herein, on January 17, 1969. As a result of the accident, claimant sustained a cerebral concussion, scalp laceration, multiple rib fractures, fractured left clavicle and sprain of the neck and low back.

Prior to his accident with American Uniform & Rental Service, hereinafter referred to as American, and at the time of his accident, claimant was concurrently employed by American and by Master Plastics. Claimant was hired by American to repair and rebuild machinery. He was employed by Master Plastics as a night foreman, whose duty it was to oversee the operators and operations of three plastic mold machines.

Claimant's employment with Master Plastics was full-time night employment from 4:00 p. m. to 12:00 p. m. His employment with American was part-time and he had only worked for two weeks at the time of the accident. His rate of pay at American was $2 per hour and he earned $36 the first pay period of one week and $65 the second pay period of one week with American. His pay at Master Plastics was $2.20 per hour or $88 each week.

The Judge of Industrial Claims found that claimant's two jobs were concurrent but not similar and therefore the wages could not be combined to give claimant a higher weekly wage under the authority of *J. J. Murphy and Son, Inc. v. Gibbs.*[14] The Judge of Industrial Claims also found that none of the methods of arriving at a proper average weekly wage under § 440.14(1), (2), (4), and (5), applied so that only § 440.14(3) would apply. That subsection of the act states that:

> If either of the foregoing methods cannot reasonably and fairly be applied the full-time weekly wages of the injured employee shall be used, except as otherwise provided in subsections (4) or (5) of this section.

---

[14] *(Court's footnote)* 137 So. 2d 553 (Fla. 1962).

The Judge of Industrial Claims found that claimant had an average weekly wage of $80 with American, based upon $2 per hour for a forty-hour week, making him entitled to a compensation rate of $48 per week. The Judge also found that claimant suffered a 25% permanent partial functional disability and a 40% permanent partial loss of future earning capacity.

The Full Commission affirmed per curiam without opinion.

In *J. J. Murphy and Son, Inc.*,[15] this Court first enunciated the rule that wages in concurrent *similar* employments may be combined for the purpose of arriving at the average weekly wage under Florida Statutes § 440.14, F.S.A. In the *J. J. Murphy* case, claimant held one job working in the school cafeteria, as an employee of the Dade County School Board, preparing food and operating the cash register and another job, with a printing company, operating a machine which bound together invoice forms. Her two jobs were found to be dissimilar so that the wages could not be combined.

On re-examination of the *J. J. Murphy* case, we find that the frequently inequitable results arising from the rule of that case, prohibiting a combination of wages from concurrent dissimilar employment, are not required by Florida Statutes § 440.14, F.S.A., or any other section of the Workmen's Compensation Act.

If the injury occurring on the part-time job has disabled the employee from working at his full-time job, his capacity as a wage earner is impaired beyond the limits of his part-time job and his compensation should be based on the combined wages. The purpose of the Act is to compensate for loss of wage earning capacity due to work-connected injury. It is the capacity of the "whole man" not the capacity of the part-time or full-time worker that is involved.

We are aware of the arguments of "unfairness" to the employer and his carrier who may be called upon to provide compensation in excess of wages actually earned by the part-time worker. This argument would apply equally to the employer-carrier of the part-time worker who holds a concurrent *similar* full-time job, but this view has not prevented the combination of wages from *similar* employments. The problem is analyzed by Larson as follows.[16]

> Of course, it can be argued that it is unfair to one employer and his carrier to burden them with a liability, out of proportion to his own payroll and premium computed thereon, arising from a risk not associated with his type of employment. . . .

> On closer examination, however, the primary objection . . . does not seem to be the argument that the insurer has not had a chance to collect a premium on the entire wage so adopted, since this argument applies as strongly to related as to unrelated concurrent jobs. The objection, then, must be that one industry may ultimately be required to bear part of the burden of an injury produced by another. This may or may not be true in a particular case, *but the harm done is so remote and theoretical that it hardly seems to offset the very real injustice of relegating a disabled man accustomed to full earnings to a benefit level below that of destitution because of the circumstance that he happened to earn his living in two "dissimilar" jobs.*

We conclude that the similar-dissimilar distinction has little to commend it from a practical point of view and has resulted in much litigation. An employee does not consider whether his jobs are similar and he often will not know until after an accident whether compensation will be limited because based on his part-time earnings. In close cases a court test inevitably results. Further, the employer and his carrier cannot protect themselves by obtaining prior information on the employee's other jobs and

---

[15] *(Court's footnote) Ibid.*

[16] *(Court's footnote)* 2 Larson, Workmen's Compensation Law, § 60.31 at p. 88.219

perhaps collecting increased premiums since it is difficult to determine beforehand whether concurrent employments will be held sufficiently similar to allow combination of wages.

We note that prior to the decision in *J. J. Murphy*, the Commission had taken the view that wages from dissimilar employments could be combined in *Alexander v. Rolfe Armored Truck*,[17] and *Barnes v. White's Superette*.[18] These decisions were disapproved in *J. J. Murphy* but not without some reluctance, as stated:[19]

> In view of the fact that the benefits of the Act are designed to compensate workers for loss of earning capacity it may well be that to refuse to allow combination of wages in dissimilar employment will in some instances result in an inequity to a worker since his compensation may be based on wages which do not accurately reflect his actual earning capacity.

Further dissatisfaction with the rule in *J. J. Murphy* was expressed by this Court in *Central Welding and Iron Works v. Renton*,[20] wherein the Court reluctantly reversed an award of compensation based on the combined weekly wages earned in dissimilar jobs, and stated:[21]

> We are not unaware of the hardship that would result were a workman, who had been forced to follow two unlike vocations in order to provide for his family, so injured in one of them that his income in the one would be greatly reduced, while the income from the other would be entirely lost.

In summary, we herewith broaden the rule in *J. J. Murphy, supra,* to provide prospectively that wages from concurrent employments shall be combined without regard to similarity of jobs.

The case before us must be remanded for determination of the average weekly wage, a determination which will include the employee's combined wages for the thirteen weeks preceding the accident. The method of computation used by the Full Commission in *Watson v. Merrill-Stephens Drydock and Repair Co.*,[22] in combining wages from concurrent similar employments is approved. In that case the average weekly wage was stated to be one-thirteenth of the total amount of wages actually earned in both employments during the thirteen weeks immediately preceding the injury. In *Watson*, as in the instant case, the employee had worked less than thirteen weeks in one of his jobs, and the Commission held:[23]

> One-thirteenth of the total amount of wages he actually earned in both employments during the thirteen weeks preceding his injury is a realistic representation of his average weekly wage for substantially full-time employment, i.e., employment "during substantially, the whole of thirteen weeks" within the contemplation of Section 440.14(1), *supra.*"

What we have said does not change the rule of *Jacquette Motor Co. v. Talley*,[24] that wages from employments outside the operation of the Workmen's Compensation Act may not be used in determining average weekly wage under the Act.

We also note that in determining a claimant's loss of wage-earning capacity, his

---

[17] *(Court's footnote)* Decision No. 2-718, cert. denied without opinion, Rolfe Armored Truck Service v. Alexander, 105 So. 2d 927 (Fla. App. 3rd dist. 1958).

[18] *(Court's footnote)* Decision No. 2-909, *cert. denied*, without opinion, White's Superette v. Barnes, 125 So. 2d 875 (Fla. 1960).

[19] *(Court's footnote)* J. J. Murphy & Son, Inc. v. Gibbs, 137 So. 2d 553, 563 (Fla. 1962).

[20] *(Court's footnote)* 145 So. 2d 876 (Fla. 1962).

[21] *(Court's footnote) Id.* at 877.

[22] *(Court's footnote)* 1 F.C.R. 355 (1956).

[23] *(Court's footnote) Id.* at 357.

[24] *(Court's footnote)* 134 So. 2d 238 (Fla. 1961).

ability, after the accident, to earn in either or both of his concurrent employments will be considered as bearing on the extent of disability under Florida Statutes § 440.02(9), F.S.A., which provides:

> (9) "Disability" means incapacity because of the injury to earn in the same *or any other employment* the wages which the employee was receiving at the time of the injury. (e.s.)

Thus, a claimant who injured his back on his job as a construction worker and is unable to do heavy work, may still be able to work at his desk job. Wages from both jobs, even though dissimilar, may now be combined to determine "average weekly wage," but any earning capacity remaining after the accident in either job would go to reduce the claimant's disability rating. This has been the general rule and is not altered by our decision here.[*(Court's footnote)*See, Parrott v. City of Fort Lauderdale, 190 So. 2d 326 (Fla. 1966).]

Accordingly, certiorari is granted, the decision of the Full Commission is quashed and the cause remanded with directions to remand to the Judge of Industrial Claims for further proceedings in accordance herewith.

It is so ordered.

ERVIN, CARLTON and ADKINS, JJ., concur.

ROBERTS, C.J., dissents.

§ 17.04 MAXIMUM AND MINIMUM LIMITS ON WEEKLY BENEFITS

After the wage formula has been applied, the result is still subject to maximum limits. Until comparatively recently, these limits were expressed in terms of dollar figures. With the advent of chronic inflation, the hardship wrought by the fixed maximum limits became intolerable, what with the legislatures, some meeting only every two years, finding it impossible to legislate appropriate increases promptly enough to keep pace with the cost of living. Accordingly, following the pioneering lead of Connecticut, most states adopted a sliding-scale maximum tied to the state's average weekly wage. By 1999, the device in some form was in use in over 40 states. The Longshore Act is tied to the national average weekly wage, the Federal Employees' Compensation Act to the Consumer Price Index, and the Texas Act to the average wage of manufacturing production workers. As of January 1999, the commonest percentage figure applied to the state average weekly wage to produce the compensation maximum was 100 percent, in use in about half of the states. Several were higher: 110 percent in Alabama, and 200 percent in Iowa, 133 1/3 percent in Illinois, 200 percent in the Longshore Act.

The constitutionality of this type of flexible maximum has been upheld, as against the charge that it impaired the obligation of contracts because of uncertainty as to the amounts to be paid.[25]

As to the minimum benefit figure, over a dozen states employ a flexible figure tied to the state's average weekly rate, with the percentages ranging from 20% to 50%. Most of the rest specify a minimum dollar amount. Usually there is also a proviso, something like "employee's actual average wage if less." If this proviso has been omitted, as it has in some states, the danger of benefits exceeding actual wage is obvious, particularly as to part-time employment and as to partial disability.

---

[25] Wien Air Alaska v. Arant, 592 P.2d 352 (Alaska 1979).

§ 17.05 TIME AS OF WHICH LEGISLATIVE OR AUTOMATIC BENEFIT INCREASES APPLY

The general rule is that benefit increases, whether automatic under escalator clauses or legislatively enacted, are not retroactive,[26] and that the benefit level in effect at the time of injury controls.[27] Alaska, on the strength of the doctrine of liberal construction, applies the benefit level prevailing at the time the disability was rated.[28]

§ 17.06 COST OF LIVING ADJUSTMENTS IN EXISTING BENEFITS

A second by-product of the era of chronic inflation, in addition to the flexible maximum for new awards, was the cost-of-living adjustment for past awards. Some such adjustment provision been enacted in close to two dozen states.[29] Because of the relative novelty of this type of provision, no standard pattern has appeared — indeed, the provisions vary so widely that it is almost impossible to frame any general rules or observations applicable to them. Some are extremely limited in scope — for example, California's applies only to temporary total awards existing for more than two years; Rhode Island's statute applies only to the Second Injury Fund's liability. A number are limited as to the time of injury.[30]

Most of the adjustment clauses cover only total disability — often only permanent total — and death. Many call for direct payment of the supplement by the employer or carrier, with reimbursement by a special fund or sometimes the second injury fund.

Adjustments are frequently annual and automatic, and usually keyed to the state's average weekly wage, although a few are tied to the national Consumer Price Index.[31]

The constitutionality of cost-of-living adjustment statutes has been challenged in several states, and has been upheld in most cases. The leading case, decided by the Delaware Supreme Court, is *Price v. All-American Engineering Co.*[32] The court's rationale can be summarized as follows: the statute, although retroactive, did not impair the obligation of contracts, because workers' compensation rights and obligations are based on status, not contract; but even if it were a matter of contract, the carriers and employers suffered no impairment, because they had a right to be reimbursed for their supplementary outlay; but even if their rights were impaired, the provision was valid as a reasonable exercise of the state's police power.

---

[26] *E.g.*, State *ex rel.* Briggs & Stratton v. Noll, 302 N.W.2d 487 (Wis. 1981). A statute passed May 12, 1980, raised compensation benefits for injuries occurring on or after January 1, 1980. The Wisconsin Supreme Court held retroactivity unconstitutional under the Wisconsin Constitution. The right to receive compensation fully accrued at the time of injury, and benefits were set by the law as of the date of the injury.

[27] *E.g.*, E.I. duPont de Nemours & Co. v. Green, 411 A.2d 953 (Del. 1980).

[28] Hood v. State Workmen's Compensation Board, 574 P.2d 811 (Alaska 1978).

[29] *E.g.*, California, Connecticut, Illinois, and New York.

[30] *E.g.*, Delaware, Florida, and Wisconsin.

[31] *E.g.*, California, Ohio, Rhode Island, and Virginia.

[32] Price v. All-American Engineering Co., 320 A.2d 336 (Del. 1974).

Chapter 18
MEDICAL BENEFITS AND REHABILITATION

§ 18.01 INTRODUCTION

All states now provide medical and hospital benefits, including artificial members and aids, that are either unlimited as to time and amount, or, if limited, can be extended indefinitely by administrative authority. Under the usual statute, the employer is required to furnish the necessary medical services, and it is only if after notice it fails to do so within a reasonable time that the employee is entitled to incur medical expense on his or her own behalf.

Medical benefits ordinarily include not only medical and hospital services, but necessary incidentals such as transportation, apparatus, and nursing care, which may be compensable even when supplied at home by a member of claimant's family. Palliative measures are included under the decisions of most jurisdictions, to relieve pain even after all hope of cure is gone.

Rehabilitation is becoming an increasingly important part of the compensation program, under special provisions supplying additional maintenance and compensation during the rehabilitation period as well as curative and retraining centers to restore earning power to disabled workers.

§ 18.02 HOSPITAL AND MEDICAL BENEFITS

[1] In General

An integral and important part of the benefit scheme of all compensation acts is the provision of hospital and medical benefits. These benefits account for about one-third of the total benefits paid to injured workers.

In 48 states such benefits are essentially unlimited as to duration and amount. In the remaining two — Arkansas and New Jersey — the administrator can extend benefits without limit.

[2] What Are Medical Services?

KUSHAY v. SEXTON DAIRY COMPANY
394 Mich. 69, 228 N.W.2d 205 (1975)

LEVIN, JUSTICE.

John Kushay became totally and permanently disabled as the result of a work-related injury. Workmen's compensation benefits were paid by his employer, Sexton Dairy Company.

This appeal concerns Kushay's claim that Sexton Dairy is liable for services rendered in the Kushay home by Kushay's wife, Daisy.

The Workmen's Compensation Appeal Board rejected the claim for funds to compensate Daisy Kushay on the ground that her services were those "any conscientious wife would give her husband." The Court of Appeals denied leave to appeal.

We reverse and remand to the Appeal Board for determination of the amount payable for services rendered by Daisy Kushay.

The statute provides that an employer shall provide an employee injured in the course of his employment with "reasonable medical, surgical and hospital services and medicines or *other attendance* or treatment recognized by the laws of this state as legal, when they are needed."[1] (Emphasis supplied.)

Sexton Dairy contends that the issue is factual, not legal. The Appeal Board's determination that the services performed by Daisy Kushay were those a dutiful wife would perform for her husband is said to be a factual determination, dispositive of the issue and binding on this Court in the absence of fraud.[2]

There are factual questions which, on remand, it will be the function of the Appeal Board to resolve. The construction to be given the statute and whether particular services fall within that construction are, however, questions properly reviewable by this Court.[3]

I

In January, 1961, while employed by the Sexton Dairy Co., John Kushay injured his back lifting a 130 pound can of cream. He was operated on in February and again in June of that year. The Appeal Board found that Kushay became totally and permanently disabled[*(Court's footnote)* M.C.L.A. § 418.361; M.S.A. § 17.237(361).] due to the industrial loss of use of both legs following the June surgery. The nature of Kushay's disability is pain in the lower back and legs caused by the formation of scar tissue around his spinal cord.

Kushay spends 90% of his time in bed. He moves about in a wheel chair or with the aid of two canes. He claims that he suffers "intense, unremitting" pain, a "burning sensation" and "numbness" in his legs, caused by the scar tissue pulling and squeezing the spinal nerves radiating into his legs, and that walking with his canes requires tremendous effort.

The Appeal Board has in other cases made awards for care rendered by a member of the family as "other attendance" within the meaning of the statute.

In *Dunaj v. Harry Becker Co.*, 1972 WCABO 2781, *aff'd* 52 Mich. App. 354, 217

---

[1] *(Court's footnote)* M.C.L.A. § 418.315; M.S.A. § 17.237(315).

[2] *(Court's footnote)* Const. 1963, art. 6, § 28.

[3] *(Court's footnote)* Cf. DeGeer v. DeGeer Farm Equipment Co., 391 Mich. 96, 214 N.W.2d 794 (1974); Zaremba v. Chrysler Corp., 377 Mich. 226, 139 N.W.2d 745 (1966).

N.W.2d 397 (1974), the claimant lost the industrial use of his legs due to a back injury. He suffered periods of severe pain and spent much time in bed. His wife bathed him, changed his clothes, administered medication and helped him to the bathroom; compensation was awarded for these services.

Daisy Kushay bathes her disabled husband, helps him dress, gives him medication, serves meals in bed, helps him to the bathroom, occasionally gives him enemas, clips his toenails and drives him to appointments.

In *Anttonen v. Cleveland Cliffs Iron Co.*, 1962 WCABO 152, payment was awarded for services rendered by the wife of a worker who had lost a leg and the industrial use of an arm. She helped him dress, bathe, assisted him in the bathroom and in attaching and removing his artificial leg.

Similarly, the claimant in *Ertel v. Chrysler Corp.*, 1972 WCABO 1662, lost the industrial use of his right arm and leg due to pain associated with a spinal injury. His wife helped him dress and bathe, massaged his back and put him in traction; payment was awarded for these services [*(Court's footnote omitted.)*]

II

The irreconcilability of the results in these cases with the result in this case may be attributable to the standard — whether the services are "beyond ordinary wifely duties"[4] or, conversely, those "which any conscientious wife would give her husband"[5] — employed by the Appeal Board.

The language of the statute, "reasonable medical, surgical and hospital services and medicines or other attendance or treatment," focuses on the nature of the service provided, not the status or devotion of the provider of the service. Under the statute, the employer bears the cost of medical services, other attendance and treatment. If services within the statutory intendment are provided by a spouse, the employer is obligated to pay for them.

Ordinary household tasks are not within the statutory intendment. House cleaning, preparation of meals and washing and mending of clothes, services required for the maintenance of persons who are not disabled, are beyond the scope of the obligation imposed on the employer. Serving meals in bed and bathing, dressing, and escorting a disabled person are not ordinary household tasks. That a "conscientious" spouse may in fact perform these services does not diminish the employer's duty to compensate him or her as the person who discharges the employer's duty to provide them.

Under the statute it is the employer's duty to provide medical services "or other attendance or treatment . . . *when they are needed.*"[6] (Emphasis supplied.) The Appeal Board did not find that the services rendered by Daisy Kushay were not "needed."

III

Professor Larson writes that the early case law denied payment for services performed by a claimant's wife on the ground that she "did no more than she was bound to do as an affectionate spouse. Later cases, however, have permitted the charge, on the reasoning that the employer, by statute, has the affirmative duty of furnishing these services."[7]

The claimant in *A. G. Crunkleton Electric Co., Inc. v. Barkdoll*, 227 Md. 364, 371, 177

---

4 *(Court's footnote)* Anttonen v. Cleveland Cliffs Iron Co., 1962 WCABO 152.

5 *(Court's footnote)* The formulation in this case.

6 *(Court's footnote)* See footnote 1.

7 *(Court's footnote)* 2 Larson, Workmen's Compensation Law, § 61.13, p. 10-470.

A.2d 252, 256 (1962), suffered the amputation of both arms due to extensive burns. The statute provided that " . . . the employer shall promptly provide for an injured employee such medical, surgical or other attendance or treatment, nurse and hospital services, medicines, crutches, apparatus, artificial hands, arms, feet and legs as may be required by the Commission." The highest court of Maryland, without discussing the nature of the services performed by the claimant's wife, affirmed an award:

> The services rendered by the wife were not minor in character, or of such a nature so as to be classified as ordinary household duties. We think it is clear that the duties performed by the wife in this case were extraordinary, unusual, and clearly above and beyond the usual call of any marital obligation.

In an earlier case, *Daugherty v. City of Monett*, 238 Mo. App. 924, 938, 192 S.W.2d 51, 56 (1946), the wife of a worker paralyzed from his waist down was awarded compensation for services "in addition to her ordinary [household] duties" under a statute requiring the employer to furnish "such medical, surgical, and hospital treatment, including nursing," as may reasonably be required for the first 90 days, and "such additional similar treatment as the commission by special order may determine to be necessary."

In *Western Alliance Insurance Co. v. Tubbs*, 400 S.W.2d 850 (Tex. Civ. App., 1965), the services performed by the claimant's wife "consisted of feeding, bathing, shaving and turning claimant, taking him to the doctor and generally 'taking care of' him in his home while he was an invalid." The court held that she was properly awarded compensation for rendering services which the employer had a statutory duty to provide . . .[8]

Remanded to the Workmen's Compensation Appeal Board for further proceedings. The Appeal Board shall determine the amount payable for services rendered by Daisy Kushay. Costs to appellant.

T. G. KAVANAGH, C. J., and WILLIAMS, FITZGERALD and SWAINSON, JJ., concur.

COLEMAN, J., concurs in result.

PROBLEMS

(1) Does "all reasonable and necessary medical expenses" include a heart transplant? *See* Bill Hodges Truck Co. v. Gillum, 774 P.2d 1063 (Okla. 1989). A penile implant? *See* Jackson v. Greyhound Lines, Inc., 734 S.W.2d 617 (Tenn. 1987).

(2) As a result of a workplace injury a worker becomes quadriplegic. Can an employer be required to furnish that worker with a laptop computer under a state's workers' compensation act? *See* Stone Container Corp. v. Castle, 657 N.W.2d 485 (Iowa 2003).

[3] Choice of Medical Provider

During the 1990s the focus on prevention of fraud, medical incompetence, and "doctor shopping," together with broader efforts to reduce costs, produced a trend toward restricting the worker's choice of medical provider. Pennsylvania, New York and Nebraska have, for example, enacted legislation limiting the injured worker's choice of doctor in the workers' compensation setting.

But the issue of choice of medical provider has troubled workers' compensation long before this recent legislative activity. The tendency to limit employee choice derives from a fundamental feature of workers' compensation, namely, that it is the employer

[8] *(Court's footnote) Contra*, Bituminous Casualty Corp. v. Wilbanks, 60 Ga. App. 620, 4 S.E.2d 916 (1939); Graf v. Montgomery Ward & Co., Inc., 234 Minn. 485, 49 N.W.2d 797 (1951), on the ground that the services were performed by the injured worker's wife.

who is legally obligated to provide adequate medical treatment to the injured worker. It is hard to see how an employer can satisfy this obligation if it has no say in what treatment is provided or who is providing it. Moreover, the employer which is also paying wage loss benefits has a legitimate interest in encouraging rehabilitation and prompt return to work. At present only a few jurisdictions give a worker receiving medical benefits the unfettered right to choose his or her physician. Some states, like North Carolina, give the choice to the employer outright. Others have intermediate schemes. A few states, Alaska for example, allow the employee an initial choice but limit his or her right to *change* doctors. In other states, a worker may choose from a list of doctors prepared by the state agency or, as the case may be, the employer. There are also efforts to import the managed care concept into workers' compensation, although there are problems with this, not the least of which is the potential incompatibility of managed care's cost-cutting approach and "wait and see" strategy with the employer's interest in getting the employee back to work and off compensation as quickly as possible.

Some studies suggest that allowing the employer to choose the doctor may not have the intended effect. According to one study, which came out in 1993, states where employers choose the doctor had medical costs that were 24% higher than states where they do not.[9]

PROBLEM

Claimant, a Mexican citizen and resident of Tijuana, injured his back in a fall while picking fruit. Since the physicians provided by the employer were unable to help him, he independently sought and obtained successful medical treatment by a Mexican physician in Tijuana. Should the employer be liable for the Mexican physician's charges?

§ 18.03 REHABILITATION

[1] Introduction

The typical workers' compensation statute contains rehabilitation provisions designed to restore the injured worker, where possible, to an income earning status. This can include physical therapy, prosthetics, and medical treatment whose purpose goes beyond health restoration in that it is specifically to restore work capability. It can also include vocational rehabilitation as well as job placement assistance. In general, although the states differ somewhat on this point, the employer is not obligated as a part of rehabilitation to provide formal education or training for an entirely new type of job or career.[10]

Generally speaking, the injured worker's cooperation with rehabilitation and job placement efforts is mandatory, and refusal to cooperate can result in termination of compensation. Within certain limits, employers may offer light duty work as a way of easing their burden of paying compensation, and the worker's refusal to accept such work when capable of performing it may also be grounds to discontinue compensation benefits.

---

[9] *Workers' Comp: A Complex Adaptation for Managed Care*, Medicine & Health, April 28, 1997, citing a report published in John Burton's Workers' Compensation Monitor in 1993.

[10] *See, e.g.*, City of Salem v. Colegrove, 228 Va. 290, 321 S.E.2d 654 (1984).

[2]   What is Rehabilitation?

GRANTHAM v. CHERRY HOSPITAL
98 N.C. App. 34, 389 S.E.2d 822 (1990)

This workers' compensation case was first tried on 3 March 1988 with Deputy Commissioner Richard B. Ford presiding. An opinion and award for the plaintiff were filed on 24 August 1988. Defendant appealed in timely fashion to the Full Commission, which affirmed and adopted as its own the deputy commissioner's opinion and award with one commissioner dissenting. Defendant appealed to this court.

It is undisputed that on 25 November 1984 Donald Grantham suffered a closed-head injury, an accident that arose out of and occurred in the course of his employment with Cherry Hospital. Mr. Grantham is now permanently and totally disabled from his injuries. He suffers from expressive dysphasia (extreme difficulty in speaking), hemiparesis (weakness) of his upper and lower right extremities, attention and memory lapses, depression and "persistent cognitive, psychological and behavioral difficulties."

The plaintiff claims that prior to his injury he worked two jobs, and that as a result of his injury and disability, his and his wife's combined income fell for over two years by nearly $ 1,100 a month. Mr. Grantham did not begin receiving disability retirement income until December 1987. The record indicates that as a consequence of his injuries, certain family debts were incurred totaling $ 27,865.07. These debts were as follows:

1. Wayne Oil Company	$ 969.69
2. Wayne County Tax Collector's Office	$ 267.80
3. Howard Brothers Food	$ 83.87
4. Heilig-Meyers (furniture)	$ 3,469.00
5. State Employee's Credit Unit	$ 16,592.82
6. Musgrave Tire and Gas	$ 428.30
7. Pate's Service Station and Garage	$ 533.59
8. Babysitter (138 wks. at $ 40/wk)	$ 5,520.00
TOTAL	$ 27,865.07

None of this debt involved medical expenses attributable to the plaintiff's injuries.

It is also clear from the record that through his own highly commendable efforts and the work of his neuropsychiatrist, Dr. Thomas Gualtieri, Mr. Grantham has begun to rehabilitate himself. These efforts at self-help probably have saved the State of North Carolina the expense of placing Mr. Grantham in a rehabilitation residence, which could cost as much as $30,000 a month. The doctors who treated Mr. Grantham immediately after his injury recommended his placement in an inpatient unit.

At the hearing before the deputy commissioner, Dr. Gualtieri testified that payment of the debts and relief from the burden and worry of the indebtedness would be "the best thing for Donald's rehabilitation that we could do." The debt and resulting depression were interfering with Mr. Grantham's rehabilitation, Dr. Gualtieri said.

After the hearing, Deputy Commissioner Ford made the following findings and conclusions of law:

9. The Plaintiff, as of the date of the hearing on March 3, 1988 had incurred a family indebtedness of $27,865.07 as the result of his injury, his inability to earn income and the mental, psychological and physical disabilities which he suffers.

10. This indebtedness is of great concern to the Plaintiff, causes him stress, and effects his mental and emotional well-being and is efficient in preventing his recovery from the mental and psychological depression and illness from which he suffers as a result of the injury on November 24, 1984.

. . . .

12. While there is no cure for the Plaintiff's physical condition, the payment of his indebtedness will tend to effect a cure and give him relief from the mental and emotional depression and illness from which he suffers as a result of this injury on November 25, 1984 and the resulting indebtedness; and is a reasonable and necessary rehabilitative service and care for the Plaintiff's well-being.

. . . .

14. Further the Plaintiff is entitled to be relieved from the indebtedness . . . in an amount not to exceed $27,865.07 as a rehabilitation service which may reasonably be required to effect . . . a cure or give the Plaintiff relief from the injury related psychological and emotional problems caused by the brain damage resulting from the injury occurring on November 25, 1984.

ARNOLD, JUDGE.

In this case we must decide if N.C. Gen. Stat. § 97-29 of the Workers' Compensation Act authorizes the Industrial Commission to order an employer to pay an employee's common consumer debts as a "rehabilitative service." N.C. Gen. Stat. § 97-29 requires that "[i]n cases of total and permanent disability, compensation, including reasonable and necessary nursing services, medicines, sick travel, medical, hospital, and *other treatment or care or rehabilitative services* shall be paid for by the employer during the lifetime of the injured employee" (emphasis added). N.C. Gen. Stat. § 97-29 (Supp. 1989). (In the original statute, the word between care and rehabilitative services is "of." This is a misprint. It should be "or." *See* 1973 N.C. Sess. Laws ch. 1308, § 2. The mistake has been corrected in the statutory supplement that we cited.)

A decision of the Industrial Commission will not be overturned on appeal absent an abuse of discretion. . . .

We recognize the general principle that the provisions of the Workers' Compensation Act should be construed liberally so that benefits are not denied to an employee based on a narrow or strict interpretation of the statute's provisions. *See Petty v. Transport, Inc.*, 276 N.C. 417, 173 S.E.2d 321 (1970). We also realize that this case arises in an important and dynamic area of workers' compensation law — defining the parameters of employer responsibility for employee rehabilitation. As one commentator has noted: It is too obvious for argument that rehabilitation, where possible, is the most satisfactory disposition of industrial injury cases, from the point of view of the insurer, employer and public as well as of the claimant. Apart from the incalculable gain to the worker himself, the cost to insurers and employers of permanent disability claims under a properly adjusted system is reduced; and, so far as the public is concerned, it has been said on good authority that for every dollar spent on rehabilitation by the Federal Government it has received back ten in the form of income taxes on the earnings of the persons rehabilitated (citation omitted). It is probably no exaggeration to say that in this field lies the greatest single opportunity for significant improvement in the benefits afforded by the workmen's compensation system. Larson, 2 Workmen's Compensation Law § 61.25 (1987). Furthermore, Mr. Grantham's request falls into one of the most controversial corners of rehabilitation compensation — providing services of a non-medical nature that somehow might be relevant to the employee's rehabilitation. *See id.* at § 61.13(a).

It may be true in this case that the most cost-effective decision would be to uphold the Commission's award. Such a determination might stave off the much more expensive possibility of placing Mr. Grantham in an inpatient rehabilitation program. Nevertheless, cost-effectiveness is not the sole goal of our Workers' Compensation Act, and as the Act is presently written, we hold that it is not a reasonable interpretation of the statute to classify the payment of consumer debt as a rehabilitative service. We believe that any other decision undermines the integrity of the Act.

We base our conclusion on an analysis of the structure of the Act, case law that develops the relevant provisions, and also on common sense. We simply fail to see how the term "services," in the context of medical rehabilitative services, can reasonably be read to encompass a monetary payment for basic necessities.

Furthermore, the structure of the Workers' Compensation Act indicates the decision below is incorrect. The Act provides a dual approach to employee compensation. *Derebery v. Pitt County Fire Marshall*, 318 N.C. 192, 205–06, 347 S.E.2d 814, 822 (1986) (Billings, J., dissenting in part). First, disability compensation, which is calculated based upon the individual employee's earning power, is provided as a substitute for the wages lost due to the injury. This compensation is the employer's contribution for items that wages ordinarily purchase — the basic necessities of life such as food, clothing and shelter. *Id.* The Act, however, also requires employers to compensate injured employees for medical costs related to their injuries; specifically, employers must pay a permanently disabled employee such as Mr. Grantham for "necessary nursing services, medicines, sick travel, medical, hospital, and other treatment or care or rehabilitative services. . . . " N.C. Gen. Stat. § 97-29. In the case before us, we believe the Commission erroneously attempted to engraft one prong of the Act onto the other. By ordering a payment to cover the injured employee's expenses for basic necessities under the guise of "rehabilitative services," the Commission has turned the statute on its head.

In two limited situations, our Supreme Court has upheld payments under the language of "other treatment or care or rehabilitative services" to claimants for medically related expenses that are not listed in the statute. But neither of these cases attempts to stretch the language of the statute as far as the plaintiff here, and we see no conflict between those holdings and our decision in this case. In all, three North Carolina cases have interpreted the questioned language of N.C. Gen. Stat. § 97-29. In *Godwin v. Swift & Co.*, 270 N.C. 690, 155 S.E.2d 157 (1967), the Supreme Court held that the phrase "other treatment or care" covered compensation to pay in-laws of a claimant who needed around-the-clock attention and care. *Id.*

In *McDonald v. Brunswick Electric Membership Corp.*, 77 N.C. App. 753, 336 S.E.2d 407 (1985) (Wells, J., dissenting), this Court held that the statute could not be interpreted to include compensation for a specially equipped van for a wheelchair-bound claimant. The employee in *McDonald* sustained an employment-related injury which resulted in amputation of both of his legs and left arm. Although the employee could drive a specially adapted car that could carry a regular wheelchair, he wanted the van to transport himself and his motorized wheelchair. Claimant's employer agreed to pay for the special adaptive equipment installed in the van, but balked at paying for the van itself. *Id.* at 754, 336 S.E.2d at 408. At the hearing before the deputy commissioner, the employee's rehabilitation nurse testified it was important for the claimant's rehabilitation that he learn to do things independently and therefore the specially equipped van was necessary to fully rehabilitate the employee. His physician also testified that the van was an important and necessary part of his rehabilitation. The deputy commissioner concluded that the specially equipped van was a rehabilitative service within the meaning of N.C. Gen. Stat. § 97-29 and ordered the employer to reimburse the claimant for the cost of the van itself. *Id.* On appeal, the Full Commission affirmed and adopted the Opinion and Award of the deputy commissioner. In reversing the Commission, we stated in *McDonald*:

> [N]either the phrase "other treatment or care" nor the term "rehabilitative services" in G.S. 97-29 can reasonably be interpreted to include a specially-equipped van. This language in the statute plainly refers to services or treatment, rather than tangible, non-medically related items such as van; thus, it would be contrary to the ordinary meaning of the statute to hold that it includes the van purchased by plaintiff.

McDonald, at 756–57, 336 S.E.2d at 409. Our decision in *McDonald*, which follows the majority rule in this country, was not appealed.

In *McDonald*, we relied in part on another Court of Appeals decision, the third case in our jurisdiction to interpret this section of N.C. Gen. Stat. § 97-29, *Derebery v. Pitt County Fire Marshall*, 76 N.C. App. 67, 332 S.E.2d 94 (1985). In *Derebery*, this Court held that an employer's statutory duty to provide "other treatment or care" did not extend to furnishing a wheelchair-accessible mobile home for an injured employee. However, with three justices dissenting, the Supreme Court overturned that opinion and ordered the employer to pay for the residence. *Derebery*, 318 N.C. 192, 347 S.E.2d 814; *accord Squeo v. Comfort Control Corp.*, 99 N.J. 588, 494 A.2d 313 (1985). Nevertheless, *Derebery* does not control on the facts before us, and we believe that the holding of the Industrial Commission in this case strays far beyond the boundaries of the statute as outlined by *Derebery* and *Godwin*.

Whether or not specially adaptive vehicles and wheelchair-accessible housing are compensable under the statute are debatable issues, as the four dissents in *Derebery* and *McDonald* indicate. We can see a strong nexus between the words "other treatment or care or rehabilitative service" and requiring adaptive vehicles and housing for wheelchair-bound persons. The connection between that language and paying compensation for consumer debt, on the other hand, is much more tenuous, and we believe not reasonable.

A survey of holdings from other jurisdictions reinforces our determination here. To our knowledge no other court has come close to holding that "rehabilitative services" could encompass consumer debt. The outer limits of this concept are much narrower than the plaintiff before us argues. The Florida Court of Appeals, which has been one of the most generous courts in interpreting the scope of medical services, ordered an employer to pay the nursery school costs for the child of a woman who had to spend much of the day in traction. *Doctors Hosp. of Lake Worth v. Robinson*, 411 So. 2d 958 (1982). The court cautioned, however, that child care expenses would not be construed as a medical necessity in cases involving "less extreme" circumstances. *Id.* Even Florida, however, refused to provide compensation for paying workplace assistants to perform the part of a job that a claimant was unable to do because of her work-induced disability. *Ulmer v. Jon David Coiffures*, 458 So. 2d 1218 (1984). The court recognized that under certain circumstances medical allowances had been made for vehicles, pools, child care and the like, but that no cases authorized compensation for the cost of aid in performing the job functions of a disabled worker. *Id.*

One purpose of the Workers' Compensation Act is to insure a limited and determinate liability for employers. To this end, courts must not legislate expanded liability under the guise of construing a statute liberally. *McDonald*, 77 N.C. App. at 756, 336 S.E.2d at 409. While the Act should be liberally construed to benefit the employee, the plain and unmistakable language of the statute must be followed. *Hardy v. Small*, 246 N.C. 581, 99 S.E.2d 862 (1957). We do not believe that the General Assembly intended to include compensation for an employee's consumer debt within the meaning of "rehabilitative services." The Industrial Commission, therefore, was without authority to require the defendant to bear that responsibility. Accordingly, we reverse the opinion and award below.

Reversed.

PROBLEM

Claimant, who weighed 422 pounds and who had been chronically overweight since childhood, slipped and injured his back and elbow at his job in California. Three physicians recommended that he lose weight in order to facilitate recovery from his injuries. He enrolled in a weight loss program at Duke University Medical Center's live-in obesity clinic in Durham, North Carolina. Was he entitled to reimbursement from the California compensation system for the cost of this program? *See* Braewood Convalescent Hospital v. Workers' Comp. Appeal Board, 34 Cal. 3d 159, 193 Cal. Rptr. 157, 666 P.2d 14 (1983).

[3] Prosthetic Devices, Modified Vans, and the Like

STRICKLAND v. BOWATER, INC.
322 S.C. 471, 472 S.E.2d 635 (1996)

HEARN, JUDGE.

In this workers' compensation case, the appellant, Richard Strickland, a quadriplegic, argues the commission erred when it failed to require the respondents, Bowater, Inc. and Liberty Mutual Insurance Company (Bowater), to pay the full cost of an unmodified van for Strickland. We affirm.

Strickland sustained an admitted accident to his head and neck on March 17, 1992, during the course of his employment with Bowater. Strickland was not initially disabled, but underwent surgery to remove a herniated disc from his cervical spine. As a result of complications during the surgery, he was rendered a quadriplegic. By a previous commission decision, Strickland was awarded permanent and total lifetime disability benefits.

Bowater stipulated a modified van was medically necessary for Strickland and agreed to pay for the modifications necessary to specially equip the van to accommodate Strickland's quadriplegia. The parties dispute, however, whether or not Bowater must reimburse Strickland for the "base cost" of an unmodified van. In other words, Strickland contends Bowater should be responsible for providing the full cost of an unmodified van plus the costs associated with its modifications. Bowater asserts it should be required to pay only the difference between an unmodified van and a mid-range automobile of the same year.

The single commissioner, affirmed by the commission and the circuit judge, ordered Bowater to reimburse Strickland $4,338.90. This amount represents the cost difference between an unmodified van and a mid-range automobile of the same year. Strickland had purchased a 1993 van for $23,338.90. The parties stipulated the average price for a 1993 automobile was $19,000.00, thus creating a difference of $4,338.90. The only issue before this court, therefore, is whether or not Bowater is responsible for the full cost of an unmodified van.

Strickland relies on S.C. Code Ann. § 42-15-60 (1976) as the basis for requiring Bowater to pay for the van. Section 42-15-60 states, in part:

> In cases in which total and permanent disability results, reasonable and necessary nursing services, medicines, prosthetic devices, sick travel, medical, hospital and other treatment or care shall be paid during the life of the injured employee, without regard to any limitation in this title including the maximum compensation limit. (Emphasis added).

Strickland contends the full cost of a modified van constitutes "other treatment or care" necessary to lessen his disability. Therefore, Strickland asserts Bowater should be held liable for all costs associated with a modified van, including the initial cost of an unmodified van.

Whether or not the legislature intended a vehicle that enables an injured worker to be mobile to constitute "other treatment or care" is a novel issue in South Carolina. Other courts, considering the language in the context of their states' statutes, have reached varying results on this question.

Maryland, New York, North Carolina, and South Dakota have denied reimbursement for specially-equipped automobiles or vans for similarly disabled claimants. See *R & T*

Construction Co. v. Judge, 323 Md. 514, 594 A.2d 99 (1991); *Nallan v. Motion Picture Studio Mechanics Union*, Local # 52, 49 A.D.2d 365, 375 N.Y.S.2d 164 (1975), *rev'd on other grounds*, 40 N.Y.2d 1042, 391 N.Y.S.2d 853, 360 N.E.2d 353 (1976); *Kranis v. Trunz*, Inc., 91 A.D.2d 765, 458 N.Y.S.2d 10 (1982); *McDonald v. Brunswick Elec. Membership Corp.*, 77 N.C. App. 753, 336 S.E.2d 407 (1985); *Johnson v. Skelly Oil Co.*, 359 N.W.2d 130 (S.D.1984).

In McDonald the North Carolina Court of Appeals construed a provision very similar to the South Carolina statute, and held the phrase "other treatment or care" did not include furnishing a claimant with a wheelchair-accessible van. Thereafter, however, the North Carolina Supreme Court reversed the Court of Appeals decision that "other treatment or care" did not include furnishing a claimant with a wheelchair-accessible place to live. See *Derebery v. Pitt County Fire Marshall*, 318 N.C. 192, 347 S.E.2d 814 (1986). This subsequent decision by the North Carolina Supreme Court, wherein it found an employer responsible for providing a claimant with wheelchair-accessible housing, casts doubt on the viability of the Court of Appeals' restrictive interpretation of "other treatment or care" in McDonald. [footnote omitted]

Courts in Arizona, Florida, North Dakota and West Virginia have held that a specially-equipped automobile or van is compensable under certain circumstances and conditions. See *Terry Grantham Co. v. Industrial Comm'n of Arizona*, 154 Ariz. 180, 741 P.2d 313 (Ct. App. 1987); *Fidelity & Cas. Co. v. Cooper*, 382 So. 2d 1331 (Fla. Dist. Ct. App. 1980); *Meyer v. North Dakota Workers Compensation Bureau*, 512 N.W.2d 680 (N.D.1994); *Crouch v. West Virginia Workers' Compensation Commissioner*, 184 W.Va. 730, 403 S.E.2d 747 (1991). These courts have construed provisions such as "medical treatment" more broadly in favor of the claimant, and have allowed this expenditure where the evidence showed the van to be medically necessary.

In support of its position that an employer should be responsible for a portion but not all of the costs associated with a van, Bowater presents the West Virginia decision in Crouch as persuasive authority. Under similar facts, the West Virginia Supreme Court of Appeals held a modified van was "reasonably required" for a quadriplegic worker, and, therefore, compensable under their statute. However, the employer was entitled to offset the cost of the unmodified van with the cost of an average, mid-priced automobile of the same year. Thus, the West Virginia court required the employer to pay what the employer in this case has agreed must be paid, that is, the difference between the cost of an unmodified van and the average cost of a mid-sized automobile.

In this case, however, it is not necessary for us to reach the question of whether an employer should be responsible for providing the difference between an unmodified van and an average mid-sized automobile since Bowater agrees with the commission's decision to do this. Similarly, we need not decide whether an employer is also responsible for paying the costs associated with modification of the van because Bowater has agreed to do so in this case.

Strickland urges this court to require Bowater to pay the full cost of an unmodified van. While the provisions of the workers' compensation law are entitled to a liberal construction in favor of the employee, we do not believe that under our present statute an employer could be required to pay for such an expenditure. The General Assembly, rather than this court, should address this matter.

Given Bowater's willingness to provide the costs of modification and its acquiescence in the commission's decision that it should pay the difference between an unmodified van and an average mid-sized automobile of the same year, the commission's decision is

Affirmed.

HOWELL, C.J., and ANDERSON, J., concur.

Chapter 19
DEPENDENCY AND DEATH BENEFITS

SYNOPSIS

§ 19.01   STATUTORY CATEGORIES OF RELATIONSHIP

[1]   Introduction

The analysis of almost all dependency questions is a weighing of two factors: claimant's compliance with statutory requirements of relationship to the deceased, and dependency in fact. Under most statutes, a surviving spouse and young children living with the deceased need prove only this relationship, but if not living with the deceased must prove dependency in fact. Other eligible claimants must usually prove actual dependency. When the rights of a widow, widower, or children are based by statute on relationship alone, the rights are absolute, and are not detracted from by proof of misconduct, nondependency, attempted invalid divorce, impending divorce and the like. Questions affecting relationship, such as validity of marriage or divorce, legitimacy, and obligation to support, are determined by the usual statutory and decisional domestic relations law of the jurisdiction, but a slight beginning may be observed of a tendency to decide such questions in such a way as to effectuate the policies of workers' compensation even at the expense of literal compliance with domestic relations precedents in other fields.

[2]   Classification of Dependency Statutes and Problems

All statutes provide death benefits for the dependents of deceased workers. About two thirds of the states[1] pay benefits to a widow or widower for life or until remarriage, and to children until they reach a specified age. Of these, about a quarter impose some sort of limitation in terms of dollar amounts.[2]

Although the dependency statutes differ considerably in detail, it is possible to categorize and classify their common features.

Most statutes contain some kind of list of relatives, which includes the widow, widower, children under 16 or 18, and dependent parents, and may go on to add brothers, sisters, grandchildren and many other named categories, sometimes concluding with some general phrase like "other members of the family" or "other members of the household."

---

[1] Including, *e.g.*, Florida, Illinois, Maryland, New York, and Texas. The same is true for the District of Columbia, the Longshore and Harbor Workers' Compensation Act, and the Federal Employees' Compensation Act.

[2] *E.g.*, California, Florida, Illinois, Indiana, Mississippi, North Dakota, and Tennessee.

Where such a list exists, the initial task of the claimant is to bring himself or herself within one of the named categories. Under some statutes, if the claimant can establish status as widow or widower or child of deceased, dependency is conclusively presumed and the question of factual dependency never arises. And under some statutes, occupancy of one of the named categories of relationship is an absolute condition precedent to recovery of death benefits — in other words, even a claimant who can prove dependency in fact would nevertheless have no rights unless he or she had first shown that he was within one of the specified categories.[3]

[3] Establishment of Statutory Relationship to Deceased

HEATHER v. DELTA DRILLING COMPANY
533 P.2d 1211 (Wyo. 1975)

RAPER, JUSTICE.

"The status of illegitimacy has expressed through the ages society's condemnation of irresponsible liaisons beyond the bonds of marriage. But visiting this condemnation on the head of an infant is illogical and unjust." *Weber v. Aetna Casualty & Surety Company*, 1972, 406 U.S. 164, 175, 92 S.Ct. 1400, 1406, 31 L.Ed.2d 768. Thus, we must reopen and reexamine the judicial treatment of the illegitimate child in the application of Wyoming's workmen's compensation laws.

Heather, the appellant, is admitted by appellee to be the illegitimate child of Bryan. When she was only a few months old, her father was killed instantly while employed by the employer-appellee. She has claimed benefits as the dependent child of the deceased workman and the claim was disapproved by the employer. The trial judge held that the status of illegitimacy deprived Heather of any entitlement to death benefits under § 27-89, W.S. 1957, C.1967.

In re Dragoni, 1938, 53 Wyo. 143, 156, 79 P.2d 465, 468, very positively held that the word "children," as used in the workmen's compensation act with respect to awarding compensation in their favor for death or injury to parent means "legitimate children" and illegitimate children are not entitled to benefits under the workmen's compensation law of Wyoming.[4] We must set aside *Dragoni* on that issue for the reason that its interpretation establishes a discriminatory classification which is justified by no legitimate state interest and violates the equal protection clause of the Fourteenth Amendment to the constitution of the United States. *Weber*[5] in arriving at this conclusion, while dealing with Louisiana's workmen's compensation law and by which we are similarly bound, went on to say:

> . . . It would, indeed be far-fetched to assume that women have illegitimate children so that they can be compensated in damages for their [fathers'] death. [Citing case.] "Nor can it be thought here that persons will shun illicit relations

---

[3] *E.g.*, Browning v. City of Huntsville, 244 So. 2d 378 (Ala. App. 1971).

[4] *(Court's footnote)* Appellee also cited Smith v. National Tank Co., Wyo. 1960, 350 P.2d 539, as authority for the proposition that illegitimate children are not under any theory, potential beneficiaries under the compensation laws of Wyoming. However, the facts of that case are nothing like the facts of our case here. In Smith, the employee's wife made claim for benefits for her daughter, sired by a stranger to the marriage, conceived and born while the deceased workman was incarcerated and never supported by him. The question we have in the case now before us is whether or not the illegitimate child of a deceased workman is entitled to benefits. The basis for that decision was that "Eleanor's child was the result of her adulterous relation with another man. To award compensation for her child would be to forget, forgive and, in fact, put a premium upon, adultery." We do not disturb the holding of Smith.

[5] *(Court's footnote)* 406 U.S. 173, 92 S. Ct. 1405, 31 L. Ed. 2d 777–778.

because the offspring may not one day reap the benefits of workmen's compensation."[6]

Illegitimate and legitimate children are now entitled to the same treatment without regard to their legitimacy, under the workmen's compensation law.

Having decided that an illegitimate child of an employee is entitled to the same consideration as a legitimate child of an employee under the workmen's compensation laws of Wyoming, we move to a consideration of the second question raided in this appeal. Is the child of the deceased workman entitled to benefits even though she was never actually furnished any specific financial or other support by her father, as she admits?

While we are elevating the status of the illegitimate child to that of the legitimate child, we are not approving the life style of those responsible for bringing such children into the world. An abnormal and generally unsatisfactory family relationship is created, lacking stability and guidance for the youngster. Our sole interest is in protecting the child of the union in only this one particular before us.

The specific statutory provisions controlling the answer to the question are found in § 27-49(II), W.S. 1957, C.1967:

> (d) *"Dependent families"* means the spouse, or children under eighteen (18) years of age of the workman who are wholly or in part actually dependent upon the workman for support at the time of the injury, . . .

> (e) *"Child or children"* means the immediate offspring, stepchild or stepchildren or legally adopted child or children of the injured workman, under eighteen (18) years of age or under twenty-one (21) years of age (if physically or mentally incapacitated from earning) and shall also include legitimate children of the injured workman born after his death or injury. In other cases, questions of family dependency in whole or in part shall be determined in accordance with the fact, as the case may be, at the time of the injury, . . .[7]

---

[6] *(Court's footnote)* 2 Larson, The Law of Workmen's Compensation, § 62.22, p. 11-35 (Rel. No. 17-1974) reconstructs the crucial episode referred to, more melodramatically:

On a summer night, under a full moon, in a secluded Louisiana bayou, Marvin and Julia are about to embark upon a meretricious relationship. Suddenly Julia thrusts Marvin away.

Julia: "No, Marvin, No — we mustn't."

Marvin: (perplexed and slightly angry) "But why, why, why? What's the matter?"

Julia: "I just remembered that under Stokes v. Aetna Casualty & Surety Company, if we should have an illegitimate child because of this meretricious conduct, and if you should get killed in an industrial accident before the child was born, this posthumous illegitimate offspring would be subordinated to your legitimate children in any claim for workmen's compensation dependency benefits."

Marvin: . . .

At this point the author, not being a dramatist, is at a loss how to continue the colloquy — at least if the time were pre-1972. After 1972, Marvin's response is obvious.

Marvin: (chuckling with relief) "Oh, is that all? Well, it might interest you to know that *Stokes* was reversed by the Supreme Court of the United States in Weber v. Aetna Casualty and Surety Company (Justice Rehnquist dissenting), and that any discrimination against illegitimates in workmen's compensation dependency benefits is now forbidden as a violation of the Equal Protection Clause of the Fourteenth Amendment."

Julia: "Well, in that case . . . " (Slow Curtain)

---

[7] *(Court's footnote)* The balance of the subsection goes on to say:

. . . the foregoing definition of "dependent families" shall not include any of the persons named, who are aliens residing beyond the jurisdiction of the United States of America, except a surviving widow or a child or children under eighteen (18) years of age, or parent or parents, and as to such non-resident aliens the rate of compensation shall not exceed thirty-three and one-third percent

Appellee-employer argues that the trial judge correctly decided that since no support had been actually received by Heather in the shape of money, payment of doctor or hospital bills at the time of birth, or contribution by food or otherwise, she failed the test of dependency set out in 2 Larson, The Law of Workmen's Compensation, § 63.00, p. 11-58.[8] We disagree and hold that § 27-49(II)(e) grants a conclusive presumption of dependency to a child of the covered workman. This is a new guideline in Wyoming jurisprudence, though possibly practiced administratively, thereby not previously bringing the matter before the courts.

A careful, analytical and thoughtful study of the foregoing statutory definition of "a child or children" in § 27-49(II)(e) calls to our attention that after the definition in the first sentence, the second sentence qualifies the first by saying, "*In other cases*, questions of family dependency in whole or in part shall be determined in accordance with the fact, as the case may be, at the time of the injury; . . . " (Emphasis supplied.) To tell it differently but with and in the same sense, the subsection is saying, "Except in the case of a child or children, questions of family dependency, in whole or in part, shall be determined in accordance with the fact, as the case may be, at the time of the injury." The conclusive presumption of dependency is thereby fixed and it is unnecessary to explore any effect of § 27-49(II)(d).

This becomes more apparent when we look into the history of this phase of the workmen's compensation law. By chapter 79, Session Laws of Wyoming, 1913, the legislature passed, "AN ACT to submit to the qualified voters of the State of Wyoming an amendment to the Constitution of the State of Wyoming adding to Section 4 of Article 10 of the Constitution a provision authorizing and requiring Workmen's Compensation Acts." By vote of the people, the proposed amendment was ratified on November 3, 1914, and proclaimed in effect December 26, 1914. Records of the Secretary of State. The authority for our workmen's compensation law as a result of the amendment is now found in § 4 of Art. X of the Wyoming constitution, wherein the following pertinent provision appears:

> . . . As to all extra hazardous employments the legislature shall provide by law for the accumulation and maintenance of a fund or funds out of which shall be paid compensation as may be fixed by law according to proper classifications to each person injured in such employment or to the dependent families of such as die as the result of such injuries, except in case of injuries due solely to the culpable negligence of the injured employee. . . .

By chapter 124, Session Laws of Wyoming, 1915, our workmen's compensation law came into being. Subsections 6(j) and (k) contained essentially the same language as subsections 27-49(II)(d) and (e) now in effect.

But from what did Wyoming model its act? We find quite a number of other contemporary state workmen's compensation laws with respect to dependency that

---

(33 1/3%) of the rates of compensation herein provided.

---

[8] *(Court's footnote)* "Dependency in fact must be established in order to qualify for death benefits in all cases except those involving a conclusive presumption of dependency. Proof of actual dependency does not require a showing that the claimant relied on the deceased for the bare necessities of life and without his contribution would have been reduced to destitution; it is sufficient to show that the deceased's contributions were looked to by claimant for the maintenance of claimant's accustomed standard of living. Hence a claimant may be dependent although receiving other income from claimant's own work, from property or from other persons on whom claimant is also dependent. Usually, actual contribution to claimant's support is enough to establish dependency without evidence of legal obligation to support. Proof of bare legal obligation to support, unaccompanied by either actual support or reasonable expectation of support, is ordinarily not enough to satisfy the requirement of actual dependency. Under the general principle that morality is not an inherent ingredient of dependency, a statute based on dependency in fact is none the less satisfied when actual dependency accompanies unconventional domestic arrangements."

carry marks of being a source for the particular sections in which we are interested; it is impossible to determine its exact origin. Notice many of the same words and phrases and their arrangement, for example, out of Massachusetts, L.1911, C. 751:

> Part II, § 7. The following persons shall be conclusively presumed to be wholly dependent for support upon a deceased employee:
>
> . . . .
>
> (c) A child or children under the age of eighteen years (or over said age, but physically or mentally incapacitated from earning). . . .
>
> In all other cases questions of dependency, in whole or in part, shall be determined in accordance with the fact, as the fact may be at the time of the injury; . . .[9]

Wyoming could have used this as a sample and mutilated it but it is still capable of identification and failed to lose its vigor in spite of parts that were hacked out and rearranged.

Under quite a number of decisions in states having statutes practically like that of Wyoming or the law of origin, whatever it might have been, where children under a particular age are conclusively presumed dependents, there is no necessity to prove any actual dependency and the right to recover is fixed.[10] We hold that to be the rule in Wyoming.

Such a presumption is founded on reason, is the result of common observation and follows from experience. As said in *Gulf States Steel Co. v. Griffin, supra*: (p. 128 of 214 Ala., p. 900 of 106 So.)

> . . . children under the age of 16 are not acquainted with or capacitated to compete with the necessities of life or the customs and requirements of business and social conditions, and are not acquainted with the laws protecting their rights and governing the family relations. . . .

It further makes good logic for the workmen's compensation law to ensure support to those normally entitled to parental maintenance because there is an obligation of support that rests upon a father of either illegitimate or legitimate children and the courts have not hesitated to make reference to that obligation in approving the award, without reference to what actual support was being given at the time of the injury. The legislature has manifested the public policy of this State. Wyoming has the Uniform Illegitimacy Act, § 14-59 *et seq.*, W.S. 1957, C.1965, by which the obligation of support may be enforced not only by the mother but by the child, through its guardian or next friend, or by public authorities. Failure to support an illegitimate child is a crime, punishable by fine and jail sentence. §§ 14-87, 88. Since the mother and child were in Colorado and the father was in Wyoming, the Revised Uniform Reciprocal Enforcement of Support Act was available to enforce support. § 20-105 *et seq.*, W.S. 1957, 1973 Cum. Supp. It is a felony for a parent, without just cause, to fail or refuse " . . . to provide adequately for the care, support and maintenance of his child . . . under the age of 18 years." § 20-71, W.S. 1957, 1973 Cum. Supp. A separate civil action for support is authorized by § 14-18, W.S. 1957, C.1965.

---

[9] *(Court's footnote)* Taken from Bradbury's Workmen's Compensation and State Insurance Law, 1912, p. 326. In the same work it is shown that California, 1911, p. 324, Michigan, 1912, p. 327, Rhode Island, 1912, p. 329, and Wisconsin, 1911, p. 331, also had identical provisions.

[10] *(Court's footnote)* Day v. Town Club, 1950, 241 Iowa 1264, 45 N.W.2d 222; Morris v. Glen Alden Coal Co., 1939, 136 Pa. Super. 132, 7 A.2d 126; Armour and Company v. Strickland, Okl. 1966, 413 P.2d 320; Atkinson v. Atkinson, 1933, 47 Ga. App. 345, 170 S.E. 527; Larson v. Independent School District No. 11J of King Hill, 1933, 53 Idaho 49, 22 P.2d 299; Pruden Coal & Coke Co. v. Johnson, 1932, 167 Tenn. 358, 53 S.W.2d 384; Gulf States Steel Co. v. Griffin, 1926, 214 Ala. 126, 106 So. 898; State v. District Court of Hennepin County, 1919, 143 Minn. 144, 172 N.W. 897; and Holmberg's Case, 1918, 231 Mass. 144, 120 N.E. 353.

The deposition of the mother discloses that the father of this child was honorable to the extent that he admired and visited the little girl and took pride in claiming her as his. He was a very young man, going to college under the G.I. Bill, at the time of the conception. The mother was convinced that "he couldn't afford to do anything." The youngster was born in May and her father was killed instantly in November of the same year by being hit on the head by a fitting under pressure blown from an oil drilling rig. The probability of collecting support was good, if ever undertaken on behalf of the child. An infant of tender years should not be robbed of whatever rights might arise as a result of its relationship with its parents. The courts go far to bestow their compassion upon children.

In *McGarry v. Industrial Commission of Utah*, 1925, 64 Utah 592, 232 P. 1090, 39 A.L.R. 306, the father of a minor had furnished no support to his son after the latter was about six months old and his wife obtained a divorce, giving her the custody and maintenance of the child. The court observed that:

> . . . The child was only 3 or 4 years of age at the most when its father entirely abandoned it and its mother. Human experience teaches us that a child of that age, or even of the age it is now, is practically helpless, and lexicographers of the English language generally give to the word "dependent' a definition which covers and includes a helpless infant. The Industrial Act of Utah does not state the circumstances and conditions under which an actual dependency may be established. It does not make actual dependency depend upon some support furnished the applicant by deceased down to a recent date, nor has any respectable authority had the temerity to so interpret industrial acts unless the act itself prescribed such limitation, as in most of the states of the Union. . . .

In the same case, a concurring judge stated:

> . . . To hold that a mere infant, only 7 years of age when it makes its application, is not a dependent because it did not take some steps to enforce its father's legal duty in his lifetime, or because its father did not contribute or promise to contribute to its support down to within a recent date, where there is no positive law making such element an essential factor in such case, is well-nigh shocking to the judicial conscience. The fact that the mother of the child may have had the opportunity to attempt the enforcement of the father's duty when she knew of his whereabouts during the first 4 years of the child's life and failed to do so, certainly should not be assigned as a reason for annulling the award allowing the child compensation. . . .

In *Ocean Accident & Guarantee Corporation v. Industrial Commission of Arizona*, 1928, 34 Ariz. 175, 269 P. 77, the deceased workman was divorced from his wife and ordered to pay $75 per month for the support of his children. He moved away and ignored the obligation of support. The claim was made that the children were at the time of their father's death totally dependent upon their stepfather and thus could not be dependent upon their natural father. The court observed that at no time did the minor children or their mother release the father from his obligation to support them. The court held that under such circumstances the children are dependent upon him for support and entitled to workmen's compensation benefits.

In *Borgmeier v. Jasper*, Mo. App. 1934, 67 S.W.2d 791, the claimant was born at a time when her parents were living apart. When she was about one year of age, her parents were reconciled and they lived together for several months, when a second final separation occurred, without there ever being a divorce. Claimant never lived under the same roof with her father and she was supported entirely by her mother and her relatives, other than a $10 or $12 contribution. The daughter had no independent means of her own and had never earned anything on her own account. Missouri had a statute in which there would have been a presumption of dependency if the child had been living with her father at the time of his death. It was there said:

. . . Clearly claimant was dependent upon some one, her circumstances being such that she was in no wise self-sustaining; and in so far as the question of legal dependency is involved, it was her father upon whom she was dependent, he being the one person legally liable for her support. . . .

After favorably citing a case, the opinion went on to say:

. . . it was held not to be absolutely essential upon the issue of dependency to show that the deceased parent had actually contributed to his child's needs during the parent's lifetime. Rather it was held to satisfy the requirements of due proof to show that there was some reasonable probability that the deceased father's legal duty would thereafter have been fulfilled by him.

Webster defines dependent as lacking the necessary means of support and receiving aid from others. The fact that such reliance is misplaced, or that such other might fail or be unable in his duty in the premises, would not and should not make a dependent non-dependent. The dependency exists whether it is recognized or not by him who owes the duty to support. To say that a child is not dependent upon her father because he fails or is unable to support her and she is obliged to appeal to the charity of others is to permit his conduct to determine the fact, rather than the justice and right of the case as well as the law. A little baby is not capable of supporting itself and not competent either to claim or waive a right under the law. Such a child upon her father's death, within the boundaries of the Wyoming Workmen's Compensation Act, becomes an actual dependent without regard to the question whether she has received or had any promise of support or must speculate in that regard, in whole or in part. A child must not be left unattended to spite normal human concupiscence.

The motion for summary judgment by the employer should have been overruled.

Reversed and remanded with directions to the trial court to vacate the summary judgment and set the matter for hearing on issues remaining, if there are any, and final disposition.

[4] Conclusive Presumption of Spouse's or Child's Dependency

In many statutes, the right of the spouse and often of the young children to recover death benefits is made absolute, if they were living with the deceased. In some, even the requirement of living with the deceased is absent.

WENGLER v. DRUGGISTS MUTUAL INSURANCE CO.
446 U.S. 142, 100 S.Ct. 1540, 64 L.Ed.2d 107 (1980)

MR. JUSTICE WHITE delivered the opinion of the Court.

This case challenges under the Equal Protection Clause of the Fourteenth Amendment a provision of the Missouri workers' compensation laws, Mo. Rev. Stat. § 287.240 (Supp. 1979), which is claimed to involve an invalid gender-based discrimination.

I

The facts are not in dispute. On February 11, 1977, Ruth Wengler, wife of appellant Paul J. Wengler, died in a work-related accident in the parking lot of her employer, appellee Dicus Prescription Drugs, Inc. Appellant filed a claim for death benefits under Mo. Rev. Stat. § 287.240 (Supp. 1979), under which a widower is not entitled to death benefits unless he either is mentally or physically incapacitated from wage earning or proves actual dependence on his wife's earnings. In contrast, a widow qualifies for death benefits without having to prove actual dependence on her husband's earnings.[11]

Appellant stipulated that he was neither incapacitated nor dependent on his wife's earnings, but argued that, owing to its disparate treatment of similarly situated widows and widowers, § 287.240 violated the Equal Protection Clause of the Fourteenth Amendment to the United States Constitution. The claim was administratively denied, but the Circuit Court of Madison County reversed, holding that § 287.240 violated the Equal Protection Clause because the statutory restriction on a widower's recovery of death benefits did not also apply to a surviving wife. Dicus and its insurer, appellee Druggists Mutual Insurance Co., were ordered to pay death benefits to appellant in the appropriate amount. App. to Juris. Statement A22-A25.

The Missouri Supreme Court, distinguishing certain cases in this Court, reversed the Circuit Court's decision. The equal protection challenge to § 287.240 failed because "the substantive difference in the economic standing of working men and women justifies the advantage that [§ 287.240] administratively gives to a widow." 583 S.W.2d 162, 168 (1979).

Because the decision of the Supreme Court of Missouri arguably conflicted with our precedents, we noted probable jurisdiction. 444 U.S. 924 (1979). We now reverse.[12]

II

The Missouri law indisputably mandates gender-based discrimination. Although the Missouri Supreme Court was of the view that the law favored, rather than disfavored, women, it is apparent that the statute discriminates against both men and women. The provision discriminates against a woman covered by the Missouri workers' compensation system since, in the case of her death, benefits are payable to her spouse only if he is mentally or physically incapacitated or was to some extent dependent upon her. Under these tests, Mrs. Wengler's spouse was entitled to no benefits. If Mr. Wengler had died, however, Mrs. Wengler would have been conclusively presumed to be dependent and would have been paid the statutory amount for life or until she remarried even though she may not in fact have been dependent on Mr. Wengler. The benefits, therefore, that the working woman can expect to be paid to her spouse in the case of her work-related death are less than those payable to the spouse of the deceased male wage earner.

It is this kind of discrimination against working women that our cases have identified and in the circumstances found unjustified. At issue in *Weinberger v. Wiesenfeld*, 420 U.S. 636 (1975), was a provision in the Social Security Act, 42 U.S.C. § 402(g), that granted survivors' benefits based on the earnings of a deceased husband and father covered by the Act both to his widow and to the couple's minor children in her care, but that granted benefits based on the earnings of a covered deceased wife and mother only to the minor children and not to the widower. In concluding that the provision violated the equal protection component of the Fifth Amendment, we noted that, "[o]bviously, the notion that men are more likely than women to be the primary supporters of their spouses and children is not entirely without empirical support." *Weinberger v.*

---

[11] *(Court's footnote)* At the time of her death Mrs. Wengler's wages were $69 per week. Had appellant prevailed in his attempt to receive full death benefits under the statute, his compensation would have been $46 per week. App. to Juris. Statement A23; see Mo. Rev. Stat. § 287.240(2) (Supp. 1979). These benefits would have continued until appellant's death or remarriage. § 287.240(4)(a).

[12] *(Court's footnote)* Recent decisions in three States have held unconstitutional workers' compensation statutes with presumptions of dependency identical to that at issue in this case. Arp v. Workers' Compensation Appeals Board, 19 Cal. 3d 395, 563 P. 2d 849 (1977); Passante v. Walden Printing Co., 53 App. Div. 2d 8, 385 N. Y. S. 2d 178 (1976); Tomarchio v. Township of Greenwich, 75 N. J. 62, 379 A. 2d 848 (1977). The workers' compensation laws of the vast majority of States now make no distinction between the eligibility of widows and widowers for death benefits.

Wiesenfeld, supra, at 645, citing *Kahn v. Shevin,* 416 U.S. 351, 354, n.7 (1974).[13] But such a generalization could not itself justify the gender-based distinction found in the Act, for § 402(g) "clearly operate[d] . . . to deprive women of protection for their families which men receive as a result of their employment." 420 U.S., at 645. The offensive assumption was "that male workers' earnings are vital to the support of their families, while the earnings of female wage earners do not significantly contribute to their families' support." *Id.,* at 643 (footnote omitted).

Similarly, in *Califano v. Goldfarb,* 430 U.S. 199 (1977), we dealt with a Social Security Act provision providing survivors' benefits to a widow regardless of dependency, but providing the same benefits to a widower only if he had been receiving at least half of his support from his deceased wife. 42 U.S.C. § 402(f)(1)(D). Mr. Justice Brennan's plurality opinion pointed out that, under the challenged section, "female insureds received less protection for their spouses solely because of their sex" and that, as in *Wiesenfeld,* the provision disadvantaged women as compared to similarly situated men by providing the female wage earner with less protection for her family than it provided the family of the male wage earner even though the family needs might be identical. *Califano v. Goldfarb, supra,* at 208. The plurality opinion, in the circumstances there, found the discrimination violative of the Fifth Amendment's equal protection guarantee.

Frontiero v. Richardson, 411 U.S. 677 (1973), involved a similar discrimination. There, a serviceman could claim his wife as a dependent without regard to whether she was in fact dependent upon him and so obtain increased quarters allowances and medical and dental benefits. A servicewoman, on the other hand, could not claim her husband as a dependent for these purposes unless he was in fact dependent upon her for over one-half of his support. This discrimination, devaluing the service of the woman as compared with that of the man, was invalidated.

The Missouri law, as the Missouri courts recognized, also discriminates against men who survive their employed wives' dying in work-related accidents. To receive benefits, the surviving male spouse must prove his incapacity or dependency. The widow of a deceased wage earner, in contrast, is presumed dependent and is guaranteed a weekly benefit for life or until remarriage. It was this discrimination against the male survivor as compared with a similarly situated female that Mr. Justice Stevens identified in *Califano v. Goldfarb, supra,* as resulting in a denial of equal protection.[14] 430 U.S., at 217–224 (opinion of Stevens, J.).

---

[13] *(Court's footnote)* In Kahn v. Shevin, the Court upheld a Florida annual $500 real estate tax exemption for all widows in the face of an equal protection challenge. The Court believed that statistics established a lower median income for women than men, a discrepancy that justified "a state tax law reasonably designed to further the state policy of cushioning the financial impact of spousal loss upon the sex for which that loss imposes a disproportionately heavy burden." 416 U. S., at 355. As in Kahn we accept the importance of the state goal of helping needy spouses, see *infra,* at 151, but as described in text the Missouri law in our view is not "reasonably designed" to achieve this goal. Thus the holding in Kahn is in no way dispositive of the case at bar.

[14] *(Court's footnote)* As noted previously, see n.3, *supra,* three state courts have recently held unconstitutional workers' compensation statutes with presumptions of dependency identical to that at issue in this case. In each of the three cases the court characterized the statute's discrimination as against both working wives and surviving husbands. See Arp v. Workers' Compensation Appeals Board, 19 Cal. 3d, at 406, 563 P. 2d, at 855 ("[I]t is noteworthy that the conclusive presumption in favor of widows discriminates not only against the widower but against the employed *female* as well"); Passante v. Walden Printing Co., 53 App. Div. 2d, at 12, 385 N. Y. S. 2d, at 181 (the statute "compels dissimilar treatment both for surviving husbands and working wives, respectively, vis-a-vis widows and working males"); Tomarchio v. Township of Greenwich, 75 N. J., at 75, 379 A. 2d, at 854 (statute unconstitutionally discriminates against both working women and surviving husbands).

III

However the discrimination is described in this case, our precedents require that gender-based discriminations must serve important governmental objectives and that the discriminatory means employed must be substantially related to the achievement of those objectives. *Califano v. Westcott*, 443 U.S. 76, 85 (1979); *Orr v. Orr*, 440 U.S. 268, 279 (1979); *Califano v. Webster*, 430 U.S. 313, 316–317 (1977); *Craig v. Boren*, 429 U.S. 190, 197 (1976).

Acknowledging that the discrimination involved here must satisfy the *Craig v. Boren* standard, 583 S.W.2d, at 164–165, the Missouri Supreme Court stated that "the purpose of the [law] was to favor widows, not to disfavor them" and that when the law was passed in 1925 the legislature no doubt believed that "a widow was more in need of prompt payment of death benefits upon her husband's death without drawn-out proceedings to determine the amount of dependency than was a widower." *Id.*, at 168. Hence, the conclusive presumption of dependency satisfied "a perceived need widows generally had, which need was not common to men whose wives might be killed while working." *Ibid.* The survivor's "hardship was seen by the legislatur[e] as more immediate and pronounced on women than on men," and "the substantive difference in the economic standing of working men and women justifies the advantage that [the law] administratively gives to a widow." *Ibid.*

Providing for needy spouses is surely an important governmental objective, *Orr v. Orr, supra,* at 280, and the Missouri statute effects that goal by paying benefits to all surviving female spouses and to all surviving male spouses who prove their dependency. But the question remains whether the discriminatory means employed — discrimination against women wage earners and surviving male spouses — itself substantially serves the statutory end. Surely the needs of surviving widows and widowers would be completely served either by paying benefits to all members of both classes or by paying benefits only to those members of either class who can demonstrate their need. Why, then, employ the discriminatory means of paying all surviving widows without requiring proof of dependency, but paying only those widowers who make the required demonstration? The only justification offered by the state court or appellees for not treating males and females alike, whether viewed as wage earners or survivors of wage earners, is the assertion that most women are dependent on male wage earners and that it is more efficient to presume dependency in the case of women than to engage in case-to-case determination, whereas individualized inquiries in the postulated few cases in which men might be dependent are not prohibitively costly.

The burden, however, is on those defending the discrimination to make out the claimed justification, and this burden is not carried simply by noting that in 1925 the state legislature thought widows to be more in need of prompt help than men or that today "the substantive difference in the economic standing of working men and women justifies the advantage" given to widows. 583 S.W.2d, at 168. It may be that there is empirical support for the proposition that men are more likely to be the principal supporters of their spouses and families, *Weinberger v. Wiesenfeld*, 420 U.S., at 645, but the bare assertion of this argument falls far short of justifying gender-based discrimination on the grounds of administrative convenience. Yet neither the court below nor appellees in this Court essay any persuasive demonstration as to what the economic consequences to the State or to the beneficiaries might be if, in one way or another, men and women, whether as wage earners or survivors, were treated equally under the workers' compensation law, thus eliminating the double-edged discrimination described in Part II of this opinion.

We think, then, that the claimed justification of administrative convenience fails, just as it has in our prior cases. In *Frontiero v. Richardson*, 411 U.S., at 689–690, the Government claimed that, as an empirical matter, wives are so frequently dependent upon their husbands and husbands so rarely dependent upon their wives that it was cheaper to presume wives to be dependent upon their husbands while requiring proof of dependency in the case of the male. The Court found the claimed justification insufficient to save the discrimination. And in *Reed v. Reed*, 404 U.S. 71, 76 (1971), the Court said "[t]o give a mandatory preference to members of either sex over members of the other, merely to accomplish the elimination of hearings on the merits, is to make the very kind of arbitrary legislative choice forbidden by the Equal Protection Clause. . . . " *See also Califano v. Goldfarb*, 430 U.S., at 219–220 (opinion of Stevens, J.). It may be that there are levels of administrative convenience that will justify discriminations that are subject to heightened scrutiny under the Equal Protection Clause, but the requisite showing has not been made here by the mere claim that it would be inconvenient to individualize determinations about widows as well as widowers.

IV

Thus we conclude that the Supreme Court of Missouri erred in upholding the constitutional validity of § 287.240. We are left with the question whether the defect should be cured by extending the presumption of dependence to widowers or by eliminating it for widows. Because state legislation is at issue, and because a remedial outcome consonant with the state legislature's overall purpose is preferable, we believe that state judges are better positioned to choose an appropriate method of remedying the constitutional violation. Accordingly, we reverse the decision of the Supreme Court of Missouri and remand the case to that court for further proceedings not inconsistent with this opinion.[15]

So ordered.

PROBLEMS

(1) In complying with the *Wengler* mandate of equality between widows and widowers, which is the preferable course — to extend the conclusive presumption of dependency to widowers, or to abolish that presumption as to widows? Does the Supreme Court care which way it is done? *See, e.g.*, Passante v. Walden Printing Co., 53 A.D. 2d 8, 385 N.Y.S. 2d 178 (1976).

(2) In a New York case, the claimant widow had procured a Mexican divorce (invalid in New York), and also had got an interlocutory decree of divorce in New York. Before the divorce became final, the husband died. Should the claimant be heard to claim benefits as a widow?

(3) The claimant's child's father and mother were both employed and both were killed in an employment-related plane crash. Under a statute containing a conclusive

[15] *(Court's footnote)* Appellees attempt to draw support from the fact that Goldfarb and Wiesenfeld arose in the context of the Social Security program. First, they argue, the statute at issue here, unlike a social insurance system that provides blanket survivorship benefits, seeks to compensate for specific economic loss to the worker or his dependents, and appellant can claim no such loss. Relatedly, a widower who suffers and can prove any loss of support is entitled to a corresponding level of benefits under § 287.240, whereas Mr. Goldfarb, under the Social Security Act provision, had to show that he had received at least one-half of his support from his wife at the time of her death. These arguments rely on the fact that covered widowers suffering provable economic loss will receive benefits corresponding to that loss under § 287.240, but they ignore the statute's discriminatory effect on working women by providing them with less protection for their families than working men. Appellees also argue that, unlike the Social Security program, the workers' compensation system is not based on mandatory contributions from past wage earnings of the employee. Thus appellant's late wife was not deprived of a portion of her earnings to contribute to a fund out of which her husband would not benefit. But we have before rejected the proposition that "the Constitution is indifferent to a statute that conditions the availability of noncontributory welfare benefits on the basis of gender," Califano v. Westcott, 443 U.S. 76, 85 (1979), and we refuse to part ways with our earlier decisions by applying a different standard of review in this case simply because the system is funded by employer rather than employee contributions.

presumption of a child's dependency on a "parent," should the child be entitled to double death benefits? *See* U.S. National Bank v. Industrial Comm'n, 128 Colo. 417, 262 P.2d 731 (1935).

(4) May a same-sex partner to a state-sanctioned civil union, such as that prescribed by Vt. Stat. Ann., tit. 15, § 1201, be awarded workers' compensation death benefits as a "spouse?" *See* Matter of Langan v. State Farm Fire & Casualty, 48 A.D.3d 76; 849 N.Y.S.2d 105 (3d Dept. 2007).

[5] What Constitutes "Living With" Deceased

MCDONALD v. CHRYSLER CORPORATION
68 Mich. App. 418, 242 N.W.2d 810 (1976)

R. B. BURNS, JUDGE.

Plaintiff appeals from an adverse decision of the Workmen's Compensation Appeal Board reversing its hearing referee and denying dependency benefits.

Plaintiff's left hand was amputated as the result of a die press accident while he was working for defendant. At the time of the accident, plaintiff had been living apart from his wife for two or three years. Plaintiff's uncontroverted testimony was that this separation was amicable and motivated by economic considerations; specifically, that he absented himself from the home in order to enable his family to establish eligibility for public assistance. He testified that he regularly visited his family and that he gave his wife whatever money he could manage from his sporadic employment throughout the period of separation. . . .

We next consider the Appeal Board's holding that plaintiff was not "living with" his wife and children within the meaning of the statute.

We are aware of the generally accepted legal fiction recited in 2 Larson's Workmen's Compensation Law, § 62.40, pp. 11-48, 11-50.

> The phrase "living with" has usually been given a constructive meaning going well beyond physical presence under the same roof. . . . Separation for economic reasons, because of the husband's inability to provide adequate residence and support, is not voluntarily living apart.

Nevertheless, this principle is clearly inconsistent with the specific language of Michigan's law. Again, M.C.L.A. § 418.331; M.S.A. § 17.237(331) provides the presumption for widows "living with" or "living apart for justifiable cause", while M.C.L.A. § 418.353; M.S.A. § 17.237(353) simply states "living with". The legal maxim that the inclusion of one is the exclusion of another leads to the obvious conclusion that the Legislature's intent was not to indulge the fiction that "living with" could include "living apart". We must conclude that the Legislature varied these sections intentionally. *Holden v. Gifford Lumber Co.*, 231 Mich. 532, 204 N.W. 689 (1925), emphasized by the hearing referee, is a death benefits case, and inapposite.

The Appeal Board's decision that the conclusive presumption does not apply in this case is affirmed. The case is remanded to the Appeal Board to enable plaintiff an opportunity to present proofs as to dependency in fact.

PROBLEM

If a wife is living in a hospital or sanitarium for reasons of physical or mental illness, should she be deemed to be "living with" her husband? *See* Delaware County Trust Co. v. General Chem. Co., 44 Del. 598, 64 A.2d 608 (1949) and Gibbs Gas Engine Co. v. Jackson, 159 Fla. 86, 31 So. 2d 51 (1947).

§ 19.02   DEPENDENCY IN FACT

Dependency in fact must be established in order to qualify for death benefits in all cases except those involving a conclusive presumption of dependency. Proof of actual dependency does not require a showing that the claimant relied on the deceased for the bare necessities of life and without that contribution would have been reduced to destitution; it is sufficient to show that the deceased's contributions were looked to by claimant for the maintenance of claimant's accustomed standard of living. Hence a claimant may be dependent although receiving other income from claimant's own work, from property, or from other persons on whom claimant is also dependent. Usually, actual contribution to claimant's support is enough to establish dependency without evidence of legal obligation to support. Proof of bare legal obligation to support, unaccompanied by either actual support or reasonable expectation of support, is ordinarily not enough to satisfy the requirement of actual dependency. Under the general principle that morality is not an inherent ingredient of dependency, a statute based on dependency in fact is none the less satisfied when actual dependency accompanies unconventional domestic arrangements.

WILLIAMS v. CYPRESS CREEK DRAINAGE
635 S.W.2d 282 (Ark. App. 1982)

MAYFIELD, CHIEF JUDGE.

This is an appeal from a decision of the Workers' Compensation Commission denying dependency benefits.

James Williams began working for Cypress Creek Drainage on June 13, 1980, and worked until he died in an accident on the job on August 6, 1980. At the time of his death, the decedent was 20 years old, unmarried, and left no surviving children. Annie Mae Williams, his mother, filed a workers' compensation claim for dependency benefits under Ark.Stat.Ann. § 81-1315 (Repl. 1976).

The administrative law judge held that appellant failed to prove that she was partially dependent on the decedent but we are troubled by the law judge's opinion in which he took his definition of the word "dependent" from Webster's Seventh New Collegiate Dictionary instead of the Arkansas Workers' Compensation Act and the appellate cases which have construed and interpreted that Act.

Since the commission specifically stated that it adopted the law judge's opinion as its own, we are forced to conclude that the decision appealed from was not based upon the law.

We, therefore, remand this matter for a determination based upon the law as we now review it.

In *Crossett Lumber Co. v. Johnson*, 208 Ark, 572, 187 S.W.2d 161 (1945), the court quoted with approval from a treatise on workers' compensation by Honnold as follows:

> Partial dependency, giving a right to compensation, may exist, though the contributions be at irregular intervals and of irregular amounts, and though the dependent have other means of support, and be not reduced to absolute want.

In *Smith v. Farm Service Cooperative*, 244 Ark. 119, 424 S.W.2d 147 (1968), the court said, "Dependency is a fact question. It is to be determined in the light of surrounding circumstances." And the court quoted with approval from Larson's treatise on workers' compensation. The full paragraph from Larson now reads:

> Partial dependency may be found when, although the claimant may have other substantial sources of support from his own work, from property, or from other persons on whom claimant is also dependent, the contributions made by

the decedent were looked to by the claimant for the maintenance of his accustomed standard of living.

2 Larson's Workmen's Compensation § 63.12(a) (Nov. 1981 Cum. Supp.).

A factor to be considered is the claimant's "reasonable expectation of future support." *Roach Mfg. Co. v. Cole*, 265 Ark. 908, 582 S.W.2d 268 (1979); *Doyle's Concrete Finishers v. Moppin*, 268 Ark. 167, 594 S.W.2d 243 (1980). Obviously, the support being furnished at the time of the worker's injury is important but conditions prior to the injury should be considered, *Nolen v. Wortz Biscuit Co.*, 210 Ark. 446, 196 S.W.2d 899 (1946); a reasonable period of time should be used, *Smith v. Farm Service Cooperative;* dependency is not to be controlled by an unusual temporary situation, *Roach Mfg. Co. v. Cole.*

Also in the instant case, it would be appropriate to consider the amount of any contribution the decedent made to his mother's support in the light of the amount of any contribution she made to his support. *Pufahl v. Tamak Gas Products Co.*, 238 Ark. 895, 385 S.W.2d 640 (1965); *Sherwin-Williams Co. v. Yeager*, 219 Ark. 20, 239 S.W.2d 1019 (1951).

This matter is remanded for a decision based upon the law as set out above. We leave to the commission's discretion the question of whether another hearing should be had.

Remanded.

GLAZE, J., not participating.

STATE COMPENSATION INSURANCE FUND v. WORKERS' COMPENSATION APPEAL BOARD (ASHER)
19 Cal. App. 4th 1645, 24 Cal. Rptr. 2d 67 (1993)

PUGLIA, PRESIDING JUSTICE.

Labor Code section 4703.5 obligates an employer to pay a special death benefit to the "totally dependent minor children" of an employee who dies as the result of a work-related injury. In this petition for writ of review, we affirm the Workers' Compensation Appeals Board's (Board's) interpretation of section 4703.5 as extending this special death benefit to a totally dependent minor grandchild. [Court's footnote omitted]

I

Albert Asher (decedent) was electrocuted during the course of his employment on August 9, 1990. Decedent and his widow, respondent Connie Asher (widow), cared for and provided a home and total financial support for their grandson, respondent Justin Anthony Bernal (Justin), from the moment of Justin's birth on March 20, 1990. Since decedent's death, widow has provided sole support for her grandson. State Compensation Insurance Fund (petitioner) concedes Justin was a minor totally dependent upon decedent at the time of decedent's death.

On December 13, 1990, widow and Justin filed an application for adjudication of claim, seeking death and other benefits. On July 20, 1992, a worker's compensation judge (WCJ) approved the parties' compromise and release, in which, inter alia, widow and Justin released their claims for dependents' death benefits under sections 4702 and 4703, and the parties agreed the Board would determine the sole remaining issue in the case, Justin's entitlement to the special death benefit under section 4703.5.

. . . .

The Legislature has provided for workers' compensation death benefits in section 4701 et seq. Section 4701, subdivision (b), makes the employer liable for "[a] death benefit, to be allowed to the dependents when the employee leaves any person dependent upon him or her for support." Sections 4702 and 4703 set out the monetary amounts and allocation of death benefits, drawing distinctions based primarily on total as distinct from partial dependency. Section 4703.5 provides: "In the case of one or more totally dependent minor children, after payment of the amount specified in Section 4702, and notwithstanding the maximum limitations specified in Sections 4702 and 4703, payment of death benefits shall continue until the youngest child attains age 18 in the same manner and amount as temporary total disability indemnity would have been paid to the employee, except that no payment shall be made at a weekly rate of less than two hundred twenty-four dollars ($224)."

Sections 3501 to 3503 define dependency for purposes of workers' compensation death benefits. Generally, minor children, disabled adult children, and, with certain exceptions, spouses are conclusively presumed to be wholly dependent upon a deceased employee parent. (§ 3501.)[Court's footnote omitted] In all other cases, "questions as to who are dependents . . . shall be determined in accordance with the facts as they exist at the time of the injury of the employee." (§ 3502.) Section 3503 provides: "No person is a dependent of any deceased employee unless in good faith a member of the family or household of the employee, or unless the person bears to the employee the relation of husband or wife, child, posthumous child, adopted child or stepchild, grandchild, father or mother, father-in-law or mother-in-law, grandfather or grandmother, brother or sister, uncle or aunt, brother-in-law or sister-in-law, nephew or niece."

III

Petitioner contends the plain language of section 4703.5 and the statute's relationship to other death benefit provisions of the Labor Code demonstrate the Legislature intended to extend the special death benefit of section 4703.5 only to those persons who are "totally dependent minors" and also "children" of the decedent. We disagree. Petitioner's contention ignores nearly a half century of judicial construction of the term "dependent minor children," and the Legislature's acquiescence in that judicial construction by its use of the term in section 4703.5.

In 1947, the Legislature amended section 4702 to provide an augmented death benefit for "a surviving widow with one or more dependent minor children." (Stats. 1947, ch. 1031, § 1, p. 2302, emphasis added.) Until 1980, subsequent amendments to section 4702 retained this augmented death benefit. A 1979 amendment substituted "spouse" for "widow" and expanded the death benefit to make it applicable also to "two or more surviving dependent minor children." (Stats. 1979, ch. 749, § 4, p. 2600.) In 1980, the Legislature deleted the augmented death benefit for dependent minor children. (Stats. 1980, ch. 1042, § 4, p. 3329.)

In *Industrial Indem. Co. v. Ind. Acc. Com.* (1950) 98 Cal. App. 2d 741, 220 P.2d 765, the court construed the term "dependent minor children" to include dependent minor grandchildren. There, the decedent's two grandchildren had been made wards of the welfare department and were then placed with decedent and his wife. The court upheld the maximum death benefit award to the widow and grandchildren under former section 4702. Quoting the Board's predecessor, the Industrial Accident Commission, the court said: "It is common knowledge that many homes today include minor children who are not the immediate progeny of the husband and wife. Divorces, second marriages, death of parents, desertions by parents, unfitness on the part of parents, and other factors constantly are creating situations in which minor children are given into the care and custody of couples other than their own parents. Upon the death of the breadwinner of such a family group, the problem of economic readjustment is just as great to the dependent minor children as if a parental relationship had existed between themselves and the decedent." (98 Cal. App. 2d at p. 742, 220 P.2d 765.)

Another appellate decision has since consistently construed the phrase "dependent minor children." In *Gonzalez v. Workmen's Comp. Appeals Bd.* (1975) 49 Cal. App. 3d 280, 122 Cal. Rptr. 515, the Board awarded the augmented death benefit then provided by section 4702 to the decedent's widow and two dependent minor step-grandchildren. The court affirmed the augmented award, explaining: "The Board also upheld the award to the minor step-grandchildren as within the Labor Code section 4702 classification of 'dependent minor children,' relying on Argonaut Ins. Co. v. I.A.C., 30 Cal. Comp. Cases 260, where the section was interpreted to 'include all minors who are dependent members of decedent's household regardless of the relationship to the deceased.'" (Gonzalez v. Workmen's Comp. Appeals Bd., *supra*, 49 Cal. App. 3d at p. 282, 122 Cal. Rptr. 515.)

The Legislature is presumed to have full knowledge of judicial decisions and to have enacted legislation in light thereof. (*In re Misener* (1985) 38 Cal. 3d 543, 552, 213 Cal. Rptr. 569, 698 P.2d 637; *Stafford v. Realty Bond Service Corp.* (1952) 39 Cal. 2d 797, 805, 249 P.2d 241.) "When legislation has been judicially construed and a subsequent statute on the same or an analogous subject is framed in the identical language, it will ordinarily be presumed that the Legislature intended that the language as used in the later enactment would be given a like interpretation." (*Los Angeles Met. Transit Authority v. Brotherhood of Railroad Trainmen* (1960) 54 Cal. 2d 684, 688, 8 Cal. Rptr. 1, 355 P.2d 905; see also *Estate of McDill* (1975) 14 Cal. 3d 831, 839, 122 Cal. Rptr. 754, 537 P.2d 874; *People v. Curtis* (1969) 70 Cal. 2d 347, 355, 74 Cal. Rptr. 713, 450 P.2d 33; *Estate of Sax* (1989) 214 Cal. App. 3d 1300, 1304, 263 Cal. Rptr. 190.)

We presume the Legislature knew that appellate decisions are in agreement with the Board's construction of the term "dependent minor children" to include all minor dependent members of a decedent's household, including grandchildren. The augmented death benefit for totally dependent minor children provided by section 4703.5 applies to precisely the same class of beneficiaries as the augmented death benefit formerly extended by section 4702 to dependent minor children. There is nothing in the language of section 4703.5 or its legislative history that suggests a contrary legislative intent. Accordingly, Justin is a "dependent minor child" within the meaning of section 4703.5 and is entitled to a death benefit thereunder.

IV

The December 10, 1992, decision denying reconsideration by respondent Workers' Compensation Appeals Board is affirmed.

SPARKS and NICHOLSON, JJ., concur.

§ 19.03 DEATH BENEFITS

The dependent's right to death benefits is an independent right derived from statute, not from the rights of the decedent. This principle leads to several conclusions of practical importance. First, it can even lead to the recovery of death benefits by some who appear to be less than fully deserving. Thus, a divided New York appellate court held that a "deadbeat dad" was entitled to one-half the workers' compensation death benefit award regarding a 30-year-old employee killed as a result of the September 11, 2001 terrorist attack on the World Trade Center. Affirming a decision of the state Workers' Compensation Board that held the term "parent" meant simply the biological or adoptive father and mother of a child, the appellate court indicated there was nothing in N.Y. Workers' Comp. Law § 16(4-b) to indicate the meaning of "parent" to vary from the obvious and commonly accepted definitions.[16]

---

[16] Caldwell v. Alliance Consulting Group, Inc., 6 A.D.3d 761, 775 N.Y.S.2d 92 (2004). The fact that the deceased's father voluntarily left the marital home approximately one month after his son was born, that the decedent had contact with his father on only two occasions: spending one night at his father's home when decedent was six years old and seeing his father, although not speaking to him, at the funeral of decedent's maternal grandmother in January 1984, and the fact that decedent's father provided no financial support for

Second, death benefits are not affected by compromises or releases executed by decedent, or by an adverse holding on decedent's claim, or by claimant's failure to claim within the statutory period.

Death benefits consist of fixed percentages of weekly wage for specified statutory periods.

Since the total amount of the death benefit is under most statutes confined to a fixed maximum, priorities and rules for allocation are necessary in cases of multiple dependency. Usually total dependents, if any, take to the exclusion of partial dependents. Multiple total dependents may share equally, or in proportions fixed by statute. Partial dependents, if there is anything left for them, may get a fraction of the total death benefit corresponding to the fraction they received of deceased's earnings. When a surviving spouse's payments are terminated by remarriage (as they usually are), the unexpended balance may be awarded to other dependents who were lower in priority.

Status as a dependent is usually determined as of a point in time fixed by the statute, such as date of injury or date of death; changes occurring after that point in time, such as ceasing to live with deceased after the accident, or marriage to deceased after the accident in states making the time of accident controlling, cannot ordinarily affect claimant's rights. A fortiori, changes occurring after the making of the award, with the usual statutory exception of remarriage or attainment of a specified age, are usually immaterial.

---

his children and may have owed as much as $20,000 in unpaid child support at the time of the decedent's death did not prevent an equal division of the $50,000 death benefit between the decedent's mother and so-called father. Had the legislature intended differently, it could have so provided.

Part 7

EFFECT OF MISCONDUCT

Chapter 20

MISCONDUCT OF EMPLOYEE

§ 20.01 GENERAL IRRELEVANCE OF EMPLOYEE FAULT

Misconduct of the employee, whether negligent or wilful, is immaterial in compensation law, unless it takes the form of deviation from the course of employment, or unless it is of a kind that has been made a specific statutory defense in the jurisdiction in question.

Although it is frequently observed that "negligence is irrelevant" in compensation law, this statement is apt to be misleading because it is too narrow. The correct statement is that employee fault of any character is irrelevant, with a few exceptions to be noted presently. Misconduct of the employee, whether negligent or wilful, is immaterial not because it is affirmatively stated to be so in the statutes (although a few contain such language), but because the basic test of coverage is relation of the injury to the employment, with no reference to the personal merits of the parties. The Compensation Act marks out a circle whose boundaries are fixed by the "arising out of" and "in the course of" employment concept. Within that circle there is compensation. Outside there is not. Most acts are simply silent on the entire question of general fault in the employee. There is therefore no occasion to distinguish between negligent fault and wilful fault, since fault itself has no bearing on the process of drawing the boundaries of compensability.

The effect of a given act of misconduct by an employee must be judged against a background of three different kinds of statutes:

    (1) the commonest kind of statute, in which there are no affirmative defenses based on misconduct (except perhaps self-injury and intoxication);

    (2) statutes making wilful misconduct a defense; and

    (3) statutes making particular kinds of misconduct, such as wilful failure to use safety devices or violation of law, either a complete defense or a ground for reduction of the amount of the award.

Thus, the act of deliberately removing safety goggles in violation of regulations may give rise to the contention that this takes the employee out of the course of employment in the absence of any affirmative defense in the statute, or the contention that such intentional violation of a safety rule amounts to wilful misconduct under a statute making wilful misconduct a defense, or the contention that this act is a clear example of the specific defense of wilful failure to use a safety device.

HAWK v. JIM HAWK CHEVROLET-BUICK, INC.
282 N.W.2d 84 (Iowa 1979)

McGIVERIN, JUSTICE.

Mary Jean Hawk claims workers' compensation death benefits based upon the injury and death of her husband, James Hawk II, on September 28, 1973 in a private airplane crash near the Council Bluffs airport. The main question in this appeal is whether commission of "an unusual and rash act" by an employee which results in injury causes that injury not to arise out of and in the course of the employment within the meaning of the workers' compensation law. The deputy industrial commissioner held the death compensable. In a review decision, however, the industrial commissioner applied the unusual and rash act doctrine to deny compensation. On judicial review the district court reversed the industrial commissioner. We affirm the district court. . . .

To assist in understanding the issues, we state the operative facts on which there is no substantial disagreement among the parties and commissioner.

The decedent, James Hawk II, was president, sole stockholder, chief operating officer and an employee of Jim Hawk Chevrolet-Buick, Inc., an automobile sales dealership in Denison that sold vehicles throughout southwest Iowa. He lived in Denison with his wife, Mary Jean Hawk, and two children.

On September 27, 1973 Hawk flew his private plane to Council Bluffs on business for his company. On September 28, at about 2:30 a.m., Hawk was killed when his plane crashed shortly after takeoff on an intended return trip to Denison.

At the time of the fatal crash Hawk held a student pilot certificate. He had logged 53.9 hours of flight time involving 20.2 solo hours and .8 nighttime hours. He was restricted by his student certificate to a radius of 25 miles from the Denison airport, although he could be "signed off" by the instructor for solo cross country flights. On the days relevant here, however, Hawk had not been "signed off." Log books show Hawk had been last authorized for cross country flight on September 4, 1973.

On September 27 Hawk and his business associate, Mark Crampton, drove to the Denison airport. Each drove a separate car in order that a car could be left at the airport for Hawk's use the next day. According to Crampton, Hawk planned to return to Denison in the early morning hours and use the waiting vehicle to return to his home where Crampton would meet him and accompany him to work for a sales meeting at 9:00 a.m.

Hawk left the Denison airport that afternoon and arrived in Council Bluffs around 5:45 p. m. He was met at the airport by Robert McIntyre, a car dealer. They proceeded from the airport to McIntyre's place of business where they examined two cars Hawk was considering for his customers.

After discussing the cars, McIntyre and Hawk went to the Lakeshore Country Club for dinner. Upon arrival the two men encountered friends with whom they ate and drank. Before dinner Hawk discussed the sale of two vehicles with William Cutler, another friend and business associate, with whom he had planned to meet in Council Bluffs.

While at the club Hawk and McIntyre were invited to a stag party for a friend in Omaha. McIntyre declined but Hawk left with Harry Sayers, another auto dealer. Before Hawk left, McIntyre offered him a place to stay for the night.

Sayers testified he and Hawk stayed at the party about one hour until 11:30 or 12:00 p.m. when they left for Sayers' office. Although both men had drinks at the party, neither continued drinking thereafter. Sayers and Hawk visited at Sayers' office on auto sales conditions and other matters until 1:30 a.m. when Hawk decided to return to the airport and fly back to Denison. The two men argued over whether Hawk should fly back at that hour. Because Hawk insisted on leaving, Sayers agreed to take him to the airport.

Weather conditions at the Council Bluffs airport in the early morning hours of September 28, 1973 were not good for flying. Although ground visibility was between four and five miles, the sky was overcast with rain and fog. Hawk told his friend Sayers to wait while Hawk circled the airport to check out the weather. The plane disappeared up into the fog and then crashed. Hawk was dead at the scene.

Analysis of body fluid drawn from Hawk's body showed a blood alcohol content of. 147 per cent ethyl alcohol. FAA regulations prohibit flight within eight hours following alcohol consumption.

Charles Hawley, Hawk's flight instructor, testified Hawk was not instructed to fly by instruments and could not have interpreted any instrument readings. Hawley further testified that, according to FAA studies, non-instrument pilots who fly without the horizon in sight inevitably develop vertigo and lose control of the craft regardless of prior consumption of alcoholic beverages.

Mary Jean Hawk filed an application for arbitration of her claim for dependent's workers' compensation benefits with the industrial commissioner. After receiving an adverse review decision from the commissioner who had reversed the deputy, she filed petition for judicial review in district court. The court ruled workers' compensation should be awarded. Appeal to us by the employer and insurance carrier is under section 17A.20, The Code 1977. . . .

The usual and rash act doctrine. On judicial review to the district court the commissioner's application of the unusual and rash act doctrine to bar Hawk's widow's benefits was reversed. In this appeal we are asked to review the continued vitality of this doctrine.

The statutory defenses to recovery of worker's compensation benefits are set out in section 85.16, The Code, which provides:

No compensation under this chapter shall be allowed for an injury caused:

1. By the employee's willful intent to injure himself or to willfully injure another.

2. When intoxication of the employee was the proximate cause of the injury.

3. By the willful act of a third party directed against the employee for reasons personal to such employee.

Appellants raised the defenses stated in section 85.16(1) and (2) before the deputy and commissioner and received adverse rulings. They do not urge those statutory defenses before us.

The thrust of appellants' position before this court is that Hawk's death did not arise out of and in the course of his employment due to his "unusual and rash act" of flying his plane in the early morning hours of September 28.

Although the statute does not address the impact of unusual and rash acts on the part of employees, case law has addressed this issue. The leading case in this jurisdiction is *Christensen v. Hauff Brothers*, 193 Iowa 1084, 188 N.W. 851 (1922). In *Christensen* a Hauff employee made a business trip from Struble, Iowa, to Hinton. It was understood Christensen would return to Struble by train. Christensen did not catch the early morning passenger train but, nevertheless, decided to take a freight train scheduled to leave about one and one half hours later. The freight consisted of twenty eight freight cars and one caboose designed to accommodate passengers. Christensen was discussing business nearby when the freight began to pull out at between eight and ten miles per hour. Although the caboose, alone, had steps and a handrail for boarding, Christensen did not wait for the caboose. He attempted to board a flat car and was thrown under the wheels and killed. This court denied compensation for the death saying:

> There was no justification for Christensen's attempt to board the freight train by mounting the flat car in a most unusual manner, and for reasons wholly unjustifiable. In attempting to jump onto the flat car, he was not at a place where he might reasonably be, doing what a man so employed might reasonably do. We cannot conceive that Christensen's employment contemplated or comprehended any such unusual and rash act. . . . *We think it could not have been contemplated in this relationship of employer and workman, disclosed by the facts and circumstances in this case, that Christensen would do the hazardous and rash act which he did.* There was nothing in his engagement requiring such an act. We think it cannot with any reason be said that the injury and consequent death of the workman arose out of his employment.

Id. at 1089–92, 188 N.W. at 853–54. (Emphasis added.)

Under the *Christensen* reasoning, an employee who, by an unusual and rash act, exposes himself to a risk not occasioned by the nature of the employment and sustains injury, acts outside the scope of his employment. Since articulation of the principle in 1922, however, this case has been frequently distinguished. . . . *(citations omitted.)*

Other jurisdictions have declined to apply reasoning similar to *Christensen*. . . .

California rejected a rationale substantially similar to the *Christensen* rationale in *Associated Indemnity Corp. v. Industrial Accident Commission*, 18 Cal. 2d 40, 112 P.2d 615 (1941). In *Associated* a dock superintendent frequently traveled along and across railroad tracks en route from dock to a freight depot. In making a routine trip from depot back to his office, the superintendent asked permission to catch a ride on an engine about to take off. The superintendent, as well as other employees, frequently rode on the engines. On this occasion the engine stopped about halfway to "blow steam." The superintendent stepped off to avoid the steam and fractured his leg. The court held the injury arose out of the employment and said:

> Petitioner contends, however, that (claimant) in riding on the switch engine adopted such an unreasonable and hazardous method of traveling from the depot to the dock that it constituted an abandonment of his employment- . . . . The doctrine urged by petitioner must be applied with extreme caution for the reason that it is barely distinguishable from the rules of contributory negligence and assumption of risk which are not applicable in compensation cases.

> Indeed, it may well be asserted that the doctrine of "added risk," that is, where an employee assumes a risk greater than that usually incident to his employment, he cannot recover, cannot be followed in California because it is in effect nothing more than contributory negligence.

112 P.2d at 619. . . .

. . . .

The "added risk" or "added peril" doctrine is discussed in Larson IA *The Law of Workmen's Compensation*, § 30.22, at 6-4 and 6-5. Larson points out the doctrine is frequently applied where the employee performs activities incidental to the main job in a needlessly dangerous manner. Larson states:

> The so-called "added risk" or "added peril" doctrine has been based almost entirely upon this type of case. In other words, *it is very doubtful whether, except in a few jurisdictions, there ever was a rule of general applicability to the effect that an employee forfeited his coverage by doing his job in a needlessly dangerous way.* The doctrine in practice was usually pressed into service only in the incidental-activity cases. . . . The "added peril" doctrine —

in the sense of a doctrine that a needlessly dangerous method of doing the employee's active work takes him outside the range of compensation protection — is of no current importance.

(Emphasis added.)

Since the added risk doctrine, kin to the unusual and rash act doctrine, is a minority position and the Iowa case of *Christensen* has been distinguished rather than expanded since its announcement in 1922, the present appeal presents this court with the opportunity to put the doctrine to rest. Section 85.16 clearly does not contemplate such a bar to recovery of benefits. Judicial engrafting of the unusual and rash act doctrine to workers' compensation law distorts the statute by inserting a defense which, as the California court noted in *Associated Indemnity*, is barely distinguishable from the admittedly inapplicable rules of contributory negligence and assumption of risk.

As we stated in *Cady*, 278 N.W.2d 299:

> In keeping with the humanitarian objective of the workers' compensation statute, we apply it broadly and liberally. The legislation is primarily for the benefit of the worker and the worker's dependents. Its beneficent purpose is not to be defeated by reading something into it which is not there, or by a narrow and strained construction.

We hereby overrule the "unusual and rash act" doctrine of *Christensen v. Hauff Brothers,* and hold the doctrine cannot bar recovery of workers' compensation benefits.

We conclude, based on the undisputed facts, that Hawk's death arose out of and in the course of his employment.

The district court is affirmed and the case is remanded to the commissioner for award of appropriate workers' compensation benefits as provided by law.

We have considered all contentions raised by appellants and find them without merit.

Affirmed.

All Justices concur except LEGRAND and REES, JJ., who dissent. . . .

§ 20.02   MISCONDUCT APART FROM STATUTORY DEFENSES

When misconduct involves a prohibited overstepping of the boundaries defining the *ultimate work* to be done by the claimant, the prohibited act is outside the course of employment. But when misconduct involves a violation of regulations or prohibitions relating to *method* of accomplishing that ultimate work, the act remains within the course of employment. Violations of express prohibitions relating to incidental activities, such as seeking personal comfort, as distinguished from activities contributing directly to the accomplishment of the main job, are an interruption of the course of employment.

HOYLE v. ISENHOUR BRICK & TILE CO.
55 N.C. App. 675, 286 S.E.2d 830 (1982)

Appeal by guardian ad litem Ernest Hoyle on behalf of the minor children of deceased Gerald Allen Hoyle in an action seeking death benefits under G.S. 97-38 and -39. The Deputy Commissioner's award denying benefits was adopted by the full Industrial Commission and affirmed by a split panel of the Court of Appeals, Vaughn, J., with Wells, J., concurring, and Martin (Harry C.), J., dissenting. The appeal is pursuant to G.S. 7A-30(2).

The evidence before the Commission was to the effect that deceased had been employed by Isenhour Brick & Tile as a cull brick stacker. He removed imperfect bricks from a conveyor after which he would "band them up, like a box." A forklift operator would then remove the culls.

Deceased was killed when a forklift he was operating overturned, pinning him underneath it.

The employer had a rule against unauthorized personnel operating forklifts. Supervisory personnel who testified at the hearing explained that the employer had such a rule because of the dangerous propensities of forklift machinery. Deceased was not authorized to operate a forklift. Several employees testified that unauthorized personnel used the forklifts and the supervisors admitted this, although one noted that he did not recall ever finding an unauthorized employee operating a forklift after being warned against the practice.

On two occasions prior to the accident, one occurring several months before and another occurring about two weeks before, deceased was observed by different supervisors using a forklift to move his bricks. On each occasion the supervisor verbally reprimanded deceased, advised him of the rule against operating forklifts without authorization, and warned him that if caught again he would be disciplined, either suspended or terminated. Neither of the supervisors was aware until after the fatal accident that the other had previously caught deceased operating a forklift.

On the night of the accident, the forklift operator who was to have moved deceased's stack of cull bricks was busy helping another employee. The forklift operator, Larry Rollins, testified at the hearing that although "[t]here was not really any limit as to how many culls he [deceased] could stack out there before I moved the culls," on that particular night, deceased *"didn't have no more place to put them."* [Emphasis added.] The forklift operator described deceased's cull stacking operation as follows: "He'd band them up, *like a box*, like you stack them culls in there and you band them up. *The box was full* [that night]." [Emphasis added.] When it became necessary to move the stack of culls, Rollins, being otherwise occupied, told deceased he could use the forklift to move the bricks. Rollins admitted he had no authority to let deceased use his forklift, but observed, "No one had ever told me not to let [deceased] use the forklift." No supervisor was present on the night of the accident.

Deceased loaded the stack of cull bricks and moved them away from his work station. He conversed with another forklift operator as they drove along a paved road to an area where bricks were stacked in storage. The forklift operator deposited his load and went back for another. When he returned he found deceased pinned under the overturned forklift, and the stack of cull bricks deceased had been carrying was stacked in an area reserved for good bricks.

. . . .

The Court of Appeals held that deceased's operation of the forklift, after prior warnings and in the face of rules against the practice, constituted a departure from the job for which deceased had been employed and affirmed the award of the Industrial Commission denying death benefits. Judge Harry C. Martin dissented, asserting that the actions of deceased had not been "so extreme as to break the causal connection between his employment and his death."

BRANCH, CHIEF JUSTICE.

The parties stipulated in instant case that the employee "was injured by accident on June 9, 1978," and that he "died on the same date as a result of those injuries."

Our Workers' Compensation Act affords compensation only for those injuries resulting from accidents "arising out of and in the course of the employment. . . . " G.S. 97-2(6). . . .

. . . .

Professor Larson, in his treatise on Workers' Compensation Law, addresses the general situation before us and is quoted by both the majority and the dissent in the Court of Appeals in support of their respective positions. In order to place these quotations in context and to get a better understanding of the position Larson posits, we quote the treatise more fully:

> It has already been observed that the modern tendency is to bring within the course of employment services outside regular duties performed in good faith to advance the employer's interests, even if this involves doing an unrelated job falling within the province of a co-employee. This, of course, assumes that no prohibition is thereby infringed. But if the unrelated job is positively forbidden, all connection with the course of the claimant's own employment disappears, for he has stepped outside the boundaries defining, not his method of working, but the ultimate work for which he is employed. Decisions on this topic have consistently denied compensation on these facts when the extraneous job was in no sense auxiliary to claimant's own task. . . .
>
> It frequently happens that an employee will have his work stopped by some clogging, lack of oil, or disrepair of his machine. Quite commonly, also, there will be a company rule forbidding the operator to attempt to deal with the situation, and requiring him to wait until the specialists — whether oilers, electricians, or other repairmen — arrive on the scene. Sometimes the operator decides he can make the repair without the delay involved in calling the experts, and sometimes he gets hurt because he underestimated the expertness required or overestimated his own versatility. Now, the question is: has he departed from the course of his employment? He has attempted another person's job in violation of instructions. Yet the fact remains that he is attempting to get his own work done, although in forbidden fashion. Cases presenting these facts have gone both ways, depending on whether attention was focused on the fact that the job belonged to another or the fact that the action was a method of advancing the employer's work. . . .
>
> As a matter of compensation theory, it is quite permissible to treat the incidental invasion of another employee's province as merely a forbidden route on the main journey to the ultimate objective, the performance of claimant's work. Realistically, in some circumstances it is quite unfair to the claimant to penalize him for his well-meant short-cut, since in the everyday operation of a factory it is not uncommon and is probably often to the interest of the employer for employees to take direct action rather than "going through channels" when confronted with some minor adjustment which technically they are not permitted to undertake. On the other hand, it is equally true that risk of industrial accident may be increased when amateur electricians and repairmen take upon themselves dangerous jobs for which they have no qualifications. Most of the cases, however, seem to be of the former sort.

1A A. Larson, The Law of Workmen's Compensation § 31.14(a) & (b) (1979).

The above quotation from Larson, while instructive is not dispositive of the question before us. It speaks in terms of *unrelated* jobs. The question of whether deceased's operation was or was not related to the job for which he was hired is at the heart of this appeal. Moreover, the statement about forbidden activities is not fully in accord with our case law. Our decision in this case must be guided by the decisions of this Court construing our own Workers' Compensation Act.

Several opinions of this Court have dealt with situations similar to the facts of instant case. While the older cases often viewed acts outside the employee's job description as being outside the scope of the employment, the more recent cases have not viewed minor deviations from the confines of a narrow job description as an absolute bar to the recovery of benefits, even when such acts were contrary to stated rules or to specific instructions of the employer where such acts were reasonably related to the accomplishment of the task for which the employee was hired. We examine the cases, five of which were cited and discussed in the Court of Appeals' opinion in instant case.

In *Teague v. Atlantic Co.*, 213 N.C. 546, 196 S.E. 875 (1938), an employee was killed attempting to ride a conveyor belt intended to convey empty crates from the basement of the employer's plant to the first floor. Stairs were provided for this purpose and generally used by the employees. Deceased employee had been instructed by his foreman not to ride the conveyor. In a Per Curiam opinion, citing no authority, the Court held that deceased had disobeyed his orders and exceeded the scope of his employment by attempting a hazardous feat for the thrill of it or for his own convenience and affirmed the Industrial Commission's denial of death benefits.

That same year the Court affirmed the Industrial Commission's denial of death benefits to a painter who drowned in the Catawba River. *Morrow v. Highway Commission*, 214 N.C. 835, 199 S.E. 265 (1938). The deceased had dropped his paintbrush from a bridge he was painting. His foreman was present and ordered deceased not to go into the water to retrieve the brush. Deceased jumped in the river and was drowned. In a Per Curiam opinion of less than fifty words, and again citing no authority, the Court affirmed the Industrial Commission's conclusion that the accident did not arise out the employment.

In *Taylor v. Dixon*, 251 N.C. 304, 111 S.E.2d 181 (1959), plaintiff was hired to cut down trees in a logging operation. On the day of the accident, he refused to cut trees and announced he was going to drive the tractor instead. Plaintiff was ordered by his employer to get off the tractor, to which he replied, "Old man, I will get down and whip your . . . if you don't hush up. I know what I am doing. . . . " *Id.* at 304, 111 S.E.2d at 182. The employer stated in the hearing that, "He [the injured employee] was employed to run the chain saw — not to operate the tractor. . . . I didn't hire him as a tractor driver." *Id.* at 305, 111 S.E.2d at 182. This Court reversed an award of compensation on the ground that the Industrial Commission erred in failing to find facts concerning whether plaintiff's operation of the tractor in defiance of the orders of his employer to the contrary constituted a departure from the employment sufficient to take plaintiff out of the Act. The Court quoted 1 Larson's Workmen's Compensation Law 463 to the effect that "if . . . the *unrelated job* is *positively forbidden*, all connection with the claimant's own employment disappears, for he has stepped outside the boundaries defining, not his method of working, but the ultimate work for which he is employed." [Emphasis added.] *Id.* at 308, 111 S.E.2d at 185.

In *Hartley v. Prison Dept.*, 258 N.C. 287, 128 S.E.2d 598 (1962), plaintiff, a prison guard, was called to relieve another guard in a nearby tower. To get to the tower, plaintiff had to walk 100 yards to a gate, and 100 yards back to a point just on the other side of the fence from where he was when called. Instead of walking the 200 yards to use the gate, he tried to climb the fence, fell, and was hurt. It was *against prison rules* for the guards to climb the fence.

Reasoning that the employee's purpose for climbing the fence was to relieve the guard on duty in the next tower, which was the thing he had been ordered to do, the Court noted that, although plaintiff had been negligent to climb the fence, "not even gross negligence is a defense to a compensation claim." *Id.* at 289, 128 S.E.2d at 600. The Court went on to state, "Only intoxication or injury intentionally inflicted will defeat a claim," *id.*, and observed that even the willful violation of an employer's rule does not defeat compensation, but may result in a ten percent reduction *if* the rule has been approved by the Industrial Commission. G.S. 97-12. The Court then affirmed the award of compensation, stressing that the purpose of the Worker's Compensation Act was "to eliminate the fault of the workman as a basis for denying recovery." *Id.* at 290, 128 S.E.2d at 600.

The most recent case to deal with facts similar to those in the case *sub judice* was *Hensley v. Carswell Action Committee*, 296 N.C. 527, 251 S.E.2d 399 (1979). In *Hensley* the deceased was employed to cut weeds around a lake. He was specifically instructed not to go into the water. After finishing the job, he spotted an area he had missed. The supervisor who had ordered deceased not to go into the water was not then present.

Against these prior orders, deceased attempted to wade across the lake to cut the weeds he had missed. He drowned.

. . . The Court followed *Hartley, supra,* holding that the deceased's disobedience of his supervisor's order was not such a departure from his employment as to destroy the causal connection between the accident and the employment. . . .

In addition to the five cases cited and relied upon by the Court of Appeals in the majority and dissenting opinions filed below, we find four other cases instructive.

Archie v. Lumber Co., 222 N.C. 477, 23 S.E.2d 834 (1943), does not involve an employee stepping outside the bounds of his job description; yet it does provide the definitive answer to the question of whether prior orders or rules of the employer may constitute an absolute bar to the recovery of compensation. The case involved a deceased employee who had worked as a logger for defendant Lumber Company. Defendant provided its employees with a specially equipped "safety car" which took them to and from their work site along the company's railroad line. The company had a rule against employees riding in the log cars; nevertheless, on occasion employees would ride the log cars to get from the work site. Deceased employee had been specifically instructed not to ride the log cars. Apparently, on the day of the accident, the safety car was a little slow departing the work site to take the employees back to the camp. Deceased attempted to board a log car and was mortally injured.

This Court, 55 N.C.App. 675, 286 S.E.2d 830 reversed the Superior Court's reversal of the Industrial Commission's award of benefits despite the deceased's violation of both a rule of his employer and a specific instruction warning him not to ride the log car. The Court held that denial of benefits was inconsistent with the intent of the Act to eliminate fault as a basis for determining compensation in industrial injury cases. The Court noted that the violation of an *approved* safety rule is covered in G.S. 97-12 and that the penalty for violation is a ten percent reduction and not a denial of compensation. In so holding, the Court expressly disapproved cases from other jurisdictions holding to the contrary as not in accord with the "proper interpretation" of the North Carolina Worker's Compensation Act.

. . . .

Parsons v. Swift & Co., 234 N.C. 580, 68 S.E.2d 296 (1951), involves a deceased employee who had been specifically prohibited by company rule from operating a tractor. His job was to haul filler in a wheel barrow. Upon finding a tractor blocking his path, the employee asked two tractor operators to move it. Both refused. The employee then attempted to move the tractor and was killed when the tractor rolled over crushing him. The Industrial Commission found that the employee was acting in furtherance of his employer's business in seeking to move the tractor and that the deceased employee had moved similar tractors on prior occasions in violation of the company's rule to the contrary. This Court held that the evidence supported the award of compensation and affirmed.

. . . .

Summarizing the legal principles gleaned from these pertinent cases, we find that thrill seeking which bears no conceivable relation to accomplishing the job for which the employee was hired moves the employee from the scope of his employment. *Teague v. Atlantic Co., supra.* Likewise, disobedience of a direct and specific order by a then present superior breaks the causal relation between the employment and the resulting injury. *Taylor v. Dixon, supra; Morrow v. Highway Commission, supra.* This is patently so; the employee's subjective belief concerning the advisability of his course of action becomes irrelevant since there would be no room for doubt as how best to serve his employer's interest in the face of the employer's direct and immediate order. Conversely, when there is a rule or a prior order and the employee is faced with the choice of remaining idle in compliance with the rule or order or continuing to further his employer's business, no superior being present, the employer who would reap the benefits of the employee's acts if successfully completed should bear the burden of injury resulting from such acts. Under such circumstances, engaging in an activity which is outside the narrow confines of the employee's job description, but which is reasonably related to the accomplishment of the task for which the employee was hired, does not ordinarily constitute a departure from the scope of employment. *Parsons v. Swift & Co., supra; Hensley v. Carswell Action Committee, supra; Hartley v. Prison Department, supra.*

Here all of the evidence discloses that the employee did *not* disobey a direct, immediate, and specific order by a then present superior not to operate the forklift. Rather the evidence shows that employee was faced with the choice of abandoning the furtherance of his employer's business or acting in controvention of a previous order. There was no superior present to forbid or permit his operation of the forklift. We are therefore of the opinion that employee's election to disobey a prior given order did not break the causal connection between his employment and his fatal injury if the disobedient act was reasonably related to the accomplishment of the task for which he was hired. We believe that the evidence disclosed that the employee's action was reasonably related to his employment. The single statement in the record to which defendant-employer points to support a contrary conclusion does not in fact support the employer's position. The authorized forklift operator testified, "[t]here was not really any limit as to how many culls he [deceased] could stack out there before I move the culls." In the next breath, the witness testified that deceased "didn't have no more place to put the cull bricks" and that "the box was full." When taken in context, the first statement obviously was directed to the forklift operator's job description and does not suggest that the stacking area was unlimited. All the competent evidence tended to show that deceased could not continue the task for which he was hired until the bricks were removed. Thus, the removal of the bricks was reasonably related (indeed necessary) to the accomplishment of the task for which deceased had been hired.

Because of their striking factual similarity, we emphasize the compelling authority in *Hensley v. Carswell Action Committee, supra,* and *Parsons v. Swift & Co., supra.* In both *Hensley* and *Parsons,* this Court held that the deceaseds were acting in the course and scope of their employment when fatally injured. In each case the Court, in finding for the plaintiff, based its decision on the fact that the employee was acting in furtherance of the employer's business, albeit in disobedience of the employer's rule or order.

It is neither the role of the Industrial Commission nor of this Court to enforce the employer's rules or orders by the denial of Worker's Compensation. Enforcement of rules and orders is the responsibility of the employer, who may choose to terminate employment or otherwise discipline disobedient employees. This Court will not do indirectly what the employer failed to do directly.

For the reasons stated, we hold that the Industrial Commission erred in concluding that deceased's injury did not arise out of and in the course of his employment.

This case is reversed and remanded to the Court of Appeals with direction that it be remanded to the Industrial Commission for entry of an award consistent with this opinion.

Reversed and Remanded.

MEYER, JUSTICE, dissents.

§ 20.03 STATUTORY DEFENSE OF WILFUL MISCONDUCT

The statutory "wilful misconduct" defense, whatever its actual general definition might be, has in practical application been largely limited to the deliberate and intentional violation of known regulations designed to preserve the employee from serious bodily harm.

The "wilful misconduct" defense is of less importance in compensation law than its sweeping title might indicate. For one thing, only about a third of the statutes have the defense in any form. Among those the most common wording is "wilful misconduct;"[1] Other variations include "serious and wilful";[2] "intentional and wilful";[3] "wilful negligence";[4] and "deliberate and reckless indifference to danger."[5] In addition, California reduces compensation by 50 percent for serious and wilful misconduct.[6]

The other reason for the relative unimportance of the defense is that its application has been nothing like as broad as the term itself might lead one to expect. After all, "wilful misconduct" could mean almost anything. But an analysis of the cases shows that the defense has been generally successful in only one narrow field, that of intentional violation of safety regulations. It would not be much wide of the mark to say that almost every case in which the wilful misconduct defense succeeded would also have succeeded under a statute making wilful violation of safety regulations a defense.

PROBLEM

Claimant, exasperated when his wheelbarrow tipped, slammed his hand against a van door, breaking a bone. What result? *See* Cunningham v. Industrial Comm'n, 78 Ill. 2d 256, 399 N.E.2d 1300 (1980).

§ 20.04   STATUTORY DEFENSE OF FAILURE TO OBEY SAFETY RULES

The statutory defense of wilful disobedience of safety rules or wilful failure to use a safety device will succeed only if the employee is given actual (as distinguished from constructive) notice of the rule and an understanding of the danger involved in its violation, if the rule is kept alive by bona fide enforcement, and if the employee had no valid excuse for the violation.

The special defense of failure to observe safety rules and use safety devices appears in some form in the statutes of over twenty states. Some of those states make complete defenses of both safety regulation and safety device violations;[7] some make only failure to use a safety device a defense;[8] and some, for injuries involving safety rule or safety device offenses, reduce compensation by specified percentages.[9]

Like the wilful misconduct defense, these defenses have received strict construction by the courts, although when the penalty is a mere reduction rather than a forfeiture of compensation the construction tends to be slightly less exacting.

There are very few cases in which the defense of wilful disobedience of a safety *rule* (as distinguished from failure to use a safety *device*) has in itself produced a denial of compensation.[10] But cases can be found in which a reduction of compensation for this

---

[1] *E.g.*, Alabama, California, and Maryland.

[2] Massachusetts. *See also* the Connecticut statute, which uses "wilful and serious."

[3] Michigan.

[4] Nebraska.

[5] Delaware.

[6] Cal. Labor Code § 4551. The reduction does not apply in case of death, 70% disability, employer's misconduct, or where claimant is under 16 years of age. There appears to be an inconsistency between this section and Section 5705(c), which makes a wilful misconduct a complete defense.

[7] *E.g.*, Georgia, Indiana, and Virginia.

[8] *E.g.*, Alabama, Kansas, and Oklahoma.

[9] *E.g.*, North Carolina (10%,); Utah (15%); Nevada (25%) and Colorado (50%).

[10] One such case is Gregory v. McKesson & Robbins, Inc., 54 So. 2d 682 (Fla. 1951). Claimant violated the

cause has been ordered.[11] And there are cases of complete denial of compensation for failure to use a safety device, where, for example, an experienced worker disdained the use of a safety rope while working on a scaffold,[12] or where an employee deliberately refused to wear safety goggles.[13]

But the majority of cases in this area have rejected these statutory defenses for one or another of the reasons mentioned in the first sentence of this section.

PROBLEM

Claimant, working in an excavation where light was poor, momentarily lifted his goggles the better to give directions to a crane operator. Does this excuse violation of the safety rule? *See* American Steel Foundries v. Fisher, 106 Ind. App. 25, 17 N.E.2d 840 (1938). What if the reason for removal was frequent steaming-up? *See* Carrico v. State Compensation Comm'r, 127 W. Va. 463, 33 S.E.2d 281 (1945).

§ 20.05 INTOXICATION

In some jurisdictions intoxication is an explicit statutory defense. Among those statutes the requisite causal connection between intoxication and the injury varies widely, ranging from mere existence of intoxication at time of injury to the requirement that intoxication be the sole cause.

In the absence of this kind of special statute, evidence of intoxication at the time of injury is ordinarily no defense, except that voluntary intoxication to such an extent as to render the employee incapable of performing the work is considered a departure from the course of employment.

FLAVORLAND INDUSTRIES, INC. v. SCHUMACKER
32 Wash. App. 428, 647 P.2d 1062 (1982)

McINTURFF, CHIEF JUDGE.

Was Ervin Schumacker acting within the scope of his employment when he left a business meeting in a highly intoxicated state in a company car which subsequently left the road, causing his death?

Mr. Schumacker was the assistant manager of the Flavorland Meat Packing Plant in Toppenish, Washington. He was salaried, worked irregular hours, was provided an automobile and all operating expenses of the auto were paid by Flavorland. His public relations duties required him to socialize with the local livestock buyers and sellers. While engaged in these duties, Mr. Schumacker, on Thursday, January 29, 1976, attended the weekly area livestock auction. Afterwards, Mr. Schumacker and many of the cattle sellers and buyers gathered in the lounge of the Squeeze Inn, a restaurant and bar in Zillah, Washington. Flavorland expected him to attend these weekly gatherings which had become a tradition among the cattle people. In fact, a charge account had been established by Flavorland to pay for the drinks and dinners charged by Mr. Schumacker for himself and others over the previous 3 1/2 to 4 years. Mr. Schumacker occasionally overindulged in alcohol at these gatherings, but his wife said he usually arrived home between 10 p.m. and midnight.

On the night in question, Mr. Schumacker drank more than usual. He left the

---

state speed law by driving at 70 to 80 miles per hour. *Held*, he was wilfully refusing to observe a safety rule required by statute.

[11] *E.g.*, Bennett Properties Co. v. Industrial Comm'n, 165 Colo. 135, 437 P.2d 548 (1968) (entering an elevator pit without informing anyone, in violation of an oral safety rule.

[12] Carter v. Christ, 148 So. 714 (La. App. 1933).

[13] Nashville C. & St. L. Ry. v. Coleman, 151 Tenn. 443, 269 S.W. 919 (1924).

restaurant in his company car about 9:30 p.m. and while proceeding through the city of Zillah, his car struck the extended bumper of an angle-parked pickup truck. Mr. Schumacker drove slowly after the accident, then suddenly accelerated out of town. Approximately 1/10 mile out of Zillah, his automobile, traveling at 70–90 miles per hour around a curve, left the road and he was killed. His blood alcohol level was .28.

Mrs. Schumacker's claim for a widow's pension was rejected by the Department of Labor & Industries (DLI) on July 20, 1976. She appealed to the Board of Industrial Insurance Appeals, which reversed DLI and allowed her claim for benefits. Flavorland, a self-insurer, appealed to the superior court. The jury determined Mr. Schumacker was acting within the scope of his employment at the time of his death. The jurors also answered a special verdict form which stated he was intoxicated at the time of his death; that he became intoxicated during the course of his employment; and that his intoxication was a proximate cause of his death.

Flavorland moved for judgment notwithstanding the verdict. This motion was granted after the trial judge concluded, as a matter of law, Mr. Schumacker was not acting within the scope of his employment. The trial court made three rulings. First, there was insufficient evidence to permit a finding that Mr. Schumacker was on his way home when the accident occurred. Second, Mr. Schumacker's failure to stop after striking the pickup was an attempt to escape apprehension and therefore a purely personal act. Finally, if Mr. Schumacker was so intoxicated he was not aware he had been involved in the accident with the pickup, he had become too intoxicated to be considered as remaining within the scope of employment.

Flavorland argued to the jury that Mr. Schumacker was acting outside the scope of his employment on the night in question. He had recently notified Flavorland of his intention to terminate his employment. Flavorland maintains Mr. Schumacker's attendance at the meeting was to celebrate his impending termination of employment. Flavorland presented testimony that the majority of Mr. Schumacker's evening was spent soliciting business for his new employer, one of Flavorland's competitors. However, Mr. Van Monson, a cattle seller who was present at the meeting, said Mr. Schumacker spent only 5 to 10 minutes of the evening discussing his new employment. Flavorland further contended that even if Mr. Schumacker was at the gathering on company business, his degree of intoxication constituted such a deviation from the scope of his employment that he could not have been furthering any of Flavorland's interests. Flavorland urges that Mr. Schumacker's failure to stop after hitting the pickup amounted to his fleeing the scene of a hit-and-run accident which takes him outside the scope of his employment.

The Industrial Insurance Act was promulgated to provide sure and certain relief for workers injured in their work. RCW 51.04.010. A worker is entitled to compensation if injured in the course of his employment. RCW 51.32.010. A worker acts within the course of his employment when acting at his employer's direction or in the furtherance of his employer's business. RCW 51.08.013.

The general rule is that a worker is not, under ordinary circumstances, in the course of employment while going to or from his place of employment. *Aloha Lbr. Corp. v. Department of Labor & Indus.*, 77 Wash. 2d 763, 766, 466 P.2d 151 (1970); *Superior Asphalt & Concrete Co. v. Department of Labor & Indus.*, 19 Wash. App. 800, 802, 578 P.2d 59 (1978). The well-established exception to this rule is that a worker is within the course of employment when going to or from work in a vehicle furnished by the employer as an incident of employment pursuant to custom or contractual obligation, express or implied. *Westinghouse Elec. Corp. v. Department of Labor & Indus.*, 94 Wash. 2d 875, 880, 621 P.2d 147 (1980); *Aloha Lbr., supra.*

In ruling on a motion for judgment notwithstanding the verdict, the court must view the evidence in a light most favorable to the nonmoving party. . . .

In viewing the evidence and all reasonable inferences therefrom in a light most favorable to Mrs. Schumacker, the jury could have reasonably found Mr. Schumacker's attendance at the Thursday night gatherings to have been a long-standing practice; that his attendance was to perform the public relations function of his job; that Flavorland knew he drank and expected him to buy drinks for others; that Flavorland not only condoned this practice but encouraged it;[14] that he had been known to drink to excess in the past; that Flavorland paid for Mr. Schumacker's drinks and the drinks he bought for others; that Flavorland provided him with a car to drive to and from work; and when Mr. Schumacker left the gathering at his usual time, he was on his way home when the accident occurred. The findings by both the Board and the jury that Mr. Schumacker was acting within the scope of his employment at the time of his death are supported by substantial evidence.

Flavorland contends there was no evidence Mr. Schumacker was headed home at the time of his death and such a conclusion is speculation. Testimony was presented that Mr. Schumacker left the gathering at his regular time and was on the highway from Zillah to Toppenish which was a direct route to his home. This evidence is sufficient to support a jury finding he was on his way home at the time of his death.

Flavorland also argued to the jury that even if Mr. Schumacker was acting within the scope of his employment when he left the Squeeze Inn, his failure to stop after striking the pickup truck was an attempt to flee a hit-and-run accident which constituted an abandonment of his employment. It bases the abandonment theory on the premise that a worker is no longer in the scope of his employment when he departs from its purpose to such an extent the deviation could constitute an abandonment of his employment. *Tilly v. Department of Labor & Indus.*, 52 Wash. 2d 148, 324 P.2d 432 (1958). Whether Mr. Schumacker departed from the course of his employment to the extent necessary to constitute an abandonment of that employment was a factual determination for the jury which specifically found Mr. Schumacker to be acting within the scope of his employment at the time of his death. This finding, which is supported by substantial evidence, precludes Flavorland's abandonment theory. (*Court's footnote omitted*)

Flavorland next argues Mr. Schumacker's level of intoxication constitutes, as a matter of law, an abandonment of his employment. We disagree.

Intoxication is a defense, in the absence of an applicable statute, only when the claimant has become so intoxicated he abandons his employment. 1A A. Larson, Workmen's Compensation § 34.21, at 6-72 (1979). Whether Mr. Schumacker's intoxication constituted an abandonment of his employment was for the jury to decide. The jury heard the testimony, viewed the demeanor of the witnesses, and was instructed that:

> A workmen [*sic*] may be acting in the course of his employment even though he may be intoxicated or under the influence of intoxicating liquor.

(Instruction 7.)

> A worker otherwise acting in the course of his employment deviates and departs therefrom during such time as he engages in a course of action which is entered into for his own purposes and which is neither incident to his employment nor in furtherance of his employer's interests.

(Instruction 12.)

Flavorland argued to the jury that Mr. Schumacker's intoxication took him outside the scope of his employment. The jury disagreed and found he was acting within the scope of his employment at the time of his death. As previously noted, this finding is

---

[14] (*Court's footnote*) Prior to Mr. Schumacker's death, a company directive questioned the amount of money being expended at these Thursday gatherings. Although Mr. Schumacker was told to "slow down a little", Flavorland continued to pay for dinners and drinks charged by him and other Flavorland employees. The practice was discontinued following Mr. Schumacker's death.

supported by substantial evidence. We decline the invitation to invade the province of the jury.

The present case must be distinguished from those where the consumption of alcohol is unrelated to the worker's job activities. *M & M Parking Co. v. Industrial Comm'n*, 55 Ill.2d 252, 302 N.E.2d 265 (1973); *Richard v. George Noland Drilling Co.*, 79 Wyo. 124, 331 P.2d 836 (1958); *O'Neil v. Fred Evens Motor Sales Co.*, 160 S.W.2d 775 (Mo. App. 1942). In those cases, the worker became intoxicated either prior to or during his working hours. There was no anticipation by the employer that the worker would be consuming alcohol. Here, Mr. Schumacker's job included socializing where alcohol was served.

If an employer continually encourages and finances an employee's attendance at weekly functions which expose that employee to an atmosphere which results in the employee becoming intoxicated, he may not then disclaim liability after that employee is killed on his way home while driving his company car. In the case at bench, we hold that Mr. Schumacker's intoxication was not an abandonment of his employment.

. . . .

The judgment of the Superior Court granting judgment notwithstanding the verdict is reversed. This case is remanded for the issuance of an order allowing Mrs. Schumacker's claim for widow's benefits.

MUNSON and ROE, JJ., concur.

HAYNES v. R. B. RICE, DIVISION OF SARA LEE
783 S.W.2d 403 (Mo. Ct. App. 1989)

GAITAN, JUDGE.

Claimant, Craig F. Haynes, appeals from the denial of worker's compensation benefits.

Haynes was injured on April 19, 1986, while at work on the premises of his employer R. B. Rice Company. The duties of his employment included cleaning metal chili tubs by using 180 degree Farenheit water directed into the tubs with a high pressure hose.

It is critical to note the following scenario regarding the events that preceded Haynes injury. On the evening and early morning hours preceding his injury, Haynes had intravenously injected approximately 1-1/2 grams of cocaine into his bloodstream in a series of injections over a four hour period. Additionally, he drank from four to six beers. Further, he had not eaten nor slept the night prior to this incident.

Haynes was addicted to cocaine; his habit cost him nearly all his weekly paycheck. Within weeks of this injury he admits having blacked out as a consequence of excessive use or overdose of cocaine. Additionally, six weeks prior to this incident he nearly died from an overdose.

On the morning of this incident, Haynes was driven to work by a friend, Eddie Salter, who was with him the preceding night. They arrived at approximately 6:00 a.m. Haynes was seen trying to walk into the plant by a co-worker, James Jamison. Mr. Jamison testified as follows: . . .

> A. Got him back to the car, which took a lot of time to do because he couldn't walk, he just keep slumping down and you'd have to keep picking him up, and practically toting him.

> Q. All right. So then you got to the car, what happened then?

> A. I opened the door latch, see, I had his arm with this hand and this arm around him and then I just reached out and got the door latch and then he just

kind of saddled down and set down on his hind end and looked up at me and grinned and just laughed.

Haynes was found lying unconscious in scalding water in the chili room at 8:15 or 8:30 a.m., after he had been at work from 90 minutes to two hours. The fall was caused by, or caused, a loss of consciousness. As he lay unconscious on the floor, his head, face, right arm and buttocks were severely burned by the scalding water from the open hose. No one witnessed the fall. However, Haynes told a paramedic that he had not ingested any drugs for twenty-four hours prior to his injury. . . .

Missouri courts have long held that if an injured employee is intoxicated at the time of his injury to the extent that he cannot physically and mentally perform his job duties, then his claim is to be denied. *Phillips v. Air Reduction Sales Co.*, 337 Mo. 587, 85 S.W.2d 551 (Mo. 1935); *O'Neil v. Fred Evens Motor Sales Co.*, 160 S.W.2d 775 (Mo.App. 1942).

The uncontradicted facts in this case are convincing and compelling. Haynes was a cocaine addict, and he intravenously injected cocaine repeatedly into his veins up and until several hours before reporting to work. In addition, he did not take nourishment nor did he sleep the night prior to his injury. He was seen stumbling around, falling to his hands and knees, and was carried back to Salter's car. The testimony of Mr. Jamison, an unbiased, independent Union co-employee, was that Haynes, "looked out of his mind, it would have been impossible for him to work that morning." Cocaine, in the quantitative amount of 2.8 micrograms per milliliter, was found to be present in Haynes' urine and Dr. Oxley, a board certified pathologist, testified that given this high dosage, it would have been impossible for Haynes to have been performing his work duties. Finally, there were Haynes' statements made prior to trial in which he stated that he did not remember what had happened.

In *O'Neil*, an employee was found unconscious next to his car with the engine running. At trial, the employee testified that his foot slipped off the clutch, the car jerked and he fell on his left side and head rendering him unconscious. It was established on cross-examination that the employee had told doctors and other witnesses that he had no specific recollection of how the injuries occurred. The Court of Appeals in *O'Neil* denied the claim and held that the claimant had not met his burden of establishing that his injuries arose out of and in the course of his employment. *Id.* at 780.

The similarities between *O'Neil* and the instant case are obvious. In both cases, there were no witnesses, and the employee had given conflicting stories of how he was injured. In fact, the only difference between *O'Neil* and the instant case is that in the instant case, a witness, Jim Jamison, actually saw Haynes prior to his injury and testified to his drugged condition. Mr. Jamison's testimony was then corroborated by Dr. Oxley and another co-employee, Melody Pease, who stated that Haynes had not rinsed out any of the chili tubs in the chili room even though he had been somewhere on the premises for approximately an hour and a half. . . .

The accident occurred on April 19, 1986. His hearing was February 2 and 3, 1987. There was adequate time for him to prepare his case including the presentment of these witnesses.

In summary, there was sufficient competent evidence for the intravenous use of narcotics that it would have been impossible for him to perform his work duties, and therefore, his injury did not occur by accident arising out of and in the course of his employment.

Accordingly, the judgment of the Commission is affirmed. Claimant is denied worker's compensation benefits.

KENNEDY, C.J. dissents in separate opinion.

KENNEDY, CHIEF JUDGE, dissenting.

. . . Only by ignoring the evidence and by substituting its own assumptions about the effects of cocaine use could the Commission deny compensation to claimant.

The Commission's alternative finding . . . that the claimant was so intoxicated at the time of his fall "that it would have been impossible for the claimant to engage in his employment" is based upon speculation. . . . So far as this record shows (and it includes the testimony of three experts — two pathologists and the claimant), cocaine does not intoxicate. I use the term "intoxicate" to mean something resembling alcoholic intoxication, manifested in its advanced stages by lack of coordination and by stupefaction the kind of disabling intoxication, in other words, which would make it impossible for one to do his work, so that he could be said to have abandoned his employment. . . .

. . . .

Eliminate the basic premise that cocaine intoxicates like alcohol intoxicates, however, and the conclusion fails that claimant's condition was cocaine-induced intoxication. The evidence is quite clear and undisputed that there are no similarities between alcohol and cocaine in their effects upon the user. Our knowledge of the familiar alcoholic intoxication is irrelevant in dealing with a case of cocaine usage. There is no evidence whatever that cocaine would have any tendency to cause a person to act in the way claimant was acting as he arrived at work on the morning of his injury.

. . . .

It seems to me (if I may speculate along with the Commission) that the Commission was on the right track when it found that claimant's fall was caused by an "idiopathic fall or blackout" which was "likely related to cocaine injections". The condition earlier observed by Jamison was also an idiopathic fall likely related to cocaine injections. Claimant had omitted the evening meal the evening before and had had no breakfast on the morning of his fall. He had not slept the night before, although he had lain in bed. He was addicted to cocaine. This was not an isolated instance of abuse of his body; it represented a pattern. Fatigue and malnourishment caused the "idiopathic fall or blackout", and also caused the earlier behavior observed by Jamison. In that way claimant's actions were "related" to his cocaine use. But that is not to say that he was at any time "intoxicated."

. . . .

I would reverse the Commission's award and would remand to the Commission for determination of benefits owing to claimant.

THOMAS v. HELEN'S ROOFING COMPANY, INC.
199 Ga. App. 161, 404 S.E.2d 331 (1991)

COOPER, JUDGE.

We granted this discretionary appeal from a decision of the full board of workers' compensation affirmed by operation of law pursuant to OCGA § 34-9-105 (b).

The transcript from the hearing before the ALJ shows that appellant was replacing a roof on a building when he lost his footing and fell off the roof. It is undisputed that appellant was in the course of his employment with appellee at the time of the accident. Appellant was immediately taken to the hospital and was admitted for four days. The medical history taken from appellant indicated that he had used marijuana and cocaine in the past, and laboratory results revealed the presence of cocaine in appellant's urine. Appellant testified that he had used drugs in the past; that he did not remember the last time he used cocaine; but that he did not use any cocaine the day of his injury.

Appellant's supervisor testified that he did not see the accident; however, he examined the roof and the area where appellant fell after the accident and in his opinion appellant had to have jumped from the roof. He also testified that he had worked with appellant on another job where he witnessed appellant jump from a roof. The ALJ found that appellant's injury was caused by his intoxication from the use of cocaine and denied appellant's claim pursuant to OCGA § 34-9-17.

1. OCGA § 34-9-17 formerly provided that compensation would be denied for injuries due to intoxication. The statute was amended, effective July 1, 1990, to provide that no compensation would be allowed for injury due to intoxication by alcohol or "being under the influence of marijuana or a controlled substance. . . . " Appellant, whose injury occurred prior to the effective date of the amendment contends that the ALJ erred in finding that he was "intoxicated" as defined by Georgia law. Regardless of whether at the time of appellant's injury "intoxication" referred only to being under the influence of alcohol, previous case law indicates that it meant something more than having merely ingested alcohol or drugs. *See Parks v. Maryland Cas. Co.*, 69 Ga. App. 720(3), 26 S.E.2d 562 (1943). There was no evidence that appellant was under the influence of cocaine to the extent that he was not entirely himself or that his judgment was impaired or that his actions and conduct were noticeably affected. *Parks v. Maryland Cas. Co., supra.* "It is axiomatic that any finding of fact by the board, if supported by any evidence, is conclusive and binding upon the superior court and this court. [Cits.]" *Henry Gen. Hosp. v. Stephens*, 189 Ga. App. 619, 620(1), 376 S.E.2d 705 (1988). However, we do not find that the presence of cocaine in appellant's urine constitutes evidence of appellant's intoxication at the time of his injury. The record being devoid of any evidence that appellant's behavior or conduct was visibly or noticeably affected by the presence of cocaine in his urine, the ALJ erred in finding that appellant was intoxicated.

2. Appellee also failed to meet its burden of proving that the presence of the cocaine in appellant's urine proximately caused the accident. Appellant's supervisor testified that he did not see the accident, yet opined that appellant must have jumped from the roof. Appellant testified that he did not jump off the roof but that he slipped and fell. Appellee argues that the mere ingestion of cocaine should be considered wilful misconduct sufficient to deny compensation under OCGA § 34-9-17. However, "to deny compensation it is not sufficient for [the] employer to show wilful misconduct; the employer also has the burden of proving [that] the employee's misconduct proximately caused his injury. [Cits.]" *City of Buford v. Thomas*, 179 Ga. App. 769, 770(1), 347 S.E.2d 713 (1986). Appellee having failed to meet its burden under OCGA § 34-9-17, the ALJ erred in denying compensation.

Judgment reversed.

BANKE and BIRDSONG, P.JJ., concur.

PROBLEMS

(1) An intoxicated employee's verbal abuse led a coemployee to assault him. Was the assault "caused by" the intoxication? *See* Conley v. Travelers Ins. Co., 53 So. 2d 681 (La. App. 1951).

(2) What if the alcohol causes the death directly, as by pulmonary edema or asphyxiation, as distinguished from causing an accident? *Compare* Bullington v. Aetna Cas. & Sur. Co., 122 Ga. App. 842, 178 S.E.2d 901 (1971), *rev'd on other grounds*, 227 Ga. 485, 181 S.E.2d 495, *with* Herman v. Greenpoint Barrel & Drum Reconditioning Co., 9 A.D.2d 572, 189 N.Y.S.2d 353 (1959), *aff'd* 8 N.Y.2d 880, 203 N.Y.S.2d 922, 168 N.E.2d 721 (1960).

§ 20.06 VIOLATION OF STATUTE OR COMMISSION OF CRIME

[1] Introduction

The violation of a law or the commission of a crime in the performance of duties does not *per se* remove the offending employee from the course of employment. It may amount to "wilful misconduct" in states having this defense, if the employee knew and understood the statute, if its violation was intentional, and if the injury was of the kind which the statute aimed to prevent. Several states have specific statutory defenses of "violation of law" or "commission of crime," which have generally received strict construction.

[2] Varieties of Law-Violation Problems

The defense of violation of law may arise against several types of compensation statute background. Under the great majority of statutes, which create no defenses based on employee misconduct, the defense would have to take the form of a contention that the violation constituted a deviation from the employment. Under statutes containing "wilful misconduct" or "violation of safety law" defenses, the issues would be similar to those dealt with in Ch. 20, §§ 20.03 and 20.04, *above*. And under statutes making violation of law or commission of crime specific defenses, the issue becomes one of determining by judicial decision how broad a sweep was intended to be given to the language of the defenses, which, taken literally, might work forfeitures for any number of relatively trivial offenses.

[3] Violation of Statute in Absence of Statutory Defense

It is well established that violation of statute or commission of crime does not affect a compensation claim when the illegal feature of the conduct was not the causative factor in producing the injury. The most obvious illustration is the violation of Sunday blue laws. A longshoreman was injured while unloading scrap iron on Sunday, contrary to a provision of the penal code, and payment of compensation was resisted on this ground. The fine for breach of this penal law was $10 to $50, and the court pointed out that to deny compensation for the same offense might amount to a fine of $25,000, although there was no causal relation between the doing of the work on Sunday instead of Monday and the occurrence of the injury.[15]

But even if there is a causal connection between the illegal feature of the conduct and the injury, there is still no basis for denial of an award in the usual statute which contains no defenses based on employee misconduct.[16] It should be obvious that a truck driver, fluctuating between 50 and 60 miles an hour in a 55-mile speed zone is not automatically leaving and re-entering employment each time the speedometer needle crosses the 55 mark.[17]

The weight of authority is represented by *Moore v. J.A. McNulty Company*,[18] which awarded compensation to an employee who was injured while attempting to climb

---

[15] Texas Employers' Ins. Ass'n v. Peppers, 133 S.W.2d 165 (Tex. Civ. App. 1939).

[16] *E.g.*, Kemp v. Evening Star Newspaper Co., 533 F.2d 1224 (D.C. Cir. 1976). Violation of the District of Columbia Code provision prohibiting the carrying of a firearm did not bar recovery under the District of Columbia Workmen's Compensation Act for the death of an employee caused by the accidental discharge of such a firearm.

[17] Chaffee v. Effron, 1 A.D.2d 197, 149 N.Y.S.2d 115 (1956). Driving at 45 miles per hour in a 30-mile zone and crossing over the center line did not bar recovery.

[18] Moore v. J.A. McNulty Company, 171 Minn. 75, 213 N.W. 546 (1927).

aboard a moving freight train in violation both of city ordinances and state statutes. The court distinguished between prohibitions which limit the scope of employment and those which limit conduct within that area. The illegal conduct here was ruled to be a *method* of doing the man's work, and not a deviation from the area of employment.

[4] Violation of Statute as Wilful Misconduct

The modern rule is that violation of a statute is not wilful misconduct *per se*. There must be the intentional doing of something of a quasi-criminal nature, either with knowledge that it is likely to result in serious injury, or with a wanton disregard of probable consequences.

A striking illustration of the relation between the statutory offense and the compensation defense is afforded by the decision in *Day v. Gold Star Dairy*,[19] in which the claimant, having been involved in a collision resulting from his attempt to pass a truck at the crest of a hill on a wet day, was convicted of reckless driving by a jury. Nevertheless, his award of compensation was affirmed under the Michigan statute making wilful and intentional misconduct a defense. The court held that the compensation department was entitled to determine for itself whether the claimant's conduct was merely a high degree of negligence as distinguished from wilful and intentional misconduct.

The great majority of cases involving simple violation of traffic ordinances and statutes, such as speed or stop laws, similarly have failed to find wilful misconduct on the strength of the violation.[20]

If, however, the violation of statute is so extreme as to satisfy the language of the statutory defense by its intrinsic character, and not merely by the technicality of law violation, the defense will apply. Thus, under the Wyoming defense of "culpable negligence," driving 80 to 90 miles per hour in a 45-miles-per-hour zone was held to bar compensation to the driver.[21]

[5] Statutory Defense of Violation of Statute or Commission of Crime

Several states[22] make violation of law a separate ground of defense. Indiana[23] and Washington[24] deny compensation if the injury was incurred in the course of commission of a crime. The general tendency has been to give these statutes as narrow a construction as the words themselves will bear. In Indiana, one of the commonest methods used to by-pass the statute is a finding that the offense was not the proximate cause of the injury. This type of finding has been upheld when the violation took the form of failing to stop at a railroad crossing when the train had whistled.[25] Another way to neutralize the defense is to hold that the employer was aware of and condoned the conduct.[26]

In Georgia, it has been held that "wilful failure to perform a duty required by statute" is more than a mere careless failure to observe a traffic statute. Thus, a truck driver's conduct in attempting to pass another vehicle on the left, when he did not have

---

[19] Day v. Gold Star Dairy, 307 Mich. 383, 12 N.W.2d 5 (1943).

[20] *E.g.*, In re Pearson's Case, 341 Mass. 576, 170 N.E.2d 917 (1960).

[21] Weidt v. Brannan Motor Co., 72 Wyo. 1, 260 P.2d 757 (1953).

[22] Including, *e.g.*, Pennsylvania, Georgia, and Delaware.

[23] Ind. Ann. Stat. § 22-3-2-8 (1999).

[24] Wash. Rev. Code § 51.32.020 (1999).

[25] Hayes Freight Lines v. Martin, 119 Ind. App. 97, 84 N.E.2d 205 (1949).

[26] *E.g.*, Motor Freight Corporation v. Jarvis, 324 N.E.2d 500 (Ind. App. 1975).

enough vision ahead, although a technical violation of a traffic statute for which he pleaded guilty in a traffic court, was not the kind of wilful conduct contemplated by the statute.[27] But a subsequent case applying the defense to a case in which the employee was killed while jaywalking — a misdemeanor under the Georgia Code — appears to shift the emphasis from the real seriousness of the offense to the technical nature of the conduct as violation of a penal statute.[28]

The experience of states having the broad defense of crime or statute violation indicates the undesirability of a defense couched in sweeping terms. What with the proliferation of statutes and regulations having the force of law, it is probably fair to say that each one of us violates some law almost every day, if only by shifting into second instead of making a perfect stop at every stop sign.[29] Undoubtedly such offenses deserve penalties. But there is no justification for a compensation law provision that may have the effect of transforming a $10 fine into a $10,000 fine by the device of an absolute defense based on violation of statute.

RICHARDSON v. FIEDLER ROOFING, INC.
67 N.Y.2d 246, 502 N.Y.S.2d 125, 493 N.E.2d 228 (1986)

SIMONS, JUDGE.

Claimant's decedent, Norman Richardson, was employed by appellant, Fiedler Roofing, Inc. as a waterproofer and roofing mechanic. On January 20, 1981 he fell seven stories from the roof of a building near his jobsite sustaining head injuries which resulted in his death. Immediately before the accident, Richardson and a co-worker were at their work place on the roof waiting for material to arrive with no assigned work to do. While waiting, they moved some distance over the roof and across party walls to another part of the structure and removed some copper downspouts from the building to sell as salvage. While doing so, Richardson slipped on a patch of ice and fell to his death. Respondent Workers' Compensation Board affirmed a finding of the Administrative Law Judge that the accident occurred during the course of decedent's employment and that death was causally related to it and awarded benefits to decedent's five minor children. A divided Appellate Division 491 N.Y.S.2d 489, 112 A.D.2d 551 affirmed the decision of the Board, and the employer and its insurer appeal. They claim that the employer should not be required to pay benefits because decedent was actually engaged in a theft at the time of his accident, and thus his death resulted not from his work duties, but from "decedent's purely personal act of stealing copper downspouts."

To be compensable, an injury must arise out of and in the course of employment (Workers' Compensation Law § 10). Activities which are purely personal pursuits are not within the scope of employment and compensation may not be recovered for injuries sustained while engaging in them (*Matter of Pasquel v. Coverly*, 4 N.Y.2d 28, 31, 171 N.Y.S.2d 848, 148 N.E.2d 899). The test for determining whether specific activities are within the scope of employment or purely personal is whether the activities are both reasonable and sufficiently work related under the circumstances (*Matter of Capizzi v. Southern Dist. Reporters*, 61 N.Y.2d 50, 55, 471 N.Y.S.2d 554, 459 N.E.2d 847; *Matter of Davis v. Newsweek Mag.*, 305 N.Y. 20, 24, 110 N.E.2d 406; *Matter of Tyler v. Gilbert*, 29 A.D.2d 591, 285 N.Y.S.2d 452). It has been held that an employee directed to wait for a specified period of time until materials arrive, is not required to stand by idly but is free to engage in any reasonably related activity while waiting (*Matter of Anadio v. Ideal Leather Finishers*, 32 A.D.2d 40, 42, 299 N.Y.S.2d

---

[27] Reid v. Raper, 86 Ga. App. 277, 71 S.E.2d 735 (1952).

[28] Pacific Indem. Ins. Co. v. Eberhardt, 107 Ga. App. 391, 130 S.E.2d 136 (1963).

[29] Mudlin v. Hills Materials Co., 698 N.W.2d 67 (2005).

489, lv. denied 25 N.Y.2d 737, 304 N.Y.S.2d 1025, 251 N.E.2d 556; see also, *Matter of Capizzi v. Southern Dist. Reporters, supra,* 61 N.Y.2d p. 53, 471 N.Y.S.2d 554, 459 N.E.2d 847). Momentary deviation from the work routine for a customary and accepted purpose will not bar a claim for benefits. The determination of what is reasonable activity and what is unreasonable, and thus a deviation, is factual and the Board is afforded wide latitude in deciding whether the employee's conduct is disqualifying (*Matter of Anadio v. Ideal Leather Finishers, supra,* 32 A.D.2d p. 42, 299 N.Y.S.2d 489).

The Board found from the evidence in this case that it was common practice in the industry for roofers to remove copper downspouts and sell them for scrap. It further found that this employer not only knew of the practice but also frequently had been required to pay for or replace downspouts stolen by its employees. Despite this experience, the employer had never disciplined or discharged an employee for these thefts, and after it learned that decedent and his co-worker had been stealing downspouts on the day of the accident, it did not discipline or discharge the coemployee. Accordingly, the Board found that decedent's activities while waiting for necessary work materials to arrive did not constitute a deviation from, or an abandonment of, his employment and that the death arose out of and in the course of decedent's employment. These findings are supported by substantial evidence and thus are conclusive on the court (*Matter of Capizzi v. Southern Dist. Reporters,* 61 N.Y.2d 50, 54, 471 N.Y.S.2d 554, 459 N.E.2d 847, *supra*).

Indeed, appellants do not now challenge the Appellate Division's finding that there was substantial evidence to support the award. They contend in this court, for the first time, that a claimant is excluded from compensation benefits, as a matter of law, if he is engaged in an illegal activity at the time of the accident. Normally, they would not be permitted to raise the issue when they challenged only the factual basis of the Administrative Law Judge's finding that decedent had not deviated from the scope of his employment before the Board (see, *Matter of Middleton v. Coxsackie Correctional Facility,* 38 N.Y.2d 130, 132–133, 379 N.Y.S.2d 3, 341 N.E.2d 527; Workers' Compensation Law § 23). The argument raises solely a question of statutory interpretation, however, which we may address even though it was not presented below (see, *Telaro v. Telaro,* 25 N.Y.2d 433, 439, 306 N.Y.S.2d 920, 255 N.E.2d 158; Cohen and Karger, *Powers of the New York Court of Appeals,* at 627–628 [rev ed]).

Appellants base their argument on policy grounds, urging that an employee who engages in illegal activity during his employment should not receive benefits. Appellants note that Workers' Compensation Law article 9, the disability benefits section, expressly precludes benefits for non-work-related injuries caused by a claimant's illegal acts (see, Workers' Compensation Law § 201[9][A]; § 205[3]), and they contend that section 10 of the statute, the liability provision for work-related injuries, should be interpreted as containing a similar limitation. [footnote omitted] The history and nature of these two clauses prove otherwise.

In 1913, the Bill of Rights of the 1894 New York State Constitution was amended to give the Legislature the power to enact workers' compensation legislation (see, 1894 N.Y. Const., art. I, § 19) and the next year the Legislature did so. The resulting statute provided that employees were to be compensated on a "no-fault" basis, regardless of any negligence on their own part, for all injuries "arising out of and in the course of" their employment (see, Workers' Compensation Law § 10). To further the claimant's ability to establish his right to benefits, the statute creates a presumption that the injuries are compensable (see, Workers' Compensation Law § 21). The statute was enacted for humanitarian purposes, framed, in the words of Chief Judge Cardozo, to insure that injured employees might "be saved from becoming one of the derelicts of society, a fragment of human wreckage" (see, *Surace v. Danna,* 248 N.Y. 18, 20–21, 161 N.E. 315; see also, *Matter of Winfield v. New York Cent. & Hudson Riv. R.R. Co.,* 168 App. Div. 351, 352–353, 153 N.Y.S. 499, affd. 216 N.Y. 284, 110 N.E. 614; and see,

Minkowitz, *Practice Commentary, McKinney's Cons. Laws of N.Y.*, Book 64, Workers' Compensation Law § 10, pp. 126–127 [1986 Cum. Ann. Pocket Part]). To further that purpose, we have held that the statutory obligation to compensate injuries sustained in the course of employment which are causally related to it does not depend on the equities of a particular case, nor may it be avoided because of the workers' fraud or wrongdoing: it is absolute (see, *Matter of Sackolwitz v. Hamburg & Co.*, 295 N.Y. 264, 268, 67 N.E.2d 152, [construing § 14-a]).

The exceptions to this broad statutory liability are found in section 10, derived from the 1913 amendment to the Bill of Rights. They bar compensation when the injury has been occasioned solely by intoxication of the injured employee while on duty or by willful intention of the injured employee to bring about injury or death (Workers' Compensation Law § 10; compare, N.Y. Const., art. I, § 18; *Matter of Sackolwitz v. Hamburg & Co., supra*; and see, Minkowitz, Practice Commentary, op. cit., p. 127). Neither is applicable here.

The disability benefits provisions have an entirely different history and purpose. They were enacted in 1949 to expand the scope of the Workers' Compensation Law by providing short-term weekly benefits to employees for sickness or disability not arising "out of or in the course of" employment. We discussed the nature of article 9 in *Matter of Flo v. General Elec. Co.*, 7 N.Y.2d 96, 99, 195 N.Y.S.2d 652, 163 N.E.2d 876): "The Disability Benefits statute is broad in concept and general in terms. It was designed to assist the employee of the State who suffered disability by bridging the gap between the Workmen's Compensation Law and the Unemployment Insurance Law. Unlike the Workmen's Compensation Law, the Disability Benefits Law contains no requirement that the cause of a disability arise out of and in the course of employment. It contemplates a broad social coverage to protect the employee against the hazard of sickness and disability which interfere with and prevent his continuance in active employment and which can occur and do occur both within and outside of working hours."

Article 9 excludes benefits for several disabilities and disability periods (see, Workers' Compensation Law § 205) and one of its provisions, section 205(3), provides that benefits shall not be paid for a disability occasioned by the "perpetration by the employee of an illegal act". That limitation is not duplicated in the provisions of the statute dealing with work-related injuries. Indeed, the only exception to liability that the disability benefits provisions and workers' compensation provisions have in common is the provision which bars recovery for injuries caused by the employee's willful intention to bring physical harm to himself or another (compare, Workers' Compensation Law §§ 10 and 205). It is not claimed that that provision has application to this case and there is nothing else in the text of the statute, its legislative history, or in our case law, that supports the appellants' claim that section 10 should be read to foreclose work-related death benefits in the same way that section 205 forecloses benefits for non-work-related injuries.

We have previously emphasized that the Workers' Compensation Law is remedial in nature and must be "construed liberally to accomplish the economic and humanitarian objects of the act" (*Matter of Holcomb v. Daily News*, 45 N.Y.2d 602, 607, 412 N.Y.S.2d 118, 384 N.E.2d 665). It is significant that although we have consistently interpreted the statute in this way (see, e.g., *Matter of Sackolwitz v. Hamburg & Co.*, 295 N.Y. 264, 67 N.E.2d 152, *supra*, and cases cited therein), and the Legislature has amended and revised it repeatedly (see, Millus and Gentile, Time to Recodify the New York Workmen's Compensation Law, 47 NYSBJ 655), the list of activities which will disqualify an employee from compensation for work-related injuries has remained unchanged for over 70 years. Indeed, despite this long history of liberal interpretation, when section 205(3) was subsequently enacted barring disability benefits for injuries resulting from illegal acts, there was no effort to change section 10 to include a similar exception for work-related injuries. It is reasonable to assume from all of this that the

Legislature did not intend section 10 to be similarly limited. And there is good reason why it should not. It is one thing to disqualify a claimant for injuries he sustains during the course of an illegal activity pursued on his own time, an activity unknown to the employer and one which it cannot control. It is quite another to deprive dependents of benefits because the employee's death results from misconduct during the course of employment when the employer knows about the illegal activity and tolerates it (compare, *Matter of Chaffee v. Effron*, 1 A.D.2d 197, 198–199, 149 N.Y.S.2d 115).

Although the appellants' argument is based on moral grounds — the need to prevent parties from profiting from illegal acts — the suspicion is that the concern has more to do with dollars and cents than morality. The way for an employer to express dissatisfaction with its employees' acts and also avoid paying benefits for such claims, however, is not for the Board to disqualify innocent dependents but for the employer to make clear to its employees that illegal conduct on the job will not be tolerated.

Accordingly, the order of the Appellate Division should be affirmed, with costs.

TITONE, JUDGE (dissenting):

The majority holds that where an employer tolerates conduct blatantly in violation of the Penal Law, that conduct arises out of and in the course of employment within the meaning of Workers' Compensation Law § 10. Because I find that holding totally unacceptable, I must dissent.

. . . .

When the decedent chose to steal — which by no stretch of the imagination can be deemed a "reasonable" activity in any civilized society — he removed himself from his employment and acted at his own peril (*Matter of Goldfine v. Barsol [Parson] Cab Operating Co.*, 19 A.D.2d 672, 241 N.Y.S.2d 273).

. . . .

Here, decedent not only strayed from the roof on which he was supposed to wait to a different one but also proceeded to engage in a theft and then a cover-up of his actions leading him to pretend to inspect the icy edge of the unrelated roof. This was a completely unreasonable personal, dangerous and illegal indulgence which substantially increased his risk of injury (*Matter of Pasquel v. Coverly, supra*, 4 N.Y.2d p. 30, 171 N.Y.S.2d 848, 148 N.E.2d 899).

. . . .

The majority notes that it is the policy of this State to award compensation on a "no-fault" basis. It must also be recognized that this policy must be balanced with a strong policy against rewarding crime. I, too, sympathize with the plight of the innocent children who would suffer financially from the transgressions of their father. It is most unfortunate that children must bear the brunt of the nearsighted choices that their parents make. While it is true that we often disregard these "victims" of crime, this State has not seen fit to enact a workers' compensation law for the dependents of criminals who sustain injuries in the course of and arising out of their chosen "profession."

Accordingly, I would reverse the order of the Appellate Division and dismiss the claim.

§ 20.07   SUICIDE OR INTENTIONAL SELF-INJURY

Suicide under the majority rule is compensable if the injury produces mental derangement and the mental derangement produces suicide. The minority rule is that suicide is not compensable unless there has followed as the direct result of a work-connected injury an insanity of such severity as to cause the victim to take his own life through an uncontrollable impulse or in a delirium of frenzy without conscious volition to produce death.

Suicide may be made the basis of a defense against a compensation claim in several ways. The most direct is reliance on the specific defense, present in most state statutes, of suicide or intentional self-injury. It may also be argued that suicide does not arise out of the employment, since the source of harm is personal. It can also be said that suicide is not accidental, but rather intentional. It can even be argued that suicide is a departure — indeed the most irrevocable and final of all possible departures — from the course of employment.

At the outset, there must be found an injury which itself arose out of and in the course of employment, and then the suicide must be traced directly to it. If there is no such employment-connected injury setting in motion the causal sequence leading to the suicide, the suicide is a complete defense. Thus, when an employee was observed running through the plant clutching his head in pain, and was later found to have thrown himself out of a window, compensation was denied because there was no industrial injury as the initial cause.[30]

Most cases of this kind present the same pattern of facts: a severe, or extremely painful, or hopelessly incurable injury, followed by a deranged mental state ranging from depression to violent lunacy, followed in turn by suicide. The basic legal question is whether the act of suicide was an intervening cause breaking the chain of causation between the initial injury and the death. The controversy involves the kind or degree of mental disorder which will lead a court to say that the self-destruction was not an independent intervening cause.

At one time the field was dominated by the "voluntary wilful choice" test, sometimes called the "Sponatski rule," under which compensation in suicide cases was not payable unless there followed as the direct result of a physical injury an insanity of such violence as to cause the victim to take his own life through an uncontrollable impulse or in a delirium of frenzy without conscious volition to produce death. This doctrine was gradually displaced as majority rule by the "chain-of-causation" test, which found compensability if the injury caused the deranged mental condition which in turn caused the suicide.

Under the chain-of-causation test there remains, however, some room for uncertainty on precisely how deranged the decedent's mind must have been. New York has repeatedly emphasized the necessity for some "brain derangement" as distinguished from severe melancholy. Other "chain-of-causation" jurisdictions have employed varying terms to describe the requisite mental condition, sometimes similar to those used by New York, sometimes not as exacting. Moreover, even in states that might normally still appear to adhere to the *Sponatski* rule, the application of the rule in practice may produce results difficult to distinguish from those in "chain-of-causation" jurisdictions.

KAHLE v. PLOCHMAN, INC.
85 N.J. 539, 428 A.2d 913 (1981)

CLIFFORD, J.

The Workers' Compensation Act precludes an award of compensation "when the injury or death is intentionally self-inflicted." N.J.S.A. 34:15-7. Petitioner's decedent was injured in an accident arising out of and in the course of her employment. Ten years later she committed suicide. The judge of compensation dismissed petitioner's dependency claim petition on the ground that the employee's death was "intentionally self-inflicted" within the meaning of the statutory preclusion. We ordered direct certification of petitioner's appeal pending unheard in the Appellate Division, 84 N.J.

---

[30] Joseph v. United Kimono Co., 194 App. Div. 568, 185 N.Y. Supp. 700 (1921).

417, 420 A. 2d 331 (1980); R. 2:12-1, and now reverse.

I

On February 11, 1966 Rosalie Kahle (employee) was seriously injured in the course of her employment when a skid fell on her back at respondent's mustard-packing plant in Vineland, New Jersey. Employee was twenty-six years old, was married, had one child, and was three months pregnant with her second child at the time of the accident. She sustained injuries to her back and left leg which over the course of the next several years required hospitalization surgical removal of a lumbar disc and spinal fusion, and the prescription of medication for pain and depression. In 1971 a judge of compensation awarded 66 2/3% permanent partial disability for the orthopedic, neurological and psychiatric consequences of her work-connected accident.

The years of Mrs. Kahle's life following the compensation award continued to be dominated by unremitting pain and increasing disability. She never returned to work. Her medications included anti-depressants, pain relievers and sleeping pills. She was diagnosed as suffering at various times from a convulsive disorder caused by drug withdrawal, severe compressive lumbar and dorsal arachnoiditis (inflammation of the membrane of the spinal cord), a neurogenic bladder, anemia, iron deficiency and chronic cystitis. Mrs. Kahle was rehospitalized in 1972 for spinal injections and again in 1973 for the surgical implant of a dorsal column stimulator (a battery operated electrode positioned below the collarbone and intended to eliminate pain electronically), a measure later conceded to have been unsuccessful. There were further hospitalizations in 1974 and on three occasions in 1975. Dorsal nerve blocks were performed and Mrs. Kahle was reduced to using crutches. In late 1975, trying to negotiate some cellar stairs she fell and injured her head, neck and back, resulting in additional hospital confinement. Thereafter the treating physician prescribed foot drop braces for both feet. A month before her death Mrs. Kahle received a nerve block for chest pain and two weeks later a renewal of a narcotic prescription.[31]

During the night preceding her death petitioner's decedent complained of pain and slept fitfully. Sometime after four o'clock in the morning of May 2, 1976 she wrote two poignant notes, one to her husband and the other to her treating physician of ten years. Shortly thereafter she ended her life with a single rifle shot to her head. The notes make it abundantly clear that Mrs. Kahle was no longer able to bear her pain, anxiety and depression.

II

Petitioner, widower of the deceased employee and father of their two young sons, filed a claim for death benefits for himself and on behalf of the children. The dependency claim petition alleged that Mrs. Kahle's suicide was the result of the severe pain, anxiety and depression caused by the work-connected injuries sustained in the accident at respondent's plant. Respondent denied the compensability of the suicide.

At the ensuing hearing petitioner produced Dr. Theodore Kushner, a neuropsychiatrist who had examined the decedent on two occasions, the second being in January 1976, approximately three months prior to her death. Dr. Kushner testified that at the last examination he found Mrs. Kahle to be depressed and anxious. He diagnosed her psychiatric condition as post-traumatic anxiety depressive reaction, which he assessed at a 40% psychiatric disability rating. He described her psychiatric

---

[31] *(Court's footnote)* The employee's last compensation payment was received from respondent on October 25, 1975. On March 5, 1976, Mrs. Kahle filed a First Application for Review or Modification claiming an increase in disability. On June 18, 1976, six weeks after the employee's death, respondent filed an Answer admitting that the disability had increased since the date of the original award to the point that the employee had become totally disabled prior to her death.

condition at that time as "chronically anxious and moderately depressed" but "free of psychosis." Dr. Kushner proffered his medical opinion that when he examined the employee in January 1976, "she was totally disabled with no possibility of recovery or rehabilitation." In response to a detailed hypothetical question put forth by counsel for petitioner, the neuropsychiatrist concluded that Mrs. Kahle's suicide was a direct consequence of the work-connected injury she sustained on February 11, 1966, after ten years of unusual suffering, increasing disability, chronic unremitting pain, depression, drug dependency, "and finally the knowledge that she would never recover." Respondent introduced no evidence at the hearing and produced no witnesses of its own, being content to rely on the legal argument that by virtue of N.J.S.A. 34:15-7 suicide is not a compensable death under New Jersey law of workers' compensation.

In ruling that Mrs. Kahle's suicide was "intentionally self-inflicted" within the meaning of N.J.S.A. 34:15-7 and therefore not a compensable death, the compensation judge relied upon the standard announced in the case of *In re Sponatski*, 220 Mass. 526, 108 N.E. 466 (Mass.1915), adopted *sub silentio* in *Konazewska v. Erie R.R. Co.*, 132 N.J.L. 424, 41 A. 2d 130 (Sup.Ct.1945), aff'd, 133 N.J.L. 557, 45 A.2d 315 (E. & A.1946). Under the *Sponatski* rule, a suicide following a work-connected injury is compensable only "where there follows as the direct result of a physical injury an insanity of such violence as to cause the victim to take his own life through an uncontrollable impulse or in a delirium of frenzy 'without conscious volition to produce death, [without] having knowledge of the physical consequences of the act'. . . . " 220 Mass. at 530, 108 N.E. at 468 (quoting *Daniels v. New York, New Haven & Hartford R.R.*, 183 Mass. 393, 67 N.E. 424 (Mass.1903)). Or, as the judge of compensation put it, an employee's suicide is not compensable unless the worker (1) as the direct result of a physical injury, (2) was possessed of an uncontrollable impulse to commit suicide or was in a delirium of frenzy, (3) did not consciously intend to kill himself, and (4) did not realize the consequences of his act of self-destruction. Because the petitioner's proofs fell short of satisfying the *Sponatski* test, judgment was entered in favor of the employer.

In applying the *Sponatski* formula to the plight of the employee in the instant case, the judge recognized that Mrs. Kahle unquestionably suffered intense pain from the date of her work-connected injury through the time of her death, and that the mental consequences of this prolonged suffering required two hospitalizations for psychiatric examination. Of greater importance to the judge, however, were the negating facts that employee did not require active psychiatric care, had no diagnosed psychosis, and was 60% functional psychiatrically. He also determined that the employee's conduct immediately prior to her death, particularly the writing of farewell notes to her husband and her physician, evidenced conscious volition to produce death and knowledge of the consequences of her act — factors militating against recovery under the *Sponatski* rule.

The compensation judge was guided by the general statement from Professor Larson's treatise that under *Sponatski*, "[t]he compensable cases are frequently marked by some violent or eccentric method of self-destruction while the noncompensable cases usually present a story of quiet but ultimately unbearable agony leading to a solitary and undramatic suicide." *See* 1A Larson, Workmen's Compensation Law § 36.21 (1978). It is apparent that under *Sponatski* the suicide of the employee in the present case falls within the latter category of tragic but noncompensable cases.

III

Petitioner's appeal does not challenge the compensation judge's findings of fact. Nor does it disagree that the *Sponatski* formula is currently recognized as controlling law in New Jersey as to the circumstances under which an employee suicide is an "intentionally self-inflicted" death for the purposes of the statutory exclusion in N.J.S.A. 34:15-7. *See Konazewska, supra; Kazazian v. Segan*, 14 N.J.Misc. 78, 182 A. 351 (N.J. Dept. Labor 1936). Rather, petitioner's brief urges us to overrule "this antiquated [*Sponatski*] doctrine to bring New Jersey in line not only with the modern view in other states, but also with the spirit of our court's prior interpretations of our compensation law."

At the time the *Konazewska* decision was affirmed by the Court of Errors and Appeals in 1946, the *Sponatski* test was the standard followed by the majority of states in suicide-compensation cases. This standard, however, has been gradually displaced as the majority rule by the "chain-of-causation" test, under which death benefits may be awarded to dependents of employees whose suicides are shown to be causally related to a disturbance of mind arising from the pain, despair and psychiatric consequences of work-connected injuries. *See* 1A Larson, *supra*, at § 36.10. The leading case espousing the chain-of-causation rule is *Whitehead v. Keene Roofing Co.*, 43 So. 2d 464 (Fla.1949), in which the Supreme Court of Florida reviewed a widow's claim for death benefits under a statutory provision that precluded compensation for injuries "occasioned primarily . . . by the wilful intention of the employee to injure or kill himself." 43 So. 2d at 465 (quoting Fla. Stat. Ann. § 4440.09(3) (West 1941)). Concluding that the suicide of the deceased employee was directly attributable to the mental disturbance that arose out of physical injuries he sustained in a fall from a roof on which he was working, the *Whitehead* court posed what has since become the classic statement of the rule:

> We believe that in those cases where the injuries suffered by the deceased result in his becoming devoid of normal judgment and dominated by a disturbance of mind directly caused by his injury and its consequences, his suicide cannot be considered "wilful" within the meaning and intent of the Act. [43 So. 2d at 465.] *(court's footnote omitted)*

The issue of the compensability of an employee suicide under the *Whitehead* standard turns not on the employee's conscious volition or knowledge of the consequences of his act, but rather on the existence of an unbroken chain of causation from the work-connected injury to the suicide. *See* 1A Larson, *supra*, at § 36.30.

. . . .

We hold that the chain-of-causation test is a more realistic and reasonable standard than the *Sponatski* rule. It is to be incorporated henceforth in the New Jersey law of workers' compensation. Under the rule we adopt today an employee's death by suicide is compensable where the original work-connected injuries result in the employee's becoming dominated by a disturbance of mind directly caused by his or her injury and its consequences, such as extreme pain and despair, of such severity as to override normal rational judgment. A suicide committed by an employee suffering from such disturbance of mind is not to be considered "intentional" within the meaning and intent of N.J.S.A. 34:15-7, even though the act itself may be volitional. . . . The *Sponatski* rule's emphasis on the employee's conscious volition and knowledge of the physical consequences of his or her act virtually ignores the role that severe pain, anxiety, despair and prescribed psychotropic drugs may play in breaking down a rational mental process. . . .

Today's decision not only falls in line with the trend of enlightened judicial determinations in other jurisdictions, but also is in accordance with the often expressed intent and purpose of New Jersey Worker's Compensation Act. It has long been axiomatic to this Court that the Act is remedial social legislation and should be given liberal construction in order that its beneficent purposes may be accomplished. *Panzino v. Continental Can Co.*, 71 N.J. 298, 303, 364 A.2d 1043 (1976); *Torres v. Trenton Times Newspaper*, 64 N.J. 458, 461, 317 A.2d 361 (1974); *Petrozzino v. Monroe Calculating Machine Co., Inc.*, 47 N.J. 577, 580, 222 A.2d 73 (1966). It is for this reason that in construing the statutory exclusion of benefits for "intentionally self-inflicted" injury or death, N.J.S.A. 34:15-7, this Court is not bound by its coldly literal import. *Paul v. Baltimore Upholstering Co.*, 66 N.J. 111, 136, 328 A.2d 610 (1974). Rather, by holding compensable those suicide cases in which work-connected injury causes such disturbance of mind as to impair the employee's capacity for normal reason and rational judgment, we honor the legislative purpose of relieving society as a whole of the burden of supporting dependents of those whose death is caused by work-connected injuries. *See Petrozzino, supra,* 47 N.J. at 580, 364 A.2d 1043.

. . . .

Reversed and remanded for further proceedings consistent with this opinion. We do not retain jurisdiction.

For reversal and remandment — CHIEF JUSTICE WILENTZ and JUSTICES SULLIVAN, PASHMAN, CLIFFORD, SCHREIBER, HANDLER and POLLOCK — 7.

For affirmance — None.

PROBLEMS

(1) What if acute worry over some work-related matter is the cause of the suicide — should this be subject to the same chain-of-causation test? More specifically, suppose an employee of a state home and training school commits suicide after learning that a legislative committee is investigating his possible responsibility in the death of a patient at the home. Compensable? *See* Trombley v. State of Michigan, 366 Mich. 649, 115 N.W.2d 561 (1962). *But cf.* Hyde v. New York State Dept. of Mental Hygiene, 39 N.Y.2d 854, 386 N.Y.S.2d 214 (1976), reaching a result *contra* to *Trombley* on somewhat similar facts.

(2) In the *Bullington* case, Section 20.05, Problem 2, *above,* one defense advanced was that of intentional self-injury. What result?

(3) Suppose that the injury, physical or psychological, that caused decedent to take his own life, was a matter of decedent's subjective perception rather than actual fact. *See* Lopucki v. Ford Motor Co., 311 N.W.2d 338 (Mich. Ct. App. 1981).

(4) Suppose that an injured male worker committed suicide shortly after he received a Notice of Contest from his employer's workers' compensation claims administrator stating that his claim was being contested pending completion of an investigation. Can his widow recover against the employer and the claims administrator for an alleged breach of defendants' duty of good faith and fair dealing? *See* Moore v. Western Forge Corp., 2007 Colo. App. LEXIS 2199 (November 15, 2007).

§ 20.08 EMPLOYEE FRAUD

The discussion found thus far within this chapter has generally focused upon the activity of the employee at or near the time of the employee's claimed injury and, while acknowledging the general irrelevance of employee fault within the workers' compensation system, has elicited examples of employee misconduct that are sufficiently egregious so as to remove the employee's activities (at the time of the alleged injury) from the course and scope of the employment. Thus, certain employee activities — e.g., the violation of some statutes, the commission of certain crimes, the failure to obey some safety rules or regulations, the act of being intoxicated or under the influence of drugs, or the commission of suicide can sometimes be sufficient to defeat the claim of the employee or the employee's dependents for workers' compensation benefits.

A different type of employee misconduct arises when an employee makes false statements or engages in other types of fraudulent behavior in order to obtain workers' compensation benefits. This sort of misconduct may be far removed, in terms of time and place, from the claimed injury itself. It may take the form of making false statements on a benefits application, giving false symptoms and other medical information to a treating or examining physician, presenting false testimony or medical evidence regarding a work-related injury, or intentionally mis-characterizing the extent and nature of the employee's injuries or post-injury earnings. Employee misconduct of this sort, like the sorts of misconduct discussed in previous chapters, can have the effect of limiting a claimant's benefits or barring them altogether.

In order to impose a penalty upon a claimant for workers' compensation fraud or to disqualify that claimant from receiving workers' compensation benefits, the false statement, representation, or omission must be related to a material fact. Thus, in the first case to reach the New York appellate courts after the enactment of the state's 1996 anti-fraud provisions, *Phelps v. Phelps*,[32] the court held that a landscaper who testified that he was unable to find work and that he had not worked due to a work-related spinal injury could be disqualified from receiving any additional wage replacement benefits when videotape evidence showed that the landscaper was sufficiently fit to lift large tree limbs and carry them on his shoulders. The court agreed with the state's Workers' Compensation Board that the landscaper's false statements were material.

Other material misrepresentations that have resulted in the sanctioning of workers' compensation claimants include lying about the compensable circumstances of the injury itself,[33] the giving of false information to treating physicians,[34] the filing of false medical mileage reimbursement forms,[35] and the giving of false statements or testimony regarding a claimant's post-injury physical capabilities,[36] or regarding the existence or non-existence of prior injuries.[37]

A rather common example of employee misconduct warranting the forfeiture of workers' compensation benefits is the failure on the part of the injured worker to disclose post-injury earnings, particularly if the worker is drawing disability benefits. Examples include a worker who failed to tell the Board that he enjoyed an annual salary of $25,000 as a minister while also receiving disability benefits,[38] a claimant who drew temporary total disability benefits and also worked at a pizzeria/deli,[39] a worker who neglected to inform his employer that he had received the sum of $270 through a sale of crack cocaine,[40] and a "disabled" worker who helped out at his brother's business,[41] Finally, it should be observed that while an employee's material false statement made in connection with his or her workers' compensation claim may result in the forfeiture of lost wage benefits, it does not necessarily result in a forfeiture of future medical benefits related to the original, legitimate injury.[42]

---

[32] Phelps v. Phelps, 277 A.D. 2d 736, 716 N.Y.S. 2d 160 (3rd Dept. 2000).

[33] Tensfeldt v. Workers' Comp. Appeals Bd., 66 Cal. App. 4th 116, 77 Cal. Rptr. 2d 691 (1998).

[34] Dishaw v. Midas Serv. Experts, 27 A.D.3d 921, 810 N.Y.S.2d 600 (App. Div. 2006).

[35] St. Bernard Parish Police Jury v. Duplessis, 2002-0632 (La. 12/4/02), 831 So. 2d 955. In conjunction with his disability claims, the claimant turned in mileage reimbursement forms which listed a travel distance of 4,354 miles. When his employer's insurer traced the claimant's alleged routes, it arrived at a figure of 1,114. Both the employer and its insurer filed a petition for forfeiture of the claimant's benefits. The claimant argued that his misstatements were not intentional or willful, as he miscalculated due to his limited education. The court refused to accept this argument, particularly since the claimant was employed as a truck driver and thus was familiar with logging miles. The court found the presence of willfulness and ordered forfeiture.

[36] Passari v. New York City Hous. Auth., 13 A.D.3d 853, 786 N.Y.S.2d 254 (2004).

[37] Bibbins v. Sonny's Pizza, Inc., 2001-1524 (La. App. 1 Cir. 6/21/02), 822 So. 2d 79.

[38] State *ex rel.* Jerdo v. Pride Cast Metals, Inc., 2002 Ohio 1491, 95 Ohio St. 3d 18, 764 N.E.2d 1021.

[39] Woods v. New York State Thruway Auth., 27 A.D.3d 933, 810 N.Y.S.2d 580 (App. Div. 2006).

[40] Johnson v. New York State Dep't of Transp., 305 A.D.2d 927, 758 N.Y.S.2d 870 (2003).

[41] Bottieri v. New York State Dep't of Taxation & Fin., 27 A.D.3d 1035, 811 N.Y.S.2d 493 (App. Div. 2006).

[42] Rodriguez v. Burn-Brite Metals Co., Inc., 300 A.D.2d 904, 754 N.Y.S.2d 682 (2002), *aff'd mem.*, 1 N.Y.3d 553, 772 N.Y.S.2d 236, 804 N.E.2d 400 (2003). *See also* Vanostrand v. Felchar Mfg. Corp. 306 A.D.2d 770, 761 N.Y.S.2d 535 (2003), *appeal dismissed*, 100 N.Y.2d 615, 767 N.Y.S.2d 397, 799 N.E.2d 620 (2003). Applying *Rodriguez*, the court held that the claimant did not forfeit the reimbursement she had obtained by overstating and double charging two employers for the mileage traveled for medical appointments. The court held that while a workers' compensation carrier might suspend wage replacement benefits to an employee who made

false representations to receive benefits under the state compensation act, it could not terminate the injured employee's right to medical treatment causally connected to the original compensable accident.

Chapter 21
MISCONDUCT OF EMPLOYER

SYNOPSIS

§ 21.01 INTENTIONAL INJURY BY EMPLOYER OR EMPLOYER'S AGENT

Intentional injury inflicted by the employer in person on his or her employee may be made the subject of a common law action for damages on the theory that, in such an action, the employer will not be heard to say that such an intentional act was an "accidental" injury and so under the exclusive provisions of the compensation act. The same result may follow when the employer is a corporation and the assailant is, by virtue of control or ownership, in effect the alter ego of the corporation. But when the intentional injury is committed by a coemployee the better rule is that an action in damages will not lie against the employer merely because the coemployee occupied supervisory status in relation to the claimant. "Intentional" injury does not include accidental injury caused by the gross, wanton, wilful, deliberate, intentional, culpable, or malicious negligence, breach of statute, or other misconduct of the employer short of genuine intentional injury.

KITTELL v. VERMONT WEATHERBOARD, INC.
138 Vt. 439, 417 A.2d 926 (1980)

PER CURIAM.

This is an appeal from a decision of the Lamoille Superior Court that dismissed plaintiff's complaint on the ground that Vermont's Workmen's Compensation Act, 21 V.S.A. ch. 9, provides the exclusive remedy for his injury. In his complaint, plaintiff alleged that he was an inexperienced workman set to work without instruction or warnings at a multiple saw and trim from which the defendant employer had stripped all safety devices. While operating the saw, a splinter flew into plaintiff's eye and penetrated his head, causing severe injuries. These injuries, plaintiff alleges, were due solely to defendant's wanton and wilful acts and omissions.

The question presented is not whether plaintiff can recover an award for these injuries in any forum, but whether his complaint pleads a cause of action outside the scope of the Workmen's Compensation Act, thus entitling him to an award in the common-law courts. Section 622 of Title 21 makes the Workmen's Compensation Act the exclusive remedy for all injuries within the scope of the Act. The Act's coverage extends to "personal injury *by accident* arising out of and in the course of . . . employment. . . . " 21 V.S.A. § 618 (emphasis added). Therefore, we must determine whether plaintiff's allegation of wilful and wanton conduct leading to a sudden but foreseeable injury constitutes "personal injury by accident" within section 618. If it does, the Act applies and the case was properly dismissed; if not, the Act would not apply, and plaintiff would be entitled to his common-law remedy.

The Legislature has provided the following guidance for construing the Workmen's Compensation Act:

> In construing the provisions of this chapter, the rule of law that statutes in derogation of the common law are to be strictly construed shall not be applied. The provisions of this chapter shall be so interpreted and construed as to effect its general purpose to make uniform the law of those states which enact it.

21 V.S.A. § 709. The fact that workmen's compensation is in derogation of common-law remedies is not, therefore, grounds for limiting the scope of the Act. Furthermore, any construction we place on this Act should serve the general purpose of harmonizing the law of workmen's compensation.

The overwhelming weight of authority in other jurisdictions is that "the common-law liability of the employer cannot be stretched to include accidental injuries caused by the gross, wanton, wilful, deliberate, intentional, reckless, culpable, or malicious negligence, breach of statute, or other misconduct of the employer short of genuine intentional injury." 2A A. Larson, Workmen's Compensation Law § 68.13, at 13-5 (1976), and cases cited *id.* at n.11. Nothing short of a specific intent to injure falls outside the scope of the Act. 2A A. Larson, *supra,* § 68.13; accord, *e.g., Duncan v. Perry Packing Co.*, 162 Kan. 79, 86, 174 P.2d 78, 83 (1946); *Wilkinson v. Achber*, 101 N.H. 7, 9-10, 131 A.2d 51, 53 (1957); *Santiago v. Brill Monfort Co.*, 10 N.Y.2d 718, 718, 219 N.Y.S.2d 266, 266, 176 N.E.2d 835, 835 (1961); *Duk Hwan Chung v. Fred Meyer, Inc.*, 276 Or. 809, 813, 556 P.2d 683, 685 (1976); *Foster v. Allsop Automatic, Inc.*, 86 Wash.2d 579, 581–84, 547 P.2d 856, 857–59 (1976) (en banc); *see* Annot., 96 A.L.R.3d 1064 (1979). *But see Mandolidis v. Elkins Industries, Inc.*, W.Va., 246 S.E.2d 907, 96 A.L.R.3d 1035 (1978). Absent such specific intent, the right to benefits under the Act, and thus the triggering of the exclusivity rule of section 622, "depends on one simple test: Was there a work-connected injury?" 1 A. Larson, *supra,* § 2.10 (1978). Plaintiff's complaint admits that there was.

"The purpose of the workmen's compensation law is to provide, not only for the employees a remedy which is both expeditious and independent of proof of fault, but also for employers, a liability which is limited and determinate." *Morrisseau v. Legac*, 123 Vt. 70, 76, 181 A.2d 53, 57 (1962). These purposes are best served by allowing the remedial system which the Legislature has created a broad sphere of operation. We are not unmindful that in individual cases this may work some hardship, but where the Legislature has determined that the benefits derived from quick and certain basic compensation outweigh those from delayed and contingent full compensation, we are unwilling to disturb this choice.

Judgment affirmed.

WOODSON v. ROWLAND
329 N.C. 330, 407 S.E.2d 222 (1991)

Exum, Chief Justice.

This is a wrongful death action arising from a work-related trench cave-in which killed Thomas Alfred Sprouse on Sunday, 4 August 1985. Plaintiff is the administrator of Sprouse's estate. The principal question is whether the exclusivity provisions of the Workers' Compensation Act limit plaintiff's remedies to those provided by the Act. The courts below concluded plaintiff was so limited in her choice of remedies. We disagree. Other issues in the case concern the viability of certain theories of liability plaintiff asserts: the nondelegability of duties of safety owed to plaintiff's intestate, and the negligent hiring and retention of a subcontractor.

I.

Defendant Pinnacle One Associates ("Pinnacle One") was the developer on a construction project for IBM in Research Triangle Park. It retained defendant Davidson & Jones, Inc. ("Davidson & Jones") as general contractor. One aspect of the project required construction of a sanitary sewer line on Chin Page Road in Durham County. Davidson & Jones hired defendant Morris Rowland Utility, Inc. ("Rowland Utility" or "employer") to dig the line. Defendant Neal Morris Rowland ("Morris Rowland") has at all relevant times been the president and sole shareholder of Rowland Utility. Decedent Thomas Sprouse was Rowland Utility's employee.

On defendants' motions for summary judgment, plaintiff's forecast of evidence tends to show the following:

On Saturday, 3 August 1985, workers from both Rowland Utility and Davidson & Jones were digging trenches to lay sewer lines. The Chin Page Road project required two separate trenches. Although Rowland Utility was hired to dig both, in the interest of time a Davidson & Jones crew provided men to work in one of the trench sites.

Because the trenches were not sloped, shored, or braced, and did not have a trench box, Lynn Craig, the Davidson & Jones foreman, refused to let his men work in them. The Occupational Safety and Health Act of North Carolina ("OSHANC") and the rules promulgated thereunder required such safety precautions for the trenches in question. N.C.G.S. § 95-136(g); 13 N.C. Admin. Code 7E.1400 et seq; cf. 29 C.F.R. § 1926.650–.653. Because of the soil conditions and geography, Craig believed that a trench box was the best means of ensuring his workers' safety. Morris Rowland procured a trench box for Craig and the Davidson & Jones crew, which commenced work inside the trench after receiving the safety device on the morning of Saturday, 3 August. Morris Rowland did not acquire a trench box for his own crew.

Charles Greene, a member of the Davidson & Jones crew, was operating a backhoe at the Rowland Utility site that Saturday. Craig checked on the site's progress several times. Morris Rowland asked Craig if he could put a Rowland Utility man on the job because he believed that Greene was not operating the backhoe fast enough. Several times Craig denied these requests. Once, Craig operated the machinery himself for a few minutes and concluded that Greene's progress had been adequate. In his deposition, Craig testified that by the end of the day the sides of the Rowland Utility trench were not being adequately sloped, and that it "could have been a little safer." At that point, the trench construction violated OSHANC regulations. [footnote omitted]

On Sunday, 4 August, the Davidson & Jones crew did not work, and its trench box lay idle. However, the Rowland Utility crew reported to the site to continue digging its trench. A Rowland Utility man, rather than Greene, was now operating the backhoe. Morris Rowland and project supervisor, Elmer Fry, discussed whether to use the trench box in their ditch. They decided not to use it, indicating in deposition that they had believed the soil was packed hard enough so the trench would not cave in.

A backhoe worked in front of of decedent Sprouse and his coworkers, who were laying pipe inside the freshly dug trench. A piece of heavy machinery called a front-end loader drove along the edge of the ditch and followed their progress, dumping loads of gravel onto the newly laid pipe. Workers tamped the gravel using a device similar to a jackhammer. Sprouse was the closest person in the trench to the front-end loader.

At about 9:30 a.m. one side of the trench collapsed, completely burying Sprouse and burying the man closest to him up to his armpits. The partially buried man was Alan Fry, son of project supervisor Elmer Fry. The workers pulled Alan Fry out of the trench, and Morris Rowland took him to the hospital.

Morris Rowland did not return to the site for several hours after the cave-in. The remaining workers continued to dig Sprouse out. They refused several offers of help given by Jennifer Spencer, a security guard for another company, who was then on duty and who volunteered to call a rescue squad. By the time the workers had finished digging Sprouse out, he was dead.

The trench was approximately fourteen feet deep and four feet wide with vertical sides at the point of the cave-in. Craig, who saw the site later and commented on a photograph of it at his deposition, stated that the trench was being sloped less than it had been at the end of the previous day's work. He characterized it as "unsafe" and stated that he "would never put a man in it."

Pursuant to N.C.G.S. § 28A-18-2, plaintiff filed civil suits against Rowland Utility; Morris Rowland in his individual capacity; Davidson & Jones; and Pinnacle One Associates. In July 1987, plaintiff filed a Workers' Compensation claim to meet the filing deadline for compensation claims. In order to avoid a judicial ruling that she had elected a workers' compensation remedy inconsistent with the civil remedies she presently seeks, plaintiff specifically requested that the Industrial Commission not hear her case until completion of this action. The Commission has complied with her request, and plaintiff has received no benefits under the Workers' Compensation Act.

In the civil actions before us, the trial court granted all defendants' motions for summary judgment; and the Court of Appeals affirmed, with Judge Phillips concurring in part and dissenting in part. Plaintiff appealed of right on the basis of Judge Phillips' dissent, and we granted her petition for discretionary review as to additional issues. We now affirm in part and reverse in part.

II.

We first decide whether the forecast of evidence is sufficient to survive Rowland Utility's and Morris Rowland's motions for summary judgment, which are based on the ground that Sprouse's death was caused only by "accident" under the Workers' Compensation Act ("the Act"). If the death can only be considered accidental, defendants' summary judgment motions were properly allowed because Sprouse's death would fall within the Act's exclusive coverage, and no other remedies than those provided in the Act are available to plaintiff either against his employer, *Hicks v. Guilford County*, 267 N.C. 364, 148 S.E.2d 240 (1966), or a co-worker, *Strickland v. King*, 293 N.C. 731, 239 S.E.2d 243 (1977). On the other hand, if the forecast of evidence is sufficient to show that Sprouse's death was the result of an intentional tort committed by his employer, then summary judgment was improperly allowed on the ground stated, because the employer's intentional tort will support a civil action. See *Pleasant v. Johnson*, 312 N.C. 710, 325 S.E.2d 244 (1985), and cases cited therein.

We conclude, for reasons given below, that the forecast of evidence is sufficient for plaintiff to survive defendants' motions for summary judgment because: (1) it tends to show that Sprouse's death was the result of intentional conduct by his employer which the employer knew was substantially certain to cause serious injury or death; and (2) this conduct is tantamount to an intentional tort committed by the employer. We conclude, further, that plaintiff may pursue simultaneously her workers' compensation claim and her civil action without being required to elect between them because the forecast of evidence tends to show that: (1) Sprouse's death was the result of both an "accident" under the Act and an intentional tort; and (2) the Act's exclusivity provision does not shield the employer from civil liability for an intentional tort. Plaintiff is, of course, entitled to but one recovery.

A.

. . . .

The [North Carolina Workers' Compensation] Act seeks to balance competing interests and implement trade-offs between the rights of employees and their employers. It provides for an injured employee's certain and sure recovery without having to prove employer negligence or face affirmative defenses such as contributory negligence and the fellow servant rule. *Pleasant v. Johnson*, 312 N.C. 710, 325 S.E.2d 244. In return the Act limits the amount of recovery available for work-related injuries and removes the employee's right to pursue potentially larger damages awards in civil actions. Id. at 712, 325 S.E.2d at 246–47 (citing 1 A. Larson, The Law of Workmen's Compensation § 2.20 (1984)). "[W]hile the employer assumes a new liability without fault he is relieved of the prospect of large damage verdicts." 2A A. Larson, The Law of Workmen's Compensation § 65.11 (1989) (hereinafter "Larson"). Notwithstanding these important trade-offs, the legislature did not intend to relieve employers of civil liability for intentional torts which result in injury or death to employees. In such cases the injury or death is considered to be both by accident, for which the employee or personal representative may pursue a compensation claim under the Act, and the result of an intentional tort, for which a civil action against the employer may be maintained. See *Pleasant v. Johnson*, 312 N.C. 710, 325 S.E.2d 244, and cases cited therein.

In *Pleasant*, which involved co-employee liability for recklessly operating a motor vehicle, we concluded that "injury to another resulting from willful, wanton and reckless negligence should also be treated as an intentional injury for purposes of our Workers' Compensation Act." 312 N.C. at 715, 325 S.E.2d at 248. The *Pleasant* Court expressly refused to consider whether the same rationale would apply to employer misconduct. Id. at 717, 325 S.E.2d at 250. Nonetheless, *Pleasant* equated willful, wanton and reckless misconduct with intentional injury for Workers' Compensation purposes.

The plaintiff in *Barrino v. Radiator Specialty Co.*, 315 N.C. 500, 340 S.E.2d 295 (1986), urged us to extend the Pleasant rationale to injuries caused by an employer's willful and wanton misconduct. The plaintiff, administrator of the estate of the deceased employee, alleged in part that the decedent died as a result of severe burns and other injuries caused by an explosion and fire in the employer's plant. On the employer's motion for summary judgment, the plaintiff's forecast of evidence, which included the allegations of the complaint, tended to show as follows: the employer utilized ignitable concentrations of flammable gasses and volatile flammable liquids at its plant, violated OSHANC regulations in the use of these substances, covered meters and turned off alarms designed to detect and warn of dangerous levels of explosive gasses and vapors — all of which resulted in the explosion and fire which caused the employee's death.

A majority of this Court in Barrino refused to extend the Pleasant rationale to employer conduct, but only two of the four majority justices expressed the view that the plaintiff's injuries were solely by accident and that the remedies provided by the Act were exclusive. These two justices relied in part on *Freeman v. SCM Corporation*, 311 N.C. 294, 316 S.E.2d 81 (1984), a per curiam opinion which concluded that a complaint alleging injuries caused by the willful and wanton negligence of an employer should be dismissed for lack of subject matter jurisdiction under Rule 12(b)(1) of the North Carolina Rules of Civil Procedure because exclusive jurisdiction rested under the Workers' Compensation Act with the Industrial Commission.

The other two justices in the Barrino majority concurred on the ground that the plaintiff, having accepted workers' compensation benefits, was thereby barred from bringing a civil suit. *Barrino*, 315 N.C. at 514–15, 340 S.E.2d at 304 (Billings, J., concurring).

The three remaining justices dissented on the ground that the plaintiff's forecast of evidence was sufficient to raise a genuine issue of material fact as to whether the defendant-employer's conduct "embodies a degree of culpability beyond negligence" so as to allow the plaintiff to maintain a civil action. Id. at 521, 340 S.E.2d at 307 (Martin, J., dissenting). Believing the plaintiff's forecast of evidence was sufficient to survive summary judgment on the question of whether the employer was guilty of an intentional tort, the *Barrino* dissenters said:

> As Prosser states: "Intent is broader than a desire to bring about physical results. It must extend not only to those consequences which are desired, but also to those which the actor believes are substantially certain to follow from

what he does." W. Prosser, Handbook of the Law of Torts § 8 (4th ed. 1971). Accord Restatement (Second) of Torts § 8A and comment b (1965). The death of Lora Ann Barrino [the employee] . . . was, at the very least, "substantially certain" to occur given defendants' deliberate failure to observe even basic safety laws. Id. at 518, 340 S.E.2d at 305 (Martin, J., dissenting). As discussed in a subsequent portion of this opinion, the dissenters also concluded that the plaintiff was not put to an election of remedies. They thus would have allowed the plaintiff's common law intentional tort claim to proceed to trial on the theory that the defendant intentionally engaged in conduct knowing it was substantially certain to cause serious injury or death. They would also have allowed the plaintiff to pursue both a workers' compensation claim and a civil action.

Today we adopt the views of the *Barrino* dissent. We hold that when an employer intentionally engages in misconduct knowing it is substantially certain to cause serious injury or death to employees and an employee is injured or killed by that misconduct, that employee, or the personal representative of the estate in case of death, may pursue a civil action against the employer. Such misconduct is tantamount to an intentional tort, and civil actions based thereon are not barred by the exclusivity provisions of the Act. Because, as also discussed in a subsequent portion of this opinion, the injury or death caused by such misconduct is nonetheless the result of an accident under the Act, workers' compensation claims may also be pursued. There may, however, only be one recovery. We believe this holding conforms with general legal principles and is true to the legislative intent when considered in light of the Act's underlying purposes.

Our holding is consistent with general concepts of tort liability outside the workers' compensation context. The gradations of tortious conduct can best be understood as a continuum. The most aggravated conduct is where the actor actually intends the probable consequences of his conduct. One who intentionally engages in conduct knowing that particular results are substantially certain to follow also intends the results for purposes of tort liability. Restatement (Second) of Torts § 8A and comment b (1965) (hereinafter "Rest. 2d of Torts"). "[I]ntent is broader than a desire to bring about physical results. It extends not only to those consequences which are desired, but also to those which the actor believes are substantially certain to follow from what the actor does." W. Keeton, D. Dobbs, R. Keeton, & D. Owen, Prosser and Keeton on Torts § 8, at 35 (5th ed. 1984) (hereinafter "Prosser"). This is the doctrine of "constructive intent." "As the probability that a [certain] consequence will follow decreases, and becomes less than substantially certain, the actor's conduct loses the character of intent, and becomes mere recklessness. . . . As the probability decreases further, and amounts only to a risk that the result will follow, it becomes ordinary negligence." Rest. 2d of Torts § 8A, comment b.

Prosser discusses the tortious conduct continuum:

> Lying between intent to do harm, which . . . includes proceeding with knowledge that the harm is substantially certain to occur, and the mere unreasonable risk of harm to another involved in ordinary negligence, there is a penumbra of what has been called "quasi-intent." To this area, the words "willful," "wanton," or "reckless," are customarily applied; and sometimes, in a single sentence, all three.

Prosser § 34, at 212 (footnotes omitted).

In North Carolina we follow, applying our own terminology, the basic rules discussed in the Restatement and Prosser. We have recognized the doctrine of "constructive intent" and have generally applied it where willful and wanton conduct is present. For a full, scholarly discussion of this doctrine, see *Pleasant*, 312 N.C. 710, 325 S.E.2d 244. This discussion in *Pleasant* makes clear that an actual intent to cause injury is not a necessary element of an intentional tort generally, nor is it required for intentional tort claims based on work-related injuries.

Though the reasons in *Pleasant* for holding co-employees civilly liable for injuries caused by willful and wanton misconduct are sound, it is also in keeping with the statutory workers' compensation trade-offs to require that civil actions against employers be grounded on more aggravated conduct than actions against co-employees. Co-employees do not finance or otherwise directly participate in workers' compensation programs; employers, on the other hand, do. N.C.G.S. § 97-93 (1985). This distinction alone justifies the higher "substantial certainty" threshold for civil recovery against employers.

The substantial certainty standard satisfies the Act's purposes of providing trade-offs to competing interests and balancing these interests, while serving as a deterrent to intentional wrongdoing and promoting safety in the workplace. N.C.G.S. § 95-126(b)(2) (1985).

Other jurisdictions which have considered how egregious employer misconduct must be in order to justify a worker's civil recovery against the employer extraneous to workers' compensation statutes have reached different results. Some require that the employer actually intend to harm the worker, as in a classic assault and battery suit. *See, e.g., Griffin v. George's, Inc.*, 267 Ark. 91, 589 S.W.2d 24 (1979); see generally 2A Larson § 68.13 and cases cited therein. Others require the employer's misconduct to be willful and wanton. *See, e.g., Mandolidis v. Elkins Industries, Inc.*, 161 W.Va. 695, 246 S.E.2d 907 (1978). Still others require intentional conduct which the employer knows is "substantially certain" to cause injury or death. *Bazley v. Tortorich*, 397 So. 2d 475 (La. 1981); *Beauchamp v. Dow Chemical Co.*, 427 Mich. 1, 398 N.W.2d 882 (1986); *Jones v. VIP Development Co.*, 15 Ohio St.3d 90, 472 N.E.2d 1046 (1984); *Blankenship v. Cincinnati Milacron Chemicals, Inc.*, 69 Ohio St.2d 608, 433 N.E.2d 572 (1982); *VerBouwens v. Hamm Wood Products*, 334 N.W.2d 874 (S.D.1983).

It is true that some of the cases adopting the willful and wanton misconduct or substantial certainty standard have been modified by statute. Legislation enacted in Michigan modified the decision in *Beauchamp v. Dow Chemical Co.*, 427 Mich. 1, 398 N.W.2d 882. The legislation provides:

> The only exception [to the exclusivity of workers' compensation] is an intentional tort. An intentional tort shall exist only when an employee is injured as a result of a deliberate act of the employer and the employer specifically intended an injury. An employer shall be deemed to have intended to injure if the employer has actual knowledge that an injury was certain to occur and willfully disregarded that knowledge. Mich. Comp. Laws § 418.131 (Supp. 1990) (emphasis added).

Effective in 1986, the Ohio legislature amended its workers' compensation law in an apparent response to cases such as *Blankenship v. Cincinnati Milacron Chemicals, Inc.*, 69 Ohio St. 2d 608, 433 N.E.2d 572, and *Jones v. VIP Development Co.*, 15 Ohio St.3d 90, 472 N.E.2d 1046. The Ohio statutory amendments provide for civil recovery outside workers' compensation for acts "committed with the intent to injure another or committed with the belief that the injury is substantially certain to occur." 41 Ohio Rev. Code Ann. § 4121.80 (1990). Although the Ohio amendments equate substantial certainty with the "deliberate intent to cause an employee to suffer injury . . . or death," *id.*, they also treat certain unsafe acts as if they were done with the intent to injure another.

While generally moving away from the willful and wanton misconduct standard enunciated in *Mandolidis v. Elkins Industries, Inc.*, 161 W. Va. 695, 246 S.E.2d 907, and toward a standard requiring "deliberate intention to injure," W.Va.Code § 23-4-2 (1983), the West Virginia legislature has set out an important exception. The exception allows plaintiffs to recover outside workers' compensation where the employer is aware that there is a high degree of risk of serious harm, and that the conditions creating the risk violate specific safety statutes. *Id.*

On the basis of these kinds of statutory modifications, Rowland Utility urges us to conclude that the willful and wanton misconduct and substantial certainty standards should be rejected as inconsistent with the legislative purpose of North Carolina's Workers' Compensation Act. We do not read the statutory modifications of judicial decisions in other jurisdictions to repudiate the standards adopted in those decisions. The statutory modifications seem more to narrow the application of, rather than to abolish, these standards. The Michigan legislature provided that "an employer shall be deemed to have intended to injure if the employer had actual knowledge that an injury was certain to occur and willfully disregarded that knowledge." Mich.Comp.Laws § 418.131 (Supp. 1990). This amounts only to a rejection of the substantiality aspect of the substantial certainty standard. The Ohio and West Virginia legislatures essentially redefined what employer conduct will allow tort recovery. These legislative modifications confirm, rather than reject, the proposition that, in those states, actual intent to injure is not required in order for an employer to be civilly liable outside workers' compensation statutes.

At least two other states, Louisiana and South Dakota, continue to apply the substantial certainty standard adopted by their judiciaries, *Bazley v. Tortorich*, 397 So. 2d 475 (La.); *VerBouwens v. Hamm Wood Products*, 334 N.W.2d 874 (S.D.), without legislative modification.

Thus, both courts and legislatures in a fair number of other jurisdictions have rejected the proposition that actual intent to harm is required for an employer's conduct to be actionable in tort and not protected by the exclusivity provisions of workers' compensation. Our adoption of the substantial certainty standard does the same.

B.

We now apply the substantial certainty standard to the facts. We emphasize that in a summary judgment proceeding, the forecast of evidence and all reasonable inferences must be taken in the light most favorable to the non-moving party. *Wilkes County Vocational Workshop v. United Sleep*, 321 N.C. 735, 365 S.E.2d 292 (1988).

A corporation can act only through its agents, which include its corporate officers. *Raper v. McCrory-McLellan Corp.*, 259 N.C. 199, 130 S.E.2d 281 (1963). For purposes of this appeal plaintiff has forecast sufficient evidence that at all relevant times Morris Rowland as chief executive officer was exercising corporate authority in directing the trenching operations. We thus examine Morris Rowland's conduct and attribute it to his principal, Rowland Utility. If plaintiff's forecast of evidence is sufficient to show that there is a genuine issue of material fact as to whether Morris Rowland's conduct satisfies the substantial certainty standard, then plaintiff is entitled to take her case against Rowland Utility to trial.

We conclude that plaintiff's forecast of evidence is sufficient to raise such a material issue of fact against Rowland Utility. Agronomist James Rees, offered as an expert in soil and environmental analysis, submitted an affidavit on the status of the soil where the cave-in occurred. He stated:

> Based on my review of the physical conditions existent at the time of the trench collapse, as nearly as they can be determined, and on the nature and physical conditions of the surface and subsurface materials, my conclusion is that the trench as constructed by Morris Rowland Utility, Inc. consisting of sheer, vertical walls approximately fourteen feet deep, had an exceedingly high probability of failure, and the trench was substantially certain to fail. From this evidence, a reasonable juror could determine that upon placing a man in this trench serious injury or death as a result of a cave-in was a substantial certainty rather than an unforeseeable event, mere possibility, or even substantial probability.

There is also evidence to indicate that Morris Rowland knew of this substantial certainty. Neither we, nor later the jury, need accept his characterization of his state of mind at face value. Other evidence is available from which his state of mind can be inferred. See, e.g., *Waste Management of Carolinas, Inc. v. Peerless*, 315 N.C. 688, 700 n.6, 340 S.E.2d 374, 383 n.6 (1986) (recurrent evidence of "accidental" toxic emissions allows inference that they were intentional). There is evidence that Morris Rowland was capable of discerning extremely hazardous ditches. His career had been excavating different kinds of soil. He knew the attendant risks. He had been cited at least four times in six and one-half years immediately preceding this incident for violating multiple safety regulations governing trenching procedures. He was aware of safety regulations designed to protect trench diggers from serious injury or death. He knew he was not following these regulations in digging the trench in question.

Davidson & Jones foreman Lynn Craig testified that the trench at point of collapse was "unsafe" and that he would "never put a man in it" without a trench box or other precautions. Craig was an experienced construction worker with knowledge about soil composition and the dangers associated with deep-ditch trenching. His emphatic indication that the trench was unsafe could lead reasonable jurors to conclude that Morris Rowland, who was also at the trench and equally capable of observing its dangerous tendencies, shared Craig's knowledge and disregarded the substantial certainty of a cave-in resulting in serious injury or death. Rowland's attempts to rush Greene the previous day and his commencement of hasty, unsafe procedures, including his failure to use the available trench box, would offer the jury a motive for his conduct-swift completion of the project, whatever the risk.

Morris Rowland's knowledge and prior disregard of dangers associated with trenching; his presence at the site and opportunity to observe the hazards; his direction to proceed without the required safety procedures; Craig's experienced opinion that the trench was unsafe; and Rees' scientific soil analysis converge to make plaintiff's evidentiary forecast sufficient to survive Rowland Utility's motion for summary judgment.

We reject Rowland Utility's reasons for concluding to the contrary. Rowland Utility contends that no reasonable business person would knowingly engage in conduct that is substantially certain to cause a trench cave-in because of the significant delay in work and additional cost that such an event would cause. This argument is more properly directed toward the jury at trial rather than to the Court on summary judgment.

At least one court has indicated that a trench cave-in may satisfy the substantial certainty standard. In *Beauchamp v. Dow Chemical Co.*, 427 Mich. 1, 398 N.W.2d 882, the Michigan Supreme Court discussed the trench cave-in case of *Serna v. Statewide Contractors*, 6 Ariz. App. 12, 429 P.2d 504 (1967). The Beauchamp Court indicated that the failure to observe trenching safety procedures and the resulting cave-in discussed in *Serna* would likely have presented a valid claim had the *Serna* court applied the substantial certainty standard. Beauchamp, 427 Mich. at 23, 398 N.W.2d at 892.

Rowland Utility also argues that its placing Alan Fry, son of project supervisor Elmer Fry, into the trench with the acquiescence of Elmer Fry is inconsistent with Rowland Utility's knowledge that a cave-in was a substantial certainty. The argument is that Elmer Fry would never have agreed to put his son in the trench had he appreciated the danger and that since Elmer Fry did not appreciate the danger, neither did Morris Rowland. Again, this is an argument more properly directed to the jury, which on all the evidence can determine whether the state of Morris Rowland's knowledge and appreciation of the risk was more like Elmer Fry's on the one hand or Lynn Craig's on the other.

C.

Plaintiff next asks us to hold that the forecast of evidence is sufficient to survive Morris Rowland's motion for summary judgment in his individual capacity. She contends that the forecast of evidence at least raises a genuine issue of material fact as to whether Morris Rowland was acting as her decedent's co-employee and is, therefore, liable under Pleasant for willful and wanton misconduct. Morris Rowland contends that since the forecast of evidence shows without contradiction that he is president and sole shareholder of Rowland Utility, he cannot be held liable individually as a co-employee of the decedent. He must, rather, be treated as the "alter ego" of the corporation itself.

Since the evidentiary forecast shows that Morris Rowland was at all material times the president and sole shareholder of Rowland Utility, and was acting in furtherance of corporate business, we conclude that any individual liability on his part must be based on the same standard as that applied to the corporation.

. . . .

D.

Although, for the reasons stated, plaintiff may continue to pursue her civil action, we also conclude she is not barred from simultaneously pursuing her workers' compensation claim because the injury to her intestate was the result of an "accident" as that term is used in the Act. A claimant may, but is not required to, elect between these remedies but, in any event, is entitled to but one recovery.

"Accident" under the Act means "(1) an unlooked for and untoward event which is not expected or designed by the injured employee; (2) a result produced by a fortuitous cause." *Harding v. Thomas & Howard Co.*, 256 N.C. 427, 428, 124 S.E.2d 109, 110–11 (1962); see *Rhinehart v. Market*, 271 N.C. 586, 157 S.E.2d 1 (1967). Because employees do not expect to suffer intentional torts committed against them while on the job, such injuries are "unlooked for and untoward events . . . not expected or designed by the injured employee," *Harding*, 256 N.C. at 428, 124 S.E.2d at 110–11. The employee may treat these injuries as accidental and accept workers' compensation benefits. See *Pleasant*, 312 N.C. 710, 325 S.E.2d 244, and cases cited therein; *Warner v. Leder*, 234 N.C. 727, 69 S.E.2d 6 (1952); *Andrews v. Peters*, 55 N.C. App. 124, 284 S.E.2d 748 (1981), *disc. rev. denied*, 305 N.C. 395, 290 S.E.2d 364 (1982) (cited with approval in *Pleasant*).

While plaintiff has pursued her civil suit, she has received no benefits for accidental injury under the Act. Thus, there is not the election of remedies problem presented in *Barrino*. Nonetheless, insofar as *Barrino*; *Wesley v. Lea*, 252 N.C. 540, 114 S.E.2d 350 (1960); and *Warner v. Leder*, 234 N.C. 727, 69 S.E.2d 6 (1952), [footnote omitted can be read to hold that simultaneous pursuit of civil and workers' compensation remedies are inherently inconsistent and an election of remedies is required, these cases are overruled.

From the standpoint of the injured party, an injury intentionally inflicted by another can nonetheless at the same time be an "unlooked for and untoward event . . . not expected or designed by the injured employee." *Harding*, 256 N.C. at 428, 124 S.E.2d at 110. It is, therefore, not inherently inconsistent to assert that an injury caused by the same conduct was both the result of an accident, giving rise to the remedies provided by the Act, and an intentional tort, making the exclusivity provision of the Act unavailable to bar a civil action.

Allowing an injured worker to pursue both avenues to relief does not run afoul of the goal of the election doctrine, which is to prevent double redress of a single wrong. *Smith v. Oil Corp.*, 239 N.C. 360, 79 S.E.2d 880 (1954). Although the worker may pursue both statutory and common law remedies, the worker ultimately is entitled to only one recovery. Double recovery should be avoided by requiring the claimant who recovers civilly against his employer to reimburse the workers' compensation carrier to the extent the carrier paid workers' compensation benefits, or by permitting the carrier to become subrogated to the claimant's civil claim to the extent of benefits paid.

. . . .

III.

We next decide whether plaintiff may proceed to trial against Davidson & Jones and Pinnacle One on her claims that they breached nondelegable duties of safety owed to plaintiff's decedent. We hold plaintiff may take her case against Davidson & Jones to trial, but summary judgment was properly allowed on her claim against Pinnacle One.

A.

Generally, one who employs an independent contractor is not liable for the independent contractor's negligence unless the employer retains the right to control the manner in which the contractor performs his work. *Mack v. Marshall Field & Co.*, 218 N.C. 697, 12 S.E.2d 235 (1940). Plaintiff can recover neither from Davidson & Jones nor from Pinnacle One unless the circumstances surrounding the trench cave-in place her claim within an exception to this general rule.

Plaintiff contends her action falls within such an exception. She argues that Davidson & Jones and Pinnacle One breached nondelegable duties of safety owed to decedent because the trenching project was an "inherently dangerous activity" and these defendants failed to take adequate measures to correct Rowland Utility's poor safety practices.

. . . .

One who employs an independent contractor to perform an inherently dangerous activity may not delegate to the independent contractor the duty to provide for the safety of others: "The liability of the employer rests upon the ground that mischievious [sic] consequences will arise from the work to be done unless precautionary measures are adopted, and the duty to see that these precautionary measures are adopted rests upon the employer, and he cannot escape liability by entrusting this duty to another as an 'independent contractor' to perform." *Thomas v. Lumber Co.*, 153 N.C., 351, 69 S.E., 275. *Evans*, 220 N.C. at 259, 17 S.E.2d at 128–129. The party that employs the independent contractor has a continuing responsibility to ensure that adequate safety precautions are taken. *Dockery v. World of Mirth Shows, Inc.*, 264 N.C. 406, 142 S.E.2d 29.

The rule imposing liability on one who employs an independent contractor applies "whether [the activity] involves an appreciable and foreseeable danger to the workers employed or to the public generally." *Evans*, 220 N.C. at 260, 17 S.E.2d at 129. The employer's liability for breach of this duty "is direct and not derivative since public policy fixes him with a nondelegable duty to see that the precautions are taken." *Dockery*, 264 N.C. at 410, 142 S.E.2d at 32; *Evans*, 220 N.C. at 259, 17 S.E.2d at 129.

Imposition of this nondelegable duty of safety reflects "the policy judgment that certain obligations are of such importance that employers should not be able to escape liability merely by hiring others to perform them." *Daye*, § 23.31, at 393 (citing *Royal v. Dodd*, 177 N.C. 206, 209–11, 98 S.E. 599, 600–02 (1919)). By holding both an employer and its independent contractor responsible for injuries that may result from inherently dangerous activities, there is a greater likelihood that the safety precautions necessary to substantially eliminate the danger will be followed.

. . . .

In determining whether the trenching process which killed Thomas Sprouse was inherently dangerous, the focus is not on some abstract activity called "trenching." The focus is on the particular trench being dug and the pertinent circumstances surrounding the digging. It must be shown that because of these circumstances, the digging of th e trench itself presents "a recognizable and substantial danger inherent in the work, as distinguished from a danger collaterally created by the independent negligence of the contractor." *Evans*, 220 N.C. at 259, 17 S.E.2d at 128.

We conclude the forecast of evidence is sufficient to survive summary judgment on the question of whether the trenching in this case was "inherently dangerous."

. . . .

B.

If the jury finds that the trenching in question here was or had become at the time of the cave-in an inherently dangerous activity, then Davidson & Jones, if it knew of the circumstances creating the danger, cannot escape liability by merely relying on the legal ground that Rowland Utility was an independent contractor. Rather, it would have a nondelegable duty to exercise due care to see that plaintiff's intestate was provided a safe place in which to work and proper safeguards against any dangers as might be incident to the work. *Greer v. Construction Co.*, 190 N.C. 632, 130 S.E. 739; cf. *Brown v. Texas Co.*, 237 N.C. 738, 76 S.E.2d 45. If Davidson & Jones did not exercise such care to ensure safety, it is liable.

Plaintiff's forecast of evidence on the issue of Davidson & Jones' negligence is sufficient to survive summary judgment. This forecast tends to show as follows: Davidson & Jones knew on Saturday, 3 August, that the trench in which plaintiff was working was unsafe in that it was not being properly sloped, shored, or braced, and that a trench box was not being used. It knew these precautions were required by OSHANC for the safety of the workers. Craig had asked Morris Rowland to procure a trench box for the Davidson & Jones crew. Knowing of the dangers associated with the Rowland Utility ditch, Davidson & Jones did not itself act to ameliorate the dangers.

. . . .

C.

Plaintiff also seeks to hold Pinnacle One liable on a theory of breach of a nondelegable duty to her intestate to provide him with a safe working environment. Pinnacle One was the developer on this project, in which capacity it hired Davidson & Jones as general contractor. We need not decide whether Pinnacle One, like Davidson & Jones, owed a nondelegable duty to plaintiff's intestate. Assuming that it did, we find nothing in the forecast of evidence to show that such a duty was breached by Pinnacle One. There is nothing in the forecast indicating that Pinnacle One or any of its representatives knew or should have known that Davidson & Jones had hired Rowland Utility, much less of the trenching activity in which plaintiff's intestate was engaged or the dangerous propensities of the particular trench in question. There is no forecast that Pinnacle One had any knowledge or expertise regarding safety practices in the construction industry generally or in trenching particularly. So far as the forecast of evidence shows, Pinnacle One justifiably relied entirely on the expertise of its general contractor Davidson & Jones.

IV.

[The court here concludes that the general contractor Davidson & Jones could not be held liable for negligently selecting and retaining Rowland Utility as its subcontractor. The evidence showed that because of its past direct experience with Rowland Utility, Davidson & Jones was justified in not investigating Rowland Utility's safety record.]

V.

In conclusion, and for the reasons given, we reverse the Court of Appeals' decision insofar as it affirms summary judgments in favor of Rowland Utility and Morris Rowland, and in favor of Davidson & Jones on plaintiff's claim for breach of nondelegable duty of safety, and we remand for further proceedings against these defendants consistent with our opinion. We affirm the Court of Appeals' decision insofar as it allows summary judgments in favor of Pinnacle One, and in favor of Davidson & Jones on the negligent hiring and retention claims.

The result is

Affirmed in Part; Reversed in Part; Remanded.

MITCHELL, JUSTICE, concurring in part and dissenting in part. . . .

An activity is either inherently dangerous or it is not. If an activity may be conducted in an entirely safe manner when ordinary safety precautions are taken but may be hazardous if performed in a negligent manner, it is not an "inherently dangerous" activity in my view. See Black's Law Dictionary 782 (6th ed. 1990). Here, the record reveals and the majority concedes that the trenching activity leading to the cave-in which killed the plaintiff's decedent could have been performed safely if ordinary safety precautions, such as sloping the shoulders of the trench or the use of a trench box, had been employed. Therefore, it would seem to follow ipso facto that the trenching was not inherently dangerous. For that reason, I dissent from the majority's conclusion that this claim by the plaintiff may be found to fall within an exception to the general rule that an employer is not liable for its independent contractor's negligence where, as here, it has not retained the right to control the manner in which the work undertaken is to be performed. I would affirm the holding of the Court of Appeals that the trial court properly entered summary judgment for the defendant Davidson & Jones, Inc. with regard to this claim for relief.

Finally, for reasons fully set forth in the thoughtful opinion of Judge Eagles (Judge Parker concurring) in the Court of Appeals, I dissent from Part II of the opinion of the majority of this Court. *Woodson v. Rowland*, 92 N.C. App. 38, 40–42, 373 S.E.2d 674, 675–77 (1988). In Part II, the majority holds that the exclusivity provision of the North Carolina Workers' Compensation Act, N.C.G.S. § 97–10.1, does not apply here and that the plaintiff may recover in a civil action against the defendants Morris Rowland and Morris Rowland Utility, Inc. for conduct substantially certain to cause injury. Although I concede that the majority's holding represents reasonable and perhaps desirable social policy, I must agree with the Court of Appeals that to give an employee, in addition to the rights available under our Workers' Compensation Act, a right to bring a civil action "against his employer, even for gross, willful and wanton negligence, would skew the balance of interests inherent in [the] . . . Act. Changes in the Act's delicate balance of interests is more properly a legislative prerogative than a judicial function." *Id.* at 42, 373 S.E.2d at 677. See generally *Pleasant v. Johnson*, 312 N.C. 710, 325 S.E.2d 244 (1985) (describing the Act's balance of interests between employers and employees). Therefore, I would affirm the holding of the Court of Appeals that the trial court properly entered summary judgment for the defendants Morris Rowland and Morris Rowland Utility, Inc.

MEYER, J., joins in this concurring and dissenting opinion.

PROBLEMS

(1) Do you agree with the *Woodson* court that the kind of behavior engaged in by the defendants should subject them to tort liability? Or does this decision represent an unfortunate and misguided erosion of the principle of workers' compensation exclusivity?

(2) Under the "substantially certain" test articulated in *Woodson*, isn't the outcome of that case incorrect? That is, was it really "substantially certain" that death or serious injury would occur? Or was there not a real possibility, or even a likelihood, that the cave-in would have occurred at a time when no one was in the trench, or that it would never have occurred at all?

(3) When any large project, such as a dam, is undertaken, it can be predicted statistically that a certain number of workers will be killed or seriously injured. Under *Woodson*, wouldn't the employer of any such large project be held to have intended those injuries and deaths?

SITZMAN v. SCHUMAKER

221 Mont. 304, 718 P.2d 657 (1986)

Harrison, Justice.

This is an appeal from a summary judgment of the District Court in the Seventh Judicial District of the State of Montana, in and for Prairie County. We reverse and remand for trial.

The plaintiff, James Sitzman, worked for the defendant, Jake Shumaker, performing general ranch labor. The two men did not get along. Shumaker often called Sitzman a "son-of-a-bitch" and "idiot." Sitzman did not respond to these names at first, but eventually began shouting back.

The day Sitzman was injured, he and Shumaker were working together. Shumaker asked Sitzman if the calf feeders were full. Sitzman responded by telling Shumaker that the first one was half full, the second about three-quarters full, and the third one was about two-thirds full. Shumaker exploded, saying "I believe you, you god damn idiot. Can't you just say 'yes' or 'no'?" Later in the morning, Shumaker asked Sitzman if he wanted to work on the tractor. Sitzman responded, "Yeah, sure, no problem. Let's go to work on it." Shumaker again exploded, saying, "you god damn son-of-a-bitch. Why can't you just say 'yes' or 'no'?" When Sitzman replied, "Don't call me an s.o.b.," Shumaker walked over to him and struck him several times in the face. Sitzman pushed Shumaker to the ground. Shumaker then picked up a four-foot length of two-inch pipe and held it over his head. Sitzman asked Shumaker not to hit him, and turned to walk away. Shumaker hit Sitzman on the back of the head and when Sitzman turned to protect himself, hit him on the front of the head, knocking him to the ground, unconscious. Sitzman suffered severe injuries, including a fractured skull. The extensive head injuries have altered the course of his life.

Sitzman applied for and was granted temporary total disability wage and medical benefits under the Workers' Compensation Act. He brought this action in the District Court to recover damages caused by Shumaker's attack. His wife, Barbara, brought an action for loss of consortium, society, support, comfort and companionship of her husband due to his injuries. Shumaker moved for summary judgment.

Judgment was granted in both actions for the stated reason that because of Sitzman's application for and receipt of Workers' Compensation benefits, their remedies were exclusive to the Workers' Compensation Act. Upon stipulation of the parties, the Sitzmans' actions were consolidated for purpose of appeal.

The issue presented for review by Sitzmans is whether receipt of Workers' Compensation benefits by them results in an election pursuant to § 39-71-411, MCA, thereby barring them from a common law tort action against employer Shumaker.

Summary judgment is proper only when there is no genuine issue of material fact and the movant is entitled to prevail as a matter of law. *Cereck v. Albertson's* (1981), 195 Mont. 409, 411, 637 P.2d 509, 510. The lower court, in granting summary judgment, reasoned that by filing for benefits under the Workers' Compensation Act "Sitzman became subject to the provision of the Act and more specifically § 39-71-411, MCA."

The exclusivity clause, found in § 39-71-411, MCA, provides in pertinent part: For all employments covered under the Workers' Compensation Act or for which an election has been made for coverage under this chapter, the provisions of this chapter are exclusive. . . .

The election referred to in § 39-71-411, MCA, however, is the election to come under the Act made by an employer not specifically covered by the Act pursuant to § 39-71-401(2), MCA. It has no reference to an employee seeking to recover for injuries suffered as a result of an assault and battery committed personally by the employer upon the employee who also may have filed for and received Workers' Compensation benefits.

Ordinarily, when an employee is injured in the work place due to negligence or accident, his remedy is exclusive to the Workers' Compensation Act. *Noonan v. Spring Creek Forest Products* (Mont. 1985), 700 P.2d 623, 625, 42 St. Rep. 759, 762. Common law damages are not available under § 39-71-411, MCA, for injuries negligently or accidentally inflicted by an employer. Negligence claims should be dismissed on this ground. Such are not the facts in this case — Sitzman's injuries are not the result of negligence or accident.

The question then becomes whether there is a permissible exception under § 39-71-411, MCA, for the tort inflicted by Shumaker upon Sitzman.

This Court has said: The "intentional harm" which removes an employer from the protection of the exclusivity clause of the Workers' Compensation Act is such harm as is maliciously and specifically directed at an employee . . . out of which such specific intentional harm the employee receives injuries as a proximate result. *Great Western Sugar v. District Court* (1980), 188 Mont. 1, 7, 610 P.2d 717, 720. There is evidence that Sitzman suffered intentional harm maliciously and specifically directed at him by Shumaker. It is not reasonable to suppose the legislature intended to give statutory protection in the form of immunity from suit to an employer who hits his employee in the head with a pipe while the employee is carrying out his employment duties.

The egregiousness of these circumstances removes the exclusivity bar for an employee. In a manner similar to injury by a fellow employee, § 39-71-413, MCA, where the legislature provided for coverage from an intentional injury, under the facts of this case, we provide for such coverage where the injury is by the employer.

There are sound policy reasons for reaching this decision. The purpose of the Workers' Compensation Act is to protect both the employer and the employee by incorporating a quid pro quo for negligent acts by the employer. The employer is given immunity from suit by an employee who is injured on the job in return for relinquishing his common law defenses. The employee is assured of compensation for his injuries, but foregoes legal recourse against his employer. To allow an employer to personally commit an assault and battery upon an employee and hide behind the exclusivity clause of the Workers' Compensation Act is to disregard the purpose of the Act. Other employers would have to pay for his protection. In effect, he would have bought the right to hit his employees. That is not a quid pro quo. The law does not allow a wrongdoer to benefit from his wrongs.

Consequently we hold that a narrow exception to the exclusiveness of the compensation remedy exists where the employer personally commits an assault and battery upon an employee.

The summary judgment is reversed and the case is remanded for trial consistent with the findings of this Court.

TURNAGE, C.J., and MORRISON, WEBER, SHEEHY, GULBRANDSON and HUNT, JJ., concur.

JETT v. DUNLAP
179 Conn. 215, 425 A.2d 1263 (1979)

LOISELLE, ASSOCIATE JUSTICE.

The plaintiff instituted this action against his work supervisor, Lester F. Dunlap, and their employer, Farrel Corporation, to recover damages in common-law tort for an alleged battery which occurred at the workplace.

The plaintiff alleged that Dunlap accused him in a profane and insulting manner of being away from his machine. When he responded to Dunlap in a similar manner, Dunlap struck him, pushing him backwards and knocking off his hat. The plaintiff sued Dunlap and the Farrel Corporation, under a theory of respondeat superior, for the ensuing depression, disruption of his home life and humiliation among his fellow employees who harassed him for his failure to strike back.

. . . .

There is a distinction between an assault directly committed or authorized by the employer and an assault committed by a supervisory employee. Moreover there are strong arguments against entertaining a common-law tort action against an employer for a supervisory employee's intentional assault. The first is that to allow such suits would mean that "in all assault cases by one co-employee on another, of which there are hundreds, [the] claimant would have only to show that the assailant was one notch higher on the totem-pole than the victim, and the compensation act would go out the window. So, in a large factory, with layer upon layer of foremen, supervisors, managers, executives and officers, the exclusiveness of compensation would no longer depend on whether the assault was merely another work-connected quarrel, but would turn on the relative rank of the participants — a consideration which has no bearing on work-connection at all." 2A Larson, op. cit. § 68.21, p. 13-13. Furthermore, the righteous indignation one feels when one employee deliberately injures another is inadequate justification for awarding a common-law tort remedy against an innocent employer.

The correct distinction to be drawn in this case is between a supervisory employee and a person who can be characterized as the alter ego of the corporation. If the assailant is of such rank in the corporation that he may be deemed the alter ego of the corporation under the standards governing disregard of the corporate entity, then attribution of corporate responsibility for the actor's conduct is appropriate. It is inappropriate where the actor is merely a foreman or supervisor. 2A Larson, op. cit. §§ 68.21–68.22. Courts in other jurisdictions have adopted this distinction. *Heskett v. Fisher Laundry & Cleaners Co., Inc.*, 217 Ark. 350, 355–56, 230 S.W.2d 28 (1950); *Boek v. Wong Hing*, 180 Minn. 470, 471–72, 231 N.W. 233 (1930); *Thompson v. Jones Construction Co.*, 199 S.C. 304, 310, 19 S.E.2d 226 (1942); *Garcia v. Gusmack Restaurant Corporation*, 150 N.Y.S.2d 232, 234 (City Ct. N.Y., 1954). The distinction is based on identification, not agency. If the assailant can be identified as the alter ego of the corporation, or the corporation has directed or authorized the assault, then the corporation may be liable in common-law tort; if the assailant is only another employee who cannot be so identified, then the strict liability remedies provided by the Workmen's Compensation Act are exclusive and cannot be supplemented with common-law damages.

The pleadings do not indicate that the employer directed or authorized the assault or that the assailant was of such a status in the defendant's organization as to be characterized as the alter ego of the corporation. The plaintiff, however, did plead that the acts of the supervisor were subsequently "condoned" by the employer. Although we assume this pleading to be true, such condoning is not an intentional tort on the part of the employer and does not relate back to make it such. In *Bakker v. Baza'r, Inc.*, 275 Or. 245, 253–54, 551 P.2d 1269 (1976), it was held that Oregon's statutory exception to the Workmen's Compensation Act, which permits a worker to sue the employer in common-law tort for an intentional injury, did not encompass an employer's ratification of another employee's intentional tort because the plaintiff's injury, if any, did not result from the subsequent ratification but from the tortious act. Therefore, when we consider the case as pleaded, the trial court's judgment for the employer upon the demurrer was proper.

The plaintiff next claims that if his remedies under the Workmen's Compensation Act are exclusive, then the act violates the federal constitutional guarantee of equal protection under the fifth and fourteenth amendments, because, under § 31-284(a), the "wilful and serious misconduct of the injured employee" deprives him of his right to compensation, but the wilful and serious misconduct of the employer does not subject it to a penalty. This claim is inappropriate. There is no allegation that the plaintiff was denied statutory compensation as a result of wilful and serious misconduct, nor did the employer engage in wilful or serious misconduct by directing or authorizing Dunlap to strike the plaintiff. Where a fellow employee engages in wilful or serious misconduct resulting in personal injury or death to a plaintiff, which arises out of and in the course of a plaintiff's employment, then a plaintiff's remedy lies within the Workmen's Compensation Act. *Willis v. Taylor & Fenn Co.*, 137 Conn. 626, 79 A.2d 821 (1951). Where such wilful or serious misconduct is engaged in by an employer, as identified by the standard set forth today, then a plaintiff may pursue common-law remedies.

(The court next rejects the plaintiff's contention that since the workers' compensation statute does not afford "an adequate remedy" to the plaintiff, the common-law action is not replaced.)

There is no error.

In this opinion the other Judges concurred.

§ 21.02 NONPHYSICAL-INJURY TORTS

[1] Introduction

Whether nonphysical-injury torts, such as defamation, false imprisonment, and deceit, are barred by the exclusive-remedy provision usually depends on whether the essence of the damage for which a remedy is sought is nonphysical rather than physical. In some cases a second (and actionable) cause of action may arise, as when the employer deceives the employee about his or her legal rights or his or her physical condition under a compensable injury, or when a carrier or employer intentionally harrasses a compensation claimant. Retaliatory discharge for filing a compensation claim is now actionable in most states that have dealt with the subject.

[2] Fraud and Conspiracy

JOHNS-MANVILLE PRODUCTS CORPORATION v. CONTRA COSTA SUPERIOR COURT (RUDKIN)
27 Cal. 3d 465, 165 Cal. Rptr. 858, 612 P.2d 948 (1980)

Mosk, Justice.

Section 3600 of the Labor Code provides that an employer is liable for injuries to its employees arising out of and in the course of employment, and section 3601 declares that where the conditions of workers' compensation exist, the right to recover such compensation is the exclusive remedy against an employer for injury or death of an employee. The issue to be decided in this proceeding is whether an employee is barred by these provisions from prosecuting an action at law against his employer for the intentional torts of fraud and conspiracy in knowingly ordering the employee to work in an unsafe environment, concealing the risk from him, and, after the employee had contracted an industrial disease, deliberately failing to notify the state, the employee, or doctors retained to treat him, of the disease and its connection with the employment, thereby aggravating the consequences of the disease.

We conclude that while the workers' compensation law bars the employee's action at law for his initial injury, a cause of action may exist for aggravation of the disease because of the employer's fraudulent concealment of the condition and its cause.

Reba Rudkin, real party in interest (hereinafter plaintiff), brought an action against Johns-Manville Products Corporation, his employer for 29 years (defendant) and others, alleging as follows:

> Defendant is engaged in mining, milling, manufacturing, and packaging asbestos. Plaintiff worked in its Pittsburg, California, plant for 29 years beginning in February 1946, and he was continuously exposed to asbestos during that period. As a result of the exposure, he developed pneumonoconiosis, lung cancer, or other asbestos-related illnesses.

> The defendant corporation has known since 1924 that long exposure to asbestos or the ingestion of that substance is dangerous to health, yet it concealed this knowledge from plaintiff, and advised him that it was safe to work in close proximity to asbestos. It failed to provide him with adequate protective devices and did not operate the plant in accordance with state and federal regulations governing dust levels.

> In addition, the doctors retained by defendant to examine plaintiff were unqualified, and defendant did not provide them with adequate information regarding the risk of asbestos exposure. It failed to advise these doctors of the development of pulmonary disease in plaintiff or of the fact that the disease was the result of the working conditions at the plant, although it knew that his illness was caused by exposure to asbestos. Finally, defendant willfully failed to file a First Report of Occupational Injury or Illness with the State of California regarding plaintiff's injury, as required by law. Had this been done, and if the danger from asbestos had been revealed, plaintiff would have been protected. Each of these acts and omissions was done falsely and fraudulently by defendant, with intent to induce plaintiff to continue to work in a dangerous environment. Plaintiff was ignorant of the risks involved, and would not have continued to work in such an environment if he had known the facts.

In a separate cause of action plaintiff alleged that defendant knowingly conspired with others to perpetrate the acts set forth above.

The complaint sought compensatory and punitive damages, including compensation for the cost of medical care which plaintiff was required to obtain in order to treat his illness.

Defendant filed an answer alleging, inter alia, that the action was barred under section 3601. It requested the trial court to take judicial notice of an application filed by plaintiff seeking workers' compensation benefits for disability caused by "[e]xposure to asbestos." Defendant moved for judgment on the pleadings on the ground that section 3601 bars the action. The trial court denied the motion. In this proceeding for a writ of mandate, defendant seeks to set aside the trial court's order.

According to a brief filed on plaintiff's behalf, he died of lung cancer after the petition for writ of mandate was filed. The issues presented are not moot, however, since an action for personal injuries survives the death of the plaintiff. (Prob. Code, § 573.)

For purposes of reviewing the trial court's denial of defendant's motion, we must accept as true the allegations of plaintiff's complaint. (*Colberg, Inc. v. State of California* (1967) 67 Cal. 2d 408, 411–412, 62 Cal. Rptr. 401, 432 P.2d 3.)

The primary focus of the dispute between the parties centers upon the question whether section 4553 is intended to cover the intentional acts of employers which cause employee injuries. The section provides that "compensation otherwise recoverable shall be increased one-half where the employee is injured by reason of the serious and willful misconduct" of the employer, not to exceed $10,000. Defendant urges that the penalty imposed upon employers by this section is a substitute for a common law right of action against an employer whose intentional misconduct results in injury, while plaintiff argues that such misconduct is distinguishable from the "serious and willful misconduct," described in section 4553, and therefore his complaint alleging intentional acts by defendant is cognizable in an action at law.

Defendant relies upon both the legislative history of the Workers' Compensation Act and cases interpreting the words "serious and willful misconduct" in support of its position.

Prior to 1917, the law allowed an employee a choice of remedies if an injury was caused by an employer's gross negligence or willful misconduct. He could either claim workers' compensation benefits or maintain an action at law for damages. (Stats. 1913, ch. 176, § 12(b), pp. 283–284.) In that year, however, this provision was deleted and a new section added specifying a one-half increase in compensation in the event of serious and willful misconduct by the employer. (Stats. 1917, ch. 586, § 6(b), p. 834.) This history, contends defendant, demonstrates that the right to seek additional compensation for injuries caused by the serious and willful misconduct of the employer was intended by the Legislature as a substitute for the right to seek damages in an action at law for such conduct.

Plaintiff claims that the reason for the amendment was a desire by the Legislature to equalize the treatment of employer and employee with regard to the commission of the acts of serious and willful misconduct.[1] However, the argument is not convincing because it does not account for the repeal of the provision allowing an employee to bring an action at law for the employer's willful misconduct.

We find the historical background cited by defendant to be persuasive. The clear implication is that the addition in 1917 of the "exclusive remedy" limitation and the provision for a penalty for the willful misconduct of the employer was a substitute for the previous right of an employee to bring an action at law.

Next, defendant contends that the term "serious and willful misconduct" as used in section 4553 has the same meaning as intentional misconduct, and plaintiff may not avoi d the bar of section 3601 merely by characterizing defendant's conduct as intentional. Defendant relies on *Mercer-Fraser Company v. Industrial Accident Commission* (1953) 40 Cal. 2d 102, 117, 251 P.2d 955, 962, in which the term "willful misconduct" as used in section 4553 was defined as conduct which "necessarily involves deliberate, intentional, *or wanton* conduct in doing or omitting to perform acts, with knowledge or appreciation of the fact . . . *that danger is likely to result therefrom.*" "Willfulness necessarily involves the performance of a deliberate or intentional act or omission regardless of the consequences."[2] This definition expressly includes intentional conduct

---

[1] (*Court's footnote*) The act provided that an employee who is guilty of serious and willful misconduct would have his compensation reduced by 50 percent. (Stats. 1917, ch. 586, § 6(a)(4), p. 834.) That provision appears in section 4551, which sets forth some exceptions to the reduction penalty.

[2] (*Court's footnote*) Plaintiff asserts that decisions both before and after Mercer-Fraser found serious and willful misconduct on facts which did not meet the strict definition set forth in that case. (*Citing, e.g., Rogers Material Co. v. Ind. Acc. Com.* (1965) 63 Cal. 2d 717, 723, 48 Cal. Rptr. 129, 408 P.2d 737; Vega Aircraft v. Ind. Acc. Com. (1946) 27 Cal. 2d 529, 533–534, 165 P.2d 665; Parkhurst v. Ind. Acc. Com. (1942) 20 Cal. 2d 826, 829, 129 P.2d 113; E. Clemens Horst Co. v. Ind. Acc. Com. (1920) 184 Cal. 180, 189, 193 P. 105.) We fail to comprehend how this circumstance assists plaintiff's argument that intentional acts may be distinguished from

within the purview of section 4553.

Plaintiff counters that the Legislature recognized a difference between intentional misconduct and serious and willful misconduct because it has provided that an employee who is guilty of the former is precluded from recovering workers' compensation (§ 3600, subd. (d), (e), (f), (g)), whereas if he is injured as the result of his own serious and willful misconduct he only suffers a one-half reduction in compensation benefits (§ 4551).

The contention misconstrues these provisions. The only intentional misconduct of an employee which excludes his right to compensation is the deliberate infliction of injury upon himself, his participation in an altercation in which he is the aggressor, or where his injuries are caused by intoxication. (*See* fn. 1, *ante*, pp. 859, 860 of 165 Cal. Rptr., pp. 949, 950 of 612 P.2d.) These provisions were obviously designed, at least in part, to prevent an employee from injuring himself in order to collect compensation, to deter physical aggression by employees, and to prevent injuries due to intoxication. The fact that the Legislature chose to except these particular types of intentional acts from compensation coverage does not imply that all types of employee misconduct which may be described as intentional will preclude recovery of compensation. If, for example, the employee deliberately performs an act "with knowledge or appreciation of the fact . . . *that danger is likely to result therefrom*" — conduct which constitutes serious and willful misconduct under section 4551 (*Mercer-Fraser Company v. Ind. Acc. Com., supra*, 40 Cal. 2d 102, 117, 251 P.2d 955, 962) — he is not precluded from recovering compensation but is only subject to a reduction of his recovery by one-half.[3]

In sum, the provisions of section 4553 were designed to penalize intentional misconduct of an employer, and the injuries which result from such acts are compensable under that section.

However, while the case law cannot be described as consistent, it reveals that in some exceptional circumstances the employer is not free from liability at law for his intentional acts even if the resulting injuries to his employees are compensable under workers' compensation. Indeed, in one unusual situation, despite the "exclusive remedy" provision of section 3601, an action at law was allowed for injuries incurred in the employment where the employer's conduct was negligent rather than intentional.[4]

First we consider cases in which the intentional acts of the employer have been held not to justify an action at law. Compensation was determined to be the exclusive remedy for injuries suffered in a case in which the employer concealed the dangers inherent in the material the employees were required to handle. (*Wright v. FMC Corporation* (1978) 81 Cal. App. 3d 777, 779, 146 Cal. Rptr. 740) or made false representations in that regard (*Buttner v. American Bell Tel. Co.* (1940) 41 Cal. App. 2d 581, 584, 107 P.2d 439.) The same conclusion was reached on the basis of allegations that the employer was guilty of malicious misconduct in allowing an employee to use a machine without proper instruction. (*Law v. Dartt* (1952) 109 Cal. App. 2d 508, 509, 240 P.2d 1013.)

The reason for the foregoing rule seems obvious. It is not uncommon for an employer to "put his mind" to the existence of a danger to an employee and nevertheless fail to

---

willful misconduct. In virtually all of the cases cited by plaintiff, it is recognized that an employer is guilty of serious and willful misconduct under section 4553 if he knows he is placing his employees in a dangerous position and fails to take precautions for their safety.

[3] (*Court's footnote*) Hawaiian Pineapple Co. v. Ind. Acc. Com. (1953) 40 Cal. 2d 656, 664, 255 P.2d 431, holds that the term "serious and willful misconduct" is to be given the same meaning in sections 4551 and 4553. However, it does not discuss the provisions of subdivisions (d), (e), (f), and (g) of section 3600 or their relationship to section 4551.

[4] (*Court's footnote*) In Duprey v. Shane (1952) 39 Cal. 2d 781, 793, 249 P.2d 8, a nurse who was employed by a chiropractor was treated by him for an industrial injury. We held that she could sue her employer for malpractice because in committing the tortious acts he was acting in his capacity as a doctor rather than as an employer. (See also Baugh v. Rogers (1944) 24 Cal. 2d 200, 214, 148 P.2d 633; Douglas v. E. & J. Gallo Winery (1977) 69 Cal. App. 3d 103, 110, 137 Cal. Rptr. 797.)

take corrective action. (*See, e.g., Rogers Materials Co. v. Ind. Acc. Com., supra*, 63 Cal. 2d 717, 723, 48 Cal. Rptr. 129, 408 P.2d 737.) In many of these cases, the employer does not warn the employee of the risk. Such conduct may be characterized as intentional or even deceitful. Yet if an action at law were allowed as a remedy, many cases cognizable under workers' compensation would also be prosecuted outside that system. The focus of the inquiry in a case involving work-related injury would often be not whether the injury arose out of and in the course of employment, but the state of knowledge of the employer and the employee regarding the dangerous condition which caused the injury. Such a result would undermine the underlying premise upon which the workers' compensation system is based. That system balances the advantage to the employer of immunity from liability at law against the detriment of relatively swift and certain compensation payments. Conversely, while the employee receives expeditious compensation, he surrenders his right to a potentially larger recovery in a common law action for the negligence or willful misconduct of his employer. This balance would be significantly disturbed if we were to hold, as plaintiff urges, that any misconduct of an employer which may be characterized as intentional warrants an action at law for damages. It seems clear that section 4553 is the sole remedy for additional compensation against an employer whose employee is injured in the first instance as the result of a deliberate failure to assure that the physical environment of the work place is safe.

Thus, if the complaint alleged only that plaintiff contracted the disease because defendant knew and concealed from him that his health was endangered by asbestos in the work environment, failed to supply adequate protective devices to avoid disease, and violated governmental regulations relating to dust levels at the plant, plaintiff's only remedy would be to prosecute his claim under the workers' compensation law.

But where the employer is charged with intentional misconduct which goes beyond his failure to assure that the tools or substances used by the employee or the physical environment of a workplace are safe, some cases have held that the employer may be subject to common law liability. A physical assault by the employer upon the employee has been held to justify an action at law against the employer. (*Magliulo v. Superior Court* (1975) 47 Cal. App. 3d 760, 779, 121 Cal. Rptr. 621; *see Meyer v. Graphic Arts International Union* (1978) 88 Cal. App. 3d 176, 178, 151 Cal. Rptr. 597; *contra, Azevedo v. Abel* (1968) 264 Cal. App. 2d 451, 458–460, 70 Cal. Rptr. 710.) In *Ramey v. General Petroleum Corporation* (1959) 173 Cal. App. 2d 386, 402, 343 P.2d 787, it was held that an action for fraud could be maintained against an employer who made misrepresentations regarding the employee's right to medical care and conspired with a third party to conceal from the employee that his injuries, which occurred while he was working, were caused by the third party against whom he had recourse. And in *Unruh v. Truck Insurance Exchange* (1972) 7 Cal. 3d 616, 630, 102 Cal. Rptr. 815, 498 P.2d 1063, we allowed an action at law against an insurer for assault, battery, and intentional infliction of emotional distress, based upon its deceitful conduct in investigating a workers' compensation claim.[5]

The reasons given in these cases for allowing a common law action for intentional misconduct of the employer vary. In *Magliulo* the rationale was based, at least in part, on the ground that since an employee may sue a fellow employee at law for assault (§ 3601, subd. (a)(1)), he should have the same right against his employer, and that an

---

[5] *(Court's footnote)* It has also been held that damages for intentional infliction of emotional distress unaccompanied by physical injury may be sought in an action at law as an implied exception to the exclusive remedy provisions of the workers' compensation law because that system provides no remedy for a non-physical injury in the employment. The court reasoned that the Legislature did not intend to deny an employee all redress for that tort. (Renteria v. County of Orange (1978) 82 Cal. App. 3d 833, 841–842, 147 Cal. Rptr. 447.) Conversely, cases holding that workers' compensation is the sole remedy for such an injury are based upon the fact that physical injury resulted from the tort, and therefore the injury was compensable under workers' compensation. (Gates v. Trans Video Corp. (1979) 93 Cal. App. 3d 196, 206, 155 Cal. Rptr. 486.)

intentional assault by the employer has a questionable relationship to the general conditions of employment.

Ramey held that even though the employee had previously recovered workers' compensation for the physical injury arising from the employment, the injury from the fraudulent concealment of his cause of action was distinct from the industrial injury and did not occur while he was performing services growing out of or incidental to his employment. The court declared that the Legislature never intended that an employer's fraud was a risk of the employment.

In *Unruh*, we recognized that an insurer ordinarily stands in the shoes of the employer when it investigates a claim for compensation (§§ 3850, 3852), and that its negligence in carrying out this duty must be remedied under the compensation law. However, we held that the immunity from common law liability was lost insofar as the insurer did not "remain in its proper role" but, rather, acted deceitfully in investigating the claim. A separate cause of action was allowed against the insurer for aggravation of the initial industrial injury, for which the plaintiff had already received compensation.[6]

The parties attempt to distinguish, harmonize, or explain these holdings. While we do not purport to find in them a tidy and consistent rationale, we perceive in *Magliulo, Meyer* and *Unruh* a trend toward allowing an action at law for injuries suffered in the employment if the employer acts deliberately for the purpose of injuring the employee or if the harm resulting from the intentional misconduct consists of aggravation of an initial work-related injury. In *Magliulo, Meyer, Unruh,* and *Ramey*, the alleged misconduct consisted of assault or fraud and deceit. *Ramey* and *Unruh* distinguished between an initial injury and a later injury which is separate from but related to the first injury (*Ramey*) or aggravates the initial injury (*Unruh*).

In the present case, plaintiff alleges that defendant fraudulently concealed from him, and from doctors retained to treat him, as well as from the state, that he was suffering from a disease caused by ingestion of asbestos, thereby preventing him from receiving treatment for the disease and inducing him to continue to work under hazardous conditions. These allegations are sufficient to state a cause of action for aggravation of the disease, as distinct from the hazards of the employment which caused him to contract the disease.

This approach is not inconsistent with cases which hold that aggravation of an industrial injury by negligent treatment or the negligent failure to provide treatment may not be made the basis of an action at law against the employer or its insurer. (*Deauville v. Hall* (1961) 188 Cal. App. 2d 535, 543–544, 10 Cal. Rptr. 511; *Noe v. Travelers Ins. Co.* (1959) 172 Cal. App. 2d 731, 735–737, 342 P.2d 976; *Hazelwerdt v. Industrial Indem. Exchange* (1958) 157 Cal. App. 2d 759, 761–765, 321 P.2d 831.) *Unruh* distinguished between negligent and intentional misconduct in this regard holding, as we have seen, that an insurer which engages in intentional misconduct following a compensable injury may be held liable in an action at law for aggravation of the injury. (7 Cal. 3d 616 at pp. 626–628, 102 Cal. Rptr. 815, 498 P.2d 1063.)

In *Magliulo* it was said that although an employee might be willing to surrender his

---

[6] (*Court's footnote*) The holding that the insurer could be sued as a "person other than the employer" (§ 3852) was based upon the "dual capacity" doctrine enunciated in Duprey v. Shane, *supra*, 39 Cal. 2d 781, 249 P.2d 8, and followed in Douglas v. E. & J. Gallo Winery, 137 Cal. Rptr. 797, *supra*, 69 Cal. App. 3d 103. By analogy to Duprey, it was determined that the insurer in Unruh was "invested with a dual personality" so that while it was performing its proper role within the compensation system it stood in the position of plaintiff's employer and was immune from suit, but when it stepped outside that role by committing an intentional tort, it "became a 'person other than the employer'" like the doctor in the Duprey case, and subject to liability at law. We recognize that Unruh involved the liability of the insurer as the alter ego of the employer rather than, as here, the employer itself. Nevertheless, the distinction between liability for negligent conduct which aggravates an industrial injury and intentional conduct which has the same result is significant in the context of the present case.

right to an action at common law for the ordinary type of work-related injuries, it is not equally clear that when he accepts employment he contemplates his employer might assault him or if an assault occurs he must be satisfied with the additional compensation provided by section 4553. So, here, it is inconceivable that plaintiff contemplated defendant would, as he alleges, intentionally conceal the knowledge that he had contracted a serious disease from the work environment, thereby aggravating the disease, and by accepting employment he would surrender his right to damages at law for such conduct.[7]

Moreover, defendant's alleged actions are more blameworthy than the insurer's conduct in using "evidence perfidiously" procured in *Unruh*, and, if established at trial, are so egregious and the societal interest in deterring similar conduct in the future is so great that there is justification for awarding punitive damages. Such a penalty, however, may be afforded only in an action at law.[8]

PROBLEMS

(1) When the employer's fault takes the form of negligence in not disclosing the existence of a *noncompensable* disease discovered in the course of an examination in the company clinic, should a tort action be barred by the exclusiveness principle? *See* Reid v. United States, 224 F.2d 102 (5th Cir. 1955). *But cf.* Tourville v. United Aircraft Corp., 262 F.2d 570 (2d Cir. 1959).

(2) In *Unruh*, referred to in *Rudkin*, the court resorted to the dual-capacity doctrine. But if the carrier was not acting in its capacity as carrier when it carried on an improper investigation, what was it acting as? Can you formulate a better rationale for this undoubtedly appealing result?

---

[7] (*Court's footnote*) Although our holding herein is based in part on an analogy to the Magliulo-Ramey-Unruh line of decisions, we are not to be understood thereby as resolving any conflict between Magliulo and Azevedo v. Abel (1968), 264 Cal. App. 2d 451, 458–460, 52 Cal. Rptr. 283, as to an employee's right to maintain an action at law against his employer for a physical assault by the latter related to the employment. That issue is not presented in this case, and we do not purport to address it.

Since the question at issue here was decided on the pleadings the record contains no evidence as to the difficulty of separating the damage caused by the onset of the disease suffered by plaintiff from its subsequent aggravation. There is a considerable body of medical literature regarding disease caused by the ingestion of asbestos (see Borel v. Fibreboard Paper Products Corporation (5th Cir. 1973) 493 F.2d 1076, 1083–1085), and at trial the parties will undoubtedly introduce medical evidence in support of their contentions regarding causation and aggravation. We note for the guidance of the court on retrial that if plaintiff is successful in establishing that his injury was aggravated by the wrongful acts of defendant as alleged in the complaint, the burden of apportioning damages between the initial contracting of the disease and its subsequent aggravations is upon defendant, since the problem of apportionment emanates from defendants' wrongful acts. (*Cf.* Pullman Kellogg v. Workers' Comp. App. Bd. (1980) 26 Cal. 3d 450, 455–456, 156 Cal. Rptr. 851; Summers v. Tice (1948) 33 Cal. 2d 80, 88, 199 P.2d 1.)

[8] (*Court's footnote*) The 50-percent increase in the award authorized by section 4553 is additional compensation and does not represent exemplary damages. (State Dept. of Corrections v. Workmen's Comp. App. Bd. (1971) 5 Cal. 3d 885, 891, 97 Cal. Rptr. 786, 489 P.2d 818; E. Clemens Horst Co. v. Ind. Acc. Com., *supra*, 184 Cal. 180, 193, 193 P. 105.)

[3]   Sexual Harassment

ACCARDI v. SUPERIOR COURT OF CALIFORNIA
17 Cal. App. 4th 341, 21 Cal. Rptr. 2d 292 (1993)
As Modified on Denial of Rehearing Aug. 20, 1993

GILBERT, ASSOCIATE JUSTICE.

Sexual harassment does not necessarily involve sexual conduct. It need not have anything to do with lewd acts, double entendres or sexual advances. Sexual harassment may involve conduct, whether blatant or subtle, that discriminates against a person solely because of that person's sex.

In this writ proceeding, we hold that sexual harassment occurs when an employer creates a hostile environment for an employee because of that employee's sex. We also hold that a claim for sexual harassment is not time-barred when there are continuous acts of discrimination over a period of time provided that some of those acts fall within the limitations period. We further hold that a claim of emotional distress arising out of sexual harassment is not preempted by workers' compensation law.

Petitioner, Debbra J. Accardi, was at one time employed as a police officer with the City of Simi Valley. On October 11, 1991, she filed sexual discrimination complaints with the California Department of Fair Employment and Housing (DFEH). On October 17, 1991, Accardi obtained a "right to sue letter" from DFEH. On March 13, 1992, she filed a lawsuit against real parties, the City of Simi Valley, James Bartholomew, Richard Wright, Anthony Harper, III, and Mark Layhew, and others. Her complaint alleges causes of action for sexual harassment in violation of Government Code section 12940 et seq., constructive discharge, intentional interference with business relationship, and intentional infliction of emotional distress.

Real parties demurred upon the ground that the causes of action for sexual harassment and intentional infliction of emotional distress are preempted by the exclusive provisions of workers' compensation laws. (Lab. Code, §§ 132a, 3601; *Cole v. Fair Oaks Fire Protection Dist.* (1987) 43 Cal. 3d 148, 151, 233 Cal. Rptr. 308, 729 P.2d 743.) They also asserted that the cause of action for sexual harassment was barred by the statute of limitations. (Gov. Code, § 12960.)

. . . .

Accardi alleges in her amended complaint that she was hired as an officer of the police department of the City of Simi Valley in November 1980. During her tenure, between November 1980 and July 1991, she claims to have been subjected to numerous and continuing episodes of discrimination and harassment because of her sex. The misconduct she specifies includes, among other things, spreading untrue rumors about her abilities, deliberately singling her out for unfavorable work assignments and work shifts, making unsubstantiated complaints about her performance, making statements that her baton was only useful to perform sex acts, stuffing her shotgun barrels with paper so that the weapon would explode if fired, spreading rumors that she had slept with superior officers in order to receive favorable assignments, and threatening to disrupt her wedding.

The amended complaint also alleges such events as: deliberately overburdening her with double work assignments; denying assistance when she requested it; deliberately circumventing established procedures when she was assigned to duty as a court officer in order to make her work more difficult; excluding her from group activities; mimicking and making fun of her before her peers in the unit; admitting to her that there were double standards and telling her she must live with them; allowing threats of bodily harm to be made to her in front of a room filled with officers; allowing derogatory and condescending remarks to be made about her, and women in general; and making sexual advances to her.

Accardi complains that her superiors ratified the actions of her fellow officers by: advising her to accept the double standard and not doing anything about the harassment; allowing the filing of false reports; assigning duties to her only because she was a woman; causing false and misleading medical reports to be filed alleging that petitioner was 100 percent fit notwithstanding a permanent Workers' Compensation Appeals Board declaration that she was 28 3/4 percent disabled; excluding her from work details to which all other partially disabled officers were assigned; ordering her to either declare herself 100 percent fit, or file for early retirement; and telling petitioner she would be eligible for early retirement only if she were 30 percent disabled.

Accardi alleges that each of the defendants was acting in concert as the representative, employee, or agent, of the other defendants.

DISCUSSION

No preemption for discrimination claim

Discrimination in employment is not a normal incident of employment. (*Jones v. Los Angeles Community College Dist.* (1988) 198 Cal. App. 3d 794, 244 Cal. Rptr. 37.) A claim for damages under FEHA is not preempted by the Workers' Compensation Act. (*Meninga v. Raley's, Inc.* (1989) 216 Cal. App. 3d 79, 90, 264 Cal. Rptr. 319.)

Real parties also argue that Accardi's exclusive remedy lies within the provisions of Labor Code section 132a. This section provides remedies for employees whose employers have retaliated against them for filing a workers' compensation claim. The intent of the statute is to deter employers from discriminating against injured employees who assert their rights under the workers' compensation laws. (*Judson Steel Corp. v. Workers' Comp. Appeals Bd.* (1978) 22 Cal. 3d 658, 668, 150 Cal. Rptr. 250, 586 P.2d 564.) A claim under section 132a lies within the exclusive jurisdiction of the Workers Compensation Appeals Board. (*Portillo v. G.T. Price Products, Inc.* (1982) 131 Cal. App. 3d 285, 182 Cal. Rptr. 291.

Labor Code section 132a is not applicable here. Accardi does not claim her employer retaliated against her because she filed a workers' compensation claim. She claims she is the victim of sexual harassment.

Sexual harassment — the creation of a hostile work environment because of a person's sex

It is unlawful for an employer to discriminate against an individual because of their sex. (42 U.S.C. § 2000e-2(a)(1); Gov. Code, § 12940 et seq.) Article 1, section 8 of the California Constitution prohibits the discrimination in employment based on "sex, race, creed, color, or national or ethnic origin."

Sexual harassment is a form of sex discrimination. (*Meritor Savings Bank v. Vinson* (1986) 477 U.S. 57, 67, 106 S.Ct. 2399, 2405, 91 L.Ed.2d 49; *Katz v. Dole* (4th Cir.1983) 709 F.2d 251, 254; Lindemann et al., Sexual Harassment in Employment Law (1992) pp. 9–10.) There are two actionable types of sexual harassment:

1. Quid pro quo harassment. This form of harassment occurs when a term of employment is conditioned upon unwelcome sexual advances. (*Highlander v. K.F.C. Nat. Management Co.* (6th Cir.1986) 805 F.2d 644.)

2. The creation of a hostile work environment for the employee because of that employee's sex. (*Chamberlin v. 101 Realty, Inc.* (1st Cir.1990) 915 F.2d 777, 782, quoting 29 C.F.R. § 1604.11(a) (1983).) Hostile environment and quid pro quo harassment claims are not always separate and distinct, but in this case the sexual harassment claim arises out of a hostile work environment. (*Fisher v. San Pedro Peninsula Hospital, supra,* 214 Cal. App. 3d at p. 607, 262 Cal. Rptr. 842.)

The term "sexual harassment" may lead many people to think of the first type of sexual harassment, that which involves unwelcome sexual advances. For example, in *Henson v. City of Dundee* (11th Cir. 1982) 682 F.2d 897, a female police dispatcher stated a claim for sexual harassment where she alleged she had been denied promotion because she had rejected her supervisor's request for sexual favors. (See also *Sampayo-Garraton v. Rave, Inc.* (D.P.R.1989) 726 F. Supp. 18.)

But sexual harassment of the second type, the creation of a hostile work environment, need not have anything to do with sexual advances. (*Andrews v. City of Philadelphia* (3d Cir. 1990) 895 F.2d 1469, 1485; *McKinney v. Dole* (D.C. Cir. 1985) 765 F.2d 1129, 1138; see *Lindemann & Kadue*, Sexual Harassment in Employment Law (1992) p. 174.) It shows itself in the form of intimidation and hostility for the purpose of interfering with an individual's work performance. (*Chamberlin v. 101 Realty, Inc., supra*, 915 F.2d at p. 782, quoting 29 C.F.R. § 1604.11(a) (1983).) To plead a cause of action for this type of sexual harassment, it is "only necessary to show that gender is a substantial factor in the discrimination, and that if the plaintiff 'had been a man she would not have been treated in the same manner.'" (*Tomkins v. Public Serv. Elec. & Gas Co.* (3d Cir. 1977) 568 F.2d 1044, 1047, fn. 4.)

This type of harassment can occur in a variety of ways. (*Andrews v. City of Philadelphia* (3d Cir. 1990) 895 F.2d 1469, 1485 ["the pervasive use of derogatory and insulting terms relating to women generally and addressed to female employees personally may serve as evidence of a hostile environment."]; *Hall v. Gus Const. Co., Inc.* (8th Cir.1988) 842 F.2d 1010 [incidents of cruel practical jokes, although not conduct of a sexual nature, may be properly considered to constitute sexual harassment]; *Broderick v. Ruder* (D.D.C. 1988) 685 F. Supp. 1269 [supervisor obtains sexual favors from subordinates other than complainant].)

As the Fisher court pointed out, "[s]exual harassment creates a hostile, offensive, oppressive, or intimidating work environment and deprives its victim of her statutory right to work in a place free of discrimination, when the sexually harassing conduct sufficiently offends, humiliates, distresses or intrudes upon its victim, so as to disrupt her emotional tranquility in the workplace, affect her ability to perform her job as usual, or otherwise interferes with and undermines her personal sense of well-being. [Citation.]" (*Fisher v. San Pedro Peninsula Hospital, supra*, 214 Cal. App. 3d at p. 608, 262 Cal. Rptr. 842.)

Statute of limitations

[The court here ruled that the complaint could be shown to be timely, because the plaintiff was entitled to prove that a deliberate pattern of discrimination had continued during the entire period of her employment.]

Intentional infliction of emotional distress — not arising out of employment

Emotional distress caused by misconduct in employment relations involving, for example, promotions, demotions, criticism of work practices, negotiations as to grievances, is a normal part of the employment environment. A cause of action for such a claim is barred by the exclusive remedy provisions of the workers' compensation law. (Lab. Code, § 3601, subd. (a); *Cole v. Fair Oaks Fire Protection Dist., supra*, 43 Cal. 3d at p. 160, 233 Cal. Rptr. 308, 729 P.2d 743.) The Legislature, however, did not intend that an employer be allowed to raise the exclusivity rule for the purpose of deflecting a claim of discriminatory practices. (*Flait v. North American Watch Corp.* (1992) 3 Cal. App. 4th 467, 480, 4 Cal. Rptr. 2d 522; *Goldman v. Wilsey Foods, Inc.* (1989) 216 Cal. App. 3d 1085, 1095–1096, 265 Cal. Rptr. 294.)

Thus, a claim for emotional and psychological damage, arising out of employment, is not barred where the distress is engendered by an employer's illegal discriminatory practices. (*Watson v. Department of Rehabilitation, supra,* 212 Cal. App. 3d at pp. 1285–1286, 261 Cal. Rptr. 204.) " . . . A responsible attorney handling an employment discrimination case must plead a variety of statutory, tort and contract causes of action in order to fully protect the interests of his or her client . . . [Citation.] Although the common law theories do not per se 'relate to discrimination,' they are nonetheless a standard part of a plaintiff's arsenal in a discrimination case." (*Rojo v. Kliger* (1990) 52 Cal. 3d 65, 74, 276 Cal. Rptr. 130, 801 P.2d 373.)

Real parties cite *Davaris v. Cubaleski* (1993) 12 Cal. App. 4th 1583, 16 Cal. Rptr. 2d 330, in support of their assertion that the exclusivity provision of the Workers' Compensation Act bars petitioner's claim. In Davaris, the plaintiff claimed that she had been discriminated against when, after informing her employer that she needed time off in order to have a hysterectomy, she was terminated from employment.

The trial court sustained defendant's demurrer to the cause of action for intentional infliction of emotional distress. It ruled that the injuries alleged fell within the purview of the exclusivity provision of the Workers' Compensation Act. Plaintiff appealed. She asserted that her employer's conduct violated "the public policy of this state to encourage proper medical care." (*Davaris v. Cubaleski, supra,* 12 Cal. App. 4th at p. 1589, 16 Cal. Rptr. 2d 330.)

The Court of Appeal rejected plaintiff's assertion. It held that plaintiff had failed to allege a recognizable public policy which was violated by her termination. (*Davaris v. Cubaleski, supra,* 12 Cal. App. 4th at p. 1589, 16 Cal. Rptr. 2d 330.) It concluded that plaintiff's emotional distress injuries are subsumed under the exclusive remedy provisions of workers' compensation. (Id., at p. 1588, 16 Cal. Rptr. 2d 330.)

In contrast to the plaintiff in Davaris, Accardi alleges that she suffered emotional distress because of the pattern of continuing violations which were discriminatory; her cause of action for emotional distress is founded upon actions that are outside the normal part of the employment environment and violate this state's policy against sex discrimination. As such, her claim for emotional distress arising out of sexual harassment is not barred by the exclusivity provisions of workers' compensation laws. (*Gantt v. Sentry Insurance* (1992) 1 Cal. 4th 1083, 1100, 4 Cal. Rptr. 2d 874, 824 P.2d 680.)

Accardi's cause of action for emotional distress relates to the same set of facts as alleged in the claim of discrimination. Her discrimination claims are based upon allegations of actions outside the normal part of her employment environment. Therefore, her claim for discrimination is not barred by the exclusivity provisions of workers' compensation law.

. . . .

Conclusion

The right to earn a living is not predicated upon the condition that one " . . . run a gauntlet of sexual abuse . . . " (*Meritor Savings Bank v. Vinson, supra,* 477 U.S. at pp. 66–67, 106 S.Ct. at p. 2405, quoting *Henson v. Dundee, supra,* 682 F.2d at p. 902.) Accardi alleges that because of her sex she was forced to suffer sexual harassment for 11 years while employed with the Simi Valley Police Department. She shall have the opportunity to prove these allegations.

. . . .

STEVEN J. STONE, P.J., and YEGAN, J., concur.

PROBLEM

A former employee brought an action for damages against her employer to recover for an acute nervous breakdown, subsequent hospitalization and inability to secure employment along with humiliation, embarrassment, and loss of self-esteem resulting from an alleged denial of promotion and discharge on the basis of sex. Should all or part of this action be barred by the exclusive remedy clause? *See* Stimson v. Michigan Bell Telephone Co., 77 Mich. App. 361, 258 N.W.2d 227 (1977).

[4]   Intentional and Negligent Infliction of Emotional Distress

LIVITSANOS v. SUPERIOR COURT
2 Cal. 4th 744, 7 Cal. Rptr. 2d 808, 828 P.2d 1195 (1992)

ARABIAN, JUSTICE.

We granted review to consider whether the exclusive remedy provisions of the Workers' Compensation Act apply to bar an employee's claims for intentional and negligent infliction of emotional distress, where no physical injury or disability is alleged. We hold that claims for intentional or negligent infliction of emotional distress are preempted by the exclusivity provisions of the workers' compensation law, notwithstanding the absence of any compensable physical disability. We further conclude that, for unrelated reasons, the case must be remanded to the Court of Appeal for further proceedings consistent with the views set herein.

FACTS

Because the matter reaches us after the sustaining of a demurrer, all well-pleaded allegations of the complaint are taken as true. (*Ephraim v. Metropolitan Trust Co. of California* (1946) 28 Cal. 2d 824, 838, 172 P.2d 501; see *Foley v. Interactive Data Corp.* (1988) 47 Cal. 3d 654, 663, 254 Cal. Rptr. 211, 765 P.2d 373; *Tameny v. Atlantic Richfield Co.* (1980) 27 Cal. 3d 167, 170, 164 Cal. Rptr. 839, 610 P.2d 1330.)

Plaintiff Apostol Livitsanos began his employment at Continental Culture Specialists, Inc. (Continental), a yogurt manufacturing company owned by Vasa Cubaleski (Cubaleski), in 1976 in the shipping department. Two years later, plaintiff was promoted to supervisor of the department and in 1980 he was made manager, with attendant salary increases. Plaintiff alleges that, as an inducement to remain at Continental, an oral employment agreement with Continental included a provision, repeated by defendant Cubaleski on many occasions to plaintiff and other employees, that "Continental is your future" as long as plaintiff followed proper procedures, and that "if Continental makes money, so will you." Plaintiff believed his employment was of indefinite duration, and would not be terminated without good cause.

In 1982, plaintiff was promoted to general manager and received a 1.25 percent share of Continental's gross sales in addition to an increased salary. As general manager, plaintiff worked sixteen hours a day on weekdays and three or four hours a day on weekends. In 1987, Continental introduced an employee profit-sharing plan as an inducement to employees to remain with the company. Pursuant to the plan, plaintiff was entitled to receive a share of Continental's profits so long as he was an employee.

In 1984, Continental's regular distributor went out of business, leaving Continental without a distributor. Plaintiff and another Continental employee, Andy Stylianou, formed a company, known as ABA, exclusively to distribute Continental's products. Plaintiff and Stylianou operated the distributorship with full knowledge and approval of defendants Continental and Cubaleski.

Throughout plaintiff's term of employment, defendant Cubaleski praised plaintiff's performance, telling him that he had "saved the company," and that he would "someday own Continental."

In late 1988 or early 1989, for no apparent reason, Cubaleski began a campaign of harassment against plaintiff. This campaign took several forms. Cubaleski falsely accused plaintiff, along with Continental's office manager, of writing fraudulent checks to an outside contractor as part of a scheme to siphon funds away from Continental. Cubaleski communicated this charge to other Continental employees, as well as to an employee of an outside accounting firm. In addition, Cubaleski told Continental employees and others that $800,000 was "missing" from Continental, implying that plaintiff had stolen the money. Cubaleski threatened to have plaintiff "put in jail" because of the "missing" money.

In December 1988, Cubaleski borrowed $100,000 from plaintiff and promised to repay the entire amount by January 9, 1989. By March 15, 1989, Cubaleski still had not repaid plaintiff. When plaintiff asked Cubaleski for the money, Cubaleski became angry. Instead of repaying the loan, Cubaleski falsely told others that plaintiff owed him $24,000. Cubaleski knew there was no such debt owed to him by plaintiff. Cubaleski eventually repaid the $100,000 debt by paying $50,000 to plaintiff and by assuming a $50,000 debt plaintiff owed to Continental.

In or about April 1989, plaintiff took a four-week vacation. While plaintiff was on vacation, Cubaleski told other Continental employees that plaintiff had given himself an unauthorized pay raise, that money was missing from Continental (implying that plaintiff had stolen it), and that plaintiff was trying to sabotage Continental by telling certain employees to decrease the amount of fruit in the yogurt. When plaintiff returned, Cubaleski instructed Andy Stylianou, Continental's sales manager, to telephone plaintiff and accuse him of taking an unauthorized pay raise and sabotaging Continental.

In August 1989, Cubaleski insisted that plaintiff and Stylianou sell their distributorship company, ABA, to another distributor that Continental wished to employ. At the time, one of the clients of ABA was indebted to the company because Continental had asked ABA to extend $100,000 credit to this customer. Cubaleski promised that, if plaintiff sold ABA, Continental would assume responsibility for the $100,000 credit. After plaintiff agreed to sell ABA, Cubaleski demanded that plaintiff sign a promissory note for the $100,000 credit and agree to personal liability or he would "be in trouble." Plaintiff signed the note. Approximately two weeks later, plaintiff was terminated.

Plaintiff was discharged with no warning, no explanation and no severance pay. After the termination, Cubaleski told other Continental employees that plaintiff's company had been improperly buying fruit toppings to resell, using Continental's money. The accusations were false. After the termination, Cubaleski also told other Continental employees that plaintiff had stolen $800,000 from Continental and that plaintiff was blackmailing Cubaleski.

Plaintiff filed suit against Continental and Cubaleski for breach of contract, defamation, intentional infliction of emotional distress, negligent infliction of emotional distress, and money lent. [footnote omitted] He alleged that defendants engaged in a campaign of harassment resulting in the wrongful termination of his employment. Defendants demurred to the causes of action for defamation and negligent and intentional infliction of emotional distress. [footnote omitted] The trial court sustained Continental's demurrers without leave to amend, apparently on the ground that the employer's conduct was "a normal part of the employment relationship" and therefore barred by the Workers' Compensation Act (*Cole v. Fair Oaks Fire Protection Dist.* (1987) 43 Cal. 3d 148, 160, 233 Cal. Rptr. 308, 729 P.2d 743 (hereafter Cole). Cubaleski's demurrers were also sustained, but leave to amend was granted as to limited issues. The Court of Appeal, citing *Cole, supra,* 43 Cal. 3d 148, 233 Cal. Rptr. 308, 729 P.2d 743, summarily denied plaintiff's petition for writ of mandate. . . .

DISCUSSION

1. Intentional Infliction of Emotional Distress [footnote omitted]

Plaintiff contends that because he did not allege any physical injury or disability resulting from defendants' conduct, his cause of action for intentional infliction of emotional distress is outside the scope of the workers' compensation law, and thus not governed by *Cole*, . . . 43 Cal. 3d 148, 233 Cal. Rptr. 308, 729 P.2d 743. He relies principally on *Renteria v. County of Orange* (1978) 82 Cal. App. 3d 833, 838, 147 Cal. Rptr. 447 (hereafter *Renteria*), which held that a cause of action for intentional infliction of emotional distress is outside the scope of the workers' compensation scheme where the injury is purely "emotional," and no "physical" disability is alleged.

We have not heretofore been called upon to reconcile the principles of *Cole* and *Renteria*. In Cole, the employer engaged in a campaign of harassment which caused the plaintiff severe physical injury and disability. We held that the injuries were compensable under workers' compensation notwithstanding the egregious nature of the employer's misconduct, because such actions "are a normal part of the employment relationship." (43 Cal. 3d at p. 160, 233 Cal. Rptr. 308, 729 P.2d 743.) There was no allegation, however, that the plaintiff had suffered a "purely emotional" injury. (*Id.* at p. 153, 233 Cal. Rptr. 308, 729 P.2d 743.) Although we took note of certain problems posed by the reasoning in *Renteria, supra*, 82 Cal. App. 3d 833, 147 Cal. Rptr. 447, we did not address them. (43 Cal. 3d at p. 156, 233 Cal. Rptr. 308, 729 P.2d 743.) Subsequently, in *Shoemaker v. Myers* (1990) 52 Cal. 3d 1, 276 Cal. Rptr. 303, 801 P.2d 1054, and *Gantt v. Sentry Insurance* (1992) 1 Cal. 4th 1083, 4 Cal. Rptr. 2d 874, 824 P.2d 680, we considered the relation between workers' compensation and an injured employee's civil damage claims, but because both of the plaintiffs there alleged mental and physical disability, we were not required to address the so-called *Renteria* "anomaly." (*Cole, supra*, 43 Cal. 3d at p. 156, 233 Cal. Rptr. 308, 729 P.2d 743.) Here, plaintiff has not alleged any physical injury or disability resulting from the employer's conduct. [footnote omitted] Thus, for the first time, we are called upon to construe the principles we adduced in *Cole* in the context of a case of purely emotional injury.

We begin with a review of *Renteria, supra*, 82 Cal. App. 3d 833, 147 Cal. Rptr. 447. The plaintiff filed a civil action against his employer and fellow employees alleging numerous acts of harassment designed to discriminate against him because of his Mexican-American ancestry. The defendants successfully demurred on the ground the action was barred by the exclusive remedy provisions of the workers' compensation law. The Court of Appeal reversed, holding that the cause of action for intentional infliction of emotional distress was not barred. [footnote omitted]

The court first rejected the defendants' claim that emotional distress damages are generally recoverable in a workers' compensation proceeding. Although physical injury (*e.g.*, a heart condition) caused by mental and emotional stress, or disabling mental illness caused by job pressures are compensable, the court held that "mental suffering, as such," without accompanying physical injury or disability, was not a compensable injury. (*Renteria, supra*, 82 Cal. App. 3d 833, 839, 147 Cal. Rptr. 447; italics in original.) The court noted that the fact that an injury was noncompensable did not, "by itself, abrogate the exclusive remedy provisions of the Workers' Compensation Act." (*Id.* at p. 840, 147 Cal. Rptr. 447.) It determined, however, that the plaintiff's action was "not an isolated instance of a physical injury which is noncompensable, but an entire class of civil wrongs outside the contemplation of the workers' compensation system. [Citation.]" (*Id.* at p. 841, 147 Cal. Rptr. 447.)

It reached this conclusion, evidently, in large part because the alleged wrong involved intentional injury. As the court stated: "While it is possible to believe that the Legislature intended that employees lose their right to compensation for certain forms of negligently or accidentally inflicted physical injuries in exchange for a system of workers' compensation featuring liability without fault, compulsory insurance, and prompt medical care, it is much more difficult to believe that the Legislature intended the employee to surrender all right to any form of compensation for mental suffering caused by extreme and outrageous misconduct by an employer." (*Renteria, supra*, 82 Cal. App. 3d 833, 841, 147 Cal. Rptr. 447.)

The *Renteria* court therefore concluded that the cause of action for intentional infliction of emotional distress constituted an implied exception to workers' compensation exclusivity under conditions where the "essence of the tort, in law, [was] non-physical. . . . " (*Renteria, supra*, 82 Cal. App. 3d 833, 842, 147 Cal. Rptr. 447.)

In many respects the *Renteria* opinion (*supra*, 82 Cal. App. 3d 833, 147 Cal. Rptr. 447) is instructive; for example, the notion that certain wrongs lie wholly outside the contemplation of the workers' compensation scheme presaged our holding in *Gantt v. Sentry Insurance, supra*, 1 Cal. 4th 1083, 4 Cal. Rptr. 2d 874, 824 P.2d 680, concerning claims for discharge in contravention of fundamental public policy. (See *Tameny v. Atlantic Richfield Co., supra*, 27 Cal. 3d 167, 164 Cal. Rptr. 839, 610 P.2d 1330.) However, the analysis was also in several respects fatally flawed.

In the first place, the proposition that intentional or egregious employer conduct is necessarily outside the scope of the workers' compensation scheme is erroneous. This was the precise problem which we addressed in *Cole, supra*, 43 Cal. 3d 148, where we noted that many intentional acts by an employer could be expected to cause emotional distress and yet do not lie outside the proper scope of workers' compensation. Even intentional "misconduct" may constitute a "normal part of the employment relationship." (*Id.* at p. 160, 233 Cal. Rptr. 308, 729 P.2d 743.) As we subsequently observed in *Shoemaker v. Myers, supra*, 52 Cal. 3d 1, 276 Cal. Rptr. 303, 801 P.2d 1054, "Even if such conduct may be characterized as intentional, unfair or outrageous, it is nevertheless covered by the workers' compensation exclusivity provisions." (Id. at p. 25, 276 Cal. Rptr. 303, 801 P.2d 1054.)

Furthermore, as we observed in *Cole, supra*, 43 Cal. 3d 148, 156, 233 Cal. Rptr. 308, 729 P.2d 743, the *Renteria* court's distinction between "physical" and "emotional" injury presents a glaring anomaly: If the employer's misconduct causes "purely emotional" distress, then the employee may maintain a civil action with full tort remedies; if the employer's conduct is so outrageous as to cause actual physical disability, however, the employee is limited to the recovery of workers' compensation. Thus, the more reprehensible the employer's conduct, the more likely that such conduct would be shielded by the workers' compensation exclusivity rule. It would then be in the employer's best interest to make conditions so intolerable for an employee and to cause such a level of emotional distress that the employee could not work as a result. Thus, the employer could avoid civil liability for the most egregious misconduct. (*Meninga v. Raley's, Inc.* (1989) 216 Cal. App. 3d 79, 89, 264 Cal. Rptr. 319.)

Clearly, the law should not, and need not, countenance such paradoxical results. The "physical" versus "emotional" dichotomy is logically insupportable. More importantly, it is contrary to the text and purposes of the workers' compensation law.

The touchstone of the workers' compensation system is industrial injury which results in occupational disability or death. (*Shoemaker v. Myers, supra*, 52 Cal. 3d 1, 16, 276 Cal. Rptr. 303, 801 P.2d 1054; *Union Iron Wks. v. Industrial Acc. Com.* (1922) 190 Cal. 33, 39, 210 P. 410.) Labor Code section 3208 defines "injury" as "*any* injury or disease arising out of the employment. . . . " (Italics added.) Labor Code section 3208.1 describes "specific" injuries "occurring as the result of one incident or exposure *which causes disability or need for medical treatment*" and "cumulative" injury as "occurring as repetitive mentally or physically traumatic activities extending over a period of time, the combined effect of which *causes any disability or need for medical treatment.*" (Italics added.) Thus, as the court in *Coca-Cola Bottling Co. v. Superior Court* (1991) 233 Cal. App. 3d 1273, 286 Cal. Rptr. 855, observed, "a compensable injury is one which causes disability or need for medical treatments." (*Id.* at p. 1284, 286 Cal. Rptr. 855.)

Moreover, the workers' compensation system is designed to compensate only for such disability or need for treatment as is occupationally related. "Temporary disability" benefits are a substitute for lost wages during a period of temporary incapacity from working; "permanent disability" payments are provided for permanent bodily impairment, to indemnify for impaired future earning capacity or decreased ability to compete in an open labor market. (*Russell v. Bankers Life Co.* (1975) 46 Cal. App. 3d 405, 120 Cal. Rptr. 627; see Lab. Code, § 4660, subd. (a).) The basic purpose of the Workers' Compensation Act is to compensate for the disabled worker's diminished ability to compete in the open labor market, not to compensate every work-related injury. (*Mercier v. Workers' Compensation Appeals Bd.* (1976) 16 Cal. 3d 711, 716, 129 Cal. Rptr. 161, 548 P.2d 361.)

Thus, compensable injuries may be physical, emotional or both, so long as they are disabling. (See *Hart v. National Mortgage & Land Co.* (1987) 189 Cal. App. 3d 1420, 1428–1430, 235 Cal. Rptr. 68 [rejecting the "physical versus emotional harm" test, but finding multiple acts of offensive touching were not a risk incident to or a normal part of the employment relationship].) Recognition of compensable psychiatric injury is contained, for example, in Labor Code sections 3209.3, 3209.7, and 3209.8, which expressly permit "therapy" as a compensable means of treatment, and define licensed psychologists and counselors as qualified providers of treatment. Labor Code section 3208.3, added by Statutes 1989, chapter 892, Section 25, presently provides that a psychiatric injury "shall be compensable if it is a mental disorder which causes disability or need for medical treatment" and it is diagnosed under prescribed criteria. (Lab. Code, § 3208.3, subd. (a).) "In order to establish that a psychiatric injury is compensable, an employee shall demonstrate by a preponderance of the evidence that actual events of employment were responsible for at least 10 percent of the total causation from all sources contributing to the psychiatric injury." (Lab. Code, § 3208.3, subd. (b).)

Compensation for psychiatric injury is not new; rather, in enacting Labor Code section 3208.3, the Legislature intended simply to require a higher threshold of compensability for psychiatric injury. (Lab. Code, § 3208.3, subd. (c).) An employee who suffers a disabling emotional injury caused by the employment is entitled, upon appropriate proof, to workers' compensation benefits, including any necessary disability compensation or medical or hospital benefits. (See, e.g., *Albertson's, Inc. v. Workers' Comp. Appeals Bd.* (1982) 131 Cal. App. 3d 308, 313–314, 182 Cal. Rptr. 304; *City of Los Angeles v. Workers' Comp. Appeals Bd.* (1981) 119 Cal. App. 3d 355, 365–366, 174 Cal. Rptr. 25; see also *Pichon v. Pacific Gas & Electric Co.* (1989) 212 Cal. App. 3d 488, 496–498, 260 Cal. Rptr. 677.)

Thus, the Renteria court plainly erred in suggesting that emotional injury which results in an industrial disability is not compensable under the Workers' Compensation Act. So long as the basic conditions of compensation are otherwise satisfied (Lab. Code, § 3600), and the employer's conduct neither contravenes fundamental public policy (*Tameny v. Atlantic Richfield Co., supra,* 27 Cal. 3d 167, 164 Cal. Rptr. 839, 610 P.2d 1330) nor exceeds the risks inherent in the employment relationship (*Cole, supra,* 43 Cal. 3d 148, 233 Cal. Rptr. 308, 729 P.2d 743), an employee's emotional distress injuries are subsumed under the exclusive remedy provisions of workers' compensation.

The conclusion that emotional injury lies within the scope of the workers' compensation law does not complete the analysis, however. For injury must also result in an industrial disability compensable under workers' compensation. (Lab. Code, § 3208.1; *Coca-Cola Bottling Co. v. Superior Court, supra,* 233 Cal. App. 3d at p. 1284, 286 Cal. Rptr. 855.) It is theoretically possible to incur a work-related injury that results in no compensable industrial disability. Indeed, this was one of the concerns originally addressed in *Renteria.* And *Renteria* itself contains the answer: "The existence of a noncompensable injury does not, by itself, abrogate the exclusive remedy provisions of the Workers' Compensation Act." (82 Cal. App. 3d at p. 840, 147 Cal. Rptr. 447.)

This proposition was more fully explained by the court in *Williams v. State Compensation Ins. Fund* (1975) 50 Cal. App. 3d 116, 123 Cal. Rptr. 812, where an employee who allegedly suffered a loss of sexual function as the result of an industrial injury asserted that his civil claim should go forward because such losses were not compensable under workers' compensation. The court rejected the argument, explaining as follows: "Plaintiff is correct in arguing that the statutory emphasis on occupational disability as a rating factor denigrates the compensability of nonoccupational handicaps. Decisions in other states hold that the workers' compensation law provides the exclusive remedy for industrial injury even though the resulting disability — for example, sexual impotence — is noncompensable. (See cases cited, 2 Larson, *Workmen's Compensation Law*, § 65.20.) . . . The theory underlying the out-of-state decisions is that the workers' compensation plan imposes reciprocal concessions upon employer and employee alike, withdrawing from each certain rights and defenses available at common law; the employer assumes liability without fault, receiving relief from some elements of damage available at common law; the employee gains relatively unconditional protection for impairment of his earning capacity, surrendering his common law right to elements of damage unrelated to earning capacity; the work-connected injury engenders a single remedy against the employer, exclusively cognizable by the compensation agency and not divisible into separate elements of damage available from separate tribunals; '*a failure of the compensation law to include some elements of damage recoverable at common law is a legislative and not a judicial problem*. [Citations.]' " (Id. at p. 122, 123 Cal. Rptr. 812, italics added.) [footnote omitted]. . . .

In sum, where the employee suffers annoyance or upset on account of the employer's conduct but is not disabled, does not require medical care, and the employer's conduct neither contravenes fundamental public policy nor exceeds the inherent risks of the employment, the injury will simply not have resulted in any occupational impairment compensable under the workers' compensation law or remediable by way of a civil action. To be sure, the theoretical class of cases which fit these criteria, in which there will be no remedy, would appear to be rather limited. Nevertheless, the possibility of a lack of a remedy in a few cases does not abrogate workers' compensation exclusivity. Not every aggravation in normal employment life is compensable. [footnote omitted]

The question remains whether, in light of the foregoing principles, the demurrers to plaintiff's causes of action for intentional and negligent infliction of emotional distress were properly sustained. As discussed above, there is no merit to plaintiff's assertion that purely emotional injuries lie outside the scope of the workers' compensation system. The mere failure to allege physical disability will not entitle the injured employee to a civil action. To this extent, the demurrers were properly sustained.

Plaintiff's contention that defendants' misconduct exceeded the normal risks of the employment relationship is another matter. Plaintiff has alleged that defendants engaged in a campaign of outrageous and harassing conduct, which included falsely claiming that plaintiff embezzled money from Continental and tried to sabotage the company's product; compelling plaintiff to sell his independent distribution company, ABA, and demanding possession of its books and records; and forcing plaintiff to sign a $100,000 promissory note for a debt owed to ABA under threat of retaliation if he refused. The circumstances of the discharge were further complicated by the fact that plaintiff apparently occupied a dual status in his relationship with defendants: as employee, and as independent distributor of Continental's product.

In summarily denying plaintiff's petition for writ of mandate, the Court of Appeal cited *Cole, supra*, 43 Cal. 3d 148, 233 Cal. Rptr. 308, 729 P.2d 743. In so doing, however, it is unclear whether the court was concerned with the *Renteria (supra*, 82 Cal. App. 3d

833, 147 Cal. Rptr. 447) issue or the nature of defendants' alleged misconduct. *Cole*, of course, addressed both issues. Its central holding that workers' compensation provides the exclusive remedy for torts that comprise "a normal part of the employment relationship" (43 Cal. 3d at p. 160, 233 Cal. Rptr. 308, 729 P.2d 743) has been discussed. However, as also noted, while *Cole* did not resolve the *Renteria* issue it acknowledged the "anomaly" which that decision had engendered. (Id. at p. 156, 233 Cal. Rptr. 308, 729 P.2d 743.)

Whatever the Court of Appeal's intentions in issuing a summary denial, it plainly failed to render a decision on the merits. In light of the serious allegations set forth in plaintiff's complaint, however, we conclude that the issue is an important one which should be addressed in a written opinion by the Court of Appeal. Accordingly, we shall remand the matter to the Court of Appeal with directions to consider whether, in this regard, the demurrers to the causes of action for negligent and intentional infliction of emotional distress were properly sustained. (Cal. Rules of Court, rule 29.4(b).)

2. Defamation

In addition to his claims of intentional and negligent infliction of emotional distress, plaintiff asserted a cause of action for defamation based on defendants' allegedly false statements accusing plaintiff of embezzlement and other misconduct against the company. Plaintiff claimed that the statements were slanderous per se, that he was "shocked and humiliated" by their publication, and that he suffered general damages to his reputation of $1 million. [footnote omitted]

We have not heretofore ruled on the question whether defamation claims arising out of the course and scope of employment are barred by the exclusive remedy provisions of the Workers' Compensation Act. [footnote omitted] We need not do so here. For even assuming, without deciding, that certain defamatory remarks in the employment context may be subject to workers' compensation, as we noted in the previous section the seriousness of the allegations in plaintiff's complaint and the hybrid nature of the relationship between plaintiff and defendants raise the further issue whether defendants' conduct was outside the scope and normal risks of employment. Therefore, on remand the Court of Appeal is directed to address these issues. (Cal. Rules of Court, rule 29.4(b).)

DISPOSITION

Plaintiff's contention that *Renteria, supra,* 82 Cal. App. 3d 833, 147 Cal. Rptr. 447 compels reversal of the order of the superior court sustaining the demurrer to his causes of action for negligent and intentional infliction of emotional distress is without merit. Nevertheless, the judgment of the Court of Appeal summarily denying plaintiff's petition for writ of mandate for relief from that order is reversed, and the case is remanded to the Court of Appeal to consider on the merits the remaining issues identified herein.

LUCAS, C.J., and MOSK, PANELLI, KENNARD, BAXTER and GEORGE, JJ., concur.

[5]   Retaliatory Termination of Employment

KELSAY v. MOTOROLA, INC.
74 Ill. 2d 172, 23 Ill. Dec. 559, 384 N.E.2d 353 (1979)

RYAN, JUSTICE.

Plaintiff, Marilyn Jo Kelsay, filed a complaint in the circuit court of Livingston County, seeking compensatory and punitive damages against her ex-employer, Motorola, Inc. The plaintiff alleged that her employment with defendant had been terminated as retaliation for her filing a workmen's compensation claim. The trial court directed a verdict in plaintiff's favor and the jury assessed damages in the amount of $1,000 compensatory damages and $25,000 punitive damages. The court remitted the compensatory damages to $749, which represents the wages plaintiff lost between the time she was discharged and the time she found a new job. On appeal, the Fourth District Appellate Court reversed the judgment of the trial court, holding that an employee has no cause of action against an employer for retaliatory discharge. (51 Ill. App. 3d 1016, 9 Ill. Dec. 630, 366 N.E.2d 1141.) Because a different panel of the same court reached a contrary result in an opinion filed on the same day (*Leach v. Lauhoff Grain Co.* (1977), 51 Ill. App. 3d 1022, 9 Ill. Dec. 634, 366 N.E.2d 1145), the appellate court issued a certificate of importance to this court (*see* 58 Ill. 2d R. 316) so that we may resolve the conflict.

Plaintiff suffered a cut to her thumb while working at the Motorola factory in Pontiac. She received immediate medical attention at a local hospital, where her thumb was stitched. She returned to work later that same afternoon. Shortly thereafter, plaintiff sought advice of counsel regarding a workmen's compensation claim for her thumb injury. Counsel sent notice of the impending claim to the employer, Motorola, Inc.

Plaintiff spoke with the personnel manager at the Motorola plant, Donald Aherns, after he received notice of the workmen's compensation suit. Aherns told plaintiff that the corporation was aware of the situation, that she would be "more than adequately compensat[ed]" by the corporation for her thumb injury, and that there was no need for her to follow through with her claim. He also informed the plaintiff that it was the corporation's policy to terminate the employment of employees who pursued workmen's compensation claims against it, and advised the plaintiff to "think about it" a little longer. Plaintiff, however, decided to proceed with her claim and, after informing Aherns of her final decision, was discharged. Her compensation claim against Motorola was eventually settled. Subsequently, as noted above, plaintiff sought relief in the Livingston County circuit court against defendant, Motorola, for her retaliatory discharge by the corporation.

This appeal raises several issues. First, should this State recognize a cause of action for retaliatory discharge? If so, is such an action one which may give rise to a claim for punitive damages, and, if so, was the jury's award of $25,000 punitive damages proper in the instant case?

The employer argues that no cause of action should exist in this State for the retaliatory discharge of an employee. He contends that, as of the time of plaintiff's discharge, there was nothing in the Workmen's Compensation Act (Ill. Rev. Stat. 1973, ch. 48, par. 138.1 *et seq.*) that impinged on the employer's unfettered right to terminate without cause an employee whose employment contract was at will. Further, the employer argues that recognition of a cause of action for retaliatory discharge is totally inconsistent with the exclusivity provision of the Act itself, which specifically provides:

> The compensation herein provided, together with the provisions of this Act, shall be the measure of the responsibility of any employer engaged in any of the enterprises or businesses enumerated in Section 3 of this Act. . . . (Ill. Rev. Stat. 1973, ch. 48, par. 138.11.)

Finally, the employer argues that the legislature's decision to provide solely for criminal punishment of employers who, after 1975, "discharge or . . . threaten to discharge . . . an employee because of the exercise of his rights or remedies granted to him by [the] Act" (Ill. Rev. Stat. 1975, ch. 48, par. 138.4(h)), without providing for a *civil* remedy for employees who are so discharged, precludes the plaintiff's action in the instant case.

The Workmen's Compensation Act (Ill. Rev. Stat. 1973, ch. 48, par. 138.1 *et seq.*) substitutes an entirely new system of rights, remedies, and procedure for all previously existing common law rights and liabilities between employers and employees subject to the Act for accidental injuries or death of employees arising out of and in the course of the employment. (37 Ill. L. & Prac. Workmen's Compensation sec. 2 (1958).) Pursuant to the statutory scheme implemented by the Act, the employee gave up his common law rights to sue his employer in tort, but recovery for injuries arising out of and in the course of his employment became automatic without regard to any fault on his part. The employer, who gave up the right to plead the numerous common law defenses, was compelled to pay, but his liability became fixed under a strict and comprehensive statutory scheme, and was not subjected to the sympathies of jurors whose compassion for fellow employees often led to high recovery. (Sec. 81 Am. Jur. 2d Workmen's Compensation sec. 1 *et seq.* (1976).) This trade-off between employer and employee promoted the fundamental purpose of the Act, which was to afford protection to employees by providing them with prompt and equitable compensation for their injuries. *See O'Brien v. Rautenbush* (1956), 10 Ill. 2d 167, 139 N.E.2d 222.

The Workmen's Compensation Act, in light of its beneficent purpose, is a humane law of a remedial nature. (*Shell Oil Co. v. Industrial Com.* (1954), 2 Ill. 2d 590, 119 N.E.2d 224.) It provides for efficient remedies for and protection of employees and, as such, promotes the general welfare of this State. Consequently, its enactment by the legislature was in furtherance of sound public policy. (*Deibeikis v. Link-Belt Co.* (1914), 261 Ill. 454, 104 N.E. 211.) We are convinced that to uphold and implement this public policy a cause of action should exist for retaliatory discharge.

While noting that in 1975, subsequent to plaintiff's discharge, the Workmen's Compensation Act was amended making it unlawful for an employer to interfere with or to coerce the employee in the exercise of his rights under the Act (Ill. Rev. Stat. 1975, ch. 48, par. 138.4(h)), the employer argues that as of the time of plaintiff's discharge, the legislature had neither prohibited nor provided for any remedy for a discharge resulting from the filing of a workmen's compensation claim. As such, its authority to terminate the employee, whose contract was at will, was absolute. In this regard he cites various statutes in which the legislature has seen fit to limit the employer's right to discharge (the wage assignment act (Ill. Rev. Stat. 1975, ch. 48, par. 39.11), the Service Men's Employment Tenure Act (Ill. Rev. Stat. 1973, ch. 126 1/2, par. 33), and the Fair Employment Practices Act (Ill. Rev. Stat. 1973, ch. 48, par. 851 *et seq.*)), and correctly notes that none of these limitations are applicable to the instant case.

We are not convinced that an employer's otherwise absolute power to terminate an employee at will should prevail when that power is exercised to prevent the employee from asserting his statutory rights under the Workmen's Compensation Act. As we have noted, the legislature enacted the workmen's compensation law as a comprehensive scheme to provide for efficient and expeditious remedies for injured employees. This scheme would be seriously undermined if employers were permitted to abuse their power to terminate by threatening to discharge employees for seeking compensation under the Act. We cannot ignore the fact that when faced with such a dilemma many employees, whose common law rights have been supplanted by the Act, would choose to retain their jobs, and thus, in effect, would be left without a remedy either common law or statutory. This result, which effectively relieves the employer of the responsibility expressly placed upon him by the legislature, is untenable and is contrary to the public policy as expressed in the Workmen's Compensation Act. We cannot believe that the legislature, even in the absence of an explicit proscription against retaliatory discharge, intended such a result.

We recognize that the Court of Appeals for the Seventh Circuit has reached a contrary conclusion in construing the Illinois Workmen's Compensation Act. In *Loucks v. Star City Glass Co.* (7th Cir. 1977), 551 F.2d 745, the court considered the question without the benefit of any prior decision of this court on the question involved and held that inasmuch as the legislature had not provided for a prohibition against retaliatory discharge, the employer was free to exercise its traditional right to discharge at will.

Decisions of the Federal courts in construing statutes of this State are not binding on this court. For the reasons above stated, we believe that the construction adopted in *Loucks* contravenes the public policy of this State.

Two recent cases in other States have held that an employee has a cause of action against an employer for retaliatory discharge. *Frampton v. Central Indiana Gas Co.* (1973), 260 Ind. 249, 297 N.E.2d 425, and *Sventko v. Kroger Co.* (1976), 69 Mich. App. 644, 245 N.W.2d 151.

In *Frampton*, the plaintiff had been injured on the job, and received workmen's compensation. Later, she made a claim for increased disability and received a settlement. Soon thereafter she was fired without cause, and brought an action for retaliatory discharge against the employer. In sustaining the cause of action, the Indiana Supreme Court noted that to prohibit a cause of action under such circumstances would be to sanction the ability of employers to coerce employees into forgoing their rights and by so doing unilaterally defy and destroy the function of the State's workmen's compensation act. *See* 2A A. Larson, Workmen's Compensation sec. 68.36 (Supp. 1978).

Similarly, in *Sventko*, the plaintiff was discharged for filing a workmen's compensation claim against her employer. The Michigan Appellate Court, in holding that the employee should have an action for retaliatory discharge, stated that an "employer at will is not free to discharge an employee when the reason for the discharge is an intention on the part of the employer to contravene the public policy of [the] state." 69 Mich. App. 644, 647, 245 N.W.2d 151, 153.

There are decisions of other State courts that have held to the contrary (*see* Annot., 63 A.L.R.3d 979, 983 (1975)). We believe, however, that the reasoning in *Frampton* and *Sventko* is persuasive and conforms with the public policy expressed by the legislature in our workmen's compensation act. Concerning the decision of *Frampton v. Central Indiana Gas Co.*, we agree with the comment of Professor A. Larson that "[i]t is odd that such a decision was so long in coming." (2A A. Larson, Workmen's Compensation sec. 68.36 (Supp. 1978).) We do not agree with the employer's argument that *Frampton* is distinguishable from the instant case because the Indiana Supreme Court "placed express reliance on Indiana's statutory language prohibiting any 'device' to circumvent employers' liabilities under the Act," (*Loucks v. Star City Glass Co.* (7th Cir. 1977), 551 F.2d 745, 748), and because no analogous language can be found in the Illinois statute. While the Indiana Supreme Court may have used the statutory language to buttress its decision, the overriding principle enunciated by the court is that the workmen's compensation statute embraced the important public policy that compensation should be available to injured workers. Certainly it cannot be argued that the absence of any language from the Act prohibiting devices whereby employers may circumvent their duties under the Act can be interpreted to mean that retaliatory discharge is less repugnant to the public policy of this State than it is to that of Indiana.

The employer argues that the exclusivity provision of section 11 of the Act, which provides that the provisions of the Act "shall be the measure of the responsibility of any employer" (Ill. Rev. Stat. 1973, ch. 48, par. 138.11) precludes an action for retaliatory discharge. Motorola argues that this conclusion is compelled because the section clearly shows that the legislature intended that the Act should be exclusive in providing for employees' rights and remedies. We do not agree. First, that section was meant to limit recovery by employees to the extent provided by the Act in regard to work-related injuries, and was not intended to insulate the employer from independent tort actions. Second, we cannot accept a construction of section 11 which would allow employers to put employees in a position of choosing between their jobs and seeking their remedies under the Act. As we have already discussed, to prevent such anomalous results it is necessary to allow an action for retaliatory discharge. It would be illogical to bar the action on the basis of language of the Act itself, the fundamental purpose of which is to ensure rights and remedies to employees who have compensable claims. Accordingly, we feel it is improper to interpret section 11 in the manner suggested by the employer. . . .

. . . .

In summary, the judgment of the appellate court denying plaintiff a cause of action for retaliatory discharge is reversed. Plaintiff's award in the amount of $749 compensatory damages by the trial court is affirmed, but the trial court's order for $25,000 punitive damages is reversed.

Appellate court reversed; circuit court *affirmed in part and reversed in part.*

KLUCZYNSKI, J., took no part in the consideration or decision of this case.

UNDERWOOD, JUSTICE, concurring in part and dissenting in part:

[Dissenting opinion omitted.]

PROBLEMS

(1) Should the retaliatory discharge exception be extended to situations in which the injured worker is not discharged, but is only demoted in retaliation for filing a claim? *See* Trosper v. Bag 'N Save, 273 Neb. 855, 734 N.W.2d 704 (2007).

(2) In a jurisdiction such as Mississippi, which does not recognize the tort of retaliatory discharge, can the employee successfully argue that the retaliatory firing resulted in a "change of circumstances" that should allow the reopening of his or her workers' compensation claim in order to allow additional disability benefits? *See* Sims v. Ashley Furniture Industries, 964 So. 2d 625 (Miss. Ct. App. 2007)

§ 21.03 STATUTORY PROVISIONS ON EMPLOYER'S MISCONDUCT

Several states provide an election to sue at common law, or a percentage increase in compensation, as the penalty for employer misconduct, such as wilful intent to cause injury, failure to provide safety devices, or wilful misconduct generally.

The option to sue at common law is given by statute for employer's intentional injury in several states,[9] for the employer's wilful misconduct in Arizona, and for wilful act or gross negligence causing death in Texas. Failure to provide safety devices or to obey safety regulations, or failure to comply with duties imposed by statute or regulation, result in percentage increases in several states.[10] Increased awards of 50 percent in California, and 100 percent in Massachusetts, are assessed as penalties for serious and wilful misconduct of the employer or its supervisory personnel.

---

[9] *E.g.*, Oregon and West Virginia

[10] *E.g.*, North Carolina (10%), Arkansas (15%), and Ohio (15–50% in discretion of Board).

Part 8

EXCLUSIVENESS OF COMPENSATION REMEDY

Chapter 22

NONCOMPENSABLE INJURIES OR ELEMENTS OF DAMAGE

§ 22.01 INTRODUCTION

One of the major exceptions to exclusiveness of the compensation remedy — intentional injury by the employer — has already been covered in the preceding chapter. This and the two chapters that follow address the concept of exclusiveness in a broader context.

The compensation remedy is exclusive of all other remedies by the employee or his or her dependents against the employer and insurance carrier for the same injury, if the injury falls within the coverage formula of the act. If it does not, as in the case where occupational diseases are deemed omitted because not within the concept of accidental injury, the compensation act does not disturb any existing remedy. However, if the injury itself comes within the coverage formula, an action for damages is barred even although the particular element of damage is not compensated for, as in the case of disfigurement in some states, impotency, or pain and suffering.

§ 22.02 COVERAGE OF INJURY VERSUS COMPENSABILITY OF DAMAGE

Once a workers' compensation act has become applicable either through compulsion or election, it affords the exclusive remedy for the injury by the employee or the employee's dependents against the employer and insurance carrier. This is part of the *quid pro quo* in which the sacrifices and gains of employees and employers are to some extent put in balance, for, while the employer assumes a new liability without fault, it is relieved of the prospect of large damage verdicts.

If this is the justification for the exclusive remedy rule, it ought logically to follow that the employer should be spared damage liability only when compensation liability has actually been provided in its place, or, to state the matter from the employee's point of view, rights of action for damages should not be deemed taken away except when something of value has been put in their place.

A distinction must be drawn, however, between an injury which does not come within the fundamental coverage provisions of the act, and an injury which is in itself covered but for which, under the facts of the particular case, no compensation is payable.

The most troublesome cases are those in which the act clearly covers the injury and thereby bars all common law rights, but because of the failure of the compensation system to award benefits for the particular kind of harm, gives the worker nothing in return.

The commonest and most striking illustration of this unhappy combination is the well-established rule that work-connected injury to sexual or child-bearing organs or capacity, although of itself entitling claimant to no compensation benefits, cannot ground a damage suit.[1] The leading case is *Hyett v. Northwestern Hospital*,[2] in which claimant, as a result of an injury arising out of and in the course of employment, suffered an injury to the pubic nerve, rendering him impotent. The court denied the right to bring a common-law action, although this item of damage, not being of a disabling character, would also entitle plaintiff to nothing in a compensation claim.[3]

Similarly, loss of the sense of taste or smell, although ordinarily not compensable,[4] confers no common-law right of action.[5] As for physical pain and suffering, unless it interferes with earning capacity, no allowance can be made in a compensation award;[6] nevertheless, a common-law suit for pain and suffering from a work-connected injury will not lie.[7]

Up to this point, the examples of loss of common-law remedies with no gain of actual compensation benefits have involved fact situations in which the particular element of damage was not compensable. The same result has emerged when the claimant's compensation rights were foreclosed altogether because of the operation of a statutory period of limitations. In *Kane v. Durotest Corporation*,[8] the employee was exposed to highly toxic beryllium compounds which ultimately resulted in her death from beryllium poisoning. The disease did not manifest itself until seven and one-half years after her employment had terminated. Death occurred one year later. The common-law action against the employer was held barred by the exclusive-remedy provisions of the compensation act, although the compensation claim was itself barred by provisions requiring claims be filed within five years from the date of exposure.

Under some statutes, death benefits are payable only if the death occurs within a specified period, such as two years after the injury. In a Louisiana case,[9] decedent Hawkins died more than two years after the injury, and, although the widow and children could recover no compensation, because of this type of two-year statute, it was also held that the survivors could not bring a wrongful death action, because of the exclusive-remedy rule.

In principle, these two cases may seem to resemble the more numerous cases involving noncompensable elements of damage. In one important respect, however, they are different: The reason why the impotency, taste and pain cases are noncompensable is a reason that goes to the heart of the compensation act's purpose, which is to deal with the problem of loss of earning capacity. The noncompensability in the *Kane* and *Hawkins* cases, by contrast, had nothing to do with the theory or objectives of workers' compensation, but was the product of an arbitrary and unnecessary technicality. In the *Kane* type of case, there was never any moment in time when claimant had a compensation right she could enforce, although all elements of compensability were present in the most intense degree. The claim could obviously not have been brought

---

[1] *E.g.*, Williams v. State Comp. Ins. Fund, 50 Cal. App. 3d 116, 123 Cal. Rptr. 812 (1975).

[2] Hyett v. Northwestern Hospital, 147 Minn. 413, 180 N.W. 552 (1920).

[3] Note, however, that in one case, Berglund Chevrolet v. Landrum, 43 Va. App. 742, 601 S.E.2d 693 (2004), a finding by the state Workers' Compensation Commission that a worker had sustained sexual disfunction related to his compensable back injury was affirmed. The employer was ordered to underwrite the cost of Viagra.

[4] Arrington v. Stone & Webster Eng'g Corp., 264 N.C. 38, 140 S.E.2d 759 (1965).

[5] Scott v. C.E. Powell Coal Co., 402 Pa. 73, 166 A.2d 31 (1960).

[6] Blancett v. Homestake-Sapin Partners, 73 N.M. 47, 385 P.2d 568 (1963).

[7] Landry v. Acme Flour Mills Co., 202 Okla. 170, 211 P.2d 512 (1949).

[8] Kane v. Durotest Corporation, 37 N.J. 552, 182 A.2d 559 (1962).

[9] Hawkins v. Employers Cas. Co., 177 So. 2d 613 (La. App. 1965).

during the limitations period since, the disease not having produced disability, there was nothing to base a claim on. The fundamental vice here, however, is the senseless and inexcusable cruelty of dating the limitations period from a point in time, such as time of accident or termination of employment, earlier than the moment when the claimant knew or should have known the nature of her condition and its connection with the employment.

§ 22.03   DISFIGUREMENT

Disfigurement cases are another example of this kind of harsh result. A typical case is *Morgan v. Ray L. Smith & Son, Inc.*, [10] in which claimant had suffered severe third degree burns leaving him permanently disfigured. He received compensation for his actual disability, of course, and hospital and medical expenses, but no compensation allowance for the disfigurement was possible under the Iowa statute. The worker then sued at common law for the disfigurement, contending that it was an item not covered by the compensation act and therefore not within the area of barred actions; but the court held that the exclusive remedy rule extends to the entire injury with all its elements of damage.

§ 22.04   DEGREE OF DISABILITY NOT COMPENSATED

When a previously omitted kind of damage or injury is added legislatively, but compensation is limited to cases in which the injury is disabling, an action for the same kind of injury in nondisabling form is barred.[11] Thus, the Minnesota statute provides compensation only for disabling disfigurement, and this has been held to bar a common law suit for a nondisabling disfigurement.[12] Similarly, when an occupational disease statute permits an award for silicosis only when it has reached the stage of total disability, an employee suffering from partially disabling silicosis cannot sue at common law.[13] The New York Court of Appeals has held that an act producing such a result is not unconstitutional.[14]

§ 22.05   ANTIDISCRIMINATION LAWS AND THE EXCLUSIVITY DEFENSE

[1]   Sexual Harassment and Other Sex Discrimination Claims

It is now well established that sexual harassment in the workplace can constitute unlawful sex discrimination in violation of Title VII of the Civil Rights Act of 1964,[15] as well as of the sex discrimination provisions of numerous state antidiscrimination laws.

Illegal sexual harassment can take the form of conditioning employment or employment opportunities on compliance with sexual demands, or of the employer's creating or tolerating an atmosphere of sexual innuendo or intimidation.[16] For sexual harassment to be unlawful under Title VII, the conduct complained of must be unwelcome. Harassment of an employee because he or she is male or female is also

---

[10]   Morgan v. Ray L. Smith & Son, Inc., 79 F. Supp. 971 (D. Kan. 1948).

[11]   Repka v. Fedders Mfg. Co., 239 App. Div. 271, 267 N.Y. Supp. 709 (1933), *aff'd*, 264 N.Y. 538, 191 N.E. 553 (1934), involving an occupational disease recognized by statute, but in nondisabling form.

[12]   Breimhorst v. Beckman, 227 Minn. 409, 35 N.W.2d 719 (1949).

[13]   Cope v. General Elec. Co., 101 N.Y.S.2d 46 (1950), *aff'd sub nom.* Cifolo v. General Elec. Co., 305 N.Y. 209, 112 N.E.2d 197 (1953).

[14]   Cifolo v. General Elec. Co., 305 N.Y. 209, 112 N.E.2d 197 (1953).

[15]   Meritor Sav. Bank v. Vinson, 477 U.S. 57, 106 S. Ct. 2399 (1986).

[16]   Meritor Sav. Bank v. Vinson, 477 U.S. 57, 106 S. Ct. 2399 (1986).

illegal, even when sexual behavior or sexual demands are not present; this kind of sexual harassment is akin to harassment on the grounds of race or ethnic origin.

Sexual harassment in some instances results in physical or emotional injury requiring medical attention and/or resulting in inability to work. When a workers' compensation claim either is, or could be, filed, the argument has sometimes been made that the sexual harassment claim is barred by workers' compensation exclusivity.

To begin with, many kinds of sexual harassment don't seem very "accidental." Indeed, in a Wisconsin case,[17] the court held that the harassing employer was in no position to plead that it was an accident. So this is one route by which application of the exclusivity principle may be avoided. Similarly, the personal character of sexual harassment, and the lack of any connection to advancing the purposes of the employment, has led some courts to rule that this kind of behavior is outside the scope of the employment and therefore not subject to workers' compensation.[18]

Other courts have stressed public policy in refusing to bar sex discrimination claims on exclusivity grounds. Notably, the Michigan Supreme Court in *Boscaglia* [19] adopted the rationale that to apply the exclusivity provision to a discrimination claim would be to allow one statutory scheme to frustrate the goals and objectives of the other. And at least one court has refused to bar a Title VII claim, explicitly invoking the Supremacy Clause of the U.S. Constitution.[20]

Sexual harassment injuries are often psychological or emotional rather than physical. In jurisdictions which bar any compensation for emotional injury unless there is a physical component, harassment may be ruled to lie outside the reach of workers' compensation exclusivity.

This large heap of rationales, all leading to the same conclusion, sends a strong signal that workers' compensation was never designed to redress the types of injuries at which the sex discrimination laws are directed. Barring discrimination claims because they involve compensable injury would indeed frustrate the purpose of those laws.

PROBLEM

If a victim of sexual harassment who prevails in a discrimination suit is also allowed to collect workers' compensation, doesn't this create a double recovery problem? How might this problem be addressed?

[2]   Claims Under the Americans With Disabilities Act and Similar Statutes

The Americans With Disabilities Act of 1990 (ADA) prohibits employment discrimination against the disabled, and it requires "reasonable accommodation" of workers' physical and mental disabilities.[21] Its coverage is both broader and narrower than workers' compensation: broader, in that the protected disability need not have arisen from a work-related injury; narrower, in that many injuries and conditions which are compensable would not, perhaps because of their temporary or minor nature,

---

[17] Lentz v. Young, 195 Wis. 2d 451, 536 N.W.2d 451 (1995).

[18] *See, e.g.,* Schweitzer v. Rockwell International, 402 Pa. Super. 34, 586 A.2d 383 (1990). This was a common law action for rape arising out of sexual harassment.

[19] Boscaglia v. Michigan Bell Telephone Co., 420 Mich. 308 (1984). The Michigan fair employment practices law that was at issue in this case was superseded by a newer Civil Rights Act (1976 PA 453), but the principle for which the case is cited here presumably remains good law.

[20] Lopez v. S.B. Thomas, Inc., 831 F.2d 1184,1190 (2d Cir. 1987), *abrogated on other grounds*, Patterson v. McLean Credit Union, 491 U.S. 164, 109 S.Ct. 2363 (1989).

[21] 42 U.S.C. §§ 12101 *et seq.* (1995).

qualify as disabilities under the ADA. Also, there can be no successful ADA claim if the injury or condition is so severe that the employee cannot work at all, with or without reasonable accommodation. Nevertheless, there is a large area of overlap, consisting of injured workers who are entitled to workers' compensation and who may also have rights and remedies under the ADA.

Again, in these kinds of situations, the argument has arisen that ADA claims are preempted by the exclusive remedy provisions of the applicable workers' compensation statute. Courts that have addressed the issue have ruled, relying on the Supremacy Clause of the U.S. Constitution, that the ADA preempts the exclusivity provisions of a conflicting state workers' compensation law.[22]

What is interesting, though, is that the same result has not uniformly occurred when the disability discrimination claim is based on state law. Here the results are mixed: at least one court has barred state law disability discrimination claims due to workers' compensation exclusivity,[23] while at least one court has allowed both claims to co-exist.[24]

PROBLEM

How do you explain the apparent difference in the courts' attitudes between sex discrimination and disability discrimination cases? Do the policy considerations militating against barring sexual harassment claims on exclusivity grounds have the same force when applied to a claim by a disabled person under an ADA-like state statute?

---

[22] Mangin v. Westco Security Systems, Inc., 922 F. Supp. 563 (M.D. Fla. 1996); Wood v. Alameda, 875 F. Supp. 659 (N.D. Cal. 1995).

[23] Karst v. F.C. Hayer Co., Inc., 447 N.W.2d 180 (Minn. 1989).

[24] Mangin v. Westco Security Systems, Inc., 922 F. Supp. 563 (M.D. Fla. 1996).

Chapter 23

EXCLUSIVENESS AS TO PERSONS OTHER THAN EMPLOYEE

SYNOPSIS

§ 23.01 INTRODUCTION

Under the working of most "exclusive remedy" clauses, any common law right of a husband or wife to sue for loss of the wife's or husband's services and consortium, or of a parent to sue for loss of a minor child's services, is barred. In rare and unusual circumstances, however, it may be possible to show that the injury to the spouse or parent was such an independent violation of duty that its abrogation was not contemplated by the exclusive-remedy provision.

§ 23.02 EXCLUSIVE-REMEDY PROVISIONS CLASSIFIED

There are three general types of "exclusive liability" clauses which, for present purposes, must be carefully identified with the cases that depend upon them; from the narrowest to the broadest, they are as follows:

(1) the *Massachusetts type*, which says that only the employee, by coming within the act, waives common law rights;

(2) the *California type*, which says that the employer's liability shall be "exclusive," or that it shall have "no other liability whatsoever"; and

(3) the *New York type*, which carries this kind of statute one step further by specifying that the excluded actions include those by "such employee, his personal representatives, husband, parents, dependents or next of kin, or anyone otherwise entitled to recover damages, at common law or otherwise on account of such injury or death."

§ 23.03 ACTIONS BY SPOUSES, PARENTS, OR CHILDREN

Under the second and third type of statute, which are the commonest type of exclusive remedy clause, the cases with near-unanimity have barred suits by husbands for loss of the wife's services and consortium,[1] by wives for loss of the husband's services and consortium,[2] by parents for loss of minor children's services,[3] by children for death of a parent,[4] and by next of kin under wrongful death statutes.[5]

The leading cases[6] permitting such a suit by parents were concerned with interpreting the first type of statute — the unusually narrow Massachusetts statute — and have repeatedly been distinguished in states having statutes of the more familiar sort.

---

[1] Guse v. A.O. Smith Corp., 260 Wis. 403, 51 N.W.2d 24 (1952). Loss of consortium of paralyzed wife; action barred.

[2] Wright v. Action Vending Co., 544 P.2d 82 (Alaska 1975).

[3] Stample v. Idaho Power Co., 92 Idaho 763, 450 P.2d 610 (1969).

[4] Leech v. Georgia-Pacific Corp., 485 P.2d 1195 (Or. 1971).

[5] Jordan v. C.A. Roberts Co., 379 Mich. 235, 150 N.W.2d 792 (1967).

[6] *E.g.*, King v. Viscoloid Co., 219 Mass. 420, 106 N.E. 988 (1914).

New Hampshire, with a similarly narrow statute, originally reached the same result as to a wife's consortium action and a parent's wrongful death action. The statute was amended in 1971 to bar a spouse's consortium action, and again in 1978 to bar wrongful death actions by personal representative in cases covered by the compensation act. The latter amendment was held unconstitutional as a violation of the state's equal protection clause.[7] But in the great majority of cases, all such restrictions have survived constitutional attack.[8] As in the case of uncompensated elements of damage, the remedy is barred, and constitutionally so, even if the parent or spouse, being nondependent, gets no valuable compensation rights in place of the common law or statutory death-action rights destroyed.[9]

The principal justification for these decisions usually lies in the explicit wording of the clause barring any noncompensation liability for damages on account of the injury or death. Even without the additional precaution of a list of third persons barred, the sweeping language used in describing the employer's immunity seems to indicate a legislative intention that is accurately reflected in the majority rule.

SNYDER v. MICHAEL's STORES, INC.
16 Cal. 4th 991, 68 Cal. Rptr. 2d 476, 945 P.2d 781 (1997)

WERDEGAR, ASSOCIATE JUSTICE.

Plaintiff Mikayla Snyder, a minor, alleges she was injured in utero when her mother, Naomi Snyder, breathed carbon monoxide gas in amounts toxic to both Naomi and Mikayla. The injury occurred at Naomi's workplace, a store owned and operated by defendant Michael's Stores, Inc., during Naomi's employment. The trial court granted Michael's Stores' demurrer on the ground the action was barred by Labor Code sections 3600–3602, [footnote omitted] providing that workers' compensation proceedings are the exclusive remedy for injuries to employees arising out of their employment. The court so ruled under the compulsion of *Bell v. Macy's California* (1989) 212 Cal. App. 3d 1442, 261 Cal. Rptr. 447 (Bell), which held fetal injuries are, as a matter of law, derivative of injury to the pregnant mother. (*Id.* at pp. 1453–1454, 261 Cal. Rptr. 447.) The Court of Appeal in the present case reversed, explicitly rejecting *Bell's* rationale and holding.

We agree with the appellate court below and will affirm its judgment. Section 3600 bars personal injury actions against an employer only "for any injury sustained by his or her employees arising out of and in the course of the employment." Mikayla's action is for her own injuries, not her mother's. The trial court therefore should have overruled Michael's Stores' demurrer.

FACTUAL AND PROCEDURAL BACKGROUND

In reviewing a dismissal following the trial court's sustaining of a demurrer, we take the properly pleaded material allegations of the complaint as true; our only task is to determine whether the complaint states a cause of action. (*ABC Internat. Traders, Inc. v. Matsushita Electric Corp.* (1997) 14 Cal. 4th 1247, 1253, 61 Cal. Rptr. 2d 112, 931 P.2d 290; *Aubry v. Tri-City Hospital Dist.* (1992) 2 Cal. 4th 962, 967, 9 Cal. Rptr. 2d 92, 831 P.2d 317.)

Plaintiffs are Mikayla Snyder, a minor, by and through Naomi Snyder, her mother and guardian ad litem, Naomi Snyder personally, and David Snyder, Mikayla's father. Defendants are Michael's Stores, Inc., and Dennis Cusimano, the manager of the store

---

[7] Park v. Rockwell Int'l Corp., 483 A.2d 1136 (N.H. 1981).

[8] Slagle v. Reynolds Metals Co., 344 So. 2d 1216 (Ala. 1977).

[9] Mullarkey v. Florida Feed Mills, Inc., 268 So. 2d 363 (Fla. 1972).

where Naomi worked (hereafter collectively Michael's). (Two additional nonemployer defendants are not involved in this appeal.) Mikayla seeks damages for her physical injuries resulting from Michael's negligence; Naomi and David seek economic damages for the increased medical, educational and other expenses they have incurred and will incur due to Mikayla's physical injuries.

Plaintiffs allege that on October 2, 1993, Michael's negligently allowed a janitorial contractor to operate a propane-powered floor-buffing machine in the store without adequate ventilation, resulting in hazardous levels of carbon monoxide. Several customers and employees fainted from the fumes. Some, including Naomi, were taken to the hospital with symptoms of nausea, headaches and respiratory distress. Plaintiffs allege that both Naomi and Mikayla, then in utero, were exposed to toxic levels of carbon monoxide, which impairs the ability of red blood cells to transport oxygen. As a result, Mikayla suffered permanent damage to her brain and nervous system, causing her to be born with cerebral palsy and other disabling conditions.

The trial court sustained Michael's demurrer without leave to amend, citing *Bell*, *supra*, 212 Cal. App. 3d 1442, 261 Cal. Rptr. 447, as binding, and dismissed the action as to Michael's. The Court of Appeal reversed as to Mikayla's cause of action and her parents' cause of action for Mikayla's expenses of treatment and care. Because Mikayla's injuries were not derivative of Naomi's, but the result of her own exposure to toxic levels of carbon monoxide, the Court of Appeal reasoned, the exclusive remedy provisions of the workers' compensation law (§§ 3600–3602) were not applicable to Mikayla's injuries. Hence, neither Mikayla's cause of action for her own injuries nor her parents' cause of action for the expenses of her treatment was barred by those provisions.

We granted Michael's petition for review in order to resolve the conflict between the appellate decision in this case and that in *Bell*.

DISCUSSION

That Mikayla's complaint would state a cause of action had she been negligently exposed to toxic fumes outside the context of her mother's employment is undisputed. Under California law, "[a] child conceived, but not yet born, is deemed an existing person, so far as necessary for the child's interests in the event of the child's subsequent birth." (Civ. Code, § 43.1.) The quoted provision, originally enacted in 1872 as Civil Code section 29, gives a child the right to maintain an action in tort for in utero injuries wrongfully or negligently caused by another, a right that did not exist at common law. (*Young v. Haines* (1986) 41 Cal. 3d 883, 892, 226 Cal. Rptr. 547, 718 P.2d 909; *Scott v. McPheeters* (1939) 33 Cal. App. 2d 629, 631–633, 92 P.2d 678.) In light of this authority, Michael's does not contend that, the workers' compensation law aside, Mikayla's complaint fails to state a cause of action for her prenatal injuries.

The only question presented, therefore, is whether fetal injuries in the mother's workplace are remediable solely, if at all, through the workers' compensation system, We begin with the statutes establishing the exclusive jurisdiction of that system. Section 3600, subdivision (a), setting forth the conditions of compensation under the workers' compensation system, provides:

> Liability for the compensation provided by this division, in lieu of any other liability whatsoever to any person except as otherwise specifically provided . . . , shall, without regard to negligence, exist against an employer for any injury sustained by his or her employees arising out of and in the course of the employment and for the death of any employee if the injury proximately causes death, in those cases where the following conditions of compensation concur: . . .

Section 3602 provides, in relevant part:

(a) Where the conditions of compensation set forth in Section 3600 concur, the right to recover such compensation is, except as specifically provided in this section and Sections 3706 and 4558, the sole and exclusive remedy of the employee or his or her dependents against the employer. . . .

In terms similar to those of section 3602, section 3601 provides that, for a covered injury, the employee generally does not have a civil cause of action against a fellow employee.

A fundamental condition of compensation under section 3600 and, hence, a fundamental premise of the exclusivity provided in all three sections, is that the compensation sought is for an injury to an employee. In some circumstances, however, the bar on civil actions based on injuries to employees extends beyond actions brought by the employees themselves. The employers' compensation obligation is "in lieu of any other liability *whatsoever to any person*" (§ 3600, italics added), including, but not limited to, the employee's dependents (§ 3602) for work-related injuries to the employee. This statutory language conveys the legislative intent that "the work-connected injury engender a single remedy against the employer, exclusively cognizable by the compensation agency." (*Williams v. State Compensation Ins. Fund* (1975) 50 Cal. App. 3d 116, 122, 123 Cal. Rptr. 812).

Based on the statutory language, California courts have held worker's compensation proceedings to be the exclusive remedy for certain third party claims deemed collateral to or derivative of the employee's injury. Courts have held that the exclusive jurisdiction provisions bar civil actions against employers by nondependent parents of an employee for the employee's wrongful death (*Treat v. Los Angeles Gas etc. Corp.* (1927) 82 Cal. App. 610, 615–616, 256 P. 447), by an employee's spouse for loss of the employee's services (*Gillespie v. Northridge Hosp. Foundation* (1971) 20 Cal. App. 3d 867, 868–870, 98 Cal. Rptr. 134) or consortium (*Cole v. Fair Oaks Fire Protection Dist.* (1987) 43 Cal. 3d 148, 162–163, 233 Cal. Rptr. 308, 729 P.2d 743; *Casaccia v. Green Valley Disposal Co., Inc.* (1976) 62 Cal. App. 3d 610, 612–613, 133 Cal. Rptr. 295; *Williams v. State Compensation Ins. Fund, supra*, 50 Cal. App. 3d at p. 123, 123 Cal. Rptr. 812), and for emotional distress suffered by a spouse in witnessing the employee's injuries (*Cole v. Fair Oaks Fire Protection Dist., supra*, 43 Cal. 3d at p. 163, 233 Cal. Rptr. 308, 729 P.2d 743; *Williams v. Schwartz* (1976) 61 Cal. App. 3d 628, 631–634, 131 Cal. Rptr. 200). It was primarily on the " 'derivative' injury doctrine" drawn from these cases (*Bell, supra*, 212 Cal. App. 3d at pp. 1453–1454, 261 Cal. Rptr. 447) that the Bell court relied in holding fetal injuries barred by the exclusive remedy provisions. (*Id.* at pp. 1452–1455, 261 Cal. Rptr. 447.) As will appear, we agree with plaintiffs that the *Bell* court misapplied the rule the cited decisions drew from the statutory language.

In *Bell*, a pregnant worker complained, during work, of severe abdominal pain. A nurse provided on premises by the employer misdiagnosed the worker's condition as gas pains and delayed calling for an ambulance. When the mother was finally taken to the hospital, she was found to have suffered a ruptured uterus, and her baby, delivered live by Cesarean section, had suffered consequential injuries including brain damage. Evidence accepted by the appellate court for purposes of the appeal from summary judgment in favor of the employer showed that the nurse's delay in calling an ambulance caused a significant portion of the fetal injuries. (*Bell, supra*, 212 Cal. App. 3d at pp. 1446–1447, 261 Cal. Rptr. 447.)

The appellate court concluded the derivative injury rule barred the tort claims of the child (called Baby Freytas in the opinion) because the child's prenatal injury "was a collateral consequence of the treatment of Bell [the mother]." (*Bell, supra*, 212 Cal. App. 3d at p. 1453, 261 Cal. Rptr. 447, italics added.) "*[B]ecause the injuries to Baby Freytas were the direct result of Macy's work-related negligence towards Bell, they derived from that treatment and are within the conditions of compensation of the workers' compensation law.*" (*Ibid.*, italics added.) More generally, the *Bell* majority reasoned that, even if the employee mother was not herself injured, a "central physical fact . . . compels application of the [derivative injury] doctrine: that the fetus in utero is inseparable from its mother. *Any injury to it can only occur as a result of some condition affecting its mother. When, as in the case at bench, the condition arises in the course of employment, the derivative injury doctrine would apply.*" (*Id.* at p. 1453, fn. 6, 261 Cal. Rptr. 447, italics added.)

The above italicized passages clearly reveal the *Bell* majority's critical error. Assuming it true that all fetal injuries occur as a result of some maternal "condition," to conclude the derivative injury rule applies to all such fetal injuries occurring in the maternal workplace is a non sequitur. Neither the statutes nor the decisions enunciating the rule suggest workers' compensation exclusivity extends to all third party claims deriving from some "condition affecting" the employee. Nor is a nonemployee's injury collateral to or derivative of an employee injury merely because they both resulted from the same negligent conduct by the employer. The employer's civil immunity is not for all liability resulting from negligence toward employees, but only for all liability, to any person, deriving from an employee's work-related injuries. (§ 3600.) In the words of the dissenting justice in *Bell*, the derivative injury rule governs cases in which "the third party cause of action [is] derivative of the employee injury in the purest sense: It simply would not have existed in the absence of injury to the employee." (*Bell, supra*, 212 Cal. App. 3d at p. 1456, 261 Cal. Rptr. 447 (conc. and dis. opn. of White, P.J.).) As plaintiffs' attorney explained in remarks at oral argument, the rule applies when the plaintiff, in order to state a cause of action, must allege injury to another person — the employee.

In barring certain third party civil actions, the derivative injury cases do not depart from the language of section 3600; they merely apply the statutory language to actions that are necessarily dependent on the existence of an employee injury. In *Treat v. Los Angeles Gas etc. Corp., supra*, the parents sought their own damages for the work-related death of thir minor son. (82 Cal. App. at p. 613, 256 P. 447; see Code Civ. Proc., § 376.) The court held this claim within the exclusivity rule because it existed "by reason of the injury accruing to the employee." (82 Cal. App. at p. 616, 256 P. 447.) In a similar way, claims for loss of services or consortium by a nonemployee spouse are necessarily dependent on the employee injury; the claim could not exist without an injury to the employee spouse. In *Cole v. Fair Oaks Fire Protection Dist., supra*, 43 Cal. 3d at page 162, 233 Cal. Rptr. 308, 729 P.2d 743, it is true, we acknowledged that consortium claims are not "merely derivative or collateral to the spouse's cause of action," but at the same time we held the exclusivity provisions applied because the consortium claim is "based on the physical injury or disability of the spouse." (*Id.* at p. 163, 233 Cal. Rptr. 308, 729 P.2d 743.) While the losses for wich damages are sought in a consortium action may properly be characterized as "separate and distinct" from the losses to the physically injured spouse (*Rodriguez v. Bethlehem Steel Corp.* (1974) 12 Cal. 3d 382, 405, 115 Cal. Rptr. 765, 525 P.2d 669), the former are unquestionably dependent, legally as well as causally, on the latter. One spouse cannot have a loss of consortium claim without a prior disabling injury to the other spouse.

Similarly, a claim for negligent or intentional infliction of emotional distress, based on the plaintiff's having witnessed the physical injury of a close relative, is logically dependent on the prior physical injury. Thus the claim is "due to the employee's injury" (*Cole v. Fair Oaks Fire Protection Dist., supra*, 43 Cal. 3d at p. 163, 233 Cal. Rptr. 308, 729 P.2d 743), and the action is barred as "deriv[ing] from injuries sustained by an employee in the course of his employment." (*Williams v. Schwartz, supra*, 61 Cal. App. 3d at p. 634, 131 Cal. Rptr. 200.) [footnote omitted]

The question the *Bell* court should have asked, therefore, was not whether Baby Freytas's injuries resulted from the employer's negligent treatment of Bell or from "some condition affecting" *Bell (Bell, supra*, 212 Cal. App. 3d at p. 1453, fn. 6, 261 Cal. Rptr. 447), but, rather, whether Baby Freytas's claim was legally dependent on Bell's work-related injuries. From the appellate opinion, no evidence of such dependence appears. Although the fetal injuries resulted in part from the mother's ruptured uterus, the appellate court and the parties all assumed that "Bell's ruptured uterus was unrelated to her employment save only that it occurred during working hours and on Macy's premises." (*Id.* at p. 1447, 261 Cal. Rptr. 447.) As to the nurse's delay in summoning an ambulance, the majority's recitation of the evidence indicates simply that the delay "caused significant injury to Baby Freytas" (*ibid.*); nothing in the majority opinion suggests Baby Freytas's claim depended conceptually on injuries the delay caused to Bell. The majority, in other words, says nothing to contradict the dissent's assertion that "the nurse's negligence caused an injury to Baby Freytas which was not dependent on or derived from any injury to the mother." (*Id.* at p. 1456, 261 Cal. Rptr. 447 (conc. and dis. opn. of White, P.J.).)

The *Bell* court's observation that "the fetus in utero is inseparable from its mother" (*Bell, supra,* 212 Cal. App. 3d at p. 1453, fn. 6, 261 Cal. Rptr. 447), while tautologically true, falls far short of dictating application of the derivative injury rule to all fetal injuries. Biologically, fetal and maternal injury have no necessary relationship. The processes of fetal growth and development are radically different from the normal physiological processes of a mature human. Whether a toxin or other agent will cause congenital defects in the developing embryo or fetus depends heavily not on whether the mother is herself injured, but on the exact stage of the embryo or fetus's development at the time of exposure, as well as on the degree to which maternal exposure results in embryonic or fetal exposure. (See 7 Encyclopedia of Human Biology (1991) Human Teratology, pp. 411–418.) Even when the mother is injured, moreover, the derivative injury rule does not apply unless the child's claim can be considered merely collateral to the mother's work-related injury, a conclusion that rests on the legal or logical basis of the claim rather than on the biological cause of the fetal injury. For all the above reasons, we disapprove both the result and reasoning of the *Bell* decision, 212 Cal. App. 3d 1442, 261 Cal. Rptr. 447, on exclusivity of workers' compensation as a remedy for fetal injuries.

Having clarified the scope of the derivative injury doctrine, we turn to the case at bench. Michael's demurrer should have been sustained only if the facts alleged in the complaint showed either that Mikayla was seeking damages for Naomi's work-related injuries or that Mikayla's claim necessarily depended on Naomi's injuries. (See *Arriaga v. County of Alameda* (1995) 9 Cal. 4th 1055, 1060, 40 Cal. Rptr. 2d 116, 892 P.2d 150 [complaint subject to demurrer only if it affirmatively alleges facts showing workers' compensation is exclusive remedy].) The facts alleged here did not so demonstrate. Plaintiffs alleged simply that both Naomi and Mikayla were exposed to toxic levels of carbon monoxide, injuring both. Mikayla sought recompense for her own injuries. Since Mikayla was not herself breathing at the time of the accident, that her exposure to carbon monoxide occurred through Naomi's inhalation of the fumes and the toxic substance conveyed to her through the medium of her mother's body can be conceded. As we have emphasized above, however, the derivative injury doctrine does not bar civil actions by all children who were harmed in utero through some event or condition affecting their mothers; it bars only attempts by the child to recover civilly for the mother's own injuries or for the child's legally dependent losses. Mikayla does not claim any damages for injury to Naomi. Nor does the complaint demonstrate Mikayla's own recovery is legally dependent on injuries suffered by Naomi. For that reason, sections 3600–3602 did not defeat Mikayla's cause of action for her own injuries (the first cause of action) or her parents' claim for consequential losses due to Mikayla's injuries (the third cause of action).

Our conclusion the derivative injury rule does not apply in these circumstances accords with the view of every other court that has considered the question, with the exception of *Bell*. Thus, in *Ransburg Industries v. Brown* (Ind. Ct. App. 1995) 659 N.E.2d 1081 (hereafter *Ransburg Industries*), a child was severely injured in utero, and died shortly after birth, as a result of his mother having inhaled paint fumes in her workplace. The Indiana workers' compensation law precludes all civil actions by employees' family members "on account of" the employee's injury (Ind. Code, § 22-3-2-6, quoted in *Ransburg Industries, supra*, 659 N.E.2d at p. 1082), and Indiana courts had previously recognized the derivative injury doctrine as applicable to claims for loss of consortium (id. at pp. 1084–1085). Nevertheless, the appellate court concluded the parents' wrongful death suit for the son's death "is not derivative of his mother's claim for injuries. Unlike a loss of consortium claim, the action does not seek compensation for damages suffered by the claimant which arose on account of the injury sustained by the employee. Rather, this action seeks to recover for the injury sustained by Brandon himself while in utero, which ultimately resulted, it is claimed, in Brandon's death." (*Id.* at pp. 1085–1086.)

Similarly, in *Pizza Hut of America, Inc. v. Keefe* (Colo. 1995) 900 P.2d 97, the Colorado Supreme Court rejected application of the derivative injury doctrine to prenatal injuries allegedly suffered as a result of the mother's performance of various work tasks negligently ordered by her employer. "[T]he injury to the child was separate and distinct and subjects the employer to separate liability. In this case, the child's right of action arises out of and on account of her own personal injuries, and not any injury suffered by the mother." (*Id.* at p. 101.) That the mother also claimed injury from the same events did not alter the court's conclusion: "The exclusivity provisions do not constitute a bar to a claim asserted by a third-party victim, even though both the employee and the victim were injured together as a result of the same negligent act in a single transaction." (*Ibid.*)

Substantially the same analysis led the court in *Cushing v. Time Saver Stores, Inc.* (La. Ct. App. 1990) 552 So. 2d 730, to conclude that a child's suit for in utero brain injuries, allegedly caused by his mother's accidental workplace fall, was not barred by an exclusive remedy provision that, like our own section 3600, granted the employer civil immunity in actions "for" an employee's compensable injury. (552 So. 2d at p. 731, quoting La. Rev. Stat. § 23:1032.) While prior Louisiana decisions had barred civil actions for third party derivative injuries, in all those cases the claimant's injury "hinged upon the injuries of the employee. Because Dad or Mom suffered an injury, the family suffered a loss based on that injury." (552 So. 2d at p. 732.) The collateral loss might be economic, as in a claim for loss of support, or intangible, as in a claim for loss of consortium based on the employee's inability to continue participating in family life. (*Id.* at pp. 731–732.) In contrast, the fetal injuries at issue in Cushing were not logically derivative of the mother's injury: "Whether Mom is there to continue bringing home a paycheck or to participate in the child's life has no relevance to this child's alleged brain damage." (*Id.* at p. 732.)

Other courts considering the issue have reached the same conclusion. (See *Thompson v. Pizza Hut of America, Inc.* (N.D. Ill. 1991) 767 F.Supp. 916, 918 [Illinois law: child's suit for in utero injuries, allegedly caused by mother's workplace exposure to carbon monoxide and other fumes, not barred by Illinois workers' compensation law]; *Namislo v. Akzo Chemicals, Inc.* (Ala. 1993) 620 So. 2d 573, 575 [child's claim for in utero mercury poisoning at mother's workplace not barred]; *Jackson v. Tastykake, Inc.* (Pa. Super. Ct. 1994) 437 Pa. Super. 34, 648 A.2d 1214, 1216–1217 [injury to child, whose mother went into premature labor at workplace, not within exclusive remedy provision]; *Hitachi Chem. Electro-Products, Inc. v. Gurley* (1995) 219 Ga. App. 675, 466 S.E.2d 867, 869 [child's suit for in utero injuries caused by exposure to chemicals in parent's workplace not barred].) [footnote omitted]

The merit or lack thereof in *Bell's* reasoning aside, Michael's maintains the failure of the Legislature to abrogate that decision in the intervening eight years, coupled with its amendment of sections 3600 and 3602 in other respects, constitutes an implied endorsement of *Bell's* holding. We discern no cause to find a presumption of legislative approval in the present case. Bell was a single decision on a question of first impression, not a "consistent and long-standing judicial interpretation" of the statutory language. (*People v. Escobar* (1992) 3 Cal. 4th 740, 750, 12 Cal. Rptr. 2d 586, 837 P.2d 1100.)

Moreover, the intervening amendments to sections 3600 and 3602 have been to other portions of the statutes (see Historical and Statutory Notes 44A West's Ann. Cal. Codes (1997 Pocket pt.) foll. § 3600, pp. 34–35; id., foll. § 3602, p. 46); they did not constitute reenactments of the language construed in *Bell*. (See *People v. Escobar, supra*, 3 Cal. 4th at p. 751, 12 Cal. Rptr. 2d 586, 837 P.2d 1100.) Under these circumstances, the claim of legislative inaction is truly a "weak reed upon which to lean." (Ibid., internal quotation marks omitted.) [footnote omitted]

As an alternative ground, distinct from the derivative injury doctrine, for bringing Mikayla's injuries within sections 3600 to 3602, Michael's argues Mikayla herself — in utero — was an employee of Michael's. This novel theory, [footnote omitted] on first encounter merely implausible, proves on further examination to be utterly without merit. Although we have interpreted the statutory definitions of employee liberally to extend beyond traditional contracts of hire (see e.g., *Arriaga v. County of Alameda, supra*, 9 Cal. 4th at pp. 1061–1063, 40 Cal. Rptr. 2d 116, 892 P.2d 150; *Laeng v. Workmen's Comp. Appeals Bd.* (1972) 6 Cal. 3d 771, 776–783, 100 Cal. Rptr. 377, 494 P.2d 1 (*Laeng*)), we have never suggested a claimant might be considered an employee while failing to satisfy the basic statutory requirement of being "in the service of" (§ 3351) or "rendering service for" (§ 3357) another. Indeed, in *Laeng, supra*, 6 Cal. 3d at page 783, 100 Cal. Rptr. 377, 494 P.2d 1, we reaffirmed that "rendition of such service [is] a crucial criterion of liability under the act." Michael's, of course, does not and cannot assert that Mikayla, before her birth, rendered Michael's any service.

In *Laeng* we held that a job applicant, injured while performing a physical agility test required by the potential employer, was in the service of the potential employer and was therefore its employee at the time of the injury, even though the applicant had, of course, not yet been hired. We reasoned that the "tryout" was performed for the benefit of the employer, which was thereby able to hire better qualified workers. (*Laeng, supra*, 6 Cal. 3d at pp. 781–782, 100 Cal. Rptr. 377, 494 P.2d 1.) In addition, we observed that the applicant at a tryout is also in the service of the employer in that the applicant "subjects himself to the employer's control" and "undertak[es] a 'special risk of employment.'" (*Id.* at pp. 782–783, 100 Cal. Rptr. 377, 494 P.2d 1.)

Extracting these phrases from their factual context, Michael's argues the fetus, too, is under the employer's control (because the mother is under her employer's control) and subject to the special risks of the workplace (again because the mother is subject to these risks). Wordplay can only take one so far, however; the language of an opinion is not some kind of magical putty, to be stretched as long and thin as needed for the task at hand. The question in *Laeng* was whether the "inchoate" employment relationship (*Laeng, supra*, 6 Cal. 3d at p. 783, 100 Cal. Rptr. 377, 494 P.2d 1) between applicant and potential employer was sufficient to bring the applicant within workers' compensation. We held it was because "given the act's purpose of protecting individuals from any special risks inherent in employment, the act's coverage may at times properly precede the actual formation of an employment contract when those special risks are present at an early stage." (*Id.* at p. 782, 100 Cal. Rptr. 377, 494 P.2d 1.) The relationship between Michael's and Mikayla at the time of the latter's injury bore no relationship to that between applicant and potential employer. It was not an early stage of employment; in fact, no employment relationship existed between them, inchoate or otherwise. [footnote omitted]

The concerns raised by Michael's may be substantial, but are more properly addressed to the Legislature than to this court. The "compensation bargain" to which Michael's alludes is between businesses and their *employees* and generally does not include third party injuries. The workers' compensation law " . . . imposes reciprocal concessions upon employer and employee alike, withdrawing from each certain rights and defenses available at common law. . . . " (*Williams v. State Compensation Ins. Fund, supra*, 50 Cal. App. 3d at p. 122, 123 Cal. Rptr. 812, italics added.) The employee's "concession" of a common law tort action under sections 3600 to 3602 extends, as we have seen, to family members' collateral losses deriving from the employee's injury . Neither the statutory language nor the case law, however, remotely suggests that third parties who, because of a business's negligence, suffer injuries — logically and legally independent of any employee's injuries — have conceded their common law rights of action as part of the societal "compensation bargain." As the *Bell* court acknowledged, even close family members of employees are third parties entitled to sue when their claims are independent of and not collateral to an employee injury; the employer is not relieved of tort liability to such family members injured while visiting the work site. (*Bell, supra*, 212 Cal. App. 3d at 1451, 261 Cal. Rptr. 447; see, e.g., *Robbins v. Yellow Cab Co.* (1948) 85 Cal. App. 2d 811, 813–814, 193 P.2d 956 [workers' compensation not exclusive remedy for plaintiff injured while picking up her husband's paycheck].)

Generally speaking, businesses, like other actors, must bear the costs of accidents caused by the negligent conduct of their activities; when the injured person is not an employee, and the person's claim does not derive from an employee's injury, the costs are assessed and recovered through the civil justice system. (Civ. Code, § 1714, subd. (a).) The third parties to whom businesses may be civilly liable include, of course, the conceived but unborn child of a nonemployee "in the event of the child's subsequent birth." (Civ. Code, § 43.1.) Nothing in sections 3600 to 3602, or in any other statutory source Michael's cites, suggests a legislative intent that prenatal injuries to the children of employees be any different.

Section 3600 provides civil immunity to an employer for liability "for any injury sustained by his or her employees arising out of and in the course of employment." As we have seen, the immunity so provided includes collateral or derivative losses to family members from employee injuries, but does not include logically independent claims by family members or other third parties. We cannot legitimately rewrite the statutory grant of immunity to include a particular class of such third party injuries (prenatal injuries to employees' children), any more than we could rewrite it to include, for example, a particular class of injuries arising outside the course of employment.

Our conclusion is reinforced if one considers the policy choices this court would have to make in formulating a rule of civil immunity for fetal injuries. Should the new rule of civil immunity be coupled with a provision giving injured children, or their parents, compensation through the workers' compensation system? The *Bell* court conceded the current workers' compensation system provides little if any compensation to parents for birth defects or other harms their child suffers as a result of injury in the mother's workplace; of course, the system provides none to the child. (*Bell, supra*, 212 Cal. App. 3d at p. 1455, fn. 7, 261 Cal. Rptr. 447.) [footnote omitted] If compensation is to be given, to whom should it be directed, what elements of loss should be included, and how should they be estimated? These are questions that only the political branches of government can answer.

Michael's points out that, under federal antidiscrimination law, employers are generally prohibited from implementing broad "fetal protection" policies excluding fertile women from potentially hazardous jobs. (*United Automobile Workers v. Johnson Controls, Inc.* (1991) 499 U.S. 187, 206–207, 111 S.Ct. 1196, 1207–1208, 113 L.Ed.2d 158 (*Johnson Controls*).) Michael's suggests employees' children should therefore be treated differently than those of nonemployees because, while businesses can control most third party liability for workplace accidents by excluding nonemployees from the workplace, biology and federal antidiscrimination law prevent them from excluding the employee's child in utero. (See also *Pizza Hut of America, Inc. v. Keefe, supra*, 900 P.2d at p. 104 (dis. opn. of Rovira, C.J.) [making the same argument].)

Again, Michael's argument is directed at policy decisions beyond our realm of authority in a case of statutory interpretation. Our focus has been and must be on sections 3600 to 3602 of the Labor Code, not on what might be the fairest or economically most beneficial policy for the state to pursue in light of federal law. We observe, however, that the scope of the problem presented by Johnson Controls may be narrower than Michael's suggests.

Although real, the distinction between employees' children and others is easily overstated. Much of what businesses do is done, and must be done, in the presence of third parties, including pregnant women, thus putting the women's unborn children at risk for accidental injury and exposing the business to possible civil liability. The same threats to fetal health identified in *Bell, supra*, 212 Cal. App. 3d at page 1454, 261 Cal. Rptr. 447, as risks to which an employee's child is subject — "[t]rips and falls, car accidents, explosions, fires . . . poisoning by exposure to toxic substances, genetic damage caused by radiation," etc. — can also cause prenatal injury to children of nonemployees. For example, Michael's, like most other retail and service establishments, necessarily conducts its business in the presence of nonemployees — customers — including pregnant women. According to the instant complaint, use of a propane-powered machine in the store, coupled with inadequate ventilation, resulted in carbon monoxide poisoning to "approximately 21 employees and customers." At least one of the employees, Naomi, was pregnant. But one or more of the affected customers could also have been pregnant, and her child could have suffered the same injuries as Mikayla allegedly did. Michael's could no more exclude fertile female customers than it could exclude fertile female employees.

Regardless of whether *Bell's* rule stands or falls, therefore, a retail store cannot operate without running the risk of civil liability if its negligence causes a fetal injury. In the same way, businesses in such diverse and populous categories as hospitals and clinics, common carriers, trucking companies, theaters, law firms, health clubs and restaurants all must conduct significant portions of their activities with, or in the presence of, customers and other nonemployees, including pregnant women. None of these businesses can, by controlling who comes into the workplace, preclude the possibility they will negligently cause prenatal injuries to a nonemployee's child. All they can do is attempt to conduct their businesses safely and insure themselves against the remaining risks of accident. The *Bell* rule thus makes at most a quantitative, not a qualitative, difference to the exposure of businesses to tort liability for fetal injury. Neither a flood of new personal injury cases nor a greatly increased pressure to discriminate against women in employment would seem, as to these employers, a likely outcome of overruling *Bell*.

There may be certain businesses, primarily manufacturers, that conduct the major part of their operations away from the presence of customers and other members of the public and routinely expose their employees, through these operations, to agents causing fetal injury. Even as to these employers, however, it is not clear overruling *Bell* will create significant new tort liability. As the high court explained in *Johnson Controls*, federal antidiscrimination law would likely preempt state tort law to the extent the employer's actions were required by federal law. (*Johnson Controls, supra*, 499 U.S. at p. 209, 111 S.Ct. at p. 1208–1209.) Thus, the possibility that an employer that merely allowed women to occupy jobs involving exposure to teratogens, while fully informing them of the risks, would face tort liability "seems remote at best." (*Id.* at p. 208, 111 S.Ct. at p. 1208.) Liability could rest only on the employer's actual negligence in exposing the pregnant employee's unborn child to an unreasonable risk of injury. Whether society would enjoy a net benefit by barring tort actions in such cases is a question we will not even try to answer.

CONCLUSION

Up to this time, the Legislature has made workers' compensation the exclusive remedy for work-related injuries to employees and for collateral losses deriving from those injuries, but not for legally independent claims by nonemployees for their own injuries. The decision whether to go beyond that point, to provide civil immunity — and perhaps a corresponding remedy in the workers' compensation system — for a particular class of such independent third party injuries, is not ours to make.

The judgment of the Court of Appeal is *affirmed*.

GEORGE, C.J., and MOSK, KENNARD, BAXTER, CHIN and BROWN, JJ., concur.

PROBLEMS

(1) Isn't the argument made by Michaels' regarding *Johnson Controls* a telling one? If indeed the fetus in utero is a separate person with legal rights independent of the mother, and the exclusive remedy provision is inapplicable thus permitting the unborn child to sue the employer in tort, shouldn't an employer be able to protect itself from that kind of liability by excluding pregnant women from workplaces that involve toxic exposure?

(2) Decedent's widow sued the employer, seeking damages on an independent federal cause of action for defendant's negligent violation of the federal Occupational Safety and Health Act. Does the state's exclusive remedy bar the federal action? *See* Byrd v. Fieldcrest Mills, 496 F.2d 1323 (4th Cir. 1974).

Chapter 24
UNINSURED OR NONELECTING EMPLOYERS

SYNOPSIS

§ 24.01   INTRODUCTION

The small minority of compensation acts permitting election generally provide that an employer who elects to reject compensation coverage is subject to common law suit without benefit of the defenses of fellow servant, assumption of risk and contributory negligence. Most acts give a similar action against a covered employer who fails to secure payment of compensation by carrying insurance or qualifying as a self-insurer. This has been construed in a few states to put the employee to a strict election between common law and compensation remedies, so that even a fruitless suit may deprive the employee of compensation. However, the majority rule appears to be that a choice of what proves to be a nonexistent remedy is no election at all. Because of this problem and others of the same sort, the entire device of election in workers' compensation and the practice of using resort to common law rights as a penalty are unsatisfactory in practice and should be replaced by compulsory provisions, with additional penalties within the framework of the compensation system itself, in the form of increased compensation and criminal sanctions.

§ 24.02   ACTION AGAINST NONELECTING EMPLOYER

All but two compensation acts are compulsory as to the major part of industrial employment, and those two are elective.[1]

As a sort of club to drive employers into election of coverage, the typical act makes the noncovered employer subject to common law liability without benefit of the defenses of fellow servant, assumption of risk and contributory negligence.

When acceptance of coverage is presumed by statute in the absence of rejection, the rejection must be in strict conformity with statutory requirements, whether by employer or employee. When the question is what will amount to affirmative election of coverage, most courts are less exacting as to formalities, and will accept any realistic evidence of intent to accept coverage, such as the taking out of workers' compensation insurance[2] or filing a bond securing payment.[3]

---

[1] The list of "elective" states, which is rapidly dwindling, at this writing includes only New Jersey and Texas.

Note that some of the cases in this section are from states that have since made their acts compulsory. These cases are retained for whatever value they might have in states still having elective acts.

The New Jersey act is compulsory as to public employment.

[2] Horton v. Foster-Glocester Regional School Dist., 103 R.I. 410, 238 A.2d 53 (1968).

[3] Garrison v. Bonfield, 57 N.M. 533, 260 P.2d 718 (1953).

§ 24.03   ACTION AGAINST UNINSURED EMPLOYER

A common exception to the exclusiveness of the compensation remedy is the right of suit against an employer who fails to secure its compensation liability by taking out insurance or qualifying as a self-insured. In interpreting what is meant by "securing" compensation, courts are inclined to give the benefit of the doubt to an employer who has in substance if not in form provided the secured protection contemplated by the act. A mere omission to prepare the insurance policy or file it has been held not to amount to a failure to secure compensation, so long as insurance coverage was actually in effect.[4] But when an employer is unable in spite of its best efforts to get insurance, its good intentions can not overcome the fact of absence of insurance coverage.[5]

Occasionally the penalty of liability to common law suit will result from other related kinds of noncompliance with the act, such as omission to post notices informing employees of their compensation rights. This is not, as may at first appear, a mere formality, since one purpose of posting the notice is to inform employees of the employer's election, so that they in turn may exercise their right of rejection if they choose.[6]

Since 1949, no American jurisdiction gives a covered employee the option to sue for damages in the absence of one of these specific acts of noncompliance or misconduct on the part of the employer.

The abolition of defenses applicable to the nonelecting employer is also applicable to the noninsuring employer. In addition, criminal penalties are sometimes imposed, to meet the problem of fly-by-night businesses whose general cloak of irresponsibility would make them as insensitive to the sting of common law liability as to that of compensation liability.

§ 24.04   ELECTION OF REMEDIES BY EMPLOYEE

The most troublesome question that emerges from the various situations in which an action at law may lie against the employer, as when a statute giving the employee an option to claim either common law damages or compensation from the uninsured employer, is this: Is the employee who pursues one remedy to a fruitless conclusion barred by his election from pursuing the other? The majority of cases have held that an unsuccessful damage suit does not bar a compensation claim,[7] and that an unsuccessful compensation claim does not bar a damage suit.[8] The correct theory, which has its beneficent counterpart in almost any other field of law where the harsh old Roman doctrine of election rears its head, is that an election of a remedy which proves to be nonexistent is no election at all.[9] Election, according to this view, is a choice between two valid but inconsistent remedies; it is not the mistaken pursuit of a misconceived right when only one right in fact existed.

Unquestionably this is the only view which effectuates the purposes of the legislation, whatever arguments may be raised against it based on literal wording of statutes[10] or on the technical application of the election doctrine at some stages of the common law. Workers' compensation is above all a security system; a strict election doctrine transforms it into a sort of double-or-nothing gamble. Such gambles are appealing to

---

[4] *E.g.*, Mirabal v. International Minerals & Chem. Corp., 77 N.M. 576, 425 P.2d 740 (1967).

[5] McCoy v. Cornish, 220 Miss. 577, 71 So. 2d 304 (1954).

[6] Herring v. Lawrence Warehouse Co., 222 S.C. 226, 72 S.E.2d 453 (1952).

[7] *E.g.*, Virginia Used Auto Parts, Inc. v. Robertson, 212 Va. 100, 81 S.E.2d 612 (1971).

[8] *E.g.*, Carter v. Ferris, 337 S.W.2d 852 (Tex. Civ. App. 1960).

[9] American Lumbermen's Mut. Cas. Co. v. Lowe, 70 F.2d 616 (2d Cir. 1934).

[10] Tocci's Case, 269 Mass. 221, 168 N.E. 744 (1929).

those who still think of the judicial process as a game in which formal moves and choices are made at peril, and in which the ultimate result is spectacular victory for one side and utter defeat for the other. The stricken worker is in no mood for this kind of play, and should not be maneuvered into the necessity for gambling with his or her rights, under the guise of enforcing a supposed penalty against the employer.

This line of argument is less cogent when the alleged election takes the form of a successful rather than an unsuccessful achievement of either the compensation or the damages remedy. A successful compensation claim will ordinarily bar a subsequent damage suit,[11] and a successful damage suit will ordinarily bar a subsequent compensation claim.[12] The situations resulting from these two kinds of prior claim are not precisely symmetrical, however. If the first remedy sought is that of damages, even if successful, there still remains the argument — which has no counterpart the other way round — that the employee entitled to workers' compensation by statute cannot waive the right to compensation by anything he or she does.[13] There is also the practical distinction that, while a prior compensation remedy may be assumed to be subject to some control as to adequacy, a prior damages recovery or settlement may be totally inadequate, leaving the basic function of the compensation system unperformed. Moreover, a distinction should be observed between the mere passive acceptance of benefits that the employee has not claimed, and the active prosecution of a compensation claim, since the former has much less content of deliberate and conscious election and pursuit of a particular remedy.

The attempt to mix the common law with compensation is no more successful here than at the other points where it has been attempted. There are two principal weaknesses: From the employer's point of view, as we have seen, the threat of common law liability is not always a sufficient incentive to compel compliance with the act; and from the employee's point of view, the option to seek damages sometimes turns out to be a perilous gamble, dependent on his or her ability to prove actionable negligence attributable to the employer. In addition, the election procedure produces much uncertainty and litigation about the technicalities of what constitutes a binding election, what mistakes or frauds or coercions will avoid the election, and so on.

§ 24.05   UNINSURED EMPLOYER FUNDS

The most satisfactory solution of the uninsured employer problem is to provide an uninsured employer fund, as is done in a substantial and steadily growing number of states. The fund pays compensation to the employee of the uninsured employer, then turns upon the employer and calls it to account, armed with a battery of penalties, sometimes including fines and imprisonment,[14] which cannot fail to impress the most elusive and irresponsible of employers.

The Fund's liability is identical to that of the uninsured employer — no more[15] and no less.[16] Thus, although this might seem a bit surprising, the Fund has consistently been held liable for penalties assessed against the employer.[17] However, the surprise diminishes when one remembers that the Fund's subrogation rights against the

---

[11] *E.g.*, Biner v. Dynalectron Corp., 85 Nev. 539, 458 P.2d 616 (1969).

[12] *E.g.*, Martin v. C.A. Prods. Co., 8 N.Y.2d 226, 168 N.E.2d 666 (1960).

[13] Worthington v. Industrial Comm'n, 85 Ariz. 310, 338 P.2d 363 (1959).

[14] *E.g.*, Ohio Rev. Code §§ 4123.50 and 4123.99 (1965): $500 fine, 90 days' imprisonment.

[15] Candee v. State Acc. Fund, 40 Or. App. 567, 595 P.2d 1381 (1979).

[16] Uninsured Employers' Fund v. Booker, 13 Md. App. 591, 284 A.2d 454 (1971).

[17] *E.g.*, Flores v. Workmen's Comp. App. Bd., 113 Cal. Rptr. 217, 520 P.2d 1033 (1974).

employer includes these penalties.[18] Generally, the Fund is bound by decisions holding the employer liable.[19] The employer, however, remains directly liable to the employee.[20]

§ 24.06 PERCENTAGE INCREASE IN COMPENSATION AS PENALTY FOR NONINSURANCE

In some states, there is a penalty for noninsurance in the form of a percentage increase in compensation payments. In Colorado, the payments may be increased by fifty percent.[21] In Alabama, the penalty is a double award, and it is mandatory.[22] Another type of intra-compensation penalty is that in Missouri, where the entire amount of compensation becomes due instantly in a lump sum.[23]

---

[18] Flores v. Workmen's Comp. App. Bd., 113 Cal. Rptr. 217, 520 P.2d 1033 (1974).

[19] Barth v. Cassar, 357 N.Y.S.2d 46 (App. Div. 1974).

[20] Davis v. Turner, 519 S.W.2d 820 (Ky. App. 1975).

[21] Colo. Rev. Stat. § 8-43-408 (1999).

[22] Ala. Code § 25-5-8(e) (1999); Hester v. Ridings, 388 So. 2d 1218 (Ala. App. 1980). The statute providing for an award of double compensation against an employer who fails to secure his compensation liability is constitutional.

[23] Mays v. Williams, 494 S.W.2d 289 (Mo. 1973).

Part 9

THIRD-PARTY ACTIONS

Chapter 25
THEORY OF THIRD-PARTY ACTIONS

§ 25.01 INTRODUCTION

When compensable injury is the result of a third person's tortious conduct, the tortfeasor remains liable in tort, since the compensation system was not designed to extend immunity to strangers. To avoid a double recovery by the employee, the great majority of statutes provide varying systems with the general effect of reimbursing the employer for its compensation outlay and giving the employee the excess of the damage recovery over the amount of compensation. However, the carrier generally has no right to reimbursement out of the proceeds of the claimant's uninsured motorist policy. As to automobile no-fault policies, the typical policy provides that the no-fault insurer may reduce the no-fault benefits by the amount of workers' compensation payable. But jurisdictions are split on the right of compensation carriers to reimbursement out of the excess in the claimant's third-party recovery above economic loss.

§ 25.02 REACHING THE ULTIMATE WRONGDOER

The concept underlying third party actions is the moral idea that the ultimate loss from wrongdoing should fall upon the wrongdoer. Every mature loss-adjusting mechanism must look in two directions: It must make the injured person whole, and it must also seek out the true wrongdoer whenever possible. While compensation law, in its social legislation aspect, is almost entirely preoccupied with the former function, it is not so devoid of moral content as to overlook the latter. It should never be forgotten that the distortions of our old-fashioned fault concepts that have been thought advisable for reasons of social policy are exclusively limited to providing an assured recovery for the injured person; they have never gone on — once the injured person was made whole — to change the rules on how the ultimate burden was borne.

Similarly, in compensation law, social policy has dispensed with fault concepts to the extent necessary to ensure an automatic recovery by the injured worker; but the disregard of fault goes no further than to accomplish that object, and, with payment of the worker assured, the quest of the law for the actual wrongdoer may proceed in the usual way.

So, it is elementary that if a stranger's negligence was the cause of injury to claimant in the course of employment, the stranger should not be in any degree absolved of the normal obligation to pay damages for such an injury.

§ 25.03   AVOIDING DOUBLE RECOVERY

[1]   Introduction

It is equally elementary that the claimant should not be allowed to keep the entire amount both of a compensation award and of a common law damage recovery for the same injury.[1] The obvious disposition of the matter is to give the employer so much of the negligence recovery as is necessary to reimburse it for its compensation outlay, and to give the employee the excess. This is fair to everyone concerned. The *employer*, who, in a fault sense, is neutral, comes out even. The *third party* pays exactly the damages that would normally be paid, which is correct, since to reduce the third party's burden because of the relation between the employer and the employee would be a windfall which the third party has done nothing to deserve. And the *employee* obtains a fuller reimbursement for actual damages sustained than is possible under the compensation system alone.

[2]   Specific Double-Recovery Situations

But now and then a peculiar combination of facts will occur producing a double recovery that is allowed to stand. One situation in which a double recovery has been upheld is in the case of an uninsured employer, the justification being that such an employer's liability is in the nature of a penalty.[2] The double recovery came about in this fashion: the employer, being uninsured, was entitled to none of the normal rights of an employer under the Act. Therefore, when the employee obtained a third-party recovery, the employer had no right to reimbursement from it, just as it had no right of subrogation. Moreover, the Act absolutely required the employer to pay compensation as a penalty for failure to comply with the insurance provisions of the Act.

However, the policy of avoiding double recovery is a strong one, and has on occasion been invoked to override a result that might be thought required by a literal or technical interpretation of statutes or insurance policies. In an interesting New York case,[3] the decedent had been killed in a car leased by the employer, due to the negligence of his coemployee. The accident occurred in Connecticut, which allows suit against a coemployee, while the employment was covered by the New York Act, which does not allow such actions. Death benefits were paid by the employer under the New York Act. A recovery in a wrongful death action was had in Connecticut against the coemployee and the employer, who was liable under an indemnity agreement with the lessor. The compensation carrier was held entitled to a lien against the recovery for the amount of its obligation, although the statutory provision only applied to cases in which the third party was one other than a coemployee. The decision was squarely based on the legislative intent not to allow double recovery in such situations.

[3]   Coordination of Uninsured Motorist Insurance and Workers' Compensation

A comparatively recent problem in double recovery presents the question whether a carrier that has paid compensation benefits should have a lien upon the proceeds of the claimant's private uninsured motorist policy. At this writing, the case law disfavors any such lien.[4]

---

[1] Richardson v. U.S. Fid. & Guar. Co., 233 Miss. 375, 102 So. 2d 368 (1958).

[2] State *ex rel.* Woods v. Hughes Oil Co., 58 N.D. 581, 226 N.W. 586 (1929).

[3] Petterson v. Daystrom Corp., 17 N.Y.2d 32, 268 N.Y.S.2d 1, 215 N.E.2d 329 (1966).

[4] *See, e.g.*, The Travelers Ins. Co. v. National Farmers Union Property & Cas. Co., 252 Ark. 624, 480 S.W.2d 585 (1972).

[4]   Coordination of Automobile No-Fault Insurance and Workers' Compensation

[a]   In general

Another relatively recent problem is that of coordinating automobile no-fault insurance with workers' compensation. Here, too, although some broad lines of principle are discernible, substantial differences from state to state have also appeared, due in part to variations in the statutes themselves.

The typical no-fault statute provides that the no-fault carrier may reduce the no-fault benefits by the amount of workers' compensation payable.[5] This deduction has been held constitutional as having a rational basis.[6]

Since the no-fault insurer's right to the deduction turns on the compensability of the worker's injuries, awkward problems may arise on how the compensability of the injuries and the amount of compensation payable is determined. Much depends on the wording of the particular no-fault statute. In some acts,[7] the deduction clause speaks of compensation benefits "received" or "recovered." Colorado's reduction applies to benefits "actually available" under the compensation act — which arguably could mean either "provided for" or actually paid.[8] Several other states[9] use such phrases as "compensable," "collectible," or "entitled to receive." Under this type of clause, the obvious next question is: If the claimant has not obtained the compensation benefits to which he or she is entitled, what can the insurer do to establish that the benefits are indeed payable?

New Jersey has held that, to protect its right to reimbursement, the no-fault insurer can initiate, in its own name, a petition in workers' compensation to determine what amount was collectible from workers' compensation as a collateral source.[10]

But in New York, when the claimant had made a compensation claim, which was disallowed, the court was less solicitous of the carrier's interests. In *Lotito v. Salt City Playhouse*,[11] the Insurance Department had issued a rule that, in a case where both no-fault and controverted compensation liability are involved, the no-fault carrier must first pay, getting from the claimant an agreement to pursue the compensation claim diligently and to reimburse the no-fault carrier from the compensation proceeds.[12] The no-fault carrier had accordingly paid the full no-fault liability, and received the agreement to press the compensation claim and reimburse the no-fault carrier. The compensation claim was disallowed. But the no-fault carrier was held to have no standing in the compensation proceeding, in spite of its interest in possible reimbursement, since the statute had given the carrier no enforceable interest in the compensation claim.

In several cases, no-fault carriers have contended that the compensation amount should be deducted, not from plaintiff's actual wage loss, but from the no-fault policy ceiling on wage-loss replacement. This contention has been consistently rejected: courts in several states[13] have held that the deduction should be applied to actual wage loss.

---

[5] Wagner v. National Indem. Co., 492 Pa. 154, 422 A.2d 1061 (1980).

[6] Aetna Insurance Co. v. Smith, 263 Ark. 849, 568 S.W.2d 11 (1978).

[7] *E.g.*, South Carolina and Maryland.

[8] Colo. Rev. Stat. Ann § 10-4-707(5).

[9] *E.g.*, New Jersey and Connecticut.

[10] Aetna Cas. & Sur. Co. v. Para Mfg. Co., 176 N.J. Super. 532, 424 A.2d 423 (1980).

[11] Lotito v. Salt, 66 A.D.2d 437, 414 N.Y.S.2d 44 (1979).

[12] 11 N.Y.C.R.R. Sec. 65.6(p)(3)(i).

[13] *E.g.*, Pennsylvania: Adams v. Nationwide Ins. Co., 285 Pa. Super. 79, 426 A.2d 1150 (1981).

So, if the actual weekly wage loss were $400, the worker's compensation benefit $225, and the no-fault policy limit $300, the $225 would be subtracted from the $400, not the $300. The no-fault benefit would then be, not $75, but $175.

What happens if the compensation act applies but no benefits are payable? In *Carey v. Electric Mutual Liability Ins. Co.*,[14] Carey was injured while making deliveries for his employer in a truck owned by it. He had proceeded into a railroad crossing after the warning light had operated and crossing gates had descended. When struck by the oncoming train, he had had a high blood alcohol level. The court found that he was covered by Pennsylvania's compensation act, but that benefits had been denied because the injuries were caused by his violation of the law. However, because Carey was covered by the Act (although without receiving benefits), the employer's no-fault insurance carrier escaped liability.

Michigan[15] and New York[16] have held that the exclusive remedy clause does not bar an action by the employee based on his employer's no-fault insurance. The principal reason for this result is that the no-fault carrier's liability is a direct one, created by statute, and thus not subject to the employer's exclusive liability defense. But both states have also gone on to hold that an employer with self-insured no-fault coverage is also subject to suit.[17] The courts evidently thought it would be incongruous to have the result turn on whether the employer secured its statutory no-fault liability by insurance or self-insurance.

Pennsylvania has reached the opposite conclusion, holding that the exclusive remedy clause controls[18] — even when the plaintiff, although covered by the compensation act, in fact received no benefits under it.[19]

[b] Third-Party Suit Beyond No-Fault Limits: Rights of Carrier

Suppose that the employee has obtained a third-party no-fault recovery which, even after deducting "economic loss" in the form of wage loss and medical expense, contains a substantial balance. Can the compensation carrier claim reimbursement for its compensation outlay from this balance? New York, in *Granger v. Urda*,[20] held that it can. The claimant was injured in an automobile accident which arose out of and in the course of his employment, and received from his employer's compensation carrier a total of about $9,000 in compensation and medical payments. In a subsequent negligence action against other parties to the accident, the claimant received a judgment for about $31,000, which pursuant to the no-fault automobile statute excluded his "basic economic loss" (lost past and future wages and medical payments). The defendants paid the claimant all but the amount that he had previously collected under his compensation claim, and then deposited the remaining sum with the court, being unable to determine the proper party to pay. The Court of Appeals held that the compensation carrier had an absolute lien against all the proceeds of the judgment. The court recognized that this had the effect of making the employee a self-insurer of his or her economic loss, but concluded that the remedy for this "harsh, unintended result" lay with the legislature.

---

[14] Carey v. Electric Mutual Liability Ins. Co., 500 F. Supp. 1227 (W.D. Pa. 1980).

[15] Mathis v. Interstate Motor Freight Sys., 408 Mich. 164, 289 N.W.2d 708 (1980).

[16] Carriers Ins. Co. v. Burakowski, 93 Misc. 2d 100, 402 N.Y.S.2d 333 (N.Y. Sup. Ct. 1978).

[17] Ryder Truck Co. v. Maiorano, 44 N.Y.2d 364, 405 N.Y.S.2d 666, 376 N.E.2d 1311 (1978); Mathis v. Interstate Motor Freight Sys., 408 Mich. 164, 289 N.W.2d 708 (1980).

[18] Wagner v. National Indem. Co., 422 A.2d 1061 (Pa. 1980).

[19] Turner v. Southeastern Pennsylvania Transp. Auth., 256 Pa. Super. 43, 389 A.2d 591 (1978).

[20] Granger v. Urda, 44 N.Y.2d 91, 404 N.Y.S.2d 319, 375 N.E.2d 380 (1978).

Pennsylvania has reached the opposite result.[21] Its principal rationale is that, since no-fault insurers are liable only for amounts beyond basic loss benefits, and since compensation benefits are by definition basic loss benefits, there is nothing left of the tortfeasor's liability to which the compensation carrier's subrogation rights could attach.

§ 25.04 DOUBLE RECOVERY APART FROM SUBROGATION STATUTE

In the small handful states that have no third-party statutes, it appears to be accepted that the injured employee can keep both compensation payments and whatever he or she can get from the tortfeasor.[22] The employer gets no subrogation or reimbursement, on the theory that such rights are purely statutory, and that the doctrine of equitable subrogation does not apply.[23] This view misconceives the fundamental nature of workers' compensation, referring to it as equivalent to accident insurance, and applying precedents denying equitable subrogation under such insurance. It is nothing of the sort. In accident insurance, the insured buys and pays for a certain kind of payment upon the occurrence of a stipulated contingency; on the happening of the contingency, the insured has a proprietary right in the insurance proceeds. But in workers' compensation, the employer pays the premium, not the employee and, thus, no such personal proprietary interest in the employee exists.

---

[21] Brunelli v. Farelly Brothers, 266 Pa. Super. 23, 402 A.2d 1058 (1979).

[22] *E.g.*, Trumbull Cliffs Furnace Co. v. Shakovsky, 111 Ohio St. 791, 146 N.E. 306 (1924).

[23] Liberty Mut. Ins. Co. v. Georgia Ports Auth., 155 Ga. App. 940, 274 S.E.2d 52 (1980).

Chapter 26
WHO ARE "THIRD PERSONS"?

§ 26.01   INTRODUCTION

In around six jurisdictions, the concept of "third persons," against whom common law actions may be brought for compensable injuries, includes all persons other than the injured person's own employer; i.e.; it includes coemployees, employers of employees working on the same project, and physicians whose malpractice aggravates the compensable injury. However, both by statute and by judicial decision, the class of persons amenable to third-party suit has in most jurisdictions been narrowed to exclude sometimes coemployees and sometimes persons working on the same project. If an employer has a second legal persona creating completely independent duties, a few jurisdictions have held that the employer may be sued as a third person for violation of those duties. Apart from statutes identifying the carrier with the employer or expressly granting the carrier immunity from suit, the carrier has been held a third party vulnerable to suit for negligent safety inspections or medical treatment in a number of cases, but there is substantial authority to the contrary.

The first question that must be examined is the range of persons considered "third parties" and as such amenable to common law suit.

The variants here fall into three categories, granting immunity from third-party suit to the following: (1) the employer only; (2) the employer and coemployees in the same employment; (3) the employer, coemployees, and all contractors and their employees engaged upon a common employment. For reasons of historical interest, it may be noted also that at one time three states extended immunity to all persons subject to the state's compensation system.

§ 26.02 EMPLOYER ALONE IMMUNE

In around six jurisdictions, immunity to common law suit is extended only to the employer.[1] An injured employee can therefore sue a *coemployee* for the latter's negligence,[2] and it follows logically that the employer can exercise subrogation rights against its own tortfeasor employee.[3]

As to *corporate officers, stockholders, and directors*, most courts have held that such status is not in itself a bar to liability as a coemployee,[4] since the corporate entity is the employer. The clearest case for liability is that in which the corporate officer is acting in his capacity as an employee — even a managerial employee — and in which the conduct involved is the kind of negligence or misconduct that would normally make any coemployee liable.[5] At the other extreme, the clearest case for immunity is that in which the defendant's alleged liability is predicated entirely upon status as stockholder, rather than active conduct.[6]

Between these two extremes are various shades of close cases. Most courts will hold the individual defendant immune if the act with which the defendant is charged is an act done in his or her official capacity as an agent or representative of the corporation,[7] or if the duty allegedly violated was a nondelegable duty of the corporation, such as the duty to provide a safe place to work.[8]

Like corporate officers, and with even stronger reason, a supervisor or foreman is entitled to no general immunity under outmoded concepts such as the vice-principal doctrine.[9] On the other hand, a member of a partnership, even if a "working partner," is still in law the employer of employees of the partnership and cannot be sued.[10]

---

[1] Including, *e.g.*, Arkansas, Missouri, Maryland, and Vermont.

A strong tide toward coemployee immunity has been running for some years. As recently as 1974, a majority of states permitted suits against coemployees.

Note that a number of decisions referred to in this subsection are from states that have since amended their statutes to immunize coemployees.

[2] Markle v. Williamson, 518 P.2d 621 (Wyo. 1974).

[3] Zimmer v. Casey, 296 Pa. 529, 146 A. 130 (1929).

[4] Barnette v. Doyle, 622 P.2d 1349 (Wyo. 1981).

[5] West v. Jessop, 339 So. 2d 1136 (Fla. App. 1976).

[6] Steele v. Eaton, 285 A.2d 749 (Vt. 1971).

[7] Kruse v. Schieve, 61 Wis. 2d 421, 213 N.W.2d 64 (1973).

[8] Cunningham v. Heard, 134 Ga. App. 276, 214 S.E.2d 190 (1975).

[9] Tully v. Estate of Gardner, 169 Kan. 137, 409 P.2d 782 (1966).

[10] Daniels v. Roumillat, 264 S.C. 497, 216 S.E.2d 174 (1975).

§ 26.03   EMPLOYER AND COEMPLOYEES IMMUNE

[1]   Summary of Coemployee Immunity Statutes and Decisions

The great majority of states[11] and the Longshore Act now exclude coemployees from the category of "third persons." Of these, over 30 recognize an exception for intentional wrongs.[12] A typical general provision is as follows:

> If an injury or death is compensable under this article, a person shall not be liable to anyone at common law or otherwise on account of such injury or death for any act or omission occurring while such person was in the same employ as the person injured or killed, except for intentional wrong.[13]

It is now well established that the effect of this general type of clause is to bar all suits against coemployees by injured employees or by subrogated employers.[14] The barring of suits against a coemployee has been held not an unconstitutional deprivation of the common law rights of the injured worker.[15]

This legislative extension of immunity to the coemployee may be justified within the bounds of compensation theory. The reason for the employer's immunity is the *quid pro quo* by which the employer gives up its normal defenses and assumes automatic liability, while the employee gives up the right to common law verdicts. The tortfeasor coemployee, too, is involved in this compromise of rights: one of the things, so the argument runs, such a coemployee is entitled to expect in return for what he or she has given up is freedom from common law suits based on industrial accidents in which he or she may be at fault.

[2]   Necessity that Coemployee Be Acting in Course of Employment

It must be observed, however, that the immunity attaches to the coemployee only when the coemployee is acting in the course of his employment.[16]

The commonest question that arises in these cases is: Which test of "course of employment" applies? Is it the workers' compensation test, or the vicarious liability test? The answer may be dictated by the wording of the immunity clause itself. In California, for example, under the statutory phrase "acting within the scope of his or her employment," suit is barred against the coemployee only if at the time of the injury he or she was actively engaged in some service for the employer.[17] Accordingly, it can readily happen in California — indeed has happened — that in a marginal course of employment situation an employee will be held to have been sufficiently within the course of employment to receive workers' compensation, but not sufficiently actively engaged in service for his employer to enjoy immunity from suit. In one such case, an employee who was struck by a coemployee's automobile after work on the employer's parking lot was held not barred from suing the coemployee, although the coemployee had actually been awarded workers' compensation benefits as for an injury in the

---

[11] *E.g.*, California, New York, and Texas.

[12] *E.g.*, California, Massachusetts (by judicial decision), and Pennsylvania.

[13] N.J. Stat. § 34:15-8.

[14] Liston v. Hicks, 243 App. Div. 159, 277 N.Y. Supp. 19 (1935), *aff'd* 269 N.Y. 535, 199 N.E. 523.

[15] Lowman v. Stafford, 226 Cal. App. 2d 31, 37 Cal. Rptr. 681 (1964).

[16] D'Agostino v. Wagenaar, 183 Misc. 184, 48 N.Y.S.2d 410 (1944), *aff'd*, 268 App. Div. 912, 51 N.Y.S.2d 756, *appeal denied*, 268 App. Div. 986, 52 N.Y.S.2d 784.

[17] McIvor v. Savage, 220 Cal. App. 2d 128, 33 Cal. Rptr. 740 (1963).

course of employment.[18] The more satisfactory test, unless expressly ruled out by statute, is that adopted by New Jersey and the majority of states that have confronted the issue, which simply uses the regular workers' compensation course of employment standard for this purpose.[19]

[3] Who Are "Persons in the Same Employ"?

The concept of "all persons in the same employ" or its equivalent has received some interpretation. A corporate officer is a coemployee for this purpose.[20] Michigan has even included within the term "a natural person in the same employ" the president, manager, and sole stockholder of the corporation.[21] And a physician who is also a coemployee may be exempt from suit in his or her capacity as coemployee.[22] But in general subcontractors on the same project and their employees are not immune as coemployees of an employee of the general contractor,[23] nor is a wholly-owned subsidiary of the corporate employer, conducting business for the employer.[24]

CREES v. CHILES
437 N.W.2d 249 (Iowa Ct. App. 1989)

HAYDEN, JUDGE.

Plaintiffs appeal the ruling of the district court granting summary judgment for defendant Richard L. Heideman on the ground he was the alter ego of the corporation which employed plaintiff Barry A. Crees, and thus was immune from suit under Iowa Code section 85.20(2). Plaintiffs claim the trial court erred as a matter of law in finding Heideman was the alter ego of the corporate employer and therefore not subject to the court's jurisdiction under section 85.20(2). We reverse and remand for trial.

Plaintiff Barry A. Crees was employed by Heideman Drywall, Inc. Defendant Richard L. Heideman and his wife were the sole stockholders and officers of the corporation. Defendant Heideman and Vern Chiles were also employees of the corporation.

In the course of his employment with Heideman Drywall, Inc. Barry Crees operated a flat bed truck and he stopped at a pay telephone to call the company's office to get further instructions about the job he was on. While he was talking on the phone, the brakes or the clutch of the truck failed and, the truck rolled from where it was parked, struck him, and pinned him to the phone booth and ground. He was severely injured.

Both defendants were supervisory coemployees of Barry Crees and responsible for the truck. Both were previously warned and advised of the truck's dangerous condition, and were aware of the brake and clutch deficiencies in the truck.

In their petition, plaintiffs alleged specific and individual acts of gross negligence against both defendants as coemployees.

Defendant Heideman filed a motion for summary judgment on the ground he was the alter ego of the corporation and so should be considered Crees's employer. Iowa Code section 85.20(2) permits suits only against coemployees whose gross negligence amounts to a wanton disregard for the safety of another. The district court found

---

[18] Saala v. McFarland, 63 Cal. 2d 124, 45 Cal. Rptr. 144, 403 P.2d 400 (1965).

[19] Konitch v. Hartung, 81 N.J. Super. 376, 195 A.2d 649 (1963).

[20] Samuel v. Baitcher, 247 Ga. 71, 274 S.E.2d 327 (1981), rev'g 154 Ga. App. 602, 269 S.E.2d 96 (1980).

[21] Pettaway v. McConaghy, 367 Mich. 651, 116 N.W.2d 789 (1962).

[22] Hayes v. Marshall Field & Co., 351 Ill. App. 329, 115 N.E.2d 99 (1953).

[23] State v. E.W. Wylie Co., 79 N.D. 471, 58 N.W.2d 76 (1953).

[24] Daisernia v. Co-Operative G.L.F. Holding Corp., 26 A.D.2d 594, 270 N.Y.S.2d 542 (1966).

Heideman ran the corporation as if he were the sole proprietor or sole manager. The court relied on the case of *Pappas v. Hughes*, 406 N.W.2d 459 (Iowa App. 1987), for the proposition that an individual who is the sole shareholder of a corporation is in fact the alter ego of such a corporation and is protected as the "employer" under Iowa law by the exclusive remedy provision of Iowa Code section 85.20, even though the shareholder was also an employee of the corporation. The court granted the motion for summary judgment as to Heideman only.

Crees claims the trial court erred in considering Heideman to be the alter ego of Heideman Drywall, Inc. He states a corporation is treated as a separate entity from its shareholder, and a shareholder who created a corporate status would be to his disadvantage. Crees argues the Iowa workers' compensation statutes do not allow the court to construe an employee shareholder to be the corporation's alter ego, exempt from coemployee liability. He claims the court ignored the definition of "employer" and "employee" found in section 85.61, and the court improperly imposed an amendment to the statutory definitions.

This court in *Pappas* held that defendant Hughes, who was the sole shareholder, sole director, and sole officer of Mondo's Restaurant, Inc., was the alter ego of that corporation. The fact he was also employed by the corporation does not change this conclusion. *Pappas v. Hughes*, 406 N.W.2d 459, 461 (Iowa App. 1987).

The *Pappas* court relied upon the 1969 Arkansas case of *Neal v. Oliver*, 246 Ark. 377, 438 S.W.2d 313 (Ark. 1969), for authority. In *Neal* the court held:

> Under compensation coverage the employer gives up the defense of contributory negligence and the injured employee is relieved of the burden of proving negligence but he gives up the right to sue his employer in a court of law. A president of a corporation or the owner of a business may or may not be an employee of the corporation, or in the business, for the purpose of determining liability for compensation benefits under the Workmen's Compensation Law. That would depend on what he does.
>
> In the case at bar Mr. and Mrs. Oliver owned the corporate business and they, as well as the corporation, were the employers.

Neal v. Oliver, 246 Ark. 377, 438 S.W.2d at 318 (citations omitted).

The *Pappas* court also noted a comment from 2A Larson's Workman's Compensation Law, section 72.13 (1983), as follows:

> If the defendant so dominates the corporation, perhaps as stockholder, president, and manager, that he can honestly be said to be the alter ego of the corporation, this in itself may suffice to bar any action against him.

The *Pappas* court did not look any further than *Neal* or that sole comment from Larson in arriving at its decision.

In the case before us, we first look at section 85.61 of the 1985 Iowa Code entitled "Definitions." In this section the Iowa Legislature has defined employer, worker, or employee for the worker's compensation chapter. We set out the relevant portions as follows:

> 85.61 Definitions. In this and chapters 86 and 87, unless the context otherwise requires, *the following definitions of terms shall prevail*:
>
> 1. *"Employer"* includes and applies to any person, firm, association, or *corporation*, state, county, municipal corporation, school corporation, area education agency, township as an employer of volunteer firemen only, benefited fire district and the legal representatives of a deceased employer.
>
> 2. *"Worker"* or *"employee"* means a person who has entered into the employment of, or works under contract of service, express or implied, or apprenticeship, for an employer, *every executive officer elected or appointed and empowered under and in accordance with the charter and bylaws of a*

corporation, including a person holding an official position, or standing in a representative capacity of the employer, and including officials elected or appointed by the state, counties, school districts, area education agencies, municipal corporations, or cities under any form of government, and including members of the Iowa highway safety patrol and conservation officers, except as hereinafter specified.

. . . 3. The following persons *shall not* be deemed "workers" or "employees":

. . . c. Partners; *directors of any corporation who are not at the same time employees of such corporation*; or directors, trustees, officers or other managing officials of any nonprofit corporation or association who are not at the same time full-time employees of such nonprofit corporation or association. [Emphasis ours.]

It is clear to us the Iowa Legislature has, by definition, included corporations as employers. It has also included every executive officer, elected or appointed and employed under and in accordance with the charter and bylaws of a corporation, including a person holding an official position, or standing in a representative capacity of the employer, as a worker or employee. We note with interest our State's legislature in section 85.61(3) has expressly excluded directors of any corporation who are not at the same time employees of such corporation as workers or employees.

The definition statute makes no mention of shareholders or sole shareholders of corporations as employers or workers or employees. It makes no mention of "alter ego" of a corporation or employer.

In the field of statutory interpretation, legislative intent is expressed by omission as well as by inclusion. The express mention of certain conditions of entitlement implies the exclusion of others. *Barnes v. Iowa Department of Transportation,* 385 N.W.2d 260 (Iowa 1986). *See also In re Estate of Wilson,* 202 N.W.2d 41, 42 (Iowa 1972).

We hold here the legislature did not intend a person lose his or her status as an employee merely because he or she is a shareholder of a corporate employer. Consequently, the legislature did not intend any person who may be determined an "alter ego" of a corporate employer to be immune from suit for gross negligence by a coemployee.

Appellant claims the *Pappas* decision is wrong and should be reversed. Appellee contends the *Pappas* case should not be overruled as it comports with the overall philosophy of the Iowa Workers' Compensation Laws to limit an employee's remedy against an employer to the benefits provided by statute. Both sides have cited us cases from other state jurisdictions in support of their respective positions. We have studied those cases, but do not set out our analysis of each of those cited cases.

We note with interest the case of *Barnette v. Doyle,* 622 P.2d 1349 (Wyo. 1981). In that Wyoming case: Doyle was injured when an unattended truck ran over him, crushing his legs. He brought suit against Lenise Williams, the driver of the truck and a fellow employee, and Gibson A. Barnette, the president, director, shareholder of plaintiff's corporate employer and a fellow employee. The jury found Barnette was 100 percent culpably negligent and awarded Doyle $84,000.00 in damages.

Barnette argued an appeal that he as shareholder, director, and president of the corporate employer of plaintiff, a family-owned corporation, and he was not an employee of the corporation as required by the Wyoming Worker's Compensation Act. Doyle argued Barnette was not immune because he was in charge of the day-to-day operation of the company and Barnette failed to have the emergency brake on the truck repaired after he was advised the brake was not working.

The Supreme Court of Wyoming rejected Barnette's argument and held as follows:

In raising the contention that he is immune from suit because of the Wyoming Worker's Compensation Act, Barnette has ignored the legal entity of

Barnette Enterprises, Inc. Presumably, Barnette and his wife created this legal entity for the purpose of protecting themselves from personal liability for the obligations of the corporation, the acts of the corporation's employees, and worker's compensation benefits. After the corporation was formed, Barnette undertook to work for Casper Mud Service, a division of the corporation, and he received a salary from that company. Therefore, when Barnette became an employee of his corporation, he assumed the additional role of a coemployee. And as a coemployee, he is liable for the breach of any duty that he owes to his fellow employees. (Citations omitted.)

Id. at 1353. That court further held at pages 1354 and 1355:

[W]hen the corporate alter ego becomes an employee of his corporation, he assumes the additional role of a fellow employee. As a fellow employee, he then becomes liable for the breach of any duty he owes to his colleagues who are also employed by the corporation. . . . "Employee," as the term is used in § 27-12-102, includes corporate officers. This Act does not bar an injured employee from bringing an action against a coemployee who is also a corporate officer, if that coemployee was culpably negligent and he owed the plaintiff a duty of care. This result is consistent with the majority of courts that have considered the issue. As stated in 2A Larson, Workmen's Compensation Law § 72.10, p. 14-34 (1976): " . . . In the present setting, modern cases usually hold that a person who is a corporate officer, director, stockholder, or all three can still be treated merely as a coemployee for purposes of being held accountable in a damage suit, although there is *contra* authority. . . . " An officer, director and shareholder of the corporate employer who is also a coemployee is not granted immunity by the worker's compensation act because such immunity would "confer upon a workman freedom to neglect his duty towards a fellow employee and immunize him against all liability for damages proximately caused by his negligence."

We determine here the coverage provisions of our Worker's Compensation Act should be liberally construed and the immunity provisions should be narrowly construed. *See Boggo v. Blue Diamond Coal Company*, 590 F.2d 655, 659 (1979).

We hold defendant Richard L. Heideman, who is a shareholder, officer, and director of Heideman Drywall, Inc., is not immune from a suit, permitted by our Workman's Compensation Act, by an employee of that corporation if he is also employed by the same corporate employer. The fact defendant Heideman may be considered the "alter ego" of the corporate employer does not make him immune from suit by a third party co-employee. [Text Deleted by Court Emendation.] He remains an employee as long as he is employed and paid by the corporation he works for. Any changes in or amendments to the Iowa Worker's Compensation Act should be considered and accomplished by the Iowa Legislature and not mandated by this court.

To the extent *Pappas v. Hughes*, 406 N.W.2d 459 (Iowa App. 1987), is in conflict with or contrary to our holding today, it is reversed.

This case is reversed and remanded to the district court for trial.

Reversed And Remanded For Trial. . . .

DONIELSON, J. (dissenting)

I believe that Richard L. Heideman is immune from suit by his employee. This result does not require a legislative act but results from interpretation of the existing statute.

Iowa Code section 85.61 defines the terms employer and worker for purposes of Chapters 85, 86, and 87. The statute expressly states: *"unless the context* otherwise requires, the following definitions of terms shall prevail. . . . "

Because there are many possible combinations of titles one may possess in a small business, the statute allows the court to interpret the *context* of a situation to determine whether an individual is functionally more like an employer or a worker. Heideman is more like an employer and Crees should be limited to recovering under the workers compensation statute.

Heideman and his wife are the only two shareholders and officers of the corporation. The district court found that Heideman ran the business as if he were the sole proprietor or sole manager. Heideman is functioning as the employer.

This is similar to the situation in *Pappas v. Hughes*, 406 N.W.2d 459 (Iowa App. 1987). There we quoted Professor Larson's treatise on Workmen's Compensation which says: If the defendant so dominates the corporation, perhaps as stockholder, president and manager, that he can honestly be said to be the alter ego of the corporation, this in itself may suffice to bar any action against him. 2A Larson's Workmen's Compensation Law § 72.13 (1983).

The alter ego serves the purpose of the worker's compensation statutes. It provides coverage under the act for situations that do not fit within the clear definitions of the terms. There is no reason to overturn the *Pappas* case as it is consistent with the intent of the worker's compensation statute and the legislature has not amended that part of the statute since the *Pappas* decision was announced. Therefore, I would affirm the ruling of the district court granting summary judgment for defendant Richard L. Heideman.

SACKETT, J., joins this dissent.

[4] Kinds of Action Barred

The kind of suits barred by the exclusive-remedy clause are not limited to common law actions, but embrace statutory rights of action as well, such as a vehicle owner's liability law. New York, for example, not only has held that a suit against a coemployee in his capacity as owner of a car driven by still another coemployee was barred,[25] but also has barred a suit against a complete stranger who owned the car driven by a coemployee.[26]

[5] The "Intentional Wrongs" Exception to Coemployee Immunity

As previously noted,[27] in a majority of states the immunity of a coemployee is subject to an exception for intentional wrongs or the equivalent. Iowa, Minnesota and Wyoming withhold coemployee immunity in cases of gross negligence.

Most of the decisional law here consists of repeated affirmations that "intentional" means "intentional" and not merely gross or wanton negligence.[28] The defendant must have entertained a desire to bring about the injurious result and must have believed that the result was substantially certain to follow.[29] Thus, failure to equip a police officer's motorcycle with a siren, although a siren might have helped prevent the accident, was not such an intentional act.[30] And the fact that an injury was caused by the defendant's intoxication did not make it intentional.[31]

---

[25] Naso v. Lafata, 4 N.Y.2d 585, 152 N.E.2d 59 (1958).

[26] Rauch v. Jones, 4 N.Y.2d 592, 176 N.Y.S.2d 628, 152 N.E.2d 63 (1958).

[27] *See* Ch. 26, § 26.03[1] n.12, *above.*

[28] Keating v. Shell Chemical Co., 610 F.2d 238 (5th Cir. 1980).

[29] Bazley v. Tortorich, 397 So. 2d 475 (La. 1981).

[30] Bourgoyne v. City of Baton Rouge, 380 So. 2d 131 (La. App. 1979), *cert. denied*, 382 So. 2d 164 (La. 1980).

[31] Eisnaugle v. Booth, 226 S.E.2d 259 (W. Va. 1976).

Aliter, by statute, in California.

O'CONNELL v. CHASDI
400 Mass. 686, 511 N.E.2d 349 (1987)

Before HENNESSEY, C.J., and WILKINS, ABRAMS, NOLAN, and LYNCH, JJ.

HENNESSEY, CHIEF JUSTICE.

The plaintiff brought this action in the Superior Court against the defendants, alleging assault and battery, intentional infliction of emotional distress, and violation of her civil rights under G. L. c. 12, § 11 (1986 ed.). After the jury returned verdicts for the plaintiff on her claims against Chasdi for assault and battery and intentional infliction of emotional distress, the judge granted Chasdi's motion for judgment notwithstanding the verdicts on the ground that those claims were barred by the exclusivity provisions of the Workers' Compensation Act, G. L. c. 152, §§ 15 and 24 (1986 ed.). In addition, the judge ordered judgment for the defendants on the plaintiff's claims under the Massachusetts Civil Rights Act, G. L. c. 12, § 11.

In the spring of 1980, the plaintiff, Kathleen O'Connell, was hired as assistant to the director of the Institute for International Education Programs, Inc. (Institute). The defendant, Shimon Chasdi, was the director of the Institute. Shortly thereafter, Chasdi and O'Connell departed on a business trip to South America. Beginning on the airplane flight at the start of the trip, Chasdi engaged in a series of sexual advances and other objectionable actions of a sexual nature. On the airplane, Chasdi asked O'Connell to share a hotel room with him. When she refused Chasdi said that it was "rigid and inflexible" on her part. He repeated this request in the taxi from the airport. Again she refused.

During the business trip, Chasdi repeatedly made physical advances toward O'Connell placing his hand on her knee, hugging her, stroking her hair and face, and attempting to hold her hand. O'Connell resisted his advances, telling him that such contact was unwelcome. Nevertheless, Chasdi persisted. He renewed his request that O'Connell share his hotel room, and when she refused, Chasdi said that she "was very unsophisticated. It was probably because of [her] Catholic background, and that kind of thing is very common when you're working internationally, and that [she] would have to learn how to deal with these things in a more sophisticated way."

As O'Connell resisted Chasdi's advances, he became increasingly critical of her, and began to threaten her job. During one taxi ride from a meeting, Chasdi attempted to hold O'Connell's hand. When she withdrew her hand, Chasdi said, "I think you should go back to Boston. When I get back, we can discuss whether you should continue to work for the organization." Soon thereafter, however, Chasdi changed his mind about having O'Connell return to Boston. O'Connell felt that her job was in jeopardy if she did not continue on the trip.

Chasdi's behavior did not improve. He questioned O'Connell about her personal life, and criticized her for her morals, calling her "rigid and Catholic." Chasdi continually tried to touch O'Connell, and became angry and critical when she resisted. Chasdi told her, "You have no quality in your thinking. I'm eliminating you." Another time, Chasdi punished O'Connell for resisting his advances by not allowing her to attend meetings that day, and later told her "he didn't know if [she] was capable of the close working relationship you needed in this job." Once, when Chasdi visited O'Connell in her hotel room because she was ill, Chasdi lifted the bedcovers and stroked her thighs. Finally, when Chasdi had a maid let him into O'Connell's room while she was sleeping, O'Connell decided to return to Boston alone. She left the next day. When Chasdi returned to Boston a few days later, O'Connell confronted him. He denied that anything had happened, and said that nobody would believe her. O'Connell resigned shortly thereafter.

O'Connell brought this action against Chasdi and the Institute, asserting claims against Chasdi for assault and battery and intentional infliction of emotional distress, and against Chasdi and the Institute for violation of her civil rights under G. L. c. 12, § 11. The judge ruled that G. L. c. 12, § 11, did not entitle the plaintiff to a jury trial, and therefore instructed the jury only on the assault and battery and intentional infliction of emotional distress claims against Chasdi. The jury returned a verdict for damages of $25,000 for assault and battery and $100,000 for intentional infliction of emotional distress. In response to a special question, the jury indicated that the damages awarded for intentional infliction of emotional distress included the amount awarded for assault and battery.

As to the claims for assault and battery and intentional infliction of emotional distress, the judge granted Chasdi's motion for judgment notwithstanding the verdicts. As to the claim under the Civil Rights Act, the judge, who was hearing that matter without jury, ordered the entry of judgment for the defendants.

In granting Chasdi's motion for judgment notwithstanding the verdicts on the claims of assault and battery and intentional infliction of emotional distress, the judge reasoned that the exclusivity provisions of the Workers' Compensation Act precluded separate, common law claims against Chasdi. The judge relied on *Foley v. Polaroid Corp.*, 381 Mass. 545 (1980), S.C., ante 82 (1987), and *Tenedios v. Wm. Filene's Sons Co.*, 20 Mass. App. Ct. 252 (1985). We disagree, and conclude that the judge erred.

General laws c. 152, § 15 (1986 ed.), provides in part:

> Where the injury for which compensation is payable was caused under circumstances creating a legal liability in some person other than the insured to pay damages in respect thereof, the employee shall be entitled, without election, to the compensation and other benefits provided under this chapter. . . . Nothing in this section . . . shall be construed to bar an action at law for damages for personal injuries or wrongful death by an employee *against any person other than the insured person* employing such employee and liable for payment of the compensation provided by this chapter for the employee's personal injury or wrongful death *and said insured person's employees* (emphasis added).

The precise question before us is whether the act bars an action against a fellow employee who commits an intentional tort which was in no way within the scope of employment furthering the interests of the employer.[32] We have stated that "an employee injured in the course of his employment by the negligence of a fellow employee may not recover from that fellow employee if he also was acting in the course of his employment." *Saharceski v. Marcure*, 373 Mass. 304, 306 (1977), citing *Murphy v. Miettinen*, 317 Mass. 633, 635 (1945). *See Mendes v. Tin Kee Ng*, ante 131, 134–135 (1987).

Where a fellow employee commits an intentional tort not related to the interests of the employer, on the other hand, the policies behind the act would not be served by immunizing the coemployee.[33] Two purposes of immunizing coemployees have been suggested. First, employee immunity might be considered a quid pro quo, part of the general compromise of employer and employee rights involved in the act. Second, the act might be considered to protect employees not only from being injured themselves, but also from the risk of personal liability for negligently injuring others as part of the

---

[32] *(Court's footnote)* Because the judgments for intentional infliction of emotional distress and assault and battery were against Chasdi only, we need not express an opinion whether, under the facts of this case, O'Connell's injuries are compensable under the Workers' Compensation Act, and whether a separate action against the employer would be barred by the exclusivity provisions of the act. Cf. Foley v. Polaroid Corp., *supra*; Tenedios v. Wm. Filene's Sons Co., *supra*.

[33] *(Court's footnote)* We need not discuss here the argument that an intentional tort (*e.g.*, assault and battery) by an employee (*e.g.*, a security officer) against a coemployee might, in some circumstances, be so related to the employer's interests as to immunize the offending employee. In the case before us, the torts were not remotely related to the employer's interests.

circumstances of employment. 2A A. Larson, Workmen's Compensation Law § 72.10 (1987). L. Locke, Workmen's Compensation § 662, at 802 n.9 (2d ed. 1981). Neither of those policies supports immunizing coemployees for intentional torts not related to the interests of the employer. We do not think that the right to commit such acts with impunity was part of the general compromise of rights involved in the act. Moreover, liability for such intentional torts is not part of the circumstances of employment, unlike liability for negligently injuring others in the course of employment. Such intentional torts are not an accepted risk of doing business. *See, e.g., Elliott v. Brown,* 569 P.2d 1323 (Alaska 1977); *Maines v. Cronomer Valley Fire Dep't.,* 50 N.Y.2d 535 (1980); *Williams v. Smith,* 222 Tenn. 284 (1968); *Bryan v. Utah Int'l,* 533 P.2d 892 (Utah 1975); 2A A. Larson, Workmen's Compensation Law, *supra.* In all respects, the evidence was sufficient to warrant the jury verdicts. Therefore, we conclude that the judge erred in granting Chasdi's motion for judgment notwithstanding the verdicts on O'Connell's claims for assault and battery and intentional infliction of emotional distress. . . .

§ 26.04 EVERYONE IN "COMMON EMPLOYMENT" IMMUNE

[1] "Statutory Employer" as Third Party

All but about half a dozen states[34] now have "statutory-employer" or "contractor-under" statutes — i.e., statutes which provide that the general contractor shall be liable for compensation to the employee of a subcontractor under it, usually when the subcontractor is uninsured, but sometimes without reference to the insured status of the subcontractor, doing work which is part of the business, trade or occupation of the principal contractor. Since the general contractor is thereby, in effect, made the employer for the purposes of the compensation statute, it is obvious that it should enjoy the regular immunity of an employer from third-party suit when the facts are such that it could be made liable for compensation; and the great majority of cases have so held.[35]

But when the facts necessary to the general contractor's liability are not complete, as when the subcontractor is insured under a statute limiting the general contractor's liability to uninsured subcontractor situations, there is a sharp split of opinion. For many years, a comfortable majority of jurisdictions held that the general contractor in these circumstances remained a third party subject to common-law liability.[36] But there has been a marked trend in more recent times toward granting immunity to the general contractor when the subcontractor was insured,[37] and even when compensation has been actually paid under the subcontractor's policy.[38]

The cases denying immunity to the general contractor whose subcontractor is insured proceed on the theory that the general contractor's status should be tested by its actual relation to the subcontractor's employee on the given facts and at the specific moment of the accident, not by its potential liability if, for example, the subcontractor failed to carry insurance. In one sense, this is rather harsh on the general contractor. The object of the "contractor-under" statutes is to give the general contractor an incentive to require subcontractors to carry insurance. But if the general contractor does conscientiously insist on this insurance, its reward, under these cases, is loss of exemption from third-party suit. A sounder result would seem to be the holding that the overall responsibility of the general contractor for getting subcontractors insured, and its latent liability for compensation if it does not, should be sufficient to remove it from the category of "third party." The general contractor is under a continuing

---

[34] Among the exceptions are California, Delaware, and Iowa.

[35] *See, e.g.,* Jackson v. J.B. Rush Constr. Co., 134 Ga. App. 445, 214 S.E.2d 710 (1975).

[36] *E.g.,* Baldwin Co. v. Maner, 224 Ark. 348, 273 S.W.2d 28 (1954).

[37] Wright Assn. Inc. v. Rieder, 247 Ga. 474, 277 S.E.2d 41 (1981).

[38] Wright Assn. Inc. v. Rieder, 247 Ga. 474, 277 S.E.2d 41 (1981).

potential liability; it has thus assumed a burden in exchange for which it might well be entitled to immunity from damage suits, regardless of whether on the facts of a particular case actual liability exists.

The most extreme holding on this point is the ruling in several jurisdictions[39] that the general contractor remains liable to a common law suit even if it is also liable for compensation, its only comfort being that the amount of the compensation is deducted from the damages to prevent a double recovery. The theory of this extraordinary holding is that the general contractor does not in any sense become the "employer"; but rather becomes an insurer of the subcontractor's compensation obligations.

WASHINGTON METROPOLITAN AREA TRANSIT AUTHORITY v. JOHNSON ET AL.
467 U.S. 925, 104 S. Ct. 2827, 81 L. Ed. 2d 768 (1984)

JUSTICE MARSHALL delivered the opinion of the Court.

Section 4(a) of the Longshoremen's and Harbor Workers' Compensation Act (LHWCA or Act), 44 Stat. (part 2) 1426, 33 U.S.C. § 904(a), makes general contractors responsible for obtaining workers' compensation coverage for the employees of subcontractors under certain circumstances. The question presented by this case is when, if ever, these general contractors are entitled to the immunity from tort liability provided in § 5(a) of the Act, 33 U.S.C. § 905(a).

I

Petitioner Washington Metropolitan Area Transit Authority (WMATA) is a government agency created in 1966 by the District of Columbia, the State of Maryland, and the Commonwealth of Virginia with the consent of the United States Congress.[40] WMATA is charged with the construction and operation of a rapid transit system (Metro) for the District of Columbia and the surrounding metropolitan region. Under the interstate compact that governs its existence, WMATA is authorized to hire subcontractors to work on various aspects of the Metro construction project.[41] Since 1966 WMATA has engaged several hundred subcontractors, who in turn have employed more than a thousand sub-subcontractors.[42]

Of the multifarious problems WMATA faced in constructing the Metro system, one has been ensuring that workers engaged in the project in the District of Columbia are covered by workers' compensation insurance. Under § 4(a) of the LHWCA,[43] general contractors "shall be liable for and shall secure the payment of [workers'] compensation to employees of the subcontractor unless the subcontractor has secured such payment." 33 U.S.C. § 904(a). A company "secures" compensation either by purchasing an insurance policy or by obtaining permission from the Secretary of Labor to self-insure and make compensation payments directly to injured workers. 33 U.S.C. § 932(a). The

---

[39] *See, e.g.,* Laffoon v. Bell & Zoller Coal Co., 65 Ill. 2d 437, 3 Ill. Dec. 715, 359 N.E.2d 125 (1926), *rev'g* 27 Ill. App. 3d 472, 327 N.E.2d 147 (1975).

[40] *(Court's footnote) See* Washington Metropolitan Area Transit Authority Interstate Compact, Pub. L. 89-774, 80 Stat. 1324; D.C. Code § 1-2431 (1981); 1965 Md. Laws, ch. 869; 1966 Va. Acts, ch. 2.

[41] *(Court's footnote) See* 80 Stat. 1329.

[42] *(Court's footnote)* For the remainder of this opinion, the term "subcontractor" will be used to include both subcontractors and sub-subcontractors.

[43] *(Court's footnote)* District of Columbia Code § 36-501 (1973) incorporates the LHWCA, 33 U.S.C. § 901 et seq., to cover employees "carrying on any employment in the District of Columbia." In the other two jurisdictions in which WMATA operates, state statutes place general contractors under similar duties to ensure that subcontractor employees are covered by worker's compensation insurance. See Md. Ann. Code, Art. 101 et seq. (1979 and Supp. 1983); Va. Code § 65.1-30 et seq. (1980).

effect of § 4(a) is to require general contractors like WMATA[44] to obtain workers' compensation coverage for the employees of subcontractors that have not secured their own compensation. *See infra*, at 938.

During the initial phase of Metro construction, which ran from 1969 to 1971, WMATA relied upon its subcontractors to purchase workers' compensation insurance for subcontractor employees. However, when the second phase of construction began, WMATA abandoned this policy in favor of a more centralized insurance program. As a financial matter, WMATA discovered that it could reduce the cost of workers' compensation insurance if it, rather than its numerous subcontractors, arranged for insurance. Practical considerations also influenced WMATA's decision to change its workers' compensation program. Requiring subcontractors to purchase their own insurance apparently hampered WMATA's affirmative action program, because many minority subcontractors were unable to afford or lacked sufficient business experience to qualify for their own workers' compensation insurance policies.[45] Moreover, as the number of Metro subcontractors grew, it became increasingly burdensome for WMATA to monitor insurance coverage at every tier of the Metro hierarchy. Periodically, subcontractors' insurance would expire or their insurance companies would go out of business without WMATA's being informed. In such cases, a group of employees went uninsured, and WMATA technically breached its statutory duty to ensure that these employees were covered by compensation plans.

For all of these reasons, WMATA elected to assume responsibility for securing workers' compensation insurance for all Metro construction employees. Effective July 31, 1971, WMATA purchased a comprehensive "wrap-up" policy from the Lumberman's Mutual Casualty Co. Under the policy, WMATA paid a single premium and, in return, Lumberman's Mutual agreed to make compensation payments for any injuries suffered by workers employed at Metro construction sites and compensable under the relevant workers' compensation regimes.[46] After arranging for this "wrap-up" coverage, WMATA informed potential subcontractors that WMATA would "for the benefit of contractors and others, procure and pay premiums" for workers' compensation insurance and that the cost of securing such compensation insurance need no longer be included in bids submitted for Metro construction jobs. App. 104, 106. Subcontractors, however, were also advised that, if they deemed it necessary, they could "at their own expense and effort" obtain their own workers' compensation insurance. *Id.*, at 104. Once subcontractors were awarded Metro contracts, Lumberman's Mutual issued certificates of insurance confirming that the subcontractor's employees were covered by WMATA's policy. On these certificates, both WMATA and the subcontractor were listed as parties to whom the insurance was issued. *Id.*, at 225.

Respondents are employees of subcontractors engaged in the Metro project. Each respondent filed a compensation claim for work-related injuries. Most of these claims alleged respiratory injuries caused by high levels of silica dust and other industrial pollutants at Metro sites. None of respondents' employers had secured its own workers' compensation insurance, and respondents' claims were therefore handled under the

---

[44] *(Court's footnote)* Despite contrary findings by the District Courts and Court of Appeals, respondents persist in arguing that WMATA is not a general contractor for purposes of the LHWCA. Whether WMATA serves as the general contractor for the entire Metro construction project turns on a factual inquiry into WMATA's responsibility for supervising project construction. Because the lower courts' findings have ample support in the record, see, *e.g.*, App. 163-184, 276–280, we accept their conclusion that WMATA is a general contractor for purposes of § 4(a) of the LHWCA. See Rogers v. Lodge, 458 U.S. 613 (1982).

[45] *(Court's footnote)* As a result of its federal funding, WMATA is charged with ensuring that minority business enterprises have a full opportunity to participate in the Metro construction project. See Urban Mass Transportation Act of 1964, § 12, 49 U.S.C. § 1608(f); 49 CFR § 23.1 et seq. (1983).

[46] *(Court's footnote)* WMATA's own employees were not covered by the Lumberman's Mutual policy. For these employees, WMATA has qualified as a self-insurer under § 32(a)(1) of the LHWCA, 33 U.S.C. § 932(a)(1).

Lumberman's Mutual policy purchased by WMATA. Lumberman's Mutual paid five of the respondents lump-sum compensation awards in complete settlement of their claims. The remaining two respondents received partial awards from Lumberman's Mutual.

The instant litigation arose when respondents attempted the supplement their workers' compensation awards by bringing tort actions against WMATA. These suits, which were filed before five different judges in the United States District Court for the District of Columbia, involved the same work related incidents that had given rise to respondents' LHWCA claims. In each of the actions, WMATA moved for summary judgment on the ground that it was immune from tort liability for such claims under § 5(a) of the LHWCA, 33 U.S.C. § 905(a). In all of the District Court cases, WMATA's motions for summary judgment were granted, each judge agreeing that, by purchasing workers' compensation insurance for the employees of its subcontractors, WMATA had earned § 5(a)'s immunity from tort suits brought for work-related injuries.

In a consolidated appeal, the United States Court of Appeals for the District of Columbia Circuit reversed. *Johnson v. Bechtel Associates Professional Corp.*, 717 F. 2d 574, 230 U.S. App. D.C. 297 (1983). The Court of Appeals reasoned that § 5(a) of the LHWCA grants general contractors immunity from tort actions by subcontractor employees only if the general contractor has secured compensation insurance in satisfaction of a statutory duty. According to the Court of Appeals, WMATA had not acted under such a duty in this case. Had respondents' employers actually refused to secure the worker's compensation insurance, then WMATA as general contractor would have had what the Court of Appeals considered a statutory duty to secure insurance for respondents. However, WMATA never gave respondents' employers the opportunity to default on their statutory obligations to secure compensation; WMATA pre-empted its subcontractors through its unilateral decision to purchase a "wrap-up" policy covering all subcontractor employees. The Court of Appeals concluded that, by pre-empting its subcontractors, WMATA acted voluntarily, and was therefore not entitled to § 5(a)'s immunity. We granted WMATA's petition for a writ of certiorari, 464 U.S. 1068 (1984), and we now reverse.

II

Workers' compensation statutes, such as the LHWCA, "provide for compensation, in the stead of liability, for a class of employees." S. Rep. No. 973, 69th Cong., 1st Sess., 16 (1926). These statutes reflect a legislated compromise between the interests of employees and the concerns of employers. On both sides, there is a quid pro quo. In return for the guarantee of compensation, the employees surrender common-law remedies against their employers for work-related injuries. For the employer, the reward for securing compensation is immunity from employee tort suits. *See Morrison-Knudsen Construction Co. v. Director, OWCP*, 461 U.S. 624, 636 (1983); *Potomac Electric Power Co. v. Director, OWCP*, 449 U.S. 268, 282, and n.24 (1980); *see also* 2A A. Larson, Law of Workmen's Compensation § 72.31(c) (1982).

In the case of the LHWCA, § 4(a)(b) and § 5(a) codify the compromise at the heart of workers' compensation. The relevant portions of these provisions read as follows:

> SEC. 4. (a) Every employer shall be liable for and shall secure the payment to his employees of the compensation payable under sections 7, 8, 9. In the case of an employer who is a subcontractor, the contractor shall be liable for and shall secure the payment of such compensation to employees of the subcontractor unless the subcontractor has secured such payment.
>
> (b) Compensation shall be payable irrespective of fault as a cause for the injury.

44 Stat. (part 2) 1426, 33 U.S.C. §§ 904(a), (b).

> SEC. 5. (a) The liability of an employer prescribed in section 4 shall be exclusive and in place of all other liability of such employer to the em-

ployee . . . , except that if an employer fails to secure payment of compensation as required by this Act, an injured employee . . . may elect to claim compensation under this Act, or to maintain an action at law or in admiralty for damages. . . .

86 Stat. 1263, 33 U.S.C. § 905(a).

I

The current case stems from an ambiguity in the wording of these sections. It is unclear how § 5(a)'s grant of immunity applies to the contractors mentioned in § 4(a). This interpretative question divides into two distinct inquiries. First, does § 5(a)'s grant of immunity ever extend to general contractors? And second, if § 5(a) can extend to general contractors, what must a contractor do to qualify for § 5(a)'s immunity? We will consider these questions in turn.

A

The language of § 5(a)'s grant of immunity does not effortlessly embrace contractors. Section 5(a) speaks in terms of "an employer" and, at least as far as the employees of subcontractors are concerned, a general contractor does not act as an employer.

A few courts have accepted a literal reading of the language of § 5(a) and analogous state immunity provisions. For instance, in *Fiore v. Royal Painting Co.*, 398 So. 2d 863, 865 (1981), a Florida appellate court concluded: "Only the actual employer . . . may get under the immunity umbrella of [33 U.S.C.] § 905." Similarly, in interpreting an almost identical provision of New York workers' compensation law,[47] the New York Court of Appeals has reasoned that tort immunity should not apply to contractors because "[t]he word "employee' denotes a contractual relationship" and a contractor never is contractually bound to the employees of a subcontractor. *Sweezey v. Arc Electrical Construction Co.*, 295 N.Y. 306, 310–311, 67 N.E. 2d 369, 370–371 (1946) (quoting *Passarelli Columbia Engineering and Contracting Co.*, 270 N.Y. 68, 75, 200 N.E. 583, 585 (1936)).

The more widely held view, however, is that the term "employer" as used in § 5(a) has a statutory definition somewhat broader than that word's ordinary meaning. The majority of courts considering the issue, including the Court of Appeals in this case, have concluded that § 5(a)'s tort immunity can extend to general contractors, at least when the contractor has fulfilled its responsibilities to secure compensation for subcontractor employees in occurrence with the requirements of § 4(a). *See, e.g., Johnson v. Bechtel Associates Professional Corp., supra*, at 302, 717 F. 2d, at 581; *Thomas v. George Hyman Construction Co.*, 173 F. Supp. 381, 383 (D.C. 1959); *DiNicola v. George Hyman Construction Co.*, 407 A. 2d 670, 674 (D.C. 1979).[48]

In choosing between these conflicting interpretations of § 5(a), we are predisposed in favor of the majority view that tort immunity should extend to contractors. This position is presumptively the better view because it is more consistent with the compromise underlying the LHWCA. The reward for securing compensation and assuming strict liability for worker-related injuries has traditionally been immunity from tort liability. *See, supra*, at 931-932. "Since the general contractor is [by the operation of provisions like § 4(a) of the LHWCA], in effect, made the employer for the purposes of the compensation statute, it is obvious that he should enjoy the regular immunity of an employer from third-party suit when the facts are such that he could be made liable for compensation." 2A Larson, *supra*, § 72.31(a), at 14-112.

---

[47] *(Court's footnote)* 1922 N.Y. Laws, ch. 615, § 56; see H.R. Rep. No. 1190, 69th Cong., 1st Sess., 2 (1926) ("The [LHWCA] follows in the main the New York State compensation law. . . . ").

[48] *(Court's footnote)* As discussed below, courts have differed as to what it means for a general contractor to secure compensation in accordance with § 4(a). *See infra*, at 936–940.

Our only difficulty in adopting the majority view is that it requires a slightly strained reading of the word "employer." As we have repeatedly admonished courts faced with technical questions arising under the LHWCA, "the wisest course is to adhere closely to what Congress has written." *Rodriguez v. Compass Shipping Co.*, 451 U.S. 596, 617 (1981); *see Director, OWCP v. Rasmussen*, 440 U.S. 29, 47 (1979). Absent convincing evidence of contrary congressional intent, we are reluctant to depart from this sound canon of statutory construction. However, upon reviewing the use of the term "employer" elsewhere in the Act, we find ample evidence to infer that Congress intended the term "employer" to include general contractors as well as direct employers.

The second sentence of § 4(a) provides that "unless the subcontractor has secured [worker's] compensation," the contractor "shall secure the payment of such compensation." This section clearly assumes that contractors have the capacity to secure compensation for subcontractor employees. Securing compensation is a term of art in this area of law. Under the LHWCA, compensation can be secured only through the procedures outlined in § 32(a) of the LHWCA. *See supra*, at 928. However, § 32(a) speaks only of insurance being secured by an "employer." 33 U.S.C. § 932(a). Because the LHWCA requires that contractors secure compensation for subcontractor employees under certain circumstances, the term "employer" as used in § 32(a) must be read to encompass general contractors.

Similarly, under § 4(a), contractors are made liable for payment of "compensation payable under sections 7, 8, and 9." These three sections refer exclusively to employers' making payments; they contain no references to contractors. *See* 33 U.S.C. §§ 907(a), 908(f). For purposes of these sections as well, contractors would appear to qualify as statutory employers.

Further evidence that contractors can be employers under the LHWCA is found in § 33(b), which governs the assignment of an injured worker's right to recover damages from third parties to the worker's "employer." 33 U.S.C. § 933(b); *see Rodriguez v. Compass Shipping Co., supra*. It is difficult to believe that Congress did not intend for contractors making compensation payments under § 4(a) to receive assignments under § 33(b) or that Congress wanted the assignment to run to a worker's actual employer, who may never have secured any compensation insurance. Accordingly, it seems highly probable that "employer" as used in § 33(b) also covers contractors.

Finally, there are the enforcement provisions of § 38 of the Act, 33 U.S.C. § 938. It is generally assumed that contractors who fail to comply with the requirements of § 4(a) may be liable for § 38's criminal penalties. App. 263–265, 299. This assumption seems reasonable, for, if contractors are not covered by § 38, then the LHWCA contains no apparent mechanism for enforcing the second sentence of § 4(a). But, once again, § 38 refers only to "[a]ny employer required to secure the payment of compensation under this Act." If contractors are truly liable under § 38, then contractors must be considered statutory employers.

From the foregoing examples, it is clear that Congress must have meant for the term "employer" in other sections of the LHWCA to include contractors.[49] It is reasonable to infer that Congress intended the term "employer" to have that same broad meaning in § 5(a). This is particularly so inasmuch as granting tort immunity to contractors that comply with § 4(a) is consistent with the *quid pro quo* underlying workers' compensa-

---

[49] *(Court's footnote)* In Probst v. Southern Stevedoring Co., 379 F. 2d 763, 767 (1967), the Fifth Circuit characterized a contractor's duty to secure compensation for subcontractor employees as "secondary, guaranty-like liability." See also Johnson v. Bechtel Associates Professional Corp., 717 F. 2d 574, 582, 230 U.S. App. D.C. 297, 305 (1983). This characterization is apt to the extent that general contractors do not have to secure compensation for these workers "unless the subcontractor" fails to provide insurance. 33 U.S.C. § 904(a). However, this description of contractor's duties in no way diminishes that fact that, once a statutory obligation to secure compensation attaches, the contractor must qualify as an "employer" under §§ 7, 8(f), 32(a), 33(b), and 38 in order for its obligation to make any sense under the Act.

tion statutes. For both of these reasons, we adopt the majority view that general contractors can be embraced by the term "employer" as used in § 5(a).

B

Having concluded that § 5(a) can cover general contractors, we now consider the conditions under which contractors may qualify for § 5(a)'s immunity. The Court of Appeals took the view that to qualify for § 5(a)'s grant of immunity, "WMATA must first require its subcontractors to purchase the insurance. It is only by providing compensation insurance *when the subcontractors fail to do so* that WMATA obtains immunity as a statutory employer." 230 U.S. App. D.C., at 303, 717 F. 2d, at 582 (emphasis in original). This view — that § 5(a) covers general contractors only if the contractor secures compensation after the subcontractor actually defaults — is consistent with the opinions of several other federal courts. *See, e.g., Probst v. Southern Stevedoring Co.,* 379 F. 2d 763, 767 (CA5 1967); *Thomas v. George Hyman Construction, Co.,* 173 F. Supp., at 383.

The Court of Appeals' interpretation of the LHWCA rests on the notion that general contractors are entitled to the reward of tort immunity only when the contractor has been statutorily required to secure compensation. In essence, the Court of Appeals would withhold the *quid* of tort immunity until the contractor had been legally bound to provide the *quo* of securing compensation. Though plausible given the logic of workers' compensation statutes,[50] the Court of Appeals' view is difficult to square with the language of the LHWCA.

Section 5(a) does not say that employers are immune from tort liability if they secure compensation in accordance with the Act. The section provides just the obverse — that employers shall be immune from liability unless the employer "fails to secure payment of compensation as required by this Act." Immunity is not cast as a reward for employers that secure compensation; rather, loss of immunity is levied as a penalty on those that neglect to meet their statutory obligations.

Since we have already determined that contractors qualify as employers under § 5(a), the most natural reading of § 5(a) would offer general contractors tort immunity so long as they do not fail to meet their statutory obligations to secure compensation. Under § 4(a), a contractor "shall be liable for and shall secure [compensation] unless the subcontractor has secured such payment." Contrary to the Court of Appeals' reading of the Act, this provision contains no suggestion that the contractor must make a demand on its subcontractors before securing compensation or that the contractor should forestall securing compensation until the subcontractor has affirmatively defaulted. Rather, the section simply places on general contractors a contingent obligation to secure compensation whenever a subcontractor has failed to do so. Taken together, §§ 4(a) and 5(a) would appear to grant a general contractor immunity from tort suits brought by subcontractor employees unless the contractor has neglected to secure workers' compensation coverage after the subcontractor failed to do so.

Besides being faithful to the plain language of the statute, this reading furthers the policy underlying the LHWCA, which is to ensure that workers are not deprived workers' compensation coverage. If the benefits of securing compensation insurance —

---

[50] *(Court's footnote) See supra,* at 931–932. In any workers' compensation scheme, the onus of securing compensation falls in the first instance on a worker's immediate employer, even when that employer is a subcontractor. In order to ensure that contractors do not prematurely relieve subcontractors of their responsibility for securing compensation, Congress might have tried to discourage general contractors from securing compensation unless and until a subcontractor actually defaulted on its own statutory obligation. Indeed, several States have adopted workers' compensation statutes, with such a phased obligation to secure compensation. *See, e.g.,* Neb. Rev. Stat. § 48-116 (1978); Ind. Code § 22-3-2-14 (1982). Under these regimes, it might make sense to adopt the Court of Appeals' view that tort immunity should extend only to those general contractors that secure compensation after a subcontractor defaults on its obligation.

that is, tort immunity — did not accrue to contractors until subcontractors had affirmatively elected to default, then contractors would be reluctant to incur the considerable expense of securing compensation insurance until they were absolutely convinced that subcontractors were in statutory default. Inevitably, such a rule would create gaps in workers' compensation coverage — a result Congress clearly wanted to avoid. The reason for passing the LHWCA was to bring one of the last remaining groups of uninsured workers under the umbrella of workers' compensation.[51]

A further argument in favor of accepting the natural reading of §§ 4(a) and 5(a) is that it saves courts from the onerous task of determining when subcontractors have defaulted on their own statutory obligations. If a contractor's tort immunity were contingent upon an affirmative default on the part of subcontractors, then every time a subcontractor employee sued the general contractor after recovering compensation under the contractor's compensation policy, the contractor would be forced to establish that the worker's direct employer had been given a reasonable chance to secure compensation for itself and then had failed to respond to the opportunity. Nothing in the LHWCA or its legislative history suggests that Congress intended to unleash such a difficult set of factual inquiries. And it is unlikely that Congress would silently impose such a barrier to contractor immunity.[52] As the natural reading of §§ 4(a) and 5(a) comports with the policies underlying the LHWCA and is consistent with the legislative history of the Act, there is no cause not to "adhere closely to what Congress has written." *Rodriguez v. Compass Shipping Co.*, 451 U.S., at 617. We conclude, therefore, that §§ 4(a) and 5(a) of the LHWCA render a general contractor immune from tort liability provided the contractor has not failed to honor its statutory duty to secure compensation for subcontractor employees when the subcontractor itself has not secured such compensation. So long as general contractors have not defaulted on this statutory obligation to secure back-up compensation for subcontractor employees, they qualify for § 5(a)'s grant of immunity.

III

Applying our interpretation of § 4(a) and § 5(a) to the facts of this case, we conclude that WMATA was entitled to immunity from the tort actions brought by respondents. Far from "fail[ing] to secure payment of compensation as required by [the LHWCA]," 33 U.S.C. § 905(a), WMATA acted above and beyond its statutory obligations. In order to prevent subcontractor employees from going uninsured, WMATA went to the considerable effort and expense of purchasing "wrap-up" insurance on behalf of all of its subcontractors. Rather than waiting to secure its own compensation until subcontractors failed to secure, WMATA guaranteed that every Metro subcontractor would satisfy and keep satisfied its primary statutory obligation to obtain worker's compensation coverage.[53] Due to the comprehensiveness of its "wrap-up" policy, WMATA's statutory

---

[51] *(Court's footnote)* In endorsing the LHWCA, the House Judiciary Committee recommended that "this humanitarian legislation be speedily enacted into law so that this class of workers, practically the only class without the benefit of workmen's compensation, may be afforded this protection, which has come to be almost universally recognized as necessary in the interest of social justice between employer and employee." H.R. Rep. No. 1190, 69th Cong., 1st Sess., 3 (1926); accord, S. Rep. No. 973, 69th Cong., 1st Sess., 16 (1926).

[52] *(Court's footnote)* The absence of discussion is made more telling because of industry objections to other provisions in the original LHWCA that called for companies to monitor the insurance coverage of other firms. In § 38 of the 1927 Act, Congress required that before employing a stevedoring firm, the owner had to obtain a certificate proving that the firm was insured in compliance with the Act. 44 Stat. (part 2) 1442. The administrative ramifications of this provision sparked considerable debate during congressional hearings. *See, e.g.*, Compensation for Employees in Certain Maritime Employments: Hearings on S. 3170 before a Subcommittee of the Senate Judiciary Committee, 69th Cong., 1st Sess., 48, 98, 101 (1926).

[53] *(Court's footnote)* Although the Court of Appeals left the question open, see 230 U.S. App. D.C., at 306, n.16, 717 F. 2d, at 583, n.16, the uncontested facts of this case establish that these subcontractors fulfilled their statutory obligation to secure compensation. WMATA bought its "wrap-up" policy "for the benefit of" the

duty to secure back-up compensation for its subcontractor employees has not been triggered since the second phase of Metro construction began, and WMATA has therefore had no opportunity to default on its statutory obligations established in § 4(a). Under these circumstances, it is clear that WMATA remains entitled to § 5(a)'s grant of tort immunity.

The judgment of the Court of Appeals is reversed, and the case is remanded for further proceedings consistent with this opinion.

It is so ordered.

JUSTICE REHNQUIST, with whom JUSTICE BRENNAN and JUSTICE STEVENS join, dissenting.

The Court today takes a 1927 statute and reads into it the "modern view" of workers' compensation, whereby both the contractor and the subcontractor receive immunity from tort suits provided somebody secures compensation for injured employees of the subcontractor. In practical terms, the result is undoubtedly good both for the construction industry and for our already congested district courts. The result may even make overall economic sense. *See* 2A A. Larson, Law of Workmen's Compensation § 72.31(b) (1982). But one can hardly pretend that it "adhere[s] closely to what Congress has written." *Rodriguez v. Compass Shipping Co.*, 451 U.S. 596, 617 (1981). The Court has simply fixed upon what it believes to be good policy and then patched together a rationale as best it could. Believing that it is for Congress, not this Court, to decide whether the LHWCA should be updated to reflect current thinking, I dissent. . . .

Shortly after *Johnson* was handed down, Congress in the 1984 amendments attempted to overrule it by adding the italicized portions of the following sections:

Sec. 4. (a) Every employer shall be liable for and shall secure the payment to his employees of the compensation payable under Sections 7, 8, and 9. In the case of an employer who is a subcontractor, *only if such subcontractor fails to secure the payment of compensation shall the contractor be liable for and be required to secure the payment of compensation. A subcontractor shall not be deemed to have failed to secure the payment of compensation if the contractor has provided insurance for such compensation for the benefit of the subcontractor.*

Sec. 5. (a) The liability of an employer prescribed in section 4 shall be exclusive. . . . *For purposes of this subsection, a contractor shall be deemed the employer of a subcontractor's employees only if the subcontractor fails to secure the payment of compensation as required by section 4.*[54]

The amendment also purported to apply not only to claims filed after its enactment but to claims pending at the time of enactment.

In mid-1984 a federal District Court held that, since the D.C. Act, under which *Johnson* was decided, was no longer a part of the Longshore Act, an amendment of the Longshore Act could not retroactively affect pending claims such as those in *Johnson*.[55]

The disposition of this issue from that point on proceeded on two tracks. In the D.C.

---

contractors. See *supra*, at 929-930. Respondents' employers contributed to WMATA's "wrap-up" policy by reducing the bids they submitted for work on the Metro project. Upon being awarded their jobs, these subcontractors received a certificate of insurance, naming them as insured parties. By thus participating in WMATA's "wrap-up" program, these subcontractors "in substance if not in form" secured compensation for purposes of § 32(a)(1) of the LHWCA. 2A A. Larson, Law of Workmen's Compensation § 67.22, pp. 12-83 (1982); accord, Edwards v. Bechtel Associates Professional Corp., 466 A. 2d 439 (D.C.), *cert. denied*, 464 U.S. 995 (1983). Because these subcontractors are also "employers" for purposes of § 5(a) and because they have not failed to secure the compensation required by the Act, they would also appear entitled to immunity from tort liability.

[54] *(Court's footnote)* 98 Stat. 1639 §§ 4(a) and 5(a).

[55] *(Court's footnote)* In re Metro Subway Accident Referral, 630 F. Supp. 385 (D.D.C. 1984).

court system, it took the form of an appeal to the D.C. Court of Appeals. In *O'Connell v. Maryland Steel Erectors, Inc.* that court held:

> As a result of the Council action repealing the District of Columbia 1928 Act, that act ceased to exist by 1984, when Congress amended the Longshore Act. Had it not been for the repealer, the 1928 Act would indeed have incorporated those amendments, including the revisions of Section 33 which would have benefitted appellant's cause. But as the 1928 Act was no longer on the books, what Congress subsequently did to the Longshore statute did not affect any rights created by such prior law.[56] This left the possibility of an attack through the federal courts. But the D.C. Circuit, in *Keener v. Washington Metro. Area Transit* agreed with the D.C. Court of Appeals, and that appears to be the end of the matter.

One cannot refrain from commenting on the questionable tactics of those who tried to win a private litigation by back-door politics that they had lost by the fair and open operation of the judicial system. The *Johnson* holding was endorsed by every court, except one, up to and including the Supreme Court. It had had the fullest possible public discussion and study at every court level. The losers then managed to slip this amendment, with its retroactive effect, into a wide-ranging bill that almost everyone had been waiting for years. But the amendment never had any public discussion or hearings, and the people most closely connected with the matter, including WMATA's counsel in the *Johnson* case, never knew what was going on.

There is irony in the fact that, because they had made the elementary legal blunder of overlooking the difference between the D.C. Act and the Longshore Act, the backers of the amendment never succeeded in overruling the Supreme Court's decision in their pending cases, which was their only motivation. At the same time, the irony becomes depressing when we realize that, as the incidental by-product of this shady maneuver, they have saddled the Longshore Act with an archaic rule of law that runs counter to the modern trend and to modern business necessities, and have destroyed a rule that even the dissenters in *Johnson* grudgingly conceded was "undoubtedly good for both construction industry and for our already congested courts."

[2] Subcontractor on Same Project

When the positions are reversed, and an employee of the general contractor, or the general contractor itself as subrogee, sues the subcontractor in negligence, the great majority of jurisdictions have held that the subcontractor is a third party amenable to suit.[57] The reason for the difference in result is forthright: the general contractor has a statutory liability to the subcontractor's employee, actual or potential, while the subcontractor has no comparable statutory liability to the general contractor's employee.[58]

[3] Meaning of Common Employment or Business

The North Carolina and Virginia statutes expressly makes the compensation remedy exclusive not only as to the employer but also as to "those conducting his business." This has been interpreted to bar not only tort suits against coemployees,[59] but also a suit by the employee of one subcontractor against another subcontractor on the same job, when both are under the same general contractor,[60] and a suit by the employee of

---

[56] *(Court's footnote)* 495 A.2d at 1142.

[57] Frohlick Crane Serv., Inc. v. Mack, 510 P.2d 891 (Colo. 1973).

[58] State v. Curtis, 321 S.W.2d 713 (Springfield, Mo. Ct. App. 1959).

[59] Coker v. Gunter, 191 Va. 747, 63 S.E.2d 15 (1951). Lent employee treated as coemployee.

[60] Utica Mut. Ins. Co. v. Potomac Iron Works, Inc., 300 F.2d 733 (D.C. Cir. 1962), applying Virginia law.

a subcontractor against the general contractor, who is its statutory employer.[61] The "common employment" concept is also of importance in Minnesota, but there it confers, not immunity from suit, but limitation of liability to the amounts specified in the compensation act.[62]

§ 26.05 IMMUNITY OF AFFILIATED CORPORATIONS

The commonest question arising out of relations between affiliated corporations and their employees is whether an employee of a wholly-owned subsidiary can sue the parent corporation, and whether an employee of the parent can sue the subsidiary.

Ordinarily it is the corporation that is trying to insist on its separateness from its subsidiary, and it is the plaintiff that is trying to "pierce the corporate veil." But here the positions are reversed. The parent strives to disavow its separateness so as to assume identity with its subsidiary and thus share its immunity as employer. But this makes it vulnerable to the argument that the parent, having deliberately set up the corporate separateness for its own purposes, should not be heard to disavow that separateness when it happens to be to its advantage to do so. Of course, the more evidence there is of genuine separateness in practice, as of operations, tax liabilities, loans, accounting, insurance, hiring, and payroll, the stronger the case for denying the parent immunity.

But if the parent corporation faces a dilemma in trying to deny the very corporate separateness it created, the plaintiff by the same token faces a similar dilemma in reverse. For purposes of proving his or her main case, which usually rests on the theory that the parent so completely dominated the subsidiary that it should be liable for the subsidiary's torts, the plaintiff must make the strongest possible case of domination of the subsidiary by the parent. But the more thoroughly the plaintiff succeeds in this demonstration, the more he or she also proves that the subsidiary has no real separate identity for legal purposes.[63]

Generally, common ownership, identity of management, and the presence of a common insurer are not enough to create identity between parent and subsidiary for compensation purposes.[64] Probably the most significant factor is actual control, and if the subsidiary is in practice not only completely owned but completely controlled by the parent, identity may well be found and immunity conferred.[65]

When the suit is by an employee of one subsidiary corporation against another subsidiary, the issues are somewhat different, and efforts to establish immunity here are generally unsuccessful. Even if a considerable degree of identity within the corporate family is proved, this does not necessarily make a sibling subsidiary the *employer* of the first sibling's employees — as happens in the case of the parent. Accordingly the defendant sibling subsidiary has sometimes tried to find shelter in the status of immune coemployee, but without success.[66]

---

[61] Utica Mut. Ins. Co. v. Potomac Iron Works, Inc., 300 F.2d 733 (D.C. Cir. 1962).

[62] Minnesota Workers' Compensation Act § 176.011.

[63] Beck v. Flint Construction Co., 154 Ga. App. 490, 268 S.E.2d 739 (1980).

[64] Latham v. Technar, Inc., 390 F. Supp. 1031 (E.D. Tenn. 1974).

[65] Coco v. Winston Industries, Inc., 330 So. 2d 649 (La. App. 1976), *writ issued* 332 So. 2d 864 (1976).

[66] *See* Belen v. Dawson, 52 Mich. App. 670, 217 N.W.2d 910 (1974).

§ 26.06 PHYSICIANS AS THIRD PARTIES

[1] General Liability of Physicians as Third Parties

When a physician has no special status under the act conferring immunity, almost every jurisdiction dealing with the question has recognized in some form that a suit will lie against a physician who has aggravated a compensable injury by malpractice.[67] Two states appear to allow the employee to keep the proceeds of the malpractice recovery in addition to compensation, with no obligation to reimburse the employer.[68]

[2] Immunity of Physician as Coemployee

Of course, the physician may fall within a category expressly made immune to suit, in which case he or she may base a defense, not on physician status, but rather on status as a member of the immune class. Thus, in a state whose statute excludes coemployees from the range of suable third parties, a doctor who is employed by the same employer as the plaintiff employee is usually held sheltered by the exclusive-remedy provision of the act.[69]

[3] Immunity of Employers of Physicians

Since the virtually universal rule is that the employer is liable in compensation for aggravation of a compensable injury by a physician's negligence, and since the boundaries of tort immunity normally coincide with those of compensation liability, the employer cannot ordinarily be sued as a third party for such an aggravation of the injury.[70]

One inroad into this immunity has been opened up by the dual-capacity doctrine of *Duprey v. Shane*.[71] As will be discussed at greater length, there has been a recent tendency to try to run the dual-capacity idea into the ground, by ignoring its central requirement of a second and distinct legal *persona*. So here there is a danger that the *Duprey* approach may be attempted in all kinds of situations in which the employer merely furnishes medical services, which services then result in aggravation by a doctor's negligence.

In *Duprey* there was an employer who was in the business of practicing medicine, and who personally committed the malpractice. Now let us go to the opposite extreme, and consider the familiar picture of a first-aid room maintained by the employer, with a nurse and perhaps even a company doctor. Would anyone suggest that the employer, as furnisher of these medical services, becomes liable in tort for any negligence of the nurse or doctor? Even California has said no, in *Dixon v. Ford Motor Co.*[72] Where then is the line between *Duprey* and *Dixon* to be drawn?

At the very minimum, the dual-capacity approach should be confined to cases in which, as in *Duprey*, the employer is in the business of furnishing medical services, and in which the responsibility for the malpractice is personal, not vicarious. The reason is that it is only in such limited cases that it can conceivably be said that the employer

---

[67] DeHaven v. Caulfield, 314 F.2d 269 (D.C. Cir. 1963).

[68] *Colorado:* Froid v. Knowles, 95 Colo. 223, 36 P.2d 156 (1934) (semble).

Minnesota: McGough v. McCarthy Improvement Co., 206 Minn. 1, 287 N.W. 857 (1939).

[69] *E.g.,* Garcia v. Iverson, 33 N.Y.2d 421, 309 N.E.2d 420 (1974). *See also* Fuller v. Blanchard, 358 S.C. 536, 595 S.E.2d 831 (2004).

[70] McCormick v. Caterpillar Tractor Co., 85 Ill. 2d 352, 423 N.E.2d 876 (1981).

[71] Duprey v. Shane, 109 Cal. App. 56, 241 P.2d 78 (1951), *aff'd* 39 Cal. 2d 781, 249 P.2d 8.

[72] Dixon v. Ford Motor Co., 53 Cal. App. 3d 499, 125 Cal. Rptr. 872 (1975).

assumes a second *persona*. Take, for example, the usual case of a corporate manufacturer that employs a full-time company doctor. If the doctor exacerbates a compensable injury by malpractice, it is absolutely impossible to say that the corporate employer is now "someone other than the employer." The liability of employer for the malpractice, if there were any, would be vicarious — which means it would be based on its status *as an employer*. Indeed, this would be true even if the employer were a hospital or other entity furnishing health services. Thus, the only kind of employer who could properly come within the dual-capacity concept would be one, like the doctor in *Duprey*, who personally committed the malpractice, and became liable directly as a doctor, not vicariously as an employer.

[4] Distribution of Malpractice Action Proceeds

A practical difficulty that attends the application of ordinary third-party rules to malpractice cases arises from a fundamental difference between these aggravation cases and third-party cases in which the wrongdoer caused the original injury. The difference lies in the fact that the malpractice action involves liability for only a part of the injury while every other third-party action involves liability of the third party for the entire injury. An illustration will point up the problem: suppose that the employee suffers a simple injury, for which he or she would ordinarily receive compensation in the amount of $2,000. The injury is aggravated by a physician, so that the actual compensation for which the employer becomes liable is $5,000. The compensation cost, so to speak, of the aggravation is $3,000. Now suppose, under the majority rule, the employer, having paid the employee $5,000 compensation, and having been subrogated to the employee's malpractice action, recovers $5,000 damages for the aggravation alone from the physician. Under a literal reading of most subrogation statutes, presumably the employer can keep the entire $5,000 to repay itself for his compensation outlay, and presumably there is no "excess" to be paid over to the employee. This is obviously unfair, since the $5,000 damages should be used to repay only the $3,000 outlay attributable to the malpractice, and the other $2,000 should go to the employee.

The case closest to the hypothetical facts just given is the California case of *Heaton v. Kerlan*.[73] The only difference is that here the employee rather than the subrogee had brought the third-party action, and, under the California statute,[74] the insurer had a right to a lien upon "the entire amount of any judgment" to the extent of its "expenditures for compensation." The original injury was a fractured arm; through defendant's malpractice it was permanently disabled. The insurer paid an award of compensation for the permanent disability amounting to $1,625, as well as some medical expenses. The employee recovered $8,000 from the doctor in the malpractice suit. The Supreme Court of California held that the insurer had a lien upon the $8,000 for so much of the compensation expenditure as was attributable to the malpractice. Actually, the insurer did not even attempt to claim more than this, in spite of his literal and unqualified statutory right to a lien for his "expenditures for compensation."

The best solution would be amendments to the third-party statutes making it quite clear first, that the employer, in reimbursing itself out of the malpractice damages, gets only so much of its outlay as was caused by the malpractice; and second, that if any judgment segregates noncompensable and compensable items, the employer's reimbursement must come only out of the portion of the damages attributable to compensable items.

---

[73] Heaton v. Kerlan, 27 Cal. 2d 716, 166 P.2d 857 (1946).

[74] Cal. Labor Code § 3856 (1955).

§ 26.07   THE DUAL-PERSONA DOCTRINE

[1]   Meaning of "Dual Persona"

An employer may become a third person, vulnerable to tort suit by an employee, if — and only if — it possesses a second persona so completely independent from and unrelated to its status as employer that by established standards the law recognizes it as a separate legal person.

To illustrate this principle, consider *Mercer v. Uniroyal, Inc.*,[75] in which a truckdriver, injured because of a blowout, discovered that the tire had been manufactured by his employer. He brought an action based on products liability and recovered.

There is a risk of looseness and over-extension attending this so-called "dual capacity" doctrine. In a sense, a single legal person may be said to have many "capacities," since that term has no fixed legal meaning. As a result, a few courts have stretched the doctrine so far as to destroy employer immunity whenever there was, not a separate legal person, but merely a separate relationship or theory of liability. When one considers how many such added relations an employer might have in the course of a day's work — as landowner, land occupier, products manufacturer, installer, modifier, vendor, bailor, repairer, vehicle owner, shipowner, doctor, hospital, health services provider, self-insurer, safety inspector — it is plain enough that this trend could go a long way toward demolishing the exclusive remedy principle. To get some idea of what this might lead to, one has only to look at some of the extrapolations that have been attempted. Thus, in an Illinois case[76] the employer had merely modified a machine, and the employee sued him in products liability as a "quasi-manufacturer." He did not succeed. Imagine how much would remain of employer immunity if it were forfeited every time an employer adjusted or tinkered with a machine.

Since the term "dual-capacity" has proved to be subject to such misapplication and abuse, the only effective remedy is to jettison it altogether, and substitute the term "dual persona doctrine." The choice of the term "persona" is not the result of any predilection for elegant Latinisms for their own sake; it is dictated by the literal language of the typical third-party statute, which usually defines a third party, in the first instance, as "a *person* other than the employer." This is quite different from "a person acting in a capacity other than that of employer." The question is not one of activity, or relationship — it is one of identity. The Tennessee Supreme Court, brushing aside all the fictitious sophistry of "dual-capacity," nailed down this point with breathtaking simplicity: "The employer is the employer; not some person other than the employer. It is as simple as that."[77]

Perhaps the best way to approach a correct analysis of the dual-persona concept is to provide illustrations of exceptional situations in which the concept can legitimately be employed. These will ordinarily be situations in which the law has already clearly recognized duality of legal persons, so that it may be realistically assumed that a legislature would have intended that duality to be respected. The duality may be one firmly entrenched in common law or equity. The status of a trustee or of a guardian is a familiar example of this. One can hypothesize the case of a trustee who, as trustee, is legal owner of a small business. If the question should arise whether this confers immunity on him or her as an individual for torts he or she commits upon employees of the trust business, no one would hesitate to answer in the negative.

---

[75] Mercer v. Uniroyal, Inc., 49 Ohio App. 279, 361 N.E.2d 492 (1977).

[76] Rosales v. Verson Allsteel Press Co., 41 Ill. App. 3d 787, 354 N.E.2d 553 (1976).

[77] McAlister v. Methodist Hospital of Memphis, 550 S.W.2d 240, 246 (Tenn. 1977).

The duality may also be created by modern statute, the obvious example being the one-person corporation. Here again, apart from exceptional circumstances justifying "piercing the corporate veil," it is assumed without question that the corporation is a separate legal persona — because the statute makes it so.

[2] Owner or Occupier of Land

It is held with virtual unanimity that an employer cannot be sued as the owner or occupier of land, whether the cause of action is based on common law obligations of landowners or on statutes such as safe place statutes or structural work acts.[78]

Apart from the basic argument that mere ownership of land does not endow a person with a second legal persona or entity, there is an obvious practical reason for this result. An employer, as part of its business, will almost always own or occupy premises, and maintain them as an integral part of conducting its business. If every action and function connected with maintaining the premises could ground a tort suit, the concept of exclusiveness of remedy would be reduced to a shambles.

Moreover, if the circumstances are such that a president and sole stockholder of a corporation would be immune to suit by an employee, he or she does not lose that immunity by being also the owner of the land.[79]

[3] Products Liability

An employer, who is also the manufacturer, modifier, installer, or distributor of a *product used in the work*, cannot be held liable in damages to its own employee on a theory of products liability. For example, in *Longever v. Revere Copper & Brass, Inc.*,[80] the Supreme Judicial Court of Massachusetts flatly rejected the application of the dual-capacity doctrine in a case involving an employer who was also the manufacturer of the allegedly defective product, saying:

> [I]n this case the defendant was performing its common law function as an employer in supplying equipment, tools, and machinery to the [employee's] division. The plaintiff's argument therefore must fail as he "overlook[s] the simple fact that the use of the product was a routine and integral part of the employment. . . .

California abolished the dual-capacity doctrine by statutory amendment in 1982, and Ohio achieved the same result by a 1989 decision of its Supreme Court.[81]

[4] Departments or Divisions of a Single Employer

[a] Private Employers

Dual-capacity or persona will not be found merely because the employer has a number of departments or divisions that perhaps are quite separate in their functions and operations,[82] such as a drug store and a laundromat operated by the same employer,[83] or a separate division of the employer that manufactured the machine involved in the injury.[84]

---

[78] *E.g.*, State v. Purdy, 601 P.2d 258 (Alaska 1979).

[79] Jackson v. Gibson, 409 N.E.2d 1236 (Ind. App. 1980).

[80] Longever v. Revere Copper & Brass, Inc., 408 N.E.2d 857 (Mass. 1980).

[81] Schump v. Firestone Tire & Rubber Co., 44 Ohio St. 148, 541 N.E.2d 1040 (1989).

[82] *E.g.*, Miller v. United States, 307 F. Supp. 932 (E.D. Va. 1969).

[83] Hudson v. Allen, 161 N.W.2d 596 (Mich. App. 1968).

[84] Longever v. Revere Copper & Brass, Inc., 408 N.E.2d 857 (Mass. 1980).

[b]　State and Local Governments

Attempts have several times been made to subdivide a municipality, and assert common law rights on behalf of an employee of one city department against a different city department as if it were a stranger. These attempts have also been consistently unsuccessful.[85] Thus, when a city has both a fire department and a street railway line, the widow of a fireman killed by the street railway's negligence cannot maintain a death action against the city in its capacity as street railway operator.[86]

Similarly, at the state level, an employee of the Department of Highways, who was injured when struck by an automobile driven by a state trooper of the Department of Public Safety, could not bring an action of law against the Department of Public Safety, since both employees were employees of the commonwealth.[87]

[c]　Federal Government

A version of the dual-capacity principle as to federal government employment was rejected in *Denenberg v. United States*.[88] By statute, employees of nonappropriated Fund activities, such as the P.X. in London, are to be provided workers' compensation coverage equal to the Longshore and Harbor Workers' Compensation Act benefits, and this is made the exclusive remedy for an injured employee. The court held that a claim for injuries suffered by the plaintiff which prevented her pursuing her musical career could not be sustained in the Court of Claims under the Federal Tort Claims Act, since the United States did not waive immunity when, by statute, another exclusive remedy was provided.

[5]　Automobile Owner's Liability

The New York case of *Costanza v. Mackler*[89] has some of the characteristics of a dual-persona case. The holding was that the coemployee immunity created by the New York Act did not extend to the defendant employee as owner of the truck involved in the accident, and that therefore he could be held liable under the New York vehicle owner's liability law. The defendant regularly rented two trucks to his employer. The alleged tort was based on the condition of the truck. A loose floorboard had struck the plaintiff, a fellow employee of the defendant. The court made short work of the issue by assimilating it to the situation in which the coemployee was not in the course of his employment at the time of the accident, and concluded: "The alleged tort charged of the defendant is independent of and not related to the common employment of both. . . . "[90]

§ 26.08　INSURER AS THIRD PARTY

[1]　Summary of Case and Statute Law on Insurers as Third Parties

In a dramatic and fast-moving line of cases, mostly during the 1960s, injured employees attempted to treat the compensation carrier as a third party for purposes of tort suits, usually on the basis of alleged negligence in either safety inspections or medical services. Legislatures too were busy, sometimes reversing the courts,

---

[85] Thompson v. Lewis County, 92 Wash. 2d 204, 595 P.2d 541 (1979).

[86] Walker v. City & County of San Francisco, 97 Cal. App. 2d 901, 219 P.2d 487 (1950).

[87] Osborne v. Commonwealth, 353 S.W.2d 373 (Ky. App. 1962).

[88] Denenberg v. United States, 305 F.2d 378 (Ct. Cl. 1962).

[89] Costanza v. Mackler, 34 Misc. 2d 188, 227 N.Y.S.2d 750 (1962), *aff'd* 17 A.D.2d 948, 233 N.Y.S.2d 1816.

[90] 227 N.Y.S.2d at 751.

sometimes confirming them, and sometimes doing a little of each. The net result is that, among states that have specifically dealt with the subject, by either judicial decision or legislative amendment or both, carriers are immune in over a dozen states,[91] and suable in over half a dozen.[92]

[2] Origins and Development of Carrier Liability

The modern story begins with the *Smith* case[93] in New Hampshire in 1960. The plaintiff had lost both her legs as the result of an explosion due to the alleged negligence of the insurance company in performing the function it had assumed of making safety inspections. It was held that an action would lie against the carrier, and that the carrier was not protected by the exclusive-remedy clause of the compensation act. In short, the carrier could be sued as a third party when the other facts necessary to liability were present.[94]

The opening argument in the *Smith* opinion is disarmingly simple. The question is whether the insurer is "some person other than the employer." Is the carrier a "person"? Yes, by statutory definition. Is it one "other than the employer"? Of course, if the word "other" means anything. The court then rightly proceeds on the theory that the burden from that point on would be to show a statutory intent different from the obvious meaning of the words. One by one the court briskly disposes of many of the arguments that have been worked over at great length in subsequent cases. The fact that the carrier would be subrogated to a claim against itself did not trouble the court; the amount of compensation could simply be set off, thus preventing a double recovery. The argument that the insurer has contracted to step into the employer's shoes is answered on straight contract grounds: an agreement between these two persons, to which the employee is not a party, cannot detract from the employee's rights against the carrier. The now-familiar argument that permitting recovery would have "undesirable results" — meaning discouragement of voluntary safety services by carriers — is met in one sentence: "There is force in this contention but as we have often held such a question of policy is for the Legislature and not for this court."[95]

Smith caused some consternation in the insurance community, as might have been expected. But what really set off the alarm bells was the *Nelson* case[96] the following year, in which the Illinois Supreme Court, applying the Florida statute, upheld a judgment of $1,569,400 against a carrier based on negligent performance of a gratuitous safety inspection. Perhaps the sheer size of the judgment added to the shock. The two jurisdictions involved were major ones. The *Nelson* case stands as a decision, without dissent, that a compensation carrier can be made liable as a third party in tort for negligence in safety inspections.

After *Nelson*, suits against carriers, of both safety inspection and malpractice types, appeared in jurisdiction after jurisdiction, accompanied by a corresponding burst of activity in legislatures. In particular, the Florida statute was amended to immunize insurers.

[91] *E.g.*, Arkansas, Florida, Maryland, and Massachusetts.

[92] *E.g.*, Kentucky, Iowa, Indiana, New Jersey, and New York.

[93] Smith v. American Employer's Ins. Co., 102 N.H. 530, 163 A.2d 564 (1960).

[94] The decision was shortly afterward nullified by statutory amendment, N.H. Rev. Stat. Ann. § 281:2 (1966), which provides "[e]xcept where the context specifically indicates otherwise, the term 'employer' shall be deemed to include the employer's insurance carrier."

[95] 163 A.2d 564, at 568.

[96] Nelson v. Union Wire Rope Corp., 31 Ill. 2d 69, 199 N.E.2d 769 (1964).

[3]   The Conceptual Approach: Is the Carrier a Third Party?

The commonest approach in the judicial opinions is a conceptual approach which asks: Who *is* the carrier? Is it a third party? The emphasis is on trying to extract from the language of the act any clues on whether the carrier was meant to be assimilated to the employer, or in any other way excluded from the third-party category. Many statutes virtually dispose of the issue by express language, usually either by generally identifying the carrier with the employer, or by specifically extending immunity to the carrier. Closely related are those statutes that, while not expressly identifying the carrier with the employer, employ language containing a strong implication to the effect. A good example is the Wisconsin statute which says that a claim against the employer or insurer will not bar a suit in tort against any other party. The Wisconsin court reasoned that the carrier cannot be "other" than itself.[97]

In the other opinions approaching the issue conceptually, the statutes are typically combed for whatever implications might be drawn from express mention or omission of mention of the insurer at various points other than the three affecting the issue directly, that is, the definition of employer, the exclusiveness section, and the third-party section. Thus, the familiar provisions that notice to the employer shall be notice to the carrier, that jurisdiction of the employer shall be jurisdiction of the carrier, and that an award against the employer shall bind the carrier, are invoked as evidence of the identity of employer and carrier.[98]

This type of conceptual approach is not a satisfactory way to solve so important a problem. Fictions have no place in the interpretation of a detailed modern statute.

[4]   Suggested Solution of Carrier Liability Problem

The solution here suggested is this: A distinction should be drawn between the carrier's function of *payment* for benefits and services, on the one hand, and, on the other, any function it assumes in the way of direct or physical performance of services related to the act. For negligent performance of the latter it should be liable in tort as a "person other than the employer."

These two concepts have been lumped together in almost all treatments of the problem, although on closer examination the two actions have a crucial difference. It is virtually impossible to cause physical injury by writing a check. It is very possible to cause physical injury by administering medical treatment to a patient or by making a safety inspection.

It is true that safety is a central concern of the compensation program. It is equally true that medical care is of the essence of compensation. And it is true that the insurer is a vital part of the compensation process — when it is performing its basic role of *paying*. But it is not of the essence of the compensation process that the carrier should step out of its fundamental role as financial guarantor and payor and go into the safety inspection service or medical clinic business directly. If the carrier merely puts up the money, and the employee obtains medical services from an independent physician or clinic, the employee in case of malpractice has someone to sue. But if the carrier performs the service directly, and if third-party liability is destroyed, the employee has no one to sue.

In concluding this analysis of the carrier as third party, one must note that almost every opinion on the issue as related to safety inspections has included a treatment of the element of public policy. The imposition of tort liability, so the argument runs, will impel carriers to discontinue the making of safety inspections.

---

[97]   Kerner v. Employers Mut. Liab. Ins. Co., 35 Wis. 2d 391, 151 N.W.2d 72 (1967).

[98]   Bartolotta v. United States, 276 F. Supp. 66 (D. Conn. 1967), interpreting the Connecticut act.

To this several answers have been made. One is that the carriers still have enough self-interest at stake in making inspections that they will continue the practice even under the shadow of potential tort liability. Another is that in any event no inspection at all is preferable to a negligent inspection.

But the all-purpose answer to the public policy argument, in practically every case from the *Smith* case on down, has been the familiar maxim that questions of public policy are for the legislature. Legislative attention is also desirable because the optimum solution may well be something other than a simple yes-or-no answer to carrier liability. The public policy factor is by no means completely one-sided. True, public policy would favor promotion of safety through safety inspections by insurance carriers, and would presumptively disfavor anything that would tend to discourage such efforts. At the same time, it must be asked: Does public policy generally favor relieving tortfeasors of the burden of paying for the consequences of their wrongs? If not, the issue becomes one of balancing policy considerations.

The need for legislative involvement also stems from the fact that the policy argument turns on facts that should be known rather than guessed at. Have carriers quit making inspections in states where they are vulnerable to suit? If so, have other ways been found to get the same job done?

An example of the kind of statutory amendment that gives evidence of being something more than a reflex reaction against carrier liability is the Wisconsin statute addressed, not specifically to inspection by compensation carriers, but to the liability of insurers generally for safety inspections.[99] It rules out such liability generally, but with two exceptions. The first is active negligence in creating the condition causing the injury — which seems a rather unlikely situation. The second applies to services required to be performed under a written service contract. This exception is no doubt designed to take some of the vagueness out of the relation created by voluntary and even casual inspections. This statute is evidence of a consciousness that the total subject of safety inspection liability is deserving of legislative attention.

---

[99] Wis. Stat. Ann. § 895.44 (1966).

Chapter 27
SUBROGATION

§ 27.01 INTRODUCTION

The mechanics of subrogation vary between the states, some subrogating the payor of compensation absolutely, some allowing the subrogation right and the employee's direct right to sue the third party to stand side by side, and some establishing a sequence under which first one, then the other, has the right to bring the third-party suit. Under all forms, however, the ultimate result of following out the statutory procedure is approximately the same: reimbursement of the payor of compensation, with any excess — or most of the excess — going to the employee. In most states, if the employee recovers a fund from the third party, the compensation payor is required to bear a portion of the claimant's attorneys' fees and costs out of its share in the recovery, usually in proportion to that share.

§ 27.02 THE FIVE TYPES OF SUBROGATION STATUTE

[1] The Five Types of Statute Summarized

The subrogation procedures of the different states contain many variations, but for convenience they may be grouped under the following five categories:

    1. No subrogation statute, where the payor of compensation has been held to have no right of action against the third party, on the theory that subrogation is purely the creature of statute. All states curently have some form of subrogation statute in place.

    2. A few states,[1] typically from among those requiring an election of remedies by the employee, assign the employee's cause of action to the payor of compensation unconditionally.

    3. Some statutes[2] allow either the payor or employee to sue the third party, and typically provide for joinder of one in a suit begun by the other.

---

[1] *E.g.*, Idaho.

[2] *E.g.*, California and Wisconsin.

4. The New York type of statute gives the employee six months after the "awarding of compensation" to bring a third party suit. If the employee fails to do so within this period, his or her right of action is assigned to the payor of compensation.

5. The Massachusetts type of subrogation provision is like the New York idea, except that the subrogee's turn comes first. The timing is a little different, however: If the employee has claimed or received compensation within six months of the injury, and if the insurer has not within nine months after the injury brought the third party action, the employee may proceed with the action.

[2] Merits of the Five Types of Subrogation Statute

Of the five types just identified in [1], *above,* the first, granting no subrogation, is no doubt the worst, since it does not even begin to meet the central objective of third-party procedure, and results in double recovery for the claimant.

The second type of statute, which immediately transfers the cause of action to the compensation payor and leaves it there, is not much better. Unless it is tempered by a judicial holding that a cause of action remains with the employee even after the transfer, it creates a situation in which the subrogee has no incentive to recover more than enough to offset its out-of-pocket payments for compensation. Why should a carrier undergo the effort and uncertainty of struggling for the maximum damage recovery, when the only beneficiary of its exertions will be the employee?

The third type of statute, permitting both carrier and employee to sue the third party, largely avoids this problem, but may give some advantage to the carrier in that, with its superior facilities and experience, it is apt to be the more alert and aggressive in launching the action. Moreover, there may be some advantage of simplicity in having only one cause of action in existence at a given time, and in knowing exactly whose it is.

Of the two types of priority statutes, although arguments can be made for giving either the employee or the carrier the first chance, logic would dictate that the employee should have first priority. After all, it is the employee's injury and cause of action.

[3] Conflict of Interest of Carrier

The incentive — or disincentive — problem appears in its most severe form when the insurer has a direct conflict of interest, usually as the result of being both the compensation insurance carrier and the liability insurance carrier of the third party. A court confronted with this conflict of interest will sometimes go to considerable lengths to combat its consequences. The Longshore Act prior to 1959 provided for an absolute assignment of the cause of action against a third party if the employee had accepted compensation benefits. The compensation carrier for the stevedoring company also provided that company's liability coverage. The carrier did not bring suit against the shipowner for the stevedore's injury as the result of the unseaworthiness of the vessel. The stevedore brought the action in his own name and for the use of the carrier, and the action was sustained.[3] A comparable problem arose after the Longshore Act was amended to provide that the employee's cause of action against a third party is assigned to the employer unless the employee has brought suit within six months after acceptance of a compensation award. The suit was brought after the six-month period had expired. The court held that, where there was a conflict of interest because the

---

[3] Smith v. A.H. Bull S.S. Co., 208 F. Supp. 172 (D. Md. 1962).

same carrier insured the employer and the third person, the employee could bring suit in his or her own name even after the six-month period.[4]

[4] Necessity for Employer's Consent to Employee's Settlement

Just as the employee needs to be protected from dispositions of third-party rights by compensation carriers motivated solely by carrier self-interest, so the carrier sometimes needs to be protected from improvident dispositions of third-party rights by employees. The commonest expression of this concern is the familiar rule, sometimes explicitly laid down in the statute, that if an employee settles a third-party claim without the employer's consent, the employee forfeits any right to future compensation.[5]

In the delicate balancing act necessitated by the third-party problem, the process is not necessarily complete when the carrier's consent to the employee's settlement is required. For what if the carrier unreasonably refuses to consent to the settlement? Now the law must face in the other direction and once more protect the employee. The next measure is to permit the employee to seek court approval of the settlement in lieu of carrier approval.[6]

§ 27.03 ACTS EFFECTING ASSIGNMENT

Under most statutes the operative act effecting assignment of the employee's cause of action to the employer or insurer is the payment of compensation. This result has been reached even under a statute making the assignment period date from the award of compensation. In *Juba v. General Builders Supply Corporation*, [7] the worker had been awarded compensation for injuries, but the employer was not insured, did not pay any compensation, and was insolvent. The claimant commenced his third-party suit after the six-month special limitations period, which could have meant that his rights had passed to the employer if the statute had been construed literally, since the operative fact is the award of compensation rather than its payment. But the New York Court of Appeals felt that the legislature could not have intended such a harsh and illogical result, and held that the automatic assignment does not take place where there has been no payment of compensation. The suit was held timely, since it was within the overall three-year statute for personal injury actions.

In the same spirit, under statutes which speak of "claiming compensation," it has been held that this must mean to claim it effectively by obtaining an award — otherwise the result might well be to relieve the tortfeasor of liability entirely.[8] The opposite result was reached, however, under an election-and-assignment type of statute in Massachusetts, where it was held that even an unsuccessful compensation claim constituted a binding election and at the same time assigned the employee's cause of action to the insurer.[9] Obviously the insurer has no incentive to sue the tortfeasor in such a case since, assuming there is no compensation liability, there would be no occasion for the insurer to be reimbursed out of the proceeds of the action.

Whether the payment of compensation without an award will effect an assignment to the payor may depend on the wording of the third-party statute. New York has held

---

[4] McClendon v. Charente S. S. Co., 348 F.2d 298 (5th Cir. 1965), *rev'g* 227 F. Supp. 256 (S.D. Tex. 1964).

[5] Hornback v. Industrial Comm'n, 106 Ariz. 216, 474 P.2d 807 (1970).

[6] Schnabel v. Grimes, 31 A.D.2d 375, 298 N.Y.S.2d 271 (1969).

[7] Juba v. General Builders Supply Corporation, 7 N.Y.2d 48, 194 N.Y.S.2d 503, 163 N.E.2d 328 (1959). Two justices dissented.

[8] McGonigal v. Ward Baking Co., 45 Del. 55, 67 A.2d 61 (1949).

[9] Miller v. Richards, 305 Mass. 424, 26 N.E.2d 380 (1940).

such payment sufficient,[10] but the opposite result was reached by the United States Supreme Court under the Longshore Act.[11] Unless a court believes the statute compels the latter conclusion, as happened in the Supreme Court case, the clear assumption of compensation liability without a formal award should be enough to work the assignment. The contrary view places a penalty on voluntary payment, which, from the administrative point of view, should rather be encouraged.

§ 27.04 DISTRIBUTION OF PROCEEDS OF THIRD-PARTY ACTION

[1] Summary of Reimbursement Statutes

Under most subrogation statutes the payor of compensation gets reimbursement for the amount of its expenditure as a first claim upon the proceeds of the third-party recovery, and the employee gets the excess. Some states, for reasons of incentive, have varied this slightly. In Massachusetts, for example, the employee gets only four-fifths of the excess, on the theory that the subrogee will thereby have a greater incentive to sue or settle for more than the bare amount necessary to cover the compensation expenditure.[12]

[2] Calculating Amount of Lien for Future Liability

A complication that, in the nature of things, cannot be avoided is the fact that at the time of distribution of the third-party recovery the extent of the carrier's liability for future compensation benefits often is unknown. Indeed, this would happen in almost every serious case in which the compensation payments are periodic and the third-party recovery is reasonably prompt. A well-drawn statute will anticipate this problem and spell out the steps to meet it. Under the New York statute, for example, the Board in such a case first estimates the probable future liability, using the survivors annuitants table of mortality or the Dutch Royal Insurance Institution remarriage tables. If the award is later modified either upward or downward, or if the total amount of periodical payments proves to be either greater or less than the estimate, the excess of third-party proceeds retained by the employee is credited against future compensation liability and third-party proceeds held by the carrier in excess of final compensation liability must be paid over to the employee. If the statute does not take pains to deal explicitly with the problem of future benefits, but merely credits the carrier for compensation paid, or compensation for which the carrier is liable, the correct holding is still that the excess of third-party recovery over past compensation actually paid stands as a credit against future liability of the carrier.[13]

[3] Whether Lien Attaches to Recovery for Medical Expenses, Pain and Suffering, and Punitive Damages

The "compensation" expenditure for which the insurer is entitled to reimbursement includes not only wage benefits but hospital and medical payments as well; this is usually expressly stated, but is the correct result even if the reimbursement provision speaks only of "compensation" paid.[14]

---

[10] Lumbermen's Mut. Cas. Co. v. Beschner, 198 Misc. 375, 97 N.Y.S.2d 781 (1950).

[11] Pallas Shipping Agency, Ltd. v. Duris, 103 S. Ct. 1991 (1983).

[12] Mass. Gen. Laws, Ch. 152, § 15.

[13] Richardson v. U.S. Fid. & Guar. Co., 233 Miss. 375, 102 So. 2d 368 (1958).

[14] Dockendorf v. Lakie, 251 Minn. 143, 86 N.W.2d 728 (1957).

When the third-party verdict segregates two or more items of damage, specifying a sum for each, the question arises whether the subrogee's claim attaches to the entire sum. An employer became liable for $9,000 disability benefits and $400 medical expense; the employee in a third-party action recovered $6,000 for personal injury and $1,458 for medical expense. The employer contended that it was entitled to the entire $7,458 as credit on the award. The Kentucky court held, however, that only the $400 medical expense item should come out of the $1,458 special damages for medical expense, leaving an "excess" of $1,058 which the employee was entitled to retain.[15] This appears to be the correct result, especially when an arbitrary statutory maximum on medical expenses has already relieved the employer of paying the full medical cost. The $1,058 "excess" is no windfall to the employee, who must immediately utilize it to pay the bills which he or she has already incurred and which supported the jury's verdict. On the other hand, the employee, having taken on the responsibility of achieving a third-party recovery, cannot defeat the employer's right to reimbursement for medical outlays by deliberately dropping medical expense from the items of damages claimed in his suit.

As to verdicts segregating pain and suffering, the prevailing rule in the United States refuses to place an employee's third-party recovery outside the reach of the employer's lien on the ground that some or all of it was accounted for by damages for the noncompensable item of pain and suffering.[16]

§ 27.05 SHARING ATTORNEYS' FEES IN EMPLOYEE'S THIRD-PARTY RECOVERY

In a substantial majority of states, when a third-party suit is brought or recovery effected by the employee, the employer or carrier is now obliged to pay a portion of the attorneys' fees out of its share. The emergence of this majority rule is the result both of a number of legislative amendments, not least in the major compensation jurisdictions, and of a similar trend in decisional law.

---

[15] Southern Quarries & Contracting Co. v. Hensley, 232 S.W.2d 999 (Ky. 1950).

[16] Pelkey v. Elsea Realty & Investment Co., 394 Mich. 485, 232 N.W.2d 154 (1975).

Chapter 28
THIRD PARTY'S DEFENSES

§ 28.01 INTRODUCTION

Under most statutes the third-party suit, whether brought by employee or employer, is deemed to be primarily the employee's cause of action. Therefore defenses which would be available against the employee are also available against the subrogated employer or insurer. This applies to the statute of limitations, unless modified by statute, and to the employee's contributory negligence. Conversely, when the employee is the plaintiff, the employer's concurring negligence is not a defense, and most cases reach the same result even when the employer is also the subrogee plaintiff. A substantial line of modern cases holds that the third party may not use as a defense any matter affecting the relations of employer and employee between themselves, and that therefore the statutory assignment of the cause of action to the employer cannot be raised by the third party.

§ 28.02 IDENTIFICATION OF SUBROGEE'S WITH EMPLOYEE'S CAUSE OF ACTION

The question of which defenses are available to the third party turns most frequently on the underlying theoretical issue of the extent to which the subrogee's action is deemed to be derivative from and identified with the employee's cause of action. As to this issue, the first investigation must always be the exact language of the subrogation statute in the particular jurisdiction, since this will sometimes settle the issue by the choice of words used to describe the subrogation process. For example, if the statute "assigns" the employee's cause of action to the employer, as the New York statute does, it seems beyond dispute that the cause of action remains the same.[1] But, at the other extreme, if the statute, like the Wisconsin statute,[2] merely says that the employer shall have the "right to maintain an action in tort," there is room for argument that a new and independent cause of action has been created.[3] Between these extremes are statutes using the word "subrogate" — a word not quite as unambiguous as "assign" — followed usually by the phrase "to the rights of the employee," which seems to support the usual holding that the cause of action remains the original employee's action.[4]

---

[1] Exchange Mut. Ind. Ins. Co. v. Central H.G. & Elec. Co., 243 N.Y. 75, 152 N.E. 470 (1926).

[2] Wis. Stat. Ann. § 102.29.

[3] *See* Western Cas. & Sur. Co. v. Shafton, 231 Wis. 1, 283 N.W. 806, 285 N.W. 408 (1939).

[4] General Box Co. v. Missouri Util. Co., 331 Mo. 845, 55 S.W.2d 442 (1932).

§ 28.03 CONTRIBUTORY NEGLIGENCE

The practical issue which most frequently precipitates the necessity for taking a stand on the nature of third-party actions is the question of the effect of contributory negligence in the employer and employee.

The distinctive feature of third-party compensation litigation which breeds so many troublesome questions is this: Both the employer and employee normally profit by a successful recovery against the third party. If one is innocent and the other guilty of negligence, the award of damages has the effect of rewarding the guilty; but a denial of damages has the equally unfair effect of penalizing the innocent. Since the cause of action cannot be split, a choice must be made between the two injustices.

The problem can arise in several variants:

When the employee's own contributory negligence is involved, there is very little controversy, due to the widespread acceptance of the basic conception of the third-party action as the employee's cause of action. Obviously, if the employee is the plaintiff, his or her own contributory negligence is as much a defense as it ever was, when suing a third person in an ordinary negligence action.[5] It is also held with substantial unanimity that the employee's contributory negligence is a defense in an action by the subrogated employer.[6]

When the employer's concurring negligence is involved, and the employee is the plaintiff, the decisions have similarly been dominated by the concept of the third-party action as the employee's cause of action. Consequently it is generally held that the employee cannot be met with a defense that the employer's negligence contributed to the injury.[7] Two states, however, North Carolina[8] and California,[9] have held that the third party may be permitted to plead the employer's contributory negligence as a *pro tanto* defense to the extent of the workers' compensation benefits paid to the employee.

When the question takes the form of the effect of the employer's contributory negligence in the employer's own suit, the dilemma described at the beginning of this subsection is presented in its most visible form. If one follows to its logical conclusion the theory that the employer is really asserting only an assigned cause of action belonging to the employee, one may well hold, in accord with the majority view, that the employer's own negligence is of no relevance.[10] On the other hand, it is admittedly an odd spectacle to see a negligent employer reimbursing itself at the expense of a third party; and several courts have barred the employer's recovery on these facts.[11]

§ 28.04 STATUTE OF LIMITATIONS

Under most statutes containing no special treatment of the question of limitations, the subrogated employer's cause of action is barred by the same statute of limitations that would have applied to an action brought by the employee or the employee's administrator.[12] This view has usually prevailed over the argument that the subrogee's

---

[5] Poindexter v. Johnson Motor Lines, 235 N.C. 286, 69 S.E.2d 495 (1952).

[6] Lather v. Michigan Pub. Serv. Co., 332 Mich. 683, 52 N.W.2d 551 (1952).

[7] Clark v. Chicago, M., St. P. & P. R.R., 214 Wis. 295, 252 N.W. 685 (1934).

[8] Essick v. City of Lexington, 233 N.C. 600, 65 S.E.2d 220 (1951).

[9] Roe v. Workmen's Comp. App. Bd., 12 Cal. 3d 884, 527 P.2d 771 (1974).

[10] Royal Indem. Co. v. Southern Cal. Petroleum Corp., 67 N.M. 137, 353 P.2d 358 (1960).

[11] Fireman's Fund Indem. Co. v. United States, 110 F. Supp. 937 (N.D. Fla. 1953), *aff'd* 211 F.2d 773 (5th Cir. 1954).

[12] American Mut. Liab. Ins. Co. v. Reed Cleaners, 265 Minn. 503, 122 N.W.2d 178 (1963).

action is a new cause of action created by statute and therefore subject to the special statute of limitations for statutory causes of action, and the argument that the cause of action is one for indemnity rather than for tort, thus taking the quasi-contractual rather than the delictual limitations period, and beginning to run at the time of payment rather than injury.[13]

There is a practical flaw in the majority rule: Frequently, within a one-year or even two-year personal-injury limitations period, the employer's obligation to pay compensation may not be established. Until it is established, the employer cannot sue the third party, and by the time it is established, the short personal-injury period may have run.[14]

This difficulty has been noted in some of the decisions[15] but the remedy has been said to lie with the legislature; and the legislatures of some of the states have responded by supplying appropriate amendments. Indiana, for example, amended its statute to permit the bringing of subrogation actions within one year from the date of acceptance of compensation.[16]

§ 28.05   SUBROGATION AS DEFENSE TO THIRD-PARTY SUIT BY EMPLOYEE

When, through the acceptance of compensation by the employee, the employer has acquired by subrogation or assignment the right to sue the third party, the question arises whether this creates a defense assertable by the third party if the employee himself or herself attempts to bring suit.

It might be thought to follow as a matter of course that the same act which vests the cause of action in the employer divests the employee of it, on the dictionary meanings of "assign" or "subrogate," which usually are thought of as connoting the transfer of a right away from the assignor and to the assignee. Several jurisdictions take this position.[17] Others, however, have found a legislative intention merely to give a right to the employer without taking anything away from the employee, with the result that the subrogation or assignment has the effect of creating parallel rights of action which may be asserted by either employer or employee.[18]

Apart from the operation of statutory assignment in some states, what goes on between the employer and employee is generally of no concern to the third-party defendant and cannot form the basis of a defense on its behalf. The fact that the plaintiff employee has already been paid for some of the damages through workers' compensation,[19] or has had medical expenses already paid,[20] is no ground for reducing the liability of the third-party tortfeasor. Moreover, the employee's failure to perform a duty owed to the employer, such as the duty to give the employer notice when a third-party suit is filed, cannot be raised as a defense by the third party.[21]

---

[13] Buss v. Robinson, 255 S.W.2d 339 (Tex. Civ. App. 1952).

[14] *See, e.g.,* American Mut. Liab. Ins. Co. v. Reed Cleaners, 265 Minn. 503, 122 N.W.2d 178 (1963).

[15] *E.g.,* Employers' Liab. Assur. Co. v. Indianapolis & Cincinnati Traction Co., 195 Ind. 91, 144 N.E. 615 (1924).

[16] *See* 1945 amendment to Ind. Stat. Sec. 40-1213, applied in Standard Acc. Ins. Co. v. Pet Milk Co., 118 Ind. App. 477, 78 N.E.2d 672 (1948).

[17] Taylor v. New York Central R.R., 294 N.Y. 397, 62 N.E.2d 777 (1945), *cert. denied,* 326 U.S. 786.

[18] Parkhill Truck Co. v. Wilson, 190 Okla. 473, 125 P.2d 203 (1942), applying a statute that stated that "the cause of action against such other shall be assigned to the insurance carrier."

[19] Walta v. Bayer Constr. Co., 185 Kan. 408, 345 P.2d 631 (1959).

[20] Powell v. Wagner, 178 F. Supp. 345 (E.D. Wis. 1959).

[21] Lewis v. Crews, 237 A.2d 136 (Del. Super. 1967).

§ 28.06   EFFECT OF CARRIER OR EMPLOYER CONFLICT OF INTEREST ON EMPLOYEE'S RETENTION OF CAUSE OF ACTION

Finally, it may be noted that in cases involving a conflict of interest on the part of the carrier the argument for allowing the employee to retain his or her cause of action even after assignment may have added strength. The Supreme Court of the United States in 1956 accordingly held, in *Czaplicki*[22] that, when the insurer of the employer-assignee was also the insurer of one of the defendants, the employee could maintain the action despite the assignment.

Since 1956, however, the Longshore Act, under which this case was decided, has been twice amended in ways that led the Supreme Court to hold in *Rodriguez*,[23] in May 1981, that *Czaplicki* may have lost its vitality.

One of these amendments took place in 1972. Most of the conflict of interest cases since *Czaplicki* have involved a conflict of interest, not of the carrier, but of the stevedore-employer. Before the 1972 amendments, this conflict was relatively conspicuous. It grew out of the potential liability of the employer to indemnify the third party under the theory of *Ryan Stevedoring Co. v. Pan-American S.S. Corp.*[24] For a time, it was almost routine for the shipowner, having been held liable for injuries under the unseaworthiness doctrine, to recover indemnity from the employer-stevedore, and plainly the employer-stevedore had little incentive to set in motion a chain of liability that would eventually reach right back to it.

In 1972, Congress abolished the *Ryan* recovery-over pattern. The Second Circuit, in *Rodriguez*,[25] concluded from this that the kind of conflict that had figured in *Johnson* was no longer possible. In 1981, the Supreme Court affirmed *Rodriguez*, but left "for another day" the question whether, even in an actual conflict situation, *Czaplicki* retained any validity.

---

[22] Czaplicki v. The Hoegh Silvercloud, 351 U.S. 525, 76 S. Ct. 946, 100 L. Ed. 1387 (1956).

[23] Rodriguez v. Compass Shipping Co., 68 L. Ed. 2d 472 (1981).

[24] Ryan Stevedoring Co. v. Pan-American S.S. Corp., 350 U.S. 124, 76 S. Ct. 232, 100 L. Ed. 2d 133 (1956).

[25] Rodriguez v. Compass Shipping Co., 68 L. Ed. 2d 472 (1981).

Chapter 29

THIRD PARTY'S BREACH OF SEPARATE DUTY TOWARD EMPLOYER

SYNOPSIS

§ 29.01 Introduction
§ 29.02 Question of Exclusiveness of Employer's Statutory Third-Party Remedy
§ 29.03 The *Burnside* Rule: Statutory Remedy Not Exclusive

§ 29.01 INTRODUCTION

When a third-party statute has provided a statutory method whereby the employer or insurer may be reimbursed for compensation expenditures caused by the third party's negligence, the Supreme Court of the United States has ruled that this statutory method is not necessarily exclusive, and the employer may therefore bring a separate action against a third party claiming damages to the amount of compensation paid as the result of the third party's breach of an independent duty to the employer. There is, however, some contra authority in state decisions.

§ 29.02 QUESTION OF EXCLUSIVENESS OF EMPLOYER'S STATUTORY THIRD-PARTY REMEDY

In the great majority of cases, there is no occasion for the employer who has paid workers' compensation to search beyond its rights as statutory subrogee under the act for a remedy against a third-party tortfeasor. Typically, the damages recovered from the third party in an action by the injured employee or by the subrogated employer are adequate to cover reimbursement of the employer for its compensation outlay. In some special circumstances, however, this is not true. The amount recoverable on the employee's cause of action may be less than the compensation payable, or may even be zero. The question then arises: may the employer assert an independent cause of action against the third party, grounded on breach of a separate duty running from the third party to the employer, to recover the cost of compensation which the employer has been forced to pay because of this breach?

§ 29.03 THE *BURNSIDE* RULE: STATUTORY REMEDY NOT EXCLUSIVE

In 1969 there appeared a Supreme Court decision, the *Burnside* case,[1] which answered this question in the affirmative. The peculiar circumstance inspiring the separate suit in this instance was the then-applicable arbitrary limit of $30,000 on wrongful death recoveries under Illinois law, while the potential compensation liability was $70,000.

The employee was killed by a fall into a hatch that had been left unguarded. His widow, having been awarded compensation, brought a wrongful-death action against the shipowner. The shipowner, Burnside, brought a separate action in the same federal court seeking indemnification from the stevedoring company, Marine Terminals, on the ground of breach of warranty of workmanlike performance under the *Ryan*[2] formula. The stevedore struck back with a counterclaim for "all sums which have been paid or will

---

[1] Federal Marine Terminals, Inc. v. Burnside Shipping Co., 394 U.S. 404, 89 S. Ct. 1144, 22 L. Ed. 2d 371 (1969).

[2] *See* Ch. 30, §§ 30.01 and 30.04, *below.*

be paid" as compensation benefits. The principal ground was that Burnside, as owner and operator of the vessel, owed *to the stevedoring contractor* "the duty of providing and maintaining a safe place to work so that injury to the employees . . . would be avoided." The facts alleged as showing a breach of this duty included failure to guard or cover the deep tank opening, to clear the passageways, to provide adequate lighting, and to provide a safety railing. The Federal District Court dismissed this counterclaim, and the Seventh Circuit affirmed. The ground relied on by the District Court was that that employer's rights against third parties provided by the Longshore Act were exclusive.

The Supreme Court disposed of the exclusiveness issue with refreshing forthrightness. It began by saying that the Court of Appeals had been "clearly mistaken" in asserting that the statutory remedy was exclusive. The prime ground was that, when a new right is granted by statute, it does not ordinarily cut off existing rights in the absence of clear language to that effect. The statutory language assigning the employee's cause of action to the employer contains no words of limitation. The act concerned itself only with rights between the employer and employee, and when it made the employee's compensation remedy exclusive, this was a *quid pro quo* for the employer's shouldering of absolute liability. The third party is not involved in any such *quid pro quo*, and there is therefore no reason why it should derive a new immunity from the act.

Chapter 30
ACTIONS BY THIRD PARTIES AGAINST EMPLOYER

§ 30.01 NATURE OF RECOVERY-OVER PROBLEM

[1] Introduction

The evenly balanced controversy on third party's rights over against a negligent employer requires making a distinction between recovery in the form of contribution and recovery in the form of indemnity. Indemnity may result either from express contract or from an implication raised by law.

[2] Reasons for Closeness of the Controversy

Perhaps the most evenly balanced controversy in all of compensation law is the question whether a third party in an action by the employee should get contribution or indemnity from the employer, when the employer's negligence has caused or contributed to the injury.

The typical fact situation is that in *American District Telegraph Co. v. Kittleson.*[1] Kittleson was an employee of Armour & Company. American District Telegraph Company had contracted with Armour to repair a signal system. One of American's employees fell through a skylight and landed on Kittleson, injuring him severely. Kittleson accepted compensation from Armour, and also sued American, alleging that American's employee failed to ascertain whether the skylight would carry his weight. American then brought a third-party complaint against Armour, asserting that the injury was primarily due to Armour's negligence in allowing the skylight to become so encrusted with dirt that it was indistinguishable from the roof around it. Armour moved to dismiss the third-party complaint on the ground that Armour's compensation liability was exclusive. (The compensation liability amounted to $6,800, while the judgment recovered against American was almost $60,000).

The District Court dismissed the third-party complaint. The Circuit Court of Appeals reversed, and held that Armour could be held liable to American for the damages that American had to pay Armour's employee.

Each side to this controversy has an argument in its favor which, considered alone, sounds irresistible. The employer here complains with considerable cogency that the net result is that $60,000 has been put in the employee's pocket and has left the employer's pocket, all because of a compensable injury, in spite of the plain statement in the act that the employer's liability for such an injury shall be limited to compensation payments.

Yet if the third party were made to bear the entire $60,000 damages, it would argue with equal cogency that it is unfair to subject it, the lesser of two wrongdoers, to a staggering liability which it would not have had to bear but for the sheer chance that the other parties involved happened to be under a compensation act. Why should the third party, a stranger to the compensation system, subsidize that system by assuming liabilities that it could normally shift to or share with the employer?

Because of the closeness of the issue, the number and variety of attempted solutions, both legislative and judicial, has been nothing short of breathtaking, and the end is by no means in sight. Even when deliberate legislative choices have been made, that has not necessarily been the end of the matter, for more than once the courts have had the last word by declaring the statutes unconstitutional. Indeed, few areas of law have evoked such daring displays of uninhibited judicial activism, with centuries-old doctrines being bulldozed out of the way to clear a path for an "equitable" compromise.

---

[1] American District Telegraph Co. v. Kittleson, 179 F.2d 946 (8th Cir. 1950), *rev'g* 81 F. Supp. 25 (N.D. Iowa 1948).

[3]　Reasons for Upsurge in Importance of the Issue

At the time *Kittleson* was first decided, in 1950, while the problem here at stake was a major one in the intellectual sense, it did not loom very large in the quantitative sense. The reason was that the state of the law governing the injured employee's possible third-party tort rights had not developed anything resembling the opportunities that began to appear a few years later. The employee's case would ordinarily involve plain negligence by the third party directly contributing to a collision or other typical industrial accident. But, after all, workers are not injured every day by the falling bodies of telephone repairers. And so, while the legal controversy was no less exasperating then than now, the sheer volume of hardship created was not yet sufficient to touch off the explosion of remedial efforts that came later.

Two principal developments, each vastly increasing the injured worker's possible third-party recoveries, and thus equally increasing the potential for inequity as between third party and employer, account for the recent prominence of this problem: First, the extension of the unseaworthiness doctrine to longshore workers, and then the upsurge of products liability litigation.

In *Seas Shipping Co. v. Sieracki*,[2] the Supreme Court held that the virtual nonfault liability of the ship for unseaworthiness extended to longshore workers. This laid the groundwork for *Ryan Stevedoring Co. v. Pan-Atlantic Steamship Corp.*[3] which dominated this area for about 15 years. Here the Supreme Court held that a contract to perform stevedoring operations implied an agreement with the shipowner to perform these services in a workmanlike way, and a further agreement to indemnify the shipowner for any liabilities it might incur as a result of failure to live up to this promise. Moreover, this duty, being contractual in nature, was not affected by the exclusive-remedy clause of the compensation act.

The advent of this doctrine coincided with a vast expansion of the doctrine of unseaworthiness, extending it, for example, to conditions on dry land. Indeed, at the time of *Ryan*, the Supreme Court itself had expanded the concept to include assault by a fellow worker.[4] Since the net result of all this was, in effect, to shift the full burden of the ship's damage liability to the stevedoring employer, there was mounting complaint that the employer's supposed immunity to damage liability had been in effect destroyed. The result was the congressional abolition in 1972 of both the *Sieracki* and the *Ryan* doctrines, in exchange for a dramatic liberalization of the Longshore Act. But if this was intended to put an end to controversy in the field, it was far from successful, what with the appearance of multifarious efforts to revive third-party actions against the shipowner under some rubric other than unseaworthiness, such as actual negligence, occupier's liability, and assorted other doctrines.

The second — and vigorously continuing — development contributing to the proliferation of litigation in this field is the expansion of products liability. Defective machine tools, cranes, and scaffolding, dangerous chemicals, and the like have produced many more third-party damage awards to employees than were dreamed of 30 years earlier.

This development, in turn, has understandably placed severe pressure on the classical compensation doctrine that the employer, having been relieved of all tort liability to its own employee by the exclusive-remedy clause of this compensation act, cannot be liable to the third party either for contribution or for noncontractual indemnity. Business periodicals carry repeated stories of skyrocketing costs for product liability insurance, as in the machine-tool industry, where a twenty-fold increase in a decade is not unusual. Forced liquidation is sometimes the result. This is

---

[2] Seas Shipping Co. v. Sieracki, 328 U.S. 85, 66 S. Ct. 872, 90 L. Ed. 1099 (1946).

[3] Ryan Stevedoring Co. v. Pan-Atlantic Steamship Corp., 350 U.S. 124, 76 S. Ct. 232, 100 L. Ed. 133 (1956).

[4] Ryan Stevedoring Co. v. Pan-Atlantic Steamship Corp., 350 U.S. 124, 76 S. Ct. 232, 100 L. Ed. 133 (1956).

blamed both on the increase in products liability itself, and on the traditional impossibility of transferring any of the burden to the employer, even when the employer's fault was greater.

[4] Contribution and Indemnity Distinguished

In commencing the analysis of the recovery-over problem, a distinction must be observed between recovery-over in the form of contribution and recovery-over in the form of indemnity. The right of contribution is based either upon contribution — between tortfeasor statutes or upon common law or admiralty contribution, where available and applicable. The right of indemnity is based upon an independent duty or obligation owed by the employer to the third party, either as the result of express contract or as the result of an implication raised by law.

§ 30.02 CONTRIBUTION

[1] Introduction

When the third party, in a suit by the employee, seeks recovery over against a contributorily negligent employer, contribution is ordinarily denied on the ground that the employer cannot be said to be jointly liable in tort to the employee because of the operation of the exclusive-remedy clause.

[2] Contribution: Majority Rule Banning

The great majority of jurisdictions have held that the employer whose concurring negligence contributed to the employee's injury cannot be sued or joined by the third party as a joint tortfeasor, whether under contribution statutes or at common law.[5] The ground is a simple one: The employer is not jointly liable to the employee in tort; therefore it cannot be a joint tortfeasor. The liability that rests upon the employer is an absolute liability irrespective of negligence. The claim of the employee against the employer is solely for statutory benefits; his or her claim against the third person is for damages. The two are different in kind and cannot result in a common liability.

[3] Limiting Employer Contribution to Amount of Compensation

The basic doctrine went largely unchallenged until the appearance of the Third Circuit's opinion in *Baccile v. Halcyon Lines*[6] in 1951. The views expressed in this opinion, although the case itself was reversed by the Supreme Court,[7] deserve attention, as this was the first of many attempts to work out a compromise to minimize the apparent unfairness of an all-or-nothing disposition of the recovery-over problem. The court stressed that the policy of compensation acts is not to relieve the employer of *all* liability, but rather to limit its liability to the amounts specified in the act. It concluded by allowing the third party a recovery of contribution from the employer, but limited to the sum which the employer would have been liable to pay the employee in compensation.

The court thus partly avoided the dilemma posed by the two irreconcilable positions described at the outset, for at least the third party was not left to bear the entire burden alone.

---

[5] *See, e.g.*, Seattle First Nat'l Bank v. Shoreline Concrete Co., 91 Wash. 2d 230, 558 P.2d 1308 (1978).

[6] Baccile v. Halcyon Lines, 187 F.2d 403 (3d Cir. 1951).

[7] Halcyon Lines v. Haenn Ship Ceiling & Refitting Corp., 342 U.S. 282, 72 S. Ct. 277, 96 L. Ed. 318 (1952).

The actual ground of the Supreme Court's reversal did not reach this issue, which is the one of interest to workers' compensation law, but rather involved a narrow point of admiralty law.

The second early attempt to achieve a compromise in the form of limited contribution, which similarly failed to survive, this time because of a legislative amendment, was the so-called "Pennsylvania rule." It began with the proposition that contribution between joint tortfeasors under the Uniform Act depended not on joint liability but on joint negligence. To put the matter a little more exactly, one may quote Justice Roberts of the Pennsylvania Supreme Court: "Implicit in these holdings is the view that the definition of 'joint tortfeasors' does not require that they have a common liability toward the injured party but only that their combined conduct be the cause of the injury."[8]

This rule was of course in conflict with that described earlier as the normal rule. Once the requirement of joint liability is removed, the employer's defense based on absence of liability *to the employee* collapses.

Pennsylvania, before abolishing by a 1974 amendment not only contribution against the employer but implied indemnity as well,[9] accordingly produced a series of cases allowing the third-party action over against the employer in contribution — but it also arbitrarily limited the amount of contribution to the amount of the employer's compensation liability. This result was exactly what the Third Circuit set out to produce and did produce in the *Baccile* case.[10]

The Supreme Court of Minnesota, in the 1977 case of *Lambertson*,[11] also adopted the result-oriented approach, and concluded that the result that was most equitable and most consonant with compensation policy was to allow contribution by the employer in proportion to its fault, but in no event beyond its workers' compensation liability. Acknowledging that there was no "common liability" of the kind classically required to support contribution, the court argued that the employer and third party were nevertheless both liable in their own way to the employee, that contribution was an equitable doctrine, and that outworn technical concepts like common liability should not be allowed to stand in the way of a fair result. The result was also consistent with compensation policy, in that the employer's liability remained limited to that under the compensation act.

[4] Deducting Compensation From Employee's Third-Party Recovery

If it is postulated that the compromise result temporarily achieved in Pennsylvania and in the Third Circuit by *Baccile* is desirable, there is a short cut that might at first seem to put all the parties in this same position with less waste of motion. This is the rule adopted in North Carolina,[12] California[13] and Idaho,[14] under which, when the employer's negligence contributed to the injury, the employee's third party recovery is

---

[8] Elston v. Industrial Lift Truck Co., 420 Pa. 97, 216 A.2d 318, 320, n.2 (1966).

[9] Pa. Stats. Section 303(b), as amended in 1974. The constitutionality of the amendment was upheld in Tsarnas v. Jones & Laughlin Steel Corp., 488 Pa. 513, 412 A.2d 1094 (1980).

[10] Baccile v. Halcyon Lines, 187 F.2d 403 (3d Cir. 1951).

[11] Lambertson v. Cincinnati Corp., 312 Minn. 114, 257 N.W.2d 679 (1977).

[12] Hunsucker v. High Point Bending & Chair Co., 237 N.C. 559, 75 S.E.2d 768 (1953). In North Carolina, the reduction applies when there is an actively negligent employer.

[13] *See* Tate v. Superior Court of Los Angeles, 213 Cal. App. 2d 238, 28 Cal. Rptr. 548 (1963).

[14] Under the *Witt* rule, as adopted in Idaho, a non-negligent employer is entitled to the reimbursement of its compensation outlay, while in the case of a negligent employer, the third party is entitled to deduct the employer's compensation outlay from the plaintiff's recovery. The manipulation of this rule by the insurers was

merely reduced by the amount of compensation. This is the rule adopted in North Carolina and California under which, when the employer's negligence contributed to the injury, the employee's third-party recovery is merely reduced by the amount of compensation.

To illustrate, suppose the third-party verdict is $10,000 and the compensation outlay is $3,000. Under the former Pennsylvania contribution rule, the employer would pay the employee $3,000, the third party would pay the employee $10,000, the employee would pay back the $3,000 to the employer, and the third party would recover $3,000 from the employer as contribution. At the end of the process, the employee would have $10,000, the employer would have parted with $3,000, and the third party would have paid $7,000. Under the North Carolina rule, the employee would merely keep the $3,000 and then collect $7,000 from the third person.

But if the California approach was intended to save wasted motion, in practice it did just the opposite, setting off a flood of confusion and litigation that continues to this day. Several courts, including the U.S. Supreme Court, have deliberately declined to emulate California's well-intended effort.[15]

[5] The New York Rule in *Dole*

The next entry in the Equitability Sweepstakes was the New York Court of Appeals decision in *Dole v. Dow Chemical Company*.[16] This case held that the third-party defendant in a suit by the employee's widow could implead the employer, which was partially responsible for the employee's death, and recover from the employer an amount proportionate to the employer's share of fault. For all the Court's repeated references to "indemnity," it has in effect revolutionized the sharing of damages between joint wrongdoers in New York. Previously, New York had employed the "active-passive" negligence test in deciding when indemnification would be allowed. Now there appears to be an implied contract of indemnity in favor of any tortfeasor by any other tortfeasor, whatever their degree of responsibility.

In other words, *Dole* strikes two resounding blows in favor of flexibility. First it replaces contribution, and its rigid *pro rata* rule on sharing liability, with indemnity, at least in any case in which a party has insisted on having indemnity determined in the judgment. Second, it replaces the previous all-or-nothing outcome in indemnity with proportionate-responsibility sharing.

In a typical case, here is how the *Dole* rule attempts to achieve a rough equity among the parties. Suppose the total damages were $20,000, and suppose claimant has received $9,000 in workers' compensation. The third party, let us assume, was 40 percent responsible for the loss, and the employer 60 percent. The employee would recover its full $20,000 from the third party in the tort suit. Out of this, the third party would eventually pay only $8,000, which is calculated in relation to its fault. The employer would pay $12,000, which is also calculated in relation to its fault. But in New York, fault or no fault, employer would have a right to reimbursement of its compensation

allowed by the Supreme Court of Idaho in Schneider v. Farmers Merchant, Inc., 106 Idaho 241, 678 P.2d 33 (1983).

[15] Edmonds v. Compagnie Generale Transatlantique, 443 U.S. 256, 99 S. Ct. 2753, 61 L. Ed. 2d 521 (1971); Schweizer v. Elox Division of Colt Industries, 70 N.J. 280, 359 A.2d 857 (1976); and Stroud v. Dorr-Oliver, Inc., 112 Ariz. 403, 542 P.2d 1102 (1975).

[16] Dole v. Dow Chemical Company, 30 N.Y.2d 143, 331 N.Y.S.2d 382, 282 N.E.2d 288 (1972).

However, in September of 1996, New York enacted a comprehensive workers' compensation reform package. The new legislation limits the ability of third parties to recover over and against a negligent employer except in cases of serious injury. Among its provisions was a reduction in the scope of the *Dole v. Dow Chemical Co.* doctrine. The act repeals employer liability to third parties in all cases except those involving grave injury. Grave injury ranges from death and quadriplegia to loss of an index finger, nose, or ear. (1996 N.Y. Laws 635).

outlay from the proceeds of the third party suit, and so it would get back $9,000 from the employee. This prevents a double recovery by the employee, who is now left with $20,000, the exact amount of his or her loss. The employer has finally paid out a total of $12,000, which is a little more than it would have paid under a castiron exclusiveness rule, but much less than it would have paid out if its 60 percent negligence had been called the "active" and "primary" negligence, saddling it with the entire tort liability under the old rule.

[6]   The Illinois Rule in *Skinner* and 1979 Amendment

It remained for the Illinois Supreme Court, in *Skinner*,[17] to go all the way in demolishing the familiar no-contribution rule, by decreeing contribution, as contribution and not as indemnity, in proportion to fault, and without limitation to the amount of compensation liability.

Perhaps the most serious single blind spot in this otherwise understandable attempt to find an equitable compromise is the almost complete failure to give any weight to the component of exclusiveness of the compensation remedy. Here we have a field of law that is entirely statutory in origin, with an intricate legislative balancing of interests of employer, employee, and third party, one keystone of which is the exclusiveness principle. It is no light matter for a court, after 65 years, to take it on itself to alter drastically that balance of interests at the expense of one party to the system, however appealing to the court the final result might be.

Shortly after *Skinner*, the Illinois legislature adopted a general statute on contribution among joint tortfeasors.[18] It authorizes contribution "where 2 or more persons are subject to liability *in tort* arising out of the same injury. . . . "[19] Although the effective date of the amendment was September 14, 1979, it applied to causes of action arising on or after March 1, 1978 — the exact final date of the *Skinner* decision.

At first it seemed self-evident that the effect of the amendment was to rule out contribution on the *Skinner* facts. But, incredibly, the Supreme Court of Illinois managed to produce the opposite result, with a morsel of semantic hair-splitting that would make any medieval theologian green with envy. In effect, the court said that the employer was indeed "subject to liability in tort" — unless it alleged and proved the employment relation as an affirmative defense![20] In the instant case, however, the fact of employment relation was undisputed throughout. The moral is: Never underestimate the determination and resourcefulness of a court of last resort when it sets out to protect its own brainchild from an attempted change by the legislature.

§ 30.03   EXPRESS INDEMNITY

[1]   Introduction

If the employer can be said to have breached an independent duty toward the third party, recovery in the form of indemnity may be allowed. The right to indemnity is clear when the obligation springs from a separate contractual relation, such as an employer-tenant's agreement to hold the third-party landlord harmless.

---

[17] Skinner v. Reed-Prentice Division Package Machinery Co., 70 Ill. 2d 1, 374 N.E.2d 437 (1978) (3 dissents), *cert. denied*, 436 U.S. 946.

[18] Ill. Rev. Stats., Ch. 70, Sec. 302 (1979). The right is only in favor of a tortfeasor who has paid more than his or her *pro rata* share, and is limited to the amount paid in excess of the *pro rata* share.

[19] Ill. Rev. Stats., Ch. 70, Sec. 302 (1979). Italics supplied.

[20] Doyle v. Rhodes, 461 N.E.2d 382 (Ill. 1984).

[2] General Statutory Language Underlying the Independent-Duty Issue

The third party may recover over against the employer whenever it can be said that the employer breached an independent duty toward the third party and thus acquired an obligation to indemnify the third party.

The initial question is whether the exclusive-remedy clause is broad enough to grant immunity to the employer for all causes of action growing out of the accident, regardless of the question of independent breach of duty. This issue requires careful examination of the language used in the particular exclusive-liability provision. The statutory language directly relevant in most of these cases is a familiar passage similar or identical to that in the New York Act, and many of the other acts applied in these cases:

> The liability of an employer prescribed by the last preceding section shall be exclusive and in place of any other liability whatsoever, to such employee, his or her personal representatives, spouse, parents, dependents, distributees, or any person otherwise entitled to recover damages, contribution or indemnity at common law or otherwise, on account of such injury or death. . . .[21]

At first glance, this language seems broad enough to cover almost any claim against the employer relating to the injury, what with phrases like "any other liability *whatsoever*, to . . . *anyone* otherwise entitled to recover damages, at common law *or otherwise*. . . . " This has been taken by several judges to be broad enough to embrace any recovery over against the employer by the third party, on the theory that it must have been intended to limit the employer's overall liability to exactly the same degree that it limited the employee's rights against the employer.

A closer reading of the passage, however, makes this interpretation questionable, and the majority of courts have preferred a narrower construction. They reason as follows: The immunity conferred is only against actions for damages on account of the employee's injury; a third party's action for indemnity is not exactly for "damages" but for reimbursement, and it is not "on account of" the employee's injury, but on account of breach of an independent duty owed by the employer to the third party.[22]

[3] Express Indemnity Contract as Clear Exception to Exclusiveness Defense

The clearest exception to the exclusive-liability clause is the third party's right to enforce an express contract in which the employer agrees to indemnify the third party for the very kind of loss that the third party has been made to pay to the employee.[23] A familiar example is the situation in which an employee is injured because of the condition of the premises, and recovers from the landlord who leased the premises to the employer; if the landlord in the lease has exacted a covenant from the employer to hold the landlord harmless in the event of such claims, the enforcement of this covenant does not violate the exclusive-remedy provision of the compensation act.[24] Another increasingly familiar example is the hold-harmless agreement assumed by a contractor

---

[21] N.Y. Work Comp. Law § 11.

[22] Ryan Stevedoring Co. v. Pan-Atlantic Steamship Corp., 350 U.S. 124, 76 S. Ct. 232, 100 L. Ed. 133 (1956).

[23] Porello v. United States, 153 F.2d 605 (2d Cir. 1946), *aff'd in part and rev'd in part and remanded sub nom.* American Stevedores, Inc. v. Porello, 330 U.S. 446, 67 S. Ct. 847, 91 L. Ed. 1011 (1947).

Contra: Alabama, in Paul Krebs & Assocs. v. Matthews & Fritts Constr. Co., 356 So. 2d 638 (Ala. 1978).

[24] Clements v. Rockefeller, 189 Misc. 889, 70 N.Y.S.2d 146 (1947).

doing work for an owner,[25] or by a subcontractor for the benefit of the general contractor.[26]

[4] Specific Statutory Treatment of Express Indemnity

Several state statutes[27] specifically provide that there shall be no right of recovery over against the employer by a third person, whether by indemnity or contribution, in the absence of a written agreement entered into before the injury.

Express statutory treatment may also take the form, not of authorizing the express-indemnity exception, but of forbidding it, in whole or in part. An example of forbidding it wholly may be the sweeping Nevada provision stating: "A contract of employment, insurance, relief benefit, indemnity, or any other device, does not modify, change or waive any liability created by chapters 616A to 616D."[28] The Nevada Supreme Court has indicated in a dictum that an express contract of indemnity given by the employer would be void under this clause.[29]

§ 30.04 IMPLIED INDEMNITY

[1] Introduction

If the third party and the employer stand in a special legal relationship, such as bailor-bailee, that carries with it the obligation of the employer to indemnify the third party, an exception to the exclusive-remedy clause may be found. And when the employer's relation to the third party is that of a contractor doing work for the third party, some courts, including the United States Supreme Court, have found an independent duty to perform the work in a workmanlike manner. But the great majority of courts now reject the idea that the employer as a primary wrongdoer may have an implied obligation to indemnify a secondary wrongdoer, or that an employer as purchaser of a product owes the manufacturer an independent duty not to use it in such a way as to bring liability on the manufacturer.

[2] Indemnity Growing Out of Separate Duty Based on Relationship

One relationship under which a relational right of indemnity may be enforced without offending the exclusive-remedy clause is that of a bailee to a bailor. In a leading California case,[30] the employer, driving a car belonging to the third party, ran into his own employee. The employee sued the third party as owner of the car, under an owner's liability statute. The third party then claimed the right of reimbursement from the employer, whose negligence was the actual cause of the injury. It was held that the bailee of an automobile had a separate obligation to hold the bailor harmless from damage arising out of the bailment, and this obligation extended to indemnification for imposition of third-party liability on the owner in the present circumstances.

---

[25] Republic Steel Corp. v. Glaros, 12 Ohio App. 2d 29, 230 N.E.2d 667 (1967).

[26] Western Contracting Corp. v. Power Eng'g. Co., 369 F.2d 933 (4th Cir. 1966).

[27] Including California, North Carolina, Pennsylvania and Texas.

[28] Nev. Stats. Ch. 616B.609.

[29] Corrao Constr. Co. v. Curtis, 94 Nev. 569, 584 P.2d 1303 (1978) (rehearing denied).

[30] Baugh v. Rogers, 24 Cal. 2d 200, 148 P.2d 633, 152 A.L.R. 1043 (1944).

[3]   Implied Contractual Indemnity Under the Longshore Act

[a]   Introduction

When the employer's relation to the third party is that of a contractor doing work for the third party, there may be an implied obligation to perform the work with due care. If, by failing to use such care, the employer causes an accident injuring its own employee, it may be said that the employer has simultaneously breached two duties of care. The one is toward the employee, and it is for this breach that compensation bars any common law remedy. The other is toward the third party contractee, and among the damages flowing from the breach of this separate duty are any damages the third party may be forced to pay the employee because of their relation.

[b]   The *Ryan* Doctrine

Between 1955 and 1972, this doctrine was associated with and strongly influenced by the decision of the United States Supreme Court in *Ryan Stevedoring Company v. Pan-Atlantic Steamship Corporation.*[31]

This case held that in a contract to perform stevedoring operations, the stevedoring company impliedly agreed with the shipowner both to perform these services in a workmanlike way and to indemnify the shipowner for any liabilities it might incur as the result of the stevedoring company's failure to live up to this promise.

[c]   Abolition of the *Ryan* Doctrine by the 1972 Amendments

This *Ryan* type of liability, together with dozens of cases stemming from the *Ryan* precedent, was abolished by Congress late in 1972. The abolition was in two steps, one affecting the employee's cause of action against the ship in the first place, the other affecting the *Ryan* liability-over of the longshoring employer. As to the first, it should be pointed out that the groundwork of this line of cases had been laid when the Supreme Court held in the *Sieracki*[32] case that the virtual nonfault liability of the ship for "unseaworthiness" extended to longshore workers. The 1972 amendment strikes directly at this beginning-point by providing:

> The liability of the vessel under this subsection shall not be based upon the warranty of seaworthiness or a breach thereof at the time the injury occurred. The remedy provided in this subsection shall be exclusive of all other remedies against the vessel except remedies available under this Act.[33]

There remains, of course, the possibility of a suit by the employee against the ship based on negligence rather than seaworthiness. The amendment recognizes this, but then, while placing a special limitation on such liability, proceeds immediately to knock out any derivative *Ryan*-type recovery over by the ship against the longshoring employer.

Despite the conspicuous place occupied by the *Ryan* line of cases in this field, the recovery-over problem after the demise of *Ryan* remains an important and active one both in federal cases other than those directly covered by the amendment, and in state cases.

---

[31] Ryan Stevedoring Company v. Pan-Atlantic Steamship Corporation, 350 U.S. 124, 76 S. Ct. 232, 100 L. Ed. 133 (1956).

[32] Seas Shipping Co. v. Sieracki, 328 U.S. 85, 66 S. Ct. 872, 90 L. Ed. 1099 (1946).

[33] Longshore and Harbor Workers' Compensation Act, Sec. 5(b), as amended by P.L. 92-576, effective November 26, 1972.

[d] Remaining Grounds of Vessel's Liability to Employee

The 1972 amendments were intended to break the *Ryan* cycle at two points. The one break was at the point of recovery-over by vessel against the employer; efforts to thwart this break failed completely. The other break was at the point of the employee's recovery from the vessel for unseaworthiness, leaving intact, however, its action for "negligence." Here the plaintiffs' efforts took the form of trying to maximize the grounds for the vessel's liability, if possible, stretching them to include some kind of strict liability other, of course, than unseaworthiness. An enormous volume of litigation and reported case law developed, but here again the Supreme Court went a long way toward clearing the decks, with its 1981 opinion in *Scindia Steam Navigation Co. v. Santos.*[34]

Santos was a longshoreman unloading cargo when sacks of wheat fell on him from a pallet overhead. The winch used in unloading the wheat had a brake mechanism which had malfunctioned on the date of the accident as well as on the previous two days. The District Court had applied the Restatement (Second) of Torts land-based rules for invitees: The shipowner was not liable for dangerous conditions caused by the stevedore's negligence while in exclusive control of the work. Nor was it under a duty to warn the stevedore of open or obvious dangers and defects. The Ninth Court of Appeals reversed a summary judgment for Scindia. It rejected the land-based Restatement standards as incorporating such notions as contributory negligence and assumption of the risk. It held the shipowner liable if the owner was aware of an unreasonable risk to the longshore workers and failed to use reasonable care to protect them.

The Supreme Court disagreed with both courts, holding that the shipowner had a duty to exercise reasonable care and warn the stevedore of defects known to him which would not be obvious to the stevedore, even though the shipowner did not supervise the stevedoring operation.

> Absent contract provision, positive law or custom to the contrary . . . the shipowner has no general duty by way of supervision or inspection to exercise reasonable care to discover dangerous conditions that develop within the confines of the cargo operations that are assigned to the stevedore. . . . [T]he shipowner is not liable to the longshoremen for injuries caused by dangers unknown to the owner and about which he had no duty to inform himself.[35]

However, the shipowner may have a duty to intervene when a dangerous condition existed in the cargo operation, such as the malfunctioning winch, which was known by the stevedore and dangerous to longshore workers. The Court said an inquiry into safety statutes, regulations, and customs was necessary to determine whether the ship had a duty to repair the winch. The case was remanded to discover whether the shipowner had actual knowledge or was chargeable with knowledge of the defective winch.

[4] Implied Contractual Indemnity Under State Law

A sharp divergence of opinion exists between the small minority of jurisdictions holding that, when the relation between the parties is based on contract, an obligation of care with accompanying indemnity obligation can be implied which survives the exclusiveness defense,[36] and the majority that reject the implied indemnity doctrine.[37]

The greater part of the controversy between these cases has been supplied, not by the issue whether an independent duty to indemnify based on contract is free of the

[34] Scindia Steam Navigation Co. v. Santos, 451 U.S. 156, 101 S. Ct. 1614, 68 L. Ed. 2d 1 (1981).

[35] 101 S. Ct. at 1624.

[36] *See, e.g.*, Blackford v. Sioux City Dressed Pork, Inc., 254 Iowa 856, 118 N.W.2d 559 (1962).

[37] *E.g.*, Outboard Marine Corp. v. Schupach, 561 P.2d 450 (Nev. 1977).

compensation exclusiveness principle, but by the issue whether under the law of the jurisdiction there is an implied obligation of care and indemnity in the circumstances.

[5] Noncontractual Indemnity

[a] No Contract Whatever Between Parties

The final combination to be examined is that in which there is no such contractual or special relation, the simplest illustration being that of a collision between strangers. If the form of the recovery-over by third party against employer sounds in tort, as in a claim for contribution, the near-universal rule bars the action under the exclusive-remedy principle. There remains the question whether, by clothing its claim in the form of indemnity, the third party can surmount the exclusiveness barrier.

The third-party plaintiff here has not one hurdle but two to leap. Such a plaintiff must first establish that the law implies an agreement by the primary tortfeasor to indemnify the secondary. Second, it must show that this liability, even if contractual in form, is not on account of the injury. As a consequence of this dual obstacle, the great majority of cases hold that, when the relation between the parties does not spring from a contract or special position such as bailee or lessee, the third party cannot recover indemnity from the employer.[38] The reason is that an active or primary wrongdoer does not have an implied obligation, capable of penetrating the exclusiveness rule of workers' compensation law, to indemnify a passive or secondary wrongdoer. In a leading case establishing this rule, Judge Learned Hand gave the following reason for the holding:

> [W]e shall assume that, when the indemnitor and indemnitee are both liable to the injured person, it is the law of New Jersey that, regardless of any other relation between them, the difference in gravity of their faults may be great enough to throw the whole loss upon one. We cannot, however, agree that that result is rationally possible except upon the assumption that both parties are liable to the same person for the joint wrong. If so, when one of the two is not so liable, the right of the other to indemnity must be found in rights and liabilities arising out of some other legal transaction between the two.[39]

[b] No Contractual Relation Along Which Implied Obligation Can Travel

There may also be a contractual relation of sorts, but not one along which an implied obligation can travel, or at least travel in the necessary direction. In *Bertone*,[40] the third party was the manufacturer and the employer the purchaser of a dangerous solvent. If the positions had been reversed, a separate implied duty running with the goods might have been found. But when buying a product, does a purchaser make an implied contract with the manufacturer to use the goods in such a way as not to bring liability upon the manufacturer? This would be stretching the concept of contract out of all relation to reality. The court's approach to the matter assumed that the employer's duty to the manufacturer, if any, would have to be one based on its relative negligence, and on that basis could not survive the exclusive-liability clause.

As an Ohio court said, in a typical chemicals case:[41]

> The mere fact that a product has been sold by a vendor to a vendee does not per se make the vendee of the product primarily liable and the vendor

---

[38] *E.g.*, Hysell v. Iowa Pub. Serv. Co., 534 F.2d 775 (8th Cir. 1976).

[39] Slattery v. Marra Bros., 186 F.2d 134, 139 (2d Cir. 1951).

[40] Bertone v. Turco Prods., Inc., 252 F.2d 726 (3d Cir. 1958), applying New Jersey law.

[41] Williams v. Ashland Chem. Co., 52 Ohio App. 81, 368 N.E.2d 304, 311 (1976).

secondarily liable, and thereby establish an implied contract of indemnity running in favor of the vendor.

MYCO, INC. v. SUPER CONCRETE CO., INC.
565 A.2d 293 (D.C. Ct. App. 1989)

GALLAGHER, SENIOR JUDGE:

In this appeal we are called upon to determine the effect of the District of Columbia's Workers' Compensation Act[42] on the right of a third party to indemnity from the employer of an injured worker seeking recovery in tort from that third party. Appellant Myco, Inc., appeals from an order of the Superior Court dismissing its amended third-party complaint for indemnity against appellee, Super Concrete Company.

Appellant argues that the trial court erred in determining that Myco failed to allege a cognizable cause of action. We disagree and affirm.

I

Reviewing the facts in the light most favorable to appellant,[43] the record shows that in October, 1985, Super Concrete Co. contracted with appellant Myco, Inc., an electrical service and supply company incorporated in Maryland and doing business in the District, for Myco to convert a power washer on Super Concrete's business premises from a gasoline driven pump to an electric motor drive. The washer was located outdoors and used to wash trucks utilized in transporting concrete. Myco completed the conversion, and the two companies had no further business contacts.

On June 10, 1987, Thomas Fugitt — employed by Super Concrete as a truck driver — was using the washer to wash cement off the axle of his cement truck. When he picked up the metal spray wand, he was electrocuted. Fugitt's wife filed a workers' compensation claim for death benefits with the District of Columbia Department of Employment Services on June 19, 1987. As a result, Super Concrete's insurer, the PMA Group, has been paying weekly death benefits to Fugitt's estate.[44]

Fugitt's wife later filed a wrongful death action against Myco. The complaint alleged that Myco had been negligent in installing a non-watertight starter box on the power washer and in installing only a single clamp attaching the power cord to that starter box, thereby allowing water to seep into it. On April 7, 1988, Myco filed a third-party complaint against Super Concrete. Myco alleged that Super Concrete, in contravention of Myco's instructions, "altered, modified, changed or otherwise tampered with the power washer . . . said alteration including" replacing the original five-foot power cord with one thirty feet long, as well as altering the "plug, strain relief clamp and other equipment" installed by Myco. The third-party complaint sought contribution or indemnification from Super Concrete "for all sums of money which may be adjudged against . . . Myco . . . plus costs and attorney's fees."*(Court's footnote omitted)*

II

In reviewing the propriety of an order granting a motion for summary judgment, we are guided by the principle that the entry of summary judgment is proper if "there exists no genuine issue of material fact and the movant is entitled to judgment as a matter of law." *Wolf v. Regardie*, 553 A.2d 1213, 1216 (D.C. 1989); *see Nader v. de*

---

[42] *(Court's footnote)* D.C. Law 3-77, 27 D.C. Reg. 2503 (1980) (codified at D.C. Code §§ 36-301 to -345 (1989 Repl.)).

[43] *(Court's footnote)* See Leichtman v. Koons, 527 A.2d 745, 746 (D.C. 1987); Taylor v. Eureka Inv. Corp., 482 A.2d 354, 357 (D.C. 1984).

[44] *(Court's footnote)* See D.C. Code § 36-309 (1989 Repl.).

Toledano, 408 A.2d 31, 42 (D.C. 1979), cert. denied, 444 U.S. 1078 (1980); Super. Ct. Civ. R. 56 (c). As the parties have failed to allege the existence of a disputed material fact, we focus solely on the latter portion of this principle, that is, whether there exists a viable legal theory which, if proved, would entitle appellant to judgment in the trial court. *See Williams v. Gerstenfeld*, 514 A.2d 1172, 1177 (D.C. 1986). We must therefore determine whether a third party, in an action against it by or on behalf of an injured or deceased employee, is entitled to indemnity from the employer whose negligence is alleged to have contributed to the employee's injury. A leading authority has noted that the issue is "[p]erhaps the most evenly balanced controversy in all of [workers'] compensation law. . . . " 2B A. Larson, Workmen's Compensation Law § 76.11, at 14-644 (1989); *see* Comment, *The Effect of Workers' Compensation Laws on the Right of a Third Party Liable to an Injured Employee to Recover Contribution or Indemnity from the Employer*, 9 Seton Hall L. Rev. 238, 297–300 (1978) (hereinafter Effect of Workers' Compensation Laws). Each of the parties to this dispute makes a strong argument. We conclude that the objectives underlying the Act, as well as the great weight of case law, oblige us to answer the question in the negative on the indemnity issue.

A.

The triadic relationship between an employer, an injured or deceased employee, and a third party is governed by the District of Columbia Workers' Compensation Act, D.C. Code 36-301 et seq. (the Act), which establishes a no-fault means of recovery for accidental injuries occurring in the course of employment. . . . § 36-304 (a) of the Act provides:

> The liability of an employer prescribed in Section 36-303 *shall be exclusive and in place of all liability* of such employer to the employee, his legal representative, husband or wife, parents, dependents, next of kin, *and anyone otherwise entitled to recover damages from such employer at law on account of such injury or death (Court's footnote omitted)*

(Emphasis added.)

. . .

Though workers' compensation statutes typically govern only the employee-employer relationship, in many instances the injury results from the exclusive or concurrent fault of a third party. Because an employee is prevented from seeking a tort award from the employer, *see* D.C. Code § 36-304 (a), and because workers' compensation benefits often fall far short of those potential awards,[45] *see Castro v. State*, 114 Cal. App. 3d 503, 515, 170 Cal. Rptr. 734, 741 (4th Dist. 1981), suing the third party becomes an attractive alternative to make up the difference.

In such cases, nothing precludes the employee from seeking injury-related damages from that third-party tortfeasor. . . . However, when the third party, to protect against an adverse monetary judgment, seeks indemnity from the employer for having contributed to or caused the injury for which the employee seeks damages, that cause of action runs head-on into the exclusivity provision of the Act.

To illustrate, in this case the estate of the injured employee sued Myco, which in turn joined Super Concrete as a third-party defendant seeking indemnification (or contribution). Myco alleged that Super Concrete was negligent in maintaining and

---

[45] *(Court's footnote)* For comparisons of compensation awards with the amount of total damages, see Dodge v. Mitsui Shintaku Ginko K.K., Tokyo, 528 F.2d 669, 670 (9th Cir. 1975) (compensation: $ 1,454.92; damages: $ 9,000), cert. denied, 425 U.S. 944 (1976); Newport Airpark, Inc. v. United States, 419 F.2d 342, 344 (1st Cir. 1969) (compensation: $ 8,600; settlement: $ 50,000); Stark v. Posh Constr. Co., 192 Pa. Super. 409, 411, 413, 162 A.2d 9, 10–11 (1960) (compensation maximum: $20,000; judgment: $ 111,123.42).

modifying the washer. Although Myco later conceded that the exclusivity provision of the workers' compensation statute bars an action for contribution, *(Court's footnote omitted)* it continues to assert its "right" to indemnification. Super Concrete, on the other hand, contends that the exclusivity provision of the Act precludes an action for indemnity. We turn, then, to examine this contention.

B.

Indemnity is a common law remedy which shifts a monetary loss from one compelled to pay it to another whom equity dictates should bear it instead. W. Prosser, The Law of Torts § 51 (4th ed. 1971); *see McFall v. Compagnie Maritime Belge, S.A.*, 304 N.Y. 314, 328, 107 N.E.2d 463, 471 (1952). A right to indemnity may either be express, arising out of a written agreement, or implied, arising out of a relationship between the parties.

In addition to barring contribution from an employer, the exclusivity provisions of state workers' compensation statutes are generally held to preclude indemnity in all but a few specified instances. This is due, in part, to a recognition that there is little appreciable difference between requiring an employer to reimburse a third party's payment to a worker in separate litigation and requiring the employer to pay the worker that amount in damages directly, an action explicitly precluded by the exclusivity provisions of most workers' compensation laws.

1. Express Indemnity

It is well settled in most jurisdictions that when the third party's claim against the employer is for indemnity pursuant to an express contractual provision, the exclusivity provisions of workers' compensation laws do not bar the indemnification. *See, e.g., Superior Companies v. Kaiser Cement Corp.*, 152 Ariz. 575, 733 P.2d 1158 (Ct. App. 1987); *Republic Steel Corp. v. Glaros*, 12 Ohio App. 2d 29, 31, 230 N.E.2d 667, 669, 41 Ohio Op. 2d 86 (1967). This is because the duty involved is one voluntarily accepted by the employer and existing separate and apart from either of the parties' relationships with the injured employee. Consequently, the duty is not one which arises "on account of" the employee's injury and thus is not covered by the statute. As there exists no such contractual provision in the case before us, we need not further discuss the issue.

2. Implied Indemnity

Implied indemnity is essentially an equitable remedy that "arise[s] without agreement, and by operation of law to prevent a result which is regarded as unjust or unsatisfactory." W. Prosser, D. Dobbs, R. Keeton & D. Owen, Prosser & Keeton on the Law of Torts § 51, at 341 (5th ed. 1984). Under this theory, indemnification may rest essentially on one of two concepts. The first, the "active/passive" theory, permits indemnity when the relationship between the employer and third party is that of joint tortfeasors, and is "based squarely upon the theory that an 'actively' negligent tortfeasor has an implied obligation to indemnify a 'passively' negligent tortfeasor." *Effect of Workers' Compensation Laws, supra*, 9 Seton Hall L. Rev. at 256.[46] This is, however, a minority position. *See id.* at 256–60. The second — and more widely accepted — is based on the well-established theory that if one breaches a duty owed to another and the breach causes injury, the former should compensate the latter. *See* Prosser & Keeton on the Law of Torts, *supra*, § 53, at 356–59. This is often referred to as the "independent duty" theory.

a. The active/passive theory of indemnity

Under the "active/passive" theory, also called the "primary/secondary" theory, a few courts have allowed indemnification when the third party's conduct "passively" contributes to an injury while the employer's acts "actively" cause the injury. *See, e.g., American District Telegraph Co. v. Kittleson*, 179 F.2d 946, 952–53 (8th Cir. 1950);

---

[46] *(Court's footnote)* At times, a contractual relationship between the parties exists. *Id.* at 258.

Coates v. Potomac Electric Power Co., 96 F. Supp. 1019, 1021 (D.D.C. 1951); *Jones v. McDougal-Hartman Co.*, 115 Ill. App. 2d 403, 406, 253 N.E.2d 581, 583 (1969). Passive negligence is characterized by non-feasance, such as the failure to perform some duty imposed by law. *See Adler's Quality Bakery Inc. v. Gasteria, Inc.*, 32 N.J. 55, 79–80, 159 A.2d 97, 110 (1960). Active negligence, on the other hand, is misfeasance, such as an affirmative negligent act. *See Rossmoor Sanitation, Inc. v. Pylon, Inc.*, 13 Cal. 3d 622, 629, 119 Cal. Rptr. 449, 453, 532 P.2d 97, 101 (1975); *State Farm Fire & Casualty Co. v. Home Insurance Co.*, 88 Wis. 2d 124, 130–31, 276 N.W.2d 349, 352 (Wis. Ct. App. 1979). Thus,

> indemnification of a concurrently negligent tortfeasor is said to be based upon a disparity of duties of care owed by the tortfeasors to the injured party, the doctrine of last clear chance or discovered peril, a disparity of gravity of the fault of the tortfeasors, or a combination of these.

United Air Lines, Inc. v. Weiner, 335 F.2d 379, 399 (9th Cir.) (footnotes omitted), *cert. denied*, 379 U.S. 951 (1964).

. . . .

The basis for recovery under the "active/passive" theory is, in reality, the joint liability of the employer and third party — albeit in differing degrees. *See Arcell v. Ashland Chemical Co.*, 152 N.J. Super. 471, 489, 378 A.2d 53, 62 (Law Div. 1977); *Slattery v. Marra Brothers*, 186 F.2d 134, 139 (2d Cir.) (L. Hand, C.J.), *cert. denied*, 341 U.S. 915 (1951). However, under the exclusivity provision of the Act the employer cannot be liable in tort to the employee for the injury, *see* D.C. Code § 36-304 (a), and therefore cannot be jointly liable with a third party, *see Santisteven v. Dow Chemical Co.*, 506 F.2d 1216, 1219 (9th Cir. 1974).

To conclude otherwise would be to sanction a form of indemnity that is, in actuality, solely "an extreme form of contribution." *Slattery, supra*, 186 F.2d at 138. Yet, joint tortfeasor contribution as a form of recovery is barred by the exclusivity portion of the Act. *See* 2B A. Larson, *supra*, § 76.20, at 14-654 & n.24.[47] So far as we can see therefore there is no body of sure authority for saying that differences in the degrees of fault between two tortfeasors will without more strip one of them, if he is an employer, of the protection of the compensation act; and we are at a loss to see any tenable principle which can support such a result. *Slattery, supra*, 186 F.2d at 139. Consequently, Myco's right to indemnity must be found — if at all — in the second concept of implied indemnity: the "independent duty" theory.

b. The independent duty theory of indemnity

Under this theory, the third party is entitled to indemnity from the employer if the two "stand in a special legal relationship that carries with it the obligation to indemnify the third party" and this right of indemnity "may be enforced without offending the exclusive-remedy clause." Larson, *Third-Party Action Over Against Workers' Compensation Employer*, 1982 Duke L.J. 483, 505–06; "[I]t is the fact situation in its entirety, consensual and non-consensual elements both included, which gives rise to the obligation. . . . " Leflar, *Contribution and Indemnity Between Tortfeasors*, 81 U. Pa. L. Rev. 130, 147 (1932).

In order to establish the right to this particular type of implied indemnity, the obligation must arise out of a specific duty of defined nature — separate from the injury to the employer — owed to the third party by the employer. *See Hysell v. Iowa Public Service Co.*, 534 F.2d 775, 782 (8th Cir. 1976) (applying Iowa law); *Ramos v. Browning Ferris Industries of South Jersey, Inc.*, 103 N.J. 177, 188–89, 510 A.2d 1152, 1158 (1986). The legal basis for this exception is fairly straightforward. The immunity from liability conferred on employers by the Act and other similar provisions is only against actions

---

[47] *(Court's footnote)* See *supra* p. 8 & note 12.

for damages "on account" of the employee's injury or death. *See* D.C. Code § 36-304 (a). Consequently, a suit in which "a third party's action for indemnity is not exactly for 'damages' but for reimbursement, and . . . is not 'on account of' the employee's injury, but on account of breach of an independent duty owed by the employer to the third party" avoids the exclusivity provision. 2B A. Larson, *supra*, § 76.41, at 14-733 to -734; *cf. Holden v. Placid Oil Co.*, 473 F. Supp. 1097, 1100–01 (E.D. La. 1979) (LHWCA). Thus, when the indemnity is based on a special legal relationship existing separate and apart from any liability which the employer might have had to the injured employee, indemnity is allowed. *See Bonus-Bilt, Inc. v. United Grocers, Ltd.*, 136 Cal. App. 3d 429, 437, 186 Cal. Rptr. 357, 361 (1st Dist. 1982).

Examples of the special legal relationships that have been held to support a third-party claim for indemnification include that of bailor and bailee and lessor and lessee, *see* 2B A. Larson, *supra*, § 76.51, at 14-763 to -767; *see, e.g., Baugh v. Rogers*, 24 Cal. 2d 200, 214–15, 148 P.2d 633, 641–42 (1944); principal and agent, *see, e.g., Hagen v. Koerner*, 64 N.J. Super. 580, 586–87, 166 A.2d 784, 787 (App. Div. 1960).

Myco contends that Super Concrete owed it a legal duty to use and maintain the power washer so as to "prevent injury and protect Myco from any future legal action." Myco asserted below that when it converted the washer it "properly performed the necessary work in accordance with the then-existing practice in the industry," and that it instructed Super Concrete "in the safety precautions necessary in the proper maintenance of the equipment, specifically in regard to any alteration or replacement of the electric power cord." Thus, Myco argues, Super Concrete had a duty to follow those instructions, and its failure to do so was a breach of a legal obligation giving rise to a right to indemnification.

Put another way, Myco's argument is that when an employer has a previously-purchased product serviced or modified, there is an implied contract with the seller to use the product in such a way as not to bring liability upon the service provider. We have not previously considered the question. However, courts have almost unanimously rejected the analogous argument that when a buyer purchases a product he impliedly contracts with the manufacturer to use the product so as to avoid the imposition of liability on the manufacturer. *See, e.g.*, Drake v. Raymark Industries, Inc., 772 F.2d 1007, 1010 (1st Cir. 1985), *cert. denied*, 476 U.S. 1126 (1986); *Decker v. Black & Decker Manufacturing Co.*, 389 Mass. 35, 39., 449 N.E.2d 641, 644 (1983); *Williams v. Ashland Chemical Co.*, 52 Ohio App. 2d 81, 90–91, 368 N.E.2d 304, 311, 6 Ohio Op. 3d 56, 61 (1976); *Olch v. Pacific Press & Shear Co.*, 19 Wash. App. 89, 93–94, 573 P.2d 1355, 1357 (1978). We find the two arguments sufficiently comparable so as to conclude that the holding in these latter cases support the rejection of appellant's argument.

We agree with the authorities that conclude the imposition of such a duty would stand "indemnity on its head." *Santisteven, supra*, 506 F.2d at 1219. The employer's duty of proper use and care of the washer extends solely to its employees; Super Concrete's liability for a breach of that duty was satisfied, pursuant to the Act, by payment to Fugitt's estate of the compensation award. *See* D.C. Code § 36-304 (a); *Therrien v. Safeguard Manufacturing Co.*, 35 Conn. Supp. 268, 270, 408 A.2d 273, 275 (1979), *aff'd*, 180 Conn. 91, 429 A.2d 808 (1980).

That liability being extinguished, we would not conclude that the employer, Super Concrete, had an independent duty to Myco to protect it from liability. Absent a much closer relationship than that which exists between the parties here,[48] *cf. Roy v. Star Chopper, Inc.*, 442 F. Supp. 1010 (D.R.I. 1977) (relationship between manufacturer and purchaser/employer supporting indemnity may be more in nature of co-manufacturers), *aff'd*, 584 F.2d 1124 (1st Cir. 1978), *cert. denied*, 440 U.S. 916 (1979), any other

---

[48] *(Court's footnote)* A different question may be presented, possibly, after the evidence is adduced, if this case goes to trial.

determination would "be stretching the concept of contract out of all relation to reality," 2B A. Larson, *supra*, § 76.84, at 14-871.

We thus conclude that Super Concrete owes no independent duty to Myco which would serve to entitle the latter to indemnification. Rather, Super Concrete owed Myco

> only the general duty that every member of society owes to every other member — the duty not to harm him through tortious acts. Such a general duty does not support a right to indemnity in a case where the would-be indemnitor is an "employer" covered by the Work[ers'] Compensation law.

Western Casualty & Surety Co. v. Grolier, Inc., 501 F.2d 434, 438 (8th Cir. 1974) (interpreting Iowa statute similar to exclusivity provision of D.C. Code); *accord, Hysell, supra*, 534 F.2d at 782.

Consequently, because there exists no legal basis for Myco's complaint, no reasonable juror, acting reasonably, could find for Myco as a matter of law. The trial court therefore properly granted summary judgment for Super Concrete. *See Nader, supra*, 408 A.2d at 42.

III.

. . . .

Despite equities in favor of each of the parties in this case, the weight that tips the scales against Myco is the exclusivity provision of the Act, which we conclude compels the decision we reach. While we recognize it is conceivable that the end result of this litigation for Myco could turn out to be harsh, *(Court's footnote omitted)* any other solution would require a significant change in the statute as it presently exists.

In other words, we consider that the legislation compels us to conclude that the exclusivity provision requires us to rule against the allowance of indemnity here. A conclusion that a right of implied indemnity exists here, "in the absence of an independent duty, would subvert the [present] legislative intent to restrict the employer's liability to the Workers' Compensation Act." *Ramos, supra*, 103 N.J. at 188–89, 510 A.2d at 1158; *see Rupe v. Durbin Durco, Inc.*, 557 S.W.2d 742, 750 (Tenn. Ct. App. 1976), overruled in part on other grounds by *Crosslin v. Alsup*, 594 S.W.2d 379 (Tenn. 1980). Allowance of such a recovery would allow the employee to accomplish indirectly what cannot be done directly and thereby evade the legislation. It tends to impair "the balance of the workers' compensation system by subjecting the employer to unlimited liability."[49]

Given this legislative intent, the nature and extent of the statutory change necessary to effectuate a workable restructuring and reform of the present system, and the important public policy considerations behind the Act, any expansion in the availability of indemnification in cases such as this is not for us to fashion, but must be left to the legislative branch. *District of Columbia Department of Corrections v. Teamsters Union Local No. 246*, 554 A.2d 319, 326 (D.C. 1989) ("If this result seems unsatisfying, then it is up to the Council of the District of Columbia to amend the statute.") In the meantime, the courts are bound by the legislation.

Affirmed.

---

[49] *(Court's footnote)* 9 Seton Hall L. Rev. at 300.

§ 30.05   POLICY ARGUMENTS AND MERITS OF VARIOUS SOLUTIONS

[1] Introduction

Choice of a solution to the recovery-over problem will depend on which of three values is rated highest: stability, fairness, or simplicity. The rich and rapidly changing array of solutions, actual or proposed, to this "most evenly-balanced" problem, will now be arrayed depending on which of these values is favored.

[2] Solutions Arrayed According to Values Served

[a] Introduction

In the world of everyday law, by contrast with the world of abstract ethics, decisions often involve the balancing of values other than pure equity — even if pure equity could be discovered. A legal system must have some element of constancy and predictability, which means that it cannot necessarily be swayed by whatever seems to be the fairest result from one moment to the next. Moreover, a legal system must be administrable, in the sense that it must be able to translate concepts of justice into decisions of actual cases involving an almost infinite variety of complications. And so, in an issue as close as the one we are dealing with, choice of a solution will ultimately depend on the relative weight given to three competing values: stability, equity, and simplicity.

[b] Solutions Favoring Stability

Most courts have chosen the course which respects the value of stability; that is, they have adhered to several time-honored doctrines: the rule of exclusiveness of the employer's compensation liability and its right to reimbursement for his compensation outlay; the rule that contribution between joint tortfeasors requires joint tort liability; the rule that a fictional indemnity obligation will not be implied because of varying degrees of fault of tortfeasors, and that even if it were, it would still be "on account of the injury"; and the rule that a separate duty of care does not run "upstream" from a purchaser to a manufacturer of a product.

A clear illustration of the deliberate honoring of the value of stability may be seen in the decision of the Supreme Court of New Jersey in *Schweizer*,[50] as it refused to emulate the North Carolina-California approach. The New Jersey Court observed that it would be inappropriate at this late date to make drastic judicial changes in a "carefully articulated scheme of adjustment" of the relative rights of all the parties that had stood for 60 years without legislative alteration.

[c] Solutions Favoring Fairness

When courts have decided to elevate fairness above all other considerations, including stability, the result has usually been to proportion the ultimate liability of employer and third party to their relative fault, as for example in New York.[51]

Appealing as this is on first look, it is subject to question in at least three respects — leaving aside the damage done to the concept of *stare decisis*, which the courts in these instances plainly felt was outweighed by the injustice being perpetuated.

The first observation is that the New York-Illinois approach gives zero weight to the factor of the employer's traditional immunity to liability beyond its compensation

---

[50] Schweizer v. Elox Div. of Colt Indus., 70 N.J. 280, 259 A.2d 857 (1976).

[51] *See* Ch. 30, § 30.02[5], *above*.

obligation. In other words, fairness is appraised as if between two equal strangers, ignoring the fact that one, the employer, has already made concessions and assumed liabilities to the employee, for which his immunity was the *quid pro quo*. The Minnesota formula at least recognizes this factor and attempts to do something about it, by placing an absolute ceiling on the employer's liability in the amount of its compensation liability.[52] It is thus possible to say that the employer, in the end, pays out no more than it expected to under the compensation act.

The second comment is that fairness, in this context, is even more elusive than usual, because it involves a complex mix of different kinds of fault — some real moral fault, some merely fictitious, vicarious or technical. The employer's fault is usually not personal but vicarious; the third party's fault is often virtually absolute, as in unseaworthiness, products liability, automobile owner's liability, and the like. It is no wonder that a strange kind of balancing of fault often results, when the fault being balanced is no-fault on both sides.

The third criticism is that the price of equity will inevitably be the sacrifice of the third value — simplicity. Litigation will be complicated. It would appear that all three parties will have to be involved in practically all cases, with percentage assessments of fault for each.

[d]   Solutions Favoring Simplicity

There is a possible solution that would achieve maximum simplicity without, perhaps, too shocking a departure from equity. It is a sort of adaptation of the North Carolina-California approach, with some important alterations designed in part to avoid the appalling complexities that bedeviled the California courts:

(1) Reduce the employee's recovery against the third party by the amount of compensation *in all cases*, not just in those involving employer negligence. And, of course, the employee keeps his or her compensation, thus coming out whole. Note that one complication has already been eliminated — that of determining the relative fault of employer and third party.

(2) Abolish subrogation in all cases, and of course abolish reimbursement of the employer by the employee, since the employee has not recovered the equivalent of the compensation from the third party. The advantage here is that the employer and the carrier are out of the third-party picture altogether.

(3) Abolish all recovery-over by the third party.

There is something for everybody in this wholesale compromise. The employee comes out with full damages, with less complications and delays, and without the possible prejudice to his or her interests attendant on the presence of the employer in the litigation. The employer loses some opportunities for reimbursement from the third party, but in jurisdictions in which some kind of recovery-over by the third party against the employer is possible, the employer would be relieved of any such possible liability. The third party, in turn, would have its liability reduced below what it now is in most jurisdictions, and in all jurisdictions in cases in which the employer was not at fault.

In short, there would be only one lawsuit and only one issue: Was the third party at fault? The problem that caused the most difficulty in California is avoided, since it is not necessary to try the issue of the employer's negligence in the employee's suit against the third party — or at any other time.

---

[52] *See* Ch. 30, § 30.02[3], *above.*

[3] General Conclusions

No solution is clearly optimal, but there are several choices depending on the values to be served. The solution should be based on what is good for compensation law. If products liability law has got out of hand, the necessary corrections should be made within the boundaries of products liability law, not by distorting long-standing compensation principles.

Finally, in choosing between the values identified, recall that one of the important values stressed by the early founders of workers' compensation was getting rid of the uncertainties and complications of common law litigation and substituting simple, near-automatic remedies. This ideal, as it turned out, was not to be realized, but at least it can be said that any step in the direction of simplicity is a step toward one of the oldest and finest traditions of workers' compensation.

Part 10
OTHER TOPICS

Chapter 31
PROCEDURE

§ 31.01 INTRODUCTION

Each jurisdiction has its own procedures, defined by statute and regulations, for the filing and processing of workers' compensation claims, for hearing contested cases, and for judicial review. Since these procedures vary greatly from state to state, it would be pointless to attempt to cover them in detail here. Instead, we will briefly survey the major procedural features commonly found in state administrative systems.

The procedural law of workers' compensation, like the substantive, takes its tone from the beneficent and remedial character of the legislation. Procedure is generally summary and informal. The initial handling of claims and the first review are administrative in all but a few states. The whole idea is to get away from cumbersome procedures and technicalities of pleading, and to reach a right decision by the shortest and quickest possible route. On the other hand, as every lawyer knows, there is a point beyond which the sweeping-aside of "technicalities" cannot go, since evidentiary and procedural rules usually have an irreducible hard core of necessary function that cannot be dispensed with in any orderly investigation of the merits of a case. The question that constantly recurs in a survey of the procedural side of workers' compensation is whether, in any particular case involving a loss of benefits for procedural reasons under an otherwise meritorious claim, the indispensability of the procedural purpose so served outweighs the thwarting of the protective functions of the act.

§ 31.02 NOTICE AND CLAIM PERIODS

[1] Summary

Under most acts, the employee must (1) give the employer notice of injury as soon as practicable, or within a specified number of months, and must also (2) file any claim for compensation with the administrative agency within a fixed period, usually one to two years.

Since the purpose of the notice requirement is to enable the employer to protect itself by prompt investigation and treatment of the injury, failure to give formal notice is usually no bar if the employer had actual knowledge or informal notice sufficient to indicate the possibility of a compensable injury, or if the employer furnished medical service or paid some compensation, or, in many jurisdictions, if the employer was not prejudiced by the lack of notice.

[2] Excuses for Late Notice — In General

Moreover, since the law does not exact the impossible of the employee, lateness of both notice and claim may be excused for various reasons, including the following: impossibility of knowing that an apparently minor accident would later develop into a compensable injury; reasonable inability to recognize a disease or disabling condition in an early or latent stage; medical opinion that the injury is not serious or is non-industrial; voluntary payment of benefits by the employer, or assurances that the employee will be taken care of, inducing the employee to refrain from making claim; and disability preventing the making of the claim, due to mental or physical incapacity, minority, and the like. Some statutes, however, by making the claim period run from the date of "accident," have produced holdings that an injury which manifests itself for the first time after the period has expired is nevertheless barred. The right to assert the statutory bar can, in most jurisdictions, be lost by waiver, through the payment of compensation, the failure to raise the defense promptly, or the admission of liability.

EVJEN v. NORTH DAKOTA WORKERS COMPENSATION BUREAU
429 N.W.2d 418 (N.D. 1988)

LEVINE, JUSTICE.

Paul Evjen appeals from a district court judgment affirming a North Dakota Workers Compensation Bureau decision dismissing his claim for benefits because it was not timely filed. *We affirm.*

Evjen began working at the North Dakota State Hospital on December 27, 1982. In 1983 he suffered the onset of headaches that lasted eight or ten hours once or twice a month. He first consulted a doctor about the headaches in November of 1983. On August 1, 1984 Evjen's doctor suggested that he not work the afternoon shift because of his headaches. The headaches worsened until Evjen quit his job on November 11, 1985, because, as he testified, "[t]hey were just so strong that it hurt so much and I was not able to function in a job situation."

Evjen applied for benefits on March 13, 1986. . . .

The Bureau dismissed Evjen's claim, concluding that it lacked jurisdiction because the claim was not timely filed. Evjen appealed to the district court, which affirmed the Bureau's decision.

While Evjen has raised several issues on appeal, we deem the dispositive issue to be whether his claim was timely filed. We conclude that the claim was not timely filed and that determination of the other issues raised is unnecessary.

Section 65-05-01, N.D.C.C., provides in part:

> 65-05-01. *Claims for compensation — When and where filed.* All original claims for compensation shall be filed within one year after the injury or within two years after the death. The date of injury for purposes of this section shall be the actual date of injury when such can be determined with certainty by the claimant and bureau. When the actual date of injury cannot be determined with certainty the date of injury shall be the first date that a reasonable person knew or should have known that the injury was related to employment. . . .

The Bureau construed the statute as depriving it of jurisdiction over Evjen's claim because the claim was filed more than one year after Evjen's injury and more than one year after he knew or should have known that the injury was related to employment. The statute must, of course, be construed liberally in favor of injured workers so that the benefit provisions of the Workers Compensation Act may be extended to all who can fairly be brought within them. See *Kroeplin v. North Dakota Workmen's Compensation Bureau*, 415 N.W.2d 807 (N.D. 1987); *Lass v. North Dakota Workmen's Compensation Bureau*, 415 N.W.2d 796 (N.D. 1987).

In using "a reasonable person" standard in § 65-05-01, N.D.C.C., "the Legislature had in mind the ordinary reasonable lay person and not a person learned in medicine." *Teegarden v. North Dakota Workmen's Compensation Bureau*, 313 N.W.2d 716, 718 (N.D. 1981). Thus, under § 65-05-01, N.D.C.C., the time period within which to file a claim relating to an injury whose date of occurrence is uncertain, begins on the first date that a reasonable lay person, not learned in medicine, knew or should have known that the injury was related to his or her employment.

In *Teegarden, supra,* we concluded that because the claimant was not informed by his physician or anyone else that his disease was either caused by or related to his work, and because there was no evidence that "a worker comparable to the one in question here under the conditions of employment should have known that his injury or disease was caused by work or was work-related," the Bureau erred in finding untimely the filing of the claim. *Teegarden, supra,* at 719.

The record in this case shows that Evjen knew he was having headaches that were causally related to his employment by August 1, 1984, and that his physician recommended that he stop working the afternoon shift because of his headaches. In an August 13, 1984, letter that Evjen kept and a copy of which he provided to his employer, Evjen's physician referred to Evjen's headaches as a "significant health problem . . . caused by significant stress on the job" and stated that he "would like to see him transferred to a different Unit at the State Hospital and also recommend that he not work the afternoon shift."

Unlike the claimant in *Teegarden,* Evjen received specific medical advice that his injury was related to his employment and also that it was a significant health problem. Without that advice, this would be a different case because headaches are fairly common afflictions often suffered by many from job stress. A reasonable lay person would not immediately file a claim for compensation upon learning that occasional headaches were work-related.

From the evidence before it, the Bureau found that Evjen's "claim was filed more than one year after the date of injury and/or the date that he knew or should have known that the condition was related to his employment." From our review of the evidence, we conclude that "a reasoning mind reasonably could have determined that the factual conclusions reached were proved by the weight of the evidence from the entire record." *Power Fuels, Inc. v. Elkin,* 283 N.W.2d 214, 220 (N.D. 1979).

Evjen's reliance upon *Beauchamp v. North Dakota Workmen's Compensation Bureau,* 126 N.W.2d 417 (N.D. 1964), is misplaced. In *Beauchamp* we held that under § 65-05-01, N.D.C.C., an injury which results from a progressive disease, fairly traceable to employment and culminating in a compensable disability, dates from the time that it results in incapacity for work. At the time of the *Beauchamp* decision, § 65-05-01, N.D.C.C., provided in relevant part:

> All original claims for compensation for disability or death shall be made within sixty days after injury or death. For any reasonable cause shown, however, the bureau may allow original claims for compensation for disability or death to be made at any time within one year after the injury or death.

Section 65-05-01, N.D.C.C., was amended in 1967 (S.L. 1967, ch. 484, § 1) by the addition of the following language:

> The date of injury for purposes of this section shall be the actual date of injury when such can be determined with certainty by the claimant and bureau. When the actual date of injury cannot be determined with certainty the date of injury shall be the first date the injury or diseased condition culminates in a need for medical attention or an incapacity of the employee for work.

The effect of the 1967 amendment was to incorporate *Beauchamp's* incapacity-for-work trigger and add to it an alternative need-for-medical-attention standard.

Section 65-05-01 was again amended in 1977 (S.L. 1977, ch. 579, § 8) to provide, as it now does, that:

> When the actual date of injury cannot be determined with certainty the date of injury shall be the first date that a reasonable person knew or should have known that the injury was related to employment.

Thus, the 1977 amendment eliminated not only the 1967 amendment's need-for-medical-attention test, but also *Beauchamp's* incapacity-for-work test. Evjen knew by August 1, 1984, that his headaches were "related to employment." We are not permitted to disregard the clear and unambiguous statutory language requiring that the period within which to file a claim begin to run at the point that Evjen knew or should have known that his headaches were related to employment.

While "[t]he justice, wisdom, necessity, utility and expediency of legislation are questions for legislative, and not for judicial determination" [Syllabus P11, *Asbury Hospital v. Cass County*, 72 N.D. 359, 7 N.W.2d 438 (1943)], we invite legislative reconsideration of § 65-05-01, N.D.C.C. To begin the running of a claim period, the claimant should have had reason to be aware of the seriousness of his injury or disease, "since any other rule would force employees to rush in with claims for every minor ache, pain, or symptom." 3 A. Larson, Workmen's Compensation Law § 78.41(e), p. 15-213. *See also* 3 A. Larson, *supra*, § 78.52. Starting the period within which to file a claim at "the first date that a reasonable person knew or should have known that the injury was related to employment" encourages employees to "rush in with claims for every minor ache, pain, or symptom" in order to make sure that any future claim for compensation will not be deemed untimely. The present statute imposes an unnecessary burden on the Bureau, the workers compensation fund, employers and employees. At the same time, the statute discourages and penalizes employees who attempt to keep working, rather than filing a claim, after learning that an injury is related to employment. "[I]t seems to us palpably unjust to the employee to deny him compensation because he has tried to keep his place on the employer's pay roll by doing his regular work." *Baldwin v. Scullion*, 50 Wyo. 508, 62 P.2d 531, 539 (1936).

Affirmed.

[3] Long-Latency Injuries or Diseases

A rigid claims period may operate unfairly not only because the nature, seriousness and work-connection of the injury could not reasonably be recognized by the claimant, or perhaps even by his or her doctor, but in many cases because the injury itself does not exist in compensable degree during the claims period. This latent or delayed injury problem presents in the sharpest relief the senselessness of uncompromising time periods. The classic illustration is that of the apparently trivial accident that matures into a disabling injury after the claim period has expired. A worker is struck in the eye by a metal chip, but both he and the company doctors dismiss the accident as a petty one, and of course no claim is made, since there is no present injury or disability. Eighteen months later a cataract develops as the direct result of the accident. If the statute bars claims filed more than one year after the "accident," and if the courts apply the statutory language with medieval literalism, workers can never collect for injuries no matter how diligent they are: they cannot claim during the year, because no compensable injury exists; they cannot claim after the year, because the statute runs from the accident.[1]

About half of the states date the claim period from the "accident"; most of the rest date it from the "injury." Under the "injury" type of statute, there is now almost complete judicial agreement that the claim period runs from the time compensable injury becomes apparent. But the "accident" type of statute produced in some older cases some very harsh rulings: for example, compensation was denied to a worker whose cataract developed 18 months after getting a steel chip in his eye.[2] Similarly, under the "exposure" type of provision, compensation has been denied to asbestos

---

[1] Whitted v. Palmer-Bee Co., 228 N.C. 447, 46 S.E.2d 109 (1948).

[2] Whitted v. Palmer-Bee Co., 228 N.C. 447, 46 S.E.2d 109 (1948).

workers who, because of the extremely long latency period of some asbestos-related diseases, never could have brought a claim within the statutory period.[3]

It is odd indeed to find, in a supposedly beneficent piece of legislation, the survival of this fragment of irrational cruelty surpassing the most technical forfeitures of legal statutes of limitation. Statutes of limitation generally proceed on the theory that one forfeits rights only when inexcusably delaying assertion of them. But here no amount of vigilance is of any help.

[4] Voluntary Payment of Compensation or Furnishing of Medical Services

When an employer voluntarily makes compensation payments, the period for filing a claim usually dates from the last payment.[4] The general idea is that an employee who has been receiving compensation for 11 months cannot reasonably be expected to have made claim during that period, and should not, upon cessation of voluntary payments at the end of the 11th month, be allowed only 1 month in which to file the claim.

A common controversy under this rule is the question whether medical "payments" are the kind of payments that toll the statute. The great majority of courts include such services,[5] on the theory that the furnishing of any kind of benefit required by compensation law indicates an acceptance of liability, but a few courts have interpreted their claim period statutes to exclude medical services entirely.[6]

BLAKELEY v. WORKMEN'S COMPENSATION APPEALS BOARD
3 Cal. 3d 320, 90 Cal. Rptr. 429, 475 P.2d 661 (1970)

BURKE, JUSTICE.

Petitioner seeks review of the appeals boards' opinion and order denying reconsideration of the referee's findings and award which disallowed petitioner's claim for compensation benefits for permanent disability. We have concluded that petitioner's application for benefits was timely filed and that the board's decision should be annulled.

Petitioner testified that on June 5, 1967, she was employed as a potato chip packer, and that on that date she slipped and fell during the course of her employment, injuring her knees, elbow, pelvis and rib cage. She further testified that the following day she showed her injuries to the company nurse, who examined her and told her to take some aspirin, but who did not advise her to see a doctor; that petitioner, having already taken some aspirin at her home, declined the offer of aspirin, telling the nurse that she could obtain more aspirin from the "chip room" cupboard if she needed them; that the nurse told petitioner to take the aspirin that was so provided; and that subsequently petitioner did take some aspirin from the cupboard. Petitioner completed an accident report the day following her fall, and she continued to see the nurse for three or four days thereafter, but her condition did not improve. She continued working until

---

[3] *See, e.g.*, National Gypsum Co. v. Bunker, 441 N.E.2d 8 (Ind. 1982), *appeal dismissed*, 460 U.S. 1076 (1983). The Indiana Occupational Disease Act provision, IC 22-3-7-9(f), barring claims unless brought within three years of exposure, was held constitutional as to asbestos workers, in spite of the long latency period. *But see* Stone v. State Acc. Ins. Fund Corp., 57 Or. App. 808, 646 P.2d 668 (1982). The absolute five-year limitations period was not constitutional as applied to asbestos-related diseases.

[4] *See, e.g.*, Sturgill Lumber Co. v. Maynard, 447 S.W.2d 638 (Ky. App. 1969).

[5] *See, e.g.*, Mihesuah v. Workmen's Comp. App. Bd., 29 Cal. App. 2d 337, 105 Cal. Rptr. 561, 37 Cal. Comp. Cas. 790 (1972).

[6] *See, e.g.*, Franklin v. Blue Grass Cooperage Co., 447 S.W.2d 621 (Ky. App. 1969).

November 14, 1968, and filed her claim for compensation benefits on April 7, 1969, 22 months after the date of her injury.

The referee and board denied petitioner's claim solely on the basis that it was barred by the one-year limitations period under Labor Code, section 5405, [Court's footnote omitted] and held that the mere furnishing of aspirin to petitioner did not constitute medical treatment which would have entitled her, under section 5410, [Court's footnote omitted] to a five-year period for claiming benefits for new and further disability.

The rule as established by the cases is that before an employee is entitled to the advantage of the five-year period under section 5410, he must have been furnished workmen's compensation benefits by the employer either voluntarily or pursuant to a commission award. (*Standard Rectifier Corp. v. Workmen's Comp. App. Bd.*, 65 Cal. 2d 287, 290, 54 Cal. Rptr. 100, 419 P.2d 164.) The rationale of this rule is that the "new and further disability" to which section 5410 refers is a disability in addition to that for which the employer previously provided benefits as required by the statute. The furnishing of medical treatment for an industrial injury constitutes such a benefit. (*Standard Rectifier Corp. v. Workmen's Comp. App. Bd., supra,* pp. 290–291, 54 Cal. Rptr. 100, 419 P.2d 164.)

In Standard Rectifier, we held that the furnishing of "gray pain pills" by the employee's supervisor, with knowledge that they were to alleviate a condition caused by work, constituted the furnishing of medical treatment. We stated further that

> We are persuaded that this view is sound and accords with the intent of the Legislature that provisions of the workmen's compensation act be liberally construed "with the purpose of extending their benefits for the protection of persons injured in the course of their employment." (§ 3202; * * *.) (65 Cal. 2d at p. 291, 54 Cal. Rptr. at p. 103, 419 P.2d at p. 167.)

Respondents rely upon Stevens v. Industrial Acc. Com. (1963) 28 Cal.Comp. Cases 39, wherein the mere offer of aspirin to the employee by a foreman was held not to constitute the furnishing of medical treatment. In Standard Rectifier, we distinguished Stevens, stating that

> But in Stevens the employee replied in the negative to the foreman's inquiry whether he wished to go to a doctor, and whether the proffered aspirin was accepted does not appear * * *. (65 Cal. 2d at p. 291, 54 Cal. Rptr. at p. 103, 419 P.2d at p. 167.)

In the instant case, petitioner was not offered the services of a doctor; instead, the nurse recommended that petitioner take aspirin for her injury, and she followed that advice and subsequently took the aspirin furnished by her employer. That the source of the aspirin was a cupboard accessible to all employees rather than the nurse's own cabinet is irrelevant, for aspirin was the form of medical treatment prescribed to petitioner and followed by her. Nor do we think that a meaningful distinction can be made between the "gray pain pills" furnished in the Standard Rectifier case and the aspirin furnished herein. Aspirin, being a known analgesic, [footnote omitted] is in fact a "pain pill," and to sanction any distinction between the two types of pills would exalt form over substance, contrary to the statutory injunction of liberal construction set forth above.

The decision of the appeals board is annulled and the case remanded for further proceedings consistent with the views expressed herein.

WRIGHT, C.J., and McCOMB, PETERS, TOBRINER, MOSK and SULLIVAN, JJ., concur.

[5] Excuses Based on Employer Fault

A familiar defense to assertion of the bar of late claim is the plea that the lateness was the result of the employer's assurances, misrepresentations or even deliberate deceptions or threats. In the states having statutes permitting the excusing of late claims for good cause or mistake, the issue is simply whether the facts satisfy the statute; in other states the issue usually takes the form of the question whether the employer should be held estopped to invoke the bar. The commonest type of case is that in which a claimant, typically not highly educated, contends that he or she was lulled into a sense of security by statements of employer or carrier representatives that "he or she will be taken care of" or that his or her claim has been filed for him or her or that a claim will not be necessary because he or she would be paid compensation benefits in any event. When such facts are established by the evidence, the lateness of the claim has ordinarily been excused.[7] The Supreme Court of California has gone even further and has held that the employer has an affirmative duty to notify the employee that he or she might have a compensation claim for his or her heart attack; failure to give such notice prevented reliance on the statute of limitations.[8]

[6] Mental or Physical Incompetence as Excuse

Mental or physical incompetence is a common excuse for lateness in filing a claim, in the absence of appointment of a conservator or guardian. For this purpose extreme illiteracy[9] or a "beclouded mind"[10] have been brought within the reach of the mental incompetency principle.

[7] Mistake of Law

A mistake of law is no more an excuse in connection with a late compensation claim than anywhere else.[11] For example, it has been ruled that filing a claim in a state not having jurisdiction does not toll the statute.[12]

[8] Waiver of Limitations

The majority rule is that strict compliance with notice and claim requirements may be waived by the employer or insurer.[13] Many of the relaxations of notice and claim periods discussed above have been the result, in whole or in part, of a theory of waiver. Thus, actual knowledge of the injury, or any conduct indicating that the employer has such knowledge, is sometimes said to amount to a waiver of formal notice; and voluntary payment of compensation is often said to constitute a waiver of formal claim.

A valid waiver may also take procedural form, the commonest example being the holding that the right to rely on lateness of notice or claim may be lost by failure to raise it promptly.[14] Here again the waiver is more than merely technical; it serves the

---

[7] See, e.g., Thorn v. Strawbridge & Clothier, 191 Pa. Super. 59, 155 A.2d 414 (1959).

[8] Reynolds v. Workmen's Comp. App. Bd., 12 Cal. 3d 726, 527 P.2d 631 (1974).

[9] J. E. Green Co. v. Bennett, 207 Tenn. 635, 341 S.W.2d 751 (1960).

[10] Corporate Group Serv. Inc. v. Lymberis, 146 So. 2d 745 (Fla. 1962).

[11] Inland Gas Corp. v. Flint, 255 S.W.2d 1006 (Ky. 1953).

[12] Sherrill v. U.S. Fid. & Guar. Co., 108 Ga. App. 591, 133 S.E.2d 896 (1963).

[13] Lindskog v. Rosebud Mines, Inc., 84 Idaho 160, 369 P.2d 580 (1962).

[14] Bethlehem Steel Co. v. Carter, 224 Md. 19, 165 A.2d 902 (1960).

important procedural end of ensuring that such defenses will not be raised for the first time in the appellate stages of the controversy.

§ 31.03 EVIDENCE

[1] Introduction

The evidence problem in workers' compensation is not the admissibility of evidence incompetent by common law standards, but the ability of such evidence to support an award. The majority rule is the "residuum" rule, which permits incompetent evidence to be received and considered, but requires that there be at least a residuum of competent evidence upon which the Commission's findings may rest. On either side of this rule are two minority lines of opinion, the one permitting an award to stand on the strength of technically incompetent evidence alone, if in the circumstances it is deemed to be of sufficient probative value to guide a reasonable person in the conduct of his or her affairs, the other reversing an award whenever it affirmatively appears that the Commission relied upon incompetent evidence and would not have reached the conclusion it did but for that evidence.

In line with the general tendency of administrative law to recognize the expertise of specialized tribunals, compensation boards may rely to a considerable extent on their own knowledge and experience in uncomplicated medical matters, and in such cases awards may be upheld without medical testimony or even in defiance of the only medical testimony.

[2] Admissibility Versus Ability to Support Award

If one leaves out of account those few jurisdictions having court administration of workers' compensation, as will be done for the most part in the ensuing discussion of evidence, it can be confidently said that the admission of evidence which is incompetent under common law rules is not in itself ground for reversal of an award.[15] This narrows and simplifies the evidence problem: essentially, we are here dealing with an issue, not of conduct of a trial or hearing, but of review.

True, there is much talk of admissibility in compensation cases, but close examination will usually reveal that the underlying issue is the extent to which the "inadmissible" evidence figured in the production of the commission's decision. Ordinarily the only way in which a mistake on admissibility as such could amount to reversible error would be by the exclusion of admissible evidence, rather than by the admission of incompetent evidence. In other words, a compensation board that wants to avoid reversal on admissibility-of-evidence grounds can best do so by admitting everything and excluding nothing. It can be presumed to discount hearsay, but it cannot be presumed to have reached a right result if some important piece of evidence that might have swayed the result has been erroneously excluded.

[3] Extent to Which "Incompetent" Evidence Can Support Award

The cases that have dealt with the effect of incompetent evidence, such as hearsay, may be divided into the following four lines of decision, ranging from the least to the most strict:

> (1) Hearsay evidence is both admissible and capable alone of supporting an award.

---

[15] *See, e.g.*, Bushnell v. City of Duluth, 241 Minn. 189, 62 N.W.2d 813 (1954).

(2) Hearsay evidence is admissible, but alone cannot support an award; there must be a residuum of legal evidence (the so-called "residuum rule").

(3) Admission of hearsay evidence is not in itself reversible error, but the award will be reversed if it appears that the commission relied on such evidence and would not have made the award but for such evidence.

(4) The admission of hearsay evidence is in itself reversible error. This line of decision is of contemporary interest only under some court-administered systems.

Of these rules, the "residuum rule" has been followed in the majority of jurisdictions, although it has been under constant attack ever since it was announced. The residuum rule, as Wigmore has pointed out,[16] assumes flatly that all legally admissible evidence is reliable and that all other evidence is unreliable. Both assumptions are contradicted by common experience: All kinds of deceptive evidence gets into trials operated under the strictest evidence rules, while, on the other hand, some evidence is barred upon which any prudent person would readily base an important judgment affecting his private affairs. Of course, much hearsay is worthless rumor or gossip, but there is also such a thing as "persuasive hearsay," as when a number of independent hearsay accounts corroborate each other.

Inroads into the residuum rule have been made both legislatively and judicially. The New York statute was amended, as some others have been, to permit reliance on corroborated hearsay statements by deceased employees.[17] It was recognized that in many typical industrial accidents there is no independent witness, and the only account of the origin of the injury is the deceased's story to his wife or doctor. The judicial development of most interest is the *Altschuller*[18] case, which upheld an award based on hearsay statements made by an employee who later became "mentally dead," because the "established 'facts and circumstances' leave little reasonable doubt that the narration is substantially true."

The rigors of the hearsay rule are also sometimes tempered by a generous application of its exceptions. *Res gestae* utterances have been treated as such although made after an interval that would seem excessive in a common-law case; for example, a statement by claimant several hours after the accident that he had bumped his head has been accepted.[19] Statements to doctors for purposes of treatment are admitted. Hospital or physician's records have been accepted, sometimes under the rubric of the business record exception to the hearsay rule, but reports and letters of doctors have elicited a difference of view. Generally, statements of persons to whom the accident was reported have been held to be competent.[20]

[4]   Effect of Statutes Abolishing Evidence Rules

More than half of the state statutes provide that common law and statutory rules of evidence shall not apply to compensation proceedings. It might be thought that this kind of provision would sweep aside all disputes about the competence of testimony, and would usher in the era of uninhibited technicality-free fact investigation that reformers have so long dreamed of. The intermediate appellate court that dealt with what was

---

[16] WIGMORE, EVIDENCE 41 (3d ed. 1940).

[17] N.Y. Workmen's Compensation Law, § 118, as amended in 1922.

[18] Altschuller v. Bressler, 289 N.Y. 463, 46 N.E.2d 886 (1943).

[19] Ogden Iron Works v. Industrial Comm'n, 102 Utah 492, 132 P.2d 376 (1942).

[20] *See, e.g.*, Fagan v. City of Newark, 78 N.J. Super. 294, 188 A.2d 427 (1963).

destined to be the leading case on the subject, *Carroll v. Knickerbocker Ice Company*,[21] did indeed so read the statute, saying:

> [T]hese two sections wholly abrogate the substantive law of evidence — abrogate the common law, the statute law, the rules of procedure formulated by the courts, and all the technicalities respected by the legal profession. The commission is authorized . . . to make its investigation in any manner that it chooses, wholly unfettered by any law previously invented by man.[22]

The heady exhilaration of this manifesto of freedom was short-lived; the majority of the Court of Appeals viewed the statute as intended only to facilitate the unrestricted introduction of evidence, leaving untouched the entire question of the quality of evidence that will sustain an administrative finding of fact on review. For the latter purpose, as has been shown, the court insisted upon a "residuum" of evidence that would be considered competent by common law standards.

The New York view was generally accepted, and the result was that the final state of the law in most states came to be about the same whether the rules of evidence had expressly been made inapplicable or not. This is not particularly surprising since, even without special statutes, it has been generally accepted that administrative tribunals are not bound by the rules of evidence applicable to courts.[23] One cannot help wondering, however, whether the legislatures really meant to produce a hybrid situation in which commissions could freely hear all the incompetent evidence they pleased, but could make no legal use of it.

[5]　Admissions and Signed Statements

The employer's report of the accident, which in most states is required to be filed with the commission, is competent as an admission against interest. This is so even if the report itself is based upon hearsay, for by incorporating it in his report, the employer transforms it into an admission. For example, in a New York case, an award for death benefits was sustained on the strength of the employer's first report of injury, which stated that decedent scratched his foot while unloading billets and developed blood poisoning.[24] It was shown at the hearing that the report was made out by a clerk of the employer entirely on the strength of the decedent's own declarations. However, the statement became the admission of the employer, and what lay behind that admission was deemed immaterial.

Payment of compensation,[25] or furnishing or offering of medical services,[26] is not in itself an admission of liability.

As to admissions by the employee, a scene that has been many times re-enacted in compensation practice is this: The insurer's investigator obtains a signed written statement from the injured worker describing the circumstances of the accident; at the hearing the claimant contradicts the written statement; the insurer then offers the statement to discredit the oral testimony and to support a different version of the facts. In these circumstances, commissions will usually receive the statement and use their discretion as to the relative weight to be given to the oral and written stories. The

---

[21] Carroll v. Knickerbocker Ice Company, 169 App. Div. 450, 155 N.Y. Supp. 1, *rev'd*, 218 N.Y. 435, 113 N.E. 507 (1916).

[22] 155 N.Y. Supp. at p. 2.

[23] Interstate Commerce Comm'n v. Baird, 194 U.S. 25, 24 S. Ct. 563, 48 L. Ed. 860 (1904).

[24] Anthus v. Rail Joint Co., 193 A. D. 571, 185 N.Y.S. 314, *aff'd*, 231 N.Y. 557, 132 N.E. 887 (1921).

[25] Frasure v. Agripac, Inc., 290 Or. 99, 619 P.2d 274 (1980).

[26] Texas Employers' Ins. Ass'n v. Shelton, 339 S.W.2d 519, 161 Tex. 259 (1960).

commission may, of course, disregard the statement and believe the oral testimony. Or it may find the written statement convincing, particularly when corroborated, and base a denial of compensation on it.

[6] Medical Evidence

[a] Introduction

In compensation law, the administrative-law-evidence problem of expert opinion and official notice finds its principal application in the handling of medical facts. The usual question is the extent to which findings of the existence, causation or consequences of various injuries or diseases can rest upon something other than direct medical testimony — the claimant's own description of his or her condition, for example, or the commission's expert knowledge acquired not by formal medical education but by the practical schooling that comes with years of handling similar cases.

[b] Award Without Definite Medical Testimony

It is first necessary to dispel the misconception that valid awards can stand only if accompanied by a definite medical diagnosis. One of the best opinions on this subject is that in a Rhode Island case,[27] in which the undisputed testimony of claimant showed that she had been struck a sharp blow on the nipple of the left breast by a bobbin, that about two weeks later a lump had formed at that exact spot and pus was beginning to come off, and that shortly after, on the advice of doctors, the breast was removed. The award was attacked on the ground that there was no direct medical testimony fixing the pathological nature of the condition that necessitated the operation, and no medical testimony connecting the blow with the growth. The Supreme Court of Rhode Island rejected this argument and ordered an award to be made. As to the necessity of medical diagnosis in the record, the court said:

> . . . medical evidence, although highly desirable, is not always essential for an injured employee to make out a prima facie case, especially if the testimony is adequate, undisputed and unimpeached. Thus where, as in the instant case, injury appears in a bodily member reasonably soon after an accident, at the very place where the force was applied and with symptoms observable to the ordinary person, there arises, in the absence of believed testimony to the contrary, a natural inference that the injury, whatever may be the medical name, was the result of the employment.[28]

A decision of unusual interest applying this principle is *McAllister v. Workmen's Compensation Appeals Board*.[29] Decedent, a firefighter for 32 years, as well as a pack-a-day smoker, died of lung cancer. The Supreme Court reversed a denial of an award. Petitioner presented medical testimony that it was "probable" that the smoke inhaled by decedent in fighting fires contained carcinogens, and that the carcinogens in cigarette smoke "may well" be present in smoke from tar and creosote, of the kind encountered by decedent. Defendant presented no evidence. The court held that the exact causal mechanism by which smoke inhalation induces lung cancer need not be shown, nor the present toxicity of each kind of pollutant. It was enough to show that industrial causation was reasonably probable.

---

[27] Valente v. Bourne Mills, 77 R.I. 274, 75 A.2d 191 (1950).

[28] 75 A.2d 191 at 194.

[29] McAllister v. Workmen's Compensation Appeals Board, 69 Cal. 2d 408, 71 Cal. Rptr. 697, 445 P.2d 313 (1968).

[c] Award Contradicting Medical Testimony

Even more striking is the holding that, if the circumstances themselves are persuasive enough, a conclusion supported by no medical testimony may stand in defiance of medical testimony to the contrary. As in the case of awards without medical testimony, two main categories may be discerned into which these special circumstances fall: those involving matters of observable causation, and those involving existence or degree of disability.

An example in the causation category is a Wisconsin case,[30] in which claimant, who previously had suffered no shoulder ailment, experienced severe pain after a day or two on a new job in which his arm was repeatedly jolted by a drop forge. The condition progressed steadily until it resulted in loss of use of the arm, and the cause was found to be atrophy of the deltoid muscle due to a nerve injury. The medical testimony was all to the effect that it would be pure speculation to attribute that injury to the jolting effect of the machine; but the award was upheld on the strength of the sequence of facts pointing to industrial causation.

It has also been held that the fact-finders may find disability when the medical testimony denies its existence,[31] or may find a degree of disability different from any degree supported by medical testimony,[32] or, in the case of conflicting medical testimony, adopt a percentage of disability somewhere between the figures favored by the doctors.[33]

[d] Reasons for Relaxing Rule

In arriving at the rule permitting awards in the absence or even in contradiction of medical testimony, two underlying reasons may be discerned: The first is that lay testimony, including that of claimant himself or herself, is of probative value in establishing such simple matters as the existence and location of pain, the sequence of events leading to the compensable condition, and the actual ability or inability of claimant to perform the work; the second is that industrial commissions generally become expert in analyzing certain uncomplicated kinds of medical facts, particularly those bearing on industrial causation, disability, malingering and the like. These considerations apply with particular force to the issue of disability. As has been stressed at length earlier,[34] disability is not a purely medical question. It is a hybrid quasi-medical concept, in which are commingled in many complex combinations the inability to perform, and the inability to get, suitable work.

[e] When Is Medical Testimony Indispensable?

Since these are the reasons for the rule relaxing the necessity for medical testimony, they should set the boundaries of the rule; in other words, reliance on lay testimony and administrative *expertise* is not justified when the medical question is no longer an uncomplicated one and carries the fact-finders into realms which are properly within the province of medical experts. For example, in a Texas case,[35] an award was made on the theory that claimant's disability was due to a heat stroke, which contributed to his contraction of polio, in spite of the fact that the only medical testimony repeatedly denied that claimant had suffered a heat stroke. The award was reversed, on the ground that as difficult an analysis as distinguishing heat stroke from the first

---

[30] Nash-Kelvinator Corp. v. Industrial Comm'n, 253 Wis. 618, 34 N.W.2d 821 (1948).

[31] Hamlin & Allman Iron Works v. Jones, 200 Tenn. 242, 292 S.W.2d 27 (1956).

[32] McManus v. Southern United Ice Co., 243 Miss. 576, 138 So. 2d 899 (1962).

[33] Porter v. Continental Bridge Co., 246 N.W.2d 244 (Iowa 1976).

[34] *See* Ch. 14, *above.*

[35] Travelers Ins. Co. v. Blazier, 228 S.W.2d 217 (Tex. Civ. App. 1950).

symptoms of polio, or of appraising the possible causal connection between the two, was peculiarly within the realm of scientific knowledge, and not the sort of determination of a trier of facts could make independently in defiance of the only expert testimony in the record.

The increasing tendency, then, to accept awards unsupported by medical testimony should not be allowed to obscure the basic necessity of establishing medical causation by expert testimony in all but the simple and routine cases, and even in these cases such evidence is highly desirable and is part of any well-prepared presentation.

[7] Nonrecord Evidence and Official Notice

Conceding that expert commissions should be allowed, on the strength of their own experience, to supply some deficiencies in medical testimony, and even to disregard the only medical testimony and substitute their own medical opinions, one is still entitled to ask whether the fact of such self-reliance should not be revealed to the parties as the basis of the commission's findings, in time for them to meet and counteract these opinions by appropriate evidence just as they would deal with any other opposing evidence on the record.

In other administrative law fields, the United States Supreme Court has repeatedly held that all evidence relied upon for an administrative finding of fact must be in the record or identified there with particularity. The leading case[36] holds that the Interstate Commerce Commission cannot consider data from annual reports unless they are so included or identified. The same principle applies when the agency relies, not on particular data, but upon its specialized experience in general.[37]

A commission's expert knowledge and experience may be put to use in two different ways — one improper and the other proper — which are sometimes difficult to distinguish. The improper use is the non-record supplying of essential evidentiary *facts* from the reservoir of the commission's fund of knowledge, including reports, technical data, statistics, or other information in its files; the other is the supplying of *judgment* in the form of weighing and even rejection of expert testimony by checking it against the commission's own cumulative experience. A Wisconsin case will serve to illustrate how what might at first glance seem to be a matter of expert judgment may actually be found to be a matter of nonrecord evidence. In the *Milwaukee Corrugating Company* case,[38] a 15-percent penalty had been assessed against the employer for failure to provide a basket guard for a drop hammer, on the assumption, nowhere supported by evidence in the record, that such a guard was in existence, commercially available, and practical. The employer was using a rather clumsy and uncomfortable harness guard, which snatched the operator's hand away when the hammer dropped, and which was therefore often left off by employees. The penalty was evidently based on the commission's knowledge, as admitted experts in the field of accident prevention, of the existence of a better type of guard; but there had been no evidence that the employer knew of any better guard. The court ruled that such knowledge was an evidentiary fact that must appear on the record where the employer could have an opportunity to meet it with rebuttal evidence or appropriate explanation.

A high degree of probability is not sufficient to justify official notice; the fact must be so notoriously true and capable of immediate demonstration that it is subject to no reasonable dispute. Thus, the characteristics of the disease of byssinosis cannot be the subject of judicial notice.[39]

---

[36] United States v. Abilene & S. Ry., 265 U.S. 274, 44 S. Ct. 565, 68 L. Ed. 1016 (1924).

[37] Securities & Exch. Comm'n v. Chenery Corp., 318 U.S. 80, 63 S. Ct. 454, 87 L. Ed. 626 (1943); 332 U.S. 194, 67 S. Ct. 1575, 91 L. Ed. 1995 (1947).

[38] Milwaukee Corrugating Co. v. Industrial Comm'n, 197 Wis. 414, 222 N.W. 251 (1928).

[39] Wood v. J.P. Stevens & Co., 297 N.C. 636, 256 S.E.2d 692 (1979).

As to secret *ex parte* investigations or examinations made by the commission, it has repeatedly been held in compensation cases that use of such evidence, without inclusion in the record, is a violation of due process,[40] even when the statute expressly permits the taking of such evidence.[41] The basic right to confront, cross-examine and refute must be respected.[42] An award, for example, based on unsworn testimony taken before a special investigator with no notice to the other party cannot stand.[43] Under the increasingly common practice of referral of claimant to an official medical examiner or an independent physician chosen by the commission, it is particularly important that commissions not lose sight of the elementary requirement that the parties be given an opportunity to see such a doctor's report, cross-examine him or her, and if necessary provide rebuttal testimony.

[8] Best Evidence Rule

The best evidence rule, in compensation practice, appears to be invoked most frequently in foreign dependency cases. Commissions are inclined to be rather suspicious of affidavits coming from remote areas purporting to establish crucial facts of relationship, no matter how loaded the affidavits may be with ribbons and wax. Affidavits unsupported by official records will usually be rejected as evidence of relationship and dependency.[44]

[9] Moving Picture Evidence

The decision whether to admit motion picture evidence and the weight to be accorded such evidence is usually held to be discretionary with the commission. It is not error to refuse to view such pictures offered for the purpose of proving claimant's disability to be less than that claimed.[45] Although on the surface it might appear that nothing could be more cogent and even dramatic refutation of a disability claim than motion pictures of claimant jacking up a car or playing tennis, the courts have rightly observed that such evidence must be used with great caution. For example, in a Louisiana case,[46] the insurer had managed to take pictures showing claimant doing certain heavy work. What the pictures did not show was that claimant had to rest between the scenes shown in the films, that he was in constant pain, and that he had to go to bed the next day. While it is not error to admit such films, and to rely on them in proper cases, the commission may decline to assign much weight to them, and may make a finding of disability in spite of pictures showing claimant engaged in activity which appears to be inconsistent with such disability.[47]

BRIGGS v. CONSOLIDATED FREIGHTWAYS
234 Neb. 410, 451 N.W.2d 278 (1990)

BOSLAUGH, JUSTICE.

The plaintiff, Napoleon J. Briggs, has appealed from the award on rehearing of the Nebraska Workers' Compensation Court.

---

[40] Carstens v. Pillsbury, 172 Cal. 572, 158 P. 218 (1916).

[41] Gauthier v. Penobscot Chem. Fiber Co., 120 Me. 73, 113 A. 28 (1921).

[42] Chavez v. Industrial Comm'n, 5 Ariz. App. 294, 425 P.2d 864 (1967).

[43] Bereda Mfg. Co. v. Industrial Bd., 275 Ill. 514, 114 N.E. 275 (1916).

[44] Bass Foundry & Mach. Co. v. Christopoulos, 119 Ind. App. 568, 88 N.E.2d 692 (1949).

[45] Wallace v. Bell Aircraft Corp., 276 App. Div. 800, 3 N.Y.S.2d 162 (1949).

[46] Gagliano v. Boh Bros. Constr. Co., 44 So. 2d 732 (La. App. 1950).

[47] De Battiste v. Anthony Laudadio & Son, 167 Pa. Super. 38, 74 A.2d 784 (1950).

The plaintiff was injured on January 23, 1988, while employed by the defendant, Consolidated Freightways, as a truckdriver. While attempting to install chains on the truck tractor that he was driving, the plaintiff injured his back. The plaintiff did not feel any pain immediately, but by the time he arrived at his destination, Cheyenne, Wyoming, he was cold, and his back and neck were sore and stiff. The next morning his condition was worse, but he was able to make the return trip.

The plaintiff did not report his injury to his supervisor until making two more trips. His last trip was on January 31, 1988, and he has not worked since then. . . .

The matter was heard by a single judge of the compensation court on November 1, 1988. The court found that the plaintiff was temporarily totally disabled from February 1 to November 1, 1988, that the plaintiff may not have reached maximum medical improvement, and that the plaintiff was entitled to recover his medical expenses.

. . . .

The plaintiff contends the evidence was insufficient to support the finding on rehearing that he was no longer temporarily totally disabled. He alleges the evidence did not show he had reached maximum medical healing. The plaintiff challenges the court's reliance on surveillance videotapes in its determination that he is no longer temporarily totally disabled. He claims to be temporarily totally disabled because he can no longer work as a truckdriver. . . .

Videotapes taken by a private investigator who observed the plaintiff's activities on April 25, 28, 29, and 30, 1988, were received in evidence. These tapes show the plaintiff driving a car and a pickup truck, moving an approximately 25-pound chest of drawers with help from a friend, going to yard sales and test starting lawnmowers, mowing his yard, and engaging in horseplay with his children. His gait appears to be normal, and he is seen bending, pulling, and squatting a number of times.

The compensation court found that the activity level of the plaintiff which was demonstrated on the videotapes established that the plaintiff was not totally disabled. To the extent that the opinions of Drs. Fulcher and Gross were at variance with the conclusions drawn by the court after viewing the videotapes, it disregarded their opinions.

Triers of fact are not required to take the opinions of experts as binding upon them. *Mulder v. Minnesota Mining & Mfg. Co.*, 219 Neb. 241, 361 N.W.2d 572 (1985).

In *Harpham v. General Cas. Co.*, 232 Neb. 568, 441 N.W.2d 600 (1989), the plaintiff alleged the compensation court erred in relying on videotapes to reach its award in light of contradictory testimony from his doctors. As in this case, the tapes were properly admitted as competent evidence of the plaintiff's physical capabilities.

By challenging the court's reliance on the videotapes, plaintiff is challenging the court's evaluation and weighing of the evidence. "As the trier of fact, the compensation court is the sole judge of the credibility of witnesses and the weight to be given testimony." *Harpham, supra* at 573, 441 N.W.2d at 604.

The record shows there are no objective medical conditions to be eliminated with treatment regarding plaintiff's injury. He has been given a permanent disability rating. The only further treatment recommended is to reduce subjective pain in plaintiff's back and legs. According to *Pollard v. Wright's Tree Service, Inc.*, 212 Neb. 187, 322 N.W.2d 397 (1982), under these circumstances, there is no uncertainty that plaintiff's injury is permanent and that he is no longer entitled to temporary total disability benefits. See, also, 2 A. Larson, The Law of Workmen's Compensation § 57.12(c) at 10-25 to 10-29 (1989), where the author states: The fact that some treatment is still necessary, such as physical therapy or drugs, does not necessarily rule out a finding that the condition has become stabilized, if the underlying condition causing the disability has become stable and if nothing further in the way of treatment will improve that condition. . . . The persistence of pain may not of itself prevent a finding that the healing period is over, even if the intensity of the pain fluctuates from time to time, provided again that the underlying condition is stable.

The plaintiff argues that the compensation court was wrong in not finding him to be totally disabled and finding that he had only a 20-percent loss of earning capacity. He contends that he is permanently totally disabled on the basis of the definition of that term in *Minshall v. Plains Mfg. Co.*, 215 Neb. 881, 886, 341 N.W.2d 906, 909 (1983), which states: "A workman who is unable to perform or to obtain any substantial amount of labor, either in his particular line of work or in any other for which he would be fitted except for the injury, is totally disabled within the meaning of the Workmen's Compensation Act."

The plaintiff claims that there was no competent evidence his earning capacity was reduced by only 20 percent and that the evidence clearly shows he is totally disabled because he is 61 years old, black, limited in his education and training, and unable to return to work as an over-the-road truckdriver. The record does not show that the plaintiff is unable to obtain employment in any other job for which he is suited.

The plaintiff has the burden to prove his claimed disability. *See Parrish v. Karl Kehm & Sons Contractors*, 186 Neb. 252, 182 N.W.2d 422 (1970). He presented no evidence that he is unable to obtain any employment.

The videotapes convinced the compensation court that the plaintiff is not totally disabled. The 20-percent permanent partial disability rating to the body as a whole was the only expert testimony as to the extent of his permanent disability.

In *Gardner v. Beatrice Foods Co.*, 231 Neb. 464, 436 N.W.2d 542 (1989), the plaintiff claimed that the compensation court had erred in determining his loss of earning capacity to be the same as his functional disability. In that case, the evidence showed that the plaintiff could not return to his former job and that the only jobs he could qualify for with his education would have a low starting pay. The court stated: "Earning power is synonymous neither with wages . . . nor with loss of physical function. . . . Nonetheless, loss of physical function may affect a worker's eligibility to procure and hold employment, his or her capacity to perform the required tasks, and the ability to earn wages in employment for which he or she is engaged or fitted. Thus, while there is no numerical formula for determining one's earning power following an injury to the body as a whole . . . the extent of such impairment or disability may provide a basis for determining the amount of that worker's loss of earning power." *Gardner, supra* at 469, 436 N.W.2d at 545 (quoting *Thom v. Lutheran Medical Center*, 226 Neb. 737, 414 N.W.2d 810 (1987)).

In this case, the record is sufficient to support the compensation court's finding that the plaintiff's loss of earning capacity was 20 percent. . . .

Affirmed.

§ 31.04   RES JUDICATA AND JUDICIAL ESTOPPEL

The general principal of *res judicata* appears in many connections both in compensation proceedings, and, even more often, in noncompensation suits growing out of or associated with compensation situations. The beginning point is recognition of the proposition that res judicata does apply to the decisions of compensation boards and commissions no less than to the decisions of a court.[48]

The application of res judicata when the subsequent proceedings are themselves compensation proceedings is found in several situations, in addition to the interplay

---

[48] Scott v. Industrial Acc. Comm'n, 46 Cal. 2d 76, 293 P.2d 18 (1956).

between injury and death claims noted earlier.[49] Most obvious is the holding that prior decisions by the tribunal on earlier aspects of the same case are binding on it.[50]

The sequence of a court decision in a common law suit followed by a compensation claim by the same employee against the same employer for the same injury is illustrated by the Indiana case of *Garrigus v. Kerns*,[51] which held that an employer who had successfully defeated a truck driver's action for damages on the ground that the plaintiff was an employee was estopped from alleging that the plaintiff was not an employee but an independent contractor in a workmen's compensation hearing before the Industrial Board. But in a Washington case,[52] when the claimant had first taken the position that he was an independent contractor in a tort suit against the employer, and lost the case for failure of proof of negligence, it was held that he was not barred from alleging that he was an employee in his subsequent compensation claim. The reason — which indicates that the court was thinking in res judicata and not estoppel terms — was that there had been no specific determination of his relationship in the tort case.

The sequence in which the issue of res judicata is most frequently encountered is that of a compensation claim followed by a common law suit. If the conventional elements of res judicata are present, a prior decision or finding on any relevant issue in a compensation proceeding is res judicata as to the same issue in a subsequent suit at law to recover for the same injury or death, whether the effect is to defeat the suit or to defeat a defense to the suit.[53]

The normal rule of res judicata, which requires identity or privity between the parties to the two proceedings, applies of course to compensation-related applications of the doctrine.[54] Thus, although a compensation award may have been based in part on a finding that the injury was aggravated by the negligence of a physician, that finding is not res judicata in a later action against the physician, who was not a party to the compensation proceedings.[55]

The classical res judicata doctrine requires identity not only of parties but of issues. A mere holding in a compensation case that the injury was not work-connected cannot control a damage suit in which the issue is negligence, since negligence was immaterial in the compensation proceeding.[56]

§ 31.05 JUDICIAL ESTOPPEL AND THE AMERICANS WITH DISABILITIES ACT

Judicial estoppel precludes a party from gaining an advantage by taking one position, and then seeking a second advantage by taking an inconsistent position.[57] The doctrine is intended to prevent a litigant from "playing fast and loose with the courts."[58]

Typically, in a proceeding under the Americans With Disabilities Act of 1990 (ADA), the aggrieved party is claiming that he or she, despite a disability, is capable of working, if given reasonable accommodation. But what if the worker is receiving wage replace

[49] *See* Ch. 19, § 19.03, *above.*

[50] Waller v. Industrial Comm'n, 6 Ariz. App. 249, 431 P.2d 689 (1967).

[51] Garrigus v. Kerns, 134 Ind. App. 240, 178 N.E.2d 212 (1961).

[52] Risher v. Department of Labor & Indus., 55 Wash. 2d 830, 350 P.2d 645 (1960).

[53] Trautman v. Standard Oil Co. of Ind., American Oil Div., 263 N.W.2d 809 (Minn. 1978).

[54] Finnerman v. McCormick, 499 F.2d 212 (10th Cir. 1974), cert. denied, 419 U.S. 1049 (1975).

[55] Bryant v. Dougherty, 270 N.C. 748, 155 S.E.2d 181 (1967).

[56] Katzenmeier v. Doeren, 150 Minn. 521, 185 N.W. 938 (1921).

[57] *See, e.g.*, Helfand v. Gerson, 105 F.3d 530, 534 (9th Cir. 1997).

[58] Russell v. Rolfs, 893 F.2d 1033, 1037 (9th Cir. 1990), *cert. denied*, 501 U.S. 1260, 111 S. Ct. 2915, 115 L. Ed. 2d 1078 (1991).

ment workers' compensation, based on representations of inability to work? Is the worker estopped from asserting otherwise in the ADA context? Conversely, should a worker who has asserted in an ADA proceeding that he or she is capable of working with reasonable accommodation be barred, based on estoppel, from receiving wage loss compensation?

At first glance, an ADA claim, which requires proof of ability to perform the essential functions of a job, appears to be in direct conflict with a claim for disability benefits based on inability to work. Thus, judicial estoppel has been applied to preclude an ADA claim when the claimant made a prior worker's compensation,[59] social security disability,[60] eight or disability insurance claim.[61] Application of the doctrine has not been uniform, however. The circuits are split, with courts taking several distinct approaches in determining whether respective claims are in fact inconsistent.

A few courts have held that judicial estoppel is applicable only when the prior representation was made in a judicial or quasi-judicial proceeding.[62] Those courts refuse to apply the doctrine to bar claims of disability discrimination when a plaintiff merely applied for and received disability benefits. Other courts have taken a strict estoppel approach, maintaining that an individual can never claim disability benefits on the basis of inability to work and also claim the ability to perform the essential functions of a job for purposes of the ADA. These courts hold that mere application for or receipt of disability or workers' compensation benefits is sufficient to estop a plaintiff from bringing an ADA claim.[63] It should be noted that there is no consistency in how the courts address this issue, some courts being much more willing to utilize estoppel than the *Sumner* court below.[64]

SUMNER v. MICHELIN NORTH AMERICA, INC.
966 F. Supp. 1567 (M.D. Ala. 1997)

Memorandum Opinion

Myron H. Thompson, Chief Judge.

In this lawsuit, plaintiff Robert Sumner claims that Uniroyal Goodrich Tire Company failed to accommodate his disability at its plant in Opelika, Alabama, in violation of the Americans with Disabilities Act of 1990 . . . Sumner has sued defendant Michelin North America, Inc., Uniroyal's successor at the Opelika plant. . . .

(Sumner, a tire builder, suffered a serious on-the-job injury which left him with

---

[59] *See, e.g.:* Cline v. Western Horseman, Inc., 922 F. Supp. 442, 5 AD Cases 714 (D. Col. 1996). Lamruy v. Boeing Co., 5 AD Cases 39 (D. Kan. 1995). Hensley v. Punta Gorda, 686 So. 2d 724 (Fla. Dist. Ct. App. 1997).

[60] *See, e.g.*, McNemar v. Disney Store, Inc., 91 F.3d 610, 5 AD Cases 1227 (3d Cir. 1996), cert. denied, 117 S. Ct. 958 (1997).

[61] *See, e.g.:* Bollenbacher v. Helena Chemical Co., 934 F. Supp. 1015, 5 AD Cases 1404 (N.D. Ind. 1996). Trotter v. B & S Aircraft Parts & Accessories, Inc., 1996 WL 473837, 5 AD Cases 1584, 8 NDLR P 287 (D. Kan. 1996). Harden v. Delta Air Lines, Inc., 900 F. Supp. 493, 4 AD Cases 1241 (S.D. Ga. 1995).

[62] *See, e.g.:* Mohamed v. Marriot, 944 F. Supp. 277, 6 AD Cases 562 (S.D.N.Y. 1996). Dockery v. North Shore Med. Ctr., 909 F. Supp. 1550, 5 AD Cases 1443 (S.D. Fla. 1995).

[63] *See, e.g.:* Violette v. International Business Machines Corp., 962 F. Supp. 446, 7 AD Cases 395 (D. Vt. 1996), *aff'd*, 116 F.3d 466, 7 AD Cases 544 (2d Cir. 1997). Farrow v. Bell Atlantic, 1996 WL 316798, 5 AD Cases 793 (W.D. Pa. 1996), *aff'd*, 107 F.3d 7 (3d Cir. 1997). Lowe v. Angelo's Italian Foods, Inc., 966 F. Supp. 1036, 6 AD Cases 1761 (D. Kansas 1997).

[64] *Compare, e.g.*, Garcia-Paz v. Swift Textiles, Inc., 873 F. Supp. 547 (D. Kan. 1995), which takes a strict estoppel approach, *with* Reigel v. Kaiser Foundation Health Plan, 859 F. Supp. 963 (E.D. N.C. 1994), which takes a content-based estoppel approach.

physical and mental limitations. In 1991 he filed a complaint in state court seeking worker's compensation benefits. In 1992 he returned to work and performed light-duty tasks at the plant. In 1993 he received state-court approval to settle his workers' compensation lawsuit. According to Michelin, the settlement amount "was greater than what he could have recovered for a 99% permanent loss of earning capacity disability." Nevertheless, Sumner continued until December 1993 to perform "make-shift" light-duty tasks at the plant. Thereafter he engaged in various discussions with management regarding available positions at the plant and whether, given his limitations, he could perform the essential functions of these positions. After efforts failed to identify any jobs Sumner could do, he was placed on extended unpaid leave of absence for three years. Alternatively, Sumner was told that he could elect to apply for disability retirement and its concomitant benefits. In 1994 Sumner applied for and was denied Social Security disability benefits. Two years later, he filed the current suit.)

. . . Michelin asserts that it is entitled to judgment as a matter of law on two grounds: First, the company contends that Sumner is precluded from seeking relief by the doctrine of judicial estoppel. Second, the company contends that Sumner's claim is time barred.

A. Judicial Estoppel

The doctrine of judicial estoppel is a vintage doctrine whose popularity varies from court to court nearly as greatly as its contours do. And yet. it is gaining renewed currency. The Ninth Circuit Court of Appeals is one of the courts to have infused it with renewed life and vigor. That court applied judicial estoppel most recently to an estate planning case in Hawaii. The court wrote: "Judicial estoppel, sometimes also known as the doctrine of preclusion of inconsistent positions, precludes a party from gaining an advantage by taking one position, and then seeking a second advantage by taking an incompatible position." *Helfand v. Gerson*, 105 F.3d 530, 534 (9th Cir. 1997) (quoting *Rissetto v. Plumbers and Steamfitters Local* 343, 94 F.3d 597, 600 (9th Cir. 1996)). The doctrine is intended to prevent a litigant from "playing fast and loose with the courts." *Russell v. Rolfs*, 893 F.2d 1033, 1037 (9th Cir. 1990), *cert. denied*, 501 U.S. 1260, 111 S. Ct. 2915, 115 L. Ed. 2d 1078 (1991)

Michelin contends that the doctrine erects a bar to Sumner's ADA claim because Sumner previously took the position that he was permanently and totally disabled when he filed for state workers' compensation benefits and took the position that he was totally disabled when he filed for Social Security disability benefits.

1.

The first question is whether Sumner has, in fact, previously asserted that he is totally and permanently disabled. The record is replete with evidence that he has.

. . . *(The court reviews the various assertions made by Sumner in those two proceedings)*

The record leaves no doubt that Sumner has previously sworn to being totally and permanently disabled. Before the court can decide whether these assertions should preclude, or at least weigh heavily against, Sumner's ADA claim, it will have to address two antecedent questions: Under what conditions, that is to say, for what purposes, should a court apply the equitable doctrine of judicial estoppel to prevent a party from proceeding with a lawsuit before it? And do the circumstances in this case satisfy those conditions, or advance those purposes, sufficiently to outweigh the policies driving the ADA?

2.

Michelin suggests that, under the judicial estoppel doctrine, a plaintiff who has previously sought workers' compensation or Social Security benefits based on a representation that he is totally and permanently disabled is per se barred from seeking relief under the ADA. The court rejects this argument, for, as will be demonstrated below, the positions a party might take in applying for workers' compensation and Social Security benefits are not necessarily inconsistent with the position he might take in pursuing an ADA claim.

The ADA is a sweeping civil rights law designed "to provide a clear and comprehensive national mandate for the elimination of discrimination against individuals with disabilities." 42 U.S.C.A.§ 12101(b)(1). It is designed "to provide clear, strong, consistent, and enforceable standards addressing discrimination against individuals with disabilities." § 12101(b)(2). The ADA prohibits employers from discriminating against "qualified individuals with disabilities" in all aspects of employment.§ 12111(8). To be protected by the Act, a person must meet the definition of the term "qualified individual with a disability." A "qualified individual with a disability" is "an individual with a disability who satisfies the requisite skill, experience, education, and other job-related requirements of the employment position such individual holds or desires, and who, with or without reasonable accommodation, can perform the essential functions of such position." 29 C.F.R. § 1630.2(m) (emphasis added). By including the phrase "qualified individual with a disability," "Congress intended to reaffirm that the ADA 'does not undermine an employer's ability to choose and maintain qualified workers.'" EEOC Enforcement Guidance on the Effect of Representations Made in Applications for Benefits on the Determination of Whether a Person Is a "Qualified Individual with a Disability" Under the Americans with Disabilities Act of 1990(ADA), EEOC Notice No. 915.002, at E-13 n.2, released February 12, 1997, reprinted in BNA's Daily Labor Report, No. 1418-2693/97 (Feb. 14, 1997) (hereinafter EEOC Enforcement Guidance) (quoting S.Rep. No. 101-116 at 26 (1989)).

The ADA, therefore, requires employers to provide a "reasonable accommodation" to "known physical or mental limitations" of otherwise qualified individuals with disabilities unless doing so would result in "undue hardship." 42 U.S.C.A. §§ 12111(10), 12112(b)(5)(A); 29 C.F.R. §§ 1630.2(p), 1630.9(a). This reasonable accommodation requirement, which is critical to achieving the goals of the Act, includes "modifications or adjustments to the work environment, or to the manner or circumstances under which the position held or desired is customarily performed, that enable a qualified individual with a disability to perform the essential functions of that position." 29 C.F.R.§ 1630.2(o)(1)(ii). Some of the most common accommodations an employer may be required to provide are reassignment to vacant positions, job restructuring, part-time or modified work schedules, modification of equipment or devices, and other similar accommodations. § 1630.2(o)(2).

To be sure, within the definitional structure of the ADA statute and regulations, someone who is totally and permanently disabled cannot be a "qualified individual with a disability." But the question is far less straightforward whether being totally and permanently disabled, as defined in other statutory or regulatory contexts, such as under workers' compensation or Social Security laws, is intrinsically incompatible with any level of disability that would still permit an employee to perform the essential functions of any job, with accommodations.

Unlike the ADA definition, the definition of disability under the Social Security Act does not consider whether the individual can work with reasonable accommodation. Titles II and XVI of the Act provide benefits to persons determined to be "disabled" and entitled to benefits under the Social Security Disability Insurance (SSDI) and Supplemental Security Income (SSI) programs. 42 U.S.C.A. §§ 401–433, 1381–1385. Under both Titles, disability is defined as "inability to engage in any substantial gainful activity by reason of any medically determinable physical or mental impairment which can be expected to result in death or which has lasted or can be expected to last for a continuous period of not less than twelve (12) months." 42 U.S.C.A. §§ 423(d)(1)(A), 1382c(a)(3)(A). According to the Supreme Court, "the Secretary has promulgated regulations creating a five-step test to determine whether an adult claimant is disabled. . . . The first two steps involve threshold determinations that the claimant is not presently working and has art impairment which is of the required duration and which significantly limits his ability to work. . . . In the third step, the medical evidence of the claimant's impairment is compared to a list of impairments presumed severe enough to preclude any gainful work. . . . If the claimant's impairment matches or is 'equal' to one of the listed impairments, he qualifies for benefits without further inquiry. . . . If the claimant cannot qualify under the listings, the analysis proceeds to the fourth and fifth steps. At these steps, the inquiry is whether the claimant can do his own past work or any other work that exists in the national economy, in view of his age, education, and work experience. If the claimant cannot do his past work or other work, he qualifies for benefits." *Sullivan v. Zebley*, 493 U.S. 521, 525–526, 110 S. Ct. 885, 888–889, 107 L. Ed. 2d 967 (1990) (citations and footnote omitted).

In light of this definitional and assessment structure, an "interpretative guidance" issued by the Social Security Administration addressing the effect of the ADA on the Social Security disability determination process states as follows: "The fact that an individual may be able to return to a past relevant job, provided that the employer makes the accommodations, is not relevant to the issue(s) to be resolved. . . . [H]ypothetical inquiries about whether an employer would or could make accommodations that would allow return to a prior job would not be appropriate." EEOC Enforcement Guidance at E-5 (quoting "Americans with Disabilities Act of 1990-INFORMATION," Memorandum from the Associate Commissioner, Social Security Administration 1 (June 2, 1993). Thus, the Social Security Administration may find that a person is unable to do any work that exists in the national economy even though that person can work with a reasonable accommodation. In those instances the person is both a person with a total disability under the Social Security Act and a yet "qualified individual with a disability" under the ADA. Accordingly, a person claiming to be totally disabled or found to be totally disabled under the Social Security Act still may be entitled to protection under the ADA.

Similarly, unlike the ADA definition for "qualified individual with a disability," state workers" compensation law definitions of "disability" — and Alabama's in particular — do not consider whether an individual can work with a reasonable accommodation. *See, e.g.*, 1975 Ala. Code §§ 25-5-1 to 25-5-318. In many workers' compensation cases, a person has a "disability" when he is unable to do certain tasks — that is, has lost some or all earning capacity; there is no requirement of, or allowance for, reasonable accommodation by the employer. *See, e.g.*, § 25-5-57(a)(4)d ("[A]ny physical injury or mental impairment resulting from an accident which . . . permanently and totally incapacitates the employee from working at and being retrained for gainful employment, shall constitute . . . the sole basis on which an award of permanent total disability may be based.") § 25-5-57(a)(2)a ("For temporary partial disability, the compensation shall be 66 2/3 percent of the difference between the average weekly earnings of the worker at the time of the injury and the average weekly earnings he or she is able to earn in his or her partially disabled condition."). Thus a person may be totally and permanently disabled for workers' compensation purposes and yet still be able to perform a position's essential functions with or without reasonable accommodation. [Court's footnote omitted]

Courts have recognized this important difference between the ADA definition of "qualified individual with a disability" and other definitions of "disability." For example, in *D'Aprile v. Fleet Services Corp.*, 92 F.3d 1 (1st Cir. 1996), the First Circuit Court of Appeals reversed a district court's grant of summary judgment on a claim for reasonable accommodation under a state handicap law where the plaintiff had sought insurance disability benefits. The court found that plaintiff's contention that she was unable to work because her employer had refused her request for a modified schedule was "entirely consistent with her claim of totally disabled" within the meaning of the insurance policy. Id. at 5. The court noted that plaintiff asserted that she could work on a part-time basis and that she in fact had worked part time. The court therefore found that there existed a genuine issue of material fact as to whether the plaintiff could have worked with a reasonable accommodation. See also *Mohamed v. Marriott Intern.*, Inc., 944 F. Supp. 277, 281–82 (S.D.N.Y.1996) ("[I]t would be inappropriate to invoke the fact-sensitive and limited doctrine of judicial estoppel to erect a per se bar to ADA protection for individuals who have also applied for and/or received SSDI benefits. Such uncritical application of judicial estoppel fails to recognize significant differences in . . . the applicable legal standards of the ADA and the Social Security Act."); *Pegues v. Emerson Elec. Co.*, 913 F. Supp. 976, 980 (N.D. Miss. 1996) ("[T]he court does not believe that a finding of disability by the Workers' Compensation Commission or the Social Security Administration necessarily forecloses an ADA claim."); *Smith v. Dovenmuehle Mortgage, Inc.*, 859 F. Supp. 1138, 1141–43 (N.D. Ill. 1994) (plaintiff's prior: representation of disability to SSA did not judicially estop him from raising subsequent ADA claim); *Labonte v. Hutchins & Wheeler*, 424 Mass. 813, 678 N.E.2d 853, 856 (1997) ("A majority of courts have rejected a defendant's claim that seeking benefits automatically disqualifies a plaintiff from pursuing a handicap discrimination claim."); EEOC Enforcement Guidance; Anne Beaumont, This Estoppel Has Got to Stop: Judicial Estoppel and the Americans with Disabilities Act, 71 N.Y.U.L. Rev. 1529 (1996). [footnote omitted]

Here, the simple fact that Sumner claimed he was disabled under the Social Security Act and permanently and totally disabled under Alabama's Workers' Compensation Act is not necessarily inconsistent with his claim for relief under the ADA. Indeed and ironically, the circumstances surrounding Sumner's receipt of workers' compensation benefits demonstrate this conclusion dramatically. By Michelin's own admission, Uniroyal settled Sumner's workers' compensation claim for more than he would have received for 99% permanent loss, and yet both Uniroyal and Sumner informed the state judge at the time of settlement that Sumner would continue the next day with the light-duty work he had been given because of his injury. Thus, it appears that Uniroyal, Sumner, and even the state judge all recognized that Sumner was disabled for workers' compensation purposes and yet still able to return to work at Uniroyal with some accommodation.

The EEOC appears to suggest, based in large measure on public policy considerations, that the judicial estoppel doctrine is not only not a per se bar to an ADA claim, it has no application at all in the fact-intensive inquiry into whether a person is entitled to relief under the Act. EEOC Enforcement Guidance at E-9. . . .

The court need not reach the question of whether the doctrine has no application at all under the ADA, for, assuming that the doctrine applies to ADA claims, the doctrine does not apply to Sumner's.

3.

As the Eleventh Circuit Court of Appeals has explained, "Judicial estoppel is a doctrine whereby a party is estopped from asserting a proposition in the present proceeding 'merely by the fact of having alleged or admitted in his pleadings in a former proceeding under oath' an allegation to the contrary," *Bregman v. Alderman*, 955 F.2d 660, 664 n.3 (11th Cir. 1992) (citing a case from Texas, *Long v. Knox*, 155 Tex. 581, 291 S.W.2d 292 (1956)). "Judicial estoppel is applied to the calculated assertion of divergent sworn positions. The doctrine is designed to prevent parties from making a mockery of justice by inconsistent pleadings." *McKinnon v. Blue Cross and Blue Shield of Ala.*, 935 F.2d 1187, 1192 (11th Cir. 1991). . . .

These are the broad strokes of the doctrine. It is the fine lines courts draw around and between them that leave the doctrine with a rather uncertain outline. [footnote omitted] And where these fine lines are to be appropriately drawn has direct bearing on this case.

When emphasis is put on the "litigant's relationship to the court," *Donaldson v. Bernstein*, 104 F.3d 547, 555–556 (3rd Cir. 1997), whether or not a prior representation to the court ultimately was accepted by the court recedes in importance, as does identity between the opposing party in the prior litigation and the party seeking to estop a claim in the later litigation, since detrimental reliance is not of primary concern. *See, e.g.*, *Bregman*, 955 F.2d at 664 n.3. However, when the factfinding function of the court is highlighted, judicial estoppel is often applied more "judiciously" to cases in which a previous court made a finding or decision that was favorable to a litigant or actually yielded an advantage, particularly where the opponent was identical in both cases, or each was in privity with the other. [footnote omitted] * * * [See] *Teledyne Indus., Inc. v. NLRB*, 911 F.2d 1214, 1217–18, 1217 n.3 (6th Cir. 1990) [other citations omitted]. These two underlying theories of judicial estoppel have been glossed as the "sanctity of the oath" approach and the "prior success" rule. *Reynolds v. Commissioner of Internal Revenue*, 861 F.2d 469, 475 (6th Cir. 1988) (Kennedy, J., dissenting).

While, under the "prior success" rule, judicial acceptance of a stated position does not occur only where a party ultimately prevails on the merits, it does mean, at least, that "the first court has adopted the position urged by the party, either as a preliminary matter or as part of a final disposition." Teledyne, 911 F.2d at 1218 (quoting *Edwards v. Aetna Life Ins. Co.*, 690 F.2d 595, 599 n.5 (6th Cir. 1982)). Certainly, for judicial estoppel to apply as a result of a negotiated settlement approved by the court, or an agreed order entered by the court, there must at least have been a finding by the court, a stipulation, or an assertion or admission by the party against whom estoppel will later be sought. But most commonly, in civil actions, when parties petition the court to approve a settlement or enter an agreed order, there is no implication that the court has accepted whatever terms it contains. Therefore, in that situation, since the court has not accepted or endorsed anyone's position, there can be no recourse to judicial estoppel in a letter proceeding. *Reynolds*, 861 F.2d at 473; Edwards, 690 F.2d at 600.

On this version, Sumner could not be estopped because the petition for settlement of his workers' compensation case was approved by the court without a ruling on or acceptance of Sumner's position that he was totally disabled, since the parties merely stipulated that they subscribed to different positions on this issue. [Court's footnote omitted]

There is little precedent in this area from the Eleventh Circuit Court of Appeals. . . .

Without further guidance from precedent in this circuit, and with fealty to the instruction to apply the doctrine of judicial estoppel flexibly to protect the court's integrity against those ready to play fast and loose within its sanctum, the court reaches its own conclusion, as an initial matter, that the prior success rule is not entirely coherent, risks collapsing judicial estoppel into equitable estoppel, and partially defeats its own avowed purpose of protecting the integrity of the courts. If judicial estoppel should be "applied with caution to avoid impinging on the truthseeking function of the court because the doctrine precludes a contradictory position without examining the truth of either statement," *Teledyne*, 911 F.2d at 1218, then it should be applied regardless of whether a position succeeded or not, since truth and success are not always commensurate. This is particularly true in the area of on-the-job injury, where the long-term medical prognosis may be anything but apparent at the time an injured worker must expediently decide what forms of benefits and compensation to seek in order to pay medical bills and meet living expenses. The court only damages its own integrity when it refuses to reconsider whether it (or another court or agency, or the party) was, in fact, mistaken or misled the first time around. The "prior success rule" amounts to a "saving judicial face" version of the doctrine, which is hardly tantamount to preserving the court's integrity.

For instance, the Teledyne court observed that the doctrine, to be consistent, should not, in the name of averting damage to the integrity of courts, allow exceptions in cases where the prior position was the result of inadvertence or mistake, because "a party inherently argues that a prior position was false if the new position contradicts it," and so the exceptions would swallow up the rule. 911 F.2d at 1218 n.4. The court did not see the irony in its own position, because in allowing exceptions to correct previous blunders, whoever's they may be, the integrity of the judicial system is preserved. In that regard, prior success is immaterial. The court should not use an equitable doctrine to estop itself from exercising its judgment, but rather to estop parties from taking bad faith positions before it. Clearly then, neither the court's desire to leave a position undisturbed once it or another court has accepted it, nor the reliance upon that position, to its detriment, of another party, as required for equitable estoppel, is crucial. [Court's footnote omitted] What the doctrine does demand of the court is careful attention to the totality of the facts of each case before it, to see not only whether a party is advocating a position that is inconsistent with a position it has previously taken under oath, [footnote omitted] but also to see whether, in doing so, that party is engaging in "cold manipulation and not an unthinking or confused blunder." *Johnson Serv. Co. v. Transamerica Ins. Co.*, 485 F.2d 164, 175 (5th Cir. 1973). . . .

Therefore, the court believes it best to address a defense of judicial estoppel to ADA claims in the following way: first, the court should conduct a detailed inquiry into whether the plaintiff really did make inconsistent claims in separate judicial or administrative proceedings, by looking closely at the pertinent legal, statutory, or regulatory frameworks, along with the totality of factual circumstances, surrounding the claims in each proceeding; next, the court should make a fact-sensitive determination of the true circumstances surrounding the plaintiff's averments of disability and employability, to decide whether the plaintiff intended to mislead, or otherwise proceeded in bad faith. No two cases will be exactly alike, and the court will retain the flexibility to set the bar of judicial estoppel at the height appropriate to each plaintiff.

Toward this and, the following factors (borrowed from the discussion above) seem appropriate and should be considered: (1) the definition of disability, or total disability, under the relevant statute or contract; (2) the specific content of the representations (in particular, whether they were qualified), who made them, and the purpose for which they were made; (3) whether the representations are in the claimant's own words; (4) the period of time to which the representations refer, when they were made, and whether the claimant's mental or physical condition might legitimately have changed since; (5) whether the claimant was in fact working during the period of time referenced as a period of total disability; (6) whether the employer suggested that the claimant apply for benefits; (7) whether claimant asked for and was denied a reasonable accommodation; (8) when the employer learned of the representations; and (9) other relevant factors, such as advances in technology or changes in the employer's operations that may have occurred since the representations were made that make it possible for the claimant to perform essential functions of a position with or without reasonable accommodation.

With the above factors in mind, the court turns to the question of whether the conditions for just application of judicial estoppel are satisfied in this case.

i.

First, the circumstances surrounding Sumner's original complaint for workers' compensation benefits must be looked at more carefully. As suggested earlier, in the area of on-the-job injury, where the long-term medical prognosis may be anything but apparent at the time an injured worker must expediently decide what forms of benefits and compensation to seek in order to pay bills and meet expenses, a claim of total disability must be regarded as provisional, in keeping with the liberal pleading requirements of Rule 8 of the Federal Rules of Civil Procedure. [footnote omitted] There is no reason why an injured employee should be held to a stricter standard in an original application or complaint for statutory benefits than a civil litigant is in other kinds of lawsuits. If the latter may amend a complaint, once as a matter of course, and subsequently upon leave of the court, [footnote omitted] as facts develop and understanding dawns, then an injured employee should enjoy the same privilege and right. In fact, the Alabama Worker's Compensation Act itself allows for that possibility. Section 25-5-57(a)(4)b of the 1975 Alabama Code says: "At any time, the employer may petition the court . . . to alter, amend, or revise the award or approval of the compensation on the ground that as a result of physical or vocational rehabilitation, or otherwise, the disability from which the employee suffers is no longer a permanent total disability." If the Alabama law of workers' compensation will allow that what was once permanent may no longer be, then so should this court. That is why this court sees no justice in a blanket rule barring applicants for total disability benefits from subsequently bringing ADA lawsuits.

Sumner filed his complaint seeking workers' compensation benefits from his employer long before he underwent rehabilitation, let alone returned to work. From this filing alone, therefore, the court can also infer little in the way of intent to undermine the integrity of the court. Sumner continued to undergo regular medical and vocational evaluation throughout 1993; thus no conclusions were reached about his capacity to return to full employment status until December 1993, when he was put on extended leave. A June 1993 report from a vocational consultant hired by Sumner's attorney in the worker's compensation case opined that Sumner would be unable to find employ outside of Uniroyal, that his "light-duty" tasks at Uniroyal were not real work at all, and that his vocational disability rating was 100%. [footnote omitted] And yet, in deposition testimony taken in that same lawsuit, also recorded in June of 1993, Sumner responded to the question whether he felt like he would be able to do more things if Uniroyal had the work to give him, "Sometimes, yes." [footnote omitted] Sumner also testified in this case that it was always his hope and desire to return to full employment at Uniroyal, and that he has said so consistently throughout. [footnote omitted] No evidence to contradict that statement has emerged. The picture presented by the evidence in this case, viewed as a whole, is hardly that of a person trying to play fast and loose with the courts.

ii.

The court must next address in more detail the events that framed the settlement of Sumner's workers' compensation lawsuit. There is uncontroverted evidence in the record that, at a settlement conference before the state court judge in the workers' compensation case, the judge asked Sumner whether he was satisfied with the settlement, to which Sumner responded that he was, because he was going back to work. The state court judge also asked Uniroyal whether Sumner would return to work, and was told that he would. Although Sumner did return to his light-duty tasks the very next day, he had understood, based on representations from Richard Lynn, the Safety Director at Uniroyal, that after settlement he would be placed in a permanent job. [Court's footnote omitted]

Furthermore, although detrimental reliance by another party, as was said earlier, is not an element of judicial estoppel, in equity the court must determine what is fair and just treatment of the parties before it. In this case, where Uniroyal took the position in the settlement petition, and maintained to the state judge, that Sumner could and would return to work, and then ultimately decided that Sumner was too severely disabled to qualify for employment with reasonable accommodation, Michelin should show greater humility about condemning anyone else's inconsistency. Had Uniroyal truly believed Sumner was ready and able to return to work in some meaningful capacity, surely, at some point between late 1991, and the commencement of this lawsuit, it would have found a position for him. Managers at Uniroyal continued to discuss potential jobs with Sumner, and to commission and review medical and vocational evaluations of his condition, up until December 1993, and even beyond. If the court is to be generous with Michelin, and grant that Uniroyal truly did not know throughout that period whether or not a suitable position would eventually be found for Sumner, then it should be no less generous with Sumner, who is the less sophisticated party.

iii.

The final issue for the court is whether Sumner's application for Social Security disability benefits should bar his ADA claim. Sumner was told that, in order to apply for his retirement benefits as a totally disabled employee, he would first have to apply for Social Security benefits. The amount of his pension benefits would depend on whether he received Social Security. These applications postdated the relevant conduct in this lawsuit, which was Sumner's constructive termination, and thus are largely not determinative. Sumner's case depends on his ability to argue that he was a qualified individual with a disability when wrongfully terminated; not after he was terminated, and given the choice of seeking retirement and insurance benefits as someone with total disability, or receiving no salary at all.

Sumner's position regarding his disability was, at worst, ambiguous, but hardly so inconsistent and duplicitous that it warrants outright estoppel in this action. In addition, Sumner regularly attested to the fact that he relied on his attorney's counsel and language — thus any representations of total disability were not in his own words. Uniroyal also encouraged Sumner to apply for retirement disability and other benefits. Clearly, then, many of the other specific factors listed above by the court militate against estopping Sumner's ADA claim.

Sumner will not be judicially estopped from bringing this ADA action against Michelin. [Court's footnote omitted]

(The court determined, however, that the ADA claim was not timely filed with the EEOC, and entered judgment for Michelin as a matter of law.)

§ 31.06 REVIEW OF AWARDS

[1] Introduction

Judicial review of awards is usually confined to questions of law. Except in a minority of jurisdictions, the evidence supporting fact findings is not weighed on review, such findings being conclusive if supported by any substantial evidence. Awards cannot, however, be based on speculation and conjecture, nor on a "preponderance of possibilities"; the distinction between preponderance of "probabilities" and "possibilities" should not follow too slavishly the exact choice of words used by cautious medical witnesses.

[2] Normal Review: Substantial-Evidence Rule

Compensation acts now provide in detail for judicial review of awards, but with or without such provisions, there is an inherent right to the judicial review of questions of law[65] Complete destruction of the right of review would be unconstitutional,[66] except

---

[65] Crowell v. Benson, 285 U.S. 22, 52 S. Ct. 285, 76 L. Ed. 598 (1932).

[66] Meunier's Case, 319 Mass. 421, 66 N.E.2d 198 (1948).

under the Federal Employees' Compensation Act, which is treated as creating outright grants to which Congress can attach any conditions it pleases.[67]

A finding of fact based on no evidence is an error of law.[68] Accordingly, in compensation law, as in all administrative law, an award may be reversed if not supported by any evidence. Conversely, since the compensation board has expressly been entrusted with the power to find the facts, its fact findings must be affirmed if supported by any evidence, even if the reviewing court thinks the evidence points the other way. This statement is the number one cliche of compensation law, and occurs in some form in the first paragraph of hundreds of compensation opinions almost as a matter of course.

Whatever adjectives are chosen to describe the minimum quantity, as distinguished from quality, of evidence necessary to support an award, the net result is about the same. Among the phrases encountered are "any evidence," "some evidence," "any credible evidence," "any substantial evidence,"[69] and many others. The United States Supreme Court has expressly held that "substantial evidence" is not a larger quantity than "any evidence,"[70] and since these two phrases sound like the largest and smallest quantum described in the various phrases, presumably the others represent the same concept.

One comes back to this same standard of review whether the statute expressly adopts the substantial-evidence rule, or is silent on review, or even says that the commission's findings of fact shall be conclusive. The frequently heard statement that such findings are "conclusive" must always be taken subject to the implied qualification "if supported by any evidence," since, in the absence of such evidence, as indicated above, there is an error of law, and the court, without disturbing the commission's absolute preeminence in the realm of fact-finding, can still reverse for legal error.[71]

There is in compensation review procedure, just as in any other judicial review procedure, such a thing as a completely unreviewable matter, as in the case of interlocutory decisions that are unreviewable for lack of finality,[72] or incidental decisions that involve details committed to the absolute discretion of the lower tribunal.[73] Ordinarily an order is reviewable only at the point where it awards or denies compensation.[74] Accordingly, review has been denied of orders allowing claimant to

[67] Calderon v. Tobin, 187 F.2d 514 (D.C. Cir. 1951). The Federal Employees' Compensation Act makes the administrator's decision final as to both law and facts, and forbids review by any official or court by mandamus or otherwise. 5 U.S.C.A. § 793 (1964).

[68] Crowell v. Benson, 285 U.S. 22, 52 S. Ct. 285, 76 L. Ed. 598 (1932).

[69] Colonna's Shipyard Inc. v. O'Hearne, 200 F.2d 220 (4th Cir. 1952). The Administrative Procedure Act, 5 U.S.C. § 1001 et seq., governs the Longshore and Harbor Workers' Compensation Act, and makes the ground for reversal failure of the finding to be supported by substantial evidence on the record considered as a whole.

[70] Del Vecchio v. Bowers, 296 U.S. 280, 56 S. Ct. 190, 80 L. Ed. 229 (1935).

[71] Craddock's Case, 310 Mass. 116, 37 N.E.2d 508, 146 A.L.R. 116 (1941).

[72] E.g., Webster v. Indiana Dep't of Pub. Instruction, 132 Ind. App. 595, 178 N.E.2d 909 (1962). The court would not hear an appeal alleging an error of law when the Board had not made an award for or against compensation.

[73] E.g., Boggetta v. Burroughs Corp., 368 Mich. 600, 118 N.W.2d 980 (1962). Granting of claimant's petition for interrogatories as to facts surrounding her husband's death was not reviewable by the court. Appeal dismissed.

[74] Armour & Co. v. Moore, 206 Okla. 72, 240 P.2d 1113 (1952). Order of full commission vacating order of trial commissioner denying compensation and holding case in abeyance for further hearing is not reviewable, since it neither awards nor denies compensation.

amend the claim,[75] denying a motion to receive further evidence,[76] and directing the claimant to be medically examined.[77]

Under the typical compensation system there is usually some sort of review at the administrative level; a single examiner or referee or commissioner makes findings which are then confirmed, modified or rejected by the full board or commission. An appeal to the courts from the decision of an examiner or referee in this kind of system is premature; generally the courts have jurisdiction to hear appeals only from the board, director, or other final administrative decision-maker.[78]

It follows logically that the rule of conclusiveness of administrative findings of fact should apply to the final action of the director or full board rather than to the decision of the referee.

In most jurisdictions the court can not take a finding by a single commissioner, which had been reversed by the full commission, and reinstate that single commissioner's findings on the ground that it was supported by substantial evidence.[79]

Seven states[80] and the Longshore Act take the opposite approach.

In 1972, Congress created an administrative Benefits Review Board to review awards under the Longshore Act. The title of deputy commissioner was abolished, with their functions being assumed by hearing examiners whose findings of fact are conclusive if supported by substantial evidence.[81]

Although, Pennsylvania amended its workers' compensation statute to reflect the minority position, under the state's Occupational Disease Act, the basic fact-finding responsibility does not shift to the referee unless the Board takes new evidence.[82]

Normally the powers of the reviewing commission, board, or director are quite broad, as befits its ultimate responsibility for the final findings. Some states treat the referee's findings as no more than a recommendation to the full board, and hold that the board on review exercises an original jurisdiction and is in no way bound by the referee's findings.[83] When it believes it necessary in the furtherance of justice, the full commission may, on petition,[84] or without petition and on its own motion,[85] order additional testimony.

A corollary of the rule making administrative findings of fact final if supported by evidence is that those findings and that evidence must be in the record. This is only common sense, for if the findings and supporting evidence are not clearly laid before the reviewing court, its review function becomes meaningless.

---

[75] Big Vein Coal Co. of Lonaconing v. Leasure, 192 Md. 435, 64 A.2d 563 (1949).

[76] Creech v. Roberts, 362 S.W.2d 734 (Ky. App. 1962).

[77] Ocean Acc. & Guar. Co. v. Hulsey, 108 Ga. App. 8, 131 S.E.2d 806 (1963). Board order directing the claimant to be X-rayed and medically examined to determine his disability was not an appealable final order. Writ of error dismissed.

[78] Bammes v. Viking Mfg. Co., 192 Kan. 616, 389 P.2d 828 (1964).

[79] Garbo v. P. M. Burner Granitoid Co., 249 S.W.2d 477 (Mo. Ct. App. 1952).

[80] Arizona, Colorado, Florida, Kentucky, Michigan, Oklahoma, and Pennsylvania.

[81] Longshore and Harbor Workers' Compensation Act, Sec. 21(b)(3), as amended by P.L. 92-576.

[82] See Universal Cyclops Steel Corp. v. Workmen's Comp. App. Bd., 9 Pa. Cmwlth. 176, 305 A.2d 757 (1973).

[83] Beck v. Industrial Comm'n, 32 Ill. 2d 148, 204 N.E.2d 7 (1965).

[84] Carter v. City of Detroit, Bd. of Educ., 66 Mich. App. 128, 238 N.W.2d 419 (1976).

[85] Rehberg v. Board of Educ. of Melvindale Ecorse Township School Dist. No. 11, Wayne County, 330 Mich. 541, 48 N.W.2d 142 (1951).

[3] Court's Inability to Weigh Evidence

Except in a minority of jurisdictions that have adopted a different standard of review,[86] the reviewing court will not ordinarily weigh the evidence nor substitute its judgment for that of the commission on findings of fact or choices between conflicting testimony or inferences, even when it is convinced that the weight of the evidence is contrary to the commission's findings.[87] It is the commission's function to weigh the evidence and make findings on questions of fact, which includes such matters as the credibility of witnesses, causal relation, the business or personal character of a trip, extent of disability, ability to return to work, suitability of offered work, average weekly wage, and, most common of all, medical causation.

The rule in its undiluted form requires that, when the particular finding is supported by credible evidence, it must be affirmed when contrary, not only to the weight, but even to the clear preponderance of the evidence.[88] If the commission chooses to believe the one doctor who testifies that the injury is work-connected, and not the ten who testified the opposite, the court has no power to reverse its determination. California has supplied an illustration of how one-sidedly noncompensable a record can appear and still survive on appeal. Experts who took a blood analysis of decedent testified that he must have been dead drunk, indeed gutter drunk and semi-conscious at the time of the accident. His wife, however, apparently testified that he was not drunk, and this was said by the court to create a conflict of evidence which it was for the commission to resolve.[89]

The commission may even refuse to follow the uncontradicted evidence in the record;[90] but when it does so, its reasons for rejecting the only evidence in the record should appear.[91] Unless some explanation is furnished for the disregard of all the uncontradicted testimony in the record, the commission may find its award reversed as arbitrary and unsupported.[92] This sometimes occurs when the commission denies compensation on a record that contains nothing but testimony favorable to claimant, with no indication whether all or part of the testimony was disbelieved, and if so why.[93]

[4] Speculation and Conjecture Rule

The phrase "supported by some evidence" is often found contrasted with its opposite, "based on speculation and conjecture." Another pair of phrases, which come perilously close to sheer word-play, is "preponderance of probabilities," which will support an award, as against "preponderance of possibilities," which will not. The general idea, of course, is that a fact is not proved by a showing of its possibility, no matter how strong

---

[86] *E.g.*, in Illinois an award is affirmed, unless "manifestly contrary to the weight of the evidence." Boutwell v. Industrial Comm'n, 408 Ill. 11, 95 N.E.2d 916 (1951).

Several states authorize trial *de novo* in the courts in compensation cases. *See, e.g.*, Knight Broadcasting v. Kane, 109 N.H. 565, 258 A.2d 355 (1969). Appeal from Labor Commission to Superior Court held to be a *de novo* hearing, and claimant required to carry the burden of proof even though he had prevailed in the first hearing.

[87] Cardillo v. Liberty Mut. Ins. Co., 330 U.S. 469, 67 S. Ct. 801, 91 L. Ed. 1028 (1947).

[88] R. T. Madden, Inc. v. Department of Indus., Labor & Human Relations, 43 Wis. 2d 520, 169 N.W.2d 73 (1969).

[89] Industrial Indem. Co. v. Industrial Acc. Comm'n, 108 Cal. App. 2d 632, 239 P.2d 477 (1952).

[90] *E.g.*, Kwasizur v. Cardillo, 175 F.2d 235 (3d Cir. 1949). Claimant's uncontradicted story disbelieved.

[91] Dole v. Industrial Comm'n, 115 Utah 311, 204 P.2d 462 (1949).

[92] Gomez v. Industrial Comm'n, 72 Ariz. 265, 233 P.2d 827 (1951). The Commission may choose between conflicting inferences, but it may not arbitrarily disregard the only reasonable inference which can be drawn from the uncontradicted testimony.

[93] Arvas v. McNeil Coal Corp., 119 Colo. 289, 203 P.2d 906 (1949).

that showing is. Thus, if a traveling man contracts undulant fever, and shows that in one of the cities he visited there was an unusually high incidence of the disease, he has established the possibility of his having contracted it there, but no more — since it is equally possible that he contracted it through his own personal use of meat or dairy products. However, if it can be shown that the work-connected origin is distinctly more probable, as when the disease normally is contracted only in the area through which the man's travels required him to go, this probability will support an award, even though it falls short of an absolute proof of the crucial fact.

The distinction between probability and possibility should not follow too slavishly the witnesses' choice of words, as sometimes happens in respect to medical testimony. A doctor's use of such words as "might," "could," "likely," "possible" and "may have," particularly when coupled with other credible evidence of a non-medical character, such as a sequence of symptoms or events corroborating the opinion, is in most states sufficient to sustain an award.[94] It is a common experience of compensation and personal injury lawyers to find that the more distinguished a medical witness is, the more tentative and qualified are the witness' statements on the stand. The weight of such testimony, however, should not be too sharply discounted because of the disposition of the highly trained scientific mind to refrain from unqualified statements or opinions on such matters as causation.

The weakest type of case is that in which the proffered evidence of "possibility" turns out to be a concession on cross-examination wrung from a doctor who has just testified positively to the opposite effect on direct examination.[95] At the other extreme, if the tentative medical testimony is completely uncontradicted, it has its best chance to survive. The remarkable California case[96] reversing a denial of an award to a fireman, on the strength of testimony that the smoke he inhaled on the job "may well" have contained the same carcinogens as the smoke he inhaled from a pack of cigarettes every day, is explainable mainly by the curious fact that the defendant chose to present no evidence at all.

The compensation process is not a game of "say the magic word," in which the rights of injured workers should depend on whether a witness happens to choose a form of words prescribed by a court or legislature.[97] What counts is the real substance of what the witness intended to convey, and for this purpose there are more realistic approaches than a mere appeal to the dictionary.

§ 31.07   REOPENING AWARDS

[1]   Summary of Reopening Problem

In all states, some kind of provision is made for reopening and modifying awards. This provision is a recognition of the obvious fact that, no matter how competent a commission's diagnosis of claimant's condition and earning prospects at the time of hearing may be, that condition may later change markedly for the worse, or may improve, or may even clear up altogether. Under the typical award in the form of periodic payments during a specified maximum period or during disability, the

---

[94] Dillow v. Florida Portland Cement Plant, 258 So. 2d 266 (Fla. 1972). Pathologist's statement that "this cancer, once begun, could very probably have been irritated and caused to accelerate and grow faster" by the conditions of employment was held to support an award for disability from removal of one lung for treatment of cancer.

[95] Frisbie v. Boffer Business Serv., 5 A.D.2d 1038, 173 N.Y.S.2d 148 (1958). When a doctor who says the accident "could" have produced a particular result also says that in his opinion it did not, this testimony will not support an award.

[96] McAllister v. Workmen's Comp. App. Bd., 69 Cal. 2d 408, 71 Cal. Rptr. 697, 445 P.2d 313 (1968).

[97] Oklahoma Gas & Elec. Co. v. State Indus. Court, 366 P.2d 609 (Okla. 1961).

objectives of the legislation are best accomplished if the commission can increase, decrease, revive or terminate payments to correspond to claimant's changed condition. Theoretically, then, commissions ought to exercise perpetual and unlimited jurisdiction to reopen cases as often as necessary to make benefits meet current conditions. But the administrative and practical difficulties of such a course have led to severe limitations on the power to reopen and alter awards. The most serious administrative problem lies in the necessity of preserving the full case records of all claimants that have ever received any kind of award, against the possibility of a future reopening.[98] Moreover, any attempt to reopen a case based on an injury 10 or 15 years old must necessarily encounter awkward problems of proof, because of the long delay and the difficulty of determining the relationship between some ancient injury and a present aggravated disability.[99] Another argument is that insurance carriers would never know what kind of future liabilities they might incur, and would have difficulty in computing appropriate reserves.[100]

[2] Time Limits on Reopening

In spite of these administrative considerations, an important minority of states[101] permits reopening for changed condition at any time, subject to various qualifications and restrictions, such as the Delaware provision that modifications cannot be made more often than once every six months. The remaining states limit the reopening period in a wide variety of ways, some setting a fixed period of limitation running from the injury[102] or award,[103] some limiting continuing jurisdiction to the duration of the original award,[104] and some extending the period to a specified number of months or years after the last payment of compensation[105] or the expiration of the award.[106] The periods themselves range from as little as one year to as much as ten.

The questions that arise in connection with time periods for reopening are similar to those examined in connection with time periods for the original notice and claim,[107] having to do with what starts and what tolls the running of the period, and whether the defense can be waived. One distinctive limitations question that may arise as to reopening petitions is whether, when the event starting the time period is the award, the first award controls or the most recent. Oregon has repeatedly held that its two-year period runs from the first award, even if there has subsequently been a successful petition for rehearing resulting in modification of the award.[108]

---

[98] *See* Dodd, Administration of Workmen's Compensation, at p. 203, reporting the difficulties of this kind experienced in New York and Massachusetts, where jurisdiction is continuing.

[99] *See, e.g.*, Metropolitan Cas. Ins. Co. v. Industrial Comm'n, 260 Wis. 298, 50 N.W.2d 399 (1951). An insurance company was called upon in 1949 to defend a further claim dating from an injury on which it had made voluntary payment in 1928.

[100] New York has attempted to meet some of these difficulties by creating a Special Fund for Reopened Cases, N.Y. Workmen's Comp. Law § 25-a (1965).

[101] *See, e.g.*, Delaware, Kentucky, Minnesota, and Nevada.

[102] *E.g.*, Cal. Labor Code § 5410.

[103] *E.g.*, 820 Ill. Comp. Stat. Ann. 305/19(h).

[104] *E.g.*, Conn. Gen. Stat. Ann. § 31-315.

[105] White v. Shoup Boat Corp., 261 N.C. 495, 135 S.E.2d 216 (1964).

Intercounty Constr. Co. v. Walter, 422 U.S. 1, 95 S. Ct. 2016, 44 L. Ed. 2d 643 (1975).

[106] *E.g.*, Ohio Rev. Code § 4123.52 (1965).

[107] *See* Ch. 31, § 31.02, *above, passim.*

[108] Marsh v. State Indus. Acc. Comm'n, 235 Or. 297, 383 P.2d 999 (1963).

[3]   Reopening for Change in Condition

The "change in condition" which justifies reopening and modification is ordinarily a change, for better or worse, in claimant's physical condition. The fact that the change necessitates making an award in an entirely different category, as when an original award was one of temporary benefits for time loss and the award on reopening would be for total permanent disability, is no obstacle to reopening.[109] Indeed, it is one of the main advantages of the reopening device that it permits a commission to make the best estimate of disability it can at the time of the original award, although at that moment it may be impossible to predict the extent of future disability, without having to worry about being forever bound by the first appraisal.[110] Although the beginning point and usually the main concern of an inquiry into change in condition for reopening purposes is claimant's relative physical condition, it should not be forgotten that disability in the compensation sense has an economic as well as a medical component;[111] accordingly a change in claimant's ability to get or hold employment, or to maintain the earlier earnings level, should be considered a "change in condition," even though claimant's physical condition may have remained unchanged.[112]

In a reopening proceeding for change in condition, the issue before the board is sharply restricted to the question of extent of improvement or worsening of the injury on which the original award was based. That is, no matter who brings the reopening proceeding, neither party can raise original issues such as work connection, employee or employer status, occurrence of a compensable accident, and degree of disability at the time of the first award.[113]

Moreover, a claimant who knew of injuries at the time of the original action but failed to include them in the claim, cannot for the first time assert disability from these injuries in a petition based on "change of condition."[114] But if the claimant did not know of the other injuries at the time of the original claim, he or she is not barred from asserting them in a reopening petition.[115]

[4]   Reopening of Agreement Awards

Under most reopening statutes, the power to reopen is unaffected by the distinction between awards based on agreement and awards in contested cases.[116] In some jurisdictions, however, because of particular reopening or agreement statutes, an approved settlement that by its terms disposes of all the rights of the parties is final and cannot be reopened.[117] In states following the latter rule, courts are inclined to be

---

[109] Parsons v. State Indus. Ct., 372 P.2d 27 (Okla. 1962).

[110] Malmedal v. Industrial Acc. Bd., 135 Mont. 554, 342 P.2d 745 (1959).

[111] See Ch. 14, § 14.01, above.

[112] Levesque v. Shorey, 286 A.2d 606 (Me. 1972).

[113] Charles F. Trivette Coal Co. v. Hampton, 509 S.W.2d 280 (Ky. 1974).

[114] Krell v. South Carolina State Highway Dep't, 237 S.C. 584, 118 S.E.2d 322 (1961).

[115] Gosek v. Garmer & Stiles Co., 158 N.W.2d 731 (Iowa 1968).

[116] Novak v. C.J. Grossenberg & Son, 232 N.W.2d 463 (S.D. 1975). A claimant can reopen a claim in spite of a full release based on the existence of no injuries at the time of the release. The court said that "there is no statutory mandate against setting aside a release where consequences of an injury were not discoverable until sometime in the future." 232 N.W.2d at 467.

[117] Durham v. Gulf Interstate Eng'r Co., 74 N.M. 277, 393 P.2d 15 (1964). Claimant received a lump-sum judgment based upon a stipulation of the parties. Held, it could not be reopened for aggravation or increase in disability.

exacting about the formal character of the settlement and its approval. Thus New Jersey refused to consider an agreement final that was not approved in open court.[118]

[5] Reopening Apart From Change in Condition

Apart from reopening for change in conditions where available under the foregoing analysis, and apart from express statute, awards and settlements cannot be disturbed[119] except upon a showing that they were procured by fraud.[120] This remedy may be based either on specific provision of the compensation act or upon the general power of courts to set aside judgments obtained by fraud.[121]

Fraud may be in the form of intentional deception, as when the employer dishonestly induced the signing of an agreement by telling the employee that this was necessary if the employee was to have his or her medical expenses paid.[122] But the "fraud" may also be constructive, and may even consist, for example, in the honest but entirely erroneous opinion, expressed by the insurance representative and insurance doctor in the agreement negotiations, that claimant's condition would clear up in 60 days, when that opinion induced claimant to acquiesce in the agreement.[123]

A number of statutes have extended the power of reopening beyond change of condition by express statute. Such statutes sometimes specify additional grounds, such as mistake,[124] or newly discovered evidence.[125] The concept of "mistake" requires careful interpretation. The kind of mistake that will warrant reopening is ordinarily a mistake on the part of the factfinder,[126] not on the part of one of the witnesses.[127] But when a key medical witness, whose testimony was relied on, later testifies that his earlier diagnosis as to this particular case was mistaken, reopening may be in order.[128]

§ 31.08 AGREEMENTS AND SETTLEMENTS

[1] Introduction

The great majority of compensation claims are disposed of without contest either at the administrative or at the judicial level. As to both uncontested and contested claims, some states forbid agreements by which the claimant gets less than the amount specified in the statute; but in other jurisdictions claims involving controversial issues of liability may be compromised and settled like any other claim, usually subject to approval by the compensation commission.

---

[118] Bisonic v. Halsey Packard, Inc., 58 N.J. Super. 166, 155 A.2d 797 (1959), aff'd, 62 N.J. Super. 365, 163 A.2d 194 (1960).

[119] State Comp. Fund v. McComb, 492 P.2d 1241 (Ariz. App. 1972).

[120] Woods v. Hobbs, 75 N.M. 588, 408 P.2d 508 (1965). Claimant executed a release of further workmen's compensation benefits, relying on his supervisor's misrepresentation that he would be able to retain his old job. This was held to be sufficient grounds for setting aside the release.

[121] Pellet v. Industrial Comm'n, 162 Wis. 596, 156 N.W. 956 (1916).

[122] Iacoponi v. Plisko, 412 Pa. 576, 195 A.2d 362 (1963).

[123] Texas State Highway Dep't v. Kinsler, 230 S.W.2d 364 (Tex. Civ. App. 1950).

[124] See Banks v. Chicago Grain Trimmers Ass'n, Inc. 390 U.S. 459, 88 S. Ct. 1140, 20 L. Ed. 2d 30 (1968).

[125] See Borum v. Industrial Comm'n, 13 Wis. 2d 570, 108 N.W.2d 918 (1961).

[126] International Metal Prod. v. Industrial Comm'n, 6 Ariz. App. 543, 434 P.2d (1967). In a series of awards, the commission set claimant's average weekly wage at an incorrect figure. The court held that since the incorrect figure was the result of mutual mistake, the commission retained jurisdiction to correct the error, although the awards had otherwise become final.

[127] Sauder v. Coast Cities Coaches, Inc., 156 So. 2d 162 (Fla. 1963).

[128] Stimburis v. Leviton Mfg. Co., 5 N.Y.2d 360, 184 N.Y.S.2d 632, 157 N.E.2d 621 (1959).

[2] Volume of Claims Disposed of Without Contest

Although compensation law produces a tremendous number of contested and litigated cases, it should never be forgotten that they represent but a small fraction — something like one-tenth to one-fifteenth — of the claims that are disposed of without contest.[129]

It has been rightly observed that "the successful administration of a compensation law depends to a much greater extent upon the machinery adopted for disposing of the undisputed claim than upon the methods of procedure employed in the litigation of the contested case, important as the latter undoubtedly is."[130]

[3] Fairness and Adequacy of Settlements

It has been charged that claimants in uncontested cases do not get what they are entitled to by statute, and that this is a serious defect in the uncontested claims procedure of most states.[131] Whether this is currently true cannot be determined from any available studies. If it should be true that the purposes of the act are not being fully realized at the uncontested-case level, the answer may lie partially in the question whether agreements for payment of less than the statutory amount are legally valid; for if they are not, the evil can be corrected by enforcement of the law as it stands, without resort to corrective legislation.

[4] Legality of Compensation Compromises

The question whether compensation claims can be compromised arises in this simple fact pattern: Claimant has received an injury which, if compensable at all, calls for 400 weeks' compensation; his wage basis clearly produces the maximum benefit of $270 a week; there is, however, a serious question whether the injury arose out of and in the course of employment; can the claimant accept, for example, 200 weeks' compensation at $270, or 400 weeks' at $135, or a lump sum of $54,000?

---

[129] DODD, ADMINISTRATION OF WORKMEN'S COMPENSATION, gives the following figures for 1929–1930, at 117:

State	Total Compensable Injuries	Uncontested
Illinois	56,100	53,300
Massachusetts	41,000	37,000
Pennsylvania	85,000	80,000
Wisconsin	21,700	19,800
Ohio	64,000	57,600

Thus, in Dodd's sample, something like one-tenth to one-fifteenth — of the claims are disposed of without contest.

A more recent survey indicated that only 9.8% of "accident" cases were controverted by the insurer and that 55.4% of these controverted cases were eventually settled by agreement. (Not surprisingly, the percentage of controverted cases was much higher in occupational disease (62.7%) and heart (55.2%) cases, but large percentages of these cases were also eventually settled — 66.7% for controverted occupational disease cases and 63.5% for heart cases.) Cooper & Co., Report on Closed Case Survey for the Interdepartmental Workers' Compensation Task Force (1976) reported in P. Barth & H. Hunt, Workers' Compensation and Work-Related Illnesses and Diseases, ch. 5 (1980).

[130] DODD, ADMINISTRATION OF WORKMEN'S COMPENSATION, at 118.

[131] Richter & Forer, *The Railroad Industry and Work-Incurred Disabilities*, 36 CORN. L.Q. 203, 223, 227 (1951). "In the vast majority of cases, being unable to litigate, he settles for less than his legal due." *Id.* at 229.

This problem is encountered in both uncontested and contested claims. In the great majority of states, the uncontested claims procedure takes the form of agreement between the parties subject to the approval of the compensation board. However, at any stage in a contested, litigated or appealed case, the parties may decide to effect a settlement, and, when they do, the amount agreed upon — by the very nature of the compromise process — is apt to be less than the full statutory amount. In fact, an official award may already have been made and may be pending on appeal; if the claimant compromises away part of this award to get rid of the appeal, the question of the right to bargain away what the statute says he or she should have is presented in its sharpest form.

In the absence of a statutory provision prohibiting the waiving or altering of statutory compensation rights by agreement, some courts have held that a claimant cannot validly agree to take less compensation than that specified by the statute.[132] Other courts have taken the position that a claim for compensation rights may be compromised like any other claim.[133]

Where there is a specific statutory provision prohibiting waiver of compensation rights by agreement, the same split of opinion appears. Such a provision can usually be construed to mean either (a) that compensation rights may not be contracted away before any claim has arisen, or (b) that, in addition, the employee cannot, after a claim has arisen, compromise his or her rights to the full benefits specified in the act. Here again the majority view appears to forbid the agreement to take less than the statutory amount,[134] although there is authority to the contrary.[135]

[5] Pros and Cons of Permitting Compromise

Apart from variations in the language of the statutes applied in these cases, which undoubtedly account in part for the disparity in results, the underlying issue is once more the choice between viewing a compensation claim as a sort of private tort right and recognizing the social-protection character of the compensation system. If one thinks of a compensation claim as a private, personal, adversary money claim against the particular employer and his insurance carrier, one will go on to conclude, as the Kansas court did, that workers "are not in any respect under guardianship or other disability; they and their employers are free agents; they may release their employers from liability for injuries on any agreed terms set forth."[136] To permit compromises will also enable claimants to get at least something in the many controversial cases where there is serious doubt whether fundamental conditions of liability can be established.

The other view is that the entire compensation system has been set up and paid for, not by the parties, but by the public, which is bearing the cost of compensation protection in the price of the product with the purpose of avoiding having the disabled victims of industry thrown on private charity or public relief. So the employer and employee have no private right to thwart this objective by agreeing between them on a disposition of the claim that may, by giving the worker less than this amount, make him a potential public burden.[137]

The question differs depending on the seriousness of the injury. When the claimant continues to have an income earning capability at or above the subsistence level, it would not appear to thwart statutory policy to allow settlement and compromise on a

---

[132] American Cas. Co. of Reading v. Kligerman, 365 Pa. 168, 74 A.2d 169 (1950).

[133] Cannon v. Folsom, 401 A.2d 977 (Me. 1979).

[134] International Coal & Mining Co. v. Industrial Comm'n, 293 Ill. 524, 127 N.E. 703, 10 A.L.R. 1010 (1920).

[135] Brigham Young Univ. v. Industrial Comm'n, 74 Utah 349, 279 P. 889, 65 A.L.R. 152 (1929).

[136] Dotson v. Procter & Gamble Mfg. Co., 102 Kan. 248, 169 P. 1136 (1918).

[137] Nagy v. Ford Motor Co, 6 N.J. 341, 78 A.2d 709, 713 (1951).

liberal basis. But where, say, long-term total disability is involved, commissions will take a harder look at any proposed settlement and will not approve a compromise that involves payment at a sub-subsistence level.

[6]   Commission Approval of Settlements

If the statute requires that a settlement have commission approval, a settlement lacking such approval amounts to nothing more than a voluntary payment of compensation.[138] As such it may toll the running of the statute of limitations on claims,[139] but it does not give rise to an "award" upon which procedures for reopening[140] can be based, nor is it a waiver of the right to controvert the claim.[141]

If the settlement is approved, it takes on the quality of an award, and the parties can no more back out of it than out of any other kind of award.[142]

[7]   "Lump-Summing"

The lump-summing problem, which is often encountered with and sometimes confused with the compromise problem, is basically a separate issue. Lump-sum settlements, when they are authorized by statute, are not compromises in the usual sense;[143] that is, they do not assume concessions and adjustments in the amount of payment because of the existence of a disputed issue. Rather, they are essentially commutations, and should be calculated on a sound annuity basis in accordance with any statutory rules provided.[144] Thus, a claim for total permanent disability could not be disposed of for a lump-sum settlement of $900.[145] Although there need not be agreement of both parties to the lump-sum disposition,[146] at least one of them must have petitioned for it,[147] and there must be either an agreement settlement or an award fixing a definite period of disability on which the commutation is to be based.[148]

The excessive and indiscriminate use of the lump-summing device can reach a point at which it threatens to undermine the real purposes of the compensation system. Since compensation is a segment of a total income-insurance system, it ordinarily does its share of the job only if it can be depended on to supply periodic income benefits replacing a portion of lost earnings. If a partially or totally disabled worker gives up these reliable periodic payments in exchange for a large sum of cash immediately in hand, experience has shown that in many cases the lump sum is soon dissipated and the worker is right back where he or she would have been if workers' compensation had never existed. One reason for the persistence of this problem is that practically everyone associated with the system has an incentive — at least a highly visible short-term incentive — to resort to lump-summing. The employer and the carrier are glad to get the case off their books once and for all. The claimant is dazzled by the vision of perhaps the largest sum of money he or she has ever seen in one piece. The claimant's

---

[138] Bisonic v. Halsey Packard, Inc., 58 N.J. Super. 166, 155 A.2d 796, *aff'd*, 62 N.J. Super. 365, 163 A.2d 194 (1960).

[139] Little v. Persun Constr. Co., 332 S.W.2d 647 (Ky. App. 1960).

[140] Chamberlain v. Brown & Sharpe Mfg. Co., 92 R.I. 132, 167 A.2d 237 (1961).

[141] Nacirema Operating Co. v. O'Hearne, 217 F. Supp. 332 (D. Md. 1963).

[142] Argonaut Ins. Co. v. Hix, 120 Ga. App. 415, 170 S.E.2d 762 (1969).

[143] Baham v. Raziano, 58 So. 2d 341 (La. App. 1952).

[144] Brevard County School Bd. v. Walters, 396 So. 2d 1197 (Fla. App. 1981).

[145] Southern v. Department of Labor & Indus., 39 Wash. 2d 475, 236 P.2d 548 (1951).

[146] Paltsios's Case, 329 Mass. 526, 109 N.E.2d 163 (1952).

[147] Spitzer v. Wolff Bros., 80 S.D. 187, 121 N.W.2d 7 (1963). A lump-sum award cannot be ordered by the board unless the employer, employee or beneficiaries so petition.

[148] Lowery v. Iowa Packing Co., 252 Iowa 112, 106 N.W.2d 71 (1960).

lawyer finds it much more convenient to be paid promptly out of a lump sum than protractedly out of small weekly payments. The claimant's doctor, creditors, and wife and family, all typically line up on the side of encouraging a lump sum settlement. Who then is to hold the line against turning the entire income-protection system into a mere mechanism for handing over cash damages as retribution for industrial injury? It should be the administrator, but even he or she all too often is relieved to get the case completely removed from his or her docket. With all these pressures pushing in the direction of lump-summing, it is perhaps surprising that the practice has not become even more prevalent than it already has.

The only solution lies in conscientious administration, with insistence that lump-summing be restricted to those cases in which it can be demonstrated that the purposes of the act will best be served by a lump-sum award. The clearest cases for lump-summing are those in which the rehabilitation of the worker would genuinely be promoted. Although the claimant who wants a lump sum to start a chicken farm[149] is almost a standing joke among compensation lawyers, there are of course *bona fide* instances in which a small capital investment may help to make the worker self-sufficient in operating a farm[150] or business.[151] A lump sum has also been found warranted to support a training program that would enable claimant to qualify for a job within his or her limited physical capacity.[152] And finally, in cases where the claimant has regained the ability to work and earn income at some respectable level, lump-sum settlements would appear to do little harm, allowing the carrier/employer to close their files on a large volume of smaller cases which otherwise would require continuing administration.

HERNANDEZ v. JENSEN
236 Mont. 210, 770 P.2d 502 (1989)

McDONOUGH, JUSTICE.

This appeal from the Montana Workers' Compensation Court concerns the court's denial of a request to lump sum benefits. Claimant, R. Gail Hernandez, petitioned to lump sum the majority of her entitlement alleging that financial hardship had created a pressing need for more household income. By placing the lump sum of benefits in various types of mutual funds and one real estate limited partnership, Hernandez hoped to increase her income by drawing a monthly rate of return from the investments. She also proposed that a portion of the lump sum benefits he used to establish funds generating a rate of return for her children's post secondary education, emergencies, protection from inflation, and a down payment for the purchase of a house. The increase in income from her various investments would in part be used to made house parents. The lower court held that the proposal failed to overcome the presumption in the Montana Workers' Compensation Act against lump summing benefits. We affirm.

Hernandez's monthly income from bi-weekly payments totals $579.00. Hernandez also receives food stamps and lives in federally subsidized housing. Her food stamp entitlement fluctuates between $150.00 and $190.00 per month, and monthly rent for her four bedroom apartment totals $104. Hernandez does not qualify for Aid to Families with Dependent Children or Social Security Disability benefits. Her attorney will begin collecting a portion of her benefits each month to pay her agreed attorney fees. Hernandez's husband lives in Peru and contributes little to the family income.

---

[149] Malmedal v. Industrial Acc. Bd., 135 Mont. 554, 342 P.2d 745 (1959).

[150] Chatfield v. Industrial Acc. Bd., 140 Mont. 516, 374 P.2d 226 (1962).

[151] Texas Employers' Ins. Ass'n v. Rollins, 257 S.W.2d 851 (Tex. Civ. App. 1953).

[152] Chevrolet, Atlanta Div. v. Dickens, 86 Ga. App. 18, 70 S.E.2d 515 (1952).

Hernandez attempts to support five children and her sister-in-law using her benefits. The family income places the household well below the federal poverty line.

Evidence in the record established that lack of funds adversely affects Hernandez and her family. Hernandez must borrow money to provide for adequate medical care. Her eldest son works to provide money to attend college part-time. Hernandez testified she could not afford to provide high school graduation expenses for her eldest daughter.

Hernandez also testified to housing problems due to low income. Her third story apartment is too small and makes coming and going difficult because she suffers from a bad back. Hernandez believes that some of her neighbors exert a bad influence on her children. She has investigated the feasibility of obtaining better housing using the proposed fund for making a down payment on a home. However, she revealed no definite plan for obtaining the financing needed to complete a home purchase.

Hernandez contends on appeal that she demonstrated that a lump sum entitlement satisfied a pressing need and served her best interest. Thus, according to Hernandez, the lower court erred in denying her request. Hernandez also contends that the lower court's decision is not supported by substantial evidence, and that the lower court denied her equal protection of the laws through its erroneous reasoning.

The State Compensation Insurance Fund (Fund) responds that Hernandez failed to make a showing sufficient to overcome the presumption favoring bi-weekly payments. For example, the Fund contends that evidence in the record demonstrates Hernandez exaggerated her financial problems. The Fund points out that Hernandez pays $20.00 per month for cable T.V., spends another $50.00 per month renting video tapes, and has already received lump sums to provide for medical debts and future medical expenses.

The Fund also contends Hernandez exaggerated her budget needs for medical expenses, and failed to pursue available programs for help in meeting her medical needs. The Fund also argues that the decision of the lower court may be justified by the negative impacts of Hernandez's plan. Hernandez's rent subsidy and food stamps could likely decrease with an increase in income. The Fund further asserts that an award of a lump sum to provide for educational expenses for Hernandez's children fails to overcome the presumption favoring periodic benefit payments.

There exists a high probability that in inflationary times the rate of return from investments purchased with a discounted lump sum of benefits will exceed the income generated by bi-weekly payments. 3 A. Larsen, The Law of Workmen's Compensation § 82.72(d) (1988). However, Montana law requires more than a showing of increased income through a feasible investment plan. *LaVe v. School District No. 2* (1986), 713 P.2d 546, 548, 43 St. Rep. 165, 168. Otherwise, bi-weekly benefits could become the exception and lump sums the rule. *LaVe*, 713 P.2d at 548.

In passing on any lump sum proposal, the lower court must consider the best interests of the claimant, the claimant's family, and the public. *Komeotis v. Williamson Fencing* (Mont. 1988), 756 P. 1153, 1155–56, 45 St. Rep. 1098, 1101. In weighing these interests, the presumption favors bi-weekly payments. *Komeotis*, 756 P.2d at 1156. This Court affords the lower court with aide discretion in reviewing lump sum decisions because the lower court occupies the best position to familiarize itself with the needs of the claimant and the results which could probably follow granting or denying the petition for a lump sum. *Komeotis*, 756 P.2d at 1156.

In this case, an investment plan accompanies a strong showing of financial need. However, the increase in income would probably be accompanied by loss of subsidies. The proposed investment plan has an element of risk. The house purchase plan necessitates a large debt which will further increase the claimant's expenses. The lower court considered the advantages and disadvantages of the plan and decided the presumption against lump summing controlled under these circumstances, we hold that the lower court acted within its discretion and that substantial evidence supports its decision.

Claimant's equal protection argument also fails. Hernandez contends that the lower court's decision rests on the classification of individuals. According to Hernandez, under the lower court's reasoning, individuals with business acumen may receive lump sum benefits, and individuals without business acumen may not. Hernandez argues that this classification improperly infringed on the "fundamental right to receive workers' compensation benefits."

First, a review of the decision of the Workers' Compensation Court reveals that the decision rested on the particular facts of this case. Most importantly, the lower court considered the interests of Hernandez, her family, and the public. The lower court concluded that in light of the particular facts of this case, the legal presumption favoring bi-weekly benefits controlled. Thus, there exists no issue here on whether or not a classification based on possession of business acumen may survive equal protection analysis.

Affirmed. . . .

HUNT, JUSTICE, specially concurring:

I concur in the result reached by the majority here for the reasons that it has long been the policy (albeit a policy without a purpose) for the State of Montana to refuse its injured workers a lump sum that can be invested for their benefit. The proposals set forth in the dissent of Mr. Justice Sheehy are well worth consideration by the legislature.

The plight of this claimant demonstrates that being an injured worker in Montana is no big financial deal. To those who assume that there is rocking chair money in Workers' Compensation benefits, I recommend reading the facts of this case.

SHEEY, JUSTICE, dissenting:

Under this incredible Opinion, it is the decision of the Court that it is better to keep this woman on public assistance and food stamps than to invest the monies *to which she is entitled* to give her an adequate living income.

Dear reader, look at the background of exploitation and carelessness that we sanction in the Workers' Compensation system.

On September 21, 1984, R. Gail Hernandez suffered an injury arising out of her employment with Acme Press in Missoula County. The Fund, as the insurer, accepted liability for her injury and has paid her weekly disability benefits from April 22, 1985 through the present. In her employment with Acme, she was receiving on-the-job training but in the ten months she worked there, her pay never increased from $5.00 an hour for a 40-hour week. She learned no skill while on the job, her employment having confined her to menial tasks in the printing shop.

Following her injury, her condition gradually deteriorated so that she was unable to continue her work with Acme. She reached maximum healing in the fall of 1986. The Compensation Fund refused to acknowledge that she was permanently totally disabled. She requested a determination of her permanent disability from the Workers' Compensation Court, as well as a lump sum distribution of a portion of her Workers' Compensation benefits. On September 22, 1987, a pretrial conference before the Workers' Compensation Court was held. There the Fund denied that she was permanently totally disabled and denied that it should pay any amount to the appellant in a lump sum. Three days before the trial, however, which took place on November 2, 1987, the Fund finally admitted that her disability was permanent and total.

For the dispute as to her permanent disability, she has received no attorney fees as far as I can determine. Her monthly benefits of $579.00 per month are apparently now reduced by 25% because of her attorney fees to the sum of $434.25 per month. Why the Fund should not bear the attorney fees, I am unable to determine from the record.

At the time of the hearing, Mrs. Hernandez was a 41 year old married female. She is a high school graduate and an honorably discharged veteran who served in the United States Navy. She is married, but her husband lives in Peru, and does not send support on any regular basis. She has four children, ages 20, 18, 7 and 6, all of them live with her in federally-subsidized housing. She is their sole support and also the sole support for her sister-in-law and her sister-in-law's infant baby.

The children have dental problems, and a daughter is having medical problems involving fainting and stomachaches, but all dental and health care must be postponed because she is unable to provide medical insurance for herself or her children nor can she afford the deductible for Medicaid.

Her oldest son is 20 years old. He is presently attending the University of Montana on a part-time basis and is working part-time. All of the income which he earns goes toward his education and he cannot afford to go to school on a full-time basis. The oldest daughter is 18, and hopes to go either to a trade school or to college but she has no funds with which to pursue her education beyond high school. The position of the Fund is that she ought to go out and borrow the money.

This family's income places it at 53% of the poverty level established for a family of that size. Janet L. Finn, a licensed social worker testified in detail about the problems that face low income families. Extended poverty leads to feelings of hopelessness and helplessness with little opportunity for future progress because the focus has to be on day-to-day survival. Such families experience a high drop-out rate in high school, are more likely to face educational difficulties in school and are also more likely to suffer from health problems. The apartment in which this family lives is a third floor apartment, with no elevator, in a neighborhood where frequent vandalism occurs.

The Workers' Compensation found that her lifetime benefits entitlement if she lived through her life expectancy is $246,050.99, less $23,651.82 which she has received in the past. Before the Workers' Compensation Court, she requested a lump sum advance of $170,065.00, of which $123,065.00 would be used to fund a monthly income for her of $1,500.00. There were other proposals for a downpayment on a modest home, a reserve fund, a minimal education fund for the children and protection against inflation. Two expert witnesses testified that the money could be invested and provide such benefits if the request were granted by the court.

Even deducting the amounts objected to by the Fund in this cause, her monthly budget approximates $600.00 per month, which obviously she is unable to meet with the income now provided her from her compensation benefits.

Why did the Workers' Compensation Court refuse her request which might give her at least an approach to the federal poverty income level? It said:

> The lump sum requested by the claimant not only seeks to ensure her of an income that she enjoyed prior to her injury, but in fact will increase her earnings by 50 percent and double her budget. The proposal of claimant here does not merely seek to allow her to sustain herself financially or return her to her asset situation as prior to her injury but will completely alter her economic status above that which she was enjoying at the time of her injury.

If this claimant had not been injured in the course of her employment, if that employment had not given her a degenerative disc condition at several levels, if she had not traded her lifetime working ability for the paltry benefits of the Workers' Compensation system, the foregoing statement of the Court might be tolerated. Her injury denied her every possibility of ever improving her situation and reduced her to grinding poverty. When she presents a plan that could offer some relief, she is denied because she might improve her income from a menial job and because of the policy of the Court and of the legislature respecting "passive income."

As I dictate this dissent, three-month treasury bills backed by the United States Government are yielding 8.5% interest per year. Two-year notes are yielding approxi mately 9% per year. By simply taking $100,000.00 of her entitlements and placing it under supervised investment in government securities, her present income could easily be doubled, and the whole principal saved. In the guise of preserving the "best interests of the claimant," this Court, hemmed in by prior caselaw that cannot logically be supported is actually adverse to her best interests.

Years ago, when much of the cash of the state was languishing around the country in no-interest bank accounts, it was decided to take advantage of investment of these monies through the Board of Investments. I suggest that section 39-71-2324, in cases such as this, allows funds to be transferred to the Board of Investments, supervised by the Board, and used to produce income from investments which would relieve the payments due from the fund. I see no legal reason why we could not order, in the best interests of this claimant, that the Fund itself invest these monies on behalf of this claimant to provide her a living income.

Things have come to a pretty pass when this Court decides that it is better to keep a person on food stamps and public assistance than to relieve her situation through the proper use of her benefits. There is a hollow echo of Marie Antoinette in this Opinion: Let them eat foodstamps.

[8] Mediation of Contested Compensation Claims

Mediation is a process in which a neutral third party assists in the settlement of a dispute. The mediator is unlike a judge or arbitrator in that he or she has no power to decide the controversy. The mediator does, however, control the course of the settlement discussions, encouraging discussion and behaviors that move the parties toward agreement, and discouraging those that do not.

Mediation has been common for some time in labor-management disputes and divorce litigation, but in recent years it has been incorporated into many other areas of our legal system. Workers' compensation is one of these newer areas. As previously mentioned, by 1995, at least seventeen states had incorporated some form of mediation into their contested claims process.

One of the motivations behind this trend was the increasing cost, length, and complexity of processing contested claims. Settlement at an early stage in the process can alleviate these problems.

When mediation is installed as a formal part of the contested hearing process, usually the parties are required to attend, but they are not required to compromise their positions. If the case does not settle, the administrative process simply moves on as if the mediation had never occurred. If the case does settle in mediation, the nature of the agreement is really no different than if the parties had reached agreement themselves without the help of a mediator. When under the applicable law settlements must be approved by the commission, then that will be true for mediated settlements.

There are major differences in how the states go about their programs. Some, for example, use commission employees as mediators; in contrast, the North Carolina Industrial Commission uses private mediators whose fees are paid directly by the parties. Whatever form they take, these programs seem to have been highly successful in reducing the administrative hearing load. For example, in North Carolina, in 1998 over 70 percent of the contested cases were settled in mediation, and the average disposition time, from hearing request to resolution of the claim (not counting appeals), was reduced from 260+ days in 1994, to 130 days in 1999.[153]

By making mediation a formal part of the process, the commission which is administering the program is unquestionably sending the message that settlement is to be encouraged. This can be a big step for a system that regards compromise of

---

[153] Data supplied by John Schafer, North Carolina Industrial Commission Mediation Coordinator, July 1999.

compensation benefits with suspicion. In other words, all the issues discussed in the immediately preceding subsections, concerning the desirability of compromising compensation claims, apply as well to mediated settlements.

Perhaps the most important issue is the potential for unfair settlements. Consider, for example, a construction worker with a serious back injury who has a $300,000 claim. The carrier, which has previously cut off benefits, offers $20,000. The worker, because of his injury, has no income and no compensation, and cannot feed himself and his family. Even if he is clearly entitled to the $300,000, he might jump at the $20,000 just to survive if the alternative is a year of administrative litigation to establish his rights.

The potential for this kind of unfairness is reduced if, as is usually the case, the claimant has an attorney. Moreover, the commission, in reviewing any such settlement, will usually look much harder at an agreement executed by an unrepresented claimant. Even so, our example illustrates that putting a mediation system in place should never be an excuse for an agency's relaxing its efforts to reduce the time, cost and complexity of its more formal procedures.

And despite the various cautions discussed above, one important benefit seems clear. In the usual employment setting, both the employer and the employee have made substantial investments in a working relationship. By moving the workers' compensation claim from a forum of litigation to one of settlement, tensions are lessened and the relationship can often be guarded. That is, the mediation stage, properly positioned early in the compensation claims process, will reduce not only regulatory workload but also the human toll extracted by protracted litigation.

§ 31.09   FEES, EXPENSES, AND PENALTIES

[1]   Introduction

Legal and medical fees and other expenses incurred in connection with a compensation hearing must ordinarily be borne by the party incurring them, although by express statute a substantial and growing number of jurisdictions make an allowance for them in addition to the award. On appeal, costs can usually be assessed against the losing party under general costs statutes, and a substantial number of states allow a reasonable attorney's fee to the successful party. Some states apply a penalty in cases of nonpayment or unreasonable delay in payment of compensation, in the form sometimes of a percentage addition to the award, sometimes of assessment of claimant's attorneys' fees against the employer, and sometimes both.

[2]   Attorneys' Fees

The basic rule applicable to a compensation case is the same as that for any other kind of case: Each party pays his or her own lawyer, win or lose. The inability of a prevailing litigant who has incurred legal expenses to shift those expenses to the opponent has always been a somewhat paradoxical tradition of the American legal system. The successful plaintiff, whose recovery was supposed to "make him or her whole," is made something less than whole by the time the lawyer is paid. A vindicated defendant emerges from his supposedly successful legal contest with considerably less money than he or she had when he or she entered it. The obligation to bear one's own legal fees, then, has become established as a necessary evil, which each client must bear as cheerfully as he or she can.

When, however, this practice is superimposed upon a closely calculated system of wage-loss benefits, a serious question arises whether the social objectives of the legislation may to some extent be thwarted. The benefit scales are so tailored as to cover only the minimum support of the claimant during disability. There is nothing to indicate that the framers of the benefit rates included any padding to take care of legal and other expenses incurred in obtaining the award.

There are two directions from which this problem has been approached: first, to add to the successful claimant's award a reasonable allowance for an attorney's fee; or second, while preserving the principle that the claimant pays his or her own attorney, to reduce the amount as far as possible by strict supervision and maximum limitations. The first approach has been used in some form at the hearing or trial level in a substantial and growing number of states[154] and in the Longshore Act[155] by express statute; attempts to reach this result by judicial decision have been unsuccessful.[156] The second is the older and still more prevalent response to the problem. About three-fourths of the states have express statutory provisions subjecting claimants' attorney's fees to the supervision of the commission or court handling compensation administration. This supervisory control may consist of fixing the fees, or approving them, or fixing general schedules of fees, or perhaps of passing on them only if controversy about the fee develops between claimant and his or her counsel. When the commission is entrusted with the task of fixing or approving fees, this does not mean that it has power to decree arbitrary amounts in its own unexplained discretion. As with any other findings, the evidence and reasons supporting the decision on amount of legal fees must appear in the record.[157] In suitable cases the fee may be set as a percentage of the award, and approved contingency fee agreements or awards of 25 percent,[158] or 33 1/3 percent,[159] are not untypical. Contingency fee agreements as such have generally been upheld, as against the contention that they are against public policy in compensation cases.[160] A majority of states have enacted statutes that fix maximum fees, sometimes accompanied by general commission supervision of fees and sometimes not. These, too, vary markedly. No two are quite alike. They range from 15 percent[161] 2 to 30 percent with no dollar maximum.[162] Several allow 15 to 30 percent on the first $300, $500 or $1,000, then a smaller percent, such as 10 percent, on the excess.[163] Alaska is unique in that its statute[164] sets a minimum fee, but no maximum. And Kentucky sets different limits for contested and uncontested cases.[165]

The problem of the claimant's attorney's fee is an important and serious one, and one which is far from satisfactory solution. The origin of the difficulty lies in the incompatibility between the original idealized theory of compensation administration, which was that benefits would issue automatically according to the clear specifications of the statute, and the actualities of modern compensation administration, in which

[154] *See, e.g.*, Florida (original provision was first and most comprehensive of add-on fees; sharply restricted in 1979), Maine, New Jersey, Rhode Island, and Washington.

[155] The Longshore Act joined the list of statutes with add-on attorney's fees, by virtue of an amendment adopted in 1972. Longshore and Harbor Workers' Compensation Act, Sec. 28, as amended by P.L. 92-576.

[156] *See, e.g.*, Bowman v. Comfort Chair Co., 271 N.C. 702, 157 S.E.2d 378 (1967).

[157] Salmons v. E.L. Trogden Lumber Co., 1 N.C. App. 390, 161 S.E.2d 632 (1968).

[158] Sanderson v. Producers Comm'n Ass'n, 241 S.W.2d 273 (Kansas City, Mo. Ct. App. 1951).

[159] Vestal & Vernon Agency v. Pittman, 219 Miss. 570, 70 So. 2d 74 (1954).

[160] Clark v. Sage, 629 P.2d 657 (Idaho 1981).

[161] Ala. Code § 25-5-90.

[162] Wash. Rev. Code Ann. § 51.52.120.

[163] Norsworthy v. Georgia-Pac. Corp., 249 Ark. 159, 458 S.W.2d 401 (1970). Arkansas provides a sliding scale for attorneys' fees, reaching a minimum rate of 10% on all sums in excess of $2,000. Claimant received an award in excess of $2,000 and after his condition worsened a second award was made. Attorneys' fees were held limited to 10% of the second award, against the contention that the sliding scale should be applied anew to each award.

[164] Alaska Stat. § 23.30.145. The minimum fee which may be awarded is 25% of the first $1,000 of benefits and 10% of all other benefits.

[165] Ky. Rev. Stat. § 342.320. In uncontested cases, $750 is the maximum fee. In contested cases, the maximum is set on a sliding scale with an upper limit of $15,000.

lawyers are employed by claimants in a majority of compensation cases in many jurisdictions. A corollary of this incompatibility is a continuing lack of agreement as to the part, if any, that lawyers should play in compensation administration. Some administrators feel that legal fees unnecessarily cut down the worker's net recovery, that the worker would frequently do just as well without the lawyers since the board will always look after his or her interests, and that most compensation claims present no issues calling for the exercise of the lawyer's talents anyway.[166] The lawyers reply that compensation practice is unavoidably replete with controversial issues and problems of proof, that, with the best intentions in the world, commissions loaded down with thousands of claims cannot possibly look after the interests of any particular claimant as well as a lawyer could, with the result that an unrepresented claimant may be subjected to delays that would not happen to a claimant whose lawyer is constantly pushing his or her case forward, and that, all in all, the claimant who pays a lawyer gets more than his or her legal expenditure back in the form of higher awards, better settlements and greater chance of success.

Once legal representation of the claimant is recognized to be one of the given facts of present compensation practice, allowance of fees above the basic award would seem to follow as the fair solution. Some legislatures and commissions, in their zeal to save the claimant from diminution of his or her net benefits through legal fees, have carried restrictions on fees to the point where they may well injure claimants as a class both by hindering the growth of an able compensation bar and by making it economically impossible for claimant's lawyers to give the necessary time to the preparation of each case.

[3] Medical Witness Fees and Other Expenses

Like attorneys' fees, other fees and expenses must be borne by the parties themselves, in the absence of a statute shifting the incidence of such expenses.[167]

At the original hearing level, the largest single expense, after attorneys' fees, is usually the expense of medical testimony. A few states diminish this deduction from net compensation by making specific statutory allowances for witness fees above the amount of compensation.[168] California allows reimbursement for medical expenses reasonably and necessarily incurred in an attempt to prove a claim even if it is unsuccessful,[169] and has further allowed the claimant his expense and loss of wages resulting from securing his or her own doctor's examination and report used to prove his or her claim.[170]

The claimant's burden of expense for medical testimony is also lightened in some states by the supplying of impartial medical examination by the state,[171] and by the broadening judicial recognition of administrative expertise as a substitute for medical testimony in uncomplicated cases, as shown by the growing number of cases in which awards unsupported by expert medical testimony have been upheld.[172]

---

[166] *See* Edward O. Allen, Fixing of Attorney's Fees by the Industrial Accident Commission, 7 Cal. State Bar Journal 234 (1932).

[167] Claim of Brannan, 455 P.2d 241 (Wyo. 1969).

[168] This group includes California, Florida, Louisiana, Massachusetts, New Mexico, and New York.

[169] Subsequent Injuries Fund v. Industrial Acc. Comm'n, 59 Cal. 2d 842, 31 Cal. Rptr. 477, 382 P.2d 597 (1963).

[170] Caldwell v. Workmen's Comp. App. Bd., 268 Cal. App. 2d 912, 74 Cal. Rptr. 517 (1969).

[171] *See, e.g.*, Mass. Ann. Laws, Ch. 152, § 9 (1965) and N.Y. Workmen's Comp. Law, § 13(d) (1965).

[172] *See* Ch. 31, § 31.03[6], *above*.

[4]　Penalties and Interest

A number of states apply a penalty in cases of unreasonable nonpayment or delay in payment of compensation, in the form sometimes of a percentage addition to the award, sometimes of assessment of claimants' attorneys' fees against the employer, and sometimes of both.

The most common question under such statutes is: What conduct on the part of the employer justifies imposition of the penalty? Although there are somewhat varying answers from state to state, due in part to variations in statutory language, generally a failure to pay because of a good faith belief that no payment is due will not warrant a penalty. In Minnesota, where an employer who believes that the claimant's entitlement to benefits has ended may discontinue payments on notice to the commission, the court has ruled that such a discontinuance, although mistaken, is not ground for a penalty in the absence of bad faith.[173]

The issue of good faith usually arises when the employer contends that it acted in reliance upon responsible medical opinion in refusing or terminating benefits, or when there was conflicting medical opinion; in such cases penalties are not ordinarily imposed.[174] But mistake of law,[175] and reliance on advice of counsel,[176] have been found inadequate defenses to an application for imposition of penalties.

An employer or carrier must be conceded a reasonable time in which to investigate and make a decision,[177] but if it is dilatory about investigating,[178] or perhaps makes no investigation at all,[179] a penalty may be in order.

As to the right to interest on compensation payments, there is considerable difference among the states as to the date from which interest should run. Minnesota has held in a death case that interest should run only from the date of the claim, not from the date of the death;[180] but Michigan, by judicial decision, has decreed that interest is payable from the date of death, that is, from the date each compensation payment "would have been due if it had been paid voluntarily," rather than from the date of death or the date of the highest appellate decision.[181]

---

[173] Springborg v. Wilson & Co., 255 Minn. 119, 95 N.W.2d 598 (1959).

[174] LaFavor v. Aetna Cas. & Sur. Co., 117 Ga. App. 873, 162 S.E.2d 311 (1968).

[175] Bassemier v. W.S. Young Constr. Co., 110 So. 2d 766 (La. App. 1959).

[176] Darby v. Johnson, 118 So. 2d 707 (La. App. 1960).

[177] Vidrine v. Argonaut-Southwest Ins. Co., 246 La. App. 668, 166 So. 2d 287 (1964).

[178] Harmon v. Mid-South Gen. Contractors, Inc., 218 So. 2d 390 (La. App. 1969).

[179] Barham v. Mathieu, 198 So. 2d 145 (La. App. 1967).

[180] Younger v. State, 275 Minn. 340, 147 N.W.2d 354 (1966).

[181] Wilson v. Doehler-Jarvis Div. of Nat'l Lead Co., 358 Mich. 510, 100 N.W.2d 226 (1960).

Chapter 32
CONFLICT OF LAWS

§ 32.01 NATURE OF COMPENSATION CONFLICTS PROBLEM

[1] Introduction

The conflict of laws rules applicable to workers' compensation have developed not as a mechanical extension of general conflicts principles but as a special adaptation of these principles, recognizing such distinctive features of the compensation problem as the possible simultaneous social interest of several states in a single compensation claim, the marked difference in generosity of benefits between statutes which might be applicable, and the characteristic disadvantage of injured workers in making an informed election between such statutes.

Generally the conflicts issue in workers' compensation cases takes the form of the question of which statute applies, not of which state has jurisdiction, although the two usually coincide.

[2] Reason for Importance of Conflicts Issue

The kind of fact situation that gives rise to the distinctive compensation conflicts problem is exemplified by the case of *Daniels v. Trailer Transport Company*.[1] Claimant, a resident of Illinois, made a contract of employment in Texas with an employer whose home office was in Michigan, but who engaged in operations in various states. Claimant signed a contract in which it was agreed that the workmen's

---

[1] Daniels v. Trailer Transport Company, 327 Mich. 525, 42 N.W.2d 828 (1950). The Michigan statute was held inapplicable.

compensation law of Michigan should apply to his employment. He then worked for the employer in several states, not including Michigan, Illinois, or Texas. He suffered a compensible accident in Tennessee.

This sort of tangle, which almost sounds as if it had been invented for an examination question in Conflict of Laws, is by no means unusual, what with truck, bus and air lines, construction companies, and many other industries operating on a nationwide or even worldwide basis.

If there were substantial uniformity between the different statutes, the problem would be less acute; but the maximum available benefits may vary radically from state to state. Moreover, when the compensation claim is made in one state and a third-party damage action is brought in another, lack of uniformity on the question of what third persons may be sued at common law by a compensation claimant or subrogee frequently means that the very existence of the right of action depends on the treatment of the conflicts problem.

[3] Statutory Application Versus Jurisdiction

It may be noted that this discussion is entirely in terms of "which statute applies" and not of "which state has jurisdiction." However, the two usually coincide, since, under the rule that a claim, to be valid, must follow the designated procedure, and under the requirement that only the special tribunal created by the particular state can administer claims thereunder, rights created by the compensation act of one state cannot ordinarily be enforced in another state or in a federal court.[2]

There is a strong practical reason underlying this "special remedy" rule. In most acts administered by commissions, the substantive rights created by the Workers' Compensation Act involve more than a certain number of dollars. The purpose of commission administration is not merely to settle disputes and award sums of money, but also to maintain supervision over the entire process of seeing that the claimant receives the full benefits of the Act, including medical care and rehabilitation, with whatever adjustments from time to time might become necessary. This is undoubtedly the practical reason for the holding that compensation acts will not be applied in foreign states.

MILLS v. TRI-STATE MOTOR TRANSIT COMPANY
541 So. 2d 557 (Ala. Ct. App. 1989)

INGRAM, JUDGE.

The defendant, Tri-State Motor Transit Company (Tri-State), petitions this court to issue Writs of mandamus directing the trial court to dismiss two pending workmen's compensation suits for lack of subject matter jurisdiction. Our scope of review is limited to deciding whether the trial court is legally required to dismiss either case for lack of subject matter jurisdiction. *Ex parte CSX Transportation, Inc.*, 533 So. 2d 613 (Ala. Civ. App. 1987); *Ex parte State Health Planning and Development Agency*, 500 So. 2d 1149 (Ala. Civ. App. 1986).

The record reveals that Tri-State, a Delaware corporation headquartered in Missouri, hired two Alabama residents, James Tucker and Ronald Mills (claimants), as over-the-road drivers. The claimants' jobs entailed hauling specialized freight cross-country from a dispatch point in Tennessee. In 1987, the claimants sustained alleged injuries in Tennessee and Illinois, respectively, but filed separate workmen's compensation suits in Alabama.

The claimants' right to workmen's compensation benefits under Alabama law is

---

[2] *E.g.*, Green v. J.A. Jones Constr. Co., 161 F.2d 359 (5th Cir. 1947).

governed by § 25-5-35, Ala. Code 1975. Under this statute, an employee who sustains an alleged job-related injury out of state is entitled to benefits provided by Alabama's workmen's compensation act only if he meets certain prerequisites set forth in § 25-5-35(d), Ala. Code 1975 (1986 Repl. Vol.). This section reads, in pertinent part, as follows:

> If an employee, while working outside of this state, suffers an injury . . . [he] shall be entitled to the benefits provided by this article and article 3 of this chapter, provided that at the time of such injury:
>
> (1) His employment was principally localized in this state; [or]
>
> (2) He was working under a contract of hire made in this state in employment not principally localized in any state. . . .

Under § 25-5-35(d)(1), a claimant's employment must be "principally localized" in Alabama. This term is defined in § 25-5-35(b) as follows:

> (b) For the purposes of this section, a person's employment is principally localized in this or another state when his employer has a place of business in this or such other state and he regularly works at or from such place of business, *or if he is domiciled and spends a substantial part of his working time in the service of his employer in this or such other state.*

> (Emphasis added.)

We note that the phrase "spends a substantial part of his working time in the service of his employer in this . . . state," which is set forth in § 25-5-35(b), "implies a current, ongoing employment status where it is foreseeable that the employee will continue to spend a substantial part of his working time in this state." *Seales by Seales v. Daniel Construction Co.*, 469 So. 2d 629 (Ala. Civ. App. 1985).

The claimants, seeking jurisdiction under § 25-5-35(d)(1), contend they spent a substantial part of their employment with Tri-State in Alabama. The evidence, however, does not support this contention. The record indicates Mills spent only 5 days in Alabama of the 341 days he hauled freight for Tri-State. The record further indicates that Mills spent only 42 days at his home in Cordova, Alabama, on stand-by status. No freight was hauled from Cordova. There is also evidence that only 3 percent of Tucker's trips were made to destinations in Alabama. He, like Mills, also spent part of his time on stand-by at his home in Alabama.

In the alternative, the claimants argue they can invoke jurisdiction by way of § 25-5-35(d)(2). This section, as noted previously, allows recovery for out-of-state injuries when (1) the contract of hire is made in Alabama; and (2) the employment is not principally localized in any state.

It is clear that claimants' contracts of hire were subject to approval in Missouri, not Alabama. The employment applications filled out by the claimants were expressly conditioned upon the following language set forth in the contract:

> Your references will not be checked until you attend our orientation school and if your references or qualifications do not check out to Tri-State's standards, you will not be qualified to drive a tractor leased or owned by Tri-State.

After completing the applications in Alabama, the claimants forwarded them by mail to Joplin, Missouri, for approval and acceptance by Tri-State. The claimants subsequently attended orientation school at Tri-State's home office in Missouri. This court has held that contracts subject to approval in foreign states are deemed completed in that foreign state. *Genesco Employees' Credit Association v. Cobb*, 411 So. 2d 151 (Ala. Civ. App. 1982). It follows then that the contracts of hire were made in Missouri.

It is clear that the claimants have failed to meet the prerequisites set forth in § 25-5-35 and are, thus, not eligible for benefits under Alabama law. We must, therefore, determine whether the courts of this state can enforce the workmen's compensation laws of Missouri.

Missouri entrusts the administration of its workmen's compensation act to a commission. As a rule, courts of one state will not enforce the workmen's compensation laws of another jurisdiction where the other state has provided a special tribunal, such as a commission, to administer such claims. 4 Larson Workmen's Compensation Law § 84.20, at 16-3 (1987). The Fifth Circuit Court of Appeals subscribed to this rule in *Crider v. Zurich Insurance Co.*, 348 F.2d 211 (5th Cir. 1965). There, an Alabama resident sued his employer, a Georgia corporation, in an Alabama state court for an injury sustained in Alabama. This action was brought under Georgia's workmen's compensation act, which provides for exclusive enforcement by a Georgia commission. The court in *Crider v. Zurich Insurance Co., supra*, denied Alabama courts jurisdiction over cases arising under the Georgia act. It based its decision in part on *Singleton v. Hope Engineering Co.*, 223 Ala. 538, 137 So. 441 (1931), which prohibited a claimant from seeking compensation in Alabama under Georgia's workmen's compensation act since such a remedy was vested exclusively with Georgia's workmen's compensation commission. In light of the above, we must conclude that the courts of Alabama cannot grant relief under Missouri's workmen's compensation act.

We note that the claimants may seek relief in Missouri under the Missouri workmen's compensation act since this act grants jurisdiction "to all injuries received . . . outside of [Missouri] under contract of employment made in [Missouri], unless the contract of employment in any case shall otherwise provide." In view of the foregoing, the writs of mandamus are to be granted unless, within ten days from the date of this opinion, the trial court dismisses both workmen's compensation actions for lack of subject matter jurisdiction.

Writs Granted Conditionally.

§ 32.02   SUCCESSIVE AWARDS IN DIFFERENT STATES

[1]   Introduction

More than one statute can apply to a single compensible injury, so long as each state has a relevant interest in the case. Successive awards can be made in different states, deducting the amount of the first award from the second.

[2]   The "Magnolia" Doctrine

The present rule on successive awards in different states derives from two Supreme Court decisions, the *McCartin* [3] case and the *Magnolia* [4] case, which had held on its facts that a prior Texas award was a constitutional bar to an award in Louisiana of the amount by which the Louisiana benefits exceeded those allowed by Texas.

[3]   The *McCartin* Doctrine

Four years later, the *McCartin* case, in practical effect, recognized the principle of successive awards and thereby discredited the *Magnolia* case. An Illinois resident had made a contract of employment with an Illinois employer in Illinois, pursuant to which he did some work in Wisconsin, in the course of which he was injured. He began compensation proceedings in both states. While the Wisconsin proceedings were pending, the Illinois commission issued a formal order approving a settlement agreement under Illinois law, and full payment was made under the order. The settlement contract, however, contained this sentence: "This settlement does not affect

---

[3] Industrial Comm'n v. McCartin, 330 U.S. 622, 67 S. Ct. 886, 91 L. Ed. 1140, 169 A.L.R. 1179 (1947).

[4] Magnolia Petroleum Co. v. Hunt, 320 U.S. 430, 64 S. Ct. 208, 88 L. Ed. 149, 150 A.L.R. 413 (1943).

any rights that applicant may have under the Workmen's Compensation Act of the State of Wisconsin." The Supreme Court of Wisconsin, on the strength of the *Magnolia* doctrine, had denied a supplementary recovery in Wisconsin after an Illinois award. The Supreme Court of the United States reversed, by unanimous vote, reinstating the Wisconsin award and distinguishing the *Magnolia* case. The ground of distinction was not, however, the express reservation of Wisconsin rights, but the absence in the Illinois statute or case law of an explicit prohibition against seeking additional or alternative relief under the laws of another state. Since the vast majority of compensation laws resemble the Illinois law in this respect, the decision means that for all practical purposes successive awards are now sanctioned.

[4] What States Are Affected by *McCartin* Rule

The critical question therefore is: Does the statute of a given state forbid relief under the laws of another state? It is clear that the normal exclusive-coverage clause does not have this effect, as the *McCartin* opinion itself recognizes. The exclusive coverage clause of Texas was not significantly different from that of Illinois. Texas did, however, have an express statutory provision, existing in very few other states, that an employee who *first* obtains compensation in another state for an out-of-state injury shall not *thereafter* get an award in Texas. Note that this is not the present situation, but its reverse. The statute does *not* go on to say what the *Magnolia* opinion reads into it, that an employee who first obtains compensation in Texas shall not thereafter get compensation outside of the state.

[5] Application of *McCartin* Rule by States

The above analysis of the *McCartin* decision's effect has been confirmed, not only by a subsequent Supreme Court decision,[5] but by the Restatement,[6] and also by the great majority of later state cases. *Cook v. Minneapolis Bridge Construction Company* is typical.[7] Here the employer's business, the employee's residence, and the place of contracting were in Minnesota, while the place of injury was in North Dakota. Benefits were first received under a North Dakota award. The exclusive-remedy clause of the North Dakota statute was admittedly even stronger than that of Illinois, for it provided that injured employees "shall have recourse . . . only to the fund and not to the employer" and in another section that "the payment of compensation . . . shall be in lieu of any and all rights of action whatsoever." But since the statute did not explicitly preclude proceedings in another state, the Minnesota Supreme Court held that the *McCartin* rule permitted a supplementary award in Minnesota.

[6] Prior Voluntary Payment or Prior Denial

Several cases have held that a prior voluntary payment of compensation accepted by the employee under the laws of one state does not detract from the employee's statutory right to an award in another state, whether the agreement for compensation had received commission approval or not.[8] Similarly, when the employee has not applied for compensation, but an award has been entered at the *ex parte* request of the

---

[5] Thomas v. Washington Gas Light Co., 448 U.S. 261, 100 S. Ct. 2647, 65 L. Ed. 2d 757 (1980).

[6] Restatement of the Law Second, Conflict of Laws:

§ 182. **Effect of Two Statutes Governing Injury:** Relief may be awarded under the workmen's compensation statute of a State of the United States, although the statute of a sister state is also applicable.

[7] Cook v. Minneapolis Bridge Construction Company, 231 Minn. 433, 43 N.W.2d 792 (1950).

[8] *E.g.*, Industrial Indem. Exch. v. Industrial Acc. Comm'n, 80 Cal. App. 2d 480, 182 P.2d 309 (1947).

employer, even Texas, with its express statute forbidding an award to one who has "elected to pursue his remedy" in another state, permits a supplementary award.[9]

Moreover, a denial of compensation in the first state does not necessitate a denial in the second state.[10]

[7] Policy Desirability of Successive Awards

An argument against the supplementary-award procedure is that it may subject the employer and carrier to repeated claims in different jurisdictions, protracting litigation and making it impossible for the employer and carrier to know with assurance when a claim has been fully satisfied. On the other side it is urged that employees typically are at a disadvantage in learning of their potential rights under various statutes of other states, especially since complex conflict-of-laws issues may sometimes be involved; hence they may quite forgivably make an unfortunate choice at the time of filing the first claim. In any case, the worst that can happen to the defendants, apart from the inconvenience mentioned above, is that they will have to pay no more than the highest compensation allowed by any single state having an applicable statute — which is the same amount that would always be payable if the claimant made the best-informed choice the first time.

[8] Double Recovery

Double recovery is not possible except in a few rare fact combinations. One of them occurs when an employee is injured or killed while performing services simultaneously for two employers located in two different states under circumstances making both states' statutes apply. A widow collected full death benefits in both Ohio and Indiana on these facts.[11] Another, which is not a double recovery for a single injury, but has somewhat the same effect, occurs when an employee is injured first in one state, and while drawing compensation for that injury suffers a second injury in another state. Even if the latter state sets a maximum benefit for total permanent disability, it can award the maximum without deducting what the first state is already paying — although it would have been deductible if both injuries had occurred in the same state.[12]

§ 32.03 LIMITS ON APPLICABILITY IMPOSED BY FEDERAL CONSTITUTION

[1] Introduction

Any state having a more-than-casual interest in a compensible injury may apply its compensation act to that injury without violating its constitutional duty to give full faith and credit to the compensation statutes of other states also having an interest in the injury.

[2] Summary of Grounds Supporting Applicability

There are six grounds on which the applicability of a particular compensation act has been asserted; they are that the local state is the:

(1) Place where the injury occurred;

(2) Place of making the contract;

---

[9] Standard Acc. Ins. Co. v. Skidmore, 222 S.W.2d 344 (Tex. Civ. App. 1949).

[10] Loudenslager v. Gorum, 355 Mo. 181, 195 S.W.2d 498, *cert. denied*, 331 U.S. 816, 67 S. Ct. 1301, 91 L. Ed. 1834 (1946).

[11] Shelby Mfg. Co. v. Harris, 112 Ind. App. 627, 44 N.E.2d 315 (1942).

[12] Mavroulias v. Mugiana, 155 Pa. Super. 573, 39 A.2d 263 (1944).

(3) Place where the employment relation exists or is carried out;

(4) Place where the industry is localized;

(5) Place where the employee resides; or

(6) Place whose statute the parties expressly adopted by contract.

When one of these falls within the local state, and some or all of the others occur in another state, the question arises whether the local state can apply its statute without being accused of denying full faith and credit to the statute of the other. As matters now stand, it is clear that the state which was the *locus* of any one of the first three items — contract, injury or employment — and probably also of the next two — employee residence and business localization — can constitutionally apply its statute if it wants to.[13]

[3] The "Legitimate Interest" Rule

The *Alaska Packers* case,[14] began to develop the general test which inquires whether any incidents of the injury that are important and relevant to workers' compensation fall within the local state. The injury in this case occurred in Alaska, but not, this time, on a temporary or incidental mission; the work was entirely to be performed within Alaska. But the contract was made in California, which was the base of operations; transportation to and from Alaska was provided, and the employee expected to return to California on completion of the work. The parties had agreed that the Alaska act should apply. The Supreme Court held that California's interest in the injury was sufficient to justify its application of its own statute. Of special significance is the Court's observation that the claimant, if not compensated in California, might well become a public charge there, since he probably could not go back to Alaska at his own expense to seek compensation under Alaska's act. In other words, a major purpose of compensation legislation is to prevent the throwing of such injured workers on local charity, and therefore California had a highly relevant interest in forestalling that event by utilizing its own compensation law.

Any impression that locus of injury was alone insufficient to support coverage was dispelled in 1939 by the *Pacific Employers* case.[15]

§ 32.04 LIMITS ON APPLICABILITY IMPOSED BY STATE LAW

[1] Summary of State Statutes

[a] States in Compliance With National Commission Standard

Almost all states now have express statutory provisions on the conflicts question. Over half, following the 1972 recommendation on this point by the National Commission on State Workmen's Compensation Laws, give the employee or the employee's survivor the choice of filing a workers' compensation claim in the state where the injury or death occurred, or where the employment was principally localized, or where the employee was hired.

The conflicts question takes two forms: first, when are out-of-state injuries covered? and second, when, if ever, are in-state injuries excluded? The Commission's answer as

---

[13] *See* RESTATEMENT OF THE LAW SECOND, Conflict of Laws, § 181.

[14] Alaska Packers Ass'n v. Industrial Acc. Comm'n, 294 U.S. 532, 55 S. Ct. 518, 79 L. Ed. 1044 (1935).

[15] Pacific Employers Ins. Co. v. Industrial Acc. Comm'n, 306 U.S. 493, 59 S. Ct. 629, 83 L. Ed. 940 (1939).

to the first is: when *either* the hiring *or* the principal localization of the employment is in the state. Its answer to the second is: never. Thus, a state may follow the Commission's formula to the letter on the first question, but may fail to qualify because of some small exception to complete coverage of in-state injuries, or perhaps because such coverage is not sufficiently clear.

[b] Coverage of Out-of-State Injuries

The Commission's formula for out-of-state injury coverage — whenever either the hiring *or* the principal localization of the employment is in the state — has been adopted (with an exception or variant here and there) by a majority of the states. In a handful of states[16] there is a single central requisite for coverage of out-of-state injuries: the making of the contract of hire within the state. In one jurisdiction the single basic requisite is principal localization of the employment within the jurisdiction.[17] Indiana's coverage appears to be the broadest of any: all injuries in the state or outside the state or country. And there are a number of other variants.

[c] Coverage or Exclusion of In-State Injuries

About half the states cover all in-state injuries.[18] A few are silent on the matter of in-state injuries to transients,[19] but this does not necessarily mean they will not be deemed covered. A handful cover such injuries subject to some conditions or reservations.[20] Several exclude in-state injuries to transients if there is coverage in the other state and if the other state grants reciprocity.[21] And again there are other variations.

[2] Place of Injury

The most controversial question concerning the place-of-injury factor is this: Does the bare fact that the injury occurred within the local state, while the employee was present on a strictly temporary mission, make the local statute apply, even if all the other features of the employment are in a foreign state?

This precise question was answered in the affirmative in the *Bagnel* case.[22] The court reasoned that *Gould's Case*,[23] by adopting the place-of-injury test for the negative purpose of destroying local jurisdiction over foreign injuries, also established the corollary that all injuries occurring within the state are covered by the local act, without regard to the location of other employment elements.

Even in states with no such background but with specific statutory provisions on applicability, there is usually a strong implication to the same effect. Most such statutes begin with some such phrase as "If the injury occurs outside the state, this statute shall apply only when the contract was made within the state, etc." By limiting the requirements of local contract, local residence and the like to out-of-state injuries, the statute seems to say that for in-state injuries no such conditions apply — in other words, no special conditions at all.

---

[16] *See, e.g.*, Connecticut, Maine (unless the contract provides otherwise), and South Dakota.

[17] District of Columbia.

[18] *See, e.g.*, Georgia, New Jersey, and Wisconsin.

[19] *See, e.g.*, Arkansas and Michigan.

[20] *See, e.g.*, Arizona (if the other state's laws can be dealt with by the Arizona Commission and courts), and Illinois (if the contract was made outside the state).

[21] *See, e.g.*, California, Montana, and Nevada.

[22] Bagnel v. Springfield Sand & Tile Co., 144 F.2d 65 (1st Cir. 1944).

[23] *In re* Gould, 215 Mass. 480, 102 N.E. 693 (1913).

There is an important practical argument in favor of unqualified assumption of coverage by the state of injury: the possibility in a serious percentage of cases that, if the state of injury does not afford protection, no one will. In *House v. State Industrial Accident Commission*,[24] the deceased was hired in Oregon by an Oregon company, and was sent to manage a branch office in California. He was called to Oregon to attend a brief dealers' meeting, and in the course of this temporary visit was accidentally killed in Oregon. Unfortunately for his dependents, California required the place of contract to be in California, and Oregon at that time required the place of regular employment to be in Oregon. Decedent had things turned around exactly the wrong way — his place of contract was Oregon, his place of regular employment was California, and he could satisfy neither state. Compensation was denied in California because the contract was not made there. Subsequently compensation was denied in Oregon because no regular employment existed there.

[3] Place of Contract

Some early courts, attempting to adapt conventional conflicts principles to the compensation problem, and rejecting the tort theory of compensation liability, adopted the "contract theory," under which the place of making the employment contract became decisive.[25] The compensation law of the state of contract, it was said, became a part of that contract, and therefore applied no matter where the injury occurred.

In applying the place-of-contract or place-of-hiring test, whether under specific statutes or judicial decisions, the essence of the question is how technically the concept of "making the contract" will be construed. The first practical question is: Does the mere formal execution of the contract within the local state make its statute apply, even if the contract contemplates that substantially all of the work will be done elsewhere? There are decisions both ways on this point.[26]

Many other issues are raised by this place-of-contract approach. The place-of-contract test, when construed to depend upon the sheer formality of being physically present in a particular geographical subdivision when a signature is scrawled or a word spoken into a telephone mouthpiece, has an air of unreality about it. There is nothing in this technicality of relevance to the choice of an appropriate statute for practical compensation purposes. The strict contract view, therefore, has for some years been giving way to the more pertinent inquiry into the location of the employment relation that results from the contract.

[4] Place of Employment Relation

The existence of the employer-employee relation within the state gives the state an interest in controlling the incidents of that relation, one of which incidents is the right to receive and the obligation to pay compensation.[27]

The main question is: What is meant by existence or localization of the relation within the state? The location of an injury is easy to identify; the location of a contract less so; but the whereabouts of a relation between two people has a somewhat more mystic quality.

The making of the contract within the state is usually deemed to create the relation within the state.[28] The relation, having thus achieved a situs, retains that situs until

---

[24] House v. State Industrial Accident Commission, 167 Or. 257, 117 P.2d 611 (1941).

[25] Kennerson v. Thames Towboat Co., 89 Conn. 367, 94 A. 372 (1915).

[26] *Compare* Baker v. Industrial Court, 92 Ariz. 198, 375 P.2d 556 (1962) *with* Covington v. Associated Employers Lloyds, 195 S.W.2d 209 (Tex. Civ. App. 1946).

[27] Anderson v. Miller Scrap Iron Co., 169 Wis. 106, 170 N.W. 275 (1919).

[28] Houghton v. Babcock & Wilcox Co., 9 A.D.2d 575, 189 N.Y.S.2d 436 (1959).

something happens that shows clearly a transference of the relation to another state. This transfer is usually held to occur when either a new contract is made in the foreign state,[29] or the employee acquires in the foreign state a fixed and nontemporary employment situs.[30]

New York applies its act to out-of-state injuries if the contract was made in the state even if the *entire* employment is intended to be outside of the state, provided that this out-of-state employment is transitory.[31]

[5] Localization of Employer's Business

The state in which the employer's business is localized has a relevant interest in a compensible injury, since the obligation side of the compensation relation is as much a part of that relation as the benefit side, and since the burden of payment would ordinarily fall most directly on the employer and community where the industry is centered. But, except for an early period in Minnesota,[32] this factor has never been held sufficient in itself to confer jurisdiction over out-of-state injuries. In a few states, however, it is relevant in conjunction with other tests.[33]

[6] Place of Employee's Residence

The place of the employee's residence, although having a very real interest as the community which might have to support a disabled and uncompensated worker, has never either by judicial decision or statute been held entitled to apply its statute on the strength of the residence factor alone. In combination with other tests, however, it has at times played an important part.[34]

[7] Contractual Specification of Particular Statute

Express agreement between employer and employee that the statute of a named state shall apply is ineffective either to enlarge the applicability of that state's statute or to diminish the applicability of the statutes of other states. Whatever the rule may be as to questions involving commercial paper, interest, usury and the like, the rule in workers' compensation is dictated by the overriding consideration that compensation is not a private matter to be arranged between two parties; the public has a profound interest in the matter which cannot be altered by any individual agreements. This is most obvious when such an agreement purports to destroy jurisdiction where it otherwise exists.[35] The only exception occurs under several statutes which explicitly permit the parties to agree that the local statute shall not apply to out-of-state injuries.[36]

The principle is equally valid when the parties attempt to come under a statute which by its terms or by the established decisional law governing its applicability does not cover them.[37] Once more the reason is that the state's compensation protection must be accorded to those whom the state's public policy has specified as the persons covered;

---

[29] *See* Stephens v. Hudson Maintenance Co., 274 A.D. 1077, 85 N.Y.S.2d 505 (1949).

[30] Poliquin v. DeSoto Kerns Co., 118 N.H. 371, 386 A.2d 1287 (1978).

[31] Lewis v. Knappen Tippetts Abbett Eng'r Co., 279 A.D. 1107, 112 N.Y.S.2d 79, *aff'd* 304 N.Y. 461, 108 N.E.2d 609 (1952).

[32] Marrier v. National Painting Corp., 249 Minn. 382, 82 N.W.2d 356 (1957).

[33] *See* Midwest Dredging Co. v. Etzberger, 270 Ark. 936, 606 S.W.2d 619 (App. 1980).

[34] *E.g.*, Nashko v. Standard Water Proofing Co., 4 N.Y.2d 199, 173 N.Y.S.2d 565, 149 N.E.2d 859 (1958).

[35] Alaska Packers Ass'n v. Industrial Acc. Comm'n, 294 U.S. 532, 55 S. Ct. 518, 79 L. Ed. 1044 (1935).

[36] *E.g.*, Kansas and Ohio.

[37] Daniels v. Trailer Transp. Co., 327 Mich. 525, 42 N.W.2d 828 (1950).

the commission administering the compensation act has been given jurisdiction only over the persons and claims so covered, and cannot acquire jurisdiction by consent of the parties.

§ 32.05 CONFLICTS INVOLVING DAMAGE SUITS

[1] Introduction

If a common-law action against the employer is available in the state of the forum but barred by the exclusive-remedy statute of a state granting a compensation remedy for the injury, the state of the forum will usually enforce the bar on grounds of comity or policy, although it is not bound to do so by the Full Faith and Credit Clause. As to third-party actions, if compensation has been paid in a foreign state and suit is brought against a third party in the state of injury, the substantive rights of the employee, the subrogated insurance company and the employer are ordinarily held governed by the law of the foreign state, although there is contra authority. If no compensation has as yet been paid, but could be awarded just as properly in the state in which the third-party suit is brought as in the foreign state, the local statute will control the incidents of the third-party action.

[2] Exclusive-Remedy Defense of Foreign Statute in Damage Action Against Employer

The most common example of the problem of applicability of a foreign exclusive-remedy clause occurs because of varying rules as to the availability of the exclusive-remedy defense to the statutory employer. Thus, the forum state may immunize the general contractor only when the subcontractor is uninsured, while the foreign state in which compensation is payable may immunize the general contractor absolutely. It is generally held that, if a damage suit is brought in the forum state by the employee against the employer or statutory employer, the forum state will enforce the bar created by the exclusive-remedy statute of a state that is liable for workers' compensation as the state of employment relation, contract, or injury.[38] Thus, although the local state might give the affirmative benefit of its own compensation act as to this employee, thereby asserting its right to apply its own statute to the exclusion of the foreign statute, it does not follow that the foreign statute will be disregarded when the employee is trying to get out of the compensation system altogether and back into the common-law damage system. In other words, the local state may reserve the right to apply its own statute in order to ensure that its *benefits* are conferred on the employee, for when it does this, no irremediable harm can possibly ensue to either of the parties. This refusal to limit the employee to the affirmative benefits of the foreign compensation act hurts no one, for if rights exist thereunder they are now no less enforceable in the foreign state after the first award than before. But if the defenses created by the foreign state are not enforced, irremediable harm to the employer is the result. Because of this distinction, then, a foreign exclusive-remedy defense to common-law suit against the employer will usually be honored although, on the same facts, the benefits of the foreign act would be required to give way to the benefits of the local act, if the employee chose to pursue compensation rights locally.

Now, although states *may* enforce the bar of a foreign statute against a suit involving an employer, and indeed usually *will*, this is not to say that, because of constitutional compulsion, they *must*. It is now firmly established by the decision of the Supreme Court of the United States in *Carroll v. Lanza* [39] that a state may decline to

---

[38] Jonathan Woodner Co. v. Mather, 210 F.2d 868 (D.C. Cir. 1954).

[39] Carroll v. Lanza, 349 U.S. 408, 75 S. Ct. 804, 99 L. Ed. 1183 (1955). Three judges dissenting.

apply the exclusive-remedy provision of a sister state when different from its own without violating the Full Faith and Credit Clause.

[3]   Conflict of Laws in Third-Party Actions

[a]   Importance of Conflicts in Third-Party Cases

When compensation is awarded or payable in one state, and a third-party action lies in another state, the wide variance between third-party and subrogation statutes makes it important to ascertain which state's statute governs the incidents of the third-party suit. The range of possible third parties, for example, differs sharply from state to state, as do the extent and timing of the insurer's subrogation to the employee's rights on payment of compensation.

When the issue is whether the particular class of third-party defendants is completely immune to suit — as when one state immunizes co-employees, or subcontractors on the same project, or physicians, while the other does not — the result of the choice of law will ordinarily be an all-or-nothing holding that the defendant is or is not suable. But when the issue is whether the assignment or subrogation statutes of a sister state should be given effect, the result is often merely that a particular plaintiff is granted or denied standing to sue. The cause of action itself is probably not destroyed, and the proceeds of the suit may well be ultimately distributed in much the same way no matter who is plaintiff.

The scope of *Carroll v. Lanza* [40] is broad enough to suffuse all the third-party suit cases in this section. That is, the decision on whether to enforce a bar imposed by a sister state, against a statutory employer, a co-employee, or anyone else, is no longer to be made on constitutional considerations of Full Faith and Credit, but on choice-of-law grounds free of constitutional compulsion.

[b]   Conflicts as to Immunity of Particular Third Parties

In *Stacy v. Greenberg*,[41] a New Jersey case, the plaintiff was traveling through New Jersey from a work site in Pennsylvania to his home and employment base in New York. The defendant employer was a New York corporation, and the contract of employment had been made in New York. The car was being driven by a co-employee, through whose alleged negligence plaintiff was injured. New Jersey, where the tort suit against the co-employee was brought, permitted tort suits against co-employees; New York did not. The court held that the bar imposed by the New York compensation statute should be respected, and the defense was upheld.

The closeness of the legal issue in this class of cases is illustrated by the fact that the Court of Appeals of Maryland, seventeen years later, reached diametrically opposite results on substantially identical facts.[42]

In both cases it was clear both that the compensation act of the state of injury and forum did not apply to the injury, and that the compensation act of the foreign state, whose third-party clause was in question, did. But if compensation has not yet been awarded or even sought, and might be payable in the forum state as well, the question becomes much easier. In *Bagnel v. Springfield Sand & Tile Co.*,[43] the place of contract, place of regular employment, and employer's business were all in New York. The employee was injured on a temporary assignment in Massachusetts, due as he alleged, to the negligence of a subcontractor of his employer. The law of New York permits a

---

[40] Carroll v. Lanza, 349 U.S. 408, 75 S. Ct. 804, 99 L. Ed. 1183 (1955).

[41] Stacy v. Greenberg, 9 N.J. 390, 88 A.2d 619 (1952).

[42] Hutzell v. Boyer, 252 Md. 227, 349 A.2d 449 (1969).

[43] Bagnel v. Springfield Sand & Tile Co., 144 F.2d 65 (1st Cir. 1944).

third-party suit against such a subcontractor; the law of Massachusetts does not. Suit was brought in Massachusetts. The court reduced the entire question to the issue whether the Massachusetts compensation act was applicable to this injury. It concluded that it was applicable, on the strength of locus of the injury alone. The act being applicable, its third-party provisions also came into play and barred the action against the subcontractor.

OSBORN v. KINNINGTON
787 S.W.2d 417 (Tex. Ct. App. 1990)

OSBORN, CHIEF JUSTICE.

The Appellant's motion for rehearing is granted, the opinion of this Court dated December 6, 1989, is set aside and the following is the opinion of this Court.

This is an appeal from an Order of Dismissal in which the trial court dismissed a suit filed by one Alabama employee against another Alabama employee, for injuries sustained in a vehicle accident in Texas, where both were covered by workers' compensation, and the compensation statute in Texas bars suits against an employer and a co-employee. We reverse and remand.

In September 1984, Ronnie Kinnington and Willie Osborn drove a truck owned by H.D. Edgar Trucking Company, Inc., from Alabama to California and were on a return trip when the vehicle overturned near Odessa, Texas. At the time of the accident, Mr. Kinnington was driving, and Mr. Osborn was asleep in the sleeper compartment of the cab. As a result of the accident, Mr. Osborn, who was injured, filed suit against Mr. Kinnington. Although both drivers lived in Alabama, suit was filed in Texas. By way of admissions, it was established that both drivers were employed by the trucking company on the date of the accident and that the trucking company provided workers' compensation insurance for its employees on that date and that benefits were paid to Osborn as a result of the accident.

The Appellee filed what it called a motion to dismiss and sought a judgment under the provisions of Rule 166a of the Texas Rules of Civil Procedure. The motion was based upon the pleadings, depositions and files in the cause. It asserted the claim was barred as against a fellow employee. A motion was filed in response asking the trial court to take judicial notice of the laws of Alabama and permit the suit to be maintained against the co-employee. Attached to the motion was a copy of the opinion of the Supreme Court of Alabama in *Grantham v. Denke*, 359 So. 2d 785 (1978), holding that part of the state's Workmen's Compensation Act which prohibited suits against a co-employee to be unconstitutional. The Order of Dismissal does not recite any action on the motion to take judicial notice of the laws of Alabama.

The Appellant presents eight points of error in which he asserts that the co-employee defense was not established, as a matter of law, that there is no proof that the employer was a subscriber under Texas law and that the law of Alabama should control the issue of liability.

First, the admissions and the deposition testimony of the two truck drivers establish, as a matter of law, that they were co-employees, both driving the same truck for their employer, H.D. Edgar Trucking Company, at the time of the accident. The admissions establish the compensation coverage provided to these employees, and Mr. Osborn admitted in his deposition that he was drawing $194.00 per week in workmen's compensation benefits.

The Texas Workers' Compensation Act provides that the employees of a subscriber shall have no right of action against their employer or against any agent, servant or employee of said employer for damages for personal injuries. Article 8306, sec. 3; *Mobley v. Moulas*, 468 S.W.2d 116 (Tex. Civ. App.—El Paso 1971, writ ref'd n.r.e.). We conclude that Appellee did establish the bar to this suit, as a matter of law, if Texas law applies.

Appellant further asserts that there was no proof that the employer was a subscriber under Texas law, that the law of Alabama should be applied and that the cause of action against the co-employee was a valid cause of action under the law of that state. Without proper proof to the contrary, Alabama law is presumed to be the same as the law in this state. *Ogletree v. Crates*, 363 S.W.2d 431 (Tex. 1963). In this case, the motion for judicial notice was properly before the trial court, and there appearing no reason the court would not have taken judicial notice as requested, and there being nothing in the record to reflect that the trial court did not take judicial notice, we will assume that the court did as requested. Thus, the trial court was faced with the law of the forum which would preclude a suit by a co-employee where the employer was covered by worker's compensation, and the law of a foreign state, where the employees were hired and the employer had its principal place of business, which would not preclude such a suit.

Had this suit been filed in Alabama, the courts of that state would apparently follow the rule of lex loci delicti and apply the Texas rule since that was where the accident occurred. *Powell v. Sappington*, 495 So. 2d 569 (Ala. 1986). Thus, no recovery would be had in a suit between two Alabama residents in an Alabama court. The *Powell* opinion notes the Alabama law was amended after this accident to restrict suits against co-employees.

Since the decision in *Gutierrez v. Collins*, 583 S.W.2d 312 (Tex. 1979), Texas has applied the most significant relationship test of the Restatement (Second) of Conflicts (1971). Section 6 sets out the general principles by which the more specific rules are to be applied. Section 145 lists factual matters to be considered when applying the principles of Section 6 to a tort case. Section 184 sets the standards by which a court is to determine immunity from a tort suit where an employee is covered by a worker's compensation statute.

If we were only applying Section 145 of the Conflict of Laws, we would affirm the trial court. Although the four factors under that section are evenly divided, the place of injury and the place of the conduct causing the injury both being in Texas, and the place of residence and business of the parties and the place where the relationship is centered being in Alabama, the Comment on Subsection (2) states:

> When the injury occurred in a single, clearly ascertainable state and when the conduct which caused the injury also occurred there, that state will usually be the state of the applicable law with respect to most issues involving the tort.

But, see *Robertson v. Estate of McKnight*, 609 S.W.2d 534 (Tex. 1980), and *Crisman v. Cooper Industries*, 748 S.W.2d 273 (Tex. App.—Dallas 1988, writ denied).

But, Section 184, which deals with immunity from tort claims arising out of a worker's compensation statute, provides that the controlling statute should be the statute of the state under which the employer is required to provide insurance against the particular risk and under which the plaintiff has obtained an award for the injury. Larson, The Law of Workmen's Compensation, Vol. 4, Sec. 88.00 (1989), sets forth the general rule as follows:

> As to third-party actions, if compensation has been paid in a foreign state and suit is brought against a third party in the state of injury, the substantive rights of the employee, the subrogated insurance company and the employer are ordinarily held governed by the law of the foreign state, although there is contra authority.

One of the first cases to decide a similar issue was *Stacy v. Greenberg*, 9 N.J. 390, 88 A.2d 619 (N.J. 1952). In a suit filed in New Jersey as a result of an accident in that state involving New York residents who were employees of a New York corporation, the Court applied New York law which barred suit against a co-employee although the law of the forum did not. The opinion was written by Justice William J. Brennan, Jr. That holding was rejected in *Hutzell v. Boyer*, 252 Md. 227, 249 A.2d 449 (Md. 1969). Courts which have applied the law of the state where the employment relationship was created include *Hunker v. Royal Indemnity Co.*, 57 Wis. 2d 588, 204 N.W.2d 897 (Wis. 1973); *Saharceski v. Marcure*, 373 Mass. 304, 366 N.E.2d 1245 (Mass. 1977); *Connor v. Hauch*, 50 Md. App. 217, 437 A.2d 661 (Md. Ct. Spec. App. 1981); *Frassa v. Caulfield*, 22 Mass. App. Ct. 105, 491 N.E.2d 657 (Mass. App. Ct. 1986) and *Farias v. City of Tucson*, 153 Ariz. 113, 735 P.2d 143 (Ariz. Ct. App. 1986).

In *Total Oilfield Services, Inc. v. Garcia*, 711 S.W.2d 237 (Tex. 1986), the Court found that the most significant relationship test was to be applied and that Texas law was applicable in a wrongful death case where a Texas resident was killed in an industrial accident in Oklahoma.

We conclude that Willie Osborn (no relation to the author of this opinion), may maintain this suit in a Texas court even though he could not maintain it in a court of his home state of Alabama. We sustain Points of Error Nos. Two, Three, Six and Seven.

The Order of Dismissal is reversed and the case remanded to the trial court.

[c] Conflicts as to Assignment or Subrogation in Foreign State

The second major question involving conflicts as to third-party suits arises most frequently in this form: the law of the state of compensation assigns the recipient's common-law rights of action to the insurer. The employee then appears as plaintiff in the courts of the state of injury, whose laws contain no such assignment provision. It is usually held that the assignment will be enforced.[44] The assignment worked by the acceptance of compensation is an accomplished fact between the parties. By respecting it, the court is not giving extraterritorial effect to foreign laws, but is merely recognizing the adjustment of rights which the parties have brought about between themselves by their conduct. There is, however, some authority to the contrary.[45]

§ 32.06 STATE ACTS VERSUS LONGSHORE ACT

[1] Introduction

Since 1972, coverage of the Longshore's Act turns on two tests, the situs test and the status test. Under the situs test, the injury must have occurred upon navigable waters, whose meaning was expanded to include any adjoining pier, wharf, dry dock, terminal, building way, marine railway, or other adjoining area customarily used by an employer in loading, unloading, repairing, or building a vessel. Under the status test, the definition of covered employee is limited to a person engaged in maritime employment, including any longshore worker or other person engaged in longshoring operations, and any harborworker including a ship repairer, shipbuilder, and shipbreaker. The Supreme Court, in defining the limits of maritime employment status, has included all segments of the longshoring process up to movement away from the terminal for delivery to the consignee.

[2] Nature of Longshore Act Conflicts Problem

The Longshore and Harbor Workers' Act[46] is, in form, an ordinary compensation act, modelled on the New York act. There are perhaps hundreds of thousands of workers as to whom, at some time or another, a question might arise whether they fall

---

[44] Dinardo v. Consumers Power Co., 181 F.2d 104 (6th Cir. 1950), involving subrogation.

[45] Middle Atlantic Transp. Co. v. State, 206 Misc. 535, 133 N.Y.S.2d 901 (1954).

[46] 33 U.S.C.A. §§ 901–50 (1970) as amended.

under local compensation acts or under the Longshore Act: stevedores, repairers, painters, construction workers, guards, and dozens of other categories of workers, who live on shore but who work on and off vessels or installations in navigable waters. The conflicts question has proved to be a unique one. It was not approached like the state-versus-state questions dealt with up to this point, for here, instead of a competition between equal jurisdictions both subject to the full faith and credit provision, the courts saw a preeminent federal maritime power on one side. But neither was it at first solved by a simple enforcement of this preeminent federal power, as "seamen's" cases under the Jones Act might be, because the Longshore Act was originally by its terms confined to an area narrower than that of full maritime power in two respects: It applied only to injuries that occurred upon the navigable waters of the United States, and it also purported to apply only when state acts could not validly apply. The first of these two terms, as the ensuing discussion will show, eventually assumed a dominant and decisive position; the second by judicial decision became a dead letter and was deleted from the act in 1972. In 1972 Congress also expanded the situs reach of the act beyond navigable waters as such to certain "adjoining" areas, and at the same time added a completely new requirement that the claimant must have been in "maritime employment." The 1972 amendments not only opened up a wide range of questions on how broad the coverage of the new "situs" and "status" tests would prove to be, but also reopened the troublesome question whether there could be a "twilight zone" in which both state and federal acts could apply.

[3] Evolution of the Present Rule

[a] Pre-1972 Development

With the passage of the Longshore Act in 1927, its boundaries were set by the two requirements that the injury occur upon navigable waters and that state acts be incapable of applying. There followed a trend of loosening of the second requirement, signaled by the *Moores* case,[47] in which the Supreme Court upheld the application of a state act to an injury in the course of ship repair — thus making it clear that concurrent jurisdiction could extend to those areas that had been definitely identified as federal.

In the 1960s the navigable waters test emerged as the dominant test of the affirmative applicability of the Longshore Act. This came about through two Supreme Court decisions: *Calbeck*,[48] which held that the Act *always* applies to *all* injuries on navigable waters, thus judicially deleting the second condition of coverage, that compensation could not validly be provided by state law; and *Johnson*,[49] which held that the Act *never* applies to any injury that does *not* occur on navigable waters, although the situation might have been within the constitutional reach of maritime power, since the Act was explicitly limited to injuries upon navigable waters.

[b] The 1972 "Status" and Expanded "Situs" Tests

In October, 1972, Congress amended the Longshore Act to create a two-tiered test of coverage. The two components may be called the "situs" and the "status" requirements.

The "situs" test consists of the previous navigable-waters rule, expanded to embrace adjoining areas of the sort that might ordinarily be the setting for injuries in "maritime employment." It is found in the section on "Coverage," which formerly was limited to

---

[47] Bethlehem Steel Co. v. Moores, 335 U.S. 874, 69 S. Ct. 239, 93 L. Ed. 417 (1948).

[48] Calbeck v. Travelers Ins. Co., 370 U.S. 114, 82 S. Ct. 1196, 8 L. Ed. 2d 368 (1962).

[49] Nacirema Operating Co. v. Johnson, 396 U.S. 212, 90 S. Ct. 347, 24 L. Ed. 2d 371 (1969). Justices Douglas, Black and Brennan dissented.

injuries "occurring upon the navigable waters of the United States (including any dry dock)." The amendment enlarges the parenthetical passage, so that the full paragraph reads as follows:

> Compensation shall be payable under this Act in respect of disability or death of an employee, but only if the disability or death results from an injury occurring upon the navigable waters of the United States (including any adjoining pier, wharf, dry dock, terminal, building way, marine railway, or other adjoining area customarily used by an employer in loading, unloading, repairing, or building a vessel).[50]

The "status" test is entirely new. Before 1972, there was nothing in the act limiting the concept of "employee" in terms of the character of the worker's activities. After 1972, the claimant must satisfy not only the "situs" test as to the injury, but also the following "status" test embodied in the definition of "employee":

> The term "employee" means any person engaged in maritime employment, including any longshoreman or other person engaged in longshoring operations, and any harbor-worker including a ship repairman, shipbuilder, and ship-breaker, but such term does not include a master or member of a crew of any vessel, or any person engaged by the master to load or unload or repair any small vessel under eighteen tons net.[51]

The words, "if recovery for the disability or death through workmen's compensation proceedings may not be validly provided by state law," were deleted.

[c]   Reasons for the 1972 Changes

The reason for the 1972 changes was not some intellectual preference for a superior conflict-of-laws theory. The reason was money.

By 1971, there were 11 maritime states whose maximum weekly benefits for permanent total disability were higher than those afforded by the Longshore Act. The result was that, in the conflict-of-laws picture, the traffic was made up mostly of claimants trying to get out of the federal act and into a state act. But when in 1972 the maximum Longshore Act benefits were more than doubled, going initially from $70 to $167, the federal-state comparison was turned upside down. Later, as of 1975, the maximum weekly benefit for permanent total disability under the Longshore Act had reached $318.38. Only one state, Alaska, had a higher maximum; in most of the other important maritime states, the basic state maximum was now less than half of this, and sometimes a third or less.

The *quid pro quo* for this spectacular increase in compensation benefits was the abolition of the seaworthiness warranty for longshore workers together with the *Ryan* type of recovery over by the shipowner against the stevedoring firm.

From 1972 on, therefore, in almost every state, there has naturally been tremendous motivation from the claimant's point of view to broaden the reach of the Longshore Act as widely as possible, beginning with the expanded "situs" test in the amendments themselves.

---

[50] Longshore Act § 3(a), 33 U.S.C. § 903(a) (Supp. II 1972).

[51] 33 U.S.C. § 902(3) (Supp. II 1972).

[4] The "Situs" Test: "Navigable Waters"

[a] Introduction

The *Calbeck* case in 1962 and the *Johnson* case in 1969, by holding first that the Longshore Act *always* covered *all* injuries occurring upon navigable waters, and, second, that it *never* covered injuries *not* occurring upon navigable waters, obviously threw a heavy burden on the situs test. The 1972 amendments added the "maritime employment" requirement and broadened the definition of "navigable waters," but did not alter the decisive character of the navigable waters test if that test is not satisfied. This is the result of the uncompromising language employed in the section on coverage:

Compensation shall be payable . . . *only if* the disability or death results from an injury occurring upon the navigable waters of the United States etc.

[b] Meaning of Expanded 1972 Situs Coverage

As noted above, the situs test under the 1972 amendments limits coverage to injuries "occurring upon the navigable waters of the United States (*including any adjoining pier, wharf, dry dock, terminal, building way, marine railway, or other adjoining area customarily used by an employer in loading, unloading, repairing, or building a vessel*)."[52]

Both the named areas and the "other" areas are covered only if "adjoining."

If an area or facility is not specifically named, but if it is *within* an area that is specifically named and that adjoins navigable waters, this is sufficient.[53] The most common application of this generalization is that a warehouse is covered if it is within a "terminal" that adjoins navigable waters,[54] and in such a case the distance of the warehouse itself from navigable waters is immaterial.[55]

The more difficult type of problem is that in which the particular facility is neither itself contiguous to navigable waters nor within a terminal that in turn is contiguous to navigable waters. Thus, in *Santumo v. Sea-Land Service, Inc.*,[56] the warehouse in question was not "inside" a terminal but was across the street from the employer's main yard, which itself was adjacent to a navigable waterway. The Board ruled that this slight physical interruption did not rob the area as a whole of its "adjoining area" character. On the particular facts, this decision was not particularly surprising. The entire area belonged to the employer, and was known as the Sea-Land Terminal. The particular warehouse "played an integral part in the loading and unloading process." The Board first cited and relied on several cases, of the kind already mentioned, for the proposition that "terminal" includes "all the facilities within the terminal area." Obviously, "within the terminal area" is a little broader than "within the terminal," and can effortlessly be made to include a facility immediately across the street.

But the Board went further and invoked a generalization that, taken literally, could become the focal point of almost unlimited controversy and litigation: "An adjoining area as defined by the Act must be deemed bounded only by the limits of its use as a maritime enterprise."[57]

---

[52] Longshore Act § 3(a) as amended by P.L. 92-576 (1972). New material in italics.

[53] Cabrera v. Maher Terminals, Inc., 3 BRBS 297 (1976): "The word 'terminal' has been held to include all the facilities within the terminal area. Vinciquerra v. Transocean Gateway Corp., 1 BRBS 523, BRB No. 75-125 (June 5, 1975)." 3 BRBS at p. 300.

[54] I.T.O. Corp. v. Benefits Rev. Bd., 529 F.2d 1080 (4th Cir. 1975).

[55] *E.g.*, Brady-Hamilton Stevedore Co. v. Herron, 568 F.2d 137 (9th Cir. 1978).

[56] Santumo v. Sea-Land Service, Inc., 3 BRBS 262 (1976).

[57] Santumo v. Sea-Land Service, Inc., 3 BRBS 262, 266 (1976).

It does not take a particularly vivid imagination to see what this principle will lead to in practice.

The kind of minefield that lies ahead appears even more ominous when one turns to the version of the same problem presented by shipbuilding activities in general, and by parts fabrication in particular. In *Maxin v. Dravo Corp.*,[58] the situs at stake was a structural shop in which components of all kinds of maritime products were preassembled. The employer attempted to rely on the fact that a thoroughfare, Grand Avenue, ran between the structural shop and the major body of navigable water. The Board rejected this argument out of hand, calling it "illusory." It stressed that this facility was part of a large integrated shipyard, and that merely being bisected by a public road was of no consequence. The Third Circuit affirmed.

So far, so good. But inevitably will come the cases in which the parts fabrication shop is two blocks, two miles or two hundred miles away. Assuming that the parts being fabricated are identical to those fabricated in the cases already decided, how can the Board say that this fabrication is any less within the limits of maritime enterprise? And if this is the holding, again the question will be raised, "whatever happened to the word 'adjoining' "?

[c]   Constitutionality of Landward Extension of Coverage

The constitutionality of the Act's 1972 landward extension has been consistently upheld.[59]

In *Victory Carriers, Inc. v. Law*,[60] the Supreme Court had found it necessary to hold that state law rather than the federal maritime law controlled when an injury occurred on a dock as a result of an alleged defect in the employer's own forklift, and that therefore under pre-1972 law an unseaworthiness action would not lie. The Court stressed heavily that, as the law then stood, maritime law governed only those torts occurring on navigable waters. But the Court added this dictum: "[I]f denying federal remedies to longshoremen injured on land is intolerable Congress has ample power under Arts. I and III of the constitution to enact a suitable solution."[61]

The reference to these two Articles means, of course, that the extension could be supported under both the commerce power and the maritime power. In the numerous subsequent cases raising the constitutional argument, the Benefits Review Board has merely cited *Coppolino* and said that the matter was settled for the reasons there stated.

[5]   The "Status Test": Maritime Employment

[a]   Significance of 1972 Addition of Status Test

Before 1972, coverage of the Longshore Act turned exclusively on situs of injury, and that situs in turn was strictly bounded by navigable waters. In 1972, in order to get away from the undesirable effects of having longshore and harbor workers popping in and out of the federal act with every gangplank crossing, the situs test was enlarged to embrace terminals, piers, and other areas adjoining navigable waters and used for loading, unloading, building and repairing ships. If the amendments had stopped there, however, the expansion of coverage would have seriously overshot the mark. The

---

[58] Maxin v. Dravo Corp., 2 BRBS. 372 (1975), *aff'd sub nom.* Dravo Corp. v. Maxin, 545 F.2d 374 (3d Cir. 1976).

[59] *E.g.*, Pittston Stevedoring Corp. v. Dellaventura, 1976 Maritime Cases 881 (2d Cir. 1976).

[60] Victory Carriers, Inc. v. Law, 404 U.S. 202, 92 S. Ct. 418, 30 L. Ed. 2d 383 (1971).

[61] Victory Carriers, Inc. v. Law, 404 U.S. 202, 216, 92 S. Ct. 418, 30 L. Ed. 2d 383 (1971).

reason was that, before 1972, any employee injured on navigable waters was under the act, however unrelated to longshoring or other waterfront activities his or her regular work might be.

Now, the number of cases in which railway workers, outside truckers, and others crossed onto navigable waters was perhaps not large enough to cause major concern before 1972. But when the covered situs was expanded to include entire terminal and shipbuilding areas, it became obvious that some additional limitation had to be superimposed to prevent coverage of every trucker or railway worker that entered a terminal and every local materials supplier or service worker that entered a shipyard. The solution chosen was to require covered employees to be engaged in maritime employment.

The addition of the "status" test thus had both an expansive and a constrictive purpose and effect.

[b] Longshoring: "Point of Rest" Versus "Maritime Commerce" Theory

The first major controversy touching the scope of longshoring activities covered by amended act can best be described as a contest between the "point of rest" theory and the "in maritime commerce" theory.

The Supreme Court, in its unanimous opinion in *Caputo* and *Blundo*,[62] held that the Act, as amended, covered Blundo, a checker, who was injured while marking cargo that had already been stripped from a container, and Caputo, a member of a regular longshoring gang, who at the time of injury was rolling a dolly loaded with cheese into a consignee's truck. As to Blundo, the checker, the Court's principal rationale was based on the technological change in longshoring operations. With the advent of containerization, the loading and unloading of cargo had moved inshore. The Court observed that "the container is a modern substitute for the hold of a vessel." Stripping and checking cargo at this point was thus clearly part of the unloading process under modern conditions, and Congress intended to adapt the Act's coverage to these conditions.

As to Caputo, however, the Court began by saying that modern technological change was not relevant to his case, since he was engaged in the old-fashioned process of moving already-unloaded goods into a delivery truck by means of a dolly. As to him, then, a different "dominant theme" underlying the amendments was invoked: the theme that Congress intended uniformity of coverage of waterfront workers some of whose duties would previously have been covered. The facts in Caputo's case made this determination relatively easy, since he himself worked on ships as well as off, and indeed never knew on a given day whether it would be one or the other.

In so ruling, the Court firmly rejected the "point of rest" doctrine. That doctrine, which had gained favor among some courts, holds that the benefits of the Act extend only to those who unload cargo from the ship to the first point of rest at the terminal, or who load cargo from the last point of rest at the terminal to the ship. (Both the claimants were beyond that point at time of injury.) It ruled that if Congress had intended to impose such a definite and narrow limit on coverage, it surely would have said so: there is not a word about "point of rest" either in the amendments themselves or in the ample legislative history. Moreover, the limitation defies the plain intent both of coverage of longshoring workers and of achieving uniformity of coverage of waterfront employees.

---

[62] Northeast Marine Terminal Co. v. Caputo, and International Terminal Operating Co. v. Blundo, 432 U.S. 249, 97 S. Ct. 2348 (1977).

[c] Overall Duties Versus Immediate Task as Test

The Court in *Caputo* also, in effect, ruled out the "pinpoint" approach by holding that coverage of a worker depends, not on what he or she was doing at the moment of injury, but on what the worker's overall status was. Since Caputo was a longshore worker who spent at least some of his time in activities that were "indisputably longshoring operations," it did not matter what he was doing at the instant of injury, so long as he was in a covered situs. Thus a claimant's status as a covered "employee" is determined by an evaluation of his or her work activities considered as a whole, not of the activity at the moment of injury.

[6] The "Twilight Zone" and Concurrent Jurisdiction Doctrines After 1972

The question whether, after 1972, there might be a "twilight zone" between state and federal jurisdiction, as well as concurrent jurisdiction and successive awards, was for the most part put to rest by the Supreme Court's 1980 decision in *Sun Ship Inc. v. Pennsylvania*.[63] The Court there held that a state may apply its compensation law to land-based injuries that also fall within the coverage of the Longshore Act as amended in 1972. It rejectee the petitioner's argument that, by enacting the 1972 amendments to the Longshore Act, which broadened compensation coverage to include maritime workers' activities on land, Congress created a pervasive federal regulatory scheme in an attempt to achieve national uniformity in compensating maritime workers.

§ 32.07 CONFLICTS INVOLVING SEAMEN'S REMEDIES

[1] Introduction

Applicability of the Jones Act as against state or federal compensation acts turns principally on the concept of "seaman" or "member of a crew of a vessel." A worker is now generally considered a seaman if he or she was permanently assigned to a vessel, including special purpose floating structures such as drilling barges, or performed a substantial part of his or her work on the vessel, and if his or her duties contributed to the function or welfare of the vessel. Seaman status is ordinarily a question of fact for the fact finder, but may be decided as a question of law if clearly within or outside the above definition. Substantively there can be no overlap between Jones Act and Longshore Act, but there is some support for the recognition of an overlap between Jones Act and state acts. Successive recoveries are not uncommon, especially when compensation benefits are followed by a Jones Act proceeding.

[2] Nature of Seamen's Conflicts Problem

This section discusses the boundary between compensation acts, both state and longshore, on the one hand, and seamen's remedies, chiefly damages under the Jones Act.[64] That Act gives to seamen or their personal representatives a right of action against the employer for negligence. The remedy is the same as that of railroad workers under the Federal Employers' Liability Act, and the common-law defenses are similarly modified. Seamen also have the non-fault remedy of maintenance and cure, which by its nature is of no value in death cases, and a right of action for injury caused by unseaworthiness of a vessel or her tackle.

As between the Longshore Act and seamen's remedies, the distinction turns upon the particular wording of the Longshore Act exclusion clause, which exempts from

---

[63] Sun Ship Inc. v. Pennsylvania, 447 U.S. 715, 100 S. Ct. 2432, 65 L. Ed. 2d 458 (1980), *rehearing denied*, 448 U.S. 916, 101 S. Ct. 37 (1980).

[64] Merchant Marine Act, 41 Stat. 1007 (1920), 46 U.S.C.S. § 688 (1952).

coverage the "master or members of a crew of any vessel."[65] As between state acts and seamen's remedies, the beginning-point of the distinction has been the general exclusiveness of admiralty law in respect to seamen's rights, under the rule that states cannot legislate in an area occupied by preeminent federal legislation.

In practice, the problem arises most often in the form of an attempt by a worker on the borderline between the status of seaman and non-seaman to obtain damages under the Jones Act, rather than compensation, because of the higher amounts ordinarily recoverable under the former. However, if actionable negligence is not provable, the borderline seaman may be in the position of wanting to prove that he or she is *not* a seaman or crew member, so as to be able to recover non-fault workers' compensation under either the Longshore Act or a state compensation act.

[3]   Who is a "Seaman"?

[a]   Introduction

The term "seaman," which controls Jones Act coverage, is undefined in that act.[66] However, when the Longshore Act is potentially involved, there is another statutory term that must be observed. The Longshore Act specifically excludes coverage of "a master or member of a crew of any vessel." This exception was inserted to undo the effect of *International Stevedoring Company v. Haverty*,[67] which had held that a stevedore was a "seaman" under the Jones Act. For most practical purposes, there seems to be no significant distinction between the concepts of "seaman" and "crew member."[68]

[b]   Legal Elements in "Seaman" Status

Originally, in maritime usage, the term "seaman" was used to refer to a mariner — one who was trained to reef and steer and maneuver a vessel.[69] From this concept there emerged three elements[70] that were generally supposed to be present to support a finding that a person was a "seaman" or "a member of a crew": first, that the "vessel" was "in navigation"; second, that the worker had a "more or less permanent connection with the ship"; and, third, that the worker's function was "primarily to aid in navigation."

However, as the result of hundreds of decisions broadening these concepts, expressions can be found[71] to the effect that the term "seaman" has now been expanded to the point where it covers practically any worker, from helmsman to bartender,[72] who

---

[65] Longshore and Harbor Workers' Compensation Act § 903(a) (1964).

[66] The Jones Act applies to "any seaman who shall suffer personal injury in the course of his employment."

[67] International Stevedoring Company v. Haverty, 272 U.S. 50, 47 S. Ct. 19, 71 L. Ed. 157 (1926).

[68] *Cf.* language in Gahagan Constr. Corp. v. Armao, 165 F.2d 301 (1st Cir.), *cert. denied*, 333 U.S. 876, 68 S. Ct. 905, 92 L. Ed. 1151 (1948).

[69] Beddoo v. Smoot Sand & Gravel Corp., 76 App. D.C. 39, 128 F.2d 608 (D.C. Cir. 1942). The court in this same opinion goes on to point out that the term has become much more flexible and inclusive in scope.

[70] Desper v. Starved Rock Ferry Co., 342 U.S. 187, 72 S. Ct. 216, 96 L. Ed. 205, *rehearing denied*, 342 U.S. 934, 72 S. Ct. 374, 96 L. Ed. 695 (1952).

[71] Early v. American Dredging Co., 101 F. Supp. 393 (E.D. Pa. 1951).

[72] *See* McAfoos v. Canadian Pac. Steamships, 143 F. Supp. 73 (S.D.N.Y. 1956), *rev'd on other grounds*, 243 F.2d 270 (2d Cir. 1957), in which a magician's helper sought maintenance and cure. Levet, J., said that "the term, 'seaman' is not limited to those who can 'land, reef, and steer' and has been extended to include a person employed as an entertainer aboard a vessel . . . "

sustains an injury while working on almost any structure that floats, or once floated, or is capable of floating on navigable waters.[73]

The explanation of the transformation of the image of the seaman to this miscellany of assorted workers doing odd jobs on all sorts of funny-looking floating contraptions, is not to be found in a surge of permissiveness on the part of courts so much as in a fundamental change in the nature of sea-going activities. For a start, the advent of steam-powered vessels and luxury liners ushered in a period in which a large proportion of the jobs to be done on board were quite unrelated to "navigation" in the usual sense. Then, to complicate matters further, there appeared all kinds of special-purpose craft that, apart from the fact that they floated, bore little resemblance to the conventional picture of a vessel: dredges, barges, floating derricks, floating hoisters, floating pile drivers, drill scows, and, most recently, various kinds of submersible barges and other rigs used for offshore oil drilling. If the idea behind "seamen's" remedies was that those who were subjected to the hazards of life and work at sea should be entitled to special kinds of protection, it was not inappropriate to let the remedies follow the hazards. But in the process, considerable strain was placed on the wording of the second two of the three classical tests. As to "attachment" to the vessel, while this was a natural enough requirement for a ship with its crew at sea, it raised problems if interpreted too literally in the case of dredges, derricks, and the like that might not even have living quarters. Even more emphatically, the words "naturally and primarily aboard to aid in navigation" were bound to get in the way of any extension of these remedies to those who oiled the pumps on dredging scows, or who operated the pile-drivers on floating pile-driver platforms, or who worked on oil drilling machinery in submersible barges.

For these reasons, it seems desirable, although some courts still dutifully announce the three classical tests as their beginning-point, to substitute for the second two tests what might be called the "Robison tests," enunciated by Judge Wisdom in the leading case of *Offshore Company v. Robison:* [74]

> (1) [I]f there is evidence that the injured seaman was assigned permanently to a vessel (including special purpose structures not usually employed as a means of transport by water but designed to float on water) *or performed a substantial part of his work on the vessel*; and (2) if the capacity in which he was employed or the duties which he performed *contributed to the function of the vessel or to the accomplishment of its mission*, or to the operation *or welfare* of the vessel in terms of maintenance during its movement or during anchorage for its future trips.[75]

[c] "Seaman" Status as Issue of Fact

The major turning-point leading to the broadening of the reach of the terms "seaman" and "member of a crew" was the establishment of the proposition that "seaman" or "crew" status was a question of fact to be determined by the fact-finder — which is to say, in the case of the Jones Act, by the jury. The transition from court to jury determination of seaman status was the product of a series of Supreme Court

---

[73] Offshore Co. v. Robison, 266 F.2d 769, 75 A.L.R.2d 1296 (5th Cir. 1959).

See, e.g., Barger v. Petroleum Helicopters, Inc., 514 F. Supp. 1199 (E.D. Tex. 1981). A helicopter, designed for landings, takeoffs, and movements on water, equipped with pontoons, and used to take personnel to and from drilling platforms, was held a "vessel" under the Jones Act. The court observed that this holding was "no more strange than the Fifth Circuit cases holding that movable offshore drilling platforms [were] vessels for Jones Act purposes, while fixed platforms were not." 514 F.Supp. at p. 1212.

[74] Offshore Co. v. Robison, 266 F.2d 769, 75 A.L.R.2d 1296 (5th Cir. 1959).

[75] Offshore Co. v. Robison, 266 F.2d 769, 779, 75 A.L.R.2d 1296 (5th Cir. 1959). Italics supplied.

cases beginning with the Supreme Court's 1955 decision on *Gianfala v. Texas Company.* [76]

[d] What Is a "Vessel"?

Workers on dredges, barges and comparable vessels such as floating hoisters, floating pile drivers, and floating derricks, in navigable waters have been found to be seamen in numerous cases. And, beginning with *Gianfala*, the cases have now clearly established that a member of the crew of a submersible oil drilling barge or a mobile oil drilling platform is a seaman entitled to remedies under the Jones Act.

[e] Seamen Engaged in Land Activity

Until 1943, seamen's remedies were restricted to injuries actually occurring on navigable waters, on the theory that such remedies in general and the Jones Act in particular must have been intended to be confined to what was then conceived to be the area of admiralty jurisdiction. But in that year the United States Supreme Court set up a new test in *O'Donnell v. Great Lakes Dredge & Dock Company.* [77] The Jones Act was held to apply also to inland injuries if they were in the course of employment and related to the vessel's activities. In this case a deckhand had been ordered ashore to assist in the repair of an unloading device, and while so engaged was injured. The Supreme Court held that the Jones Act was applicable, and that as so applied it was constitutional.

The effect of this expansion, like the effect of the comparable expansion of the concepts of "vessel" and "seaman," is not only the affirmative conferral of seamen's remedies in a much wider range of cases, but quite probably a corresponding negative constriction of the workers' compensation remedies available. The federal jurisdiction thus assumed being exclusive of both longshore and state compensation acts, most compensation applications for inland injuries to seamen have been denied.[78]

O'Donnell was followed by a flood of cases applying maritime remedies to such shoreside activities as shore leave, recreation and going-and-coming activities. One of the most famous cases was *Warren v. United States,*[79] in which a seaman on shore leave drank a bottle of wine, leaned over an unprotected ledge in a room adjoining a dance hall, and lost his balance and fell, breaking his leg, when an iron rod he was using as a rail came off. Maintenance and cure were awarded.

In *Aguilar*,[80] the Supreme Court extended the *O'Donnell* rule to maintenance and cure cases.

The swift expansion of the category of seamen to include many land-based workers was accompanied by an equally swift expansion of the range of land-based injuries covered. In *Williamson v. Western-Pacific Dredging Corp.*,[81] decided by the federal district court in Oregon in 1969, the decedent was employed as a mate on a dredge. The dredge did not provide sleeping quarters, and consequently the decedent was required

---

[76] Gianfala v. Texas Company, 350 U.S. 879, 76 S. Ct. 141, 100 L. Ed. 776, *rehearing denied,* 350 U.S. 960, 76 S.Ct. 346, 100 L. Ed. 834, *rev'g,* 222 F.2d 382 (5th Cir. 1955).

The rule was made explicit and reconfirmed in Senko v. La Crosse Dredging Corp., 352 U.S. 370, 77 S. Ct. 415, 1 L. Ed. 2d 404, *rehearing denied,* 353 U.S. 931, 77 S. Ct. 716, 1 L. Ed. 2d 724 (1957), and Grimes v. Raymond Concrete Pile Co., 356 U.S. 252, 78 S. Ct. 687, 2 L. Ed. 2d 737 (1958), *rev'g per curiam,* 245 F.2d 437 (1st Cir. 1957).

[77] O'Donnell v. Great Lakes Dredge & Dock Company, 318 U.S. 36, 63 S. Ct. 488, 87 L. Ed. 596 (1943).

[78] *E.g.*, Rudolph v. Industrial Marine Serv., 187 Tenn. 119, 213 S.W.2d 30 (1948).

[79] Warren v. United States, 340 U.S. 523, 71 S. Ct. 432, 95 L. Ed. 503 (1951).

[80] Aguilar v. Standard Oil Co., 318 U.S. 724, 63 S. Ct. 930, 87 L. Ed. 1107 (1943).

[81] Williamson v. Western-Pacific Dredging Corp., 304 F. Supp. 509 (D. Or. 1969).

to live ashore. By virtue of the union contract, each employee was allowed four dollars a day for "travel pay," and defendant had a policy, which was not enforced, that employees should use their own automobiles in going to and coming from work. In this instance, decedent was riding to work in a car driven by a fellow-employee at the time of injury that resulted in his death. The district court held that decedent was a seaman in the "service of the ship" at the time of the accident, and that the appropriate remedies were therefore maintenance and cure and Jones Act damages, not workers' compensation under either the Longshore Act or the Oregon compensation act. The court relied heavily on shore leave decisions holding that seamen are in the course of their employment if they are answerable to the call of duty during such leave.

[4] The Local-Concern Doctrine and Seamen

The classical local-concern or maritime-but-local doctrine is that, notwithstanding the maritime nature of a tort resulting in injury or death of an employee, local rather than maritime law may constitutionally apply when the activity of the employee and the vessel on which he or she was employed is a mere matter of local concern, and when the application of local law would not work material prejudice to the characteristic features of the general maritime law or interfere with the former harmony and uniformity of the law in its international and interstate relations.[82]

The local-concern doctrine appears to have lost all vitality when the competition is between the Longshore Act and state acts. When we turn to conflicts issues between the Jones Act and state acts, once again the relevance of the local-concern doctrine has been sharply constricted, this time by the fact that the doctrine is of no importance when the case arises as an affirmative Jones Act claim. The outer boundaries of the Jones Act, as shown by the cases discussed in this section, have been almost entirely fixed by asking, not the constitutional question, "does this invade the local-concern area?" but the statutory question, "does this invade an area where the water is not navigable, or the craft is not a vessel, or the worker was not a seaman or crew member, or the seaman was not in the course of his employment?"

This, however, leaves one remaining area — that of affirmative claims under state acts, resisted on the ground that they invade the exclusive providence of federal seamen's remedies. In this category, there have been a number of cases holding that the doctrine of local concern sustained the applicability of state workers' compensation laws.[83] There can also be found cases holding that the state claim was barred by the exclusiveness of the federal remedy, since the situation was not local enough to fall within the local-concern exception.[84]

[5] Possible Jones Act Twilight Zone

Between the Longshore Act and a state compensation act the worst that can happen to a claimant is that he or she might get the lesser of two benefit scales. But if a gap is left between the Jones Act and state compensation acts, the claimant may get nothing.

The Fifth Circuit has met this issue head-on and held that the twilight-zone treatment can be applied to the borderland between the Jones Act and a state compensation act. In *Maryland Casualty Company v. Toups*,[85] the decedent was the captain and crew of a 46-foot vessel which he used to carry pilots out to sea-going ships. While sitting on a dock making fenders for use on his boat, he fell into the water and

---

[82] Alaska Packers Ass'n v. Alaska Indus. Bd., 88 F. Supp. 172 (D. Alaska 1950), *aff'd*, 186 F.2d 1015 (9th Cir. 1951).

[83] Cordova Fish & Cold Storage Co. v. Estes, 370 P.2d 180 (Alaska 1962), involving a crab fisherman injured while moving pots on a boat deck.

[84] *See, e.g.*, Valley Towing Co. v. Allen, 236 Miss. 51, 109 So. 2d 538 (1959).

[85] Maryland Casualty Company v. Toups, 172 F.2d 542 (5th Cir. 1949).

was drowned. His widow sought compensation under the Texas act, and the court held that the state act could be applied. The court stressed that the widow, if left to seamen's remedies, would have received nothing: There was no negligence on which to base a Jones Act suit, and the remedy of maintenance and cure does not arise in death cases. The court's reasoning is exactly that of the state-versus-longshore cases. It said that the accident was a matter of local concern, and that to afford compensation protection would not interfere with the uniformity of the maritime law. It conceded that if there had been negligence a Jones Act suit could have been brought, but concluded that since no such remedy was actually available on the present facts, the compensation remedy should be provided.

Theoretically, there are two possible impediments to a twilight-zone doctrine for state-Jones Act areas of overlap. The first is constitutional: the concept of maintaining the uniformity of maritime law. The short answer is that the entire rationale of *Davis* in creating the twilight zone in the first place is just as applicable to the Jones Act as to the Longshore Act. The constitutional problem is the same, and both have to do with the constitutional concept of uniformity of maritime law.

The other impediment is statutory: the argument that by passing the Jones Act the Congress has preempted the area so covered, thus excluding state remedies from that area *even if they are merely of local concern.* This is the more difficult problem. But everything points to the fact the Congress was bent on increasing the remedies available to injured seamen, not cutting them down. The Jones Act itself was passed with the object of getting rid of the fellow-servant defense in suits by the employee against his employer. Moreover, in passing the Jones Act the Congress did not displace other nonfault seamen's remedies for maintenance and cure and for unseaworthiness.[86]

As to the Longshore Act and the Jones Act, however, it is quite clear that, in any substantive sense, there can be no twilight zone between them, since the latter expressly and intentionally draws a sharp, hard line between the two by use of the "master or member of a crew" test.[87]

[6] Successive Awards Involving Jones Act

The successive-award or successive-recovery problem could occur in connection with the Jones Act in four permutations: Longshore Act followed by Jones Act; state compensation act followed by Jones Act; Jones Act followed by Longshore Act; and Jones Act followed by state compensation act.

It can be taken as universally accepted that the mere acceptance of compensation payments will not bar a Jones Act suit.[88] The compensation benefits are of course credited on the Jones Act recovery.[89]

If the claimant actively claimed compensation benefits, a new possible legal argument is added — election of remedies. Here again, however, a substantial majority of the cases hold that the claiming of compensation benefits does not in itself bar a subsequent Jones Act suit, whether or not followed by acceptance of some benefits.[90]

When the compensation process has gone beyond acceptance of benefits and even beyond the filing of a claim to the point at which a formal award has been entered, a far more formidable defense looms: that of res adjudicata or collateral estoppel. Most of the cases that have found it unnecessary to apply the bar in longshore cases have reached this result, not by attacking the applicability of res adjudicata in this context

---

[86] Panama R.R. v. Johnson, 264 U.S. 375, 44 S. Ct. 391, 68 L. Ed. 748 (1924).

[87] Norton v. Warner Co., 321 U.S. 560, at p. 569, footnote 3, 64 S. Ct. 747, 88 L. Ed. 430 (1944).

[88] Tipton v. Socony Mobil Co., 375 U.S. 34, 84 S. Ct. 1, L. Ed. 2d 4 (1963).

[89] Williams v. Offshore Co., 216 F. Supp. 98 (E.D. La. 1963).

[90] Harney v. William M. Moore Bldg. Corp., 359 F.2d 649 (2d Cir. 1966).

head-on, but by finding that for some reason the facts fall short of full compliance with the exacting requisites of the doctrine. For example, there is authority for the view that an award is not res adjudicata if the compensation tribunal's finding and award do not disclose that the crew member issue was put in issue and directly ruled upon in support of the tribunal's jurisdiction.[91]

Since recoveries under the Jones Act are typically more generous than those under compensation acts, the successive-award problem is seldom encountered in the sequence of a Jones Act recovery followed by a compensation claim. However, when the Jones Act suit has been unsuccessful, and the claimant then turns to the Longshore Act or a state compensation act, controversy may arise as to whether the first attempt has in any way prejudiced or barred the second. In such a situation, everything depends on the question: *Why* was the prior Jones Act suit unsuccessful? If it failed because the plaintiff was found not to be a seaman, this finding — far from hurting the compensation claim — would actually support it. But if the Jones Act suit failed for reasons having more to do with the merits, then the defenses of election and res judicata might well come into play.

§ 32.08 CONFLICTS INVOLVING THE FELA

The Federal Employers' Liability Act[92] (FELA) is not a workers' compensation act. It gives employees of interstate rail carriers an action in negligence against their employers, free of the fellow servant and assumption of risk defenses, and with comparative negligence put in place of common-law contributory negligence.

The line between federal remedies under FELA and the state compensation acts has been drawn not on the basis of the limits of federal constitutional power but on the basis of the extent to which Congress has, by the express language of the FELA, occupied the field and thereby excluded the states therefrom. All interstate railway employees any part of whose duties further or substantially affect interstate commerce are entitled to the benefits of the FELA. Since, for an employee who has some duties affecting interstate commerce, this removes the necessity of showing that the activity at the moment of injury was related to interstate commerce, and since the concept of "affecting interstate commerce" has been broadened to include auxiliary, maintenance and supply activities over an extremely wide area, the FELA comes very near to covering all employees of such interstate railways.

Other interstate carriers, however, such as motor and air lines, remain proper subjects for state legislation, since the federal government has for the most part made no attempt to legislate as to work injuries in such employments.

As to FELA-LHWCA conflicts, in *Pennsylvania R.R. v. O'Rourke* [93] the United States Supreme Court held that the occurrence of the injury on navigable waters was the sole criterion. Thus, a railroad brakeman who worked on a flat car situated on a car float on navigable water could not maintain suit under the FELA or the Safety Appliance Act, since his exclusive remedy was under the Longshore Act. This rule probably continues to apply despite amendments to the LHWCA that were generally thought to have overruled *O'Rourke*.[94]

---

[91] Mike Hooks, Inc. v. Pena, 313 F.2d 696 (5th Cir. 1963).

[92] Act of April 22, 1908, 35 Stat. 65 (1909), 45 U.S.C. §§ 51–59, as amended by the Act of April 5, 1910, 36 Stat. 291 (1910), 45 U.S.C. §§ 56, 59, and the Act of August 11, 1939, 53 Stat. 1404 (1939), 45 U.S.C. §§ 51, 54, 56, 60 (1964).

[93] Pennsylvania R.R. v. O'Rourke, 344 U.S. 334, 73 S. Ct. 302, 97 L. Ed. 377 (1953).

[94] *See* Director, Office of Workers' Comp. Programs (Churchill) v. Perini North Rivers Assocs., 103 S.Ct. 634 (1983) (dictum).

Chapter 33
INSURANCE

§ 33.01 THE SEMI-PUBLIC NATURE OF COMPENSATION INSURANCE

[1] Introduction

Since compensation insurance is for the benefit of the employee as well as of the employer, some of the usual incidents of insurance are modified for the employee's protection. Defenses, such as non-payment of premium or breach of policy conditions, which the insurer might have against the employer, are not available against the employee. Moreover, under many statutes a policy cannot be cancelled merely by action of the insurer, the employer or both; notice to the compensation commission is ordinarily required, followed by an interval in which replacement of the insurance can be effected. The compensation commission has jurisdiction to pass upon questions of compensation insurance when they affect the rights of the employee, while questions purely between the insurer and insured may remain within the jurisdiction of the courts.

[2] Methods of Securing Liability

All states require that compensation liability be secured. There are three methods of securing compensation liability: private insurance, "self-insurance" and insurance in state funds. Several states require insurance in exclusive state funds.[1] Over a dozen states have competitive state funds.[2] Self-insurance is permitted in most states.

The strictness of standards for self-insurance varies widely from state to state. In some, it is sufficient to give evidence of general financial responsibility; in others the posting of security or filing of a surety bond is required; and in some the present value of an installment award must be furnished at the time of the award.

Most of the special measures applied to self-insurance are, of course, designed to forestall the possibility that a claimant might lose compensation protection due to the employer's bankruptcy. For many years, this was not a major problem. But in the early 1980s the number of business failures was rising markedly, and early in 1982 eleven major self-insurers went into bankruptcy, occasioning reexamination of the adequacy of existing safeguards against the loss of the worker's compensation protection.

If there is no special back-up fund or even security deposit, the compensation claimant is relegated to the same status as any other creditor in bankruptcy.[3]

About one-fourth of the states have some kind of fund arrangement to pay claims against insolvent self-insurers. Four — Michigan, Maine, Mississippi, and Oregon — have a pre-assessment fund, which is built up by annual assessments to provide in advance a fund to pay such claims. Four states — Alabama, Florida, New York, and Wisconsin — have a post-assessment fund, which imposes assessments retroactively to cover insolvencies after they occur. In three state fund states — Nevada and Washington, which are monopolistic, and Arizona, which is competitive — the state fund pays unpaid claims against insolvent self-insurers. And in three other states — Connecticut, Hawaii, and Minnesota — such unpaid claims are handled through a fund supported by assessments against both self-insurers and insurers.

[3] Inapplicability to Employee of Insurer's Defenses Against Employer

The distinctive feature of compensation insurance is that, although it arises from a contract between the employer and the carrier, it creates a sort of insured status in the employee which comes to have virtually an independent existence. The insurance carrier stands in two relations: to the employer, to protect it from the burden of its compensation liability, and to the employee, to ensure that the employee gets the benefits called for by the statute. The former relation is governed largely by the insurance contract; the latter is governed by the statute.

As between the insurer and the employee, then, defenses based upon the misconduct or omissions of the employer are of no relevance.[4] Fraudulent statements by the employer preceding and inducing the issuance of the policy are no defenses against the employee,[5] nor does failure by the employer to report all of claimant's wages for compensation premium purposes affect claimant's right to full benefits.[6] Even non-payment of premiums by the employer does not of itself entitle the carrier to deny

---

[1] *E.g.*, Nevada, Ohio, and Washington.

[2] *E.g.*, California, Michigan, and New York.

[3] Crum v. Dependents of Reed, 241 Miss. 111, 129 So. 2d 375 (1961).

[4] This rule is incorporated in the statutes of several states, including for example Pennsylvania and Wisconsin.

[5] Aioss v. Sardo, 249 N.Y. 270, 164 N.E. 48 (1928).

[6] Goal Operators Cas. Co. v. Richardson, 414 S.W.2d 735 (Tex. Civ. App. 1967).

liability to the employee.[7] The independence of the insurer's liability to the employees is also seen in the fact that, once it is established that the carrier was on the risk at the time of the injury, the carrier is liable even if the employer corporation has dissolved and gone out of business before the claim is made or heard.[8]

Insurance can, however, be defeated for all purposes by act of the employer if the insurance is absolutely void *ab initio*, rather than voidable. This would occur for example if the employer attempted to insure against an accident that had already occurred, by pre-dating the insurance and fraudulently concealing the known existence of an accident within the period so covered.[9]

[4] Cancellation and Expiration

In view of the essential role of insurance in the compensation process, and the serious potential effects of non-insurance on both employer and employee, requirements for cancellation of insurance are generally exacting, and are strictly construed and applied.[10]

Compensation statutes often provide that the cancellation of a policy, whether by unilateral act of one of the parties or by agreement of both, does not become effective in the absence of notice to the compensation commission plus sometimes either the approval of the commission or the lapse of a specified interval of time in which provision may be made for replacement of the insurance. Under such statutes, when the insurer cancels and the insured immediately procures other insurance, if an accident occurs before the lapse of the statutory period after notice to the commission, the cancelling insurer does not remain liable along with the new insurer; the replacement insurer becomes solely liable.[11] If the policy simply expires because of the completion of the fixed term of duration, the question may arise whether the insurer has a duty to inform the insured or the commission of the expiration, at the risk of having the policy remain in force if it does not. This duty has been found in the circumstances of some cases.[12]

[5] Jurisdiction of Insurance Questions

The general rule appears to be that, when it is ancillary to the determination of the employee's rights, the compensation commission has authority to pass upon a question relating to the insurance policy, including fraud in procurement, mistake of the parties, reformation of the policy, cancellation, existence or validity of an insurance contract, coverage of the policy at the time of injury, and construction of extent of coverage. This is, of course, in harmony with the conception of compensation insurance as being something more than an independent contractual matter between insurer and insured.

On the other hand, when the rights of the employee in a pending claim are not at stake, many commissions disavow jurisdiction and send the parties to the courts for relief. This may occur when the question is purely one between two insurers,[13] or when the insured and insurer have some dispute entirely between themselves about the validity or coverage of the policy.[14]

---

[7] Home Life & Acc. Co. v. Orchard, 227 S.W. 705 (Tex. Civ. App. 1921).

[8] Metropolitan Cas. Ins. Co. v. Industrial Comm'n, 260 Wis. 298, 50 N.W.2d 399 (1951).

[9] Century Indem. Co. v. Jameson, 333 Mass. 503, 131 N.E.2d 767 (1956).

[10] *E.g.*, Pressman v. State Acc. Fund, 246 Md. 406, 228 A.2d 443 (1967).

[11] Security Ins. Co. v. Wisconsin Dep't of Industry, Labor & Human Relations, 69 Wis. 746, 233 N.W.2d 386 (1975).

[12] *E.g.*, Ebert v. Fort Pierre Moose Lodge #1813, 312 N.W.2d 119 (S.D. 1981).

[13] *E.g.*, U.S. Fid. & Guar. Co. v. Collins, 231 Miss. 319, 95 So. 2d 456 (1957).

[14] *E.g.*, United States Fid. & Guar. Co. v. Town of West Warwick, 379 A.2d 924 (R.I. 1977).

ROVIRA v. LAGODA, INC.
551 So. 2d 790 (La. Ct. App. 1989)

CHEHARDY, CHIEF JUDGE.

The worker's compensation insurer refused to defend the insured employer on a wrongful discharge claim. The district court awarded the employer attorney's fees but denied its claim against the insurer for indemnification. The insurer appeals the award, the insured answers seeking an increase. With slight amendment, we affirm the district court judgment.

FACTS

LaGoDa, Inc., is a heating and air-conditioning service and installation business. On December 29, 1986, plaintiff, Donald Rovira, experienced an on-the-job back injury while employed with LaGoDa. He claimed and collected worker's compensation benefits for six weeks' disability. Rovira returned to work on February 16, 1987 and three days later he was dismissed from his job.

Rovira brought suit against LaGoDa and its officers, Larry and Mary Bolner, seeking damages for wrongful discharge. Plaintiff alleged that he had been fired without just cause or for filing a worker's compensation claim. LaGoDa answered the petition, responding that Rovira had been discharged for cause because he had falsified his employment application, had damaged his employer's and customer's property, and for overall unsatisfactory job performance. By third-party demand, LaGoDa sought indemnity and costs of defense from its insurer, National Fire Insurance Company of Hartford, on the basis of its worker's compensation/employer's liability policy. National Fire answered, denying that Rovira's claims were covered under its policy.

Rovira amended his petition to name National Fire and claimed that the insurer was liable for LaGoDa's wrongfully discharging him. National Fire again denied coverage and claimed indemnity from LaGoDa for any sums that it might be required to pay plaintiff.

Rovira settled his claim against LaGoDa for $1,500 and dismissed the corporation as a defendant in suit. Larry and Mary Bolner were dismissed on exception. After trial the district court granted judgment in favor of National Fire against plaintiff on the main demand, finding that Rovira had not proved his claim for damages for retaliatory discharge against the insurer. Consequently the judge dismissed National Fire's third-party demand against LaGoDa as moot. On LaGoDa's third-party demand, the court granted judgment against National Fire and awarded LaGoDa $4,366.70 in attorney's fees, plus costs and interest.

National Fire appeals the fee award, arguing that because the policy issued to LaGoDa excluded coverage for Rovira's claim of retaliatory discharge, the district court acted erroneously in awarding attorney's fees. Alternatively, appellant contends that the fee award is excessive in that it includes charges unrelated to LaGoDa's defense against Rovira's claim. LaGoDa answers the appeal and seeks recovery of the $1,500 it paid in settlement of the wrongful discharge claim. Appellee prays for an additional $5,000 in fees for conduct of the trial and appeal.

DUTY TO DEFEND

National Fire argues in brief that it properly refused to defend the suit because the compensation policy issued to LaGoDa excluded coverage for Rovira's claims. The jurisprudence dictates that the onus of an incorrect denial of coverage lies with the insurer.

The insurer's duty to defend a suit brought against its insured is determined by the allegations of the plaintiff's petition. The insurer is obligated to furnish a defense unless the petition unambiguously and absolutely excludes coverage. *American Home Assurance Company v. Czarniecki*, 255 La. 251, 230 So. 2d 253 (La. 1969), *Cute-Togs of N. O. v. La. Health Ser., Etc.*, 386 So. 2d 87 (La. 1980). If the allegations made against the insured, taken as true, would result in liability on the part of the insured that is unambiguously not covered by the policy, then the insurer has no duty to defend. Otherwise the insurer must provide a defense for its insured regardless of the final outcome of the underlying suit. *Bourque v. Lehmann Lathe, Inc.*, 476 So. 2d 1129 (La. App. 3 Cir. 1985).

An interpretation of coverage under the policy is favored by law. Exclusions are read strictly in favor of the insured. Where more than one interpretation of an exclusion is reasonable, that affording coverage is adopted. Any limitation on coverage must be clear and express so as to inform the insured that it must take special measures to obtain other protection. *Hebert v. First American Ins. Co.*, 461 So. 2d 1141 (La. App. 5 Cir. 1984). Where the pleadings allege coverage, even though in fact there is no coverage, the insurer may be cast for the insured's expenses in defending the suit. *Hanover Ins. Co. v. Highlands Ins. Co.*, 511 So. 2d 1296 (La. App. 2 Cir. 1987).

In petition Rovira claimed that LaGoDa had discharged him without just cause. Alternatively, plaintiff contended that he was fired in violation of LSA-R.S. 23:1361, which imposes a civil penalty against an employer who is found to have discharged an employee for asserting a worker's compensation claim. National Fire based its refusal to defend on policy language which holds the insured responsible for payment due an employee discharged in violation of the compensation law.

The district court found that LaGoDa had proved its third-party demand. That is, it found that National Fire should have defended LaGoDa against Rovira's claims, and so awarded defense costs. This ruling presupposes a finding that the policy in question did not unambiguously exclude coverage for Rovira's claims. We find that the district court was correct in its interpretation of the policy.

National Fire's compensation policy provides:

> Workers Compensation Law means the workers or workmen's compensation law and occupational disease law of each state or territory named in item 3.A. of the Information Page. It includes any amendments to that law which are in effect during the policy period. It does not include the provisions of any law that provide nonoccupational disability benefits.
>
> . . . Terms of this insurance that conflict with the workers compensation law are changed by this statement to conform to that law.
>
> . . . We will pay promptly when due the benefits required of you by the workers compensation law.

We have the right and duty to defend at our expense any claim, proceeding or suit against you for benefits payable by this insurance. We have the right to investigate and settle these claims, proceedings or suits.

The provisions on which National Fire relied in denying coverage state:

> Payments You Must Make. You are responsible for any payments in excess of the benefits regularly provided by the workers compensation law including those required because:
>
> 1. of your serious and willful misconduct
>
> . . . 4. you discharge, coerce or otherwise discriminate against any employee in violation of the workers compensation law.

If we make any payments in excess of the benefits regularly provided by the workers compensation law on your behalf, you will reimburse us promptly.

The policy as issued is amended in all respects to comply with the worker's compensation law. Within that confine, the insurer pays benefits due an employee under the law and must defend any claim for those benefits. The insured pays excess benefits due unless the insurer pays them, in which case the insured reimburses it. Neither "benefits" nor "payment" is defined in the policy.

With respect to the petition and the policy, the following conclusions regarding coverage can be drawn. If LaGoDa fired Rovira without just cause, National Fire makes any payment due. If the absence of just cause was the result of LaGoDa's willful misconduct, either the insured makes the payment or it reimburses National Fire for payments made. If LaGoDa fired Rovira in violation of LSA-R.S. 23:1361, and the benefits recoverable by the employee are those due under the compensation law, National Fire pays them. If the benefits due are in excess of those legally provided for, then either LaGoDa pays or National Fire pays and obtains reimbursement from LaGoDa.

That the analysis of the policy provisions is convoluted serves to emphasize our conclusion: National Fire's worker's compensation policy does not unambiguously exclude coverage for Rovira's claims so as to negate the insurer's duty to defend. At the point that LaGoDa was sued and called on National Fire for a defense and coverage, the insured could ultimately have been cast for sums not resulting from retaliatory discharge National Fire had a duty to respond.

Had National Fire intended to write a policy whereby it could divorce itself from responsibility for participation in any employee discharge claim, however frivolous or brought on whatever basis, it had the power to do so. This is not strictly what the policy before us states. The limiting language is not designated as an exclusion so as to alert the insured that National Fire will not respond to any claim of discharge. The policy is ambiguous, therefore the duty to defend existed. *Armstrong v. Land & Marine Applicators*, 463 So. 2d 1327 (La. App. 5 Cir. 1984).

PUBLIC POLICY

National Fire argues that neither the law nor public policy requires insurance coverage for a retaliatory discharge claim. LSA-R.S. 23:1162 provides in part:

> No policy of insurance against liability under this Chapter shall be made unless the policy covers the entire liability of the employer provided, that as to the question of the liability as between the employer and the insurer the terms of the insurance contract shall govern. . . .

National Fire's policy is amended to adopt and to comply with all aspects of the compensation law. Preliminarily, it responds to provide coverage for the entire liability of the employer under this law, including, or at least not precluding, a claim for benefits under LSA-R.S. 23:1361. *Armstrong v. Land & Marine Applicators*, 463 So. 2d 1331 (La. App. 5 Cir. 1984) and see H. Alston Johnson, Workers' Compensation, 47 La. L. Rev. 532 (1987). The statute permits a limitation between the employer (insured) and the insurer, governed by the terms of the contract. As between the employee and the insurer, the former is entitled to full coverage the insurer must respond to any liability of the employer. *Pierson v. Aetna Casualty Surety Company*, 184 So. 2d 572 (La. App. 1 Cir. 1966). Therefore, with respect to Rovira's claims in petition, National Fire responds to any claim against LaGoDa. As between LaGoDa and National Fire, the insurer neglected to provide an unambiguous policy so as to successfully limit its liability.

Appellant cites *Vallier v. Oilfield Const. Co. Inc.*, 483 So. 2d 212 (La. App. 3 Cir. 1986), wherein the Third Circuit held that sums due an employee under LSA-R.S. 23:1361 did not constitute worker's compensation benefits. The court found that the policy did not provide coverage for plaintiff's retaliatory discharge claim under a specific policy exclusion: "[T]he insurance afforded by this endorsement does not cover fines or *penalties* imposed on the insured for failure to comply with the requirements of any workmen's compensation law." (Emphasis in original). While we express no opinion on the conclusion that employee recovery under LSA-R.S. 23:1361 is not a benefit, we do observe that the policy before that court contained a specific and unambiguous exclusion of coverage. When an insurer's liability to its insured is limited, "the terms of the insurance contract shall govern." LSA-R.S. 23:1162. In the case before us, National Fire's policy does not explicitly exclude coverage for Rovira's claims against LaGoDa.

The Employers Liability section of National Fire's policy responds to employer liability not covered by the worker's compensation act. Appleman, Insurance Law and Practice (Berdal ed.) § 4571. These are employee claims brought under the theory of maritime tort. The section is not applicable to our coverage inquiry.

ATTORNEY'S FEES

National Fire alternatively contends that if the imposition of the fee award is affirmed, the amount of the award is excessive and should be reduced. Appellant argues that LaGoDa should not recover either defense fees it incurred before notifying National Fire of Rovira's pending claim, or fees charged for other than the defense of Rovira's claim. In answer to appeal, LaGoDa seeks an increase in the fee award to include fees incurred in the trial and appeal of the suit. None of the arguments set forth in brief support a change in the district court judgment.

The duty to defend arises when the insurer receives notice of the litigation. Delayed notice of a claim relieves the insurer of the obligation if it was actually prejudiced by the delay. *Gully & Associates v. Wausau Ins.*, 536 So. 2d 816 (La. App. 1 Cir. 1988). National Fire has not shown that it was prejudiced by the 20-day lapse between Rovira's filing of suit and LaGoDa's notice of claim and request for defense. The attorney's fees that LaGoDa incurred during this time are recoverable.

National Fire argues that LaGoDa's recovery is limited to fees incurred in its own defense against the wrongful discharge claim and that recovery of fees accumulated in defending the Bolners and in prosecuting the demand for defense should be disallowed and deducted from the award. Appellant's reasoning is unpersuasive.

At trial, LaGoDa introduced four invoices reflecting professional services rendered by its attorney in defending against Rovira's claim. National Fire provided no testimony or evidence to refute the validity of the invoices, to contradict the value of the services or to rebut the contention that the fees were costs of defending the wrongful discharge claim. In this court, National Fire offers no proof that the fees are excessive. Instead, it points to isolated descriptions of services and makes vague and conclusory arguments that the services are not defense-based. The evidence that National Fire does submit copies of the invoices, bears no indication of the attorney's hourly rate charge or the number of hours he expended in defending LaGoDa.

Appellee, conversely, seeks an equitable increase in the fee award to offset its trial and appeal costs. Aside from raising the issue it offers no factual basis for an increase in the award.

Finding that National Fire had breached its defense duties, the district court awarded LaGoDa attorney's fees of $4,366.70. Considering the nature and circumstances of the principle demand, we cannot say that the award is unjust, unreasonable or erroneous. *Turner v. Winn Dixie Louisiana, Inc.*, 474 So. 2d 966 (La. App. 5 Cir. 1985) *Little v. Kalo Laboratories, Inc.*, 424 So. 2d 1065 (La. App. 2 Cir. 1982). Our independent review of the record convinces us that the sum awarded compensates LaGoDa in a more-than-adequate fashion. The district court award of attorney's fees in favor of LaGoDa is affirmed. Appellee is not entitled to recover an additional fee award. LSA-C.C.P. art. 2164.

INDEMNIFICATION

By answer to appeal LaGoDa seeks recovery of the $1,500 it paid to Rovira in settlement of the retaliatory discharge claim. The district court denied indemnification we agree.

Appellee does not cite any jurisprudence that specifically supports its recovery of the settlement sum. Where a claim is based on a written contract of indemnity or insurance, the indemnitee must show potential, rather than actual, liability on his part in order to recover from the indemnitor. *Terra Resources, Inc. v. Lake Charles Dredging & Towing Inc.*, 695 F.2d 828 (5th Cir. 1983).

LaGoDa denied liability to Rovira in its answer and third-party demand. It compromised the wrongful discharge claim with plaintiff for what it characterizes in brief as a nuisance value settlement confected primarily to halt the accrual of additional defense costs rather than to avoid the imposition of an adverse liability judgment. At trial LaGoDa's participation was confined to proof of its entitlement to defense costs. Counsel elicited testimony from the Bolners indicating that they had notified National Fire of Rovira's claim, had requested that the insurer defend the suit, and had, at least at the outset, been advised that coverage existed under the policy. Third-party plaintiff did not introduce evidence of its potential liability to Rovira for retaliatory discharge.

It is apparent that, in denying indemnification, the district court found that LaGoDa had not proved its potential liability on which to found such recovery. We agree. We also note that there has been no definitive finding that coverage under the policy exists. LaGoDa, therefore, cannot obtain reimbursement of the settlement sum on the basis that it paid a covered claim.

PENALTIES

LaGoDa did not pray for the assessment of penalties in its answer to appeal. It raises this request in brief, citing LSA-R.S. 22:658. We read the statute as allowing for the imposition of penalties against an insurer for failure to pay benefits after satisfactory proof of loss. There has been no finding of either benefits due or loss proved. The issue at trial and on appeal is the duty of defense. While *Frederick v. Electro-Coal Transfer Corp.*, 548 F. Supp. 83 (E.D. La. 1982), imposes a penalty for the insurer's failure to defend, the district court in that case found that the insurer's breach of duty was arbitrary and capricious. There has been no such finding against National Fire. LaGoDa is not entitled to an award of penalties.

CONCLUSION

For the above-outlined reasons, the district court award of attorney's fees of $4,366.70 in favor of LaGoDa is affirmed. LaGoDa's plea for increased fees and recovery of indemnification and penalties is denied. The judgment is amended to reflect that interest on the fee award runs from the date of judgment rather than from the date of judicial demand. *Bink v. Blackwell*, 432 So. 2d 296 (La. App. 5 Cir. 1983), *Alexander v. Burroughs Corp.*, 359 So. 2d 607 (La. 1978). Costs are assessed against National Fire Insurance Company of Hartford.

Amended and Affirmed.

[6]   Option to Reject Insurance Application

Since the law requires an employer to insure (or qualify as a self-insurer) before carrying on a covered business, the refusal of insurers to issue a policy to the employer amounts to an effective bar against its carrying on that business in the state. From the insurer's point of view, it is quite understandable that, as far as possible, the good risks will be accepted and the bad ones rejected. On the basis of its experience, a company may adopt a policy of insuring drilling operations, for example, only when the drilling is for water and not when it is for oil. Yet oil drilling is an essential business just as water drilling is, and needs the protection of compensation even more acutely. It is not the function of the compensation system to shut down extra-hazardous operations, but this might well be the result if direct private insurance were left to select its own risks.

A few states at first set out to meet this problem by the forthright device of a statutory requirement that insurers accept all applications for compensation insurance presented by qualified employers.[15] But the more common approach is assigned-risk practice.[16]

In states with competitive state funds it is usually assumed that the fund should solve the undesirable-risk problem by acting as residual legatee of risks that private carriers do not want, although this does not always occur. Monopolistic state funds, however, seem to accept all applications from qualified employers as a matter of routine practice, and the question of their right to reject risks does not appear to have arisen.

The most common approach to the rejected-risk problem is statutory provision for assignment or apportionment of the rejected risk either by action of the industrial commission or rating board,[17] or by voluntary agreement among insurers under administrative supervision.[18]

Such a voluntary agreement constitutes a third-party beneficiary contract which may be enforced by the insured. Each insurer, in consideration of the identical agreement of the others, has agreed to insure the risks assigned to it. The compulsion of this arrangement does not stem from governmental authority, but from the contract itself, and the insured, whose relief was the principal object of the plan, can apply to court for specific enforcement. This kind of policy may not be cancelled by the assigned insurer since cancellation would be a breach of the assigned-risk agreement.

[7] Rate Making

Rate making is now entrusted in practically all states to official rating bureaus established by the states themselves, or to the National Council on Compensation Insurance, which has been licensed as a rating body in most of the remaining states. The National Council, which is made up of hundreds of companies and state funds, and which works closely with the state rating organizations, makes the studies and calculations on which the classification pure premium is based. This figure is designed to represent the premium necessary in a given state to pay the losses in the particular industrial classification, there being something over 600 such classifications. To this is added the expense loading factor, the pure premium representing about seven-tenths and the expense loading about three-tenths of the total. This may then be adjusted for a plant-inspection factor and for an occupational disease factor, to produce the final manual rate. The premium so produced may next be adjusted by an experience or merit rating plan for the industrial risk.

Rate making is an administrative function.[19] Judicial interference is justified only when the rates are discriminatory, unreasonable or confiscatory,[20] or when clear legal errors appear in the rating method adopted.[21]

§ 33.02   CONSTRUCTION OF POLICY COVERAGE

Many statutes expressly provide that compensation insurance contracts shall be construed to cover the entire liability of the assured; some provide that coverage shall be complete as to the named business or named location, including all activities incident to that business; and some contain no specific treatment of the subject. Under the

---

[15] *E.g.*, Tex. Rev. Civ. Stat. Ann., Art. 8308 § 7, Art. 8309 § 1 (1967).

[16] Tex. Rev. Civ. Stat. Ann., Art. 8309, § 2, and Tex. Ins. Code, Art. 5.76.

[17] *See, e.g.*, Arkansas.

[18] *See, e.g.*, New Jersey.

[19] U.S. Wall Paper Co. v. Industrial Comm'n, 132 Ohio St. 372, 7 N.E. 2d 798 (1937).

[20] State v. Hughes Elec. Co., 51 N.D. 45, 199 N.W. 128 (1924).

[21] Wisconsin Comp. Rating & Inspection Bureau v. Mortensen, 227 Wis. 335, 277 N.W. 679 (1938).

"full-coverage" statutes, while the majority rule appears to construe them to require coverage of all employees in all a given employer's businesses, there is some authority for limiting these statutes to full coverage of a particular business, location, or employment category. At the opposite extreme, under statutes having no express provision, it has been held that an employer cannot insure part of its employees in a business and leave others uninsured.[22] Under a broad interpretation of what is the employer's business, or what is incident to its business, the breadth of policy coverage so achieved can be very nearly as great as if there were a full-coverage statute.[23] Some states have taken the attitude that, in the absence of a statute on policy construction, employers can insure all or any part of their risk, with such geographical or other limitations and exclusions as they choose to adopt. Thus, exclusions of particular kinds of activities,[24] kinds of employment,[25] or kinds of employees,[26] have been upheld.

§ 33.03 RIGHTS BETWEEN EMPLOYER AND INSURER

[1] Introduction

As between the employer and insurer, the usual incidents of insurance law apply; thus insurance protection may be forfeited by breaches of policy conditions. The employer by statute is required in some states to bear personally penalties imposed for employment of minors, but in the absence of such a statute, the insurance covers the penalty. As to policy coverage construction, some courts apply their full-coverage statutes and decisions even to the interpretation of the policy as between insurer and insured, when there is any room for construction; but when the parties have inserted a point-blank exclusion clause, the insurer even under a full-coverage statute may, as against the insured, not be liable within the excluded area.

[2] Employer's Breach of Condition

Since the special incidents of compensation insurance law have arisen largely for the benefit of the employee, there is no strong reason why the rights of insurer and insured *inter se* should not be governed by ordinary insurance rules. Thus, if the employer has been guilty of a breach of the policy's notice provision, it may find his action against the insurer for reimbursement of the sum paid to the employee dismissed because of the breach.[27] *A fortiori*, if the breach is one which seriously affects the risk, such as the prohibited use of explosives,[28] the insurer, while it may have to pay the employee, is entitled to reimbursement from the employer.

[3] Insurance Coverage of Penalties

The question whether the employer must bear personally any penalty for illegal employment of a minor has received varied statutory and decisional answers. Some statutes put the penalty on the employer alone.[29] Wisconsin makes the employer

---

[22] *E.g.*, Stoltze's Case, 325 Mass. 692, 92 N.E.2d 260 (1950).

[23] *E.g.*, Employers Mut. Liab. Ins. Co. v. Merrimac Mills Co. 325 Mass. 676, 92 N.E.2d 256 (1950).

[24] National Auto. Ins. Co. v. Industrial Acc. Comm'n, 220 Cal. 642, 32 P.2d 356 (1934) (users of power shovels).

[25] Maryland Cas. Co. v. Industrial Acc. Comm'n, 209 Cal. 394, 287 P. 468 (1930) (illegal employment).

[26] Alperin v. Eagle Indem. Co., 169 Tenn. 215, 84 S.W.2d 101 (1935) (corporate officers).

[27] Wisconsin Michigan Power Co. v. General Cas. & Sur. Co., 252 Mich. 331, 233 N.W. 333 (1930).

[28] Janes Contracting Co. v. Home Life & Acc. Co., 245 S.W. 1004 (Tex. Civ. App. 1922), *aff'd*, 260 S.W. 839 (Tex. Civ. App. 1924).

[29] *E.g.*, Florida, Maryland, New Jersey, and Pennsylvania.

primarily liable and the insurer secondarily liable.[30] But in most jurisdictions having no such provisions, the courts have held that the double compensation or other penalty is merely part of the compensation that the insurer has agreed to pay.[31]

[4] Construing Coverage

When a question of construing policy coverage arises exclusively between insurer and insured, it might be thought that the terms of their contract should be allowed to control. However, if a statute expressly says that the insured's entire liability must be covered, the unqualified language of the statute is broad enough to include issues arising between insured and insurer.[32] Probably the safest generalization is this: If there is room for construction, the statutory or decisional law of the state may be invoked to enlarge the policy's coverage,[33] but if there is no margin for interpretation,[34] the exclusion clause may control between the parties, in which case the insurer, although liable to the employee, will be reimbursed by the employer.

§ 33.04   RIGHTS BETWEEN INSURERS

[1] Introduction

When a disability develops gradually, or when it comes as the result of a succession of accidents, the insurance carrier covering the risk at the time of the most recent injury or exposure bearing a causal relation to the disability is usually liable for the entire compensation. In some jurisdictions apportionment has been worked out by judicial decision, or provided for by express statute, when events within the coverage periods of successive insurers contribute causally to the final disability.

[2] Nature of Successive-Carrier Problem

The successive carrier problem arises when a worker suffers two or more episodes of disability with an intervening change of employers or change of insurance carriers by the same employer. The problem also arises in occupational disease cases when the employer has changed insurers (or the employee has changed jobs) during the period in which the employee was exposed to the disease-causing substance.

As to successive accidental injuries, the cases in which the successive carrier problem arises may be divided into three types — new injuries, aggravations, and recurrences — with the question of which insurer is liable often depending on how the injury is characterized.

[3] Last Injurious Exposure Rule

The "last injurious exposure" rule in successive-injury cases places full liability upon the carrier covering the risk at the time of the most recent injury that bears a causal relation to the disability. This rule is the majority rule in successive insurer cases, either by judicial adoption[35] or by express statutory provision.[36]

---

[30] Wis. Stat. Ann. § 102.62 (1957).

[31] Carmack v. Great Am. Indem. Co., 400 Ill. 93, 78 N.E.2d 507 (1948).

[32] Fidelity & Cas. Co. v. Hill Constr. Co., 11 N.J. Misc. 58, 164 A. 16 (1933).

[33] Employers Ins. Co. v. Lewallen, 293 Ala. 574, 307 So. 2d 689 (1975).

[34] Underwriters at Lloyds v. Munz, 224 F. Supp. 954 (D. Alaska 1963) (the policy clearly excluded piloting aircraft).

[35] *E.g.*, Ketichikan Gateway Borough v. Saling, 604 P.2d 590 (Alaska 1980).

[36] *E.g.*, Mich. Comp. Laws Ann. § 418.435 (Supp. 1983).

If the second injury takes the form merely of a recurrence of the first, and if the second incident does not contribute even slightly to the causation of the disabling condition, the insurer on the risk at the time of the original injury remains liable for the second.[37] This group typically includes the kind of case in which a worker has suffered a back strain, followed by a period of work with continuing symptoms indicating that the original condition persists, and culminating in a second period of disability precipitated by some lift or exertion.[38] The last injurious exposure rule is also utilized in occupational disease cases.[39]

Traditionally, courts applying the last injurious exposure rule have not gone on past the original finding of some exposure to weigh the relative amount or duration of exposure under various carriers and employers. As long as there was some exposure of a kind which could have caused the disease, the last insurer at risk is liable for all disability from that disease. Thus, insurers or employers who have been at risk for relatively brief periods have nevertheless been charged with full liability for a condition that could only have developed over a number of years.[40]

In contrast to this traditional rule, however, are decisions such as that in *Busse v. Quality Insulation*,[41] in which the Minnesota Supreme Court took notice of medical testimony to the effect that there is a "lag time" of five to ten years between exposure to asbestos and the development of asbestosis. The court accepted this testimony in support of a conclusion that the claimant's exposure under the last insurer, who had been at risk for only two months, was not a "substantial contributing cause" of his death. Other courts have also held that in order to impose liability on the insurer who was last at risk, the exposure during its period of risk must have been of such length or degree that it could have *actually* caused the disease.[42]

[4] Apportionment Between Insurers

The harshness of the last-exposure rule requiring that a single insurer assume the entire cost of any single injury has been tempered in some jurisdictions by a practice permitting apportionment between two carriers when two successive incidents combine to produce the final disability. The leading case establishing this practice is the *Anderson* case,[43] decided by the New York Court of Appeals in 1931. Claimant had fractured his hip in 1926. Later in 1927, when he was working for a different employer with a different carrier, he felt something crack in his hip while he was helping four or five other men lift a timber weighing about a thousand pounds. The court held that the compensation should be equally apportioned between the two insurers. However, it remarked that this kind of apportionment rule applies only when a question of sharing liability between successive carriers is involved. It does not alter the well-established rule that in all other cases an insurer is fully liable for the disability resulting from aggravation of a preexisting weakness, when that weakness itself does not constitute an actual disability.

Several statutes which place initial liability, so far as the employee is concerned, upon the employer who provided the last occupational disease injurious exposure,

[37] Willette v. Statler Tissue Corp., 331 A.2d 365 (Me. 1975).

[38] St. Paul Fire & Marine Ins. Co. v. Hughes, 125 Ga. App. 328, 187 S.E.2d 551 (1972).

[39] *E.g.*, Todd Shipyards Corp. v. Black, 706 F.2d 1512 (9th Cir. 1983).

[40] *E.g.*, Climax Uranium Co. v. Smith, 33 Colo. App. 337, 522 P.2d 134 (1974).

[41] Busse v. Quality Insulation, 322 N.W.2d 206 (Minn. 1982).

[42] *E.g.*, Fluor Alaska, Inc. v. Peter Kiewit Sons' Co., 614 P.2d 310 (Alaska 1980).

[43] Anderson v. Babcock & Wilcox Co., 256 N.Y. 146, 175 N.E. 654 (1931).

follow this provision with a procedure whereby liability may be apportioned among previous employers whose employments have contributed.[44]

---

[44] *See, e.g.*, Me. Rev. Stat. 39-A, § 354; R. I. Gen. Laws § 28-34-8.

Chapter 34

RELATION TO OTHER KINDS OF WAGE-LOSS PROTECTION

SYNOPSIS

§ 34.01   COMPENSATION AS PART OF GENERAL WAGE-LOSS SYSTEM

[1]   Comprehensiveness of American System

It is customary to assume that the United States has nothing in the way of social legislation approximating the comprehensive national programs in force in England, New Zealand, Australia and many continental countries. This inclination to underestimate the degree to which comprehensive coverage has been attained here may be due to two causes: one is the failure to realize that workers' compensation is part of the general social security system — in fact, the parent and precursor of all such legislation; the other is failure to appreciate the cumulative effect of separate items of security legislation during the past decades, including federal and state legislation on non-occupational sickness and disability.

The objective of a "comprehensive social insurance system" is to protect the breadwinner and any dependents from all the major exigencies of life which interfere with earning capacity, and at the same time to help that breadwinner bear accompanying extraordinary expenses for which the average person is presumed to be unprepared. This means that the system is aimed usually at two things: wage loss, and accompanying hospital, medical and funeral expense.

The two great exigencies that interrupt earning power are loss of physical capacity to work, and loss of economic opportunity to work. Three major categories of wage loss stem from these two misfortunes:

    (a) Physical injury, illness or death (which involves the factor of physical capacity only);

    (b) Unemployment (which involves the economic factor only);

(c) Old age and retirement (which usually involves a combination of both, i.e., an economic policy or practice destroying opportunity to work, based on a sort of presumed, but often not actual, physical incapacity after a certain age).

[2] Death and Dependency Coverage

As to death, and resulting dependency, the coverage is virtually complete when the cause is industrial, under the workers' compensation acts of the various states. When death occurs from non-industrial or natural causes, the federal Social Security[1] system provides benefits for all persons who, under the theory of the legislation, are and will remain dependent. That is, surviving spouses over 62 and surviving spouses who have dependent children in their care, as well as the dependent children themselves, receive benefits. Apparently young and middle-aged surviving spouses without dependent children are presumed to be able to look after themselves. It is interesting to note that even the British system, which is supposed to be a model of comprehensiveness, makes the same assumption and withholds benefits from widows under somewhat similar, although more restricted, circumstances. The coverage of the Social Security system is thus somewhat narrower than that of the typical workers' compensation act, which places no such age limitations on widows as beneficiaries.

[3] Injury and Illness Coverage

As to injury and illness: again coverage is in principle complete, under compensation acts, when the disability has an occupational origin. When we come to non-occupational disability and sickness, however, we encounter the principal area in which American coverage is conspicuously incomplete. Only a few states[2] have disability benefit laws. Even where these laws exist, they provide only short-term benefits and do not pay hospital and medical expenses.

As to long-term disability, the federal Social Security system pays benefits to disabled workers whose disabilities satisfy the test of inability to engage in any substantial gainful activity by reason of any medically determinable physical or mental impairment which can be expected to result in death or which has lasted or can be expected to last for a continuous period of not less than twelve months.

[4] Unemployment Coverage

As to unemployment, every state has an unemployment compensation act, but no act aspires to do more than tide the worker over temporary periods of unemployment, nine months being the longest possible benefit period. So we see one more chink in the worker's defensive armor against wage loss — long-term unemployment. But once more we also see that the criterion by which we are judging the completeness of our system, namely the British comprehensive scheme, contains the same deficiency, since unemployment insurance benefits there are normally limited to 180 days.

[5] Old-Age Coverage

As to old age and retirement: The Old Age and Survivors' Insurance system may be regarded as a thorough treatment of this category of wage loss. About nine out of ten jobs are covered under social security or the railroad retirement system, which is coordinated with social security. More than half of the rest are under various government employee systems. The uncovered jobs, about four percent of the labor

---

[1] 42 U.S.C. § 402.

[2] *E.g.*, California, New York, and Rhode Island.

force, are accounted for mainly by jobs in which people do not work long enough or earn enough to meet the minimum requirements for coverage during a particular year or calendar quarter.

[6] Hospital, Medical, and Funeral Expenses

In many other countries, there are included within the term "social security" programs that do not depend on the occurrence of wage loss at all, such as systems paying family allowances for children, or hospital and medical benefits for all, even in times of full earnings. For the most part, however, the American social insurance pattern has concentrated on income: if it is not interrupted, the worker is presumed to be able to pay his or her bills, including child support and medical expenses; if it is interrupted, the remedy is replacement of a portion of the income, with the worker or the worker's dependents once more presumed to be able to "take it from there."

An exception to this limitation occurs when the same event that produces income loss also typically produces a substantial special extra expense. In that case the system should also pay that extra expense. The clearest example is the payment of medical and hospital expenses under workers' compensation. The practical rationale for this exception to strict preoccupation with income replacement is that, if the extra accompanying expense is not paid, it will often eat up the income benefits themselves, and the whole purpose of the system will be defeated. A less important but equally relevant example is the payment of funeral expenses by both workers' compensation and social security.

Applying this same principle to medicare, hospital expenses of the aged are characteristically much greater than those of younger persons — twice or perhaps even three times as great, depending on the age groups compared. Unless the exaggerated hospital costs attending old age are paid by the system, the income benefits may themselves be consumed by these costs.

The obvious gap in the system is the omission of medicare for the disabled under social security. Disability of the gravity required to satisfy the social security test would ordinarily be accompanied by hospital and medical expenses. And yet, at this writing, medicare for the disabled has not been provided, although in principle a stronger case can be made for it than in the case of the elderly.

§ 34.02 IMPROPRIETY OF DUPLICATE WAGE-LOSS BENEFITS

Once it is recognized that workers' compensation is one unit in an overall system of wage-loss protection, rather than something resembling a recovery in tort or on a private accident policy, the conclusion follows that duplication of benefits from different parts of the system should not ordinarily be allowed.

Wage-loss legislation is designed to restore to the worker a portion, such as one-half to two-thirds, of wages lost due to the three major causes of wage-loss: physical disability, economic unemployment, and old age. The crucial operative fact is that of wage loss; the cause of the wage loss merely dictates the category of legislation applicable. If a worker undergoes a period of wage loss due to all three conditions, it does not follow that he or she should receive three sets of benefits simultaneously and thereby recover more than actual wages. The worker is experiencing only one wage loss and, in any logical system, should receive only one wage-loss benefit. The same is clearly true for medical expense or cost.

§ 34.03   COORDINATION WITH UNEMPLOYMENT COMPENSATION

The jerry-built character of American social legislation has resulted at many points in failure to anticipate and provide for appropriate coordination. Thus, several jurisdictions have permitted collection of both unemployment and workers' compensation benefits for the same period, in the absence of any statutory prohibition. The majority of unemployment statutes, however, now specifically forbid benefits to anyone drawing workers' compensation. These statutes vary in scope, some applying only to temporary workers' compensation payments and some to temporary and permanent; many make an exception of schedule benefits. Several compensation acts have recently added an offset for unemployment insurance benefits.[3]

But the original workers' compensation laws, having had no preexisting social legislation to coordinate with at the time of their enactment, usually contain no such specific provision. When, therefore, the worker collects unemployment compensation first, under an unemployment act forbidding such benefits if workers' compensation is being received or is about to be received, and later applies for workers' compensation for the same period, the court is confronted with an awkward problem: The obvious legislative intention is to prevent dual benefits, but the specific act before the court — the workers' compensation act — contains no authorization for reduction of benefits on this ground. The Supreme Judicial Court of Massachusetts, in dealing with this exact question, has read the restriction of the unemployment act into the compensation act, and held that one who has recovered unemployment benefits cannot later recover workers' compensation benefits.[4]

§ 34.04   COORDINATING WITH FEDERAL PENSION AND DISABILITY SYSTEMS

[1]   The Social Security Offset for Compensation

The coordination of workers' compensation with the federal social security system takes the form principally of the offset provision in the federal act, although offset provisions in a growing number of state acts must also be noted.

The present social security offset provision states that the social security disability benefit for any month shall be reduced to the point where the combined social security and periodic workers' compensation benefit does not exceed 80 percent of the individual's average current earnings.[5]

Late in 1971, the United States Supreme Court held the offset constitutional.[6] Of the various grounds relied upon, the one of greatest interest for present purposes was the necessity for coordination and avoidance of overlap within an essentially unitary system.

Since the purpose of the offset is to prevent actual duplication of income benefits, it is obviously only fair and logical to exclude from any compensation benefit such amounts as represent medical and legal expenses, and the regulations of the Department of Health and Human Services explicitly so provide.[7]

---

[3] *E.g.*, California, North Carolina, and Pennsylvania.

[4] Pierce's Case, 325 Mass. 649, 92 N.E.2d 245 (1950).

[5] Social Security Act § 224(a)(5).

[6] Richardson v. Belcher, 404 U.S. 78, 92 S. Ct. 254, 30 L. Ed. 2d 231 (1971).

[7] 20 C.F.R. § 404.408(d).

Is the offset provision any less applicable because the compensation award was for a scheduled injury and was therefore not based on actual wage loss? The United States Court for the Southern District of Mississippi has ruled that the scheduled nature of the injury does not change the basic nature of the benefit as a periodic payment for disability.[8]

When a lump-sum payment is a commutation of or substitute for periodic payments, the regular offset applies,[9] and the great majority of reported decisions dealing with ordinary lump-sum payments have found them to be subject to the offset for this reason. As noted earlier, so much of a compensation payment as is attributable to medical or legal expenses is not to be offset. If it appears that this adjustment has been made, the burden is on the claimant to show that the lump sum included some additional medical expense not accounted for in the adjustment. But if it is not clear that medical expenses have been separated out before the offset was applied, a specific calculation must be made of how much of the payment was for periodic benefits and how much for past and future medical expenses.

When a settlement agreement provides for a lump sum payment which is a substitute for periodic payments, SSA regulations have over the years given considerable deference, within reason, to what the agreement itself specifies as to proration period.[10] By specifying as long a period as possible, even up to the actuarially projected lifetime of the claimant, the Social Security offset may be minimized, and, in some cases, avoided completely.

The possibility of avoiding offset by including appropriate language in lump sum settlement agreements has created a trap for the unwary practitioner. Failing to include the needed language can result in the client's losing tens of thousands of dollars of Social Security disability benefits, and in a malpractice suit as well.

In September 1997, the Social Security Administration, which has never liked this situation, proposed new rules which would if enacted supply a uniform system of proration.[11] The effect of this change would be to limit severely the ability to avoid offset in the manner described above. As of this writing the proposed rules are being energetically opposed by the claimants' bar, as well as by a number of Industrial Commissions, who predict that the new rules will discourage settlement and thereby increase their caseloads.

[2] State Compensation Offset for Social Security

Over a dozen states apply some kind of deduction to compensation benefits for social security payments.[12]

It may seem odd, with the intense concern about compensation costs, that the states have been so slow to exploit this obvious way to reduce their compensation burden. The explanation probably lies in the almost irrational fear of federalization that has permeated the compensation community for many years. Applying a state offset was viewed as a pro tanto abdication of a portion of state workers' compensation to the federal government — and even this relatively minor bit of "federalization" appeared so threatening that overlapping benefits were not too high a price to pay to avoid it.

---

[8] Ladner v. Secretary of Health, Educ. & Welfare, 304 F. Supp. 474 (S.D. Miss. 1969).

[9] 42 U.S.C.A. § 424a(b).

[10] 20 C.F.R. § 404.408 *et seq.*

[11] 62 Fed. Reg. 46682 (1997) (proposed Sept. 3, 1997).

[12] *E.g.*, Colorado, Michigan, and Oregon.

The constitutionality of state offset provisions has been consistently upheld.[13] A challenge to a specific detail of the offset, that excluding cost of living increases in social security benefits, on the ground of vagueness, has also been rejected.[14]

[3] Other Federal Benefits Not Generally Subject to Offset

Apart from specific offset provisions, the receipt of federal benefits does not ordinarily affect a worker's right to workers' compensation benefits,[15] although it may be relevant to the issue of dependency when a relative is required to establish actual dependency.[16]

§ 34.05 COORDINATION WITH STATE PENSION AND DISABILITY SYSTEMS

When the pension plan and the workers' compensation act are both state-controlled, the meshing of the two is much simpler, and some states apply offsets of the one type of benefit against the other, on the pension side, on the compensation side, or on both. For example, New York's workers' compensation act provides generally that death benefits may be reduced by any amounts payable by a political subdivision under a non-contributory pension scheme.[17] New York's Civil Service Law also reduces civil service pensions by the amount of workers' compensation awards,[18] but does not apply the reduction to so much of the annuity as is payable from the civil servant's own contributions.[19]

Some states put the beneficiaries to an election between their compensation and pension rights.[20] But in the absence of such express statutory election or offset provisions, and under the familiar provision forbidding reduction of compensation because of other income or benefits, the benefits of both a public pension law and a compensation act can be simultaneously drawn.[21]

§ 34.06 COORDINATION WITH PRIVATE PLANS

As to private pensions or health and accident insurance, whether provided by the employer, union, or the individual's own purchase, there is ordinarily no occasion for reduction of compensation benefits. For example, in *Meyers v. Meyers Oil Co.*,[22] the claimant suffered a concededly compensable accident and sought compensation from his employer's insurer. The insurer refused to pay, on the ground that claimant had not incurred these costs, since his personal private insurance carrier had paid his medical expenses. The court ruled that, since accident insurance is a matter of private contract, it would not affect the rights of injured employees to recover under the compensation

---

[13] *E.g.*, Meyer v. Industrial Comm'n, 644 P.2d 46 (Colo. App. 1982).

[14] Great At. & Pac. Tea Co. v. Wood, 380 So. 2d 558 (Fla. App. 1980).

[15] *E.g.*, Cudahy Packing Co. v. Industrial Comm'n, 7 Ariz. App. 335, 439 P.2d 307 (1968). After becoming totally disabled, claimant was entitled to social security disability benefits. *Held*, these benefits were not to be considered in determining loss of wage-earning capacity.

[16] *See, e.g.*, Peterson v. Thief River Falls Welding Co., 245 Minn. 212, 72 N.W.2d 75 (1955), in which it was held that Social Security payments should be taken into account in determining dependency of parents.

[17] N.Y. Worker's Comp. Law § 30 (1965).

[18] N.Y. Civ. Serv. Law § 67 (1965).

[19] Dalton v. City of Yonkers, 262 App. Div. 321, 29 N.Y.S.2d 42 (1941), *aff'd without opinion*, 287 N.Y. 49 (1942).

[20] Ogilvie v. Des Moines, 212 Iowa 117, 233 N.W. 526 (1930).

[21] City Council of Augusta v. Young, 218 Ga. 346, 127 S.E.2d 904 (1962).

[22] Meyers v. Meyers Oil Co., 216 N.W.2d 820 (S.D. 1974).

law. That is, if a claimant chooses to pay the premium for personal insurance, the compensation carrier should not, in the event of injury, be the beneficiary of claimant's personal policy.

VARNELL v. UNION CARBIDE
29 Ark. App. 185, 779 S.W.2d 542 (1989)

CORBIN, CHIEF JUDGE.

Appellant was employed as a machine operator's adjuster for appellee, Union Carbide, on July 25, 1985, when she injured her back while stepping off a step. The employer's non-occupational group insurance carrier paid medical benefits for appellant and also, together with the employer, made payments to appellant of $300.00 per week from July 29, 1985, through November 24, 1985, and $40.00 per week from November 24, 1985, through January 27, 1986, as benefits under a sick pay plan provided by the employer.

A hearing was held before an administrative law judge on February 27, 1986, to determine appellant's entitlement to workers' compensation benefits. Appellant contended that she sustained a compensable accidental injury which entitled her to temporary total disability benefits, permanent partial disability benefits, medical expenses, and a controverted attorney's fee. Appellee contended that appellant had not suffered a compensable work-related injury but alternatively argued that if appellant sustained a compensable injury, it was entitled to credit for the weekly disability benefits and medical expenses previously paid by its group insurance carrier.

The administrative law judge concluded by opinion rendered February 23, 1987, that appellant sustained an injury arising out of and in the course of her employment and that she was temporarily totally disabled from July 26, 1985, to a date yet to be determined. The issue of permanent partial disability was premature at the time of the hearing and was held in abeyance. The administrative law judge also found that appellee was responsible for all reasonable and necessary medical expenses incurred by appellant as a result of her injury. Additionally, the law judge found that appellee was entitled to credit for all amounts previously paid by it and its group insurance carrier toward medical expenses and temporary total disability benefits. In addition, the administrative law judge awarded an attorney's fee on the amounts of weekly benefits and medical expenses previously paid to appellant under the group insurance coverage which was fully funded by appellee but limited the fee to the difference between benefits awarded and those already paid.

Appellant appealed to the Workers' Compensation Commission, contending that the administrative law judges erred in granting appellee credit for the amounts already paid toward her disability and medical expenses by appellee and its group carrier. Appellant also contended that the law judge erred in limiting the amount of attorney's fees to the difference between benefits awarded and benefits already paid. By opinion entered September 8, 1988, the Commission affirmed the opinion of the administrative law judge in all respects.

On appeal, appellant argues the same two points she argued at the Commission level. We reverse on both issues and remand.

I.

IT WAS ERROR FOR APPELLEE TO BE AWARDED CREDIT FOR ALL DISABILITY BENEFITS RECEIVED BY THE CLAIMANT AS A RESULT OF GROUP INSURANCE COVERAGE AND FOR AMOUNTS PAID IN EXCESS OF THE COMPENSATION RATE UNDER THE GROUP INSURANCE POLICY.

The issue in this point for reversal is whether the payments made by appellee were "advance payments for compensation" allowing for a setoff against previous payments or whether they were "sick pay benefits" for which no setoff is allowed. Appellant argues that the payments were not intended to be advance payments for compensation but "were strictly fringe benefits and taxable as income" to her. Appellee argues and the Commission held that the previous payments were advance payments for compensation and appellees were, therefore, entitled to a setoff against payments already made.

The statute around which this controversy centers is Arkansas Code Annotated Section 11-9-807 (1987) which provides:

> If the employer has made advance payments for compensation, he shall be entitled to be reimbursed out of any unpaid installment or installments of compensation due. If the injured employee receives full wages during disability, he shall not be entitled to compensation during the period.

The evidence reveals that Gene Bland, the employee relations manager for appellee, testified he was involved in the decision to treat appellant's injury as non-occupational based upon his belief that appellant had periodic back problems "due to whatever cause." Mr. Bland testified that an employee on non-occupational pay receives $40.00 a week from Metropolitan, one of appellee's insurance carriers, and appellee pays the remainder of money necessary to amount to a total of 85% of the employee's average weekly wages. Mr. Bland testified that the non-occupational pay plan is a noncontributory one to which the employees do not contribute. Bland testified that Blue Cross/Blue Shield of Arkansas is appellee's carrier for medical insurance and that, like the non-occupational coverage, is noncontributory.

The Commission's ruling that the payments to appellant were advance payments for compensation for which appellee was entitled to a credit was predicated upon the following reasoning contained in its opinion:

> While Varnell cites several cases in which the credit was not allowed, the monies paid in those cases did not constitute "advance payments of compensation." For example, the employer's representative in *Looney v. Sears, Roebuck & Company*, 236 Ark. 868, 371 S.W.2d 6 (1963) admitted that a gratuity was intended. Similarly, the payments in *Southwestern Bell Telephone Company v. Siegler*, 240 Ark. 132, 398 S.W.2d 531 (1966) were labeled as "benefits" in the employee's handbook. In Varnell's case, however, the payments could not have been insurance "benefits" since the group health insurance company only paid $40.00 per week and the employer made up the deficit between that and 85% of the employee's weekly wage. It is also obvious that the monies were not payments in lieu of wages since the amount was less than Varnell's wages. Neither were they gratuities since the purpose was to compensate employees for the expenses of illnesses rather than to make a gift or provide a bonus.

Having eliminated other possibilities (as required by *Siegler*), we conclude that the payments should be treated as advance payments of compensation. If such payments are not so treated, claimants who are dishonest could routinely collect from both the Workers' Compensation carrier and from the group health carrier. On the other hand, where the payment by the group carrier is the employer's mistake, the carrier would have a right of subrogation against the workers' compensation carrier, and the latter would eventually pay the same benefits twice, once to the claimant and once to the group carrier.

Finally, we find this case distinguishable from *Emerson Electric v. Cargile*, 5 Ark. App. 123, 633 S.W.2d 389 (1982), where the employee paid the entire premium, and the Court termed the plan a "private contract" having no relevance to the employees' workers' compensation rights. The plan here, by the way of contrast, was fully funded by Union Carbide. We find that Varnell's case is on all fours with *Lion Oil Company v. Reeves*, 221 Ark. 5, 254 S.W.2d 450 (1952), where the credit was allowed for payments intended to represent a percentage of wages, which is the situation here. If there is a conflict between *Reeves* and *Cargile*, a decision of the Arkansas Supreme Court obviously controls over a decision of the Arkansas Court of Appeals.

In the *Lion Oil* case relied upon by the Commission, the employer, a self-insurer, paid the employee amounts "aggregating full wages" during his injury period for which the employer received full credit for the excess of the amount paid over what the workers' compensation benefits would have been for that period of time. In making this determination to allow *Lion Oil* such credit, the court stated: "It is highly probable that Reeves [employee] thought the excess payments he received were gratuities, and certainly the oil company was endeavoring to provide for the workers' current needs." In *Looney v. Sears Roebuck*, 236 Ark. 868, 371 S.W.2d 6 (1983), the supreme court deemed it wise to limit the holding of *Lion Oil* to its own particular facts making a clear distinction between "advance payments of compensation" and payment of "wages and gratuities." *Looney* specifically held that the excess of wages paid over the weekly compensation award cannot be deducted from the award. Further, it held that the employer cannot make such payments and later claim credit for the excess against an award made. The *Looney* court declared that where it is shown that both parties intended that the payment be compensation in advance, the credit is allowed against future benefits. In the case at bar, we find no evidence suggesting such intent. At the beginning of the hearing before the administrative law judge, counsel for appellees stated that appellant had not been paid anything in the way of workers' compensation benefits and that appellant had not suffered a compensable injury.

While the reasoning by the Commission set out above may be a plausible alternative that is followed by a minority of jurisdictions, we believe the general rule set out in A. Larson, The Law of Workmen's Compensation Section 97.51(a) (1989), is the direction followed by Arkansas to wit:

> As to the private pensions or health and accident insurance, whether provided by the employer, union, or the individual's own purchase, there is ordinarily no occasion for reduction of compensation benefits.

Judge Cracraft writing for a majority in *Emerson Electric v. Cargile*, 5 Ark. App. 123, 633 S.W.2d 389 (1982) in reliance upon *Southwestern Bell Telephone Company v. Siegler*, 240 Ark. 132, 398 S.W.2d 531 (1966), noted that our supreme court adopted the above Larson's rule insofar as it dealt with health and accident insurance provided by the employer. Judge Cracraft wrote:

> We conclude that the sounder rules to apply are that where the insurance, whether private or company administered, is provided and funded by the employer the rule announced in *Southwestern Bell Telephone Company, supra,* should be followed and the employer afforded the right to show, if he can, that the payments were "payments of compensation in advance."

Emerson, 5 Ark. App. at 126, 633 S.W.2d at 391. In *Emerson*, the Commission held that payments made to the claimant were not advance payments of compensation and, therefore, no setoff was allowed. In rendering its decision, the Commission took into consideration that although the insurance was offered through the employer, the claimant paid *all* premiums on the insurance. This court affirmed the Commission's disallowance of a setoff by finding that the relationship was a private contractual one in which the employer did nothing more than make the group coverage available at the employee's sole expense.

In any event, *Southwestern Bell*, cited above, mandates a reversal in the case at bar. At this point, we note that in *Southwestern Bell* the claimant, before his award of permanent partial disability, received full wages during his permanent disability for which his employer claimed a set off. Whereas in the case at bar, the award of permanent partial disability was held in abeyance and instead deals with a set off claimed by the employer against a current award of temporary total disability. Having noted this distinction, we find that the same principles apply for purposes of allowing or disallowing set offs to employers for amounts previously paid. In *Southwestern Bell*, the employee sustained a knee injury while in the course of his employment and received his normal rate of pay ($128.00 per week) during his disability period under a "Plan" provided by the employer. The "Plan" was contained in a 28 page printed booklet and included disability payments to an injured employee during a period of disability. The "Plan" was fully funded by the employer and the employee made no contribution to it. The language of the "Plan" did not state that any benefits received under it would be considered as advanced payments of compensation.

The employee in *Southwestern Bell* suffered a residual injury and sought partial disability benefits in addition to those benefits previously received under the "Plan" claiming that one had nothing to do with the other. The employer claimed that the payments under the "Plan" represented an advance payment of compensation for disability and that it should be allowed a setoff against the workers' compensation award for any amounts paid the claimant under the "Plan."

The supreme court stated that the interpretation of the "Plan" was a question of law and also noted that without any designation in the "Plan" itself, the monies received by that employee might have been wages, gratuities, benefits or advance payment of compensation, and until the company showed that under the "Plan" such payment "could have been nothing except advance payment of compensation the company failed to establish its case." The court held that only where the employer clearly establishes that the sums paid or provided by it to an injured employee are advanced payments of compensation could it be entitled to any setoff. In all other situations, the employee could recover the full amount of his disability benefits provided under the Workers' Compensation Act.

Applying the principles established in *Southwestern Bell* to the case at bar, the evidence reveals that appellee sought through the testimony of Gene Bland to establish its case and meet its burden of proof to show that the payments received by appellant were "payments of compensation in advance." Mr. Bland's testimony generally reveals that he has a high opinion of appellant and her work ethic, and would be happy for her to return to work. He also testified that he was involved in the decision to treat appellant's claim as a non-occupational injury however, he admitted that he did not discuss this matter or his decision in this regard with appellant "at that time or even later." Furthermore, Mr. Bland stated that he acted in good faith in determining to treat appellant's injury as non-occupational and "at that time" he really thought the treatment and payments were in the proper category. Mr. Bland's testimony also revealed general information about appellee's non-occupational injury plan as well as how it is funded, the lack of employee contribution, and the treatment of appellant's claim under this plan.

Appellant's testimony revealed that at the time she filled out the report to claim benefits for her work-related accident, she was not told by appellee nor was she aware that the form she signed was for a non-occupational type incident. Also, she stated that she later refused to sign forms concerning payment of medical bills because she noticed that there was language on the forms categorizing her injury as "non-occupational." There was no viable evidence showing that both parties clearly intended that the payments were compensation in advance. In fact, the evidence bears out that the treatment of appellant's claim as a non-occupational injury was the result of a unilateral decision made by appellee and totally unbeknownst to appellant. It is apparent from case law and from statute that a clear distinction is drawn between money received as "advanced payment of compensation" and "wages and gratuities." *Southwestern Bell Tel. Co. v. Siegler*, 240 Ark. 132, 398 S.W.2d 531 (1966); *Looney v. Sears Roebuck*, 236 Ark. 868, 371 S.W.2d 6 (1963); *Arkansas Louisiana Gas Co. v. Grooms*, 10 Ark. App. 92, 661 S.W.2d 433 (1983); *Hill v. CGR Medical Corp.*, 9 Ark. App. 334, 660 S.W.2d 171 (1983); *Emerson Elec. v. Cargile*, 5 Ark. App. 123, 633 S.W.2d 389 (1982); Ark. Code Ann. § 11-9-102(8), (9) (1987). Based upon the foregoing, there is no substantial evidence to support a finding by the Commission that the payments made to appellant were payments of compensation in advance.

Our standard of review on appeal is whether the decision is supported by substantial evidence. *Boyd v. General Indus.*, 22 Ark. App. 103, 733 S.W.2d 750 (1987). Substantial evidence is such relevant evidence as a reasonable mind might accept as adequate to support a conclusion. *Phillips v. State*, 271 Ark. 96, 607 S.W.2d 664 (1980). This standard must not totally insulate the Commission from judicial review and render this court's function in these cases meaningless. We will reverse a decision of the Commission where convinced that fair-minded persons with the same facts before them could not have reached the conclusion arrived at by the Commission. *Wade v. Mr. C. Cavenaugh's*, 25 Ark. App. 237, 756 S.W.2d 923 (1988). In the instant case, we cannot say that fair-minded persons would have reached the same conclusion about granting appellee a setoff against "advance payments for compensation." For the reasons discussed, we reverse on this point. . . .

Although avoidance of duplication cannot ordinarily be achieved under American statutes in these cases by, so to speak, trimming at the compensation end, it is frequently achieved by express language trimming at the private-plan end, that is, by reducing the private benefits by the amount of any compensation payments.[23] Even when the language of the plan is not specific, a court may give the benefit of the doubt to a construction that will avoid overlapping payments. In a New York case,[24] the employer had unilaterally promised its employees the benefits of its retirement plan, not only on reaching retirement age, but also when retirement had been recommended by the company's medical staff "for reasons of ill health." Claimant suffered a heart attack in the course of his employment, and received workers' compensation and medical benefits. He also applied for retirement benefits under the employer's plan, but the court denied him these, saying:

> Plaintiff was not retirable for "ill health" within the meaning of the provision of the plan above quoted. That provision to make any sense must be deemed to refer to ill health not compensable under the Workmen's Compensation Law. Otherwise there is a duplication of benefits.

On the other hand, if the health or accident insurance policy contains no express reduction of benefits for workers' compensation,[25] or contains merely the familiar "other insurance" clause, there is nothing to prevent enforcement of the insurer's liability under the policy even after receiving workers' compensation payments for the same injury.[26]

Dissatisfaction with the level of benefits afforded by statute had led to the appearance of a large number of collectively-bargained contracts under which the employer agrees to supplement compensation benefits and bring them up to an agreed level. There is, of course, no impediment in the compensation act to the contractual provision of supplemental benefits or relaxation of statutory requirements of the act in favor of the employee.[27]

It is possible to imagine a number of troublesome legal questions that might emerge from the type of contracts in which the employer agrees to pay, say, $350 a week benefits instead of the $250 specified by statute. One cardinal principle, however, should ordinarily settle most such questions. That principle is the simple proposition that the contractual excess is not workers' compensation. It performs the same functions, and is payable under the same general conditions, but legally it is nothing more than the fruit

---

[23] *See* Alessi v. Raybestos-Manhattan, Inc., 451 U.S. 504, 101 S. Ct. 1895, 68 L. Ed. 2d 402 (1981).

[24] Bromberg v. United Cigar Whelan Stores Corp., 125 N.Y.L.J. 687, 19 Labor Cases 66,203 (1961).

[25] Schrieder v. National Distillers & Chemical Corp., 51 A.D.2d 1068, 380 N.Y.S.2d 805 (1976).

[26] Inter-Ocean Cas. Co. v. Lenear, 95 S.W.2d 1355 (Tex. Civ. App. 1936).

[27] Baltimore Transit Co. v. Harroll, 217 Md. 169, 141 A.2d 912 (1958).

of a private agreement to pay a sum of money on specified conditions.

TABLE OF CASES

[References are to pages]

[References are to pages]

C

[References are to pages]

[References are to pages]

M

[References are to pages]

[References are to pages]

[References are to pages]

[References are to pages]

[References are to pages]

INDEX

[References are to page numbers.]

[References are to page numbers.]

[References are to page numbers.]

[References are to page numbers.]

[References are to page numbers.]

[References are to page numbers.]

[References are to page numbers.]

[References are to page numbers.]

[References are to page numbers.]

[References are to page numbers.]

[References are to page numbers.]